EXECUTIVE BRANCH OF THE GOVERNMENT

From the Bureau of the Budget, *The Federal Budget in Brief, Fiscal Year 1951.*

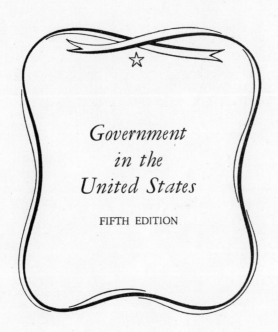

Government
in the
United States

FIFTH EDITION

Government in the United States

United States

FIFTH EDITION

CLAUDIUS O. JOHNSON

Professor of Political Science and
Chairman of the Department of History and Political Science
The State College of Washington

New York

THOMAS Y. CROWELL COMPANY

1952

FIRST EDITION

First Printing, October, 1933
Second Printing, May, 1934
Third Printing, July, 1934
Fourth Printing, September, 1934
Fifth Printing, March, 1935
Sixth Printing, September, 1935

SECOND EDITION

First Printing, June, 1937
Second Printing, January, 1938
Third Printing, September, 1938
Fourth Printing, August, 1939
Fifth Printing, August, 1940
Sixth Printing, August, 1941

THIRD EDITION

First Printing, October, 1944
Second Printing, December, 1944
Third Printing, September, 1945
Fourth Printing, February, 1946
Fifth Printing, August, 1946
Sixth Printing, August, 1946
Seventh Printing, September, 1946

FOURTH EDITION

First Printing, July, 1947
Second Printing, May, 1948
Third Printing, February, 1949

FIFTH EDITION

First Printing, April, 1951
Second Printing, August, 1951
Third Printing, August, 1952

MANUFACTURED IN THE UNITED STATES OF AMERICA
BY THE VAIL-BALLOU PRESS, INC., BINGHAMTON, N.Y.

In Memoriam

WINSTON B. THORSON
Master teacher, mature scholar,
inspiring colleague

Preface to the Fifth Edition

It is perhaps an act of supererogation to remark that the "term" of any particular edition of a textbook on American Government is somewhat shorter than that of the President of the United States. The Taft-Hartley Law, the Social Security Act Amendments, the Hoover Reports, progress and retrogression on the civil liberties front, political victories that fooled most of the experts, and international crises the solution of which seems to baffle all the experts are among the developments that constitute compelling reasons for this Fifth Edition of *Government in the United States.*

My efforts have been concentrated upon writing a book that students may find of interest, and if, on occasion, a student may read a particular section with enjoyment, I shall not plead guilty to overshooting my mark. In pursuance of this aim to engage the student's interest, I have unhesitatingly made liberal use of text space for purely illustrative purposes. Similarly, I have yielded considerable space for charts and tables, a synoptic view of which often conveys more information than the well-executed paragraph. Finally, the Questions and Problems that accompany each chapter have been designed to stimulate student response beyond the mere acquisition of facts.

Although this Edition contains the same general plan of organization as the Fourth, numerous changes in arrangement have been made within the chapter and section structures. Such changes may be particularly noticeable in the chapters on "The President's Executive Powers," "The National Administrative System," "Government and Labor," and "National Defense." No alterations have been made simply for the sake of change, but the endless quest for effectiveness of expression, new and challenging situations, and recent political policies and judicial decisions have led to well over a hundred significant changes and additions. A new chapter, "The Conduct of Foreign Relations," has been included in the present volume.

The chapter on "The United States and International Organization," originally written for the Fourth Edition by my able colleague, the late Winston B. Thorson, has been thoroughly revised by another colleague, Professor H. Paul Castleberry, to whom I am greatly indebted. My warm appreciation goes also to a third associate, Dr. Daniel M. Ogden, Jr., who generously prepared the major part of the material on water-power development. It is always a pleasure to acknowledge my obligations to my colleagues Professors Herman J. Deutsch and Paul Beckett, whose general counsel and specific suggestions are invariably worthy of attention. To those teachers of government in other institutions who have sent me helpful criticisms and suggestions and to those students who have given me pleasant occasions by mailing to me their comments or penetrating questions I extend hearty thanks.

Appreciation to teachers who have used the earlier editions is hereby acknowledged, and the fact that their generous acceptance of my offering periodically imposed upon me the obligation of revision does not lessen that appreciation. A "state of servitude" thus imposed is easily borne.

C.O.J.

March 28, 1951

Contents

PART TWO

Governmental Structure and Procedure

PART THREE

Government and the Economic and Social Order

PART FOUR

Government and the World Community

PART FIVE

The Obligations of Citizenship

Charts and Tables

Charts

xv

Tables

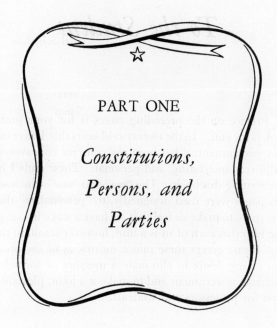

PART ONE

Constitutions,
Persons, and
Parties

To the Student

THE Preface on the preceding pages is for your professor. The book is for you. In the twenty-odd years that I have taught American government, it has been my constant endeavor to make the subject clear, direct, interesting, and personal. These ends I have held in view as I was writing this book. The "we" and "our" which so frequently appear on its pages were used designedly, to "personalize" the subject, to bring it home to us, to make us feel that we have a stake in our government, to convey the idea that each of us is a unit, however small, in the process of government. Please accept these minor intimacies of the printed page as an indication of my desire to eliminate a measure of formality from the study of American government and to make it a joint, pleasant, and profitable excursion for professors and students.

C.O.J.

☆ 1 ☆

The Foundations of American Government

HE large majority of the American colonists were English, and the influence of the mother country remains strong among us to this day. In the language of Professor Allan Nevins: "An American may have not a drop of British blood; he may evince a distinct prejudice against the British; yet he is molded in a way of life which owes far more to Britain than to any other source." [1] The American colonists brought with them and retained their British ideas concerning government and other institutions when, in search of religious freedom, or in pursuit of economic gain, or in quest of adventure, they left civilization and settled in a land inhabited by savages. For that reason the history of American institutions begins, not with those who braved the dangers and endured the hardships of early colonial life, but in England with the Saxons, the Danes, and the Normans.

Our political background. Four hundred years before venturesome Englishmen planted colonies along the Atlantic seaboard the enraged King John was forced to affix the Great Seal to the document in which he promised, among other things, that "no freeman shall be taken, or imprisoned, or disseised,[2] or outlawed or banished, or anyways destroyed, . . . unless by the legal judgment of his peers, or by the law of the land." [3] So, too, in those far-off days, our English forbears were establishing many another civil liberty, among which are the right of trial by jury, the right to petition a government for a redress of grievances, and the privilege of the writ of *habeas corpus*.

Long before the earliest English settlers in America deprived the Indians

---

[1] *The Saturday Review of Literature,* August 20, 1949, in a review of Gerald W. Johnson's *Our English Heritage* (1949).

[2] Ousted from the possession of an estate.

[3] *Magna Charta,* Article 46.

3

of their hunting ground and began to till the soil, their ancestors in England had curbed the powers of kings, made government officials obey the laws, and established a representative government that carried the principle of "no taxation without representation." The common law and equity grew up in England in mediaeval times as did the English system of courts. The sheriff, the coroner, the justice of the peace—officers so familiar in America today—come to us from feudal England. Thus, although the Englishmen who cleared the wilderness in America had to make their own economic future, nearly all their important political institutions were ready-made. They brought with them a practical knowledge of a system of government that had been in operation for centuries. They brought also the Englishman's conception of the limits of government, and a jealous regard for his liberties under government.[4]

THE INHERITANCE MODIFIED BY ENVIRONMENT. American political institutions as they operate in the twentieth century are modifications, in some cases very slight modifications, of English practices of the seventeenth and eighteenth centuries, plus important features that we have added from time to time to suit our environment.[5] In making our changes, we have followed the practice usually adhered to by the English of making them by evolution rather than by revolution. Even our Revolutionary War brought few immediate changes in addition to establishing our independence as a nation. Indeed, in the controversies that led up to that war, leading Americans denied that they were asking for any changes and insisted that they were asking only for the rights due them as Englishmen. We have never torn down one system to erect another; but, instead, we have always built upon what we had, thus giving a unity and a continuity to our political structure that would have been impossible otherwise. The Constitution adopted in 1789 contains many provisions shaped from English practice and from the experience of the states.

Even this brief discussion of the background of American political institutions must include reference to our indebtedness to peoples other than British. The political philosophy of Continental Europe was influential in America in colonial times and in the revolutionary period. Particularly did the French ideas and theories of the eighteenth century influence our Founding Fathers. Perhaps no other European engaged the attention of American constitution-makers as did the celebrated French jurist and philosopher the Baron de Montesquieu, who elaborated the doctrine of the separation of powers.

[4] C. E. Merriam, *American Political Theories* (1903), pp. 4–5, 27, 44–45. See also A. T. Mason, *Free Government in the Making* (1949), Ch. II and F. G. Wilson, *The American Political Mind* (1949), Ch. 2.

[5] M. W. Jernegan, *The American Colonies* (1929), p. 25.

I. THE SEPARATION FROM GREAT BRITAIN[6]

Clash of colonial and British interests. The growth of the colonies, their increased self-reliance because of that growth and the important part they played in the French and Indian War, and the additional security they enjoyed with the French expelled from America, all tended toward the development of an autonomous spirit. Nevertheless, there was no movement toward independence until Great Britain decided to take a more active hand in the regulation of colonial affairs. Shortly after the conclusion of the French and Indian War, the English ministers decided to enforce the laws that were applicable to the colonies—especially those relating to colonial trade—to station British troops in America for defense purposes, and to levy certain taxes on the colonies for the purpose of providing revenue to meet a part of the cost of their defense.

ARGUMENTS FOR AMERICAN RESISTANCE. The colonies objected to any such acts of the British government, and in particular to the requirement that they pay taxes levied three thousand miles away by a Parliament in which they had no representation. They claimed that they owed their fealty and allegiance to the King and not to Parliament, and that Parliament had no authority to levy an internal tax on the colonies.[7] They maintained also that they were entitled to all the rights and privileges of Englishmen and that one of the rights most dear to the heart of an Englishman was that he should not be taxed unless he was represented in the taxing body. These arguments were not the most effective, for it was pointed out by able jurists that the authority of Parliament did extend to the colonies and it was a notorious fact that citizens and taxpayers in a number of the important English cities were unrepresented in Parliament.

An argument that was used more effectively and more frequently than the others as the differences between the colonies and the English government became more pronounced was best set forth in the Declaration of Independence, which states as a self-evident truth that all men are "endowed by their Creator with certain unalienable rights; that among these are life, liberty, and the pursuit of happiness; that to secure these rights, governments are instituted among men, deriving their just powers from the consent of the governed; that whenever any form of government becomes destructive of these ends, it is the right of the people to alter or abolish it, and to institute new government." This was perfectly

[6] Merriam, *op. cit.*, Ch. II; Mason, *op. cit.*, Chs. III–IV; Wilson, *op. cit.*, Chs. 3–4; A. M. Schlesinger, *New Viewpoints in American History* (1922), Ch. VII.

[7] The majority of American historians hold that the colonists' position here was legally wrong. A few historians say that their claim was well founded. For the latter view, see C. H. McIlwain, *The American Revolution: A Constitutional Interpretation* (1923).

good English political theory—the theory by which Englishmen had over-thrown two kings in the seventeenth century; indeed, the theory by which George III came to occupy the British throne. When the colonies claimed the right of revolt because of the arbitrary acts of the King and Parliament, they were simply following English precedent.[8] Small wonder that they had so many sympathizers and well-wishers in Great Britain!

The colonies reluctantly dissolved the political bands that had connected America and Britain, for the American leaders had great admiration for English political institutions and were led to the separation primarily because they were not given what they conceived to be the full advantage of them. With the war in progress, however, some leaders who had no respect for the English system gained the ascendancy, and so many others were won over to their point of view that practically all the erstwhile cherished features of the British political system were assailed. Thomas Paine led the attack in 1776 with his *Common Sense*. He demolished monarchy in the eyes of the Americans with the assertion that "of more worth is one honest man to society, and in the sight of God, than all the crowned ruffians that ever lived." He proceeded with equal vigor against other British institutions. According to Professor Charles E. Merriam, Paine's attack upon all things English, and especially upon the King, gave new vigor to the cause of American independence.[9] The more re-strained constitutional and philosophical arguments of the leading states-men made good state papers and turned the sympathy of liberals the world over toward the American cause, but Thomas Paine's bold and somewhat irresponsible assertions, written in a "spicy" style, revived the spirits of freezing and hungry soldiers.

II. THE CONTINENTAL CONGRESS AND THE CONFEDERATION [10]

The Continental Congress. At the suggestion of the Massachusetts Assembly, delegates from all the colonies except Georgia met in Phila-delphia on September 5, 1774, for the purpose of devising means for re-storing harmony with Great Britain. This first Continental Congress sat from time to time for about seven weeks. It stated the rights of the colonies in an impressive manner, and, for the purpose of bringing the King and Parliament to terms, agreed to boycott British trade. At this Congress there was little or no thought of independence. A second Con-gress was called with the idea that it continue the work of the first; but

[8] Merriam, *op. cit.*, pp. 38 ff.

[9] *Ibid.*, pp. 69–74.

[10] Merrill Jensen, *The New Nation: A History of the United States During the Confedera-tion* (1950); A. C. McLoughlin, *The Confederation and the Constitution* (1905), Chs. III–XI.

when it met on May 10, 1775, the war had already begun. Since there was no other national organization, this body took control and directed affairs until March 1, 1781, thus carrying us almost to Yorktown.

The Continental Congress labored under many difficulties. (1) It had no authority except what it assumed and what thirteen independent states allowed it to exercise. It began as a voluntary conference for the discussion of grievances, and during its existence it rested on no legal basis (had no constitution) and received support only as a *de facto* and revolutionary body. (2) The states conceived of themselves as thirteen independent states, co-operating temporarily for the purpose of winning independence. To be sure, ardent nationalists like J. W. Burgess assert that we became a nation with the Declaration of Independence, but the records of the period hardly sustain this contention. (3) The delegates, frequently changed in personnel, came as ambassadors from the states, and voted by states, not as individuals. (4) The states frequently asserted their sovereignty, even going so far as to meddle occasionally in foreign affairs.

The Articles of Confederation. Leaders soon came to the conclusion that this informal league of states was entirely inadequate for the work to be accomplished. Consequently, in June, 1776, acting upon a motion of Richard Henry Lee, the Continental Congress appointed a committee to draft a declaration of independence and another committee to draw up articles of confederation. Because the states were extremely jealous of their sovereignty, it was found very difficult to devise a plan that would be acceptable to all of them. The Articles of Confederation, an instrument that left as much to the states as possible, was finally put through Congress in November, 1777; but, since it carried the provision that it would not go into effect until all the states had ratified it, and Maryland withheld her approval for more than three years, it did not go into effect until 1781.

Achievements of the Confederation government. Despite the difficulties and blunders of the Continental Congress and its successor, the Congress of the Confederation, they recorded several substantial achievements. (1) They managed in one way or another to keep armies in the field until the war was brought to a successful conclusion. (2) They sent out some of the ablest diplomats this country has ever produced—men who, in the face of some opposition from France and Spain, succeeded in negotiating with Great Britain a treaty of peace that gave us everything to which our military success had given us any substantial claim. Some favorable treaties were negotiated with other countries during the period of the Confederation. (3) Realizing that administrative duties could not be well performed by the whole body of the delegates or by a committee of them, Congress established (1781) four executive departments that were the forerunners of our present Departments of State, Treasury, Army, and Navy. The office of Postmaster-General, inherited from colonial times, existed from the beginning of the Revolution. (4) The Northwest Ordinance of 1787, one of the later measures of the Confederation Congress, is ranked with the greatest documents of American history. It was the first territorial government act to go into effect, and its wise and liberal provisions have been generally adhered to since in the government of our territories,[11] particularly those within our continental domain.

Reasons for failure of the Confederation government: 1. THE STATES RETAINED THEIR SOVEREIGNTY. The insufficiency of the Articles was apparent to some leaders even before the new government started to function. The states retained their "sovereignty, freedom, and independence" when they entered this "firm league of friendship." It was agreed that no changes should be made in the Articles unless such changes were approved by Congress and by the legislatures of every state. As a further concession to the states, Congress was denied the right to declare war, make treaties and alliances, borrow money, or exercise a number of other important powers unless nine states gave their assent. Although the states agreed "to abide by the determinations of the United States in Congress assembled" on all questions arising under the Articles, and to "inviolably observe" the terms of the union, which was several times declared by its constitution to be "perpetual," the fact remains that the union was only a loose confederation composed of thirteen sovereign states.[12]

2. IT HAD NO CONTROL OVER INDIVIDUALS. Since the Confederation government was only a loose league of states, it followed logically that it could deal only with the states, not with individuals. Thus, while Congress could fix the amount of money to be raised, it could do no more than apportion the tax among the several states "in proportion to the value of all land within each state." The taxes for paying that proportion were laid and levied by the authority and direction of the legislatures of the states. Congress could fix the quota of soldiers to be raised by each state; but the states appointed the regimental officers, and raised, clothed, armed, and equipped the men "in a soldierlike manner," at the expense of the United States. The provisions of Article IV did give individuals the right to move freely from one state to another and to enjoy "all privileges and immunities of free citizens in the several states," but such provisions gave the national government no control over persons in the states.

---

[11] McLaughlin, *op. cit.,* Chs. I and VI, and pp. 51–52, 120–122.

[12] These articles are given in C. A. M. Ewing and R. J. Dangerfield, *Documentary Source Book in American Government and Politics* (1931), p. 10, and in other source books on American government.

3. THE POWERS OF CONGRESS WERE INADEQUATE. The central government, if such it may be called, consisted of just one body, a unicameral Congress, with executive rather than legislative powers. This Congress was given the authority to declare war and to conclude peace; to make treaties and alliances, with certain limitations; to fix the amount of money to be raised for the services of the United States, and to appropriate the same; to coin money; to borrow money; to build up and equip a navy; to agree upon the number of land forces, and to make requisitions from each state for its quota; to settle disputes between the states, but in a manner prescribed in Article IX; to regulate Indian affairs; to establish a postal system; and to exercise a few other powers. The states thought they had given Congress quite extensive powers; but the powers were fatally defective because Congress was given no means of enforcing the powers delegated, and no power to tax nor to lay tariff duties nor to regulate commerce.

In noting the constitutional disabilities of Congress, we should recall here, a fact mentioned above, that Congress could not exercise her more important powers unless nine of the thirteen states assented. Delegates representing five of the smaller states—a small part of the country—could, and frequently did, prevent the passage of most essential measures. Perhaps the caustic comment made some fifty years ago by Secretary of State John Hay, that thirty-four per cent of the American Senate would "always be found on the blackguard side of every question," might be more appropriately applied to the obstructing five-thirteenths minority in the Confederation Congress.

4. CONGRESS COULD NOT GET MONEY. We have just observed that Congress lacked essential financial powers. Yet money was needed to pay the troops, the civil servants, the interest on the public debt, and for various other purposes. Congress had three ways of attempting to get money: it could beg alms abroad, requisition the states, and ask the printer to issue paper money. No one of these methods produced money. Foreign governments were very slow to advance money to a government that was powerless to do more than make recommendations; the states did not honor more than one fourth of the amounts requisitioned; and the printer's paper was not money. The states were asked as early as 1781 to strengthen the financial position of the Confederation by authorizing Congress to levy a five per cent duty on imports. Assent was given to this proposal by most of the states; but Rhode Island, an important commercial state, refused to accede on the grounds that the import duties would bear most heavily upon the commercial states and that her liberties might be impaired. Virginia, a short time thereafter, jealously guarding her

sovereignty, repealed the act by which she had given Congress the authority requested. Similar attempts to get authority for Congress to levy import duties met with failure. Faced with these conditions, Robert Morris, the Superintendent of Finance, in 1783 stated emphatically, "It can no longer be a doubt to Congress, that our public credit is gone." [13]

Its paper money was worthless. During the Revolution, Congress issued quantities of paper money. By the end of 1781, according to Jefferson, a thousand dollars of this currency was worth about one dollar in specie. A barber who had no delusions about its value used it to paper his shop; a crowd of men and boys parading in Philadelphia decorated their hats with it, and in their company was a wretched dog pitched with tar and plastered from head to tail with Continental paper dollars.[14] The origin of the expression, "isn't worth a Continental," is now explained. To add to the currency chaos, ignorant men and demagogues in the states persuaded the people that their economic salvation was to be found in paper money; and the majority of the state governments issued such paper, which, of course, rapidly depreciated.[15] Jefferson once paid a workman $450 in Virginia currency—fifty cents in specie—for a day's work.

5. CONGRESS COULD NOT REGULATE COMMERCE. Closely linked with the financial impotency of the Confederation was its inability to regulate commerce. The treaty-making power could be used by Congress to regulate commerce indirectly, but there was no way to force the states to observe the treaties. We have already noted the failure of Congress to get the authority from the states to levy a small import duty. In 1784 Congress passed a resolution declaring that the trade restrictions of England should be met with counter-restrictions, and asked for the authority to pass a navigation act, to be effective for fifteen years. The states received this request as they did the other requests of Congress, with coolness and suspicion. They acted as if the request had come from some foreign power rather than from their own representatives in Congress. They burdened their assent with so many qualifications and conditions that the whole matter fell through.[16]

And the states regulated commerce ruinously. Since the states refused to give Congress any authority over commerce, it was not to be expected that they would, by independent action, reach any adequate solution of the problem of its regulation. Their efforts were more frequently directed by jealousy and the desire to take trade from each other than by a genuine

13 McLaughlin, *op. cit.,* pp. 53 ff., 79–80.
14 *Ibid.,* pp. 55–56.
15 *Ibid.,* pp. 140 ff.
16 *Ibid.,* pp. 84–86.

interest in reaching a common basis for the regulation of trade and the levying of duties on imports.[17]

When three other New England states placed severe restrictions on
British shipping in their ports in the hope Britain would feel the pinch and
relax her commercial restrictions against the states, Connecticut promptly
took advantage of this move by immediately giving English vessels the
widest rights in her ports, and followed this up by levying duties upon
imports from Massachusetts. When New York passed acts forcing Connecticut and New Jersey vessels to pay entrance fees and obtain clearance
papers at her customhouses, as if they had been ships from foreign countries, New Jersey retaliated by laying a heavy tax on a lighthouse owned
by New York City but happily, thought the Jerseymen, located on their
soil. As for Connecticut, her businessmen unanimously agreed to suspend
all commercial intercourse with New York; and each merchant signed an
agreement, under a penalty of $250 for the first offense, not to send any
goods to New York for a year. Pennsylvania's discriminations against
her two small neighbors, New Jersey and Delaware, were met by prompt
retaliations from those sovereign states. The situation, then, was simply
this: the states, refusing to give the central government authority to regulate
commerce in the only way it could be adequately regulated, proceeded to
set each other by the ears with discriminations and retaliations, thus dis-
rupting both foreign and domestic commerce.[18]

6. CONGRESS HAD NO COERCIVE POWER. It has been shown that the
authority of Congress did not extend to individuals, but only to the states.
Yet Congress had no power to force the states to respect her authority,
and the "state of the Union" was revealed as sad indeed. Congress "could
ask for money," says Professor A. C. McLaughlin, "but not compel payment; it could enter into treaties but not enforce their stipulations; it could
provide for raising of armies but not fill the ranks; it could borrow money
but take no proper measures for repayment; it could advise and recommend
but not command. In other words, with some of the outward seemings
of a government, and with many of its responsibilities, it was not a government." [19]   Noah Webster wrote in 1785: "A law without a penalty is mere
advice; a magistrate, without the power of punishing, is a *cypher.*" [20]
Congress was becoming more impotent daily because it had no coercive
power.

[17] *Ibid.,* p. 86.

[18] J. Fiske, *Critical Period of American History* (1888), Ch. IV.

[19] McLaughlin, *op. cit.,* pp. 50–51. Quoted by permission of Harper and Brothers publishers.

[20] Quoted, *ibid.,* p. 177.

The menace of a social upheaval. The period of the Confederation is characterized as the critical period of American history not only because of the inadequacy of the Articles and the consequent helplessness of Congress to exercise essential powers of government over thirteen states jealous of their newly won sovereignty, but also because of a very serious economic depression—a condition that challenges the best of governments—that followed the Revolution. These difficulties were accompanied by a general weakening of respect for government, a growing hostility to the most reasonable taxation, a disposition to set private rights aside lightly, and even a feeling on the part of a small minority that property ought to be common. Resistance to government and opposition to taxation were, unfortunately, survivors of the Revolution. The laxity and extravagance attending that struggle further contributed to the social unrest. The war had brought forward some men who were unfit to lead; but they nevertheless had a large following, in which were included the vicious, the restless, the ignorant, and the foolish, although, excepting the vicious, they were for the most part honest and with few exceptions in real distress.[21]

SHAYS'S REBELLION. In Massachusetts, Daniel Shays, a man of no great talent, who had seen service in the Continental Army, assumed the leadership of a populist group that had grievances against the judges and the lawyers, whom they regarded as unholy allies of the creditor class. Shays's followers complained also of taxation and of extravagance in government; and, being in the debtor class, they wanted more paper money, and some even said the time had come to wipe out all debts. During the winter of 1786–7 Shays led his forces in a rebellion, which was put down by the firm hand of Governor Bowdoin.

Shays's Rebellion caused all thoughtful men to take stock of the situation in other states. "There are combustibles in every state," Washington wrote, "which a spark might set fire to. . . . I feel . . . infinitely more than I can express to you, for the disorders which have arisen in these states." [22] While the rebellion was in progress, Congress raised some troops for the assistance of Massachusetts, but it did not dare to take this step until it had been assured that "money holders" would take up a loan to pay the troops. Congress, having no money with which to pay soldiers for suppressing a rebellion, feared that the soldiers might turn upon it and demand their pay. Congress was clearly reduced to the shadow of a self-respecting government. Events in Massachusetts, the justifiable fear of similar events in other states, the evidence that Congress was reduced to a cipher,

---

[21] This is the conventional picture of the "critical period."   C. A. and M. R. Beard consider it overdrawn—*Rise of American Civilization* (1930 ed.), pp. 297 ff.   Merrill Jensen, *op. cit.*, takes the side of the Beards against the more conventional historians Fiske and McLaughlin.

[22] Quoted, McLaughlin, *op. cit.*, p. 166.

all strengthened the reactionary movement against the excesses of democracy that had been let loose by the Revolution. With the exception of Jefferson there were not many important leaders left who held to the theory that the best government was that which governed least. The movement to give the Union strength and vigor gained force and gave promise of success.

III. STEPS TOWARD A NATIONAL GOVERNMENT [23]

Failures of earlier attempts. From the very first, clear heads had little hope that the Articles would be a success. The practical and direct Washington stated that a government should have coercive power and that the states would not respond to the requests of Congress. Hamilton, then a statesman twenty-three years of age, spoke of the need of a "solid coercive union" and of the necessity of giving Congress the authority to levy taxes and regulate commerce. Under his influence, in 1782, the New York Legislature proposed a convention of the states for the purpose of revising the Articles, but Congress took no action on the proposal. Early in 1781 Madison was working for the adoption of an additional Article that would give Congress the authority to employ force against the states that did not fulfill their federal obligations. This and similar efforts to amend the Articles came to naught. We have already noted the failure to adopt the amendments that would have given Congress some revenue and some control over commerce. The jealousy of the states and the slow and circumspect action of their mediocre delegates in Congress spelled defeat for every suggestion.[24]

The Virginia-Maryland conference. As the position of the Confederation became more and more hopeless, men like Washington, Madison, Hamilton, and Jay redoubled their efforts to revive it. Their opportunity came almost by chance. Virginia and Maryland appointed commissioners to arrive at an agreement between the two states concerning the navigation of the Potomac. The commissioners reached an agreement at Mount Vernon in the spring of 1785. Maryland then proposed a new conference on commercial affairs to include Pennsylvania and Delaware. Madison, hard at work in the Virginia Legislature, labored earnestly for this and similar movements, and on the last day of the legislative session a resolution was passed authorizing the appointment of commissioners to meet with such commissioners as other states might appoint for the

---

[23] B. J. Hendrick, *Bulwark of the Republic: A Biography of the Constitution* (1937), pp. 9–64; McLaughlin, *op. cit.*, Ch. XI; C. B. Swisher, *American Constitutional Development* (1943), Ch. I.

[24] McLaughlin, *op. cit.*, p. 85.

purpose of considering uniformity in commercial regulations. Madison was the directing power in the Virginia commission that invited the other states to send delegates to a convention to be held at Annapolis in September, 1786.

The Annapolis Convention. Only five states were represented at the Convention, thus making it impossible to carry out the purposes for which it was called. But the Convention took a bold step and adopted unanimously a report, framed by Hamilton, which was to lead ultimately to happy results. The report stated that the critical times called for the "united virtue and wisdom of all the members of the confederacy," and it proposed that a convention of delegates from all the states be held in Philadelphia in May, 1787, "to take into consideration the situation of the United States, to devise such further provisions as shall appear to them necessary to render the constitution of the federal government adequate to the exigencies of the Union; and to report such an act for that purpose to the United States in Congress assembled as, when agreed to by them, and afterwards confirmed by the legislatures of every state, will effectually provide for the same." [25]

The call for the Philadelphia Convention. This report was transmitted to Congress and to all the states. Some months later, Congress came to life sufficiently to issue the official call for a convention to meet at the time and place mentioned in the report of the Annapolis Convention, "for the sole and express purpose of revising the Articles of Confederation." All the states appointed delegates to the convention except Rhode Island. Although leading men were not particularly optimistic over the possibilities of such a convention, it was clear to them that now was their chance, if ever.

Reading List

R. G. Adams, *The Political Ideas of the American Revolution* (1922).

C. M. Andrews, *Colonial Background of the American Revolution* (1924).

——, *The Colonial Period of American History,* 4 vols. (1934–1938).

C. A. and M. R. Beard, *The Rise of American Civilization* (1930), pp. 33–309.

C. Becker, *The Declaration of Independence* (1922).

B. J. Hendrick, *Bulwark of the Republic: A Biography of the Constitution* (1937), Ch. I.

H. C. Hockett, *The Constitutional History of the United States, 1776–1826,* 2 vols. (1939).

Merrill Jensen, *The New Nation: A History of the United States during the Confederation* (1950).

[25] *Documents Illustrative of the Formation of the Union of the American States.* 69th Cong., 1st sess., House Document No. 398, pp. 39–43.

A. Johnson, *Readings in American Constitutional History, 1776–1876* (1912), Chs. I–II.

Gerald W. Johnson, *Our English Heritage* (1949).

A. T. Mason, *Free Government in the Making* (1949), Chs. II–IV.

Wm. MacDonald, *Select Charters and Other Documents Illustrative of American History* (1904).

C. H. McIlwain, *The American Revolution: a Constitutional Interpretation* (1923).

A. C. McLaughlin, "The Background of American Federalism," *Am. Pol. Sci. Rev.* (1918), XII, 215–240.

——, *The Confederation and the Constitution* (1905), Chs. III–XI.

——, *A Constitutional History of the United States* (1935), Chs. I–XIII.

C. E. Merriam, *A History of American Political Theories* (1903), Chs. I–II.

W. C. Morey, "The Genesis of a Written Constitution," *Annals of the Am. Acad. of Pol. and Soc. Sci.* (1891), I, 4.

A. M. Schlesinger, *New Viewpoints in American History* (1923), Ch. VII.

C. B. Swisher, *American Constitutional Development* (1943), Ch. I.

C. H. Van Tyne, *The American Revolution* (1905), Chs. IX, XI.

——, *The Causes of the War of Independence* (1922).

F. G. Wilson, *The American Political Mind* (1949), Chs. 2–4.

Questions and Problems [1]

1. Show that the study of American government appropriately begins in Great Britain.
2. Can it be said that the American Revolution was essentially a conservative one?
3. How do you account for our measure of success under the Articles of Confederation?
4. Could you reason that there was an element of strength in the weakness of the Articles of Confederation?
5. Trace the steps that led to the calling of the Philadelphia Convention.

---

[1] These questions do not by any means cover the entire subject matter of this text. They are intended to be representative and suggestive, not exhaustive.

The Federal Constitution

THE statement is sometimes made that the English Constitution is unwritten, the Constitution of the United States written. This is not merely over-simplification but is inaccurate. True it is that the English Constitution as a single document does not exist, but much of it is written. Other parts consist of usages and practices, "customs and conventions." Not all of the Constitution of the United States is written, that is, not all of our fundamental law appears in the document printed in the back of this book. A great deal of this law is found in statutes, judicial decisions, executive precedents, and in the practices of political parties. For that reason reference to the written instrument alone does not provide complete understanding of the nature of the American constitutional system.[1] Consequently, although this chapter contains considerable discussion of the written document, it gives special attention to what has been added to that document by Congress, courts, Presidents, and "time and habit."

I. THE FRAMING OF THE CONSTITUTION [2]

The personnel of the Convention. The fifty-five delegates who represented the twelve [3] states at the Philadelphia Convention in the summer of 1787 were above the average of those who had been sent to the Confederation Congress. About half of them were college graduates, representing

[1] Brief and profitable discussions of constitutions, written and unwritten, may be found in many volumes. Mention here is made only of R. G. Gettell's *Political Science* (1949 ed.), Ch. XV, and W. F. Willoughby's *Government of Modern States* (1936), Chs. X–XI.

[2] C. A. and M. R. Beard, *The Rise of American Civilization* (1930), pp. 309–335; M. Farrand, *The Framing of the Constitution of the United States* (1913); B. J. Hendrick, *Bulwark of the Republic: A Biography of the Constitution* (1937), pp. 11–99; A. C. McLaughlin, *The Confederation and the Constitution* (1905), Chs. XII–XVIII.

[3] Rhode Island sent no delegates.

a degree of academic training that few, if any, previous political assemblies could boast; some of them were learned in the law and political institutions. A fairly high percentage of them had ability—a number of them marked ability—which had been demonstrated by practical experience. Washington, who hoped that the Convention would "adopt no temporizing expedients," was elected president of the body; and, although he took no great part in its deliberations, his prestige and character were of infinite value. The sage Franklin, a world figure, now mellow with years, let the younger men do most of the talking; but his mere presence was worth a great deal, and his kindly humor and wide experience in diplomacy helped ease some of the clashes among the other delegates.

James Madison was not only a practical young statesman who had seen service with the Virginia government and in the Congress of the Confederation, but he was also a thorough student of politics and history who had prepared himself for the Convention by reading everything he could find which had any bearing on American problems. A colleague described him as "a Gentleman of great modesty—with a remarkably sweet temper," and who, "from a spirit of industry and application which he possesses in a most eminent degree, . . . always comes forward the best informed man on any point in debate." [4] To this same industrious and painstaking Madison, although he was not the official secretary, we are indebted for the best report of the work of the Convention, which deliberated in profound secrecy. New York sent as delegates the able Hamilton and two mediocre men. Hamilton's part in the framing of the Constitution has frequently been overestimated because of the very important part he took in the campaign for its ratification and in putting the new government on its feet after the Constitution had been adopted. His position at the Philadelphia Convention was ultra-conservative, and his extreme ideas were not shared by his fellow delegates.

Gouverneur Morris of Pennsylvania was able and daring, and he saw clearly the need for a national government. It was he who, after the provisions of the Constitution had been agreed upon, put it in final form with his direct and forcible English. James Wilson of the same state, a learned lawyer and scholar, labored indefatigably for the national idea. Another Pennsylvania delegate, Robert Morris, had the national viewpoint and experience in public affairs; but he took no part in the discussions in the Convention. The three delegates from Connecticut—Johnson, Sherman, and Ellsworth—were men of very high caliber; and to the list of alert and able delegates we should add Paterson of New Jersey, Dickinson of Delaware, Randolph of Virginia, and the two Pinckneys of South Carolina. Probably half of the delegates were just average men

[4] Pierce's notes, *Am. Hist. Rev.* (1898), III, 331.

who could contribute little to the work of the Convention, although some of these voted with the constructive statesmen on important questions before that body.[5]

Character of the delegates. A number of the delegates were owners of considerable property[6] and had the very natural conservative leanings of their class. Nearly all of them had had considerable experience in both private and public affairs, an experience quite likely to banish radical political and economic ideas even from the tenets of enthusiastic reformers. Furthermore, this experience had made men who were naturally practical more practical, leaving little room for theories and dogmas on government. They had "lived a long time" during the critical and momentous years following 1775. They had seen the Declaration of Independence signed, its main purpose served; and now they saw some of their fellow citizens interpreting it too literally, and even thinking darkly and speaking threateningly about private property. They were dismayed at the possibilities suggested by Shays's Rebellion; they had seen enough of the "levelling spirit." The greater number of the delegates still professed to be believers in democracy, but in a democracy restrained by law, and a government with power to enforce the law. The men of 1776 had torn down the old structure—an essential performance in establishing our national existence; and now the Convention delegates, meeting in the same city, in the very same building, were to erect the new structure—a task infinitely more difficult. Very naturally, the Constitution they drafted contained no radical pronouncements on liberty; its purpose, declared in its Preamble, was to "*secure* the blessings of liberty," to "insure domestic tranquillity," and to "establish justice," through the medium of "a more perfect union." This purpose the framers were able to achieve while, at the same time, they established a government more democratic than any of its contemporaries.

The Virginia Plan. When the time set for the Convention arrived, only a few of the delegates had appeared, and some days passed before a quorum was present. The delegates who arrived on time were those who advocated a strong government, and they spent the days before the Convention could be formally opened in very important preliminary discussions as to how their aim could best be achieved. Consequently, on May 29, just four days after the Convention met for the first time, the Virginians, led by Madison but using Randolph as a spokesman, presented a plan, taken

[5] McLaughlin, *op. cit.*, pp. 184 ff.

[6] See C. A. Beard, *Economic Interpretation of the Constitution* (1913), for a full discussion of the delegates' private interests and an estimate of the extent to which these interests influenced their work in the Convention. For a severe criticism of Beard's analysis, see the review of his book by E. S. Corwin, *History Teacher's Magazine* (1914), V, 65–66.

as a basis for the work of the Convention, that contained a number of important features later given place in the Constitution.

ITS PROVISIONS. The Virginia resolutions [7] called for representation in a bicameral legislative body either in proportion to the amount of money contributed by the states to the national government or to the number of free inhabitants in the states, "as the one or the other way may seem best in different cases." They stated that election to membership in the first branch of the national legislature should be by the people, and that the members of the first branch should choose the members of the second branch. This national legislature was to have all the powers the Confederation Congress held; other powers which the states were incompetent to exercise; the authority to negative state laws contravening national laws; and the power to use the armed force of the union against any state which failed in its obligations to that union. The resolutions declared for a national executive, to be chosen by the national legislature, who should "receive punctually" a fixed compensation, whose duties should be to execute the laws and act with some members of the national judiciary as a council of revision on legislative matters. This plan also called for a national judiciary with limited jurisdiction, but included among its powers the right to try suits in which foreigners were interested and all cases of impeachment. The resolutions stated further that state officers should take an oath to support the union; that the United States should guarantee the republican form of government to each state; and that new states should be admitted to the union by less than a unanimous vote of the national legislature. The sort of union thus proposed meant a great deal more than an amendment to the Articles of Confederation. It was no "temporizing expedient," but looked to the establishment of a strong national government.

ITS PROGRESS IN THE CONVENTION. The plan for a national government as proposed by the Virginia delegation was the basis of discussion in the Convention for several weeks. Its main features were acceptable to the majority of the state delegations, although the provision for coercing the states was not preserved; for even its author, Madison, thought that "the use of force against a state, would look more like a declaration of war, than an infliction of punishment" [8] and hoped that a better method of enforcing national authority would be found. The delegates of a minority of the states—New York,[9] New Jersey, Delaware, and Maryland—were

[7] J. Elliot, *The Debates . . . on the Federal Constitution*, I, 143–145.

[8] Elliot, *Debates*, V, 140.

[9] The New York delegates, Hamilton excepted, held essentially the same views as the delegates from the small states. It is interesting to note also that New York was not the most populous state in 1787.

not in favor of so firm a union, and in their opposition to the principle of representation in proportion to free inhabitants or to funds contributed to the national government they were joined by the Connecticut delegates. These delegates were rather slow in formulating a plan of their own; but, on June 15, Paterson of New Jersey introduced a plan of union that represented the ideas of the greater number of the small-state delegates.

The New Jersey Plan. The New Jersey Plan [10] was "purely federal" in character, offering important amendments to the Articles of Confederation, but leaving the states in their position of equality in the matter of representation. By the scheme proposed, Congress would have the authority to levy duties on imports, to regulate commerce, and to make requisitions on the states for money and direct its collection in case a state should not pay. There was to be, in addition to Congress, a plural executive and a judiciary. The most important proposal of the New Jersey Plan was that all acts of Congress and all treaties made and ratified under the authority of the United States "shall be the supreme law of the respective states." In this proposal the Convention later found the method by which national authority could be enforced without resorting to the cumbersome and dangerous method of coercing the states. The advocates of the New Jersey Plan probably did not see the significance of this part of their scheme of government, for they advocated that the federal executive be authorized to use force against states opposing or preventing the operation of federal laws.

The compromises in the Constitution. The large states wished to establish a new government, whereas the small states wished to remodel the old. The battle between them was primarily on the question of representation: the large-state delegates contended earnestly, cogently, and sometimes acrimoniously for proportionate representation as set forth by the Virginia Plan; while the small-state delegates used every resource at their command for the principle of equal representation. When the Virginia proposal on representation was accepted for the first legislative body, the Southern states, naturally desiring as many representatives as possible, wanted the slaves counted as part of the population. Other states, having few slaves, did not want them counted. The commercial states wanted to give Congress considerable power over commerce, but the agricultural states were afraid Congress would levy export duties on their products. Then, there was the question of the slave trade: the majority of the delegates were ready to abolish it—some of them were eager to do so—but the spokesmen of North Carolina, South Carolina, and Georgia, supported by some of the

10 Elliot, *Debates*, I, 175–177.

New England delegates whose fellow citizens were profiting by the slave trade, took a firm stand on the "right to import slaves."

Clearly, if the Convention was to accomplish any useful purpose, these differences between the large states and the small states, between the commercial states and the agricultural states, between the slave states and the states in which there were few slaves, and between the states which wanted to stop the importation of slaves and those which wished it continued, had to be compromised. Had the delegates been a body of theorists, each group in the Convention would have insisted upon the correctness and morality of its position and would have made no compromises; then there would have been recriminations, the Convention would have broken up in disorder, and the situation in our country would have been hopeless. Some of the delegates did leave the Convention because they could not endorse its proposals; but nearly all of the statesmen remained, spoke their minds freely and sometimes heatedly, compromised on numerous points in the end, and brought forth the Constitution.

1. THE CONNECTICUT COMPROMISE. Over the question of representation in Congress, the debate went on and on, with the discussion apparently leading nowhere. Wilson, speaking vehemently for proportionate representation, asked the small-state men if one hundred fifty citizens of Pennsylvania were required to balance fifty citizens of New Jersey;[11] while Martin wearisomely argued that "the corner stone of a federal government is equality of votes,"[12] and Franklin urged the Convention to implore "the assistance of Heaven." Franklin's solemn proposal was not followed for fear this tardy action would arouse suspicion on the outside that there was dissension among the delegates.[13] Finally, the Connecticut delegates, who wanted a strong government but who were determined to secure some recognition of the states, came forward with very able arguments in support of a plan for representation in proportion to the population of the states in the first branch of Congress and equal representation in the second branch. The large-state delegates, seeing no other solution of the problem, accepted the scheme reluctantly and with misgivings; but, just the same, the most stubborn difficulty the Convention encountered was removed. This compromise had been previously proposed; but because of the fact that the Connecticut delegates were chiefly responsible for its adoption, it is frequently called the "Connecticut compromise."

2. THE SLAVE THREE FIFTHS OF A MAN. As to the vexing question of how to count the slaves in determining a state's quota of representatives in the first branch of Congress, the delegates agreed that each slave should be

[11] Madison, *Writings* (Hunt's ed.), III, 135.
[12] Elliot, *Debates,* I, 454.
[13] *Ibid.,* V, 254.

counted as three fifths of a man.   This solution of the problem had been
proposed by Congress several years before in its recommendation to the
states on the subject of the apportionment of the revenue.[14]   Nothing came
of it at the time; but now it was brought out and accepted as a compromise
between counting the slave one or zero, both in fixing the quota of representatives and in apportioning the direct taxes among the states.   In speaking of the illogic of this arrangement, Wilson pointed out that, if the slaves
were people, then they should be counted as such; if property, then other
property should be counted in making the apportionment.   He admitted,
however, and expressed the practical opinions of his colleagues in doing
so, that compromise was the only solution for such difficulties.[15]

3. THE REGULATION OF COMMERCE.   The interests of the Eastern and
Southern states may not have been "as different as the interests of Russia
and Turkey," as Butler put it; [16] yet essential differences were clearly revealed as the delegates tried to arrive at an agreement on the regulation
of commerce.   Mason of Virginia said that the Southern states would be
in a minority in both houses of Congress, and it was feared that the commercial states of the East would discriminate against the agricultural states
of the South.   One Eastern delegate stated frankly, but no doubt with
exaggeration, that the sole motive for union in that section was a commercial one.[17]   As a result of these differences, Congress was given the
very necessary power to regulate commerce and lay duties on imports; but
the authority to lay export duties was denied in order to placate the Southerners, who feared that this power would be used to give Eastern merchants
a monopoly on their staples.

4. THE SLAVE TRADE.   An important phase of the commerce question had
to do with the importation of slaves.   Many members of the Convention
thought that Congress should have the power to prohibit their importation.   Madison was opposed to an admission in the Constitution "that
there could be property in men." [18]   Mason, the owner of many slaves,
spoke earnestly against the system, declaring that it robbed labor of dignity,
discouraged arts and manufactures, made every master a petty tyrant.   To
him the slave trade was a "nefarious traffic," and he regretted that the
merchants of the Northeast had been drawn to it "from a lust of gain." [19]
But the states south of Virginia insisted that their economic development
depended upon the importation of more slaves.   The New England delegates were equally insistent that a simple majority of Congress be em-

[14] Elliot, *Debates,* I, 95.
[15] Madison, *Writings* (Hunt's ed.), III, 407.
[16] Madison, *op. cit.,* IV, 329.
[17] McLaughlin, *op. cit.,* p. 262.
[18] Madison, *Writings* (Hunt's ed.), IV, 306.
[19] *Ibid.,* 265, 267.

powered to pass navigation acts and that the two-thirds requirement in the preliminary draft of the Constitution be stricken out. The states of the far South supported New England's demand in return for New England's support of a provision permitting the slave trade to continue until 1808.[20]

A government over men and not over states. It will be recalled that the Articles of Confederation provided for a government with no authority over individuals, and that Congress could do little more than make requests of the states. As the work of the Convention progressed, the idea was clearly developed that the national government should have direct control over individuals and not be dependent upon the states in any way. There were to be two governments: a national government, with certain powers it would exercise quite independent of the states; and the states, independent of the nation, to be left to exercise the many powers remaining to them. The important point to note is that Congress would make laws on subjects of national competence which would apply to individuals; that national courts would interpret and apply these laws to individuals; and that a national executive would back the other arms of the government by seeing to it that individuals observed the laws. This arrangement meant that the national government would be a government worthy of the name; that it could levy taxes on individuals and enforce payment; that it could compel men to do military service when necessary; that it could try in its own courts individuals who violated its laws. It was no longer necessary to talk about coercing states; that cumbersome blunderbuss was dropped with sighs of satisfaction because a better method had been found.[21]

The law of the land. But what was to be done in case a state should pass a law in contravention to the national Constitution or laws? An early proposal was that the national authorities be given the right to veto such laws. This was discarded as impracticable and contrary to the general principles of the Constitution as they were being worked out. The New Jersey proposition with regard to the binding effect of national laws was now brought forward and unanimously adopted. The clause in its finished form reads: "This Constitution, and the laws of the United States which shall be made in pursuance thereof; and all treaties made, or which shall be made, under the authority of the United States, shall be the supreme law of the land; and the Judges in every State shall be bound thereby, anything in the Constitution or laws of any State to the contrary notwithstanding." [22] Thus the Constitution was made a law binding upon

[20] On the compromises discussed above and on others not mentioned see Farrand, *op. cit.*, Chs. VII, X, XI.

[21] McLaughlin, *op. cit.*, pp. 241 ff.

[22] Art. VI, sec. II.

state judges, a law they must enforce in their own court rooms, even as against conflicting laws of their own state. The next clause of the Constitution provides that all officers, both of the nation and the states, shall take an oath to support the "supreme law." The decisions to apply national laws to individuals and to establish the Constitution as law, binding on all officers, were among the most important decisions of the Convention, for without these arrangements it is not likely that the government would have long survived.[23]

Other work of the Convention. Only a few of the more important questions before the Convention have been considered. The delegates agreed readily that there should be a national judiciary, but there was some difficulty in securing an agreement relative to inferior federal courts. Some said that the state courts could serve as such courts; others feared to trust the state courts. The result was another compromise. It was agreed that Congress should not be *required* but only *permitted* to establish inferior federal courts.[24]

Another problem that sorely perplexed the Convention was that of determining how the President should be chosen. Provision was made for choice by electors, each state to have electors equal to the number of its representatives and senators in Congress—a point won by the large states. But in the event no candidate received the vote of a majority of the electors, then the House of Representatives should proceed to elect the President, the delegation from each state having one vote. The agreement that the vote in the House should be by states was a concession to the small states.

The Convention had still other perplexing problems to decide. What powers should be given to the executive, legislative, and judicial departments? What should be the relation of these departments? What obligations should the central government assume for the states? What restrictions should be placed upon the states? Just how these and other points were decided by the Convention will appear in following chapters that explain the Constitution in some detail.

The attitude of the delegates toward their creation. The delegates probably had no idea that the Constitution they drafted would have such permanence; that it would be venerated by millions of Americans a century and a half later. The majority of the members could feel only that the Convention had done its best under the circumstances and that the country should ratify the Constitution they proposed. To those who hesitated to sign the instrument because of its defects, as they saw them, Franklin told a humorous story of a French lady who said she never met

[23] McLaughlin, *op. cit.,* pp. 245 ff.
[24] Farrand, *op. cit.,* pp. 79–80.

anyone but herself who was always in the right. As for himself, he admitted that he had often had cause to question his own judgment and to change his opinion on important matters. "I confess," said he, "that there are several parts of this Constitution which I do not at present approve, but I am not sure I shall never approve them. . . . I cannot help expressing a wish that every member of the Convention, who may still have objections to it, would with me, on this occasion, doubt a little of his own infallibility, and, to make manifest our unanimity, put his name to this instrument." [25] All except three of the delegates present signed. The Convention gave the appearance of unanimity by adopting a resolution drawn up by Gouverneur Morris and proposed by Franklin: "Done in Convention by the unanimous consent of *the states* present." [26]

Doctor Franklin sees the sun rise. As the thirty-nine hopeful delegates were putting their signatures to the Constitution, "Dr. Franklin, looking towards the president's chair, at the back of which a rising sun happened to be painted, observed to a few members near him, that painters had found it difficult to distinguish, in their art, a rising from a setting sun. 'I have,' said he, 'often and often, in the course of the session, and the vicissitudes of my hopes and fears as to its issue, looked at that behind the president, without being able to tell whether it was rising or setting; but now, at length, I have the happiness to know that it is a rising, and not a setting sun.'" [27]

Distinctive features of the Constitution. The Constitution that saw the light of day at Philadelphia had certain distinctive, if general, features that may well be emphasized at this point. (1) The work of the delegates was so well done that the Constitution has survived to this day and is the oldest written constitution in the world. It has stood the test of time because it was made by wise and practical men to meet particular needs, and because these men made it sufficiently flexible to meet new conditions. (2) It is one of the briefest of all constitutions in operation at the present time. The seven articles of the American instrument, establishing the three departments of government and outlining their powers, fixing the position of the states, decreeing national supremacy, providing for amendments, and prescribing the method of ratification by the thirteen original states, cover scarcely a dozen pages. (3) Although a pedant might criticize the arrangement of material in the Constitution, it stands as one of the best written of all instruments of government. The fact that there have been numerous heated disputes and almost innumerable litigations over the meaning of a number of its provisions is due much more to the im-

[25] Elliot, *Debates*, V, 554–555.

[26] *Ibid.*, 555.

[27] Elliot, *Debates*, V, 565.

portance of the Constitution—to the fact that it touches so many phases of our economic and social life—than to possible defects in its composition. (4) Certain intentional omissions of the framers should receive notice. Did the states retain sovereignty? The Constitution gave no clear answer. Could a state secede from the Union? Only an ardent nationalist could find in the Constitution an unmistakably negative answer to this question. The framers avoided pronouncements on these points because they felt sure that denials of state sovereignty would ruin the prospects of ratification by the states. These questions were settled by the Civil War. (5) Finally, the Constitution contained very little that can be characterized as new. Practically all of its provisions were drawn from English laws and practice, colonial experience, state constitutions adopted during the Revolution, the Articles of Confederation, and so on.[28] Indeed, the language of the Constitution cannot be understood except by reference to the sources of the document. For example, the Constitution specifies that trials shall be by jury. But the Constitution does not define "trial by jury." We must look to British and American practice in 1789 to learn that trial by jury meant a trial by a jury of *twelve* men, under the direction of a judge, and a unanimous verdict.

II. THE ADOPTION OF THE CONSTITUTION

Submission of the Constitution to the states. With the "salvation of the republic" at stake, the framers had not hesitated to go beyond their powers. They had been called to propose amendments to the Articles of Confederation, but in the Convention hall they worked a quiet revolution, devising an entirely different plan of government. They paid no attention to that provision of the Articles which specified that amendments could be made only by the consent of the legislatures of all the states; but they boldly presented their Constitution carrying the provision that when it had been ratified by conventions chosen by the people in as many as nine states it should go into effect between the states so ratifying. The framers believed that conventions were more likely to pass affirmatively upon their handiwork than were the legislatures, and they were determined that a few sovereign-conscious states should not prevent the majority from securing "the blessings of liberty" under the Constitution. The proposed Constitution, containing these important provisions for its ratification, was sent by the Convention to the Confederation Congress. It received a cool reception in that body; but after some discussion it was transmitted, without favorable comment, to the states for action by the state conventions.

[28] W. B. Munro, *The Government of the United States* (1946 ed.), pp. 63–64.

Ratification of the Constitution by the states. Some of the states were prompt in ratifying the Constitution, but Virginia ratified only after a bitter fight against it led by the Revolutionary orator Patrick Henry. Without New York, the Union could hardly be expected to prosper, and the opposition in that state was very determined. Hamilton, Madison, and Jay wrote articles which were signed "Publius," and gave them to the leading newspapers of the state in the hope that the public could be brought to accept the Constitution after reading a systematic exposition of it. These campaign documents, known collectively as *The Federalist,* were written in haste, but this did not impair their quality. The authors stated the case for the Constitution vigorously, clearly, and convincingly. We sometimes speak ironically of campaign "literature" in our day, but *The Federalist* is a classic and the term "literature" suffers no violence in being applied to it. Although the popular vote in New York was against ratification, the state convention, earnestly importuned by Hamilton, Jay, and Livingston, and influenced by the fact that ten states had decided for the Union, gave the Constitution a narrow margin in July, 1788. In November, 1789, a few months after the new government had been organized, North Carolina came into the Union. The hope that the "inconsiderate people" of Rhode Island would not "fill up the measure of Iniquity" was fulfilled when that state ratified in May, 1790.[29]

III. AMENDING THE CONSTITUTION [30]

The amending clause of the Constitution. Article V provides that "the Congress, whenever two thirds of both houses shall deem it necessary, shall propose amendments to this Constitution, or, on the application of the legislatures of two thirds of the several states, shall call a convention for proposing amendments, which in either case shall be valid to all intents and purposes as part of this Constitution, when ratified by the legislatures of three fourths of the several states, or by conventions in three fourths thereof, as the one or the other mode of ratification may be proposed by the Congress . . . provided that no State, without its consent, shall be deprived of its equal suffrage in the Senate." It will be noticed that the framers threw aside the unanimity rule which applied to amendments to the Articles of Confederation, and that the supposedly "unamendable" provision with regard to equal representation in the Senate rendered the amending clause less objectionable to the smaller states.

SOME LEGAL QUESTIONS. From the above-quoted provision for amend-

---

[29] A. J. Beveridge, *The Life of John Marshall* (1919), I, 319–480; A. C. McLaughlin, *A Constitutional History of the United States* (1935), Ch. XV.

[30] R. E. Cushman, *Leading Constitutional Decisions* (1950 ed.), pp. 1–8.

ment it is clear that amendments may be brought about by four different combinations of procedure: (1) proposal by Congress and ratification by state legislatures; (2) proposal by Congress and ratification by state conventions; (3) proposal by a national convention and ratification by state legislatures; and (4) proposal by national convention and ratification by state conventions. In practice, however, except in the case of the Prohibition Repeal proposal of 1933, only one method has ever been used—proposal by two thirds of both Houses of Congress and ratification by the legislatures of three fourths of the states.

Certain legal questions have been raised in connection with this process. (1) Does two thirds of both Houses mean two thirds of the entire membership or just two thirds of a quorum? In 1920 the Eighteenth Amendment was attacked because the vote for it in the House of Representatives was less than two thirds of the membership of that body. The Court held that the affirmative vote of two thirds of a quorum met the requirement of the Constitution.[31]

(2) Does the President have the authority to veto a proposal for amendment submitted by Congress? This question was answered in the negative very early in our national history.[32] The Constitution gives the President no part in the amending process. Executive vetoes extend only to legislation. In proposing an amendment to the Constitution, Congress is not legislating but is exercising what is called a constituent power.

(3) How long does a proposal for an amendment "stand"? It stands until ratified by three fourths of the states. Of course, it may never be ratified by the requisite majority; but, technically, it is a standing proposal from Congress to the states. A state may reject the proposal and later reconsider and ratify. In Coleman v. Miller [33] the specific question was: Could the Legislature of Kansas, having rejected the Child Labor Amendment in 1925, ratify it in 1937? The Supreme Court of the United States held that the effect of the previous rejection upon the later ratification was a political question, and therefore a question not for the Court but for the Congress to answer. Since Congress had taken no action concerning the reversal of the Kansas Legislature, it can be assumed that the legislative change of heart met with the approval of Congress. If, however, Congress desires to place a time limit on its proposals to the states, it may do so. As a part of the Eighteenth, Twentieth, Twenty-first, and Twenty-second Amendments Congress submitted a clause that would make them inoperative if they were not ratified by the states within seven years.

[31] National Prohibition Cases, 253 U.S. 350 (1920).
[32] Hollingsworth v. Va., 3 Dallas 378 (1798).
[33] 307 U.S. 433 (1939).

The Supreme Court declared this limitation valid.[34] Further, in Coleman v. Miller, noted above, the Court strongly intimated that Congress had the power to declare dead, because of the passage of time or changed conditions, an unratified proposal in which Congress, at the time of presenting it, had not specified the number of years the states might have to ratify it.

(4) May a state having ratified an amendment rescind its action, provided three fourths of the states have not ratified? The answer is "No." Ohio and New Jersey attempted to rescind their approval of the Fourteenth Amendment, and they were answered by a concurrent resolution of Congress binding them to their previous ratification. Many years later (we must refer once more to Coleman v. Miller) the Court seemed of the opinion that Congress had acted quite within the sphere of its authority in its action concerning these two states. In other words, the Supreme Court is content to designate as political, and therefore within the power of Congress to determine, the question of the validity of a state ratification, whether the question is one of the validity of a ratification after an earlier rejection or of the validity of an attempt to withdraw a previous ratification.

Attempts to give the ratification process a more popular basis. In 1918 the voters of Ohio ratified an amendment to the constitution of that state that purported to give the people of the state a "referendum on the action of the general assembly ratifying any proposed amendment to the Constitution of the United States." The Supreme Court of the United States held that the process of ratification of amendments was limited to the two methods prescribed in the Constitution, viz., to ratification by state legislatures or by state conventions, and that the action of Ohio in attempting to prescribe a third method was contrary to this provision of the Constitution.[35] However, there could be no objection on constitutional grounds to giving the people of the states an "advisory referendum" on the question of the ratification of a proposed amendment to the federal Constitution. This method has been employed in some states.[36] Tennessee attempted to give the people a more direct voice in the ratification of an amendment to the national Constitution by inserting in her own constitution a provision that no legislature should act on a proposed amendment to the national instrument unless elected after the proposal was submitted. But the Supreme Court held that the states had no au-

---

[34] Dillon v. Gloss, 256 U.S. 358 (1921).

[35] Hawke v. Smith, 253 U.S. 221 (1920).

[36] See W. A. Robinson, "Advisory Referendum in Massachusetts . . . ," *Am. Pol. Sci. Rev.* (1925), XIX, 69–73.

thority to limit the ratification process in this way.[37] Here, as in the case of Ohio, we must observe that states can accomplish by informal action the purpose attempted by Tennessee. All that is necessary is that there be a "gentlemen's agreement" among members of state legislatures that they will take no action on a proposed amendment unless elected after the proposal is submitted.

The amending process alleged to be undemocratic. The illustrations just cited add considerable weight to the charge that the method employed in amending the Constitution is undemocratic. Furthermore, it is pointed out that it is mathematically possible for the legislatures of thirteen states, containing less than ten per cent of the population of the country, to defeat an amendment that is acceptable to thirty-five states containing more than ninety per cent of the inhabitants. On the other hand, it is possible for thirty-six states, with about one half the total population, to secure the adoption of an amendment which is opposed by the other half of the population residing in twelve states. This criticism of the system of amendment is not so serious as it might seem, for the sparsely settled states are not formed into a perpetual league against the more populous states or *vice versa*. Then, too, we should bear in mind that amendments are not determined by states alone, but by the states and Congress, in the lower house of which the states are represented in proportion to their population.

Many people have felt that the Congress and the state legislatures are not sufficiently responsive to the public demands for amendments. This, of course, is another phase of the alleged undemocratic character of the process of amendment. Figures are advanced to prove this point: the Sixteenth Amendment was introduced in Congress forty-two times before it was favorably voted upon by two thirds of both houses, and the Seventeenth was voted down one hundred ninety-nine times before it was finally approved and sent to the states for ratification. It took nearly twenty years to get the Income Tax Amendment and more than three quarters of a century to secure the constitutional provision for the direct election of senators. To these figures the other side answers: almost any member of Congress will introduce a proposal for an amendment to satisfy a few voters in his constituency, and a few score premature introductions is no argument against the amending system established by the framers of the Constitution. They answer further that, in recent years, there has been no undue delay in the adoption of amendments.

---

[37] Leser v. Garnett, 258 U.S. 130 (1922). It is possible that, should the questions raised in the Ohio and Tennessee cases be presented again, the Court would hold that they are for Congress, not the Court, to decide. At any rate, in Coleman v. Miller (1939) the Court leaned strongly to the view that the entire ratification process is subject only to the control of Congress.

The democracy of convention ratification. Various proposals have been made looking to a more democratic method of proposing and adopting constitutional amendments, but none of them have aroused general interest. It may be that the great majority of citizens are satisfied with the degree to which democratic participation is possible in the amending process. In 1933, in the case of the Prohibition Repeal Amendment, Congress for the first time designated that ratification should proceed by the state convention method. There was general satisfaction with this plan, and it is probable that Congress will resort to it more in the future. It has an advantage over the legislative method in that the convention delegates are chosen for the sole and specific purpose of passing upon a proposed amendment. Furthermore, in choosing the delegates the people vote for avowed proponents or opponents of the amendment. The result is that the state conventions serve merely to ratify the popular will as expressed in the election of delegates. Thus, for all practical purposes ratification by state conventions is the same thing as ratification by popular referendum.

The twenty-two amendments. Although nearly three thousand amendments have been proposed in Congress, that body has passed favorably upon but twenty-seven, of which number the states have ratified twenty-two. These the student will find printed with any copy of the Constitution as parts thereof (see pages 1024–1030). Discussion of them will occur when we reach the topics to which they relate.

IV. THE CONSTITUTION VITALIZED [38]

The Constitution of the United States consists of much more than the original instrument and its twenty-two amendments. Nearly all countries in this twentieth century have certain parts of their constitutions reduced to writing; but other and very important parts of these constitutions are found in statutes, judicial decisions, executive acts, and customs and practices. In the broader sense a constitution is that set of laws, rules, principles, practices, and understandings which determines the structure of a government, outlines its powers, and fixes the position of the individual in relation to that government.

For convenience we designate our written instrument of government the "Constitution," but its articles and sections and clauses, significant as they are, fall far short of revealing the American constitutional system in

---

[38] R. E. Cushman (ed.), "Ten Years of the Supreme Court: 1937–1947," *Am. Pol. Sci. Rev.,* Dec., 1947, pp. 1142–1181; Feb., 1948, pp. 32–67; C. E. Merriam, *The Written Constitution and the Unwritten Attitude* (1931); W. B. Munro, *The Makers of the Unwritten Constitution* (1930).

its entirety. A person unfamiliar with our plan of government would get a very incomplete understanding of it from a reading of the written Constitution. He would assume that the two Houses of Congress legislated with very little direction from the White House, and he would get not a suspicion of the activities of committees and caucuses. He would consider the presidential electors to be men charged with the very grave responsibility of electing the President, while in fact they are men of straw who register the popular will. He would not get much light on the President's use of the veto power, his war power, and his appointing power. A careful reader of the Constitution might get the impression that there are certain administrative departments, but he would get no information concerning departmental organization and powers, and the fact that the heads of the departments constitute the President's Cabinet would remain a deep secret. The Constitution would tell him very little about our judicial system, and would not inform him that the courts set aside statutes of Congress which in judicial opinion extend beyond constitutional bounds. And what would this stranger reading our written instrument of fundamental law learn of our political parties, their organizations, conventions, and primaries? Obviously he would have to look beyond the written Constitution, as we do, in order to get an adequate conception of the American political system.

Clarification, elaboration, and modification of the Constitution: 1. By statutes. The framers of the Constitution very wisely left many important details of governmental organization to be worked out by Congress and, to some extent, by state legislatures. The number, organization, duties, and relationships of the great executive departments were left to Congress to determine. The Interstate Commerce Commission, the Tariff Commission, and all similar administrative bodies were created by Congress and are not mentioned in the Constitution. The Constitution left the time, place, and manner of choosing members of Congress to the state legislatures and to Congress. The Twelfth Amendment, dealing with the electoral vote, is hardly more important than the act of Congress of 1887, which provides in detail for the counting of that vote and for the settling of disputes incident thereto. The Constitution provides that the presidential electors shall be chosen as the state legislatures may direct; the fact that these legislatures have directed the people to choose them would be regarded almost as a revolution by the framers of the Constitution.

Some acts of Congress occupy as high a place in the public mind as do articles of the Constitution. The repeal of the Missouri Compromise (1854) aroused as much popular protest as would have a resolution of Congress canceling its constitutional obligation to guarantee to every state the republican form of government. By act of Congress the number of judges of the Supreme Court is fixed at nine, and by the same authority that number can be changed at any time; but when, in 1937, the President asked Congress to authorize an increase in the number of judges to fifteen (under certain contingencies), it was discovered that a very large segment of the public regarded the statutory requirement of nine as sacred. If Congress should repeal the civil service laws, a much more violent protest would go up from the public than is heard against such infractions of the Constitution as a failure to reapportion the seats in the House of Representatives following the decennial census. And what would the people's reaction be if the state legislatures should deprive them of their "right" to vote for presidential electors? So firmly is this popular method of choosing a President fixed in our constitutional system that the average citizen does not know that the state legislatures have any authority in the matter; he thinks that the Constitution of the United States gives him the privilege of voting for the President.

2. BY JUDICIAL INTERPRETATION. The courts have played a very conspicuous rôle in developing the Constitution, for the reason that they have been frequently called upon to interpret its meaning. The Constitution delegates certain powers to Congress, the President, and the courts; it places some limitations upon the powers of the states; and it explicitly guarantees a number of rights to individuals. A document that delegates and limits powers and declares specific rights very naturally lends itself at many points to judicial interpretation. The courts in this country have not been slow to assume this task—a matter that is explained in a later chapter. The court having the final word on constitutional questions is, of course, the Supreme Court of the United States.

a. By the courts acting with Congress. The courts have gone a long way in helping Congress expand the Constitution. That joint participation has come about in this way. Congress enacts a statute on a new subject, or acts upon an old subject in a new way. Some interested party will very likely contest the validity of this statute in court. The court usually sustains the act of Congress and lays down the principles on which it is sustained. Acting under the principle thus announced, Congress will pass other statutes still further extending its powers. These, in turn, will probably be upheld by the Supreme Court, which, at the same time, may announce additional principles, broadening the meaning of the Constitution. And thus the Constitution is expanded and developed "from precedent to precedent" by Congress and the Supreme Court. A few examples of this expansion are given in the next chapter, under the title "implied powers of the national government."

But let no one suppose that the Court has always been ready to join Congress in a project to expand the Constitution. Our highest judicial tribunal has placed its veto upon an act of Congress levying an income tax, an act taxing employers of child labor, the National Industrial Recovery Act, an Agricultural Adjustment Act, and some three score other acts of Congress. In none of these cases was the Court giving the Constitution a broader meaning. There were always distinguished authorities on constitutional law who insisted that the Court gave the Constitution an unduly restrictive interpretation in a few of these cases. For example, Professor Edward S. Corwin in his *The Commerce Power versus States Rights* (1936) attacked with clarity and vigor judicial decisions that narrowly interpreted the power of Congress to regulate interstate commerce, maintaining that such decisions gave the Constitution a narrow meaning never intended by its framers. Since 1937, however, the Supreme Court has almost invariably gone along with Congress in a broader interpretation of the Constitution.[39]

b. By independent action of the courts. The action of the courts is not always dependent upon initial action by Congress. The courts may interpret and expand (or contract) parts of the Constitution on which Congress has little or no authority to legislate. One example will illustrate this point. The Constitution forbids the states to pass any law impairing the obligation of contracts. This restriction does not give Congress the authority to legislate on contracts, but it does give the federal courts jurisdiction over cases arising under this clause. In 1769 Dartmouth College was chartered by the English Crown. Some forty years later, the state legislature of New Hampshire passed a law changing the charter of the college. Up to that time few people had thought of a charter of a college as a contract; but the Supreme Court, speaking through Chief Justice Marshall, held that such charters are contracts.[40] By the rule laid down in this decision charters of business corporations became contracts that would be protected by the federal courts against interference on the part of state legislatures.

3. BY EXECUTIVE ACTION. All of our great Presidents have given meaning to the Constitution; some have shaped it with vigor and gusto. The first President naturally fixed his stamp upon our system of government. Our policy of neutrality proclaimed by him was changed but little until the rise of Hitler. And who does not know that he originated the two-term tradition, which remained unbroken until 1940? Jefferson had scruples concerning the constitutionality of the Louisiana Purchase, but he closed the deal, thus establishing a precedent. Jackson developed the veto and the removal powers, being the first President to use them freely;

---

[39] Cushman, *op. cit.* See especially articles in the symposium by David Fellman and Vincent M. Barnett, Jr., at pp. 1142 and 1170 respectively.

[40] Dartmouth College v. Woodward, 4 Wheat. 518 (1819).

and his vigorous action against Nullification in South Carolina furnished Lincoln with an example for dealing with recalcitrant states. Theodore Roosevelt interpreted the executive powers liberally, and Lincoln, Wilson, and Franklin D. Roosevelt, not without the approval of Congress, developed the President's war powers.

4. BY CUSTOM AND USAGE. Our Constitution is made a living instrument, adaptable to the needs of successive generations, not only through its expansion and modification by the specific acts of those charged with the responsibility of government but also by the play of social and economic forces, the march of time, and even by accidents. The President's Cabinet —not mentioned in the Constitution and almost an accident in its origin— is a product of the years. The Constitution gives the President the power, "by and with the advice and consent of the Senate," to appoint various officers; but, as we shall learn in due time, practical politics has led to almost as many different interpretations of this power as there are different offices to be filled. The Constitution, except in its provision for impeachment, makes no mention of methods by which misfits may be removed from office. That process has been worked out by trial and error, by time and custom, and only in 1935 can it be said that the Supreme Court spoke something approximating the final word on the subject. The strength of precedent was well illustrated by the opposition in many quarters to a third term for President Franklin D. Roosevelt and perhaps still better illustrated by his abandonment, in the face of popular disapproval, of his plan to have the nation celebrate Thanksgiving one week earlier. He won his third term (and his fourth) for the Presidency but lost his third Thursday for Thanksgiving!

Political parties have made revolutionary changes in the system as outlined by the Constitution. The President's power has grown primarily through his position as party leader—a position that frequently enables him to play the dominant rôle in legislation and to win an organized support for his policies throughout the country. Although aggressive Chief Executives would have lifted the office of President above the minimum stipulations of the Constitution in any case, no doubt can exist that party leadership has made his position increasingly powerful. The organization and the procedure of Congress are shaped largely by the exigencies of party politics. Parties have made the caucuses, the conventions, the primaries— institutions that have so much to do with the process of government, that are, in fact, parts of any realistic picture of government.

Slavery profoundly influenced the interpretation of the Constitution, produced a constitutional crisis, and precipitated the Civil War. Complete legal freedom was granted to the Negro by three constitutional amendments; but so strong was (and is) tradition against the legal equality thus guaranteed that even today the solemn words of the Constitution, particularly those of the Fourteenth and Fifteenth Amendments, are only partially effective in those states in which the Negro was once a slave. The Eighteenth Amendment prohibited the transportation and sale of alcoholic beverages. It developed that the beverage habits of many of the people and hostility on the part of others to the principle of Prohibition were stronger than the Eighteenth Amendment. Its failure led to its repeal. We may conclude, then, that usage has shaped our constitutional system hardly less than statutes of Congress and judicial decision; and further, that even the words of the written Constitution may not prevail against tradition, time, and habit.

5. BY CHANGING CONDITIONS. Some years ago Chief Justice Hughes stated, "While emergency does not create power, emergency may furnish the occasion for the exercise of power." [41] To put it concretely, war does not create the war powers of the national government, but calls for the exercise of war powers long ago delegated by the Constitution to the national government. Chief Justice Hughes' statement is completely accurate if we consider the question only in the legal sense. But, as a practical matter, we may suggest that emergency powers exercised on one occasion will be more naturally and fully exercised in the next crisis. It requires no profound thinking to arrive at the conclusion that the war power would not be what it is if we had not had three major wars in the last hundred years, or that the emergency powers which the national government exercised during the last economic crisis will not be the more quickly and fully resorted to when a new crisis arises. In other words, if we reason from the lines of the Constitution, we may follow Chief Justice Hughes; if we consider the practical effect of emergencies, the possibilities of developing a power through use, we may not follow him.

Walter F. Dodd makes the point that national power under the Constitution has also been expanded by the development of transportation and communication, thus bringing under the control of the national government innumerable transactions in interstate and foreign commerce. The same authority emphasizes the significance of the rapid "development of social and economic problems which require a national as distinct from a state solution." [42] Here again it might be claimed that such developments do not create power, but the fact that they do call for the exercise of powers, even though they already exist, certainly makes those powers actualities.

"The Living Constitution." "The Constitution of the United States is not a mere lawyer's document," said Woodrow Wilson: "it is a vehicle of

[41] Home Building and Loan Asso. v. Blaisdell, 290 U.S. 398 (1934).
[42] *Cases and Materials on Constitutional Law* (1949 ed.), p. 435, note.

life, and its spirit is always the spirit of the age." It might be argued that this scholar was stating his ideal rather than a fact. Yet during the greater part of our history that ideal has been measurably attained. Even those who are concerned only with the written instrument must admit that its meaning is changing somewhat from time to time. There are few who will not agree that "due process of law," for example, has quite a different meaning today from what it had a hundred years ago. Judicial decisions, acts of the President and Congress, declarations of political parties, and even public opinion, change the meaning of the Constitution. Statutes of Congress are giving the Constitution a wider scope; practices and habits are changing it imperceptibly from year to year but quite perceptibly from generation to generation. The Constitution is changing and must change to meet the demands of the time. Naïve indeed is the American who imagines that the Constitution of his country is finished and immutable; fortunate is the country that such a Constitution exists only in the imagination of ignorant or simple-minded persons.

Reading List

C. A. Beard, *An Economic Interpretation of the Constitution* (1913).

A. J. Beveridge, *The Life of John Marshall,* 4 vols. (1919).

Irving Brant, *James Madison: Father of the Constitution, 1787–1800* (1950).

J. Bryce, *American Commonwealth* (1913 ed.), Vol. I, Chs. XXIII, XXXI–XXXV.

E. S. Corwin, *Constitutional Revolution* (1941).

R. E. Cushman, *Leading Constitutional Decisions* (1950 ed.), pp. 1–8.

———, (ed.), "Ten Years of the Supreme Court: 1937–1947," *Am. Pol. Sci. Rev.,* Dec., 1947, pp. 1142–1181 and Feb., 1948, pp. 32–67.

J. Elliot, *Debates in the Several State Conventions on the Adoption of the Federal Constitution . . .* 5 vols. (2nd ed., 1891).

M. Farrand, *The Fathers of the Constitution* (1919).

———, *The Framing of the Constitution* (1913).

———, (ed.), *The Records of the Federal Convention,* 4 vols. (1937 ed.).

B. J. Hendrick, *Bulwark of the Republic: A Biography of the Constitution* (1937).

H. C. Hockett, *The Constitutional History of the United States* (1939).

H. W. Horwill, *The Usages of the American Constitution* (1925).

E. Latham (ed.), *The Declaration of Independence and the Constitution* (1949).

B. Long, *The Genesis of the Constitution of the United States* (1925).

W. MacDonald, *A New Constitution for a New America* (1921).

J. M. Mathews and C. A. Berdahl, *Documents and Readings in American Government* (1940 ed.), Ch. II.

H. L. McBain, *The Living Constitution* (1927), Ch. I.

A. C. McLaughlin, *The Confederation and the Constitution* (1905), Chs. XII–XVII.

———, *A Constitutional History of the United States* (1935), Chs. XIV–XVIII.

C. E. Merriam, *The Written Constitution and the Unwritten Attitude* (1931).

W. B. Munro, *The Makers of the Unwritten Constitution* (1930).

D. P. Myers, *The Process of Constitutional Amendments* (76:3, S. Doc. No. 314), Nov. 29, 1940.

C. Read (ed.), *The Constitution Reconsidered* (1938).

C. E. Stevens, *Sources of the Constitution of the United States* (1894).

C. B. Swisher, *American Constitutional Development* (1943).

———, *The Growth of Constitutional Power in the United States* (1946).

C. Van Doren, *The Great Rehearsal: the Story of the Making and Ratifying of the Constitution of the United States* (1948).

Questions and Problems

1. Write a critical discussion of this statement: *No constitution is either wholly written or unwritten.*
2. Write an essay on the framers of the Constitution.
3. Leaving Madison with the qualities he possessed and adding to them those of Franklin, what additional information would we probably find in Madison's notes on the Convention?
4. Compare and contrast the Virginia and New Jersey Plans.
5. Discuss the compromises of the Philadelphia Convention.
6. Did the delegates in their attitude toward the Constitution they had drafted give us a guide to a healthy attitude toward it for our own time?
7. Can it be said that the Constitution has been changed much more by informal than by formal amendment?
8. Discuss Woodrow Wilson's comment: "The Constitution . . . is a vehicle of life, and its spirit is always the spirit of the age."

☆ 3 ☆

The Distribution of Governmental Powers

ALTHOUGH effective government must have a high degree of unity, the powers of government must be distributed both territorially (among the national government and smaller divisions) and functionally (among the several branches—executive, legislative, and judicial). This chapter is designed to show how this distribution is effected in the American system.

I. TERRITORIAL DISTRIBUTION OF POWERS [1]

Two types of government: UNITARY GOVERNMENTS. In all countries the powers of government are territorially divided; that is to say, the central governments exercise certain powers, and local governments exercise certain other powers. If the central government has the authority to alter, change, or abolish the local government units, we say that the country has the *unitary* type of government. France and England are examples of this type of government. France has her local government areas—the départments, arrondissements, cantons, and communes; but the national government may do with them as it sees fit at any time. In like manner the central government in England has complete authority over counties, cities, and other districts of local government. Such local areas are neces-

[1] James Bryce, *The American Commonwealth* (1913 ed.), Vol. 1, Chs. XXVII–XXX; R. E. Cushman, *Leading Constitutional Decisions* (1950 ed.), 9–35; David Fellman, "Federalism," in "Ten Years of the Supreme Court: 1937–1947" (R. E. Cushman, ed.), *Am. Pol. Sci. Rev.*, Dec. 1947, pp. 1142–1160, and "Postwar American Federalism," in T. C. T. McCormick, *Problems of the Postwar World* (1945), Ch. VIII; R. G. Gettell, *Political Science* (1949 ed.), Ch. XIV; H. L. McBain, *The Living Constitution* (1927), Ch. II; W. F. Willoughby, *The Government of Modern States* (1936), Chs. XII–XIII; W. W. Willoughby, *Principles of the Constitutional Law of the United States* (1930 ed.), Chs. IV–X.

sary for the proper administration of government, but they exist only under the authority of the central governments.

FEDERAL GOVERNMENTS. If the local government units of a country have powers independent of the national government, if the constitution of the country establishes them as entities and protects them from possible encroachments of the central authority, then we say that the country has a *federal* system of government. To this class belong the United States, Canada, Switzerland, and a number of other countries. The states in the United States, the provinces in Canada, and the cantons in Switzerland have powers independent of the national governments of those countries. The degree of independence these local units enjoy is, to borrow a word from Professor McBain,[2] "frozen" into the constitutions of the respective countries.

Advantages and disadvantages of the federal plan. Publicists have written learnedly about the advantages and disadvantages of the federal scheme of government. Its advocates, among whom are numbered Montesquieu, John Fiske, and Lord Bryce, assert that it makes possible the union of commonwealths with somewhat dissimilar backgrounds and interests into a powerful state; and that these commonwealths, while retaining their local autonomy, secure the advantage of protection, commerce, and other services that a strong government is able to offer. They claim further that this distribution of powers between the nation and the commonwealths prevents the rise of a single despotism, and that the people are thus able to protect their liberties. The commonwealths, being left to themselves in local affairs, serve as training schools in self-government. Experiments that the nation would hesitate to attempt may be worked out in the local field, as has been demonstrated in the United States, notably in North Dakota.

On the other hand, many regard the federal system as cumbersome and complex, as lacking necessary unity, as likely to be too rigid and, therefore, too slow in adapting itself to the needs of the time. Furthermore, the advantages claimed for local autonomy under the federal system may be had under the unitary system, if the central government prefers to be liberal with the local units, as is the case in England.[3]

SIMILARITIES OF UNITARY AND FEDERAL GOVERNMENTS. The difference between federal and unitary governments is more in fiction than in fact. Unitary England with her omnipotent Parliament cannot abolish the counties and boroughs as very active units of government—the people would not stand for it. Congress and the courts in the federal United States do quietly assume powers for the nation that the states formerly

[2] *Op. cit.*, p. 34.
[3] Gettell, *op. cit.*, pp. 237 ff.

exercised, and only a few authorities hold that the liberties of the people are in danger. Finally, the tendency is away from federalism in all countries that have started with that type of government.[4]

Reasons for adoption of federal plan by the United States. The statesmen at Philadelphia in 1787 did not adopt the federal system of government because they considered it superior to the unitary model. They established the federal system because it was the only type their countrymen would accept. Here were thirteen practically independent states who had, under the stress of war, entered a league of friendship; but with the conclusion of peace they became increasingly jealous of the "sovereignty, freedom, and independence" they had retained under the Articles of Confederation. Obviously, the only sort of government they would accept was one that delegated a few powers to a central body and left the others to the states—a federal government. And it may be appropriate to add that when the nations of the world, or any group of them, unite to form an effective government (the UN is not) they will be impelled, as were the American states and for the same reasons, to organize a federal system of government.

Powers delegated to the national government. The Constitution delegates certain powers to the national government. All other powers, subject to certain exceptions and limitations to be noted later, are left to the states; and to make this more certain the Tenth Amendment stipulates that "powers not delegated to the United States by the Constitution, nor prohibited by it to the states, are reserved to the states respectively, or to the people." The central government's powers are chiefly enumerated in Article I, section VIII, of the Constitution. Included among them are the powers to tax, borrow money, coin money and regulate its value, declare war, maintain armies and a navy, regulate interstate and foreign commerce, control foreign relations, and establish post offices. In addition to these and a few other specific powers, Congress is given the authority "to make all laws which shall be necessary and proper for carrying into execution the foregoing powers, and all other powers vested by this Constitution in the government of the United States, or in any department or officer thereof." [5]

Implied powers of the national government. Over the meaning of the clause just quoted, one of the greatest of political controversies was almost immediately started. Did the clause mean that Congress could pass only those laws that were absolutely necessary for carrying into execution its

---

[4] McBain, *op. cit.,* pp. 36–37. For a discussion of recent developments in the United States *see* W. B. Graves, "What Is Happening to Our Federal System?" *State Government,* Nov., 1949, pp. 255–259, 270.

[5] Art. I, sec. VIII, cl. 18.

enumerated powers? Jefferson and his followers, who placed a strict construction upon the powers of Congress, vigorously affirmed that it did. Hamilton and his fellow nationalists liberally construed the powers of Congress and said that Congress might pass any laws which in its judgment were proper for carrying into execution those powers expressly granted to it. They cogently argued that Congress, having been given the power to legislate for specified *ends,* was authorized by the clause in question to use any *means* not prohibited by the Constitution for accomplishing those ends; that by implication Congress was authorized to use its discretion in passing laws which would give it the most effective control over the important matters submitted by the Constitution to its charge. In vain the Jefferson crowd pointed out that such an interpretation of the Constitution would give the national government almost unlimited power and would lead to encroachment upon the powers reserved to the states. The nationalists, or Federalists, as they are commonly called, had their way, and under this doctrine of "implied powers" chartered the First Bank of the United States in 1791.

McCULLOCH v. MARYLAND. The charter of the Bank expired in 1811 without its constitutionality ever having been tested in court. The Second Bank of the United States was chartered in 1816, and it very quickly incurred the enmity of large sections of the country as a "money trust" and what not. Eight states passed laws restricting the activities of the Bank in various ways. Maryland placed a heavy tax upon the notes of all banks not chartered by the state. The cashier of the branch Bank of the United States in Baltimore, McCulloch, refused to pay the tax, and the State of Maryland sought to recover the penalties prescribed for nonpayment. When the case came to the Supreme Court of the United States, it was argued for nine days by six of the ablest American lawyers.[6]

Chief Justice Marshall's decision. The decision in this case is probably the ablest of all opinions delivered by John Marshall, America's greatest Chief Justice. In answering the question, "Has Congress the power to incorporate a bank?" he stated that "the government of the Union, though limited in its powers, is supreme within its sphere of action." "Although, among the enumerated powers of government," he continued, "we do not find the word 'bank' or 'incorporation,' we find the great powers to lay and collect taxes; to borrow money; to regulate commerce; to declare and conduct war; and to raise and support armies and navies. . . . It may, with great reason, be contended, that a government, intrusted with such ample powers, on the due execution of which the happiness and prosperity of the nation so vitally depends, must also be intrusted with ample means for their

[6] Cushman, *op. cit.,* p. 10, note.

execution. The power being given, it is the interest of the nation to facilitate its execution. It can never be their interest, and cannot be presumed to have been their intention, to clog and embarrass its execution by withholding the most appropriate means." He goes on to say that the Constitution "does not profess to enumerate the means by which the powers it confers may be exercised; nor does it prohibit the creation of a corporation, if the existence of such a being be essential to the beneficial exercise of those powers. . . . We think the sound construction of the Constitution must allow to the national legislature that discretion, with respect to the means by which the powers it confers are to be carried into execution, which will enable that body to perform the high duties assigned to it, in the manner most beneficial to the people. Let the end be legitimate, let it be within the scope of the Constitution, and all means which are appropriate, which are plainly adapted to that end, which are not prohibited, but consistent with the letter and spirit of the Constitution, are constitutional."

Significance of the decision. In holding that the Congress might charter a corporation—in this case a bank—as a means of facilitating the execution of her express powers with regard to revenues, the post office, war, and other matters, Chief Justice Marshall gave the highest judicial sanction to a principle of constitutional construction that has been of incalculable value in expanding the powers of the national government. Without the acceptance of this principle, it is difficult to see how we could have developed into a strong nation. We have noticed that very strong arguments were made against the doctrine of implied powers, and we cannot say that they did violence to the actual words of the Constitution; but had this opposing interpretation of national powers prevailed, we would have been turned back toward the Confederation and the national government might have come to be helpless and contemptible under certain contingencies. At any rate, the doctrine is firmly fixed in our constitutional system, and it was given the widest application under the New Deal. It is a matter of particular interest that the New Dealers based the constitutionality of their legislation upon the reasoning of Hamilton and Marshall, authorities almost invariably cited by conservatives.

ILLUSTRATIONS OF IMPLIED POWERS. Exercising its implied powers, Congress has established postal savings banks as one of the means of exercising its delegated financial powers; it has created such parks as the Gettysburg Park, presumably as a means of carrying its war power into execution; it has excluded objectionable matter from the mails as a means of carrying into execution its postal power; it has made paper money legal tender as a part of its power to borrow money; it has even aided the federal banks (a means) in their competition with state banks by giving the former the authority to execute wills; and in almost innumerable other ways has turned to good advantage the theory so ably expounded by Marshall.[7] The layman has some difficulty at times in finding the particular delegated power that is served by an act of Congress that is supposed to be a means of carrying it into execution; but he should avoid the common error of assuming that under implied powers Congress may do anything it pleases. Congress cannot pass a uniform marriage and divorce law, a general law regulating the incorporation of cities, a law limiting state debts, or laws relating to a wide variety of other subjects, and it cannot do so because there is no clause in the Constitution from which the power to take such action can be implied.

Powers of the states. Although the national government has acquired by a liberal construction of the Constitution a great many powers that our forefathers probably had no idea it would ever possess, there is no truth in the assertion commonly made that the states have practically no powers left. The nation has those powers that are delegated to it and those that are fairly implied from those delegated; the states have all other powers except those few that they are prohibited from exercising. The powers of the states are largely inherent and undefined. Because the Constitution deals almost entirely with national powers and because its powers over foreign relations and war furnish a great deal of the drama of government, we are likely to forget the great number of important powers left to the states. The states have the power to tax; to borrow money; to make and administer our great bodies of civil and criminal law; to exercise very wide powers in connection with the health, safety, and well-being of their inhabitants; to establish schools and supervise education; to charter and control corporations; to make practically all of the suffrage and election laws; to administer charities and correction; to regulate trade within the state; and to make all rules and regulations respecting local government. This recital by no means exhausts the list of the powers of the states, but it is sufficient to show that they are comprehensive and important.

State government close to the individual. Despite the rapid growth of the powers of the national government in the last fifty years, the individual still has much more contact with his state and local government. His state government is with him from the cradle to the grave. It issues his birth certificate and his burial permit; and between the Alpha and Omega of his mortal existence it protects his rights, penalizes his delinquencies, and regulates his conduct in various ways. If he goes hunting, it is under state authority. If he gets married, he must have a state license. If he

---

[7] Some authorities refer to a particular type of implied power as a "resulting power," defining it as a power that is not implied from any particular clause of the Constitution but that may be inferred from a number of clauses grouped together.

is divorced, it is by a decree of the state court. Before he enters a profession, he must satisfy the state that he is competent. The reader may continue the enumeration!

Exclusive powers of the national and state governments. The greater number of the national government's powers are exclusive. Its powers over war and peace, treaty making, foreign commerce, coinage, and naturalization are examples of this. Certain powers of the states are exclusive also. The laws relating to wills, torts, domestic relations, and the like, are exclusively state laws. The same is true of our ordinary criminal law, although the national government prescribes penalties for those who violate its postal laws, its laws regulating interstate commerce, and so on.

Concurrent powers. Over some matters the states and the nation have concurrent powers. Obviously, both must have the power to tax and to borrow money. Then the states are permitted to exercise certain powers that are delegated to Congress, provided the states exercised these powers before 1789, and provided further that their continued exercise of them does not conflict with acts of Congress on those subjects. Thus, although the Constitution gives Congress the power to regulate interstate commerce, the states are permitted, in the absence of Congressional legislation, to enact measures that touch the current, and sometimes actually retard the flow, of interstate commerce. The clearest illustration of concurrent powers was found in the exceptional provision of the Prohibition Amendment, the enforcement clause of which read: "The Congress and the several states shall have concurrent power to enforce this article by appropriate legislation."

The limits of governmental powers: 1. ON THE NATIONAL GOVERNMENT. The English government has no legal limits; its limits are moral and physical only. In contrast to the English, we have very definite legal limits both on the national government and on the states. The national government is limited not only by the fact that it is a government of delegated powers, but also by a number of express prohibitions. These prohibitions are found in certain parts of the original Constitution, but chiefly in the first ten amendments. To mention only a few, the national authorities are forbidden to abridge the freedom of speech or of the press; to establish a religion or prohibit the free exercise thereof; to deny the right of trial by jury; to deprive any person of life, liberty, or property without due process of law; to pass any bill of attainder or *ex post facto* law.

2. ON THE STATES. The federal Constitution restricts the states by addressing to them a number of prohibitions. The states are prohibited from entering into treaties and alliances and from exercising certain other political powers that would obstruct and embarrass the central government in conducting its affairs. More important, perhaps, the Constitution places them under a number of prohibitions concerning personal and property rights. As examples of these, we cite the prohibitions against any state's passing bills of attainder, *ex post facto* laws, or laws impairing the obligation of contracts. Especially important is a provision of the Fourteenth Amendment that no state shall deprive any person of life, liberty, or property, without due process of law.

The foregoing makes clear that certain provisions of the federal Constitution impose restrictions upon the national government, that certain *other* provisions impose restrictions upon the states, and that some of these restrictions are identical, for instance, the prohibition of *ex post facto* laws.

3. POWERS RESERVED TO THE STATES AND TO THE PEOPLE. By the terms of the Tenth Amendment, "the powers not delegated to the United States by the Constitution, nor prohibited by it to the states, are reserved to the states respectively, or to the people." This provision was designed to make certain that the national government would not draw unto itself powers not granted to it. Some thirty years ago, the Supreme Court of the United States became so concerned over what it conceived to be the tendency of the national government to encroach upon the powers reserved to the states that it evolved a rather novel theory to protect them— the theory that the national government could not exercise the powers delegated to it in such a manner as to curtail the powers reserved to the states. For example, in the case of Hammer v. Dagenhart [8] the Court, in holding that Congress had not the power to exclude the articles of child labor from interstate commerce, gave as one of its reasons the fact that such exclusion would result in restrictions on the employment of children in factories, a condition with which only the states had the power to deal. To the layman and to a number of authorities on constitutional law, it seemed that the Court had said, in effect, that a power *delegated* to the national government may at the same time be *reserved* to the states, or at least limited because of the powers reserved to them. In 1941 the Supreme Court in a far-reaching decision said that the Dagenhart case "should be and now is overruled." It stated further that the Tenth Amendment does not deprive "the national government of authority to resort to all means for the exercise of a granted power which are appropriate and plainly adapted to the permitted end." [9] We are thus brought back to Chief Justice John Marshall's broad interpretation of national power.

May a subject not delegated to the control of the national government, and one not reserved for the control of the states, be dealt with by Congress? The Supreme Court answers "No," explaining that a matter not within

[8] 247 U.S. 251 (1918).
[9] United States v. Darby, 312 U.S. 100 (1941).

the regulatory authority of either the states or the nation is reserved by the provisions of the Tenth Amendment to "the people" of the United States.[10] Of course, if the people desire to do so, they may amend the Constitution, giving Congress authority over the matter in question. It should be added, however, that amendments are usually unnecessary, for a broad construction of delegated powers, a construction now followed more than ever by the Supreme Court, has the result of giving Congress the authority to take practically any action the national well-being seems to require.[11]

Supremacy of national authority. It has been shown that the Constitution establishes a federal system of government by delegating certain powers to the national government and by reserving other powers to the states. In a sense, the states are supreme in their sphere of activity, just as the national government is supreme in its sphere. But there is a difference. The Constitution, acts of Congress in pursuance thereof, and treaties are the supreme law. The national authorities, final decision usually resting with the Supreme Court, themselves determine their powers under the Constitution. But the states cannot determine the extent of their powers; they must accept the decision of national officers on these points. For example, Congress passes an act regulating commerce. Interested parties may contest the constitutionality of the act in the federal courts, arguing that it invades the states' province of government, but the decision of the Supreme Court settles the matter. On the other hand, when a state legislature enacts a measure, it is subject to review not only by its co-ordinate branch, the state courts, but it may also be carried to the Supreme Court of the United States. Thus, in conflicts of authority—and they are numerous—between the state and national governments, the national government is the judge—the judge in its own case. What, then, becomes of our theory that the national government has only delegated powers and those fairly implied from the powers delegated? Would it not be possible for Congress to enact, the Supreme Court to sustain, and the President to enforce, any law whatsoever, however much it might exceed the powers granted the national government? Theoretically, this possibility exists, and it must be admitted that the national powers have been considerably expanded already; but it can hardly be demonstrated that they have been expanded arbitrarily. The Supreme Court decisions, in particular, have often preserved the rights of the states, and not a whit less significantly in our own time than in earlier periods.[12] But, whether exercised with or without restraint, the power of the national government to judge its own

10 Kansas v. Colorado, 206 U.S. 46 (1906).
11 W. F. Dodd, *Cases and Materials on Constitutional Law* (1949 ed.), p. 441, note.
12 David Fellman, *Am. Pol. Sci. Rev.*, Dec., 1947, pp. 1145–1147.

competence as well as that of the states gives ample justification for the use of the term "national supremacy."

Means of maintaining national supremacy.   Supremacy of national authority is maintained through the authority of Congress to pass all laws necessary for promoting the activities of the central government; through the authority of the President to see that the laws are faithfully executed; and through the federal courts, whose power extends to all cases in law and equity arising under the Constitution, laws, and treaties.   The power of the federal courts to declare invalid state laws that conflict with national authority is of particular importance in this connection.   A complete explanation of the system by which supremacy is maintained would require considerable space and involve us in technicalities.   A few illustrations will serve the purpose better.

1. STATES MAY NOT TAX NATIONAL AGENCIES.   In the first part of this chapter (page 42) we learned that the state of Maryland attempted to tax the Baltimore branch of the Bank of the United States.   At that point we reviewed that part of the decision in which the authority of Congress to charter the bank was upheld.   Here we shall consider the part in which the act of the legislature of Maryland, taxing the bank, was held void. The Constitution does not expressly prohibit the states from taxing such agencies of the national government.   But Chief Justice Marshall, speaking for a unanimous Court, said that the power to tax was the power to destroy; and that, if the states may tax one instrument of the national government, they may tax any and every other instrument "to an excess which would defeat all the ends of [the national] government."   As an "unavoidable consequence of the supremacy which the Constitution has declared," he denied that the states had any power, "by taxation, or otherwise, to retard, impede, burden, or in any manner to control the operations" of the national government in carrying into execution the powers granted to it by the Constitution.[13]   Thus the states may not, even in the exercise of the very highest "reserve" power of taxation, interfere with the operation of a convenient, much less a necessary, agency of the national government.   But the rule is applied to both state and national governments.   The Supreme Court has held that Congress may not tax state governmental agencies.

2. STATES MAY NOT INTERFERE WITH NATIONAL OFFICERS.   Many years ago a federal revenue officer in Tennessee, in the discharge of his duty, killed a man and claimed it was done in self-defense.   He was indicted for murder by the state authorities and held for trial in the state courts.   But by the provisions of a statute of Congress, upheld by the Supreme Court of the United States, such cases were to be tried in federal courts.   Consequently,

[13] McCulloch v. Maryland, 4 Wheat. 316 (1819).

the federal revenue officer was able to have his case removed from the Tennessee court and tried in the federal district court.[14]

A case of much greater significance is that of Neagle, a deputy marshal of the United States in California. He had been assigned by the Attorney General, acting for the President, to protect Mr. Justice Field, whose life was threatened by a lawyer who was enraged at the judge because of an adverse decision. Finding the judge in a railroad restaurant, the would-be-murderer was about to draw his revolver; but Neagle acted more quickly and shot him dead. Neagle was arrested by California authorities and indicted for murder. He was then released upon a writ of *habeas corpus* by the federal circuit court. There was no statute of Congress that clearly authorized the sort of duty Neagle was performing in protecting Judge Field, but the Supreme Court held that the authority of the President to see that the laws of the United States were faithfully executed was sufficient authorization for Neagle's appointment to protect the judge. Said Justice Miller in giving the Court's decision: "It would be a great reproach to the system of government of the United States . . . if there is to be found within the domain of its powers no means of protecting the judges in the conscientious and faithful discharge of their duties, from the malice and hatred of those upon whom their judgments may operate unfavorably." [15]

3. STATES MAY NOT INTERFERE WITH THE TRANSPORTATION OF MAIL. Another illustration of national supremacy is found in the prosaic activity of transporting the mail. The State of Maryland passed a law requiring drivers of motor vehicles to pass an examination demonstrating their competence and to pay a license fee of three dollars. A driver of a mail truck over the post road from Mt. Airy, Maryland, to Washington, was arrested by Maryland authorities for not having complied with the provisions of this law. The Supreme Court of the United States held that the application of the requirements of the Maryland driver's license law to an employee of the Post Office Department was an unwarranted interference with the transportation of the mails, for "it lays hold" of government servants "in their specific attempts to obey orders, and requires qualifications in addition to those that the government" of the United States has deemed sufficient.[16] However, the Supreme Court might permit a state law against reckless driving to be applied to a driver of a mail truck, as the states are allowed considerable leeway in protecting the safety of their inhabitants. Indeed, in 1817, a high constable of Philadelphia was held not guilty of obstructing the mails when he stopped a mail stage

---

[14] Tennessee v. Davis, 100 U.S. 257 (1880).
[15] *In re* Neagle, 135 U.S. 1 (1890).
[16] Johnson v. Maryland, 254 U.S. 51 (1920).

"going very rapidly through Market Street . . . at a rate of eight or nine miles an hour." [17]

President Cleveland sees that the laws are "faithfully executed." When a great strike of railway employees obstructed the transportation of the mails in the vicinity of Chicago in 1894, and when Governor Altgeld, who sympathized with the strikers, would do nothing, President Cleveland sent troops to guard the mail trains and to keep open the channels of interstate commerce. Despite the severe criticism of this action by the friends of organized labor and by others who were opposed to the use of federal troops in such disturbances unless state authorities had requested the national government to intervene, the President was undoubtedly acting within his power to execute faithfully the laws of the United States.

II. FUNCTIONAL DISTRIBUTION OF POWERS [18]

The three main branches of government. Just as the powers of government are territorially divided, so are they divided according to functions. We commonly divide the work of government among the legislative, executive, and judicial branches. Many authorities, particularly French jurists, consider the judicial power as a part of the executive power and years ago F. J. Goodnow propounded a somewhat similar view; [19] another American scholar [20] added the electoral and administrative functions to the three with which every school boy is familiar. Neither of these views should be lightly put aside; but American constitutions, both national and state, follow the traditional threefold functional division of powers into legislative, executive, and judicial departments; and that method is, therefore, best adapted to the purpose of the following discussion.

Types of executive-legislative relationships: PARLIAMENTARY GOVERNMENT. In those countries in which the executive department is controlled by the legislative branch, the government is said to be *parliamentary*. England, the members of the (British) Commonwealth of Nations, and nearly all of the democracies of Continental Europe have this system. In these, the executive departments are conducted by "cabinets" or "ministries" under a more or less active control of the legislative bodies. Almost invariably the officers of the executive branch are members of one of the legislative bodies. They hold office only as long as they have the confidence of a majority in the more popular branch of the parliament. Obviously parliament is supreme in such governments and the executive department is

17 United States v. Hart, 1 Peters (U.S. Cir. Ct.), 390 (1817); Cushman, *op. cit.,* p. 21, note.
18 *The Federalist,* XLVII–LI; Gettell, *op. cit.,* Ch. XIII; W. F. Willoughby, *Government of Modern States* (1936), Chs. XIV–XV.
19 *Politics and Administration* (1900), Chs. I–II.
20 W. F. Willoughby, *op. cit.*

conducted by an executive committee or cabinet composed of members of the parliament.

PRESIDENTIAL GOVERNMENT. The parliamentary system had not been fully developed in England when our state and national constitutions were being made, nor did the Americans fully understand it as it was then operating. Furthermore, constitution-makers in America wanted checks placed on each department of government in order to prevent governmental tyranny, and conservative men wished to devise a plan of political organization that would secure private property from hasty action of legislative bodies. It was but natural, then, that the "Fathers" should cast about for a new system.

In the middle of the eighteenth century Montesquieu had written that liberty could be found only where the powers of government were distributed among the legislative, executive, and judicial departments, each having a check upon the other two. This doctrine was very influential with the framers of state constitutions during the period of the Revolution. The framers of the federal Constitution accepted it as a practical solution of the problem of the distribution of powers for the national government; and they established the three great departments, with their "checks and balances," forming our *presidential* system. A number of the South American countries have established, in theory at least, somewhat similar systems of government.

The separation of executive, legislative, and judicial powers. The complete separation of executive, legislative, and judicial powers has never prevailed in practice, despite the two-century hold the theory has upon the minds of men. Neither Montesquieu, who first gave the precept classic expression and most effectively recommended it to the attention of Americans, nor the political craftsmen who incorporated it into our constitutions believed that an absolute separation of powers was possible or desirable. In a brilliant article in *The Federalist* (XLVII) Madison demonstrated that the celebrated Montesquieu meant only that there could be no liberty if the *whole* power of one department is exercised by the same hands that possess the *whole* power of another department. Madison showed also that the framers of the state constitutions had not isolated and insulated each department of government in a corner of the governmental triangle. Madison stated in his next article that "unless these departments be so far connected and blended as to give to each a constitutional control over the others, the degree of separation which the maxim requires, as essential to free government, can never in practice be duly maintained." [21]

A number of "connections and blendings" are very definitely provided

[21] *The Federalist*, XLVIII.

for in the Constitution. Here are a few examples: The acts of Congress are made subject to the executive veto. Treaties made by the President must meet the approval of two thirds of the Senate, and his appointments must be submitted to that body for confirmation. Congress determines the appellate jurisdiction of the Supreme Court, and that Court may declare acts of Congress void. Congress has often declared a policy and left to the President or some other administrative authority the duty of promulgating rules and regulations (a legislative power) to carry that policy into effect. In like manner Congress has frequently clothed administrative bodies with powers essentially judicial. There are thousands of pages of regulatory codes promulgated by administrative authorities and so commonly do the same authorities act in a judicial capacity that they determine more civil cases than do all the federal courts.[22] In a realistic view of the total process of government there is such a blending of powers, functions, and duties that the lines separating the three branches all but fade from view. Government might be compared to a machine that functions only when it is in gear with all of its parts synchronized and in motion so that it operates as a unit.

Politics and the separation of powers. In addition to the exceptions noted above, political practice has further modified the principle of a rigid separation of powers. One branch of the government sometimes dominates another. Lincoln used almost dictatorial powers during the Civil War. Congress was in the saddle during Reconstruction days. Theodore Roosevelt occupied the center of the stage during his presidency, and Wilson dominated the scene during his administrations, even before the outbreak of the First World War. During the war he was given and exercised even greater powers than Lincoln had exercised. With the inauguration of Franklin D. Roosevelt, presidential leadership, because of unprecedented crises, reached a peak never before attained in peace time. The entrance of the United States into the Second World War was the signal for further extension of executive power.

In theory, Americans hold to the dogma of the separation of powers, but they trouble themselves little about its application in the conduct of their government. We like to have aggressive Presidents who lead Congress or even force that body to act. Democrats complain of executive usurpation when the Republicans have an occupant of the White House who takes it upon himself to be the chief legislator as well as the chief executive; Republicans, without laughing, make similar charges of presidential autocracy when the aggressive head of the government happens to be a Democrat. The truth is that American party government naturally makes the President

---

[22] Dodd, *op. cit.* (1949 ed.), p. 144 note. In one year (1936) a single department determined more than all the federal courts.

the leader; and, if the Executive relishes or has a capacity for that rôle, he often gains the ascendancy over Congress.

The future of the presidential system. For more than a century and a half the presidential system has served us. This is not conclusive proof of its adequacy. The fixed and overlapping terms of President and congressmen bring about occasional deadlocks between the two branches of government. During the century and more that we had a negative conception of government, a conception expressed in the words "that government is best which governs least," the system gave rather general satisfaction. With the growing demand, indeed with the necessity, for substituting for a government of restraint a government that would provide services, the system displayed certain weaknesses, the chief of which was that there could be no certainty that the executive and legislative branches could unite upon a program of affirmative action. As was shown above, this problem has sometimes been solved by a strong President who with popular backing took the reins. By the use of favors and threats he often succeeded in getting action from Congress. However, the method is extra-constitutional and it is improvised. If Congress will not "go along" with the President, there is nothing to do but wait for the next election. To say the least, a most regrettable situation would be created if, for example, the people and Congress wanted to change leaders in war time and could not do so because the President's term had two more years to run. To put it shortly, under our system of government there is no constitutional means by which the executive and legislative bodies can be brought to unity of action. To date the occasional deadlocks we have suffered have been irritating and embarrassing but none has been fatal. Quite possibly, however, we are no longer able to afford the luxury of a governmental stalemate and should look about for means of preventing one. Further discussion of this topic is undertaken in Chapter 12, section vi, and in Chapter 15, section viii.

III. THE PLACE OF THE JUDICIARY IN THE AMERICAN SYSTEM [23]

The judiciary fills a most important place in our governmental structure. The details of its organization and procedure are reserved for a later chapter, but it is essential to an understanding of the workings of our type of government that a few of the main functions of the judiciary be considered here.

[23] C. A. Beard, *The Supreme Court and the Constitution* (1912); C. G. Haines, *The American Doctrine of Judicial Supremacy* (1932 ed.), and *The Role of the Supreme Court in American Government and Politics* (1944); McBain, *op. cit.,* Ch. VII; A. C. McLaughlin, *A Constitutional History of the United States* (1935), Ch. XXIII.

Basic functions of the courts. In the first place, some authority must exist to draw the line between the powers of the national government and those of the states. The Constitution draws the line in general terms, but these terms are in constant need of interpretation and reinterpretation. Conceivably this function might have been entrusted to some other authority; but the wording of the Constitution, the intention of its framers, and subsequent practice appropriately make it a judicial function. An act of Congress that is alleged to encroach upon the powers reserved to the states or an act of a state legislature that is deemed to be in conflict with a power held by the national government may thus be carried to the federal courts by an interested party on the grounds of unconstitutionality.

In the second place, the courts have the function of preserving the balance among the three branches of the national government. In practice this usually means guarding against encroachments by Congress upon the powers of the other two branches.

In the third place, the federal courts have the function of maintaining private rights. It has been shown that the Constitution lays certain prohibitions upon both Congress and the states; that it guarantees civil rights. Suppose Congress should pass a law abrogating the right of trial by jury, a right granted by the Sixth Amendment. Any person denied trial by jury under this law would have the right to test its validity in a federal court, and he would have no difficulty in having it set aside as unconstitutional. A state law impairing the obligation of a contract, thus violating Article I, section x, of the Constitution, would meet with the same fate in a federal court. More will be said of the guaranty of personal and property rights in Chapter 6, "Civil Liberties." It is sufficient at this point to emphasize that any person may seek redress in the federal courts whenever Congress or the states, wittingly or unwittingly, violate any of the prohibitions laid upon them by the Constitution.

The power of the judiciary to void legislative acts: Its ORIGIN. Clearly the judiciary could not perform the important functions named above without the power to void legislative acts. What is the source of this power of "judicial review"? At the time of the Revolution and after, American thinkers and public men were thoroughly familiar with the theory that a constitution should be a paramount law, a law to govern the government. Furthermore, they had had the none-too-happy experience of seeing the English Privy Council nullify a few of the acts of colonial legislatures as being contrary to the paramount law of the mother country. And, more to the point, before the federal Constitution was framed, several of the state courts had taken it upon themselves to pass upon the constitutionality of acts of state legislatures. In theory and practice, then, there did exist, in

1787, some basis for judicial review. But the federal Constitution does not give the judiciary such authority in express language. It does proclaim, however, that "this Constitution, and all the laws of the United States which shall be made in pursuance thereof; and all treaties made, or which shall be made, under the authority of the United States, shall be the supreme Law of the Land; and the judges in every state shall be bound thereby, anything in the constitution or laws of any state to the contrary notwithstanding." It states also that the judicial power of the federal courts shall extend to all cases arising under the Constitution. But nowhere in the Constitution were the federal courts expressly given the authority to nullify acts of Congress. On the other hand, there is strong evidence that the framers expected the courts to exercise this power. Certainly the Constitution did not state that they should not exercise it, nor did it stipulate that Congress and the state legislatures should be the final judges of their own competence.[24] Chief Justice Marshall, applying judicial logic to the provisions of the Constitution, in the celebrated case of Marbury v. Madison,[25] came out with the conclusion that the courts have the power to pass upon the constitutionality of acts of Congress. His decision was largely political, not one of his judicial masterpieces, and even to this day there are those who are not convinced by his reasoning nor by the logic of the hundreds who support his opinion with additional arguments. To some Americans, a few of whom are learned men, judicial review is still judicial "usurpation." [26]

MARSHALL'S OPINION. The view of Marshall on the power of the courts to void acts of Congress may be summarized as follows: (1) The Constitution is a superior law. (2) A legislative act contrary to the Constitution is, therefore, not a law. (3) It is always the duty of the court to decide between two conflicting laws. (4) If a legislative act conflicts with the superior law, the Constitution, it is clearly the duty of the court to refuse to apply the legislative act. (5) If the court does not refuse to apply such legislation, the foundation of all written constitutions is destroyed. But the Constitution proclaims that all laws made "in pursuance" of it as well as the Constitution itself shall be the supreme law. Why, then, say those who criticize Marshall, should the courts any more than Congress, the lawmaking body, determine when a law is made in pursuance of the Constitution? Marshall said that there would be no purpose to the limits on the powers of government if those limits may be passed by those intended to be restrained. But, of course, he may be answered by the statement that the Supreme Court, in voiding an act of Congress, was going beyond

---

[24] McBain, *op. cit.*, pp. 237 ff.

[25] 1 Cranch 137 (1803).

[26] For a very critical analysis of the explanations of the origins of the power, including Marshall's reasoning, see L. B. Boudin, *Government by Judiciary* (1932), I, 51–66, 531–563.

those very limits to which the Chief Justice referred. The Constitution limits both Congress and the courts. If the courts may void acts of Congress, they are surely superior organs of government and there is no practical limit upon their powers. These and other flaws are found in Marshall's decision; but the right of judicial review as announced in that decision is accepted by the great majority of Americans today as the practical solution of the problem of keeping the national and state governments in their proper spheres and preserving the "checks and balances" in our somewhat complicated political system.[27]

The power of the judiciary to void provisions of state constitutions and laws. The provisions of the "Law of the Land" clause, quoted above, make fairly clear that the framers of the Constitution believed the national as well as the state courts should disregard any part of a state constitution or law that was contrary to the federal Constitution, laws, or treaties. Furthermore, the twenty-fifth section of the Judiciary Act, passed by the First Congress in 1789, provided that the Supreme Court of the United States might review any case in which a state court had upheld a state law alleged to be in conflict with the federal Constitution. The Court early intimated that it would exercise the authority to declare a state law void, although the first clear case of its use was not until 1810.[28] Since then it has been used a great many times.

State courts and judicial review. Judicial tribunals in the states disregard state laws when they are in conflict with the state constitutions; and, as we have seen, they are obligated to declare void provisions of state constitutions and laws that contravene any part of the federal Constitution or laws. As the fear of a strong central government vanished, conservative state courts were not slow to set aside state laws on the alleged ground that they conflicted with national authority. To prevent state judges from using their judicial power to thus void state laws that might conflict with their personal views on social and economic questions, Congress passed a law, in 1914, providing that such cases might be reviewed by the Supreme Court at Washington at its discretion. At the present time, therefore, state laws may be carried to Washington whether state courts sustain or reject the claim that they conflict with provisions of the federal Constitution. It is difficult, however, to get a review of a state law that has been held void by a state court as conflicting with the federal Constitution.[29] This is all that need be said about judicial review at present. Further discussion of its operation and of the conflicts that have raged around

---

27 McBain, *op. cit.*, pp. 240–242.
28 Fletcher v. Peck, 6 Cranch 87 (1810).
29 McBain, *op. cit.*, pp. 249–251.

it may be more appropriately deferred for Chapter 17, "The Federal Judicial System."

Reading List

C. A. Beard, *The Supreme Court and the Constitution* (1912).

J. M. Beck, *The Constitution of the United States* (1924), Chs. XVI–XIX.

A. J. Beveridge, *Life of John Marshall* (1919), Vol. III, Chs. I–III, Vol. IV, Chs. V–VI, VIII.

L. B. Boudin, *Government by Judiciary* (1932).

J. Bryce, *The American Commonwealth* (1913 ed.), Vol. I, Chs. XXV–XXX.

H. S. Commager, *Majority Rule and Minority Rights: A Study in Jeffersonian Democracy and Judicial Review* (1944).

J. A. Corry, *Elements of Democratic Government* (1947), Chs. 2, 14.

E. S. Corwin, *Court over Constitution: A Study of Judicial Review as an Instrument of Popular Government* (1938).

R. E. Cushman, *Leading Constitutional Decisions* (1950 ed.), Ch. II.

The Federalist, Nos. XL–XLVIII.

R. G. Gettell, *Political Science* (1949 ed.), Chs. XIII, XIV, XX.

C. G. Haines, *The American Doctrine of Judicial Supremacy* (1932 ed.).

——, *The Role of the Supreme Court in American Government and Politics, 1789–1835* (1944).

—— and B. M. Haines, *Principles and Problems of Government* (1934 ed.), Chs. VIII, IX, XIII, and XV.

H. J. Laski, *The American Presidency* (1940), Ch. III.

R. Luce, *Congress—An Explanation* (1927), Ch. IV.

H. L. McBain, *The Living Constitution* (1927), Chs. II, IV, V, VII.

A. C. McLaughlin, *A Constitutional History of the United States* (1935), Chs. XVI, XXIII, XXX, XXXIV.

W. M. Meigs, *The Relation of the Judiciary to the Constitution* (1920).

B. F. Moore, *The Supreme Court and Unconstitutional Legislation* (1913).

C. Warren, *Congress, the Supreme Court, and the Constitution* (1936 ed.).

K. C. Wheare, *Federal Government* (1946).

W. F. Willoughby, *Government of Modern States* (1936), Chs. XII–XV.

W. W. Willoughby, *Principles of the Constitutional Law of the United States* (1930 ed.), Chs. II–XII.

Questions and Problems

1. Show that there is no necessary relationship between unitary and parliamentary government; between federal and presidential forms of government.

2. Would the decision of the Supreme Court in the case of McCulloch v. Maryland have been, of necessity, quite different from what it was had there been no "necessary and proper" clause in the Constitution?

3. Make a list of functions still reserved to the states.
4. Make a list of functions the national government has entered upon since 1932.
5. Does an increase in national functions necessarily mean that state functions are decreased?
6. Make a clear statement of what is meant by "national supremacy."
7. Discuss this statement: *The principle of "the separation of powers" is as essential to good government today as it was 175 years ago.*
8. Consider the accuracy of this statement: *Judicial review is entirely an American invention.*
9. Indicate the strength and weakness of Chief Justice Marshall's reasoning in Marbury v. Madison.

☆ 4 ☆

State Constitutions

ALTHOUGH the Constitution of the United States lays some significant limitations [1] upon the states and provides for the essential phases of interstate relations,[2] it makes no specific requirement concerning the form of state government beyond the rather vague one that it shall be republican in character.[3] Each state is thus left essentially free to provide through its own constitution for government of its own choosing, with only one limitation—its constitution shall not violate the federal Constitution or the treaties or laws made under the authority of that instrument.[4] As our present-day state governments had their origin deep in English and colonial laws and practices, it is essential to begin the discussion of state constitutions with a brief sketch of colonial developments. Long ago a wise man said, "We cannot escape history." Certainly no student of government should make the attempt.

I. COLONIAL GOVERNMENT [5]

Different types of colonies. The thirteen colonies were founded at different times, Virginia being the first, in 1607, and Georgia the last, in 1732. Not only did the regions in which the colonists settled differ in climate, terrain, and in other respects, but the settlers themselves differed in background, purpose, and capacity. Moreover, the rights granted the colonies by the British crown also differed, although there was a strong tendency toward uniformity in the later colonial period. Eight of the colonies ultimately became royal colonies, that is, colonies governed by the "royal will and pleasure." Maryland, Pennsylvania, and Delaware continued under

---

[1] See the discussion on this point in this volume, pages 82–90, and Chapter 6, especially in sections IV and V.

[2] Below, pages 93–101. [3] Below, pages 91–93. [4] Ant. VI, 11.

[5] M. W. Jernegan, *The American Colonies* (1929); A. H. Kelley and W. A. Harbison, *The American Constitution* (1948), Chs. 1–2; C. E. Merriam, *A History of American Political Theories* (1903), Ch. I; Gerald W. Johnson, *Our English Heritage* (1949).

their proprietors and were called proprietary colonies. These proprietors
held their grants in a semi-feudal fashion, administering them personally
or through agents, but always under the general supervision of the British
crown. The corporate colonies, Rhode Island and Connecticut, went their
own way for a time under temporary provisions for government that were
very democratic; the "Fundamental Orders of Connecticut" is one of the
great documents of free institutions. Later, both of these colonies received very liberal charters from the king, charters that gave legal sanction
to the forward civil and political views of the founders of those colonies.[6]

Extent of control by the British crown. Each of the thirteen colonies
was allowed a measure of self-government. The extent to which the
colonies regulated their own affairs varied with the terms on which the
crown authorized their establishment, with the interest of the British government in asserting its authority, and with the ability of the king's officers
in restraining colonial legislatures, which were nearly always active in extending the sphere of their own authority. In general, the London government retained the right to revoke or alter the charters (constitutions) of
the colonies that possessed them; to veto, except for Maryland,[7] Rhode
Island, and Connecticut, the laws enacted by their legislative bodies; to
appoint or confirm the appointment of their governors, except in Rhode
Island and Connecticut; and to hear appeals from the colonial courts. It is
hardly necessary to add that no colony was supposed to pass any act contrary
to the laws of Great Britain.

Although there was no question concerning the complete legal authority
of the British government over the American colonies, in the course of
time these colonies came to regard themselves as practically independent
of the mother country in their domestic affairs, and only grudgingly admitted the authority of the British to regulate their external affairs. Facing this attitude, the officers of the crown frequently found it unwise and
sometimes impossible to exercise their authority in the colonies. It may
be said, then, that although Britain had a rather strict control over the
colonies on paper, in practice the colonies often had their own way, even
to the extent of violating orders of the crown or of forcing governors to
break the instructions of the crown.

Authority of the colonial governor. The governor was the most important official in the colonies, although his powers were much more limited
in some colonies than in others. He was the agent of the British crown,
and as such it was his duty to issue all the orders of the crown and see that
they were enforced, to supervise the work of other officers of the crown

---

[6] Jernegan, *op. cit.,* pp. 134 ff., 149–150, 273.

[7] Maryland was supposed to send her laws to England for approval, but this requirement
was seldom obeyed. *Ibid.,* pp. 273–274.

who were located in the colony, and to make reports and recommendations to the government at London. His duties to the colony, as distinguished from those he owed the crown, were very similar to those of our present-day governors. He enforced the laws enacted by the colonial assembly, was empowered to pardon all offenders except murderers and traitors, appointed various officers, was the head of the militia, and acted as official spokesman for the colony. His authority in legislative matters was also similar to but greater than that exercised by state governors in our own day. He convoked assemblies, adjourned them, dissolved them, exercised an absolute veto on their bills, and even appointed the "upper house" in a number of the colonies. As a judicial officer he was the head of the colonial court. In Connecticut and Rhode Island, however, the governors were elected by the assembly, were very definitely responsible to that body, and, therefore, exercised no such wide powers as those named above.[8]

The governor's council. Councils of about a dozen men advised and in some cases, particularly in Rhode Island and Connecticut, directed the governors. In these two colonies the council was elected by the assembly, in Massachusetts by the assembly and the old council; but in the other colonies, council membership was determined by the crown and the governor or proprietors. In addition to giving the governor advice and direction, the council, or individual members of it, assisted the governor in various phases of his administrative work in some such manner as the secretary of state, the treasurer, the auditor, and other executive officers assist in state administration at the present time. The council served with the governor as the highest court in nearly all the colonies; and in all except Pennsylvania, Delaware, and Georgia it sat as the upper house of the legislative body, thus performing the duties now discharged by our state senates. The council, with executive, legislative, and judicial functions to perform, thus defied the "separation of powers" that later came to be such an important theory and principle in American government.

Establishment of representative government. Representative government started early in the colonies. The same year (1619) that twenty slaves were sold by the Dutch to English planters at Jamestown, twenty burgesses met with the governor and his council in the church of that capital city and drew up laws designed to prevent idleness, drunkenness, and gaming; sought to curb the extravagance in dress of those days by taxing wearing apparel; and passed laws for the encouragement of agriculture.[9] In the course of time every colony had an assembly. Only those who possessed considerable property were eligible to the assemblies in the greater number of the colonies, and, in addition, a religious test was usually imposed. The men who voted for assemblymen had to show

[8] Jernegan, *op. cit.*, pp. 273–276.
[9] L. G. Tyler, *England in America* (1904), pp. 79–81.

that they possessed a small amount of real property, and in some colonies they had to show further that they were correct in religion and morals.

In New England the basis of representation was the town, and in other colonies the county was generally used as the unit. At first each area had representation roughly proportional to its population; but, with the growth of settlements in the interior, the inhabitants of these "back-country" districts made frequent complaints against the original apportionments, which left them without their fair share of representation. By denying to these districts the number of representatives to which their population entitled them, the more conservative elements on the seaboard kept the liberals in the back country from getting control of the legislative bodies.[10]

GAIN IN POWER BY THE ASSEMBLIES. In spite of the several undemocratic features of the colonial assemblies as judged by present-day standards, these bodies led in the movement for colonial rights—a movement the ultimate result of which was separation from Great Britain. Through their control of finance, which they early secured, they forced governors, who had the authority on paper to nullify their acts, to do their bidding or find no money appropriated to carry on the government. A governor of New York wrote in 1741: "If a governor will not blindly consent to their bills, however unreasonable or contrary to [the governor's] instructions, they will starve him into compliance." A member of the New Jersey assembly expressed the view of a number of his fellow legislators in these words: "Let us keep the dogs poore, and we'll make them do what we please." [11] The assemblies claimed the right to legislate on all the internal affairs of the colonies and regarded themselves as parliaments. An English officer in Virginia complained in 1703 that "the Assembly conclude themselves entitled to all the rights and privileges of an English Parliament, and begin to search into the records of the honorable house for precedents to govern themselves by." [12]

Significance of the rise of the assembly. Although there is no doubt that some of the assemblymen were crude, self-seeking demagogues who secured their election by means not dissimilar to those employed by their kind in our own day, such qualities did not detract from the fact that they were paving the way for ultimate independence and to some extent fighting the battle for the people. When the governor's council of New York, in 1711, sharply reproved the assembly for not allowing it to amend money bills, a power it claimed as a grant from the crown, the assembly made reply in a spirit that breathed of the free air of '76: " 'Tis true, the share the Council have (if any) in Legislation, (comes) only from the meer Pleasure of the Prince . . . On the contrary, the *inherent Right* the

---

[10] See Jernegan, *op. cit.*, pp. 288–291, for these inequalities.

[11] Quoted, *ibid.*, p. 285.

[12] Quoted, *ibid.*, p. 287.

Assembly have to dispose of the money of the Freemen of this Colony, does not proceed from any commission, Letters Patent or other Grant from the Crown; but from the free Choice and Election of the People: who ought not to be divested of their Property (nor justly can) without their consent." [13]   When the British Parliament, in 1764 and following years, challenged the rights claimed by the colonial assemblies, asserting that it had the power to make all laws for the colonies if it cared to exercise it, the break between the colonies and the mother country was made almost inevitable.

The colonial judiciary.   Law and justice in the colonies followed the English models very closely.   Indeed, the law enforced was for the most part the common law of England.   It was supplemented by those statutes of Parliament that were made applicable to the colonies, and by an increasing number of laws enacted by the local assemblies.   As in England, the justice of the peace was chosen from capable men of wealth who had the respect of the community.   Sitting alone, one of these justices could hear and determine petty cases; sitting in a body, the justices of a county formed an intermediate or county court and heard the greater number of civil cases and criminal cases not involving loss of life or limb.   The sheriff helped them in such matters as summoning juries; and constables made arrests, collected the fines imposed, and administered floggings.

The highest court in a colony was composed of the governor and his council or of a body of judges appointed by the governor.   This court was primarily a court of appeals.   It was not a court of final appeal, however, for cases might be carried from the supreme court of a colony to the Judicial Committee of the Privy Council in London.   Decisions by this body three thousand miles away were frequently no more popular in the colonies than they are in some of the British self-governing colonies today, and in some cases the colonies successfully evaded them.[14]

Local government in the colonies: THE COUNTY.   As the people in a colony extended their settlements beyond the original location, the establishment of local government became necessary.   The Virginia Assembly created counties as early as 1634.   The county was the important unit of local government in the Southern Colonies and to a considerable extent in the Middle Colonies.   County government in these colonies followed the English system very closely.   It is an interesting fact that county government in some of the Southern states today is more like the English practice of the seventeenth century than is the present county system in England. In the counties the justices of the peace were the "statesmen of all work." Their part in the administration of justice has already been mentioned.

[13] Quoted, *ibid.*, pp. 286–287.
[14] *Ibid.*, 77, 277 ff.; J. M. Mathews, *American State Government* (1934 ed.), pp. 387–388.

In addition to their judicial duties, the justices of the peace administered practically all the other affairs of the county. Among their general duties may be mentioned the appointment of a number of officers of the county, the issuing of licenses, the letting of contracts for the construction of roads and bridges, the paying of bounties for the destruction of wild beasts, and the making of the county levies. The counties were divided into parishes governed by a vestry of twelve Anglican gentlemen. The vestry performed various local duties, including the supervision of the churches and the administration of poor relief. There was nothing of democracy in this local government. The justices of the peace and the vestrymen were appointed by the governor, and frequently an individual held several offices. This sort of government was, however, suited to the people and the times, and was reasonably good government.[15]

THE TOWN. The town was the important unit of local government in New England. It was an area of land, usually about forty square miles, granted to a small group of proprietors, who held it in common. The proprietors were entitled to send representatives to the colonial legislative body, and they were allowed very extensive privileges in governing their own town. They levied taxes, elected officers, imposed fines and penalties, made rules for the good order and well-being of the town, and admitted new arrivals to citizenship. The government of these towns in time came to be essentially democratic, in sharp contrast to the system in the Southern counties, where all the important officers were named by the governor.[16] The town meetings, at which practically all matters of political or economic interest were attended to by the citizens in a body, won the praise of the great Virginia democrat, Thomas Jefferson, who saw them as splendid training schools for popular government, as indeed they were.[17]

Democratic tendencies in the colonies. The statement that there was little democracy in the colonies has been made frequently, and it is true in the main. Certainly the Cavaliers, who dominated the Southern Colonies and kept the offices and as many other good things as possible for themselves, were not democratic. Governor Spotswood of Virginia, one of the good colonial governors, was no more democratic than the others, and expressed the strongest disapproval of the growing tendency of the people to choose, as their representatives, persons of small means and low intelligence and those who inflamed the people with talk about the ruin of their liberties. Even William Penn recorded his disapprobation of the rank and file of Americans who were trying to obtain political power and who, having secured some recognition, thought nothing taller than themselves but the trees. The Puritans were very little, if any, more

---

[15] Jernegan, *op. cit.,* pp. 76–78.

[16] *Ibid.,* pp. 166–168.

[17] Merriam, *op. cit.,* pp. 159, 160.

democratic than those who controlled the other colonies. They believed in spiritual equality but not in political equality. They were ready to oppose with vigor the attempts of the British crown to impose its authority over them, but they were not much concerned about the liberties of the individuals in their midst.[18]

There were, however, very definite signs of democracy in the colonies. We have just indicated that New England town government contained democratic features. Rhode Island and Connecticut had liberal governments. The complaints of Spotswood and Penn noted above bear witness to the fact that there was a general movement toward a more popular control of government. The frontier has ever been fertile soil for the growth of democratic ideas, and the back country in the colonies proved no exception to that rule. The people who lived beyond the tidewater were to a considerable degree economically and socially equal, and they very naturally wanted to apply the principle of political equality as well.

The Great Awakening, which began in 1734, was essentially religious in character, but it reached into the whole life of the people. Its appeal was primarily to the inarticulate masses, to whom it gave hope, emotional stimulation, and ideas on political subjects as well as on those of religious and moral import. Opposition to this movement by the conservative and privileged classes had the very natural result of making its followers, the Methodists, Baptists, and Presbyterians, hostile to the aristocratic order, thus furthering the cause of democracy. The individualistic spirit of many of the colonists, their self-reliance, their remoteness from England, and the migration to the colonies of Scotch-Irish, Irish, and Germans were other factors that contributed to the growth of the democratic spirit. In the growing spirit of resistance to what they considered arbitrary government, the colonists found very encouraging examples in such English documents as the Petition of Right, the Grand Remonstrance, and the Bill of Rights.[19]

II. THE FIRST STATE GOVERNMENTS [20]

The separation from England led ultimately, in 1789, to the establishment of our federal system of government. But before this change was completed we passed through a period of transition. During this time the colonial governments became state governments, and a makeshift Continental Congress carried the country nearly through the Revolution and was then succeeded by a government under the Articles of Confederation that kept us in an uncertain national existence until the Constitution was

---

[18] *Ibid.*, pp. 15–16, 23–26, 32–34.
[19] Jernegan, *op. cit.*, pp. 134–135, 271–272, 280–281, 407–412.
[20] A. Nevins, *The American States during and after the Revolution* (1924), Chs. IV, V, X; Merriam, *op. cit.*, pp. 74–95; F. G. Wilson, *The American Political Mind* (1949), Ch. 4.

adopted. But here our discussion will be limited to the establishment of state governments during the Revolution.

Drafting and adoption of the first state constitutions. When the Revolutionary War began in 1775, the colonial governments crumbled one after the other. At first their places were taken by irregular authorities. Later, acting upon the rather vague advice of the Continental Congress of May 15, 1776, that they "adopt such government as shall in the opinion of the representatives of the people, best conduce to the happiness and safety of their constituents in particular, and America in general," [21] the states began to adopt constitutions. Eleven states had new constitutions in operation by 1780. Rhode Island and Connecticut considered their liberal colonial charters good enough for use in statehood.

In drafting their constitutions the statesmen of 1776, except in Massachusetts and New Hampshire, did not follow the method of having them prepared by conventions chosen by the people for that one purpose, as is the practice today. Ordinarily, they had this work done by their assemblies. Nor was the later method of submitting constitutions to the will of the voters commonly employed. Only in Massachusetts and New Hampshire was approval by the people regarded as essential, although in four other states the constitutions were submitted to popular referendum.

Principles embodied in the original constitutions: PROVISIONS FOR AMENDMENT. What were the characteristics of these, our first, state constitutions? Present-day state constitutions make very careful provisions for their amendment, but the framers of the early constitutions did not give this matter a great deal of attention. Five states made no provision for amendments, acting presumably on the theory that the legislatures or conventions would take care of amendments when the need for them arose—in a sense a recognition of the sovereignty of the people. Other states provided for amendment by legislatures, by conventions, or by modifications of these methods.

GUARANTY OF CIVIL RIGHTS. In these early constitutions civil liberties, such as the right of trial by jury, the prohibition of excessive bail, the guaranty against irregular search and seizure, the right of assembly and petition, religious toleration, and various guaranties for the protection of private property, were secured. As a measure of the importance attached to these guaranties, they were given first place in the new political systems.

LIMITATION OF POLITICAL PRIVILEGES TO PROPERTY HOLDERS. Political privileges, however, were not conferred so freely as civil rights were guaranteed. Although the authors of the constitutions denounced through the paragraphs of these instruments the hereditary and aristocratic principle in government, they, nevertheless, kept public affairs in the hands of the

[21] *Journals of the Continental Congress,* IV, 342.

upper classes. In a number of the states the governor was required to show that he possessed landed property to the value of $5,000, or $25,000, and in South Carolina the value was fixed at $50,000. For the lesser offices a smaller estate was satisfactory, and for some offices there was no property qualification. By constitution or by statute enacted in pursuance to the constitution, the makers of our states limited the right to vote to those who held property, although the amount fixed as the qualification was usually not over two or three hundred dollars. Even such men as Franklin held the idea that a man with no property was a very irresponsible citizen and should be denied the ballot.[22]

APPLICATION OF RELIGIOUS TESTS. Although freedom of worship was recognized by the new states, there was no considerable opposition to the governments' imposition of a religious test upon those who held office or upon the voters. Officers were commonly required to be Christians, frequently Protestants. No one could vote in Pennsylvania and South Carolina who did not believe in a future state of rewards and punishments. It might be added that the good people of those days considered the belief in future punishment a much more salutary influence toward political righteousness than the belief in future rewards. Only Protestants could vote in North Carolina and Georgia, and Delaware required its voters to believe in the Trinity and in the inspiration of the Scriptures. Rhode Island, Connecticut, New York, and Virginia made the nearest approaches to absolute religious freedom.[23]

INCONSISTENCY OF THE "FATHERS." Although those who established our first governments are supposed to have subscribed to the doctrine that all men were created equal, they obviously felt that certain modifications of the doctrine should be made in practice. The property qualifications and religious tests they imposed so commonly for officeholding and voting would seem to indicate that they believed in the equality of man as an aspiration for the future, not as a reality for immediate application. As for the Negro in bondage, only a few like Jefferson thought of his condition as otherwise than natural; to the great majority he was not in the picture.[24]

Yet we should not say that the "Fathers" were not democratic. The institutions they were establishing were democratic for their day. We have since gone beyond them and abolished the property qualifications and the greater number of the religious tests, but it is worth while for us to note that Pennsylvania and Tennessee still close their public offices to those who do not believe in a future state of rewards and punishments; that in a half-dozen other states officeholders must believe in God. In

[22] Merriam, *op. cit.*, pp. 84–86.
[23] *Ibid.*, pp. 86–87.
[24] *Ibid.*, pp. 87–88.

1929, a judge in North Carolina, acting under a statute of 1777, stated that a witness's disbelief in a punishing God should lessen the force of her testimony, and added: "If I believed that life ends with death and that there was no *punishment* after death, I would be less apt to tell the truth." [25]

THE FEAR OF STRONG GOVERNMENT. The framers of the first state constitutions regarded government as an unreliable and untrustworthy servant of the people. Government was a necessary evil that must be watched at all times to prevent it from becoming oppressive and destructive of individual liberty. In order to hold government in check it was given the minimum number of powers. Everywhere there was fear of strongly organized central governments.[26] The statesmen of '76 emphasized local government as the unit that would best secure their liberties; they were suspicious of state governments and fearful of a national government.

CHECKS ON GOVERNMENT THROUGH FREQUENT ELECTIONS. The new state constitutions further protected the people from arbitrary government by providing for frequent election of officers. John Adams once said that tyranny begins where annual elections end. Nearly all the state constitutions declared that long continuance in office was dangerous to liberty, and stated the principle of frequent elections and rotation in office as the best means of preventing those in authority from becoming oppressors of the people. In some of the states the annual changes in office were assured by constitutional provisions against officers' succeeding themselves. Despite the likelihood that such provisions will impair the efficiency of the government, a fact of which the patriots were doubtless aware, their first concern was to prevent governments from getting out of bounds.[27]

THE SEPARATION OF POWERS. The principle of separating executive, legislative, and judicial powers was perhaps not thoroughly understood by our statesmen of the Revolutionary period. Nevertheless they usually placed an announcement of that doctrine in their constitutions, seemingly with the idea that by this division of the functions of government the people would be protected from the arbitrary whims of those who held power. Thus, the Massachusetts Constitution of 1780 states that no one of the three departments shall exercise any of the functions of either of the other two, to the end that the government may be one of laws and not of men.

Legislative supremacy in practice. In the actual construction of the framework of the government, however, the powers were not effectively distributed except in New York, Massachusetts, and New Hampshire.[28] During colonial times the governor was the officer against whom com-

[25] *Time,* Oct. 28, 1929.
[26] Merriam, *op. cit.,* pp. 76–78.
[27] *Ibid.,* pp. 82–83.
[28] A. N. Holcombe, *State Government in the United States* (1931 ed.), pp. 54 ff.

plaints of arbitrary conduct were frequently made, while the popular assemblies usually resisted the governor and the English crown and won
the distinction of being the champions of liberty. It was but natural, then,
that the legislatures of the new states should have the confidence of the
people and that the governors should inherit, in the form of grave suspicion, the enmity formerly shown toward the chief executives in the colonies. As we have seen, the legislatures usually made the state constitutions, and they were thus able to take full advantage of the good esteem in
which the people held them. They placed practically no limits upon their
own power. Where the limitations embodied in the bills of rights were
not so vague and general as to be inapplicable to any arm of the government, they applied primarily to the courts and executive officers, seldom
to the legislatures.

SEVERE LIMITATIONS OF THE GOVERNOR'S POWERS. The governor was limited to a very short term of office—only one year in seven states. In all states
except Massachusetts and New York, where he was elected by the people, the governor was chosen by the legislature. Only in Massachusetts
was the governor given the qualified veto power, but in New York he
could exercise that power acting with his council. He had very little of
the influence in connection with legislation that he enjoys today. His
appointing power was severely limited, as were any other powers granted
him. In spite of the limits placed upon the governor, several states took
the rather unnecessary precaution of providing for his impeachment.

FEW CHANGES IN THE JUDICIARY. Few changes were made in the judiciary as the colonies passed into statehood. The law to be applied was
still the common law and equity, and the statutes as enacted by the legislative bodies. The only changes necessary were those that had to do with
the selection and tenure of judges. Judges had been appointed by the
crown. The states provided for their appointment by the chief executives
acting alone or with their councils, or for their selection by legislative bodies.
Georgia alone adopted the method of popular election that has since come
to be one of the generally approved methods of choosing state judges.
Appointment was commonly for short terms, and judges were usually
subject to removal by the legislatures—another manifestation of legislative
supremacy.

Observations on the first state governments. As a conclusion to this
discussion of our early state constitutions, a few observations on the type
of governments established should be made. (1) The elective officers were
not numerous. Legislatures were, of course, elected in all states, and in a
few states important executive officers were elected; but other officers were
chosen by the legislatures or appointed by executive authorities. The idea
that practically all officers should be chosen by the people is a later democratic development. (2) The governments established were representative

in character. Direct government through the use of such instruments of democracy as the referendum and the initiative was not seriously considered. (3) The constitutions were very short, probably averaging less than ten pages, and dealt, for the most part, with fundamentals. State constitutions of our own day, with their many detailed provisions and regulations, frequently cover fifty pages. (4) After making due allowance for English examples and colonial experience, we should still give our early statesmen credit for originality and good common sense for drafting in war time practical schemes of government that served most of the states adequately until the next century was well advanced. For their varying in some instances from liberal democratic theory to conservative practice, we might let them be judged by a practical political standard—"Consistency is the virtue of fools."

III. MODERN CONSTITUTIONAL CONVENTIONS [29]

The discussion in the preceding section makes clear that our first state constitutions were commonly made by legislative assemblies, or by conventions of more or less irregular character. In some states, constitutions may still be made or completely revised by the legislatures; but the common practice is to assign these tasks to conventions chosen by the people for the sole and express purpose of drafting a constitution. The constitutions of about a fourth of the states do not provide for the calling of constitutional conventions; but it is held that, even where the provision is not made, the legislature may take the necessary steps for calling the convention.[30] Since the states, unlike the nation, have not been slow to revise completely their fundamental laws, the number of such conventions has passed well beyond the two hundred mark. Among recent constitutional conventions, we may mention those in Massachusetts (1917–1919), Illinois (1920), Louisiana (1921), Missouri (1943), New York (1938), Rhode Island (1944), New Jersey (1947), and New Hampshire (1948).

Calling the convention. A constitutional convention is called in accordance with provisions of the existing constitution, or by an act of the state legislature. The constitutions of New York and seven other states provide that the people shall vote on the question, "Shall a constitutional convention be called," at regular intervals, varying from seven to twenty

[29] F. G. Bates and O. P. Field, *State Government* as revised by Field, P. S. Sikes, and J. E. Stoner (1949), Ch. 4; J. E. Dovell, *Modernizing State Constitutions* (pamphlet, Public Administration Clearing House, University of Florida, 1950); W. B. Graves, *American State Government* (1946 ed.), Ch. 3; Austin F. Macdonald, *American State Government and Administration* (1950 ed.), Ch. 4. See also article and table by W. B. Graves, "Constitutions," *Book of the States* (1950–1951), pp. 81–95.

[30] In Illinois, Michigan, and several other states it is difficult to call a convention because of the large affirmative vote (a majority of those voting in a general election) required. See *National Municipal Review*, Ed., Nov., 1949.

years. Although the question of a constitutional convention was in no sense a live issue in the campaign, the people of New York voted in 1936 for a convention in 1938.

Selection of delegates. Usually, delegates are chosen from state legislative or senatorial districts. Sometimes a few delegates are chosen at large, that is, by the voters of the entire state. By the latter method it is possible to secure the talent of several outstanding individuals who might live in the same district. In any case, the personnel of a convention is usually somewhat higher than that of the ordinary legislature, for the reason that men who can ill afford to sit regularly in legislative bodies are willing to serve in this important capacity.

Organization and procedure of conventions. A convention, on the average, has around two hundred delegates. Its organization is not unlike that of the typical lower house of a state legislature. The delegates elect a presiding officer and arrange for the various clerks and assistants needed by such bodies. Rules of procedure are adopted, and a number of committees are appointed. Each committee is made responsible for certain parts of the constitution.[31] Committees receive proposals from members of the convention or from individuals outside the convention. They listen to the exhortations and warnings of interested citizens whom they allow to appear before them. From the mass of proposals and suggestions made and from the ideas of its own members, a committee prepares an article or sections of an article, which it presents to the whole body of delegates. Here the proposal is discussed and possibly accepted. It is more likely, however, to be adopted with amendments or returned to the committee for further consideration. This process goes on until at length a constitution is drafted.

Popular ratification of constitutions. Although there are a few exceptions to the rule, the common practice is to refer the work of a convention to the people for their approval. The simplest method of doing this is to submit the whole constitution as a unit and let the voters accept or reject it as such. This method of submission is not altogether satisfactory, for the reason that an instrument containing a few features that do not commend themselves to the voters may result in the defeat of a constitution they would otherwise be pleased to accept. This method proved disastrous to the constitutions submitted by the New York Convention of 1915 and by the Illinois Convention of 1920–1922, and it has not been commonly followed since the 1920's. It should be noted, however, that constitutions submitted

---

[31] Missouri, New Jersey, New York, Georgia, and a few other states have appointed constitutional commissions for the purpose of making preliminary investigations on proposed constitutional changes. See Graves, *American State Government*, pp. 86–89; William Miller, "The Report of New Jersey's Constitutional Commission," *Am. Pol. Sci. Rev.*, XXXVI, 900 (October, 1942); and Bill Logan, "Constitutional Revision for Oklahoma," *State Government*, June, 1949, pp. 155–156, 161–162.

as single units were approved by the voters of Missouri in 1944 and of New
Jersey in 1947. A plan highly favored by a number of authorities and now
in rather general use is that of submitting to the voters the proposed constitutions in a number of parts. Thus, in 1938, New York submitted the
work of its constitutional convention to the people in nine proposals. One
was an omnibus proposal including forty-nine miscellaneous and relatively
noncontroversial provisions. The eight other proposals were specific and
highly controversial. The omnibus proposal and five of the specific proposals were approved by the voters. Three of the specific proposals were
rejected. In this manner New York secured a new constitution.

IV. AMENDING STATE CONSTITUTIONS [32]

Legislative proposals. Amendments may be proposed by constitutional
conventions, and sometimes are so proposed, but simpler processes are
commonly employed—proposals by the legislatures or by the voters. The
method of amendment by legislative proposal dates from the time of the
adoption of the first state constitutions. At the present time its use is
authorized in all states except New Hampshire, in which state amendments
may be originated only by a constitutional convention. The New Hampshire restriction does not, however, unduly impede the amending process,
for the question of calling a constitutional convention must be submitted
to the voters every seven years, and the old (1784) constitution has been
amended more than ninety times.

The process of legislative proposal varies somewhat, some constitutions
requiring that proposals shall receive majority votes in the legislature,
others three fifths of the votes, and still others two thirds. But whatever
may be the legislative vote required, nearly all the constitutions stipulate
that the vote shall be based on the number of members *elected to* the legislature, not simply on the number which happens to be present when the
vote is taken. Furthermore, a few states require the affirmative action of
two successive legislatures. In some states there are even more severe restrictions as to the manner of making proposals. For examples, the Vermont constitution prohibits the submission of amendments more frequently
than once in ten years, and the constitution of Tennessee fixes the period
at six years and requires the affirmative action of a majority of the members of the legislature in one session and a two-thirds majority of such
membership at the next succeeding session. One is quite prepared for
the fact that the Tennessee constitution (adopted 1870) has never been
amended.

Popular approval of legislative proposals. When a proposed amendment to a state constitution has passed a legislature in accordance with

[32] See references for Sec. III.

the requirements of the state constitution, it is then necessary, except in Delaware, to submit it to the people for approval. The prevailing practice is that approval by a majority of those voting on the amendment makes it a part of the state constitution. There are exceptions to this rule, however. Six or more states require a majority of all those voting in a general election, a majority much more difficult to win than a majority on the amendment; for many people who will not take the trouble to vote on amendments submitted in the same election will vote for candidates for office. It happened in Illinois a number of times that an amendment which received, let us say, 600,000 affirmative votes and 200,000 negative votes was nevertheless defeated because 2,000,000 people voted in the same election for candidates, thus leaving the 600,000 far short of the required majority of all votes cast in the election. Other states, following the procedure required in Illinois before 1951, have found it difficult to get amendments approved. Special elections in which constitutional amendments alone are submitted would, of course, secure the ratification of amendments, if a majority of those voting approved them. A less expensive solution of the problem would be for the states that require a majority of those voting in the *election* to join the ranks of the greater number of the states that require only a majority of those voting on the *amendment*. For a number of years the tendency has been in this direction.

Amendment by popular initiative. Oregon having blazed the trail in 1902, thirteen states [33] now have constitutional provisions that authorize the amendment of their fundamental laws by popular initiative. An individual or a group may draft a proposal. The next step is to have the proposed amendment endorsed by the requisite number of petitioners. In Massachusetts and North Dakota the number required to make the petition effective is definitely fixed. Other states require a number of petitioners equal to a certain percentage of the vote cast in the last state election. This percentage is eight in California and Oregon, but the average requirement is about ten per cent. In order to insure against proposals having a purely local basis, several states require that signatures shall be secured in a number of counties or districts. For example, Nebraska requires ten per cent of the voters of the state and five per cent in each of two fifths of the counties for an effective petition.[34]

When a proposal has received the required number of signatures, it is then submitted to the voters of the state for their approval or rejection,[35] usually on a regular election date. In ten states, a proposed amendment

[33] They are: Arizona, Arkansas, California, Colorado, Massachusetts, Michigan, Missouri, Nebraska, Nevada, North Dakota, Ohio, Oklahoma, and Oregon.

[34] *Book of the States,* pp. 88–94.

[35] In Massachusetts the petition must first be referred to the legislature, and it must be approved by one fourth of the members in two successive sessions before it may be referred to the people.

is adopted if it is approved by a majority of those voting on it. But in Oklahoma and Nevada a majority of all those voting in the election is required, and the constitution of Massachusetts provides that the majority voting affirmatively on an amendment shall secure its adoption only when such majority is at least thirty per cent of the total votes cast in an election.[36]

Number and character of amendments. Most of the states use the amending process frequently. This practice prevails largely because state constitutions, particularly those of the newer states, contain so many specific provisions that amendments are necessary to accomplish even the simplest changes in governmental organization or policy. Since 1879 some 800 amendments have been proposed in California alone, and nearly half of them were approved. It is a "poor" election year (the even year) if less than a hundred amendments are proposed to the people of the several states. If less than half that number is adopted, amending state constitutions still remains an active political industry; a state that has not during the last forty years amended its constitution twenty times is lagging behind the procession. Some amendments deal with affairs of significance, but the greater number relate to trivial matters or to minor phases of important matters. Amendments of consequence are those that relate to basic questions of state and local finance, the popular control of government, corporations, labor, education, industrial undertakings of the state, social security, and similar policy. Trivial amendments deal with such propositions as increasing the salaries of state officials, authorizing counties to combine functions of certain offices, and changing the debt limit of some municipality, questions, that along with many others, the constitution should have left to the discretion of the legislature.

V. CONTENT OF STATE CONSTITUTIONS [37]

In later discussions of the framework and functions of state government we shall have occasion to give further consideration to specific constitutional provisions, but a brief summary of the content of state constitutions may be helpful at this point.

The Bill of Rights. Every state constitution contains a bill of rights. These rights include such cherished guaranties as indictment by grand jury, trial by a jury of twelve individuals, freedom of speech and of the press, and the right of petition. Several of these rights have been modified in a number of the states, especially in the newer states. A few examples of

---

[36] *Book of the States,* pp. 88–94.

[37] C. A. Beard, *American Government and Politics* (1949 ed.), pp. 539–545; Dodd, *State Government,* Ch. III, and pp. 78–92; Graves, *American State Government,* pp. 58–63; A. N. Holcombe, *State Government in the U.S.* (1931 ed.), Chs. IV–V. All state constitutions may be found in Vol. III, New York State Constitutional Convention Committee, *Reports* (1938).

these changes are submitted. As long ago as 1879, the California constitution provided that an accused might be held for trial upon information furnished by a magistrate, as well as by the time-honored method of indictment by a grand jury. Other states have adopted this simplified process. The jury trial itself has been modified. Utah authorizes the trial of cases by a jury of eight persons, whereas the old common law requires twelve. Oklahoma authorizes a verdict in some cases by three fourths of the jurors, in place of the unanimous verdict required by the common law. The old constitutions commonly provided that the privilege of the writ of *habeas corpus* should not be suspended except in case of rebellion or invasion, whereas some of the newer constitutions stipulate that it shall never be suspended by the state authorities. Several recent constitutions, including those of New Jersey and New York, contain specific provisions designed to prevent various types of racial and religious discrimination.

RESTRICTIONS ON CORPORATIONS. Many of the rights guaranteed to natural persons are also enjoyed by corporations or artificial persons. Some states have felt that corporations reap too many advantages from these rights, and they have restricted their application to these business concerns. For example, the Oklahoma constitution, while it amply safeguards the people of the state against unreasonable search and seizure, expressly states that the books and records of corporations shall be open at all times to public officers who are charged with the responsibility of seeing that they conduct their business in conformity with the laws. We should add that, for the purpose of protecting their people from what they regard as exorbitant rates charged by corporations and also for the purpose of supplying services for their citizens that privately owned corporations do not ordinarily provide, a few states have through constitutional provisions authorized their governments to engage in various occupations and businesses. North Dakota has owned and operated—among other establishments—banks, grain elevators, and flour mills.[38]

HORTATORY CLAUSES. Although the greater number of clauses in the bills of rights are of substantial nature and are enforceable in court, some are simply expressions of social philosophy and have no material value. The Vermont constitution supports virtue in the following language: "Every sect or denomination of Christians ought to observe the Sabbath or Lord's day, and keep up some sort of religious worship, which to them shall seem most agreeable to the revealed will of God"; and the whole body of inhabitants are advised "that frequent recurrence to fundamental principles, and a firm adherence to justice, moderation, temperance, industry, and frugality, are absolutely necessary to preserve the blessings of liberty, and

[38] For examples of the newer provisions in bills of rights, see the constitutions of Georgia, New Jersey, New York, North Dakota, and Oklahoma.

keep government free." A number of other constitutions contain similar provisions that have no legal effect.

The three branches of government. The second general division of a state constitution deals with the legislative, executive, and judicial departments. In the course of this work a full chapter is devoted to each of these three arms of state government. Discussion of them is therefore deferred until we reach those chapters.

Taxation and public debts. In addition to the bill of rights and the articles dealing with the three historic departments, present-day state constitutions usually contain other important articles dealing with finance, public and private corporations, education, the suffrage, and so on. Typical restrictions concerning taxation and state debts run as follows: Revenue shall not "exceed in any one year four mills on the dollar of the assessed valuation of all taxable property in the state. . . . Taxes shall be uniform upon the same class of property." State "debts shall never in the aggregate exceed the sum of $200,000 exclusive of what may be the debt at the time of the adoption of this constitution. . . . The debt of any county, township, city . . . or any other political subdivision, shall never exceed five per centum upon the assessed value of the taxable property therein; provided, that any incorporated city may by a two-thirds vote, increase such indebtedness three per centum." [39]

Corporations. We have already learned that a number of states expressly restrict the method of chartering corporations and subject them to various conditions not required of individuals. Thus the constitution of Ohio stipulates that corporations shall not be formed except by general laws, and that all such laws may from time to time be altered or repealed; that corporations may be classified and be made subject to supervision and regulation by officers of the state; that no right of way shall be appropriated to the use of any corporation unless full compensation be paid. Other restrictions of a similar nature are imposed, covering about a page in the constitution. Some of the newer constitutions, especially those of the Southern and Western states, regulate corporations in much more detail. They impose restrictions with regard to rates and charges for service, make specifications concerning the quality of the service to be performed, forbid the granting of passes to public officers, prohibit monopolies, attempt to prohibit "stock watering," and establish corporation commissions to administer these and many other provisions which relate to incorporated enterprises. In addition to these regulations vitally concerning corporate business, state constitutions commonly contain restrictions with regard to municipal corporations. These have to do with the manner in which city charters may be issued, and with such matters as the limits of the city

[39] Constitution of North Dakota, Articles XI and XII.

authorities to tax, borrow money, and engage in business usually reserved for private individuals or corporations.

Education. State constitutions almost invariably contain sections with reference to education. Such sections are found even in some of the older constitutions. For instance, Vermont's fundamental law, proclaimed in 1793, declared that "laws for the encouragement of virtue and prevention of vice and immorality, ought to be constantly kept in force, and duly executed; and a competent number of schools ought to be maintained in each town." The newer constitutions almost invariably provide in some detail for public education. Thus the constitution of North Dakota requires the legislature to establish and maintain "a uniform system for free public schools throughout the state, beginning with the primary and extending through all grades up to and including the normal and collegiate course." Other provisions concerning the administration of schools and school lands cover four or five pages.

Labor. The states in our day not infrequently give labor some special consideration in their constitutions. For instance, in Oklahoma child labor is prohibited in hazardous employment; the eight-hour day is established for work underground; the right to contract for convict labor is denied; and other protection is extended to laborers. The constitution of New Jersey gives persons in private employment the right to organize and bargain collectively, and public employees the right to organize and present "their grievances and proposals through representatives of their own choosing."

Miscellaneous provisions. A great variety of other matters are touched upon in the typical state constitution. These include banking and insurance, state institutions, the civil service, agriculture, public highways, city, county and township government, to mention some of the more important items. Then, constitutions often make provision for various executive boards, such as boards of pardon, railway commissions, tax commissions, and boards of education. Finally, we have the provisions for constitutional amendment, which provisions, as we have learned from previous discussion of the amending process, are rather elaborate in some states.

Length of state constitutions. The older constitutions are relatively brief, as instanced by the fact that Vermont's constitution of 1793 (still in force) and its amendments would occupy about twenty pages of this text. The newer instruments of government are ordinarily much longer, that of California, to take an extreme example, occupying space equivalent to about two hundred pages of this book. The difference in the length of constitutions does not necessarily indicate any great difference in the structure of state governments, for states with short constitutions frequently deal by statute with matters that are cared for in other states by constitutional provisions. If, for instance, the state's fundamental law does not contain elaborate provisions concerning the regulation of corporations, it does not follow that the state allows such organizations to follow their own sweet will in all things. It may quite adequately regulate corporations by statutes alone.

Constitutions and statutes. This brings us to a brief consideration of the wisdom of detailed provisions in constitutions. Originally, constitutions laid down the fundamental principles of government and left to the state legislatures the authority to fill in the detail by the enactment of statutes. For a number of years, the tendency has been more and more to place this detail in the constitutions. Constitutions of this type must be frequently amended, if they are to keep abreast of changing conditions; and it is not possible to amend them often, if the methods of amendment are not made simple and easy. Unfortunately, framers of constitutions with these detailed and temporary provisions have not always arranged for the simple amending process that should accompany them. Consequently, a few states have found themselves seriously handicapped with constitutions badly in need of amendments difficult to obtain.[40] Perhaps we should have no quarrel with states who distrust their legislatures and for that reason place rather trivial matters in the constitutions instead of leaving them to be disposed of by statute; but such states should follow the example of Oregon and California and some other commonwealths and make their constitutions easy to amend.

Reading List

F. G. Bates and O. P. Field, *State Government,* as revised by Field, P. S. Sikes, and J. E. Stoner (1949), Ch. 4.
Book of the States, 1950–1951, pp. 81–95.
J. Bryce, *American Commonwealth* (1913 ed.), I, Chs. XXXVII–XXXVIII.
Commonwealth of Massachusetts, *Bulletins for the Constitutional Convention* (1918).
W. F. Dodd, "The Functions of a State Constitution," *Pol. Sci. Quar.* (1915), XXX, 201–222.
———, *The Revision and Amendment of State Constitutions* (1910).
———, *State Government* (1928 ed.), Chs. III–IV.
J. E. Dovell, *Modernizing State Constitutions* (pamphlet, Public Administration Clearing House, University of Florida, 1950).

[40] Under the constitutional requirement that an amendment is lost unless it receives affirmative votes equal to a majority of all votes cast in an *election,* the Illinois constitution of 1870 stood unamended from 1908 to 1950. In November of 1950, with both major political parties actively supporting the proposal, the so-called Gateway Amendment was approved. Under its provisions constitutional amendments may now be adopted with the approval of a majority of those voting in the election or by the affirmative vote of two-thirds of those voting on the amendment.

C. R. Erdman, *The New Jersey Constitution* (1934).

W. B. Graves, *American State Government* (1946 ed.), Chs. II–III.

C. G. Haines and B. M. Haines, *Principles and Problems of Government* (1934 ed.), Ch. XIV.

R. S. Hoar, *Constitutional Conventions: their Nature, Powers, and Limitations* (1917).

A. N. Holcombe, *State Government in the United States* (1931 ed.), Chs. II–V.

Illinois Legislative Reference Library, *Constitutional Convention Bulletins* (1920).

M. W. Jernegan, *The American Colonies* (1929).

Gerald W. Johnson, *Our English Heritage* (1949).

A. H. Kelley and W. A. Harbison, *The American Constitution* (1948), Chs. 1–4.

C. Kettleborough, *Constitution-Making in Indiana,* 2 vols. (1916).

I. Loeb, *Constitution and Constitutional Conventions in Missouri* (1922).

A. F. Macdonald, *American State Government and Administration* (1950 ed.), Ch. IV.

J. M. Mathews, *American State Government* (1934 ed.), Ch. VI.

—— and C. A. Berdahl, *Documents and Readings in American Government* (1940 ed.), Ch. XIX.

M. B. McCarthy, *The Widening Scope of American Constitutions* (1928).

C. E. Merriam, *A History of American Political Theories* (1903), Chs. I–II.

National Municipal League, *A Model State Constitution* (1948 ed.).

National Municipal Review, issue for March, 1948, "Modernizing State Constitutions."

A. Nevins, *The American States during and after the Revolution* (1924).

New York State Constitutional Convention Committee, *Report,* 12 vols. (1938).

V. A. O'Rourke and D. W. Campbell, *Constitution-Making in a Democracy: Theory and Practice in New York State* (1943).

B. M. Rich, "A New Constitution for New Jersey," *Am. Pol. Sci. Rev.,* December, 1947, pp. 1126–1129.

B. F. Shambaugh, ed., *The Constitution of Iowa* (1935).

C. F. Snider, *American State and Local Government* (1950), Ch. I.

F. G. Wilson, *The American Political Mind* (1949), Ch. 4.

Questions and Problems

1. Show that the study of American government appropriately begins in Great Britain.

2. Make a list of present-day organs of state government that had their origin in colonial times.

3. Discuss this statement: *American democracy had its beginnings in the colonies.*

4. How did the framers of the first state constitutions seek to guard against governmental "tyranny"?

5. Indicate the appropriate functions of constitutional commissions; conventions.

6. What are the provisions for constitution-making in your state? Suggest any needed changes in the process.
7. Prepare and defend what you consider a desirable method of amending state constitutions. Wherein does it differ from the system in your state?
8. What would be the nature of a state constitution that would need relatively infrequent amendment?
9. List the provisions of your state constitution that have no legal significance; that duplicate provisions of the federal Constitution.
10. What inconsistencies do you find in the constitution of your state?
11. What provisions of the constitution of your state would be more appropriate in statutes?

☆ 5 ☆

Intergovernmental Relations

HAVING in previous chapters examined constitutions, national and state, and having learned something of the division of powers between the nation and the states, we are ready to discuss intergovernmental relations. Here we shall consider the place of the states in the Union—their legal position, the restrictions upon them in respect to commerce and taxation, their trade barriers that represent an abuse of the commerce and taxing powers, the obligations of the central government to them, their obligations to each other, and national-state co-operation, particularly through the "federal aid" system. A final section deals briefly with the territories.

The legal equality and indestructibility of the states. The Constitution authorizes Congress to admit new states to the Union, and in pursuance of this power Congress has admitted thirty-five states, thus forming a continental empire of free and equal "republics." Rhode Island has the same right to order her internal affairs as has New York—the same right to be different, a right she has at times guarded with some jealousy. When North Dakota wants to establish state-owned mills and elevators, she may do so. If a Pennsylvania coal baron has unprintable opinions of Wisconsin's political and economic system, it is certainly in part because the constitutionally guaranteed equality of the states permits Wisconsin to go one way and Pennsylvania another. California may sue Nevada and vice versa. Several of the original states moved their capitols; therefore, Oklahoma could move hers, although at the time she was admitted to the Union she agreed not to move it.[1]

The states are not only legally equal, but they are also legally inviolable and indestructible. The Constitution prohibits the creation of a state within the territory of any other state and the forming of any state "by the junction of two or more States or parts of States, without the consent of

[1] Coyle v. Smith, 221 U.S. 559 (1911).

the legislatures of the States concerned as well as of the Congress."[2] In a legal sense the states are as secure as the Union itself. Although one may have a very strong suspicion that General Grant and his armies were not without influence in determining the matter, the Supreme Court of the United States has said that "The Constitution, in all its provisions, looks to an indestructible Union, composed of indestructible states."[3]

I. CONSTITUTIONAL RESTRICTIONS UPON THE STATES [4]

The standing restrictions imposed by the Constitution upon all the states may be divided into two classes—those that are political in character and are for the purpose of giving the national government a free hand in the exercise of some of its very essential powers, and those that protect personal and property rights from possible encroachment on the part of the states. The protection of private rights is discussed in Chapter 6. In this section we shall limit ourselves to a discussion of those restrictions that are primarily political in character.

Limitations upon compacts between the states. The Constitution provides that "no State shall enter into any treaty, alliance, or confederation," and that "no State shall, without the consent of Congress . . . enter into any agreement or compact with another State or with a foreign power."[5] The courts of the United States have been very liberal in interpreting the powers of the states under the second clause just quoted. They have held that on a number of matters the states may make agreements without even asking the assent of Congress. In the case of Virginia v. Tennessee,[6] the Court said: "If, for instance, Virginia should come into possession and ownership of a small parcel of land in New York which the latter state might desire to acquire as a site for a public building, it would hardly be deemed essential for the latter state to obtain the consent of Congress before it could make a valid agreement with Virginia for the purchase of the land. . . . If the bordering line of two states should cross some malarious and disease-producing district, there would be no possible reason, on any conceivable public grounds, to obtain the consent of Congress for the bordering states to agree to unite in removing the disease."

For what sort of compacts or agreements between states must the assent of Congress be obtained? In the same case the Court answers this question. "It is evident that the prohibition is directed to the formation of

---

[2] Art. IV, sec. III.

[3] Texas v. White, 7 Wall. 700 (1869).

[4] C. K. Burdick, *The Law of the American Constitution* (1922), pp. 242–254 and Ch. XX; *Book of the States*, 1950–1951, pp. 22–51.

[5] Art. I, sec. x.

[6] 148 U.S. 503 (1893).

any combination tending to the increase of political power in the states, which may encroach upon or interfere with the just supremacy of the United States." If, for example, two states are establishing a boundary, and the line is run in such a way "as to cut off an important and valuable portion of a state, the political power of the state enlarged would be affected by the settlement of the boundary; and to an agreement for the running of such a boundary, or rather for its adoption afterward, the consent of Congress may well be required." But where a boundary, which actually existed before, is simply being marked and defined, the action on the part of the states does not require for its validity the consent of Congress.[7]

Although compacts may not play a large part in the solution of interstate problems, they are in rather common use. One of the most conspicuous examples of a thoroughly satisfactory interstate compact is that under which New Jersey and New York established the Port of New York Authority, a compact approved by Congress in 1921. More recent compacts have to do with such topics as crime prevention, oil and gas conservation, flood control, and division of waters. One of the most significant of the last type mentioned is the upper Colorado River Basin Compact (approved 1949) between Arizona, Colorado, New Mexico, Utah, and Wyoming.[8]

Limitations in respect to foreign commerce. Very material limitations are placed upon the states with regard to commerce. Not only is the power given to Congress to regulate commerce "with foreign nations, and among the several States, and with the Indian tribes" (Art. I, sec. VIII, cl. 8); but "no State shall, without the consent of the Congress, lay any imposts or duties on imports or exports, except what may be absolutely necessary for executing its inspection laws"; nor may a state lay a duty of tonnage without the consent of Congress (Art. I, sec. x, cl. 10).

An inspection tax, for example, a tax or fee to cover the cost of inspecting the quality of tobacco intended for export, may be levied or imposed by a state without the consent of Congress, but it seems that it is for Congress to determine whether or not the charge made is more than is "absolutely necessary" to cover the cost of the inspection.[9] If a state wishes to levy a duty or tonnage (the latter is a tax on the carrying capacity of a vessel entering or leaving a port), it may do so only after the assent of Congress has been given. Frequently, during the early years of the Republic, Congress permitted the states to make such levies for the purpose of improving local port facilities.

[7] 148 U.S. 503 (1893).

[8] See Jean S. Breitenstein, "The Upper Colorado River Basin Compact," *State Government*, Sept., 1949, pp. 214–216, 225.

[9] Patapsco Guano Co. v. N.C. Bd. of Agri., 171 U.S. 345 (1898). The Chief Justice cites Justice Bradley, on circuit, in Neilson v. Garza.

The prohibition of the Constitution regarding the imposition of import duties by the states is given a broad judicial interpretation. It is construed to mean not only that the states shall not impose duties on articles at the time of their importation, but also that the states may not tax imported articles as long as they have not become a part of the general property in the state. Thus, articles that remain the property of an importer in his warehouse are not subject to state taxation, for such a tax "is too plainly a duty on imports to escape the prohibition in the Constitution." [10] States may, of course, tax imported articles along with other property after such articles have become commingled (placed on store shelves for sale, for example) with the general property in the state.

Limitations in respect to interstate commerce. The Constitution gives Congress the power to regulate interstate commerce. The grant of this power to Congress does not exclude the states from passing considerable legislation on the subject, but it does limit the authority of the states in two significant ways. First, when Congress acts to regulate a particular type of transaction in interstate commerce or an interstate carrier, the railroads, for example, all state law inconsistent with the national regulations must give way. Second, even in the absence of any congressional legislation, state laws are regularly declared void if they relate to interstate transportation or trade that admits of only one uniform (and therefore national) system of regulation. Then what power over interstate commerce is left to the states? The answer is, a great deal. Long ago the courts held that the states, exercising their police powers, could make regulations in the interest of local health and safety, even though such regulations might incidentally interfere with interstate commerce. Thus, when an epidemic of anthrax was raging among Louisiana livestock, the State of Texas prohibited the transportation of such stock from Louisiana into Texas, and the Supreme Court of the United States sustained this act.[11] Similarly, the Court has upheld the right of a state to require locomotive engineers to be examined and licensed; to regulate the heating of passenger cars; to require guard posts on bridges; and to limit the speed of trains at grade-crossings.[12] The proudest of the many interstate "cannon balls," "flyers," "rockets," and "zephyrs" may be validly required by city ordinance to slow down within the corporate limits and to refrain from making unnecessary noises. Many other state and local regulations promulgated in the interest of the health, safety, and convenience of the public have been sustained. Indeed, the delegation of the interstate commerce power to Congress, as that power

[10] Brown v. Maryland, 12 Wheat. 419 (1827).
[11] Smith v. St. L. & S.W.RR. Co., 181 U.S., 248 (1901).
[12] Southern Ry. Co. v. King, 217 U.S. 524 (1910).

has been interpreted by the courts, has not prevented the states from imped-
ing and obstructing the flow of trade between the states.

INTERSTATE TRADE BARRIERS AN ABUSE OF STATE POWER: *Quarantine
Laws.* Moved by the understandable and commendable desire to improve
the economic lot of their citizens, and urged by special interest groups, state
legislatures have used their police and taxing powers to prohibit or restrict
the sale in local markets of out-of-state products. Quarantine laws as a
protection from insects and plant diseases that might be carried in the
products of other states are desirable, and all the states have them on
their statute books. But those who have made careful studies of this legislation have a decided inclination to share the opinion of irate haulers of
produce that it is more often intended for the purpose of barring perfectly
good produce from other states than for keeping out insect pests and plant
diseases. States have quarantined the fruits of other states for diseases
that have not existed in those states for years. Such quarantines are for
the purpose of protecting local fruit growers and forcing local consumers
to eat state-grown fruits or go without.

Highway traffic regulation. States have the right to regulate highways
in the interest of safety and to require payment for their use. This right is
also abused. The height, width, load per tire, and overall gross weight
of trucks permitted by law vary greatly among the states, and some states
almost certainly lay down these and other specifications for commercial
trucks with an eye to keeping out trucks from other states. Taxes, or the
charges for the use of the highways, are sometimes so levied as to discriminate against out-of-state commercial vehicles.

Food-grading laws. Food-grading laws for the protection of the consumer against unscrupulous and careless dealers are necessary and desirable. But many states have used such laws to discriminate against the
food that might be brought in from other states. A law or ordinance that
on its face is designed for the entirely proper purpose of insuring pure milk
to the consumer may be and often is primarily for the benefit of local dairymen, and a law that is supposed to guarantee to the consumer fresh eggs
may do no more than require that out-of-state eggs be branded "shipped
eggs," while local hens may be permitted to cackle over labels suggesting
the super-freshness of their output. A number of dairy states have taxed
margarine, a perfectly good article of diet, so heavily that it cannot compete
with butter. Some Southern states are even more discriminating in their
discrimination. They tax only margarine that is not made exclusively from
cottonseed oil and other home-produced oils and fats.

California's "indigent persons" barrier. Even before John Steinbeck
wrote *The Grapes of Wrath,* it was common knowledge that large segments

of the population of less-favored states were migrating to states in which they hoped to find better economic opportunities. In the case of California this huge influx of migrants unquestionably placed a strain upon the state's resources and presented her with new problems of health and morals. Consequently, that state by law declared any person who brought an indigent person into it, knowing him to be indigent, guilty of a misdemeanor. The Supreme Court of the United States was not impressed with the old argument that a person without employment or funds constitutes a "moral pestilence." "Poverty and immorality are not synonymous," said Justice Byrnes, speaking for the majority of the Court. The California statute was declared to be an invalid exercise of the police power, an unconstitutional burden upon interstate commerce. Several of the justices gave a broader basis for their opinion, holding that one of the privileges and immunities of a citizen of the United States is that of moving freely from state to state.[13]

Effect of trade barrier laws. These and many other trade barrier laws are directly in conflict with the policy of a free exchange of goods among the states that our forefathers thought they had written into the Constitution, the policy that goes far to explain the national prosperity enjoyed during the greater part of our history. The new war between the states, this economic war born of the depression beginning in 1929, is even less sensible as a solution of our present economic ills than was the Civil War a sane solution of the problems of 1860. Trade barriers help only a few groups in particular states. The consumers are not benefited, the states are not benefited, and even the state producers who are supposed to be favored may not profit in the long run. Certainly most producers want to sell outside their own state. But the restrictions the home state puts on the transportation and marketing of out-of-state goods meet with speedy retaliation from other states, so that trade is interrupted and even brought to a standstill in certain commodities. If one wants to sell, one must buy. It is as simple as that. Buy American, buy New Mexican, buy Oshkosh do not, "begosh," make sense as an economic argument. The last step in this argument is—do not buy at all; if you want something, make it or grow it yourself. Trade is an exchange of goods, and it is promoted by laws that encourage that exchange, not by laws that restrict it.

Moves to reduce trade barriers. The federal courts seem to be without sufficient power to prevent the erection of these interstate trade barriers because in erecting them the states have used powers they undoubtedly possess, the police and taxing powers. Furthermore, the Twenty-first Amendment expressly permits the states to pass restrictive legislation concerning interstate trade in intoxicating liquors. Of course this provision

[13] Edwards v. California, 314 U.S. 160 (1941).

was inserted in the amendment to enable the "dry" states to protect themselves from floods of liquor from other states, but it has been used primarily as a means of forcing individuals who drink wine and beer to
purchase wines and beers made locally from home-grown products.

Yet something is being done about these trade barriers. The Council
of State Governments has attacked them with intelligence and energy.
Various departments of the federal government, many editors, and some
enlightened state officials and legislators have become interested. Since
1939 the state legislatures have shown some tendency to resist proposals that
would increase trade restrictions among the states, and when legislatures
have not been able to resist temptation or withstand pressure (it is usually
the latter failing) governors have sometimes been found equal to the occasion.[14]

There have been some instances of the repeal of restrictive measures; and,
in 1942, in response to an emergency request from the President, the states
unanimously agreed to a uniform standard with respect to widths, lengths,
and weights of commercial motor vehicles. This agreement, to be sure,
was only for the period of the war, but the states are not now imposing
restrictions, the wartime agreement has been substantially observed, and
the Governors' Conference is definitely interested in maintaining the free
flow of interstate commercial vehicles.[15] Despite this encouraging report
the large-scale removal of barriers by state action will be a long and tedious

[14] A conspicuous example of executive action against the erection of a trade barrier is
found in Governor Arthur B. Langlie's veto (March 21, 1949) of a bill submitted by the
Washington legislature prohibiting the sale of out-of-state wines in taverns. The veto message
reads in part as follows: ". . . It is legislation which discriminates against out-of-state wines
and its effect is to set up an interstate trade barrier. . . . As such it is in my judgment inherently bad legislation. It has far-reaching implications in that it sets both a precedent
and a pattern for further trade barriers of this kind here and for retaliatory measures against
Washington products elsewhere. In my judgment no state should embark on a program of
trade barriers unless it is prepared to follow it through to its logical conclusion, which is
self-sufficiency. It should be self-evident that there can be no such thing as self-sufficiency
in this or any other state. . . . Prosperity for the great majority of producers and consumers
can be achieved, not by trade barrier laws, but by the free exchange of goods across all
political boundaries. The only restrictions which, in my judgment are warranted, are those
which protect the public health and safety. . . .

"Being fully aware of the importance of this legislation to the wine growers of this state
and being completely sympathetic to their problems, I have not taken this matter lightly. I
have taken occasion to discuss the entire problem with the governors of several of our sister
states, among them New York and California, and with the Council of State Governments.
Not only have I found a complete unanimity concerning the dangerous aspects of this type of
legislation, but I am convinced from my investigations that my signature on this bill would
not be serving the best interests of the state as a whole."

[15] "Here Is the Story," *State Government*, July, 1942, pp. 135-136, 145; "Motor Carrier
Taxes," *ibid.*, Dec., 1948, p. 237; Resolutions Adopted by the Governors' Conference, June
19-22, 1949 and June 19-21, 1950.

process. National legislation alone could do it properly, but Congress, ever concerned about states' rights, is slow to make the necessary use of its power over interstate commerce.[16]

Limitations on state monetary and taxing powers: 1. STATE BANKS AND BANK NOTES. "No state shall . . . coin money; emit bills of credit; [or] make anything but gold and silver coin a [legal] tender in payment of debts" (Art. 7, sec. x, cl. 1). This provision of the Constitution owes its origin to the unfortunate paper money experiments of the states during and immediately following the Revolution. The commercial classes were fully persuaded that the national government alone should have monetary powers.

We must note that the restrictive clause does not prohibit the states from chartering banks that compete with the national banks; nor does it prevent states from authorizing their banks to issue bills that may circulate as currency, although not as legal tender. State bank notes are kept out of circulation, however, by a statute of Congress that imposes a heavy tax upon their issue.

2. BILLS OF CREDIT. The courts have been liberal with the states in interpreting the prohibition with regard to bills issued on the credit of the state and designed to circulate as money. In only one case have state obligations been held void as bills of credit. This invalidation occurred when Missouri, more than a hundred years ago, made loans to her citizens in the form of certificates that were to be accepted as money for taxes and for salaries and fees of state officers. The more liberal view is illustrated by the following: Texas issued state warrants to pay its debts. They were made receivable for all taxes and public dues, and the law authorized state officers to pay public creditors with them if such creditors would receive them. When this paper was received back by the state, it was not to be reissued. Since it was not to circulate as money in ordinary business transactions, the Court held that the issue did not constitute bills of credit.[17]

3. INTERGOVERNMENTAL TAXATION. In the discussion on national supremacy, reference was made to Chief Justice Marshall's opinion in which

[16] There is much literature on the subject. A few titles are as follows: F. E. Melder, *State and Local Barriers to Interstate Commerce in the United States* (1937); Melder, "State Trade Walls," *Public Affairs Pamphlet* No. 37, 1939; Melder, "Trade Barriers between States," *Annals of the American Academy of Political and Social Science*, January, 1940, pp. 54–61; R. L. Buell, "Death by Tariff," *Fortune*, August, 1938; J. T. Flynn, "Shove Thy Neighbor," *Collier's*, April 30, 1938; *Trade Barriers among the States,* published by the Council of State Governments, 1939; R. C. Hendrickson, "Trade Barriers and National Unity," *State Government*, April, 1941; O. K. Armstrong, "Barriers between the States Must Go," *Reader's Digest*, April, 1942 (condensed from *The Rotarian* of the same month); "More Color in Oleo v. Butter Fight," *Investor's Reader* (published by Merrill Lynch, Pierce, Fenner & Beane), Feb. 5, 1947.

[17] Huston, etc., Ry. Co. v. Texas, 177 U.S. 66 (1900).

he laid down the rule that the states could not tax the operations of the national banks.[18]   Following the principle enunciated by Marshall, the Supreme Court has held that the states may not tax the property of the national government, its bonds, its franchises, the salaries of its officers, or otherwise by taxation obstruct the operations of the national government.   However, Congress may authorize the states to levy certain taxes that might otherwise fall within the list of prohibitions.   For example, the states are permitted to tax the real property of national banks as they tax other real property, and they may tax the stockholders.   When the national government attempted to tax the salaries of state officers, the Supreme Court originally imposed the same rule of implied prohibition, holding that the central authority had no more right to interfere with the functioning of the state governments than those governments had to interfere with the processes of the central government.

Taxation of public salaries.   Formerly the Supreme Court made much of Marshall's extreme statement in McCulloch v. Maryland—"the power to tax involves the power to destroy"—and was quick to declare invalid any act of a state legislature that imposed a tax upon national agencies or officers on the theory that such a tax was the entering wedge that would "destroy" the national government.   Recently the Court has been less under the influence of Marshall's absolutes and it has been more under the guidance of the legal wisdom of the late Justice Holmes, who recognized few absolutes.   Holmes maintained that "distinctions of the law are distinctions of degree" and that "the power to tax is not the power to destroy as long as this Court sits." [19]

Approaching the problem of intergovernmental taxation with the distinctions of degree in mind, the Court now takes the view that a state tax, nondiscriminatory in character, that falls upon an agency or officer of the national government is valid if it is not an economic burden passed on to that government.   It no longer holds that taxing the salary of a government official has the same result as a tax on the government itself.   In Graves v. New York [20] the Court held that the New York State income tax law was valid when applied to the salary of an examining attorney for the Federal Home Owners' Loan Corporation.   This tax, said the Court, "is laid upon income which becomes the property of the taxpayer when received as compensation for his services; and the tax laid upon the privilege of receiving it is paid from his private funds and not from the funds of the government, either directly or indirectly."   By the same reasoning the national government was given the green light to tax the salaries of

[18] McCulloch v. Maryland, 4 Wheat. 316 (1819).
[19] Dissenting in Panhandle Oil Co. v. Mississippi, 277 U.S. at 223 (1928).
[20] 306 U.S. 466 (1939).

state officers. In the Public Salary Act of 1939 Congress brought the salaries of state officers and employees within the federal taxing area, and authorized the states to impose nondiscriminatory taxes upon the salaries of officers and employees of the United States. The demise of the old practice of intergovernmental salary tax exemption finds few mourners. It was of no clear benefit to any government and it gave those receiving salaries for government services a privileged position.

Taxation of public enterprises. The national government taxes state activities that are of a nongovernmental, or, to use the term generally employed, "proprietary" character. The terms "governmental" functions and proprietary functions were invented by the courts; and, in the course of time, the tribunals listed as governmental the states' courts, the police systems, the public schools, the public hospitals, and waterworks under state ownership. These things, said the courts, the national government may not tax. The courts also, in cases appropriately before them, ruled as proprietary the states' liquor business, state or municipally owned street railways, state banks, publicly owned wharfs, and state university football contests (but not the university—that was governmental). These things the national government may tax. The distinctions were not always convincing, but the general rule seemed to be that an activity of a state or one of its subdivisions that historically had been in the domain of private business could be taxed by act of Congress. But in 1946 the Supreme Court held that the State of New York must pay a federal gallonage tax on the sale of mineral water taken from Saratoga Springs.[21] This decision was, of course, not in accord with the classification that put waterworks down as governmental and nontaxable functions. As a matter of fact, the decision pretty well discards the classifications so painfully built up and seems to rely more upon whether the subject of the tax is traditionally within the national taxing power and whether the tax bears alike upon states and citizens.[22]

This sort of confusion has never arisen in respect to national functions or the state's power to tax them. Because the national government has only those powers delegated to it by the Constitution, and, therefore, maintains the Supreme Court, its "every action within its constitutional power is governmental action." [23] A critical student might ask (and he should), Why are not all state actions within their constitutional power also governmental? The lame answer that he must receive is that the Supreme Court has not so decided. Proceeding on the basis of what the Court has

[21] New York v. United States, 326 U.S. 572.
[22] David Fellman, "Federalism," in "Ten Years of the Supreme Court, 1937–1947" (R. E. Cushman, ed.), *Am. Pol. Sci. Rev.*, Dec., 1947, pp. 1157–1159.
[23] Graves v. New York, 306 U.S. 466 (1939).

decided, we find that a state may not, without the consent of Congress, tax a function of the national government even though Congress may tax state governments performing the same functions. But a state tax that is not a burden on the national function is commonly sustained. Among such valid state taxes are the following: a nondiscriminatory state privilege tax on gross receipts, an occupation tax on gross income, and a net income tax on contractors with the federal government; an unemployment insurance tax from persons conducting business in national parks; and a sales tax on the purchase of materials for use in fulfilling cost-plus contracts with the federal government.[24] These and similar taxes the states are permitted to impose because the burden of such taxation falls upon others, and not upon the United States.

II. OBLIGATIONS OF THE NATIONAL GOVERNMENT TO THE STATES [25]

The national government is under some specific obligations to the states. Article IV, section IV, of the Constitution reads: "The United States shall guarantee to every state . . . a republican form of government, and shall protect each of them against invasion, and on application of the legislature, or of the executive (when the legislature cannot be convened), against domestic violence."

The guaranty of the republican form of government. The Constitution nowhere defines what is meant by the republican form of government. Undoubtedly the framers were sure that the state governments as they were constituted in 1787 were republican. Certainly also Congress, by her acceptance of the constitutions of the new states, recognized them as having the essential features of republicanism. Republican government is thus understood to be a government in which a substantial body of the people have the right to choose their representatives and, in American practice, the right directly or indirectly to choose their executive.[26]

WHO APPLIES THE TEST FOR REPUBLICANISM? As the Constitution fails to define republican government, so it fails to specify what branch of the national government shall apply the republican test to a state's political institutions. Applying the test is rather obviously a political matter and, therefore, a power that naturally belongs to the political arms of the government—Congress and the President. Congress, through its power to admit new states and by its authority to exclude representatives from

---

[24] Fellman, *op. cit.*, pp. 1155–1156.

[25] J. M. Mathews, *The American Constitutional System* (1940 ed.), pp. 57–63; W. W. Willoughby, *Principles of the Constitutional Law of the United States* (1930 ed.), Ch. XI.

[26] Willoughby, *op. cit.*, pp. 139–140.

its membership, is in the best position to determine whether a state is republican and to enforce its ideas as to what constitutes that type of government. The courts have taken this view, at least; and they accept as republican any and all state governments that are expressly or tacitly recognized as such by Congress, or by the President acting under the authority of Congress and the Constitution.

Examples of the application of the test. Rhode Island, continuing under her old colonial charter, had a very restricted suffrage, of which the more democratic element in the state complained incessantly, insisting upon a constitutional amendment to broaden the franchise. Invariably blocked by the legal voters of the state, who constituted a relatively small group of the population, the reformers took matters into their own hands and in 1841, under the leadership of Thomas Dorr, established a competing "state government" along more democratic lines. Upon an appeal of the regular authorities of the state, President Tyler took steps to put down Dorr's rebellion, and his irregular government then collapsed. In the course of time the question as to which government of Rhode Island was republican in form came before the Supreme Court. The Court held that it was bound to accept the acts of the political departments of the national government as conclusive on that question, and that the President's action in assisting the regular authorities in the state was a recognition of their government as the republican government.[27]

A very interesting case arose over whether Oregon's initiative and referendum system violated the principles of republican government. Some alleged that republican government was *representative* government, and that laws enacted directly by popular vote were therefore in violation of the republican guaranty of the Constitution. The Court held again that the question was political in character, and dismissed the case for want of jurisdiction. The Court indicated, however, that Congress, in admitting representatives from the state, tacitly affirmed that the initiative and referendum did not contravene republican principles.[28]

Protection of the states against invasion and domestic violence. Closely connected with the guaranty of the republican form of government in the states is the guaranty that the national government shall protect the states against invasion and domestic violence. There is no difficulty in interpreting the meaning of this obligation with regard to invasion, for an invasion of a state by a foreign army would be at the same time an invasion of the United States, and no question exists as to the right and duty of the national government to resist such an attack. But when the internal

---

[27] Luther v. Borden, 7 Howard 1 (1849). It ought to be stated that Rhode Island has long since liberalized her suffrage.

[28] Pacific States Tel. & Tel. Co. v. Oregon, 223 U.S. 118 (1912).

order of a state is disturbed by rebellion or riot, the obligation of the national government is not so clear. The Constitution says that aid shall be extended to the states when the state authorities request it. This was done in the Rhode Island case noted above. If, however, the President feels that the state is capable of maintaining order and that it makes a request for national intervention because of timidity or for political reasons, he may refuse to send aid. For some such reasons President Harding at first hesitated to accede to the request of West Virginia for federal support in reducing disorders incident to a coal strike in that state. On the other hand, when domestic disturbances in a state reach such proportions that the national property is in danger or the national services are interrupted, the President may send federal troops to the scene of the disorder, even against the protest of state authorities, as President Cleveland did in 1894 on the occasion of the serious railway strike in the Chicago vicinity.

III. INTERSTATE RELATIONS [29]

The states, when acting within their spheres of government, are, in a legal sense, foreign to one another except where the Constitution of the United States specifies to the contrary. To be sure, foreign countries co-operate to a considerable extent under the rules of international law, but, in four important particulars, the Constitution establishes a much closer relationship among the states than is to be found between foreign states. These relate to public acts, privileges of citizens, extradition, and the settlement of controversies.

Full faith and credit. In the first place, "full faith and credit shall be given in each State to the public acts, records, and judicial proceedings of every other State." [30] In colonial times one colony treated the judgments of the courts of another as foreign judgments, allowing them to be re-examined on their merits and to be impeached for fraud or prejudice. Such procedure operated as a considerable handicap upon intercolonial relations; and the men who drew up the Articles of Confederation, as well as those who drafted the Constitution, inserted the provision quoted above in order to establish more satisfactory legal relationships among the new states.

GENERAL ILLUSTRATIONS. The "full faith and credit" clause does not require the courts of one state to enforce the penal laws of another. The requirement covers only civil matters, and there are definite limitations

[29] Burdick, *op. cit.,* Chs. XXIII–XXV; W. F. Dodd, *Cases on Constitutional Law* (1949), 391–410; Mathews, *op. cit.,* Ch. VI; Willoughby, *op. cit.,* Chs. XIII–XV.

[30] Art. IV, sec. I.

even here. For example, a state is not expected or required to enforce in its courts a contract made under a law of another state when to do so would be repugnant to good morals or lead to disturbance and disorganization of the local law. But in an appropriate case the courts of one state must enforce the law of another. Here are two concrete cases: A New York law imposed "double liability" upon owners of stock in New York banks. When, in the great depression period (1929–1933), the superintendent of banks of the State of New York sought to collect the double liability from New Jersey residents who owned stock in a New York bank, the courts of New Jersey declined to entertain the action, holding that a New Jersey law protected the residents of the state from this sort of proceeding. The Supreme Court of the United States decided otherwise, however, declaring that the subject matter was peculiarly within the regulatory power of the State of New York, and that New Jersey could not enable its residents "to escape the performance of a voluntarily assumed statutory obligation, consistent with morality, to contribute to the payment of depositors of a bank of another state of which they were stockholders." [31] An electric light company and an individual made a contract of employment in Vermont, accepting the employment compensation act of that state. The company had lines running into New Hampshire, and there the employee in the performance of his duties was killed. It was held that the Vermont compensation act, not the compensation act of New Hampshire, should apply.[32]

These illustrations relate to the application, in appropriate cases, of the laws of one state in the courts of another. More significant and more commonly observed in operation is the requirement that the judgment of a court in one state shall receive "full faith and credit" in the courts of every other state. If the duly attested record of the court giving the judgment in state A is presented, and if the court had jurisdiction (authority to hear and determine the case), the court in state B, in which the enforcement of the judgment is sought, is obligated to carry out the judgment of the court in state A. To be sure, there are various complicating factors, but the basic rule is simple enough. An individual wins a suit in one state, but before the judgment of the court is satisfied the defendant leaves the state, taking his property with him. The successful litigant may then take the judgment to the state in which the elusive defendant is found and there institute suit upon the judgment. It is not necessary for him to begin all over again—he simply brings a suit for the enforcement of the judgment. It may happen that a litigant may win a judgment in state A

[31] Broderick v. Rosner, 294 U.S. 629 (1935).
[32] Bradford Electric Company v. Clapper, 286 U.S. 145 (1932).

and later have it enforced by a court in state B, even though under the laws of state B he could not have won the original judgment.[33]

APPLICATION OF FULL FAITH AND CREDIT TO DIVORCE. A divorce granted to a spouse by a court of a state in which husband and wife are domiciled is a valid divorce anywhere, because there is no question of the jurisdiction of such a court. Suppose that a spouse, a wife, let us say, leaves the state in which she was domiciled with her husband, takes up residence in another state, works as a secretary, and, after some years, gets a divorce in this state. Does she have a decree that must be accepted as valid in the first state? It would seem that the answer is "yes," for she had established bona fide (in good faith) domicile in the second state (not just a fake domicile for the purpose of a divorce). Suppose, on the other hand, she did not establish bona fide domicile in the second state, but simply resided there the necessary 42 days, or whatever its law requires, in order to get the divorce. Must the state in which she lived as a wife recognize her divorce? The answer appears to be "no." Here is such a case and the decision of the Supreme Court thereon: In 1940 the Nevada divorce mill granted decrees to husband A and wife B, who had motored from North Carolina and stopped for six weeks in a Nevada auto camp to establish domicile. They married the same day they were divorced, and they returned immediately to North Carolina, where the former spouse of each resided. Here they were convicted of bigamous cohabitation and sentenced to jail. The Supreme Court of the United States set aside their conviction, holding that North Carolina, not having questioned the good faith of the Nevada domicile, must respect the divorce decrees.[34] The Tar Heel State lost no time in setting the matter right. It proceeded against the parties and clearly established the fact that they had gone to Nevada solely for the purpose of getting a divorce, that they had not taken up residence in Nevada in good faith. From these facts it contended that the accommodating state therefore had no jurisdiction to grant the divorces. This argument satisfied the Supreme Court.[35] The situation seems, then, to be this: a state may refuse to recognize a decree of divorce granted by another state, provided the first state can convince the Supreme Court of the United States that the second state assumed jurisdiction over a party who was not in fact a bona fide resident of the state, but had only remained in it long enough to get a "migratory" divorce.

This scant page on full faith and credit and divorce is an over-simplification of the subject. The problem has many angles, and Supreme Court

[33] Dodd, *op. cit.,* p. 402 n.
[34] Williams v. North Carolina, 317 U.S. 287 (1942).
[35] Williams v. North Carolina, 325 U.S. 226 (1945).

decisions in the cases are difficult to reconcile. It is as hard to keep abreast of the judicial application of "full faith and credit" to divorce as it is to be informed of the name of the latest spouse of some of our celebrities! For example, in a recent case a wife had been awarded maintenance and support by a decree in New York and her husband later obtained a divorce in Nevada without provisions for alimony. A majority of the Supreme Court held that the Nevada decree was valid for the divorce but ineffective on the issue of alimony.[36]

Privileges and immunities. The second particular in which the Constitution brings about a much closer relationship among the several states than is found among foreign states is expressed in the provision that "the citizens of each State shall be entitled to all privileges and immunities of citizens in the several States."[37] The importance of preventing unjust and arbitrary discriminations by the states to the advantage of their own citizens and against citizens of other states was recognized from the first, for the Articles of Confederation contained a provision similar to that just quoted.

The object of the clause is to place the "citizens of each state upon the same footing with citizens of other states, so far as the advantages resulting from citizenship in those states are concerned. It relieves them from the disabilities of alienage in other states; it inhibits discriminating legislation against them by other states; it gives them the right of free ingress into other states, and egress from them; it insures to them in other states the same freedom possessed by the citizens of those states in the acquisition and enjoyment of property and in the pursuit of happiness; and it secures to them in other states the equal protection of their laws. It has been justly said that no provision in the Constitution has tended so strongly to constitute the citizens of the United States one people as this."[38] The provision does not mean, of course, that a citizen of Texas who goes to California carries the laws of Texas along with him; but that when he is in California he must be treated by that state as it treats its own citizens,[39] and we shall presently find that even this is subject to certain modifications.

ILLUSTRATIONS: *1. Invalid discriminations.* Maryland passed a law requiring persons not permanent residents of the state to take out licenses for the sale of goods. In declaring the law invalid the Court said: "The defendants might lawfully sell . . . any goods which the permanent resi-

---

[36] Estin v. Estin, 334 U.S. 541 (1948). See also *U.S. News & World Report,* June 18, 1948, p. 24 (This publication will be cited hereafter as *U.S. News*).

[37] Art. IV, sec. II.

[38] Paul v. Virginia, 8 Wall. 168 (1869).

[39] Neither aliens nor corporations reap any advantage from the clause under discussion, for neither are citizens.

dents of the state might sell . . . without being subjected to any higher tax or excise than exacted by law of such permanent residents." [40] Not only may a state not require a special license tax for the sale of goods by nonresidents, but such nonresidents may not be taxed on their general property in the state except as permanent residents of the state are taxed. Again, if a state permits its citizens to act as trustees of property within the state, it must extend the same privilege to nonresidents. In like manner, statutes that confine to residents the right to take property by will are invalid.[41]

2. *Valid discriminations.* Various types of discrimination are, however, permitted. Said the Court in Blake v. McClung: "There are privileges that may be accorded by a state to its own people, in which citizens of other states may not participate, except in conformity to such reasonable regulations as may be established by the state. For instance, a state cannot forbid citizens of other states from suing in its courts, that right being enjoyed by its own people; but it may require a nonresident, although a citizen of another state, to give bond for costs, although such bond be not required of a resident. . . . So, a state may, by rule uniform in its operation as to citizens of the several states, require residence within its limits for a given time before a citizen of another state, who becomes a resident thereof, shall exercise the right of suffrage or become eligible for office." [42]

Concerning common property. It has never been held that a state must allow the citizens of other states to share the common property of its citizens. More than a century ago New Jersey passed a law forbidding any person not a resident of the state from gathering oysters therein. This was upheld on the ground that the state was exercising ordinary property rights.[43] The same rule is applied with regard to wild game, fish, and common grazing land. By the same principle, students who are not permanent residents of a state are usually charged higher fees in public institutions of learning, such institutions being the common property of the people of the state. It might be argued also that a state could charge nonresidents more for the use of property connected with its courts and police protection, but these are such essential functions of government that discriminating rates in respect to them would doubtless be held to violate the privileges and immunities clause.[44]

Concerning professions and occupations. A citizen of one state may

[40] Ward v. Maryland, 12 Wall. 418 (1871).
[41] J. P. Hall, *Cases on Constitutional Law* (1926 ed.), pp. 204, 205, notes.
[42] 172 U.S. 239 (1898).
[43] Corfield v. Coryell, 4 Wash. C.C. 371 (1825).
[44] J. P. Hall, *Constitutional Law* (1910), p. 339.

not claim an unrestricted right to practice his profession or engage in his occupation in another state if it can be shown that residence in the state or residence for a certain period better qualifies him for following such profession or occupation in the state. Lawyers, being officers of the courts, in a technical sense at least, are reasonably required to be residents of the state.[45] A Nevada statute restricted the practice of medicine in the state to regular graduates in medicine and to those who had practiced in the state for ten years next preceding the enactment of the statute. It was contended by counsel for a Dr. Spinney, who had violated this statute, that ten years of practice in any other state was just as good experience as practice for that length of time in Nevada, and that the statute was, therefore, unreasonable. The court sustained the statute on the ground that different types of diseases and vocations in the several states rendered experience gained in medical practice in other states less valuable than experience gained in Nevada.[46] Statutes imposing somewhat similar restrictions upon the practice of dentistry and requiring bankers to be residents of the state have been upheld. States commonly require the proprietors of saloons to be residents.[47] These and similar regulations respecting various callings that have to do with the safety, health, and vital interests of citizens are permitted because the states would be under great difficulties in controlling nonresidents or in learning essential facts about newcomers seeking to engage in those callings.

In final analysis, then, the privileges and immunities guaranties of the Constitution "forbid only such legislation affecting citizens of the respective states as will substantially or practically put a citizen of one state in a condition of alienage when he is within or when he removes to another state, or when asserting in another state the rights that commonly appertain to those who are part of the political community known as the people of the United States." [48]

Interstate rendition. A third particular in which the states are brought a little closer together than are foreign states is in the matter of handling fugitives from justice. The nations commonly regulate the extradition of fugitives by treaty agreement. Our Constitution provides that, "a person charged in any State with treason, felony, or other crime, who shall flee from justice, and be found in another State, shall, on demand of the executive authority of the State from which he fled, be delivered up to be removed to the State having jurisdiction of the crime." [49] Thus the in-

---

[45] Hall, *Constitutional Law*, p. 341.
[46] Ex parte Spinney, 10 Nev. 323 (1875).
[47] J. P. Hall, *Cases on Constitutional Law* (1926 ed.), p. 212, note.
[48] Blake v. McClung, 172 U.S. 239 (1898).
[49] Art. IV, sec. II, cl. 2.

ternational practice of extradition is made constitutional law in the American states. As between our states, it is commonly referred to as "interstate rendition."

THE RENDITION PROCESS. The process of rendition is regulated by an act of Congress that is supplemented by local statutes in most states. It operates about as follows: A crime of robbery is committed in Maryland, and the person alleged to have committed the crime flees to New York. His whereabouts having become known to Maryland authorities, the Governor of Maryland notifies the Governor of New York, who causes the arrest of the alleged fugitive. The Governor of Maryland must present to the chief executive of New York a certified copy of the indictment or affidavit charging the person demanded with having committed the crime of robbery in Maryland. If the Governor of New York (assisted, of course, by his legal advisers) is satisfied with the regularity of these papers, and if it appears that the individual demanded is probably a fugitive from Maryland justice, he will have him surrendered to an officer of the State of Maryland, to be carried back to that state for trial.[50]

RENDITION NOT COMPULSORY. Ordinarily the requisitions of one governor to another are honored and the process of rendition works smoothly, but in no case may a governor be compelled to comply with a demand for an alleged fugitive. Speaking of the rendition clause of the Constitution and of the act of Congress relating to it, Chief Justice Taney said: "Looking to the subject-matter of this law, and the relations which the United States and the several states bear to each other, the Court is of opinion the words 'it shall be the duty' were not used as mandatory and compulsory, but as declaratory of the moral duty which this command created, when Congress had provided the mode of carrying it into execution. The act does not provide any means to compel the execution of this duty, nor inflict any punishment for neglect or refusal on the part of the executive of the state; nor is there any clause or provision in the Constitution which arms the government of the United States with this power. Indeed, such a power would place every state under the control and dominion of the General Government, even in the administration of its internal concerns and reserved rights."[51]

REASONS FOR NONCOMPLIANCE: *1. Unreasonable delay in making the requisition.* There are several types of cases in which, on more or less justifiable grounds, a governor has refused to comply with a requisition

[50] Roberts v. Reilly, 116 U.S. 80 (1885). Once back in Maryland, the accused may be tried for crime other than that specified in the request for his rendition. Furthermore, he has no redress, even if he has been kidnapped and returned without lawful authority. Willoughby, *op. cit.,* p. 173.

[51] Kentucky v. Dennison, 24 How. 66 (1860).

from the governor of another state. A Mr. Wurtsbaugh, for many years
a resident of Iowa, was wanted in Kentucky, where he was alleged to have
committed the crime of bigamy eighteen years before. The Attorney
General of Iowa, in advising the Governor not to comply with the requisition of the Governor of Kentucky, said: "It is repugnant to every sense of
justice to say that where a person leaves a state in the ordinary course of
affairs without any attempt of concealment, and for eighteen years lives
an upright life, he may be arrested and returned to the state where the
crime is claimed to have been committed eighteen years before, to be put
on trial for that offense, unless he is charged with murder [52] or treason.
. . . If the authorities of Kentucky desired to try Mr. Wurtsbaugh for the
offense of bigamy, an application for his return to that State should have
been made with reasonable promptness after the offense was committed.
Under all the circumstances of this case, I am of the opinion that Wurtsbaugh cannot now be held to be a fugitive from justice under the provisions of the federal Constitution." [53]

2. *Belief that fair trial will not be granted.* Governors have also refused
to honor requisitions from chief executives of other states in cases in which
it was felt that the fugitives would not be given a fair trial if delivered up.
For this reason, in 1918, Governor McCall of Massachusetts failed to comply with the request of the West Virginia authorities for a Negro alleged
to have committed a crime in the latter state. This refusal was, of course,
a great affront to West Virginia; but, as we have learned, a decision like
Governor McCall's is final.

West Virginians may have found some comfort in the letter of Governor
(Mrs.) Ferguson of Texas to Governor Fuller of Massachusetts, in which
she refused to deliver up A. P. Russell, wanted in Massachusetts for wife
desertion. "I have many precedents, either right or wrong," she wrote,
"but the most vivid to my memory of them all is the action of a Governor
of Massachusetts a short time ago in refusing to honor the requisition of
Governor John J. Cornwell of West Virginia for the interstate rendition
of a Negro charged with a felony in West Virginia, who sought a haven of
safety in your state and found it." [54]

---

[52] Governor Cullom of Illinois once refused to honor a requisition for two men wanted in
Pennsylvania for murder. His chief reason for refusal was that they had lived in Illinois for
fourteen years as respectable citizens. R. L. Mott, *Materials Illustrative of American Government* (1925), p. 48.

[53] C. A. Beard, *Readings in American Government and Politics* (1913), p. 149.

[54] J. M. Mathews and C. A. Berdahl, *Documents and Readings in American Government*
(1940 ed.), p. 102. In 1949 the Governor of the State of Washington requested the extradition from New York of George Hewitt, who was wanted in Washington for second-degree
perjury in connection with testimony he had given before the Washington un-American
Activities Committee in Seattle. Hewitt was discharged by Supreme Court Justice Aaron J.
Levy on a writ of habeas corpus. It is by this writ that an individual whose extradition

3. Political reasons. In international practice, extradition is commonly refused where an alleged fugitive is wanted for a political offense, such as participating in a rebellion. It would seem that the American states may apply the same principle in connection with crimes associated with politics. When former Governor Taylor of Kentucky was indicted in that state for participation in the murder of Governor Goebel, he took refuge in Indiana and the chief executive of that state would not deliver him to the Kentucky authorities.

Controversies between states. The fourth constitutional provision that brings the states into a closer degree of relationship than is enjoyed by foreign powers is that clause which calls for judicial settlement of interstate controversies. Sovereign states, such as the United States and Great Britain, may not sue each other unless both parties consent. Where they are unwilling to submit their differences to an international court, they may exhaust the arts of diplomacy and risk the force of arms in reaching a settlement. The states of the United States are forbidden to make war. They must settle all of their disputes by agreement or judicial means. Although many interstate disputes are settled by agreements between the states, the great majority of the more serious differences are brought to a solution through the operation of that incalculably valuable provision of the Constitution that extends the judicial power of the United States to controversies between the states.

ILLUSTRATIONS. In a number of cases the Supreme Court of the United States has been called upon to settle boundary disputes between the states. Many cases of other types have been similarly adjudicated. Missouri sued Illinois when the Sanitary District of Chicago, acting under state authority, constructed a drainage canal that carried sewage to the Mississippi, thus polluting the water supply for inhabitants of Missouri.[55] Some years ago, Colorado took so much water from the Arkansas River for irrigation purposes that Kansas felt deprived of her share, and the Supreme Court upheld the right of Kansas to sue Colorado.[56] When West Virginia came into the Union, she agreed to pay a fair part of the debt of Virginia as it stood January 1, 1861. It was necessary for Virginia to institute a number of suits in the courts of the United States before West Virginia would make

---

is sought tests the validity of the demand for him). Said the Judge in ordering the discharge of Hewitt: "There is nothing to warrant my sending this man to slaughter." The Judge thought that the Communists in Washington were in an almost impregnable position! He further objected to honoring the Washington requisition because Hewitt had not been indicted in that state by grand jury but by "information." He took this stand despite the fact that the latter method of indictment is common in many states and as long ago as 1884 was sustained as a fair proceeding by the Supreme Court of the United States. (On Hewitt's case see *AP* dispatch, May 12, 1949).

[55] 180 U.S. 208 (1901) and 200 U.S. 496 (1906).
[56] 185 U.S. 125 (1902) and 206 U.S. 46 (1907).

a settlement. This long-standing controversy over some $12,000,000 illustrates not only the importance of cases settled by judicial means, but also the rare tact and good judgment exercised by the Court in deciding such cases.[57]   A more recent case that aroused considerable interest was Arizona's unsuccessful attempt to secure a Court injunction to prevent California, certain other states, and the Secretary of the Interior from carrying out the Boulder Dam project.[58]

IV. FEDERAL AID TO THE STATES [59]

The topic to be discussed at this point differs materially from the preceding ones.   The subjects discussed in the preceding sections are primarily legal and political in character.   The present one, federal aid, has its legal and political aspects, to be sure; but its economic and social bearings are of much greater significance.   Here we find the nation and the states cooperating in various governmental functions, and we find the lines that divide national and state activities a trifle dim in some cases.   Federal aid to the states is not a new adventure in our system of government; but in recent decades it has increased both in amount and kind.   The states are now commonly required to "match the federal dollar," and, at the same time, federal control over the functions for which the money is appropriated has increased.   Federal aid presents an interesting problem in intergovernmental relationships.

The authority for federal aid.   In 1859 President Buchanan had before him for his approval or rejection the Morrill Bill (very similar to the measure passed in 1862 and signed by President Lincoln).   President Buchanan expressed strong disapproval of the policy to be effected by the bill.   He wrote: "Should the time ever arrive when the State governments shall look to the Federal Treasury for the means of supporting themselves and maintaining their systems of education and internal policy, the character of both Governments will be greatly deteriorated."

Then he turned to the main question, that of constitutional authority: ". . . The general proposition is undeniable that Congress does not possess the power to appropriate money in the Treasury [and not without logic he placed land grants in the same category as money] . . . for the purpose of educating the people of the respective States. . . . Should Congress exercise such a power, this would be to break down the barriers which have

[57] 246 U.S. 565 (1918).

[58] 283 U.S. 423 (1931).

[59] The Council of State Governments, *Federal Grants-in-Aid* (1949); Joseph P. Harris, "The Future of Federal Grants-in-Aid," *The Annals* . . . , Jan., 1940, pp. 14–26; V. O. Key, Jr., *The Administration of Federal Grants to the States* (1937); A. F. Macdonald, *Federal Aid* (1928).

been so carefully constructed in the Constitution to separate Federal from State authority. We should then not only 'lay and collect taxes, duties, imposts, and excises' for Federal purposes, but for every State purpose which Congress might deem expedient or useful." [60] President Buchanan has been dead for a long time!

The authority to make such appropriations has been found long since. Indeed, Alexander Hamilton and John Marshall, although they might have objected to federal grants-in-aid on the grounds of policy, would have had no scruples on the question of the authority of Congress to make such grants. The authority comes from several provisions of the Constitution, the particular provision covering a specific grant depending upon the purpose of the appropriation. Congress has the power to regulate interstate commerce, and it follows from this power, for example, that Congress may make grants of money to protect the forests that hold the waters that feed the interstate rivers. Another example: Congress has the authority to "lay and collect taxes, duties, imposts, and excises" for "the general welfare of the United States." Congress has decided that appropriations for land-grant colleges, old-age assistance, and a host of other things are for the "general welfare of the United States." The Supreme Court has upheld the constitutionality of such acts of Congress.[61]

Aid without strings attached. Earlier federal aid to the states was usually in the form of land grants, which were received subject only to the understanding that they were to be used for specified purposes. This system had its origin in 1785, when the old Congress of the Confederation decreed that certain lands of the Northwest Territory should be set aside for public schools. When Ohio was admitted to the Union in 1802, Congress granted one section of land in each township for schools, a practice that was continued for states admitted thereafter. In 1848 the grant was increased to two sections, and even this was doubled for Arizona, New Mexico, and Utah. Higher education also received assistance, the common practice until 1889 being to grant to each newly admitted state at least two townships for a university. States were also given lands for their seats of government, for building canals, for the stimulation of railroad construction, and for other purposes.

But these early grants contained no stipulations as to the minimum price the states should receive for the lands, nor were directions given for the administration of the funds thus acquired. The result was that the state authorities did as they pleased; and what most of them pleased to do causes us to deplore the lack of foresight, to put it mildly, of the rugged individuals who sat in high places a few generations ago. Often the land

---

[60] J. D. Richardson, *Messages and Papers of the Presidents*, Vol. V., pp. 545, 547.
[61] Council of State Governments, *op. cit.*, pp. 15 ff.

was sold at rates so low that the suspicion of corruption was persistent. The best that can be said is that it was parted with light-heartedly and with the unjustified optimism that there would always be more. In 1875, when much of the loss had already occurred, Congress began the practice of fixing a minimum price per acre at which the states might sell the lands, and from time to time has added more restrictions respecting sale and the administration of funds received.

Aid with supervision. As just noted, supervision of the type of grant mentioned above came too late to conserve the grant in most states. A new policy of "locking the stable before the horse was stolen" had its inception with the far-reaching Morrill Act of 1862, by which each state received 30,000 acres of land for each of its senators and representatives in Congress—such lands to be used for the establishment of colleges in which agriculture, mechanic arts, and other subjects should be taught. Safeguards in the use of the lands were few and ineffective as measured by present standards of federal regulation of subsidies to the states, but a beginning was made. Although failing to fix a minimum price at which land might be sold, Congress did establish requirements respecting the investing of the money obtained from sales and stipulated that the principal should not be expended. Another important provision prohibited the use of any of the money for college buildings, building construction being fixed as the obligation of the states. Here we see the beginning of the principle that a state, in order to receive federal aid, must itself assume a financial obligation.

The second Morrill Act (1890) provided cash appropriations for the land-grant colleges. Appropriations under this act, the Nelson amendment (1907), and the Bankhead-Jones Act (1935) now average about $100,000 annually for each state. Expenditure of any of this money for buildings is prohibited, as in the original act. But the most important feature of the act of 1890 is that the Secretary of the Interior may withhold the allotment from any state that does not fulfill its obligations under the act. At this point we see the introduction of the now very familiar and very powerful means of federal supervision. When the kindly central government approached them "with its hand in its pocket," states found it expedient to forget their right of freedom from federal interference in their local affairs and accept the supervision. Three years prior to the passage of the Second Morrill Act, Congress provided in the Hatch Act for cash contributions to the states and territories, the funds to be used for agricultural experiment stations. Under this act and later supplementary acts, particularly the Bankhead-Jones Act (1935) and Public Law 733 (1946), each state and territory now receives an annual appropriation averaging approximately $200,000 for experiment stations established in connection with the agricultural colleges. Although no adequate means of federal supervision of the expenditure of funds was provided for in the Hatch Act, federal authority in this direction was considerably strengthened by the Adams Act (1906).

Aid on the fifty-fifty basis plus federal supervision. Some authorities have considered the Weeks Act (1911), which provided small federal payments to the states for protection from fire of the forested watersheds of navigable streams, as marking the beginning of modern federal-aid policy. But a measure that appears to have the better claim to the honor is the Smith-Lever Act (1914), which provided for agricultural extension work through the co-operation of the federal government and the land-grant colleges. Under this law each state was to receive a uniform lump sum grant of $10,000 each year, but a much larger amount (about $4,000,000) was to be apportioned among the states on the basis of rural population. More significantly, no state could get "its share" of the money so apportioned unless it matched the federal appropriation. Furthermore, in order to get the money, a state had to secure approval of its plans of expenditure from the federal government.

In 1924 the Weeks Act was superseded by the Clarke-McNary Act, enlarging the scope of forest protection and requiring a state to match the federal allotment, an allotment to be determined by the Secretary of Agriculture on the basis of need. The act further provided that funds were to be expended under the direction of state officials, but that federal inspectors were to audit accounts and in certain other particulars strive to keep state standards up to a satisfactory minimum. The Federal Aid Road Act of 1916 authorized annual appropriations up to $25,000,000 for roads over which the mails were transported. Dollar-for-dollar matching was required, and funds were allocated to each state as follows: one third according to population, one third according to area, and one third according to rural delivery mileage. In addition, the act made provisions for advance federal approval of highway projects and for continuing federal supervision, and required each state to set up a department of highways.

The preceding paragraphs give examples of the standard type of federal aid. The federal-grant policy has a certain flexibility, but it will be noticed that each grant mentioned above contained three basic features: apportionment of funds among the states on some reasonable and fair basis (for example, agricultural extension funds on the basis of each state's rural population), state matching of the federal appropriation, and federal approval and inspection of state projects supported by the grant. There are exceptions to these general requirements, particularly to the matching requirement, as instanced by the Bankhead-Jones Act of 1935, which very liberally supplemented the earlier grants for agricultural extension and omitted any state-matching-of-funds requirement.

Emergency grants. During the depression years of the 'thirties the matching requirement was greatly relaxed and in a number of instances abandoned. In 1930 the federal government advanced $80,000,000 to the states to *enable them to match* the federal highway grants; two years later the Reconstruction Finance Corporation was authorized to advance $120,000,000 for similar purposes; and between 1933 and 1936 the National Industrial Recovery Administration and other relief agencies expended one billion dollars for highway purposes without any matching requirement. Between 1933 and 1935 the Federal Emergency Relief Administration distributed some three billion dollars (no matching requirement) among the states for relief. Thus the emergency grants made the regular grants puny by comparison.

FEDERAL RECOGNITION OF CITIES. Of more than passing significance was the increased co-operation between the federal authority and the cities that was brought about by emergency grants to the municipalities. Up to the period of the depression grants-in-aid had always been made to the states and through them they were passed down (a large part of them were) to local communities in the form of such benefits as schools, agricultural extension services, and roads. Public officials and careful observers of the realities of government had for a long time been aware of city-federal associations in a number of functions, such as police protection, traffic control, and health administration, but it was the large federal loans and *direct* grants to cities during the depression that caused the rank and file of citizens to become thoroughly familiar with the fact that the cities and the federal government were on intimate terms; that the cities had a rich Uncle Sam who would hand money to them, if such direct subsidy seemed advantageous. Under the National Industrial Recovery Act loans were made available to cities for public works and publicly owned instrumentalities and facilities, and the NIRA came also bearing *gifts* up to 30 per cent of the cost of labor and materials for any such project. The Public Works Administration built city halls, hospitals, and schools, and constructed water and sewage disposal plants. To be sure, PWA construction was chiefly through private contractors, but the cities profited to the extent that PWA carried a part of the cost of labor and materials. These and other federal aids to cities no doubt had a permanent effect upon the relationships of the two governments concerned. Some proof of a closer relationship is adduced by the fact that the Federal Aid Highway Acts of both 1944 and 1948 authorize specific and large sums for highway construction in urban areas, thus establishing a sort of urban federal-aid system. But the Federal

Airport Act of 1946, providing for an annual appropriation not to exceed $100,000,000 for airport construction on a federal-aid basis, goes the whole way. This act authorizes the Civil Aeronautics Administration to deal directly with any city, county, village, or magisterial district, and it is the first continuing grant-in-aid act so to provide.

Social security through federal aid. Space cannot be provided for a discussion of each of the programs supported in part by federal aid, but the most significant federal-aid development must have attention. The Social Security Act of 1935 carried provisions that revived grants for venereal disease control and for maternal and child health services and established other and new grant programs in public health. But these provisions were hardly more than incidental when the main sections of the act are considered. The act calls for grants for old-age assistance, aid to dependent children, aid to the blind, unemployment compensation, employment offices, child welfare, and crippled children services. Every program authorized by the act, with the exception of the old-age annuity plan, is carried by the grants-in-aid system, that is, by federal and state appropriations and state administration in accordance with federal standards.

An examination of the trends in the amount of federal aid appropriations reveals that relatively large sums have been made available for highways since 1916, when the highway aid program got under way, and that appropriations for this function far exceeded those made for any other function until 1936, when the national government entered the social security field. In 1950 approximately one half billion was appropriated for highways and roughly three times that amount for social security. Aside from emergency grants, federal aid appropriations to the states clearly constitute very low percentages of the total federal appropriations.

Probable future of federal aid. Federal aid has been opposed on various grounds: that the wealthy states pay much more in taxes to support the system than they receive back in grants-in-aid; that it leads to extravagant spending on the part of both the states and the national government (because pressure groups urge the Congressional appropriations and the states appropriate more money in order to get the "free" federal money); that federal supervision and direction (inseparable, and properly so, in any aid program) means federal control in state and local activities; and that it will eventually lead to federal monopolization of the taxing power. The majority of students of the subject are not greatly impressed with these and other objections; and, as a matter of fact, one hears them brought forward less frequently now than formerly. Opposition to specific grants remains, but the dire prophecies of the speedy end of state sovereignty *via* the federal grant route are seldom heard. The public seems to favor the grant-in-aid system. And a large majority of the state officials who administer the

grants have put themselves on record to the effect that the grants stimulate
state activity for a program; that federal supervision has improved state
standards of administration; that federal aid has not led to interference
in state affairs; and that they (slightly more than a majority of them) want
more of it.[62]

Almost certainly federal aid is here to stay.   But its relative permanence
should not cause us to throw up our hats for any aid program that may
be suggested.   Caution should be the watchword, and it is not better expressed by anyone than by a scholar, Professor Joseph P. Harris, whom the
Committee on Federal Grants-in-Aid of the Council of State Governments
cites [63] with approval.   Professor Harris writes:

Federal aid is neither wholly good nor wholly bad, and a discussion of its
merits and faults without attention to the provisions and the operation of
individual grants is of little merit.   The formulation of a rational, consistent
national policy must await a more discriminating consideration of the practical
operation and problems which experience has indicated. . . . Federal aid
should not be adopted indiscriminately for any state and local service which
can command a powerful enough lobby to force through the necessary legislation.   It is by no means clear that it is suitable to all activities alike.   In some
instances Federal aid ought to be refused because the service can be rendered
effectively and economically only by the Federal Government.   If new Federal
aid is provided, careful consideration should be given to the provisions of the
law which govern it, the allocation of aid to the several states, and the administration of the grants.   Some of the important older grants need to be reconsidered
in the light of actual experience, and defects corrected as far as possible.

Professor Harris makes further suggestions, as follows:

1. States appropriate money for particular services in order to get the "free"
federal money, with the result that other state services, services for which no
federal grants are made, may suffer for lack of funds.   It is suggested that this
condition might be avoided by the granting of federal aid to most of the more
expensive state functions.   This need not increase the total amount granted to
the states.

2. Little attempt has been made to determine in a scientific manner the
amount the federal authority should appropriate for each aided function.   The
result has been that pressure groups have had an undue influence over Congress in the matter of particular appropriations.   It is essential that there be
assembled factual data of the need for each aided service throughout the country.

3. The method of distribution of federal aid among the states needs more
careful attention.   Distribution on the basis of population is a very poor basis
for apportionment.   The method of distribution of highway grants, based in
equal proportion upon population, area, and mileage of post roads, approximates
a scientific approach, while a still more acceptable method, that of distributing

---

[62] Council of State Governments, *op. cit.*, pp. 273 ff.
[63] *Federal Grants-in-Aid*, p. 50.

a part of the money for forestry aid upon the basis of what adequate protection would cost in each state, is followed by the United States Forest Service.

4. Reasonable standards of administration are not maintained by the simple expedient of requiring the states to pay half, or a lesser part, of the cost of the aided function. The federal authorities should insist upon nonpolitical administration in the states, professional standards and techniques, and other features of efficient administration.[64]

V. CO-OPERATION BETWEEN GOVERNMENTS

As we think back over federal-state and interstate relations, we must conclude that there is a great deal of co-operation between governments. Some of it is required by the Constitution and laws, but much of it is voluntary. Certainly, if the voluntary element were removed, our Union could soon be appropriately styled these dis-United States. The federal grants to the states have been discussed as outstanding examples of federal-state co-operation. From among many other examples a few are selected.

The first Congress under the Constitution, although it had the power to regulate pilots, simply adopted the existing state laws on pilotage, acting upon the very sound principle that the states were more competent to cope with local conditions. In 1913, in deference to the dry states, Congress prohibited the shipment of liquor into their borders, a policy made permanent by the second section of the Twenty-first Amendment of the Constitution. In matters over which national standards are desirable, the states often adopt a national law or regulation. A majority of the states have found it advantageous to require all airplanes and pilots operating within their jurisdiction to possess federal licenses. State and federal law-enforcement officers co-operate in making arrests. In this connection the Federal Bureau of Investigation with its experts and their collection of fingerprints and other criminal identification records affords invaluable aid to local officers. State courts enforce certain types of federal law, and federal courts apply state laws in particular cases. In general administration the two governments often work together, as in public health, vocational rehabilitation, agricultural extension, and employment services.[65] Perhaps the most significant illustration of such co-operation is the administration of the Federal Social Security Act of 1935, the provisions of which are outlined in a later chapter of this volume. During the Second World War there was a relatively high degree of co-operation among governments—national, state, and local. This was particularly noticeable in the administration of Selective Service and price control. Although the

[64] Joseph P. Harris, "The Future of Federal Grants-in-Aid," *The Annals,* January, 1940, pp. 14–26.
[65] Mathews, *American State Government* (1934 ed.), Ch. III.

national government and the states exhibit a notable lack of "team work" in some activities, particularly in the matter of taxation, on the whole the advantages of co-operation are recognized and applied in an encouraging number of instances.

Interstate co-operation has also made some progress, but it has been slow. As long ago as 1892 the American Bar Association started a movement for uniform state laws, and the National Conference of Commissioners on Uniform State Laws was created. The commissioners have drafted some fifty model statutes to date; but the discouraging feature is that not many of them have been adopted by a majority of the states. In the matter of admission to certain professions, such as medicine and law, many states now recognize one another's certificates of admission—a matter of concern to a relatively small group, to be sure, but indicative of a desirable spirit of co-operation. The Conference of Governors had its inception in 1908. Designed to consider such matters as uniform laws, taxation, and the appropriate sphere of state government, its earlier annual meetings turned out to be little more than polite speechmaking parties, but with the expert assistance of the Council of State Governments it now serves a most useful purpose.[66] This Council of State Governments is the outstanding organization for interstate co-operation and the improvement of state government generally. It is the secretariat for the Governors' Conference and several other similar associations of state officials. It compiles information and distributes it to state agencies; it publishes a valuable monthly magazine, *State Government,* and a biennial volume, *The Book of the States,* that is full of facts and figures. During the Second World War the Council was essentially a defense and war agency, playing, for example, a significant part in securing the removal of dimension restrictions on commercial motor vehicles operating in interstate commerce.

The future of the states. For some years, but particularly during the last twenty-five, some very distinguished authorities have questioned the capacity of the states to discharge the functions for which our governmental system makes them responsible.[67] The proposals of these authorities vary somewhat, but in general it may be said that their idea is that the states should give way to "regions," as a New England Region, a Pacific Northwest Region. Some propose that the great metropolitan areas, often

[66] See "Governors' Conference," *State Government,* Aug., 1948, Aug., 1949, and Aug., 1950.
[67] Frank Bane, "Mr. Bane and States Rights," *State Government,* Mch., 1945, pp. 48–49; Donald Davidson, "Political Regionalism and Administrative Regionalism," *The Annals,* Jan., 1940, pp. 138–143; W. Y. Elliott, *The Need for Constitutional Reform* (1935); Rudolf Heberle, "Regionalism: Some Critical Observations," *Social Forces,* Mch., 1943, pp. 280–286; C. E. Merriam, "Urbanism," *American Journal of Sociology,* Mch., 1940, pp. 720–730; D. W. Robinson, "Voluntary Regionalism in the Control of Water Resources," *The Annals,* Jan., 1940, pp. 116–123.

spreading into several states, be cut away from state authorities and established as city-states. It is a fact that present state boundaries do not conform in many cases to economic organization, political interest, social custom, and so on. It is also a fact that the states have come to lean more and more heavily upon the national government, particularly for money. Professor Charles E. Merriam is probably right when he says that the states have been singularly ill-equipped and ill-qualified to serve as guides and guardians to the metropolitan areas. Regionalism, which is suggested to supplant or partially supplant the states, is nothing new. It existed in Italy under the Romans, in Manchuria under the Chinese, and the United States government makes extensive use of administrative districts of varying sizes for its Federal Reserve Banks, its Home Loan Banks, its internal revenue collection, its Food and Drug Administration, and its scores of other services. The advocates of regionalism would carry this principle much further, divesting the states of all or nearly all their powers, and transferring them to the regions. It may be that we are coming to some such arrangement. But there are many obstacles in the way. Just where are the boundaries of the regions to be drawn? How can the people be persuaded to accept them after they have been drawn? The states have not been conspicuously successful as units of government, but the people in them still have civic cohesion, state pride, and many other sentiments that are likely to obstruct the proposal of the regionalists. Furthermore, the states still have innumerable and indispensable functions to perform. The federal government has not so much encroached upon the states' powers as it has joined with the states in grants-in-aid programs and otherwise to make more effective the powers the states possess. Evidence is lacking to prove that regions could perform many services any better than they are now administered by the states. We may expect to see more of the sort of regionalism we are now experiencing under the national administration; we may have more regionalism under interstate co-operation; but regionalism that envisages the abolition of the states, or anything approximating it, is largely a dream.

VI. GOVERNMENT OF THE TERRITORIES [68]

One other topic may be appropriately considered in this chapter—the territories of the United States. Under its power to carry on war and make treaties the United States has ample authority to acquire territory. The Constitution gives Congress full authority to govern such possessions

---

[68] E. G. Arnold, "Self-Government in U.S. Territories," *Foreign Affairs*, 1947, pp. 655–666; Mathews, *op. cit.*, Ch. XX; U.S. State Department, *The United States and Non-Self-Governing Territories*, Publication No. 2812 (1947); Willoughby, *op. cit.*, Chs. XXII–XXVIII.

through the provision that it "shall have power to dispose of and make all needful rules and regulations respecting the territory or other property belonging to the United States." [69]   Vast areas of our continental Republic were acquired by war and treaties, and, with the admission of the forty-eighth state to the Union in 1912, the last territorial government in the continental United States disappeared.   Beginning with the purchase of Alaska in 1867, lands beyond the sea have been acquired, lands that are still governed as territories.   Besides Alaska, the principal territories and the dates of acquisition are as follows: Hawaii, Puerto Rico, and Guam (1898); American Samoa (1899); Panama Canal Zone (1904); Virgin Islands (1917).   A number of small islands in the Pacific Ocean have been acquired at various times by discovery, occupation, and conquest.

The Constitution in the territories.   Does the Constitution of the United States apply in its entirety to the territories?   Does it "follow the flag"?   Many of its provisions show in clear terms that they apply only to national and state relationships.   But what of the provision respecting trial by jury, and other provisions designed to protect persons and property?   For a long time authorities supposed that these provisions applied in all territory governed by the United States.   But a problem arose in 1898 when we annexed territory in which the inhabitants were wholly unfamiliar with American institutions and in which some of the natives were only a short distance removed from savagery.   Manifestly, indictment by grand jury, trial by jury, and certain other features of Anglo-Saxon legal procedure could not be made to operate among these peoples.   What was to be done?   The Supreme Court of the United States was equal to the emergency.   In cases before it arising out of the annexations of 1898 the Court prepared the ground by ruling in effect that there were three "United States": (1) that formed by the states of the Union; (2) the same plus the territory incorporated into the Union ("incorporated" is a term applied to those territories, at present Alaska and Hawaii, that by act of Congress enjoy a status designed to fit them for statehood); and (3) the states of the Union, plus incorporated territory, plus unincorporated territory, that is, territory under the jurisdiction of the United States but to which some provisions of the Constitution need not be applied.   Upon the basis of these distinctions the court held that mere procedural regulations, such as indictment by grand jury and trial by jury, did not bind Congress in establishing government for the unincorporated territories.   The court also held, however, that the fundamental substantive provisions of the Constitution, such as the prohibition against taking property for public use without just compensation and depriving an individual of life, liberty, or property with-

[69] Art. IV, sec. III, cl. 2.

out due process of law, did apply.[70]   The decisions are not altogether convincing from the constitutional standpoint, but they have the merit of practicality.

Territories with representative government.   As previously stated, Congress has plenary powers to govern the territories. Congress may allow them local autonomy or not, as it sees fit. It has given all the more important territories some form of representative government. By several acts, of which that of 1912 is most significant, Congress gave Alaska a territorial legislature of two houses, elected by citizens of the United States (Alaskans are such citizens) who are twenty-one years of age and who can read and write English. The legislature is authorized to exercise such powers as are not forbidden by the Constitution of the United States and Congress. Its acts are subject to veto by the governor, but this veto may be overridden by a two-thirds majority. The territorial governor and other administrative officers, judges, attorneys, and marshals are appointed by the President and the Senate for a term of four years. General administrative matters are under the supervision of several of the great departments in Washington, the Department of the Interior carrying the greater part of the responsibility. The only part the territory takes in the government of the United States is through its popularly elected delegate or commissioner, who sits in the House of Representatives at Washington. The part is extremely small, for the delegate has no vote. The Hawaiian territorial government need not detain us. It is the same in all essentials as that of Alaska. Strong movements are on foot to bring both of these territories into the Union. Although there are "cons" as well as "pros" on the subject, and not every citizen of either territory prefers statehood, admission to the Union quite probably will be accomplished in the foreseeable future.

Although unincorporated, both Puerto Rico and the Virgin Islands have representative government that does not differ materially from that of Alaska and Hawaii except that the Puerto Ricans now elect their governor and the Virgin Islands has slightly less local autonomy than the other three territories that have representative government. Puerto Rico's "resident commissioner" joins the "delegates" of Alaska and Hawaii in the national House of Representatives and like those delegates he has no vote. The Virgin Islands has no delegate or commissioner in Congress. The inhabitants of both Puerto Rico and the Virgin Islands are, by act of Congress, citizens of the United States.

Government of other areas.   Representative government does not obtain in any appreciable degree in the other territories and domains over which our flag flies. These areas include the territories of American Samoa,

---

[70] Willoughby, *op. cit.*, Ch. XXVII, and cases there cited.

Guam, several other small islands in the Pacific, and the Panama Canal Zone (to be strictly accurate this area is not a territory but is under perpetual lease to the United States). Then there are the Carolines, Marshall, and Mariana Islands, formerly administered by Japan for the League of Nations and now governed by the United States under a trusteeship arrangement with the United Nations.[71] The Guantanamo Bay naval base we hold under lease from Cuba, and we have 99-year leases for bases in Newfoundland, the Bahamas, Bermuda, and several other islands in the West Indies, bases that President Roosevelt took in exchange (1940) for fifty old destroyers when Britain was making her magnificent stand against Hitler. Of course the naval bases must be strictly under naval control. The same sort of government is commonly thought to be necessary in American Samoa, Guam, and our other Pacific islands. At any rate that is essentially what they have. The Panama Canal Zone, vital to our defense, is under the control of the Army. As for the islands we now administer under trusteeship, there is little self-government as yet except in local community matters, but the United States obligates itself "to develop self-government" among these peoples, "to take due account" of their political aspirations, and to assist them in the development of free political institutions.

Philippine independence. Practically everyone knows that the United States took the Philippines at the end of the Spanish-American War, but not everyone knows that Presidents and other high officials dangled the tempting prize of ultimate independence to the Filipinos for thirty years and that independence seemed as "ultimate" in 1929 as it had in 1899. True, we gave them self-government not unlike that enjoyed by the "incorporated" territories, but when they asked, How about independence? we always replied, You are not quite ready; not just yet. It seems fair to say that in a very literal sense our depression of the 'thirties gave the Filipinos independence. American laborers on the Pacific Coast, where there were considerable numbers of Filipinos, resented their competition. Then the goods coming duty free from the Philippines stirred to action American sugar producers, dairy husbandmen, cordage fabricators, and others. These new-found proponents of independence were joined by those who on broader grounds had always advocated it, and in January, 1933, Congress passed an independence bill. President Hoover gave the measure a vigorous veto, and Congress immediately overrode it. But the measure was not acceptable to the Filipinos, and in 1934 a new one was enacted. This bill provided for independence after a ten-year transition period, after which the United States would relinquish all military bases, but the matter of naval bases was left for later agreement. When, in 1941, the Japanese occupied the Philippines, the United States gave its pledge

[71] Francis B. Sayre, "The Pacific Islands We Hold," *Atlantic*, Jan., 1950, pp. 70–74.

that the invader would be driven out and independence granted as scheduled. The loyalty of the great majority of the Filipinos to the United States
and their courage in defending their homeland made the fulfillment of this
pledge (July 4, 1946) a most pleasant national duty. Under provisions of
the Philippine Independence Act and later arrangements the United States
may maintain in the Philippines naval, military, and air bases and for a
period of years the Philippines shall have trade concessions in the United
States. But the Philippine Republic is not altogether happy. It has
serious economic and political difficulties, and large grants of money from
the United States have not appreciably aided in their solution.[72]

The District of Columbia. The government of the capital city stands
in a class by itself. The Constitution gives Congress the authority to decide upon the place for the seat of the government of the United States
and to exercise exclusive legislation over such district. For a long time
the inhabitants of the District of Columbia were allowed to manage their
local affairs, but since 1874 Congress has exercised complete control.
Three commissioners, two civilian residents of Washington, and an army
engineer, appointed by the President and the Senate, are in direct charge
of administration. Congress, as the "City Council," must concern itself
with such matters as the granting of power to the city commissioners to
regulate goats in the District of Columbia and the posting of prices in
Washington barber shops. The people of Washington are not officially
consulted about their government. Even the taxes they must pay for
local enterprises are determined by the commissioners, subject to the approval of Congress. But since so many people from all over the country
go to Washington on various missions and make use of its public services, Congress appropriates a part of the local budget from the national
treasury.

Not only do residents of Washington have little part in their local government, but they have no part in the national government. They have no
representatives in Congress, and they have no voice in electing the President.
They are disfranchised. Of course, many of the inhabitants retain a legal
residence in some other place and may vote there, as does President Truman,
who votes in Independence, Missouri. But this arrangement is decidedly
inconvenient for the majority of Washington people; and, even if they all
managed to vote elsewhere, they would still have no control over their
local government.

In truth the government of the world's greatest democracy is undemocratic "in its heart," affording its capital city's inhabitants no substantial
opportunities to participate in either national or local affairs. Agitation
breaks out from time to time against this "taxation without representation,"

[72] *United States News* . . . , Nov. 18, 1949, pp. 24–25.

and the demand is made for the suffrage and home rule. The latter is particularly to be desired because as matters now stand the District is poorly governed and its affairs take the precious time of Congress and President. In 1950 the Senate passed a home rule bill for the District of Columbia, but it remained bottled up in a house committee.[73] Just how long Congress will go on with the near folly of serving as a board of aldermen for the capital city no one knows.

Reading List

Blake Clark, *Hawaii: The 49th State* (1947).

Jane P. Clark, "Interstate Compacts and Social Legislation," *Pol. Sci. Quar.* (1935), L, 502–525 (1936), LI, 36–61.

V. S. Clark and Others, *Puerto Rico and Its Problems* (1930).

The Council of State Governments, *The Book of the States, 1950–1951*, Sec. I.
———, *Federal Grants-in-Aid* (1949).

R. E. Cushman, *Leading Constitutional Decisions* (1950 ed.), pp. 262–268, and Chs. IX and X.

W. F. Dodd, *Cases and Materials on Constitutional Law* (1949 ed.), 307–434.

W. Y. Elliott, *The Need for Constitutional Reform* (1935).

L. H. Evans, *The Virgin Islands: From Naval Base to New Deal* (1945).

E. D. Fite, *Government by Co-operation* (1932), especially Chs. III–VII.

F. Frankfurter, "The Compact Clause of the Constitution—A Study in Interstate Adjustments," *Yale Law Review* (1925), XXXIV, 685–758.

W. B. Graves, "The Future of the American States," *Am. Pol. Sci. Rev.* (1936), XXX, 24–50. *Uniform State Action* (1934).

W. H. Haas, *The American Empire* (1940).

J. R. Hayden, *The Philippines: A Study in National Development* (1942).

V. O. Key, Jr., *The Administration of Federal Grants to the States* (1937).

G. L. Kirk, *Philippine Independence* (1936).

A. F. Macdonald, *Federal Aid: A Study of the American Subsidy System* (1928).

J. M. Mathews, *The American Constitutional System* (1940 ed.), Chs. V–VI, XX.

N. J. Padelford, *The Panama Canal in Peace and War* (1942).

Harvey S. Perloff, *Puerto Rico's Economic Future* (1949).

J. A. Scott, *Law of Interstate Rendition* (1917).

G. W. Spicer, "The Constitutional Status and Government of Alaska," Johns Hopkins University Studies . . . (1927), XLV, 450–567.

Tax Institute, *Tax Barriers to Trade* (1941).

R. G. Tugwell, *Stricken Land: The Story of Puerto Rico* (1947).

U.S. Department of State, *The United States and Non-Self-Governing Territories*, Publication No. 2812 (1947).

C. Warren, *The Supreme Court and Sovereign States* (1924).

[73] *New York Times*, ed., Aug. 16, 1950.

W. W. Willoughby, *The Principles of the Constitutional Law of the United States* (1930 ed.), Chs. XI–XVI, XXI–XXVIII.

Questions and Problems

1. Upon what constitutional authority do the states erect barriers to interstate trade? Explore the "economics" of these trade barriers.
2. Discuss the origin, the use, and abuse of the principle that the states may not tax the United States and that the United States may not tax the states.
3. Did Louisiana have a republican form of government when practically every officer of the state did Huey Long's bidding?
4. How do you square the refusal of a state to recognize certain out-of-state divorces with the "full faith and credit" requirement?
5. Show the extent to which the provision that "the citizens of each state shall be entitled to all privileges and immunities of citizens in the several states" means less than it appears to mean.
6. A fugitive from justice escaped from the penitentiary in state A eight years ago, and he has since resided as a good citizen in state B. His extradition is now sought by the governor of state A. What is the best course for the fugitive to follow?
7. Discuss the developments in federal aid to the states since the Second Morrill Act.
8. Give a critical analysis of this statement: *If the United States and the states should operate in strict accordance with the Constitution we would have perfect government.*
9. Holding in mind the conduct of the United States toward its territories and dependencies, advance reasons for charging it with imperialism; for maintaining that it has been anti-imperialistic.

☆ 6 ☆

Civil Liberties

IN any democratic country individual liberties or rights are secured by constitutions, statutes, customs, and public opinion. In our own country we lay considerable stress upon the guaranties of written constitutions. Since the civil rights provisions of the federal and state constitutions are so closely related, the essential civil liberties can better be understood by a discussion based upon the significant provisions of both federal and state constitutions. That is the plan followed in this chapter.

I. CIVIL LIBERTIES IN AMERICAN CONSTITUTIONS

A bill of rights in each of our constitutions. The state constitutions adopted in the period of the Revolution, a time when liberals in the Western World were thinking and writing a great deal about the rights of man under government, included, as one of their most important sections, a bill of rights. The states admitted to the Union since 1789 have followed the example of the original states. The framers of the federal Constitution did not incorporate a bill of rights into that instrument because a number of the members of the Philadelphia Convention felt that, since the national government was to be one with expressly delegated powers, no limitations were necessary. Their idea was, of course, that delegation was itself a limitation in that it implicitly denied to the national government the right to exercise any powers other than those delegated.[1] On the other side, it was ably shown by popular leaders that the government might become offensive in the exercise of those powers that were delegated to it.[2] Furthermore, in those days the people were fearful of a central government and especially jealous of their liberty. Then there was the powerful influence of example. The state constitutions contained bills of rights. Why should

[1] Hamilton's argument—*The Federalist*, No. LXXXIV.
[2] Madison's argument—*Annals of Congress*, Vol. I, pp. 440 ff.

the federal Constitution be a notable exception? In 1791, in response to the popular demand, the desired restrictions upon the national government were added to the Constitution in the form of the first ten amendments.

Protection of the individual by two constitutions. Clearly, from the above, a person residing in one of the states of the United States is protected from government encroachment by two constitutions—by the federal Constitution and by the constitution of the state in which he resides. The separate spheres of these constitutions in giving one personal security can be understood by illustration. Let us take the case of Olaf Hansen, a resident of North Dakota. He is protected in four ways. *First,* the first eight amendments[3] (the ninth and tenth are not important in this connection) of the federal Constitution, plus Article I, section ix, clauses 2 and 3; and Article III, section ii, clause 3; and Article III, section iii, enumerate the rights in which he is secured against the national government and against the national government *only.* *Second,* Article I, section x, clause 1, and the Fourteenth Amendment, section 1 (the second sentence), represent the civil rights in which he is secured against any arbitrary act of the State of North Dakota. *Third,* the Thirteenth Amendment affords him protection from both the national government and his state. *Fourth,* the bill of rights in the Constitution of North Dakota protects him against the government of that state.

Duplicate and supplementary guaranties. The bill of rights of Olaf Hansen's North Dakota duplicates to some extent those provisions of the federal Constitution that protect him against his state government: for example, the federal Constitution prohibits his state from passing an *ex post facto* law; the Constitution of North Dakota carries the same prohibition. For the most part, however, his rights under the federal Constitution are supplemented, not duplicated, by his state constitution: for example, the Constitution of the United States gives him the right of trial by jury in the *national* courts, whereas the state constitution gives him that right in the *state* courts. It is apparent that Olaf Hansen's civil rights differ from those of John Austin in Kentucky only in so far as the bills of rights of the two states differ. Since there are seldom any essential differences between the bill of rights of one state and that of another the people in the several states of the Union enjoy substantially the same civil liberties. It is understood, of course, that while our constitutional liberties are essentially the same, the degree to which they are actually enjoyed may vary somewhat with race, color, nationality, economic status, or other factors that commonly draw lines even in our democratic society.

---

[3] The student should turn to the Constitution at the back of this book and read these parts as they are referred to.

II. FREEDOM OF THE PERSON AND OF EXPRESSION [4]

1. Personal freedom. The right of a man to be free, a right so fundamental as not to call for any positive expression concerning it in most
countries, was not established in our country until 1865, when the Thirteenth Amendment gave freedom a constitutional basis in the following
language: "Neither slavery nor involuntary servitude, except as a punishment for crime whereof the party shall have been duly convicted, shall
exist within the United States or any place subject to their jurisdiction."
A great many of the state constitutions contain this clause against slavery at the present time, but since the Thirteenth Amendment prohibits
slavery in any part of the United States or its territory, the state guaranties are simply duplications.

ITS LIMITATIONS. Basing his argument on the Thirteenth Amendment,
one Robertson, a seaman who had deserted his vessel, claimed that the
statute of the United States under which he had been arrested and returned to his ship was unconstitutional in that it forced him to "involuntary servitude." According to the Supreme Court, the words "involuntary servitude" were used in the Thirteenth Amendment in addition to the
word "slavery" in order to cover possible attempts to introduce the Mexican
peonage system and the Chinese coolie trade, either of which would amount
to practically the same thing as slavery. The Court further pointed out
that neither the Amendment in question nor any other civil rights provisions of the federal Constitution were "intended to lay down any novel
principle of government," and that since seamen had been forced to live
up to their agreements in other countries from time immemorial and in
the United States since our government was founded, "it cannot be open
to doubt that the provision against involuntary servitude was never intended
to apply to their contracts." [5]

Nor did the newly emancipated Negro find any novel principles in
the Amendment. When Congress passed an act for the purpose of preventing any discrimination against Negroes at inns, theaters, and similar
public places, the Supreme Court held that discrimination on account of
race or color did not constitute slavery and that the act therefore went
beyond any power granted to Congress by the Thirteenth Amendment. [6]
If, however, a state by legislative act attempts to force a laborer, who
is a debtor to his employer or prospective employer, to pay his debt, work

---

[4] Z. Chafee, Jr., *Free Speech in the United States* (1941 ed.); W. F. Dodd, *Cases and
Materials on Constitutional Law* (1949 ed.), pp. 811–863; *To Secure These Rights,* The Report of the President's Committee on Civil Rights (1947); S. P. Weaver, *Constitutional Law
and Its Administration* (1946), Chs. 20, 23.

[5] Robertson v. Baldwin, 165 U.S. 275 (1897).

[6] Civil Rights Cases, 109 U.S. 3, 20–25 (1883).

out the debt in the service of his employer, or go to jail,[7] such action is held
to be contrary to the Thirteenth Amendment, since a statute of this kind
would make a peon of the debtor—reduce him to involuntary servitude.[8]
In such cases the creditor may, of course, seek redress through civil action
for breach of contract. This action against a debtor with no property
may not satisfy the creditor, but the courts, acting under the Thirteenth
Amendment, have decided that liberty for the debtor is better than the
pound of flesh for the creditor.[9]

2. Religious liberty. If we regret that our country was one of the last
to abolish personal slavery, we may pride ourselves that we led in the movement for freedom of conscience. There was considerable religious toleration in several colonies even in the seventeenth century, and Rhode Island
permitted full religious freedom. During the period of the Revolution
the idea of religious freedom grew along with other democratic principles
and came to receive general acceptance. It is not surprising, therefore,
that the first provision of the First Amendment of the Constitution is that
"Congress shall make no law respecting an establishment of religion, or
prohibiting the free exercise thereof." Though this restriction does not
operate against the states, the Supreme Court of the United States has held
that religious liberty is one of the liberties the Fourteenth Amendment
secures against state encroachment. Furthermore, the constitutions of the
states regularly carry a declaration for religious liberty.

THE MEANING OF RELIGIOUS LIBERTY. What does religious liberty mean?
It means that no church shall be established or directly aided by a government; that an individual may have any religion he prefers and exercise it
freely; that he may have no religion at all and strive to "convert" others to
it. But the prohibition respecting an establishment of religion is not commonly interpreted to prevent indirect government aids to religion, such as
the adoption and enforcement of Sabbath observance laws and supplying
free transportation of pupils to parochial schools, where such service is
furnished to those attending public schools. And the "religious freedom"
of individuals is not infringed by statutes against blasphemy, nor does a

---

[7] Such statutes were passed by some of the Southern states for the purpose of getting easy
control over the colored labor.

[8] Bailey v. Alabama, 219 U.S. 219 (1911). A somewhat similar statute was still on the
books in Georgia until quite recently, when the Supreme Court of the United States declared
it void. Taylor v. Georgia, 315 U.S. 25 (1942). A Florida "peonage" statute met the same
fate in the Supreme Court of the United States in 1944. Pollock v. Williams, 322 U.S. 4.

[9] It seems, however, that a unique performer, for example, a star baseball player, who
has agreed to serve a particular person or organization for a specified period and to serve no
other during the period, may be forced to live up to his contract to the extent of not serving
another during the period agreed upon. But he cannot be forced to "play ball" for a particular person or club. See C. K. Burdick, *The Law of the American Constitution* (1922),
pp. 499–500.

religious sanction of plurality in wives save the joint spouse from prosecution for bigamy. In other words, one may not invoke the guaranty of religious freedom against laws established by society for the maintenance of the public peace and morality.

LEGISLATION AND COURT DECISIONS RELATING TO RELIGIOUS LIBERTY. Since 1937 we have had a number of interesting and significant cases on the subject of religious liberty. Jehovah's Witnesses, fortified with stout beliefs and armed with their sectarian literature and phonographs, go about spreading their beliefs on street corners and from door-to-door. They decry any form of religious ceremony, and they refuse to salute the flag because they believe that in doing so they would violate the commandment against bowing down to any "graven image." Numerous local ordinances have been enacted to curb their activities.

A small city in Georgia (the action is almost invariably taken by a small city or town) by ordinance made it a nuisance to distribute literature within the city limits without first obtaining permission of the city manager. A Witness was convicted of violating the ordinance, and the Supreme Court of the United States held the ordinance void as being in violation of the freedom of the press, of speech, and of religion.[10] A Connecticut law required that before money might be solicited for a religious cause the local public welfare council should pass upon the question of whether the cause is religious. Witnesses were convicted of violating this law, but the Supreme Court again decided for the Witnesses, holding that the law was invalid in that it authorized the welfare councils to censor religion.[11]

The flag salute cases. Jehovah's Witnesses were expelled from school in a Pennsylvania district because they would not comply with an order of the local school board that all pupils must salute the flag. The Supreme Court, eight-to-one, sustained the school board, holding that cohesive patriotic sentiments and national unity were more important than the protection of the non-conformist views of the Witnesses, and that the school boards were the appropriate authorities to determine the means by which unifying sentiment was to be developed in the schools.[12] But Mr. Justice Stone dissented; and, in a later case, three of the justices who had decided with the majority took the unusual step of saying they had been wrong on the flag salute issue.

On December 22, 1942, Congress, with the encouragement of the Ameri-

[10] Lovell v. Griffin, 303 U.S. 444 (1938). On May 3, 1943, the Supreme Court went even further, holding void an ordinance imposing a flat license tax for the privilege of selling literature from door to door, on the ground that, as applied to religious literature, the ordinance invaded the freedom of religion. Murdock v. Pennsylvania, 319 U.S. 105.

[11] Cantwell v. Connecticut, 310 U.S. 296 (1940).

[12] Minersville District v. Gobitis, 310 U.S. 586 (1940).

can Legion, adopted a sensible resolution (House Joint Resolution 359) concerning respect to the flag. The resolution states that "civilians will always show full respect to the flag when the pledge is given by merely standing at attention, men removing the headdress." The resolution did not, of course, prevent state and local authorities from requiring students to salute the flag, but it did indicate an encouraging degree of enlightenment among congressmen.

The compulsory flag salute, as decreed by a school board or some other official body of the state, was finally disposed of by the Supreme Court of the United States in a notable opinion written by Mr. Justice Jackson. This decision, which overruled the decision in the Pennsylvania flag salute case, was that the compulsory salute was nothing less than a forced declaration contrary to the religion of Jehovah's Witnesses and was in violation of religious liberty as guaranteed under the First and Fourteenth Amendments of the Constitution.[13] Is it not passing strange that school boards should have thought that a "stiff-arm" salute, enforced by expulsion from school, would teach students to respect and love their country? Compulsion has been known to inspire fear and hatred, but never a healthy loyalty or any sort of affection.

Religious instruction in the public schools. In 1940 the Board of Education in Champaign, Illinois, made an arrangement under which Jews, Protestants, and Roman Catholics might give instruction in their respective faiths for a short period each week, in the public school buildings and on school time, to students whose parents approved. Students not taking the religious instruction were required to leave their classrooms and go to some other place in the building for continued pursuit of their secular studies. The Supreme Court held such a religious instruction program to be in violation of the First and Fourteenth Amendments.[14] This decision does not, the Court was careful to point out, "manifest a governmental hostility to religion," but rather a determination to preserve the wall between Church and State. A slightly different situation is presented when arrangement is made for the release of public school pupils to attend religious instruction classes outside school buildings and off school grounds. At least a New York court has held that this "released time" does not violate the religious liberty guaranty.[15]

The wartime conscientious objector. For centuries there have been citizens who on religious and other grounds of conscience have refused to participate in war. Many of them have been persons of the highest character. The best known of them are the Quakers, who have played a notable

---

[13] W. Va. State Bd. of Educ. v. Barnette, 319 U.S. 624 (1943).
[14] McCollum v. Bd. of Educ., 333 U.S. 203 (1948).
[15] Lewis v. Spaulding, 85 N.Y. S.2d 682 (1948).

part in the development of American institutions and to whose qualities of mind and heart we pay unstinted tribute.

Although the constitutional guaranty of religious liberty does not include exemption from service in the armed forces on grounds of religion, American practice has been to deal moderately with conscientious objectors. The provision of grace in our Selective Service Act of 1940 exempted from combat training and service any person "who, by reason of religious training and belief, is conscientiously opposed to war in any form." The selective service officials interpreted this as exempting not only the conscientious objectors who were members of recognized religious sects, but also those who had other moral and philosophical grounds against bearing arms. Under this act, exemptees who were willing to perform noncombatant duty were assigned to medical or other non-combat units of the services. Exemptees who refused to participate in noncombatant activities were assigned to work of national importance under civilian direction. Such work included soil conservation, irrigation, forestry and wild life protection, rural rehabilitation, and public health service.[16] For its part, then, the government was liberal in the provisions it made for accommodating the relatively few persons who had conscientious scruples against bearing arms. For their part, many of the "CO's" performed essential or important services, as instanced by their submission to starvation rations in an experiment at the University of Minnesota.

3. Freedom of speech and the press. Although relatively new, one of the most cherished rights of a free people is that of the freedom of speech and of the press. One of the provisions of the First Amendment of the Constitution of the United States is that Congress shall make no law "abridging the freedom of speech, or of the press," and the state constitutions contain similar guaranties against restrictions by state legislatures. Furthermore, the Fourteenth Amendment of the Constitution denies to any state the right "to deprive any person of life, liberty, or property, without due process of law." The Supreme Court has repeatedly held that the freedom of speech and of the press (and of religion, as noted on page 121) are among the "liberties" protected by the Amendment. Not infrequently one of the forty-eight states or one of the thousands of local government units enacts a statute or ordinance curbing the cherished freedom under discussion, and with encouraging regularity the Supreme Court of the United States strikes down such enactments on the ground that they are contrary to the due process provision of the Fourteenth Amendment.

The freedom here under discussion must not be interpreted to mean that one is permitted to publish libels and indecent articles or is given the

[16] J. W. Masland et al., "Treatment of the Conscientious Objector," *Am. Pol. Sci. Rev.*, XXXVI (Aug., 1942), p. 697.

license to send out publications that subvert public morals or injure private reputations. The purpose of these guaranties is to protect and encourage full and free discussion of public questions. The individual is given the right to have his say and relieve his mind and conscience, and the public is given the right to hear him in order to help it make up its mind on public questions. Free speech may lead to grotesque absurdities at times, but certainly without it we would have less assurance that truth was not on the scaffold and wrong not on the throne. The right to speak freely either in praise or blame of a government and its officers creates a wholesome atmosphere and inspires confidence in and respect for government, whereas a substantial curtailment of this right creates suspicion, distrust, and furtive whisperings in the dark, and may become a strong contributing factor toward a revolt.

FREE SPEECH AND FREE PRESS IN PEACETIME. A Minnesota statute authorized the abatement, as a public nuisance, of any "malicious, scandalous, defamatory" newspaper. A Minneapolis paper ran a series of articles in which the charge was made that certain officers were grossly negligent in performing their duties. For these publications Minnesota authorities proceeded to "abate" the newspaper. The publisher carried an appeal to the Supreme Court of the United States. The Court held that the law under which publishers could be prohibited from printing newspapers was an infringement of the liberty of the press guaranteed by the Fourteenth Amendment.[17] The decision does not mean that such a publisher shall not be liable, both civilly and criminally, for any abuse of the freedom of the press, but only that the state has no right to prohibit publication. In other words, a newspaper publisher has the right to publish at his own risk, the risk of civil and criminal action for abuse. But the Supreme Court of the United States is very reluctant, laudably reluctant, to find abuse. The Miami *Herald* launched some vigorous editorials and telling cartoons at Florida's Dade County Circuit Court for failure to deal with criminals. Florida authorities cited the publishers for contempt, but the Supreme Court at Washington held that the criticism, being only of judicial action already taken, was within the realm of permissible public comment.[18] Mr. Justice Murphy, in a concurring opinion, said that the freedom of the press "covers something more than the right to approve and condone insofar as the judiciary and the judicial process are concerned. It also includes the right to criticize and disparage, even though the terms be vitriolic, scurrilous, or erroneous."

The freedom of the press took an interesting turn in connection with Marshall Field's efforts to get AP rights for his Chicago *Sun*. The AP

[17] Near v. Minnesota, 283 U.S. 687 (1931).
[18] Pennekamp v. Florida, 328 U.S. 331 (1946).

rules made it relatively easy for a newspaper with no competitor to acquire membership; difficult for one with a competitor. The *Sun* had a very strong competitor, and it could therefore obtain membership only by paying a large sum of money. For maintaining these restrictive arrangements the AP was prosecuted under the Sherman Antitrust Act, and the Supreme Court enjoined the continued enforcement by AP of the restrictive regulations. To the argument of the AP that this injunction was an abridgement of the freedom of the press, the Court said: "Freedom to publish is guaranteed by the Constitution, but freedom to combine and to keep others from publishing is not." [19]

The case of Hague v. CIO has an importance as large as the wide public interest it aroused. Mayor Hague, backed by various conservative forces, was determined to prevent the CIO from getting a foothold in Jersey City. In pursuance of this policy he had caused the City Council to enact an ordinance and his police officers to take action under it that resulted in the closing of meeting halls to CIO organizers, the prohibition of CIO meetings on the streets and in the parks, and in preventing the distribution of CIO papers and pamphlets on the streets. An imposing array of legal talent represented the CIO and other organizations in carrying the issue through the courts. The Supreme Court, by a majority of five to two, decided against Mayor Hague.[20]

FREE SPEECH AND FREE PRESS IN TIME OF WAR. As a nation we are none too proud of our restrictions on these civil liberties during the First World War. In 1917 Congress passed the Espionage Act and followed it the next year with the Sedition Act. Under the sweeping provisions of these laws harmless "crackpots" and others who criticized the government were gathered up along with the dangerous enemies of the Republic and given long prison sentences. As we entered the Second World War there still appeared on the federal statute books the Espionage Act of 1917 and it was accompanied by the Alien Registration Act of 1940. The title of the latter is incomplete and misleading. It should have some such title as the Alien Registration and Sedition Act, for section 2 covers sedition and it makes criminal a speech or publication that might possibly tend to produce results that the law forbids and makes a crime of membership in a society that may later be found to have subversive purposes. These statutes might have been so interpreted that freedom of speech and the press would have been as limited during the Second World War as they were in 1917–1918, but the Attorney General of the United States forcefully declared he would use the authority and influence of his office to prevent "the disgraceful

[19] Associated Press v. United States, 326 U.S. 1 (1945).

[20] 307 U.S. 496 (1939). A Texas statute provided that labor organizers should register with the secretary of state before soliciting union members in that state. It was declared to be in violation of due process of law. Thomas V. Collins, 323 U.S. 516 (1945).

hysteria of witch-hunts, strike breakings, and minority persecutions" of the First World War.[21]

The Supreme Court did its part to maintain civil rights during the Second World War. In 1919 Mr. Justice Holmes made this statement, one of the many that place him at the top of the list of jurists: "The question in every case is whether the words used are used in such circumstances and are of such a nature as to *create a clear and present danger* (italics mine) that they will bring about the substantive evils that Congress has a right to prevent." [22] This "clear and present danger" rule was soon abandoned by the majority of the Supreme Court, but it was later restored. The test of guilt in the Second World War was approximately this: Did the accused utter or write a statement that was liable to cause direct and serious interference with the conduct of the war? And not: Did he make a statement that by a broad construction of a statute might be labeled criminal? [23] Under this test an individual who urged men not to register for the draft, or industriously circulated defeatist literature to the armed forces, or who systematically opposed the sale of war bonds, or who harbored enemies of the United States would in all probability have been sent to prison. On the other hand, the man who in a moment of irritation loudly complained of his income tax bill, or who quietly advised a friend to invest less in war bonds, or who at a dinner party said the Commander-in-Chief of the armed forces of the United States was incompetent would go free. In other words, both the executive department and the courts were interested in the real obstructionists, not in perfectly decent and patriotic people who happened to have "tempers," who made indiscreet chance remarks, or who were just preposterous, "queer," or "nutty."

It is thus apparent that the government was disposed to follow a relatively liberal policy in maintaining the freedom of expression during the last war. If it is suggested that the government should have gone even further to preserve this freedom, the answer is that it went further than was entirely pleasing to a large segment of the public. The citizens of many communities would classify as a seditious utterance a statement that law-enforcement officers would consider only annoying or irritating; and the same citizens might on their own initiative take such action against a "preacher of sedition" as would call down upon them the gravest rebuke from the Attorney General or other responsible officials. Citizens who had an itch to serve as wartime detectives did well to heed the urgent advice of the Department of Justice: that they could serve best by reporting all suspicious cases to officers of the law and let the matter rest at that.

[21] *New York Times Magazine*, Sept. 21, 1941, p. 8, and New York *Times*, Dec. 17, 1941, p. 24. See also R. E. Cushman, "Civil Liberties," *Am. Pol. Sci. Rev.*, XXXVI, 49 (Feb., 1943).
[22] Schenck v. U.S. 249 U.S. 47 (1919).
[23] See Hartzel v. United States, 322 U.S. 680 (1944).

Wartime censorship. A nation at war must make every effort to keep its enemies from learning of its troop movements, its weapons, its shipping, its losses in men and equipment, or anything else that may enable those enemies more effectively to establish their defense or plan their attacks. Censorship of communications is one of the chief means of preventing information from reaching the adversaries. During the last war several thousands of men and women located at the principal ports and border cities carefully examined all foreign communications. All communication with enemy countries was prohibited, and cables and letters to and from other countries were examined with care, even suspicious care. The censor had to be on the look-out for messages in code as well as for those that were directly expressed. Whenever he found something suspicious, he passed it on to other officials for further investigation. Censorship not only served as a means whereby we prevented some information from reaching the enemy but also as a means by which we gained information about the enemy.

There were, however, no censors in our schools, churches, fraternal organizations, theaters, broadcasting stations, or press rooms. We could say and write what we pleased, subject only to prosecution for violating the sedition act. Our two great sources of information, the radio and the press, were naturally of great concern to the government, but even they were under only voluntary censorship. The Office of Censorship sought their co-operation and together with them drafted a voluntary censorship program. The radio and the press were asked not to publish certain types of information except when it was made available through official sources. The restriction applied to various matters relating to troops, ships, planes, fortifications, productions, photographs and maps, the weather, and the movements of the President or of other high officials. On the whole the plan worked satisfactorily.

The Post Office Department is responsible for one kind of censorship that is far from voluntary. Under the provisions of the Espionage Act of 1917 and the Alien Registration Act of 1940, this department must prevent the use of the mails to interfere with a war program. Writing forbidden by these acts is nonmailable, and the Postmaster General is given broad powers of enforcement. Newspapers that publish forbidden matter may find the mails closed to them, not only to particular offending issues, but also to their future issues as well, presumably on the ground that recurring violations constitute sufficient reasons for denying future privileges. Thus, during the First World War, the mails were closed to the Milwaukee *Leader* and the New York *Call,* and the second-class mail privilege was not restored to them until several years after that war.[24]

[24] Z. Chafee, Jr., *Free Speech in the United States* (1941 ed.), pp. 298 ff.

4. The right of assembly. The provision of the First Amendment of the federal Constitution that Congress shall make no law abridging "the right of the people peaceably to assemble, and to petition the government for a redress of grievances," is supplemented by state constitutions imposing the same restrictions upon state legislatures. Furthermore, the freedom of assembly is another of the liberties secured from state encroachment by the due process clause of the Fourteenth Amendment. Obviously, the right of assembly cannot be construed to mean the right of disorderly assembly, although those holding an assembly and the officers who break it up may sometimes disagree as to what constitutes a disorderly assembly. Neither does the right of assembly mean that one may be held at any place. A perfectly orderly group, meeting on a corner of a busy street for the purpose of hearing the Declaration of Independence read, may be dispersed for obstructing the traffic. But a "radical" assembly is sometimes unfairly and illegally broken up by the police or by enraged citizens.

In September, 1946, after Jehovah's Witnesses had held a religious meeting in a town park in Iowa, the town council passed a resolution prohibiting the use of the park for any meeting unless it was approved by the council.[25] This resolution was probably in violation of the freedom of assembly. The Witnesses planned to proceed with their scheduled meetings without obtaining permission of the council to use the park. Now Sunday afternoons are often dull and here was a chance for some excitement, real rough fun, in preventing Jehovah's Witnesses from having a Bible lecture! On Saturday night the inhabitants held an anti-Witness mass meeting in the park (whether or not the promoters of this meeting sought and obtained the consent of the council for the use of the park the record does not disclose). At this Saturday night meeting the sheriff announced that there would be no meeting of any kind in the park on Sunday. But the Witnesses had previously announced that they were coming. To prevent their arrival the sheriff, with the assistance of scores of special deputies and some state highway patrolmen, blocked the highways and turned back all who approached the town, except a doctor and a few other natives. The reason behind such high-handed tactics was that if the meeting were held there would be serious trouble, *trouble that would be caused by the local inhabitants' attack on Jehovah's Witnesses at their afternoon religious service.*

The townsmen seem to have forgotten that it was the duty of the officers of the law to protect the peaceful assembly of Jehovah's Witnesses against the unlawful efforts of the local citizenry to disperse it. Fortunately, the Federal Circuit Court of Appeals took a different view. In declaring void the town ordinance in question and otherwise sustaining the freedom of assembly, the court quoted with approval from the brief filed in Hague v.

[25] As reported by H. H. Votaw in *Liberty*, 1948, fourth quarter, pp. 16–20.

CIO[26] by the Committee on the Bill of rights of the American Bar Association. The quotation is in part as follows:

It is natural that threats of trouble should often accompany meetings on controversial questions. But meetings may not be suppressed on that account. The practice under ordinary conditions in our large cities is for the authorities to arrange with the applicants to have the meeting held in a suitable place, and to have enough policemen on hand to quell apprehended disturbances. [This is precisely the protection Mayor LaGuardia of New York arranged for a Nazi mass meeting in that city prior to the Second World War.] To "secure" the rights of free speech and assembly against "abridgement" it is essential not to yield to threats of disorder. Otherwise these rights of the people to meet and of speakers to address the citizens so gathered, could not merely be "abridged" but could be destroyed by the action of a small minority of persons hostile to the speaker or to the views he would be likely to express.

III. THE RIGHTS OF PERSONS ACCUSED OF CRIME [27]

The rights of an accused person are established in our constitutions because in less enlightened days such persons were often treated very unfairly. Everyone will agree that an innocent man, when accused of crime, is entitled to all the safeguards against conviction that the law can give him. Furthermore, the most hardened criminal is entitled to fair treatment —to protection against arbitrary conviction and punishment. The law-abiding citizen is sometimes very much out of patience because of the seeming ease with which notorious felons may escape punishment, and he may conclude that the constitutions have done too much in the way of providing protection for such individuals. We should bear in mind, however, that the enemies of society who escape punishment usually escape by some method other than reliance upon constitutional guaranties.

1. **Safeguards against accusation and conviction of treason.** Treason is defined in the federal Constitution in order to prevent Congress from passing any sweeping legislation that would classify as traitors those persons who might happen to be merely obstructionists or a source of annoyance to the United States in one way or another. According to the Constitution, "treason against the United States shall consist only in levying war against them or in adhering to their enemies, giving them aid and comfort." The Constitution goes still further and establishes safeguards for persons who may be accused of treason: "No person shall be convicted of treason unless

[26] 307 U.S. 496, 679–680 (1939).

[27] E. S. Corwin and J. W. Peltason, *Understanding the Constitution* (1949), pp. 91–103. Dodd, *op. cit.,* pp. 1358–1412; J. M. Mathews, *The American Constitutional System* (1940 ed.), Ch. XXIII; Weaver, *op. cit.,* Ch. 24; W. W. Willoughby, *Principles of the Constitutional Law of the United States* (1930 ed.), Ch. LV.

on the testimony of two witnesses to the same overt act, or on confession in open court."

In the first treason case the Supreme Court ever reviewed, that of a German-American who, in 1942, had a few drinks and conversation with a Nazi saboteur who with others had landed in the United States from a German submarine, the Court showed a scrupulous regard for the constitutional guaranties against arbitrary conviction, holding that there was no proof of "aid and comfort" to the enemy in the offering of these social amenities.[28] But the father (an American resident) of another of the Nazi saboteurs helped his son get a job in a factory that was making the Norden bombsight, helped him pay for an automobile, and for a time sheltered him. These acts, said the Supreme Court, constituted overt acts of aid and comfort to the enemy. A difficulty was experienced in the matter of "two witnesses to the same overt act." The government had the witnesses, but their testimony was not identical. The Court resolved the difficulty with the statement: "While two witnesses must testify to the same act, it is not required that their testimony be identical." [29] Broadcasting for the enemy is treason no less than is physical aid and comfort, as England's Lord Haw-Haw and our Tokyo Rose and Axis Sally discovered following the Second World War.

2. **The right to the writ of habeas corpus.** "The privilege of the writ of habeas corpus shall not be suspended, unless when in cases of rebellion or invasion the public safety may require it." The federal Constitution directs this prohibition to the national government. The state constitutions give the people similar protection from the state government. Any person under arrest and confined has the right under this writ to have an immediate hearing before a court in order that the sufficiency of the cause for which he is being held may be examined. If such a person is held by state officers and for an offense presumably falling under state law, he will apply to a state court for the writ. If he is held by national officers or state officers for an offense with which the national government is concerned, he will apply to a federal court for the writ. The writ is issued by the court to the officer who has custody of the prisoner, and it directs the officer to bring the prisoner before the court. The judge will then examine the facts of the case, and hear such testimony and arguments as seem necessary to the establishment of the facts. If it then appears that the prisoner is being detained in violation of law, he will be released; otherwise he will remain a prisoner and await regular trial.

The federal Constitution clearly states that the writ of habeas corpus may not be suspended except in cases of rebellion or invasion. Suspension

[28] Cramer v. United States, 325 U.S. 1 (1945).
[29] Haupt v. United States, 330 U.S. 631 (1947).

is held to be a legislative power, although Lincoln suspended the writ in certain sections of the country during the Civil War.[30]   Some state constitutions, in order to prevent possible abuse in exercising the power of suspending the writ, prohibit its suspension altogether.

3. **The prohibition against bills of attainder.**   The federal Constitution prohibits both the national and state governments from passing a bill of attainder or an ex post facto law.   The state constitutions regularly duplicate this guaranty with respect to the states.   A bill of attainder is a legislative act by which accused persons are declared guilty and punishment is prescribed without judicial trial.   To be sure, a legislature in our day certainly would not pass a bill declaring John Doe guilty of robbery and sending him to prison without judicial trial.   But on occasion a legislature might enact a less obvious bill of attainder.

The most famous case of a bill of attainder in recent times arose out of Dies Committee witchhunting.   Three Government employees—Robert Morss Lovett, Goodwin B. Watson, and William E. Dodd, Jr., all men of some distinction—had been found wanting in Mr. Dies' kind of Americanism.   These men were named in a rider to the Urgent Deficiency Appropriation Act of 1943, and the stipulation was made that they should be paid no salary after November 15 of that year.   Said Mr. Justice Black, speaking for the majority of the Court,

> No one would think that Congress could have passed a valid law, stating that after investigation it had found Lovett, Dodd, and Watson "guilty" of the crime of engaging in "subversive activities," defined that term for the first time, and sentenced them to perpetual exclusion from any Government employment. Section 304, while it does not use that language, accomplishes that result.   The effect was to inflict punishment without the safeguards of a judicial trial. . . .[31]

The New York Feinberg law directs the Board of Regents of that state to compile a list of subversive organizations, and to consider membership in any such organization "prima facie evidence of disqualification for appointment to or retention in any office or position in the public schools of the state."   On November 28, 1949, a lower court in Albany declared: "The statute . . . violates the constitutional proscription of bills of attainder.   It is a legislative finding of guilt of advocating the overthrow of government by unlawful means without a judicial trial." [32]

4. **The prohibition against ex post facto laws.**   The words ex post facto mean "after the fact."   The constitutional prohibition of ex post facto laws

---

[30] R. E. Cushman, *Leading Constitutional Decisions* (1950 ed.), pp. 65–67 n.

[31] United States v. Lovett, 328 U.S. 303 (1946).

[32] New York *Times*, Nov. 29, 1949, p. 1.   The decision of this court is still of interest, despite the fact that it was overruled (March 9, 1950) by New York Appellate Division judges.

is against the enactment of any law that makes a deed done before its passage, and innocent at the time, a crime. Furthermore, an act increasing a penalty, or changing a method of trial in such a way as to make conviction more certain, would be ex post facto for any person accused of having committed a crime covered by the act on a date prior to its passage.

EXAMPLES. These points can be made clear by illustrations. If we assume that conducting a gambling establishment is no crime in your state in December, a man who conducts one in that month could not be convicted under an act passed by the legislature the following January; for, obviously, as applied to him, that law would be "after the fact." [33] In like manner, if a law on the statute books in December fixes a penalty of one year in jail for the offence, a law passed in January increasing the penalty to two years would be ex post facto as applied to all persons who were being tried for committing the crime in December, or at any other time before the January act was passed. Similarly, any act passed in January altering the rules of evidence in such a way as to require materially less or different testimony for conviction than required in December would be held to be ex post facto and invalid as applied to anyone being tried for operating a gambling establishment in December, or at any other time prior to the enactment of the new law. Suppose your state law provides that trial in such cases shall be by a jury of twelve persons. A law passed fixing the number at eight would be ex post facto for one accused of having committed the crime before its enactment, for it is assumed that eight men will agree to a conviction more readily than twelve. But any law that lessens the rigors of criminal justice is valid. Thus, the repeal of a statute under which an individual is held for trial could result in his release. It is important to note that the ex post facto provision refers only to criminal matters; it does not apply to civil cases.

5. **Security against search and seizure.** The Fourth Amendment of the Constitution of the United States gives security to one against certain arbitrary acts of the national government and its officers by providing that "the right of the people to be secure in their persons, houses, papers, and effects, against unreasonable searches and seizures, shall not be violated, and no warrant shall issue, but upon probable cause, supported by oath or affirmation, and particularly describing the place to be searched, and the persons or things to be seized." The state governments and their officers are under the same restrictions by the terms of the state constitutions. These provisions form the legal basis for the statement that a man's home is his castle. The Supreme Court has strictly construed the prohibition, holding, for example, that it was violated when officers who smelled opium

---

[33] But, of course, such a law would be valid against him and all others who operate such establishments after its passage.

smoking entered the premises without a warrant.[34]   When a warrant is issued for the arrest of an individual, he must be named or described in the warrant.   If his papers are to be searched and seized, whether they are at his home, in his office, in the mails, or elsewhere, the warrant must conform to the terms of the constitutions, showing the "probable cause."

6. The right of accused to refuse to testify.   Under our legal system no person "shall be compelled in any criminal case to be a witness against himself."   The state constitutions carry provisions similar to that just quoted from the Fifth Amendment of the Constitution of the United States. This immunity means that a person cannot be made to testify against himself when he is on trial; that he shall not be compelled, as a witness in any proceedings (before a Dies or Thomas Committee, for example), to give testimony that may be used later by the government conducting such proceedings, in a criminal prosecution against him; that he cannot be forced to produce private books and papers that might contain evidence against him; and probably that he may not be required to remove his clothing and expose parts of his body or clothing, since such exposure may incriminate him.   Years ago, in Tennessee, it was held that a man on trial could not be compelled to place his naked foot in a pan of mud in order to enable the jury to compare the footprint with another left at the scene of the crime.[35]

The guaranties against unreasonable search and seizure and compulsory self-incrimination are closely linked.   If federal officers illegally seize in an individual's home his papers, the Fourth Amendment has been violated; and if in a prosecution the government attempts to use such illegally obtained evidence against an accused, the prohibition against self-incrimination of the Fifth Amendment stands in the way.   The federal courts thus interpret the guaranty against self-incrimination.   Many state courts, however, including New York courts, will admit evidence unlawfully obtained, and even the Supreme Court of the United States will admit such evidence when it has been secured by state officers and turned over to federal officials.[36]

7. Prohibition of double jeopardy.   No person shall be subject "for the same offense to be twice put in jeopardy of life or limb," declares the Fifth Amendment of the federal Constitution.   State constitutions invariably carry the same provision.   The term "limb" has survived from the days when penal amputations were sometimes ordered.   In our time it is liberally interpreted to mean liberty.   The clause means not only that one shall not be punished twice for the same offense but also that one may not be

---

[34] Johnson v. United States, 333 U.S. 10 (1948).
[35] Stokes v. State, 5 Baxt. 619 (1875).
[36] Dodd, *op. cit.*, p. 1399 n.

tried twice for the same offense. Here, as in practically every clause of our constitutions, many nice questions arise. When is an accused placed in jeopardy? In general, when he has been put on trial before a competent court. However, if the jury cannot agree and is discharged, the double jeopardy plea does not avail against trial by a new jury. Similarly, if a juror's official conduct is found to be improper, a jury may be discharged and a new trial ordered. An accused waives his immunity against double jeopardy when he asks for a retrial or appeals. Waiver is a privilege that rests solely with the accused and, consequently, if he is acquitted in the original trial, the government is blocked from ordering a new trial or making an appeal. It is important to notice that immunity against double jeopardy is granted by the federal Constitution in federal cases only. In state cases the accused must look to state constitutions. It happens, therefore, that an individual whose offense violates both state and federal law may be tried by both governments, the double jeopardy plea availing him nothing.[37]

8. Indictment and trial by jury. Everyone knows something about the right of trial by jury. The Fifth Amendment of the federal Constitution requires indictment by grand jury in capital or otherwise infamous crimes. This old common law procedure was formerly stipulated in all state constitutions, but the tendency is very definitely away from it today. In its place many states substitute indictment by an "information" filed by a prosecuting attorney against a person suspected of a crime. In two places,[38] the federal Constitution states that offenders against federal laws shall have the right of trial by jury. Here again, some states have broken away from the requirements of the common law and modified the jury trial by constitutional provisions. Unless a constitution specifies otherwise, "trial by jury" means trial by a jury of twelve persons, under the direction of a judge, and an unanimous verdict.[39] It is clear, of course, that in the indictment, whether by grand jury or information, an individual is formally charged with a crime, and that the function of the trial (or petit) jury is to decide whether he is "guilty as charged" or innocent.

9. Other rights of persons accused of crime. Constitutions list several other rights of persons accused of crime. One is the right of "speedy and public trial." Speedy trial is just what malefactors do not want. They attempt and often succeed in bringing about delay, knowing well that it is one of the surest methods of eluding justice. Another right of accused persons is that trial shall be in the district where the offense was committed. Where local opinion is such that an accused is not likely to re-

---

[37] Mathews, *op. cit.,* pp. 391 ff.
[38] Art. III, sec. II, cl. 3, and the Sixth Amendment.
[39] Weaver, *op. cit.,* pp. 449–450.

ceive a fair trial, a state case may be transferred from one county to another, but the terms of the federal Constitution are too rigid to permit a federal case to be transferred from one state to another. Constitutions regularly prohibit excessive bails and fines. With respect to bail, the prohibition does not mean that bail must always be allowed. It is almost never allowed for capital offenses. It means that, if it is allowed, it shall not be out of proportion to the offense and the financial resources of the accused. Fines must be in rough proportion to the offense of which one is convicted. Accompanying the prohibition just mentioned is another against "cruel and unusual punishments." The death sentence as ordinarily carried out does not, of course, fall within the prohibition. The Supreme Court of the United States has held that hard and painful labor in chains for falsification of public records is a cruel punishment within the meaning of the prohibition.[40] This is a rather impressive but not an exhaustive list of the rights of persons accused or convicted of crime. The discussion of due process of law in the next section and the later chapter on the courts shed a little more light on the subject.

IV. DUE PROCESS OF LAW AND THE EQUAL PROTECTION OF THE LAWS [41]

The Fifth Amendment of the Constitution prohibits the national government from depriving any person "of life, liberty, or property, without due process of law." The Fourteenth Amendment lays the same prohibition upon the states and adds that they shall not deny to any person within their jurisdiction "the equal protection of the laws." The former prohibition practically includes the latter, since most violations of equal protection also violate due process. The fundamental provision, then, is that respecting due process, a provision duplicated in all state constitutions. There has been more litigation under this clause of the federal Constitution than any other. Its significance will appear as we proceed.

The meaning of due process. The term "due process of law" is hoary with age, being accepted as the equivalent of the "law of the land" as used in Magna Charta. Our constitutional system contains no broader or more fundamental safeguard than the due process provision. Probably because of the breadth and importance of due process, plus an earnest desire not to limit its application, the courts have refused to give a complete definition of its meaning, leaving them with their theory that "the full meaning should be gradually ascertained by the process of inclusion and exclusion

---

[40] Mathews, *op. cit.,* pp. 394 ff.

[41] H. C. Black, *Handbook of American Constitutional Law* (1927 ed.), Chs. XVI, XIX–XX; C. K. Burdick, *The Law of the American Constitution* (1922), Chs. XXVIII–XXXIII; Mathews, *op. cit.,* Chs. XXVI–XXXI; Weaver, *op. cit.,* Chs. 21–22.

in the course of decisions in cases as they arise." [42]   However, a broad working definition of due process of law can be given.   It is this: the due process
of law prohibition prevents our governments from taking *arbitrary* action
against an individual's life or body, or against his fundamental liberties,
or against his property rights.   Corporations and other organizations are
also protected, except as to "life," by due process of law.   The preceding
section made clear that freedom of religion, speech, press, and assembly
are among the "liberties" protected by the due process clause of the Fourteenth Amendment.   Other rights secured by due process include the right
to a fair trial, to contract, to labor, to acquire property, to marry, and to acquire knowledge.

It must not be assumed that the due process provision of the Fourteenth
Amendment has the effect of requiring the states to observe the federal
bill of rights.   Such an assumption is, however, based upon this fact: some
of the fundamental rights of persons that due process requires the states to
respect are included in the federal bill of rights—the freedom of speech and
of the press and the right to counsel when on trial, for example.   The due
process provision of the Fourteenth Amendment forces the states to observe
these individual rights not because they are listed in the federal bill of
rights, but because they are essential to due process itself.   On the other
hand, indictment by grand jury and trial by jury are also demanded of the
national government by the federal bill of rights, but due process of the
Fourteenth Amendment does not require the states to follow these procedures because they are not essential to a fair trial.

Procedural rights: 1. In criminal cases.   In an earlier section of this
chapter the rights of persons accused of crime are discussed.   The due
process clauses of the constitutions secure to such persons additional rights.
Unlawful arrest on a criminal charge is contrary to due process, for such
arrest deprives one of his liberty.   A penal statute so vague in its meaning
that men with ordinary intelligence could only guess at its application is
contrary to due process.   A formal and definite accusation must be furnished the person to be tried; he must be given adequate opportunity to
defend himself in a court having jurisdiction, that is, the authority to try
the case; and he must be allowed adequate counsel for his defense.   The
Supreme Court recently held that due process is violated when evidence is
obtained from an accused by a coercive method—thirty-six hours of continuous questioning under powerful electric lights.[43]   Thus, the third
degree is legally banned.

The safeguards listed above are among the essential requirements of due
process in criminal cases.   Due process does not require indictment by

[42] Twining v. New Jersey, 211 U.S. 78 (1908).
[43] Ashcraft v. Tennessee, 322 U.S. 143 (1944).

grand jury or trial by jury.   Nor is due process violated if a person on trial is compelled to give testimony against himself, or if appeal is not allowed. If an accused has the rights just mentioned, and a number of others commonly associated with the rights of accused persons, he has them not because due process secures him in them, but because they are given to him by other provisions of the constitutions or by statutes.

One Hurtado had by the constitution and laws of California been examined and committed by a magistrate, tried, convicted, and sentenced to be hanged for murder.   He attempted to escape the noose by an appeal to the United States Supreme Court, basing his appeal on the ground that his being held for trial, without the ancient procedure of indictment by a grand jury, was about to deprive him of his life without due process of law.   The Court took a different view of the matter, holding that, although a method which had been followed for centuries was due process, it did not follow that other and new methods of procedure are not due process. To hold that a judicial practice must have its origin in the dim past in order to meet the requirement of due process of law "would be to deny every quality of the law but its age, and to render it incapable of progress or improvement.   It would be to stamp upon our jurisprudence the unchangeableness attributed to the laws of the Medes and the Persians." [44]

Although honest and humane individuals supposed that the Fourteenth Amendment would give the Negro civil rights, many denials of such rights have proved that their hopes were optimistic.   Yet due process has often been successfully invoked by members of the colored race.   Seven Negro boys—"the Scottsboro boys"—were arrested in Alabama for a capital crime.   They were brought into court for trial before they had any counsel and the counsel appointed at the beginning of the trial had no time to prepare for their defense.   The Supreme Court of the United States held that such a proceeding does not give the customary right of counsel, and that such right is one of those fundamental liberties guaranteed by the due process clause of the Fourteenth Amendment. [45]   In these two foregoing illustrations we have specific examples of the types of cases in which due process may not be and may be successfully invoked.

2. IN CIVIL CASES.   Due process of law in judicial action in civil cases is held to require a regular proceeding before a court duly authorized to hear the case, and full hearing for the parties in defense or in rebuttal.   As in criminal cases, due process does not mean the right of a hearing before a jury or other specific rights.   Any proceeding that gives notice, fair hear-

[44] Hurtado v. California, 110 U.S. 516 (1884).
[45] Powell v. Alabama, 287 U.S. 45 (1932).

ing, and security of essential rights meets the requirements of due process of law.[46]

Obligation of administrative officers to observe due process. Administrative officers, as well as judicial officers, are bound to observe the provisions of due process. Revenue and tax commissioners, boards of health, and any other administrative officers may not deprive a person of his property or rights in an arbitrary manner. Due process requires that a proper notice be given to the persons whose rights are concerned and that a fair hearing be had before the proper administrative officials or before a court on appeal. A state board may revoke a license to practice medicine, but the revocation may not be made without giving the doctor due notice and a hearing before the board.[47]

Substantive rights. Up to this point in this section we have discussed due process of law as it is applied in matters of procedure, such as forms of trial. In section II those paragraphs relating to freedom of expression point out that the due process clause, as judicially interpreted, protects those liberties not only by preventing arbitrary procedures that would curtail them, but also, and much more important, by striking down statutes that would muzzle the press, gag speakers, force stout witnesses for Jehovah to "worship idols," and otherwise interfere with substantive rights. Here we shall consider the operation of due process of law in relation to other substantive rights, such as the right to make contracts, the right to possess property, and the right to operate private schools.

DUE PROCESS AND THE POLICE POWER. Governments exercise certain powers, rather broadly termed "police powers," which relate to the safety, health, morals, and general welfare of the public. Obviously the field of legislation under such powers is very wide. All laws enacted with regard to these matters must meet the demands of due process of law. Right here the great controversies concerning the proper application of due process have been carried on. Here we have to fix a line between the somewhat vague police power of the governments and the not-fully-defined individual rights to liberty and property under the due process clause. Fixing a line between two uncertainties is of necessity a matter of opinion, and the line established is still a boundary fixed by opinion, even though it is laid down by a formal judicial decision. Some concrete cases will illustrate the relation of due process to the police power.

Maximum hour cases. Some years ago the state legislature of New York, in the interest of the health, safety, and general welfare of its bakers, passed a law prohibiting their employment for more than sixty hours a

[46] Black, *op. cit.,* pp. 616 ff.
[47] Weaver, *op. cit.,* pp. 348 ff.

week. In the case of Lochner v. New York,[48] the Supreme Court of the United States decided, by a five-four majority, "that there can be no fair doubt that the trade of a baker, in and of itself, is not an unhealthy one to that degree which would authorize the legislature to interfere with the right to labor, and with the right of free contract on the part of the individual, either as employer or employee." Thus, five judges decided that the law in question represented abuse rather than a use of the police power. There is some humor in the statement of the Court with regard to there being no fair doubt that the trade of a baker is not unhealthy, for three of its four dissenting judges decided "that the question is one about which there is room for debate and for an honest difference of opinion." Mr. Justice Holmes, the other dissenting judge, differed with the majority still more vigorously: "I think that the word 'liberty' in the Fourteenth Amendment is perverted when it is held to prevent the natural outcome of a dominant opinion, unless it can be said that a rational and fair man necessarily would admit that the statute proposed would infringe fundamental principles as they have been understood by the traditions of our people and our law. It does not need research to show that no such sweeping condemnation can be passed upon the statute before us. A reasonable man might think it a proper measure on the score of health."

The majority opinion of the Court in the Lochner case came in for a great deal of criticism. Some sport was made of the liberty of a laborer, under the due process provision, to contract to work eighteen hours a day if he cared to do so. Three years later, in 1908, the Court decided that an Oregon statute which fixed a ten-hour day for women was a proper exercise of the police power and, therefore, did not arbitrarily deprive women of the liberty to make a contract to work for as many hours a day as they pleased.[49] In 1917 another Oregon statute was contested before the Supreme Court. This statute, which established the ten-hour day for industry generally, was also sustained by the Court on the ground that it was a fair use of the police power of the state.[50]

Minimum wage cases. The Court was slow to sanction the regulation of wages as a legitimate exercise of the police power. A minimum wage law for women and children in the District of Columbia was declared by the Supreme Court to be in contravention to the provision of the Fifth Amendment that "no person shall be deprived of life, liberty, or property, without due process of law." The statute required a wage adequate "to supply the necessary cost of living to women workers" and took no account of the reasonable value of the service rendered. This failure to take into

[48] 198 U.S. 45 (1905).
[49] Muller v. Oregon, 208 U.S. 412 (1908).
[50] Bunting v. Oregon, 243 U.S. 426 (1917).

consideration the value of the service the Court found particularly objectionable.[51] In 1933 the New York legislature enacted a minimum wage statute for women and minors and placed in it the provision that the wage should not be above the reasonable value of the service, thus seeking to save the statute from a judicial veto. But in Morehead v. Tipaldo [52] (1936) the Supreme Court of the United States, in a five-four decision, following its decision in the earlier case, held the law invalid as an unnecessary interference with the liberty of contract guaranteed by the due process clause of the Fourteenth Amendment. Chief Justice Hughes dissented, holding that the objections to the statute for the District of Columbia had been met in the New York law. Justice Stone, in his dissenting opinion, went much further than the Chief Justice. "There is grim irony," he said, "in speaking of the freedom of contract of those who, because of their economic necessities, give their service for less than is needful to keep body and soul together!" In 1937 the Supreme Court executed a remarkable about-face on minimum wage laws.[53] Mr. Justice Roberts took his place with the four Justices who had voted to sustain the New York law and the five upheld the validity of a similar law of the State of Washington. The earlier adverse decisions were thus overruled.

The Oregon school law. The liberty of individuals and organizations to operate private schools and to determine the subjects to be taught in them, and the liberty to receive instruction in private schools are essential rights that have often been before the courts. In 1922 the people of Oregon by a popular vote adopted a statute requiring that all children between the ages of eight and sixteen who had not completed the eighth grade should attend the public schools, thus practically abolishing all the private schools at one fell swoop. A Roman Catholic school and a secular military academy contested the constitutionality of the act. The Supreme Court of the United States decided unanimously that the act of the people of Oregon was in violation of the due process clause of the Fourteenth Amendment in that it "unreasonably interferes with the liberty of parents and guardians to direct the upbringing and education of children under their control" and denies to persons engaged in private school management or instruction the liberty of following a vocation "not inherently harmful, but long regarded as useful and meritorious." [54] This decision must not be understood to deny to the states the right to regulate, in a reasonable manner, all schools, public and private, and to require attendance at some school. The decision does deny to the states a monopoly on education.

[51] Adkins v. Children's Hospital, 261 U.S. 525 (1923).
[52] 298 U.S. 587.
[53] West Hotel Co. v. Parrish, 300 U.S. 379.
[54] Pierce v. Society of the Sisters, 268 U.S. 510 (1925).

Re-emphasis on personal rights under due process of law. At the time the Fourteenth Amendment was adopted it was generally supposed to be designed to protect persons primarily and property secondarily. As it was applied, however, property rights were often secured at the expense of personal rights, and the Amendment came to be looked upon as the chief bulwark for the defense of property against regulatory state legislation. During the past twenty years a change has come about; there is a definite trend in the direction of extending protection to personal rights as distinct from the rights of property. In particular has the Supreme Court of the United States placed freedom of speech and of the press, the right of assembly, and similar "human" rights under the ample folds of due process of law. In 1945 the very significant, if somewhat confusing, case of Screws v. United States [55] was decided. The Court seems to have taken the position that a state or local officer acting under state law or "under pretense of law" (and thus acting for the state, to which due process applies) may be punished for violating a right an individual possesses under the Fourteenth Amendment, namely, "the right not to be deprived of life without due process of law." Thus, an officer who under state law arrests a Negro and beats him up and kills him under the pretense that he was trying to escape has denied to the Negro due process of law and is subject to punishment. It is under the theory that the national government may punish state and local officers for denying to persons their rights under the Fourteenth Amendment that the perennial federal anti-lynch bills are framed. No such bill has been enacted because of the violent and outspoken opposition of Southern senators and the relatively silent opposition of a number of other senators.

Equal protection of the laws. The provision of the Fourteenth Amendment that "no state shall deny to any person within its jurisdiction the equal protection of the laws" is, as previously stated, closely associated with the due process clause. The equal protection provision in the federal Constitution is duplicated by a similar provision against arbitrary class legislation in the constitutions of most of the states. Corporations, as well as natural persons, enjoy the benefits of equal protection as they do the benefits of due process.

THE MEANING OF THE GUARANTY: *Does not prohibit reasonable classification.* The requirement of equal protection of the laws does not mean that all persons and businesses shall be treated alike. Obviously regulations for children must differ from those for adults and the business of mining needs a set of regulations that differ from those for banking. Equal protection of the laws means that all persons and businesses similarly situ-

[55] 325 U.S. 91 (1945).

ated shall be treated alike. A few illustrations of classifications will make this point clear.

The various state unemployment compensation laws exclude employers of less than eight employees and do not cover certain types of employment, such as agriculture. The Supreme Court had no difficulty in finding that making classifications on the basis of the number of employees and the type of occupation was not unreasonable, and therefore not in violation of equal protection.[56] A Michigan statute required that all bartenders be licensed in cities having a population of 50,000 or more, and specified that no woman should be licensed unless she be the wife or daughter of the male owner. Here again we have two bases of classification—the size of the cities and the relationship of women to male owners of saloons. The classification was sustained.[57] There is a reasonable basis for having different saloon regulations for cities of different size, and all cities in specified sizes are treated alike. There is a reasonable basis for granting barkeepers' licenses to wives and daughters of a male saloon owner and withholding such licenses from women in general, and all women in each group are treated alike.

Under the Indiana chain store tax law of 1929, the first store paid $3 per year; the next four, $10 each; the next five, $15 each; the next ten, $20 each; and all above that, $25 each. An owner of 225 chain stores alleged he was being denied the equal protection of the laws, in that his tax amounted to $5,443, while the same number of individual stores paid only $675. In a five-four decision the Supreme Court held that "the fact that a statute discriminates in favor of a certain class does not make it arbitrary if the discrimination is founded upon a reasonable distinction. . . . The statute treats upon a similar basis all owners of chain stores. . . . This is all the Constitution requires."[58]

But requires that classification laws be fairly applied. It is not enough that a classification law be reasonable and founded on a sound principle of government policy. Such laws must be reasonably and fairly enforced in order to satisfy the requirements of equal protection. Years ago, the city of San Francisco passed an ordinance prohibiting the operation of laundries in frame buildings without a permit from a city inspector. This was a perfectly valid ordinance by its terms. Such buildings clearly present more danger of fire than do buildings of brick and stone. But the city inspector gave natives permits to operate laundries in the frame buildings and refused to give permits to Chinese. Yick Wo, acting for himself and other Chinese, accepting the advice of good counsel, went to court with

[56] Carmichael v. Southern Coal and Coke Co., 301 U.S. 495 (1937).
[57] Goesaert v. Cleary, 335 U.S. 464 (1948).
[58] State Board of Tax Commissioners of Indiana v. Jackson, 283 U.S. 527 (1931).

the plea that the enforcement of the ordinance amounted to a denial of his constitutional right to the equal protection of the laws. The Supreme Court of the United States took the same view, expressed in this language: "Though the law itself be fair on its face and impartial in appearance, yet, if it is applied and administered by public authority with an evil eye and an unequal hand, so as practically to make unjust and illegal discriminations between persons in similar circumstances, material to their rights, the denial of equal justice is still within the prohibition of the Constitution." [59]

THE NEGRO AND EQUAL PROTECTION: *Criminal cases.* Our discussion of due process brought out the fact that in the first "Scottsboro case" the Negroes were held to have been denied due process of law because they were not given a fair opportunity to retain counsel. After this decision they were again tried and convicted. They again appealed (1935) to the Supreme Court, this time on the ground that Negroes had been systematically excluded from service on both the grand jury and the trial jury. The Court examined the evidence and found that Alabama courts in the counties having jurisdiction of the accused Negroes followed the unvarying practice of excluding members of that race from jury service. This practice was declared to be in violation of the equal protection clause of the Fourteenth Amendment.[60] In 1948, a very similar case came to the Supreme Court from Mississippi, and the Court reaffirmed its earlier decision.[61]

Civil cases. The equal protection requirement of the Constitution means that persons shall be given equality of rights under the laws, not identity of rights. Hence, although state and local governments may not exclude Negroes from the public schools, they may force them to attend schools established especially for Negroes. A law requiring railway companies to provide separate, but equal, accommodations for the white and colored races meets the demands of the "equal protection of the laws" provision. Members of the Negro race ordinarily make no complaint against the separate accommodation practice, but they often bitterly complain that the accommodations furnished are not equal.

Congressman Mitchell, a Negro representing a Chicago district, was traveling from Chicago to Hot Springs, Arkansas, on a ticket that entitled him to Pullman accommodations. Upon reaching the Arkansas border he was compelled to leave the Pullman and ride in a day coach reserved for members of his race. All of this was in compliance with the Arkansas segregation law. The railroad showed that very few Negroes traveled by Pullman, and claimed that it was unreasonable to require it to provide separate and equal Pullman accommodations for them. Nevertheless, the

---

[59] Yick v. Hopkins, 118 U.S. 356 (1885).
[60] Norris v. Alabama, 294 U.S. 587.
[61] Patton v. Mississippi, 332 U.S. 463.

Supreme Court of the United States was unanimous in holding that Mitchell was a victim of discrimination and entitled to relief.[62] It is true that Mitchell presented his case under a federal law, the Interstate Commerce Act, but it is possible that the decision would have been the same had he sought his relief under the "equal protection" clause.

Virginia and a number of other states have the well-known Jim Crow laws. A Negro woman riding an interstate bus from Norfolk to Baltimore refused to change her seat when requested to do so by the driver, who was exercising his authority under the Virginia law. Upon being fined ten dollars, she carried her case through the state supreme court and to the Supreme Court of the United States. There it was held that the Virginia Jim Crow law was an undue burden on interstate commerce, that segregation on interstate buses was illegal.[63] Notice that the Court did not touch the validity of the Jim Crow law in respect to intrastate traffic. It did not hold the law, as such, invalid. It was declared to be invalid only as it constituted an interference with interstate commerce.

Segregation in cities usually works out naturally or by private arrangement, but occasionally a city will legislate. An ordinance of the city of Louisville which provided that Negroes should not occupy a residence in a block in which the greater number of houses were occupied by white people was declared void because, in the opinion of the Court, it could not be sustained under the police power, and unreasonably interfered with the liberty of property ownership and occupancy.[64] But suppose individuals made an agreement not to sell property in a particular area to people of the Negro or Mongolian race. For years these "restrictive covenants" were assumed to be valid and binding legal agreements, enforceable in court. In Shelley v. Kraemer [65] the Supreme Court of the United States declared that a state in enforcing such an agreement is violating the equal protection of the laws requirement. The point is this, and it is a material one: when a state uses the "full coercive power of government" to enforce a restrictive covenant, the state becomes a party to the discrimination embodied in the agreement and thus denies the equal protection of the laws. This decision was justly celebrated as a significant victory for civil liberties.

Negroes have had difficulty in a number of states in finding institutions in which they could take professional courses. The State of Missouri

[62] Mitchell v. United States, 313 U.S. 80 (1941).

[63] Morgan v. Virginia, Supreme Court of the United States, June 3, 1946. In 1950 the Supreme Court, again applying the Interstate Commerce Act and not the Fourteenth Amendment, held that an arrangement under which Negroes were served in dining cars at reserved tables screened off from white passengers subjected passengers to undue and unreasonable prejudice and disadvantage, contrary to the Interstate Commerce Act (Henderson v. United States et al, June 5, 1950).

[64] Buchanan v. Warley, 245 U.S. 60 (1917).

[65] 334 U.S. 1 (1948).

maintained Lincoln University for Negroes and it provided tuition in out-of-state universities for Negro residents of Missouri who desired and were qualified to take courses not offered at Lincoln University. Law was one of the courses not given at Lincoln, and a properly qualified Negro student sought admission to the Law School of the University of Missouri. He was refused admission, his attention being called to the arrangement under which the State would pay his tuition in an adjacent state. The Negro claimed, nevertheless, that the action of the University of Missouri in not admitting him was a denial of the equal protection of the laws. The Supreme Court of the United States, speaking through Chief Justice Hughes, agreed with him. It was no answer, he reasoned, for the state to say it would pay his tuition elsewhere. "By the operation of the laws of Missouri a privilege has been created for white law students which is denied to Negroes by reason of their race." Nor was the fact that there was but a limited demand for legal education among Negroes any answer. The constitutional right does not depend upon the number of persons who may be discriminated against; the essence of such right is that it is a personal one.[66] The State of Missouri then proceeded, at considerable expense, to establish professional courses at Lincoln University, but it is probably not unfair to say that these courses are not of the same degree of excellence as similar courses at the University of Missouri.

In 1950 the Negro in his fight for equal opportunity in education won two significant victories in the Supreme Court. Texas, reading the signs of the times, had set up a law school (a very inadequate one) for Negroes. Not impressed with the opportunity offered members of his race and insisting that the Negro law school was grossly inferior to the University of Texas Law School, a Mr. Sweatt sought admission to the latter. The Supreme Court accepted his contention and ordered the University of Texas to admit him.[67] The University of Oklahoma had recently admitted Negroes to its privileges, but required them to sit apart from white students in classrooms, in the library, and in the cafeteria. "Having been admitted to a state-supported graduate school," said the Court, "[Negroes] must receive the same treatment at the hands of the state as students of other races."[68] In this case the Court held, in effect, that segregation within a mixed school was a denial of the equal protection of the laws. The end of Jim Crow is not yet, although he is losing more and more of his feathers.

Equal protection of the laws in the District of Columbia. We have seen that Congress has no adequate authority to legislate for the protection of individuals against discrimination in the states; that persons who are the

---

[66] Missouri ex rel. Gaines v. Canada et al., 305 U.S. 337 (1938).
[67] Sweatt v. Painter, U.S. Supreme Court, June 5, 1950.
[68] McLaurin v. Oklahoma, U.S. Supreme Court, June 5, 1950.

THE NATION'S CAPITAL — A SYMBOL OF FREEDOM AND EQUALITY?

A NEGRO TRAVELING
FROM NORTH TO SOUTH

MUST CHANGE TO JIM CROW
TRAINS IN WASHINGTON D.C.
SOUTH

NORTH

WASHINGTON, D.C.

IF HE DECIDES TO REMAIN IN D.C. OVERNIGHT HE WILL FIND THAT:

HE CANNOT EAT IN A
DOWNTOWN RESTAURANT

HE CANNOT ATTEND A
DOWNTOWN MOVIE OR
PLAY.

HE CANNOT SLEEP IN
A DOWNTOWN HOTEL.

IF HE DECIDES TO STAY IN D.C.

HE USUALLY MUST FIND A HOME IN AN OVERCROWDED, SUB-STANDARD,
SEGREGATED AREA:

NEGRO-OCCUPIED
DWELLINGS

40% SUBSTANDARD

WHITE-OCCUPIED
DWELLINGS

12% SUBSTANDARD

HE MUST SEND HIS CHILDREN
TO INFERIOR JIM CROW SCHOOLS:

HE MUST ENTRUST HIS FAMILY'S
HEALTH TO MEDICAL AGENCIES WHICH
GIVE THEM INFERIOR SERVICES

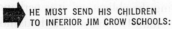

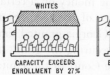

WHITES

NEGROES

CAPACITY EXCEEDS
ENROLLMENT BY 27%

ENROLLMENT EXCEEDS
CAPACITY BY 8%

WHITE

NEGRO

HOSPITALS IN THE DISTRICT OF
COLUMBIA EITHER DO NOT ADMIT
NEGROES OR ADMIT THEM ON A
SEGREGATED BASIS

From *The Report of the President's Committee on Civil Rights* (1947), p. 88.

victims of such discriminations can find relief only in the courts. In other words, the federal guaranty of equal protection of the laws in the states is essentially a negative one. But in areas over which the national government has exclusive jurisdiction there is no lack of authority to afford protection by legislation. Congress can by law prohibit specific discriminations in the territories and the District of Columbia. The extent to which such legislation may be necessary or desirable for the District of Columbia is indicated in part by the chart on the preceding page.[69]

V. THE PROTECTION OF CONTRACTS [70]

The Constitutional guaranties. In that part of the preceding section that covers briefly the restrictions laid upon the police power by the due process provision it is noted that one of the liberties included in due process is the "liberty of contract," and that laws which unreasonably prevented the making of contractual engagements, such as a law that would place a ban on railway companies selling tickets to women, would be in violation of that liberty. At this point we consider a somewhat different and more specific guaranty respecting contracts, the guaranty that a contract made in accordance with law shall not have its obligations impaired by a subsequent law. The language of the federal Constitution is that no state shall pass any "law impairing the obligation of contracts." The constitutions of nearly all the states address the same prohibitions to state legislatures. The Congress of the United States is not so restricted. Congress may not impair the obligation of contracts entered into by the United States (except by withholding consent to suits against the United States for impaired contracts), but it may and does enact laws, such as bankruptcy and currency measures, that impair the obligation of private contracts.

Types of engagements to which guaranties apply. Before an attempt is made to explain what is meant by "impairing the obligation" it is perhaps desirable to explain just what a contract is. John Doe borrows a thousand dollars from Richard Roe and agrees to pay back the money on a certain date, with interest at 6 per cent. This is a clear case of contract. Some other cases are not so clear. The state legislature of Georgia granted some land to one Gunn. Because of his alleged fraud in securing the grant, the legislature tried to rescind the grant. The Supreme Court of the United States held that the grant was a contract, and that the state could not reassert title without impairing the obligation of that contract.[71] When a

---

[69] See also Howard Whitman, "Washington—Disgrace to the Nation," *Woman's Home Companion*, February, 1950.

[70] Dodd, *op. cit.*, pp. 1281–1341; Mathews, *op. cit.*, Ch. XXV; Weaver, *op. cit.*, Ch. 25.

[71] Fletcher v. Peck, 6 Cranch 87 (1810).

state issues a charter for a business corporation, it has made a contract, although it is not easy for the ordinary person to understand just why such charters should be classed as contracts. The ordinary marriage is not a contract, but a status. Laws regulating marriage relationships do not, therefore, run the risk of impairing the obligation of contracts. Gratuitous promises to give another a thousand dollars or a car are not contracts, for valid contracts must be entered into for a consideration. Oral agreements for important transactions are usually not enforceable as contracts, for important agreements are required to be in writing in order to be enforceable.

Laws that impair the obligation. Now let us return to John Doe, who borrowed a thousand dollars from Richard Roe and agreed to pay interest at the rate of 6 per cent. Suppose the state legislature later passes a law that fixes the interest rate at 5 per cent. This law would impair the rights of Richard Roe under his contract, and it would be declared inapplicable to his case. Such a law would, however, properly apply to similar contracts made after its passage.

If the debtor does not pay the creditor, the latter may go to court and have the debtor's property sold to satisfy the debt. Suppose, after the contract is made, the state legislature passes a law providing that no debtor's property shall be sold for less than two thirds of its appraised value. This law will impair the creditor's rights under the existing contract, as it will make it more difficult to sell the debtor's property and, therefore, more difficult for the creditor to collect his money.[72]

But it should not be concluded from these simple illustrations that a legislature may not pass laws that affect existing contracts. Said Chief Justice Hughes: "The question is not whether the legislative action affects contracts incidentally, or directly or indirectly, but whether the legislation is addressed to a legitimate end and the measures taken are reasonable and appropriate to that end." [73] And in accordance with this principle the Chief Justice, speaking for himself and four of his associates, upheld the validity of an emergency measure, the Minnesota Mortgage Moratorium Law, that delayed the enforcement of mortgagees' contractual rights.

Limitations upon charter privileges. If the legislature is prohibited from impairing the obligations of a contract, what remedy is there for the public if the legislature should improvidently and contrary to good public policy grant a valuable privilege to a corporation or an individual? One safeguard is this: any privilege that has not been expressly granted by a government shall be held to have been denied.

The leading case in which this method of interpretation was applied arose

[72] Bronson v. Kinzie, 1 Howard 311 (1843).
[73] Home Building and Loan Asso. v. Blaisdell, 290 U.S. 398 (1934).

in Massachusetts more than a century ago. The state legislature had given a company the right to build a toll bridge across the Charles River, with the privilege of collecting the tolls for seventy years. Some years later the legislature gave another company the privilege of building a toll bridge a short distance from where the first bridge was located, this bridge to become free in six years. The first company complained that this free bridge would ruin its business and that the grant of a charter to build a bridge and collect tolls was an *implied* contract that the state would not thereafter cause to be erected a competing or free bridge. The Court held that, since the state had not expressly given the original company a monopoly, no such monopoly could be *implied*.[74]

The second limitation that protects the public is found in the ruling of the courts that a legislature cannot, even by express agreement, contract away its governing power in important matters. For instance, when Mississippi forbade lotteries, the law was held valid even when applied to a company that had just been chartered by the state to engage in the lottery business for twenty-five years, the basis of the decision being that the state could not contract away its power to regulate public morals.[75] The same rule is applied with regard to the public health, public safety, and to other important matters touching the general welfare. In other words, the legislature may not contract away the police power.

Another method by which the states commonly limit the operation of corporate charters is through provisions in the state constitutions and laws that the states shall have the power to alter or repeal such charters at any time. Such provisions are, of course, a part of the contract. Corporations cannot, therefore, claim that contracts are impaired when the states choose to alter or amend their charters.

VI. CIVIL LIBERTIES: THE CITIZENS' UNFINISHED BUSINESS

"But the laws which proclaim liberty do not assure it," wrote the late Charles A. Beard, and he quoted Alexander Hamilton who said: "Whatever fine declarations may be inserted in any constitution respecting it, [liberty] must altogether depend upon public opinion and on the general spirit of the people and of the government."[76] How well have we met this test? Giving due regard to human frailties and considering that there have been individuals who do not believe in liberty, it may be said that we have met it fairly well—but only fairly well.

In the first months of the Second World War we evacuated from the

---

[74] Charles River Bridge v. Warren Bridge, 11 Peters 420 (1837).
[75] Stone v. Mississippi, 101 U.S. 814 (1879).
[76] *A Charter for the Social Sciences in the Schools* (1932), pp. 116–117.

Pacific Coast and held in detention camps more than one hundred thousand persons of Japanese blood, about two thirds of whom were American citizens. On this subject Dr. Morton Grodzins has made an exhaustive study and reported his findings in a book.[77] His opinions we may accept with reservations, but his fully and carefully documented facts should not escape our mind, even though their retention may hold the evacuation of the Japanese in our conscience. If the military, the top executives of the government, and the Congress honestly believed that evacuation was necessary for national defense, that is understandable and forgiveable; and if we now feel certain that it was not necessary, we should take little credit that our hindsight leads to a happier disposition of the problem than was made by those responsible for our defense when so many of our ships lay in the bottom of Pearl Harbor. If the decision was brought about in part by race prejudice, by a desire to get possession of other men's property, or to dispose of them as competitors, it was shameful. Dr. Grodzins' facts prove all too fully that these latter considerations were present in the determination of the policy.

The Supreme Court held,[78] in effect, that the political departments had sole responsibility in the matter, that the power to wage war carried with it the authority to determine what must be done to wage it successfully. There were three dissents, however. Justice Murphy said that the evacuation fell "into the ugly abyss of racism," and Justice Jackson stated that the Court "may as well say that any military order will be constitutional and have done with it." Certainly when due process of law and a number of other civil liberties guaranties came into conflict with the war power, the latter won.

To be sure, the evacuation and detention were conducted in such a way as to reduce hardship to a minimum; and as soon as the situation had clarified, steps were taken to release loyal Americans of Japanese ancestry. The War Relocation Authority, the civilian agency that was given the responsibility for resettlement of Japanese Americans, is to be particularly commended for its work. Furthermore, Congress has established a claims commission to settle property losses resulting from the evacuation. But there is no adequate compensation for the evacuation and detention. If at any time we might become smug about the manner in which we maintain civil liberties, we should recall the wartime evacuation of the Japanese Americans and wonder . . . and wonder whose turn it might be next!

How stand our liberties today? Are we *In the Shadow of Fear?* The American Civil Liberties Union thus captions its report for 1949, and opens the report with this sentence: "The imagined insecurity of the strongest

[77] *Americans Betrayed* (1949).
[78] Korematsu v. United States, 323 U.S. 214 (1944).

democracy in the world in the face of the cold war with Communism has created an atmosphere in which fear makes the maintenance of civil liberties precarious." The report does not by any means maintain that the record is entirely bad; on the contrary it notes a number of satisfactory judicial decisions and commendable legislative actions. On the whole, however, the Union considers that civil liberties are not being satisfactorily maintained.

"Four times in our history," writes Professor Henry Steele Commager, "we have given way to fear of ideas and indulged in measures of suppression and oppression": [79] in the early days of the Republic, when, fearing the excesses of the French Revolution, we enacted the Alien and Sedition Laws; in the middle of the nineteenth century, when the Southern States gagged the press, purged college faculties, and adopted similar repressive measures in order to prevent criticism of slavery; in the 'nineties, when a large element of the population regarded labor leaders and Populists as anarchists; and in the period following the First World War, when bolshevism furnished the excuse for deporting harmless aliens and subjecting equally harmless American teachers to oath laws. Professor Commager intimates, to put it mildly, that we are now in a fifth such period, and he takes notice of "the stir and bustle of federal and state un-American activities committees," of "loyalty investigations" in the public service and in the schools, and of "witch-hunting and censorship" in general.

It is quite unnecessary to agree with all the implications of Professor Commager's excellent article for us to ask ourselves the question: Are we afraid of ideas? Surely we should not be; in a democracy we have no right to be. Read what the late Justice Oliver Wendell Holmes said: "Time has upset many fighting faiths . . . the ultimate good desired is . . . reached by free trade in ideas. . . . The best test of truth is the power of thought to get itself accepted in the competition of the market." He said further that the Constitution "is an experiment, as all life is an experiment. Every year if not every day we have to wager our salvation upon some prophecy based upon imperfect knowledge. While that experiment is part of our system I think that we should be eternally vigilant against attempts to check the expression of opinions that we loathe and believe to be fraught with death, unless they so imminently threaten immediate interference with the lawful and pressing purposes of the law than an immediate check is required to save the country." [80]

Executive officials have an obligation to use their authority and influence for the protection of individual liberties, but there have been instances when they displayed all the temper and prejudice of a Klansman toward an

[79] *New York Times Magazine,* June 26, 1949.
[80] Dissenting in Abrams v. United States, 250 U.S. 616 (1919).

OUR FEDERAL CIVIL RIGHTS MACHINERY NEEDS STRENGTHENING

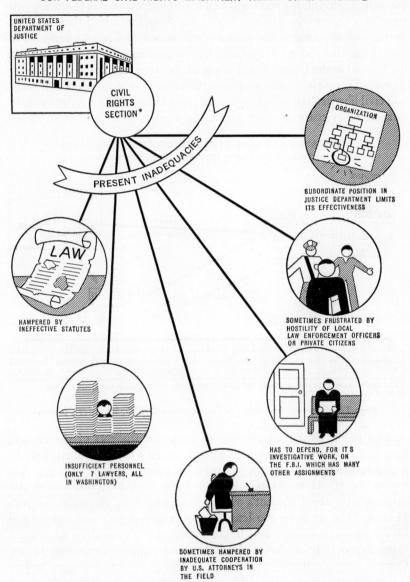

UNITED STATES
DEPARTMENT OF
JUSTICE

CIVIL
RIGHTS
SECTION*

PRESENT INADEQUACIES

ORGANIZATION

SUBORDINATE POSITION IN
JUSTICE DEPARTMENT LIMITS
ITS EFFECTIVENESS

LAW

HAMPERED BY
INEFFECTIVE STATUTES

SOMETIMES FRUSTRATED BY
HOSTILITY OF LOCAL
LAW ENFORCEMENT OFFICERS
OR PRIVATE CITIZENS

INSUFFICIENT PERSONNEL
(ONLY 7 LAWYERS, ALL
IN WASHINGTON)

HAS TO DEPEND, FOR ITS
INVESTIGATIVE WORK, ON
THE F.B.I. WHICH HAS MANY
OTHER ASSIGNMENTS

SOMETIMES HAMPERED BY
INADEQUATE COOPERATION
BY U.S. ATTORNEYS IN
THE FIELD

* THE MAINTENANCE OF CIVIL RIGHTS IS ONLY ONE OF MANY FUNCTIONS OF THE
CRIMINAL DIVISION OF THE DEPARTMENT OF JUSTICE.

From *The Report of the President's Committee on Civil Rights* (1947), p. 115.

unpopular minority. One of the best examples in our time of the use of executive responsibility was furnished by President Truman in the appointment of a Committee on Civil Rights. It should be added that the Committee took the assignment seriously and presented a most significant report,[81] one that did not fail to criticize governments nor to point out that the Capital of the United States is one of the worst examples of race segregation. Of course, legislatures have the obligation to establish and maintain civil liberties, but on occasion their proper concern for national security or some other essential factor may cause them to strike a blow at liberty.

FOR STRONGER CIVIL RIGHTS ENFORCEMENT MACHINERY
THE PRESIDENT'S COMMITTEE RECOMMENDS

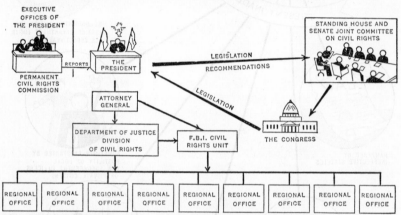

A PLAN ALONG SIMILAR LINES IS RECOMMENDED FOR STATES GOVERNMENTS WITH INCREASED PROFESSIONALIZATION OF STATE AND LOCAL POLICE FORCES

From *The Report of the President's Committee on Civil Rights* (1947), p. 150.

Among public officials of the highest rank and students of government there is a difference of opinion on whether or not a threat to liberty may be found in the Internal Security (Anti-Communist Bill) Act of 1950. On September 22, six weeks before the fall elections, Congress passed this measure over the President's veto by overwhelming majorities in both Houses. The act is far too long (it covers fifty pages) and complicated for discussion here, but it may be characterized as a great drag-net to catch Communists. "In so far as the bill would require registration by the Communist party itself," wrote the President in his veto message, "it does not endanger our traditional liberties. However, the application of the registration requirements to so-called Communist-front organizations can be the greatest danger to freedom of speech, press, and assembly, since the Alien and Sedition Laws of 1798. This danger arises out of the

[81] *To Secure These Rights* (1947).

criteria or standards to be applied in determining whether an organization is a Communist-front organization.

"The bill would permit such a determination," the President continued, "to be based solely upon the extent to which the positions taken or advanced by it from time to time on matters of policy do not deviate from those of the Communist movement. This provision could easily be used to classify as a Communist-front organization any organization which is advocating a single policy or objective which is also being urged by the Communist party or by a Communist foreign government. . . . Thus, an organization which advocates low-cost housing for sincere humanitarian reasons might be classified as a Communist-front organization because the Communists regularly exploit slum conditions as one of their fifth-column techniques."

But time will tell whether the statute is repressive or unconstitutional. If it is either or both, the fact remains that legislative bodies commonly show restraint in enacting repressive legislation. For example, in 1949 Congress enacted only one measure that the Civil Liberties Union considered an encroachment on liberty. It has been made abundantly clear that the courts stand as guardians of liberty, but they have been known to fail in their duty. Besides, there are many cases of violated rights that never get to court.

When a "radical agitator" is taken for a ride and thrown into the sage brush, "that is that." Almost never do we learn who did it. When an "un-American" speaker is met at the bus by the local patriots, who may understand not the first principle of decent Americanism, and given fifty cents and ordered to take the bus to the next town, "that is some more of that." On the Fourth of July (note the day), 1946, the National Opinion Research Center, University of Denver, published the results of a poll on this question: "In peacetime, do you think people in this country ought to be allowed to say anything they want to in a public speech?" In reply 32 per cent of those polled said "No." [82] No wonder persons so frequently violate the civil rights of others with impunity.

Broadly speaking, whatever diminishes the civil liberties of one man or group lessens the liberties of us all. Is it not true that where the Negro is subject to the most discrimination, the white share-cropper and laborer suffer only a little less? When Jews are persecuted, are not Catholics in danger? When Jehovah's Witnesses are assaulted, are not other religions threatened? And when an American-Japanese was slapped, did not the face of every American sting? Fortunately there are many citizens who recognize these facts or who from a sense of common decency fight for the maintenance of the other man's rights. It is indeed encouraging that

[82] *Time*, July 15, 1946, p. 26.

throughout the land today, South as well as North, there are millions of whites who champion the cause of the Negro; Catholics who ably and eloquently defend the rights of the Jews; Protestants who do no less for the atheists; and people of good will of every race, cast, and creed who are insistent that justice be done for American citizens of Japanese ancestry.

When, in December, 1944, a local American Legion post erased from its war memorial the names of native-born American citizens of Japanese ancestry who were serving in the armed forces of the United States, a protest went up from all over the country. In a technical sense, no civil liberty was violated, for the Legion was simply exercising its power as a private organization. But the criticisms came in, nevertheless, protests like this one: "Dear Comrade Commander: As one who like yourself wore the uniform of his country in 1917–1918, permit me to say that I think you have made a mistake. The Constitution of the United States, which all of us are supposed to follow, makes these people citizens. The law of the United States puts them in military service. By accident of birth they happen to be of Japanese rather than German or French or Swedish or English ancestry. In my opinion it is not good Americanism to discriminate against them." Such protests had their effect, and the wrong that had been done was righted.

No less effective than the protest against the un-American activities of the Legion post was the public outcry against the unjust penalties imposed upon four Indian boys by an Idaho court. In a car and under the influence of liquor (that had no doubt been sold to them by white men in violation of law), the Indians playfully picked up a wandering sheep and put it in the back of their car. Without counsel and at the urgent suggestion of the state prosecutor they pleaded guilty, and were sentenced to *fourteen years* in the penitentiary. Public protests in Idaho and other states and an organized effort to assist the boys resulted in their conviction being set aside by the supreme court of the state of Idaho.[83]

From time to time we hear used the vague term "Americanism." We even hear of "100 per cent Americanism," also a vague and undefined term. Here is a definition that might prove useful: Americanism is that quality of mind and heart that causes a citizen to fight for the right of another man to be free. Surely this quality constitutes an essential ingredient in the foundation of liberty.

Reading List

American Civil Liberties Union, *In the Shadow of Fear* (Report, 1949).
Annals of the American Academy of Social and Political Science, "Essential Human Rights," January, 1946.

[83] *New York Times,* editorial, June 30, 1950.

C. L. Becker and Others, *Safeguarding Civil Liberty Today* (1944).

H. C. Black, *Handbook of American Constitutional Law* (1927 ed.), Chs. XVIII–XXIV.

C. K. Burdick, *The Law of the American Constitution* (1922), Chs. XXVI–XXXIII.

R. K. Carr, *Federal Protection of Civil Rights: Quest for a Sword* (1947).

Z. Chafee, *Free Speech in the United States* (1941 ed.).

Earl Conrad, *Jim Crow America* (1947).

E. S. Corwin, *Liberty against Government: The Rise, Flowering and Decline of a Famous Judicial Concept* (1948).

―――― and J. W. Peltason, *Understanding the Constitution* (1949), pp. 87–123.

R. E. Cushman, *Leading Constitutional Decisions* (1950 ed.), Chs. III and IV.

―――― and Others, *The Impact of War on America* (1942), Ch. I.

W. F. Dodd, *Cases and Materials on Constitutional Law* (1949 ed.), pp. 811–1412.

O. K. Fraenkel, *Our Civil Liberties* (1944).

Walter Gellhorn, *Security, Loyalty, and Science* (1950).

Morton Grodzins, *Americans Betrayed* (1949).

A. W. Johnson and F. H. Yost, *The Separation of Church and State in the United States* (1950).

M. R. Konvitz, *The Constitution and Civil Rights* (1947).

H. D. Laswell, *National Security and Individual Freedom* (1950).

J. M. Mathews, *The American Constitutional System* (1940 ed.), Chs. XXIII–XXXI.

H. L. McBain, *The Living Constitution* (1927), Ch. III.

Carey McWilliams, *Witch Hunt* (1950).

C. E. Merriam, *American Political Ideas* (1920), Ch. V.

R. L. Mott, *Due Process of Law* (1926).

B. H. Nelson, *The Fourteenth Amendment and the Negro since 1920* (1946).

A. R. Ogden, *The Dies Committee* (1945 ed.).

To Secure These Rights, Report of the President's Committee on Civil Rights (1947).

George Seldes, *You Can't Do That: A Survey of Towns Attempting, in the Name of Patriotism, to Make a Desert of the Bill of Rights* (1938).

S. P. Weaver, *Constitutional Law and Its Administration* (1946), Chs. 20–26, 29.

Ruth G. Weintraub, *How Secure These Rights* (1949).

W. W. Willoughby, *Principles of the Constitutional Law of the United States* (1930 ed.), Chs. LV–LIX, LXXVIII–LXXXVII.

Questions and Problems

1. List the provisions of the federal Constitution that are designed primarily to protect "human" rights; property rights.
2. Show the relation of freedom of speech and of the press to religious liberty.
3. Show the extent to which "due process of law" of the Fourteenth Amendment applies the federal bill of rights to the states.

4. Can you reason that the Supreme Court of the United States is a "watch-tower" for Jehovah's Witnesses?
5. What functions do despised minorities perform in developing our civil rights?
6. What protection has the Negro received from the "equal protection of the laws" provision?
7. Is this statement in accordance with our constitutions? *Only citizens are entitled to civil rights.* Give conclusive proofs.
8. What is the significance of the assertion that civil rights are the citizen's business?
9. Is there evidence that our constitutional guaranties of civil liberties run ahead of our convictions respecting them?
10. Draw up a list of our successes and failures in maintaining civil liberties during the Second World War.
11. Discuss this statement: *Only a people socially and politically mature can maintain civil liberties.*

☆ 7 ☆

Citizenship and the Suffrage

IN the preceding chapter our attention was directed to the civil liberties of persons. In this chapter our concern is with the rights and the privileges of citizenship. Although from the beginning of our national history all persons (except Negroes and Indians) born in the United States were generally understood to be citizens, the Fourteenth Amendment gives citizenship a definite constitutional basis in the declaration that "all persons born or naturalized in the United States, and subject to the jurisdiction thereof, are citizens of the United States and of the state wherein they reside."

I. NATIVE-BORN CITIZENS [1]

Who are native-born citizens? Everyone knows that the main purpose of the Constitutional provision just quoted was to give the Negroes citizenship. But it does more than that. It declares that *all* persons born in the United States, and subject to the jurisdiction thereof, are citizens. Wong Kim Ark was born in California of alien Chinese parents. As an adult he went to China on a temporary visit. When he returned to the United States, the Collector of the Port of San Francisco denied him admission on the ground that such admission would be in violation of the Chinese exclusion law. The Supreme Court of the United States held that the citizenship of the child did not follow that of the parents, and that Wong Kim Ark, having been born in California, was a native-born American citizen and entitled to admission to his country.[2]

[1] Luella Gettys, *The Law of Citizenship in the United States* (1934); C. C. Hyde, "The Nationality Act of 1940," *Am. Journal of International Law*, XXXV, 314 (April, 1941).

[2] United States v. Wong Kim Ark, 169 U.S. 649 (1898). This is the Anglo-American doctrine, known as *jus soli*. It is adhered to by about a third of the nations. Other countries hold that a child's citizenship is in the country to which his father owes allegiance. This is the principle of *jus sanguinis*. We should add, however, that few countries, not even the United States and Great Britain, adhere exclusively to either principle.

Persons born in the United States who are not citizens. Persons born in the United States are not citizens if they are not "subject to the jurisdiction." By long-established rules of international law, several classes of persons are not subject to the jurisdiction. Diplomatic officials and executive officers of foreign governments are not under the jurisdiction of the United States, although they may be in the United States; consequently, their children who are born in the United States are not American citizens, but citizens of the countries their fathers represent. Public vessels, usually war vessels, are always under the jurisdiction of the country that owns them; hence, children born on such ships in the territorial waters of the United States are not American citizens. Another exception is found in the case of children born to enemy families in hostile occupation of American territory.

Persons born abroad who are citizens at birth. The United States has always classed as citizens children born abroad of American parents, but in the Nationality Act of 1940 this government gives a broad extension of the privilege. Persons declared to have American citizenship at birth include (1) any person born outside the United States and its outlying possessions of parents *both* of whom are citizens of the United States and *one* of whom has resided in the United States or one of its outlying possessions prior to the birth of such person; (2) any person born outside the United States and its outlying possessions of parents *one* of whom is a citizen of the United States who, prior to the birth of such person, has had *ten years'* residence in the United States or one of its outlying possessions, at least *five years* of which were after attaining the age of sixteen years. But, in order to retain citizenship acquired from the one parent, a person must reside in the United States or one of its possessions for a period of *five years* between the ages of thirteen and twenty-one.

RECIPROCITY. This rule regarding the citizenship of children born abroad of American parents operates both ways. Consequently if the country to which aliens in the United States owe allegiance claims that the citizenship of the children of such aliens must follow that of the parents, our government does not claim that such children must be American citizens. Here is a concrete case. Hans is born in the United States of Danish parents. By the Fourteenth Amendment he is a *native*-born citizen of the United States. If he goes to Denmark, that government may claim him as a *natural*-born citizen. Such a person is said to have dual nationality. Obviously, this flexible rule serves a very practical purpose in this day when so many citizens reside in foreign lands.

Subject to the exceptions just noted, all persons born in the United States and abroad of American parents are citizens. Women, as well as men, are citizens and have been all through our history. Children are citizens.

The baby's citizenship dates from the time that he first serves as the family alarm clock. A very common error is the assumption that persons are not citizens until they reach the voting age.

II. IMMIGRATION AND NATURALIZATION [3]

Perhaps strict logic would require us to proceed at once from our review of citizenship by birth to citizenship by naturalization. But since immigration must come before naturalization, it seems practical to give it precedence in the discussion.

American immigration policy. A brief consideration of our immigration policy is in order. It was most liberal until after the Civil War. We needed immigrants to help develop our vast resources and, besides, we had a feeling of pride in being the refuge of peoples held down by the social structure and political "despotism" of the Old World. The first restrictive legislation came in 1882, when Congress denied admission to paupers, lunatics, and Chinese coolies. Agitation for greater restriction, largely promoted by labor organizations, has since been almost unabated, and, in recent years, very successful. Diseased persons, criminals, Communists, and aliens objectionable for various other reasons have been placed on the ineligible list. In 1917 persons who could not read some language were debarred. Fearing a flood of immigrants following the First World War, Congress (1921) restricted the number that might enter annually from any country to three per cent of the number of persons of that nationality who resided in the United States in 1910, and by an act of 1924 changed the number to two per cent of those residing in the country in 1890.

A policy that was announced as permanent, but that is not altogether satisfactory, went into effect in 1929. Under this plan, we will admit from certain countries, chiefly European, as many as 153,000 immigrants per annum. The proportion of this 153,000 which may be admitted from any such country is determined by the proportion in which that country has contributed to our national stock. Thus, since the greater part of our population traces its ancestry back to the British Isles, those Islands have the lion's share, about 83,000. This immigration system is known as the "national origins plan." Few if any countries have supplied their full quota, and the countries of northwestern Europe have supplied less than one fifth of their quota. The quota does not apply to American peoples— Canadians, Mexicans, Cubans, and others; they may enter freely. Until 1943, no Orientals, except certain professional classes and students, were

[3] W. S. Bernard and others (eds.), *American Immigration Policy: A Reappraisal* (1950); Gettys, *op. cit.,* Chs. III–VII; Hyde, *op. cit.;* L. Adamic, "Aliens and Alien-Baiters," *Harper's,* Nov., 1936, pp. 561–574; (Judge) Phillip Forman, "Citizenship Ceremonies," *Monthly Review* (Immigration and Naturalization Service), July, 1949.

permitted to enter; but Chinese, Filipinos, and "persons of races indigenous to India" are now on the quota basis. Broadly speaking, our present immigration policy amounts to this: Some Asiatics and all Europeans are placed on a quota basis, and peoples of the American countries are admitted without numerical restriction. Of course, illiterates, anarchists, criminals, and individuals who are objectionable on various other grounds are denied admission regardless of the country of origin. The result of these changes in our immigration policy is shown by the fact that in the 'thirties less than 250,000 immigrants, including those from the non-quota American countries, were admitted annually whereas prior to the First World War, before percentage restrictions were imposed, nearly a million were admitted annually. The Second World War reduced immigration almost to a trickle.

HOW OUR POPULATION GREW

	THROUGH EXCESS OF BIRTHS OVER DEATHS	THROUGH IMMIGRATION
1860-1870		
1870-1880		
1880-1890		
1890-1900		
1900-1910		
1910-1920		
1920-1930		
1930-1940		

EACH SYMBOL REPRESENTS AN INCREASE OF ONE MILLION PEOPLE

In the first ten years of the present century, our population increased more from immigrants than from our own births. Since 1930, immigration has all but ceased.

From Twentieth Century Fund, *U.S.A.: Measure of a Nation* (Macmillan, 1949), p. 10.

POSTWAR IMMIGRATION PROBLEMS. We are not now receiving as large a flow of immigrants as we did following the First World War. The restrictive measures enacted in the early 'twenties are still in force. Our main concern now is, or should be, that of reconsidering our immigration policy. Should it be more restrictive? Should the quota system be more flexible? Should the quota system be extended to all countries? Should we be less restrictive and more selective, that is, consider such matters as occupations and needs of prospective immigrants instead of adhering to the strict quota system? Should we abolish all racial and nationality discriminations? And what solution should we offer for the problem (a temporary one, we hope) of nearly a million persons displaced by the war? These are some of the questions. The last two seem relatively easy to answer. Students of immigration and persons moderately well informed on contemporary American foreign policy do not hesitate to recommend that racial and nationality discriminations be abolished. Such discriminations are inconsistent with our international obligations and our democratic principles. If we are troubled about numbers, we can find consolation in the fact that the quota system would give no Asiatic country more than 100 immigrants a year. In 1948 Congress passed the Displaced Persons Act, a measure designed to admit to the United States 205,000 of the war's homeless (other countries were admitting their share). The title of the act read well, but in its text it revealed racial, religious, and occupational discriminations that brought strong condemnation.[4] It is, however, fair to report that about 100,000 DP's were admitted to the United States during the first year the act of 1948 was in operation. On June 16, 1950, the President signed a bill that about doubles the number of DP's who may be admitted and that removes the injustice and inadequacy of the DP Act of 1948.

Administration of immigration laws. The immigration laws are administered by the Immigration and Naturalization Service of the Department of Justice. Its two main functions in this connection are to determine the right of aliens to enter the United States and to deport those who have entered illegally. Formerly, aliens seeking admission were examined only at the ports of entry and were turned back in great numbers as being ineligible. This system often brought great hardship to rejected aliens, and it was not a very businesslike method. In recent years we have followed the plan of sending immigration inspectors abroad, who interview prospective immigrants in their own country, advise them, and determine in a preliminary way whether they will be admitted to the United States. As a consequence of this enlightened policy, only a very few immigrants from overseas are now turned back at our ports of entry. Every year thousands of aliens are deported: those who have entered surreptitiously, criminals, persons previously debarred or deported, and others. Tens of thousands (195,880 in 1947) adjudged deportable are allowed to depart at their own expense and without a warrant of deportation. Back in the 'twenties and early 'thirties, when the immigration laws were administered by the Department of Labor, the authorities were often criticized for acting arbitrarily in deportation proceedings. Particularly did this charge have justification in the period immediately following the First World War.

[4] *See New York Times,* editorials, Dec. 17, 1948, Nov. 1, and Nov. 11, 1949.

It is fair to add, however, that, beginning with 1933, the Labor Department followed a much more restrained practice and that its successor in administering the immigration laws, the Department of Justice, shows every desire to pursue a humane policy.

The Alien Registration Act of 1940. In the midst of a world upheaval Congress enacted the Alien Registration Act of 1940 as a means of protecting the American people from "fifth columnists," saboteurs, and other subversive elements. Its administration is in the hands of the Alien Registration Division of the Immigration and Naturalization Service. The act requires the registration of all aliens in the United States and the registration of all aliens entering the country, the registration of the latter to take place at American consulates abroad at which aliens obtain their entry visas (permits). The law requires also that all aliens above the age of fourteen be fingerprinted. On its face the statute seems harsh, contrary to American traditions; but its desirability would be easy to prove, and Americans are proud that it has been administered in a tolerant spirit. Moreover, the law serves not only as a protection to the United States, but also to the aliens themselves. For one thing, registration establishes proof of entry to the United States, and for another, it might save an innocent person from conviction of crime.

Naturalization. Now we are ready to consider the process of naturalization. Groups of aliens, without any affirmative act on their part, may be collectively naturalized by treaties and acts of Congress; or the individual alien, upon his own initiative, may be admitted to citizenship under the ordinary naturalization laws.

1. COLLECTIVE NATURALIZATION. The first method is commonly employed in bestowing citizenship upon "subjects" or "nationals" who reside in territory newly acquired by the United States. Prior to 1898 we naturalized the inhabitants of ceded territories collectively at the time of cession or shortly thereafter. But since 1898, when we began acquiring territory inhabited by peoples unfamiliar with our political institutions, we have pursued a more cautious policy. Several islands were added to our domain on the date mentioned. In 1900 Hawaiians were made citizens of the United States; but not until 1917 were Puerto Ricans accorded that privilege. As for the Filipinos, they were never citizens of the United States, although they were "nationals" of the United States and therefore entitled to about the same protection by its government as were citizens. The annexation of the Virgin Islands, in 1917, was followed ten years later by the collective naturalization of their inhabitants as citizens of the United States.

2. INDIVIDUAL NATURALIZATION. When we speak of naturalization, we generally have in mind the process by which aliens may obtain citizenship

individually. In 1790 Congress enacted its first legislation on the subject, and from time to time has passed other such measures, the most recent and comprehensive being the Nationality Act of 1940. Our discussion of naturalization is based primarily upon this act.[5]

Persons eligible for naturalization. Until 1870 only "free" white persons were eligible for citizenship by naturalization, but at that time persons of African nativity or descent were made eligible. To this list the act of 1940 adds "descendants of races indigenous to the Western Hemisphere." Chinese, Japanese, and other Asiatics were long ineligible, but recent legislation (1943 and 1946) authorizes the naturalization of Chinese, Filipinos, and natives of India. No person is eligible for naturalization who cannot speak English; who advocates opposition to organized government; who would overthrow by violence the Government of the United States; or who (by a Nationality Act amendment of 1950) is affiliated with any Communist organization. It is not without interest that an alien enemy may be naturalized if he has declared his intention to become a citizen of the United States not less than two years prior to the declaration of war.

Naturalization procedure. Naturalization has always been under the jurisdiction of the district courts of the United States and state courts. For many years the process was often a scandal, particularly in the metropolitan areas. Since citizenship has always been a common, although not a universal, requirement for voting, the political organizations were very active in securing the naturalization of aliens. This was accomplished by outright fraud in some cases, but a more common method was to rush through hundreds of aliens just prior to an election. At such times the courts would administer the naturalization law in a most perfunctory way, sometimes operating at the rate of a naturalization a minute. Under such conditions many persons were admitted to citizenship who were not entitled to it. The law of 1906 corrected some of these abuses, and the designation of examiners to assist the courts with naturalization cases helped to prevent others. The Nationality Act of 1940 marks a still further advance toward a better administered system.

DECLARATION AND PETITION. A person seeking naturalization must have reached the age of eighteen. His first step toward his goal is to sign a declaration of intention to become a citizen of the United States. This declaration, which contains eighteen items, should show that he has the qualifications which, with the expiration of time, will make him eligible for citizenship. Not less than two and not more than seven years after he has filed the declaration of intention, and not less than five years after his arrival in the United States, he may file his petition for naturalization. This petition must describe the applicant, give complete information con-

[5] 54 Stat. 1137.

cerning his former residence and his residence in the United States, be accompanied by a certificate of his arrival in this country, state that he is "well disposed to the good order and happiness of the United States," and contain various other facts and declarations. The petition must be accompanied by the affidavits of at least two credible witnesses, citizens of the United States, stating that they have known the petitioner during the six months preceding the filing of the petition and that he is a person of good moral character and attached to the principles of the Constitution of the United States. The five years of continuous residence in the United States required by law must also be proved by witnesses who are citizens of the United States.

Willingness to take up arms. Until 1946 applicants who did not give an affirmative answer to the question, "If necessary, are you willing to take up arms in defense of this country?" were denied citizenship. This question, framed by administrative authorities, was based on a provision of the naturalization law that reads: "I will support and defend the Constitution and laws of the United States of America against all enemies, foreign and domestic." By majority decisions the Supreme Court had sustained the action of immigration officials, but there were vigorous dissents in the Court and out. Consequently, there was no general surprise when, in 1946, the Court reversed its position, holding that one need not give an affirmative answer to the "take up arms" question in order to be naturalized. The majority of the Court took the position that the oath administered to public officers imposed no such test, and emphasized, as the dissenting judges had in earlier cases, that some of the most desirable and useful native-born citizens were opposed to bearing arms.[6] As amended in 1950, the Nationality Act requires applicants to disclose their willingness to bear arms or perform noncombatant service unless they can show such service is contrary to their religious belief, in which case they are not required to make the declaration.

ADMISSION TO CITIZENSHIP. Upon receipt of the petition for naturalization, an officer of the Immigration and Naturalization Service of the United States Department of Justice conducts hearings on it. The examiner is authorized to take testimony concerning any matter touching the admissibility of the petitioner for naturalization, to subpoena witnesses, and to administer oaths. The examiner makes his report to a court, recommending that the petition be granted, or denied, or continued, giving reasons. The final hearing on the petition is held by a judge in open court, and the judge makes the final order on the petition. If the petition is approved, the petitioner is then permitted to take the oath of allegiance to the United States. The final ceremony of admission to citizenship has not always

---

[6] Girouard v. United States, 328 U.S. 61 (1946).

been such as to impress the new citizens. It was often done in haste and without dignity. "When do I get to be a citizen?" asked a bewildered petitioner who was told to go. "You are a citizen now, you dope," replied an attendant.

The ceremony of induction into citizenship has been greatly improved in recent years. This proceeding, like the ceremony of marriage, should be solemn, dignified, and at the same time radiate cheering prospects of a new life. It is gratifying to report that many local communities now work with the Naturalization Service in organizing appropriate ceremonies for those being inducted into citizenship.[7] In some communities rather elaborate and effective annual celebrations are held for foreign-born who became citizens during the preceding year.

Education for citizenship. Infinitely more significant than any ceremony of induction is the education of the applicant for citizenship. Long conscious of the gross inadequacy of the training given most applicants (often they had none), both the government and public-spirited citizens have started to do something about it. The late President Franklin D. Roosevelt approved a Citizenship Education Program, a logical sequence of the registration of nearly five million non-citizens of this country. The Nationality Act of 1940 authorizes the Commissioner of Immigration and Naturalization to promote instruction and training in the citizenship responsibilities of applicants. Under the authority of this act the Commissioner has prepared and distributed citizenship textbooks, supplied the public schools with names of candidates for naturalization, obtained the aid of state and local authorities in promoting the program of education, and otherwise facilitated the instruction of future citizens. As no plan of this kind will bring about important results unless local nonpaid citizens take an active interest in it, the sharing of educational authorities, teachers, and civic and patriotic organizations in its development is encouraging.

Derivative citizenship. Formerly, alien women who might lawfully become naturalized, automatically became American citizens upon marriage to such citizens. This automatic acquisition of citizenship is no longer possible for such persons, but citizenship by naturalization is made easy for them. The Cable Act of 1922 authorized women of a race eligible for naturalization who married American citizens to obtain citizenship after one year of residence in the United States. Later statutes modified the plan slightly and extended essentially the same privilege to aliens who married American women. Without going into the details of the latest legislation on the subject, the Nationality Act of 1940, it may be said that

---

[7] Phillip Forman, a federal district judge in New Jersey, gives a very interesting contrast between the old and new naturalization ceremonies in his "Citizenship Ceremonies," *Monthly Review* (Immigration and Naturalization Service), July, 1949.

any alien (male or female) who marries an American citizen may within a period ranging from one to three years, depending upon circumstances, become a naturalized citizen. Formerly, children born outside of the United States acquired citizenship through the naturalization of their fathers but not through the naturalization of their mothers. Under the present law, alien children under the age of eighteen and residing in the United States become American citizens upon the naturalization of both parents, or upon the naturalization of the surviving parent or the parent having legal custody of the child. The law provides also that a child born outside of the United States, one of whose parents is a citizen at the time naturalization is sought for the child (the child being under eighteen), may be naturalized without a declaration of intention, provided he is residing in the United States with the citizen parent.

Denaturalization. Disloyalty on the part of certain naturalized citizens in time of war lends interest to the fact that the government may cancel the certificates of citizenship obtained by illegal or fraudulent means, and since 1906 it has provided by statute for such cancellation. Furthermore, the Nationality Act, as amended in 1950, specifically provides that a naturalized citizen who becomes affiliated with a Communist organization within five years after naturalization shall forfeit his citizenship. In such a case, the assumption is that he obtained his certificate by fraud or illegal procurement.

An individual who renounces allegiance to his old country, takes his oath as an American citizen, and then shows a preference for the land of his origin over the land of his adoption is likely to find himself deprived of his citizenship in the latter on the ground that he obtained it by fraudulent means—that he made mental reservations when he took the oath of allegiance to the United States. Thus, a native of Germany, naturalized in the United States in 1882, who made repeated statements to the effect that he did not wish to see the United States victorious in the First World War was deprived of his citizenship. This policy was followed in a number of similar cases during both the world wars,[8] although during the second war the Supreme Court of the United States displayed commendable hesitation in sustaining cancellations of naturalization certificates. In Baumgartner v. United States [9] the Supreme Court held that denaturalization could be sanctioned only upon a convincing showing that the holder of a naturalization certificate had consciously withheld allegiance to the United States at the time of his naturalization. Said Mr. Justice Frankfurter, speaking for the Court: "One of the prerogatives of American

---

[8] Lawrence Preuss, "Denaturalization on the Grounds of Disloyalty," *Am. Pol. Sci. Rev.,* XXXVI, 701 (August, 1942).

[9] 322 U.S. 665 (1944).

citizenship is the right to criticize public men and measures—and that means not only informed and responsible criticism but the freedom to speak foolishly and without moderation." We should not penalize "a naturalized citizen for the expression of silly or even sinister-sounding views which native-born citizens utter with impunity." In a concurring opinion Mr. Justice Murphy stated that "In the instant case the failure of the Government to present evidence of a 'clear, unequivocal, and convincing' nature that petitioner fraudulently or illegally procured his naturalization certificate in 1932 is patent. With one unimportant exception, the Government proved only that petitioner displayed certain Nazi sympathies and was critical of the United States several years after 1932."

In April, 1950, the citizenship of Harry Bridges was revoked because at his naturalization hearings, in 1945, he had falsely sworn that he was not a Communist.

Expatriation. Despite the fact that civilized nations have for centuries extended the privilege of naturalization, the right of an individual to expatriate himself, to renounce his allegiance to a country without its government's consent and swear exclusive allegiance to another country, is of relatively recent origin. One might become a citizen of another country, but the land of his first allegiance might still claim him as her own and, what is more, make matters distinctly unpleasant for him if he should happen to set foot again in her territory. During the nineteenth century the United States granted citizenship to many Europeans who came to her shores, and these "citizens by adoption," upon the occasion of a visit to the old homeland, frequently discovered that their rights as American citizens were not recognized by the government of their native land. Against this disregard of the rights of her naturalized citizens the United States made protests, sometimes vigorous and effective, but not until 1868 did Congress by law proclaim the right of an individual to expatriate himself. As the matter now stands, the United States asserts the right of an alien to renounce his allegiance to his native land, with or without the consent of its government, and by the same token it concedes the right of an American citizen to change his allegiance from the United States to another country. Not only does the United States support expatriation as the right of an individual, but it also designates a number of circumstances, such as voting in a foreign election, under which a citizen of the United States forfeits any claim he may have to such citizenship.[10] (In respect to special conditions

[10] During the Second World War native-born American citizens of Japanese ancestry, in our relocation centers and in Japan, sometimes under duress renounced their allegiance to the United States and assumed the obligations of Japanese citizens. It seems now that they might be able to recover American citizenship by submitting proof that it was renounced under duress. *See* Inoue v. Clark, U.S. Dist. Ct., S.D. Calif., 73 Fed. Supp. 1000, and *American Journal of International Law*, July, 1948, p. 492, and *ibid.*, July, 1949, p. 441.

under which naturalized citizens forfeit claim as citizens, see paragraphs 2 and 3 of the next section.)

III. THE PRIVILEGES OF CITIZENS

Limitations on privileges of naturalized citizens: 1. INELIGIBLE FOR THE PRESIDENCY. The naturalized citizen has the same privileges as the native citizen, with three exceptions. The first exception is that he is not eligible for the presidency of the United States. This constitutional provision has deprived a few of our foremost naturalized citizens, a number of whom have been governors and members of Congress, of a chance to reach the White House.

2. NO ASSURANCE OF PROTECTION AGAINST CLAIMS OF FORMER COUNTRY FOR MILITARY SERVICE. The second exception is found in the somewhat limited protection we give naturalized citizens when on visits to their old countries. Our government is often unable to prevent such citizens from being forced into the military service of the country of former allegiance or to prevent their being punished for an earlier evasion of military service. Under naturalization treaties with some countries, fairly satisfactory arrangements have been made respecting military obligations; but in those countries with which no such treaties have been made, naturalized citizens are advised that they cannot rely with assurance upon the protective arm of the United States, that before visiting such countries they should inquire of the appropriate authorities thereof whether they will be held for military service. Native-born American citizens whose parents are unnaturalized, since they may also be considered citizens of the country of their parents' origin, are similarly advised to ascertain their status before visiting the parents' homeland. Under the Nationality Law of 1940 a citizen who was born in the United States is presumed to have forfeited any claim to the protection of the United States from enforced military service in a foreign country, if he or either parent has ever been a citizen of that country, and if he remains in that country for six months or longer.

3. LOSS OF CITIZENSHIP THROUGH RESIDENCE ABROAD. A naturalized citizen who returns to the land of his fathers and there resides for two years loses his American citizenship, if he acquires through such residence citizenship in the old country by the laws thereof. Regardless of the laws of such country, he loses his American citizenship, with certain exceptions, if he resides in it for a period of three years. Loss of citizenship, again with certain exceptions, is sustained by any naturalized citizen who resides continuously for five years in any other foreign country.

With regard to the three exceptions noted, we should bear in mind that the great majority of naturalized citizens are never in a position where any one of the exceptions will apply to them, and we may conclude that their privileges are essentially the same as those of the native-born citizens.

Double citizenship under the Fourteenth Amendment. The first sentence of the Fourteenth Amendment makes it clear that we have two citizenships. We are citizens of the United States and, if we live in some state, as nearly all of us do, we are citizens of that state by virtue of our national citizenship. Because the states are compelled to accept as their citizens any citizens of the United States who choose to reside in them, we commonly regard state citizenship as of little importance. But it exists just the same. There are privileges and immunities that we enjoy as citizens of the United States and there are other privileges and immunities that we enjoy as citizens of the states, even if we do get the latter through our possession of the wider national citizenship.

1. SOME PRIVILEGES INCIDENT TO STATE CITIZENSHIP. The clause of the Fourteenth Amendment that immediately follows the sentence announcing the law of citizenship prohibits the states from making or enforcing "any law which shall abridge the privileges or immunities of citizens of the United States." Many privileges one enjoys are privileges that are incident to state citizenship and, therefore, do not fall within the terms of the prohibition. Marriage, divorce, control of children, property rights, and nearly all other rights connected with life, liberty, and the pursuit of happiness are rights over which states have control. When the State of Louisiana conferred upon a company a slaughterhouse monopoly within the city of New Orleans, some independent butchers went to court with the argument that the state, in not permitting them to carry on their business within the city, had abridged their privileges and immunities as citizens of the United States. In a much-criticized decision the Court held, five-to-four, that the privilege of slaughtering stock in a city was not a privilege conferred by United States citizenship, but was a subject within the jurisdiction of the states.[11]

2. PRIVILEGES INCIDENT TO NATIONAL CITIZENSHIP. In the same decision relating to the slaughterhouses, the Court enumerated some of the privileges incident to national citizenship. The citizen of the United States may "demand the care and protection of the federal government over his life, liberty, and property when on the high seas or within the jurisdiction of a foreign government; . . . use the navigable waters of the United States"; enjoy all rights secured to citizens by treaties with foreign nations; and, of his own volition, become a citizen of any state, by a bona fide residence therein. The Court has mentioned other privileges of the citizens of the United States; but, upon examination, it appears that they are not the

[11] Slaughterhouse Cases, 16 Wall. 36 (1873).

exclusive privileges of citizens, being enjoyed by aliens and citizens alike. For example, the privilege of seeking the protection of the government and to use its courts can hardly be said to be exclusive privileges of citizens of the United States.

If "privileges or immunities" of citizens of the United States mean anything, they mean that citizens enjoy rights or privileges that aliens do not enjoy. There are few such privileges, and they are all, or nearly all, specified above. In reality the clause of the Fourteenth Amendment under discussion gives the citizen of the United States no special status or advantages he did not have before the Amendment was adopted. In 1935 the Supreme Court seemed ready to give a much broader meaning to the privileges and immunities clause, for in Colgate v. Harvey [12] it held that the right to carry on business across state lines was a privilege of citizens protected by the Fourteenth Amendment. But in later cases [13] the Court returned to its original and restrictive interpretation of the clause. In 1941 four of the justices declared that the California law designed to prevent indigent persons from entering the state was in violation of the privileges and immunities of citizens of the United States as protected by the Fourteenth Amendment, but the majority of the Court took the view that the California statute was bad because it imposed an undue burden upon interstate commerce.[14]

IV. THE SUFFRAGE [15]

The privilege of voting is commonly associated with citizenship. Not all citizens have the privilege, but in all states voters must be citizens of the United States. The Constitution of the United States, which lays down the basic law of citizenship, leaves the matter of suffrage qualifications, with certain exceptions, to the states.

The suffrage provisions of the federal Constitution. In congressional elections all persons who by state law have the privilege of voting for members of the lower house of a state legislature may vote for Congressmen.[16] We note that this provision simply accepts the qualifications which the states establish.

A section of the Fourteenth Amendment, adopted in 1868, carries the

[12] 296 U.S. 404 (1935).

[13] Madden v. Kentucky, 309 U.S. 83 (1940); Snowden v. Hughes, 321 U.S. 1 (1944).

[14] Edwards v. California, 314 U.S. 160 (1941).

[15] R. C. Brooks, *Political Parties and Electoral Problems* (1933 ed.), Ch. XIV; V. O. Key, Jr., *Politics, Parties, and Pressure Groups* (1947 ed.), Ch. 16; D. D. McKean, *Party and Pressure Politics* (1949), Ch. 3; K. H. Porter, *History of the Suffrage in the United States* (1918); E. M. Sait, *American Parties and Elections* (H. R. Penniman's ed.—1948), Chs. II–IV.

[16] Art. I, sec. II, cl. I, and the Seventeenth Amendment.

threat that states which deny the right to vote to male citizens who have attained the age of twenty-one will have their representation in Congress reduced in the proportion which the number of such male citizens bears to the total number of male citizens twenty-one years of age residing in such states. This provision marks an attempt to force the states, especially the Southern states, to give the emancipated Negro the franchise. It has never been enforced and is probably unenforceable. No person is enfranchised by it, either in fact or in law.

The Fifteenth Amendment, ratified in 1870, provides that the right of citizens of the United States to vote shall not be denied or abridged by the United States or by any state on account of race, color, or previous condition of servitude. Notice that the Amendment does not positively place the ballot in the hands of the colored man. It provides only that the ballot shall not be withheld from him because of his race or color or because he has been a slave. If it is withheld for other reasons (and we shall presently learn that they are easily found), the Negro's case is not covered by the Amendment.

The Nineteenth Amendment, adopted in 1920, carries the provision that citizens shall not be denied the right to vote on account of sex. Its phraseology is exactly the same as that of the Fifteenth Amendment.

It would be interesting, even entertaining, to trace the history of the extension of the suffrage in the United States, for it is a part of the story of American democracy. But since the states have had a major part in this development, and since the story has already been told by competent authorities whose books are readily accessible,[17] a brief discussion of the present qualifications for voting is sufficient for this volume.

State qualifications for voting: CITIZENSHIP. In national, state, and local elections, throughout the United States, the requirements for the suffrage are essentially the same. Citizenship in the United States is required in every state. Formerly, about twenty states allowed certain classes of aliens to vote; but because of the abuses that grew up around this practice, and because of the nationalistic and nativistic spirit that has prevailed in recent years, all of these states have now abandoned the practice.

AGE. All the American colonies, and later the states, fixed the voting age at twenty-one years, following early English practice. The age requirement is not the same in all countries, but twenty-one seems to meet with the most general endorsement. In recent years compulsory military service for men in the United States who have reached their eighteenth birthday led to a strong movement to lower the age limit for the suffrage to eighteen. In 1943 Georgia, by constitutional amendment, extended the voting privilege to those citizens who had attained this age.

[17] See the authorities cited in note 15.

RESIDENCE. The state laws vary in the requirement of residence from three months to two years, one year being the most common specification. Shorter periods are required in the counties and cities, where the time varies from ten days to one year, and still shorter periods of residence are required in the precincts. The place of legal residence is not necessarily the same as the actual place of residence. A voter may spend the greater part of the time in some place other than that of his legal residence, but as long as he shows some interest in his legal residence, his act of voting from that address is not ordinarily questioned.

LITERACY TEST IN SOME STATES. Two qualifications for voting, literacy and tax paying, have a limited application. About a third of the states apply some sort of literacy test, a common form of which is reading the Constitution and writing one's name. In the South it excludes a high percentage of the Negroes from the exercise of the suffrage.[18] Eight states outside the South employ the test, but it is estimated that it disqualifies very few citizens in those states. Some would apply a more exacting educational test to all who seek the privilege of voting. There is little likelihood, however, that more rigorous tests will be applied in the near future, for the cry of politicians that democracy is threatened would have great weight. Besides, a plausible argument is made against any literacy test by those who say that many illiterates have keener perceptions and are better judges of men than their fellow citizens who read the comics and the sports pages.

THE POLL TAX. In the late 'twenties some fifteen states required all voters to pay an annual poll tax ranging from one to two dollars. At the present time, it is imposed in only six states, all of them in the South.[19] The reason for this tax is obvious. It is to keep Negroes away from the polls. It also disfranchises tens of thousands of "poor whites," but this does not disturb the dominant element in those states, for its members would probably admit, in private, that poor whites have no particular claim as citizens. Furthermore, if it becomes desirable to permit some of these people to vote, it can be arranged by paying the poll tax for them, or even by issuing poll tax receipts "wholesale and free" to party workers for discriminating distribution among the voters. Many Southerners who stand in opposition to the reactionaries who control their states have become very active in organized efforts to repeal the tax.[20] In recent years Florida,

---

[18] In 1950 South Carolina tightened her voting restrictions with the requirements, among others, that a voter must be able "both to read and write" any section of the state constitution submitted to him by a registration official, or must have paid all taxes due on property in the state assessed at $300 or more. Persons familiar with the state estimated that these and other restrictions would keep from 50,000 to 60,000 Negroes from the primaries and the general election.

[19] They are: Alabama, Arkansas, Mississippi, Tennessee, Texas, and Virginia.

[20] See Jennings Perry, *Democracy Begins at Home* (1944).

Georgia, Louisiana, North Carolina, and South Carolina (1950) have repealed it. But the poll-taxers die hard. In 1943 Tennessee repealed its law, but her supreme court took the absurd position that the constitutional mandate to enact a poll tax law, having been carried out by an act of the legislature, could not be repealed by any subsequent legislature.[21] But six years later, the Tennessee legislature abolished the poll tax requirement for participation in primary elections and exempted women, war veterans, and the blind from the requirement in general elections. In 1949 the voters of both Texas and Virginia rejected a proposal to repeal the poll tax. In Virginia, however, the proposal was so tied up with accepting or rejecting various reactionary provisions respecting registration and election laws that leaders who would have advocated straight poll tax repeal used all their efforts to defeat this particular type of "repeal."

Congress has seriously taken up the matter of outlawing the poll tax in national elections. An act of Congress would stipulate "That the requirement that a poll tax be paid as a prerequisite to voting or registering to vote at primaries or other elections" for national officers, "is not and shall not be deemed a qualification of voters . . . but it shall be deemed an interference with the manner of holding primaries and other elections." [22] By the statement that the tax shall not be deemed a *qualification,* Congress is trying to get around the provision of the Constitution (Art. I, sec. I, cl. I) that gives the states the authority to fix the "qualifications requisite for electors (voters)"; and by calling the poll tax an interference with the manner of holding elections, Congress is attempting to bring the abolishment of the tax under its constitutional authority (Art. I, sec. IV, cl. I) to prescribe the "manner of holding elections." The mere declaration by Congress, however, that a poll tax is not a qualification for voting but an interference with the manner of holding elections does not set aside history, nor does it preclude the Supreme Court of the United States from taking a different view. Up to this time the issue remains with Congress, for several Southern senators (the late Senator Bilbo in particular), with the tacit support of a few Republicans of impeccable respectability, have thus far been able, by filibuster or threat of filibuster, to block action by the Senate. In any event, a national antipoll tax law would certainly offend the South. It may be better to await the slower but less disturbing method of abolition by the individual states.

DISQUALIFICATIONS. Felons, idiots, and the insane are regularly denied the ballot, and in many states persons guilty of election offenses are disqualified from voting. Paupers, vagrants, and persons under guardian-

[21] Biggs v. Beeler, 173 S.W. 2d 144 (1943).
[22] H.R. 7, 79th Congress, 1st Session.

State	Estimated civilian population of voting age, July 1, 1948*	Vote cast for Presidential electors, November 2, 1948
Alabama	1,584,000	214,980
Arizona	374,000	177,065
Arkansas	1,100,000	242,475
California	6,714,000	4,021,538
Colorado	721,000	515,237
Connecticut	1,376,000	883,518
Delaware	196,000	139,073
Florida	1,465,000	577,643
Georgia	1,917,000	418,760
Idaho	318,000	214,816
Illinois	5,896,000	3,984,046
Indiana	2,557,000	1,656,214
Iowa	1,718,000	1,038,264
Kansas	1,294,000	788,819
Kentucky	1,618,000	822,658
Louisiana	1,495,000	416,326
Maine	568,000	264,787
Maryland	1,363,000	596,735
Massachusetts	3,228,000	2,155,347
Michigan	3,981,000	2,109,609
Minnesota	1,906,000	1,212,226
Mississippi	1,155,000	192,190
Missouri	2,623,000	1,578,628
Montana	319,000	134,278
Nebraska	846,000	488,939
Nevada	90,000	62,117
New Hampshire	365,000	231,440
New Jersey	3,255,000	1,949,555
New Mexico	295,000	185,767
New York	10,035,000	6,274,527
North Carolina	2,049,000	791,209
North Dakota	332,000	220,716
Ohio	5,189,000	2,936,071
Oklahoma	1,438,000	721,599
Oregon	1,109,000	524,080
Pennsylvania	7,111,000	3,735,149
Rhode Island	503,000	326,098
South Carolina	1,029,000	142,571
South Dakota	387,000	250,105
Tennessee	1,840,000	550,283
Texas	4,311,000	1,147,245
Utah	370,000	276,305
Vermont	238,000	123,382
Virginia	1,772,000	419,256
Washington	1,649,000	905,059
West Virginia	1,103,000	748,750
Wisconsin	2,147,000	1,276,800
Wyoming	169,000	101,425
TOTALS	93,118,000	48,743,680

* The population figures for all states except Georgia relate to civilians 21 years of age and older. For Georgia the figures are for the civilian population 18 years old and over.

The author is indebted to the Legislative Reference Service of the Library of Congress for these figures.

ship are not allowed to vote in many states. There are still other disqualifications, but those mentioned are the most common.

REGISTRATION. If an individual meets all of the qualifications as outlined above, he must still comply with a formality before he can vote—he must go before registration officials and have his name placed on the list of voters. The purpose of registration is to ascertain in advance of elections whether those desiring to vote actually possess the qualifications established by law. It is one of the principal safeguards against illegal voting. The method of registration usually employed calls for the actual presence before registration officials of persons who wish to qualify for voting. In about half the states, one such personal registration is sufficient, as long as the voter resides in the same precinct, for all succeeding elections; but other states require annual or biennial personal registration in cities, and some require the same periodic registration in the rural districts. Permanent registration is certainly satisfactory in the rural areas, and most authorities favor it for cities. Periodic registration is inconvenient, and many potential voters forget or neglect to register.

In communities where persons are usually known to the officials, registration is a relatively simple process, the name and residence of the individual often being all that is required. In cities a great deal more information is usually required, such as statements concerning age, length of residence in particular places, occupation, location of employment, and signature. In some places, a description of personal appearance is required, the purpose of this being to prevent impersonation of voters at election time.

The voting population. The accompanying chart, "Voters—Potential and Actual," shows the estimated civilian population of voting age and the actual number of voters in the presidential election of 1948. The difference between the number of persons of voting age and the number who voted is explained in part by the fact that many persons of voting age could not meet the qualifications for voting as outlined above. A much larger group of non-voters (it is impossible to say how large) are in that class because of illness, temporary absence, and indifference.

Reading List

L. Adamic, *A Nation of Nations* (1945).

W. S. Bernard and Others (eds.), *American Immigration Policy: A Reappraisal* (1950).

R. C. Brooks, *Political Parties and Electoral Problems* (1933 ed.), Ch. XIV.

L. G. Brown, *Immigration* (1933).

H. R. Bruce, *American Parties and Politics* (1935 ed.), Ch. XVI.

C. C. Catt and N. R. Shuler, *Woman Suffrage and Politics* (1923).

F. P. Cavanaugh, *Immigration Restriction at Work Today* (1928).

A. H. Eaton, *Immigrant Gifts to American Life* (1932).

J. P. Gavit, *Americans by Choice* (1922).

L. Gettys, *The Law of Citizenship in the United States* (1934).

J. P. Harris, *Registration of Voters in the United States* (1929).

A. N. Holcombe, *State Government in the United States* (1931 ed.), Chs. IV, VII.

I. A. Hourwich, *Immigration and Labor* (1922).

I. H. Irwin, *The Story of the Woman's Party* (1921).

F. R. Kent, *The Great Game of Politics* (1923), Appendix, Chs. I–V, X.

V. O. Key, Jr., *Politics, Parties, and Pressure Groups* (1947), Ch. 16–17.

————, *Southern Politics in State and Nation* (1949).

P. Lewinson, *Race, Class and Party: A History of Negro Suffrage and White Politics in the South* (1932).

A. J. Lien, *Privileges and Immunities of Citizens of the United States* (1913).

D. D. McKean, *Party and Pressure Politics* (1949), Ch. 3.

R. D. McKenzie, *Oriental Exclusion* (1928).

P. H. Odegard and E. A. Helms, *American Politics: A Study in Political Dynamics* (1947 ed.), Chs. XI–XIII.

Jennings Perry, *Democracy Begins at Home* (1944).

K. H. Porter, *History of Suffrage in the United States* (1918).

Recent Social Trends in the United States (1933), Vol. I, Chs. I and XI.

F. W. Riggs, *Pressure on Congress: A Study of the Repeal of Chinese Exclusion* (1950).

E. M. Sait, *American Parties and Elections* (H. R. Penniman's ed.—1948), Chs. II–IV.

C. Seymour and D. P. Frary, *How the World Votes* (2 Vols., 1918), Chs. IX–XIV.

A. H. Shaw, *The Story of a Pioneer* (1915).

W. T. Stone and Others, *Americans by Choice* (pamphlet, 1942).

W. W. Willoughby, *Principles of the Constitutional Law of the United States* (1930 ed.), Chs. XVIII–XX, XXVIII.

Carl Wittke, *We Who Built America* (1939).

Questions and Problems

1. A son is born to a Latin American ambassador in Washington, D.C. Later, the ambassador returns to his own country and leaves the son permanently in the United States. Is the son a citizen of the United States?

2. Discuss American immigration policy in relation to international good will.

3. Outline what you consider would be an appropriate program for the conclusion of naturalization proceedings.

4. Upon what grounds may a naturalized citizen lose his citizenship?

5. To what extent does the federal Constitution regulate or authorize Congress to regulate the suffrage?

6. Give reasons for or against the constitutionality of a federal antipoll tax law.
7. *The hundreds of thousands of nonvoters in the South are in that class because of the poll tax.* Discuss.
8. Is universal suffrage essential to democratic government?

☆ 8 ☆

Political Parties and Pressure Groups

A GREAT deal is said in previous chapters about our written Constitution as an instrument of government. At the same time, emphasis is given to the fact that the written Constitution by no means outlines the entire system of government. One of the most fundamental features of our political system, one that exerts a marked influence upon the whole democratic order, is the political party, a product not of written constitutions or laws but of political experience.

Importance of political parties. "Political parties are . . . indispensable instruments of government," reads A Report of the Committee on Political Parties of the American Political Science Association.[1] More than a hundred years ago the American people recognized the essential need for these organizations, and the voters divided into camps of more or less equal strength and fought their party battles, usually with something approaching patriotic zeal and sometimes with moral fervor. Party sentiment became strong, and the great-grandchildren of men who had voted for Jackson and the grandchildren of those who had supported Lincoln carried the torches of the respective parties and harbored warm party loyalties. With a large segment of the electorate such sentiments still prevail, but the segment is growing smaller as the number of people who are skeptical of party promises and suspicious of party leaders grows larger. Nor is this changing attitude toward political parties without substantial basis. Party organization is essentially what it was a hundred years ago. (Imagine a business corporation the organization of which had undergone no change in that time!) Parties have only a loose system for preparing their pro-

---

[1] "Toward a More Responsible Two-Party System," A Report of the Committee on Political Parties, American Political Science Association, *Am. Pol. Sci. Rev.* supplement, XLIV (September, 1950), Part 2, p. 15.

grams (platforms) and, having prepared them, they have no effective means of pushing them to fulfillment.

Yet parties are more needed now than ever. The larger the electorate the greater the need. Furthermore, government has more functions to perform now than formerly, many more positive functions, and the decisions to be made are fraught with much graver consequences now than formerly. These considerations make imperative the operations of vital political parties. To make democracy work in these critical times we need to make our party system more accountable to the public, better adapted to formulating and presenting the issues, and more able to deal with the great problems of our day. In the discussion of "parties as they are" that follows we should not lose sight of their present limitations and the worthy goal set for them by the Committee of Political Parties upon the report of which these introductory words are based.

Although space limitations require its omission here, it will be profitable to consult other authorities [2] for the story of the rise and development not only of the major political parties in the United States but also of the minor, or third, parties, several of which have contributed much more to American political life than "good" Democrats and Republicans commonly appreciate. This chapter presents the subjects of party organization, leadership, and functions, and stresses the methods and power of pressure groups that operate behind and within the parties and upon and within the government.

I. PARTY ORGANIZATION [3]

The necessity for organization. In the earlier days party organization was not so important; but with the extension of the suffrage, the rapid increase in the number of elective officers, and the growing complexities of government, the party found that only the most complete organization could serve its needs. How could the party nominate and elect candidates to office, raise and expend large sums of money for campaign purposes, appeal to each voter, distribute patronage, and do all the other things it does in nation, state, county, and city, without the most complete organization?

[2] H. A. Bone, *American Politics and the Party System* (1949), Chs. 11–15; R. C. Brooks, *Political Parties and Electoral Problems* (1933 ed.), Chs. IV–VII; H. R. Bruce, *American Parties and Politics* (1936 ed.), Chs. IV–VII; A. N. Holcombe, *The Political Parties of Today* (1925 ed.), Chs. I–X; V. O. Key, Jr., *Politics, Parties, and Pressure Groups* (1947 ed.), Chs. 8–9; S. Lewis, *Party Principles and Practical Politics* (1928), Chs. II–XI; E. M. Sait, *American Parties and Elections* (H. R. Penniman's ed.—1948), Chs. VIII–XI; J. A. Woodburn, *Political Parties and Party Problems in the United States* (1924 ed.), Chs. I–XI.

[3] Bone, *op. cit.,* Ch. 16; Brooks, *op. cit.,* Ch. VIII; Key, *op. cit.,* Chs. 10–11; E. B. Logan, (Ed.), *The American Political Scene* (1936), Ch. II; D. D. McKean, *Party and Pressure Groups* (1949), Ch. 9; C. E. Merriam and H. F. Gosnell, *The American Party System* (1949 ed.), Ch. VIII; Sait, *op. cit.,* Chs. XII–XV; "Toward a More Responsible Two-Party System," *op. cit.*

Party Committees. Probably the best-known party institution is the convention, and close to it in the popular mind is the primary election. Conventions, whether local, state, or national, have to do with the drafting and adoption of platforms and the nomination of candidates; the primaries serve only the latter function. The convention is composed of representatives who act for the party; the primary is the whole body of party members acting for themselves. Since conventions meet only for a brief period preceding elections, and primaries are equally temporary and intermittent, they clearly are not, however sovereign they may be, the organs that keep the party running.[4] From what we have already learned of the functions for which a party is responsible, we know that it must ever be on the alert to fulfill them. The necessary ceaseless activity of the party is performed by permanent committees, a hierarchy of committees, one for each political unit from the precinct to the nation.

THE NATIONAL COMMITTEE. At the head of the party committee system is the national committee, composed in both the major parties of a man and a woman from each state and territory, who serve four-year terms. Each state and territory designates its representatives on the national committee, common methods of designation being by state or territorial party convention and by the state or territorial delegates at the national convention. The national convention commonly confirms the persons so designated. The national convention chooses its own chairman, almost invariably the chief backer and promoter of the man who has just won the nomination for President and always the personal choice of the nominee. This custom makes sense because the organizer and promoter and fixer who has won a nomination for his candidate ought to be the man who can be of most service to him in the campaign for election.

The national committee has no authority in the convention that chooses it. Its duties begin when that convention adjourns. Its immediate responsibility (the chairman carrying the major part) is to conduct the presidential campaign and raise the millions of dollars necessary for that purpose. In the event of victory the committeemen (particularly the chairman, who will probably become Postmaster General) will have considerable influence in the matter of appointments to office. During the four-year interval until the next national convention the committee has the more prosaic task of serving the party's welfare in such matters as quieting dissenters (a difficult task if the party has lost the election), raising more money, assisting in the off-year congressional elections, and finding weak spots in the armor of the opposing party. In this period life is relatively sweet for the committee that has the Big Chief in the White House, but the

---

[4] Brooks, *op. cit.,* pp. 156–157.

committee that does not have the winner often has to submit to much outside criticism, and is the victim of internal dissensions that may result in the chairman's resignation. Almost a year before the time for the next national convention, the committee must begin planning for it. This phase of the committee's work is better left for the next chapter.

CONGRESSIONAL CAMPAIGN COMMITTEES. Each party has a congressional committee and a senatorial committee. The Republican congressional committee is composed of a member from each state that has a Republican in the House. The Democratic committee is the same in composition, with the exception that the chairman is empowered to name a woman member from each state and to appoint a member from any state that has no Democratic representation in the House. The principal interest of these committees is to secure the election of members of the party to the House of Representatives. To this end they are very active in the biennial congressional elections, particularly in election years when there is no presidential election. The Democratic and Republican senatorial committees are composed of six and seven members respectively, and their chief concern is, of course, with senatorial elections. Although the congressional and senatorial committees have no formal connection with the national committees, they are bound to them by partisan interests, look to them in particular for financial aid, and are quite likely to be rather completely overshadowed by them in presidential election years.

STATE COMMITTEES. At the head of a state party organization is the state central committee, composed of members chosen by direct primary, by committees of various districts of the state, or by the state convention, and varying in membership from ten or twelve in some states to several hundred in others. These committees are charged by law with certain responsibilities in respect to primaries and conventions. Formerly, in some of the Southern states they could fix the qualifications for voters in the primary elections, but the courts of the United States have ended this practice.[5] In all the states the committees may fill vacancies caused by the death or withdrawal of candidates for state office. It is, of course, in connection with the state campaigns that the committee, its operations directed by a chairman, makes its most determined efforts. It heals factional quarrels, determines the tactics to be followed, after consultation with the leading candidates, raises and spends money, sends out speakers, distributes "literature," and what not.

The national committee has considerable influence over the state organizations at all times, but especially in presidential years. Co-operation between the two organizations is mutually advantageous, for success or

[5] Rice v. Elmore, Cir. Ct. of Appeals, Fourth Cir., 165 F. 2d 387 (1947); U.S. Sup. Ct. denied certiorari, 333 U.S. 875 (1948).

failure in one unit nearly always vitally affects the other. The state committee attempts to secure co-operation among other party committees, such as the district and county committees; but unless the state has a very definitely recognized party leader, the relations of the various committees are not likely to be entirely harmonious.

LOCAL COMMITTEES. Each state has many local committees. Although the number varies considerably in the several states, those commonly found are county, city, ward, town, and precinct committees. They are chosen by the voters in many jurisdictions, but in others they are chosen by conventions or they are appointed by individual party workers of higher rank. As mentioned above, the state committees usually have no very definite control over the local committees, and the higher local committees generally have little authority over the lower ones. Contrariwise, some urban organizations, of which Tammany Hall is the best illustration, at times have sufficient discipline and power to control the state party organization. The local organizations promote the interests of their party in the various local areas by calling conventions, conducting primaries, distributing patronage, and looking after the needs of the voters in a more direct manner than is possible for the national and state committees.

THE PRECINCT COMMITTEEMAN. The strength of organization is determined in a large measure by the structure and activities of their smallest units, for these units alone are able to reach every individual directly. The smallest political unit is the precinct, of which there are approximately 135,000. Each of the great parties has an organization in practically every precinct, and the minor parties are active in many of them. The head of the precinct organization is the precinct committeeman (frequently called "captain" or "leader"), with whom is often associated a woman. Other workers may assist, who, according to Merriam and Gosnell, bring the number of active local partisans above the million mark around election time.[6]

The precinct committeeman works 365 days in the year. He helps newcomers to get settled in the neighborhood; befriends the poor; "sees" police officers and judges on behalf of those who have been careless about law observance; finds jobs for those who want them; secures innumerable favors from the government for practically every class in his precinct; looks after the naturalization of foreigners; keeps after voters until they register; and delivers the votes to the "organization" in the primaries and to the party at the regular elections. Obviously the last-mentioned function is his most important one and his other activities are incidental to it. If he fails in this, he fails as committeeman and his place is taken by another. If he succeeds notably, his "organization" is pretty sure to advance him. James A. Far-

[6] *Op. cit.,* p. 178.

ley's estimate in 1936 that Roosevelt would carry every state except Maine and Vermont was more than just a lucky guess. He had reports every day based upon the reports of tens of thousands of precinct workers.

II. PARTY LEADERSHIP [7]

Although a great deal of leadership is furnished by the various committees and committeemen discussed in the preceding section, these by no means represent the whole directing force of the party. Presidents, governors, congressmen, local officeholders of almost every conceivable type, and those who have no office and no place on a party committee are potent factors in shaping the policies, conducting the campaigns, and fixing the destiny of the party.

Leadership of the President. By virtue of his position the President is usually the leader of his party. Of course the degree to which the President may control his party varies in accordance with such factors as his inclination and capacity for leadership, the number of other national and state party leaders, and the extent to which his party is in control of the legislative branch of the government. In any case, the President is a power in the party because of the prestige of his position as Chief Executive. He is the leader of the nation as well as the leader of his party. An open repudiation of the President invites defeat for the party in a national election, and is quite likely to jeopardize party success in state and local campaigns. Local candidates of the President's party make every effort to secure his good wishes and to spread the word around that they are endorsed by the nation's Chief. Mayor Carter H. Harrison I, an able executive and probably the most astute politician who has ever been mayor of Chicago, was simply illustrating his political wisdom when, upon his nomination for his fourth term as mayor, he asked President Cleveland to wire him his congratulations.[8]

Leadership comes to the President also through his wide appointing power. Congressmen frequently find that they must follow the President, or allow their friends and supporters to go without jobs that are within the gift of the Big Chief. Likewise, state and local party organizations are very chary of incurring the President's displeasure because appointment to federal office is a reward for which many a party worker aspires.

Again, presidential leadership is evidenced in the presentation of issues. The President's position as head of the nation and his reception of

---

[7] Bone, *op. cit.*, Chs. 17–18; Brooks, *op. cit.*, Ch. IX; McKean, *op. cit.*, Chs. 11–12; Merriam and Gosnell, *op. cit.*, Ch. VII; W. B. Munro, *Personality in Politics* (1934); Sait, *op. cit.*, Chs. XIV–XVII; "Toward a More Responsible Two-Party System," *op. cit.*

[8] C. O. Johnson, *Carter H. Harrison I: Political Leader* (1928), p. 154.

almost unlimited publicity enable him not only to appeal directly to the rank and file of his party but to the whole people. A wise President can determine a number of issues for his party and practically force the other party to meet him on these issues. If he has followed a constructive program in office, he and his party will reap the reward for this in securing the votes of many independents in the next election. Clearly the party with the President has a big advantage in leadership.

Leadership in the opposition party is usually uncertain and divided. A defeated presidential candidate usually retains only a nominal leadership during the ensuing four years. Said Henry Watterson after Grover Cleveland's defeat in 1888: He "reminds one of a stone thrown into a river. There is a 'plunk,' a splash, and then silence." [9] Of course Cleveland "came back" in 1892. We should add also that Bryan, in spite of his three defeats, was a power in the Democratic party for a generation, and that Smith had a large following for several years after his defeat in 1928.

Leadership of other officeholders. Elective officers other than the President frequently stand high in party councils. Members of either House of Congress furnish a large part of the leadership for the party out of power, and the President must usually share leadership with members of his party who hold seats in Congress. On occasion, representatives and senators of the President's party have transferred the center of activity from the White House to the Capitol. The House of Representatives has contained such leaders as Blaine, Garfield, McKinley, Reed, Clark, Garner, and Bankhead. The Senate list is much longer, and we mention only Sherman, Depew, Allison, Hiram Johnson, Underwood, Thomas J. Walsh, Borah, Norris, the two La Follettes, Wagner, and Vandenberg.

Governors are frequently leaders in the states; but the brevity of their terms (two years in half the states), the law or custom in a number of states against re-eligibility, and their detachment from national affairs, all tend to lessen their opportunities for leadership. A United States senator is under none of these handicaps. Consequently, one of the familiar sights in American politics is a senator leading or bossing the party in his state. Yet the position of governor is one with excellent political opportunity, for a number of governors have become President and many have become senators. Various other officeholders, state and local, through perfecting combinations, aggressive leadership, or efficient discharge of duties, may become important factors in directing the party in their own or wider areas. The greater number of our state and national leaders have had their start in these minor offices. The local units are to a considerable extent the proving ground for those who have higher political aspirations.[10]

[9] Quoted in Sait, *op. cit.,* p. 328.
[10] Merriam and Gosnell, *op. cit.,* pp. 185 ff.

Unofficial leadership. Party control is by no means the exclusive possession of those who hold official positions in the party or public office. Bryan, holding no office of any kind, was the leading spirit in the Democratic party during the greater part of the period from 1896 to 1912. In office or out, many of our public men wield an important influence. Great journalists, leaders in commerce and industry, indeed, men from practically every calling are numbered among those who shape party policy and interpret it to their own circle or to the people as a whole.[11]

The boss. Some leaders who dominate the party in a state, county, or city, and who are considered not overly scrupulous in their methods, are called bosses. Distinguishing between a boss and a leader is not easy, perhaps impossible; for the boss is simply a type of leader, and a great deal of his technique is similar to that of the leader. Bosses are supposed to rule by secret and corrupt means; to employ violence and trickery; to strive for power for its own sake or for financial profit; and to make no moral or intellectual appeal to the voters.[12] But there are bosses and bosses. Some are certainly not personally corrupt or violent; others on occasion make a moral or intellectual appeal. Many of them may "work for their own pockets all the time," but others hold the place because they enjoy the eminence of their position—love to "see themselves pass by." Yet it is fair to say that some leaders have several of the unethical characteristics mentioned above and that the term "boss" as used in common parlance may be appropriately applied to them.

A number of explanations have been offered for the existence of the boss, of which the most significant is that our complicated constitutional systems, with their diffusions of power, their many elective officers, their provisions for short terms of office, have left us in great need of some more permanent central and controlling authority. The boss is such an authority.

Examples of bosses. From a long list of bosses, let us consider a few. Perhaps our most notorious boss was William M. Tweed of Tammany Hall, described as "a chairmaker by trade, a vulgar good fellow by nature, a politician by circumstances, a boss by evolution, and a grafter by choice."[13] Eighty years ago he and his "ring" robbed the city of New York of millions. Tweed typifies the boss to the average man, but there are many other types. Senator Boies Penrose, a scholar and a "highbrow," was the Republican boss in Pennsylvania from 1904 to 1921. Then there is Senator Harry F. Byrd of Virginia, who can match ancestors with most any American, and who, at the time of this writing, makes manifest the qualities of his progenitors in the management of his state

---

[11] Merriam and Gosnell, *op. cit.*, pp. 193–195.
[12] Summary of Roosevelt's and Stanwood's observations in Sait, *op. cit.*, pp. 359–360.
[13] S. P. Orth, *The Boss and the Machine* (1919), p. 70.

machine, "the most urbane and genteel dictatorship in America." [14]
George Brennan, coal miner, head of a bonding company, millionaire,
loved the "great adventure," the "thrill," of politics, and, seemingly for
no other reason, ran the Democratic party in Chicago and Illinois during
the eight years preceding his death in 1928. The glum Charles F.
Murphy, who was in the saloon business in a big way, exercised his superb
executive talents as "leader" of Tammany Hall, and for some twenty
years following 1902 had control of New York City, and during a part of
that time controlled the state as well. To Governor Sulzer, who resisted
his power, he said: "You are going to be governor? Like hell you are." [15]
And Sulzer was removed from office by impeachment.

Perhaps the most modern and conspicuous example of the municipal boss
of the older style is Frank ("I am the law") [16] Hague of Jersey City. Until
recently the undisputed boss of the Democratic party in his city and
state, he was not much more than annoyed when the Supreme Court of the
United States enjoined the enforcement of his ordinance that deprived
the CIO and similar "radical" organizations of their civil rights in Jersey
City.[17] The cornerstone of Hague's power was his working understanding with industrial and financial interests, and in carrying out his part of the
arrangement he waged war against the CIO, the American Civil Liberties
Union, and all other "radical" organizations. This conduct gave him
almost the unanimous support of the rank and file of "patriots" of practically every hue save red and pink. By no means insignificant was the
political strength he received as a result of his success in bringing millions
in federal funds to his county, his WPA ball park, his maternity hospital,
and his generous personal gifts to the Roman Catholic Church. But the
man Hague was the decisive factor—his will to rule through intrigue and
fear.

Rural communities and states are not, as is commonly assumed, always
free from bosses or leaders of the boss type. North Dakota was for several
years (1916–1921) under the rule of A. C. Townley, the skillful organizer
and president of the Non-partisan League, an organization that received
thousands of eighteen-dollar subscriptions from the farmers of the state.
Whatever type the boss may be, he rules largely through his knowledge of
human nature, his capacity as an organizer, his industry and tenacity, and
through his power to dispense jobs and grant favors.

---

[14] McKean, *op. cit.,* p. 269 n.   See also V. O. Key, Jr., *Southern Politics* (1949), Ch. 2.
[15] G. Myers, *History of Tammany Hall* (1917 ed.), p. 368.
[16] Hague's own words.
[17] In 1941 Hague's iron grip on New Jersey was weakened somewhat by Governor Charles
Edison, who was able to put through a legislative program despite Hague's strenuous opposition. In 1943 he received a further setback through the defeat of his candidate for governor.
In 1949 the same thing happened and more decisively.

A NEW TYPE OF BOSS. There are acute observers of the political scene who think the political boss of the Hague variety is on his way out.[18] Such a conclusion may not be warranted, yet it is encouraging to note that in 1949 bosses and machines went down (temporarily, at least) in Boston, Jersey City, and Philadelphia. We should probably be on safer ground to suggest that, although the old type of city boss is not by any means extinct,[19] his domain and powers are being reduced somewhat. The declining influence of the city boss is not being brought about primarily through an aroused civic conscience, but rather by new forces. There is a shift in the bases of political power.[20] The long arm of the federal government now reaches into the cities from a number of angles. Not so long ago Boss Pendergast of Kansas City was sent to the penitentiary for evading his federal income tax, a crime that has led to the downfall of a number of political crooks and private gangsters since the late 'twenties. During the greater part of the New Deal period Tammany Hall was far from the seat of power in New York City. The eclipse of Tammany may be attributed to a number of factors, and not the least of these was the personal magnetism and administrative activities of reform Mayor La Guardia (1934-1946); but the growth of organized labor accompanied by an increase in its political power was not an insignificant factor—one that contributed greatly to La Guardia's strength. Furthermore, since 1933 relief has been largely in the hands of the federal government, with the result that the petty charities through which city machines endeared themselves to the poor have lost much of their political value.

It may be premature to hold obsequies for the old municipal boss who ruled his city and sometimes his state through a careful cultivation of the friendship of all racial and religious groups, granting favors to businessmen in return for substantial contributions, and keeping the poor in line with Christmas baskets, sacks of coal, clam bakes, and marshmallow roasts; but it is doubtful if there is prematurity in the warning that new forces are developing a new type of boss, the boss who makes his appeal to old age pension organizations and other groups in quest of security. In the future we may have to give our attention to the demagogue-boss who comes forward as a "friend of the people" and promises "ham and eggs to all," or who would "share the wealth," and make "every man a king." The longing for security in an unstable world plays right into the hands of such a demagogue. To him Germans, Italians, and other peoples who had lost hope turned, surrendered their liberties and their right to think. The boss is the dictator in a totalitarian country. The late Senator and "Kingfish"

---

[18] Pendleton Herring, *The Politics of Democracy* (1940), p. 138.

[19] *See* Robert S. Allen (ed.), *Our Fair City* (1947).

[20] Herring, *op. cit.,* pp. 138-140.

Huey Long of Louisiana had many of the characteristics of such a boss. He had the brains, the will, the gift of oratory, the dramatic quality, and the ruthlessness of a dictator; and like all "good" dictators he constructed roads and erected magnificent public buildings for the people to enjoy. Possibly, however, he had too much sense of humor for a dictator and was too wise to convince himself that he had a divine mission to perform.

Interdependence of party organizations and leaders. Although the various party committees, organizations, and leaders have no organic relationship to each other, they often work together; and such co-operation is the ideal of good organization men. All of them would like to do what James A. Farley, Chairman of the Democratic National Committee (1932–1940), practically succeeded in doing: tie all the committees and leaders—national, state, and local—together, to the advantage of each, in the joint (and "glorious") enterprise of winning elections. At the beginning of this section reference is made to the service a local organization or candidate might receive from the President of the United States. This is a matter of common knowledge. Equally true, the services of local party organizations and leaders are indispensable to the national party command. Impeccable gentlemen high in the councils of the national organization who may loathe the state or city boss may nevertheless deferentially and earnestly urge him to come to the aid of the party, and these spokesmen are probably authorized by the presidential candidate to promise patronage and other favors in return for this "patriotic service." Even such an idealist as Henry A. Wallace, when Vice President, sat down and broke bread with city bosses. The politically righteous citizen should not be too much dismayed (at least he should be prepared for it) when a President who ordinarily measures up to his standards passes a few political plums to a city or state boss.

Of course the national leaders and the state (or local) leaders cannot always reach a working agreement. Except in a few one-party states the national organization always needs the state and local support. On the other hand, a state or city group may feel secure—know that they can win alone—and if the party's national program or its presidential candidate should not arouse their enthusiasm, little or no support will be forthcoming. Thus it happened that neither the New Deal nor the Fair Deal received any particular support from Senator Byrd's Virginia machine. Also, but less seldom, because of fundamental disagreement on policy or notorious state or local corruption, a President may decline to co-operate with a particular organization or individual. Even the best of relationships among the various party organizations and leaders is informal, undefined, and uncertain. Lack of intraparty co-ordination was one of the several defects of the major political parties that the Committee on Political Parties of the American Political Science Association singled out for attention. The committee would remedy the situation in part by party councils, authorities that would be empowered to settle the larger problems of party organization and chart its direction.

III. FUNCTIONS OF THE PARTY [21]

Authorities on political parties list their important functions about as follows: (1) the formulation of public policies; (2) the selection of official personnel; (3) the conduct or criticism of the government; (4) political education; (5) intermediation between the individual and his government; (6) the performance (in cities) of a type of social service; (7) the unification of the departments of government; and (8) the unification of the nation.

1. Formulates policies. Parties have their origin in principles and issues, and the party that does not add new ones to its program cannot hope to survive. Although the party's interest in the formulation of policies may be motivated primarily by the earnest desire for victory at the polls, it nevertheless performs a genuine public service in sifting the issues and presenting them to the people. For fear of the political consequences, parties have neglected important issues, such as woman's suffrage and Prohibition, and for the same reason they have spoken in ambiguous language upon taxation, the national debt, and other public questions. But at times they have made clear declarations of policy, as the two leading parties did in 1896 when they stated opposite convictions on the money question, and in 1920 when they differed on the League of Nations, and again in 1948 when they took basically opposite positions on housing and essentially the same position on civil rights. Parties are most actively engaged in forming policies in the months preceding elections, but the process goes on in an abated form and less dramatically around the council tables of their leaders during the relatively quiet periods between elections.

Let no one assume that parties present all the issues. As just noted, parties are afraid to make issues of some questions; others they may take up half-heartedly; a few may escape their notice. Furthermore, since parties are national in character, they do not function actively in forming state policies and they are even less active in forming local policies. Many issues are consequently presented by other organizations, such as the National Association of Manufacturers, the American Medical Association, the American Farm Bureau Federation, the American Legion, the Congress of Industrial Organizations, and others.

2. Selects official personnel. The chief interest of the party is in securing the election or appointment of its men to public office. Where two or three organization men are gathered together, especially if an election is

---

[21] H. R. Bruce, *American Parties and Politics* (1936 ed.), Ch. II; McKean, *op. cit.,* pp. 23–30, 87–102; Merriam and Gosnell, *op. cit.,* Ch. XXI; "Toward a More Responsible Two-Party System," *op. cit.*

in the offing, the conversation is likely to come to the question of available candidates for various elective offices. In official party councils, no other matters are considered with as much care. An individual is proposed as a candidate for a particular office. Immediately there arise such questions as the following: Can he carry the Negro vote? Will he support the organization, or will he be too independent? How does he stand on public utilities? Possibly it will seem advisable to endorse him for the nomination, or it may be thought best to name him for a less conspicuous office, or he may be dropped from consideration for any elective post. In like manner, the party leaders are much concerned over filling the appointive offices. In some cases elected officers who are supposed to make the appointments practically abdicate and allow the "organization" to name them; seldom, indeed, do the legal appointing authorities show decided independence in making appointments. We should add that, where the merit system is in operation, the influence of party in making appointments is limited, and that such influence is likewise limited in many local areas whose governments operate to some extent on the nonpartisan basis.

3. **Conducts and criticizes the government.** In general, the majority party may be said to conduct the government. We should bear in mind, however, that many public matters are nonpartisan or bipartisan in character; that party plays a diminishing part in government as we proceed from the nation to the state and local government; and that even in the national government the President and a majority of the Senate and the House of Representatives are not of the same party much more than half the time. Yet the party with the majority of the offices of a government is primarily responsible for the conduct of that government, whereas the other party is primarily the critic of the party in power. The former "points with pride" to its achievements in office and asks to be retained in office on its accomplishments; the latter "views with alarm" the alleged subservience of its office-holding rival to this or that, its "saturnalia of corruption," and all the rest. There is a lot of sham to the claims and counterclaims, charges and countercharges of the parties; but, broadly speaking, the fact remains that one party does conduct the government, while the other supplies the almost equally important public service of careful and constant scrutiny of its rival's stewardship. Criticism of the government is, of course, not the exclusive privilege of the party out of power; various organizations and individuals frequently make loud and well-founded complaints, and sometimes there is an outcry against both parties.

4. **Contributes to political education.** The schools, the press, the forum, and other agencies contribute very substantially to the cause of political education; but the political party is the most inclusive, continuous, and probably the most effective institution in arousing and holding the interest

of the people in public affairs. To be sure, much of the material released by the party is not of any great value in advancing a desirable type of political wisdom. The party, or influential members of it, may appeal to the religious sentiment, class prejudice, or race hatred of a group—types of appeal that are clearly pernicious. But, on the other hand, honest and courageous leaders, of whom we have a goodly number despite the sweeping declarations of cynics to the contrary, have a powerful influence in inspiring, elevating, and educating the voter. Who can calculate the effect of the addresses and public conduct of such men as William E. Borah, Herbert Hoover, Charles Evans Hughes, Theodore and Franklin D. Roosevelt, Alfred E. Smith, and Woodrow Wilson! Men of this type have the nation for their audience and following, whereas the artifices of the demagogue, however clever, are seldom effective beyond his local community, although they may give him national and even international notoriety.

5. Serves as intermediary between the citizens and the government. Governments are somewhat impersonal; perhaps a little cold and unsympathetic. Furthermore, their intricacies are beyond the ken of the great majority. The honest and the dishonest, the worthy and the unworthy, the rich and the poor, frequently feel the need of a mediator in their relations with the government of the nation, state, or city. If an oil baron wants a valuable government lease, if a manufacturer thinks his establishment is assessed too high, if a widow has a claim against the government, if a millionaire's son is in difficulties for reckless driving, if a pushcart peddler is being annoyed by police, the individuals concerned are likely to seek an interview with a man who has standing with the party in power and, hence, influence with the government. In the days when William M. Tweed held New York City in the palm of his hand, Judge Barnard asked a candidate for admission to the bar how he would proceed if he had a claim of $50,000 against the city. "I'd see Bill Tweed," replied the candidate, who understood fully the process we are here discussing.[22] Obviously party men acting as go-betweens and buffers may be honestly performing a worthy service, or they may be aiding and abetting unscrupulous persons and out-and-out crooks. At any rate, they perform a service that is well-nigh indispensable, governments and human nature being what they are.

6. Dispenses social service. Not only does the party organization serve as an intermediary between the citizen and his government, but it performs many direct social services. This type of service is offered especially by municipal party organizations. Party workers visit and send doctors to the sick, secure employment for those who want work, provide temporary

[22] Sait, *op. cit.,* p. 370.

shelter for poor families who have been burned out, promote athletics in their neighborhood, give picnics, establish clubs, and in various other ways meet the social needs of the rank and file of citizens. Today, however, government agencies for employment, social security, and relief are performing a number of the services that in the days of "rugged individualism" were assumed by political organizations and private charity. Yet the city party worker may still find useful the methods of George Washington Plunkitt. Some fifty years ago he listed a typical day's activities as follows: furnished bail for a saloon keeper who had been arrested for violating the excise law; secured the discharge of four of six "drunks" by a timely word with the judge, and paid the fines for the others; arranged for temporary quarters for several families who had been burned out; paid the rent of a poor family and gave them a dollar for food; spent nearly three hours in finding jobs for four men, but succeeded in each case; attended the funeral of an Italian and hurried back to appear at the funeral of a Jewish constituent; presided over a meeting of district captains who reported on voters who were in need or in trouble; went to a church fair—took chances on everything, bought ice cream for the girls, and took their fathers out for liquid refreshments at the corner; bought tickets for a baseball game between two teams in the district; spent ten dollars on tickets for a church excursion; graced a wedding reception with his presence, having previously sent a handsome present to the bride.[23]

7. Helps unify the government. In addition to the more or less direct functions we have mentioned, the party may be said to perform certain incidental functions. The party is a unifying agency in the government.[24] It partially breaks down the somewhat artificial "separation of powers," and to some extent gives a uniform program and concerted action to the executive and legislative branches. This process is most obvious when an executive endowed with qualities of leadership secures the enactment of a constructive program by legislative bodies in which his party has majority membership. Doubtless a Cabinet member was thinking wishfully of the unifying power and the smooth driving force of a properly functioning party when he said that he (a Republican) "would rather be in hell without a fan than Secretary of the Interior with a Democratic House of Representatives."

8. Operates as a nationalizing agency. "This great and glorious country was built up by political parties," declared the irrepressible Plunkitt in his "sillygism" on patronage.[25] We must, of course, modify this state-

---

[23] W. L. Riordon, *Plunkitt of Tammany Hall* (1905 and republished in 1948 with an introduction by Roy V. Peel), pp. 123–126.

[24] Bruce, *op. cit.*, pp. 39–41.

[25] Riordon, *op. cit.*, p. 18.

ment; but we may certainly say that parties, along with such agencies as wars, improved communications, schools, and churches, have made us a nation.[26] Parties have lessened the disintegrating force of sectionalism. They have made national appeals from the beginning; even the Jeffersonian Democrats, preaching the gospel of states' rights, perforce addressed their message to the entire country. As parties have developed their histories and traditions, sentiment for them has increased. The average citizen has a love for his party somewhat akin to his love for his country; his loyalty to his party is a close second to his patriotism.

It is not surprising, therefore, that party faith usually brings about a measure of harmony between sections of the country that have quite dissimilar economic and social interests. The farmer of the West may at least co-operate with the industrialist of the East in securing the election of Republicans to office, and the courtly Southerner will found his Democratic hopes on an alliance with a lowly urbanite of New York or Chicago. The unifying tendency of parties, with their members and organizations in practically every community, would seem to be almost aviomatic. It is very significant that, in the years preceding the Civil War, the party ties remained unbroken until some time after several of the Protestant churches had split into Northern and Southern branches: and it is equally noteworthy that parties were among the first institutions to be renationalized at the conclusion of the struggle.[27] We should not attribute any particular virtue to the party for its national scope, for party expediency necessitates an appeal to the whole people.

IV. PRESSURE GROUPS AND PROPAGANDA [28]

However significant the party's function in conducting the government may be, there are many other organizations or groups that participate in the governing process. Every unit of government (the judiciary to a lesser extent than the others) and the party itself is subject to constant request, entreaty, and threat from the very widest variety of interested groups, each seeking to make its own particular program or issue a government policy.

Our total of laws and the degree of law enforcement we enjoy are largely

[26] Merriam and Gosnell, *op. cit.,* pp. 475–477; Bruce, *op. cit.,* pp. 49 ff.

[27] We should note, however, that the Civil War and the Reconstruction policy of the Republican party long prevented that group from gaining a substantial foothold in the South and that the national civil rights program of the Democrats caused a serious political revolt among Southern democrats in 1948.

[28] *The Annals,* May, 1935; Bone, *op. cit.,* Chs. 5–10; Mary E. Dillon, "Pressure Groups," *Am. Pol. Sci. Rev.,* June, 1942, p. 471; F. C. Irion, *Public Opinion and Propaganda* (1950); Key, *op. cit.,* Chs. 2–7, 18; McKean, *op. cit.,* Chs. 5–8, 18–29; P. H. Odegard and E. A. Helms, *American Politics* (1947 ed.), Chs. VIII–XI, XXII; S. M. Rosen, *Political Processes* (1935); Wilbur Schramm (ed.), *Mass Communications* (1949).

the result of these conflicting pressures. The laws of physics are not the laws of politics in any strict sense, but an analogy is suggestive. If north and east exert equal pressure on a light object, it will move southwest. If east and west exert equal pressures, there is no movement, but a new pressure from the north will send the object south. Regardless of the number and direction of the pulls and pressures, the mathematical physicist can calculate to an exact degree the direction the object will move. We have the pulls and pressures in politics as in physics, but they are economic and social forces, not physical forces. We can see many of them at work, but we have not yet found a means of measuring them with scientific exactitude. Our task is doubly difficult because the objects upon which these social forces play have ambitions, prejudices, consciences, and all the other attributes of man. Yet as we congratulate the physicist upon the simplicity of his problem, we must seek to solve our own. Recent literature on the subject indicates that the psychologist and the political scientist are in quest of a solution.

Who applies the pressure. There are hundreds of groups pushing, shoving, pressing, pulling, hauling, milling, and mauling in a grand scramble to control the government. No enumeration of them would be complete, nor is a listing necessary.[29] A rough classification of them, based upon their objectives, with a few examples of each class will serve our purpose. At the top of the list we might place good government associations. Municipal voters' leagues have sought to improve the quality of city government, approaching the problem primarily from the angle of personnel, giving their endorsement to candidates of competence and integrity and seeking to accomplish the defeat of those lacking these qualities. Other organizations have sought to establish and improve the merit system in government. Of these organizations, the National Civil Service Reform League takes the highest rank, numbering among its past leaders Theodore Roosevelt and Woodrow Wilson, and among its achievements a large part of the credit for the progress of the merit system. There are organized groups to prevent war, such as the National Council for the Prevention of War; and there are groups that champion large armaments, such as the Navy League. The country has experienced the force of various organizations that concern themselves with the personal habits of citizens, the Anti-Saloon League easily winning chief recognition in this field. Not numerous as individuals, but powerful because of their array of talent, finance and business exert their pressures through the American Bankers Association, the National Association of Manufacturers, the Chamber of Commerce of the United States, and similar organizations. Labor meets capital through the American Federation of Labor, the Con-

[29] A long list is supplied by Irion, *Public Opinion and Propaganda*, pp. 759–764.

gress of Industrial Organizations, and some independent unions. The farmers have had numerous pressure organizations—the Grange, the Farmers' Union and others. The American Farm Bureau Federation is the most powerful of the farm organizations at the present time. Then there are articulate and persuasive professional associations, of which the American Medical Association furnishes the best example at this writing. Former soldiers can make very effective demonstrations of strength through such organizations as the American Legion, the Veterans of Foreign Wars, and the American Veterans Committee. Civil service employees seek to make secure their tenure of office and to improve the conditions of their employment through the National Federation of Post-Office Clerks, the National Federation of Federal Employees and similar organizations, national, state, and local. In short, every group which has an objective that may be obtained in whole or in part through governmental action has an organization through which action is sought.

Where the pressure is applied. Interested groups seek not only to control every unit of government, but also to bring under their influence the political parties and the party nominees for public office. Each pressure group, with varying degrees of energy and success, presents its program to political conventions, and makes every possible effort to bring about the nomination of candidates favorable to its cause. This activity is particularly noticeable at a national convention, and it is publicized in the great metropolitan dailies, but it goes on with equal intensity in policy-forming and nominating activities in small towns. During the election campaigns these groups busily occupy themselves with the task of keeping their candidates "right" on the issues and furnishing campaign support, often financial as well as oratorical and printed, to candidates who make the requisite promises. A powerful pressure group is often able to force candidates of both the leading parties to make a declaration favorable to its cause. This was a notable achievement of the Anti-Saloon League in state and congressional elections from about 1916 to 1930.

The organized group knows all about the "separation of powers" in our governmental structure, but no such separation of powers existed in the group's own organization. It works as a unit upon whatever organ or organs of the government it must influence in order to effectuate the group policy. It presses Congress, a state legislature, or a city council for legislation (Chapter 13, section VI), and it follows the statute or ordinance to the administrative departments and commissions charged with the duty of law enforcement. Of course, an organization often fights against the enactment of one law as assiduously as it champions the enactment of another, and it might endeavor to obstruct the operation of one law with an ingenuity equaled only by its zeal in urging the enforcement of another. Much of the time of the typical congressman is spent at the behest of groups and individuals, in urging administrative officers from the President down to "go easy" on enforcing certain laws, to enforce others vigorously, to speed up the operation of some laws, to defer the date for others, to make exceptions in enforcement in certain cases, and so on. Here we see the congressman acting before an administrative department, unwittingly perhaps, in the capacity of agent for a pressure group.

The judicial arm of the government is not so much subject to pressure as the legislative and administrative departments, but some notable controversies have arisen over the selection of judges. Many leading citizens and organizations opposed (1916) the confirmation of Louis D. Brandeis as Associate Justice of the Supreme Court and almost succeeded in preventing it. Negro and labor organizations did prevent (1930) the confirmation of John J. Parker as Associate Justice.

The courts may have subtle group pressures exerted upon them. One group may praise them as the bulwarks of our liberties, thereby indirectly thanking the judicial tribunals for having declared some radical legislation unconstitutional, and at the same time expressing the hope that they will strike down other and similar legislation. If that is a form of pressure, other groups exert it in like manner, praising liberal judges who have broad social viewpoints and who express them in vigorous opinions.

But, after all, influencing the government is neither the beginning nor the end of the activities of the pressure groups. The government will not move far unless the public supports it. The thing for a pressure group to do, then, is to win the support of the public to its cause. The "public be damned" may still be the basis upon which some concerns act as they exploit that public, but every effort is made to conciliate the public, to "educate" it, to make the dose more palatable. Winning the public to this or that view of a business, a movement, or a cause is a function that yields handsome salaries to some of the best brains of the country. Legislative lobbying has been present in the American system of government since 1789, and it still goes on, but since the First World War the control of the minds of the masses has been given great emphasis.

How the pressure is applied. A few concrete cases will give us the best indication of the methods by which interested groups seek to win a favorable public and control government action. In the days preceding the repeal of Prohibition, a leader of the Anti-Saloon League proposed this program for the Drys: *Educate* by sermons, lectures, dinners, dramatic debates, pageants, and print—tons of it; by moving pictures, the radio, press publicity, and every other method of modern agitation. *Organize* local, county, state, and national committees and conventions to support all officials who are faithful to Prohibition. Everywhere recruit and enroll the voters; everywhere enlist and pledge the youth. Spread everywhere such creeds and slogans as "Obedience to law is liberty!" "The saloon must never come back!" *Finance* the League's program. The annual budget of $650,000 of recent years must be increased to $850,000. "We must have a stronger fighting front. . . . Re-elect Dry Congresses the next four years and a Dry President in 1932!" [30]

At the time of this writing the American Medical Association is engaged in a relentless struggle against national compulsory health insurance (commonly called "socialized medicine" by its opponents). In 1949 "it met its enemies in spectacular contest," declared AMA President Dr. Elmer L. Henderson, and, he continued, "the fight for compulsory health insurance was abandoned, even though the White House itself had become a sounding board for the socializers. . . . But the battle of Armageddon—the decisive struggle which may determine not only medicine's fate but whether state socialism is to engulf all America—is still ahead of us." [31] In 1948 the AMA House of Delegates voted a voluntary assessment of $25 on each of the 140,000 members of the Association, and about 75 per cent of the doctors paid. In 1949 the Association voted for the first time in its history to levy dues ($25 a year) on its members, dues that would bring in some $3,500,000 per annum. The AMA dropped Dr. Morris Fishbein, long the recognized spokesman for medicine, and with its funds engaged, for $100,000 a year, public relations experts, Whitaker & Baxter, business partners, husband and wife. They soon had something to report on what they had done since "the virus of socialized medicine had spread from decadent Europe and taken deep root here." In less than a year's time, they had, among other things, distributed 55,000,000 pieces of campaign literature, carrying the doctors' views of compulsory national health insurance, put in doctors' offices over 65,000 posters of *The Doctor,* carrying the Whitaker & Baxter caption "Keep Politics Out of This Picture." [32] The painting from which the posters were made is by Sir Luke Fildes and seems to represent the old-fashioned family doctor (complete with whiskers) keeping an all-night vigil with a sick child. There is nothing unusual or strange about these methods. The chief interest we have in them is that they furnish a contemporary example of campaigns for favorable public opinion and favorable governmental action or nonaction.

Here is a brief digest of a report made in 1929 by a publicity expert representing the sugar interests in their fight against a higher sugar tariff. He finally prevailed upon the *American Exporter's and Importer's Association*

---

[30] *Lobby Investigation, 1929–1930,* p. 4466.

[31] Associated Press, Dec. 6, 1949.

[32] *Time,* Dec. 19, 1949, p. 77. See also Milton Mayer, "The Rise and Fall of Dr. Fishbein," *Harper's,* Nov., 1949, pp. 76–84 and "The Dogged Retreat of the Doctors," same, Dec., 1949, pp. 25–37.

to pass strong resolutions, which were very influential in newspaper discussions of the tariff. He induced John Barrett to prepare a statement that strongly influenced the *Foreign Trade Council*. He persuaded the research director of the *Foreign Policy Association* to prepare a special bulletin on Cuba and the sugar tariff. Further, at the sugar expert's suggestion, the *Chamber of Commerce of the State of New York* gave a special luncheon in honor of Cuban Independence Day, and by reference to his brief it passed a resolution against the sugar tariff. Eventually he reached the *American Federation of Labor,* presenting to it material relative to child labor in the beet fields in the United States, material that prompted Mr. William Green to write a strong letter to Representative Frear. He induced a representative of *Time* to make a trip to Cuba and arranged for his reception. He managed to have audience with four of the principal executive officers of the *Federal Council of Churches* and interested them in his project of abolishing child labor in the American beet fields by securing the importation of sugar free of duty. When the House of Representatives fixed the sugar duty at 2.40 cents per pound, he distributed to 1,200 newspapers a *Consumer Story* "showing exactly how much the citizens of the town in which the paper is published would have to pay merely for the privilege of buying sugar." He arranged for Governor Smith "to come out at the proper time with a statement saying that the American people will not knowingly tax themselves further to increase the exploitation of child labor in the beet fields. . . . This plan is highly confidential." He reported that Senator Capper had been sounded out and that suitable articles were being prepared for his farm papers.[33] Notice how much of the activity of this publicity agent was directed at the public and how little of it was aimed directly at Congress, the tariff-making authority. This is the method of the twentieth century lobby, the lobby of propaganda—to persuade the public to bring influence to bear upon the government. Notice also how skillfully he used other organizations and pressure groups to promote the purpose of his own special sugar group.

Of the many handy illustrations of the specific application of pressure on Congress, we select two. When the Muscle Shoals question was before Congress in 1920, every member of the House of Representatives received a letter on the same day, the sort of letter that causes the more timid congressman to have cold chills and the best of them to think twice. It read:

All competent and impartial inquirers have agreed that the Muscle Shoals project would result in greatly increased nitrate supplies and materially decrease costs. Hence the farmer as well as the consumer is intensely interested.

It is evident to the farmer that the Muscle Shoals appropriation yesterday was

[33] *Lobby Investigation, 1929–1930,* p. 1978.

defeated through the influence of large corporations who have a selfish interest in maintaining fertilizer costs.

The American Farm Bureau Federation has a paid-up membership exceeding 1,500,000 active farmers. These farmers expect us to keep them informed on legislative matters.

We regret that the vote yesterday was not one of record. In order that we may do justice both to Representatives in Congress and to our membership, will you kindly notify our Washington Representative Mr. Gray Silver, 1411 Pennsylvania Avenue—whether you voted for or against this proposition.

The letter was signed by the president of the Farm Bureau.[34]

"O God . . . thy enemies have made a noise," prayed Father Charles E. Coughlin, reciting over the radio the 83rd Psalm, with his interpolations, the night before the Senate took its vote on American membership in the World Court, in February, 1935. "They have said: Come and let us destroy them, so that they may not be a nation, and let the name of Israel (America) be remembered no more. For they have contrived with one consent: they have made a covenant (League of Nations) against thee." The Father urged his countless hearers to wire their Senators to vote against the Court. They wired with a vengeance. Fifty extra telegraph clerks had to be hired to receive the messages. The vote was taken; it stood 52 for and 36 against, seven votes short of the required two-thirds majority.[35] To be sure, there is no proof that the deluge of telegrams caused the unfavorable Senate action on the Court, but many competent observers in Washington believed that it did.

The press and propaganda. Since the modern pressures are exerted on the masses as much as or more than upon governing authority, it is pertinent to mention the chief vehicles that convey the pressure to the public. Those vehicles are the newspapers and the radio. Newspapers are indispensable to the operation of a democracy; they give the news by which a people judge governmental policies. But they give both more and less than the news, and public conduct may be influenced by the omission of news and the coloring of news as well as by "pure" news. Of course, there is practically no such thing as news that does not contain some distortions, some bias. The reporter himself will have his peculiarity as an observer, his set of attitudes. He may seek out the sensational rather than the basic forces behind men and events. His story may be revised by a "re-write" man and pass through the hands of an editor. As finally printed, it must conform to the policy of the newspaper; and even the greatest of our dailies have some very definite policies that may be detected in their news columns.

Try as they may, the publishers of papers that print all the news "that's

[34] O. M. Kile, *The American Farm Bureau Movement* (1921), p. 173.
[35] *Time*, February 11, 1935.

Lehman Hails Welfare State; Dulles Makes Economy Plea

Democrat Asserts Industry Owes Record Prosperity to Party's Program

Senator Says That Running Government Should Be Like Running House

By CHARLES GRUTZNER
Special to THE NEW YORK TIMES.

ROCHESTER, N. Y., Oct. 25— Profits have reached an unprecedented peacetime level and the private enterprise system has gained new strength because of Democratic measures that constitute the "welfare state," former Gov. Herbert H. Lehman declared tonight.

The Democratic-Liberal candidate for United States Senator made his bid for support of business men and investors at a dinner sponsored by the Monroe County Democratic Committee. Replying to the charge by Senator John Foster Dulles, his Republican opponent, that Democratic policy was making this country into a "welfare state" threatening individual freedom, Mr. Lehman said:

"We are proud that during the Roosevelt and Truman Administrations the Reconstruction Finance Corporation was expanded to help all legitimate private business in need of additional financing

Continued on Page 22, Column 4

By KALMAN SEIGEL

Senator John Foster Dulles, Republican candidate to succeed himself, pleaded for greater government economy yesterday. Addressing 2,000 women at the Astor Hotel, he likened the task of running a government to that of running a household.

"In managing your own homes," he told a reception on behalf of his wife, "you couldn't continue to overspend day in and day out, year in and year out, and expect to raise and take care of your family. That is just simple economics. You have to keep your own home budget balanced or go into the red."

Senator Dulles charged the Washington Government with "doing just the opposite."

"They are wasting billions of dollars a year running into deficits, and then they expect that all of us will just dig down deeper itno our own pockets and get them out of their troubles," he said.

Continued on Page 22, Column 2

An Example of Fair Reporting, *New York Times,* Oct. 26, 1949.

fit to print" do not thoroughly succeed in giving "simple news." Faults in physical perception, emotional responses, the hurry of getting news published, the desire to make a good story, and other influences will shade and color the news published by the most respectable press. In the case of newspapers other than the most respectable, there is hardly a pretense that the news is not distorted. The race to increase circulation, to secure and hold advertisers (the profit of the newspaper comes from this source), and the lust for power, political or otherwise, result in the grossest distortions of the news, sometimes in the total elimination of significant news items. Everyone understands that the editorial columns of a newspaper are given over to propaganda, much of it noble in motive, but not everyone realizes that there is much propaganda in the news columns as well. This propaganda in the news is largely unintentional with the more ethical papers, but with other papers, particularly with the "yellow" press, it is intentional. Yet, in all fairness, it must be said that the American press comes as near giving unbiased news as the press of any other country in the world.

Although the influence of the press cannot be accurately estimated, everyone agrees that it is prodigious. The "yellow" press played a large part in bringing on the Spanish-American War, and the press in the Allied Countries, not always scorning lies, shared a major part of the credit for keeping up the morale of the peoples of those countries during the First World War. Some reforms have been engineered largely by the press and some signal failures of the press to achieve attempted reforms must be recorded. In political campaigns the press may exercise its minimum influence. Time and time again city organizations have won elections in the face of practically unanimous press opposition. Without doubt a factor, the press is certainly not a decisive factor in determining a national election. At times we are tempted to think the political influence of the press is tremendous, but that is when the press happens to be on the political bandwagon, as in 1924. The influence of the press in national elections since 1930, with at least two thirds of the papers on the losing side, seems to have reached an all-time low. Intense partisanship pleases only the intense partisan. It would seem logical to assume that partisanship irritates the very persons who must be won in order to insure success, namely, independent voters. The man who had never voted a straight ticket in his life but who made up his mind to do so to spite his "screaming" morning paper is probably not an isolated case.

The radio as a vehicle of propaganda. The radio as an instrument for creating mass impressions will outdistance, if it has not already outdistanced, the press. In European countries it is operated by governments, and in the countries ruled by dictators radio programs are hardly anything more than sustained governmental propaganda. Under private ownership in the United States the radio is nevertheless subject to governmental control through a license system, and the possibility of government ownership is one of the reasons why American radio stations give their programs careful scrutiny. Communists, pacifists, and "radicals" seldom have an opportunity to use the facilities of the radio. Intentionally or unintentionally the radio champions the *status quo*. Broadcasting companies will turn down programs that would yield them large revenues if the material to be broadcast is offensive to large groups or is of such a nature as to disturb conventional attitudes. In political campaigns an effort seems to be made to give all parties, within the limits of their budgets, opportunities to present their programs and candidates. But even in campaigns the radio corporations exercise an anxious care. Thus, when Senator Arthur H. Vandenberg, in the campaign of 1936, started a radio "debate" with President Roosevelt by an ingenious arrangement in which he had reproduced the voice of the President from his previous speeches, the broadcasting system took him off the air.

The possibilities of the use of radio by the government is well illustrated by the success with which President Franklin D. Roosevelt resorted to it. "The Nation will recall with kind memory that momentous night [in March, 1933] when the President sat in his study and first told a listening public over the radio what he proposed to do in aiding to solve the problems of a troubled nation," said General Hugh Johnson. "You will likewise recall," he continued, "the news of the speed of Congress in passing bills that carried out the President's program and how the stories of these events were disseminated through the radio and public press." [36] And many of us still recall the monumental campaign the General put on over the radio and through the press for his own organization—the National Recovery Administration! And all of us know something of the extent and intensity to which the warring nations employ the radio.

Summary on pressure groups and propaganda. In summary, our few observations on pressure and propaganda come to this: (1) Pressure groups representing every variety of interest busy themselves in their attempts to control political parties, the public authorities, and the masses. (2) The platforms of political parties, the policies of governments, and the attitudes of the public are to a considerable extent determined by the programs of "education" and advertising promoted by the pressure groups. (3) Without underestimating the significance of motion pictures, billboards, sky writing, parades, and other vehicles of propaganda, students of pressure activities generally agree that newspapers and radio are perhaps its principal vehicles. (4) Political parties are most assiduous in the use of propaganda, and governments themselves rely upon it and will probably place greater reliance upon it in the future. (5) Some pressure is for "good" causes and some is for "bad" causes, with the common man strongly inclined to place in the former category the ideas and movements he endorses and in the latter those he opposes. (6) Pressures are perhaps eternal and inevitable. Groups have always fought for the control of

[36] Quoted in Rosen, *op. cit.*, p. 160.

government. The coming of democracy has simply brought the contest into the open, made the struggle more obvious, the problem of reaching the masses having been met by new propaganda techniques that operate on a very wide scale.

The public opinion poll: a possible antidote to propaganda. It may be that a modern device, the scientific public opinion poll, will help those who are responsible for government to determine the extent to which the program of a pressure group represents the will of the American people. In 1934 and 1935 the Townsend Plan to pay $200 a month to every person over sixty years of age appeared to be in process of taking the country, beginning in California, extending up the Pacific Coast, and then moving East on a wide front. Congressmen were worried; there were more than a few members who "thought there might be something to it," and less than a few who openly called it fantastic. Dr. Townsend, sure of his backing, came to Washington to get action. He was received with great courtesy and the Senate Finance Committee, under the chairmanship of the affable Senator Harrison, day after day held hearings on *The Plan.* At least the hearings might give public men time to think of something else! Then Dr. George Gallup came to the rescue with a poll, showing that not quite 4 per cent of the American people endorsed the Townsend Plan. Congressmen breathed a long sigh of relief. In the course of time they even cited Dr. Townsend for contempt of a committee. Of course the poll was not alone in concluding the issue for Congress; there was never any likelihood that Congress would enact the Townsend Plan, pressure or no pressure, but the poll was a distinct aid to Congress, and was one of the factors which enabled that body to proceed unharried with the significant social security legislation of 1935. Then, at the same time, it may be said that the pressure of the Townsendites probably had some influence in the passage of the Social Security Act. The Townsend movement was a symptom not to be ignored. If the poll helped to kill the Townsend Plan, the Townsend idea helped make alive a social security program.

It would be an error to suppose that public opinion polls will resolve all questions of public policy so neatly, or that Congress, or any other legislative body, will shape its actions after consulting such polls. Examples of contrary action are at hand in the removal of price controls and the granting of a loan to Britain (both in 1945) in the face of adverse poll majorities. The poll is one factor, however, and it ought to be a significant one. Legislators make up their minds on the basis of many considerations. A few (who probably could be counted on one's fingers) will follow their personal convictions regardless of what the external influences might be; but the great majority are influenced by their convictions, their mail (the degree of influence here depends upon who is writing), their callers, their observations in their constituencies, the wishes of party leaders, opinion polls, and other factors as varied as are the problems and the leading personalities in our national life.

Reading List

Herbert Agar, *The Price of Union* (1950).

S. K. Bailey, *Congress Makes a Law: The Story Behind the Employment Act of 1946* (1949).

E. L. Bernays, *Public Relations* (1950).

Hugh A. Bone, *American Politics and the Party System* (1949).

D. W. Brogan, *Government of the People* (1933), Pts. 2 and 8.

R. C. Brooks, *Political Parties and Electoral Problems* (1933 ed.), Chs. I–IX.

H. R. Bruce, *American Parties and Politics* (1936 ed.), Chs. I–X, XVIII–XIX.

Hadley Cantril, *Gauging Public Opinion* (1944).

Stuart Chase, *Democracy under Pressure: Special Interests vs. the Public Welfare* (1945).

K. G. Crawford, *The Pressure Boys* (1939).

Virginius Dabney, *Dry Messiah: The Life of Bishop Cannon* (1949).

Economic Power and Political Pressures. TNEC Monograph No. 26, 1941.

J. A. Farley, *Behind the Ballots* (1938).

E. J. Flynn, *You're the Boss* (1947).

George Gallup and S. F. Rae, *The Pulse of Democracy* (1940).

Ray Ginger, *The Bending Cross* (1949).

P. Herring, *The Politics of Democracy* (1940).

W. E. Hocking, *Freedom of the Press* (1947).

A. N. Holcombe, *The Political Parties of Today* (1924).

———, *The New Party Politics* (1933).

Frederick C. Irion, *Public Opinion and Propaganda* (1950).

H. T. Kane, *Louisiana Hayride* (1941).

V. O. Key, Jr., *Politics, Parties, and Pressure Groups* (1947 ed.).

———, *Southern Politics in State and Nation* (1949).

H. D. Lasswell, *Power and Personality* (1948).

House Select Committee on Lobbying Activities, General Interim Report. 81st Cong., 2[n] ses., House Report No. 3138 (1950).

D. D. McKean, *Party and Pressure Politics* (1949).

N. C. Meier and H. W. Saunders (eds.), *Polls and Public Opinion: The Iowa Conference on Attitude and Opinion Research* (1949).

C. E. Merriam and H. F. Gosnell, *The American Party System* (1949 ed.).

Raymond Moley, *Twenty-Seven Masters of Politics* (1949).

Olga Moore, *I'll Meet You in the Lobby* (1950).

Warren Moscow, *Politics in the Empire State* (1948).

W. B. Munro, *Personality in Politics* (1924).

G. Myers, *History of Tammany Hall* (1917 ed.).

P. H. Odegard and E. A. Helms, *American Politics* (1947 ed.), Chs. VIII–XI.

M. B. Ogle, Jr., *Public Opinion and Political Dynamics* (1950).

W. M. Reddig, *Tom's Town: Kansas City and the Pendergast Legend* (1947).

W. L. Riordon, *Plunkitt of Tammany Hall* (with an introduction by Roy V. Peel—1948).

S. M. Rosen, *Political Process: A Functional Study in American Government* (1935).

E. M. Sait, *American Parties and Elections* (H. R. Penniman's ed.—1948), Chs. V–XVII.

Sir Arthur Salter, *Personality in Politics* (1947).

J. T. Salter, *Boss Rule* (1935).

———, *The Pattern of Politics* (1940).

———, ed., *Public Men in and out of Office* (1946).

E. E. Schattschneider, *Politics, Pressure and the Tariff* (1935).

———, *Party Government* (1943).

Carl Schriftgiesser, *This Was Normalcy . . . 1920–1932* (1948).

C. S. Siepmann, *Radio, Television, and Society* (1950).

B. L. Smith, H. D. Lasswell, and R. D. Casey, *Propaganda, Communications, and Public Opinion* (1946).

T. V. Smith, *The Promise of American Politics* (1936).

M. S. Stedman, Jr., and Susan W. Stedman, *Discontent at the Polls* (1949).

"Toward a More Responsible Two-Party System," A Report of the Committee on Political Parties, American Political Science Association, *Am. Pol. Sci. Rev.*, XLIV (1950), No. 3, Pt. 2.

Questions and Problems

1. Lincoln once said to a young man, a candidate for office, "Ask Mr. So-and-so to vote for you. He does not even know that you want his vote unless you ask him." What is the significance of this advice?
2. Name your top four American party leaders and explain why you list them as such.
3. Is the boss a leader?
4. Compare the pressure methods of old-age pension groups with those of the American Medical Association.
5. Discuss the problem of regulating pressure groups.
6. How could the press improve its usefulness in a democracy?
7. What are the best safeguards against the pernicious influence of propaganda?

☆ 9 ☆

Nominations for Elective Office

WE HAVE learned that the most important functions of the political parties are those of choosing candidates for public office and conducting campaigns for their election. In this chapter, our chief concern is with nominations.

I. NATIONAL CONVENTIONS [1]

Forces that produced the convention system. By far the most important public officer to be nominated and elected is the President. The Constitution makes no provision for nominations for the presidency. It stipulates only that the President shall be chosen (elected) by electors to be named in each state as the legislature thereof might see fit. The Fathers of this Republic hoped and fully expected that the President would be chosen by a quiet body of well-bred electors, appointed by state legislatures, and far removed from the influence of the "madding crowd." But political parties and the growth of democracy have altered their plans beyond all recognition. Parties brought caucuses, conventions, and primaries for nominating purposes; and a democratic host fifty millions strong participates in the choice of a President and reduces the constitutional electors to a row of ciphers.

Excepting a war, the choosing of a President is our most absorbing public

[1] H. A. Bone, *American Politics and the Party System* (1949), Ch. 20; R. C. Brooks, *Political Parties and Electoral Problems* (1933 ed.), Chs. X–XII; H. R. Bruce, *American Parties and Politics* (1936 ed.), Chs. XI–XIII; James A. Farley, *Behind the Ballots* (1938), Chs. I–II; P. Herring, *The Politics of Democracy* (1940), Ch. 16; V. O. Key, Jr., *Politics, Parties, and Pressure Groups* (1947 ed.), Ch. 13; D. D. McKean, *Party and Pressure Politics* (1949), Ch. 10; C. E. Merriam and H. F. Gosnell, *The American Party System* (1949 ed.), Ch. XV; P. H. Odegard and E. A. Helms, *American Politics* (1947 ed.), pp. 522–545; Louise Overacker, *Presidential Primaries* (1926); R. V. Peel and T. C. Donnelly, *The 1928 Campaign* (1931) and *The 1932 Campaign* (1935); E. M. Sait, *American Parties and Elections* (H. R. Penniman's ed.—1948), Chs. XX–XXI.

activity. Although we take the campaign seriously, it is at the same time a great national sport. Enormous sums of money are raised to promote it; bets are made upon candidates as upon athletic teams or race horses; and politics is for months the talk of every circle from the most exclusive "silk-stocking" clubs down to the "Wide-Awakes" or the "Dirty Dozen." There is probably no greater political contrast than is found in the difference between the simple constitutional provision for the election of the President and the actual process as it has been developed by political parties and democracy. Despite the Fathers' distrust of the people and the somewhat juvenile and primitive features of contemporary campaigns, the process of nominating and electing the President of the United States is one of democracy's grandest spectacles.

The congressional caucus. As observed above, the Constitution is silent on the subject of nomination and its framers thought that the President would be chosen without any formal preliminaries. But political parties were functioning before the end of Washington's administration. Now, if a party is to win, there must be unity. There must be an agreement to support a particular individual for the presidency, or the party's electors will scatter their votes and give no one the majority.

The congressional caucus, originating about 1796, was the institution used by the Jeffersonian Republicans [2] for the purpose of agreeing upon (nominating) party candidates. The caucus worked very simply. All the Republicans who held seats in Congress met and named their candidates. This method of nomination had certain advantages over our present convention system. (1) The caucus, composed of congressmen, was better fitted than ordinary voters or even state officers to pass upon the fitness of men for the highest office in the nation. (2) Since its members held office, the caucus could not escape responsibility for its choice of candidates, as the convention, which meets quadrennially for a few days, may so easily do. (3) The caucus did not name "dark horses," but tended to confine nominations to men of ripe experience and known opinions on public affairs. (4) Furthermore, it was likely to pick candidates acquainted with legislative temperament and methods, thus assuring some degree of harmony between Congress and the President. (5) Finally, the caucus was a very convenient means of making a nomination. It involved no expense, no choosing of delegates, and no long, tedious journeys to convention cities.[3]

The caucuses soon came to be denounced, however, as corrupt oligarchies, usurpers of power that rightfully belonged to the people, and as assemblies tending to subordinate the executive power to Congress, charges in which there was some element of truth. Andrew Jackson and his fol-

---

[2] The Federalists held one such caucus—in 1800.

[3] Sait, *op. cit.,* p. 272.

lowers dethroned (about 1824) the hated "King Caucus" as a nominating agency. For a few years thereafter candidates were endorsed by various state conventions, mass meetings, or even by caucuses of state legislatures. In a short time, however, the national convention system was evolved. Several such conventions were held in the early 'thirties, and by 1840 the national convention had become an established institution. A generation ago it was challenged as the caucus before it was challenged, but the national convention successfully rode the storm.

A. Preconvention Activities

The "call." Early in the winter preceding the summer and fall of the great party battle for the presidency, the national committees meet in Washington and issue the call for the conventions. Each call announces the time (usually about the middle of June for the Republicans and a few weeks later for the Democrats) and place fixed by the committee for holding the convention. The Democratic committee in its call gives a statement as to the number of delegates to which each state and territory is entitled; the Republican committee goes further and lays down the process by which and the time within which the delegates shall be chosen, and indicates also the procedure to be followed in forwarding the credentials of delegates and the manner in which contesting delegates or delegations shall submit their claims.

Choosing the convention city. In deciding where the convention shall meet, the national committee must consider the claims of local politicians, the inducements of business interests, and the broader questions of party advantage. Party leaders in a state want the convention in order that the party may be strengthened locally by the enthusiasm the great conclave engenders. They argue at the same time that success in the national election may depend upon a few voters who might be influenced by a convention in their state. Various business interests present the claims of their cities for the convention. They want the convention largely for the crowd and the business it brings with it, and they often pay a party as much as $200,000 for it. Location, railroad transportation facilities, hotel and convention hall accommodations, financial contributions, newspaper support and the extent of newspaper circulation, radio facilities, the local political effect of the convention, and the wishes of candidates and their backers, all determine the choice of the convention city. Chicago is the favorite convention city, although other large cities draw a convention occasionally. Sometimes strategy suggests the selection of a city well away from the center of things. Thus, the Democrats in 1928, fairly certain of the nomination of Wet and Catholic Governor Smith, picked Houston,

Texas, in the Dry and Protestant South, in the vain hope of reconciling that section to a candidate unacceptable to many Southern Democrats.

Apportionment of delegates by the Democratic party. For seventy years or more the practice in both parties, with certain exceptions to be noted, has been to give each state a number of convention delegates equal to twice its number of electors, and to give each delegate one vote. Thus a state with eight representatives and two senators in Congress, being entitled by the Constitution to ten presidential electors, is entitled by party rules to twenty convention delegates, each having one vote. In addition to the delegates from the states, each party allows a few delegates from the territories. On the basis of this method of apportionment the number of delegates in a national convention runs to about 1,200. In recent years, however, the Democratic conventions have had a considerably larger number of delegates (in 1940 the number was 1,844). This increase occurred because of the liberal policy that party has pursued in permitting states to send extra delegates.[4] Furthermore, by a rule adopted by the convention in 1940, each state that has gone Democratic in the preceding presidential election is to have two additional delegates at large. This was a concession to the Southern states for their agreement to the abolishment of the two-thirds rule (see below), a rule under which the delegates from those states had been able to veto the nomination of any candidate who might be unacceptable to them.

It may easily be shown that the Democratic party's method of apportionment is not particularly democratic. The figures assembled by the Committee on Political Parties of the American Political Science Association and published in their "Toward a More Responsible Two-Party System" (*American Political Science Review,* supplement, September, 1950) are eloquent on this point.

DEMOCRATIC NATIONAL CONVENTION, 1948

State	Democratic voters per delegate
Maine	11,191
Vermont	7,443
Connecticut	21,164
New York	28,960
Pennsylvania	26,955
Illinois	33,245
Wyoming	8,725
Nevada	3,129
Texas	15,014
South Carolina	1,721
Louisiana	5,680

[4] Such delegates do not carry any additional convention votes for their states. That is prevented by limiting certain delegates to one half votes. Thus, in 1948, the number of delegates was 1,596, but the number of votes was 1,234.

The Republicans' difficulty over apportionment. The rule that the party shall have twice as many representatives from each state as the state has presidential electors has done considerable violence to proportionate representation in the conventions. Wide disproportions have always been especially glaring in the Republican party, for it has never had, except in 1928, a substantial following in the South. From many examples of gross unfairness, we take just one. In 1908 South Carolina had eighteen delegates to the Republican convention and cast only four thousand votes for Mr. Taft in November of that year, whereas Maine had twelve delegates and cast sixty-seven thousand votes. A little arithmetic will show that in making a nomination the Republican voter in South Carolina had twenty-five times the voice of his fellow Republican in Maine. But disproportionate representation was by no means the worst feature of the system. In nearly all the Southern states the Republican organization was built up around those who held federal office. The sole interest of the organization was said to be in federal patronage. Consequently, skillful men in the national Republican organization could dispense offices in return for votes of the Southern delegates in the national conventions. The climax of this sort of manipulation was reached in 1912, when the Republican strategists, through their several hundred hand-picked delegates from the Solid South, nominated Taft and disrupted the Republican party in so doing.

Mild reforms in apportionment. The long-delayed reform in representation was made before the next (1916) Republican national convention. Under the new plan the number of delegates from the Southern states was considerably reduced. In 1921 a still more drastic (and equitable) plan of reduction was brought forward, but it was never put into operation because of opposition in the South and dire threats of revolt against the party on the part of a large number of Negro voters who held the balance of power in such border states as Missouri, Indiana, and Illinois. Three years later, ignoring the mandate of the preceding national convention, the national committee drew up a much milder plan designed to conciliate the threatening factions. The national convention of 1924, with victory in the air, was not disposed to quibble over the action of the national committee and adopted its recommendation (made contrary to the instructions of the preceding convention) without debate. In 1940 a slight modification was made in the plan of apportionment. Yet the Republican apportionment of 1948 still had the same glaring inequalities as that of 1908. For example, New York had one delegate for each 29,290 Republican voters and Mississippi had a delegate for each 630 such voters. In 1948 the delegates were apportioned as follows: four delegates at large from each state (two for each United States senator); two dele-

gates at large for each congressman at large (a congressman chosen by
the electorate of the entire state); a delegate from each congressional district that cast as many as 1,000 votes for a Republican candidate in the
last national election and two delegates if as many as 10,000 Republican
votes were cast; and each state that voted Republican in the last presidential election or subsequently elected a Republican to the United States
Senate gets a bonus of three delegates. The principal territories and the
District of Columbia are given from two to five delegates each. There
were 1,094 delegates in the convention of 1948.

Methods of choosing delegates: CONVENTIONS. Delegates to the national
conventions are chosen in two ways, by state or district conventions and
by the voters in direct primaries. More than a majority of the states still
use the convention method. A state convention may choose all of the
delegates; it may choose the delegates at large and accept the recommendations of the delegates from each congressional district attending the state
convention as to the delegates who should be chosen to represent such
districts in the national convention; or the state convention may choose
the delegates at large and conventions in each congressional district may
choose the district delegates. It should be added that the manner of
choosing delegates must conform to state law.

DIRECT PRIMARIES. Since 1900 the system of direct primaries has been
established in many states. Its purpose was to take state and local nominations out of the hands of professional politicians, machines, wirepullers,
and the like. Advocates of the direct primary soon enlarged their activities and attempted to break the power of the irresponsible national conventions through the primary system. Wisconsin (1905) was the pioneer
in this field, but Oregon (1910) enacted the first comprehensive presidential preference primary law. Other states followed quickly, so that before
the conventions of 1916 there were twenty-four states with such laws.
Since then the movement has declined, leaving only sixteen states with
some form of presidential preference primary law at the present time.
The laws vary considerably in the several states, but the most common
rule is that the party voters in a state elect the delegates to the national
convention and on the same ballot mark their choice for the presidential
nomination. The delegates elected from a state to attend the convention
are expected (in some states required) to support for the nomination the
candidate who received the highest number of votes in the state's primary.
From 1916 to 1928 more than half the delegates who sat in national conventions were chosen by the direct primary, but, beginning with 1932, the
number of such delegates has been considerably less than half.

Even in the 'twenties, the period of the maximum use of the presidential primary, it was never a controlling factor in the nominating proc-

ess. To be sure, the primary results of 1928 did foreshadow the action of the party conventions, but there is hardly any doubt that Hoover and Smith would have been nominated had there been no primaries. In 1932 the Democratic primaries somewhat vaguely indicated that Roosevelt was the popular choice. In 1936 popular approval of Roosevelt made his re-nomination a foregone conclusion. The contest for delegates in the Republican party was marked by the action of a leading candidate, Governor Alfred Landon, in *keeping out* of the primaries, and thus avoiding the danger of arousing the enmity of "favorite sons." It may be necessary to add that Landon was nominated by the convention with great enthusiasm. In 1940 uncertainty of what Roosevelt was going to do prevented any effective primary activity among Democrats. The Republican primaries developed Thomas E. Dewey as the favorite, but in the few months preceding the convention some talented young leaders groomed Wendell Willkie (whom probably not one thousand Americans had previously considered as a possibility) and won the nomination for him. Primaries meant nothing to the Democrats either in 1944 or 1948, the war giving Roosevelt a "no contest" nomination and White House incumbency the same for Truman. In both years Republican primaries pointed in the general direction of Thomas E. Dewey.

The presidential preference primary is without a doubt ineffective. Some of the principal reasons for its short-comings are as follows: (1) It is in operation in only a third of the states, and it is by no means uniform in those. (2) Not all of the candidates enter the primary race, and frequently those who do enter make a contest in only a few of the sixteen states, thus bringing about meaningless results. (3) No satisfactory method has been found for fixing the obligation of the convention delegate to support the voters' choice for presidential nominee. A further weakness of the presidential primary, but not the primary's "fault," is the conservative opposition to it in both political parties. A large number of very respectable men, leaders in politics and large private affairs, long for the earlier days when convention delegates were far removed from popular control.

Suggestions for improvements in the presidential preference primary are easy to make, and a number of excellent proposals have been made. From them the following plan is evolved: (1) It should be national, conducted in every state for all political parties on the same day. (2) Any candidate who receives the majority of the votes of his party should be declared the nominee. The national convention could then meet, "shake feathers, and brandish tomahawks," and draft the party platform. (3) In the event no candidate receives a majority in the national primary, then each aspirant for the nomination should be permitted to select a proportion of delegates corresponding to his proportion of the total party vote in each state, and the convention should proceed to nominate a candidate from one of the three highest in the national primary. This plan would spell the end of the "dark horse" and the "favorite son," although it would not entirely eliminate the "back stairs" and the "smoke-filled" conference room. To make effective the plan outlined, or one approximating it, would probably require a constitutional amendment. In any event there is no indication that any such proposal is going to be adopted, for the American people show little or no interest in widening its use.

The use of public opinion polls. Until such time as a national presidential primary system may be adopted, our scientific public opinion polls will serve us infinitely better than our present wholly inadequate primary "system." The opinion polls on the voters' preconvention preference may be taken from time to time over the period of a year or longer, thus showing the rise and decline among the people of presidential possibilities. And better still, the polls will show the popular reaction to specific activities or declarations of men seeking the nomination, as was so well demonstrated in the spring of 1948 by the poll results (favorable to Dewey) following the Dewey-Stassen debates in Oregon. The figures presented by the "pollsters" are probably well below 10 per cent in margin of error [5] and are therefore far and away better than any other guide we now have to public opinion. They can be used and doubtless are being used by convention delegates as one test of the strength of an individual's candidacy. No other test (instructed delegate or delegates obligated by a primary) not legally binding on the delegates would do much more.

Preconvention maneuvers for the nomination. Long before the delegates to the national convention have been chosen, long before the national committee has issued the call for a convention, candidates and their backers are busy. "A political campaign is a matter of years—not weeks or months," says James A. Farley, who ought to know. When did he and Franklin D. Roosevelt start their campaign to make the latter President? "Like everything else in politics," Mr. Farley explains, "the roots of this story are buried back in the annals of other years." Farley went to work in earnest on November 5, 1930, when the returns of the New York election showed that Roosevelt had been re-elected governor by the unprecedented majority of 725,001. In consultation with the Governor's closest associate, Louis McHenry Howe, he prepared a very careful statement. The statement was that Mr. Roosevelt could not escape becoming the next presidential nominee of his party, *"even if no one should raise a finger to bring it about"* [italics mine].[6] Everyone knows that Farley raised many a finger, traveled many a mile, slapped many a back, learned many a first

[5] McKean, *op. cit.,* pp. 170–174.
[6] Farley, *op. cit.,* pp. 59–62. This book is well worth reading.

name, wrote many a "keep in touch," and chewed many a pack of gum to bring about Roosevelt's nomination.

In the months when Farley was bringing his candidate into the "sunlight of popular attention," the magazine *Time* entertained its readers with an account of how all politicians who had been stung by the presidential bee in November, 1930, should, and probably would, proceed to conduct their campaigns. Following is a summary of *Time*'s handbook on "How to Become President." [7]

(1) An aspiring candidate must acquire a "wise, devoted friend" who will work and speak for him as the candidate would for himself. "The aspirant cannot go about telling people he wants to be President." He must leave that to his *alter ego*. The *alter ego* should be industrious, but not too obviously zealous; he should be distinguished, but less so than his candidate. (2) "Close in the background must be an eminent banker or financier." But the money must not be too obvious, nor should large contributions be made too early. (3) The aspirant should "find strong community of interest with the leaders of his party, . . . the permanent, entrenched leaders, rather than the party executives of the moment." (4) He should identify himself "early and firmly with a national issue"— "American Individualism," national security, etc. "The tariff should be attempted only by acknowledged economic experts." (5) "Get a press! This is accomplished in several ways. The *alter ego* must see to it that editors get courteous, efficient service when they exhibit curiosity. Friends of editors may be asked to bring the editors to call, dine. . . . Writer friends should be encouraged to undertake character sketches. . . . Anecdotes (safe, amusing ones) should be frequently dropped among newspaper men. . . . Any cartoonable physical characteristics or appurtenances should be emphasized—as were [Theodore] Roosevelt's grin and spectacles, Taft's girth, Dawes's pipe, Smith's hat." (6) "The candidate must move about the country. Not aimlessly, of course, or just hoping he will be seen. He must be supplied with places to go, people to visit, ceremonies in which to participate. Dedications of bridges, schools, memorials—especially statues of great dead leaders of the party—are especially good." (7) He must "seem always full of health. . . . Bursting, booming, up-at-seven physical condition is readily suggested by appearing on horseback, walking to the office, going swimming, playing golf. Fishing from a boat is good," but the aspirant should "*never* be seen at the wheel of a yacht." (8) He should never "go around without a ladder." He should keep handy a means of climbing down from the eminence he has achieved, for failure to descend gracefully and in good spirits when the nomination prize goes to another is likely to do irreparable damage to

[7] November 24, 1930, pp. 15–16; see also *Time*, May 18, 1936.

one's chance in any future convention. The effectiveness of this kind of strategy, particularly in the use of the press, was well illustrated by Governor Landon's managers, who in a few months' time lifted him from relative obscurity and presented him to the American people as the Republican candidate for the presidency. The case of Wendell Willkie (1940) was different. He was a national figure, but hardly considered as a candidate for the presidency until two or three months before the convention, when a few skillful leaders successfully promoted his candidacy.

B. Platforms and Candidates

Personnel of the convention. Conspicuous among the delegates in a national convention are United States senators, members of the House of Representatives, and, until the passage of the Hatch Act (1939), a number of appointive federal officeholders. The Constitution states that persons who hold any of these positions shall be ineligible to serve as presidential electors. It is, therefore, contrary to the spirit of the Constitution for any of them to be chosen as convention delegates, since the delegates have a much more important function to perform than the electors in the matter of choosing a President. Another objection to these officials serving as delegates is that largely through them "steam roller" tactics are applied in a convention. In 1912 this office-holding group and other organization men were largely responsible for the defeat of Theodore Roosevelt, the people's choice for the Republican nomination. Too long delayed was the Hatch Act, which prohibits federal administrative officers and employees from serving as convention delegates or taking any part in political campaigns.[8]

A convention commonly numbers among its distinguished delegates such elder statesmen as former ambassadors and ex-senators. Other influential delegates we find in the list of governors and state bosses. The rank and file of delegates are local officeholders or party leaders in those areas, businessmen or representatives of their interests, journalists, and so on. In recent years, women are frequently chosen as delegates, especially as alternate delegates.

Convention preliminaries. The state delegations and other interested persons travel, in many cases, to the convention city on special trains, their expenses paid out of their own pockets, by affluent supporters of particular candidates, by rich candidates, or otherwise.[9] They manifest something of the spirit displayed by students aboard a "special" leaving for the holidays

---

[8] Excepted from the provision of the law are the President, the Vice President, department heads, and a few other officials of high rank.

[9] A few states have paid a part of the expenses of delegates.

or accompanying their team to a neighboring institution for the annual
football classic. Outwardly there is usually enthusiasm, optimism, and
accord; actually one or more of these elements may be lacking. They arrive
in the convention city with a great shout; and, wearing buttons or ribbons
and carrying banners, they march to their hotel, perhaps to the tune of
martial music.

As the city and its hotels become filled with delegates, newspaper men,
and spectators, there is a continuous stir and commotion. There is much
going back and forth among delegations, especially among the leaders, in
the interest of securing votes for various aspirants for the nomination.
There is a rumor that A will be nominated on the first ballot, so why not
get on the "band wagon"? Another rumor has it that B has told his
supporters to vote for the nomination of C, and that a sufficient number
of delegates are leaving A to assure C's nomination. Propositions are stated
and promises made by one faction, to be met with evasion or counter-
proposals by another. A few leaders may know about what the situation
is; but the average delegate is more or less bewildered, and hot weather
and crowded quarters do not ease his state of mind. Practically everyone
in the city seems to be working for some candidate. Even the bootblack
is likely to importune his delegate client in the interest of a "favorite son."

When the convention is formally opened, we find the delegates seated
in groups by states and surrounded by thousands of excited spectators,
who sit in the galleries. The attention of the whole country is turned to
the work of the President-makers. Millions attend the convention's deliberations via the radio, or reflect more leisurely upon its proceedings as
they are recounted in the press.

THE "KEYNOTE" SPEECH. A temporary chairman, nominated by the national committee, and usually elected by acclamation, delivers a "keynote"
speech. Its purpose is to bring about harmony and raise party enthusiasm
to the highest pitch. The "keynoter" paints dark pictures of what the
other party has done and may do to ruin the country, and from colored
facts with admixtures of fiction produces a perfect painting of his own
party, while his audience bursts forth again and again in tumultuous approval. He is likely to make an appropriate reference to each great name
associated with the party's past, each reference being greeted with a roar
of applause. In this connection it may be mentioned that Senator Fess,
the Republican "keynoter" in 1928, somehow failed to mention Theodore
Roosevelt, and rather academically claimed the floor the next day to insert
a fitting eulogy.

Convention organization: The committees. Following this speech of
the temporary chairman, committees are appointed on credentials, on permanent organization, on rules and order of business, and on resolutions

(platform). Each state and territorial delegation names a member for each of these four committees.[10]

THE CREDENTIALS COMMITTEE. Ordinarily, the credentials committee reports to the convention first. The national committee has previously made up a temporary roll of delegates, but its decision is subject to review by the credentials committee and by the convention itself. As a rule, there are few contested seats, and passing upon credentials is a relatively unimportant matter; but on occasion, when there are a number of contests, and when the votes are fairly evenly divided between factions, decisions on these contests may be decisive in determining the whole course of the convention. This was the case in the Republican convention of 1912, when Roosevelt was deprived of his majority because the credentials committee, following the preliminary decisions of the national committee, recommended the seating of some fifty Taft delegates, against the clear claims of Roosevelt "delegates." In 1932 the forces of Franklin D. Roosevelt won initial and significant victories when they seated favorable delegates from the contested delegations of Louisiana and Minnesota. In some cases, both claimants of contested seats have been seated, each being given half a vote.

THE COMMITTEE ON PERMANENT ORGANIZATION. The convention is now ready for the report of the committee on permanent organization. This committee nominates the permanent chairman, usually agreed upon by party leaders long in advance, and the other permanent officers of the convention; and its recommendations are usually accepted by the whole body of delegates as a matter of course. An interesting contest over the committee's recommendation for permanent chairman occurred in the Democratic convention of 1932, but its nominee, Senator Walsh of Montana, was elected.

The chairman is by far the most important officer named by the committee. He is called upon to preside over the largest, and at the same time the most turbulent, of all American public bodies. He must be a master of parliamentary procedure, prompt and firm in his decisions, and urbane and dignified in his bearing. Upon his installation the permanent chairman makes a speech, often somewhat more restrained than the keynote speech.

THE COMMITTEE ON RULES. The committee on rules usually recommends that the convention follow as far as practicable the rules of the House of Representatives. In addition to the recommendations concerning convention procedure, this committee may also deal with such other matters as the composition and powers of future national committees and the mode

---

[10] Under a rule adopted in 1940 the Democratic platform committee is doubled in size, half its members being women.

of electing future delegates. Its reports, like those of the other committees mentioned above, are usually acceptable to the convention.

The platform: How it is framed. The committee on resolutions is officially charged with the responsibility of preparing the party platform. Long before the convention assembles, various leaders (including a number who will be chosen for the committee on resolutions) have been conferring informally on the subject of a platform. They have collected a great deal of data, and perhaps made a tentative draft of a platform. This material is referred to the platform committee. The committee then holds sessions, and there appear before it representatives of such organized groups as the AFL, the CIO, the American Legion, the National Association of Manufacturers, and the American Farm Bureau Federation—pleading, coaxing, and sometimes threatening the committee in the interest of getting this or that plank incorporated into the platform. Sometimes the committee has little else to do than report the platform which has already been prepared by the President or other party leaders. At other times the content of the platform may arouse vigorous disagreement; the committee may wrangle for several days over certain planks, and the fight even may be carried to the convention floor. Thus, in 1932 there were lively contests on the Prohibition repeal issue on the floor of both the Republican and Democratic conventions.

We waited, however, for 1948 to see a real sight! In that year the Democratic convention, to almost everybody's surprise, adopted a strong and unequivocal civil rights plank. The plank was won because President Truman wanted it, and because Mayor (later Senator) Hubert Humphrey and his Americans for Democratic Action and a few old New Dealers (whom the country had supposed were in hibernation) fought for it.[11] This outcome was too much for the old Confederacy. Half the Alabama and all the Mississippi delegates walked out of the hall, and soon thereafter the States' Rights ("Dixiecrat") Party was formed. Incidents of this type should help us to understand why party platforms are strong on denunciation of the opposition and relatively weak on specific proposals for government action. This particular incident should also teach the practical politician a lesson: it may pay off to face an issue squarely. It is generally agreed that the stand taken by Truman and the other civil rights advocates won many more votes for Truman in other parts of the nation than it lost for him in the South.

Content of the Platform. In convention after convention, up to 1932, platforms grew longer and longer, but since that date there has been a commendable trend toward a shorter document. A platform contains

[11] *United States News*, July 23, 1948, p. 20.

a glowing account of the party's recent achievements, praises a leader or two, and denounces the work of the opposing party. The greater part of the platform is devoted to a statement of party principles. In spite of the fact that a platform may make pronouncements on some fifty issues, it cannot be said that the policy of the party is made very clear to the voters. On some issues the platform sounds a clear note, to be sure; but on many others the language is ambiguous and evasive. Frequently, very important issues are untouched, because any mention of them is likely to alienate voters from the party. On the other hand, the platform may contain expressions of sympathy for the aspirations of unhappy people in various countries. Such solicitude for peoples in other lands is, of course, intended to win the votes of persons of those nationalities who have established themselves in the United States. It may be said that, in general, the chief purpose of the platform is to win voters to the party, rather than to state honestly and explicitly the principles the party would put into operation if entrusted with office. In consequence, few people take the trouble to read the document,[12] and the party leaders are easily forgiven for conveniently forgetting platform pledges when the election campaign is over. Party platforms are not likely to have significance until such time as they are presented after long study and research, adopted by conventions much more representative (and smaller) than the present national conventions, and the people have assurance that a party, if entrusted with office, will have a responsible leadership that will translate the platform into government policy.

Nominating speeches. With the platform adopted, the convention is ready for the main purpose for which it assembled—the nomination of a candidate for the presidency. The roll is called by states, and someone in each delegation arises and makes a nominating speech; or, in case the state has no candidate to present, yields the honor of making a nominating speech to a delegate from another state; or makes a speech seconding a nomination already made. Convention oratory in general is impassioned and flamboyant, but the climax is reached in the nominating speeches. The orators declaim the glories of their country, "peopled with the greatest race of men who have lived since the sun first kissed the horizon of time." [13] They work the delegates up to a frenzy over a candidate "who learned the simple lessons of Democratic faith in the furrowed field." [14] Since about 1924 nominating speakers have shown a little more restraint, although "Babylon and Nineveh and ancient Rome wallowed in the wealth

---

[12] In 1948 Gallup reported that 7 per cent read all the platform; 26 per cent a part.
[13] Senator James A. Reed, naming Champ Clark in 1912.
[14] Martin W. Littleton, naming Judge Alton B. Parker in 1904.

of material prosperity, stood naked and unashamed in their perdition—and succumbed" in the speech nominating Hoover for a second term.[15]

Demonstrations. The conclusion of a nominating speech is the cue for pandemonium. Formerly these "demonstrations" were spontaneous; and the parades, songs, and shouts might last from ten minutes to half an hour. Now the managers are not willing to trust to spontaneity. The demonstrations are carefully arranged in advance and put in the ice box to be brought out at the proper time.[16] The din, which has sometimes gone on from one to two hours, is made by the human voice, brass bands, and almost every conceivable mechanical instrument that will produce a noise. The idea seems to be that the delegates who are to make the nomination and the country at large will be influenced by the length and intensity of the demonstration invoked by the mention of a candidate's name. As a matter of fact, the artificiality of all this synthetic uproar is obvious to all who have ever seen the genuine article as displayed by a high school or college student body in action at a football game. Competent observers are of the opinion that, however much the convention demonstrations may do to keep alive the redskin traditions on this continent, they have no influence whatever over the hard-boiled managers of a convention and hardly any more influence over the rank and file of the delegates. These sovereign representatives of the party join in demonstrations and counter-demonstrations, each faction trying to sweep the others off their feet; but if any change their votes, it is due to clever work and quiet words behind the scenes and not to the attempts to stampede or shell-shock them by noise.

The balloting. When all the nominating speeches have been made, the convention is ready to choose the standard-bearer for the party. The roll is called by states, and the chairman of each state delegation announces the vote. In the Republican convention the delegates vote individually. For instance, ten delegates may vote for A, three for B, and one for C. When the vote of each delegation has been announced, the results are totaled; and if any person has a majority, he becomes the party's candidate for the presidency. If no one receives a majority on the first ballot, the balloting continues, and so do the informal conferences between leaders in the interest of various aspirants for the nomination, until some person wins a majority.

THE DEMOCRATIC UNIT RULE. In the Democratic convention the vote of a state is ordinarily cast as a unit. For example, twenty members of a delegation may be for A, eight for B, and six for C; but the chairman of the state delegation, acting under the unit rule, will announce the vote as

[15] Speech of Joseph Scott.
[16] Newspaper accounts of any national convention will supply examples.

thirty-four for A. In other words, the person who receives the highest number of individual votes within a delegation is given the entire vote of the delegation. There are, however, certain exceptions to this rule. It is not applied if the state convention has not instructed the state delegation to observe it, and it is not applied in any case where the laws of a state require election of delegates by congressional districts and do not subject such delegates to the authority of the state convention or state committee of the party. This unit rule, emphasizing the importance of the state rather than the individual delegates, is in keeping with the ancient, if not always honored, Democratic principle of states' rights.

Until 1936 the Democratic conventions held to the requirement that nominations should be made by two-thirds majorities. Adopted more than a century ago as a means of preventing certain individuals from winning nominations, it was criticized from time to time, particularly in 1932, when Roosevelt's manager, James A. Farley, feared he could not line up a two-thirds majority for his candidate. Criticized for attempting to change the rules while the game was in progress, the astute manager dropped the matter. In 1936 there was only one candidate for the nomination and the convention took advantage of the opportunity to rescind the rule, thus providing for nomination by simple majority.

NUMBER OF BALLOTS REQUIRED. About half the time the convention nominates a candidate on the first ballot. This result is quite likely in the event the President is nominated for another term, but it may also happen in the case of other candidates, as it did with Landon in 1936 and Dewey in 1944. At other times, candidates have been nominated without lengthy struggles, as was the case with Bryan, nominated (1896) on the fifth ballot; Hughes (1916) on the third; Franklin D. Roosevelt (1932) on the fourth; Willkie (1940) on the sixth; and Dewey (1948) on the third. Occasionally when the convention is deadlocked, that is, when delegates are so divided in their support of aspirants that no one receives the necessary majority, a large number of ballots may be necessary.

"GENERAL FAVORITES," "FAVORITE SONS," AND "DARK HORSES." A "general favorite" or "logical candidate" may not be able to secure the necessary votes because a number of other candidates with local reputations and known in political parlance as "favorite sons" are drawing too many votes. Or, and this is more probable, the vote may be divided among two "general favorites" and a few "favorite sons" in such a way as to prevent any choice. Under such circumstances, the balloting may go on and on, but fluctuating with each performance in response to the quiet work of the leaders, who influence the delegates by argument, promises of government positions, and what not. All of this is sometimes without avail, and the leaders may then agree upon a "dark horse." He is usually, though not always, a colorless, tractable, relatively obscure individual of no great talent, who has hardly been considered for the nomination until this moment; but the leaders pass the word along and he is duly nominated.

INSTANCES OF PROLONGED BALLOTING. The more recent instances of prolonged balloting have occurred in the Democratic conventions, with the nomination of Woodrow Wilson (1912) on the forty-sixth ballot, James M. Cox (1920) on the forty-fourth, and John W. Davis (1924) on the one hundred and third after nine days of balloting. The difficulties the Democrats met in getting the necessary majority for nominations led, as noted above, to rescinding the two-thirds rule. There is some doubt whether its disuse will have the desired result, for a nomination before the fifth or fiftieth ballot is not so much dependent upon the majority required to make the nomination as upon convention harmony and party leadership. The longest series of balloting the Republicans have had in recent years occurred in 1920, when, after it became apparent that neither Hiram Johnson nor Frank O. Lowden nor Leonard A. Wood, the three "general favorites," could get the nomination, the leaders turned to Harding, a "favorite son," and he was chosen on the tenth ballot.

The principle of availability. A number of motives prompt national convention delegates to nominate particular men for the presidency. They range from such a purely selfish motive as the hope of getting an appointment to federal office, to the high desire to place the best qualified man in the White House. Whatever individual motives may be, the dominant motive in practically every convention is that of nominating a man who will bring victory to the party. And what sort of candidate is most likely to win? He must have a number of desirable qualities, which are classed under the general head of "availability." Availability is obviously a very elastic term. For instance, at one time the people may want an aggressive executive—a "trust buster" or a man with a "big stick"—at which time force and vigor in an individual is a quality of availability. After an administration or two dominated by this type of man, the people may tire of "executive autocracy and usurpation" and prefer a President who will be quiet, "let business alone," and "observe constitutional restraints." It should be noted then that availability includes all the reactions of the leaders and the people of various sections of the country, as well as the personal qualities of the candidate.

THE QUALITIES OF AVAILABILITY. Following Professor Robert C. Brooks,[17] we may summarize the qualities that constitute availability for the presidency.

(1) Residence in a fairly populous pivotal or doubtful state. Such residence is desirable because a native of a state ordinarily has a better

---

[17] *Op. cit.*, pp. 318 ff.

chance to carry it and win its much-needed electoral vote than does a citizen of some other state. Here we have one of the chief reasons why New York and Ohio have so often furnished presidential candidates. Neither Republicans nor Democrats are likely to name, for instance, Georgians or Pennsylvanians as candidates; for, without regard to the candidate's personal qualities or his residence, Georgia is certain to go Democratic, and Pennsylvania went Republican from 1860 to 1936.

(2) Because of the economic importance of the East and the Old West (for example, Ohio) and the large number of electoral votes the states in these regions possess, they have had almost a monopoly on presidential nominees. Ohio has been an especially favored state because its candidates have the advantage of being considered slightly Western as well as residents of a large pivotal state. Frémont, Bryan, Hoover, Landon, and Truman are the only candidates who have resided west of the Mississippi.

(3) If a party has the President and if he wishes to continue in that office, he is almost invariably renominated. To withhold the nomination would be embarrassing to the party, for the reason that it would amount to a repudiation of its chief officeholder.

(4) A candidate once defeated is ordinarily considered not available, although the Democrats nominated Cleveland after he had been defeated in his second campaign and Bryan twice after his first defeat, and in 1948 the Republicans gave Dewey a second chance. Smith's and Willkie's failure to secure renomination in 1932 and 1944, respectively, are the more common examples.

(5) Candidates still in the vigor of manhood are preferred.[18] The presidency is a burden even to the most robust man. Since 1860 the average age at which men have been inaugurated President is fifty-one.

(6) Ability as a campaigner is highly desirable, although not indispensable. Tact, affability, and kindred traits are also qualities of availability; but so, at times, are courageous bluntness and golden silence.

(7) Personal integrity is uncompromisingly demanded. The very breath of suspicion is sufficient to blast the hopes of a candidate, as is borne out by Blaine's defeat for the nomination in 1876 and for the presidency in 1884.[19]

(8) The candidate must have a record in public service.[20] Service in

[18] But a physical handicap overcome or partially overcome, as in the case of Franklin D. Roosevelt, may not injure a candidate's chances.

[19] On the other hand, when it became known after Cleveland's nomination (1884) that he was the father of an illegitimate son, he confounded his opponents and shocked his managers (politically) by *frankly admitting* it—and won the election against Blaine who admitted nothing.

[20] Wendell Willkie (1940) was an exception to this rule, although his nationally publicized contest with the President over the public utilities issue gave Willkie a build-up similar to that which a successful term of office might have brought.

Congress or in the Cabinet may meet this demand, but nominees are less frequently chosen from these groups than one might reasonably expect. Availability may be lessened by fearless and successful service at these posts, because such service often makes bitter enemies as well as enthusiastic followers. Formerly, successful generals were frequently nominated; but the "Rough Rider" Roosevelt was the last military man to receive the nomination, and he was only incidentally a soldier. Despite the fact that neither John J. Pershing (1920) nor Douglas MacArthur (1948) could make a good showing in pre-convention campaigns for the nomination we should not rule out the generals completely. Dwight Eisenhower probably could have had (or may have) a nomination. Governors, especially governors of large pivotal states, are often chosen. They have had not only experience in large affairs; but, because of their local character, they have seldom antagonized important men, with the exception of a few local rivals, bosses, and spoilsmen.

(9) Lawyers, but not corporation lawyers,[21] are more frequently nominated for the presidency than are members of any other profession.

(10) Finally, we might observe that, however deplorable, a member of some Protestant sect has a distinct advantage over a Catholic, a Jew, or a "freethinker."

Are the best men nominated? Critics have said that nominations are made on the basis of availability rather than ability. But availability does not necessarily preclude character and ability. We must not forget that blamelesss character and a good record in public service are two very important elements of availability. As we look over the list of great men who have been passed over by conventions, we find Webster, Calhoun, Seward, Hay, Root, and a few others. On the other hand, the conventions nominated Jackson, Clay, Lincoln, Blaine, Cleveland, the Roosevelts, and Wilson—a fairly good showing. When it comes to the men whom we have actually elected to the presidency, we have probably done as well in placing great men in that office as the British have in elevating great men to the premiership—each country has had both mediocrities and towering statesmen. When the people of either country succeed in evolving a system whereby the best qualified man will always be assured of the highest place, they will be too good for this world.

Nominations for the Vice Presidency. It might not be utterly inappropriate to head this paragraph with the statement: "We almost forgot something—the nomination for Vice President," for the naming of this candidate, as the last act of the convention, seems almost an afterthought. The Vice Presidency is commonly held in light esteem, and able men are reluctant to accept the nomination. This attitude toward the office is

---

[21] Again Willkie must be excepted. As an attorney he was connected with large business.

unfortunate, for seven times the Vice President has become President through the death of the Chief Executive.

The nomination is usually made after party leaders hold a conference and pass the word around that Mr. X is the man who should be made the vice-presidential candidate. He may be chosen because his selection will assure the active support of a certain element in the party that is lukewarm toward the presidential candidate; or the choice may fall upon him because he resides in a pivotal state, or because he represents a different section of the country from that represented by the man at the head of the ticket. Usually he is named for a combination of reasons. Thus, in 1924, Charles Bryan, the brother of William Jennings Bryan, was nominated by the Democrats to run with John W. Davis in order to win the support of the influential "William J." for the Davis candidacy, to give the West representation on the ticket, and to make the conservatism of the urbane Davis more palatable to liberal Democrats. At the same time, the Republicans nominated Charles G. Dawes of Illinois because he gave the West a place on the ticket headed by Coolidge of Massachusetts and because the Republicans, having in mind Wilson's physical breakdown in the White House and President Harding's death in 1923, seemed to feel the necessity of naming a man for second place who was eminently fitted for the presidency. Perhaps, also, they felt that Dawes, with his mild but picturesque profanity and his underslung pipe (which became a symbol in the campaign) would make a splendid combination with Coolidge, the quiet doer of the day's work. In 1940 the Republicans nominated Senator Charles McNary who, with his large following of farmers, was expected to be an excellent running mate for Willkie who represented industry and business. The Democrats nominated Henry Wallace because the President wanted him and was powerful enough to force the convention to accept him. In 1948 the Republican procedure in picking the candidate for Vice President was about as follows: After Dewey had been given the first place on the ticket, he called in the leaders to confer on the selection of his running mate. Charles Halleck, a Congressman from Indiana, had a claim because he had swung the Indiana delegation to Dewey at an early stage. But the feeling was that there had been no commitment to Halleck; besides, he was too closely identified with the nationalist (isolationist) wing of the party. Harold Stassen, a rival of Dewey's for first place, had yielded gracefully, and was entitled to consideration. His selection as a running mate would appeal to young Republicans. On the other hand, there was a question about his maturity and another one respecting his capacity for team work. Maybe they should defer his honors until he matured and mellowed. Governor Earl Warren, a popular vote-getter from California, was the third possibility. The Halleck group found Warren less objectionable than Stassen, and the Stassen supporters agreed that Warren was acceptable. At this point they had arrived at four A.M. (whether or not in a "smoke-filled room" the record does not disclose), when Dewey said: "Let's get some sleep and see how we feel about it *in the morning.*" After two hours in bed Dewey declared for Warren.[22]

The suggestion that the office of Vice President be abolished is not absurd. It is no reflection on the office, or on recent incumbents of it, or on recent candidates for it to say that other methods of providing for the President's immediate successor would not be likely to result in the choice of less able men than are commonly nominated for Vice President. One might well reason that the office should be abolished or reformed (see page 286).

II. STATE CONVENTIONS [23]

The people of the United States elect 435 members of the House of Representatives, 96 senators, about 10,000 state officers—governors, legislators, and others—and some 850,000 local officers.[24] Making nominations for these offices is an essential part of the election process. To be sure, the national political classic, the presidential race, commands the citizen's first interest. Nevertheless, state and local issues are not infrequently of more immediate concern to the voter than national questions, and the diversion of the voter's attention from state and local contests created by the national quadrennial sweepstakes is most unfortunate. Yet the former sometimes command wide and eager attention.

Before the convention: the caucus. Until the Jackson Era there were not many elective officers and the number of voters constituted only a small percentage of the population. In colonial times and in the early years of our independence a candidate announced himself, perhaps with the coy statement that he reluctantly consented to run because so many gentlemen had urged him to do so, or a group of politically minded persons at a rather informal meeting might name a candidate. This latter method was known as nomination by caucus. Concerning the caucus, John Adams made an oft-quoted entry in his diary, February, 1763: "This day learned that the Caucus club meets at certain times in the garret of Tom Dawes. . . . There they smoke tobacco till you cannot see from one end of the garret to the other. There they drink flip, I suppose, and they choose a

---

[22] *United States News,* July 2, 1948, p. 13.

[23] Hugh A. Bone, *American Politics and the Party System* (1949), Ch. 19; R. C. Brooks, *Political Parties and Electoral Problems* (1933 ed.), Ch. X; H. R. Bruce, *American Parties and Politics* (1936 ed.), Chs. XI–XII; V. O. Key, Jr., *Politics, Parties and Pressure Groups* (1947 ed.), 12; C. E. Merriam and H. F. Gosnell, *The American Party System* (1949 ed.), Ch. XIV; Peter Odegard and E. A. Helms, *American Politics* (1947 ed.), XVI: E. M. Sait, *American Parties and Elections* (H. R. Penniman's Edition, 1948), Chs. XII–XIII, XVIII–XIX.

[24] Merriam and Gosnell, *op. cit.,* pp. 301–302.

moderator who puts questions to the vote regularly; and selectmen, assessors, collectors, fire-wards, and representatives are regularly chosen before they are chosen in the town." [25] In state and local political affairs the caucus became an established institution long before 1800. Local officers were nominated in some such manner as mentioned in Adams's diary; state officers by the members of a given party in the state legislature—the legislative caucus; and candidates for the presidency by the party groups in Congress after 1800.

ITS OVERTHROW. In 1824 the caucus was discredited as a method of choosing candidates for the presidency. Before this date the caucus had been greatly weakened in the states, and its life was probably not greatly prolonged by the introduction of the "mixed" or "mongrel" caucus—a caucus in which delegates from districts that had no party representatives in the state legislature would sit with their fellow partisans who held seats in that body and with them nominate candidates for office. Jacksonian Democrats opposed the caucus, whether pure or "mongrel," as undemocratic, corrupt, and as subversive of the cherished principle of the separation of powers. The triumph of Jackson meant the overthrow of "King Caucus," who had been sitting on a shaky throne for at least a decade.

The delegate convention. During the decade following 1820 the caucus ceased to be used except in the smallest political units—wards, towns, and townships. It was continued in these small districts for the purpose of nominating the party candidates for offices in these areas and for the additional purpose of naming delegates to city, county, and, in some cases, congressional district conventions. The delegates in any one of these conventions named the candidates for offices of the area that the convention represented, and selected delegates to a state convention and sometimes to a congressional district convention. These higher conventions, repeating the process of the county or city conventions, named the party candidates for elective offices within the state or district and selected the delegates for the great national convention. Thus the convention system was essentially democratic in theory, resting upon the small unit cells composed of the Toms, Dicks, and Harrys who might care to attend the local caucus. Democracy seemed to be satisfied—all candidates for elective office, from the smallest to the greatest, were nominated by the people or by their delegates, and, as the practice of adopting party platforms developed, the people's delegates drafted them.

UNFAIR AND CORRUPT METHODS OF CHOOSING DELEGATES. But the convention hierarchy soon showed decided defects from the ground up. Frequently, the local caucus that selected the first set of delegates was composed only of very small-sized politicians and the "toughs" and "bums" of

25 Quoted in Brooks, *op. cit.,* p. 254.

the community. It often met in saloons, or over livery stables, or in other places likely to discourage the attendance of the best citizens. It might meet in a room too small to hold all the voters who might try to attend; but the "gang," having been previously notified, would be there early and occupy all available space. Or the local machine might hold a "snap caucus"; that is, meet in advance of the time set, perhaps display enough conscience to turn up the clock, and complete the work at hand before the arrival of the independent voters of the community.

If the delegates to the conventions were chosen by the indirect [26] primary ballot, which became a rather common practice, the results were hardly any better. The party would keep its polls open for a few hours, and frequently ballots would be cast only by "straight organization men" and their followers. The ballot box might be stuffed; independent voters might be forcibly prevented from casting a ballot, or they might not be able to find the polling place; or fraudulent returns might be made—to mention only a few of the methods by which the professionals controlled the old indirect primaries. Of course, not all the local caucuses and indirect primaries were run by professional politicians, tricksters, and "plug-uglies," but altogether too many of them were, especially in the cities.

UNFAIRNESS AND CORRUPTION IN THE CONVENTIONS. If the very foundation of the convention system—the caucus and the indirect primary—was grossly defective, it is not surprising that the convention itself failed to attain a high level. After the delegates were chosen, various politicians attempted to secure their support in the conventions by persuasion, entreaty, threats, promises of places on the public pay roll, and actual bribery. Frequently two different factions of the party sent rival delegations to a convention, where, with scant regard for the merits of the claims of the contesting delegations, the professional group that controlled the convention would seat the claimants who seemed most useful to that group. Sometimes individuals who had no notion of attending a convention would have themselves selected as delegates for the sole purpose of selling their credentials to the highest bidder. Conventions were usually run by masters of the art of politics—men who were wise to all the weaknesses of their fellow men and who were often unscrupulous enough to turn that wisdom to their own advantage.

There was money to be made in politics by men who possessed sharp wits and dull consciences. The ever-increasing number of public offices afforded positions for party men who paid a part of their salaries into the organization treasury. More important sources of revenue for the party organizations and for the enrichment of party leaders and bosses were

---

[26] The indirect primary must be carefully distinguished from the later direct primary, a system by which voters actually nominate candidates for office.

found in the unholy alliance between business and politics. Graft in the letting of public contracts, especially in cities, in the granting of franchises for public utilities, and in affording "protection" to vice and crime ran into millions. Said Big John Kennedy, "It's a pretty good game at that, is politics, and it can be brought to pay like a bank."[27] No wonder greedy professionals made every effort to control conventions. The loss of such control would mean a pass in dividends on the "good game."

True, there were some honest conventions, and a larger number showed some evidence of responsibility to the general public. But the system taken as a whole was bad. It was bad for the reasons given above and for the important additional reason that the rank and file of citizens were busy with their private affairs and did not heed the exhortations of the clergy, the entreaties of the press, or the calls of the reformers to come out and do their duty.

III. PRIMARY ELECTIONS [28]

Following the Civil War the states made various attempts to limit abuses and corruption in the caucuses, primaries, and conventions; but gradually the idea spread that the solution of the problem lay in the direct primary, to be established by state constitutions and laws. The direct primary is a system by which the voters of a given party make their nominations directly in a party election, and it is to be distinguished from the old indirect primary in which the party voters elected delegates who then made the nominations at conventions. The direct primary is usually regulated in great detail by law; the indirect primary rested for the most part upon party rules.

Origin and development of the direct primary. The direct primary seems to have originated in Crawford County, Pennsylvania, a few years after the Civil War.[29] From there it spread to counties of the West and came into even more general use in the Southern states. After 1900 the movement for it was nation-wide; and it was championed by such men as the senior Robert M. La Follette, William Jennings Bryan, Theodore Roosevelt, and Woodrow Wilson. Today the direct primary has supplanted the convention system or seriously threatened it in nearly every state in the Union.[30] The states have widely different laws on the primary,

---

[27] Quoted in M. R. Werner, *Tammany Hall* (1928), p. xi.

[28] See references under note 23.

[29] There is proof of some use of it in the same county as early as 1842. Brooks, *op. cit.,* p. 261.

[30] Only in Connecticut is the convention still undisturbed. Rhode Island is the most recent "convert" (1948). See Richard S. Childs, "Rhode Island Tries Primary," *National Municipal Review,* March, 1949, p. 126. New York and a few other states still employ the convention for state-wide, but not for local, offices.

however, and our space permits no more than a brief discussion of its general principles.

"Designation." The process by which aspirants get their names on the official primary ballot is called "designation." In a number of states, declaration of candidacy, usually accompanied by a small fee, is all that is required. The other common method of designation is by petition. The number of signatures required varies from state to state and in accordance with the importance of the office sought; but the number required is frequently excessive, running into hundreds or even thousands. If those who seek the nomination are backed by the party organization or machine, which is often the case, they are put to no inconvenience or expense in the circulation of the petition; but an independent candidate is at the disadvantage of having to circulate the petition himself, or having friends or paid workers do it for him. When a petition has received the requisite number of signatures, it is turned over to an officer authorized by law to receive it and pass upon its legality. If, upon examination, usually a very perfunctory one, the petition is found to meet the requirements of the law, the aspirant is entitled to a place upon the primary ballot. It has been proposed that party committees be authorized to name a slate of candidates, thus obviating the necessity of petitions and primaries except where elements in the party are dissatisfied with the slate named, in which case the dissenting groups may propose other candidates by petition and run them against the committee candidates in the primary.

Positions on the ballot. In what order shall the names be placed on the ballots? One might think that an alphabetical list would take care of the matter very simply, but it does not. It has been found that those who stand at the top of the list have a much better chance of being nominated than the others. Consequently, a number of states have adopted a system of rotating the names. Assuming, for example, that Abel, Hanson, and Young are seeking the Republican nomination for governor, by this system the ballots will be so printed that each aspirant's name will appear first on one third of the ballots, second on another third, and last on the other third. In a few states the order of candidates on the ballot is determined by lot. That the position on the ballot should have anything to do with the prospects for nomination is, of course, an indication of the limitations of the direct primary.

Types of primaries: "OPEN" AND "CLOSED" PRIMARIES. Primaries are classified as "open" and "closed." Under the "open" system, which is used in only eleven or twelve states, the voter is handed the ballots of all the parties. He retires to a booth, takes the ballot of his own party, and marks the name of the person he favors as the party candidate for governor, mayor, sheriff, and so on through the list. He then folds the ballot and deposits it. The ballots of the other parties he drops in a box for "blanks." The open primary has the commendable feature of preserving the secrecy of the ballot; but it is open to objection on the ground that it is possible for persons to vote in either party without any regard to their party affiliation, and they have often done so.

The "closed" primary is used in the great majority of the states. By this plan the voter must declare his party allegiance. In a number of states a simple declaration is not sufficient—he may be required to take an oath that he has been affiliated or will be affiliated with the party. When the election officials are satisfied as to the voter's party affiliation, they give him the ballot of his party (but not the ballots of the other parties, as in the open system) and he retires to a booth and marks the names of persons he prefers as candidates for the various offices. One must not assume, however, that the closed primary is air-tight. On the contrary, we are informed that, even where the test of party affiliation is strict, it is usually possible for the determined or unscrupulous voter to step out of his own party and participate in the nominations of another.

THE "BLANKET" PRIMARY. A new form of ballot, the "blanket" primary ballot, is used in the state of Washington. All the candidates for nomination appear on the same ballot, the candidates being grouped under the title of the office to which they aspire, each candidate having his party affiliation opposite his name. Every primary voter is given this blanket ballot. He may confine his selections to one party, or he may vote for a Republican aspirant for the position of United States senator and for a Democratic aspirant for the post of governor and otherwise show his discrimination as a voter. The high man of each party for each office then appears on the ballot at the general election in November. Obviously, the blanket primary ballot makes for the greatest independence in voting in primary elections. For this reason it is very popular with the voters, and for the same reason it is very much disliked and feared by the old party "wheelhorses" and all good "organization" men.[31]

Vote required for nomination in partisan primaries. Nominations are commonly made by plurality (the greatest number) vote. If there are just two persons seeking nomination for an office, one will, of course, receive a majority. If there are three on the list, then we may find some such result as 35 per cent for A, 34 for B, and 31 for C. Under the plurality rule, applied in many states, the nomination would go to A, although it is clear that he is not the choice of a majority of the voters of his party. In order to prevent plurality nominations, several devices have been employed;

[31] Daniel M. Ogden, Jr., "The Blanket Primary and Party Responsibility in Washington," *Pacific Northwest Quarterly*, XXXIX, 33 (January, 1948); C. O. Johnson, "Washington Blanket Primary," *Pacific Northwest Quarterly*, XXXIII, 27 (January, 1942).

but the only one used extensively is the double primary, employed by some six Southern states. By this system a first, or "free-for-all," primary is held. Aspirants who receive a majority of the votes are nominated in this first primary. But in respect to those offices for which no aspirants receive a majority, a second, or "run-off," primary is held to choose between the two who stood highest in the "free-for-all." This double system is troublesome and expensive; but, since the Democratic nomination is tantamount to election in these states, they naturally prefer conclusive primaries.[32]

THE NONPARTISAN PRIMARY. Many judicial and local officers are elected, in theory at least, on a nonpartisan basis. They are therefore nominated in the primaries on a nonpartisan ballot. On this ballot all the aspirants for nonpartisan offices are listed in groups, according to the office sought. All the voters, without any regard to political affiliation, are given the same ballot. For each nonpartisan office to be filled, the voter marks the name of his choice. When the ballots are counted, the two leading aspirants for any particular office are declared nominated for that office, and they will then appear as candidates on the nonpartisan ballot at the regular election that follows. It may be unnecessary to state that the nonpartisan primary does not prevent partisans from appearing on the ballot. It is only the partisan designation that is abolished.

Comments upon the direct primary: CRITICISMS. Many of the earlier advocates of the direct primary saw in it a method by which the people would in periodic expressions of civic righteousness nominate the most capable and honest men for office, while its opponents alleged that the candidates so nominated would be much inferior to those named by the conventions. After fifty years authorities still disagree concerning the relative merits of candidates chosen by conventions and direct primaries, a disagreement that seems to warrant the conclusion that the types of candidates selected under one nominating system are about the same as those selected by the other.

In the second place the direct primary is criticized because of the added expense it entails. The government must pay the cost of the primary elec-

[32] Georgia provides for nominations by a county unit vote system, a plan under which the candidate who gets the highest popular vote in a county is awarded from 2 to 6 nominating votes, the number depending roughly upon the population of the county. The plan is weighted heavily in favor of the rural county, for no matter how small the population, it has two votes, and the largest urban county gets only six votes. Thus it happened that Eugene Talmadge, whose strength was primarily in rural communities, won the nomination for governor in 1946, although one of his opponents, James V. Carmichael, was well ahead of Talmadge in the popular vote column. But in the gubernatorial race of 1948 Herman (son of Eugene, who had died in office) Talmadge won in both popular and county unit votes over Melvin Thompson. The score was about 7 to 6 in the popular vote and 3 to 1 in the county unit vote. In 1950 the results were about the same.

tion, and the candidates and their backers must pay the cost of the primary campaign. Those who advance this criticism not infrequently assert that the high cost of campaigns gives rich candidates an advantage over the poor candidates, but many poor men have been nominated in the primaries and it is common knowledge that large expenditures either by an aspirant or by others on his behalf have often failed in their purpose. We can derive considerable encouragement from the fact that a candidate with only money to offer may lose to an opponent who has ideas and plans.

Third, other critics of the direct primary assert that it breaks down party responsibility. Such critics say that under the convention system the party leaders are responsible for the nominations made, and that under the direct primary system everybody, and hence nobody, is responsible. It is true that leaders and bosses were responsible in a sense under the convention system, but the voters found no satisfactory means of enforcing this responsibility. With our direct primaries, the leaders and bosses are still functioning; but they are subject to a much closer check by the voters than they were in the heyday of conventions.

A fourth charge against the direct primary is that, unlike the convention, it furnishes no means by which very desirable compromises may be reached between factions in the party. But the party leaders frequently hold consultations before the primary and propose candidates for the various offices, and this "organization slate" is often ratified by the voters in the primary.[33]

When all the arguments against the direct primary have been heard, it is apparent that the principal one is that there is no official way in which party responsibility for the candidates may be maintained. The central problem of the direct primary then becomes that of devising a scheme whereby the party organization and the voters will each have an appropriate and effective part in making nominations. Any plan that achieves these ends must give the party organization a right to pass on the candidates and must at the same time leave the final decision respecting nominations to the voters. Such a plan has been suggested.

A PROPOSED PRIMARY SYSTEM. The National Municipal League's Committee on the Direct Primary (Professor Joseph P. Harris, Chairman) has devised a new primary system that a number of students of government look upon with favor. The essential features of the proposed plan [34] are as follows:

1. Pre-primary conferences, under direction of the party organization, should recommend candidates to the voters, such candidates to be designated on the ballot as having the endorsement of the party leaders. The

[33] Merriam and Gosnell, *op. cit.,* pp. 307–308.
[34] *Model Direct Primary* . . . , National Municipal League (1951).

plan would also permit nominations by petition, thus avoiding the restoration of an irresponsible party oligarchy. Pre-primary recommendations by the party organizations were long ago proposed by Charles Evans Hughes, when he was Governor of New York. Such a plan has been in use in Colorado since 1912, and it was recently adopted by Nebraska, Rhode Island, and Utah.

2. Individual candidates should be permitted to file for nomination in only one political party.

3. The direct primary system should be required of all parties that polled as much as 10 per cent of the vote at the preceding general election.

4. The states could use the "closed," "open," or "blanket ballot," as they might see fit. (The writer joins Professor Harris in favoring the wide-open "blanket" system.)

5. The Committee listed as essential in its recommendations the principle of the short ballot, declaring that all offices except those responsible for the major policies of government should be filled by appointment.

As there is no doubt that the direct primary is with us to stay, it is most appropriate that our efforts should be directed at its improvement. The plan briefly outlined above contains well-considered suggestions and might be studied with profit by both friends and foes of the direct primary.

Party platforms under the direct primary. How are party platforms made under the direct primary system? Clearly, the whole body of voters cannot make them. Consequently, the work must be done by conventions or by party councils. If the convention meets before the primary is held, there is no assurance that the platform drafted will conform to the views of the candidates nominated; but if the convention meets after the primary, the platform will very properly reflect the views of the nominees who have just been named by the voters. In a number of states the platform is framed by a party council after the primary has been held. This council is ordinarily composed of the candidates for important offices and a few others, such as members of the party who hold high public office or high party office. This method of framing a platform has decided merit, in that the framers are those who are directly responsible for carrying it into execution. A plan of equal merit perhaps is one under which a pre-primary party council would draft the platform at the same time it designates the organization candidates for the primary election.

Reading List

L. H. Bean, *How to Predict Elections* (1948).
Behind the Scenes in Politics (1924).
Hugh A. Bone, *American Politics and the Party System* (1949).

D. W. Brogan, *Government of the People* (1935), Pts. 9 and 10.

R. C. Brooks, *Political Parties and Electoral Problems* (1933 ed.), Chs. X–XIII, XV–XVI.

H. R. Bruce, *American Parties and Politics* (1936 ed.), Chs. XI–XV, XVII.

W. J. Bryan, *A Tale of Two Conventions* (1912).

J. Bryce, *The American Commonwealth* (1913 ed.), Vol. I, Ch. I; Vol. II, Chs. LXIX–LXXII.

The Democratic Campaign Textbook.

C. A. M. Ewing, *Presidential Elections* (1940).

James A. Farley, *Behind the Ballots* (1938).

E. J. Flynn, *You're the Boss* (1947).

Joseph Gaer, *The First Round* (1944).

The Gallup Political Almanac for 1948.

George Gallup, *A Guide to Public Opinion Polls* (1948 ed.).

Gillette Committee (report on campaign finance), *Senate Report No. 47* (77th Cong., 1st Sess., Feb. 15, 1941).

Hearings, Select Committee on Senatorial Campaign Expenditures, U.S. Senate, 72nd Congress, 1930–31 (Nye Committee).

P. Herring, *The Politics of Democracy* (1940).

S. M. Josephson, *The President Makers* (1940).

V. O. Key, Jr., *Politics, Parties, and Pressure Groups* (1947), Chs. 13–19.

———, *Southern Politics in State and Nation* (1949).

F. R. Kent, *The Great Game of Politics* (1923).

P. F. Lazarsfeld, B. Berelson, and H. Gaudet, *The Peoples' Choice: How the Voter Makes Up His Mind in a Presidential Campaign* (1948).

P. R. Levin, *Seven by Chance: The Accidental Presidents* (1948).

J. M. Mathews and C. A. Berdahl, *Documents and Readings in American Government* (1940 ed.), Ch. VIII.

W. F. McCombs, *Making Woodrow Wilson President* (1921).

D. D. McKean, *Party and Pressure Politics* (1949), Chs. 8, 10, 15.

C. E. Merriam and H. F. Gosnell, *The American Party System* (1949 ed.), Chs. XV–XX.

C. E. Merriam and Louise Overacker, *Primary Elections* (1928).

Model Direct Primary Election System Report of the Committee on Direct Primary, National Municipal League (1951).

R. Moley, *After Seven Years* (1939).

Warren Moscow, *Politics in the Empire State* (1948).

P. H. Odegard and E. A. Helms, *American Politics* (1947 ed.), Chs. XVI–XXI.

L. Overacker, *Money in Elections* (1932).

———, *Presidential Campaign Funds* (1946).

R. V. Peel and T. C. Donnelly, *The 1928 Campaign* (1931); and *The 1932 Campaign* (1935).

J. K. Pollock, *Party Campaign Funds* (1926).

Proceedings of the Democratic National Convention.

Proceedings of the Republican National Convention.

The Republican Campaign Textbook.

E. M. Sait, *American Parties and Elections* (H. R. Penniman's ed.—1948), Chs. XX–XXVII.

George Seldes, *One Thousand Americans* (1948).

Irving Stone, *They Also Ran* (1943).

"Toward a More Responsible Two-Party System," Report of the Committee on Political Parties, American Political Science Association, *Am. Pol. Sci. Rev.,* XLIV (1950), No. 3, Pt. 2.

Questions and Problems

1. Does the caucus method of making nominations offer any suggestions for a better present-day nominating system?
2. Devise a scheme for making nominations for the presidency that would be essentially democratic without at the same time destroying party responsibility.
3. Discuss party convention procedure in relation to American life in general.
4. Make a list, giving reasons in each case, of great Americans who, in your opinion, should have been nominated for President and were not.
5. Have the qualities of presidential availability changed since 1890?
6. Assess the gains and losses resulting from the overthrow of the legislative caucus system of making nominations.
7. Is any type of nominating caucus now in operation in your state?
8. Discuss the theory and practice of the delegate convention as a nominating body. To what extent is it still used?
9. Consider these propositions respecting the direct primary: It (a) destroys party responsibility (b) enables anyone to become a candidate for office (c) makes it easier for the rich to win a nomination (d) results in the nomination of mediocre men (e) stops boss control of politics (f) makes the people politically intelligent and alert (g) prevents the drafting of satisfactory party platforms.
10. Evaluate the "Model Direct Primary Election System" as proposed by the National Municipal League.

☆ 10 ☆

Campaigns and Elections

IN THE preceding chapter we learned something of the nominating process. Our present task is to trace the course of campaigns and elections. The tactics employed in the battle for national, state, or local offices are essentially the same; and campaigns for the presidency, Congress, and many state and local offices are going on at the same time. We shall take up the campaigns in the order named, and then examine the voting process and consider the problem of money in elections.

I. THE PRESIDENTIAL CAMPAIGN [1]

Campaign workers: THE CAMPAIGN MANAGER. The chairman of the national committee is the campaign manager, a position that calls for the best talent the party can command. It requires a man of wide experience in large affairs, who is at the same time something of a diplomat. He must be a man in whom the business world has confidence, for the money and influence of this class are essential to the success of the party ticket. He must be an organizer on a big scale. He must know how to deal with men; be conciliatory and tactful, yet able to command. He must be cool under any circumstances; for the instant the general loses control of himself, his army is demoralized and goes down to defeat. Sometimes the candidate does a great deal of his own managing, as instanced by the two Roosevelts and perhaps Truman, but the more common practice is for the appointed manager to be the generalissimo.

[1] H. A. Bone, *American Politics and the Party System* (1949), Ch. 21; R. C. Brooks, *Political Parties and Electoral Problems* (1933 ed.), Ch. XII; H. R. Bruce, *American Parties and Politics* (1936 ed.), Ch. XIV; James A. Farley, *Behind the Ballots* (1938), Ch. III; P. Herring, *The Politics of Democracy* (1940), Chs. XVIII–XXI; V. O. Key, Jr., *Politics, Parties, and Pressure Groups* (1947), Ch. 14; Merriam and Gosnell, *The American Party System* (1949 ed.), Ch. XVI; Odegard and Helms, *American Politics* (1947), Chs. XX–XXI; R. V. Peel and T. C. Donnelly, *The 1928 Campaign* (1931) and *The 1932 Campaign* (1935); E. M. Sait, *American Parties and Elections* (H. R. Penniman's ed.—1948), Ch. XXII.

OTHER PARTY WORKERS. The commander-in-chief will be assisted, of course, by the officers of the party, from those of general staff rank down to the workers in the precincts. Thousands of officeholders will be of service, and tens of thousands of interested citizens can be counted upon for help. A party may have leaders of the highest quality, men of character and brains, but if they are unable to win the enthusiastic support of a very large number of the rank and file, defeat is inevitable. In general, that party wins that has the best workers.

The individual who takes only a casual view of politics sees in the papers that this or that candidate addressed so many thousands of people in an auditorium, may occasionally be one of the millions who hears a candidate over the radio, and he may from time to time smile at an effective political cartoon. He knows campaigns only as they are conducted through newspapers and over the radio. We do not mean to discount these spectacular and significant campaign techniques. But a campaign involves much more. A great deal of quiet personal work must be done. The best political brains of the party are applied to the task of winning the support of leaders of various groups. There is a chance for drama in addressing a great audience, and some speakers are exhilarated when they are greeted with applause that resembles the "roar of mighty breakers on a rock-bound coast"; but a quiet conference with an individual who has influence may secure more votes for the party than a dozen of its orators can garner. In 1916 several Democratic leaders, somewhat to the surprise of the Republicans, it seems, were able to reach the influential German-Americans and secure through them a big German vote for Wilson. Personal work with the individual voter is conducted officially by the smaller fry of party workers, such as precinct captains and lieutenants. Humble voters, in numbers running into the millions, do a certain amount of personal solicitation. This unofficial work of the ordinary voter is important in the campaign, for there are few voters indeed who do not have some influence with others.

AUXILIARY ORGANIZATIONS. In practically every campaign each party has on its list of supporters political organizations of a more or less temporary character and of varying degrees of effectiveness. Some of the organizations exist only on paper, a few big names having permitted the party to use them for publicity purposes. Other groups may be primarily social—tea-drinkers, whose only contributions to the campaign may lie in their naive hatred of the opposition candidate and their devotion to their own—who will win and save the country. Other organizations may raise some money, and still others may not only pass the hat successfully but also prove their worth by stimulating interest and winning votes. Two of the latter type are worthy of comment.

The National Citizens Political Action Committee. In 1944 the personal work of thousands of PAC (for practical purposes, an arm of the CIO) enthusiasts gave Franklin D. Roosevelt a mighty boost in the ranks of labor and in urban areas. Indeed, it is said that PAC was more effective in some cities than the organization of either major political party. The headquarters and staff of PAC were composed of men and women of education, intelligence, political sagacity, and hard common sense. The pamphlets they prepared for personal workers on door-bell ringing, registration, political conversation, and scores of related topics are models of simplicity, brevity, and humor. The PAC was so effective that some "good people" were shocked, conservative congressmen wanted an investigation, and political opponents with a practical turn of mind gave careful study to the question of adopting PAC methods.[2] The organization was less effective in the congressional campaign of 1946, but two years later it was in its stride again for Truman and congressional candidates favorable to labor. In 1948 the AF of L also had an organization, the Labor League for Political Education, working for Truman and its other friends.

The Americans for Democratic Action. According to its declared policy the ADA (organized in 1947) is a "non-Communist progressive political organization" and is "neither a political party nor a part of any political party." In 1948, under the leadership of Leon Henderson, it gave its major support to Democratic candidates. As noted earlier, ADA leaders were in the front of the fight for the civil rights plank in the Democratic platform. In the campaign they did effective work of the "grass roots" variety. For example, in the State of Washington they were invaluable supporters of Truman and liberal candidates for Congress, not only in speeches and conferences but in prosaic work in hundreds of precincts and at the polls. In Illinois they did the same kind of work and had a large part of the credit for the election of 12 out of the 14 candidates they backed, including Senator Paul Douglas. The same sort of activity was in evidence in a number of states. Organizations of the type of the two mentioned here "know politics," and their effectiveness is out of all proportion to the length of their membership rolls.

The candidate's speech of acceptance. Formerly, the presidential nominee made his speech of acceptance when, a month or more after the convention adjourned, he was formally notified of his nomination. But Franklin D. Roosevelt went before the convention to give immediate ac-

---

[2] A pamphlet, "Help Yourself to Better Government," published by the United States Chamber of Commerce in the spring of 1945, very strongly resembles a PAC pamphlet in form and style. The *New York Times* of June 27, 1946, reported that a few representatives from the National Association of Manufacturers, Wall Street firms, and Republicans registered for the PAC short course on Political Action Techniques then being given in Washington, D.C.

ceptance, and Thomas E. Dewey and Harry S. Truman adopted the same procedure. In accepting the honor, the candidate takes occasion to give his views on the issues of the campaign. He usually gives his interpretation of the party platform, and he may even go so far as to modify certain parts of that platform.[3] As we stated in the preceding chapter, the views of the candidate are more important and attract much wider attention than platform declarations; for, if he is elected, his views are more likely to prevail than platform pledges.

The candidate's strategy: "THE STRATEGY OF SUPERIOR PLACE." The presidential candidate must be given first place in the campaign. He must be kept before the people at all cost. We are told that the failure of the Republicans to observe this principle in 1916 led to the defeat of Hughes. Hughes talked about Wilson; Taft and Roosevelt talked about Wilson; and when Wilson spoke he talked about Roosevelt, Taft, and *Wilson*. Everybody was talking about Wilson, and nobody was talking about Hughes. Wilson had the advantage of "the strategy of superior place." [4] In 1920 Cox, the Democratic candidate, was seriously handicapped because everybody was still talking about Wilson. In 1924 Davis could hardly get into the fight because the Republicans ignored him. In 1928 Smith was practically ignored by Hoover. The original plan of Republican strategy for 1932 seemed to call for very little effort from Hoover; but it was later found desirable to bring him to the front to answer Roosevelt, who had early adopted the "strategy of superior place." In later campaigns against Roosevelt the Republicans attempted the strategy of attacking Roosevelt and his subordinates. The Democrats would not be drawn into any discussion of subordinates. They paid little attention to the charges against Roosevelt, but emphasized his positive achievements, his gallant leadership.

THE "WHIRLWIND" CAMPAIGN. A number of candidates and their managers have made the mistake of thinking that the best way to appeal to the voters is for the nominee to tour the country relentlessly, make as many speeches as possible, and shake hands with as many as can get to him at hotels and railway stations. Although a speaking tour may undoubtedly be of decided advantage to a candidate, the authorities on such matters are in pretty general accord that it can be easily overdone. It is a great physical strain to spend so much time on a train, to change climate frequently, to make hundreds of speeches, and to shake hands with tens of thousands.

---

[3] Just before he was nominated (1936) Governor Landon wired the Republican convention his interpretation of the party planks on child labor, the currency, and the civil service, and just after he had been nominated (1928) Governor Smith wired the Democratic National Convention that he disapproved of the plank approving prohibition.

[4] Sait, *op. cit.,* p. 515, from *Behind the Scenes in Politics.*

The candidate has no time to prepare his speeches with care, nor are facilities available for giving them adequate publicity.

When conducting a campaign of this sort, the nominee is in great danger of losing his dignity, and his speeches are almost certain to deteriorate in quality. He and his backers may be greatly impressed by the throngs that greet them at every stopping place, and they may think that victory is assured. They forget, however, as Melville Stone said, that nine out of ten who gather to see and hear the candidate would be equally excited by the visit of a circus. Stone attributed Hughes's defeat in 1916 to his "touch-and-go" talking. Arriving at a small town, he would make a hasty speech, which would be inadequately reported, and, on its receipt by the great metropolitan newspapers in the rush hour, it would be so cut down that Hughes would hardly recognize his own speech when he read it in the papers the next morning.[5] In 1940 Willkie made too many extemporaneous speeches on his tours, and at times he may have been indiscreet.

THE "FRONT-PORCH" CAMPAIGN. In striking contrast to the "whirlwind" or "swing around the circle" type of campaign is the "front-porch" method of appeal. This method was employed most successfully by McKinley in 1896 while Bryan was "stumping" the country. Mark Hanna, McKinley's campaign manager, carefully arranged to have delegations representing various interests call on McKinley at Canton. The leader of a delegation would make a speech that the candidate had seen and approved some time in advance. McKinley was therefore able to make a carefully prepared reply. In this manner the Republican nominee outlined his position on the issues and reached the American public through the press in a way that Bryan could not possibly reach them with his itinerant plan of campaign. McKinley's method was followed to a considerable extent by Wilson in 1916, by Harding in 1920, and by Hoover in 1928. Smith made rather extensive tours in 1928, but he made speeches only at important points. Four years later Franklin D. Roosevelt followed the same general tactics; but President Hoover, despite his earlier declaration that he would do little campaigning, took a number of short trips, making speeches over a national hook-up at important points and rear-platform appeals at many of the smaller cities. He concluded his campaign with a dash to California. In 1936 and again in 1940, the candidates of both parties, despite their use of radio facilities, traveled widely and used many occasions for speeches. In 1944 only the Republican candidate traveled widely. Roosevelt limited himself to a few key cities. In 1948 both Truman and Dewey took to the road with zest.

Back in the 'twenties we felt rather certain that candidates would do

. [5] See Sait, *op. cit.,* p. 530.

better to stick to their front porches; now we are not so certain. A dynamic, aggressive candidate like Theodore Roosevelt may do well for himself on circuit, and so may one with a personality like Franklin D. Roosevelt, or one who, like Harry S. Truman, can mingle with the "folks," speaking their language without effort. There is no better or best method. There is only a better or best procedure for a particular candidate, and it is for him and his managers to decide how he can most effectively reach the voters.

Campaign speakers other than the candidate. It is highly desirable that a candidate be a good campaigner, but sometimes he is not. In any event, he cannot do all the speaking. He is assisted by thousands of others. Some of them can speak to the nation, and they are heard with almost as much interest as the candidate himself. Bryan was invaluable to Wilson. William Howard Taft and Theodore Roosevelt, especially the latter, almost eclipsed Hughes. In 1928 Hughes and Borah delivered smashing blows for Hoover. A number of speakers will have no particular influence in the country as a whole and they may be unknown outside of their districts, but they have political power in these districts and their services in the campaign are indispensable. Other speakers are very carefully selected and sent out to make the candidate a place with the religious, racial, national, and economic groups.

Publicity mediums: NEWSPAPERS. Intimation has already been made of the importance of newspaper publicity. Newspapers serve as one of the best means of making an appeal. Nearly all of them are connected with some party, and a number are owned by party leaders. The great journals are given information, often advance information, about practically everything that takes place in the theater of political operations. Smaller papers are given less; but the material is specially prepared for them, sometimes in the form of ready prints. This free newspaper publicity has been reinforced in recent years by paid advertising. Even the press that is hostile to a candidate in its editorial columns must nevertheless give him news publicity, publicity that is probably not offset in the voter's mind by unfavorable editorials. Certainly the second Roosevelt won "again and again and again" in the face of the opposition of three fourths of the press.

CAMPAIGN LITERATURE. Tens of millions of documents are sent out by each party in the course of the campaign. Among them we may find millions of copies of the candidate's acceptance speech, extracts from his other speeches, and articles or speeches by various other party workers. The party has an asset in the speeches made in Congress for political purposes. These are reprinted by the government in unlimited quantities at cost, and sent through the mail free under the frank of a congressman. The most complete publication of the party is the *Campaign Textbook*.

It contains a great deal of information about all parties: the biographies of candidates, acceptance speeches, platforms, party records on important issues, and other information. It is placed in the hands of journalists and party leaders. In the language of the late Professor E. M. Sait, it is for the teacher rather than the pupil.

SLOGANS AND BILLBOARDS. Slogans have frequently proved to be telling party propaganda. A good slogan is a declaration and a challenge, containing some elements of suggestion and appeal. It may strike the public fancy as a popular song. Running through the list at random we find "Tippecanoe and Tyler too," emphasizing the character of Whig candidates in 1840; "54 40 or fight," the militant cry of the Democrats for all of the Oregon territory in 1844; and "Do we want a change?" the complacent query of the Republicans in McKinley's campaign for re-election in 1900. On fences, billboards, and in any other convenient space that could be had, regardless of the price, the Democratic manager in 1916 pasted a large poster of a happy home in peace time and with it the slogan, "He [Wilson] has kept us out of war." It made a most effective appeal at a time when all the great nations except the United States were at war. Not all slogans are sure winners. The great Republican victory of 1920 probably owed very little to the poster, "Let's Have Done with Wiggle and Wobble," that cost the party $400,000. "Keep cool with Coolidge" and "Prosperity" sounded more convincing as Republican slogans in 1924 and 1928 respectively. "Happy Days Are Here Again" may have been effective, although it was only the expression of a hope.

THE RADIO. The radio is now an indispensable feature of political campaigns. Aristotle said that a state should be so small that all of its citizens could be brought within the sound of a speaker's voice. With the radio, the United States meets what was long regarded as the great philosopher's rather impractical suggestion. Not only does the radio bring the addresses of candidates and their leading spokesmen into every man's home but, much more important, it discourages the old time oratorical method of appeal. Those most skilled in the use of the radio enter our homes unobtrusively and have a brief chat with us. We cannot be certain, but there is a very general belief that the radio is now the most effective medium of appeal to voters, more effective even than the newspapers. The appropriation for radio is commonly the largest item in the party budget. It is quite probable that the radio voice and the radio manner of potential candidates will be important considerations in choosing future nominees for the presidency.

The campaign intensive in "doubtful" states. In "doubtful" states the party goes to the greatest trouble and expense to learn how the people expect to vote. If a state seems "safe" after a canvass has been made, or a public opinion poll so indicates, the leaders will keep sufficient forces there to hold it and send their reserves to other states that the canvass or poll has shown to be doubtful. It is in the states that are fairly evenly divided between the great parties that the battles are most furiously joined, the money is most lavishly spent, and bribery and corruption are most likely to be employed.

BLUNDERS MUST BE AVOIDED. Although the campaign in doubtful states is intensive, it is at the same time extremely cautious, for a pivotal state with its entire electoral vote may be won by a clever bit of strategy or lost by a small blunder. The classical instance of a campaign blunder occurred in New York in 1884, when a group of ministers held an enthusiastic meeting to give Blaine, the Republican candidate, their endorsement and a certificate of character. Their militant chairman characterized Democracy as the party of "rum, Romanism, and rebellion," and the impertinent alliteration was received by his fellow clergymen with approval. Blaine was dozing or asleep when the speech was made, or he undoubtedly would have rebuked militant and aged Doctor Burchard for his impolitic utterance. As it was, neither Blaine nor any other Republican leader seemed to realize its significance until it appeared in the newspapers. Roman Catholics were incensed. Cleveland carried New York by the extremely small plurality of 1,149 votes, and the 36 electoral votes of that state made him President. The Burchard indiscretion has been characterized as "the most important feat of its kind since the cackling of the geese saved Rome." [6]

In 1916 organized labor in California was offended because Hughes attended a banquet in San Francisco served by "scab" waiters, and some other Californians turned against Hughes for his failure, through no fault of his own, to meet Governor Hiram Johnson when the two were in the same hotel.[7] The California vote in November stood: Wilson, 466,289; Hughes, 462,516. The 13 electoral votes of that state gave Wilson his second term.

"The illusion of victory." All through the campaign, but more especially as it draws to a close, each party makes extravagant prophecies of its sure success, hoping to create the "illusion of victory." The party is going to carry states that regularly belong to it by unprecedented majorities; it is certain to achieve success in at least three fourths of the states commonly considered doubtful; in the remaining states it will make a memorable showing! Straw votes are taken in districts or among groups known

---

[6] A. Johnston, "Political Showmen," *Forum,* July, 1932. Of course it is easy to show that prohibition or other issues defeated Blaine in New York; but certainly the Burchard incident, all other factors being what they were, was decisive.

[7] F. M. Davenport, "Did Hughes Snub Johnson?" *Am. Pol. Sci. Rev.,* Apr., 1949, pp. 321–332.

to be safe, for the purpose of carrying the illusion to the hesitant or skeptical. Bets, the prevailing odds being reported in the press, are thought by political leaders not to be without effect upon the voters. Party leaders have a strong belief that thousands of electors will jump on the winner's band wagon, and the leaders therefore employ every device to present their candidate as the winner.

Political organizations have always made use of polls as a means of testing the strength of their candidates in particular areas and as indicators of the strategy that ought to be employed. Such polls are commonly the private property of the organizations. Beginning about 1916, the *Literary Digest* and other magazines and newspapers have been taking polls of the entire nation and giving the results to the public. Perhaps the best known and the most successful of these polls are those of George Gallup (American Institute of Public Opinion) and Elmo Roper (*Fortune*). By a scientific sampling of the electorate they have been able to estimate within two or three per cent (except in 1948) the sentiment the electors later expressed in the official vote. Party leaders watch these polls closely. Unquestionably the party headquarters use them in determining their strategy, and, if a poll is favorable to a particular party, uses it to create the illusion of victory. If, on the other hand, a poll shows a party in second place, the leaders will question its validity, perhaps denounce it, or even suggest that polls are a menace to free elections. There is no proof, however, that these polls have any effect upon the voters. That no such evidence has been found, that we may have exaggerated the band wagon tendency, is an encouraging sign of independent judgment on the part of voters.

What makes up the voter's mind. All these activities of parties during the election campaign, and many more that we have not mentioned, are directed at the voter. How, in the midst of all the confusion of conflicting claims and evidence, does he make up his mind?

THE REGULARS WERE BORN THAT WAY. The great majority of voters do not make up their minds for particular candidates and elections. They are Democrats or Republicans, and they support their party regardless of candidates and issues. We may go back one step further and say that the average voter was born a Democrat or a Republican; that he took his party affiliation from his parents or playmates when he was in primary or grammar school; and that he rationalized his political faith when he grew up. Said the late General Hugh S. Johnson: "My father was a Democrat, my grandfather was a Democrat and my great-grandfather was a Democrat. They were all pretty good active and leading Democrats. So I am a Democrat by inheritance [he put that first], conviction and belief." [8]

[8] Quoted in Merriam and Gosnell, *op. cit.*, p. 141.

Merriam and Gosnell estimate that 75 per cent of the voters belong to this "hereditary" group.[9] The Gallup poll (see next page) indicates a higher percentage. To be sure, such issues as slavery, "sound money," and Prohibition have caused some of the hereditary voters to change parties temporarily or even permanently. A candidate's position on "moral" questions, his religion or lack of it, may alienate a few of the up-to-now party regulars. The economic depression during the Hoover administration seemed to cause many Republicans to desert their party in 1932. But the ordinary run of issues and candidates leaves three fourths of the voters practically unshaken in their allegiance.

THE INDEPENDENTS MAY BE INFLUENCED BY ISSUES AND CANDIDATES. But what of the 20 or 25 per cent of the voters who must make up their minds concerning issues and candidates at each election? The personalities and records of the candidates win or repel many independent voters. Thus, in 1916 Wilson received a large vote from independents and from independents with Republican leanings, and in 1928 Hoover received the bulk of the independent and much of the independent-Democratic vote. Following that date, Roosevelt had the support of independents, including a number who once were fairly good Republicans. The record of the party is also a potent factor with the independent voter. The "Let well enough alone" and "Do we want a change?" slogans may often be used with effect on conservative independents by the party in power. Independent voters may be appealed to on such points as a candidate's position on social security, civil rights, foreign policy, labor, and his conservation program. Again, the independent may be influenced by his friends, especially by those who happen to be in politics, by his clubs, by straw votes, by what he reads in the papers, and by the "illusion of victory." Many independent voters can give no more logical reason for their choice than the rabid partisans. He "just feels somehow," and his head hasn't much to do with it. The writer once asked a lady why she was supporting a particular candidate. "Oh," said she, laying her hand over her heart, "something just tells me that he is the man." A young student independent, with Phi Beta Kappa grades, said he could not vote for a particular candidate because he had dark rings under his eyes.

1948 and how we got fooled. Truman did not have a chance against Dewey. He did not have a chance even if there were no revolts in the Democratic party. But there were two revolting factions with candidates in the field. Henry A. Wallace with his Progressives (and too much Communist support) was trying to carry on for Franklin D. Roosevelt. The States' Rights (Dixiecrat) Party was outraged at the civil rights pronouncement of the Democratic national convention and was therefore trying to

[9] Merriam and Gosnell, *op. cit.*, p. 141.

INDEPENDENT VOTERS (as of June 25, 1948) *

IN COMPARISON WITH EARLIER DATES

Year	Per Cent	Number
1940	20	10,000,000
1944	20	9,000,000
1948	29 **	16,800,000 ***

PER CENT OF INDEPENDENTS BY EDUCATION

College	39
High School	31
Grade or no school	23

PER CENT OF INDEPENDENTS BY OCCUPATION

Business and professional	34
White-collar	34
Manual workers	27
Farmers	17

PER CENT OF INDEPENDENTS BY AGE

21–29 years	39
30–49 years	29
50 years and over	21

PER CENT OF INDEPENDENTS BY GEOGRAPHICAL SECTION

New England and Middle Atlantic	30
East Central	35
West Central	22
South	19
Rocky Mountain and Pacific	29

* Gallup (American Institute of Public Opinion) Poll.
** But a poll conducted about the middle of October showed that only 19 per cent of the voters classified themselves as independent. *Public Opinion News Service*, release of Oct. 20, 1948.
*** Figures based on estimate of 58,000,000 voters. Only 48,684,000 actually voted in November, 1948.

HOW INDEPENDENTS VOTE ****

	Per cent	Number	Per cent	Number	Per cent	Number
	1940		1944		1948	
Democratic	61	6,000,000	62	5,500,000	No scientific measurement but probably about as in previous elections	
Republican	39	4,000,000	38	3,500,000		

**** *The Gallup Political Almanac for 1948*, p. 10.

take the South "out of the Union" again. Besides, Truman was no leader, said first one thing and then another, could not control Congress, and he was no campaigner. Wallace would get enough votes in the cities to prevent the Democrats from carrying key industrial states and the Dixiecrats would take the electoral vote of four or five Southern states. Truman was out—so we all thought. And even the scientific opinion polls agreed with us. But the polls and ourselves were fooled by the same things. We both overestimated the strength of Wallace. We both had too much truck with professional, business, and other middle-class people, and failed to talk enough to the sturdy yeomen. To be sure, the opinion polls were trying to guard against this error, but they have always had difficulty in getting an accurate picture of the voting inclinations of the submerged one fourth or one fifth.

WHEN VOTERS MADE UP THEIR MINDS
ON PRESIDENTIAL CANDIDATES, 1948 *

	Truman	Dewey	All voters **
Before campaign started	45%	64%	54%
Early in campaign	11	12	12
First half October	4	2	3
Second half October	13	5	9
Election Day	5	3	4
Indefinite	21	14	18

* Gallup Poll, published December 5, 1948.
** Includes people who voted for other candidates as well as for Truman and Dewey.

But Truman thought he could win. A few of his close associates thought so too—that is, after they had gone out in the country and dug into the grass roots. "Who is going to win this election?" they asked, "Oh, Dewey, I guess." "How are *you* going to vote?" "Why (a little sheepishly) I'm gonna vote for Truman, I think." So the "grass rooters" went back to Truman and told him that, if he would go out and see and talk to the people, he could win the election. The President needed no particular encouragement, and he went with a vengeance. And it came to pass that when the finals were run on November 8 the man on the Donkey with two fractures (the Wallaceites and the Dixiecrats) led the field.

The polls were not so far off—Gallup 5 per cent and Crossley 4.7 per cent —but a small error may put them on the wrong side in an election that is only relatively close. Furthermore, at least 13 per cent of the voters did not make up their minds until the campaign was over or nearly over (see the table above), and when they did they were for Truman by more than 2 to 1. The fall of 1948 was a bad season for the pollsters as well as for other dopesters and predicters, scientific or otherwise.

II. THE ELECTORAL SYSTEM

The electors. The Constitution does not give the people the right to elect the President and the Vice President. It prescribes that these officers shall be chosen by electors, the number from each state to be the same as that of its senators and representatives in Congress (the electors to be named as the legislature of each state shall see fit).

THEIR NUMBER. If a state is entitled to ten representatives, these, with its two senators, entitle it to twelve electors. The whole number of representatives is 435 and the number of senators is 96, making the total number of presidential electors 531. The Constitution stipulates that a candidate who receives a majority of the electoral vote (266 of the present number of electors) shall be President.

How chosen. During the first few years of the Republic the legislatures commonly chose the electors, but with the growth of democracy they passed the privilege of choosing them to the people. After 1832 South Carolina was the only state in which electors were still chosen by the legislatures; and since Civil War days no state has employed that system, except Colorado, which reverted to it temporarily in 1876. The fact that the legislatures have given the voters the privilege of choosing presidential electors for a century places the election of the President and the Vice President in their hands.

What happens is this: Each party in each state nominates a number of individuals for electors equal to the number of electors to which the state is entitled. These nominees are usually chosen by the party convention in the state, or by a party committee. Such nominees must not be members of Congress or holders of other positions under the national government, because the Constitution excludes these classes from electoral service. Usually, persons of dignity or useful partisans are picked for the honor. On the Tuesday following the first Monday in November (the date fixed by national law for the choice of electors) the voters go to the polls and cast their ballots for the electors, not for President and Vice President.

More than a century ago the people of the whole state commonly chose two electors, and an elector was chosen by the people of each congressional district. Since districts might choose electors from different parties, the system had the political disadvantage of dividing a state's electoral vote. In order to increase the power of the parties and the influence of the state in national politics, the general ticket system was adopted. By this method of choice, every voter in the state votes for all the electors to which the state is entitled. For example, if a state is entitled to twelve electors, a Democratic voter will vote for the twelve persons his party has nominated for electors. Although an individual may divide his vote among electoral candidates of two or more parties, it is obvious that he is extremely unlikely to do so.[10]

The election. The electoral candidates who receive the greatest number of popular votes in a state are elected. For example, if the Democratic electors receive 300,000 votes, the Republican 299,000, and the Socialist

[10] More than half the states have ceased going through the empty form of printing the electors' names on the ballot. In such states a vote for the presidential candidate is counted as a vote for the electors of the party.

100,000, the Democratic electoral candidates win, in spite of the fact that they have only a plurality, not a majority, of the popular votes. It usually happens, however, that some party gets a clear majority of the popular votes in a state. Now, if Democratic electors are chosen in one state, we know that those electors, being good party men, will cast their votes for the Democratic candidates for President and Vice President when the time comes for them to do so. If Republican electors are chosen in another state, we know that they will be loyal to the Republican candidates. Consequently, when we know what electors have been chosen in each of the forty-eight states (as we do Tuesday night or Wednesday morning), we know exactly how many electoral votes each candidate for President will have. If one of them will have as many as 266 electoral votes (a majority), he is our next President. On the first Monday after the second Wednesday in December the electors meet at the various state capitols and go through the formality of voting for President and Vice President. On January 6 of the year following the votes are formally counted at a joint session of the two Houses of Congress, and the president of the Senate announces the "state of the vote."

WHAT HAPPENS IF THE ELECTORAL COLLEGE DOES NOT ELECT. If no candidate for President receives a majority vote in the electoral college, the Constitution requires that the House of Representatives shall choose a President from the three highest on the electoral list. And, furthermore, the Constitution provides that in such cases each state delegation in the House shall have one vote; that members from two thirds of the states shall constitute a quorum; and that a candidate who receives the vote of a majority of all the states shall be President. If, when the election devolves upon the House of Representatives, that body should fail to choose a President before the 20th day of January (formerly before the 4th of March), the Vice President shall act as President. Two Presidents have been chosen by the House. The electoral college tied 73–73 on Jefferson and Burr in 1801, and the House then elected Jefferson. In 1824 the electoral vote stood: Jackson, 99; Adams, 84; Crawford, 41; and Clay, 37. The House, having the authority to choose any one of the three highest on the list, elected Adams. The Hayes-Tilden election dispute (1876–1877) did not throw the election into the House because the issue was not that of no candidate having a majority but rather which candidate had it. Conflicting returns had been sent in from several states, and Congress designated a commission to determine which returns (which set of electors) should be accepted. The commission having decided (by a strict party vote) the result stood Hayes 185, Tilden 184.

If no candidate for Vice President receives a majority of the electoral votes, the Senate, each senator having one vote, chooses the Vice President from the two candidates who stand highest on the electoral list. Two thirds of the Senate constitutes a quorum for this purpose, and a candidate who receives the votes of a majority of all the senators is elected. When a President is to be chosen in the House of Representatives and a Vice President in the Senate, it is possible for a deadlock to occur in both bodies, leaving the country without a President or Vice President at the date of inauguration. This untoward occurrence is extremely unlikely, of course. In any event, the Twentieth Amendment (1933) gives Congress the authority to provide for such contingencies.

MINORITY PRESIDENTS. Although the people choose the presidential electors, it does not necessarily follow that the candidate who goes to the White House is favored by a majority of the voters. It was shown above that a candidate receives all the electoral votes of a state if the electors of his party receive a majority or a plurality of the popular votes. Now suppose that one candidate's electors receive larger majorities or pluralities in states that have less than half the total electoral vote than another candidate's electors receive in states that have more than half the total electoral vote; it is clear that the latter candidate may win the presidency on fewer popular votes than his opponent received. This was the outcome in 1876, when Tilden received 250,000 more popular votes than Hayes, and Hayes became President by an electoral vote of 185 to 184. It happened again in 1888, when Harrison was elected by an electoral vote of 233 to 168, although Cleveland had received 95,000 more popular votes. If there are three or more strong candidates in the field, we are almost certain to get a "minority" President. In 1860 the popular vote stood: Lincoln, 1,866,352; Douglas, 1,375,157; Breckenridge, 845,763; and Bell, 589,581. But Lincoln, having the plurality in many states, received 180 of the 303 electoral votes. In the interesting and stimulating triparty campaign of 1912 Wilson, with about 42 per cent of the popular votes, had 435 electoral votes; Theodore Roosevelt, with 27 per cent of the popular votes, won 88 electoral votes; and Taft's score was 23 per cent of the popular votes and only 8 electoral votes.

Proposed changes in the election system. Dissatisfaction with the system under which we elect our Presidents is almost as old as the Office of President, and many proposals have been made for its improvement.[11] Because the electors have no function other than that of registering the will of the majority or the plurality of the voters, abolition of the electoral college has been suggested. Its abolishment would not change the part of

---

11 J. E. Kallenbach, "Recent Proposals to Reform the Electoral College System," *Am. Pol. Sci. Rev.*, XXX (1936), pp. 924–929; Ruth C. Silva, "The Lodge-Gossett Resolution: A Critical Analysis," *ibid.*, XLIV (1950), pp. 86–99; Lucius Wilmerding, Jr., "Reform of the Electoral System," *Political Science Quarterly*, LXIV (1949), pp. 1–21.

the states in choosing a President. Each state would retain electoral votes, as now, equal to its number of senators and representatives in Congress. The adoption of such a proposal would leave us about where we are. A more far-reaching suggestion is that we leave the choice of President to the direct vote of the people. This plan in its simplest form would mean that the candidate with the highest number of the nation's votes, without regard to state or other divisions of the country, would be President. Neither this plan nor any substantial modification of it has much chance of adoption, for it would increase the electoral weight of the populous states and decrease that of the less populous ones. Furthermore, it would place a premium on enlarging the voting list and getting out the vote—everywhere. To the extent that any state might not use its full potential of voters it would lose its voice in the election, a factor that would reduce the voice of Southern states to something approximating a hoarse whisper.

A recent proposal for change in the electoral system that has received wide attention is the Lodge-Gossett Resolution for a constitutional amendment. Under the terms of this resolution (1) the electoral college would be abolished, but each state would retain the number of electors called for under the present system; (2) each candidate for President would be given electoral votes and fractions thereof (down to one-thousandth vote) in each state in proportion to his popular vote in the state; (3) a candidate who receives a majority or plurality of the electoral votes, provided the plurality is 40 per cent of the total, would be elected President; and (4) if no candidate receives a plurality of 40 per cent, then the two Houses of Congress in joint session, the members voting individually, would choose the President from the two candidates having the highest number of electoral votes. The resolution provides that the Vice President would be chosen in the same manner.

Earlier comment on the Lodge-Gossett plan was generally favorable, and in March, 1950, the Senate by a vote of 64 to 27 registered its approval. As the resolution received more critical study and analysis, opposition developed, an opposition that in July, 1950, culminated in the defeat of the resolution in the House of Representatives.

The chief objection to the Lodge-Gossett plan seems to be in the advantage it gives the Democrats, an advantage so decided that it would be extremely difficult *ever* for the Republicans to elect a President. The Democrats would stand to gain because the electoral votes they would lose to the Republicans in the Solid South would be several times offset by the electoral votes they would win in populous Northern states that are normally Republican. More significant, the large electoral vote (mostly Democratic) of the South rests upon (and would probably continue to rest upon) a very restricted suffrage, with the result that under the Lodge-

DEFEAT FOR FOUR PRESIDENTS
IF LODGE ELECTORAL PLAN HAD BEEN USED *

	Result under existing method	Result under proposed method		Result under existing method	Result under proposed method
1876: Hayes	185	177.1	1912: Wilson	435	246.7
Tilden	184	188.1	Taft	8	113.9
Others	—	3.8	T. Roosevelt		
1880: Garfield	214	175.1	and others	88	170.4
Hancock	155	181.9	1916: Wilson	277	284.3
Others	—	12.0	Hughes	254	222.1
1888: Harrison	233	185.8	Others	—	24.6
Cleveland	168	202.9	1928: Hoover	444	291.9
Others	—	12.3	Smith	87	231.6
1896: McKinley	271	215.3	Others	—	7.5
Bryan	176	221.3	1936: F. Roosevelt	523	340.3
Others	—	10.4	Landon	8	175.6
1900: McKinley	292	217.3	Others	—	15.1
Bryan	155	217.2	1948: Truman	303	257.8
Others	—	12.5	Dewey	189	221.4
			Others	39	51.8

* Reprinted from *U.S. News and World Report* (Feb. 17, 1950, p. 19), an independent weekly magazine on national and international affairs, published at Washington. Copyright, 1950, United States News Publishing Corporation.

DIFFERENCE BETWEEN PER CENT ELECTORAL VOTE UNDER THE LODGE FORMULA AND PER CENT POPULAR VOTE

	Democratic Party			Republican Party		
Year	Per cent of electoral vote under Lodge plan	Per cent of popular vote	Deviation	Per cent of electoral vote under Lodge plan	Per cent of popular vote	Deviation
1880	49.295	48.225	+1.070	47.453	48.308	—0.855
1884	50.000	48.842	+1.158	47.307	48.215	—0.908
1888	50.599	48.658	+1.941	46.334	47.817	—1.483
1892	45.653	46.119	—0.466	41.937	43.100	—1.163
1896	49.508	46.824	+2.684	48.166	50.934	—2.768
1900	48.591	45.530	+3.061	48.613	51.699	—3.086
1904	37.605	37.597	+0.008	56.408	56.412	—0.004
1908	46.977	43.051	+3.926	47.785	51.581	—3.796
1912	46.460	41.821	+4.639	21.450	23.178	—1.728
1916	53.540	49.265	+4.275	41.827	46.058	—4.231
1920	40.038	34.666	+5.372	56.478	61.237	—4.759
1924	36.045	28.828	+7.217	48.738	54.054	—5.316
1928	43.616	40.793	+2.823	54.972	58.110	—3.138
1932	61.695	57.411	+4.284	35.706	39.651	—3.945
1936	64.087	60.194	+3.893	33.070	36.539	—3.469
1940	58.380	53.847	+4.533	40.414	44.770	—4.356
1944	55.499	51.644	+3.855	42.147	45.869	—3.722
1948	49.190	49.363	—0.173	41.902	44.988	—3.086

Reprinted from Ruth C. Silva's, "The Lodge-Gossett Resolution: A Critical Analysis," *Am. Pol. Sci. Rev.*, March, 1950, p. 93.

Gossett plan, the Democratic electoral vote for the entire country would be high in proportion to its popular vote and the Republican popular vote would be high in proportion to its electoral vote (see accompanying chart and table). It thus appears that the suggested constitutional amendment, while calling for electoral votes in each state for each candidate in proportion to his popular votes and making no substantial provision for a broader popular participation in elections, in effect, offers the Democratic party a sort of electoral bonus.

"More than the fate of the Republican Party is involved," writes Professor Ruth C. Silva.[12] "The operation of a democratic party system, in contrast to a Democratic Party system, depends upon the existence of an opposition which has a reasonable chance of winning control of the executive. To make it virtually impossible for the Republicans to win the Presidency even when they poll substantial [popular] pluralities or even majorities is to render the Republican Party ineffective as a counterpoise."

III. CONGRESSIONAL CAMPAIGNS

One third of our senators and all of our representatives are elected biennially, on the Tuesday following the first Monday in November of the even years. Quadrennially, therefore, they must be elected at the same time the people choose the President—the presidential electors, to be more exact.

Organizations supporting candidates. Candidates for Congress are for the most part strong party men, and in consequence they receive the support of the state and national party organizations. Each party has a senatorial and a congressional committee, which help plan the campaigns and furnish speakers and "literature." These committees work in co-operation with state committees, and in very close co-operation with the national committee, for from the latter their main financial support is derived.

Influence of presidential campaigns. In "presidential years" the White House is the chief objective, and all other party activity must be in co-operation with and, to some extent, subordinate to the campaign to elect the President. In these years the fortunes of the candidates for Congress are largely tied up with the fortunes of the presidential candidates, although candidates for the House of Representatives in districts in which their party is very strong and candidates for the Senate in states in which the same situation prevails will be elected in any case. The voter will ordinarily vote a "straight ticket," which means that a "landslide" for a party's candidate for President will bring a number of men to Congress who

[12] *Op. cit.*, p. 99.

would not be sent there otherwise. There are exceptions to this rule, of course, as instanced by the fact that, in 1928, several states that gave majorities to the Hoover electors chose Democrats for seats in the United States Senate.

The congressional campaign in "off years." We can get a better picture of the congressional campaign in the off years—the election years that fall between the quadrennial struggles for the chief magistracy. The chief issue of the campaign is frequently the President's record. This emphasis was particularly noticeable in 1934 and 1938. In 1942 the issue was in part the President's conduct of the war, but perhaps more the political conduct of Congress during that war.

In 1946 (the first postwar election year) each party charged the other with the responsibility for the meat shortage, price rises, production slowdowns, and so on. The arguments were not convincing but the people wanted a change. They were tired of rationing. They wanted meat, and lots of it, fats and oils, sugar and syrup, soap, and the kind that makes the husband swoon in happiness every time he so much as looks at his wife's lovely hands. They wanted the abundant life. They wanted "firmament" as did "de Lawd" in *Green Pastures,* and not "jest a little bitty dab o' firmament, caize dey was tide of not havin' it when dey wanted it." They were irked in dozens of ways by war and postwar regulations, restrictions, controls, and shortages, and they wanted to swat the administration that, in their opinion, had unnecessarily imposed them. And so the Republicans won their first Congressional election since 1928. In the congressional election of 1950 the fight centered on such issues as the State Department's conduct of foreign policy, particularly in the Far East, the charge of communists in the government service, the Fair Deal's domestic program, and the influence of two groups, labor and corrupt city machines, in the Truman Administration. The Republicans made decided gains, but the Democrats retained control of both Houses of Congress by small majorities.

Often seats in Congress are won in states and districts on purely local issues, or personalities. Few candidates are so frank; however as W. J. Bulow, South Dakota's Democratic candidate for the Senate in 1930, who is reported to have said: "There ain't any great issues out here, I guess. Mac's [Republican Senator W. H. McMaster] got a job and I want it." [13]

Aid from general headquarters. Although the individual candidates must bear a large part of the responsibility for their election in off years, this does not mean that the national party organizations leave them to their fate. The various political leaders, committees, and experts will do their

[13] *Time,* Oct. 27, 1930, p. 16.

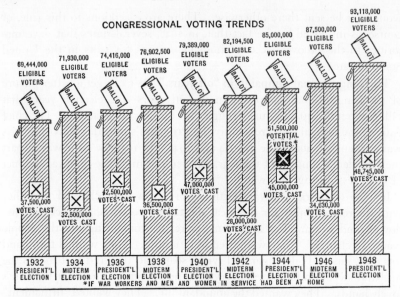

CONGRESSIONAL VOTING TRENDS

*IF WAR WORKERS AND MEN AND WOMEN IN SERVICE HAD BEEN AT HOME

Reprinted (except for votes of 1946, 1948) from *U.S. News & World Report* (Sept. 6, 1946), an independent weekly magazine on national and international affairs, published at Washington. Copyright, 1946, United States News Publishing Corporation. (An improvement is noted in the congressional election of 1950; some 41,000,000 voters participated.)

best to help party regulars all along the line. Some idea of the sort of thing that is done is furnished by *Time*'s breezy discussion of the 1930 campaign strategy.[14]

Party leaders in Washington supply the campaign words-and-music, which candidates repeat on the stump throughout the land. Chief Republican composer: James L. West, director of publicity. Chief Democratic composer: Charles Michelson, director of publicity. They write the statements that are issued under the names of party leaders. So sharp have been Composer Michelson's attacks on President Hoover that last week Chairman William Robert Wood of the Republican Congressional Campaign [Committee] cried out in hurt protest, charged the Democrats and Mr. Michelson with a "plot" to slander the President and undermine his influence. . . .

Pressagent Michelson dug through old issues of the *Congressional Record,* found where shortly after the [First] World War Mr. Wood himself had assailed Herbert Hoover, had called him an expatriate and "the most expensive luxury ever fastened on this country," had warned that he was "unfit for a responsible position of trust."

When Pressagent West brought out a fat statement listing all the party's 1928 pledges and how the G.O.P. had carried them out (except for an antilynching law), Pressagent Michelson, under the name of Congressman Cordell Hull, guyed him for omitting the party platform's preamble assuring the country of

[14] September 8, 1930, p. 14.

continued Prosperity, raised anew the deadly cry of "Hoover Panic," on which the Democrats this year have founded their campaign.[15]

In 1946 both party headquarters put out handbooks for their candidates. The Democratic handbook gave candidates source material for their speeches, 104 pages of it. The Republican volume was much thinner, but it contained many campaign phrases and catch-words. It was for "constitutional government," "individual rights," "private enterprise," and "Americanism." It was against "executive dictation," "regimentation and control," "socialistic economy," "Communism and subversive practices." Neither book contained anything original or inspiring or clever. No Charlie Michelson's hand can be seen in either of them. Let it be said to the credit of the candidates that they proceeded largely on their own; and if that was no better than what was in the book, it had at least the virtue of a trace of originality.

The President himself may take a part in the off-year campaign. He must not be too aggressive in his activity, for the voters seem to resent a President's appeal for a Congress to his liking; but he may assist individual candidates in various ways—by letters, by opportune visits to their districts, by patronage, and by other means. In 1950 President Truman made at least one major speech and Vice President Barkley a number in support of Democratic candidates, but there is no evidence that their efforts produced any results.

IV. STATE AND LOCAL CAMPAIGNS [16]

In the states the fight is on for governors, various other executive officers, legislators, and judges; in the counties, sheriffs, commissioners, surveyors, assessors, school superintendents, and coroners are among those to be elected; and in the cities, mayors, councilmen, and a number of other officers are to be chosen by the people. Not all of these officers are elected on the Tuesday after the first Monday in November in the even years, the date of the national elections; but many of them are elected at that time, and the candidates must necessarily compete for the voter's attention with candidates for national office in the unequal contest, a very unequal contest in presidential years.

Controlling factors in state and local campaigns. National issues are

[15] Charles Michelson "ghosted" for the Democratic party and individual Democrats for years. His reputation and his performance were so good that when a run-of-the-mill Democrat made a good speech, someone might remark, half in jest, half in earnest: "That was a fine speech Charlie wrote for Joe." At another time the remark might be: "That wasn't much of a speech Joe made; he ought to let Charlie write his speeches." Michelson has written an interesting book, *The Ghost Talks* (1944).

[16] Bone, *op. cit.*, Chs. 21–22; Key, *op. cit.*, 14; Merriam and Gosnell, *op. cit.*, pp. 390–392; Odegard and Helms, *op. cit.*, Chs. 17–18.

often controlling factors in state campaigns, and not infrequently in local campaigns. This unfortunate situation prevails because many state and local elections, with the exception of city elections, occur on the national election days, and national issues are usually the center of interest. The typical voter, obeying his own partisan impulses, or too much a victim of inertia to vote for candidates in different party columns, or hearkening unto the voice of party leaders to vote the ticket "straight," marks his cross in the big circle at the top of the party list, thus supporting his party for all offices from President to constable.

But at times the states and local communities have great concerns of their own; they will not subordinate their problems to the national issues. Personal or factional feuds, struggles of the public against the interests of railroads, power magnates, local public utilities, insurance companies, mining and manufacturing interests, labor unions, social security organizations, and various other groups, may temporarily or for a considerable period of time bring parties, factions, and voters to consider issues or problems in their states or counties or cities independently from those of the nation. As a result states sometimes, and cities frequently, elect the candidates of one party to national office and the candidates of another to their own offices. This division of the honors of office comes about not only for the reasons just given, but also because the ties of party do not bind the voter in state and local campaigns, particularly in the latter, as they do in national campaigns. Even in national elections a lapse of party regularity is now condoned or easily forgiven, a tolerance quite unknown thirty or forty years ago, when "scratching the ticket" in such elections was little short of treason.

Campaign methods. The methods of reaching the voter in state and local campaigns are, in general, about the same as those employed in the national contests. There are important shades of difference, however. Merriam and Gosnell tell us that personal squabbles, factional strife, class consciousness, sectional jealousies, race prejudice, and religious antipathies are found in more intense form in individual states than in the country as a whole, thus giving state campaigners more delicate problems of strategy than the national campaigners may meet. The local communities may be said to hold the same difficulties for the campaigner as the state.

Two general courses are open to the candidates: they may walk the tight rope, sidestep, wiggle, wobble, and "weasel" in the attempt to win votes from all groups or factions; or, they may pick out the classes that have the greatest number of votes, pose as the champions of their interests, and make capital of their declared hostility to, let us say, Wall Street, "bloated bondholders," "soulless corporations," and "haters of the old folks." The latter method is more likely to prove effective if the candidate is a practical psychologist. Candidates are, of course, backed by various party organizations, which help them with speakers, "literature," and money. In the local areas the candidates can do a great deal for themselves through personal contact with a large number of voters, sometimes all the voters in their district.

PETTINESS AND PERSONALITIES IN CAMPAIGNS. Sometimes state and local political contests are conducted on the somewhat dignified plane that usually characterizes the national campaigns. At other times militant gubernatorial or mayoralty candidates with burning issues and eager backers conduct "hammer-and-tongs" campaigns. Not infrequently our campaigns, other than national, degenerate to trivialities and personalities.

Here is a rather extreme example of the latter type. The fact that it comes from a Texas "run-off" primary does not impair its value as an illustration; for, there, success in the Democratic primary is equivalent to election. In 1930 Mrs. Miriam A. ("Ma") Ferguson, the state's chief executive during 1925–1927, and wealthy Ross A. Sterling were candidates for governor. Retiring Governor Dan Moody fired the heaviest projectiles against "Fergusonism" for Sterling, while Mrs. Ferguson's husband, removed (1917) from the executive mansion of the state by impeachment, championing the cause of the "common people," mixed the poison for the "millionaires." "Husband Ferguson drew enormous crowds, set them wild with denunciations of Messrs. Moody and Sterling. Newspapers were given libel law waivers by Candidate Sterling to print anything Stumpster Ferguson said against him, but Mrs. Ferguson would not grant the press the reciprocal privilege. Her husband, appealing to the 'common folks at the fork of the creek,' mocked and jibed at Candidate Sterling's handsome Bay Shore house, declared it had no less than 27 bathrooms." [17] Sterling, who was no public speaker and left the stumping to others, did feel called upon to explain just why he needed *eight* bathrooms in his home, and he expressed the hope that every citizen of Texas might have at least one bathroom. Sterling won this particular campaign, but two years later he lost to Mrs. Ferguson in a similar "run-off" contest.

V. THE VOTING PROCESS [18]

The health and strength of democracy depends in considerable measure upon the integrity of the ballot. With a large majority of the population

[17] *Time*, Sept. 1, 1930, p. 19. For a more recent example of the same sort of thing (Theodore Bilbo in Mississippi) see V. O. Key, Jr., *Southern Politics* (1949), pp. 241–243.

[18] Bone, *op. cit.*, pp. 658–679; Brooks, *op. cit.*, Ch. XV; Bruce, *op. cit.*, Ch. XVII; Key, *Political Parties*, ch. 17; Merriam and Gosnell *op. cit.*, Chs. XVII–XVIII; Sait, *op. cit.*, Ch. XXVII.

eligible to vote in nearly every section of the Union, the conduct of an election is an undertaking that calls for planning and organization, for officers and party watchers, for ballots and machines, for polling places (more than a hundred thousand of them), and above all for careful attention to details.

The polling place. The county or city is divided into precincts or districts, each of which contains several hundred voters. Each precinct has its polling place. Formerly, the prevailing practice was to rent private property for this purpose; but as this gave too much opportunity for graft and favoritism, the tendency now is decidedly in the direction of requiring the use of school buildings, police stations, or other public structures. Sometimes churches are used. A few states blessed with good climates make considerable use of tents.

Election officers. When the voter enters the polling place, he finds that several individuals, almost invariably one or two from each of the great parties, are serving as inspectors or judges of elections. These persons are responsible for the proper conduct of the election in the precinct. If they are corrupt, elections become frauds in spite of volumes of laws intended to keep them pure; for, as a learned judge once said, no statute has yet been drafted that will serve as a substitute for an honest man. The theory that dishonest inspectors of the two major parties will check each other and thus keep an election pure has some fatal defects in practice, and the soundness of the theory may well be questioned. Two dishonest men who happen to belong to different political parties are no more likely to give us an honest election than two wrongs are to make a right. These men may put personal gain above party advantage and sell out; or it may be to both their personal gain and party advantage to trade in election frauds.

A number of cases have been exposed in which party machines have reached agreements to "count out" third-party candidates. Some years ago in Chicago an election official, in imminent danger of being detected at this particular crime against the voters, actually ate twenty-eight ballots that had been cast for the "wrong" candidates. Sometimes the machines agree to trade votes, for example, presidential votes for gubernatorial votes. In such cases it may become the "duty" of the inspectors to make the exchange. It is encouraging to note that authorities are practically unanimous in the conclusion that such frauds are much less common now than they were a generation ago.

Watchers. In addition to the election officers the voter will find watchers at the polls. These individuals represent the different parties and candidates, and they have the right to see everything that is done by the election officials, in regard to both casting and counting the ballots. If they are honest, alert, familiar with the election laws, and know many of the voters, they can do a great deal to preserve the integrity of an election in their precinct.

Methods of voting: ORAL VOTING. A century and a quarter ago a number of states used the oral (*viva voce*) system of voting. The voter simply approached the county polling place, where the candidates for county and sometimes higher offices and frequently a considerable crowd had collected. Upon being recognized by the judges and being told by them to vote, he pronounced the names of his candidates, whose words of thanks were often drowned out by the applause and jeers of opposing partisans. This oral pronouncement was considered by many leading citizens to be the only manly way to vote, and it was still preserved in a few states until after the middle of the nineteenth century.

PAPER BALLOTS. The paper ballot, which was very generally substituted for oral voting a century or more ago, was no great improvement over the latter. The ballots were printed by the party, contained only the names of the candidates of the party, were distributed by the party's "ticket peddlers," and were cast in the open. The fact that a ballot contained only the names of the candidates of one party made it impossible for a voter to divide honors between parties, unless he "scratched" some names on his ticket and wrote in the names of other candidates. If he had the energy or independence or courage to do this, he was almost sure to be detected and rebuked or even slugged by party workers. The old type of ballot made machine control of elections very easy, because watchers could see how everybody voted and could therefore see that "the goods paid for were actually delivered."

THE AUSTRALIAN BALLOT. In 1888 a ballot long used in Australia, and therefore known as the "Australian ballot," was introduced in the United States. It is now used in some form by all the states except South Carolina. This ballot is printed and distributed at public expense; it bears the names of all candidates; it is given to each voter only at the polling place; it is marked by the voter in secret. The original Australian ballot did not designate the parties of the candidates. It simply listed each group of candidates under the office they sought.

Because of the multiplicity of offices, and in the interest of parties, we have modified the Australian plan. In Massachusetts and in some dozen other states the candidates for governor, Congress, and other offices are listed in separate groups; but the party of each candidate is printed after his name. According to the Massachusetts plan the voter must mark the name of the candidate of his choice for each office.

In the greater number of states the Australian ballot has been still further modified. Each party is given its own column on the ballot; and the voter, by simply putting his mark in the big circle at the top of his party column, votes for the candidates of his party for all the offices to be filled. If the voter wishes to "split" his ticket—that is, vote for candidates of another party for some of the offices, then he puts his cross in the circle of his favorite party and makes a cross opposite the name of each candidate he prefers who is in the column of another party. It is clear that the party column type of ballot makes it easier for one to vote the "straight" party ticket; that it tends somewhat to discourage independent voting; and that for these reasons it is favored by the politicians.

Nonpartisan ballots. It is generally recognized that partisanship is to be deplored in relation to judicial office and local offices. Consequently, in a number of states, candidates for such offices are now placed on the ballots in true Australian style; that is, without party designation. One would be foolish to say that this prevents all partisanship, but there is no doubt that it lessens the intensity of it and stimulates independent voting. In a few states candidates for public school superintendents are listed on a nonpartisan ballot, and in Minnesota and Nebraska candidates for the legislature are so listed.

Separate ballots. Nearly all states place the candidates for all offices on the same ballot. Several states, however, have separate ballots for different types of offices—national, state, county, and city. Thus, New York and Wisconsin use five ballots, Vermont seven; and it is said that at one time the voter had eleven different ballots in an Ohio election. Separate ballots may have some influence in the direction of independent voting, since they do in a physical sense separate candidates for the different types of offices. A number of states present initiated and referred measures to the voters on separate sheets, and thereby emphasize those questions as distinct from the election of officers.

Casting the ballot. We return now to our voter, whom we left at the polls while we were discussing ballots. When he has satisfied the election officials that he is duly qualified to vote, he is given the ballot or ballots and retires to the privacy of a booth to do the marking. An illiterate or physically incapacitated voter may have the assistance of election officials, and, in some states, the assistance of other voters, in marking his ballot. The marking being completed, the voter folds the ballot according to directions previously given and returns it to an inspector who, if he is satisfied that it is the same ballot that was given the voter, deposits it in the box.

VOTING MACHINES. In some states a mechanical device called a "voting machine" is used. It is a complicated mechanism, but like many other such mechanisms it is very easy to operate. The name of each candidate appears under a lever, and the voter indicates his choice by pulling the lever over the candidate's name. A number of states have the machines so constructed that an elector may vote the straight ticket by simply pulling down the lever of his party. As the machine is enclosed by curtains, the voter has absolute secrecy in indicating his choices. If he votes in secret, what prevents him from operating the machine several times? The answer is that the machine records only the last movement of the levers, and it will not record that until the voter opens the curtain to leave the booth. The machine adds the votes as the levers are pulled for the various candidates, parties, or measures. When the polls are closed, all that the officers have to do to learn the results of the election is to unlock the machine and read the totals. The chief advantages of the machines are: they can be operated more quickly than a paper ballot can be marked; they are accurate; they are so constructed that a voter cannot spoil his ballot; the absolute secrecy of the ballot is preserved; and they afford no opportunity for election officials to invalidate any votes as they can by mutilating or destroying paper ballots. The cost of installing machines is very high and, except in the larger precincts, this initial cost is not offset by savings on ballots and other reductions in election costs that the machine makes possible.

In spite of the obvious advantage of the voting machine over the paper ballot, it has been slow coming into general use. It is not available for any large percentage of voters, except in New York and eight or nine other states. The chief obstacles to its adoption are: its initial cost; the distrust of a mechanical device that does not show how each vote is cast; and the determined opposition of corruptionists, who find the voting machine much more rigid in resisting election trickery and fraud than the paper ballot.

Counting the votes. With the closing of the polls, the counting of votes begins. We have just observed that where a voting machine is used, the counting officers have nothing to do but unlock the machine and read the totals. Counting paper ballots is a tedious job, and it may occupy election officials, who have already been busy at the polls all day, through the better part of the night. Even honest election officials will grow weary and make mistakes. Party watchers who were annoyingly alert in the morning measurably relax their vigilance as the night advances. To lessen the strain on tired election officials, some twelve states have provided for special counting boards. These may begin their work a few hours after the polls open, and they will have the results totaled by midnight, or perhaps even earlier. The count as announced from the many precincts gives, unofficially, the results of an election. Several days later an official canvass is made by authorities, usually county officers, designated for that purpose. These canvassing boards send all the election figures that relate to the state or districts larger than the county to the state canvassing board.

Absentee voting. It always happens that many qualified voters are absent from their counties or states on election day. Nearly all of the states extend to certain classes of absentees the privilege of voting. A few states accord the privilege only to those absent in the military or naval service; a few other states allow any absentee the privilege; but the typical provision is that all those whose business or profession renders their absence necessary shall be entitled to the absent voter's ballot. About one fourth of the states allow those who are ill or physically disabled the privilege of absent voting. With respect to the distance a voter must be from his regular polling place in order to enjoy the privilege of an absent voter, the general rule is that he shall be outside his county but not beyond the boundaries of the United States.

Nine or ten states require the absentee to exercise his privilege on election day. The voter may go to any polling place in his state, make an affidavit, receive a ballot, and vote in the usual manner. The affidavit and the ballot are then forwarded to the election officers of the county in which the voter resides. The more common provision concerning the time and method of absent voting is that the absentee shall by affidavit apply to designated officers of the county in which he is a registered voter for the absent voter's ballot. The ballot is mailed to him, and he marks it. Upon receipt of the ballot, the absentee signs an affidavit and returns the marked ballot to the place of his registration, where it is counted with the other ballots on election day. The voters show scant appreciation of the legislatures' efforts, as very few of the tens of thousands who might avail themselves of the privilege of voting *in absentia* take the trouble to do so.[19]

THE ARMED SERVICE VOTE. Arrangements, usually inadequate, have been made for members of the armed forces to vote during all our major wars. In 1942 and 1944 the situation called for comprehensive plans, but the call went largely unanswered. The state laws were not practicable in this emergency, and the national government adopted only temporizing expedients. In 1942 Congress authorized members of the armed forces who were qualified (registration and poll-tax payments were expressly excepted as qualifications) to vote in their states, to vote in national elections. Servicemen had to request their state secretaries of state to send them a "war ballot." Only 28,051 members of the armed forces actually received and returned the ballots in accordance with the federal law and the laws of their states.

It was obvious that a more satisfactory arrangement should be made for 1944. But politics and constitutional questions (politics under the cover of the Constitution, one is tempted to say in this case) prevented the enactment of a comprehensive statute. Congressmen expressed the gravest con-

---

[19] Brooks, *op. cit.*, 452 ff.; Sait, *op. cit.*, 594 ff.; J. K. Pollock, *State Absentee Voting and Registration Laws, Sept., 1942* (Government Printing Office).

cern that the national government was having anything to do with the voting process, a matter heretofore left to the states, and many of them greatly feared that the soldiers and sailors would vote for Franklin D. Roosevelt, their Commander-in-Chief, as soldiers of the Civil War had voted in 1864 for Lincoln. The act that finally passed Congress gave state ballots the right of way over the ballot authorized by federal law, the latter ballot to be used only where the state ballots were not available. A number of states hastened to enact laws that would give the servicemen a reasonable opportunity to vote, and the result was a rather agreeable surprise. Approximately 2,800,000 members of the armed services voted.[20]

VI. THE VOTER'S BURDEN

The long ballot. In our country we have placed ever-increasing burdens upon the voter. He is expected to choose presidential electors, members of both Houses of Congress, several executive officers of his state, state legislators, judges in many states, and scores of county, city, and other local officers. Furthermore, we call upon the voter to nominate nearly all of these officers in the primary elections. But these electoral activities do not end his task. He must vote upon state constitutions and their amendments in practically every state. In about twenty states he must vote upon ordinary bills that have been "initiated" or "referred." He is sometimes asked to pass upon city charters and ordinances. Finally, in some states and local areas he may be summoned to the polls to vote in "recall" elections.

Formerly, a voter who did his best to exercise the privilege of the franchise in Chicago had to register twice, go to the polls five times, and weigh the merits of candidates for fifty offices within a year. The same type of voter in Colorado at a typical general election marked his ballot for candidates for thirty offices and voted on sixteen measures; and the faithful elector in Los Angeles performed the same operations for forty-five offices and fifty-eight measures.[21] The voter of San Francisco who did his full duty marked his ballot for some two score offices and thirty-nine measures, one of which was a proposed amendment to the city charter that would give a detective sergeant a right to a hearing before being transferred.[22] Of course these are rather extreme cases and there has been some shortening of the ballot in recent years, particularly in cities; but the average ballot is far too long, listing from twenty to thirty offices, the greater number of which would be much better filled by appointment than by election. In states that employ the initiative and the referendum, the ballots usually

[20] Boyd A. Martin, "The Service Vote in the Elections of 1944," *Am. Pol. Sci. Rev.*, XXXIX, 720 (August, 1945).

[21] Spencer Albright, "How Does Your Ballot Grow?" (Bulletin, Am. Legislators' Association, May 10, 1933); Sait, *op. cit.*, pp. 575–576.

[22] *New York Times*, Oct. 26, 1930.

contain some measures on which none but the most exceptional voters can express an intelligent opinion, and not infrequently they carry measures of such small consequence that they should be determined by minor public officials in the routine discharge of their duties.

Obviously, in view of the burden placed upon the voter by the long ballot, he cannot discharge his duties intelligently. He may be able to inform himself concerning the qualifications of the candidates for important offices, but even the most conscientious and intelligent voter is practically helpless in an attempt to make a wise choice of candidates for the dozens of minor offices. All the voter can do is to vote the straight party ticket and hope that the party organization which vouches for the candidates has played no trick upon him. We hear a great deal of talk about the sovereign voter; but certainly when he leaves the polls after having voted for forty or fifty candidates, four fifths of whom he knows nothing about, he must feel like a very insufficient and helpless sovereign. Many of these sovereigns, oppressed with their feeling of dependence, have abdicated in disgust. Others, equally aware of the absurdity of their positions, but endowed with a sense of humor and faith in the fundamental principles of democracy, remain on the throne in the hope that conditions will improve.

The solution. The conditions can be improved, and they have been improved to some extent. The short ballot is the remedy.[23] The ballot can be shortened by lengthening the terms of offices. Where four-year terms are substituted for two-year terms, the voter's job is cut in half. But the principal means of shortening the ballot is in the reduction of elective officers. Why should the people be asked to elect an inspector of elections, a public weigher, a clerk of a municipal court, a hide and animal inspector, and a host of others whose duties are technical and administrative? Our practical statesmen and students of government agree that there is no reason whatever for burdening the voter with such a task. They propose that the people elect such important political officers as governors, legislators, mayors, and councilmen; and that all other officers be appointed by the elected executive officers or by them in co-operation with the legislative bodies.

As everyone knows, the only national officers elected by the people are the President and congressmen—all other national officers are appointed. It is proposed that the states and the local governments follow the national plan. Some of the states have taken measurable strides in that direction;

---

[23] R. S. Childs, Short Ballot Principles (1911). Childs continues in the faith. See, for example, his "We Must Keep Ballot Short," *National Muncipal Review*, July, 1949, p. 328. See also strong endorsement of short ballot in *Model Direct Primary System*, National Municipal League, August, 1951.

many of the cities have done so. The short ballot is the only democratic ballot, if democracy has any relation to intelligent voting. The short ballot brings us responsible government, if, as is true in all business concerns, responsibility can be established by giving the chief officers the authority to name their assistants.

VII. CAMPAIGN FINANCE [24]

A fundamentally important phase of primaries and elections is that of finance. From what sources is party revenue derived? For what purposes is it expended? To what extent are campaign receipts and expenditures regulated by law?

Sources of party funds: 1. OFFICEHOLDERS. Party revenue is received from a variety of sources.[25] Those who hold office by virtue of party election or appointment usually contribute voluntarily or under pressure of the party organization. They are frequently assessed in the form of a percentage of the annual salary, 5 per cent being a commonly applied scale.[26]

2. CANDIDATES. Candidates for office are usually assessed, especially the candidates for state and local office. The assessment may amount to 5 or even 10 per cent of the salary of the office sought. If a candidate is financially independent, he is expected to bear a larger part of the campaign expenses; and, in the case of offices of great honor and trust, rich aspirants are often willing to put up large sums.

3. PUBLIC-SPIRITED CITIZENS. Many contributions are made by public-spirited citizens interested in a particular candidate, issue, or party, who have no interest in the outcome of an election beyond the belief that the choice of certain candidates will be to the advantage of the city, state, or nation. These are pure gifts, with no strings attached. In a national campaign, tens of thousands make small contributions; a few hundred make large donations; and the largess of a man of great wealth may reach or even exceed $50,000.

4. CONTRIBUTIONS FROM SPECIAL INTERESTS. A great deal of money has been contributed by individuals and corporations whose motives have been strongly questioned. Manufacturers eager for tariff protection, importers desiring the lowest tariff possible, oil men looking for government leases, railroads and other corporations wanting to be "left alone," have contributed

---

[24] Bone, *op. cit.*, Ch. 23; McKean, *op. cit.*, Ch. 14; Merriam and Gosnell, *op. cit.*, Ch. XVII; Louise Overacker, *Money in Elections* (1932) and *Presidential Campaign Funds* (1946); J. K. Pollock, "The Use of Money in Elections" in E. Logan (ed.), *The American Political Scene* (1936).

[25] See especially Merriam and Gosnell, *op. cit.*, pp. 393 ff.

[26] In 1936 the Democrats inaugurated the practice of party dinners (most of the diners being officeholders) at $100 or less per plate, the major portion of the price being turned over to the party treasurer.

handsomely to the party that seemed to offer the most direct benefits to their particular business. Concerns with business in several states have contributed liberally to the Democratic war chest in Democratic states and have served the Republicans equally as well in Republican states. Where the parties have seemed to be fairly evenly balanced in national, state, or local campaigns, some contributors have divided large sums between them, presumably with the idea of being in line for favors no matter which way the election went. E. L. Doheny and H. F. Sinclair thus helped finance the teams of both parties in the presidential campaign of 1920. In 1926 Samuel Insull was equally impartial in making contributions in an Illinois senatorial campaign.[27] And in 1944 E. F. Hutton contributed equally to the national organization of both the leading parties.[28]

Finding a strong friend in the New Deal Democratic party, labor began expressing its gratitude and perhaps laying its hopes for the future by making substantial contributions to that party. In 1936 several unions contributed in the aggregate $770,000, and in 1940 a larger amount. Although the Smith-Connally Act of 1943 contained a provision prohibiting labor union contributions to national *election* campaigns, it did not prevent such contributions in connection with primaries. Naturally enough, in 1944, organized labor used this advantage, nor was it slow to use its influence for the purpose of collecting funds for the election campaign, the result being that the Democrats may have been served as well or better in the 1944 election than in the two previous ones. In 1948 labor was instrumental in securing at least $1,250,000 toward the election of Democratic candidates. It is significant that, since 1932, contributions to the Democratic party from bankers and manufacturers have declined to approximately 10 per cent of the party's total receipts, whereas contributions from labor constitute about 16 per cent of the total.

5. CONTRIBUTIONS OF SERVICE. Parties receive a great deal of service that has money value, although it is not possible to measure it with any degree of accuracy. Nearly all the officeholders work for the parties during campaigns. Some of the time they give to the party is their own, but a great deal of it is taken from the hours in which they are supposed to be serving the public. In a national campaign the money value of the work of officeholders certainly runs well into the millions. The money value of the work of tens of thousands of enthusiastic and, for the most part, unselfish volunteers cannot be calculated. Nor can we estimate in terms of dollars and cents the value of the enormous publicity given the party and its candidates in the news columns and on the editorial pages of the press. Similarly, we cannot calculate the value of the support a

[27] H. R. Bruce, *American Parties and Politics* (1936 ed.), p. 425.
[28] McKean, *op. cit.,* p. 340.

party or some of its candidates may receive in a particular campaign from reform organizations, good government associations, groups of capitalists, laborers, farmers, and many others.

Cost of campaigns. It is estimated that a national campaign costs the major parties some $20,000,000 each. The reports of the national committees will show something like one third that amount (and since the Hatch Act, even less),[29] but these reports will not show the expenditures of political and quasi-political organizations in the states. State campaigns in commonwealths the size of New Jersey or Indiana may easily cost $100,000 or more. The cost is much higher in the largest cities, where it is said to range between $200,000 and $1,000,000.[30] Primary campaigns are sometimes as expensive as or even more expensive than election campaigns. In 1918 some $200,000 was spent by or for Truman H. Newberry in the Michigan primary. Still larger amounts were spent by McKinley and F. L. Smith of Illinois, and Pepper and Vare of Pennsylvania in the senatorial primaries of 1926.[31] And in 1930 Ruth Hanna McCormick spent nearly a half million dollars in her senatorial primary in Illinois.[32]

Where the money goes. Much more important than the amount received and certainly equal in importance to the source of party revenue are the purposes for which it is expended. Money from corrupt sources may be spent for the most legitimate purposes; donations of the most upright citizens may be distributed for the most shameful purposes. It is

---

[29] The expenditures of the national committees (not the total expenditures of the parties) in recent years has been as follows:

Year	Democratic	Republican
1928	$5,342,350	$6,256,111
1932	2,245,975	2,900,052
1936	5,194,741	8,892,972
1940	2,783,654	3,451,310
1944	2,056,122	2,828,652
1948	2,127,000	2,736,000

These figures are from Overacker, "Campaign Finance in the Presidential Election of 1940," *Am. Pol. Sci. Rev.,* XXXV, 705 (August, 1941), and "Presidential Campaign Funds, 1944," *Am. Pol. Sci. Rev.,* XXXIX, 899 (October, 1945). Grim necessity, the depression, held down the expenditures of the national committees in 1932, and the Hatch Act accounts for the reduction in 1940. In the latter year, however, much more money than usual came in from other sources. Overacker estimates that the Democratic party actually spent $5,855,082 and the Republican $14,941,142. In 1944 the Republican national committee and its affiliates received $14,601,833 and spent $13,195,375; the Democrats received $8,384,745 and spent $7,441,798. *New York Times,* March 16, 1945, p. 22. Figures for 1948 are not fully compiled, but the *National* political organizations spent $13,500,000. This figure does not include funds spent by such local organizations as the Republican Finance Committees of Pennsylvania and New York, which two committees alone spent over $2,000,000 between them (*Congressional Quarterly Almanac,* 1949, pp. 82–83).

[30] Merriam and Gosnell, *op. cit.,* pp. 403–404.

[31] Bruce, *op. cit.,* pp. 310 ff.

[32] Overacker, *Money in Elections,* p. 65.

doubtful, however, if much money is spent by either of the national committees for "shameful purposes," although some money spent by local organizations may be for such purposes, and the national organizations might reap a little benefit from such expenditures. Here are the principal items for which the national committees spent money in the campaign of 1940. Radio: Democrats $387,224; Republicans $335,000. Transportation: Democrats $57,569; Republicans $133,000. Printing: Democrats $158,527; Republicans $184,460. Salaries of clerks, copyists, messengers, and other employees ran to a large figure—to $361,986 from June to December at Republican headquarters.[33] Telephones, telegraph, advertising, rent, and many other entirely legitimate services take large sums of money. It is a fact that millions may be spent in a national campaign for purposes wholly pure and upright. At least two million dollars would be required to send a letter to every voter in the United States.

Election-day expenses run very high, in cities sometimes as high as 50 per cent of the total campaign outlay. For getting out the voters and other election expenses, a party may spend $100 or even more per precinct. It is said that much less money is used for out-and-out bribery of voters than formerly. The risks incurred and, we hope, quickened consciences, have very measurably decreased such gross forms of pecuniary corruption in elections.

Legal regulation of campaign funds. Because campaign funds were found all too often to come from organizations or individuals who seemed to expect public favors, and because a part of the funds were expended for illegitimate purposes, both the national and state governments have attempted to regulate party finance.

1. FORBIDDEN SOURCES. The first type of regulation of campaign funds is the forbidding of contributions from certain sources. Urged by Theodore Roosevelt, Congress in 1907 made it unlawful for a national corporation or a national bank to contribute money for any campaign, and for any corporation whatever to contribute for any campaign in which national office is sought. But stockholders, big and little, may, of course, contribute as individuals. Alarmed at the growing political power of labor and in particular at its financial contributions for the support of New Deal candidates, Congress extended the prohibitions respecting corporations to labor organizations. This legislation appeared first in the form of a rider to the Smith-Connally War Labor Disputes Act of 1943, and it was made applicable only for the duration of the war. The Taft-Hartley Act (1947) in Section 304 (an amendment to Section 313 of the Federal Corrupt Prac-

---

[33] Overacker, "Campaign Finance in the Election of 1940," *Am. Pol. Sci. Rev.*, XXXV, 706–707 (August, 1941). In 1944 the Democratic National Committee spent $925,000 for radio; the Republican, $841,600 (Overacker, *Am. Pol. Sci. Rev.*, XXXIX, 901, October, 1945).

tices Act) prohibits labor and corporations from making contributions or expenditures in a federal election. The prohibition of "expenditures" was immediately attacked. Did it mean that the CIO, for example, could not spend money to assist in the campaign of a Congressional candidate favorable to labor? That is what it seemed to mean. The CIO proceeded to test the meaning by supporting in *The CIO News* a candidate for Congress in a Baltimore district. When the CIO and Philip Murray, its President, were prosecuted, the federal district court declared that section 304 of the statute violated the freedom of speech and the press (the First Amendment). On appeal, the Supreme Court evaded the issue of constitutionality, holding that Congress could not have intended to prevent a journal from expressing its views on candidates for public office.[34] But may Congress validly prohibit such *indirect* expenditures on behalf of candidates and may Congress validly prohibit labor unions from making *direct* contributions to political parties or candidates? Those questions are still not clearly answered.

Approximately three fourths of the states prohibit contributions by corporations to political campaigns, and in recent years some states have prohibited labor from making such contributions. Some twelve states prohibit the assessment of officeholders.

2. LIMITATIONS ON PURPOSE OF EXPENDITURES. A second type of regulation of campaign funds is with regard to the character of expenditures. The laws vary greatly from state to state, but practically all states prohibit certain types of expenditures. Typical illegal expenditures are: purchasing votes; supplying voters with meat, drink, and entertainment during the campaign; hiring vehicles for the purpose of taking voters to and from the polls; hiring assistants other than challengers and watchers on election day; paying a voter's poll tax (in the South); purchasing the influence of a newspaper for candidates.

3. RESTRICTIONS ON AMOUNTS OF EXPENDITURES. As a third form of regulation of campaign funds, numerous laws restrict the amounts that may be spent by or on behalf of candidates. The Federal Corrupt Practices Act of 1925 limits a candidate for the Senate to $10,000 and a candidate for the House of Representatives to $2,500. The law provides an alternative plan by which a candidate for either House may spend three cents for each vote cast in the last election for the office he seeks, provided the amount does not exceed $25,000 for a seat in the Senate or $5,000 for a seat in the House of Representatives. Where a state in which a candidate seeks election to Congress has a more restrictive law relative to expenditures, then the candidate must comply with the provisions of that law.

Everyone knows that much more money is sometimes spent in senatorial

[34] United States v. CIO, 335 U.S. 106 (1948).

or congressional campaigns than the amounts fixed by the federal act. How does it happen? It happens because personal expenditures for travel, stationery, postage, telegraph, telephone, and some other items do not come under the terms of the act. Furthermore, and more important, the act does not prohibit the expenditures for campaign purposes by persons other than the candidates. Finally, the act of 1925 applies only to election campaigns.

The Newberry case,[35] decided in 1921, cast grave doubt over the question of the power of Congress to regulate its own primary elections, and Congress seems to have assumed by the act of 1925 that it had no such power. Twenty years later, when dealing with a different question, the Supreme Court of the United States took the position that Congress has ample power to regulate its primaries.[36]

Three fourths of the states have laws limiting the amount that may be spent by or for a candidate. The more rigorous provisions of the laws commonly apply, however, only to expenditures by the candidate, leaving others, either by subterfuge or by the actual terms of the law, to spend amounts many times greater than those the candidate is authorized to spend.

The Hatch Act of 1940. By far the most discussed of the acts of Congress designed to curb "pernicious political activities" is the Hatch Act of 1940. This Hatch bill was designed to prevent certain financially pernicious campaign practices. After tragic lamentations from nearly all of the senators who had the support of powerful state machines, and expressions of pure politics sentiments by senators against whom machines had operated or might operate, the Senate passed the bill. It remained in the House three months, and was assumed to be dead; but it was eventually enacted into law. In the language of the act "no political committee" shall receive contributions or make expenditures in excess of $3,000,000, and no individual may contribute to such committee a sum in excess of $5,000. But how many committees, national, state, and local, may a party have, and to how many different committees may an individual contribute $5,000? And what is to prevent a party "angel" (generous contributor) from distributing $50,000 or $100,000 among his sisters and his cousins and his aunts for $5,000 contributions to committees? These are some of the jokers in the law.

In 1940 the Republicans established fifteen state finance committees, and the Democrats proceeded along similar lines, each *party committee* adhering strictly to the prohibition against receiving and spending more than $3,000,000! The law is rather clearly a farce, and Senator Hatch ad-

---

[35] Newberry v. United States, 256 U.S. 232.
[36] United States v. Classic, 313 U.S. 299 (1941).

mits it. The combined Democratic organization and their nonparty committees and clubs raised $5,855,000 and the same type of combination raised $14,941,000 for the Republicans.[37] This process was repeated in 1944, the Republicans raising $14,601,833 and the Democrats $8,384,745. The Political Action Committee raised $1,405,120, most of which went into the Roosevelt campaign. Obviously many difficulties must be overcome in drafting a statute that will prevent the expenditure of large sums of money in elections, and the greatest obstacle to an effective measure is public indifference and congressional hostility. Furthermore, national campaigns do cost a lot of money. Expenses that most anyone would admit are legitimate run into staggering figures. One final and encouraging fact: the party that spends the most money has no assurance that it will win an election.

4. THE REQUIREMENT OF PUBLICITY. A fourth method of regulating campaign funds or holding them within reasonable bounds, and one that is receiving increasing emphasis, is the requirement of publicity. The fear of the light of day no doubt causes some party managers to leave unsolicited certain dark and odorous sources and to think twice before authorizing pernicious disbursements. The national government and practically all the states now require publicity of varying degrees of adequacy. Formerly, very few states required publicity before the election, leaving the voter without information that might have changed his vote. The national law requires publicity both before and after elections, and the present tendency in the states is in this direction.

Publicity pamphlets. Concern over the use of money in elections has not only led governments to enact legislation limiting donations and the purposes for which funds may be expended but also to suggestions that governments bear a part of the campaign expenses. It has been urged that such public appropriations for candidates or parties would give rich and poor men and parties with large war chests and parties with small ones a more nearly equal chance for office. In 1907 President Theodore Roosevelt proposed that Congress provide for the legitimate campaign expenses of each of the two major parties. In 1920 William Jennings Bryan unsuccessfully besought the Democratic national convention to advocate a national bulletin to be published jointly by the major parties at government expense and mailed to every voter. It might have been called to his attention that the *Congressional Record,* having qualities of a bipartisan bulletin, was one of the most "widely unread" publications in the United States.

Four or five states have furnished a type of indirect aid to parties and

[37] Overacker, "Campaign Finance in the Election of 1940," *Am. Pol. Sci. Rev.,* XXXV, 708, 713 (August, 1941).

candidates through the medium of publicity pamphlets. Only North Dakota and Oregon now distribute such pamphlets. In Oregon, the state that makes the more liberal use of them, both parties and candidates may have space for both primaries and elections. At a cost of $50 a page each party may have as many as 24 pages in the publicity pamphlet, setting forth its principles and promoting its candidates. Any candidate for nomination to elective office may purchase space in the pamphlet, or a supporter may do it for him, at a rather nominal cost. After the primaries and during the heat of the election campaign candidates may in like manner purchase space in the pamphlets that go to all voters. Oregon seems to be fairly well satisfied with this system, but other states do not follow her lead.[38]

For reading list, see references at the end of Chapter 9.

Questions and Problems

1. Can it be said that there are any "best methods" for conducting a presidential campaign?
2. Discuss newspaper publicity in relation to success in a political campaign.
3. Is the spirit of the Constitution maintained in our manner of selecting the President?
4. Propose a plan whereby more unity could be produced in the off-year congressional campaign.
5. Indicate a number of irrelevant factors that often influence voters.
6. To what extent do the partisan divisions in a state election campaign remain firm after the newly elected officers take over? Consider the divisions in the legislature, the alignment of legislators with the governor, etc. in your state.
7. Trace the efforts made and the progress achieved in ballot reform in the United States.
8. Should people who seldom vote be deprived of the right to vote? Should we have compulsory voting laws? Pick out six persons of different types, each of whom you consider an intelligent voter; then try to decide just what qualities make him such a voter.
9. Show how constitutions and laws might be changed to aid the voter in casting his ballot intelligently.
10. Make a list of legitimate campaign expenditures; questionable expenditures.
11. What do the Hatch (pernicious political activity) Acts and their operation tend to prove?

[38] Sait, *op. cit.*, pp. 304n, 447, 554; W. L. Josslin, "Oregon Educates Its Voters," *National Municipal Review*, July, 1943, p. 379. A number of states join Oregon in a publicity pamphlet system for initiated and referred measures, and opinions on the value of such pamphlets are generally favorable.

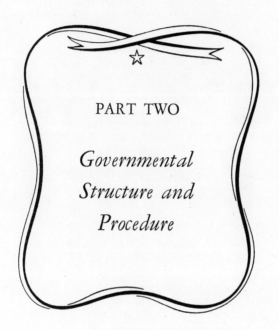

PART TWO

*Governmental
Structure and
Procedure*

☆ 11 ☆

The President: His Executive
Powers

ALTHOUGH repeated reference is made in the preceding chapters
to the executive, legislative, and judicial departments, none of
these has as yet been considered in a systematic manner. That
is the assignment for the next eight chapters. Following these are three
chapters that deal with the administrative system, that fourth branch
of the government, which operates under executive direction and performs the many services now demanded by the public. We begin, then,
with the office of President, one which is far beyond any other our democracy has to bestow, which Americans consider the best possible executive
system, but which scholars and public men of other lands consider illogical
and unworkable in theory although not without noteworthy achievement
in practice.

The presidential inauguration: THE OLD AND NEW DATES. Until the
Twentieth Amendment was adopted, the President and the Vice President,
for all practical purposes elected in November, did not take office until
the following March 4. If the incoming administration was largely committed to follow the policies of the retiring one, this delay in the transmission of powers was not serious. If, on the other hand, the old administration had been repudiated by the people and a new Moses was growing
restive waiting to lead the people to the Promised Land, the delay was
open to grave objections. Under such circumstances, the retiring President
might continue to act as if nothing had happened and risk embarrassing
his successor by committing the government on important matters; or he
might spend a very quiet winter in the White House waiting for March 4.

The country almost went to ruin waiting for Lincoln's inauguration,
while poor President Buchanan wept and prayed and wrote an essay on the
Constitution. Taft and Wilson, both repudiated at the end of their terms,

doubtless would have been just as happy to yield to the logic of events and to make way for their successors in December. President Hoover and President-elect Roosevelt made some attempts to co-operate in the winter of 1932–1933 but without conspicuous success. There was a good reason, then, for the proposal insistently made by Senator Norris and others that the inauguration date be moved up. The Twentieth Amendment, officially proposed by Congress in 1932 and adopted in 1933, brings the newly elected Congress into office on January 3 and the President-elect on January 20.

THE CEREMONY. We learned in a preceding chapter that the party gives its candidate for President a ceremonious official notice of that fact. The President-elect is not, however, officially notified that he is the choice of the American people for the highest office within their gift. But the successful candidate learns that fact from the sources open to all other Americans, and he arrives in Washington a few days before the date of inauguration. Having previously called upon the retiring President to pay his respects, he rides with him to the Capitol on Inauguration Day, followed by many another official of the nation and the states, and cheered by wildly enthusiastic throngs. Outside the Capitol, on a temporary platform erected for the purpose (in the Senate Chamber, if the weather is inclement), the President-elect becomes President by taking the oath of office, administered by the Chief Justice: "I do solemnly swear (or affirm) that I will faithfully execute the office of President of the United States, and will to the best of my ability preserve, protect, and defend the Constitution of the United States." In the inaugural address, not required by the Constitution, the President usually tries to smooth over some of the ill-feeling that recent partisan strife may have caused, appeals to the other branches of the government and all good citizens to help him in his task, and outlines his program, sometimes rather specifically. President Franklin Roosevelt clearly indicated in his brief inaugural in 1933 that he intended to ask Congress to give him sweeping powers to battle with the depression.

I. TERM, QUALIFICATIONS, IMMUNITIES, SUCCESSION [1]

The single executive. It will be recalled that the Articles of Confederation established only a Congress, and that executive powers were exercised by that Congress or its committees. This arrangement proved to be so inadequate that the members of the Constitutional Convention were prac-

[1] E. S. Corwin, *The President: Office and Powers* (1948), Chs. I–II; O. P. Field, "The Vice-Presidency of the United States," *American Law Review* (1922), LVI, 365–400; J. E. Kallenbach, "The New Presidential Succession Act," *Am. Pol. Sci. Rev.*, Oct., 1947, pp. 931–941; J. M. Mathews, *The American Constitutional System* (1940 ed.), Ch. X; Mathews and Berdahl, *Documents and Readings in American Government* (1940 ed.), pp. 207–217; C. L. Rossiter, "The Reform of the Vice-Presidency," *Pol. Sci. Qt.*, Sept., 1948, pp. 383–403.

tically unanimous in approving a separate executive branch for the national government. Although the framers of the Constitution differed materially and long on some questions relating to the executive, they experienced no great difficulty in reaching the decision to establish a single rather than a plural executive. The plural executive, or executive council, is employed in Switzerland, where the executive department is subordinate to the legislature, a plan that seems to work satisfactorily. But our executive was made co-ordinate with, not subordinate to, Congress, and to have entrusted wide and independent powers to a plural executive would have been a fatal mistake. The single executive provides at least two essentials—it unifies command, and it definitely locates responsibility.

Term and tenure. The members of the Philadelphia Convention had some difficulty in fixing the length of the term of office for the President. A few favored life tenure, but the majority favored a fixed number of years. A single term of seven years was carefully considered, but the four-year term with the privilege of election for an additional term or terms was finally agreed upon. Although the written Constitution does not limit a President in the number of terms he may serve, until 1940 custom limited his tenure of office to two terms. Washington and Jefferson both declined the honor of a third term, and thus started the two-term tradition. Grant, having served two terms (1869-1877), unsuccessfully sought the nomination in 1880 for a third. The two-term precedent was still more definitely established when Theodore Roosevelt, having served McKinley's unfinished term and the one for which he was elected in his own right (1901-1909), was rejected by his party for the nomination in the summer of 1912, and by the country in November of the same year as a Progressive candidate for President. The most recent contribution to the two-term tradition came in 1928, when Coolidge did "not choose to run." In 1940, and again in 1944, the world crisis and the political astuteness of Franklin D. Roosevelt enabled him to break the two-term tradition with relative ease. But the Twenty-second Amendment, proposed in 1947 and ratified in 1951, provides that: "No person shall be elected . . . President more than twice, and no person who has held the office of President, or acted as President, for more than two years of a term to which some other person was elected President shall be elected . . . President more than once." Thus the two-term tradition, modified only by the possible minor fraction of another term, is written into the Constitution. The incumbent, President Truman, was excepted from the provisions of this Amendment.

Removal from office. Several of our Presidents have died in office. None has resigned, although no question exists of the right to resign. Indeed, it would seem that in the case of a President who is hopelessly incapacitated, he has a duty to resign. The Chief Executive or any other civil officer of the United States may be removed from office "on impeachment for and conviction of treason, bribery, or other high crimes and misdemeanors." The House of Representatives has the sole power to impeach, that is, to make the charges; and the Senate has the sole power to try impeachments. The Chief Justice presides over the Senate when the President is tried. Andrew Johnson was the only President to be impeached, and the Senate failed by one vote to cast the necessary two-thirds majority for his conviction.

Qualifications. The Constitution states that: (1) "no person except a natural-born citizen, or a citizen of the United States at the time of the adoption of this Constitution, shall be eligible to the office of President; (2) neither shall any person be eligible to that office who shall not have attained the age of thirty-five years, and (3) been fourteen years a resident within the United States." [2] The provision "or a citizen of the United States at the time of the adoption of this Constitution" was included in order to qualify for the presidency Hamilton, James Wilson, and other founders of the Republic who were foreign-born.

We are not disposed to quarrel over the present rigid requirement of nativity; but we must observe that a foreign-born citizen may have talent and attainments and loyalty to his chosen country that in every way fit him for our highest office. There is no likelihood that the other requirements will operate to deprive the country of the services of those who are otherwise qualified. When Herbert Hoover was first discussed for the chief magistracy, a few people offered the objection that his long residence abroad during some of the fourteen years preceding the time he would take the oath of office, if elected, would disqualify him. This objection was not well founded, for the clause of the Constitution quoted above, which merely specifies "fourteen years a resident within the United States," clearly cannot be interpreted to require residence within the United States during the fourteen consecutive years preceding the date the oath of office is taken.

Compensation. "The President shall, at stated times, receive for his services a compensation, which shall neither be increased nor diminished during the period for which he shall have been elected, and he shall not receive within that period any other emolument from the United States, or any of them." [3] Congress originally fixed the salary at $25,000 a year, increased it to $50,000 in 1871 and to $75,000 in 1909. With mounting living costs and higher income taxes the $75,000 salary became inadequate, so that in 1949 Congress increased the amount to $100,000 and added $50,000 a year, tax free, for expenses, making the President's income com-

[2] Art. II, sec. 1, cl. 4. Availability, to be distinguished from legal qualifications, was discussed in Chapter 8, section IV.

[3] Constitution, Art. II, sec. 1, cl. 6.

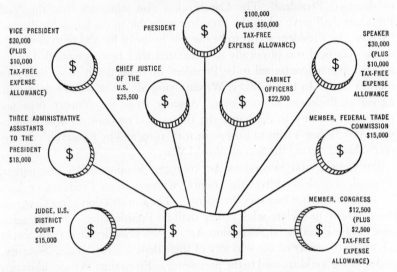

WHAT NATION'S TOP OFFICIALS GET

VICE PRESIDENT
$30,000
(PLUS
$10,000
TAX-FREE
EXPENSE
ALLOWANCE)

PRESIDENT
$100,000
(PLUS $50,000
TAX-FREE
EXPENSE ALLOWANCE)

SPEAKER
$30,000
(PLUS
$10,000
TAX-FREE
EXPENSE
ALLOWANCE

CHIEF JUSTICE
OF THE
U.S.
$25,500

CABINET
OFFICERS
$22,500

THREE ADMINISTRATIVE
ASSISTANTS
TO THE
PRESIDENT
$18,000

MEMBER, FEDERAL TRADE
COMMISSION
$15,000

JUDGE, U.S.
DISTRICT
COURT
$15,000

MEMBER, CONGRESS
$12,500
(PLUS
$2,500
TAX-FREE
EXPENSE
ALLOWANCE)

Reprinted from *U.S. News & World Report,* an independent weekly magazine on national and international affairs, published at Washington. Copyright, 1949, United States News Publishing Corporation.

parable to that of the nation's wealthiest men. The government also provides the President with a "house," yacht, plane, railroad car, and automobiles.

Personal immunities. The President, like heads of government the world over, enjoys complete personal inviolability. No officer has the authority to arrest him, no matter how grave his crimes may be; no court may subject him to its jurisdiction, not even the Supreme Court of the United States. As indicated above, he is subject to impeachment; but the Senate has no authority to compel him to appear before it in his impeachment trial. In the event that the Senate votes for conviction in an impeachment proceeding, the President becomes a private citizen, and is then subject to ordinary judicial process.

Presidential succession. Neither the German Republic, which Hitler terminated, nor the French Republic, which he crushed, had a vice president. Their constitutions stipulated that when a president resigned, or was removed, or died in office, a new president should be elected. This new president was elected for a full term (seven years), not just to complete the unexpired term of his predecessor. The constitution of the new and Fourth French Republic follows the same plan. Our Constitution provides that presidential elections shall be held only at regular four-year intervals, and this inflexible schedule necessitates the provision for a Vice

President who shall complete the unexpired term of a resigned, removed, or deceased President. The Constitution also stipulates that the Vice President shall serve when the President is unable to discharge his duties.[4] To date, the President seems to be the sole judge of his ability to discharge them. Garfield was physically incapacitated after he was wounded by an assassin, but he continued to be President until his death more than two months later. In like manner, Wilson, lying almost at death's door, continued as President in 1919–1921. Absence from the country does not constitute inability to discharge the duties of President, as was demonstrated by Wilson's trips to Europe in 1918–1919, and by Roosevelt's conferences abroad during the Second World War.

THE PRESIDENTIAL SUCCESSION ACT OF 1947. Suppose death, resignation, removal, or inability leaves the country without either President or Vice President, who then becomes President? The Constitution gives Congress the authority to declare what officer shall be President in such contingencies.[5] The Presidential Succession Act of 1886 provided that the Cabinet officers in the order of the seniority of their departments—State, Treasury, and so on—should succeed to the presidency. From time to time, however, there were objections to this arrangement—among others that it made possible, in effect, the appointment by a President (who had come into that office by the death or resignation of his predecessor) of his successor. Acting upon a strong recommendation of President Truman, Congress passed the Presidential Succession Act of 1947. This act places the succession in this order: the speaker of the House of Representatives, the president *pro tempore* of the Senate (the senator who would be presiding over the Senate when the Vice President has become President), and then the Cabinet officers as provided in the act of 1886, except that the Secretary of Defense takes the place of the Secretary of War and the Secretary of the Navy is dropped. The act of 1947 also provides that when the succession has passed to a Cabinet member, such person serves as President only until a speaker of the House or a president *pro tempore* of the Senate qualifies for the office.[6]

The Vice President. We learned in the discussion of nominations that the person named as the vice-presidential candidate is usually one who is expected to win votes from a disgruntled faction, carry some doubtful state, or serve similar political purposes. In a few cases, the office of Vice President has gone to men of the highest talents, who usually did not want

---

[4] Art. II, sec. 1, cl. 5.

[5] *Ibid.*

[6] For further details and discussion of the act of 1947, *see* J. E. Kallenbach, "The New Presidential Succession Act," *Am. Pol. Sci. Rev.,* Oct., 1947, pp. 931–941.

it. Wrote John Adams to his spouse, the equally competent Abigail: "My country has in its wisdom contrived for me the most insignificant office that ever the invention of man contrived or his imagination conceived." [7] Ordinarily the honor seems to be reserved for second-rate men. This situation is unfortunate, in view of the fact that there is considerable likelihood of the Vice President's being called upon to take over the reins of government. The salary of the Vice President is now $30,000 a year plus $10,000 in tax-free expense money, a sum sufficient to maintain the second man in the Republic on a scale befitting his position.

PRESIDENT OF THE SENATE. The Vice President has the duty of presiding over the Senate, but as its presiding officer he does not have the power or the influence the Speaker of the House of Representatives enjoys in the other wing of the Capitol. He is not a member of the Senate, nor has he a vote on its measures except in case of a tie. Mr. Dawes as Vice President did his best to make something of his position as President of the Senate, particularly in trying to get a revision of the Senate rules. But in the matter of rules the Senate refused to be led or forced, and Dawes good-naturedly gave up the attempt. In his efforts to influence legislation he was less spectacular but slightly more successful. Vice President Garner, from his long legislative experience, was of considerable aid to the President in putting his program through Congress during the first years of the New Deal. Vice President Wallace made a most serious and conscientious effort to perform his duties in the Senate, and he frequently spoke (sometimes for the administration) to the American people and to the world on matters of long-term policy.

THE EXPERIMENT OF ATTENDING CABINET MEETINGS. The Vice President's chief duty is to be in readiness to succeed the President. His position as presiding officer of the Senate does not adequately prepare him for the succession. From time to time, Presidents and candidates for that office have discussed the importance of having the Vice President in attendance at Cabinet meetings, where he would learn something of large administrative problems and get an intimate view of the work and policies of the Chief Executive he might be called upon at any time to succeed. Although Washington asked Adams at least once to sit in his Cabinet, and some other Presidents often sought the advice of Vice Presidents, no Vice President sat regularly with the Cabinet until 1921, when Harding asked Coolidge to do so. The position of Vice President Coolidge in the Cabinet was largely that of observer. There is evidence that Coolidge did not relish this position, and doubtless he had a sympathetic under-

---

[7] Quoted in C. L. Rossiter, "The Reform of the Vice-Presidency," *Pol. Sci. Qt.,* Sept., 1948, p. 384.

standing of the motives that prompted Vice President Dawes to decline his invitation to sit with the Cabinet of the 1925–1929 administration.[8] Recent Vice Presidents have sat in the Cabinet, but it is generally agreed that these efforts to increase the importance and prestige of Vice Presidents have produced no significant results. Upon being told that President Buchanan consulted Vice President Breckenridge only once, and then with regard to the phraseology of a Thanksgiving Proclamation, a later Vice President, with a saving sense of humor, is said to have replied: "Well, there is one more Thanksgiving Day before my term expires." [9]

Could the office be made effective? The problem of what to do with the office of Vice President is not a new one. There are responsible men who have suggested its abolishment, but the majority of such men want it retained and strengthened, strengthened by giving to the Vice President many of the administrative duties now performed by the President, thus relieving the President of a mass of work and increasing the dignity and power of the office of Vice President to the point where the most capable public men would welcome the opportunity to hold it. The President is probably the most over-worked man in the United States, in or out of public service, and he is thus burdened because he is responsible for too many details of administration. Relieve him of much of this burden so that he will have time to think, advise some of the thinkers in the field of administrative management. We ask the President to give us consistently intelligent and patriotic leadership, but "how much brilliant leadership," asks Professor Clinton L. Rossiter, "can a dray horse give?" [10] Perhaps a constitutional amendment would be required to transfer adequate authority to the Vice President to make that office an outstanding one and relieve sufficiently the President, but significant changes could be made by statute alone.[11]

II. THE PRESIDENT'S CABINET [12]

Before the inauguration, the President selects his Cabinet. The necessity of an advisory council did not escape the notice of the framers of the Constitution, but they thought the Senate would serve in that capacity.

[8] Mathews and Berdahl, *op. cit.*, pp. 330–331.

[9] *Ibid.*, p. 328. Quoted from (Bryan's) *The Commoner,* Nov., 1920.

[10] *Op. cit.*, p. 390.

[11] *Ibid.*, pp. 383–403.

[12] E. S. Corwin, "Wanted: A New Type of Cabinet," *New York Times Magazine,* Oct. 10, 1948, p. 14. M. L. Hinsdale, *History of the President's Cabinet* (1911); Pendleton Herring, *Presidential Leadership* (1940), Ch. V; H. J. Laski, *The American Presidency* (1940), Ch. II; H. B. Learned, *The President's Cabinet* (1912); Mathews and Berdahl, *op. cit.*, Ch. VII; Orth and Cushman, *op. cit.*, Ch. X; W. H. Smith, *History of the Cabinet of the United States* (1925).

Consequently, the Cabinet is not mentioned in the Constitution. The nearest approach to it is found in the provision that the President "may require the opinion, in writing, of the principal officer in each of the executive departments, upon any subject relating to the duties of their respective offices." [13] In addition to exercising this constitutional right, Washington soon found it convenient and desirable to take the heads of these departments into his confidence as a group. Before the end of his administration the Cabinet was established as the executive council, and the idea of using the Senate for that purpose was definitely abandoned.

Appointment to Cabinet posts. The heads of the nine [14] great executive departments who now compose the Cabinet are appointed by the President, "by and with the advice and consent of the Senate." The Senate usually accepts the President's nominations for these posts without serious question, for it realizes that if the Chief Executive is to be responsible for the administration, he must be allowed a free hand in choosing his immediate assistants. The Senate's rejection of Charles B. Warren, whom Coolidge named for Attorney General in 1925, was most unusual and almost created a sensation.

The senior executive department is the Department of State, and for this post the President usually names the man who ranks next to himself in his party. Thus, Lincoln appointed William H. Seward, his chief rival for the Republican nomination in 1860; and Wilson felt the necessity of appointing William Jennings Bryan, second to him in Democratic esteem, although he had once said that he would like to see Mr. Bryan knocked, "once for all, into a cocked hat." Other Cabinet posts go to men who have been largely responsible for the President's election (his campaign manager ordinarily becomes Postmaster General), to personal friends, to those who have marked administrative capacity, or to those whose appointment will give a particular section of the country representation in the Cabinet, or, and more commonly, to persons who fall into two or more of these classes.

Cabinet members are usually men who have been active in politics, although a relatively small number of representatives or senators are chosen. The present-day Cabinet is likely to contain some members whose interests have been primarily in private business, with only incidental or intermittent attention to politics. The personnel of a Cabinet depends, of course, to a considerable extent upon the motives and policies of the President who does the selecting. On occasion, a President may appoint men of an opposition party to Cabinet posts. The most recent example of this was

[13] Art. II, sec. II, cl. 1.

[14] Until 1947 there were ten executive departments. Under a law of that date, as amended in 1949, the Secretary of Defense took the place formerly occupied by the Secretary of War. The Secretaries of the Army, Navy, and Air Force do not have Cabinet rank. Their departments are "military," and not "executive," departments.

the appointment (1940) of Henry L. Stimson as Secretary of War and Frank Knox as Secretary of the Navy. Both men were active Republicans, but both were in harmony with the President on foreign policy and national defense. A Vice President, succeeding to the presidency upon the death of the Chief Executive, must, in common decency, retain for a time his predecessor's Cabinet. He may, however, completely reconstitute the Cabinet in the course of time, as did President Truman in 1945-1946.

Functions of the Cabinet. One must carefully distinguish between the functions of the heads of the nine executive departments, acting separately, and their functions when acting as a group—as a Cabinet. We reserve the work of the separate departments for later chapters. Here we are concerned only with the Cabinet. Its functions are purely advisory and consultative. It is the President's council. He may use it as much or little as he pleases. Jackson abandoned its use early in his administration, which he had a perfect right to do, and turned to a small group of political friends, his "Kitchen Cabinet," for advice. If the President wishes to use undersecretaries, assistant secretaries, members of independent commissions, and men with no official status as his advisers, no one may object on constitutional grounds. Wilson had his Colonel Edward M. House, Franklin D. Roosevelt his Harry Hopkins, and at various times he had much advice from certain members of the Supreme Court, the Director of the Budget, the Director of the Office of Economic Stabilization, the Commissioner of Labor Statistics, a New York state judge, and from many others not of cabinet rank or even members of the federal administration. President Truman seems to rely strongly upon his friends, although this tendency has not precluded his naming for his council board some men of unquestioned competence.

The American people complained because Wilson, during his illness, did not call Cabinet meetings for long periods of time; but he need not have called them at all. While Wilson was ill, his Secretary of State, Robert Lansing, frequently called Cabinet meetings; and when the President learned of this he accepted Lansing's resignation. We may disagree with Wilson as to the expediency of his treatment of Lansing, but we cannot deny his contention that the Cabinet belongs solely to the Chief Executive.

Cabinet meetings. The Cabinet meets when the President calls it— ordinarily twice a week; and it considers only those matters that the President lays before it or that he agrees may be laid before it by one of its members. The Cabinet may spend its time telling stories, or discussing trivial affairs, or weighing the gravest problems of state. If the President has confidence in his advisers, he will submit for their consideration important questions of policy, such as "getting tough" with or "going along" with Soviet Russia, American obligations to the United Nations, labor problems, the organization of the defense departments, or compulsory national health insurance. Sometimes, of course, there are no matters of paramount importance pending, and at other times the President may be disposed for one reason or another to keep his own counsel on important policies for which he is responsible.

In the Cabinet meetings, conditions are most favorable for the fullest and freest discussion, for the sessions are secret and no minutes are kept. Men may "get down to business" without any great concern over the political effect of their statements. Important Cabinet secrets not infrequently leak out in the course of time, however, as one did in 1830, when President Jackson promptly "excommunicated" Vice President Calhoun upon learning that in 1818, as Secretary of War under President Monroe, he had recommended that disciplinary action be taken against the then General Jackson for his high-handed conduct in his Florida expedition. Secretary of State Cordell Hull had some reticence about disclosing important secrets to the Cabinet "because there were leaks of such information to favorite news writers or broadcasters." [15] Votes are seldom taken on questions discussed in the Cabinet, and, if a vote is taken, it is only advice for the President. Following Lincoln's procedure on one occasion, a President may announce the vote: "Nine nays, one aye [the President's]; the motion is carried."

The Cabinet seems to be "on the way out" as a council, and has been since Wilson's time. More and more are other advisory bodies—the Council of Economic Advisers, the National Security Council, and others—taking over Cabinet functions, and it is reported that much of the time of the regular Cabinet is taken up with the problems of the separate executive departments and little attention given to the formulation of broad governmental policy, the appropriate function of a council.

The Cabinet and Congress. Congress has no legal control over these men sitting in a group forming the President's Council; for that Council, as we have learned, is unknown to the Constitution—is based on custom and not on law. Its deliberations are as much closed to Congress as they are to the American public. The President's communications with his Cabinet are as private, as far as the legal authority of Congress to pry into them is concerned, as his conversations with his personal friends. Jackson, who did so much to increase the power and independence of the President, had a characteristic word for the Senate, when that body asked for a copy of a statement on the removal of federal deposits from the Bank of the United States, which he was supposed to have read in a Cabinet meeting. "I have yet to learn," he wrote, "under what constitutional authority

[15] *The Memoirs of Cordell Hull* (1948), I, 204.

that branch of the Legislature has a right to require of me an account of any communication, either verbally or in writing, made to the heads of departments acting as Cabinet council." [16]   The authority of Congress in the matter of the removal of the heads of departments (Cabinet members) from office falls more appropriately into another section of this chapter.   For the present we simply state that Congress has no such authority except through impeachment.   Moreover, Congress has no authority whatever to interfere with the President's right to dismiss at any time a department head.

III. A GENERAL VIEW OF THE PRESIDENT'S POSITION AND DUTIES

The President and politics.   We will lose sight of an important fact if we do not bear in mind that the President's position is political.   In discharging his duties he must not only follow the clauses of the Constitution, the principles of sound economics, and the accepted standard of morals; but he must give attention to national tradition, sectional pride, political ambitions, and party harmony, to mention only a few items not included in any of the three categories named above.   In other words, he must consider the political effect of his acts.

It is bootless to deplore these facts; no method has yet been devised for removing the politics from a political job.   We must recognize the necessity for politics in the President's office; and as we recognize that necessity we can understand why some very fine men, exceptionally capable in large affairs other than politics, may make very poor Presidents.   Of great significance is the fact that our five great Presidents since 1860—Lincoln, Cleveland, the two Roosevelts, and Wilson—were astute politicians.

The President the center of the citizen's political interest.   The President holds the center of the political stage.   We have already given considerable space to the drama of his nomination and election.   His conduct, private as well as public, is of the greatest interest to his fellow countrymen.   His messages and addresses are heard or read by tens of millions; and so are the reports concerning his luck at fishing, his favorite exercise, his pets, and so on.   The average citizen who goes to Washington may spend hours in the hope of getting a glimpse of the President, and he returns radiant with pleasure if he manages to shake the Chief Executive's hand.   When on a tour of the country, the President will ordinarily be greeted at stopping places by great throngs; and if he should happen to toss the butt of a cigar into a gutter, he is likely to witness the unedifying spectacle of a mad scramble on the part of his admirers to recover it.

[16] J. D. Richardson, *A Compilation of the Messages and Papers of the Presidents,* III, 36.

Perhaps the citizen should be much more interested in his mayor or in his children's primary teachers; but he is not, although they touch him much more vitally than does the President.   The keen interest manifested in everything the President does arises from the fact that he not only wields large powers but also is the ceremonial as well as the actual head of the state.   He must feed the sentiment which even Americans have for the Chief of State.   He is the living symbol of the United States as the King is the symbol of the British Commonwealth of Nations.

Summary of his duties.   In the first place, and somewhat analogous to the duties that the King of England or other members of the royal family perform for Great Britain are the ceremonial and quasi-public duties of the President of the United States.   He receives and congratulates scientists, inventors, entertainers, and other public benefactors; delivers addresses before patriotic and fraternal orders; and sends greetings to scores of societies in national conventions assembled.   He must issue Thanksgiving Proclamations, and recommend the work of various charitable and humanitarian enterprises as worthy of support.   He must give state receptions and dinners, find time for an audience with small boys who have won oratorical contests or debates, and shake hands with long lines of his fellow countrymen.[17]   He is called upon to open fairs, tunnels, and bridges; to dedicate memorials and dams; and to do a host of other things, some important, some irksome and annoying, and many trivial.

In the second place, the President has duties and obligations that come to him, not from any particular clause of the Constitution, but rather from the sum total of the powers conferred upon him plus the prestige and influence his position carries.   We expect the President to take the lead in solving an unemployment problem, in encouraging manufacturing and industry, in promoting national thrift, and what not.   In the third place, the President has those great powers, executive and legislative, that are granted to him by the Constitution and by statute and that are often still further increased by aggressive executives.   His legislative powers are

[17] Hand-shaking is said to be one of the symbols of the democratic foundation of our government.   Although it is a very severe strain upon the President and the First Lady of the Land, there is no indication that it will be discontinued.   At some of these receptions three or four thousands are present and it takes them hours to pass by.   The First Lady may wear gloves, which "grow grey with the grime of democracy" as the long lines file past, but the President must take his democracy without gloves.   "The state of mind that this endless line of strangers induces in the people it passes is emphasized by everyone who has had a part in these great receptions. . . . It is told of [Theodore] Roosevelt that a man whose face seemed very familiar stood before him at a moment when the attention of the introducing aide was distracted.   Mr. Roosevelt was trying to place him, when the man leaned forward and said in a friendly whisper, 'Made your shirts, sir.'   Whereupon the President, not hearing clearly, but feeling relieved, grasped him warmly by the hand and said, 'Delighted to see you again, Major Shurtz.' "   (Mildred Adams in *The New York Times Magazine,* Nov. 30, 1930, p. 9.)   This story goes back to Andrew Jackson and his "Major Boots."

discussed in the next chapter. The remaining portion of the present chapter deals with his powers to direct administration (including the making of appointments and removals) and to grant pardons. His authority as Commander-in-Chief and to conduct foreign relations are reserved for discussion in Chapters 27–28.

IV. THE PRESIDENT AS CHIEF OF ADMINISTRATION [18]

His constitutional authority. The Constitution calls upon the President to "take care that the laws are faithfully executed." It also gives him the authority to require the opinions of the principal officers of the executive departments upon subjects relating to the duties of their offices.[19] This is as far as the Constitution goes in direct language toward making the President the director of administration. However, it gives him several other powers, such as the authority to command the Army and Navy and to make appointments to public office, which have gone far to make him the chief of administration.

His statutory authority. The earlier Congresses did not intend that the President should be the administrative chief, having authority to control and direct subordinate administrative officers of the national government. The Congress, in establishing the first executive departments, left the President a general controlling authority in the political departments— Foreign Affairs and War; but the Treasury Department was to be subject to the direction of Congress, and its Secretary was required to make his annual reports to that body, not to the President. When the Post Office Department was first organized, it was also placed under congressional direction. In other words, the original policy was that the President should be primarily a political chief, with the authority to perform political functions, that is, functions not subject to judicial review; but that Congress should be the guiding force in directing administrative affairs.

In the course of time, Congress learned that efficient government was not easy to maintain unless the President were given wide discretion in administrative affairs. Consequently, since about 1900, Congress has steadily increased the President's discretionary powers. Basic acts are passed in which only the general principles are laid down, the details of their application being left to the President. For several years Congress left the President to manage the newly acquired Philippines practically as

---

[18] Corwin, *op. cit.*, Chs. III–IV; D. K. Price, "Staffing the Presidency," *Am. Pol. Sci. Rev.*, Dec., 1946, pp. 1154 ff.; L. D. White, *Introduction to the Study of Public Administration* (1948 ed.), pp. 60–65; W. W. Willoughby, *Principles of the Constitutional Law of the United States* (1930 ed.), Chs. LXX, LXXVI; "Mr. Truman, Chairman of the Board," *United States News*, Nov. 25, 1949, pp. 17–20.

[19] Art. II, sec. II, cl. I.

he saw fit. In like manner Congress instructed the President to govern the Panama Canal Zone in his own way during the period of the construction of the Canal. Our reciprocal tariff is another illustration of the congressional practice of leaving discretion in the hands of the President. A very free rein indeed is given to the President in wartime and in periods of emergency. Thus, during the World Wars, Congress gave the President sweeping powers over the industries and resources of the country and, during the depression, gave Roosevelt most extensive authority.

His part in the administration of laws. When the citizen thinks of law enforcement, he probably thinks of the activities of the federal executive and judicial officers in bringing "dope" smugglers, interstate automobile thieves, and illegal business combinations to justice. This is, of course, a significant phase of law enforcement, but it is just one phase of the problem. Viewed broadly, law enforcement includes the administration of all laws, laws relating to the property of the United States, the promotion of health, the protection of American citizens abroad, the distribution of the mails, the construction of highways, the building of dams, the maintenance of parks, the relief of veterans, and so on to an infinite and bewildering variety of laws. Obviously, federal marshals, attorneys, and courts play only a small part in enforcing the great body of federal statutes. The services of these officers are needed only for the more extreme cases, cases in which there is definite resistance to the laws. The day-to-day administration of law is the work of department heads and their subordinates, of boards and commissions and their tens of thousands of employees, nearly all of them acting within the "chain of command" that reaches down from the White House. As Chief Administrator, the President fixes the tone and temper and spirit in which the laws are applied. He may direct that some statutes be enforced or administered with vigor, others with moderation, and some only by an occasional demonstration or example.

The President's administrative staff. The Chief Administrator has so many and such diverse duties to perform that he must have help, help far beyond that which the secretaries and clerks who have always been about the White House are able to give. He must have an administrative staff. His Committee on Administrative Management strongly recommended (1937) that one be established, and in 1939 the President carried out the essential features of that recommendation. As now constituted, the Executive Office of the President (staff) includes the White House Office, the Bureau of the Budget, the Council of Economic Advisers, and several other agencies.

In the White House Office are various secretaries and aides and five or six administrative assistants to the President. The secretaries serve the President in the more "political" aspects of his office, maintaining communication with Congress, individual congressmen, executive agencies of the government, the press, the radio, and the general public. The non-political and indispensable administrative work is performed by the administrative assistants, who are supposed to be experts and specialists and to have "a passion for anonymity." They serve the President directly, doing research, preparing reports, or whatever work the President may assign them. They are key men (salary $18,000) so far as the operation of the government is concerned, but they act only for the President and have no authority over anyone other than the personnel assigned to their office.

The Bureau of the Budget is responsible for the preparation of the financial program the President annually submits to Congress and aids in matters related to it (see Chapter 22). The Council of Economic Advisers was established by Congress in 1946 and its role is not yet fully developed, although its general function is to supply the President with information and advice on economic problems and in particular to assist him in the preparation of his annual Economic Report to Congress. The Commission on Organization of the Executive Branch of the Government (Hoover Commission) holds that the Council could much better serve the President as a staff agency if it took no public leadership on issues of policy, but confined itself to advising the President (the appropriate staff function). The Commission further holds that the economic staff work could be better performed by an Office of the Economic Adviser, headed by one individual appointed by the President, and it so recommends.[20]

EXECUTIVE OFFICE OF THE PRESIDENT

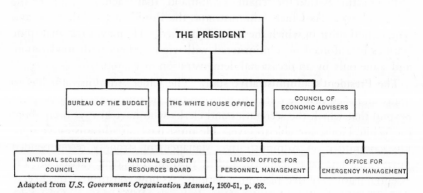

Adapted from *U.S. Government Organization Manual*, 1950-51, p. 493.

The three staff organizations mentioned do not give the President all the help he needs, but they do make it possible for him to discharge with some degree of assurance the stupendous responsibilities his office imposes.

[20] Commission on Organization of the Executive Branch of the Government, *General Management of the Executive Branch* (1949), p. 17.

The staff services collect and digest information and statistics, make and submit plans, advise and confer with the President, write administrative rules and regulations, and in various other ways, as the President may direct, serve the Executive arm of the Government. These men do not relieve the President of his responsibility as chief administrator; rather do they, by taking care of many details and supplying him with expert advice, make it possible for him to discharge his true functions as supreme administrator.

The relationship of the President and his staff is very similar to that with which the public is familiar in large business enterprises. The principal executive of the firm, relying upon his experts or "brain trusters" for facts, figures, and technical advice, makes the decisions and "takes the rap." We accept this in business without question. There is no good reason for fearing it in government.

V. THE PRESIDENT'S POWER OF APPOINTMENT AND REMOVAL [21]

Appointments. Closely associated with the President's power of Chief of Administration is that of appointment and removal. The Constitution provides that the President "shall nominate, and by and with the advice and consent [of the majority] of the Senate, shall appoint ambassadors, other public ministers and consuls, judges of the Supreme Court," and other officers of the United States. It provides further that Congress may vest the appointment of such inferior officers as it thinks proper in the President alone, or in the courts of law, or in the heads of the executive departments.

Since the Constitution does not define "inferior officers," Congress may itself determine what officers are in that class and provide for their appointment by one of the three methods just mentioned. In practice, Congress has shown a strong disposition to vest in the President and the Senate the appointment of important officers not mentioned in the Constitution. By the terms of the Constitution and acts of Congress, about 26,000 federal officers (including postmasters, who are for most purposes under the merit system) are appointed by the President and the Senate. The great majority of approximately 2,000,000 "inferior officers," who for the most part are concerned with routine and nondiscretionary administrative duties, are appointed by the heads of departments. The remainder are named by the President alone, or by the courts. We are concerned in this section with those officers who are chosen by the President and the Senate. Chapter 16 deals with the selection of the great army of federal employees.

[21] Corwin, *op. cit.*, Ch. III; Mathews and Berdahl, *Documents and Readings in American Government* (1940 ed.), pp. 246–266.

THE SENATE AND MAJOR APPOINTMENTS. Although the words of the Constitution give the Senate equal authority "to advise and consent" in respect
to any nomination the President may make, in most cases of major appointments the Senate exercises its power in considerable deference to the President. In appointing the heads of departments, ambassadors and ministers,
and high military or naval officers, the Senate gives the President practically
a free hand. Usually, even if the opposing party controls the Senate, the
President's nominees are accepted. Since the President is held responsible
for the executive and administrative functions of the government, the policy
of the Senate in allowing him the widest freedom in choosing his chief
assistants is in accordance with the basic principles of fair play.

The President's nominees for the Supreme Court are seldom rejected by
the Senate. Such nominations are usually made with care and the Senate
generally, but not always, shares the opinion of the country at large that
the game of politics should not be played too intensively over the highest
judicial appointments. The most recent exceptions to the rule of automatic confirmation of nominees for high office occurred when the Senate
rejected Charles B. Warren for Attorney General (1925), and John J.
Parker for the Supreme Court (1930). In 1946 popular protests, supported by objecting senators, forced President Truman to withdraw from
the Senate the nomination of Ed Pauley (accused by Harold Ickes and
others of attempts at political bribery) for Under Secretary of the Navy.

THE SENATE AND OTHER APPOINTMENTS. The Senate and individual
senators and representatives take a very active part in the appointment of
officers outside the class of those mentioned above. The President must
consult with members of Congress, more particularly the individual senators of his party, on the general run of appointments, because he cannot
have first-hand knowledge of the qualifications of the thousands who seek
federal office. Besides, in making an appointment, the President's task is
more than to find the best qualified person for the position—he must make
appointments that are politically good; and in that respect the advice of a
senator or representative is most useful. Furthermore, senators and representatives insist upon being consulted with regard to appointments, because
they use this patronage to build up their local political support. Let us suppose that an important federal officer, say, a district judge, is to be appointed
in a state. Various names, accompanied by many recommendations, will
be presented to the President; but the President will most probably be
guided in his selection of a candidate by the advice of a senator from the
state, provided, of course, he belongs to the same political party as the
President. When a minor federal official is to be appointed—a federal
marshal, for instance—it is the custom to allow the representative from the
district in which the appointment is to be made to make the selection, if the

representative is of the President's party and if a senator from the state endorses the representative's choice.

"SENATORIAL COURTESY." When the President sends to the Senate the name of a candidate who is recommended by a senator primarily concerned in the appointment, the Senate confirms the appointment as a matter of course. Thus, in 1936 Lamar Hardy, favored for a judicial appointment by the two senators from New York, was easily confirmed in the face of opposition led by Senators La Follette and Norris. What happens if the President does the unusual and sends in a name which has not the recommendation or endorsement of the aforesaid senator? Then, by the rule of "senatorial courtesy," which seems to have originated in Washington's administration, the Senate will stand by the senator whom the President has crossed, and will refuse to confirm the appointment. In 1939 the two Virginia senators successfully invoked the rule, thus blocking the appointment of Floyd Roberts as Federal District Judge in that state.[22] Clearly, then, where appointments are to be made in states that have a senator or senators who belong to the same political party as the President, the President has only a nominal appointing power, the actual power being exercised by one or two senators.

Senatorial courtesy may be invoked even by a senator not of the President's party. Thus, in 1950, Senator Homer Ferguson of Michigan prevented the confirmation of Frank E. Hook, his unsuccessful opponent in the election of 1948, for the Motor Carrier Claims Commission on the grounds that the appointment would be "personally obnoxious" to him.[23]

RECESS APPOINTMENTS. The Constitution gives the President the authority to fill all vacancies that may occur while the Senate is not in session, by granting commissions that expire at the end of the next session of the Senate. This authority, like most others, the Presidents have liberally construed. Thus, after the adjournment of Congress in 1949, President Truman included in a list of 23 recess appointments the name of an individual he had nominated for federal district judge but upon whose nomination a Senate committee had failed to act, the failure to act being interpreted by the President as creating a vacancy "that may happen during the recess of the Senate." In other words, if a vacancy *exists,* for whatever cause, it also *happens* within the accepted meaning of the constitutional grant of authority to make recess appointments. Recess appointments are made final if the Senate, at its next session, acts affirmatively upon them.

THE BURDEN OF APPOINTMENT. The fact that the President has the assistance, usually the very aggressive assistance, of senators, representatives, and

[22] Mathews and Berdahl, *op. cit.,* p. 252. See Borah resolution denouncing the practice, *ibid.,* p. 257.
[23] *New York Times,* August 10, 1950.

other politically minded persons in selecting nominees for thousands of federal offices, does not save the problem from being a heavy one. Numerous applications and insistent recommendations consume a great deal of the new President's time, and often fail to enlighten him as to the best-qualified candidates. Long ago (1893) Cleveland, characteristically expressing the exasperation other Presidents have probably only felt, said:

The time . . . set apart for the reception of senators and representatives has been almost entirely spent in listening to applications for office, which have been bewildering in volume, perplexing and exhausting in their iteration, and impossible of remembrance. A due regard for public duty, which must be neglected if present conditions continue, and an observance of the limitations placed upon human endurance oblige me to decline from and after this date all personal interviews with those seeking appointments to office, except as I on my own motion may especially invite them. . . . Applicants for office will only prejudice their prospects by repeated importunity and by remaining in Washington to await results.[24]

In 1933 Franklin D. Roosevelt, using the national emergency as the justification, refused to give audience to the general run of place hunters. Those who would not be put off were told to see the Postmaster General. The sordid rush for places and the strain on the President has been considerably relieved and the federal administrative services materially improved by placing the greater number of "presidential" offices under the merit system. This development is discussed in Chapter 21.

Removal from office. With regard to removal, the Constitution provides only that "all civil officers of the United States shall be removed from office on impeachment and conviction of treason, bribery, or other high crimes and misdemeanors." [25] But many officers who are guilty of none of these offenses are nevertheless unfit to continue in office. An officer who is grossly incompetent in some particular, or who is affected with "streaks of miscellaneous worthlessness," is not necessarily a traitor, or a taker of bribes, or guilty of other high crimes and misdemeanors. How, then, may he be removed? Since the Constitution is silent on the subject, one might hastily answer that he is to be removed by the power that appointed him, that is, by the President and Senate, if appointed by them. That is exactly what a number of statesmen, including Hamilton, said in 1789. Other statesmen, led by Madison, argued that the President should have the power of removal, unencumbered by the advice and consent of the Senate. The Madison view was adopted, and it has increasingly prevailed with the passing of the years.

[24] Quoted in C. A. Beard's *Readings in American Government and Politics* (1913), pp. 211–212.
[25] Art. II, sec. IV.

A little reflection will show that there is very practical reasoning behind Madison's position. The President's responsibility for administration is not seriously impaired by the requirement that his important appointments be confirmed by the Senate, for, if the Senate rejects a capable nominee, the President may submit another, and no harm is done. But, if the Senate had the right to prevent him from removing an officer, then the President might be saddled from time to time with incompetent or otherwise unsatisfactory assistants. So well understood is the necessity for the President's unrestricted right to remove his administrative officials that, when President Truman asked Henry A. Wallace to resign as Secretary of Commerce, the President was not criticized for forcing the resignation, even though it came about as a result of his own blundering.

THE REMOVAL POWER BEFORE THE COURTS. In 1867 Congress passed the Tenure of Office Act, intended to deprive President Johnson of his power to remove certain officers. Johnson and some constitutional lawyers denounced the act as unconstitutional; but the Supreme Court did not have occasion to pass upon it, although it remained on the statute books (in modified form after 1869) until 1887. Not until 1926 was the highest court asked to pass upon the authority of Congress to restrict the President's power to remove executive officers. It came about in this way. In 1917 President Wilson appointed a Mr. Myers to a first-class postmastership at Portland, Oregon. Now a statute of 1876 provided that postmasters of the first three classes should be appointed and *removed* "by the President by and with the advice and consent of the Senate and shall hold their offices for four years unless sooner removed or suspended according to law." In 1920, without consulting the Senate, Wilson removed Myers—less than three years after he had appointed him. If the Senate had confirmed the appointment of the person named as successor to Myers, as it commonly does, such confirmation would have amounted to senatorial consent to the removal. But the Senate rejected the President's new appointee. Myers therefore went to the Court of Claims, asking for the remainder of the salary for the four-year period, on the ground that he had been removed from office without the consent of the Senate, contrary to law. Losing in the Court of Claims, he appealed to the Supreme Court, where his case was argued in 1924, and, because of its great importance, reargued in 1925. In its 6 to 3 decision the Court held that the Act of 1876, "in so far as it attempted to prevent the President from removing executive officers who had been appointed by him by and with the advice and consent of the Senate," was invalid.[26]

[26] Myers v. U.S., 272 U.S. 52 (1926); R. E. Cushman, *Leading Constitutional Decisions* (1950 ed.), pp. 235–238 n. The Tenure of Office Act of 1867 was also declared invalid in this decision, although it had been repealed in 1887.

The Court based its decision on the grounds that the First Congress (1789), in which Madison and some other members of the Philadelphia Convention sat, had decided to leave the power of removal entirely in the hands of the President; that the "decision" of the First Congress had been accepted by all the Presidents and by all the Congresses, except the Reconstruction Congress, which attempted to limit Johnson's removal power; and that the President's power to remove civil officers appointed by him and the Senate might be inferred from the broad principle of the separation of powers and the provision of the Constitution concerning the President's obligation to take care that the laws be faithfully executed. The Court used the logic of history and accomplished facts in its decision. As judicial decisions go, it is not considered a masterpiece; and some authorities hold that the dissenting judges' opinions were better than the majority decision. But, at any rate, the question raised seems to be settled.

The Myers case left unanswered the question of the authority of the President to remove a member of an independent commission, such as a member of the Interstate Commerce Commission. But in 1935 this question came squarely before the Court. In 1933 William E. Humphrey, a member of the Federal Trade Commission, was "removed" by President Roosevelt. The statute under which members of this Commission served provided that they might be removed by the President for "inefficiency, neglect of duty, or malfeasance in office." The President had not sought his removal on any of these grounds. The Court held that the Congress had the power to limit the President in his authority to remove members of the independent commission, since they exercise "no part of the executive power vested by the Constitution in the President." [27] Thus, although Congress may not limit the President in removing executive officers it may limit him in removing members of the independent commissions.

CAN THE SENATE OR CONGRESS FORCE A REMOVAL? From the foregoing discussion of the President's right to remove executive officers without the advice and consent of the Senate, it follows very logically that the Senate has no authority to take the initiative and force a removal. In 1924 the Senate called upon President Coolidge to remove Edwin Denby, the Secretary of the Navy, for his connection with oil leases made "under circumstances indicating fraud and corruption." Replying to the Senate and justifying his position before the country, Coolidge quoted Presidents Madison and Cleveland on the independence of the Chief Executive, and added that "the dismissal of an officer of the Government, such as is involved in this case, other than by impeachment, is exclusively an executive function." [28]

---

[27] Rathbun v. United States, 295 U.S. 602 (1935).

[28] Mathews and Berdahl, *op. cit.*, pp. 325–326. As a matter of interest it might be added that the President's message, at his request, was written by Senator Borah, one of the Senators who opposed the resolution. See C. O. Johnson, *Borah of Idaho* (1936), pp. 287–288.

In 1943 Congress attempted to force three men out of office by inserting in an appropriation act the stipulation that the three should be paid no salary. The Supreme Court in United States v. Lovett declared this provision of the act a bill of attainder and therefore void.[29]

VI. THE PRESIDENTIAL PARDONING POWER [30]

The scope of the pardoning power. The Constitution states that the President "shall have power to grant reprieves and pardons for offenses against the United States, except in cases of impeachment." The courts have held that Congress has no power to limit the President in his use of this "benign prerogative of mercy." Until 1925 it was erroneously supposed that the President had no authority to grant pardons in cases of criminal contempt. The courts punish for contempt in order to protect themselves and further their usefulness, and it was thought that the exercise of executive clemency for contemners would seriously undermine the position of judicial tribunals. However, when Philip Grossman, of Chicago, continued to sell liquor in violation of a court injunction and was sentenced to jail for contempt, the President pardoned him, and was upheld in so doing by the Supreme Court.[31]

Although Congress has no authority to limit the President's power to grant pardons, that does not mean that the power is to be exercised exclusively by the President. Congress itself may exercise it by passing acts of general amnesty. Thus, an act granting immunity from prosecution to all witnesses testifying before the Interstate Commerce Commission was held to be valid.[32] Furthermore, the courts have held that the President's pardoning power is not so exclusive as to prevent Congress from giving other officers, such as the Secretary of the Treasury, the authority to remit certain forfeitures and penalties.[33]

ANALYSIS OF THE POWER. "A pardon reaches both the punishment prescribed for the offense and the guilt of the offender; and when the pardon is full, it releases the punishment and blots out the existence of the guilt, so that in the eye of the law the offender is as innocent as if he had never committed the offense." [34] (This judicial utterance need not prevent the layman from believing that some "moral guilt" may remain.) But a pardon does not restore offices forfeited, or property or interests vested in

---

[29] *See* page 132.

[30] Corwin, *op. cit.*, pp. 193–205; Mathews, *op. cit.*, pp. 175–179; Willoughby, *op. cit.*, pp. 623–624, 690.

[31] *Ex Parte Grossman*, 267 U.S. 76 (1925).

[32] Brown v. Walker, 161 U.S. 591 (1896).

[33] The Laura, 114 U.S. 411 (1885).

[34] *Ex Parte Garland*, 4 Wall. 333 (1866).

others in consequence of a conviction. A pardon may be granted before, during, or after a trial; that is, at any time after the offense is committed, but it usually comes after a conviction. The pardon may be a remission of the whole or a part of the penalty. Thus, an offender under a death sentence may be fully pardoned, or his sentence may be commuted to a prison term. The President may also grant a reprieve; that is, a suspension of the execution of a sentence. Finally, we must note that the President may grant general pardons or amnesties to a class of offenders; for instance, to a group guilty of insurrection.

How THE POWER IS EXERCISED. Probably the average individual has a picture of a wife, soon to be a widow, weeping with her children before the President and begging for the life of the husband and father until the President signs a pardon. This, of course, may happen, but the President is unworthy of his high office, if his pardons are determined by tears and sobs. The regular procedure is somewhat less dramatic. An application for pardon and papers bearing on the case are examined by officers of the Department of Justice. If the convicted individual has had a fair trial, if no new evidence tending to exculpate him is produced, and if the sentence is just, the President's legal advisers will in all probability recommend that the sentence be allowed to stand. The President will take this advice in most cases, although he is entirely free to use his own judgment.

Reading List

J. Alsop and R. Kintner, *Men Around the President* (1939).

W. E. Binkley, *President and Congress* (1947).

J. B. Bishop, *Theodore Roosevelt and His Times,* 2 vols. (1920).

D. W. Brogan, *Government of the People* (1935), Pt. IV.

Louis Brownlow, *The President and the Presidency* (1949).

J. Bryce, *The American Commonwealth* (1913 ed.), I, Chs. V–IX, XX–XXI, XXV.

H. J. Carman and R. H. Luthin, *Lincoln and the Patronage* (1943).

(Hoover) Commission on Organization of the Executive Branch of the Government, *General Management of the Executive Branch* (1949).

E. S. Corwin, *The President: Office and Powers* (1948 ed.).

W. Y. Elliott, *The Need for Constitutional Reform* (1936), Chs. IX–X.

O. P. Field, "The Vice-Presidency of the United States," *Am. Law Rev.* (1922), LVI, 365–400.

John Gunther, *Roosevelt in Retrospect* (1950).

J. Hart, *The Ordinance-Making Powers of the President of the United States* (1925).

———, "The Exercise of Rule-Making Power," in the *President's Committee on Administrative Management, Report With Special Studies* (1937).

Henry Hazlett, *A New Constitution Now* (1942).

S. Herbert, "The Premiership and the Presidency," *Economicia* (1926), VI, 159–169.

Pendleton Herring, *Presidential Leadership* (1940).

M. L. Hinsdale, *History of the President's Cabinet* (1911).

Richard Hofstadter, *The American Political Tradition and the Men Who Made It* (1948).

H. W. Horwill, *The Usages of the American Constitution* (1925), Chs. III–VI.

Louis Koenig, *The Presidency and the Crisis* (1944).

H. J. Laski, *The American Presidency* (1940).

H. B. Learned, *The President's Cabinet* (1912).

R. Luce, *Legislative Problems* (1935), Chs. V–IX, XVI.

Carl Marcy, *Presidential Commissions* (1944).

F. M. Marx, *The President and His Staff Services* (1947).

J. M. Mathews, *The American Constitutional System* (1940 ed.), Chs. X–XII.

—— and C. A. Berdahl, *Documents and Readings in American Government* (1940 ed.), Chs. IX–XI.

H. M. MacDonald and Others, *Outside Readings in American Government* (1949), Chs. XIII, XXI.

Allan Nevins, *Grover Cleveland: A Study in Courage* (1932).

J. E. Pollard, *The Presidents and the Press* (1947).

H. F. Pringle, *Theodore Roosevelt* (1931).

——, *The Life and Times of William Howard Taft,* 2 vols. (1939).

L. Rogers, *Crisis Government* (1934).

Eleanor Roosevelt, *This I Remember* (1949).

C. L. Rossiter, *Constitutional Dictatorship* (1948).

R. E. Sherwood, *Roosevelt and Hopkins* (1948).

W. H. Smith, *History of the Cabinet of the United States* (1925).

E. Stanwood, *History of the Presidency from 1897 to 1909* (1912), Ch. IV.

W. H. Taft, *Our Chief Magistrate and His Powers* (1916).

U.S. News and World Report. A very valuable weekly summary of government activity.

W. A. White, *A Puritan in Babylon: The Story of Calvin Coolidge* (1938).

W. W. Willoughby, *The Principles of the Constitutional Law of the United States* (1930 ed.), Chs. XXIX–XXXI, LXX–LXXI.

W. Wilson, *Constitutional Government in the United States* (1908), Ch. III.

Questions and Problems

1. Had the impeachment of President Johnson been successful, what influence do you believe it would have had upon the future of the Presidency?

2. Propose a plan that would give the Vice President a place of significance and usefulness.

3. Discuss the Cabinet in respect to origin, development, and present functions.

4. Show the part played by the Constitution and the acts of Congress in fixing the powers of the President.

5. List the types of appointments made in essential conformity to the Constitution and those made only in formal compliance with it.
6. Is there any legal means by which Congress could force the removal of an executive officer? Any political means?
7. Define the work of the President's Administrative Staff. Why is the Cabinet not an appropriate body for this work?
8. Could any criticism properly be directed toward a President who refused to grant any pardons, saying in response to each suggestion that it be exercised, "Let the law take its course?"

☆ 12 ☆

The President as Chief Legislator

T HE FRAMERS of the Constitution probably considered that their provision "he shall take care that the laws be faithfully executed" contained the substance of the President's duty; but as long ago as 1900 Admiral George Dewey, yielding temporarily to the suggestion of friends that he ought to be President, embarrassed them with a statement to the effect that all the President had to do was enforce the laws that Congress had passed. Significant as the President's executive powers are, they are probably of no more importance than his legislative powers. Although the Constitution stipulates that all legislative powers shall be vested in Congress, it nevertheless gives the President a share in legislation. Just what this share amounts to and how it has been enlarged through usage is the subject of this chapter.

A general view of the President's legislative powers. Although the framers of the Constitution accepted the theory of the separation of powers, they realized that an absolute division of authority between the two political branches of the government (executive and legislative) would be unworkable or highly unsatisfactory in practice. Consequently, they gave Congress, especially the Senate, a share in executive affairs; and they conferred upon the President some very definite legislative powers. Thus, the Constitution authorizes the President to call Congress into special session; to adjourn it when the two Houses cannot agree upon a time for adjournment; to give it information concerning the state of the Union; to recommend measures for its consideration; and to veto its bills, orders, resolutions, and votes.

But the powers enumerated do not tell the whole story of the President's authority in legislation. His power and influence over Congress have been almost steadily increased through the prestige of his office, his position as leader of his party and the nation, and his use of executive powers for legislative purposes. The President whose activity in legislative affairs does not go far beyond the clauses of the Constitution is severely criticized as being weak in the qualities of leadership.

I. PRESIDENTIAL AUTHORITY OVER SESSIONS OF CONGRESS

Calling special sessions. The Constitution requires Congress to assemble at least once a year—on January 3,[1] unless Congress by law fixes a different date. The Constitution provides further that the President may, on extraordinary occasions, convene both Houses of Congress, or either of them. The extra sessions are called entirely upon the President's responsibility, although he may be greatly influenced in his decision by the advice of leading members of Congress or even by suggestions and importunities from private sources. War, or its imminence, will quite likely lead the President to convene Congress in extraordinary session, as Wilson did in 1917.

President Truman called the Eightieth Congress into special session in November, 1947 and July, 1948, urging it to deal with housing, price rises, civil liberties and other subjects. The President has often exercised his authority to call one House into special session without the other, by convening the Senate for the special purposes of securing that body's consent to the ratification of treaties and its confirmation of appointments to office.[2]

Limited authority over adjournment. The President has constitutional authorization to adjourn Congress in case the two Houses cannot agree with respect to the time of adjournment. As the two chambers of Congress have always managed to reach an agreement, the President has never exercised this power. The Chief Executive has no more authority in adjourning a special session than he has in adjourning a regular session. As a result, an extra session that he has called to deal with inflation, for example, may get completely out of hand and spend several months in political wrangling on other affairs.

II. PRESIDENTIAL MESSAGES TO CONGRESS

Annual messages. In the language of the Constitution, the President "shall from time to time give to the Congress information of the state of the Union, and recommend to their consideration such measures as he shall judge necessary and expedient."[3] This double requirement to re-

---

[1] The Twentieth Amendment, adopted in 1933, fixes January 3 as the date. The old date of assembly was the first Monday in December.

[2] Congress was not in session in June, 1931, when President Hoover proposed the moratorium on war debts. Instead of calling a special session, the President secured, within a few hours, unofficial approval of his plan by telephoning and telegraphing members of Congress.

[3] Art. II, sec. III, cl. I.

port on the state of affairs and to recommend legislation, the Presidents invariably meet in their formal annual messages to Congress at the time it convenes. Although such messages may contain some items for political purposes, they usually relate to the problems waiting to be solved. Congress receives them seriously or lightly, depending upon the demands of the times, political relationships between the White House and the Capitol, and other factors.

Some messages have made history. Who has not heard of the Monroe Doctrine, first given formal expression in two widely separated paragraphs of Monroe's message to Congress in December, 1823! Hardly less famed is Cleveland's message of December, 1895, in which he vigorously reaffirmed and expanded the Monroe Doctrine in relation to the Venezuelan-British boundary dispute. A typical annual message is found in President Truman's communication of January 5, 1949. He reviewed and made comments and general recommendations on a number of subjects, leaving the working out of details to Congress. On other issues he made specific recommendations, for example: repeal the Taft-Hartley law; raise minimum wages from 40 to 75 cents an hour; expand the social security program and increase the benefit payments; enact a national health insurance law; keep tidelands (containing oil) for the government; restore the original provisions of the reciprocal trade law and extend the period for its operation; and enact anti-lynching, anti-poll tax, and fair employment practice measures. The budget message, submitted annually on the vital subject of national revenues and expenditures, is discussed in Chapter 22 that deals with Government Finance. The Employment Act of 1946 requires still another annual message—the economic report, which receives attention in Chapter 23 on Commerce and Business.

Other messages to Congress. The President's messages to Congress are by no means limited to the above-mentioned annual communications. The President may send a message to Congress on any subject at any time. He may ask for money with which to defray the expenses of a survey commission, or urge more speed on a revenue bill, or suggest that "the state of the Union" demands that Congress leave off investigating and discussing administrative scandals and turn to constructive legislation. President Hoover sent no less than 63 messages to Congress during its session from December 7, 1931, to June 16, 1932, suggesting, advising, and urging that action be taken on various subjects.[4] It is now the common practice of the President to speak in general terms in his annual messages and to deal with numerous specific problems in separate messages.

---

[4] Pendleton Herring, "First Session of the Seventy-Second Congress," *Am. Pol. Sci. Rev.* (1932), XXVI, 855.

How messages are delivered. Washington and John Adams delivered their important messages orally, the two Houses meeting in joint session to receive them. The method of our first two Presidents was not followed by their successors, who for well over a hundred years sent their messages to Congress, where they were droned out by clerks. In 1913 Wilson returned to the early practice. Few would deny that Wilson's rather dramatic appearances before Congress had much greater public effect, both in this country and abroad, than written messages would have produced.

President Franklin D. Roosevelt used the oral message to penetrate every cell of reason and to play upon every string of emotion. Assured of popular support and a substantial congressional majority, his tone was mandatory; uncertain of such support, he was likely to be conciliatory and emphasize partnership; he would triumphantly report achievements of his Administration, or, with his back near the wall, he might be aggressive, even defiant.

A factor of significance equal to that of the manner of delivery is the timing of a message. As observed above, the President frequently sends Congress special messages (these are usually written) on matters of importance. In 1933 when the Senate was debating the President's economy bill and while its fate was in doubt, the President sent a brief message recommending that the Volstead Act be modified to permit the sale of beer. "The public demand for economy was excelled only by its thirst for beer," comments Professor Pendleton Herring.[5] Pressure upon Congress for both measures became intense. Both Houses, long torn by dissension over the economy measure, at once enacted it and unitedly and joyously voted for beer. "Now, boys," the President had said in effect, "as soon as you get that economy bill out of the way, we can have some beer."

Effect of messages. The only obligation Congress is under with regard to a message from the President is to receive it. If, however, the majority in each House is of the same party as the President, his message will probably receive careful consideration, but the extent to which his recommendations will be followed varies considerably. Usually a majority of them fail to win legislative approval. Thus, in 1949–1950, an entirely unofficial alliance between conservative Democrats and Republicans defeated most of the program presented by the President. At times an aggressive President who is a master of the art of politics can find the means for bringing his congressional majorities to enact the major features of his program into law. If his messages express the public sentiment on old questions still awaiting settlement or reveal new problems urgently demanding solution, the force of public opinion may be so strong as to stir a reluctant Congress to action. President Wilson used his message to Congress very effectively

[5] Herring, *Presidential Leadership*, p. 62.

in getting public support for his progressive program in domestic affairs, and later in leading the country into war with the Central Powers. Indeed, his war messages were delivered not only to the American Congress and people but to the whole world, giving the President a position of leadership in world affairs that few, if any, had ever achieved. In 1933 the national emergency and popular approval of the President's leadership led Congress to adopt practically every item of Roosevelt's reconstruction program, and his messages to Congress during the Second World War probably take their place in effectiveness along with those of Wilson.

III. THE PRESIDENTIAL VETO POWER [6]

Extent of the veto power. Every bill, order, resolution, or vote passed by the Senate and the House of Representatives must be presented to the President. If he approves the act, he signs it, and it becomes a law; but if he objects to it, he may exercise his veto power, and the act does not then become a law unless Congress passes it over his veto by a two-thirds majority.

There are three matters upon which the President cannot use the veto. First, the question of the adjournment of Congress is expressly excepted by the language of the Constitution. Second, a proposed amendment to the Constitution, which requires a two-thirds vote of each House in the first instance, is not subject to the veto. Third, Congress early devised a special type of measure, called the concurrent resolution, which is not submitted to the President. In 1897 the Senate Committee on the Judiciary conceded that the language of the Constitution gave the President a veto on such resolutions; but the Committee placed what it considered a more practical construction on the veto clause, and arrived at the conclusion that "matters peculiarly within the province of Congress alone" and that "never embraced legislative decisions proper" should, in conformity to the long-established practice, continue to be exempt from executive action.[7] Thus, by concurrent resolution, the two Houses authorize joint committees, the publication of documents, payment for the same, and other expenses incident to the work of Congress for which funds have already been appropriated by law. The concurrent resolution should be distinguished from the joint resolution, which is in a real sense a legislative measure and as such is submitted to the President for his approval or rejection.

The exceptions noted above do not materially impair the veto power.

[6] E. S. Corwin, *The President: Office and Powers* (1948 ed.), Ch. VII; J. M. Mathews, *The American Constitutional System* (1940 ed.), Ch. XI; G. C. Robinson, "The Veto Record of Franklin D. Roosevelt," *Am. Pol. Sci. Rev.,* XXXVI, 75 (Feb., 1942); K. A. Towle, "The Presidential Veto since 1889," *Am. Pol. Sci. Rev.,* XXXI, 51 (Feb., 1937).

[7] Mathews, *op. cit.,* pp. 148–149.

The President may use it in connection with all measures that are definitely legislative in character. Since a two-thirds vote is necessary to override a veto, the power is a very strong defensive weapon in the hands of the President, giving him the strength of one sixth the membership of Congress.

Messaged veto. When the President receives a bill from Congress, he has ten days, not counting Sundays, in which to consider it. He may, of course, seek advice on the bill from any source; but he is most likely to consult his Special Counsel or someone else in the White House office, the Attorney General, or the head of the department primarily affected by the measure. Usually he decides to approve the bill, and affixes his signature. If he follows the very unusual procedure of neither signing nor vetoing the bill during the ten days allowed, Congress continuing in session, the bill becomes a law without his signature. When the President exercises the power of veto, he must return the bill, together with the reasons for his veto, to the House in which the bill originated. That body then proceeds to reconsider the bill, and, if two thirds of the members present approve it, it is sent to the other House, where a two-thirds vote will make it a law despite the executive veto. Obviously, if either House fails to muster the two-thirds majority, the bill fails to become a law.

The pocket veto. Suppose Congress adjourns within less than ten days after the President has received a bill and before he has acted upon it. Nonaction on the part of the President after Congress has adjourned kills the bill. This method of allowing bills to die quietly after Congress has adjourned has been used well over 700 times. It is appropriately called the "pocket veto." It should be observed that the pocket veto is an absolute veto, since Congress, being adjourned, has no opportunity to reconsider a bill so vetoed. A President sometimes places on record his reasons for a pocket veto, but his explanation is not a veto message as in the case of bills returned before the end of a session.

Approval of bills after Congress adjourns. During the ten days preceding adjournment Congress usually enacts a number of bills of which the President approves. Formerly, it was thought that all such bills should be signed before the adjournment, and Presidents, sometimes reproaching Congress for its volume of legislation near the end of its session, hurriedly signed scores of them as the session drew to a close. But Wilson, accepting the advice of his Attorney General that the adjournment of Congress did not deprive him of his constitutional right to defer action on any bill for ten days, signed some bills after the close of the session. Later Presidents have followed Wilson's example; and the Supreme Court, in 1932,[8] declared constitutional this practice that makes it possible for the

---

[8] Edwards v. U.S., 286 U.S. 482.

Chief Executive to give more deliberate attention to the dozens of bills presented to him during the hectic days immediately preceding adjournment.

The veto in practice. Early Presidents used the veto sparingly. John Adams, Jefferson, and John Quincy Adams did not use it at all. Jefferson probably expressed the opinion of his contemporaries when he said that the President should approve a bill unless it was rather clearly unauthorized by the Constitution. But Jackson, in a characteristic manner, refused to be limited by such an interpretation. Considering that only nine bills had been vetoed before 1829, his "twelve vetoes descended upon Congress like the blows of an iron flail." [9] He even went so far as to veto a bill to recharter the national bank on the grounds of unconstitutionality, although the Supreme Court had declared the original chartering act to be constitutional. Said the vigorous Executive, in part: "The Congress, the Executive, and the Court, must each for itself be guided by its own opinion of the Constitution. . . . The opinion of the judges has no more authority over Congress than the opinion of Congress has over the judges, and on that point the President is independent of both." [10]

Although later Presidents did not go to Jackson's extreme in boldly asserting that the Supreme Court had erred in interpreting the Constitution, they have followed his practice in freely exercising the veto power, particularly since the Civil War. They not only veto acts that in their opinion are unconstitutional; but they veto those they regard as extravagant, untimely, inconsistent with our treaty obligations, or otherwise inexpedient. Cleveland and Franklin D. Roosevelt share the honors as veto Presidents, their combined disapprovals representing two thirds of all measures vetoed. Cleveland concentrated his attention on pension, military, and naval relief measures. Roosevelt submitted messaged vetoes of 371 bills and pocket vetoed 260 others, a total of 631. His vetoes covered practically the entire range of congressional activity, having been employed on measures designed for agricultural relief, soldiers' bonus, flood control, the protection of fisheries, national defense, Memorial Day observance, the regulation of approaches to cemeteries, the installation of parking meters, and a host of other matters great and small.[11]

Overriding the veto. Public opinion is usually on the side of the President in his exercise of the veto, and Congress seldom finds the two-thirds

[9] Quoted in Brooks, *Political Parties and Electoral Problems* (1923 ed.), p. 55.
[10] Quoted in W. W. Willoughby, *The Constitutional Law of the United States* (1910 ed.), I, 1306–1307.
[11] G. C. Robinson, "The Veto Record of Franklin D. Roosevelt," *Am. Pol. Sci. Rev.*, XXXVI, 75 (February, 1942).

majority necessary to override it. (It should be clear that the messaged veto is the only type of veto that ever reaches Congress.) It is true that President Johnson, a Union Democrat warring with a Congress overwhelmingly Republican, saw 15 bills passed over his veto, but other Presidents have had no such experience. Not one time in ten has Congress been able to nullify the Executive veto. Only 9 of Franklin D. Roosevelt's 371 messaged vetoes were overridden. The most recent significant instances of overriding occurred in 1947, when Congress passed the Taft-Hartley law, and in 1950, when it passed the Internal Security Act, "the objections of the President to the contrary notwithstanding."

Vetoes are seldom overridden for the reason that nearly always more than one third of the members of one House or the other will agree with the President, and thus defeat a bill upon reconsideration. Taking advantage of this fact, large majorities in Congress frequently pass inadvisable bills for the purpose of pleasing their constituencies, many congressmen who vote for such bills hoping and expecting all the while that the President will show a more courageous spirit than they and kill the measures with his veto. When a presidential veto of a measure of this nature has seemed to be in danger of being overridden by Congress, some congressmen who supported the measure originally have on occasion changed sides and voted to support the Executive veto.

The threat of veto. The President may exercise a sort of veto by informing a committee of either House, or the whole Congress, of his intention to veto a pending bill. He may state that he objects to certain features of it that must be modified before he can approve it, or he may say that he is opposed to the whole purpose of the bill and will veto it in any event. When the bill authorizing an increase in veterans' loans on their bonus certificates was before the Senate Finance Committee in February, 1931, President Hoover wrote a letter to Chairman Smoot, giving his objections to the bill and warning Congress that the bill would delay the return of prosperity and place additional financial burdens upon the country. Later, when it was feared that the President would kill the bill with a pocket veto, Mr. Hoover assured Senator Reed in a telephonic conversation that he would exercise a direct veto, thus giving Congress an opportunity to pass the bill over his veto before adjournment.[12] The assurance that the veto would be exercised did not deter Congress in this particular instance, for the American Legion and other organizations exerted pressure that Congress could not resist. President Roosevelt was more successful when, in 1939, he wrote Senator Harrison, Chairman of the Senate Committee on Finance, that he would veto a pending bill if certain pro-

[12] *Time*, March 2, 1931, p. 14.

visions were incorporated in it which he regarded as certain to impair reciprocal trade agreements between the United States and several other countries.[13]

The question of the item veto. The President seems to have no authority to veto separate items of a bill. He must accept or reject the measure in its entirety. The item veto in the hands of the President would enable him to restrain congressional extravagance in the matter of appropriations. Under our present system, however much the President may preach economy and endeavor to keep expenditures down, he usually feels forced to accept an appropriation bill, even if unjustifiable items are included, because his disapproval of the bill might necessitate an extra session of Congress or lead to friction with that body, or seriously interfere with the indispensable administrative services.

More than three fourths of the states have empowered the governor to veto separate items of appropriation bills, and in a number of states he may reduce items. Although some governors have no doubt abused these powers, this additional executive discretion is generally conceded to have improved the system of appropriations in the states; and many scholars and public men propose that the President's veto power also be extended to separate items of appropriation bills.

RIDERS. Congress has sometimes tacked to appropriation bills measures relating to entirely different subjects. Frequently a President would veto such measures if they appeared in separate bills; but, since he can ill afford to veto appropriation bills to which they are attached, they "ride" to executive approval on the backs of the finance bills. Thus, a rider on an Army appropriation bill virtually deprived President Johnson of his power as Commander-in-Chief of the Army.

President Hayes earnestly contended against the use of the rider, and the House of Representatives practically conceded his point,[14] although, on occasion, Congress still arranges a "hitch-hike" for a measure. In August, 1937, Senator Tydings managed to have his Miller-Tydings Bill incorporated into a measure imposing additional taxes in the District of Columbia. This rider was really an amendment to the Sherman Antitrust Act of 1890, and it weakened that act in that it permitted manufacturers of branded and trade-marked articles destined for interstate commerce to fix retail prices in about forty states that sanctioned this procedure in intrastate business. Several months earlier the President's opposition had blocked the Miller-Tydings Bill, but now, finding it attached to a revenue measure, he had no choice but to approve it or veto the revenue law along with it. "This is

---

[13] Mathews and Berdahl, *op. cit.,* pp. 286–287.
[14] J Bryce, *The American Commonwealth* (1913 ed.), I, 214–215.

the first instance during my term of office," he complained, "that this vicious practice of attaching unrelated riders to tax or appropriation bills has occurred. . . . I have decided to sign the bill in the hope that it will not be as harmful as most people predict." [15] In the letter to Senator Harrison, referred to above, the President was objecting to proposed rider tariff legislation in a bill that was supposed to deal only with excise taxes. Prompted by the desire to outlaw the rider system and to bring individual items of appropriations bills under his scrutiny, the President, in his 1938 budget message to Congress, recommended legislation or a constitutional amendment, whichever course Congress might deem to be the correct one, to authorize the item, or selective, veto.[16] Nothing was done with this suggestion at the time, nor does the Legislative Reorganization Act of 1946 do more than restate the Senate rule prohibiting riders (only with respect to the Senate) on appropriations bills.

IV. THE PRESIDENT'S EXTRA-CONSTITUTIONAL MEANS OF INFLUENCING LEGISLATION [17]

Up to this point attention has been confined to those legislative powers that the Constitution expressly grants to the President. But the legislative power of the President rests more upon the influence he exerts through his personality, his political astuteness, his skill in working with groups and individuals, his resourcefulness, his ability to gage the public attitude, and a variety of other factors than it does upon the clauses of the Constitution. That document rather clearly stops short of making the President the chief legislator. Indeed, it may be inferred from the Constitution that the framers expected the President to go along quietly with Congress. It soon came about, however, that Congress was divided by political parties and by sectional interests stronger than those parties, interests that could wreck parties and create new parties. It became more and more difficult for Congress to legislate in the national interest, and it became necessary for the President to supply leadership on matters of national policy.

Although presidential leadership goes back to Jefferson and Jackson, Theodore Roosevelt introduced the type of executive domination with which the country has become familiar. Today the people and, to a considerable extent, Congress itself look to the President for legislative leader-

[15] *Time*, August 30, 1937, p. 11.

[16] *United States News*, January 10, 1938; Mathews and Berdahl, *op. cit.*, pp. 281–287.

[17] W. E. Binkley, *President and Congress* (1947), Chs. X–XV; Corwin, *The President*, Ch. VII; P. Herring, *Presidential Leadership: The Political Relations of Congress and the Chief Executive* (1940); H. J. Laski, *The American Presidency: An Interpretation* (1940), Ch. III.

ship. If he does not supply it, he is written down as a failure, as indeed he is. Therefore, in directing legislation the President not only uses his constitutional powers, but also employs a number of means not mentioned in the Constitution—means we may designate as extra-constitutional. Through his position as leader of his party and through the place he may win for himself as leader of the whole nation, his influence over Congress is enormously increased. He may prepare, or cause to be prepared, bills that by indirect methods he may have introduced in Congress. He can influence legislation by holding conferences with groups or individuals in Congress. At critical times he may win the favorable votes of legislators for his projects by skillfully using his constitutional power to make appointments to office.[18] To mention just one other means at his command, he may appeal to the people either directly or indirectly for their support for a particular measure or policy, or on behalf of congressmen who stand with him.

1. **Authority through party leadership.** The President, whether he likes the idea or not, is responsible for the legislative program of his party. The millions who elect him look to him to carry out the announced policies of the party and, more particularly, those he announced during his campaign for election. The people do not want a President who is timid in his relations with Congress. He is quite likely to win popular applause if he boldly takes command of the legislative bodies and pushes through his projects. Furthermore, legislators find it to their advantage to accept executive leadership. A congressman who belongs to the same party as the President can make a much more effective appeal to the voters of his district on his record in support of the President than on a record of opposition or half-hearted support. The political fortunes of senators and representatives are rather closely tied up with those of the President, and it would be the veriest folly for the majority of them to ignore this fact and chart an independent course. Presidential leadership in legislation is further strengthened because it is not possible for a single individual in either House of Congress to assume such leadership. The two Houses are equal in legislative matters, and some jealousy exists between them. A member might lead one House or the other, but not both. The President alone can supply the necessary unity of command.

SOME EXAMPLES. Without question some Presidents are more successful in directing legislation than others; but all our strong executives since the Civil War have effectively led Congress when its majorities were of the same political faith as the President. Theodore Roosevelt dominated his Congress, and Wilson's power was felt even more forcibly at the

18 The appointing power is not, of course, an extra-constitutional power; but it may be fairly classified as such when it is used for the purpose of influencing legislation.

Capitol. The Federal Reserve Act, the Income Tax Law, the Clayton Act, the Adamson Law, and many another went through Congress under the skillful direction of President Wilson. We repeat that the people expect the President to take the lead in legislation. Aggressive Presidents are glad to assume it, and those who would shun it find that they are urged from all sides to follow the example of their more "congressionally minded" predecessors. In 1921 Harding took office with the firm resolve to let Congress alone, but he had not gone far with this plan when he found that it would not work. In like manner Hoover found that he should attempt to lead Congress. In 1932 Democratic leaders in Congress turned to Roosevelt as their generalissimo immediately after his election, not waiting for the following March 4.

2. Administration measures. In a parliamentary system of government like that of Great Britain, all of the important bills are introduced in Parliament by the executive department; but our presidential system, based upon the principle of the separation of powers, did not contemplate any such procedure. The Constitution provides that the President shall from time to time recommend to Congress "such measures as he shall judge necessary and expedient," a clause that can hardly be interpreted as granting to the President the right to introduce bills. Nevertheless, a system has developed that amounts to that in practice. The procedure is for some congressman, a supporter of the President, to introduce formally the bill the administration has prepared; or the measure may be sent directly to the appropriate committee, which will probably introduce it. These administration measures, coming directly from or having the backing of the President, are usually given special consideration; and, if the President's party has a majority in Congress, they have a fair chance of being enacted into law.

Although congressmen may periodically complain of this extension of executive influence, the practice is a most logical one. The President and the officers of the departments, in their everyday task of administering the affairs of the government, learn the defects of existing laws and the need for new laws. Consequently, when they check, as they do, through the Bureau of the Budget to make sure that their proposals fit into an established program, they are in a much better position to frame bills covering the needs of the administrative services than a member of Congress or even a committee of either House. For instance, Congress might do much worse than pass a bill relating to the foreign service drafted by officers of the Department of State, or a bill relating to the public lands drafted by an upright and intelligent Secretary of the Interior.

Nearly all of the principal measures enacted during Franklin D. Roosevelt's administration were drafted by his administrative experts. Two of his notable peacetime administration measures failed to meet the approval of Congress, the bill to make the Supreme Court more amenable to presidential influence (1937) and the bill to reorganize the executive branch of the Government (1938). In the emergency years of 1941–1942 sweeping measures, accompanied by a letter from the President, were sent to some representative or senator, and by him introduced.

The committees concerned held hearings on the measures, but most of the time in each instance was consumed by Administration officials testifying in support of the legislative or appropriation bills. . . . The bills were then passed by each chamber nearly as reported. Should one chamber insist on writing in 'undesired' amendments, such provisions were more than likely to be changed or wiped out by the other body, or at least modified in conference. Thus only a few paragraphs of legislation and hardly any entire public laws were finally enacted contrary to the will of the Administration.[19]

Having followed the dictates of the Administration, senators and representatives, even members of the President's own party, complained of executive control.

Some congressmen attributed their misfortunes in the elections of November, 1942, to popular reaction against Administrative influence in Congress. It may have been, however, that the voters rebuked Congress not for following the President, but for not going beyond his relatively moderate recommendations on war finance and inflation control. Be that as it may, toward the end of the war and the tragic end of Roosevelt's tenure of office, Congress displayed a growing tendency to reject his proposals. Between January and April, 1945, Congress failed to follow his leadership on the "Work or Fight" bill, the induction of nurses into the armed forces, and peacetime universal military training. President Truman, less experienced and perhaps less inclined toward executive leadership than Roosevelt, and carrying the double handicap of sudden elevation to office and the postwar "get back to normalcy" urge in Congress and the country, has had very little success with his administration measures. His appeals to Congress have had practically no effect, and his administrative agents "lobbying" for his measures have irritated congressmen. Nor have his exhortations to the people to force Congress to act met with a large favorable response.

3. Influencing legislation by conferences. Whether the bills have emanated from executive sources or have been initiated by members or committees of Congress, the President keeps a watchful eye upon those over which he is vitally concerned. At times he is as interested in accomplishing the defeat of a particular measure as he is in securing the passage of

[19] F. M. Riddick, "First Session of the Seventy-seventh Congress," *Am. Pol. Sci. Rev.,* XXXVI, 300 (April, 1942).

another. Often leaders of his party in the House or Senate, or even leaders of the opposing party, will go of their own accord to the White House to discuss legislation. Not infrequently the President will make the first move and will summon them for a conference. "Come up some evening for a long talk," wrote Theodore Roosevelt to "Uncle Joe" Cannon, Speaker of the House. (Come) "about 9:30, if you can, so that we will be free from interruption." [20] In recent years there has been a more regular (but quite unofficial) liaison between the Capitol and the White House, the former being represented by the Big Four, consisting of the Vice President, the Speaker of the House, and the majority floor leader in each House.

At a conference the President may learn that a favorite bill has no chance of passage; that he must accept important amendments to another; that a particularly objectionable measure will probably be enacted. On the other hand, he is often able to win the leaders to his side in a number of matters and thus be assured of early and favorable action in Congress. A competent executive who knows the temper of Congress can bring many important issues to a successful termination by these informal conferences.

4. Use of the patronage. In the last chapter we learned something of the extent of the President's appointing power and of the interest of senators and representatives in securing their share of the offices for their constituents. Obviously, a politically minded President can use the large patronage at his disposal for the purpose of winning the support of congressmen of his own or of the opposing party. In 1864 Lincoln believed that the adoption of the constitutional amendment prohibiting slavery would save him the necessity of raising another million men to defeat the Confederates. A careful canvass of the states showed that the necessary three-fourths vote for the amendment was by no means certain. Consequently, it was decided that another state, Nevada, sure to vote in the affirmative, should be admitted to the Union. In order to secure the necessary majority in the House of Representatives for the admission of Nevada, Lincoln brought three representatives to his side by giving them the privilege of naming three appointees to lucrative offices.[21] Cleveland is said to have used the same tactics in bringing about the repeal of the Sherman Silver Purchase Act. A senator is reported to have declared, "Mr. President, the act will not be repealed until the nether regions freeze over." The President, having just completed a patronage agreement with some of the senator's colleagues, triumphantly asserted that the freezing would take place within two hours. Such definite bargains are probably uncommon, but congressmen are not likely to forget that the President has

[20] Herring, *Presidential Leadership*, p. 50, from L. W. Busbey, *Uncle Joe Cannon* (1927), p. 216.

[21] C. A. Dana, *Recollections of the Civil War* (1902), pp. 174–177.

the power to reward and punish them through his distribution of the patronage. In March, 1933, as the House was about to vote on the President's economy bill, a Democratic representative said: "When the *Congressional Record* goes to President Roosevelt's desk in the morning, he will look over the roll call . . . and I warn you new Democrats to be careful where your names are found." [22] Hisses and groans did not obscure the representative's point. Indeed, they added emphasis to it.

"Lame duck" appointments. Not uncommonly a defeated congressman, frequently somewhat unsympathetically referred to as a "lame duck," receives an appointment to an administrative office. In some cases the consolation prize has been more valuable than the seat in Congress. Obviously the possibility of securing through presidential appointment a place of profit and possibly a place of high honor in the event of enforced retirement from Congress may serve to keep the President's partisans at the Capitol in harmony with his program. This is not to say that many such appointees may not be quite competent to fill responsible civil offices, but only that through standing by the President they may place themselves in line for them.

5. Appeals to voters. It was pointed out above that if the President has the public on his side many congressmen will feel compelled to support him in order to square themselves with their constituents. If he does not have the confidence of the public, he can hardly hope to lead Congress. Recognizing these facts, Presidents make every effort to win popular approval for their policies. The inaugural address may do much to mollify elements disgruntled during the campaign. A message to Congress may be so skillfully framed that it strikes a popular chord. A heart-to-heart talk with the people in some anniversary address may win general admiration for the man who more than anyone else carries the public burden. In conferences with newspaper men, in interviews with influential citizens, in conversations with friends who help interpret the executive to the public, and in various other ways, appeals may be subtly made to the nation. Some Presidents have made direct appeals to the people. Jackson and Johnson both went so far as to pose as their champions against the machinations of Congress, the former succeeding and the latter miserably failing in the attempt. Theodore Roosevelt effectively appealed to the country to support Republican candidates for Congress in 1906; but Wilson's appeal for a Democratic Congress in 1918 invoked lively resentment and perhaps alienated some independent voters who otherwise would have supported the Democratic candidates. The next year Wilson went directly to the people on the League of Nations issue, but his physical collapse while on the speaking tour left the efficacy of such an appeal undecided. The Presi-

[22] Herring, *op. cit.*, p. 59.

dent who goes directly to the people in order to subject Congress to public pressure is playing a hazardous game. Even if the cause is just and the President brilliant, the public may not approve of the Executive's attempt to coerce the lawmaking bodies, especially when there are scores of congressmen, some able and others clever, who hold up the bogey of executive autocracy and usurpation.[23]

"Good evening, my friends." The possibilities of reaching the American people by radio were demonstrated most fully by President Franklin D. Roosevelt who, with the familiar greeting that heads this paragraph, caused millions of citizens to edge closer to their radios to hear his report on "the state of the Union." We quote from *Time:* [24]

For the second time [on May 7] Franklin Roosevelt was "reporting" to the country from the White House. Eight weeks prior when the country was dying by inches his first broadcast on the banking crisis had been a historic success. His second attempt to clear and steer the public mind on issues of state produced a popular reaction no less favorable.

President Roosevelt's speech, simple and sympathetic, was more than a review of his two months in office, more than a recitation of the purposes of his Civilian Conservation Corps, his Tennessee Valley Plan, his mortgage and farm relief bills, his railroad legislation. . . . Deftly he turned aside the "dictatorship" charge by pointing out that Congress still retains its Constitutional authority and has done nothing more than designate him as its agent in carrying out its will, all in keeping with U.S. tradition. As for the Government's relations with industry, agriculture, and transportation, the President explained them not as those of a Socialist State and its servants but as those of business partners, "not a partnership in profits, because the profits would still go to the citizens, but rather a partnership in planning and a partnership to see that the plans are carried out."

Congressional checks on the President. We must not exaggerate the President's power to control legislation. Although the President has many advantages over Congress, he does not easily direct the legislators along the paths he would have them follow. He cannot drive them; he must work with them. The Senate may defeat the best of treaties that the President submits for its approval, and it may withhold its assent from appointments that he regards as most desirable. The two Houses may refuse to vote appropriations for needed public services, while supplying funds for those that serve only political purposes. They may neglect to enact measures to meet new conditions, or fail to repeal laws that have proved to be in conflict with the public interest. Provided a two-thirds majority in

[23] The resentment aroused by President Roosevelt's interference in the Democratic primaries of 1938 was noted in Chapter 9, section III.

[24] May 15, 1933, p. 9.

both Houses concur, they may pass, in opposition to the President's wishes, bills that fundamentally change the organization of the administrative services and the duties of its officers. They may harass the President by repeated calls for information concerning the work of the departments, and by officially investigating their activities. The enumeration might be continued; but we conclude with the mention of the power of the House of Representatives to impeach all civil officers, the President included, and of the power of the Senate to try such impeachments.

V. THE ADMINISTRATIVE RULE-MAKING POWER [25]

Not only do the President and other high-ranking administrative officials influence the course of legislation in various ways, but they also have the authority to make rules and regulations that have the force of law. Some of this authority—for example, the authority to make codes for the government of the armed forces and for the conduct of foreign relations —comes direct from the grants of power to the President by the Constitution. The great bulk of the rule-making authority comes, however, from the statutes of Congress. That body cannot and should not provide for the details of administration. The better procedure is for Congress to pass a law declaring a *policy* and to leave with the President and other administrative officers the duty of making the necessary regulations to carry this policy into effect.

The flexible tariff law of 1922 furnishes a good example of this. The President, advised by experts, was authorized to increase or decrease the tariff rates in accordance with the declared policy of Congress to make it possible for American producers to compete in our domestic markets with foreign producers. The President was not authorized to make tariff laws; rather he was charged with the duty of making administrative regulations to put and keep in effect the tariff law that Congress had enacted.[26] The regulations so promulgated generally have the full force and effect of law.

Limits of the administrative rule-making power. The emergency that faced the country in 1933 prompted Congress not only to pass, at the President's request, unprecedented measures, but also to give the Chief Executive the most sweeping discretionary powers in putting them into effect. In some of these measures Congress announced policy only in its broadest outlines, leaving the President and his associates to work out details of policy as well as details of administration. Thus, an economy bill

[25] F. F. Blachly and M. E. Oatman, *Federal Regulatory Action and Control* (1940); James Hart, *The Ordinance-Making Powers of the President of the United States* (1925), and his "The Exercise of the Rule-Making Power," in the *Report* (with special studies) *of the President's Committee on Administrative Management* (1937); Harvey Walker, *The Legislative Process* (1948), Ch. 20.

[26] Hampton v. United States, 276 U.S. 394 (1928).

gave the President a very wide discretion in reducing salaries and pensions. Another measure gave him broad powers of control over the currency. The National Industrial Recovery Act gave him the authority to put into effect codes of fair competition. This last act was one of several that the Supreme Court held unconstitutional on the ground that legislative power had been delegated to the Executive. Said the Chief Justice, speaking for a unanimous Court: The act

. . . supplies no standards for any trade, industry, or activity. . . . Instead of prescribing rules of conduct, it authorizes the making of codes to prescribe them. . . . In view of the . . . nature of the few restrictions that are imposed, the discretion of the President in approving or prescribing codes, and thus enacting laws for the government of trade or industry throughout the country, is virtually unfettered. We think that the code-making authority thus conferred is an unconstitutional delegation of legislative power.[27]

In other words, here is the limit of the doctrine expounded in the flexible tariff case. This decision did not, however, place any serious limitation on the power of Congress to delegate to the President and other administrative officials the authority to make rules to carry legislative policy into effect.

How the rule-making power is exercised. Under powers granted to the President by the Constitution to command the Army and Navy and to conduct foreign relations elaborate codes have been promulgated for the regulation of the armed forces and the diplomatic and consular service. And under authority granted by the Constitution and more particularly by Congress the President and many other administrative officers and agencies (perhaps a hundred) prepare and promulgate codes, rules, orders, and directives on the customs service, the civil service, the postal service, agricultural production, transactions in securities, radio communications, and a wide variety of other subjects. It is perhaps unnecessary to say that the President personally attends to but little of this administrative law-making. Much of it requires his signature, but the actual work is done by others.

During the last war Congress still enacted the laws, but hundreds of Government lawyers working in scores of departments and agencies, translated these laws into active regulations touching the lives of citizens in dozens of ways. They told the manufacturer what he could make, the farmer what he might grow, the employer how he must deal with his employees, the employee how much he might earn, the housewife what she could buy, the car-owner how much gas he might use, the husband whether he might wear cuffs on his trousers or a double-breasted coat and the wife whether she could wear silk stockings or a girdle. Of course,

[27] Schechter v. United States, 295 U.S. 495 (1935).

a number of these regulations were based upon war legislation, but the process goes on in peacetime as well, the only difference being that it is slowed down a bit and the regulations may touch the average citizen in fewer particulars.

Regardless of the origin of a regulation or order, it must go to the Director of the Budget who gives it the "once over" for the President. From "the Budget" it goes to the Attorney General, who checks it for its form and legality. The Director of the Office of Price Administration, the Director of the Office of Economic Stabilization, the Chairman of the War Production Board, and such unofficial advisers as Bernard M. Baruch should be associated with the Director of the Budget and the Attorney General as the leading figures in the preparation of the wartime administrative regulations and executive orders. This group was designated the "Kitchen Congress," a term suggested by President Jackson's "Kitchen Cabinet." During one year of war 890 executive orders were prepared for President Roosevelt and received his signature. During the same period, executive agencies issued a five-foot shelf of directives, orders, and rules.

Administrative rule-making practice did not begin with any recent administration, and it will not be abolished by any change in administration. "Executive orders have long been used," declared the President's Committee on Administrative Management (1937). "They are particularly necessary in periods of emergency when there is rapid change in governmental policies and organization. Executive direction and control of national administration would be impossible without the use of this device." [28]

Distrust of the rule-making practice. The popular conception is that Congress makes the laws; and when the general body of citizens becomes aware, as it does in wartime, of the extent to which administrative departments and agencies are charged with the duty of promulgating regulations to carry laws into effect, suspicion and resentment are likely to arise. Such reaction may indicate a great deal of ignorance of the process of modern government and it may even be largely partisan in its nature. Nevertheless, the theory that Congress should not delegate power to the President and his administrative subordinates dies hard, and there are frequent orations in the Halls of Congress against such delegation of authority.

Recently, and as a necessary procedure in carrying on a great war, Congress broke the record on the matter of delegating authority to the President. To allay the misgivings of many of its members (and their constituents) it inserted in a number of enactments a clause that provided that the authority delegated to the President might be terminated by Con-

---

[28] Quoted in *United States News,* December 11, 1942, p. 13. This *News* article explains in language the layman can understand, the process of rule-making as it operates today. See also J. R. Pennock, *Administration and the Rule of Law* (1941), pp. 38–40.

gress at any time by concurrent resolution. As no such take-it-back resolution was ever passed, the issue remains in doubt. Had Congress passed such a resolution applicable, for example, to the First War Powers Act, doubtless it would have insisted upon the observance of the practice of a century and a quarter and failed to send it to the President for his approval or veto, and the President would have found the authority that had been delegated to him withdrawn without his consent.[29] Then the Attorney General and even the Supreme Court might have had to pass upon the question of whether or not a concurrent resolution of this type should be referred to the President as are ordinary laws and joint resolutions.

Further distrust of the rule-making power and administrative rule-makers is indicated by the Administrative Procedure Act (1946), which receives brief attention in Chapter 19, section III.

VI. THE QUESTION OF A CLOSER UNION BETWEEN THE EXECUTIVE AND THE LEGISLATIVE BRANCHES [30]

It is obvious to all except the most superficial observers that the national administration cannot function smoothly unless there is co-operation between the executive and the legislative branches. The absence of teamwork between President Truman and Congress has given point to this fact. The separation of powers, designed in a day when governments had little to do besides keep the peace, served very well as long as governments had only negative functions to perform. The positive functions are the all-important ones today, and they cannot be discharged under a rigid system of "checks and balances." For the purpose of carrying out the many services of modern government, co-operation of President and Congress is often achieved by informal and extra-constitutional means. In recognition of this fact and in order to strengthen the ties between the two political divisions, some statesmen and scholars have advocated the establishment of more definite and formal connecting links between the administrative and legislative branches of the government. Several of these proposals are here considered briefly.

1. **Administrative officials on the floors of Congress.** On a number of occasions the proposal has been made by responsible authorities that heads of the executive departments—Cabinet members—be admitted to each House of Congress for the purpose of giving information, advice, or participating in discussion. During Washington's administration this plan

[29] Howard White, "Executive Responsibility via Concurrent Resolution," *Am. Pol. Sci. Rev.,* XXXVI, 895 (October, 1942).

[30] E. S. Corwin, "Wanted: A New Type of Cabinet," *New York Times Magazine,* Oct. 10, 1948, p. 14; W. Y. Elliot, *The Need for Constitutional Reform* (1935), Chs. IX–X; G. B. Galloway, *Congress at the Crossroads* (1946), Ch. 7; Herring, *op. cit.,* Ch. IV; Laski, *op. cit.,* Ch. V.

was started, but it did not develop into an established practice, although the executive and legislative branches usually had various connecting lines, chiefly of a subterranean character. In 1864 a committee of the House of Representatives recommended that a law be enacted to give department heads seats (but not votes) in each House, and a committee of the Senate made a similar recommendation in 1881.[31]

Nothing having come of the proposal, President Taft took it up in his message to Congress, December, 1912. He contended that

. . . the rigid holding apart of the executive and the legislative branches of this Government has not worked for the great advantage of either. . . . The legislative and the executive each performs its own appropriate function, but these functions must be co-ordinated. Time and time again debates have arisen in each House upon issues which the information of a particular department head would have enabled him, if present, to end at once by a simple explanation or statement. Time and time again a forceful and earnest presentation of facts and arguments by the representative of the Executive whose duty it is to enforce the law would have brought about a useful reform by amendment, which in the absence of such a statement has failed of passage.[32]

2. The "question-period." Interest in administrative participation in congressional proceedings has continued, but the most popular current proposal would limit such participation to a question period. Senator Estes Kefauver and other authorities favor a plan that would bring high administrative officials to the floors of Congress once every two weeks, or once a week, for two hours of questioning. Half the time would be devoted to answering written questions and half the time to oral questions. The written questions would be approved in advance by a legislative committee and submitted in advance to the department or independent agency head, who would answer them; and the oral questions would come from members after the written ones (or some of them) had been answered.

This procedure is very similar to that employed in the English House of Commons where it has given rather satisfactory results. Its American advocates claim that it would give the whole Congress an opportunity to inform itself as to how its policies were being carried out, reduce the number of special investigating committees, give Congress a more significant place in the public mind, bring about the appointment of better department heads, and give the administrators a fair opportunity to answer criticism and to explain and clarify their actions.[33] The plan is not without merit, but the opposition to it is strong and one cannot lightly brush aside the prediction that the question period would degenerate into a "political

---

[31] *Senate Report,* No. 837, 46th Cong., 3rd Sess. (1881).

[32] Mathews and Berdahl, *op. cit.,* pp. 331 ff.

[33] Galloway, *op. cit.,* pp. 217–218, citing Kefauver.

fencing match," would become a device for partisan politics, and stir up animosities.[34] The Englishmen and the Americans do not play their games the same way, athletic or political.

3. The cabinet system. Both the seats-in-Congress and the question-period proposals have in them elements of the cabinet or parliamentary system of government. No less an authority than Woodrow Wilson, in his earlier years at least, advocated the gradual adoption of the cabinet system in America. The "illogical and tradition bound" Englishmen have a logical scheme of representative government. Its executive and legislative branches *must* work together. The members of the executive department (cabinet) are chosen from the leaders of the majority party in Parliament, and as executives and administrators they remain members of Parliament. When they fail to receive the support of Parliament, they resign from the cabinet and other members of Parliament who do have that support take their place. There is never a legislative-executive deadlock. It is just that simple.

Then why do we not adopt the cabinet system? Answer: Government is not logic, but experience. The English experience happened to give them a logical system of government. Our written Constitution and our experience have given us a somewhat illogical one. Each country must develop its own political institutions. Transplanted systems are likely to wither and die. The parliamentary system has proved notoriously unsatisfactory in a number of Continental countries that borrowed it from England. The English would no doubt come to grief if they attempted to use our presidential system, and their plan operating in Washington would in all probability give us mischievous results. Statesmen and students of government are in almost complete accord on this point.

4. An executive-legislative council. If the cabinet or parliamentary system is not for us, and if seats for department heads in Congress and the question period have their limitations, still other possibilities exist. The basic problem is to get the Administration and Congress together on policy. For this purpose a legislative-executive council holds promise. Leaders of the majority party in the House and Senate, the President, and cabinet members designated by him should form such a council. Meeting at regular intervals the council could harmonize executive and legislative proposals and elaborate a policy to be supported by President and Congress. This plan has decided merit. It is not too far removed from present practice to frighten away those who "have nothing to fear but change." It would regularize and systematize executive and legislative co-operation at the top level, and afford congressmen and administrators who are not

[34] Galloway, *op. cit.*, pp. 216–217, citing Representative Clarence Cannon.

yet at that level an opportunity to present their point of view to an established institution.

Professor E. S. Corwin proposes a "New Type of Cabinet." [35] He and other scholars agree that the present Cabinet does not in fact function as such; that very little administrative policy is actually elaborated by it; that its members are overburdened with their departmental work; and that Presidents consult frequently with other persons than Cabinet members on matters of policy. Corwin would have the President construct his Cabinet from congressional leaders of both Houses, and to this group of advisers the President might add at any time those department heads and chairmen of independent agencies who could contribute most to the matter under consideration in the Cabinet. Notice that Corwin would use the department heads who now constitute the Cabinet only in matters on which they might be particularly well advised or in which they might have a special interest. The core of the Cabinet would be the legislative leaders. The heads of the departments would normally be left free to give their entire time to administration. The President, the Congressional leaders, and such administrators as the President might call in would work out the program for administrative recommendation to Congress. Congress might not follow the program, but it is not easy to disagree with Corwin's contention that, even if the majority in Congress should be of the party in opposition to the President's, the plan proposed will bring greater co-operation than is common under the present "system."

Interest in seeking the answer to the question, How can legislative-executive co-operation be promoted? is wide-spread and persistent. Other plans than those suggested above are presented, aired, and discussed. Our search does not now lack due diligence, and an acceptable solution possibly will be found within a relatively short time. Surely the day has passed when Americans should hold to the theory that a negative government is best and accept the all-too-frequent executive-legislative impasse as a sign of rugged political health.

VII. A PRACTICAL VIEW OF THE PRESIDENT'S POWERS

As we think back over this discussion of the Chief Executive, we become clearly aware that his position and powers are not fully set forth in the Constitution. We must take notice of the provisions of statutes. Having done this, we are still a long way from understanding the office of President. To the Constitution and statutes we must add the qualities of Presidents, the temper of the American people, and the needs of the times, all of

[35] *New York Times Magazine,* Oct. 10, 1948.

which are variable quantities. When the country is tranquil and prosperous, the people are in no mood to tolerate an Executive who does not
live his official life well within the provisions of the Constitution and statutes. In less happy or in tumultuous periods, the people want action and
woe betide the President who hesitates to take it.

"He didn't do nothin', but that's what we wanted done." A popular
humorist thus characterized one of our "normalcy" Presidents who had
the country's acclaim. Even greater acclaim was accorded Roosevelt,
when, in his inaugural, in 1933, he said:

We must act, and act quickly. . . . It is to be hoped that the normal balance of
executive and legislative authority may be wholly adequate to meet the unprecedented task before us. But in the event that the Congress shall fail I shall ask
the Congress for the one remaining instrument to meet the crisis—broad executive power to wage a war against the emergency as great as the power that would
be given me if we were in fact invaded by a foreign foe.

Still greater applause greeted his action the next day, a proclamation closing
every bank in the United States in order to end the banking crisis. By
what authority was the proclamation issued? A semblance of authority
was found under the Trading-with-the-Enemy Act of 1917, and that was
all. But, in the language of Edmund Randolph at the Philadelphia Convention, "when the salvation of the Republic was at stake," neither the
President nor the country, which wanted action, was "scrupulous on the
point of power."

Meeting in special session a few days later at the President's call, Congress
approved what he had done, and, at his request, passed a measure giving
him sweeping powers over banking and currency, all within a few hours
and before many members could learn the contents of the bill they had
enacted with a "unanimous roar." The country applauded again, and
continued to applaud as the President made it clear that he intended not
only to administer the executive department but also to direct the activities
of Congress. We repeat, the powers of the President are those authorized
by the Constitution and statutes (as interpreted by the Supreme Court),
plus the capacity of the President for leadership, plus the temper of the
public, plus the demands of the times.

Essential qualities in a President. Looking back now at the office of
President, it is crystal clear that the incumbent should be a many-sided
man. He needs at least an extra five senses—of process, of history, of
timeliness, of fitness, of the possible, and the second additional five senses
might be headed by a sense of humor and concluded with a sense of fairness. He should be a judge of men and measures, a master of ways and
means. He should be a dreamer, a thinker, a planner, a promoter. He

should be the personification of "America Unlimited." [36] Mrs. Eleanor Roosevelt has some knowledge of the Presidency that should not be overlooked. H. V. Kaltenborn is reported to have asked her a question: "Which is more essential in a President, the qualities of a politician or those of an administrator?" Her reply: "The President needs both, but far more than these he needs an understanding heart."

For reading list, see references at the end of Chapter 11.

Questions and Problems

1. Compare the significance of the President's powers to call Congress into special session and to adjourn Congress.
2. Under what circumstances and with what type of message is the President most likely to influence Congress?
3. Can it be said that the President's veto power is a stronger political instrument than is indicated by the language of the Constitution?
4. Discuss the pros and cons of the proposal to give the President the item veto.
5. Show how the President's political influence over Congress may be quite different from that imagined by the framers of the Constitution.
6. Analyze this statement: *Administration measures are out of harmony with representative government.*
7. Is the following statement political "hokum" or worthy of the attention of intelligent men? *We must stop this bureaucratic rule-making and get back to legislation by Congress.*
8. To what extent do you think the parliamentary (or cabinet) system of government would solve the problem of relationship of President and Congress? What difficulties and obstacles would it likely encounter if adopted?
9. Consider the possibilities of an executive-legislative council as an agency for bringing about co-operation between President and Congress.

[36] *See also* James Reston, "The Qualities a President Needs," *New York Times Magazine,* Oct. 31, 1948, p. 7.

☆ 13 ☆

The State Executive System

C ONTINUING our examination of the executive power we come now to the executive system in the states. Unlike the President of the United States the governor must share the executive power with some half dozen (the number varies in the several states) other elected officials. President and governor do exercise essentially the same types of powers, however, and a knowledge of the Office of President makes much easier an understanding of the governor's place in the states. But we must be on the alert for differences between the two offices, and we should be mindful also that the office of governor is not exactly the same in any two states.

I. THE OFFICE OF GOVERNOR: A GENERAL VIEW

Qualifications. State constitutions commonly stipulate that the governor shall be a citizen of the United States; that he shall have resided in the state for a specified number of years—usually five; and that he shall have attained an age—thirty is the usual requirement—which is supposed to indicate maturity. None of these qualifications need be expressed in constitutions or law, for they would be enforced by the voters in any case. One can easily imagine the opposition's attacks upon the candidate who lacked them or any of them. "Are we going to let this 'foreigner' rule over us?" "Can this drawling Southerner tell us Westerners how to run our state?" "The little child shall lead them!" On rare occasions a man may move from private life to the governor's chair; but usually he has served as Congressman, or in some executive position in the state, or in the state legislature, or in some other public office.

Nomination and election. In a substantial majority of the states the candidates for governor are nominated in the direct primary. The convention system is used in the others. In every state except Mississippi the governor is elected by direct vote of the people. The Mississippi plan, somewhat on the order of our system for electing the President, calls for election by a popular and an electoral vote. Since nominations, campaigns, and elections are discussed in the preceding chapter, we do not need to deal further with them here.

Term and tenure. The framers of the original state constitutions feared "tyranny," and one of their means of guarding against it was the short term of office. Consequently, governors were commonly given one-year terms. It developed, however, that such short terms were not only unnecessary but decidedly disadvantageous, calling for frequent elections and all too frequent turnovers in state administration. During the past century the tendency has been in the direction of lengthening the terms. The term is now fixed at two years in nearly half the states, and at four years in the others. A few states, fearing the construction of a political machine by the governor and its use in continuing him in power, have made the chief executive ineligible for the term next succeeding. In other states it is not uncommon for the governor to serve two or even three consecutive terms. Smith was elected Governor of New York in 1918, 1922, 1924, and 1926, and his record was matched by Governor Herbert Lehman (1933–1942).[1]

Removal from office: IMPEACHMENT. In every state except Oregon the governor and other civil officers may be removed from office by impeachment. The charges are commonly voted in the lower house of the state legislature, and the question of guilt is decided by the state senate. Governors so removed include Sulzer of New York (1913); James E. Ferguson of Texas (1917); J. C. Walton of Oklahoma (1923), and Henry S. Johnston of the same state (1929). During North Dakota's gubernatorial tribulations of 1934, an abortive effort was made to impeach Governor Moodie, successor to Governor William Langer, who had been sentenced to a federal prison. Impeachment proceedings are frequently criticized because on occasion they are used for political reasons rather than for any high crimes or misdemeanors a governor may have committed. The impeachment method is further criticized on the ground that it is difficult to bring it into use when it is needed. Regular sessions of the legislature are ordinarily held only once in two years; and, since they are short, there is little time for an impeachment. Usually special sessions may be called only by the governor, and he is not likely to call a session to consider his own impeachment. Impeachment is a gun practically without stock or barrel as far as the governor who holds office only two years is concerned, for the legislature meets about the time he takes the

---

[1] Although elected for the same number of terms as Smith, Lehman served two years longer because, in 1938, the term was changed to four years.

oath of office and adjourns almost before he has had time to become guilty of serious misconduct in office.[2]

THE RECALL. In realization of the limits of impeachment and in accordance with democratic tendencies in government, about a fourth of the states have adopted the recall. It may be used against public officials generally, although in some states judges are excepted from its operation. In practice, executive officers, state and local, have been most likely to feel its force. After a petition for recall has been signed by the number of voters required by the constitution or law, the day is fixed for the recall election, and on that day the electors go to the polls and vote for or against an officer's removal. In respect to state executive officers the advantages of the recall over impeachment (local officers are not subject to impeachment) are that it may be invoked at any convenient time and on any charge, political or legal, whereas impeachment may fairly be used only when the executive has violated the laws respecting his duties. In 1921 Governor Lynn J. Frazier and several other officers of North Dakota were recalled. It is an interesting commentary on democracy that Frazier was elected to the United States Senate a year later.

Although Governor Frazier was guilty of no crime or misdemeanor, there is no grave charge to be lodged against the people of North Dakota for his recall. That procedure is political in its design. On the other hand, impeachment is supposed to be judicial in character, and the legislatures, which have not infrequently employed it as a political weapon, are subject to severe censure. It should be a matter of national gratification that the political impeachment of President Johnson failed to result in conviction, and a point of deep regret that political impeachments in the states have not similarly failed.

As might be expected, if, for political reasons, governors guilty of no crime have been removed by impeachment proceedings, a few crooked and jail-bird governors have, for the same reasons, been left undisturbed by the impeachment process. On occasion, the courts are called upon to take action before impeachment proceedings are instituted, or when such proceedings seem not to be contemplated. Federal courts sent a governor of Indiana, Louisiana, and of North Dakota to the penitentiary; but the courts of Illinois failed to convict a governor who was clearly guilty of having converted public funds to his own use.[3] It is a pleasure to report,

---

2 On impeachment see N. F. Baker, "Some Legal Aspects of Impeachment in Louisiana," *The Southwestern Pol. and Soc. Sci. Quart.*, X, 359 (March, 1930); F. M. Stewart, "Impeachment in Texas," *Am. Pol. Sci. Rev.*, XXIV, 652 (August, 1930); C. A. M. Ewing, "The Impeachment of Oklahoma Governors," *Am. Pol. Sci. Rev.*, XXIV, 648 (August, 1930); R. L. Miller, "The Gubernatorial Controversy in North Dakota," *Am. Pol. Sci. Rev.*, XXIX, 418 (June, 1935).

3 W. B. Graves, *American State Government* (1946 ed.), pp. 371 ff.

however, that the great majority of American governors do not merit retirement to private life by extraordinary means and that still fewer of them belong in the penitentiary. Some demagogues there are among them, but as a class they are worthy public servants.

Gubernatorial succession. The recall operates very much the same as a regular election, the governor (or any other official) against whom the recall is invoked and other candidates for that office being listed on the ballot. If the recall is successful, a new governor is elected at the same time. But in case of the impeachment, death, or resignation of a governor, the officer designated by the constitution as his successor is elevated to the place, just as the Vice President succeeds to the presidency. In some thirty-five states the lieutenant governor takes the governor's chair. In other states, the president of the senate or the speaker of the lower house takes the office.

Compensation. The governor's salary is fixed by the constitution in some states; but fortunately there is a growing tendency to leave the amount of compensation to legislative determination, which makes possible the much-needed increase without the hazard of a popular vote on the question. The salary is usually low, averaging not much more than $10,000 per annum. Four or five of the wealthier states pay salaries ranging from $20,000 to $25,000, and these may be regarded as the only states in which any liberality is shown in the matter of compensation. The states commonly furnish an executive mansion and often allow modest sums of money for expenses that are not entirely of a public nature. In spite of the relatively small compensation governors receive, the office does not go begging.

POSSIBILITY FOR FUTURE HONORS. Many able and distinguished men are glad to accept the office. In addition to being the place of highest honor in the state, it is by no means a blind alley politically. Literally scores of governors have become United States senators; a number of others have received important federal appointments; some have been made Vice President; and everyone knows that Cleveland, McKinley, the two Roosevelts, Wilson, Coolidge, and several other Presidents touched the governor's round in their climb to fame.

II. THE GOVERNOR'S EXECUTIVE POWERS [4]

The governor is not the only executive officer of the state. The executive power is divided among the governor, secretary of state, and other

---

[4] W. F. Dodd, *State Government* (1928 ed.), Ch. VIII; J. A. Fairlie, "The Executive Power in the State Constitution," *Annals of the Am. Acad. of Pol. and Soc. Sci.* (September, 1935), pp. 59–73; A. N. Holcombe, *State Government in the United States* (1931 ed.), pp. 333–352; J. M. Mathews, *American State Government* (1934 ed.), pp. 302–320.

officers. The governor is usually designated by the constitution as the "supreme executive" and charged with the duty to see "that the laws are faithfully executed"; but the courts have almost invariably held that these seemingly broad grants of power give the governor no definite authority —that his powers must come from other and definite provisions of the constitution or statutes. In other words, in construing the provisions of the constitution relating to the governor's powers, the courts have followed the principle of strict construction, with the result that the executive powers of the governor have not been developed through the years as have those of the President. We should add, however, that a number of states have been strengthening the position of the governor as an executive during the past half century. Acting primarily in the executive capacity, the governor exercises some supervision over administration, a limited appointing power, a still more limited power of removal, grants pardons and reprieves (a restricted power in some states), and performs miscellaneous duties incident to the executive power.

I. Supervision of administration. The governor's power to supervise the state administration is usually grossly inadequate. The other executive officers elected along with the governor very naturally feel their responsibility to the people rather than to him. The governor's power to appoint subordinate administrative officials is subject to considerable limitation, and his removal power is severely restricted. The duties of state executives and administrative officers are rather minutely regulated by statutes. The control over them is legislative and judicial rather than executive. In a number of states the governor may force his "subordinates" to act only by the cumbersome method of instituting court proceedings against them. Furthermore, in taking care that the laws are faithfully executed, the governor must depend not only upon state officers but upon local officers such as sheriffs and district attorneys—officers over whom he has even less control than over the state officers, except in five or six states. In short, the governor as a director of administration is far from being in the independent position occupied by the President. The national administration is largely centralized. Lower officers are responsible to higher officers, and these to still higher officers, until the responsibility rests finally with the President. In the states there is no hierarchy of administration, each office or board or commission being regulated rather minutely by law, the administrative "superiors" usually having only a shadowy directing power.

Still, the people expect the governor to see that the laws are faithfully executed, and these executives usually do the best they can with the means at their disposal. They use the powers of appointment and removal as far as they have them; they require reports from the various administrative officers concerning the work of their departments; they investigate the conduct of officers; they make use of whatever political influence they have in securing effective co-operation of officeholders; and the more skillful of them may use publicity as a means of forcing desired action on the part of officers over whom they have no definite control.

INCREASING THE POWERS OF DIRECTION. In a number of states that have reorganized their administrative system, the governor is placed in a position from which he can exercise a much more effective control. Thus, in 1917, Illinois gathered together a tangled wilderness of some sixty state agencies and placed them in nine departments (later increased to thirteen), each headed by a director appointed by the governor and senate for a term of four years. Assistant directors and bureau chiefs are appointed in like manner, but they work under the immediate supervision of the department heads. The governor directs administration through the thirteen heads of departments, and he may form a cabinet with them if he cares to do so. About half the states—including New York, Pennsylvania, Virginia, and Washington—have followed in the main the Illinois plan.

2. **Appointments.** The excesses of democracy before the middle of the nineteenth century deprived the governor of practically all the power of appointment. But the choice of administrative officers by popular election (or sometimes by legislative election) proved unsatisfactory in most cases, and in many instances notoriously corrupt. Consequently, since about 1850, the governor has been recovering his appointing power, until in most states he now names the great majority of the principal administrative officers.

LIMITATIONS ON POWER OF APPOINTMENT. It cannot be said, however, that the governor's appointing power is as large as it should be, or, relatively, as extensive as that of the President; for even in those states in which the governor's power has been recently increased, the secretary of state, the treasurer, the auditor, the attorney general, and perhaps others are commonly either elected by the people or chosen by the legislature. Furthermore, many states have administrative officers whose terms overlap the term of the governor, and, in consequence, he has subordinates who are not of his appointment. Again, in making appointments, the governor is often limited by statutes that prescribe the qualifications the appointees shall possess.

In the case of the appointment of important officials, the most common requirement is that the nomination shall be made by the governor and that confirmation shall be by the senate. The governor must name the "right" men, or the senate will not confirm his appointments. He must consult party leaders to learn who the right men are, and sometimes this consultation amounts to dictation by a leader or boss. Even Theodore Roosevelt frankly confessed that as Governor of New York he had to consult Boss Platt with regard to his appointments or find them failing of confirmation in the senate. In other words, the appointing power is not infrequently in the hands of the man who stands behind the governor's chair rather than in those of the man who sits in it. Sometimes, of course, the governor is himself the party leader in the state, in which case his appointments may be of an independent character, although that does not necessarily mean that they are any better than those an invisible leader might prompt him to make.

It seems that the more sordid type of politics is much more likely to enter into appointments by a governor than into those made by the President, for the state party organization is smaller and more unified than the national organization and therefore easier for small groups and bosses to control. In addition, the citizen is often more interested in what is taking place at Washington than he is in what his local rulers are doing, a deplorable fact which the powers that be in a state know how to use to their advantage. Conditions in respect to the choice of administrative officers in the state might be improved by vesting their appointment solely with the governor, for it is in connection with securing the confirmation of the senate that the governor often finds that he must bow to the sinister power of the boss and the machine.

3. Removals. The President may remove any executive officer or employee of the United States. This power is not held by the governors, who may remove only under authority expressly conferred by law—an authority that the states are slow to confer, although there has been some development in that direction along with the tendency to increase the appointing power. The general rule now is that the governor may remove officers whom he appoints; but that those appointed by him with the consent of the senate may be removed only upon the approval of the senate, a restriction in striking contrast to the President's independent power of removal. More extensive powers of removal are granted in Michigan, where the governor may even remove elected state officials when the legislature is not in session, and any elective county officer. In giving the governor the authority to remove local officers, usually law enforcement officers, Michigan is joined by New York, Minnesota, Wisconsin, and a few other states.[5] In 1932 Governor Franklin D. Roosevelt removed from office Thomas M. Farley, Sheriff of New York County. He seemed about to remove New York City's Mayor James J. Walker, but the Mayor's resignation forestalled that action.

4. Pardons and reprieves. The power to grant pardons and reprieves is held by the governor alone in some states; in others, a pardon may not be granted by the governor except upon the recommendation of a board of pardons; and in a third group of states, pardons are granted by a board of which the governor is simply a member. The power to grant pardons

---

[5] Fairlie and Kneier, *County Government and Administration* (1930), pp. 99–100.

has been freely exercised by governors, and in some cases it has amounted to a scandal. Governor Davis of Kansas was tried, but acquitted, when his term of office expired in 1925, for accepting a bribe for a pardon. A Governor of Arkansas liberated about three hundred prisoners at one fell swoop, in order to call the attention of the public to the evils of the system of contracting prison labor. "Ma" Ferguson of Texas has the record, with nearly four thousand convicts turned loose on society during her two-year term (1925-1927), a record that prompted the late Will Rogers to observe that her successor would have to start by catching his own prisoners. These wholesale abuses of the power should not be regarded as typical; but many governors have been too liberal in granting pardons, a condition that a number of states sought to remedy by establishing pardon boards, as mentioned above.

5. Other executive powers and duties. As the ceremonial head of the state, the governor is present at many important public gatherings, receives distinguished visitors, attends (a number of them do) the inauguration of the President, meets his fellow governors at conferences, and lends his name to numerous affairs and enterprises, public or private. Acting more definitely in an official capacity, he formally accepts the service of legal papers issued against the state, sends to and receives from governors of other states requisitions for persons alleged to be fugitives from justice, takes care of communications between the state and the national government, and performs other duties of a similar character. He is invariably the commander-in-chief of the state militia, except when it is in the service of the United States, when it is under the command of the President. The governor is empowered to call out the militia to suppress riots or prevent serious disorders. The state's chief executive is usually an *ex officio* member of a large number of boards and commissions, as is illustrated by twenty-four such memberships held by the Governor of Michigan in 1920. Many of the governor's duties, however, are petty and routine in character, consuming the major portion of his time and taking his attention from the really important problems awaiting solution. The late Governor Alfred E. Smith complained that about three fourths of his time was taken up with clerical or unimportant matters that should have been disposed of by capable administrative assistants.[6]

III. THE GOVERNOR'S LEGISLATIVE POWERS [7]

However far behind the President the governor may lag in executive and administrative powers, in most states he has authority in legislative

[6] "How We Ruin Our Governors," *Nat. Municipal Rev.* (1921), X, 277-280.

[7] Dodd, *op. cit.*, pp. 190-196; Holcombe, *op. cit.*, pp. 115-119, 352-370; Mathews, *op. cit.*, pp. 289-302; Mathews and Berdahl, *Documents and Readings in American Govern-*

matters that compares very favorably with that of the President, and in some states he has a distinct advantage over the President. Even before the executive hand was strengthened, as indicated in the last paragraph of subsection 1 above, the governor's lack of executive power failed to serve him as a defense against the people who had elected him and who wanted promises performed. Consequently, governors turned their efforts to legislation as the most promising field for achievement, and in this field a number of them won notable success. As the advantages of legislative leadership and power in the hands of the governor became apparent, more authority was vested in him, until now, even in those states that have bolstered up his administrative powers, his opportunities in legislation are probably superior to those in administration.

1. **General legislative powers.** In every state the governor may call the legislature into special session, and in a few states he must do so when petitioned by a specified number of the legislators. In about half the states he has an advantage over the lawmakers when they are in special session, in that they may not legislate upon matters other than those for which the session is called. A second legislative power of the governor is the authority to adjourn the two houses when they cannot agree upon a date for terminating their labors. This power is seldom used, because many states fix the length of legislative sessions by constitutional provision, and because in other states the houses are usually able to reach an agreement.

More important than the power either to call special sessions of the legislature or to fix the date for its adjournment, is the governor's authority and duty to send its messages. Like the President's messages to Congress, the messages of the state's chief executive are sent regularly at the beginning of a session of the legislature and at such other times as may seem desirable. The governor follows the federal model, reporting on the condition of the state and recommending needed legislation.[8] On the average, his messages are as effective in securing desired legislative action as are the messages of the President—perhaps more so—for the state assembly is usually of short duration, its deliberations must be somewhat hurried, and the majority of its members are more likely to welcome than to resent the governor's efforts to help them.

2. **The veto.** Without any question, one of the most material powers of the governor in relation to legislation is the veto power. North Carolina is the only state that has not authorized its use. When the legislature passes a bill, it is sent to the governor, who is allowed a few days, varying

---

ment (1940 ed.), Ch. XXII; F. W. Prescott, "The Executive Veto in American States," *Western Pol. Qt.* (1950), III, 97–111.

[8] H. Walker, "Governors' Messages, 1931," *Am. Pol. Sci. Rev.* (1931), XXV, 346–364, "The Results of Governors' Messages in 1931," *ibid.* (1932), XXVI, 77–84, and "Governors' Messages and the Legislative Product in 1932," *ibid.*, 1058–1075. The entire issue of *State Government*, March, 1949, is devoted to "Governors' Messages—1949."

among the states from three to ten, in which to consider it. If he signs it, it becomes a law. If he allows the allotted days to pass without acting upon it, it still becomes a law. But if he vetoes the bill, it is returned to the legislature for further consideration. In some twenty states the veto may be overcome only by a two-thirds vote of the *total* membership of each house of the legislature, and in about a dozen states the veto may be overcome by a two-thirds vote of the members *present*. All other states, except Connecticut, require a vote larger than a simple majority of the members present to "override" the governor's veto.

Originally, the governors who had the veto power used it sparingly and chiefly as a means of preventing unconstitutional legislation, as did our early Presidents. Nowadays, it is used practically without let or hindrance for any reason a governor may have in mind. At times the veto amounts to a slaughter, but it is usually a slaughter of defectives. Professor F. W. Prescott gives us some interesting figures.[9] In 1947 the Governor of New York vetoed 329 of 1245 measures; California's Governor, 175 of 1752; and governors of some other states also made high scores. Professor M. N. McGeary finds that between 1939 and 1945 the Governor of Pennsylvania vetoed 229 of 2174 bills.[10] More important than the number of vetoes is the question of their effectiveness. Does the veto axe deal a death blow to a bill? Ordinarily it does. In 1947 the legislatures were able to override only about 2 per cent of the vetoes, and about one half of such overriding occurred in two states in which the executive and legislative branches were decidedly out of harmony.[11] In Pennsylvania and some other states the veto is almost never overridden. This relatively absolute veto is made possible by the high majorities required to override it and by the fact that most bills go to the governor when the legislature is about to adjourn.[12]

THE POCKET VETO. If the legislature sends bills to the governor and then adjourns within the time allowed the governor for the consideration of bills, the governor's nonaction in reference to such "eleventh-hour" bills serves as an absolute veto, the pocket veto. Many bills come to the governor near the end of the legislative session, so many that it is impossible for him to give them anything like careful consideration. After a cursory examination of these bills and hurried consultations with advisers, he takes some long chances and signs the bills it seems desirable to approve before the time limit has expired, leaving the other bills to painless death

[9] *Op. cit.,* p. 103 (Prescott's table is reproduced on pages 444–445 below).

[10] M. N. McGeary, "The Governor's Veto in Pennsylvania," *Am. Pol. Sci. Rev.,* Oct., 1947, p. 941. The veto record of the governor of California for the legislative session of 1949 is as follows: Bills passed, 1603; bills vetoed during the session, 24 (none were overridden by the legislature); bills pocket vetoed, 86.

[11] Holcombe, *op. cit.,* p. 354; Prescott, *op. cit.,* p. 103.

[12] McGeary, *op. cit.,* pp. 944–945.

by the pocket veto. A large number of states prohibit the "pocket edition" of the veto, by providing that bills shall become a law unless actually vetoed by the governor within a stated period after the legislature has adjourned. This period varies in the several states from five to forty-five days. Obviously, this plan places the governor in a position in which he can really weigh and consider the bills that are referred to him near the end of the legislative session. It therefore enormously increases his effectiveness as a legislator. At the same time it compels him to accept a definite responsibility for his vetoes, since the indirect veto is not permitted.[13]

THE ITEM VETO. Thirty-nine states now give the governor the authority to veto separate items of an appropriation bill, and in a number of states he may also reduce such items. These powers, like the power to veto whole bills, are freely exercised. The item veto, especially when the right to reduce items is combined with it, gives the governor a broad and very useful negative in regard to appropriations [14]—a negative that legislators who for political reasons vote for extravagant appropriations often secretly hope he will exercise. This particular type of veto serves also as a most effective instrument against the mounting of "riders" on appropriation bills. Although nearly all the states feel that they have gone far enough with the item veto when the governor is empowered to strike out or reduce parts of an appropriation bill, Washington authorizes him to veto a part of any bill.

EXECUTIVE RECOMMENDATION OF AMENDMENTS. Alabama, Virginia, Massachusetts, and New Jersey (since 1947) give the governor a choice of vetoing a bill or returning it to the legislature with proposed amendments. In the latter event the legislature accepts or rejects the governor's proposal by a simple majority. In case of acceptance the amended bill goes back to the governor, who very naturally signs it. If, on the other hand, the governor's amendments are rejected, then the original bill goes back to him for his approval or veto. This plan of allowing the governor to suggest changes in a bill seems to make the occasions for the use of the veto much less frequent, and, to that extent at least, brings about a more harmonious relation between the executive and legislative branches of the state government. The same sort of plan may be used and is being used un-

---

[13] A few states follow a practice recommended by the National Municipal League; namely, that bills vetoed after the legislature has adjourned shall be filed, together with the governor's veto messages, with the secretary of state, who shall present them to the legislature at its next session for reconsideration in like manner as if they had been returned by the governor during the last session. Thus, in 1931 the secretary of state for the Commonwealth of Washington laid before the legislature 65 bills that had been vetoed by the governor after the close of the session of 1929. (*Spokesman-Review*, January 5, 1931.)

[14] R. H. Wells, "The Item Veto and State Budget Reform," *Am. Pol. Sci. Rev.* (1924), XVIII, 782–791.

officially in other states. Legislators in touch with the governor will let his views be known on projected bills; or the governor may publicly speak his mind; or the legislature may, upon the governor's request or upon its own motion, recall a bill it has sent to him. Any one of these steps may lead to the incorporation of amendments that will make a bill acceptable to the chief executive.

IMPORTANCE OF THE VETO. Few will deny that the extension of the veto power has improved our state lawmaking systems. The power has been extensively, effectively, and, on the whole, wisely used. Governors have often prevented the enactment of defective or otherwise objectionable legislation, and perhaps even more frequently they have blocked excesses in appropriations. Legislators themselves, unable to resist the pressure of powerful interests in their constituencies, not infrequently vote for an indefensible bill or item of appropriation and wait in confidence for the governor's veto. Thus, the legislator may save his head with his constituency, while the governor, who serves the whole state, incurs the wrath of some of its citizens by beheading the legislator's measures. Although it is unfair to the governor, of course, to pass such tasks to him, he can better afford to risk the hostility of voters in a particular locality than their delegate in the legislature can, for the governor's loss in one community may be made up by gains in another.

Formerly, long orations were made on the advantages of the bicameral legislative system, laying great stress upon the dogma that one house would kill the "bad" bills that emanated from the other. All too often the other chamber has failed to serve as executioner. It is the opinion of students of state government that in a number of states, including New York, the chief executive now "exerts a more powerful and beneficial check upon legislation adopted by both houses than either house does upon that adopted by the other." [15]   In those states in which he is given a few weeks' time to consider bills after the legislature has adjourned, he sits as a sort of third chamber. "He grants hearings to advocates and opponents of measures which have received legislative approval, refers legal and financial questions to his attorney general or other advisers, and in general does what he can to determine for himself whether the measures adopted by the legislature should be enacted." [16]   It would be absurd to make the governor out a hero, defending, in every instance, the interests of the people against ignorant, careless, or corrupt legislators. Governors, as well as members of the legislative branches, have sometimes failed in their trust. Nevertheless, the governor and his advisers are ordinarily better qualified to pass upon bills than is the average legislator; and when we combine the

[15] From A. N. Holcombe, *State Government in the U.S.* (1931 ed.), p. 356.   By permission of the Macmillan Company, publishers.

[16] From *ibid.*, p. 355.   Prescott, *op. cit.*, seems to agree.

State	Days after which Bill Becomes Law (before Adjournment) unless Vetoed (Sundays excepted)	Fate of Bill after Adjournment — Days after which Bill Passes unless Vetoed (Sundays excepted)	Days after which Bill Dies unless Signed (Sundays excepted)	Item Veto on Appropriation Bills	Votes Required in House and Senate to Pass Bills or Items Over Veto [a]	Constitution Prohibits Governor from Vetoing — Initiated Measures	Referred Measures
Alabama	6	..	10	★	Majority elected	(b)	(b)
Arizona	5	10	..	★	Two-thirds elected [c]	★	★
Arkansas	5	20 [d]	..	★	Majority elected	★	★
California	10	..	30	★	Two-thirds elected	★	★
Colorado	10 [d]	30 [d]	..	★	Two-thirds elected	★	★
Connecticut	5 [e]	15 [d]	..	★	Majority present	(b)	(b)
Delaware	10	..	30 [d]	★	Three-fifths elected	(b)	(b)
Florida	5	..	10 [d]	★	Two-thirds present	(b)	(b)
Georgia [f]	5	..	(g)		Two-thirds elected	(h)	..
Idaho	5	10	..	★	Two-thirds present	★	★
Illinois	10	10	..	★	Two-thirds elected	(b)	(b)
Indiana	3	5 [d, i]	..	..	Majority elected	(b)	(b)
Iowa	3	(j)	30	..	Two-thirds elected	..	..
Kansas	3	(k)	..	★	Two-thirds elected	(b)	(b)
Kentucky	10	10 [d]	..	★	Majority elected	..	..
Louisiana	10 [d, l]	20 [d]	..	★	Two-thirds elected	(b)	(b)
Maine	5	(m)	..		Two-thirds elected	★	★
Maryland	6	..	6 [n]	★	Three-fifths elected	(b)	(b)
Massachusetts	5 [e]	..	(o)	★	Two-thirds present	★	★
Michigan	10	..	5	★	Two-thirds elected	★	★
Minnesota	3	..	3 [d]	★	Two-thirds elected	(b)	(b)
Mississippi	5	(j, m)	..	★	Two-thirds elected	(b)	(b)
Missouri	(p)	..	..	★	Two-thirds elected	(b)	(b)
Montana	5	..	15 [d, q]	★	Two-thirds present	★	★
Nebraska	5	5	..	★ [r]	Three-fifths elected	★	★
Nevada	5	10	..	..	Two-thirds elected	★	★
New Hampshire	5	..	(g)	★	Two-thirds elected	(b)	(b)
New Jersey	10	..	45	★	Two-thirds elected	(b)	(b)
New Mexico	3	..	6 [q]	★	Two-thirds present	(h)	..
New York	10	..	30 [d]	★	Two-thirds elected	(h)	..
North Carolina	(s)	(s)	(s)	(s)	....	(b)	(b)
North Dakota	3	15 [d]	..	★	Two-thirds elected	★	★
Ohio	10	10 [d]	..	★	Three-fifths elected	..	..
Oklahoma	5	..	15	★	Two-thirds elected	★	★
Oregon	5	20	..	★ [t]	Two-thirds present	★	★
Pennsylvania	10 [d]	30 [d]	..	★	Two-thirds elected	(b)	(b)
Rhode Island	6	10 [d]	..	..	Three-fifths present	(b)	(b)
South Carolina	3	(m)	..	★	Two-thirds elected	(b)	(b)

State	Days after which Bill Becomes Law (before Adjournment) unless Vetoed (Sundays excepted)	Fate of Bill after Adjournment		Item Veto on Appropriation Bills	Votes Required in House and Senate to Pass Bills or Items Over Veto [a]	Constitution Prohibits Governor from Vetoing	
		Days after which Bill Passes unless Vetoed (Sundays excepted)	Days after which Bill Dies unless Signed (Sundays excepted)			Initiated Measures	Referred Measures
South Dakota	3	10 [d]	..	★	Two-thirds present	★	★
Tennessee	5	..	(g)	..	Majority elected	(h)	..
Texas	10	20 [d]	..	★	Two-thirds present	(b)	(b)
Utah	5	10	..	★	Two-thirds elected	★	★
Vermont	5	..	(g)	..	Two-thirds present	(b)	(b)
Virginia	5	..	10	★	Two-thirds present [u]	(b)	(b)
Washington	5	10	..	★ [v]	Two-thirds elected	★	★
West Virginia	5 [w]	5 [d]	..	..	Majority elected	(b)	(b)
Wisconsin	6	..	6	★	Two-thirds present	(b)	(b)
Wyoming	3	15 [d]	..	★	Two-thirds elected	(b)	(b)
Alaska	3	..	3	★	Two-thirds elected	..	..
Hawaii	10	..	10 [n]	★	Two-thirds elected	(b)	(b)
Puerto Rico	10	..	30	★	Two-thirds elected	..	..
Virgin Islands	..	30	..	..	Two-thirds elected	..	..

a Bill returned to house of origin with objections, except in Georgia, where the governor need not state his objections, and in Kansas, where all bills are returned to the House of Representatives.

b No provision for initiative or referendum in state.

c Three-fourths in case of an emergency measure.

d Sundays not excepted unless last day is Sunday.

e Sundays and legal holidays excepted.

f New constitution, passed by General Assembly, withholds right to veto constitutional amendments.

g Unsigned bills do not become laws.

h No provision for initiative in state.

i Bill becomes law if not filed with objections with secretary of state within five days after adjournment.

j Governor must act whether for or against bill within 30 days after adjournment.

k In practice, the legislature closes consideration of bills three days before adjournment sine die.

l Governor has 10 days from time bill was presented to him in which to approve or disapprove.

m Bill passed in one session becomes law if not returned within two days (Maine and Mississippi three days) after reconvening of legislature.

n Within 6 days (in Hawaii 10 days) after presentation to the governor, regardless of how long after adjournment this may be.

o Within 5 days of receipt by governor. In practice General Court not prorogued until governor has acted on all bills.

p If governor does not return bill in 15 days, a joint resolution is necessary for bill to become law.

q Governor must file his objections with secretary of state.

r Governor may not veto items in budget submitted by himself after it has passed legislature with three-fifths vote.

s No veto; bill becomes law 30 days after adjournment of session unless otherwise expressly directed.

t Also may veto items in new bills declaring an emergency.

u Including majority elected.

v Also may veto items in any bill which contains items or sections.

w Budget (appropriation) bill not submitted to governor after passage.

* Reproduced by courtesy of the Council of State Governments from The Book of the States, 1950–1951, p. 117.

governor's advantage with the fact that the eyes of the whole state are upon him, we have reason to expect that the affairs of the whole people will be better served by the governor than by individual legislators.

3. The governor and the budget. We consider the subject of state finance in a later chapter; but we must record here that the governor's part in relation to state revenues and appropriations has greatly increased in many states during the past thirty or forty years. We noted above the governor's negative and older power over appropriations through the item veto. A number of states now authorize or require him to initiate the budget, that is, the state's financial program for the ensuing fiscal period. The essence of the plan is that the governor, or officers responsible to him, collect information concerning the financial needs of the various government agencies and institutions of the state, decide how much should be appropriated for each, make an estimate of revenues to balance these appropriations, and submit the whole program to the legislature. The governor, who is actively working for the state all the time, who is in constant contact with its problems, and who bears the brunt of the responsibility for efficiency and economy, is the logical official to prepare the budget. The legislature may disregard his recommendations, but it at least has a financial program upon which to work; and if the program has public approval, the legislature will not lightly pass it by.

4. The governor's leadership in legislation. In considering the powers of the governor we must look beyond the constitutions and statutes. As the highest officeholder in the state, the governor is quite likely to be a man of considerable influence in his party, and there are many examples of governors who have dominated the party organization. Sometimes the members of his party who are in the legislature are glad to follow him; at other times they may follow him reluctantly under the dictates of political wisdom.

Governor Wilson went before the Democrats in the New Jersey legislature and said: "I have been elected Governor of New Jersey by the people of New Jersey, selected by the convention of the Democratic party, and I thereby have become the responsible leader of the Democratic party in the State. I will be held responsible by the people at the polls. . . . Each of you gentlemen will be held responsible in the districts where you were elected. I am held responsible as well as you by the same people. I am the only person in the whole State, however, to express approval or disapproval on behalf of all the people, and I will express that approval or disapproval by determining what we should do." [17] There was no denying this logic, and when Wilson immediately followed it by presenting

[17] Quoted in Ogg and Ray, *Introduction to American Government* (1945 ed.), p. 794, note, from David Lawrence in the Springfield *Republican*, Feb. 29, 1924.

a program (a thing that seldom emanates from a legislative group), the Democratic lawmakers adopted it unanimously.

It may be said that a governor has at his disposal about the same means as the President for making his influence felt in legislative chambers. Like the President, he may establish close personal relationship with legislators, judiciously use the patronage in emergencies, use his influence as the official leader of his party, and win public opinion to his side by a skillful popular appeal. Perhaps he has an advantage over the President in that there is ordinarily less party politics in a state than in the nation, a condition that enables a popular governor to carry with him a large support from all parties. Another possible advantage is found in the fact that state legislatures are usually limited to short sessions and hence not only lack the time to harass a governor as Congress sometimes harasses the President, but may actually turn with some relief to a governor who has a program prepared for their guidance during the sixty days or so they sit in biennial session.

IV. OTHER STATE EXECUTIVE OFFICERS [18]

A typical state constitution provides that "the executive department shall consist of a governor, lieutenant governor, secretary of state, auditor, treasurer, superintendent of public instruction, and attorney general," and that "the supreme executive power shall be vested in the governor." [19] In other words, although the governor is the most important executive officer, he does not hold all the executive power. These other executive officers, like the governor, are usually elected by popular vote, although there are some cases in which they are elected by the legislature or appointed by the governor.

Lieutenant governor. About three fourths of the states have a lieutenant governor, who, as we said earlier, succeeds to the governorship in case of the resignation, death, or impeachment of the governor, and in a number of states exercises the functions of governor during the temporary absence of that official from the state. Except in Massachusetts he presides over the senate. Many students of government consider the office of lieutenant governor unnecessary. Obviously, the senate would not object to choosing its own presiding officer; and it is more desirable to have as the governor's successor the secretary of state, or some other officer who is closely associated with the administrative affairs of the state.[20]

[18] W. F. Dodd, *State Government* (1928 ed.), pp. 225–231; A. F. Macdonald, *American State Government and Administration* (1950 ed.), pp. 239–249.

[19] Constitution of Illinois, Art. V.

[20] See W. R. Isom, "The Office of Lieutenant Governor in the States," *Am. Pol. Sci. Rev.*, XXXII, 921 (October, 1938).

Secretary of state. Each of the states has a secretary of state. A few of his duties are prescribed by the constitution, but most of them are imposed by legislative acts. He keeps the records of the state, supervises elections, issues certificates of incorporation and motor vehicle licenses, and does other administrative work of a similar character. His duties are numerous and often unrelated.

Attorney general. Another essential officer is the attorney general, no state being without one. Like the secretary of state, his duties are mainly prescribed by statute. It is his duty to give legal advice to the governor and other administrative officers and agencies when requested to do so, to appear in court in all cases in which the state has an interest, and to institute proceedings against violators of state law where the general public is adversely affected. In a few states he has some authority to direct the work of the prosecuting attorneys in the counties.

Superintendent of public instruction. Either the constitution or a statute provides for a superintendent of public instruction in each state. In most states his legal powers are not very comprehensive. In general, he has some authority to supervise the administration of schools in counties and other local districts, to apportion school funds among such districts, and to make various investigations. Regardless of his legal powers a high-class superintendent will have a major influence in shaping the state's educational policy.

Treasurer. A treasurer in every state receives the revenues and makes disbursements. He has little discretion beyond the authority to choose the banks in which the state funds shall be deposited, and often even this discretionary power is limited.

Auditor. The acts of the treasurer are checked by an auditor or comptroller, who is a more important financial officer than the treasurer. The auditor's chief duty is to see that the funds are being lawfully expended. A number of states have given the auditor the authority to require uniform methods of accounting in the administrative departments, and in some states he may exercise supervision over the accounts of local government agencies.[21]

Although the foregoing paragraphs include the historic executive officers of the state, there are many other officers, boards, and commissions that have a significant part in administering the state's functions. They have been created, usually by statute, during the past sixty or seventy-five years to deal with the newer social and economic conditions. There are commissioners of banking and insurance, public utilities commissioners, factory inspectors, and what not. We shall give more attention to these agencies when we take up the problem of administration; but we must at least note their existence here and, more important for present purposes,

[21] Dodd, *op. cit.*, pp. 228–229.

emphasize the fact that although the governor is called "the supreme executive," he usually has only a very limited control over such agencies.

V. THE EXECUTIVE POWER IN THE MODEL CONSTITUTION

For more than a score of years, the National Municipal League has had a Committee on State Government, which from time to time has published a Model State Constitution.[22] It is worth our while to notice briefly what the latest edition (1948) of this "Constitution" proposes on the executive department. It would make the governor the chief executive in fact as well as in name, and would establish closer and more formal relations between him and the legislature in such ways as to strengthen his leadership as a law-maker. The Model draft states that "the executive power of the state shall be vested in a governor," and it does not then proceed to parcel out executive power among other officers as do many state constitutions. It relegates to the scrap heap of "Model T" political institutions the independent executive departments with which we have too long been familiar. The Model authorizes the governor to appoint an administrative manager, to serve at the governor's pleasure, and to perform such duties as the chief executive might delegate to him. Administrative departments, not exceeding twenty, may be created by act of the legislature. Heads of departments are to be appointed and removed by the governor.

The governor, the administrative manager, and the heads of departments may sit in the legislature, introduce bills, and participate in the discussion of measures, but they are given no vote. The governor is authorized to order a referendum on any bill that fails to pass the legislature; and that body may, by majority vote, order a referendum on any measure vetoed by the governor and failing to receive the two-thirds majority in the legislature necessary to override such veto. The experts' plan gives the governor wide powers over state finance. He is required to prepare and submit to the legislature the budget, together with revenue and appropriation bills. And he is authorized to veto separate items of appropriation bills or to reduce such items. These provisions are included in the Model plan after years of careful consideration, and they are worthy of the attention of students of government and of responsible legislators and officials in the several states.

Reading List

H. Barnard, *"Eagle Forgotten": Life of John Peter Altgeld* (1938).
H. A. Barth, *Financial Control in the States, with Emphasis on Control by the Governor* (1923).

[22] The Fifth Edition, published in 1948, should be available in your university library.

G. C. S. Benson and E. H. Litchfield, *The State Administration Record in Michigan* (1938).

F. L. Bird and F. M. Ryan, *The Recall of Public Officials in California* (1930).

Book of the States, 1948–1949.

A. W. Bromage, *State Government and Administration in the United States* (1936), Ch. VIII.

F. G. Bates, O. P. Field and Others, *State Government* (1949), Ch. 11.

H. C. Black, *The Relation of the Executive Power to Legislation* (1919), Ch. VII.

F. G. Crawford, *State Government* (1931), Chs. IX–X.

W. F. Dodd, *State Government* (1928 ed.), pp. 190–196, and Ch. VIII.

J. A. Fairlie, "The State Governor," *Mich. Law Rev.* (1912), X, 370–383, 458–475.

J. H. Finley and J. F. Sanderson, *The American Executive and Executive Methods* (1907), Chs. V–XIV.

J. A. Friedman, *The Impeachment of Governor William Sulzer* (1939).

H. F. Gosnell, *Boss Platt and His New York Machine* (1924), Chs. VI–VIII.

Governors' Conferences, *Proceedings* (Annual since 1909).

W. B. Graves, *American State Government* (1946 ed.), Ch. IX.

A. N. Holcombe, *State Government in the United States* (1931), Ch. XI.

C. Jensen, *The Pardoning Power in the American States* (1922).

E. Kimball, *State and Municipal Government in the United States* (1922), Ch. VII.

R. M. LaFollette, *A Personal Narrative of Political Experience* (1913).

L. W. Lancaster and A. C. Breckenridge, *Readings in American State Government* (1950).

Leslie Lipson, *The American Governor: From Figurehead to Leader* (1939).

A. F. Macdonald, *American State Government and Administration* (1950 ed.), Ch. X.

J. M. Mathews, *American State Government* (1934 ed.), Ch. XII.

—— and C. A. Berdahl, *Documents and Readings in American Government* (1940 ed.), Ch. XXII.

National Municipal League, *Model State Constitution* (1948 ed.).

Theodore Roosevelt, *An Autobiography* (1913), Ch. VIII.

Alfred E. Smith, *Up to Now, an Autobiography* (1929).

——, *The Citizen and His Government* (1935).

C. F. Snider, *American State and Local Government* (1950), Ch. IX.

W. C. Williams, *Sweet of Colorado* (1943).

Questions and Problems

1. What are the provisions in the constitution of your state concerning the qualifications, term, and tenure of the governor?   Which of these provisions do you regard as unnecessary?

2. Show the difference in purpose and in operation between impeachment and the recall.

3. What powers as a supervisor of administration has the governor of your state?

4. What additional powers, if any, does the governor of your state need to enable him to be the chief executive in fact as well as in name?
5. How are pardons granted in your state? Is there any abuse of the power?
6. Does your governor have the item veto? The pocket veto? Look up his veto record for a recent session of the legislature.
7. What responsibilities has your governor in relation to the preparation of the budget?
8. To what extent is your governor a leader in legislation? Give specific examples of this leadership.
9. What executive officers in addition to the governor are elected in your state? Outline their duties.
10. How nearly does the distribution of executive power in your state conform to that recommended in the Model State Constitution?

☆ 14 ☆

Congress: Its Structure and Organization

IN this and the succeeding chapter we shall examine the structure, organization, procedure, and powers of Congress, not failing to take due notice of the activities of lobbies in relation to the exercise of these powers, and, finally, we shall consider that frequently-raised question, What is the matter with Congress?

The bicameral system. Since mediaeval times the English Parliament has been composed of two houses, Lords and Commons. Naturally, most of the American colonies followed the English model when they set up their legislative bodies; and when these colonies became states, only three of them, and they only temporarily, failed to adopt the bicameral principle. Of course, in deciding for two chambers, the members of the Philadelphia Convention were strongly influenced by the examples from English and American history and by the reputed advantage that one house "checks" the other. But there was a much more practical consideration. A bicameral Congress made possible an essential compromise on representation —a compromise that gave the states representation in proportion to population in one chamber and equal representation in the other. These facts alone were ample justification for the bicameral system; but it has been further justified in practice by the added consideration it brings to legislative measures and by the different character of representation in the two houses.

I. ELECTION AND LEGAL QUALIFICATIONS OF MEMBERS [1]

The House of Representatives: the popular body. The House of Representatives, commonly called the "House," is the "popular" branch of

[1] D. S. Alexander, *History and Procedure of the House of Representatives* (1916), Ch. I;

Congress. The Constitution provides that every person who shall have the right to vote for members of the most numerous branch of the state legislature shall have the right to vote for members of the House of Representatives. Since nearly all the states had adopted, even before 1789, a democratic suffrage for the election of members of the lower houses of their legislatures, the members of the lower House of Congress from the very beginning have been chosen by a democratic electorate. But the Senate is now chosen by the same electorate, so that if we are to maintain that the House is still *the* popular body we must do so on grounds other than that its members are elected by a universal suffrage. These other grounds are that the short term of two years makes its members more responsive to the people; that it represents the people of the states in proportion to their numbers; and that somehow it has come to personify many, if not all, of the American qualities.

Apportionment of representatives. The Fourteenth Amendment requires that "representatives shall be apportioned among the several states according to their respective numbers, counting the whole number of persons in each state, excluding Indians not taxed." The original provision of the Constitution relating to apportionment stated that the slave population should be counted at only three fifths of its actual number; but this provision of course became inoperative with the abolition of slavery, and the Negro became a whole man by the terms of the Fourteenth Amendment. The Amendment further provides that any state that denies the right of suffrage to any of its male citizens twenty-one years of age, shall have its representation in Congress "reduced in the proportion which the number of such citizens shall bear to the whole number of male citizens twenty-one years of age in such state." This constitutional provision represented an attempt to force the Southern states to give the Negro a vote. Although many Negroes in the South have been deprived of the right to vote by one means or another, the penalty has never been enforced. An attempt to enforce it would stir up the bitterest struggle below the Mason-Dixon line; and, besides, it would be extremely difficult, if not impossible, to determine how many persons a state had deprived of the right to vote. Furthermore, if the penalty were to be applied, it would have to be applied against those states that in good faith require voters to pass a literacy test, as well as against those that deprive persons of the franchise by subterfuge; and the penalty could not be applied in Georgia, where the voting age

G. B. Galloway, *Congress at the Crossroads* (1946), Ch. 2; G. H. Haynes, *The Senate of the U.S.* (1938), Vol. I, Chs. III–IV and Vol. II, Ch. XVI; R. Luce, *Legislative Assemblies* (1924), Chs. III–VI, X–XII, XIV–XVI; Mathews and Berdahl, *Documents and Readings in American Government* (1940 ed.), Ch. XII; L. Rogers, *The American Senate* (1926), Chs. II, IV.

is eighteen, in respect to male citizens between the ages of eighteen and twenty-one who might be deprived of the right to vote. Finally, the Woman Suffrage Amendment has rendered obsolete the penalty provision of the Fourteenth Amendment, because that provision applies only if male citizens are denied the right to vote. Since the penalty of reduction in representation for a denial of the suffrage remains a dead letter, each state has representation in the House according to population (not according to the number of citizens or voters), excluding Indians not taxed.

REAPPORTIONMENT. As shifts in population will inevitably occur, periodic reapportionments are necessary if the states are to have their fair share of representatives. The Constitution calls for a reapportionment after each decennial census. It must be said that Congress has not always hastened to carry out this constitutional mandate. Indeed, being unable to reach satisfactory agreement concerning the number of representatives and the exact method of apportioning them among the states, Congress made no reapportionment on the basis of the census of 1920. Failure to do so was, of course, contrary to the express provision of the Constitution; but nothing could be done about it, since there is no legal action which may be taken against Congress.

NUMBER OF REPRESENTATIVES. The Constitution provides that the number of representatives shall not exceed one for every thirty thousand inhabitants, but that each state shall have at least one representative. The Constitution fixed the number of representatives at 65 until the first census should be taken. After the census of 1790 Congress fixed the number at 103; and that body has increased the number following nearly every decennial census. Although the present membership of 435 is less than a tenth of the maximum number authorized by the Constitution, it is generally considered too high for the most satisfactory working of a legislative body. The explanation of the almost constant increase in the number of representatives is quite simple. The rapid increase in the population and the admission of new states accounted for a part of the increase. But the main reason was that the population of all the states did not grow in the same proportion. As a result, when Congress made a reapportionment, it either had to reduce the representation of the more slowly developing states or give the more rapidly developing states additional representatives. Since the states were naturally reluctant to see their representation decreased and since representatives were still more reluctant to vote themselves out of seats in the House, Congress usually, though not always, made the adjustment by increasing the number of seats for the rapidly developing states while leaving the representation of the other states unchanged.

THE PRESENT REAPPORTIONMENT LAW. The decennial problem of reapportionment, with the accompanying temptation to increase the number of representatives with each reapportionment, seems to have been solved by an act of 1929. This act heroically limits the membership to 435 "permanently." This limitation was made possible by the only means available, namely, by reducing the number of seats of the slow growing states and increasing the number for the other states. Thus, in the reapportionment following the census of 1940, nine states lost a seat each, six states gained a seat each, and one state (California) gained three seats. In addition to placing the total number of seats on a permanent basis, the act provides for automatic reapportionment. Following each decennial census, the Department of Commerce submits figures showing the changes in population since the last census and the proportion of the 435 representatives to which each state is entitled as a result of those changes. Congress may then act upon this information; but if it does not, the seats are automatically reapportioned according to the method of distribution Congress employed for the last reapportionment.

CONGRESSIONAL DISTRICTS. The Constitution does not lay down any rule with regard to districts. It provides only that "the times, places, and manner of holding elections shall be prescribed in each state by the legislature thereof; but the Congress may at any time by law make or alter such regulations." For about half a century, Congress allowed the states to determine how the representatives should be chosen. Some states established districts and had the voters of each district elect a representative; others employed the general ticket plan, by which each voter in the state cast his ballot for the number of representatives to which the state was entitled. The general ticket system contains a grave injustice, in that the party with a plurality of votes, however slight, will win all the representatives in the state.

To correct this evil, Congress in 1843 passed a law establishing the district plan. By later legislation the states were authorized to elect at large (on a general ticket) any additional members they may have won in a reapportionment, and, in the event of reduced representation by reapportionment, to abolish the districts and elect all of their representatives on a general ticket. Although a few states have availed themselves of one or the other of these privileges, the district system is very generally employed. This plan operates with more fairness for a minority party than the general ticket plan, in that such a party may carry one or two districts of a state that as a whole gives the other parties large majorities. But the minority voters in all districts are still, in a sense, unrepresented. For example, in a district that gives 39 per cent of its votes to a Republican, 36 per cent to a Democrat, and 25 per cent to a Socialist, the Republican is elected. It is true that the advantage a party has by virtue of a plurality in one district may be offset by a similar advantage another party has in another district, but such advantages fall to the contending parties only in rough proportions.

The gerrymander. Pursuant to authority granted by Congress, the state legislatures lay out the congressional districts. Prior to 1929 congressional reapportionment acts commonly contained an ineffective requirement that districts should be composed of "contiguous and compact territory, and containing as nearly as practicable an equal number of inhabitants." The party that happens to hold the majority in the legislature at the time of reapportionment has often yielded to the temptation to district the state in such a way as to give that party an unfair advantage over the opposing party. If a state's vote is normally, let us say, 55 per cent Democratic, a legislature in which that party has the majority might devise a set of geographical curiosities in such a way that all the districts of the state will go Democratic. Or, if the mechanicians are afraid to risk the attempt to put every district in the Democratic column, they may so change the map as to put as many Republicans as possible in one or two districts, leaving the others safe for Democracy. Some districts have resembled shoe strings, others saddlebags, still others dumb-bells.[2]

In 1811 that master political cartographer, Elbridge Gerry, carved out a Massachusetts district that left his political enemies, the Federalists, no chance of winning. "That district looks like a salamander," said a complaining Federalist. "Say rather a Gerrymander," cried another, giving the practice the name by which it has ever since been known. In our time the hand of the gerrymanderers is stayed somewhat by public opinion, but now and then the "fixers" remake the political map. In 1940 there were enough labor votes scattered among three Congressional districts around Pittsburgh to elect Democratic congressmen from all three districts. In 1943 the Republican legislature of Pennsylvania "neatly amputated these Democratic areas, added them superfluously to the safely Democratic Pittsburgh district." The legislature performed similar operations on districts in Philadelphia. "Democrats moaned in the immemorial anguish of the gerrymandered. Cried they: 'Steal,' 'dastardly,' 'foul blow.' Replied Governor Martin: 'It's just the good old American way. When we Republicans were in the minority, we bellyached when they ran over us. It just has to be done.'"[3] Some plan of proportional representation (a

---

[2] Another unfair feature in reapportionment is the frequent variation in the size of the districts. Each should contain about 345,000 inhabitants, but urban districts are often given approximately twice that number and rural districts a number much smaller than the quota. This variation, of course, represents discrimination against urban areas.

[3] *Time*, May 24, 1943, p. 17.

system under which each party gets representatives in proportion to its vote), could be adopted that would do away with the gerrymander and other evils of the district system; but our politicians are almost unanimous in approving the present plan, and the voters seem to agree with Governor (now Senator) Martin that the district system, gerrymander and all, is just the "good old American way."

The regulation of congressional elections. As Congress originally left the states to determine whether they should employ the district or the general ticket system for choosing representatives, so it left them the authority to determine other matters relating to elections, such as the date and the method of voting. Long ago, however, Congress passed a law requiring the secret ballot for the election of all representatives, and established the Tuesday following the first Monday in November as the election day.[4] Other acts of Congress relating to the election of members include the Corrupt Practices Acts and a measure designed to protect (Negro) citizens in their right to vote.

For some years it was supposed that the authority of Congress over elections did not include primary elections. At least that seems to have been the conclusion drawn from the Supreme Court's decision in the Newberry case.[5] In 1940, however, the Court held that a commissioner of elections in New Orleans, who altered and falsely counted ballots cast in a congressional *primary* election, was guilty of violating a provision of the Criminal Code of the United States which prescribes punishment for anyone "who under color of any law . . . or custom, wilfully" deprives any citizen of rights secured to him by the Constitution and laws of the United States. As noted above, persons who have the right to vote for members of the lower house of the state legislature are given the right by the federal Constitution to vote for members of the lower House of Congress. This right to vote in such elections is incomplete, says the Court, in effect, unless it is extended to cover the right to vote in primary elections.[6] Apparently, then, Congress may now enact legislation dealing specifically with congressional primaries.

The two-year term. The short term of office was the fashion when our Constitution was framed, and the more democratic element in the country complained that the two-year term for representatives was too long; that the people's liberties were in danger unless representatives were chosen annually—the practice commonly followed at that time in electing members of the lower house of state legislatures. We now regard the

[4] Maine holds her congressional election in September, being excepted from the November date because change to it would require an amendment of her constitution.

[5] Newberry v. United States, 256 U.S. 232 (1921).

[6] United States v. Classic, 313 U.S. 299 (1940). See also R. E. Cushman, "Constitutional Law in 1940–1941," *Am. Pol. Sci. Rev.*, XXXVI, 269 (April, 1942).

two-year term as too short. The disadvantage of the short term is not so serious, however, when we consider that representatives are usually re-elected several times. Indeed, the average tenure of a representative is about the same as that of a senator.

Qualifications of members. According to the Constitution any person who has attained the age of twenty-five years, who has been for seven years a citizen of the United States, and who is an inhabitant of the state that elects him, is eligible for a seat in the House.[7] Another clause of the Constitution provides, however, that no person holding any office under the United States shall be a member of either House of Congress.[8] Thus, officers of the Army and Navy and civil officers from the President on down are excluded from membership. In the matter of residence, politics and public opinion have added an additional requirement; namely, that the representative shall reside in the district by which he is elected, not simply in the state as is required by the Constitution. A few exceptions to this practice have been permitted only in metropolitan areas, where the representative may live quite close to his constituents although in a different district. We can hardly imagine a constituency in up-state New York electing a resident of New York City to the House, or a southern California constituency choosing a representative from the San Francisco Bay region.

This unwritten district inhabitancy requirement may have unfortunate results. Suppose a party has no good candidate in a district; it must nevertheless put up one of the locals and be content. Or, suppose an exceptionally good man has no chance of winning in the district in which he resides; he is cut off from any chance to serve his country in the House. In England a constituency in one corner of the country may send a man who resides in another to the House of Commons. The lack of emphasis on residence in the district is held to account in part for the broader view the average member of the House of Commons takes of national questions. Our representatives, whether they like it or not, must sometimes put aside national questions and think a great deal of the selfish desires of their constituencies, or their constituencies will forget them in the next election.

DENIAL OF SEATS TO "QUALIFIED" PERSONS. The Constitution states that each House of Congress "shall be the judge of the elections, returns, and qualifications of its own members."[9] This stipulation means that the representatives may hear and settle disputes as to who was actually elected

---

[7] Art. I, sec. II, cl. 2.

[8] Art. I, sec. VI, cl. 2. Section III of the Fourteenth Amendment, designed to keep "rebels" out of Congress, excludes from membership persons who have taken an oath to uphold the Constitution and later engaged in rebellion against the United States. It was provided, however, that Congress might remove this disability.

[9] Art. I, sec. V, cl. I.

in a particular district, and see that no person is seated who does not meet the constitutional qualifications. In passing upon the qualifications of persons duly elected, the House has on several occasions added qualifications of its own, and in so doing it may have exceeded its powers under the Constitution. In 1900 it refused to seat Brigham H. Roberts, a polygamist elected by a Utah constituency. In 1918 Victor L. Berger, famous Milwaukee Socialist, was elected to Congress; the House denied him his seat, on the grounds of his conviction on charges of sedition (of which charges the Supreme Court of the United States later cleared Berger), and more particularly for his "un-American" conduct during the First World War. The Constitution does not state that in order to be eligible for membership in the House one must have only one wife, or that one must share the patriotic sentiments of the majority of the representatives. Yet, in effect, these qualifications were respectively imposed by the House in the Roberts and Berger cases. Representatives insist that they may thus broadly interpret the term "qualifications," but some publicists are equally insistent that such denials of seats to duly elected individuals strike at the very heart of representative government; that the House, in effect, disfranchised the voters who elected these men.[10]

Expulsion a better remedy. A number of authorities argue that individuals whose delinquencies are such as to make them unworthy members of either House of Congress should be seated and then expelled. Although the difference between the refusal of a seat and expulsion might not seem material to the person directly concerned, there are, in fact, two important differences. A seat may be withheld by a majority vote, whereas a two-thirds majority is required to expel a member.[11] The more significant difference is that the Constitution, in stating the qualifications of members, thereby limits the authority to deny seats to those congressmen-elect who do not meet the qualifications; whereas it attaches no strings to the right of expulsion, and thus gives either House full power to expel a member for any reason whatsoever. It goes without saying that this power should be used only in the most extreme cases.

The Senate: equal representation of the states. The Constitution gives each state two senators, with a sort of moral guaranty that "no state, without its consent, shall be deprived of its equal suffrage in the Senate." [12] All the adults in Nevada could be accommodated in any one of our larger football stadiums; yet, through their two senators, they have equal suffrage in the upper House of Congress with the teeming millions of New York.

[10] Z. Chafee, *Free Speech in the United States* (1941 ed.), pp. 247 ff.
[11] Constitution, Art. I, sec. v, cl. 2.
[12] Art. V.

Senators from a majority of the 48 states, representing much less than half the country's inhabitants, might very easily block the efforts of the minority of the senators whose constituencies include a large majority of our population. But, contrary to the opinion entertained by a number of the framers of the Constitution, the battles in the Senate never have been joined between those who represent large populations and those who represent the small or sparsely settled states. As everyone with an elementary knowledge of American history knows, the great issues have been between the agricultural and industrial states. As a group, however, the agricultural states do have some advantage, since they are more numerous and usually less populous than the industrial states.

A CHANGE IN REPRESENTATION UNLIKELY. Voices are sometimes raised in favor of modifying the system of representation in the Senate. In all probability such voices are futilely raised; for one can hardly imagine that any state would give up its "equal suffrage in the Senate." To be sure, the pledge of equal suffrage might be removed from the Constitution by an amendment; but it is inconceivable that three fourths of the states would ratify such an amendment. Perhaps that is fortunate; for any change in representation in the Senate would undoubtedly increase the membership of that body. The House has too many members now for the most effective work, and there is every reason to believe that the Senate's usefulness would be impaired by a weight of numbers.

Election of senators: THE OLD METHOD. The framers of the Constitution finally decided that senators should be chosen by the state legislatures, and this method of choice was employed until 1913, when popular election was substituted for it by constitutional amendment. The legislatures made their selections in whatever manner suited their convenience until 1866, when Congress, exercising its constitutional power to regulate the time and manner of holding senatorial elections, laid down the rules for these electoral bodies to follow. The two houses were required to meet separately and ballot for a senator on the second Tuesday after the legislature convened. If a candidate received a majority vote in each house, he was elected. If no candidate received such majorities, then the two houses, according to law, met in joint session the next day for the purpose of electing a senator. If no candidate received a majority vote in this session, the two houses continued to take at least one vote in joint assembly every day thereafter until some candidate received a majority.

Election by state legislatures, even under this national regulation, did not prove satisfactory. It was argued that the corrupt influences of bosses and corporations too often controlled the votes in the legislatures; that men of wealth sometimes indirectly, and occasionally directly, bought their way into the United States Senate; that, when a senator was to be chosen, members of the state legislature were elected on their pledge to support this or that senatorial candidate, rather than in consideration of their stand on state policies—properly the primary concern of the legislature; that the not infrequent deadlocks in choosing a senator took valuable time which the legislature needed for the state's business, and intensified the partisan spirit which was almost invariably present during any senatorial contest; and that the choice of United States senators by legislatures was undemocratic. Refutation of any of these charges was exceedingly difficult; but many able men said that the evils of selection by legislatures were exaggerated and that popular election would bring results of a much more deplorable nature.

THE NEW METHOD—POPULAR ELECTION. The movement for popular election of senators was started long before the Civil War, and the demand for this reform became insistent during the 'eighties. In 1892 and thereafter the Populist party urged the change; the Democrats accepted it as one of their principles in 1900; and in 1908 Taft approved it as a presidential candidate. As far back as 1893 the House of Representatives had approved a resolution for a constitutional amendment that would bring direct election of senators; but the Senate withheld approval in this matter, just as the House, until 1932, acted adversely upon the Senate's resolution for an amendment that would abolish the "lame duck" sessions of Congress. But the states interested in direct election of senators did not wait for a constitutional amendment. Particularly in the Middle West and in the West, the states adopted the plan of allowing the voters to express their choice for the Senate. The legislators, under a politico-moral obligation very similar to that of the presidential electors, then legally elected the candidate who had received the largest number of popular votes. In the face of this movement, both Houses of Congress approved the Seventeenth Amendment, which was promptly ratified by the requisite number of states, and proclaimed in force (1913).

Is popular election an improvement? By the Seventeenth Amendment all persons qualified to vote for members of the lower house of a state legislature are declared to be entitled to vote for United States senator. The people have shown great interest in electing their senators. Has the popular election of senators removed the evils complained of under the old system? Certainly the state legislatures are freed of a function that often took a great deal of their time and energy and sometimes subjected them to the gravest criticism.

On other points we speak with less assurance. The fact that senators are usually nominated in direct primaries and elected by the people [13]

---

[13] The Amendment provides that vacancies which may happen in the representation of any state in the Senate shall be filled in an election called by the governor; or, that the state

(except in case of a vacancy) does not remove the boss or the machine from the picture, although they may find it a little more difficult to pull their wires. Further, money is still spent for the toga. One can easily understand how the legitimate expenditure entailed in reaching a few hundred thousand voters in a senatorial campaign may run to $90,000 or $100,000. Much larger sums have been spent in several campaigns, leaving the general public under the impression that, in spite of popular election, it is still far easier for a rich man to enter the United States Senate than it is for a camel to pass through the eye of a needle.

Do we get better senators since the adoption of the Seventeenth Amendment? Few will deny that several demagogues have been sent to the Senate as a mark of popular favor. Perhaps we have traded some of the state-boss type of senators, which legislatures not infrequently delighted to honor, for a few of the demagogue variety; but we must await further evidence before reaching a conclusion. It cannot be maintained that popular election has deterred able men from becoming senatorial candidates, or that the people are more likely to pass them by than were the legislatures. We must remember that Lincoln failed to get a seat in the Senate long before the Seventeenth Amendment was adopted. On the whole, it must be said that the Senate is about what it used to be. If it is not now the House of Webster and Calhoun, neither was it such a body during the greater part of the long period in which our elder statesmen were chosen by legislatures.

The Senate a continuous body. As we recall members of the House are elected for only two years and that every seat must be filled by election in the even year. Senators, however, are chosen for six years; and, since one third of them complete their term biennially, only one third of the seats in the Senate are filled in each Congressional election. The Senate is thus a continuous body, for two thirds of its members are always "holdovers." The House of Representatives must be reorganized after each election, but the Senate has been in organized existence since 1789. Some autumnal political revolution might completely alter the complexion of the House; but nothing less than three such revolutions, occurring at two-year intervals, could do the like for the Senate. Undoubtedly the six-year term and the provision for continuity have been important factors in making the Senate a more stable and consistent body than the House.

Qualifications of senators. The Constitution specifies that "no person shall be a senator who shall not have attained to the age of thirty years,

---

legislature may authorize the governor to make temporary appointments until the people fill the vacancies by election, as the legislature may direct. Legislatures have very generally empowered the governors to fill vacancies by appointment.

and been nine years a citizen of the United States, and who shall not, when elected, be an inhabitant of that state for which he shall be chosen." [14] Persons holding any other office under the United States are ineligible for the Senate, just as they are for the House. However, members of commissions of investigation, delegates authorized to negotiate treaties, and persons acting in similar capacities are held not to be officers of the United States within the meaning of the last-mentioned prohibition. Thus, Senators Tom Connally and Arthur H. Vandenberg served at various international conferences following the Second World War, without thereby losing their places in the Senate. Somewhat as the House, the Senate has at times been tempted, in the exercise of its power to judge of the qualifications of its members, to impose qualifications in addition to those enumerated in the Constitution. Considering the place of leadership Senator Smoot later held in the upper chamber, it is interesting to recall that, when he was first elected to that body (1903), there was a movement to refuse him a seat because of his position in the Mormon hierarchy. Wiser counsel prevailed, however, and Smoot was seated.

EXCESSIVE CAMPAIGN EXPENDITURES A POSSIBLE DISQUALIFICATION. Quite apart from the Corrupt Practices Act of 1925, which applies only to elections,[15] and for violations of which a candidate may be legally prosecuted, the Senate insists that candidates shall not spend "too much" money in the primaries. Occasionally, very large sums have been spent. In 1918 Truman H. Newberry of Michigan spent at least $195,000 in the senatorial primary, although the Michigan law then in force authorized an expenditure of only $1,875. We noted above that Newberry's conviction was set aside by the Supreme Court of the United States. But the Senate, when it finally seated Newberry in 1922, gave ominous warning of what other heavy spenders might expect. The resolution reads in part: "That whether the amount expended in the primary was $195,000, as was fully reported or openly acknowledged, or whether there were some few thousand dollars in excess, the amount expended was in either case too large, much larger than ought to have been expended." After the congressional election of 1922, in which a number of senators who had supported his claim to a seat were defeated, Newberry resigned, probably anticipating expulsion. Amounts spent by or on behalf of Frank L. Smith [16] of Illinois and William S. Vare of Pennsylvania, particularly the latter, in the primaries of 1926, caused the cynic to say that the price of nominations to

---

[14] Art. I, sec. III, cl. 3.

[15] See Chapter 10, section VII.

[16] In the case of Smith, the evil was more in his official relation to his chief contributor, Samuel Insull, than in the amount actually expended in the primary.

the Senate had skyrocketed since Newberry's sad experience. Following their nomination, these men were duly elected to the Senate; but that body, on the grounds of the staggering sums expended and the sources from which the money came, refused to seat them. In voting for such exclusions, the Senate is exercising its power to "judge of the elections" of its members.

There is now general recognition of the fact that a hard-fought senatorial primary campaign in a populous state may call for large and legitimate expenditures. The sources of the money and the purposes for which money is spent may be much more significant than the amounts involved. The Senate seems to follow a "rule of reason" in respect to the financial dealings of candidates, but that body would probably exclude as readily in the 'fifties as in the 'twenties a member-elect with the Smith-Vare type of campaign history. Lest a distorted picture of the expenditures of senatorial candidates in the primaries be given, it should be remarked that large expenditures are the exception.

II. THE REPRESENTATIVE CHARACTER OF CONGRESSMEN [17]

Back in the days when life was simple (although few people realized it was so) and the United States Senate was composed for the most part of rich men and representatives of large corporate interests, Edward Everett Hale, the author of *The Man Without a Country*, was the Senate Chaplain. One day, as he was walking toward the Chamber to offer his noonday prayer, a friend chanced to join him, and by way of passing the time of day remarked: "I suppose, Mr. Hale, that you first look at the country and then pray for the Senate." To which Hale replied: "On the contrary, I first look at the Senate, then I pray for the country." [18] This type of remark gets any platform speaker a good laugh at the expense of either House of Congress. Congressmen themselves sometimes disarm their audience with some such reference to their reputation. With us the witticism of the famous Chaplain causes us to ask, Is Congress really that bad? Just who are the congressmen? What are their qualifications, their age and experience? Whom do they represent? What is their work, and how faithfully do they perform it?

Age, education, occupation. There is a turnover of individual congressmen from one term of Congress to another ranging from one fifth to one fourth; but the type of personnel, although it may change considerably

[17] J. M. Burns, *Congress on Trial* (1949), Ch. I; G. B. Galloway, *Congress at the Crossroads* (1946), pp. 28–48, 348–349; Paul H. Douglas, "Report from a Freshman Senator," *New York Times Magazine*, Mch. 20, 1949, p. 10; Madge M. McKinney, "The Personnel of the Seventy-Seventh Congress," *Am. Pol. Sci. Rev.*, Feb., 1942, pp. 67–74; "Leftward Trend in Congress . . . ," *United States News*, Nov. 26, 1948, pp. 11–13.

[18] Quoted in Douglas, *op. cit.*, p. 76.

over a long period of time or as a result of a national crisis, probably does not change much from one Congress to another. Professor Madge M. Mc-Kinney made a study of the personnel of the Seventy-seventh Congress (January 3, 1941 to January 3, 1943), George B. Galloway of the Seventy-ninth (1945–1947), and the *United States News & World Report* of the Eighty-first (1949–1951).[19] Inasmuch as there are no material variations in the type of personnel in the three Congresses, only Professor McKinney's findings are here summarized. The reader will note from the *United States News'* chart (reproduced pages 364–365) that lawyers still constitute nearly three fifths of the membership and that veterans are there in large numbers.

Half the members of the House were fifty years of age or over; half the senators, fifty-seven or over. The personnel was certainly not youthful, although the members cannot be characterized as "531 old men—and women." Nearly all of them were born in this country, most of them in the districts and states they represent, and their sentiments and loyalties are deeply rooted in those areas. Practically all of them had some religious affiliation, with Catholics, Methodists, Presbyterians, Baptists, and Episco-palians dominating in the order named. Up to this point, notes Professor McKinney, they represented the American public in relatively fair propor-tions. They moved away, and very properly so, from this proportion in the matter of education, 88 per cent having attended college or professional schools, or both. On the score of political experience, the figures show that 156 had served in state legislatures, 109 as prosecuting attorneys, 50 as judges, and scores in various other offices. In the Senate sat 28 former mem-bers of the House and 16 former governors of states. The House claimed only two governors and one former senator. What were the former occu-pations of the members of this Congress? Insurance, publishing, real estate, lumbering and construction, merchandizing, selling, and manufac-turing all had small representation. Forty-one members had been news-paper men, 59 farmers, and 87 teachers. Few of the "teachers," however, had laid down their books to enter Congress. The great majority who indicated teaching as a former profession meant only that they had once taught (until they could find something better—probably get started in the practice of law).

WHY SO MANY LAWYERS. The great majority of congressmen (311 of the 531, or about 60 per cent, in the Seventy-seventh Congress) came from the legal profession. How is this predominance of lawyers explained? A number of explanations may be given. The lawyer's business, like that of the preacher and the teacher, is a "talking business," and, unlike that of most preachers and teachers, it brings him into frequent and fighting contact with public questions. More significant, the lawyer, even yet, often

[19] See note 17.

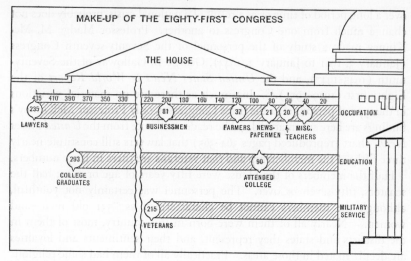

MAKE-UP OF THE EIGHTY-FIRST CONGRESS

THE HOUSE

Reprinted from the *U.S. News & World Report* (Nov. 26, 1948), an independent weekly magazine on national and international affairs, published at Washington. Copyright, 1948, United States News Publishing Corporation.

works for himself; and this independence makes it possible for him to take time out to run for public office. Still more significant, he can continue to practice law while holding his seat in Congress, and a number of the lawyers in both House and Senate do just that. In fact, it has been observed that some lawyer-congressmen have had much more lucrative practices than they ever enjoyed before they were chosen to represent the people's interest in Washington, D.C. Let it be recorded, however, that some of the ablest lawyer-congressmen have refused to have any client other than the people of the United States. The late Senator William E. Borah was the outstanding example of the latter type.[20] There is another reason for the preponderance of lawyers in Congress: the average ignorant person sees perfect logic in sending "lawyers to make the laws." Without a doubt, lawyers are most helpful, perhaps indispensable, for certain aspects of legislation; but to entertain the belief that broad economic and social problems can best be decided by lawyers and lawyers alone is an absurdity. Legislation touches the interests of the entire nation, and its intelligent formulation requires the best minds of every profession, trade, and calling.

Is Congress representative? The question whether Congress is representative could be discussed at great length, but here there is space only for a comment. If lawyers, businessmen, and farmers, who for the most part belong to the conservative and privileged classes, hold practically all

[20] C. O. Johnson, *Borah of Idaho* (1936), pp. 91–93.

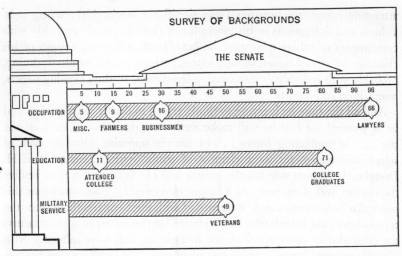

SURVEY OF BACKGROUNDS

THE SENATE

5 10 15 20 25 30 35 40 45 50 55 60 65 70 75 80 85 90 96

OCCUPATION 5 9 16 66

MISC. FARMERS BUSINESSMEN LAWYERS

EDUCATION 11 71

ATTENDED COLLEGE COLLEGE GRADUATES

MILITARY SERVICE 49

VETERANS

Reprinted from *U.S. News & World Report* (Nov. 26, 1948), an independent weekly magazine on national and international affairs, published at Washington. Copyright, 1948, United States News Publishing Corporation.

of the seats in Congress, who at the Capitol represents the teeming millions of sweating Americans? The answer is that they are not represented except to the extent that they are served by the lawyers, the businessmen, and the farmers. It must be admitted that some, perhaps many, of these congressmen have faithfully represented all classes and conditions of men, and it is also permissible to observe that the "toiling masses" have had a great deal to do with choosing the entire personnel of Congress. Here we may have a good illustration of the absence of class consciousness in America: the fact that tens of millions, presumably in one class, are relatively content to have themselves represented by men and women selected from the millions of a supposedly different class.

The congressman's job. Who has not heard the report from someone who has spent a few minutes in the gallery of the Senate or of the House that the senators or representatives are guilty of absenteeism and could not be discharging the duties they were elected to perform? Doubtless there are congressmen who shirk their responsibilities, and there are congressmen who have been convicted of crime and sent to prison, but these facts do not correctly portray the congressman. The great majority of the senators and representatives are conscientious and busy men. There are not enough hours in the day for them, even when they omit the cocktail hour (as many of them do). Your congressman's day may run something like this: Breakfast; reading the morning newspapers (one newspaper will not do); looking over mail and answering letters that require his personal attention;

attending committee hearings (very significant work, this); seeing individuals and delegations in his office; lunch (but no peace—probably with constituents or others who must be heard); attending the session of his chamber for several hours; signing letters, perhaps several hundred; dining, probably with individuals interested in legislation; reading evening papers, magazines, and reports.

And all the time he is trying to think, trying to decide what is best; and he is worried for fear he will make the wrong decision. "One feels the tug . . . of conflicting forces . . . of sharply opposing ideas, in each of which one recognizes some element of truth," writes Senator Paul H. Douglas.[21] Which side has the greater merit? Is there a way to resolve the conflict and, if so, how can it be put into effect? These questions this particular Senator asks, and "interspersed with these worries there come the reproaches of old friends who feel neglected" in the matter of appointments; the criticisms of newspapers (home newspapers that have influence with voters); citizens' letters, irate, caustic, plaintive. The result says the Senator "is a deep loneliness and also many inquietudes which at night interfere with sleep." The Senator turns to another philosopher, Shakespeare: " 'Honor alone doth not make a good surgeon.' Neither, I add, doth it make a good Senator or keep him out of trouble. Something more—and a great deal of it—is needed; something in the way of caution, physical endurance, a sense of selection, a sense of maneuver, and the inner tinkle of a bright hell's-bells air." The Senator tells us further that information and expertness on a particular problem is not enough; that one may be the world's foremost authority on a subject, "but knowledge for its own sake, and knowledge woven into a policy of legislative action are, unfortunately, two different things." This articulate freshman Senator has more to offer in his article, but we cease culling from it with the observation that he is impressed with his colleagues; that he believes the great majority of them are no less industrious and conscientious than he is.

III. COMPENSATION, PRIVILEGES, AND DISCIPLINE OF CONGRESSMEN [22]

Compensation and allowances. The Constitution stipulates that senators and representatives shall receive a compensation for their services, the amount to be fixed by law. Congressmen decide what they are worth, and pass a salary law accordingly. If they want an increase in salary, they have only to consult themselves. What is to prevent them from voting themselves "fat" salaries? The answer is fairly obvious—public opinion would

---

[21] *Op. cit.*

[22] Alexander, *op. cit.,* Chs. VIII–IX; Luce, *op. cit.,* Chs. XIII, XX–XXIII, XXV.

not permit it. The "salary grab" of 1873 [23] and its sequel of empty seats is still a familiar story in American history, and fresh in the memory of many of us is the enactment and speedy repeal (under a howl of indignation from the public) of the Annuity Act of 1942. The annuity for congressmen was only a part of a general annuity system provided for by the act. The legislation was non-pernicious, but ill-timed. The First Congress fixed the compensation at $6 for each day's attendance, and in 1818 (a $1,500 salary compensation of 1815 having greatly displeased the voters) the amount was placed at $8 per day. In 1855 an annual salary of $3,000 was voted, and in 1865 it was increased to $5,000, in 1907 to $7,500 (temporarily to this amount in 1873), in 1925 to $10,000, and in 1946 to $12,500, plus a $2,500 tax-free expense allowance. The Vice President, the President of the Senate *pro tempore* (when there is no Vice President), and the Speaker of the House receive a salary of $30,000, plus a $10,000 tax-free expense allowance. This writer does not justify the tax-free allowance. Congressmen should "pay themselves" proper salaries and then pay income taxes on them as the rest of us do. The tax-free allowance is deceptive, making the compensation seem less than the salary plus allowance, when, as a matter of fact, the tax-free feature makes the total compensation of a congressman better than a $15,000 salary and the total compensation of any of the officers named much better than a $40,000 salary.

The Legislative Reorganization Act of 1946, the Act that made the recent adjustment in salary, also provides a retirement system for congressmen. A member pays in six per cent of his basic salary, and if he serves for six years and is no longer a member of Congress or employed by the Government at the age of sixty-two, he receives an annuity based on his length of service in Congress, but in no case may the annuity exceed three fourths of his salary at the time he ceased to be a congressman. Members of Congress who retired in the year this plan was adopted were permitted to avail themselves of the annuity benefits by depositing $2,716.

It has often been stated that higher salaries and a retirement system would attract better men to Congress. This conclusion is probably valid in reference to professional administrative and judicial services, but it is doubtful whether the rate of compensation serves as any particular inducement to a high type of citizen to run for office. Capable, public-spirited men and women run for office for reasons of prestige and the services they can render. Mediocre individuals might be attracted by the compensation. But in any event, congressmen are certainly entitled to the salary and the annuity plan established in 1946.

Congressmen receive an allowance of twenty cents per mile for travel to

[23] At the end of the term Congress increased the salary from $5,000 to $7,500 and made the increase retroactive for the term.

and from the sessions, and allowances for stationery and clerical help, representatives about $10,000 for the item last mentioned, and senators twice as much or even more, the amount depending upon the size of their states. Not infrequently a member appoints to his clerical force a member, or even members, of his own family. In May, 1932, it was revealed that well over a hundred relatives of congressmen were so engaged; [24] and in December, 1949, ninety-one members of the House of Representatives alone had more than a hundred relatives on their payrolls.[25] Some working employees in this category have received valuable political lessons in this practical school of politics. Ruth Hanna McCormick, former Congresswoman from Illinois and former Senator Robert M. La Follette II both served apprenticeships as their senator fathers' secretaries. Mrs. John Nance Garner and Mrs. Harry Truman were secretaries to their congressmen husbands. No one has denied that the persons mentioned and many other relatives so employed earned their money, but in certain cases this type of employment obviously was simply a "racket" by which family income was increased. Recently one congressman, J. Parnell Thomas of New Jersey, went beyond simple nepotism, enlarging his roll of office employees (some of whom did no work) and making such financial arrangements with them as to incur the penalties of the criminal code. He was sentenced to prison for receiving "kick backs" from some of his office employees.

Under the Legislative Reorganization Act of 1946 senators receive, in addition to the amount mentioned above, $10,000 for an administrative assistant. The idea was that such assistants would be particularly capable persons who would give the senators the sort of special help they need in carrying their heavy load. Considering that more than a majority of the senators simply promoted their secretaries to this higher salary bracket, with no appreciable change in their duties, the senators do not seem to have used their opportunity to the best advantage. Under this same act of 1946 the Speaker, the majority floor leader, and the minority floor leader may each employ an administrative assistant at a salary not to exceed $8,000.

Privileges: THE FRANK. The frank, that is, the privilege of the free use of the mails, is a very valuable possession of a congressman. Not only does he use it in an official capacity; but often he uses it for his own political purposes or in the interest of his party. Speeches delivered on the floor, as well as "unspoken speeches," are printed and distributed by the ton among the voters.[26] Obviously, this privilege gives a congressman who

[24] *Time*, May 30, 1932, p. 9.
[25] Chicago *Tribune*, Dec. 31, 1949.
[26] Indulgent congressmen often permit their colleagues to have printed in the *Record* addresses which are not delivered on the floor and which are prepared only for the voters'

is a candidate to succeed himself a considerable, and rather unfair, advantage over other aspirants for the seat.

FREEDOM FROM ARREST. Senators and representatives are at all times subject to arrest for treason and felony—that is, for all indictable crimes. For such crimes they may be held and prosecuted as are other individuals. But, if they are attending the sessions of Congress, or are on their way to or from such sessions, they are not subject to arrest for minor offenses, nor may they be detained by court orders in civil cases. This exemption from arrest comes from English practice, with which all well-informed Americans were familiar in 1787, and it is, of course, one of the means of maintaining the freedom and independence of lawmakers.

FREEDOM OF SPEECH. Legislators must have the right to speak their minds freely and without fear of interference on the part of those outside the legislative halls. Members of the English Parliament won this privilege some centuries ago, and it was enjoyed by our colonial legislators. The Constitution extends this immunity to congressmen in the provision that "for any speech or debate in either House they shall not be questioned in any other place." [27] The privilege applies not only to "any speech or debate," but it applies generally to things done in a session of a House by a member in relation to the business before it. In 1913 an individual who assaulted a member of the House of Representatives was arrested, arraigned at the bar of the House, and, by direction of its members, censured by the Speaker, although the representative had been assaulted for something he had said in a debate in a previous session of Congress.[28] A congressman, in a debate on the floor, may make the most scurrilous attacks on private individuals and be perfectly secure against slander suits; or he may, even when his country is at war, deliver disloyal and "un-American" speeches without risk of prosecution, although such speeches would possibly send a private citizen to prison. Clearly, this freedom of speech may be abused; but without it, congressmen, standing in fear of civil suits and criminal prosecutions, would be all too effectively gagged for the best interests of the public.[29]

---

consumption. The Senate will not permit this practice, however, unless some of the "remarks" of a senator have been delivered on the floor.

In 1950 it was reported that millions (accounts range from 8 to 50 millions) of pieces of literature from the Committee for Constitutional Government had been mailed under the congressional frank (*New York Times,* June 28, 1950).

[27] Art. I, sec. VI, cl. I.

[28] *Cong. Record,* May 9, 1913, p. 1452, 63d Cong., 1st Sess.

[29] Alexander, *op. cit.,* p. 141. Whatever service Senator Joseph R. McCarthy may have been performing for the United States there is little doubt that he abused his immunity when, in 1950, he labeled as Communists and Communist supporters various persons whose ideas on foreign policy happened to differ from his own. One individual so attacked, Professor Owen Lattimore, replied in a book, *Ordeal by Slander* (1950). A majority of the Senate

There are, of course, practical limits to the privilege of free speech. The House to which a member belongs may discipline him for his excesses, or even expel him; or the electorate may retire him to private life, where he must assume legal responsibility for any further extravagant charges or scathing denunciations. Moreover, the privilege here under discussion does not protect a congressman in a political way. Thus, his utterances on the floor of his House may be fairly criticized by the press and by individuals, and they may be used against him in a campaign to show that he is unfit to represent the people.

The disciplining of members. Each House of Congress has the authority to "punish its members for disorderly conduct, and, with the concurrence of two thirds, expel a member." [30]   In keeping with the wide freedom guaranteed to our legislators by the Constitution, the two chambers have generally allowed their members great latitude.

1. Calling a member to order. Occasionally a member is called to order by the presiding officer, as Senator William Saulsbury was in 1863 when he referred to President Lincoln as "a weak and imbecile man." Vice President Marshall, on May 14, 1920, reminded Senator Sheppard that he had violated Senate rules by his statement that in Prohibition matters New Jersey had placed herself "on the side of revolution and anarchy." [31]

2. Censure. On rare occasions, congressmen have been censured by their colleagues. One of these rare occasions occurred on November 4, 1929, when the Senate resolved, by a vote of 54 to 22, that the action of Senator Hiram Bingham of Connecticut in placing Mr. Charles L. Eyanson of the Connecticut Manufacturers' Association on the Senate pay roll during the preparation of a tariff bill, "while not the result of corrupt motives, is contrary to good morals and senatorial ethics and tends to bring the Senate into dishonor and disrepute and such conduct is hereby condemned." [32]

3. Expulsion. As for the extreme disciplinary measure of expulsion, it has been resorted to about twenty times, usually on the ground of notorious disloyalty to the country, but in a few cases for moral turpitude. A number were expelled on the former charge during the Civil War. It is hardly necessary to add that, in relation to expulsion as well as to other

Foreign Relations subcommittee investigating Senator McCarthy's charges against particular individuals recommended that "a joint committee of the House and Senate be appointed to make a careful study of the immunity from civil suit extended members of Congress by reason of statements made by them on the floor of either House [and] before congressional committees" (*New York Times*, July 18, 1950).

[30] Constitution, Art. I, sec. v, cl. 2.
[31] Quoted in Luce, *op. cit.*, pp. 512, 646, respectively.
[32] *New York Times*, November 5, 1929.

forms of punishment, partisan strife and personal animosities are quite as likely to control the matter of discipline, or lack of it, as the actual guilt of the member disciplined. In the day when Congress and the country were much agitated over the slavery question, Senator Sumner delivered a long speech in which he insulted and ridiculed Senator Butler of South Carolina. A few days later, Representative Preston Brooks, a kinsman of Butler, entered the Senate Chamber and beat Sumner, who was sitting at his desk, into insensibility with a heavy cane. One representative even defended "the liberty of the cudgel"; another stated that Brooks "merited the highest commendation," and that Sumner "did not get a lick more than he deserved." [33] Although the majority in the House roundly denounced Brooks's conduct, the resolution for his expulsion failed to receive the necessary two-thirds vote. Had the cowardly and hot-headed Brooks used his "knock-down arguments" on any senator other than the extreme, vain, and unpopular Sumner, there is little doubt that the resolution would have been carried.

Compelling the attendance of absent members. Somewhat related to the disciplinary power is the authority of each House to compel absentees to attend its sessions. A majority of each body "shall constitute a quorum [34] to do business; but a smaller number may adjourn from day to day, and may be authorized to compel the attendance of absent members," says the Constitution.[35] In pursuance of this authority the House of Representatives empowers as few as fifteen members present, in the absence of a quorum, to send for and arrest absent members, wherever they may be found, and to secure and retain their attendance.[36] Such absentees, when presented at the bar of the House by the sergeant-at-arms or one of his assistants, are discharged from arrest.

But suppose a member brought in under arrest, or any other member, for the purpose of preventing a quorum and thereby rendering the House helpless to do business, refuses to answer to his name when called. This peculiarly annoying form of obstruction was not infrequently employed up to 1890, at which time Speaker Reed ruled that members physically present should be noted legally present. "I deny your right, Mr. Speaker, to count me as present," said a member who became angry and vocal under this ruling. "The Chair is making a statement of fact that the gentleman from Kentucky is here," replied Reed. "Does he deny it?" [37] This demon-

---

[33] Quoted in Alexander, *op. cit.*, pp. 140–141.

[34] "A quorum consists of a majority of those members chosen, sworn, and living, whose membership has not been terminated by resignation or by the action of the House." Speaker Cannon, quoted in Alexander, *op. cit.*, p. 156.

[35] Art. I, sec. v, cl. 1.

[36] Rule XV, sec. 2.

[37] Quoted in Alexander, *op. cit.*, p. 168.

strated the strength of Speaker Reed's position, a position that shortly thereafter was incorporated into the rules of the House. Without the authority
to count as present members sitting in a conspiracy of silence, the constitutional power of a legislative body to compel absent members to attend
would be hollow indeed.

The Senate also has a rule under which it compels the attendance of
absent members. In November, 1942, the Senate ordered the arrest of eight
of its members who were obstructing the business of the Senate by absenting
themselves from the Chamber. Senatorial dignity seems to have been
considerably ruffled by this procedure, several of the arrested senators being
outraged.

IV. THE SESSIONS OF CONGRESS

Regular sessions. The original clause of the Constitution relative to
sessions specified that "Congress shall assemble at least once in every year
. . . on the first Monday in December, unless they shall by law appoint
a different day." [38] As Congress never exercised its authority to appoint
a "different day," it always assembled for its regular sessions on the day
mentioned in the Constitution. The first regular session of a Congress
began in December of the odd year, *thirteen months after it was elected*.
This was called the long session, since it continued through the winter,
spring, and sometimes well into the summer. The next December, the
December of the even year, an almost incredible thing happened. In this
December, *after* we had elected all our representatives and one third of
our senators in the preceding November, the *old* Congress met for its second
regular session. Statesmen in Prince Alberts and the later cut-a-ways
solemnly assured each other and their constituents that it must be this way,
practical empire-building Americans nodded their assent, and good citizens
generally remarked, without laughing, that the newly elected congressmen
needed this thirteen months to get ready for their legislative duties. Since
this second session of Congress had to conclude its business before noon on
the fourth of the following March, when its term expired, it was politely
designated as the short session, but more commonly and irreverently dubbed
the "lame duck" session because so many casualties of the November election participated in its work.

The absurd reasoning that congressmen elected for two-year terms had
to have thirteen months to get ready to assume the legislative function or
"cool off," while many repudiated representatives of the people continued
to legislate and draw salaries, seemed to have the vitality of quack grass.
Consequently, those of us who had been somewhat critical observers of

[38] Art. I, sec. IV, cl. 2.

a Congress operating half the time with brakes on were most agreeably surprised to hear that Congress had adopted a constitutional amendment to abolish that particular nonsense. The amendment being promptly ratified by the states, congressmen's terms now begin on January 3 following the November election and the regular sessions of Congress begin January 3 of each year, "unless they shall by law appoint a different day." Congress now sits from five to seven months, or even longer, in its regular annual sessions.

Special sessions. In the earlier discussion of the legislative powers of the President we learned that the Constitution gives him the authority to convene both Houses of Congress, or either of them, on extraordinary occasions. About twenty-five special sessions of Congress have been called. Before the adoption of the Twentieth Amendment under which Congress is now in session at the time of the Inauguration, new Presidents often called special sessions at the beginning of their terms. We should add that special sessions at the beginning of administrations so frequently brought Chief Executives bad luck that they came to be "looked on with an almost superstitious aversion." [39] Some forty times the President has convoked the Senate alone for the purpose of securing action on appointments and treaties. On such occasions the members of the House are left at home, since their chamber has no legal authority in such matters.

Numbering of Congresses and their sessions. The two-year terms of Congress are numbered consecutively, the Congress which started with Washington in 1789 being designated, of course, as the First, and that which came in with President Roosevelt in 1933 as the Seventy-third. The sessions of each Congress, whether regular or special sessions, are also numbered consecutively. Thus, we refer to the Sixty-ninth Congress, Second Session; to the Eightieth Congress, First Session.

Adjournment of Congress. "Neither House, during the session of Congress, shall, without the consent of the other, adjourn for more than three days, nor to any other place than that in which the two Houses shall be sitting." [40] These limitations, relating only to separate adjournment of the two chambers, have no reference to the adjournment of the whole Congress. The Legislative Reorganization Act of 1946 provides that except in time of war or national emergency proclaimed by the President, the two Houses shall adjourn not later than the last day of July, unless otherwise provided by the Congress. If the two Houses cannot agree upon a date for adjournment, then the President may fix the time, a function that he has never been called upon to discharge. In practice, therefore, the only power the President has over the sessions of Congress is in calling a special

[39] Luce, *op. cit.,* p. 137.
[40] Constitution, Art. I, sec. v, cl. 4.

session. When in such sessions, the two Houses fix the date for adjournment just as if they were in regular session.

V. ORGANIZATION OF CONGRESS: THE HOUSE OF REPRESENTATIVES [41]

A. Officers of the House

The Speaker of the House. The first concern of a new House of Representatives, after the clerk of the preceding House has called the roll, is the election of the Speaker. It is singular that this, the most important officer of the House, who does practically no speaking except in the discharge of his duties as presiding officer, should be called "Mr. Speaker." The explanation of the title we find in the early practice of the English House of Commons, when its members, having no authority to make laws, sent one of their number to "speak" for them to the King, to ask His Majesty for redress of grievances, new laws, or amendments to old laws. This function of the Speaker ceased to be of any importance after the Commons became a lawmaking body, but the title has remained in Great Britain and in those countries and dominions that have adopted her political institutions.

Our Speaker is invariably a member of the House and one of the senior representatives of his party. The member thus honored is chosen in the House caucus of the majority party, and his election follows automatically in the House. The caucus of the minority party also names a candidate for the office, and its members go through the form of voting for him when the Speaker is elected. When the result is announced, the defeated candidate gallantly escorts the victor to the Speaker's chair, and with some gracious word presents him to the House. The "Father of the House" (the member who has had the longest continuous service as a representative), or some other member designated by the Speaker-elect, administers the oath.[42]

THE AMERICAN SPEAKER A PARTISAN OFFICER. In spite of the fact that the speakership in the lower houses of our state legislatures and in our national House of Representatives was adopted by the Americans from the practice of the English House of Commons, the institution on this side differs markedly from its English counterpart. The Speaker of the House of Commons, at his first election, is chosen by the majority party; but, once elected, he immediately divests himself of all partisanship and

---

[41] Alexander, *op. cit.,* Chs. II–VII; Galloway, *op. cit.,* Ch. 4; R. Luce, *Legislative Procedure* (1922), Chs. I–V, XIX–XXII; F. M. Riddick, *The U.S. Congress Organization and Procedure* (1949), Chs. II–VIII; *Rules of the House of Representatives;* Harvey Walker, *The Legislative Process* (1948), Chs. 9–11.

[42] Alexander, *op. cit.,* pp. 30–36.

presides over the House with the impartiality of a judge, rather than as a party man who has found a high place from which he can serve his political organization. No better conception of the political detachment of the English Speaker can be gained than by reflection upon the fact that he is re-elected from time to time, for as long a period as he is willing and able to serve, regardless of what party happens to be in power. The American Speaker is elected by the majority party, frankly uses his office to further the interests of his party, particularly its legislative program, and as soon as his party loses its majority, a Speaker is chosen from the other party. The late Speaker Longworth thus stated his own and the American conception of the Speaker's office: "I believe it to be the duty of the Speaker, standing squarely on the platform of his party, to assist in so far as he properly can the enactment of legislation in accordance with the declared principles and policies of his party and by the same token to resist the enactment of legislation in violation thereof." [43]

The difference between the American and British conceptions of the speakership is not to be explained by the doubly false statement that the Americans are unconscionable partisans and that the Englishmen in the Commons all work together for the good of their country. The explanation is rather in the fact that in the English system of government practically all of the party leaders sit in the House of Commons,[44] thus making it possible for a party to detach a Speaker; whereas our system does not permit executive officers, a number of whom are invariably important party leaders, to sit in Congress, thus making it highly desirable that the Speaker be left free to use his office in the interest of his party's legislative projects.

THE SPEAKER'S DUTIES AND POWERS. The Rules of the House require the Speaker to take the chair at the hour the House meets (usually at 12 m.), "immediately call the members to order, and on the appearance of a quorum, cause the *Journal* of the proceedings of the last day's sitting to be read, having previously examined and approved the same." He has the duty of preserving order and decorum on the floor of the House; and, in case of any disturbance in the galleries or in the lobby, he may cause the same to be cleared. He must sign all acts, addresses, joint resolutions, writs, warrants, and subpoenas that may be ordered by the House. He puts all questions, and announces the decisions of the House. He may vote in ordinary legislative proceedings if he so desires; but the rules provide that he shall not be required to vote except when his vote would be decisive, or when the voting is by ballot. Formerly, he had wide powers in the appointment of committees; but at present he appoints only the select and conference committees. The Speaker may name any member

[43] Quoted in Riddick, *op. cit.*, p. 67, from *Cong. Record*, 69th Cong., 1st Sess., p. 382.
[44] A few are in the House of Lords.

to serve in his stead for three days; and, in case of illness, he may, with the approval of the House, name someone to perform the duties of the chair for not longer than ten days. The House elects a speaker *pro tempore* if the Speaker is absent and has failed to appoint a member to serve in his place. In forming a Committee of the Whole House, the Speaker is required to leave the chair after appointing a chairman to preside.[45]

Before 1911—"Tzarism." For well over a century the Speaker had the authority to appoint committees of the House, a power that made him the master of the group over which he presided. John Quincy Adams, in righteous indignation, denounced the iniquity of the system; and in 1849, Joshua Giddings stated, quite correctly, that the Speaker's right to appoint committees gave him more influence in the government than was exercised by anyone else except the President.[46] From time to time the fight against this particular power of the Speaker was renewed, until, in 1910–1911, the authority to appoint committees, except select committees, was taken from him. In spite of this great loss of power, the Speaker was by no means reduced to insignificance. Among the important powers he still enjoys we may mention his power to decide questions of order and to recognize (or not recognize) members.

Deciding questions of order. The Rules of the House require the Speaker to decide all questions of order, subject to an appeal by any member. Under this provision, the Speaker, generally following the precedents of the House, make many decisions on points of parliamentary law in the course of a session. Sometimes he gives his reasons for his decisions; at other times he does not. A Speaker who measures up to the requirements of his office has various methods of taking the sting from his decisions. Feelings may be smoothed by an urbane compliment, a flash of wit, or similar tactics. Thus, Speaker Longworth, in "replying" to a parliamentary question asked by a Democrat for the purpose of embarrassing him, said amid laughter: "I think your question is more Democratic than parliamentary." As noted above, a member may appeal from the Speaker's ruling, but it is seldom done. Those members who are of the Speaker's party have every reason to avoid vexing him, and those who belong to the opposition are in the minority and have little hope that a vote of the House would sustain an appeal against a decision of the Speaker.[47]

The power of recognition. Another considerable power of the Speaker is that of recognizing members seeking the floor. In practice, there is no appeal from the Speaker's decision as to who shall have the floor. This

---

[45] Rules I; X, b, 1; XXIII, sec. 1.
[46] Alexander, *op. cit.,* Ch. V.
[47] Riddick, *op. cit.,* pp. 72–73.

unwritten rule does not mean, however, that the Speaker may be absolutely arbitrary in the exercise of this power. He must follow the practices of the House. For instance, when the order of business brings a particular bill before the House, the Speaker must first recognize the member who represents the committee reporting the measure. Still, the Speaker has wide discretion. Frequently, since about 1890, the Speaker has asked a very irritating question of those who have not previously arranged with him for recognition: "For what purpose does the gentleman rise?" If the gentleman is seeking recognition in order to propose a motion on a matter that, in the Speaker's opinion, is not properly before the House, he is not given the floor. When, some fifty years ago, William Sulzer stated that he rose to introduce a resolution extending sympathy to the Boers, Speaker Henderson went so far as to say that "the Chair must recognize members upon matters which the Chair thinks should be considered." On a similar occasion, Speaker Reed showed more tact in dealing with a member from Tennessee. The Speaker looked sharply at the Republican floor leader, who, quickly interpreting the look, moved to adjourn. The motion being carried, the Tennesseean was left high and dry.[48]

The refusal to entertain dilatory motions. A minority group cannot, of course, enact laws; but on many occasions such groups, skilled in the intricacies of parliamentary practice, have prevented majorities from legislating. Under the leadership of Speaker Reed, the long-suffering House, in 1890, adopted the rule that "no dilatory motion shall be entertained by the Speaker."[49] This rule has been made applicable to motions to adjourn and to lay on the table, among others. The Speaker does not exercise his authority until it becomes apparent to the House that the motion is dilatory, and he very seldom invokes the rule then unless a member raises a point of order. Obviously, the Speaker will not entertain debate or appeal on his decision as to the dilatoriness of a motion, for that would defeat the whole purpose of the rule. Since one fifth of the members present have the constitutional right to demand the yeas and nays on any question, such a motion may not be overruled as dilatory although it may be clearly of that character.[50]

IMPORTANCE OF THE SPEAKER. Despite the strong political position of Speakers, they have found the two miles of Pennsylvania Avenue that connect the Capitol with the Executive Mansion all but impassable. Only one Speaker, James K. Polk, a "dark horse" at that, has ever been able to travel them. Clay was three times a candidate for President; Blaine just missed being elected; but no other Speaker has managed to get the

---

[48] Alexander, *op. cit.,* pp. 59–60.
[49] Rule XVI, sec. 10.
[50] *House Rules and Manual,* sec. 803.

nomination. The explanations commonly given for passing over Speakers in making presidential nominations are that their views on national affairs are too well known; that they have offended too many men whose support they must have in securing a nomination; and that partisan politics, which always clings to the Speaker's chair, and the odor of "pork," which often does, do not commend the Speaker to the American people. It must be said also that many of the Speakers have been mediocre men who were elevated to the office by the rule of seniority; and, finally, that the road to the White House is paved with administrative, not legislative, experience.

The clerk. In addition to the Speaker, the House chooses a clerk, a sergeant-at-arms, a doorkeeper, a postmaster, and a chaplain.[51] We noted above that the Speaker is chosen separately and is always a member of the House. The other officers are chosen in a group by resolution and are never members. Of these officers, the clerk is the most important. His duties are to preside at the commencement of the first session of each Congress, pending the election of a Speaker; to furnish each member, at the commencement of every regular session of Congress, a list of the reports that it is the duty of any officer or department to make to Congress; to print the *Journal* of the House, and to distribute the *Journal* and all documents printed by order of either House to members and delegates; to attest and affix the seal of the House to such warrants and documents as subpoenas; to certify to the passage of all bills and joint resolutions; to make or approve all contracts for material and labor for the House; to keep and pay the stationery accounts of members and delegates; to pay the salaries of officers and employees of the House; and to perform other administrative duties of a character similar to those here enumerated.[52] In the discharge of all these duties the clerk is assisted by about a dozen subordinates appointed by himself.

The sergeant-at-arms and other officers. The sergeant-at-arms maintains order under the direction of the Speaker or chairman; executes the commands of the House in serving subpoenas on witnesses, compelling the attendance of absent members, and so on; pays the salary and mileage of members and delegates as provided by law; and controls the Capitol police. Like the clerk, he appoints the necessary assistants. The doorkeeper enforces the rules of the House relating to the privileges of the hall; assists the sergeant-at-arms in enforcing decorum on the floor; clears the floor of unauthorized persons; introduces to the House the bearers of

[51] The employees of the House, working under the direction of the Speaker, clerk, and other officers, number several hundred. The party in control of the House sees to it that the good places at its disposal go to members of the party.

[52] Rule III. Some of the duties of the clerk and other officers of the House are imposed by law as distinguished from those required by the Rules.

messages; acts as custodian of such property of the House as furniture and books; directs the work of some half a hundred messengers and other employees; and supervises the janitor service. A postmaster superintends the post office kept in the Capitol and House office building for the convenience of members. A chaplain opens each day's sitting of the House with prayer.[53]

Certain employees, appointed by the officers or key members of the House, should be mentioned. The legislative counsel, composed of lawyers and clerks, assists officers and committees with the drafting of bills and similar technical matters. A parliamentarian, an expert on legislative procedure, sits at the Speaker's right and advises him on the varied and complicated rules of the House. The parliamentarian also assists in drafting rules of procedure, and advises committees and members on methods of procedure.

B. Party Leaders in the House

Floor leaders. The Speaker, already discussed, is commonly the most influential leader of the majority party in the House. Next in importance to the Speaker, perhaps rivaling him in influence, is the majority floor leader, chosen by the party caucus or conference. The minority in like manner chooses its floor leader. Neither floor leader is an officer of the House; but, barring exceptional cases, the leader of the party in power becomes Speaker when that office becomes vacant, and the minority leader is elevated to the speakership when his party obtains a majority. The floor leader may or may not be the ablest man of his party's delegation in the House; but he must be a man of firm will, sound judgment, and good temper. Above all, he must have a capacity for appreciating and using the serviceable qualities of his colleagues. A good floor leader has the gift of clear and forceful expression, the ability to spot weak points in the arguments of opponents, and the power to safeguard the interests of his party.

The majority floor leader aids the Speaker in disentangling parliamentary snarls, in pushing the business before the House, and in checkmating any interference with the majority party's legislative program.[54] The majority leader has a great deal of influence from his position as chairman of the powerful steering committee, which selects for consideration a small percentage of the thousands of bills introduced at every session. Under normal conditions a floor leader properly qualified for the position will have considerable success in holding his party group together; but under unusual circumstances, he may fail. Thus, Underwood, the Democratic floor leader in the first years of the Wilson administration, on several occasions found

[53] Rules IV–VII.
[54] Alexander, *op. cit.*, p. 109; Riddick, *op. cit.*, pp. 94 ff.

his colleagues following the determined lead of the President rather than his own. In the case of the repeal of the clause exempting American coastwise trading vessels from the payment of tolls in the Panama Canal, the President won, not only in the face of the opposition of the floor leader, but in contravention to the provisions of the Democratic platform. On February 15, 1931, we witnessed the interesting spectacle of the House, led by Republican Speaker Longworth, voting by an overwhelming majority for increased loans to veterans on their bonus certificates despite the protests of President Hoover and the efforts of the Republican floor leader, Tilson, to prevent the passage of the measure. Off the floor of the House, the opposing floor leaders are frequently in conference on the legislative program. The minority must know the plans of the majority and the majority needs the co-operation of the minority.

Other leaders. Hardly less influential in the House than the floor leaders are the chairmen of the major committees. By long service in the House and on committees devoted to certain phases of its work they have acquired something approaching mastery of the intricacies of legislative procedure as well as of the functions of the committees of which they are chairmen. A very important committee is that on Ways and Means, and its chairmanship ordinarily goes to one of the ablest men of the majority party. The chairman of the Appropriations Committee should be ranked in importance with the chairman of the Ways and Means. The heads of six or eight other committees have considerable voice in the House. Occasionally, members who are too young in the service to be chairmen of committees but who nevertheless have marked ability may take some leading part in the proceedings. The minority party has no significant part in leading the House; but its outstanding members, in addition to the floor leader, often assist the majority leadership in matters not involving party policies. The minority has the right, indeed the duty, to scrutinize the proposals of the majority and to indicate favoritism, flaws, and inadequacies therein.

The whips. Each party has a member who carries a "whip" and who is so designated. The whip is appointed by his floor leader, and the whip in turn names a number of assistant whips. They serve the party organization, giving particular attention to orders and suggestions from the floor leader. The whips are supposed to know where all the party members are at any time; and, in the course of an hour, by a division of labor among them, they are usually able to present to party members the plans and purposes of the leaders, get an opinion of the party members on a legislative proposal, give them information, or bring them to the House for a vote.

C. The House Committees

Quite obviously the House as a whole cannot find time to consider the thousands of bills that are introduced in the course of a session. This work is done for the most part by committees, and the House simply acts upon the committee reports. In other words, the House places its official stamp upon what is unofficially agreed upon in the committees or uses the committee recommendations as bases for its action.

Types of committees. When we speak of the committees of either House of Congress, we ordinarily have in mind the regular standing committees that are reconstituted at the beginning of each Congress. First we shall refer briefly to the special committees.

1. SELECT COMMITTEES. From time to time the House directs the Speaker to appoint select committees—committees created temporarily for the purpose of considering some question that cannot be appropriately or expeditiously handled by a standing committee. The committees of investigation with which the country has grown familiar are of this type. Some of these committees are joint committees of the House and the Senate.

Conference committees. A conference committee (a special type of select committee) is appointed by the Speaker to confer with a similar committee from the Senate whenever the two Houses fail to agree upon a measure. The purpose of the conference is to effect a compromise agreeable to both branches of the Congress. Like the simon-pure select committee, the conference committee is discharged when it makes its report.

2. THE JOINT STANDING COMMITTEES. The joint standing committees are to be distinguished from the conference committees. The first-named are regular committees, formerly created by concurrent resolution of the two Houses and chosen in the same manner as were other standing committees. Today these joint standing committees are provided for by the Legislative Reorganization Act of 1946, which act specifies that the personnel of such committees shall be chosen from certain standing committees of each House. Joint committees deal with matters, chiefly of a routine character, in which both Houses are interested. The Joint Committee on the Library and the Joint Committee on the Economic Report are examples of such committees.

3. THE STANDING COMMITTEES. As noted above, the standing committees are the committees entitled to the most attention. Not so long ago there were more than sixty of these committees; in more recent years the number was reduced to some forty-five, which, despite the fact that only about a fourth of them played a significant part in the legislative process, seemed to be the irreducible number. The large number of relatively unimportant committees was continued because it was difficult to abolish a

standing committee once it was created, a fact that in turn was largely explained by the fact that the more committees there were, the more coveted chairmanships there were to distribute. The country was therefore pleasantly surprised to learn that the Reorganization Act of 1946 reduced the number of standing committees to nineteen. The more important of these are the committees on Ways and Means, Appropriations, Agriculture, Armed Services, Banking and Currency, Education and Labor, Post Office and Civil Service, Interstate and Foreign Commerce, Rules, and Veterans' Affairs. The number of members who serve on a committee is commonly twenty-five or twenty-seven, but the number is fixed at forty-three for the Committee on Appropriations, thirty-three for the Committee on Armed Services, and twelve for the Committee on Rules. With certain exceptions a member of the House is limited to service on one standing committee.[55]

We have already stated that prior to 1911 the members of standing committees were appointed by the Speaker. In that year the rule for their election by the House was adopted. As a matter of fact, each party designates its members who are to serve on committees. The Democratic caucus chooses the party's representation on the Ways and Means Committee and gives this group the authority, subject to the approval of the caucus, to select the Democratic members of all the other committees. The Republican caucus chooses a committee on committees, which in turn designates for ratification by the Republican membership the party's representatives on the committees of the House. With the committees thus chosen, the House then goes through the rather empty form of electing them.

Almost invariably, the senior member of the majority party's representation on any committee will be its chairman. When new men are elected to the House, they are assigned to the lowest places on committees; and upon their re-election they are usually reassigned to the same committees but to higher places, making room at the bottom for the latest group of new members. This process goes on in Congress after Congress, and a member's rank is gradually raised until he becomes the senior among his party colleagues on a committee, when he usually receives the chairmanship, if his party is in power. This is the well-known seniority rule. It is obvious that the rule does not necessarily mean that ability, or industry, or any other highly desirable quality, except that of experience in the House, will be found in a committee chairman. The rule does, however, have the merit of being easy to administer, and it is true that the seniors are usually among the best-qualified men for chairmanships. To abolish the rule would probably precipitate unseemly scrambles and intrigues for

[55] Rule X.

chairmanships, which would be much worse than the occasional unfortunate situations to which the present system gives rise. Few chairmen serve for a long period of time, for a change of parties in control of the House automatically puts them out of their high place. Moreover, a constituency may fail to re-elect a representative even though he is chairman of an important committee.

The Committee on Rules. The work of each committee commonly relates to a particular subject or type of subject, but the Rules Committee covers the whole matter of procedure in the House and has such far-reaching powers that we must give it special attention. Originally a small and comparatively unimportant select committee, the function of which was to report on rules at the beginning of each Congress, it became a standing committee in 1880; and later, with the Speaker as its chairman, it dominated the House. In 1910 the Speaker lost his place on it, but the Committee did not lose its power to control the House. At present there are twelve men on this Committee, four or five of them belonging to the minority party, and practically all of the dozen being seasoned veterans in legislative procedure.

THE RULES. Every legislative body that has been in existence for any length of time develops a somewhat elaborate set of rules of procedure. The lawmakers, of all men, should follow an orderly process. The House of Representatives started with a few rules (based largely upon English and colonial rules), framed by James Madison and several other distinguished parliamentarians. A few years later, Vice President Jefferson prepared his *Manual* for the Senate, and this *Manual* came to be used also in the House in all cases in which it was not inconsistent with the House rules.[56] Rules have been added more or less haphazardly from time to time, and more important still, almost innumerable precedents have been established by rulings of the Speaker, until the whole body of rules and precedents partakes of the prolixity of a legal code.[57] Few, if any, members understand them fully, and a number of members always denounce them as arbitrary and seek to have them changed.

Changing the rules. Now the most favorable time to propose a change in the rules is when a new House is being organized, for any proposals made after the organization is completed are referred automatically to the Committee on Rules, and the skillful, hard-hearted, and conservative parliamentarians who dominate this Committee are most unlikely to report any new rule that will impair their power to control the business of the House. On

---

[56] Rule XLIII.

[57] See A. C. Hinds, *Precedents of the House of Representatives*, Vols. I–IV (1907), and Clarence Cannon, same title, Vols. IV–VIII. These "precedents" are found in more than 11,000 rulings.

January 3, 1949, a majority of the House, using the advantage that the process of organizing gave them, put through a reform rule which provided that the Rules Committee may not hold for more than 21 days a bill that had been approved by one of the other committees; and that the chairman of such other committee may move for its consideration in the House despite the failure of the Rules Committee to make a report. We shall note the fate of this rule on the next page.

THE SPECIAL ORDERS OF THE RULES COMMITTEE. The Rules Committee plays a decisive part in directing the business of the House. Through its special orders it serves as an indispensable ally of the majority floor leader and his right-hand assistants, the members of the steering committee (presently to be discussed). A special order of the Committee on Rules, if approved by a majority of the House, may give precedence to particular measures; limit the time for debate on them; and specify the number and nature of amendments. Thus, if those who are supposed to control the House are temporarily out-generaled in a matter of procedure, they can rely upon the Rules Committee to come to their rescue with a special rule of some sort that will be adequate to the exigency. When a special order of the Rules Committee has been adopted, all moves for delaying the passage of a bill are blocked; and however tragic the gestures and noisy the lamentations may be against the bill in the brief period allowed for debate upon it, such stage play does not prevent the measure from having a speedy passage.

When the Independent Offices bill was under consideration in January, 1934, a rule was submitted that prohibited any amendment from the floor that would affect the economy sections of this appropriation bill or any other appropriation bill to come before that session of Congress. Republican minority leader Bertrand Snell turned white. "Just say to us that the Appropriations Committee and the President are going to do everything," he angrily cried in typical minority leader fashion. "Abolish your regular committees," he shouted. Turning to the Democrats, he exhorted: "Vote down this gag rule!" A number of disgruntled Democrats took his advice, but the rule was adopted by a narrow margin—197 to 192. The President called the steering committee to the White House. They returned to the House of Representatives and did what was expected of them; they corralled forty-one maverick Democrats and smashed an opposition move to defeat the Independent Offices bill by a vote of 240 to 141.[58]

POWER THROUGH NONACTION. The Committee on Rules makes its power felt by nonaction as well as by its special orders. The former type of power is interestingly explained by an item in one of our more critical

[58] *Time,* Jan. 22, 1934.

weeklies.[59]   The Truman 65-cent-an-hour minimum wage bill was bottled up in the Committee on Rules, where everybody talks at once, and procedure is loose and disorderly.   "Here proud and puffy chairmen of other committees, autocrats of their own little satrapies, humbly plead for a 'rule' (or legislative green light) to bring favorite measures to the floor. The Rules Committee is the traffic cop of House legislation.   It is stuffed with conservatives.   It quite frankly weighs bills in the balance of its own prejudices before letting the House debate them on their merits.   Last week, the Southerners on the committee simply said they didn't think farm 'help' should get 65 cents an hour.   So that was that"—no rule would be reported and the prospects for minimum wage legislation faded out. Representative Roger C. Slaughter was a member of the Rules Committee, and it was partly for his obstructionist tactics as a committeeman that President Truman actively and successfully opposed his renomination (1946) by the Democrats in the Fifth Missouri District.

The tactics of the Rules Committee as just described led to the adoption of the "you may stall only 21 days" rule on January 3, 1949.   The vote on that rule was rather decisive—275 to 142.   But what happened after that? The new rule had not been in operation but a year when the Rules Committee, by a vote of 9 to 2, proposed that its old power to hold up legislation indefinitely be restored.   The House rejected the proposal by a vote of 236 to 183.   It will be observed that the enthusiasm for the new rule had cooled somewhat.   Yet the House leadership in the Eighty-first Congress was eight times successful in bringing to the floor bills that had been blocked for 21 days by the Rules Committee.   In each case the bill thus brought out for consideration was subsequently passed by the House.   Conservatives heartily disliked such procedure, and on the first day of the Eighty-second Congress, the Southern Democrats and Republicans combining forces, as they often do, repealed the "21 day" rule.

The steering committees.   Each party in the House has a committee, under the slightly misleading title "steering committee," that has to do primarily with party policy.   The Democratic committee is composed of five or six House leaders and fifteen members representing geographical zones of the country.   The Republican committee is similarly constituted, although all the Republican members of the Rules Committee are included on the steering committee.[60]   Each steering committee considers policies and programs of vital interest to the party, and individual committeemen consult with rank-and-file party members, passing on information and suggestions and learning the sentiment of the members.   The steering committee of the majority party, particularly when the Republicans hold the

---

[59] T.R.B. in the *New Republic,* July 8, 1946.
[60] Riddick, *op. cit.,* pp. 109–111.

majority, has considerable influence in shaping the program of the House, advising as to what measures should be taken up and when. The details of the daily schedule are, however, left to the floor leaders. Perhaps the main function of the committee is to steer for the party once a measure or program is agreed upon.

Subcommittees. Even before the passage of the Reorganization Act of 1946 the House made some use of subcommittees; but, with the great reduction in the number of standing committees affected by that act, the subcommittees were multiplied. This outcome was natural, considering that most of the surviving committees have within their jurisdiction a variety of subjects that were formerly parceled out among several committees. Yet it may be that the subcommittees are growing too luxuriantly (there are more than a hundred of them), and the advantage of the reduction in the number of standing committees might turn out to be illusory. Before 1946 the committee prepared a measure and reported it to the House; now we often have an additional stage in the procedure-preparation by subcommittee, approval by full committee, report to the House. The House could conceivably come to a point where it would find that it had exchanged some forty-five committees for a hundred or more subcommittees, each with a position not greatly dissimilar to that of the pre-1946 standing committee.

Committee staffs. One of the most commonly mentioned defects of the "unreorganized" Congress was the lack of adequate committee staffs. The Reorganization Act, Sec. 202, gives each standing committee, except the Appropriations Committees, four professional staff members, who are to be appointed "solely on the basis of fitness to perform the duties of the office," and who may be paid a salary up to $8,000. The Appropriations Committees are authorized to appoint such staff as the majority in such committees may determine to be necessary. Each standing committee is also given a clerical staff of not more than six members. The law contains a provision that no person may be appointed to a committee staff who is detailed or assigned from any executive department or agency, except with the written permission of the Committee on Rules. This proviso was to guard against undue administrative and "bureaucratic" influence. How closely have the committees followed the provision of the law stipulating that the professional staff members shall be appointed "solely on the basis of fitness"? Some appointees meet the standard; some are personal friends of congressmen, a fact that does not preclude their meeting the fitness test; others too closely resemble what thoughtless critics think all government employees are.

D. The House Caucus (or Conference)

Mention has been made from time to time of the caucus or conference, an institution unknown to the Constitution. Perhaps the student has decided that it is the power which really directs the House of Representatives. It does, to some extent, although to a lesser degree now than formerly. Each party has its caucus, but the caucus of the majority party has a large voice in determining the organization of the House of Representatives. All the members of the House who are "reasonably regular" party men belong to their party's caucus.[61]

The work of the caucus. The caucus meets when it is called by the chairman upon his own motion, or when he is requested to call it by a group of its members or the party leader. Its principal meeting precedes the organization of a new House of Representatives. Among its chief functions we may note the following: it nominates the party's candidates for the House offices, which is tantamount to election in the case of the majority caucus; it selects the party floor leader; it provides for a steering committee; it approves assignments to the standing committees; it helps to share party policy on pending legislation; and in general tries to promote party regularity. These things are done behind the scenes. The proceedings are according to party rules; they are not covered by the Rules of the House, much less by the Constitution and laws of the United States. The caucus is a part of our extra-constitutional government. Formerly it was an essential feature of the party system, but since 1933 administrative influence has reduced the authority of the Democratic caucus.

The power of the caucus. Members of the party delegation in the House are expected to vote on party questions before that body in conformity with the decisions of the party caucus. Thus, by the rules of the Democratic caucus, members are obligated to support for offices in the House the candidates who have received a majority vote in the caucus; and

in deciding upon action in the House involving party policy or principle, a two-thirds vote of those present and voting at a caucus meeting shall bind all members of the caucus: *Provided,* The said two-thirds vote is a majority of the full Democratic membership of the House: *And provided further,* That no member shall be bound upon questions involving a construction of the Constitution of the United States or upon which he made contrary pledges to his constituents prior to his election or received contrary instructions by resolution or platform from his nominating authority.[62]

[61] C. A. Berdahl, "Some Notes on Party Membership in Congress," *Am. Pol. Sci. Rev.,* Apr., June, Aug., 1949, pp. 309, 492, 721.

[62] Mathews and Berdahl, *op. cit.,* pp. 433–434.

The caucuses do not attempt to bind members on nonessential matters; and "entire individual independence" is allowed, to quote again from Democratic rules, "in all things not involving fidelity to party principles." This provision gives the members a wide area of freedom, since perhaps 90 per cent of the measures in Congress are nonpartisan in character. The Republican caucus makes less attempt to bind its members than does the Democratic caucus; and, to indicate its liberality, the GOP in recent years has commonly used the term "conference" to designate the private meetings of its adherents in the House. But, whether the gatherings are styled conferences or caucuses, no party allows such freedom to its members that they may vote with impunity contrary to the group decisions on the choice of officers and on other matters relating to House organization.

Conclusions as to leadership in the House. At the turn of the century, in the days of Reed and Cannon, the caucus selected the Speaker and left him practically free to direct the legislative body, the caucus retaining what we might call "ultimate sovereignty." The so-called "revolution" of 1910–1911 deprived the Speaker of some of his powers, particularly of his far-reaching power to appoint committees, and gave the caucus the authority to make the committee assignments and a sort of continuing directing power over the work of the House. But the Democratic caucus, the majority group after 1911, delegated a number of its powers to the Democrats who sat on the Ways and Means Committee. In 1913 Wilson assumed and maintained the leadership of Congress, and the chief duty of party leaders in the House was to see that his legislative program was carried out. With the return of the Republicans to power in the House in 1919, the caucus of that party assumed control; but it worked largely through the Speaker, the floor leader, and the steering committee.

This system was not essentially changed when the Democrats gained a majority in 1931. But with the election of Franklin D. Roosevelt, presidential leadership of Congress was even more effectively installed than it had been in the days of Wilson. During Roosevelt's third term Vice President Wallace, Speaker Rayburn, the majority floor leaders of the two Houses, and occasionally a chairman of a principal committee held regular weekly conferences at the White House. This "legislative cabinet" assembled to hear the wishes of the President, to inform him of congressional sentiment, and, presumably, to plan with him the legislative program for the week. The "Big Four" of Capitol Hill function in the same manner with President Truman. Yet it may be said, that the majority caucus, through leaders of its own choosing, is still in ultimate control of the operations of the House. At times these leaders are allowed practically a free hand; at other times the caucus prefers to retain a share of the control of the party's legislative program and tactics. Whether the caucus controls the House directly or a few party leaders (the President and others) control both the caucus and the House, depends upon the political capacity of the leaders and upon the spirit of the caucus.

Finally, we may observe that under whatever form of effective leadership the representatives may happen to be functioning, the minority party and the insurgents in the dominant party will complain of "gag rule," the "steam roller," "dictatorship," and the like. But the occasions when the House has attempted to democratize its methods or when competent leaders have not been among its members have demonstrated the necessity for the very directing power that the minorities periodically, and sometimes hypocritically, denounce.

VI. ORGANIZATION OF CONGRESS: THE SENATE

We have already noted that the Senate is a permanent body, with the term of only one third of its members expiring every two years, whereas the entire 435 members of the House must be elected biennially. Being a permanent body and having a membership of less than one fourth that of the House, the Senators are not troubled with rules and organization to the extent the legislators in the other end of the Capitol are. The Senate does, however, have its rules and its precedents; and it makes rather liberal use of the *Manual of Parliamentary Practice* that Jefferson prepared when he presided over the Senate. In organization the Senate does not differ fundamentally from the House, although we shall note a few exceptions.

Officers and leaders of the Senate. In our discussion of the office of Vice President we noted that as President of the Senate he has no powers save those of a moderator; that he has no vote except in case of a tie; that he is not even a member of the Senate. As everyone knows, he is not of the Senate's choosing, and he is in no sense the power in the Senate that the Speaker is in the House. If the Vice President should show signs of not "knowing his place," senators would not be slow to show it to him. The Senate elects a president *pro tempore,* who presides when the Vice President is absent or when there is no Vice President. Other officers of the Senate correspond to those of the House and they are chosen in the same way, that is, in the Senate caucus of the majority party, and then formally elected by the whole body of senators. Although not an officer of the Senate, the majority floor leader, chosen by his caucus, is usually the principal figure in its deliberations. The minority caucus also chooses a floor leader, as in the House.

On January 5, 1950, a news release gave some information on the activities of the caucus and conferences relative to policy determination. At a closed conference Democratic leaders were said to have persuaded other

Senate Democrats to refrain from loading irrelevant amendments (riders) to the oleomargarine tax repeal measure or to other bills. The Senate Republicans held a conference the same day and agreed to draft a statement of policy, which they admitted would mean nothing, senators up for re-election declaring they would not be bound by it. It seems that the principal reason for any such declaration was to please financial supporters of the party.

Senate committees. Just as in the House, the caucus or conference of each party chooses a committee on committees, which supercommittee then makes the assignments to the various standing committees, subject to the approval of the caucus. The Senate then formally elects the committees. Before 1921 there were seventy-four committees, well over half of them practically useless; but in that year some two score of these were eliminated. The Legislative Reorganization Act of 1946 further reduced the number— to fifteen. The principal committees are those on Agriculture and Forestry, Appropriations, Armed Services, Banking and Currency, Civil Service, Finance, Foreign Relations, Interstate and Foreign Commerce, the Judiciary, and Rules and Administration.

The committees of the Senate have fundamentally the same functions as the similarly named committees of the House. Perhaps we should explain that the Finance Committee corresponds to the powerful House Committee on Ways and Means, and that the Senate Committee on Foreign Relations (to which must be referred all matters relating to treaties, the diplomatic service, the United Nations, and foreign relations generally) is more highly rated than the House Committee on Foreign Affairs. Thirteen senators constitute each committee, with the exception of the Committee on Appropriations, which has twenty-one members. Formerly it was not uncommon to find a senator serving on four or five committees. The Reorganization Act limits the number on which he may serve, with certain exceptions, to two. The seniority rule [63] prevails in respect to chairmanships as in the House, but in neither House does a member hold more than one chairmanship.

THE COMMITTEE ON RULES AND ADMINISTRATION AND THE STEERING AND POLICY COMMITTEES. Although the Senate has a Committee on Rules and Administration, this Committee has no such powers as are wielded by the House Rules Committee. The steering committee, like that committee in the House, consists of the principal leaders of the party. By an act of the Seventy-ninth Congress, Policy Committees of the Senate were created for both political parties. The functions of these committees is essentially

---

[63] An acute observer and Senator, Paul H. Douglas, is by no means critical of the seniority rule in the Senate, maintaining that it gives a steady flow of leaders who know the past record of legislation. *New York Times Magazine*, March 20, 1949, p. 73.

the same as that of the steering committees—"The formulation of over-all legislative policy of the respective parties." Nevertheless, the unofficial steering committees have been continued. In the Eightieth Congress the Democrats found some excuse for the two by using the steering committee exclusively for making committee appointments.

Reading List

D. S. Alexander, *History and Procedure of the House of Representatives* (1916).

American Political Science Review. Nearly every number contains an article or note on Congress.

S. K. Bailey, *Congress Makes a Law: The Story behind the Employment Act. of 1946* (1949).

C. A. Berdahl, "Some Notes on Party Membership in Congress," *Am. Pol. Sci. Rev.,* Apr., June, Aug., 1949, pp. 309, 492, 721.

J. Bryce, *The American Commonwealth* (1913 ed.), I, Chs. X–XXI.

F. L. Burdette, *Lobbyists in Action* (1950).

J. M. Burns, *Congress on Trial* (1949).

J. P. Chamberlain, *Legislative Processes, National and State* (1936).

L. H. Chamberlain, *The President, Congress, and Legislation* (1946).

Stuart Chase, *Democracy Under Pressure* (1945).

Congressional Quarterly Almanac.

M. E. Dimock, "Congressional Investigating Committees," *Johns Hopkins U. Studies in Hist. and Pol. Sci.* (1929), XLVII, 1–182.

E. J. Eberling, *Congressional Investigations* (1928).

G. B. Galloway, *Congress at the Crossroads* (1946).

J. P. Harris, "The Reorganization of Congress," *Public Adm. Rev.,* VI, 267, (Summer, 1946).

P. D. Hasbrouck, *Party Government in the House of Representatives* (1927).

G. H. Haynes, *The Senate of the United States,* 2 vols. (1938).

Robert Heller, *Strengthen the Congress.* National Planning Association (1945).

E. P. Herring, *Group Representation before Congress* (1932).

Estes Kefauver and Jack Levin, *A Twentieth-Century Congress* (1947).

F. R. Kent, *The Great Game of Politics* (1924), Chs. XLI–XLV.

Legislative Reorganization Act of 1946. Senate Report No. 1400 (to accompany S. 2177), 79th Cong. 2nd Sess. (1946).

E. B. Logan, *Lobbying* (Annals of the American Academy of Political and Social Science, Vol. CXLIV).

R. Luce, *Congress—An Explanation* (1926).

———, *Legislative Assemblies* (1924).

———, *Legislative Procedure* (1922).

J. M. Mathews and C. A. Berdahl, *Documents and Readings in American Government* (1940 ed.), Chs. XII–XIII.

Wesley McCune, *The Farm Bloc* (1943).

H. M. MacDonald and Others, *Outside Readings in American Government* (1949), Ch. IX.

Olga Moore, *I'll Meet You in the Lobby* (1950).

Fritz Nova, *Functional Representation* (1950).

A. R. Ogden, *The Dies Committee* (1945).

Organization of the Congress: Report of the Joint Committee on the Organization of Congress. Senate Report No. 1011, 79th Cong., 2nd Sess. (1946).

Political Science Quarterly. Articles on Congress from time to time.

F. M. Riddick, *Congressional Procedure* (1941).

————, *The United States Congress Organization and Procedure* (1949).

———— and G. H. Smith, *Congress in Action* (1948).

L. Rogers, *The American Senate* (1926).

Rules of the House of Representatives.

E. E. Schattschneider, *Politics, Pressure and the Tariff* (1936).

Senate Manual.

Elbert D. Thomas, "How Congress Functions Under Its Reorganization Act," *Am. Pol. Sci. Rev.,* Dec., 1949, pp. 1179–1189.

"Toward a More Responsible Two-Party System," A Report of the Committee on Political Parties, American Political Science Association, *Am. Pol. Sci. Rev.* (supplement) XLIV (1950), No. 3, Pt. 2.

Jerry Voorhis, *Confessions of a Congressman* (1947).

H. Walker, *The Legislative Process* (1948).

W. Wilson, *Constitutional Government in the United States* (1908), Chs. IV–V.

Roland Young, *This Is Congress* (1943).

Questions and Problems

1. What are the historical and practical reasons for a bicameral Congress?
2. What improvements do you suggest in the method of apportioning representatives?
3. Discuss the constitutional and political points that would arise if the House of Representatives should undertake to deny a seat to any "unpatriotic" member-elect.
4. Compare the advantages and disadvantages of the old and new methods of choosing senators.
5. Discuss the personnel of Congress, indicating what changes would produce a better balance of interests.
6. Wherein and for what purpose does freedom of speech for a legislator differ from that for the ordinary citizen?
7. Compare and contrast the American Speaker with the Speaker of the British House of Commons.
8. To what degree is there party leadership in Congress? Can you suggest improvements?
9. Explain the committee system as it existed before January, 1947; since that date.
10. Indicate the differences between organization in the Senate and the House of Representatives.

☆ 15 ☆

Congress: Procedure and Powers

CONGRESSIONAL procedure is determined to some extent by the Constitution but principally by the Rules of the two Houses and the subtle play of many forces upon congressmen. A knowledge of how laws are made may increase our respect for them and their makers; and if it does not, we are at least able to express our dissatisfaction in an intelligent manner. At any rate, the student of government must know something of how laws are made, and we take the greater part of this chapter to introduce the subject; in the last two sections we round out the discussion with a summary of the powers of Congress and a consideration of the steps for its improvement.

I. HOUSE PROCEDURE [1]

The introduction of bills. Bills may be introduced by any member of either House of Congress. Although the Constitution requires that all revenue bills shall originate in the House, the power of the Senate to amend such bills beyond all recognition operates to deprive the House of a large part of this advantage. The bills may be divided into two general classes, public and private. A public bill is one that alters or adds to the general law, or that deals with government finance; whereas a private bill is one of a purely local or personal nature, authorizing the construction of a bridge across a navigable stream, the awarding of a pension to a named individual, or damages to a person injured by some action of the Government.

The Legislative Reorganization Act of 1946 greatly restricts the introduction of private bills, but claims for which the cause of action dates prior

[1] D. S. Alexander, *History and Procedure of the House of Representatives* (1916), Ch. XIV; Galloway, *Congress at the Crossroads* (1946), Ch. 6; R. Luce, *Congress—An Explanation* (1926), Ch. I; F. M. Riddick, *The U.S. Congress Organization and Procedure* (1949), Chs. VIII–XI; and his annual article in the *Am. Pol. Sci. Rev.* on recent sessions of Congress; Walker, *The Legislative Process* (1948), Chs. 12–14.

to January 1, 1945, may still be handled by private bills. The more comprehensive public bills are commonly prepared and introduced by appropriate committees. Frequently, however, these legislative proposals come from the President or some branch of the executive department. As far back as 1926, Robert Luce, long a member of the House and an authority on its procedure, estimated that at least half of the bills came from administrative sources, and in 1940, on the floor of the House, he declared: ". . . Now almost no important bill is passed upon save upon administrative initiative or with previous approval of the Chief Executive." [2] These proposals—administration measures—are formally introduced in the House by spokesmen for the Administration, usually by chairmen of committees who may have received the bills direct from the White House or one of the subordinate administrative agencies. Other bills are introduced by rank-and-file congressmen, but, in many cases, not on their own initiative. An individual, a business concern, a labor organization, a farm association, a reform society, or what not, may originate a bill and find some obliging congressman to introduce it. A member need assume no responsibility by introducing such a bill. He may make a friend or friends by so doing. At any rate, by showing an accommodating spirit, he can avoid giving offense. This situation explains why Congress is flooded with bills at every session.

Bills in committee. All bills are referred to committees. Private bills (note restriction mentioned in preceding paragraph) are referred by the persons introducing them to the committees designated by the rules to receive them. Public bills are referred under the direction of the Speaker, as are messages from the President. Often a bill relates to subjects within the province of two or more committees, in which case it is referred to the committee having most apparent jurisdiction. Sometimes, however, the proposed legislation is so complicated and pertains to the subject matter of two or more committees in such degree that a special committee is appointed with jurisdiction over the whole problem. Separate sections of important bills, such as appropriations measures, are usually referred by the committee in charge to its subcommittees for special study and report.

COMMITTEE INTERMENT; THE DISCHARGE RULE. A committee (more particularly its chairman) does not take long to decide that the vast majority of the bills referred to it are not worthy of consideration. Such measures die quietly "in committee," and there are few indeed who mourn their passing, for nearly all of them deserve their fate. To this last sentence one might well react aggressively with the retort that committees might kill some excellent and needed measures by the same plan of non-action. In

---

[2] *Op. cit.,* pp. 3–4, and Riddick, "Third Session of the Seventy-sixth Congress," *Am. Pol. Sci. Rev.,* XXXV, 284, note (April, 1941). See also E. E. Witte, "Administrative Agencies and Statute Lawmaking," *Public Administration Review,* II, 116 (Spring, 1942).

order to prevent the committees from thus abusing their power, the House has a "discharge" rule, that is, a rule under which a bill may be taken from the jurisdiction of a committee and brought to the House.

Prior to 1931, in the years of Republican domination, the signatures of a majority of the membership were required to bring to the floor of the House a bill that a committee would not report. In 1931 this rule was changed from a majority (218) to 145. Even with the discharge rule thus liberalized, the required number of signatures was obtained in only four instances during the "long session" of the Seventy-second Congress.[3] Yet in 1935 the Democratic leaders found it necessary to make a "backward move to Cannonism" by restoring the majority discharge rule. Republicans twitted them by observing that the old rule was being restored in order to enable the Democratic leaders to control their own followers, since there were not enough Republicans to supply the 145 signatures required under the "liberal" discharge rule. The difficulty of invoking the discharge rule thus restored was illustrated by the second session of the Eightieth Congress when only once in ten tries was it found possible to get the necessary 218 signatures to discharge a committee and bring a bill to the House.[4]

COMMITTEE AIDS. In considering the bills before them committees and subcommittees (the latter being extensively used since the Reorganization Act of 1946) draw from the experience and knowledge of their members of the matter under consideration. There are almost invariably members of a committee whose term of service and application to duty have given them something approximating mastery of certain phases of the committee's work. But even the best informed will need aid from whatever source it can be derived. The Legislative Reference Service of the Library of Congress has been available for some years, but it was only in 1946, by the terms of the Reorganization Act, that sufficient funds and personnel were provided to make the Service an effective aid for committees of Congress and individual congressmen. This department of the Library of Congress advises and assists any committee of either House "in the analysis, appraisal, and evaluation of legislative proposals pending before it," compiles information of general value for legislative purposes, and in similar ways lends a helping hand.[5] Then, of course, the committees have the services of their own staffs (noted in the previous chapter), reports of other committees, documents supplied by the executive departments, and material supplied by pressure groups.

Another valuable aid in determining legislative policy is the commit-

[3] E. P. Herring, "First Session of the Seventy-second Congress," *Am. Pol. Sci. Rev.,* XXVI (1932), p. 850.

[4] Riddick, *Am. Pol. Sci. Rev.,* XLIII (1949), p. 488.

[5] W. B. Graves, "Legislative Reference Service . . . ," *Am. Pol. Sci. Rev.,* XLI (1947), pp. 289–293.

tee "hearing." Persons for or against a proposed measure may appear, voluntarily or by order of the committee, and give testimony. Some of these hearings run for several days or even weeks, with as much of the public in the committee room as can be accommodated and with the press of the country giving as much attention to the hearing as it is giving to the work on the floor of the House. Not infrequently administrative officials play the leading part at the hearings. Their participation frequently occurs when administrative bills are before a committee.

THE COMMITTEE REPORT. We noted above that thousands of bills are allowed to die without even being considered by a committee. Occasionally a bill is dropped after consideration has shown it to be unwise or inexpedient; but in the case of most bills that it considers seriously, the committee takes some form of affirmative action. It may report the bill to the House, with the recommendation that it be passed as introduced; it may report it with sections stricken out, or with additional sections, or with changes in wording; or it may frame a new bill. A report in any one of these forms gives a bill a good running chance to pass the House, but by no means insures passage.

Importance of the report. Considering the power of a committee to kill most bills by not reporting them and the tendency of the House to pass bills favorably reported by a committee, we can easily understand why committees are often called "little legislatures," as indeed they are. Although a bill is officially passed by some three or four hundred representatives, its fate is largely determined by a majority, sometimes by a bare majority, of a committee. Often the committee, in making its report, follows the decision of a subcommittee, and that body its ablest or most skillful member. Thus, the representative votes on faith, except on those few matters about which he may have more information than the rank and file of his colleagues. It should be so, for only by dividing the work among groups that contain a few specialists and then following these specialists, can the House approach intelligent action on several thousand bills in the course of a few months.

Bills on the calendars. Measures reported by committees are placed on the calendars of the House. Bills relating to revenue, appropriations, and public property are placed on the "Calendar of the Whole House on the State of the Union," commonly called the "Union Calendar." All other public bills are placed on the "House Calendar." Private bills are listed on the "Calendar of the Committee of the Whole House," more conveniently designated as the "Private Calendar." Measures are supposed to be taken up in the order in which they appear on the calendars, but there are so many bills that it is impossible to consider them all, and, in consequence, essential bills or those with a strong backing are selected with scant regard for the order of their appearance on the calendars.

The "order" of business. Rule XXIV prescribes the following as the daily order of business in the House: prayer; reading of the *Journal;* correction of reference of public bills; disposal of business on the Speaker's table, such as messages from the President; unfinished business; the "morning hour" (which may include the whole day) for the consideration of bills called up by committees; and motions to go into Committee of the Whole for the purpose of considering certain bills, particularly revenue and appropriation bills. The House is not, however, bound to this daily routine. Certain days are set aside for particular types of measures: Wednesdays for bills on the House and Union Calendars, two days a month for the Private Calendar, the second and fourth Mondays for the business of the District of Columbia. Furthermore, the regular order of business is frequently interrupted, with the consent of the majority, for such privileged matters as revenue and appropriation bills, conference reports, and special orders reported by the powerful Committee on Rules. Again, in the case of matters not privileged, any member may ask for "unanimous consent" for the consideration of a bill, and, if granted, this suspends the order of business temporarily. Finally, on certain days, a two-thirds majority of the House may suspend the rules and put a measure through almost in the twinkling of an eye.

The "regular order" is a convenient schedule to follow when possible, but in adopting it the House did not "lock itself in an iron cage and throw away the key." It wisely provided for quick and easy methods for setting the regular order aside, thus making it possible to bring matters of vital importance before it at any time.

Procedure in Committee of the Whole. Rule XXIII provides that all bills except public ones that do not raise revenue or appropriate money or property shall be first considered in Committee of the Whole.[6] This Committee is the House in personnel, but it is not officially the House. When in Committee of the Whole House on the State of the Union, the mace, the ancient symbol of authority, is removed from the pedestal at the Speaker's chair. The Speaker himself leaves the chair after appointing some other member to preside. Although a majority constitutes a quorum of the House, the Committee quorum is one hundred.

The chief purpose of the Committee is to expedite business. No time-consuming roll calls are permitted. By common practice general debate

[6] Technically, there are two Committees of the Whole: the Committee of the Whole House, for considering private bills; and the Committee of the Whole House on the State of the Union, for considering revenue and appropriation bills. Riddick, *U.S. Cong.,* 212 ff.

is had after the House "resolves" itself into the "Committee of the Whole House on the State of the Union" and before the third reading of the bill. Time for general debate is usually arranged by unanimous consent of the House upon suggestions from the Chairman and the ranking minority member of the committee reporting the bill, and the time may be fixed at one or two hours or many hours or even days. Sometimes no time limit can be fixed in the early stages of debate, in which event debate continues until members have talked themselves out, or until the House is able to reach an agreement upon time. The practice is for the time for general debate, whether limited or not, to be under the control of the ranking members of the committee reporting the bill, though variations are had and frequently some faction or group that is not in sympathy with the attitude of either the majority or the minority is granted a certain amount of time. Theoretically, this time for general debate is supposed to be on the bill under consideration. In practice, however, the debate is of wide character, sometimes on the bill and sometimes on matters that are wholly extraneous.

At the conclusion of general debate the Committee takes up the consideration of the bill under the "five minute rule," each speaker being allotted just that much time for debate. Such debate is naturally to the point and much more lively than the more formal utterances in the official sessions. With the discussion and amendment of a bill completed, the Committee "rises" and reports to the House, its official self. Affirmative action by the House gives effect to the work of the Committee.

House debates. Debate, other than that which occurs in the Committee of the Whole House on the State of the Union, ordinarily takes place on the floor of the House before the vote on the third reading [7] has been taken. Theoretically each member may speak for an hour, but a member who manages to get half an hour considers himself lucky. The Committee on Rules brings in a special order limiting the time that may be spent in debate on nearly all important measures except appropriation bills, and each side gets half the time specified. The chairman of the committee in charge of the bill divides the time among the majority members who wish to speak, and the ranking minority member of the committee apportions the time among his minority colleagues. Often so many members of the committee desire to discuss a measure that no time is left for others; and, in any case, the time allowed for a speech is likely to be limited to ten or fifteen minutes. Sometimes an understanding is reached that the five-minute rule shall apply, as in Committee of the Whole; or, that no debate shall occur and that only bills to which there is no objection be considered.

[7] The three readings are technical terms, each indicating a stage in the progress of a bill through the House.

It is a common saying that the House can do anything by "unanimous consent." Serious debate takes place on the more significant measures only, and there is practically no debate on other measures. To be specific, in 1947 the House enacted 1,029 measures but only 108 were debated for an appreciable length of time. The other 90 per cent were either not debated or debate on any one of them was insufficient to cover three pages of the *Congressional Record*.[8] In 1948 the House passed 1,191 bills and resolutions, and all but 98 of these passed without debate or with less debate than is required to occupy three pages of the *Record*.[9] This evidence indicates again that the great mass of legislation is non-partisan or at least non-controversial. But let us not be misled by these figures. A half dozen measures of fundamental character (and they are almost always controversial) could occupy the House forum for an entire session, and there are always more than a half dozen such measures.

CLOSURE. Despite the fact that relatively few measures are debated, the House does not have time to hear all the members who in good faith desire to speak; much less can it afford to give free rein to representatives who resort to obstruction tactics. Several means of securing quick action are employed. We have already learned that the rules may be suspended by a two-thirds vote; that a majority may adopt a special order of the Rules Committee limiting the time for debate; that the Speaker may refuse to put dilatory motions; and that a quorum may be compelled to attend, so that the House can transact business. All these practices save time, but the only motion used for closing debate is the handy timesaving device known as the "previous question," borrowed from the British House of Commons. A floor leader or the chairman of the committee responsible for the bill "demands the previous question," and the motion must be put at once by the Speaker. If this motion is carried, then a vote on the bill or resolution under consideration is immediately taken. If, however, there has been no debate on the subject before the House, forty minutes (usually divided evenly between the two sides) is allowed for the purpose.

How more time might be saved. Much more of the precious time of the House could be saved if the body would abandon the archaic practice of the oral reading of bills, leaving members to consult their printed copies. Years ago a Representative, Robert Luce, estimated that about a month of each term was taken up with "clerical enunciation." Still more time could be saved if the House would install a system of electric voting, now used by the legislatures in a third of the states. Several hundred times in the course of a Congress the question of the presence of a quorum is raised, and each "quorum call" consumes nearly half an hour. The for-

[8] Riddick, *Am. Pol. Sci. Rev.*, XLII (1948), p. 679.
[9] *Ibid.*, XLIII (1949), p. 489.

mality of reading the *Journal,* the toleration of irrelevant debate, and the quibbling over points of order should be added to the list of time consumers.   Remedies could be had for these delays, but inertia blocks the way.[10]

Voting in the House.   The House makes its decisions, of course, by votes.   Of the four methods employed, the chorus of ayes and noes (*viva voce*) is the most common.   Any member who feels that the Speaker's announcement of the result is incorrect may call for a rising vote.   A third method is used when a fifth of a quorum demands tellers, who count those voting for and then those voting against a measure as they pass between them in front of the Speaker's desk.   Finally, if one fifth of those present care to exercise their right under the Constitution,[11] they may require that the members vote by individual "yeas" and "nays" and that each vote be recorded in the *Journal*.   The Constitution [12] demands this method of voting when the question is: "Will the House on reconsideration agree to pass the bill, the objections [veto] of the President to the contrary notwithstanding?"   The Committee of the Whole employs the same methods of voting as the House, except for the individual yea and nay vote.

II. SENATE PROCEDURE [13]

Because, in the main, Senate procedure is similar to that of the House, we do not need to go into detail on that subject.   We shall be concerned here only with the matter of Senate debate, for that is the only essential difference between Senate and House procedure.   The first rules of the Senate adopted in 1789 provided for the "previous question," but it was used only a few times and was quietly dropped when the rules were revised in 1806.   For many years abuses of the privilege of unlimited debate were infrequent, the senators giving heed to a phrase in Jefferson's *Manual* that "no one is to speak impertinently, or beside the question, superfluously or tediously."   Obviously the freedom enjoyed by senators served as an incentive to put forth the best efforts.   No one prepared a speech with the fear that time would not be secured for its delivery, or that the time would be so limited that only an outline of the speech might be given.   Minorities were able to spend the full force of their fury upon the handiwork of the majority; independents could take the floor against the autocracy of their

---

[10] See Luce, *op. cit.,* pp. 27–29.   In the long session of 1949 the Senate scored 413 quorum calls and 226 calls for yeas and nays, each requiring from 10 to 15 minutes.   The House score was 115 quorum calls, consuming 20 or more minutes each, and 121 yea and nay votes, requiring about 40 minutes each.   Better arguments for electric roll-calls could not be found.   Jas. C. Derieux, *Collier's,* March 4, 1950.

[11] Art. I, sec. v, cl. 3.

[12] Art. I, sec. vii, cl. 2.

[13] G. H. Haynes, *The Senate of the United States* (1938), Vol. I, Chs. VII–VIII; Riddick, *U.S. Cong.,* Ch. X; L. Rogers, *The American Senate* (1926), pp. 161–190.

party; executive departments might quail under the pitiless searchlight of unhurried solons; and public opinion might be aroused by revelations in the Senate forum. Considering the opportunities there presented, it is not surprising that many of our greatest statesmen have sought places in the Senate and that other national leaders have been developed on its floor.

The filibuster. But the Senate grew larger and members were chosen who had no compunctions about speaking "beside the question, superfluously, or tediously," if they could manage by such speaking to achieve their ends. By holding the floor, a senator could delay or prevent the passage of a measure to which he was opposed. More commonly, a small group of senators worked together, delivering relays of speeches, thus holding the fort indefinitely. This oratorical obstruction in our country is known as "filibustering"; in Australia, as "stonewalling." In the winter of 1890–1891 a filibuster lasted for two months.

Individual senators have shown remarkable endurance in the rôle of filibusterers. In 1893 Senator Allen of Nebraska spoke for fourteen hours in the filibuster against the repeal of the Silver Purchase Act. A few years later Carter of Montana consumed an equal number of hours in talking a pernicious river and harbor bill to death. La Follette the elder broke the record in 1908, holding the floor for more than eighteen hours against a currency measure. This particular filibuster failed because the blind Senator Gore, a member of the relay team, ceased talking in the erroneous belief that Senator Stone, who was to follow him, was in the Chamber. The opposition was quick to take advantage of this mistake, and promptly put its measure through. Of course, in a filibuster, speeches are ordinarily of a rather poor quality, the sole object being to consume the time of the Senate and to wear out the patience of its members. In 1903 Senator Tillman of South Carolina, in lieu of a speech, threatened his colleagues with Byron's *Childe Harold* and such other poems as might be necessary to bring them to include in an appropriation bill an item settling a war claim presented by his state. The Senate soon yielded. Four years later, Senator Stone, filibustering against a ship subsidy bill, read *Pilgrim's Progress*.

THE DEBATE ON THE ARMED MERCHANT SHIP BILL. In March, 1917, the use of the filibuster to obstruct legislation was brought most forcibly to the attention of the country in the few days preceding the adjournment of Congress. President Wilson had asked Congress to pass a law authorizing him to arm merchant vessels in order that they might protect themselves from German submarines. The House passed the bill by a vote of 403 to 13. Nearly all of the senators favored the bill; but a minority of eleven held the floor until Congress adjourned, thus preventing the enactment of the measure.[14] The President, sure of popular support, then wrote one of the strongest notes of his career. "A little group of willful men, representing no opinion but their own," he declared, "have rendered the great government of the United States helpless and contemptible." He concluded by calling upon the Senate to change its rules.

THE CLOSURE RULE OF 1917. Under this pressure, the Senate adopted a mild form of closure. At any time a motion to close debate upon a measure, if signed by sixteen senators, may be presented to the Senate. Two days later the presiding officer puts the question: "Is it the sense of the Senate that the debate shall be brought to a close?" This question must be voted upon without debate; and if two thirds of the senators (under an amendment of 1949, "two thirds of the senators duly *chosen* and *sworn*") vote in the affirmative, the measure becomes the unfinished business to the exclusion of all other business until disposed of. Thereafter no senator may speak more than one hour; no dilatory motions may be put; and points of order must be decided without debate.[15]

It does not prevent filibustering. This rule has been successfully invoked only a few times. On November 13, 1919, Senator Hitchcock presented the necessary petition for securing a vote on bringing to a close the debate on the Versailles Treaty. Two days later the petition secured the two-thirds majority vote, and on November 19 the vote on the Treaty was taken. Closure was applied again in January, 1926, on the debate on American adherence to the World Court. It has been employed on several other occasions, but, in the main, the filibuster stands intact. It continues because the Senate is jealous of its long-established reputation for liberty of debate, and because it is seldom that two thirds of its membership is willing to "gag" a minority. Besides, the machinery for invoking closure is slow moving: first, the petition; then the lapse of two days before the vote upon it is taken; and, after the affirmative vote, an hour for each senator who wants it. For these reasons a filibuster started near the time set for adjournment, as nearly all of them are, will usually prove successful. As Congress approached the end of its term in March, 1919, a few senators conducted a filibuster and blocked important legislation, so that the President would be forced to call a special session. When the time for adjournment came, Vice President Marshall declared the Senate adjourned *sine Deo* (without God), instead of using the conventional phrase, *sine die.*

But a more drastic rule is not likely to be adopted. Proposals have been

---

[14] Senator Norris and other senators who opposed this bill denied with some heat that they were conducting a filibuster, maintaining, not without reason, that they were debating the measure on its merits.

[15] Rule XXII.

made for a more drastic system of closure, but without success. Vice President Dawes (1925–1929) made a dramatic attempt to force the Senate to reform itself. He met with complete failure, which he accepted with good grace. The late Senator Underwood proposed that the Senate use the previous-question device, but that each senator be allowed an hour for debate before the vote was taken. This proposition did not commend itself to his colleagues. Senator Norris held the opinion, in which many concurred, that the Twentieth Amendment, adopted January, 1933, would indirectly deal filibustering a very hard blow. Under the old system Congress had to adjourn its last session of three months' duration on March 4. We have just noted that the obstructionists found their best opportunity in the last, crowded days of this short session. The "Lame Duck" Amendment removes the time limit that so long rested upon the last session of a Congress.

Yet filibusterers still find ample opportunity for their game. One of our Founding Fathers used to say, "When in the majority vote: when in the minority talk." The rules of the Senate seem to be applied with that in mind. They give the minority's right to talk precedence over the majority's right to act. In 1936 Senator Black led a filibuster against the practice of subsidizing the merchant marine by means of exorbitant payments on ocean mail contracts. The late Senator Long conducted several one-man filibusters more or less successfully. In 1938 Senator Clark took advantage of a Senate rule that permits a quorum call (roll call) whenever the absence of a quorum is suggested, providing business has been transacted since the previous call. He obstructed the Senate for one day by alternating between making motions and compelling quorum calls. His motions were immediately laid on the table, but this action did not matter at all to him—he could then again "suggest the absence of a quorum." The Anti-lynching bills were killed by filibuster several different times. In 1942, when there were votes enough and to spare to enact a measure outlawing the poll tax as a qualification for voting in federal elections, Southern senators staged another successful filibuster. Senator Theodore Bilbo of Mississippi was their leader. His desk was piled high with reference books, including one on Japan. The Southerners were ready to talk for six weeks, and the Senate, ever carefully guarding the rights of individual senators, failed to muster enough votes to close the debate.[16] Up to the time of this writing a filibuster or a threat of one has always prevented an antipoll tax bill from coming to a vote.

And the recent change was a step backward. In 1948, when Senator Vandenberg was the presiding officer of the Senate, a motion was made to

[16] O. R. Altman, "Second and Third Sessions of the Seventy-fifth Congress," *Am. Pol. Sci. Rev.*, XXXII (1938), 1115; Haynes, *op. cit.*, Vol. I, pp. 405 ff.; *Time*, Nov. 23, 1942, p. 22.

take up an anti-poll tax bill. Southern senators started a filibuster against the motion, and they were met by an effort to invoke closure. Now the Senate closure rule as it had stood since 1917 was applicable to "any pending measure." President *pro tempore* Vandenberg ruled that a "motion to take up a measure" is not a pending measure. On this ruling the filibusterers won. The next year, with Democrats in control of the Senate again and Vice President Barkley in the Chair, the Democratic floor leader, Scott Lucas, made a motion to amend the closure rule by changing the key phrase to read "any measure, motion, or other matter pending before the Senate." The Southerners then began a filibuster against this motion. They carried it on for ten days, when the majority floor leader presented a closure petition duly signed by the requisite number of senators. The President of the Senate ruled that a "motion" was a "measure" within the meaning of the closure rule adopted in 1917. Of course there was an appeal from this ruling, and the President of the Senate was overruled, 46 to 41, some Democrats (including nearly all the Southerners) and "old guard" Republicans voting against him.[17] But a few days later (March 17, 1949) the senators adopted a "compromise" closure rule. The change in the rule provides that debate may be closed "upon any measure, motion, or other matter pending before the Senate." This was the anti-filibusterers' side of the bargain. Then the rule provides further that to close debate "two thirds of the senators duly chosen and sworn" (not just two thirds of a quorum as under the old rule) must vote to close it. This was the filibusterers' side of the bargain. One might venture to suggest that the senators are overcautious in their efforts to limit the filibuster!

A defense of the freedom of debate. There are many competent observers who justify the extreme freedom of debate in the Senate. Professor Lindsay Rogers, in his careful analysis of the Senate, justifies unrestricted debate [18] on the ground that under our system of checks and balances the Senate alone is able to serve as a check upon the autocracy of President and party. He points out also that the greater number of the bills defeated by the filibuster have deserved their fate. To the charge that the long debates prevent the Senate from disposing of a proper proportion of its business, he replies that the Senate gets much of its work done expeditiously; that the unanimous consent agreements, frequently used, are, in effect, a species of closure. Finally, he shows that senators who complain of "unrestrained garrulity" of their colleagues do not always do so in good faith. For instance, Senator Stone, who in 1907 read *Pilgrim's Progress* in a filibustering speech against a ship subsidy bill, roundly de-

---

[17] *New York Times*, March 13, 1949.
[18] *Op. cit.*, pp. 163–164, 168–169, 184 ff. Haynes, *op. cit.*, Vol. I, pp. 419 ff., is in substantial agreement with Rogers.

nounced those who in 1915 conducted "a defiant filibuster without pretense of legitimate discussion" against the Ship Purchase Bill. In other words, a "filibuster is either a reprehensible artifice of a sinister opposition, or an ingenious and patriotic device of our friends for saving the people." [19]

Concluding, we may say that the Senate is the only great forum in the United States. Freedom of debate, more than anything else, makes it so. Few there are who defend the filibuster. The question is, How can it be abolished without interfering with freedom of debate? The answer is not easy to find. But surely the present closure rule is far more restrictive than is required for full freedom of relevant debate.

III. BILLS IN CONFERENCE COMMITTEES [20]

The Conference Committee. Everyone understands, of course, that bills and resolutions must pass the two Houses in identical language. Frequently, House and Senate differ as to the details of a bill. If one House changes or amends a bill passed by the other, the body in which the bill originated may accept such changes and amendments, thus settling the differences. But the two chambers are very frequently some distance apart on the provisions of important bills, and their differences are not often composed by the simple expedient of one chamber's obligingly accepting the amendments proposed by the other. Important matters on which the Senate and the House disagree are usually settled by conference committees —special committees composed of the important members of the standing committees having the bill in charge in each House and appointed by the presiding officers. The conferees meet and go over all points at issue on a bill, seeking to find a basis of agreement. Sometimes their work is soon done; at other times they labor for days; but in the give-and-take process that characterizes a conference, they usually effect an agreement sooner or later. In 1948 the conference committees accomplished the unusual, clearing for enactment every one of the 84 bills and resolutions referred to them.[21]

ITS POWER. As long ago as 1884 John Sherman spoke out in protest against the powers of the conference committees.

I feel that both Houses ought to make a stand on the attempt to transfer the entire legislative power of Congress to a committee of three of each body, selected

---

[19] Quoted in Haynes, *op. cit.,* Vol. I, p. 418, from Edward E. Whiting, in the Boston *Herald,* Dec. 17, 1924.

[20] Alexander, *op. cit.,* pp. 283–286; Galloway, *op. cit.,* pp. 96 ff.; R. Luce, *Legislative Procedure* (1922), pp. 400–407; Riddick, *U.S. Cong.,* pp. 411 ff.

[21] Riddick, "The Second Session of the Eightieth Congress," *Am. Pol. Sci. Rev.,* XLIII (1949), p. 489.

not according to any fixed rule, but selected probably according to the favor of the presiding officer or the chairman of the committee that framed the bill; so that in fact a committee selected by two men, one in each House, may frame and pass the most important legislation of Congress.[22]

Perhaps Sherman's language was somewhat extreme, but there is no denying that the conference committees are powerful factors in shaping legislation. The power of the conference, as Robert Luce explains,[23] lies chiefly in the fact that the Houses accept its report without amendments, or reject it *in toto*. As a matter of fact, the report is quite likely to be accepted. This probability of acceptance holds true because the bills that "go to conference" are usually those that must in some form or other be enacted into law, and the rank and file of lawmakers feel that they cannot do better than take the word of the conferees as to the form in which laws should be enacted. Furthermore, many of the principal bills are referred to conference committees near the end of the session, leaving little time for any further consideration of them by the two chambers even if they are so disposed. Just as each House must leave the greater part of its work to be performed by the standing committees, so the two Houses must leave their disagreements to be settled by conference committees. For the delegation of authority in each case, the reason is essentially the same: the volume of business before Congress, a great deal of which is of a somewhat technical nature, cannot be considered in detail except by committees.

The question of using joint standing committees. The chief objection to the conference committee system is that it does not give the Houses a full opportunity to consider a matter agreed upon in conference; that the legislative bodies are practically at the mercy of the conference. If a bill were considered and reported originally by a joint committee of the two branches of Congress instead of being passed upon by separate committees of the two Houses, differences between the bodies could ordinarily be ironed out in the initial stages of a bill's history and the conference committee would have little to do. The joint committee system would give the two chambers a process for co-operative action from the time a bill reached the committee stage, thus allowing members fair opportunity, in the course of a bill's passage, to examine and discuss the propositions agreed upon in joint committee; whereas the conference committee reaches its agreements after a bill has been through both Houses, and, in practice, leaves little opportunity in either House for the consideration of amendments proposed by the other. Furthermore, the joint committee system would save some valuable time for Congress, for under our present committee system a bill must be considered and reported twice—once by the ap-

[22] Quoted in R. Luce, *Legislative Procedure*, pp. 403–404.
[23] *Ibid.*, p. 404.

propriate committee of each House. Robert Luce, long a member of the House, recommends more use of the joint committee, and he points to its satisfactory operation in several state legislatures.[24] But the great majority of the members prefer the old system because they are accustomed to it or because they fear that senators would insist upon holding the prominent places on the joint committee. There is also a feeling among many members of the House that they take their committee work much more seriously than do the senators.

IV. BILLS AND LAWS

A bill that finally winds its way through the House and Senate labyrinths and is approved by the President, or passed over his veto, becomes a law.[25] As such, it is in the select company of a very small group of measures that, out of the thousands introduced in Congress, have reached the statute books. Perhaps about one measure in five of those introduced is enacted into law. Furthermore, of the legislative proposals that reach the statute books, the great majority relate to matters of a routine character. In the course of the two-year term of Congress the great public bills passed that vitally affect the interests (chiefly economic) of the nation can usually be counted on one's fingers. It goes without saying that some measures are enacted that have little or no merit, and that not infrequently bills that seem most desirable unhappily fall by the wayside. But, considering the volume of work Congress must do, the conditions under which it must be done, and the limitations of human beings, the wonder is that legislative attainment is as high as it is.

The statute books. At the end of each session of Congress all its acts and resolutions, all treaties concluded, and all presidential proclamations issued are published in large volumes (usually two) under the title of *Statutes at Large of the United States.* One volume contains the public acts and joint resolutions; and another, the private acts and resolutions, concurrent resolutions, treaties, and proclamations. Occasionally, the statutes in force are compiled and published for the convenience of public officers, lawyers, and others. Sometimes this is done by private publishers, sometimes by the government. Recently the government published the *United States Code Containing the General and Permanent Laws of the United States in Force on January 2, 1947.* This Code is kept up to date by annual supplements.

[24] Luce, *Congress—An Explanation*, pp. 30–32. See also Galloway, *op. cit.*, p. 100.

[25] On the veto, see Chapter 12, sec. III.

V. PUBLICITY AND REPORTING OF PROCEEDINGS [26]

House sessions invariably public. Earlier legislative bodies followed the common practice of deliberating on the "mysteries of state" in secret. Our colonial assemblies very seldom made exception to this rule, but the national House of Representatives made a rather general practice of opening the galleries to the public from the beginning. Although Rule XXIX authorizes secret sessions, none has been held since 1830. Following British precedent, the House did not admit ladies as auditors in the early days; but when a fair admirer of Fisher Ames led a delegation to hear him speak, the ladies were admitted and the precedent was broken, permanently.

Senate sessions almost always public. Although the Senate did not ordinarily admit the public during the first years of its history, some members earnestly advocated open sessions. Commenting in his diary upon a resolution (1791) that the doors be opened, a senator from Pennsylvania observed:

I knew of no reason for keeping the door of any legislative assembly open that did not apply with equal force to us. The objections against it, *viz.,* that the members would make speeches for the gallery and for the public papers, would be the fault of the members. If they waged war in words and oral combats; if they pitted themselves like cocks, or played the gladiator, for the amusement of the idle and curious, the fault was theirs; that, let who would fill the chairs of the Senate, I hoped discretion would mark their deportment.[27]

This sentiment prevailed in 1794, and a resolution was passed, which provided that galleries should be constructed and opened to the public whenever the Senate should be sitting in a legislative capacity.

EXCEPT FOR SOME "EXECUTIVE SESSIONS." Until recently, in considering nominations, treaties, and other more or less confidential communications from the President, the Senate sat almost invariably in secret sessions. Many questions so considered are extremely delicate and excellent arguments for secrecy can be made, but with the increasing growth of democratic ideas the practice received severe criticism. In recent years a number of senators strenuously objected to the secret executive sessions and considered but lightly their obligation to keep secrets, as was evidenced by the fact that the public was usually informed by them through the press as to what transpired when the Senate was sitting behind closed doors. Considering that the secrets of "secret sessions" were not kept and that the prevailing sentiment in the Senate and out was against secrecy, the Senate, in 1929, voted that all business should be transacted in open session, unless the majority voted for a closed session. The resolution further provided that,

[26] Luce, *Legislative Procedure,* Ch. XIV; Walker, *op. cit.,* Ch. 15.
[27] Quoted in Luce, *Leg. Proc.,* p. 334, from the *Journal of William Maclay,* Feb. 24, 1791.

upon a majority vote, the proceedings of a secret session should be published, and that any senator was free at all times to make public his individual vote.

Reporting. The early legislative chambers permitted little or no written publicity of their proceedings. Writing of the colonial assemblies, Robert Luce informs us that in Virginia the public was not allowed to know what the laws were, that in North Carolina the public was not permitted to discuss the laws, and that in Massachusetts it was not to know how the laws were made. In the last-named colony "Mr. Speaker" and some other members of the lower House drew up an order to prevent legislators "from discloseinge any of ye private businesses thereof abroade." [28]

The Journals. The democratic spirit of the Revolution changed this, and our federal Constitution contains the requirement that "each House shall keep a journal of its proceedings, and from time to time publish the same, excepting such parts as may in their judgment require secrecy." [29] However, the *Journals* contain only records of official actions. The debates, from which the public may learn a great deal of what determines legislative action, were not and are not published in them.

Early method of reporting debates. For years the debates were not published at all, except in a haphazard and unofficial manner. Thus, Webster's great classic, the "Reply to Hayne," was not taken down verbatim; but was written out by a man who took notes on the speech and who conferred with Webster and others as to just what the Senator had said. The process of revision and correction went on for about a month, when the speech was finally published. Beginning in the 1830's, private enterprise recorded and published the debates verbatim in the *Congressional Globe;* and since 1873 Congress has itself assumed the obligation of printing the debates in the *Congressional Record*.

The Congressional Record. The *Record* does not, however, give an exact account of what takes place in Congress. Members are allowed to revise their speeches before they are published; to insert long speeches, when only a few words were actually spoken on the floor; and even to place in the *Record* speeches delivered elsewhere, magazine articles, and various types of material. In 1948 speeches and materials *not* delivered in either House occupied 5,643 pages of the *Record*—more than half as many pages as the entire proceedings of both Houses. Is there any justification for such freedom? It is often impossible for a representative to give a satisfactory statement of his views in the few minutes at his disposal, and it would seem, therefore, that he has a fair claim to the privilege of "extending his remarks," or "leave to print," in the *Record*. But everyone recognizes

[28] *Ibid.,* p. 342.
[29] Art. I, sec. v, cl. 3.

that the privilege is frequently abused, especially when a member uses it to make a political speech to his constituents, and then, under another privilege, the frank, mails it to the thousands of voters in his district. Such alleged speeches are deceptive, and they add considerably to the cost of publishing the *Record*. Congress should at least devise some means of preventing the publication and circulation at public expense of "speeches" and articles that have little or no relation to questions at issue on its floor.

VI. THE LOBBY [30]

Before leaving the subject of congressional procedure, we need to give some attention to a well-established and much-discussed institution, the lobby. We have previously stated that congressmen seldom introduce bills on their own initiative; that they introduce them at the request of individuals, social organizations, patriotic societies, economic groups, or what not. Many organizations, a number of them very powerful, maintain agents in Washington whose business it is to secure the favorable action of Congress upon measures advocated by interested groups and to accomplish the defeat of measures opposed by these groups. This business is called "lobbying," and those engaged in it are known as "lobbyists." It is not a new business; but since the national government has extended its powers over important social and economic matters, the lobby has naturally broadened its own activities and refined its processes. It is sometimes called the "Third House" of Congress. Representation in it is social and economic, especially the latter, and much more direct than in either the Senate or the House. The two constitutional Houses represent the great unorganized public, which has only hazy and conflicting notions of what it wants; whereas the lobbyists, informally, but often very successfully, represent special interests—interests that know exactly what they want— by pressing their claims upon harassed congressmen.

Types of lobbies. Organizations of manufacturers, mining industries, bankers, transportation companies, doctors, used car dealers, farmers, laborers, ex-soldiers, patriots, pacifists, Wets, Drys, and various other interests are represented in Washington by their "legislative agents." Frank R. Kent, a close observer of what goes on at the national capital, writing in 1924, fixed the number of such agencies at 145. Since Kent gave his figures, the wider activities of government, reaching significantly into every man's life, and improved communication have greatly stimulated lobbying, so that at this writing about 1,600 lobbyists are registered in Washington.

[30] F. L. Burdette, *Lobbyist in Action* (1950); Galloway, *op. cit.,* pp. 297 ff.; E. P. Herring, *Group Representation Before Congress* (1932); Frank Kent, *The Great Game of Politics* (1924), Chs. XLII–XLV; R. Luce, *Legislative Assemblies* (1924), Ch. XVII; Walker, *op. cit.,* Ch. 7.

Kent named the American Farm Bureau Federation as having the most powerful lobby (it is near the top in 1951) and gave its chief agent the credit for the very effective work of the farm bloc in Congress.[31] Another powerful lobby is that maintained by the United States Chamber of Commerce. Still another effective lobby is maintained by the American Association of Railway Executives. In the opinion of the late Senator Thomas J. Walsh of Montana and many others, the Joint Committee of National Utility Associations, often called the "power lobby," was at one time the best organized and financed of all the lobbies.[32]

The AFL and the CIO are very effectively represented by their legislative agents, and it is a matter of common knowledge that the Prohibition forces once had a powerful lobby. In every way equal to any other lobby in persistence and power is that of the veterans. In 1936 members of the House openly rejoiced that the three leading organizations of veterans had united on a bonus bill, a combination that made it possible for congressmen to please all. The entire membership of the Senate was present and voted on that bill—the first time in four years that such an attendance and vote were recorded.[33] At this writing, the farmers seem to have the most powerful lobby, with labor and manufacturers as close seconds.

TYPES OF LOBBYISTS. Some lobbyists are men of high standing in the legal profession, and they are frequently able to present to committees or individual members of Congress in a convincing manner the various aspects of proposed legislation that is of interest to their clients. A few lobbyists are recruited from the ranks of former members of Congress. They are engaged sometimes because they have a particular interest in and knowledge of the business they represent, but perhaps they are more frequently retained because of the use they are expected to make of their knowledge of congressional procedure and their friendships with former colleagues in Congress. In recent years some former journalists, skilled in the art of using the press for building up public opinion suitable to their purposes, have joined the ranks of the lobbyists. Other lobbyists are chosen primarily because they have expert knowledge of the matter they are to present to our lawmakers. Still others are not chosen by anyone; they simply go to Washington and do their own lobbying when a question of vital interest to them is before Congress, or when they feel that it should be brought before Congress.

A number of lobbyists, perhaps the majority of them, sincerely believe in the things they advocate. They are convinced that what is good for them

[31] *Op. cit.*, pp. 259–261.
[32] Walsh, "Lobbies and Lobbyists," *New York Times Magazine*, October 13, 1929.
[33] *Am. Pol. Sci. Rev.*, XXX (1936), 1102.

and their principals is good for the country. This is usually true of those who lobby for reforms, but many others are no less sincere. In 1929 Joseph R. Grundy, president of the Pennsylvania Manufacturers' Association and for many years a tariff lobbyist, frankly stated that his faith in a high protective tariff was next to his religion; that the American people believed in it too, or they would not have elected high-tariff men to office; and that the country would be better off if there were a hundred brilliant young tariff lobbyists to advise and assist congressmen in drafting a tariff bill.[34]

There are free-lance lobbyists, of course, who will advocate any cause for which they are paid, and who even go so far as to serve several organizations or groups whose interests cannot possibly be harmonized. In July, 1942, the *United States News*[35] stated that there were 628 organizations in Washington ready to supply witnesses for or against different types of legislation. One hundred eighty-two would speak for one or another kind of business or manufacturing, 24 for different phases of education, 10 for finance, 14 for youth, 27 for farming interests, 42 for labor, 43 for veterans, and so on.

The "good" lobbyist. Although there are lobbyists who are backed by so many votes that they become arrogant and even make threats, the common variety of "legislative agents" are usually very tactful. They have a wide circle of friends and acquaintances in Washington, and their personable qualities make it easy to add to this list. A newly elected congressman may rather naïvely form some very delightful friendships with persons whom he later learns to be lobbyists—a discovery that may or may not break the friendships.

Many lobbyists dispense social entertainment on a rather generous scale, a form of activity known in the "trade" as "plush-horse" lobbying. Its effectiveness has probably been greatly overrated. The expert lobbyist is thoroughly familiar with the subject or subjects on which he seeks to interest congressmen, and he often lays his cards on the table and lets the facts speak for themselves, a method quite likely to be followed by experienced representatives of well-established groups and organizations.[36]

The good lobbyist is a master of the intricacies of congressional procedure. His complete knowledge of procedure makes him a legislative strategist of the highest order: he knows when to attack and when to withdraw; when to take the citadel by storm and when to settle down to a long siege. He knows the representatives and senators—their moral and political strength, their ambitions, their mental processes—and he uses this knowledge skill-

[34] *Time,* Nov. 4, 1929, p. 13.
[35] July 24, 1942, p. 19.
[36] Robert M. La Follette, Jr., "Some Lobbies Are Good," *New York Times Magazine,* May 16, 1948, p. 15.

fully, sometimes too skillfully for the public good. His principals allow him a generous expense account and pay him a good salary, usually as much and sometimes considerably more than congressmen receive. Kent states that he knew one man whose salary was equal to the President's and that his clients received their money's worth.[37]

How the lobbyists work. Lobbyists do not bribe our representatives. At least they do not ordinarily offer direct bribes. No doubt, in some cases, an agent is in a position to offer a lucrative place in business to a congressman who will yield to his importunities, but this species of indirect bribery is probably not so common as some critics assert it to be. The strength of the lobbyist lies first in the fact that he knows infinitely more about the matter on which he attempts to influence legislation than does the average congressman. It is but natural that our legislators should listen to what he has to say. "If any person can tell me more about a pending bill than I know already, why," asked Speaker Reed, "should it be my duty to shun him?" [38] Other lawmakers of high standing have testified to the expertness of the lobbyist. Is it not to be expected that congressmen, even after making allowances for the special interests of these experts, should be greatly influenced by the materials and arguments they present? Their influence is less to be marveled at when we consider that frequently there is no lobby on the other side of the question.

But let us not credit the success of the lobbyist to his expert knowledge alone. Many of them represent powerful economic and social organizations, organizations that do or may contribute handsomely to the party war chest or to the campaign funds of particular candidates. Furthermore, some of these groups control or influence tens of thousands of voters; and in states and districts where their strength is concentrated to any degree, they may easily make or break a congressman. Thus, legislators from agricultural areas cannot ignore the farm lobby with impunity; and those in whose districts labor is strong must treat the various labor lobbies with great respect.

In 1935 the Walsh-Healey bill, regulating the conditions of employment in all firms receiving government contracts, was for ten months reposing with the House Judiciary Committee. Then William Green, President of the AF of L, wired all members of the Committee: ". . . I respectfully urge you to be present at meeting of the Judiciary Committee tomorrow morning . . . Your absence from this meeting will be construed as opposition to the measure and as unfriendly to labor. Our representative will be present at tomorrow morning's meeting. Do not fail us. Be present."

---

[37] *Op. cit.*, p. 271.
[38] Quoted in Luce, *Legislative Assemblies*, p. 395.

It is a fact that all members of the Committee were present, that they favorably reported the bill, and that the House passed it.[39] This case could easily be matched in effectiveness by a veterans' or farmers' lobby. If a member of Congress does not show interest in the cause a lobbyist promotes, word is quickly passed back to his constituents, and he is flooded with calls, telegrams, and letters. Lucky indeed is that congressman who is not menaced by the power of the lobby, and courageous is he who defies it. Fear of being voted out of office leads many of the much harassed representatives and senators to see things as the lobby sees them.

To what extent is the lobby an evil? No intelligent citizen will deny that organizations and individuals should be allowed to present their claims and programs to legislative bodies. Almost equally beyond denial, some groups and their lobbyists seek to do this with clean hands and in a straightforward manner. In fact, the motives that prompt them to act or the blameless character of their procedure may lead the public to object to the term "lobbyists" as applied to them. We can further state that the information furnished by a lobbyist, even if he is representing a very selfish interest, may be used with profit by intelligent legislators. What, then, are the evils of lobbying?

First, the organizations represented by lobbies have more than their share of influence in shaping legislation. The general public has no lobby,[40] and its interests are sometimes passed over when well-organized groups apply pressure to congressmen. Nevertheless, the power of the lobby is often overestimated. Senator Thomas J. Walsh, whose record hardly leaves him open to the accusation of having attempted to screen either the lobby or his colleagues in Congress, seemed to think that the influence of the lobby has been exaggerated, especially that influence which men who claim to have a "pull" or to be "on the inside" are supposed to exert.

A second evil of the lobby is that it carries on the greater part of its work in secret. It is thus able to resort to pressure methods that would not bear the light of day, and, in particular, to use large sums of money of which no account is given.

The third bad effect of the lobby is that it undermines the faith of the

[39] Quoted by O. R. Altman in his "Second Session of the Seventy-fourth Congress," *Am. Pol. Sci. Rev.*, XXX (1936), 1102.

[40] "The People's Lobby," whose Executive Secretary was Benjamin C. Marsh, functioned until October, 1950, but even Marsh could not go very far on a $16,000 budget. Marsh interestingly and entertainingly told how he lobbied for the Federal Regulation of Lobbying Act (1946), was the first lobbyist to register under its provisions, and thus was entitled to be called the No. 1 lobbyist, the Dean of lobbyists—on a salary of $1,800 a year. He wrote the President "to drive the rapacious horde of profiteers out of the temple of democracy," and tried to "unconfuse" senators and representatives on inflation and other problems.

people in their government. They know that the lobby is at work; they believe that it works effectively with a large portion of their lawmakers; and they become cynical on the subject of representative government. We may say, then, that, although many lobbyists neither have base motives nor use insidious methods, the lobby is an institution to be regarded with grave concern.

Means of curbing the lobby: 1. INVESTIGATION. Outcries have been made against the lobby from time to time, and these have sometimes been followed by investigations. Perhaps the most dramatic drive against it was launched by President Wilson in May, 1913, when he told the public of "extraordinary exertions being made by the lobby in Washington to gain recognition for certain alterations in the tariff bill." He denounced this lobby as numerous, industrious, and insidious. Although he made no specific charges, the Senate committee that investigated the lobby found many concrete examples that sustained his general charge. As Senator Thomas J. Walsh put it, "the President had taken a shot in the dark and brought down a whole flock of ducks." [41] Many lobbyists left Washington—for the time being. Another investigation of the lobby, again primarily a tariff lobby, was held in the fall of 1929. It revealed some questionable, if not dark, practices, as well as the fact that some concerns and individuals who employed lobbyists were duped by these hirelings to such an extent as to warrant their being placed in the "sucker" class.

These investigations may cause lobbyists to move with more circumspection for a brief period, but their permanent result is practically nil. In May, 1932, President Hoover called attention to "the locust swarms of lobbyists who haunt the halls of Congress seeking selfish privilege for special groups and sections of the country, misleading members as to the real views of the people by showers of propaganda." [42] A particularly aggressive lobby was that which operated against the utility holding company bill (1935), a lobby that led to another investigation. The Senate Committee to Investigate the National Defense Program uncovered some nasty cases of lobbying for war contracts. Several of the principals, including a congressman, were eventually given short prison sentences. While these lines are being written, a House Select Committee on Lobbying Activities is busily engaged. If lobbying continues, so do the investigations.

2. REGULATION. Presumably one of the purposes of investigation is to assemble information that may serve as a guide in drafting a corrective

[41] *Op. cit.*
[42] Quoted in Herring, "First Session of the 72nd Cong.," *Am. Pol. Sci. Rev.* (1932), XXVI, 859.

statute. But even with all the information at hand the difficulties of drafting an effective law are almost insurmountable. The problem is not unlike that which is said to have been faced by old King Canute when the tide was moving in on him. He could stop the tide not by ordering it to cease its flow, but by changing the relation of the Moon and the Earth!

Only in 1946 did Congress, in the Federal Regulation of Lobbying Act, attempt to deal with its perennial human tide, the lobby, which at times threatens to submerge it. As is indicated by the title of the act, Congress did not attempt to abolish lobbying. That would have been the veriest folly. Regulation was the aim, and the method thereof is chiefly in the provision that any person who engages himself for pay for the purpose of attempting to influence the passage or defeat of legislation shall register with the Clerk of the House and the Secretary of the Senate, giving to these officers, in writing and under oath, his name and address, the name and address of the person by whom he is employed, how much he is paid in salary and allowed for expenses, and what expenses are to be included. The lobbyist is further required to give to the Clerk and the Secretary a quarterly report "of all money received and expended by him during the preceding calendar quarter in carrying on his work; to whom paid; for what purpose; and the names of any papers, periodicals, magazines, or other publications in which he has caused to be published any articles or editorials; and the proposed legislation he is employed to support or oppose." The law specifies appropriate penalties for its violation. The lobbyists have registered, about 1,600 of them, and their business stands revealed as a multi-million dollar enterprise.

3. STRENGTHENING THE MEMBERS OF CONGRESS THROUGH PARTY ORGANIZATION. The publicity that the lobbying law requires is, of course, desirable and proper, but the only effective regulation of lobbying will come when Congress is so organized that its own efficient leadership will reduce the lobby to a relatively unimportant rôle in the legislative process. As of now each member of a party may have his own program, even his own foreign policy, and he is thus "on his own" in meeting those who seek special favors from Congress. He cannot say to the lobbyist, "Compliance with your request would be contrary to my party's program," or that, "The party is pushing a different measure to which all loyal party members in Congress are pledged." But given an integrated party, one with a clearly defined program, the member will find some protection under the wings of his party for his refusal to accommodate a selfish interest. At least the Committee on Political Parties of the American Political Science Association sees this possibility.[43] The big problem, though, is

[43] "Toward a More Responsible Two-Party System," *Am. Pol. Sci. Rev.,* Supplement, XLIV (1950) No. 3, Pt. 2, pp. 19–20.

to get the parties to adopt clear programs and to establish the discipline necessary to hold the legislators to such programs.

VII. POWERS OF CONGRESS

A. Legislative

The subjects on which Congress may legislate are enumerated in various clauses of the Constitution and in the amendments thereto, but the eighth section of Article I contains nearly all the broad grants of power. The last clause (18) of this section is of tremendous importance, for it empowers Congress "to make all laws which shall be *necessary* and *proper* for carrying into execution the *foregoing powers,* and *all other powers* vested by this Constitution in the government of the United States, or in any department or officer thereof." This is the famous "elastic" or "implied powers" clause, explained in Chapter 3, section 1. It is not necessary at this point to dwell on the legislative powers of Congress. They relate to executive organization and functions, the organization and jurisdiction of the federal courts, finance, commerce and business, labor, agriculture, conservation, health, national defense, social security, and other subjects. It is sufficient for present purposes to state that the powers of Congress, as now interpreted, reach to the daily life of the individual in various ways, although the states still have the authority, except in time of war, to regulate the normal life of the individual in most particulars.

B. Judicial

Impeachment.[44] The Constitution gives the House of Representatives the sole power of impeachment, that is, the sole authority to vote the charges against a civil officer. The person against whom charges have been made is then tried by the Senate. Impeachment proceedings have never been instituted against a military officer, and it is very generally agreed that Congress has no authority to impeach such officers. In like manner, members of Congress are not subject to impeachment—a point that was decided in 1798 when an attempt was made to impeach Senator Blount. But the President, Vice President, and all *civil* officers may be impeached for "treason, bribery, or other high crimes and misdemeanors."[45] The terms "high crimes and misdemeanors" have been given a rather broad meaning in practice. Judges have been impeached for vi-

[44] Haynes, *op. cit.,* Vol. II, Ch. XV; "Rules for Impeachment Trials," *Senate Manual;* D. Y. Thomas, "The Law of Impeachment in the U.S.," *Am. Pol. Sci. Rev.* (1908), II, 378–395; W. W. Willoughby, *Principles of the Constitutional Law of the U.S.* (1930 ed.), Ch. LXVIII.

[45] Constitution, Art. II, sec. IV.

cious personal habits and for conduct unbecoming a judge, and one of the charges against President Johnson was that his public addresses were "intemperate, inflammatory, and scandalous."

In the case of conviction in an impeachment proceeding, the penalty must be removal from office, to which may be added disqualification for holding any other office under the United States. Any officer so convicted may then be tried in the regular courts for the crime or crimes for which he was impeached, and, if found guilty, receive sentence just as an ordinary criminal. Although the President is prohibited from granting a pardon to one convicted in an impeachment, he may, of course, issue a pardon to cover the sentence of a court.

How IMPEACHMENTS ARE CONDUCTED. Impeachment procedure may be set in motion when a charge is made against a civil officer by a member of the House of Representatives, by the President in a message to the House, by the legislature of a state, or by other interested parties. A committee of the House may be asked to consider the charges; and if the committee favors impeachment, the House may then formally make the charges against the accused in a set of articles known as "articles of impeachment." A few members of the House, commonly called "managers," are then selected to conduct the trial in the Senate.

If the President is on trial, the Chief Justice presides over the Senate, since the Vice President, who would succeed to the presidency if the Senate voted for conviction, might find presiding a delicate duty. The Senate proceeds in impeachment cases very much as a court, with each senator under oath to do "impartial justice according to the Constitution and laws." The managers act as prosecuting attorneys for the House, and the accused has his defense counsel as in an ordinary trial. Witnesses are subpoenaed, examined, and cross-examined, and the trial goes on with the public in attendance. The trial ended, the Senate votes in secret on each article of impeachment and if impeachment is sustained by a two-thirds vote upon any of the articles, the accused stands convicted.

THE IMPEACHMENT RECORD. There have been thirteen impeachments (counting the abortive attempt to impeach Senator Blount) and only four convictions, although several resignations preceding the impeachment trials accomplished practically the same results as convictions. The four officers removed by impeachment were judges, and one other judge resigned after the House had voted for impeachment and just before the Senate had started the trial, with the result that action against him was dropped. Impeachment trials resulted in acquittal in the case of four judges. Likewise, W. W. Belknap, Secretary of War under Grant, was acquitted; and President Johnson was saved by one vote.

Impeachment is, and should be, a remedy of last resort. It was never intended that it should be used by Congress as a political means of controlling the executive department or the courts. Perhaps the only time the power was seriously abused was in the hectic days of Reconstruction when Congress, for political reasons, sought to remove its archenemy, President Johnson.

Power to punish for contempt. The discussion in the chapter on the structure and organization of Congress states that each House has the authority to discipline its own members. In certain cases this authority may be exercised over outsiders as well. Either House may punish an individual who physically obstructs its business, who physically assaults a member for action taken in the House, or who prevents a member from attending to his duties.[46] Of special importance is the power of either House to punish any person who fails to be present and give testimony, or who fails to bring papers and documents, when properly called upon to do so. Duly authorized investigating committees frequently have occasion to order witnesses to appear and give testimony, and the courts have held that they not only have the authority to issue such orders, but also the authority to impose punishment when the orders are not obeyed. Either House may impose the penalty, or the Congress may (it has) by general law specify the punishment in such cases, leaving the courts the duty of applying the criminal statute to recalcitrant individuals.[47]

C. Executive and Administrative [48]

Share in appointing and treaty-making powers. In the discussion of the President's powers (Chapter 11) we learned that the Senate shares with him the power to give or withhold consent to appointments to office and we shall consider in Chapter 28 the authority of the Senate to consent to the ratification of treaties. We learned also in Chapter 11 that although the House of Representatives is given no share in the matter of appointments, individual members are nevertheless not without a voice in a number of instances. In like manner, the House has no consitutional part in treaty making; but many treaties require an appropriation of money or other act of Congress to put them into effect, and in such cases the House is in a position to make its power felt. Furthermore, the House has essentially the same authority as the Senate in the matter of giving prior or subsequent approval to executive agreements. These now rival

---

[46] Marshall v. Gordon, 243 U.S. 521, 542 (1917).
[47] J. M. Mathews, *The American Constitutional System* (1940), pp. 110–111.
[48] Galloway, *op. cit.*, Ch. 8; Haynes, *op. cit.*, Vol. II, Chs. XII–XIV; A. W. Macmahon, "Congressional Oversight of Administration: The Power of the Purse," *Pol. Sci. Quar.*, LVIII (1943), 161, 380; L. Rogers, *The American Senate* (1926), Ch. VI.

treaties in number and probably in importance (see Chapter 28, section 1).

Power to prescribe executive and administrative duties. The powers and duties of the President are in a general way laid down in the Constitution; but, to a considerable extent, the nature of the President's work is determined by Congress. For instance, in the Civil Service Act of 1883, which placed a few thousand federal employees under the merit system, Congress gave the President the fundamental power of extending the merit principle to many more thousands of employees, a power that has been frequently used to the great advantage of the civil service. Again, Congress, through its powers to make laws respecting the postal service and foreign commerce, has authorized the President to make postal "treaties" and tariff agreements with foreign powers, such treaties and agreements in the individual cases to become effective *without* the advice and consent of the Senate. Taking another example, the very large responsibility of the President for the preparation and presentation to Congress of the national budget rests upon an act of Congress (1921).

Illustrations could be multiplied almost without end, particularly from the broad grants of power made to the President by Congress in 1933, as related in the chapter on the President's legislative powers; but those just mentioned are sufficient to show how wide a field of presidential activity is opened up by Congress. Not only does Congress have a most important voice in determining the President's sphere of action, but its powers are even wider in respect to the executive departments and the other institutions of national administration. More will be said of this in a later chapter. Here we shall be content to notice that the great Departments of State, Treasury, and others, and the commissions, like the Interstate Commerce Commission and the Federal Trade Commission, were brought into existence by acts of Congress.

Oversight of administration. Writing in 1925, Carl Merz stated,

Congress hurries tirelessly from one administrative problem to another: from technical details of reforestation to causes of the hoof-and-mouth disease; from the right way to protect fish in Alaskan waters to the regulation of left-hand turns in the District of Columbia; from the proper temperature for a botanical garden to the loan of the Marine Corps Band for a centennial in Florida. It is a common practice nowadays for Congress to spend days debating such administrative questions as which guns shoot best, how long paints last, how mail tubes are operated, why somebody ought to be made a captain in the Navy.[49]

A certain amount of regulation of administrative authority is, of course, necessary and desirable; but when legislative bodies concern themselves

[49] Quoted in Rogers, *The American Senate*, p. 196, from C. Merz, "Congress Invades the White House," *Harper's Magazine*, May, 1925, p. 643.

with administrative minutiæ, they are likely to do more harm than good. Congress does not now concern itself so much with regulating by law the details of administration. Many members seem to share the view of Speaker Rayburn that Congress cannot administer the laws it writes nor manage the wars it declares. Much less can Congress incorporate the rules of administration and management in its enactments. During the First World War, the crisis years following 1930, and the Second World War, Congress delegated authority to the President and other administrative officials in a most liberal fashion. Nor has this delegation of authority been limited to periods of emergency; they simply mark the high points of the practice.[50] Nevertheless, Congress, its committees, or individual members frequently take a hand in administration.

It is, of course, entirely proper for Congress to satisfy itself that the policies it fixes are carried out in good faith by administrative agencies. The appropriations committees have a regular opportunity to review the work of an administrative agency when it comes forward for funds. On occasion, appropriate legislative committees may "take a look" at the conduct of the agencies they have established. Individual members of Congress often bestir themselves over the administration of a law, the conduct of some agency, or the attitude of a particular civil officer. A congressman is likely to take action on the strength of a complaint from a friend or constituent, or from a newspaper report, or on the basis of his own observation. He may go first to the administrative agency against which complaint is made and try to get the matter corrected. Failing in this, he may report the situation to a committee, which may or may not take his view of the matter. And, finally, he may lay the case before the House of which he is a member.[51] Clearly this sort of check on administrative officials and their employees is very likely to be based on isolated cases and personal considerations. As a means of holding administration accountable to Congress it is of little value. It is sporadic and capricious. Furthermore, there is better than an even chance that it will impair rather than improve administration.

Examples of congressional outcries against the most efficient administrators are frequent. Indeed, in final analysis the charge has often been that an administrator is too good; that he will not appoint to subordinate posts the political supporters of congressmen; or that he is hewing straight to the line and letting the chips fall where they will, not responding to the pressures of powerful individuals or groups to go easy on them. It

[50] On this delegation of power see Chapter 12, section v.

[51] Elias Huzar, "Congressional Control over Administration: Congress and the WPA"; *Am. Pol. Sci. Rev.*, XXXVI, 51 (February, 1942). For the Lovett, Watson, Dodd case, see page 132.

is a matter of common knowledge that some of the best administrative officials have been forced to retire for no other reason than their resistance to unjustifiable pressure from congressmen and the selfish interests behind them.

In the Legislative Reorganization Act of 1946 Congress outlines a plan for a more systematic oversight of administration. Each standing committee of each House is authorized to "exercise continuous watchfulness of the execution by the administrative agencies concerned by any laws, the subject matter of which is within the jurisdiction of such committees." And, as noted in the preceding chapter, each standing committee is further authorized to appoint not more than four professional staff members in addition to the clerical staff. The Appropriations Committee of each House may appoint additional staff, and the House Committee on Appropriations (presumably through its professional staff) is empowered to "conduct studies and examinations of the organization and operation of any executive agency (including any agency the majority of the stock of which is owned by the Government of the United States) as it may deem necessary to assist it in connection with the determination of matters within its jurisdiction."

One might say, "This is fine! Congress now has its expert staffs, just as the administrative agencies have theirs. Congress need no longer depend upon administrative experts for information and advice." Congress cannot, however, develop staffs to match the many specialists in administration. And even if it could, the results would probably mean only rivalry and contention between the two types of staffs. Professor Joseph P. Harris, writing in 1946, expressed the fear that no good and much harm will come from the expert staffs of Congress unless such staffs are used primarily to advise administrative agencies of the information desired by the committees of Congress and the form in which it should be submitted.[52] Senator Elbert D. Thomas, naturally "congressionally" minded, nevertheless notes that the mere bulk of the executive branch outweighs Congress, and that each new function of government produces its administrative experts. The Senator believes, however, that the standing committees of Congress, assisted by their staffs, will develop legislative oversight of the administration of the laws.[53] The problem is to bring about this supervision without creating friction between administration and Congress. The two should be brought closer together, not more widely separated. Any improvement in executive-legislative relationships will probably come from a scheme

[52] "The Reorganization of Congress," *Public Administration Review*, VI, 267 (Summer, 1946).

[53] "How Congress Functions under Its Reorganization Act," *Am. Pol. Sci. Rev.*, XLIII (1949), 1179–1189.

of organization that recognizes the appropriate functions of each and thus brings them into harmonious co-operation. It is by no means certain that we now have that type of organization.

Congressional investigations. A special method, but again a hit or miss one, by which Congress seeks to maintain a degree of control over administration is that of investigation. This power is not one specified by the Constitution, but it is an indispensable part of the power to legislate. Consequently, investigations of any office or subject may be made, provided the investigation has some relation to possible legislation. Congress has resorted to sporadic but frequent investigations of official conduct. These investigations are more often undertaken by the Senate than by the House, for, as Professor Rogers points out, party control is so strong in the House that the leaders of the majority, if they are of the President's party, will usually prevent a proposal for an important investigation from coming to a vote.[54]

Investigations are roundly condemned in many quarters as being launched for partisan, or even for personal, reasons; as interfering unduly with the executive departments; and as calculated to bring those departments and their officers into disrepute, or even disgrace. These criticisms are by no means groundless, and they are often made in good faith. But some individuals oppose investigations because they happen to approve of what is being done by the departments under fire; others, because they have good reasons to fear that investigation may disclose some very nasty conditions, not only in the public service, but also in certain private business closely connected with it; still others, because they believe "everything is all right" and do not see why we should not live in a permanent state of political tranquillity. Admitting the abuses of investigations, few informed persons denounce them as unmitigated evils. Since the people's representatives have so few effective means for finding out what the departments are doing, one would be rash indeed to propose that the investigating practice be abandoned. These congressional inquiries have frequently produced salutary results of a temporary, if not of a permanent, nature. The Senate investigations of the oil and other scandals in 1924 resulted in the retirement of three Cabinet officers, several indictments, and a few convictions.[55] Of particular significance also were

[54] *Op. cit.,* p. 202. The New Deal was not, however, after Roosevelt's first term, able to hold such control over Democrats in the House. If it had been, the Dies (un-American Activities) Committee would never have been created, certainly not continued.

[55] Congressional investigations are often for other purposes than checking up on the administrative departments. One need only recall the various investigations of lobbying, banking, campaign expenditures, public utilities, munitions makers, etc. Such investigations are, broadly speaking, for legislative purposes. Occasionally they are for "political" purposes. When former Congressmen Dies and Thomas were chairmen, the Committee on un-American Activities, although not constituted primarily to investigate administration agencies, did do so,

the investigations of several committees on matters relating to war production (resulting in several prison sentences) and to the conduct of the Second World War. In 1949 the House Un-American Activities Committee (a standing committee) made public the sworn statement of Whittaker Chambers that he had received from Alger Hiss, a trusted member of the State Department, for delivery to a Russian agent, "restricted" State Department documents. This and other evidence led to the conviction of Hiss in a federal district court, a conviction that at this writing is being appealed.

THE REORGANIZATION ACT AND INVESTIGATING COMMITTEES. One of the purposes of the Reorganization Act was to bring the standing committee into its own, to give it a means of overseeing administration, as indicated above. Such a plan could be expected to result in the transfer of investigations, or most of them, to the standing committees. This aim has been accomplished in part. Of the twenty-six investigations authorized by the Senate in 1947, twenty-four were conducted by standing committees. Of twenty-seven authorized by the House, twenty-three were conducted by standing committees.[56] Following this pattern, the Senate in 1950, referred Senator Joseph R. McCarthy's broadside of charges of communist infiltration in the State Department to a subcommittee of the (standing) Foreign Relations Committee.

VIII. EFFORTS TO IMPROVE CONGRESS [57]

What is the matter with Congress? Congress is frequently criticized and ridiculed by the press and by individuals, from leading industrialists and publicists down to the keepers of the smallest shops and the possessors of the dullest wits. The reasons for the criticism of Congress are many; some are justifiable and some are not. The economic and social interests of the country are complex and diverse. Congress offends one group and pleases another by passing or failing to pass a piece of legislation. By its

---

probably for "political" purposes. For a brief but penetrating article, see Robert K. Carr, "How to Improve Congressional Inquiries," *New York Times Magazine,* Aug. 29, 1948, p. 5. For an abuse in investigations, see Louis Welborn, "The Ordeal of Dr. Condon," *Harper's,* Jan., 1950, pp. 46–53.

[56] Thomas, *op. cit.,* p. 1182.

[57] J. M. Burns, *Congress on Trial* (1949); Galloway, *op. cit.;* Robert Heller, *Strengthening the Congress,* National Planning Association (1945); Joseph P. Harris, "The Reorganization of Congress," *Public Administration Review,* VI, 267 (Summer, 1946); Estes Kefauver and Jack Levin, *A Twentieth-Century Congress* (1947); *Legislative Reorganization Act of 1946,* Senate Report No. 1400 (to accompany S. 2177), 79th Cong., 2nd Session; *Organization of the Congress: Report of the Joint Committee on the Organization of Congress,* Senate Report No. 1011, 79th Cong., 2nd Session; *The Reorganization of Congress, A Report of the Committee on Congress of the American Political Science Association,* Public Affairs Press (1945); Elbert D. Thomas, "How Congress Functions under Its Reorganization Act," *Am. Pol. Sci. Rev.,* XLIII (1949), 1179–1189.

next action or nonaction it may offend the group that was pleased by its disposition of the previous issue, and please the group that was offended. When Congress has finished a session, each interest can probably find something in the list of enactments that represents a favor or concession to it; but it will be almost certain to feel that other matters dear to its heart have been passed over or lightly considered. Such is human nature that the failure of Congress to take care of a group's interest in one case will be remembered, whereas its consideration for such interest in another will be forgotten. Congress receives criticism, not only because it must of necessity disappoint many powerful interests, but also because the public does not understand the immensity of the task that confronts Congress and the conditions under which it must work. Furthermore, the public is much more likely to notice the antics and clowning of congressmen than it is to observe their statesmanship. This unfortunate tendency is perhaps explained by the fact that the bulk of the hard work of Congress is done in committee (this is particularly true of the House) and not on the floors.

REPORT OF THE POLITICAL SCIENTISTS. In 1941 Professor Frederic A. Ogg, then President of the American Political Science Association, appointed a committee of scholars to study the problem of congressional organization and procedure and to report on the same. In 1945 the committee made its final report. In the opinion of the committee Congress was handicapped as follows: [58]

1. By being overburdened with local and private matters [of constituents] which diverts its attention from national policy making. [It is estimated that 80 per cent of a congressman's time is devoted to nonlegislative work. He has been characterized as "Uncle Sam's bellboy," running hither and yon on a wide variety of errands for his constituents. Such activities are considered by all too many congressmen as their bread and butter.]

2. By the lack of adequate, independent, technical advice necessary for wise law-making. . . .

3. By too many committees with overlapping jurisdictions. . . .

4. By inadequately developed channels of communication with the Executive, making team-work between them difficult.

5. By the lack of adequate facilities for the continuous inspection and review of administrative action.

6. By the importunities of special-interest groups [the lobbies]. . . .

7. By the need of a redistribution of power, especially in the House of Representatives.

8. By the inadequate compensation of its personnel.

To remove these handicaps the committee recommended, among other things:

[58] *The Reorganization of Congress, op. cit.,* pp. 78–80.

1. That Congress divest itself . . . of such work and activities as it can appropriately delegate to other agencies, such as the government of the District of Columbia, the settlement of private claims and pensions, and other private and local legislation. . . .

2. That the committees of Congress be adequately equipped with independent, qualified experts to aid them in making laws. . . .

3. That the appropriations to the Legislative Reference Service and to the Office of Legislative Counsel be substantially increased. . . .

4. That the committee systems of both chambers be simplified by (a) eliminating the inactive committees; (b) consolidating those with overlapping jurisdictions; (c) creating twin committees organized functionally in both houses; and (d) correlating them with major areas of public policy and administration.

5. That a Legislative Council be established, to be composed of the Vice President, the Speaker of the House, the majority leaders in both chambers, and the chairmen of the reorganized standing committees (sitting separately in each house); and that it be the duty of this Legislative Council to plan and coordinate the legislative program of Congress and to promote more effective liaison and cooperation with the Executive.

6. That the reorganized standing committees also be utilized as vehicles of communication and collaboration between Congress and the corresponding administrative agencies within their respective jurisdictions; and that the heads of the major departments and administrative agencies appoint Congressional Secretaries who shall devote full time to liaison with their corresponding committees in Congress.

7. That the function of legislative oversight of administrative performance be entrusted by Congress primarily to the subcommittees of the House Committee on Appropriations. The subcommittees should hold informal, open hearings at regular intervals, at which the heads of their corresponding administrative services should respond to questions . . . under rules of orderly procedure prescribed by Congress, and discuss the agency's problems and policies with the committee. . . .

8. That all groups, representatives of which appear before congressional committees, should register and make full disclosure of their membership, finances, etc.

9. That [some plan of rotation or other limitations on tenure for committee chairmen be established]; and that committee chairmen be required by the standing rules to (a) call committee meetings when desired by a majority of the members; (b) report bills within ten days after the committee has taken favorable action, failing which report, any member of the committee could report the bill; and (c) keep a complete public record of all committee proceedings except executive sessions.

10. That the annual salaries of Senators and Representatives be increased to $15,000; . . . [and that members of Congress be made eligible for annuities after long service].

The Legislative Reorganization Act of 1946. In the meantime other organizations were active in "investigations" of and recommendations for Congress. Not the least of these was a committee of the Congress itself, the Joint Committee on the Organization of Congress, Senator La Follette, Chairman. This committee brought in its bill in the spring of 1946, and, somewhat to the surprise of many observers, a substantial part of it was enacted into law. The Legislative Reorganization Act of 1946 contains provisions to carry out a number of the recommendations listed above. Its provisions relative to salaries, annuities, committee reorganization, private bills, the lobby (the Federal Regulation of Lobbying Act is Title III of the Reorganization Act), and committee staffs have been referred to at appropriate points in the preceding chapters. Other significant provisions of the act strengthen the Legislative Reference Service and the Office of the Legislative Counsel, authorize administrative and judicial settlement of tort claims (thus relieving Congress of this function) against the United States, and direct the revenue and appropriations committees of the two houses to give special consideration to general fiscal policy. (The two last-mentioned provisions will be discussed in Chapter 17, section II, and Chapter 22, section III, respectively.)

The reorganization proposed is probably desirable as far as it goes, but some major problems are left untouched, or practically so. Perhaps the essential task remaining is that of establishing a working relationship between the President and Congress, a meshing of the gears of the White House and Capitol, and, above all, that of elaborating the limits to which Congress should go in its oversight of administration. Other significant omissions in the Reorganization Act include the following: the selection of committee chairmen by some better method than seniority; limitations on the powers of the Committee on Rules of the House of Representatives; and abolishing or restricting the Senate filibuster. These and certain other matters not touched by the act remain to be dealt with, and some provisions of the act, such as those relating to the oversight of administration, should be reconsidered.

A standard for a Congressman. A general suggestion for the improvement of Congress may be in order. Perhaps it is too broad to be useful, too idealistic to be attainable. The suggestion is not that congressmen cease being politicians, but rather that they try a new brand of politics; that they make the national interest, by deeds as well as by words, their political program; that they go before their constituents explaining their stand on national issues with vigor and clarity and, on occasion, with a cheerful note of defiance. The average decent voter would respond favorably to a representative or senator who puts the interest of his country above that of his state or district. Voters with special interests and claims would not, but they are seldom in the majority; besides, some of them would be big enough to support a courageous man who might be against what they conceive to be their interests.

There have been, and are, men in Congress who have followed substantially the plan here suggested, and the percentage of them who have died while still in their seats or voluntarily retired is quite as high as that of the district-serving, errand-boy congressmen. The fact is that the typical member of Congress has assumed for so long that the only way to hold his place is by pandering to his district that he does not notice how many members who follow that course are repudiated by the voters, or that the few members who stand on national issues have, with an encouraging degree of frequency, experienced renewals of the voters' confidence.[59]

For reading list, see references at the end of Chapter 14.

Questions and Problems

1. Under what circumstances are administration measures most likely to win the favor of Congress?
2. Outline the stages of committee consideration of a bill.
3. Is there any good reason why the House should not adhere to the "regular order" in the consideration of measures?
4. How do you explain the Senate's reluctance to curb the filibuster?
5. Has this statement any validity? *The conference committee often plays a more significant part in legislation than either house of Congress.*
6. Write a 200-word essay on the lobby, giving particular emphasis to means by which it might be regulated.
7. What boundary should Congress set itself in the control of administration?
8. Indicate the proper limits of congressional investigations.
9. Evaluate the Legislative Reorganization Act of 1946.

[59] The defeat of Senator La Follette, who guided the Legislative Reorganization Act of 1946 through the Senate, does not lead me to modify the above statement. His defeat was due to a number of special factors. Again, in 1950 Senator Frank P. Graham was defeated in North Carolina primarily because of his work with the President's Committee on Civil Rights, an assignment he undertook and completed before he went to the Senate. My "rule" that statesmanship pays better than district politics is not discarded even though there are occasional exceptions to it.

☆ 16 ☆

State Legislatures and the Legislative Process

I N keeping with the plan of organization of this volume, we follow
the chapters on Congress with one on the state legislature. In a
number of states the Initiative and Referendum are firmly established
as supplements to the legislature, a fact which requires that these twin
instruments of democracy also be given more than passing mention in this
chapter.

The legislature is the organ of government that, within constitutional
limits, must make the decisions on what the state shall do and on where
the money is to come from. The governor recommends and advises, and
he may use the veto as a brake; pressure groups of every shade and description may play upon the legislature in a thousand ways; but the responsibility, the decision, is with the legislature. Its position is basic and
fundamental in democratic government. And in consequence its structure, organization, procedure, powers, and limitations demand careful
study.

I. LEGISLATIVE STRUCTURE, SESSIONS, AND PERSONNEL [1]

The bicameral system: POPULAR ACCEPTANCE. Nebraska is the only state
without a bicameral legislature. If an individual who is not a student
of politics thinks of the system at all, he thinks of it about as he does of a

[1] *The Annals of the Am. Acad. of Pol. and Soc. Sci.,* CVC (January, 1938), various articles
on state legislatures by leading authorities; *The Book of the States, 1948–1949,* pp. 101–114,
many facts and figures on state legislatures; F. G. Bates, O. P. Field, and Others, *State
Government* (1949 ed.), Ch. 8; W. F. Dodd, *State Government* (1928 ed.), Ch. VI; W. B.
Graves, *American State Government* (1946 ed.), Ch. VI; A. N. Holcombe, *State Government*

law of nature. It simply must be so. If one asks why there must be two chambers, the typical citizen probably regards him with mingled contempt and suspicion, and then speaks with that strong emphasis which comes from assurance: "Why, one house serves as a check upon the other. Either house might hastily pass some villainous bill; the other house will probably give the measure more consideration, defeat it, and that will be one more bad law that we won't have to bother with." If the inquirer is not made ashamed of his "ignorance" by this reply he might ask: "Why, then, should we not have three houses, or four? Certainly we have plenty of bad laws passed by the two houses. Maybe four houses, with all the checks they would provide, would succeed in checking out practically all the unwise bills." At this point the "informer" might become a bit irritated and say that every fool knows that there should be two houses, and just two; that they probably check each other as much as is desirable; that, in any case, the men who wrote the state constitution knew what they were doing when they gave the legislature an "upper" and a "lower" house, following the plan adopted by the Philadelphia Convention for Congress. At the mention of the fact that the states have the legislative system which the enlightened patriots in 1787 deemed sufficient for the needs of the national government, the inquirer is probably silenced. We, however, have the duty of pushing the inquiry a little farther.

REASONS FOR ITS ADOPTION. The student knows, of course, that most of the colonies employed the bicameral legislative system, patterned after the two Houses, Lords and Commons, of the British Parliament. Following the British and colonial models, nearly all the state governments organized during the Revolution adopted the dual plan. In some of the states the rank and file of citizens elected the members of the lower house, and the propertied classes elected the upper house. This distinction was never made in other states, and the states that adopted the plan soon gave it up and allowed the same electors to choose members of both branches of the legislature. Not only that, but, with a few exceptions, population came to be accepted as the basis of representation in the upper as well as in the lower house. There was, then, no essential difference between the two houses; and the main excuse for the two was that one would check the other, or, to put it affirmatively, that bills would be more carefully considered by two houses than by one.

The framers of the federal Constitution prescribed the bicameral system for the national government not only because past practice in Great Britain and America stamped it with approval, but also because it made possible

---

in the United States (1931 ed.), pp. 282–291; A. F. Macdonald, *American State Government and Administration* (1950 ed.), Ch. VIII; J. M. Mathews, *American State Government* (1934 ed.), Ch. X; John A. Perkins, "State Legislative Reorganization," *Am. Pol. Sci. Rev.*, XL, 510 (June, 1946); Harvey Walker, *The Legislative Process* (1948), Ch. VIII.

the great compromise on representation—representation in the House of Representatives according to population, and in the Senate an equal representation of the states. The states were strongly influenced by the federal system, and those that started with the unicameral type of legislature abandoned it for the bicameral plan.[2] With only one dissenter, the states continue with the dual type of legislature. Yet it has been discovered in recent years that ideas can be changed rather quickly, and other states may try the Nebraska experiment.

Do the houses check each other? Some studies[3] have been made of the working of the bicameral principle, and these do not show that the two houses effectively check each other, except perhaps in a few states. True, a number of bills passed by one house are killed in the other; but the killing is usually indiscriminate. True, also, one house amends many bills originating in the other; but, here again, the amending may be good, bad, or indifferent. Consideration by two houses often means only two hasty considerations, or simply a hasty consideration in the house in which a bill originates and the acceptance of its conclusions by the second house without any consideration.

It is further charged that the bicameral plan enables party leaders or the "organizations" to control legislatures in an irresponsible manner. Here is an example. The public seems to want enacted a law that the leaders secretly oppose. The leaders have a different bill introduced and passed in each house. Then a conference committee, under the control of the leaders, of course, goes through the form of attempting to agree upon a measure acceptable to both houses. By previous arrangement the conference committee fails to agree, and no law is enacted. Nevertheless, by this subterfuge, both houses go on record as approving a measure that the leaders deftly beheaded.[4] It would seem, then, that the bicameral system not only frequently fails to insure adequate consideration of bills and to accomplish the defeat of unwise ones, but also that it may be used as a means of dodging responsibility.[5]

More effective checks. After all, whether or not the houses check each other is not a very material point, for legislation is checked by a number of other means that we deem quite sufficient. The committees of each house, although far from perfect, do a great deal to improve the quality

[2] Georgia (1789), Pennsylvania (1790), and Vermont (1836). *See* D. B. Carroll, *The Unicameral Legislature of Vermont* (1933), and I. A. Watts, "Why Pennsylvania Abandoned Unicameralism," *State Government,* March, 1936, pp. 54–55.

[3] D. L. Colvin, *Bicameral Principle in the New York Legislature* (1913); Thelma I. Griswold, *Bicameralism in Ohio* (1937); Dorothy Schaffter, *The Bicameral System in Practice* (1929).

[4] Holcombe, *op. cit.,* p. 307.

[5] The typical member of the legislature usually stresses the value of the "checks" under the bicameral system, but several members have frankly told me that they need protection—the privilege of dodging responsibility.

of legislation by their preliminary studies of the bills introduced. The governor's veto, discussed in the preceding chapter, often proves to be an effective guaranty against faulty legislation. Then, we must not forget the courts with their power to nullify unconstitutional acts. In particular, we must remember that the federal courts will void state laws that violate such important provisions of the federal Constitution as the clause that prohibits the states from passing laws depriving any person of life, liberty, or property without due process of law, and the clause that prohibits the states from impairing the obligation of contracts. Considering that legislatures are held in check by these agencies, it hardly seems desirable that the bicameral check, usually fictional, seldom a positive good, and on occasion mischievous, should be retained.

The case for a unicameral legislature. With the foregoing considerations in mind it is not surprising that many students of government advocate a unicameral system for the states.[6] They argue that this system will expedite the business of the legislature; prevent the leaders from dodging responsibility; and, by reducing the number of legislators, enable states to pay adequate salaries to those remaining. They point out, further, that the single chamber has given satisfactory results in several Canadian provinces, in Swiss cantons, and in other countries. Advocates of the single chamber make a strong argument for it when they show that the cities have long since abandoned the bicameral council in favor of the single-chamber council.

The Nebraska experiment. A generation ago attempts were made in several states to secure the adoption of the unicameral plan. Constitutional amendments were submitted in Oregon (1912 and 1914), Oklahoma (1914), and Arizona (1916); but they were defeated in each case. In 1913 Governor Hodges of Kansas proposed a single chamber, to be composed of less than a score of members, who should be experts in legislation and give their full time to affairs of state. His novel and interesting proposal was not submitted to the voters.[7]

Despite the fact that ten states gave thought to the unicameral idea between 1910 and 1934, Nebraska is the only state that adopted it. The proposal was brought forward in that commonwealth from time to time for twenty years and there is little doubt that it would have remained in the proposal state for another twenty years had not Nebraska's elder statesman, the late Senator George W. Norris, in 1933 and 1934, actively sponsored the unicameral plan. Opposed by practically every newspaper of the state as "radical," "revolutionary," and "dangerous," the constitutional amendment was adopted by the voters in November, 1934—a proof of the Senator's

---

[6] See, "A Model State Constitution" (1948 ed.), Art. III.

[7] Carrol, *op. cit.*, pp. 4 ff.

influence with his constituents.[8] The amendment provides for a chamber of not less than thirty nor more than fifty members, and the legislature fixed the number at forty-three, to be chosen on a nonpartisan ballot. The plan went into operation with the legislative session of 1937. A critical evaluation of it must be deferred for some years, but Nebraskans were encouraged to note the high type of representatives elected under the new system and pleased with the record they have established.[9] Since 1934 the unicameral plan has been an issue in a score or more states.

The size of the chambers. The number of state senators and representatives is rather rigidly fixed by the constitutions in some states, but in the greater number of states the constitutions simply impose general limitations and leave the legislatures to determine the exact number. Senates vary in size from 17 in Delaware and Nevada to 67 in Minnesota, with less than half the states having as many as 40. The lower houses are considerably larger than the senates, varying in size from 35 in Delaware to 399 in New Hampshire, but the number is usually somewhere between 100 and 150. Nearly all the large lower houses are in the New England states, because the system of town representation, still in use there, necessitates a large number of representatives. It is generally agreed among authorities that the size of both the senate and the house is, in most states, larger than necessary.

The basis of apportionment. For purposes of representation the typical state is divided into two sets of districts—one set for members of the lower house, and the other for the upper house. The counties serve as convenient units for representation in the lower house in most of the states, except in New England, where the town is the unit. Counties usually have representatives in proportion to their population, but the general rule is that a county shall have at least one representative. Except in Maine and Massachusetts, the New England system of town representation pays scant attention to population, particularly in Vermont and Connecticut, the former state giving every town, regardless of size, one, and only one, representative, the latter allowing large towns a maximum of two representatives. Apportionment in the senate is usually on the basis of the population of the counties, although some of the New England states use the town as the unit, practically disregarding the difference in population. Small or sparsely settled counties may be combined to form a senate district, and densely populated counties may be divided into several districts. A few states make use of the same districts for senators and rep-

[8] J. P. Senning, "Nebraska Provides for a One-House Legislature," *Am. Pol. Sci. Rev.* (1935), XXIX, 69–74.

[9] Senning, "Nebraska's First Unicameral Sessions," *Annals of the Am. Acad. of Pol. and Soc. Sci.,* CVC, 159 (January, 1938), and "Unicameralism Passes Test," *National Municipal Review,* XXXIII, 60 (February, 1944).

resentatives. Under this plan Illinois elects one senator and three representatives from each of 51 districts.

DISCRIMINATION AGAINST CITIES. As already intimated, there are exceptions to the general rule that localities are represented in the legislature
according to population. Inequalities, sometimes amounting to gross discriminations, occur principally in those states that have large urban populations. Many authorities have discussed this problem, but this paragraph
is based upon an article by Professor David O. Walter.[10] In more than a
majority of the states the constitutions favor the rural areas in the matter
of legislative apportionment. In twenty of these states the composition of
the senate favors the less populous areas, and in twenty-seven the rural
communities are given the advantage in the lower houses. Furthermore,
legislatures, dominated by representatives from the "cow counties," often
fail to carry out the clear mandate of the constitutions to reapportion seats.
The Illinois legislature, which has not made a reapportionment since 1901,
is only one of the worst examples of this. In at least two dozen other
states the legislatures have similarly failed to carry out the requirements
of the constitutions.

The courts are powerless to correct this situation because reapportionment is a political question—one over which the courts have no jurisdiction. A member of the Texas legislature, George O. Nokes, Jr., calls attention to the fact that California, Missouri, and South Dakota secure reapportionment through a commission, should the legislature fail to act; that
boards of apportionment do the work in Arkansas and Ohio, and that in
Maine reapportionment is automatic, the population classification being
set up in the constitution.[11] But in many states the "rotten borough"
system, the scheme under which sparsely populated areas are overrepresented at the expense of the metropolitan communities, continues to
flourish. Constitutional provisions relating to senates discriminate against
Atlanta, Baltimore, Los Angeles, Providence, and other cities, and the unconstitutional failure of legislatures to do their duty add to the list Chicago,
Detroit, and other urban centers. In perhaps as many as twenty states
urban populations have only about two thirds the representation to which
their population entitles them.

Reasons for discrimination. Originally, the states were predominantly
rural and equal numbers of representatives from counties or towns, resulted in few gross disproportions. With the growth of cities, however,
"equal" representation produced the inequalities noted above. In most
states concessions were made to the urban areas by increasing their number of lawmakers, but the increase was seldom in proportion to population.

---

[10] "Reapportionment and Urban Representation," *Annals of the Am. Acad. of Pol. and
Soc. Sci.*, CVC, 11 (January, 1938). See also R. L. Neuberger, "Farmers in the Saddle,"
New Republic, Oct. 2, 1950, pp. 13–14.

[11] "Constitution and Legislature in Texas," *State Government*, July, 1948, pp. 150–151.

Delegates in legislatures and constitutional conventions, regarding cities as full of irresponsible nonproperty owners, foreigners, and radicals, or even as cesspools of iniquity, and likely to disturb the political and social order if given the power to do so, used their original advantage of numbers and voted against making fair concessions to the urban dwellers. A statesman so broad of mind as Jefferson had the gravest misgivings when he contemplated the untoward political and social damages that might be wrought by urban electorates. Discrimination continues not only because many "good" people see it as a means of curbing excesses for which large representations from cities might be responsible, but also because it is to the economic and political advantage of those who have control under the present system to continue it.

Some results of discrimination. Rural populations and their representatives, despite certain populistic tendencies, are essentially conservative on the great problems of the day; certainly more so than city people. Legislative apportionment favoring rural areas thus means that conservatism has more than its share of representation in the legislature. Whether or not this is a "good thing" depends upon one's point of view; but it is suggested that we assume a great deal when we say that a farmer and his hired man (two voters) are entitled to a voice in government equal to that of a banker, a clerk, and a factory laborer (three voters).

Another consequence of this discrimination is that a number of states may find themselves with Republican legislatures and Democratic governors, the reason being that overrepresented rural districts (outside of the South) are predominantly Republican, whereas the under-represented cities are more often Democratic. It is true that legislatures and governors of opposite political parties have, on occasion, established working relationships, but if they are of the same political persuasion "the going" is usually smoother. Still another point of significance should be mentioned. It is unfortunate that rural members of a legislature who understand nothing of the problems of municipal transportation, police, and similar complicated subjects have such a large voice in determining what shall be done about them. And it is as ridiculous as unfortunate that rural legislators should decree that there shall be no sports on Sunday, no Sunday movies, or no selling of cigarettes on any day of the week.

SHOULD REPRESENTATION BE DETERMINED ENTIRELY BY POPULATION? Despite the generally accepted principle that representation should be based on population, many students and public men argue for a modified plan. They say that there is more to be represented than numbers; that the various interests of the state should be represented as well; and that the interests of the rural sections will suffer if large cities containing over half the population of a commonwealth are given representation in that proportion in both houses of the legislature. A plan that gives such proportion in one house and limits representation in the other seems to meet with considerable favor. The criticisms made above, referring to the grosser inequalities and discriminations, are not intended to be inconsistent with a plan of representation that would contain some restrictions on urban representation in one branch of the legislature.

Do legislatures represent? It is often said that, broadly speaking, legislatures are fairly representative of the larger economic and social groups. Although few of the lawmakers carry union cards or have other direct affiliations with labor, it is stated that other voices are frequently raised on behalf of labor. There is no doubt that business and agriculture are directly and well represented in the legislature; it is certain that labor, both industrial and agricultural, and some other economic and professional groups are not directly represented in proportion to their numbers in the population, and it is debatable whether they are adequately represented by legislators who have their life among other interests and organizations. In any event, it may be argued that legislatures as now constituted are not truly representative of the many interests of the whole population of a state. This deficiency in representation is explained in part by the fact that legislators are commonly chosen by single-member districts. It is, of course, impossible for more than one to be chosen from such a district, and this means that those of the minority party, even though they may number just a few less than the majority, go unrepresented as far as that particular district is concerned. Where there are three parties in a district, it is possible for a candidate to win who has only thirty-four per cent of the votes, thus leaving sixty-six per cent of the voters unrepresented.

PROPORTIONAL REPRESENTATION. In order to give the parties fair quotas of the representatives, plans of proportional representation have been proposed. In one form or another, "P.R." is now employed in a number of European countries and in a few American cities. Without going into technicalities,[12] we will simply say here that, if applied to the election of members of the lower house of a state legislature, it would mean that our single-member districts would give way to large districts, each sending some half a dozen members to the lower house. The votes would be cast and counted in such a way that parties or groups which cast one third of the votes in the district would elect one third of the representatives, and other parties or groups would in like manner receive their fair proportion of the representatives. Of course, it would never give the parties representation in strict mathematical proportion to their voting strength, but proportions would be approximately fair—much fairer than under our present system.

---

[12] There are a number of books and articles that fully set forth the details. C. G. Hoag and G. H. Hallett, Jr., *Proportional Representation* (1926), covers the field thoroughly. Articles and items on P.R. appear regularly in the *National Municipal Review* (monthly).

Objection to P.R.   Nevertheless, the principle of proportional representation does not meet with any particular enthusiasm in this country. It is argued that, by giving smaller third parties an opportunity to elect their candidates to office, our two-party system, in which we take so much pride and in which we place so much reliance, will be disrupted. With this development, it is feared that frequently no party would have a majority in the lawmaking body, and that we would have to resort to a "bloc" system of government, the working of which in Continental European countries has not favorably impressed us. It is said further that, as between the two major parties, the present system works out with reasonable fairness in the long run; that disproportions favoring a party in one district are equalized by disproportions favoring the other party in another district. This comforting conclusion, however, is not warranted. A party with a majority will almost invariably win more than its fair quota of seats under the present arrangement. Although admitting this to be true, the advocate of party government will nevertheless say that the majority party needs this extra "unearned" majority in order to carry out its program. Even though we concede that there are certain very clear, if somewhat theoretical, advantages on the side of proportional representation, the exigencies of practical politics relegate it to the background. After all, it can hardly be said that the unfair representation of parties in legislative bodies constitutes a major problem in state government.

Legislative sessions.   Nearly all the states are now content with biennial sessions, but New York and five others hold annual sessions. In about three fourths of the states the legislatures convene in regular session in January of the odd year. The time they may remain in session is stipulated in the constitutions of approximately half the states. Sixty days is the limit fixed in the majority of these states. Sometimes, because of the mass of business to be dispatched on the last few days, the clocks are stopped or are officially ignored until the work has been finished.

SPLIT SESSIONS.   California and several other states have tried the experiment of split sessions. By the California plan, the legislature meets for not more than thirty days for the purpose of the introduction of bills and the disposition of certain preliminary matters. Then it must take a recess for not less than thirty days, the assumption being that during this period the members will mingle with their constituents and learn their will on pending legislation. When the legislature reassembles, no new bills may be introduced in either house without the consent of three fourths of the members thereof, and no member may introduce more than two bills. Although the California split sessions have not convincingly demonstrated their utility, in 1940 New Mexico adopted a similar plan.

In states that place no constitutional limit upon the length of sessions, a device known as the "adjourned" session, or recess, is sometimes resorted

to. Thus, some years ago, the Ohio legislature, with a Republican majority, adjourned several times for long periods, in order to prevent a Democratic governor from appointing men of his own party to administrative
offices held by Republicans whose terms had expired.[13] This action, of
course, represented a perversion of the idea of the adjourned session.

SPECIAL SESSIONS. Special sessions of the legislature may be called by the
governor in practically every state, and in a few states the members of
the legislature may demand a special session. More than half the states
limit the legislature as to the matters it may consider in a special session,
the common limitation being that no topics other than those proposed by
the governor shall be considered. Such sessions have not been common
except in the "depression" years of 1930–1940.

On several occasions governors have been impeached at sessions they
themselves have called. Fearing a hostile legislature, Governor Bilbo of
Mississippi (1931) refused to call a much-needed special session unless the
majority of the legislators would sign a pledge not to institute impeachment proceedings against him or other executive officers. Scorning the
pledge as dishonorable, four leaders of the legislature called an *unofficial*
session in the expectation that the governor would feel the necessity of
legalizing it by issuing a pre-dated call. The governor's reply was that only
a fool would travel to the state capital at his own expense, and he requested
the lawmakers to calculate the cost of such a trip and mail him a check,
which he would use to complete the Juniper Grove Baptist Church. "In
this way," said he, "you'll help the Lord instead of the Big Four to play
politics." [14] This comic opera proceeding is reported not only because it
illustrates one of the problems of the special session, but also because it
serves as an example of those unfortunate and all-too-frequent occurrences
that bring ridicule and contempt upon state governments and officers.

Terms, qualifications, compensation, and immunities of legislators.
Thirty-three states fix the terms of senators at four years; other states at
two years. In the lower house the term is two years in forty-three states,
and four years in four states. Nebraska elects her single chamber biennially.

Senators and representatives must meet the state constitutional requirements of citizenship in the United States, residence in the districts they
represent, and age. These requirements are of no particular importance,
for, regardless of whether or not they are fixed by a constitution, few candidates could hope to be elected who lacked such qualifications.

Compensation of state lawmakers is notoriously low. The amount is
fixed in many state constitutions, and it has been found very difficult to
secure the approval of amendments granting increases or granting the

13 Dodd, *op. cit.*, pp. 166, 168.
14 *Time*, May 4, 1931, p. 14.

legislature the authority to make highly desirable adjustments.[15] Ten dollars a day for the period of the session is, perhaps, not far below the average compensation, and it is grossly inadequate. In most states the only expense money allowed the members is for transportation to and from the capital. A few states provide a maintenance allowance while the legislature is in session.

Just as congressmen do, state senators and representatives enjoy immunity from arrest while in attendance at sessions and in going to or coming from the same, except in case of treason, felony, or breach of the peace. Again, as with their national prototypes, they are accorded freedom of speech and debate in their respective houses.

Personnel of legislatures. The composition of the typical state legislature bears a strong similarity to the personnel of Congress. Many lawyers are present, often relatively young lawyers who experience no particular difficulty in getting away from their few clients for the session and who lose no large volume of income in so doing. In fact, experience in the legislature may improve the professional status of the young attorneys and bring them more clients and larger fees. Next to the lawyers, the farmers, many of them well along in life, have the largest delegations. Then there are merchants, manufacturers, bankers, clerks, real estate men, salesmen, professional politicians, demagogues, and political "accidents." They are all there—the able, the mediocre, the selfless, the selfish, the incorruptible, and the men who have a price. In their qualifications for their duties they rise well above the general run of voters who sent them to the capitol, and their devotion to the public interest may in like manner exceed that of the electorate. The number of women serving in legislatures now varies from 125 to 150, numbers not sufficient to produce any marked changes in legislation, even if women's interests were markedly different from those of the men.

HIGH TURNOVER. The turnover in legislative personnel is very high, too high. It is often said that a member must serve in three sessions before he can hope to become effective. Professor Charles S. Hyneman has made studies of the turnover in a number of states, and his figures show that in only one fifth of the chambers studied are there majorities who have served for three sessions. In one third of the chambers he found that less than one fourth of the membership had served as many as three sessions.[16] It may be that the three-sessions test is too high, but the figures do reveal a constant and strong flow of experienced members from the legislative

[15] Five times the people of Kansas defeated a proposed amendment to increase the three-dollar-per-day allowance. A member of the legislature once facetiously proposed that a log cabin dormitory be erected on the capital grounds for the convenience of the lawmakers; that the cabin be equipped with wooden bunks; and that fresh, clean straw be supplied from time to time. Eventually, in 1948, the people approved an increase in compensation.

[16] "Tenure and Turnover of Legislative Personnel," *Annals*, CVC, 21 (January, 1938).

halls that does not augur well for any improvement in the legislative process. Yet it is encouraging to note the regularity with which certain mature members (admittedly the number is far too small) with no particular axe to grind are regularly re-elected. Practically every college student can name legislators in his own state who serve unselfishly and ably, term after term.

II. LEGISLATIVE ORGANIZATION AND PROCEDURE [17]

The speaker. The lower house in every state is presided over by a speaker. Theoretically he is chosen by the members, but actually by the caucus of the majority party—the caucus, in turn, being controlled by a few leading members of the party or even by a party boss who may not have a seat in the legislature. Occasionally the leaders of the two parties reach an understanding concerning the speakership, and in such cases the presiding officer is somewhat limited as to the extent to which he may use his office for the advantage of his own party.

In the typical state the speaker is more powerful than his counterpart in the national House of Representatives. Professor Holcombe summarizes his powers as follows: [18] the power to recognize (and, of course, to refuse to recognize) members who wish to be heard on the floor; to make rulings on points of order, subject to an appeal to the whole body of members—which appeal is usually ineffective, owing to the fact that the majority ordinarily sustains the speaker; to appoint committees—through which power he rewards and disciplines members, and largely determines the character of party leadership in the house; to refer measures to committees—a power that often enables him to determine the fate of important bills; to control the committee on rules—a power that does not exist in all legislatures, and that is important only in those in which the rules committee is a highly privileged one. In controlling the house, the speaker relies very heavily upon the majority floor leader, particularly for making the necessary motions and explanations at the proper moments to enable the party to manage the house.

The presiding officer of the senate. In about three fourths of the states there is a lieutenant governor whose duty it is to preside over the senate. He is elected by the people, and he may therefore belong to the minority party in the house over which he presides. Not being a member of the senate, he ordinarily has no vote except in case of a tie. As presiding

[17] *The Annals,* CVC (January, 1938); Bates, Field, and Others, *op. cit.,* Ch. 10; Dodd, *op. cit.,* pp. 178–190; Graves, *op. cit.,* Chs. VII, VIII; Holcombe, *op. cit.,* pp. 256–271; The Council of State Governments, *Our State Legislatures* (1948); Macdonald, *op. cit.,* Ch. IX; Mathews, *op. cit.,* pp. 249–280; Perkins, *op. cit.;* Walker, *op. cit.,* Chs. XI–XVII; C. I. Winslow, *State Legislative Committees* (1931).

[18] *Op. cit.,* pp. 294–296.

officer, his powers are similar to those of the speaker of the lower house, with the important exceptions that he usually has no power to appoint committees or to control the committee on rules. The majority party in the senate elects a president pro tempore, who presides in the absence of the lieutenant governor, and who, with other party leaders, exercises at all times the important political powers that fall to the speaker in the lower house. Under ordinary circumstances, therefore, the leading figure in the senate is not the lieutenant governor, but the president pro tempore, or some other majority party leader or leaders. In those states that have no lieutenant governor, it is, of course, the senate's privilege to elect its presiding officer, and in such states his powers are likely to be very similar to those of the speaker of the house of representatives.

Other legislative officers and employees. Each house elects a clerk, a sergeant-at-arms, a doorkeeper, a chaplain, and a postmaster. Numerous secretaries, stenographers, policemen, and pages are elected, or designated by leaders, and a few may even be selected by the rank and file of members as their part of the legislative "spoils." Frequently, legislatures have many more employees than they need, and their salaries and wages may run to exciting figures.

In 1944 a grand jury investigation in New York uncovered what was known about the State Capitol as the "wonderful lu-lu system." For years the men at Albany had voted sums of money (never a large sum at any one time) "in lieu of detailed, itemized expenditures." Some of this "lu-lu" went to certain members of the legislature, some to increase the compensation of regular employees of the legislature, and some went to individuals whose employment by the legislature was only fiction. One "employee" who had received a $1,000 "lu-lu" squirmed that he "didn't do much of anything for the state." Another whose "lu-lu" take ran to the same figure sweated but could not "recall doing a single thing for that money." This "lu-lu" sounds less like peanuts when it is totaled. In 1943 it cost the state $1,433,544.[19]

The committees. Each house of the legislature must have its committees in order to take care of the volume of work to be done. As noted above, committees of the lower house are commonly appointed by the speaker, after consultation with party leaders, or they may be agreed upon in the party caucus. The floor leader and other influential members of the minority party are usually allowed to designate their party's quota on the various committees. In the senate, committees may be chosen by the whole body upon the recommendations of the leaders of the majority party, or appointed by the president (who is commonly the lieutenant governor) or by the president pro tempore.

[19] John W. Lederle, "New York's Legislature under the Microscope," *Am. Pol. Sci. Rev.,* XL, 521 (June, 1946); and *Time,* December 18, 1944, p. 18.

Nearly all legislative bodies have more and larger committees than necessary. Thirty or more committees, with each member sitting on a half dozen or so, are not uncommon. There seem to be two reasons for this: first, members wish to increase their importance with their constituents by a chairmanship or two and by service on a number of committees; and, second, leaders find it easier to control legislation if the work is made complex by dividing it among many committees and subcommittees. Some committees seldom meet, because they have little or nothing to do; others are overworked and have difficulty in finding time for their necessary meetings.

JOINT COMMITTEES. In three or four states much use is made of joint committees—committees composed of members from both houses. Massachusetts, which has developed the joint committee system further than any other state, has about thirty such committees.[20] Under the regular committee system, each house has its own committees, which consider the bills and make their reports thereon; whereas the joint committee system requires consideration in committee only once, and the same reports are made to both houses. Furthermore, the separate committees frequently lead the houses into passing conflicting measures, but the joint committees have a decided tendency to hold them to a unified program. In further argument for the joint committee, it is often stated that the consideration such a committee gives a bill is much more complete and careful than the double consideration by a separate committee of each house. Despite these clear advantages of the joint committee system, other states appear to be in no hurry to adopt it.

The caucus. In the states the caucus is likely to function in the matter of determining the officers of the legislative bodies,[21] and it may have some influence in fixing the personnel of committees, for it is to the interest of the party to have control of the organization of the legislature. But the caucus has little to do with mapping out or pushing through a legislative program, legislation in the states being largely nonpartisan in character, and party lines being broken much more frequently and completely than in Congress. Party lines in state legislatures are usually artificial. The division in the legislatures is quite as likely to be "left wing" vs. "right wing" as it is to be Republican vs. Democrat. Sometimes the leaders of

---

[20] Luce, *Legislative Procedure*, p. 128; Graves, *op. cit.*, pp. 269–270.

[21] A very estimable lady with little knowledge of the ways of caucuses was elected to the lower house of a state legislature. Her party caucus endorsed by a very small majority a candidate for speaker who was not acceptable to her, and she had no intention of voting for him in the house. Before the vote was taken, however, she learned that the vote on the caucus nominee for speaker was an acid test of party allegiance. Quickly smothering her conscience and summoning her party loyalty, she voted for the nominee, who was easily elected speaker, since his party had a large majority. While the lady was hoping that nothing like this would happen again soon, the clerk appointed her on the committee to conduct the speaker-elect to the chair! Her lessons in practical politics were coming fast.

the two parties, ostensibly in opposition, reach an understanding, not only with regard to which measures shall be passed or defeated, but also in the matter of officers, committees, and employees. Such bipartisan combinations have produced some of the worst examples of corruption in state affairs.

The introduction of bills. Bills are introduced by individual members or by committees. The great majority of them are presented by individual members, and the overwhelming majority of these relate to some matter of interest only to the individual who introduces it, or to his constituency, or to a few voters in his constituency. Many such bills are introduced "by request," which notation on the bill indicates to the committee to which it is referred that the measure may be allowed to die in committee for all its ostensible sponsor cares. Important bills usually emanate from the powerful committees, and a number of these originate with the governor and are proposed by the committee as "administration measures."

In order to give the legislature opportunity to consider the measures before it, a time limit on the introduction of bills is fixed by the constitution or by legislative rules in some states. This limitation usually takes the form of prohibiting introductions after the legislature has been in session a specified number of days. It cannot be said that these provisions are particularly effective, for certain types of bills are ordinarily exempted from the prohibitions and others may usually be exempted with the consent of special majorities of the members.

Bills in committee. Upon the introduction of a bill, it receives its first reading, in most states, by title only. The bill is then referred to a committee, and the committee considers it or does not consider it, very much after the manner of a congressional committee. In about one third of the states all bills must be reported by the committees. But in the great majority of the states the committees may kill measures by failing to consider them or by not reporting them after consideration. True, it is ordinarily provided that the majority (one third in Missouri and in perhaps one or two other states) of the house may recall a bill from a committee; but since the principal committees are invariably controlled by the majority leaders, whom the rank and file of the party membership cannot afford to offend, this power to "discharge a committee," as it is technically called, is seldom exercised.

The common practice, then, is for the chairman and the majority of a committee to select for consideration only such bills as meet with their approval, and to report to the house only the bills they want enacted into law. In making these selections, the chairmen of the committees usually keep in close touch with the speaker of the house, or, in the case of senate committees, with the president pro tempore of the senate. Occasionally, bills are reported unfavorably; but, as we have just noted, bills not favored

LEGISLATIVE AND EXECUTIVE ACTION ON BILLS IN STATES AND TERRITORIES, 1947 **

State	Bills Introduced	Bills Passed in Both Houses	Percentage of Bills Passed	Bills Vetoed and Pocket Vetoed	Percentage of Passed Bills Vetoed	Veto Overridden	Became Law	Number of Joint and Concurrent Resolutions Adopted and in Effect	Percentage of Bills Introduced Which Became Laws	Percentage of Bills Passed Which Became Laws
Alabama	1,482	623	42.0	18	2.7		605	74	40.8	97.1
Alaska	235	101	42.9	5	5.0	1	97	5	41.3	96.0
Arizona	482	148	30.7	12	8.1	5	141	6	29.3	95.3
Arkansas	844	464	54.9	36	7.8	2	430	7	50.9	92.7
California	4,318	1,752	40.5	175	10.0		1,577	(203)	36.5	90.0
Colorado	1,629	349	21.4	6	1.7		343	(38)	20.8	98.3
Connecticut	2,348	1,076	45.8	12	1.1		1,064	—	45.3	98.9
Delaware	848	346	40.8	21	6.1		325	35	38.3	93.9
Florida	2,496	1,402	56.2	23	1.6		1,379	—	55.2	98.4
Georgia	680	404	59.4	12	3.0		392	36	57.6	97.0
Hawaii	1,504	268	17.8	24	7.5		248	25	16.5	92.5
Idaho	418	279	66.7	4	1.4		275	(16)	65.8	98.6
Illinois	1,675	738	44.0	37	5.0		701	(44)	41.8	95.0
Indiana	815	406	49.8	32	7.9		374	(19)	45.9	92.1
Iowa	1,049	358	34.1	12	3.1		347	9	33.1	96.9
Kansas	808	492	60.9	5	1.0		487	3	60.3	99.0
Kentucky (a)	794	275	34.6	32	11.6	5	248	66	31.2	90.2
Louisiana (a)	1,032	410	39.7	26	6.3		384	33	37.2	93.7
Maine	2,314	600	25.9	4	0.6		596	185	25.8	99.4
Maryland	1,418	1,011	71.3	84	8.3		927	22	65.4	91.7
Massachusetts	3,007	701	23.3	18	2.3	2	685	79	22.8	97.7
Michigan	945	381	40.3	10	2.6		371	4	39.2	97.4
Minnesota	2,960	650	22.0	8	1.2		642	(24)	21.7	98.8
Mississippi (a)	1,630	692	42.4	3	0.4		689	30	42.3	99.6
Missouri	724	221	30.5	25	11.3		196	1	27.1	88.7
Montana	603	354	58.7	13	3.6		341	26	56.5	96.4
Nebraska	568	362	63.7	6	1.7	2	358	—	63.0	98.9
Nevada	443	284	64.1	5	1.8		279	—	63.0	98.2

State	Bills Introduced	Bills Passed in Both Houses	Percentage of Bills Passed	Bills Vetoed and Pocket Vetoed	Percentage of Passed Bills Vetoed	Veto Overridden	Became Law	Number of Joint and Concurrent Resolutions Adopted and in Effect	Percentage of Bills Introduced Which Became Laws	Percentage of Bills Passed Which Became Laws
New Hampshire	616	404	65.6	2	0.5		402	*	60.6	99.5
New Jersey	846	487	57.5	70	14.2		418	10	49.4	85.8
New Mexico	566	238	42.0	16	6.7		222	32	39.2	93.3
New York	5,313	1,245	23.4	329	26.4		908	(4)	17.1	72.9
North Dakota	627	376	59.9	3	0.8		373	(39)†	59.5	99.2
Ohio	852	248	29.1	5	2.0	2	245	(16)	28.8	98.8
Oklahoma	795	389	48.1	9	2.3		380	9	47.8	97.7
Oregon	1,019	605	59.4	11	1.8		595	(58)	58.4	98.3
Pennsylvania	2,223	720	32.4	57	7.9	1	663	(77)	29.8	92.1
Rhode Island	893	326	36.4	6	1.8		320	—	35.8	98.2
South Carolina	855	606	70.8	3	0.5		603	**	70.5	99.5
South Dakota	577	430	74.5	3	0.7		427	5	74.0	99.3
Tennessee	2,774	1,120	40.4	6	0.4		1,115	37	40.2	99.6
Texas	1,335	470	35.2	12	2.6		458	(25)†	34.3	97.4
Utah	596	163	27.3	9	5.5		154	49	25.8	94.5
Vermont	403	260	64.5		0.0		260	(3)	64.5	100.0
Virginia (a)	687	406	59.1	6	1.5		400	(12)	58.2	98.5
Washington	931	309	33.2	20	6.5		289	(15)	31.0	93.5
West Virginia	834	184	22.1	1	0.5	1	183	(75)	21.9	99.5
Wisconsin	1,220	624	51.1	10	1.8		615	11	50.4	98.6
Wyoming	273	171	62.6	7	4.1	1	165		60.4	96.5
Totals	62,304	24,928	40.0	1,253	5.0	22	23,796	1,481	38.2	95.0

(a) Figures for 1946 regular sessions.

One Joint Resolution each in Alabama, Iowa, New Jersey, Tennessee, Wyoming, and four in Hawaii were vetoed and included in the number of bills vetoed.

Joint Resolutions in parentheses indicate adoption without action of governor.

* Joint Resolutions not reported separately are included in columns for "bills" and "laws" respectively.

† Indicates division between bills signed by the governor and those adopted without signature.

** From F. W. Prescott, "The Executive Veto in American States," *Western Political Quarterly* (1950), III, 102, by courtesy of the author and editors.

by the committee are usually not reported at all. Measures that are reported favorably have a good chance of passage; those reported unfavorably and those not reported have practically no chance. Thus, the committees, "little legislatures," working with the party leaders, have the power of life and death over the great majority of the bills referred to them. This system is not an unmitigated evil, for, if a house considered all the measures introduced in it, the time required would be longer than the majority of the legislatures are permitted to remain in session. Besides, many of the bills deserve no consideration, and in a number of cases their sponsors intended that they shall have none, their sole purpose in introducing them being to placate some organization or individuals having political influence.[22]

Bills before the house. When a committee reports a bill favorably, it is ordinarily placed on the house calendar and is ready for its second reading. This reading may be in full or by title only. In any case the reading is of no importance except that it indicates a stage in the advancement of the bill. It is at this time that debate on a bill ordinarily takes place, amendments are offered, and strategy for defeating it brought into play. At this stage important bills are often considered in committee of the whole, which, technicalities aside, is simply the house sitting informally. In committee of the whole there is opportunity for general debate, but the time is limited. When the house is in formal session, there is comparatively little debate, because of the pressure of time or other reasons that the leaders often have for wanting the matter disposed of with little or no debate.

When a bill has passed its second reading, it is then engrossed. This process may amount to a redrafting of the bill if many changes have been agreed upon during the second-reading stage. Engrossed bills are placed on the calendar for third reading and are taken up for consideration in the order of their appearance, unless, as is often the case with important bills, they are made the subject of a special order. Debate on third reading is ordinarily confined to the bill as a whole, not to its parts, and amendments must have unanimous consent. With the conclusion of the debate on third reading, the bill is up for final passage, and the yeas and nays on this question must be recorded in the house journal.

Time-saving devices. State legislative bodies save time and rush to a vote bills that the leaders do not want debated, in very much the same manner as our national House of Representatives. We take a few examples of these short-cut methods. The time a member may spend in debate is ordinarily limited by the rules. The presiding officer may refuse to recognize a member who wishes to speak. The "previous question" may be ordered, which means that debate must cease and the main question be

[22] Mathews, *op. cit.*, pp. 260–261.

voted upon. In many states the committee on rules brings in special rules from time to time, making a bill a special order on a given date, limiting the time that may be spent in debate, or setting the time when the final vote shall be taken. In no state is there that freedom of debate which is such a marked feature of procedure in the United States Senate. State lawmakers may object to these timesaving and often "steamroller" devices, but it is seldom that the majority will stage a protest, for the lowly member must follow the leaders, or he will have no share of the legislative patronage and no consideration will be given to the measures he proposes.

The conference committees. When a bill has passed one house, it must be sent to the other, where it runs the legislative gauntlet a second time. If the second house amends the bill, it must be returned to the first house for action upon the amendments. In case the two houses cannot agree on the amendments, the conference committee comes into play. This committee may disagree quite honestly, or it may fail to agree because the leaders find in it a convenient means of defeating the will of the members of both houses. In any case, failure of a committee to agree means that no bill will be passed. On the other hand, it may add some entirely new provisions to a measure and thus secure what the leaders were not otherwise able to get from the legislative bodies. When a bill has finally passed both houses, it is sent to the governor, whose powers of approval and veto were discussed in Chapter 13, section III.

Procedural defects and suggested remedies. From the foregoing discussion the student has no doubt gathered that legislative procedure is not all it should be. We shall attempt here to examine briefly some procedural defects, and, as far as possible, to suggest remedies.

I. SECURING INFORMATION. Those who follow the work of state legislatures often speak of the legislators' lack of information on the subjects upon which they legislate and of their lack of knowledge as to where information can be obtained. Information is needed not only on the subject with which proposed laws are to deal, but also on the type of laws that will best accomplish the purpose. Other states in the Union and legislative bodies of other countries have rich treasuries of experience from which the members of any state legislature should draw; but all too often the information is not at hand or not in convenient form, so that our lawmakers are likely to listen to advocates who have a very personal interest in proposed measures. The advocate is present and eager to "help"; the hard facts may be hidden away in uninviting volumes.

The lobby. The lobbyist "Johnny on the spot" is frequently the sole authority on which legislators base their opinions, and not infrequently legislators publicly admit their appreciation of the help of lobbyists.[23] Of

---

[23] See the articles on Lobbies and Pressure Groups in *The Annals*, CVC (January, 1938).

course lobbyists have a right to be present and to state the case for this or that interest or group; but it is not in the public interest that lawmakers, so often lacking information from unbiased sources, should rely upon them so heavily. The lobby is probably more powerful and sinister in the general run of state legislatures than it is in Congress, for the searchlight of publicity is not always glaring in state capitols and the legislators are less experienced and perhaps more likely to be influenced than congressmen. Newcomers in the legislature are easy marks for the lobbyists, often receiving from these experienced men their schooling in the intricacies of legislative organization and procedure and other "freshman days" helps and tips. It is too much to expect that none of these freshmen will in turn do their teachers a favor that may not be in the public interest.

A number of states attempt (again Massachusetts should be specifically named) to regulate the lobby, requiring registration of lobbyists, the names of firms they represent, the measures in which they are interested, and financial accounting. This type of regulation is very similar to that Congress prescribed in the recent (1946) Federal Regulation of Lobbying Act. This is perhaps as far as it is safe to go. No attempt is made, or should be made, to abolish lobbying. As long as there are powerful individuals and groups with interests at stake before a legislature there will be lobbying, legal or illegal.

More reliable information is being made available. The remedy for inadequately informed legislators lies not in a futile attempt to abolish lobbying, but in placing information from unbiased and scientific sources at the disposal of legislatures. This service is performed in part in every state through committee hearings, but here again the testimony is likely to be biased. The most promising remedy is found in legislative reference bureaus. The establishment of a legislative reference library by Wisconsin in 1901 was the signal for other states to do the same, until now about forty states have them operating with varying degrees of success. In the few states in which these organizations are functioning effectively, they are constantly collecting information on all subjects likely to be of interest to the lawmakers, and during the sessions a staff of workers is on duty day and night to assist them.[24] Since 1925 the American Legislators' Association has conducted researches, arranged regional and national conferences for legislators, and in various other ways extended a helping hand. In 1935 a more pretentious and inclusive organization, the Council of State Governments, was formed. It serves as the secretariat for the Legislators' Association and other organizations designed to improve state government. Its monthly publication, *State Government,* contains much useful material in readable form. Still other valuable aids to legislators are found in

[24] E. E. Witte, "A Law-Making Laboratory," *State Government,* April, 1930, and his "Technical Services for State Legislators," *Annals,* CVC, 137.

technical studies conducted by such organizations as the American Law Institute, the Brookings Institution, the National Institute of Public Administration, the American Society for Public Administration, and research bureaus at a number of universities. The Legislative Research Service of the Library of Congress is most useful to state legislators.[25]

2. DRAFTING BILLS. Legislators have been sadly deficient in the art of drafting bills. It is one thing to decide that a law is needed to prevent or encourage a particular thing, and quite another to draft a statute that will accomplish the purpose intended. Drafting is a technical matter. The statute must be so constructed that neither more nor less than is intended is expressed, that its meaning not only may be understood but cannot be misunderstood. Some will seek to expand the terms of a statute; others will seek to make it meaningless. A law that serves the original purpose of its makers, despite all the controversy and litigation over its meaning, is a rare product. It is obvious that the average member of a state legislature is wholly incapable of drafting a bill in the proper form; for many of them not only lack the technical knowledge necessary, but they are also deficient in the rudiments of ordinary English composition. The bill-drafting follies of legislatures are often illustrated by an extreme example: "When two trains approach each other at a crossing they shall both come to a full stop and neither shall start up until the other has gone." [26]

Lacking the qualifications of bill drafters, many legislators rely upon lawyer constituents or upon lobbyists, who are only too glad to frame statutes embodying the principles for which they are laboring. A few members, of course, are skilled in the technicalities of statutory craftsmanship, and they may not only draft their own bills but sometimes aid their colleagues and organizations or individuals who want measures drafted and introduced. Indeed, there is the belief, founded on stronger evidence than persistent rumors, that some legislators, skilled not only in bill drafting but also as advocates of the adoption of measures, have received substantial sums from outsiders for whom they exercise their talents. (Here it might be said that we have the lobbyists doing an inside job.) For the average member of the legislature, who knows few of the intricacies of statute making, more than half the states have provided help in the form of bill-drafting agencies in connection with legislative reference libraries or similar bureaus.

3. COMMITTEES. We have already noted that the typical legislature has too many committees, a situation that complicates, rather than clarifies, legislative work. There are no good reasons, other than political, for not materially reducing the number. Furthermore, the two sets of committees, one from each house, mean duplication of work; and in their hurry, com-

---

[25] Graves, *op. cit.,* pp. 328–331; Howard F. Ohm, "Legislative Reference in Wisconsin," *State Government,* Dec., 1948, pp. 240–243, 253; Walker, *op. cit.,* pp. 319–324.

[26] Bates, Field, and Others, *op. cit.,* p. 228.

mittees of both houses often do superficial work. In Massachusetts, Connecticut, and Maine joint committees do practically all of the committee work, and their demonstrated usefulness should lead to their adoption in other states.

Competent observers have often stated that in the majority of the states the committees are not the servants of the legislature, as they are supposed to be, but its masters. Rules prohibiting the reference of more than a specified number of important bills to any one committee and requiring committees to report within a specified number of days any bills referred to them would doubtless help in restoring committees to their proper spheres as servants. Hearing reports on all bills would require more time than most legislatures now have at their disposal; but electric voting devices, as used in the Wisconsin legislature and in a few others, can save a great deal of time. Some legislatures have rules similar to those just mentioned, which give them control of their committees, and the satisfactory results obtained remove our recommendations from the realm of the academic.[27]

4. END OF THE SESSION RUSH. Professor W. F. Dodd gives special attention to the great rush that, unfortunately, characterizes legislative procedure in the closing days of the session in nearly every state.[28] In the near panic of the last ten or twelve days of a four or five months' session the Illinois Legislature may pass more than half of its measures; and Pennsylvania, New York, and many other states may equal or beat that record. This last-minute rush period is the time for the making of indefensible legislative bargains, the time when members are weak and weary, and even the more conscientious ones have relaxed their vigilance; the time when the steam roller works best. Some meritorious measures are enacted, of course, but so are others of much less merit; a few may be positively vicious; and it goes without saying that many good measures may be sidetracked. A large number of members vote as they are told and hope that by so doing their own bills will be favored. There is no time to think, even if one is not too fatigued to do so.

One might assume that the rush is caused by the constitutional limitations as to the time legislatures may remain in session; but the three states just mentioned, as well as a number of others, have the rush without the time-limit excuse for it. The lawmaking sprint near the end of the sessions occurs primarily because of ineffective procedure, and secondarily because the days of so many legislatures are constitutionally numbered. The chief remedy, then, can be found in improved procedure; and here again Massachusetts points the way. Practically all bills are introduced in her legislature in the early days of the session; the committees must report

---

[27] Bates, Field, and Others, pp. 242–244; Holcombe, *op. cit.,* pp. 296–298.

[28] *State Government,* pp. 186 ff. Although Dodd made his observations some years ago, there have been no substantial improvements since.

before a given date; and committee reports are promptly considered by the house in which they are made. In some states the Massachusetts system or something approaching it would call for that anathema to many Americans, an extension of time for legislative sessions; but the results we have reason to expect would justify it.

Recommendations of the experts. *The Model State Constitution* (1948 ed.), drafted by the National Municipal League's Committee on State Government, contains several proposals on legislative procedure that are worth careful consideration.

(1) The unicameral system—the advantages of which have already been discussed—is recommended. The committee realizes, however, that the bicameral idea has professors and reformers on one side and "practical" men (whose conception of government often hovers around 1787) on the other; and that the bicameral system is likely to continue to prevail in most of the states for some time to come. Consequently, the committee urges the states that want to retain the two chambers to reduce the membership in both houses, establish more equitable systems of apportionment, set up joint legislative committees, and create legislative councils. Such states would then gain most of the advantages the Model Constitution offers.

(2) The Model would require committees to keep journals of their proceedings as public records; would authorize one third of the members of the legislature to relieve a committee of further consideration of a bill when the committee has not reported on it; and would require that notice of all committee hearings, with a statement of the subjects to be considered, be published one week in advance of the hearings.

(3) The Model provides for a legislative council consisting of not less than seven or more than fifteen members, chosen by and from the legislature. The legislature may dissolve the council at any time and elect a new one. The council is to meet as often as may be necessary to perform its duties, and its members are to receive compensation in addition to their stipend as members of the legislature. "It shall be the duty of the council to collect information concerning the government and general welfare of the state and to report thereon to the legislature. Measures for proposed legislation may be submitted to it at any time, and shall be considered, and reported to the legislature with its recommendations thereon. The council may also recommend such legislation . . . as in its opinion the welfare of the state may require. Other powers and duties may be assigned to the council by law. The legislature may delegate to the council authority to supplement existing legislation by general orders. No such general orders shall be effective until published as provided by law." Thus reads the Model.

Since 1933 more than twenty states—Kansas, Maryland, Texas, and Wisconsin, among others—have established legislative councils, although in no state is the council given quite as much range as the Model recommends. Formerly, several states had councils in which the executive was given a voice. As a matter of fact, the earlier editions of the Model Constitution gave the governor a place in the legislative council. The weight of authority now, however, favors full legislative control of the council. The fundamental duties of the council are to assemble information for and propose legislation, or alternative legislation, to the next session of the legislature. Where the councils are served by a technical and research staff, as in Kansas, the degree to which these functions are realized is very encouraging.[29]

(4) The architects of the Model Constitution would make the legislature a continuous body during the biennium for which its members are elected. The Model provides for quarterly meetings and such other meetings as may be prescribed by law and authorizes special sessions at the call of the governor or the majority of the members of the legislative council. This proposal is probably further from adoption by the states than is the unicameral system. The voters have the gravest suspicions of legislatures, and the best news they hear about them is that they have adjourned. To be sure, some of the popular distrust of lawmakers is justified, but we can hardly hope to improve their personnel and output by opposing propositions designed for those ends. The basic difficulty is that too many of us still think of government in negative terms—that that government is best which governs least; that legislature best which passes the fewest laws —a conception that has no relation to present-day functions of government and that is almost certain to defeat any proposal for improvement in the discharge of those functions.

III. LEGISLATIVE POWERS AND LIMITATIONS [30]

We have probably learned long ago that all the powers of the national government are delegated to it by the Constitution or are implied from those delegated by that instrument, and that all other powers of government are reserved to the states, subject to a few important prohibitions laid upon them by the federal Constitution. The states thus have jurisdiction over a much wider range of subjects than has the government of the United States. Each state, through its constitution, determines in the main what its governing authorities shall be, what powers they shall have, and, to a considerable extent, how these powers shall be exercised. In this division of powers within a state the legislature always receives the lion's share.

---

[29] F. H. Guild, "The Development of the Legislative Council Idea," *Annals*, CVC, 144; Graves, *op. cit.*, 343 ff. See also Guild's "Legislative Councils: Objectives and Accomplishments," *State Government*, Sept., 1949, pp. 217–219, 226.

[30] Bates, Field, and Others, *op. cit.*, Ch. 9; W. F. Dodd, *op. cit.*, pp. 173–177, 190–222; Graves, *op. cit.*, pp. 307–316; Holcombe, *op. cit.*, pp. 275–288; Mathews, *op. cit.*, pp. 242–249.

It elaborates the constitution through the enactment of innumerable statutes with respect to the functions the state shall undertake, what officers shall perform them, and how they shall perform them. Executives, administrative officers, and judges find most of their authority in these acts of the legislature.

Powers essentially legislative. Professor W. F. Dodd summarizes those powers he regards as strictly legislative as follows: [31] *First* in importance is the power to pass all revenue and appropriation bills. *Second,* all the machinery of government, except that which is provided for by the constitution, must be established by the legislature. *Third,* the legislature must enact the laws regulating the organization and powers of local governing bodies in cities, counties, and other local areas. Some states grant a measure of independence to such areas, but in only a few states is this local liberty of action sufficient to relieve the legislature of significant responsibility for local communities. *Fourth,* the legislature passes laws designed to regulate the relations of private individuals in such matters as contracts, deeds, mortgages, wills, marriages, divorces, and a host of other particulars. It protects individuals and the general public through the passage of acts defining and specifying the punishment for such crimes as murder, burglary, robbery, arson, and scores of lesser offenses; and it further looks after the safety and convenience of individuals by enacting such laws as those pertaining to motor vehicles.

Looking at the subject more broadly, we may say that the legislature very largely determines the policies of the state and the manner in which they shall be carried into execution. What system of taxation shall be employed? What highway program shall the state undertake? What educational advantages shall it offer its people, young and old? Shall child labor be prohibited? Should a workmen's compensation system be adopted? To what extent should labor unions be regulated? How much social security can the state afford? These and dozens of similar questions of the utmost importance must be decided by the legislature.[32]

Judicial powers. All state legislatures have some powers that are not legislative in character. In about half the states the legislature is authorized to decide contested elections, a power that is judicial (or should be) in its nature and from which there is no appeal from the legislative decision. In all states except Oregon[33] the governor and other civil officers may be removed by impeachment. The "articles of impeachment" are voted in the lower house and the trial is conducted by the senate, except

[31] *Op. cit.,* pp. 173 ff.

[32] Some interesting reflections on the problems the legislators face in reaching their decisions on matters of policy are found in T. V. Smith's "Two functions of the American Legislator," *Annals,* CVC, 183.

[33] In Oregon corrupt and otherwise delinquent officials are supposed to be dealt with by the courts as ordinary criminal offenders. Macdonald, *op. cit.,* p. 191 n.

in Nebraska, where the articles are voted by the one-house legislature and the trial is conducted by the state supreme court. It will be made clear in the chapter on the State Judicial System that the courts not only look to the legislature for the laws they are to enforce, but also find their organization and procedure, except as specified in the constitution, fixed by the legislature.

Executive and administrative powers. Quite commonly the governor's appointments must be validated by senatorial confirmation, and in several states certain judicial and executive officers are chosen by the whole legislature. Ordinary removals (to be distinguished from removal by impeachment) may be made in a number of states by joint action of the governor and senate or by joint action of the legislative bodies. State legislatures have fallen willing victims to a temptation to which Congress has often yielded, the temptation to regulate the details of administration. For example, legislatures not only decide what departments shall be organized, but they usually prescribe in great detail the internal organization of the departments—a function that administrative authorities could discharge much better and save the time of the legislatures while so doing. Legislatures not only enact laws for the protection of fish and game, but they may lay down the most detailed and technical regulations as to how fish and game shall be protected; and laws enacted for the purpose of eradicating or controlling the hoof-and-mouth disease may contain the most minute directions as to just how this shall be done. Now, authorities will agree that the legislature should provide for the protection of fish and game and for the eradication of the hoof-and-mouth disease, but they will also agree that the legislature should stop with the statement of the objects to be accomplished and the creation of the agencies for accomplishing them, leaving the details to be worked out by the administrative agencies. Legislatures have neither the time nor the technical information necessary for making administrative regulations.

AN ENCOURAGING DEVELOPMENT. It is indeed encouraging to see that the practice of leaving details to be worked out by administrative authorities is growing. Boards of health are being given the authority to draw up sanitary codes; industrial commissions are being empowered to make rules and regulations for guarding against fire hazards, personal injuries, disease, etc.; and public utility commissions, for some time, have been authorized not only to make ordinary rules and regulations respecting public utilities, but also to fix the rates that may be charged for services. Since about 1930 this desirable movement has proceeded at a rapid rate, leaving the legislatures more time to devote to what should be their chief function, the formulation of policies.[34]

Few limits on powers of early legislatures. In colonial times, especially

---

[34] Kansas Legislative Council, "Legislative Functions of Administrative Agencies" (1938).

during the period immediately preceding the Revolution, the people thought of their legislatures as strongholds of defense against the attacks made on their liberties by the governors who represented the British crown. When independent state governments were established after 1775, it was but natural that this confidence in the legislatures should continue, and that these bodies should retain all the powers they previously possessed and acquire a number of those formerly held by the governors. Prior to 1800 practically the only limitations on the powers of the legislatures were in the provisions for frequent elections and in the bills of rights.

FORFEITURE OF PUBLIC CONFIDENCE. The legislatures did not keep for long, however, the high place they held in public esteem. From the very first, land speculators intrigued with legislators for grants of large tracts of western lands at nominal prices—the land to be developed and advertised and sold at advanced prices, to the enrichment of the land companies and not infrequently to the profit of accommodating legislators. A little later there was great demand for roads, bridges, canals, and, after 1830, railroads. To secure their construction, legislatures granted to various concerns charters of incorporation, amounting in many cases to monopolies, and, along with the charters, most liberal, even prodigal, grants of land. In connection with these charters and grants the opportunities for corruption were too frequent and tempting to be resisted at all times by all legislators. In like manner, much unwisdom and some corruption were shown in the ease with which legislators granted bank charters to irresponsible promoters, with the result that the people suffered greatly, particularly in the West, from the operations of "wildcat" banks. Not only were the states too liberal in granting privileges to private corporations, but the states themselves went into banking and also undertook the construction of roads, canals, and railroads on a grand scale.

When the first panic struck (1837), a number of the states were heavily in debt and some of them repudiated part of their obligations. Let us not suppose that the constituents had been prophesying that dire results would follow the prodigality of their representatives. Rather was it in response to the voice of the people that these programs were undertaken. Nevertheless, when the mistakes and blunders stood revealed, the legislatures were not saved by the plea that they had given the public what it wanted.[35] Consequently, a large part of the history of state legislatures, especially since the middle of the nineteenth century, is written in the limitations placed upon them.

Present limitations and restrictions. Legislatures are now commonly limited in respect to organization and procedure by constitutional stipulations on such matters as the number of members, length of sessions, rate of pay, the manner in which bills, especially money bills, may be introduced,

[35] See discussion of abuse of legislative power in Bates, Field, and Others, *op. cit.*, pp. 204 ff.

the steps in the passage of a bill, and the method of voting. More important than these restrictions are the constitutional limitations on the scope of legislative action.

1. MATTERS OF FINANCE. The financial mistakes and excesses noted above led in many states to severe restrictions on taxation, appropriations, and debts. It is generally stipulated that taxes shall be uniform and equal on all types of property, although this provision is now frequently modified by such exceptions as the authorization of an income tax and the permission to classify property for purposes of taxation. Constitutions sometimes limit the rate of taxation, both state and local, and, in order that the rates shall be kept down and vicious favor seeking shall be avoided, frequently deny legislatures the right to exempt from taxation, persons, corporations, or localities. However, exemption is ordinarily authorized for private schools, religious, and eleemosynary institutions.

In making appropriations, legislatures must restrict themselves to those designed for a public purpose. Donations to individuals or private corporations are commonly forbidden. The form of appropriation bills is usually specified by some such provision as: "The general appropriation bill shall embrace nothing but appropriations for the different departments of the state, for state institutions, for public schools, and for interest on the public debt. All other appropriations shall be made by separate bill, each embracing but one subject." [36]

The authority of both legislatures and local governing bodies to borrow money is commonly restricted to specified amounts or to a small percentage of the assessed valuation of taxable property. However, it is usually provided that these amounts may be exceeded with the approval of the majority of the voters in the area for which the indebtedness is proposed, an approval that in practice has been relatively easy to obtain. In like manner, the constitutions usually prohibit the states and their various subdivisions from making loans to individuals, associations, or corporations.

2. SPECIAL LAWS. The majority of the states, in order to save the time of legislatures and to prevent abuses, now have constitutional prohibitions against the enactment of such local and special laws as those preventing the throwing of sawdust in Big Ivey Creek in Buncombe County and the shooting of firecrackers within one mile of the post office at Haw River,[37] reinstating a discharged fireman in Boston, granting a special privilege or franchise to a corporation, and voting a special charter to a city. A common prohibition is that no special law shall be enacted when a law of general application can be made to serve. This prohibition is ineffective in many states because the legislature itself passes upon the question of the

[36] Const. of Arizona, Art. IV, sec. 20.

[37] See Mathews, *op. cit.*, p. 247, note, for a list of such local laws enacted by a North Carolina legislature.

necessity of a special law. But in the few states in which the courts determine the matter, the restriction is usually effective.

More important than this general prohibition against special legislation, is the specific enumeration of subjects on which the legislature shall pass no special law. This list, which may run as high as thirty or more, includes such subjects as the granting of divorces, the chartering of corporations (both private and municipal), changing the rules of evidence, changing the names of individuals, the punishment of crimes and misdemeanors, locating or changing county seats, and laws affecting the estates of deceased persons or of minors. The question as to whether an act violates any of these prohibitions is determined by the courts, not by the legislature.

Another method of limiting the activities of legislatures in passing special bills is found in procedural requirements. For example, in New York a two-thirds vote of the entire membership is required to pass a special or private bill appropriating money, and in several states, including New York, acts that apply to particular localities must be referred to such areas for their approval.

It should be noted that prohibitions against special legislation do not prevent the legislatures from making reasonable classifications. For instance, a prohibition against granting special charters to cities does not prevent legislatures from classifying cities according to population and giving the different classes different charters. In like manner, the Fourteenth Amendment of the federal Constitution, which prohibits the states from denying to any person the equal protection of the laws, does not mean that the legislatures may not make reasonable classifications of persons and corporations for purposes of taxation and regulation. Thus, doctors may be subject to one set of regulations, lawyers to another, and mechanics to none at all. Railroads may be taxed by one method, and ordinary property by another.[38]

3. INDIRECT LIMITATIONS. Bates and Field [39] point out that legislatures are limited, not only by constitutional provisions that apply directly to them, but also by provisions and extraconstitutional developments that transfer power from legislatures to other organs of government. We have already learned that the veto enables the governor to wield a tremendous power over the legislature in practically every state. The growth of his authority over the budget and appointments indicates some decrease in legislative power over these subjects. With the general approval of the public, the governor frequently assumes the reins of legislative leadership in formulating and securing the adoption of policies, thereby decreasing the importance of the legislature in a field peculiarly its own.

In the early days the courts took a broad and liberal view of legislative

[38] *Ibid.,* pp. 179–181.
[39] *Op. cit.,* pp. 209 ff.

powers. Thus, in North Carolina, in 1794, the supreme court held that the people did not adopt a bill of rights "against a power they supposed their representatives might usurp, but against oppression and usurpation in general."[40]   Contrast this with the declaration of the Texas court, in 1918, to the effect that, since the constitution of that state directed the legislature to pass a local option law, it prevented the legislature from controlling the liquor traffic in any other way.   Other cases of this kind could be cited to show that, despite the theory that a legislature has all powers not denied it by the Constitution of the United States and the constitution of the state, the courts are now inclined to hold that authorization or direction to take certain action serves as a prohibition against taking other, although similar, action.[41]   Indeed, the marked tendency of the courts to apply the doctrine of "implied limitations" to legislative powers has led some authorities to say that it should be checked by constitutional means, and the constitution of Oklahoma follows this suggestion in a provision that reads: "Specific grant of authority in this constitution upon any subject whatsoever shall not work a restriction, limitation, or exclusion of such authority upon the same or any other subject or subjects whatsoever."

IV. THE INITIATIVE AND REFERENDUM [42]

In a number of states a lack of confidence in the legislatures is expressed in the initiative and referendum.   Through the initiative the voters may themselves enact a measure their representatives will not pass; through the referendum, they may defeat a measure their representatives have passed. The initiative is positive in character; the referendum is negative.   The former has been described as "a spur on the flanks," the latter as "a bit in the mouth," of the legislative steed.[43]   Manifestly, those who fear these institutions of democracy because of their alleged radical character should concentrate their efforts against the initiative, since all the referendum can do is to hold the legislature in check.   It was never intended by the most earnest advocates of the initiative and referendum that they should supplant representative (republican) government.   This was simply the time-

---

40 Quoted, Bates, Field, and Others, *op. cit.*, p. 214, from 1 Hay, N.C. 29.

41 Mathews, *op. cit.*, pp. 243 ff.

42 R. C. Brooks, *Political Parties and Electoral Problems* (1933 ed.), Ch. XVII; Colorado Legislative Reference Office, *The Initiative and Referendum in Colorado* (1940); Dodd, *op. cit.*, Ch. XX; H. F. Gosnell and Margaret J. Schmidt, "Popular Law Making in the United States, 1924–1936," in New York State Constitutional Convention Committee's, *Problems Relating to Legislative Organization and Powers* (1938); Holcombe, *op. cit.*, Ch. XVI; Claudius O. Johnson, "The Initiative and Referendum in Washington," *Pacific Northwest Quarterly*, January, 1945, pp. 29–63; V. O. Key and W. W. Crouch, *The Initiative and Referendum in California* (1939); James K. Pollock, *The Initiative and Referendum in Michigan* (Bureau of Government, University of Michigan, 1940); Waldo Schumacher, "Thirty Years of the People's Rule in Oregon," *Pol. Sci. Quar.*, XLVII, 242 (June, 1932).

43 Brooks, *op. cit.*, p. 498.

honored "scarecry" assertion of those who would frighten the electorate into voting against their adoption. The I. and R. were intended for emergency or special use, the presumption being that the legislature would ordinarily enact the laws that had popular support and refuse to enact those that had it not.

Extent of their use. Although the referendum had been in pretty general use during the nineteenth century as a means of having the people pass upon proposed state constitutions and amendments thereto, and in the local communities of some states as a means of giving them their "local option" on the saloon questions, neither the referendum nor the initiative was used for ordinary statutes in this country until 1898, when South Dakota introduced both.[44] Other states followed in rather rapid succession until about 1912, when the movement lagged. Twenty-one states [45] now have constitutional provisions authorizing direct legislation, and it is a rare election year (even year) in which the total number of amendments and statutes voted upon by the people of these states does not exceed seventy-five. The number of submissions varies considerably in the states. California, with 48 (but about half these proposals were submitted by the legislature) in 1914, seems to hold the record; but Oregon, Colorado, and some other states have made relatively high scores. A number of cities have the I. and R. for their local charters and ordinances, particularly those cities that have adopted the newer commission and manager forms of government; and as a rule the urban voters are not slow to avail themselves of their privileges. The student knows, of course, that there is no provision for the use of these direct legislative methods in our national system, and we may add that there is little or no movement for their adoption.

Referendum procedure. Although both the initiative and referendum differ in the details of their operation in the several states, the general principles are the same, and we shall describe them without greatly concerning ourselves with the variations.

1. COMPULSORY. First, we shall outline referendum procedure. Every state except Delaware has the compulsory referendum on constitutional amendments, and many states require that form of referendum on banking laws and on incurring a debt beyond a certain minimum. That is to say, constitutional amendments and statutes on the subjects mentioned, having passed the legislature, *must* be referred to the voters and be approved by

[44] Switzerland authorized the use of the referendum and initiative for statutes some years before this.

[45] South Dakota (1898); Utah (1900 but not put into operation until 1917); Oregon (1902), Nevada (R. 1904, I. & R., 1912); Montana (1906); Oklahoma (1907); Maine (1908); Missouri (1908); Michigan (1908); Arkansas (1910); Colorado (1910); California (1911); New Mexico (1911, referendum only); Arizona (1911); Idaho (1912, but not put into operation until 1933); Nebraska (1912); Ohio (1912); Washington (1912); North Dakota (1914); Maryland (1915, referendum only); Massachusetts (1918).

them before they become effective. In like manner, many cities have the compulsory referendum on charter amendments, incurring indebtedness, and other matters. The compulsory referendum, as we observed above, is not new. In fact, we have long accepted it as a matter of course, and hardly think of it as a referendum at all.

2. OPTIONAL. What we commonly have in mind when we speak of the referendum is the optional referendum, which did not come into general use until after 1900. It operates as follows. The legislature passes a statute to which some of the voters object. During the period, usually ninety days, before the statute becomes effective, the opposition circulates a petition for a referendum. If the requisite number of voters, varying in the twenty states from five to ten per cent, sign the petition, the statute must then be held in abeyance until submitted to the whole body of voters for their decision. The submission is usually made on the regular election dates.

Manifestly, some measures are designed to meet crises and are needed immediately, and a referendum on them, with the delays it entails, would be intolerable. Consequently, it is customary to give the legislatures the power to designate such bills as "emergency measures" and thus exempt them from the operation of the referendum. Legislatures sometimes abuse this privilege by designating as emergency measures, bills that are not such measures in fact. In order to correct this abuse, some states require an extraordinary majority of the legislature to attach the "emergency clause"; others allow the governor to veto the clause; still others enumerate the subjects that may not be legislated upon under the emergency classification. No system, however, will eliminate all of the abuse either on the part of legislatures or of voters who originate petitions.

Initiative procedure: 1. DIRECT. If certain voters desire a constitutional amendment which the legislature will not propose or a measure which that body will not enact, they draft it, or have it drafted, and then circulate a petition on its behalf. In the nineteen states which authorize the enactment of statutes by the initiative, the number of signers required is usually a little higher than for the referendum; and in the thirteen states (see chapter 4, sec. IV) in which the constitution may be amended by the initiative, seven require more petitioners for proposing amendments than for proposing statutes. A petition in favor of a measure, signed by the requisite number of voters, places the measure on the ballot at the next regular election, when the entire electorate determines its fate as in the case of a referred measure. This is called the direct initiative because the proposal goes directly to the voters.

2. INDIRECT. In several states, the indirect initiative is employed. The petition for a proposed measure is first submitted to the legislature; if the bill is passed by that body, the matter is settled and the necessity of a popular

vote on the question avoided. If not passed, some states require that the proposal be submitted to the people without further formalities; but in other states, additional signatures or other requirements must be met before it can be submitted.

The initiative and referendum in operation. There is no dearth of books and articles on the results achieved by the initiative and referendum, and a number of them are authoritative.[46] From these authorities we may reach several fairly safe conclusions.

1. EFFECT UPON THE LEGISLATURE. The system of direct legislation has not encroached upon the regular legislative bodies to any considerable degree. Even in those states that resort most frequently to direct legislation, the legislatures continue to enact practically all the laws. Nor does it appear that the initiative and referendum have brought about any important change in the personnel of legislatures. The caliber of our lawmakers is pretty much the same as it was a generation ago. As to whether or not the "bit in the mouth" and the "spur on the flanks" have improved the output of the duly elected legislative bodies, it is difficult to determine. Perhaps it can be said that the existence of the I. and R. has at times caused legislators to consider their responsibilities more seriously.[47]

2. EFFECT UPON THE BALLOT. Direct legislation has unquestionably added to the tasks of the voter. He must now vote on both men and measures. Although certain measures will receive a relatively high vote in many instances, the fact remains that a large number of voters do not officially express their opinions upon the ordinary measures referred to them. A business man, in telling his wife how to discharge her obligations as a citizen in a particular election, explained that she would be given two ballots; that one contained the names of the candidates, and that the other "had some laws or something on it." He advised her to follow his example and not bother about voting on the laws.

3. POSSIBILITIES OF MINORITY GOVERNMENT. The fact that a considerable portion of the electorate is not interested in referred or initiated measures often makes it possible for a minority (although a majority of those voting on a measure) to carry its point. The situation is not so serious as it may appear to be, for government policies are often determined by minorities. Those who are in any degree familiar with our history know that the federal Constitution was adopted by convention delegates chosen by a minority of the adult males of the country. A policy determined by an intelligent minority is certainly not greatly to be feared. On the other hand, however, minorities of the "lunatic fringe" variety may plague the electorate by sub-

[46] See references in note 42.
[47] On the basis of a study of my own state (Washington) I am convinced that the referendum has been used effectively and that the possibility of its use operates as a restraining influence upon the legislature.

mitting to it foolish and absurd measures, and the indifference of the rank
and file of the voters may occasionally result in the passage of a measure of
this type. Some states have guarded against this by providing that no measure shall become a law unless a certain percentage of all those voting in the
election (as distinguished from those voting on the particular measure)
shall have voted on the measures.

4. Types of laws submitted. Measures laid before the people cover
a wide range; but the greater number of them have to do with minor
changes in the organization of government, state and local. A fair number of them relate to finance—the authorization of an indebtedness, changing the system of taxation, and the like. Public utility measures have not
been so numerous; but they have usually caused the most lively interest on
the part of the electorate and, more particularly, the business group
concerned. Some important measures have related to schools, roads, alcoholic beverages, and social security. These examples by no means exhaust the list, but they do cover practically all the subjects on which important measures have been referred to the electorate. It is of interest
to note that the initiative has not deluged us with radical proposals: that
conservatives have learned to use it quite as effectively as "radicals"; and
that the groups that use it, be they the respectable or the disinherited, are
those groups that are in a minority in the legislature.

5. The question of their educational value. It is often said that the
initiative and referendum educate the electorate; that they stimulate interest in government in general. This can hardly be questioned, but the
extent to which they stimulate the voters to intelligent action is by no
means certain. In a few states "publicity pamphlets" are mailed to each
voter or household, but the evidence does not indicate that the voters
read them or any part of them with particular care. This show of indifference does not mean, however, that the citizens do not receive some civic
enlightenment from the discussions of the measures, but only that they
may rely chiefly upon the spoken rather than the written word. Written
appeals may move the educated classes, but the rank and file prefer the
oral medium. Undoubtedly direct legislation creates a greater interest
on the part of the electorate in state policies, and it cannot be said that the
interest does not run high when major questions are up for decision. Without having made any exhaustive study of the question, but having resided in states that have and in those that do not have direct systems of
legislation, the writer is of the opinion that the voters in the former states
are more intelligently concerned about public affairs than the voters in the
latter.

Probable retention of initiative and referendum. A generation ago the
lines on direct legislation were drawn, broadly speaking, between the
liberals, who favored it, and the conservatives, who opposed it. Since

neither the hopes of the former nor the fears of the latter have been realized, the lines have tended to break somewhat. It is an interesting fact
that "tories" often used the I. and R. in the New Deal period when "radicals" and "reds" controlled the legislatures! It is a matter of who controls
the legislature. If that body gives you what you want, you oppose the
I. and R.; if it doesn't, then you are for direct legislation.

Students examine the record of the I. and R., admit their shortcomings,
point out their desirable features, and give them cautious endorsement.
It is altogether probable that they will be retained by the states that now
have them, although other states will proceed with considerable circumspection in adopting them. It is also likely that changes will be made in
their operation: through authorizing a greater use of the indirect initiative
and the submission by the legislature of a substitute measure for the one
originally proposed; through lengthening the list of subjects on which the
people may not legislate directly; through providing more official help for
the drafting and scrutinizing of initiated measures; and through other
provisions of a similar character.

The 1948 edition of the *Model State Constitution* has some suggestions
relative to the initiative and referendum that public men and students of
government might well consider. One such suggestion, as explained in
the chapter on the governor, is that the chief executive be authorized to
call a referendum on any bill which fails to pass the legislature, and that
the legislature be authorized, by majority vote, to submit to the people
any measure vetoed by the governor, if, upon reconsideration by the legislature, it is not approved by a two-thirds vote but is approved by at least
a majority vote. Another suggestion is that so-called "emergency measures" be made subject to the referendum, but that such measures be
operative during the period between the filing of the referendum petition
and the date of the election. This provision would eliminate some of the
abuse to which legislature have put the "emergency clause."

A suggestion of particular significance is that "The initiative shall not be
used as a means of making appropriations of public funds, nor for the enactment of local or special legislation. No measure submitted by the
initiative shall contain therein the name of any person to be designated as
administrator of any department, office, or agency to be established by the
proposed law or constitutional amendment." The committee of experts
probably had in mind certain types of pension proposals submitted in recent years to electors in various states, and the section by which such
proposals would be rendered invalid might be characterized as the "anti-
ham-and-egg" proviso.[48]

[48] For particular reference to California's difficulties see Α. F. Smith, "Can We Afford the
Initiative," *National Municipal Review*, Oct., 1949, p. 437.

Reading List

F. G. Bates, O. P. Field, and Others, *State Government* (1949 ed.), Chs. 8–10.

A. W. Bromage, *State Government and Administration in the United States* (1936), Chs. IX and X.

A. E. Buck, *Modernizing Our State Legislatures,* Pamphlet series No. 4, the American Academy of Pol. and Soc. Sci. (1936).

D. B. Carroll, *The Unicameral Legislature of Vermont* (1933).

J. P. Chamberlain, *Legislative Processes: National and State* (1934).

Charles Childs, *The Oregon Legislature* (1937).

A. B. Clark, "The Single-Chamber Legislature of Manitoba," *Nat. Mun. Rev.* (1924), pp. 225–233.

D. L. Colvin, *The Bicameral Principle in the New York Legislature* (1913).

Council of State Governments, *The Book of the States* (biennially).

——, *Our State Legislatures* (1948).

C. E. Dagget, "Unicameral Legislatures," *Cornell Law Quar.* (1920), V, 285–301.

W. F. Dodd, *State Government* (1928 ed.), Chs. VI–VII, XX.

W. B. Graves, *American State Government* (1946 ed.), Chs. VI–VIII.

——, ed., "Our State Legislators," *Annals* (January, 1938), CVC.

Thelma I. Griswold, *Bicameralism in Ohio* (1937).

F. H. Guild and C. F. Snider, "Legislative Procedure in Kansas," *Bureau of Governmental Research and Service,* Univ. of Kans. (1930), No. 1.

F. H. Guild, "Legislative Councils: Objectives and Accomplishments," *State Government,* Sept., 1949, pp. 217–219, 226.

A. B. Hall, *Popular Government* (1921).

A. N. Holcombe, *State Government in the United States* (1931 ed.), Chs. X, XVI.

"The Initiative and Referendum," *Bulletins for the Constitutional Convention, Mass.* (1917–18), Vol. I, No. 6.

"The Initiative, Referendum, and Recall," *Illinois Constitutional Convention Bulletin* (1919), No. 2.

J. King, "The American Voter as a Lawmaker," *National Popular Government League* (1923).

J. H. Leek, *Legislative Reference Work: a Comparative Study* (1925).

"Our Legislative Mills," *National Municipal Review* (1923–24), XII–XIII. (Articles on eight states by eight authorities.)

R. Luce, *Legislative Assemblies* (1924).

——, *Legislative Procedure* (1922).

A. F. Macdonald, *American State Government and Administration* (1950 ed.), Chs. VII–IX.

J. W. Manning, *Unicameral Legislation in the States* (1938).

W. B. Munro, ed., *The Initiative, Referendum and Recall* (1912).

New York State Constitutional Convention Committee, *Problems Relating to Legislative Organization and Powers* (1938).

James K. Pollock, *The Initiative and Referendum in Michigan* (1940).

T. H. Reed, ed., *Legislatures and Legislative Problems* (1933).

P. S. Reinsch, *American Legislatures and Legislative Methods* (1907), Chs. IV–X.

Dorothy Schaffter, *The Bicameral System in Practice* (1929).

Waldo Schumacher, "Thirty Years of the People's Rule in Oregon," *Pol. Sci. Quar.*, XLVII, 242 (June, 1932).

J. P. Senning, *The One-House Legislature* (1937).

T. V. Smith, *The Legislative Way of Life* (1940).

C. F. Snider, *American State and Local Government* (1950), Chs. VII–VIII.

State Government (published monthly by the Council of State Government).

Rae F. Still, *The Gilmer-Aikin Bill* (1950). A sample of the legislative process in Texas.

Harvey Walker, *The Legislative Process: Lawmaking in the United States* (1948).

H. White, "Can Legislatures Learn from City Councils?" *Am. Pol. Sci. Rev.* (1927), XXI, 95–100.

C. I. Winslow, *State Legislative Committees* (1931).

Questions and Problems

1. Summarize the arguments for and against the bicameral state legislature.
2. How nearly does your state approximate representation according to population in the lower house? In the upper house?
3. What is the composition of your state legislature in respect to age, sex, profession, and education?
4. Comment upon the constitutional limitations as to the time a legislature may remain in session.
5. Estimate the value of joint committees in the work of the legislature.
6. What technical assistance is commonly available for a legislature? In what particulars could this service be substantially improved?
7. How far does your state constitution's provisions for the legislature fall short of those recommended in the Model State Constitution?
8. Make a list of the provisions of your state constitution that indicate a lack of confidence in the legislature.
9. Write a 200-word essay on the relation of limitations on legislatures to the problem of improving legislatures.
10. Discuss the initiative and referendum in relation to the republican form of government.
11. Can it be said that direct legislation is a tool of the "radicals" and "crack pots"?

☆ 17 ☆

The Federal Judicial System

CITIZENS generally will discuss with some assurance the activities of executives and legislators. But of judges they speak but little, finding their work too technical. It is, however, an error to assume that the common garden variety of college and university students cannot learn enough about the operation of the courts to enable them to make penetrating judgments on them. Furthermore, a review of our judicial systems is not a dreary assignment. The judges are human beings who deal with life—sometimes in the raw. With this injection of confidence we approach in this chapter the federal courts and in the next the state tribunals.

I. ORGANIZATION OF THE FEDERAL COURTS [1]

Constitutional provisions on organization. The Constitution (Article III, section 1) provides only that "the judicial power of the United States shall be vested in one Supreme Court, and in such inferior courts as the Congress may from time to time ordain and establish. The judges, both of the Supreme Court and the inferior courts, shall hold their offices during good behavior, and shall, at stated times, receive for their services a compensation which shall not be diminished during their continuance in office." Another important provision (Article II, section II, clause 2) is that judges of the Supreme Court shall be appointed by the President with the advice and consent of the Senate. Judges of the inferior courts are not inferior officers, and therefore they are appointed in like manner.

Organization of the federal judicial system by Congress. From the constitutional provisions it is quite clear that, except for the limitations relating to appointment and tenure, and the guaranty against a reduction

[1] J. M. Mathews, *The American Constitutional System* (1940 ed.), Ch. XIII; W. W. Willoughby, *Principles of the Constitutional Law of the United States* (1930 ed.), Ch. LX.

in the salary of judges, the organization of the courts is entirely within the power of Congress. The constitutional provision relating to the establishment of the courts, except the Supreme Court, is permissive, not mandatory. But not even the Supreme Court was established by the Constitution. The judiciary article simply requires Congress to establish it.

THE SUPREME COURT. In 1789 Congress established the Supreme Court with a Chief Justice and five associate justices. By later acts the number of judges was sometimes increased and sometimes decreased, but in 1869 the number was fixed at nine, where it has remained ever since.

THE CIRCUIT COURTS OF APPEALS. The First Congress (1789) established two classes of inferior courts, the district and the circuit courts. The district courts have been left substantially unchanged to this day; but the circuit courts were abolished in 1911, their original jurisdiction being transferred to the district courts, their appellate jurisdiction having been transferred to the newly created circuit courts of appeals. There are ten of these last-mentioned courts, one for each judicial circuit into which the United States is divided. There is in addition a circuit court of appeals for the District of Columbia. A circuit court of appeals has from three to nine judges.

Formerly, judges of the Supreme Court participated in the work of the circuit courts. Such assignments are still made, one justice of the Supreme Court to each circuit, and, since there are not enough justices to go around, two justices are assigned to two circuits each. But the pressure of judicial business in Washington has long since reduced the circuit work of Supreme Court judges to a pure formality.

THE DISTRICT COURTS. The lowest of the federal courts are the district courts, of which there are more than ninety. Often a state forms a single judicial district, but the larger and more populous states are divided into several districts. Some districts have two or more district judges (the southern district of New York has sixteen); and, for convenience, some districts are divided into several divisions. District courts have been established for Alaska, Hawaii, the Virgin Islands, the Canal Zone, and Puerto Rico. A judge is required to reside in the district for which he was appointed, although from time to time he may be assigned to assist in judicial work outside his own district.

The judicial council. Formerly the district courts and circuit courts of appeals were practically independent units. That is, the judges dispatched the business of the courts in the respective districts and circuits as best they could, with little aid or advice from the outside. In some districts the work was relatively light and easily disposed of, but in others the great number of cases caused congestion and delay. In 1922 a remedy was provided by an act of Congress. By this act, the Chief Justice is required to call the senior judge of each circuit court of appeals to an annual conference, which conference shall advise with the Chief Justice "as to any matters in respect to which the administration of justice in the courts of the United States may be improved." The senior district judge of each district court is required to make a report to this conference through the senior circuit judge of the circuit in which his district is located. This report must set forth the condition of judicial business in the district, including the number and character of cases on the docket, the business in arrears, and similar information.

On the basis of facts before it, the conference then prepares plans "for assignment and transfer of judges to or from circuits or districts where the state of the docket or condition of business indicates the need thereof, and shall submit such suggestions to the various courts as may seem in the interest of uniformity and expedition of business." [2]　The federal courts are thus unified to the extent of the powers of this conference to bring about such unification. The plan for the transfer of judges is of particular merit, since the tens of thousands of cases commenced each year in the federal courts do not obligingly distribute themselves among the districts in accordance with the capacity of the several courts to dispose of them.[3]

Administrative Office of the United States Courts.　By an act approved August 7, 1939, Congress created the Administrative Office of the United States Courts. The Director of the Office has no administrative duties relating to the Supreme Court, but, under the supervision and direction of the conference of senior circuit judges, he has charge of various administrative matters touching the operation of the other courts. His duties include administrative supervision of the offices of clerks and other administrative personnel of the courts, but not their appointment nor interference with the authority of the Attorney General over district attorneys and marshals; examination of the dockets of the courts and securing information as to their needs for assistance, and the preparation of statistical data and reports of the business transacted by the courts; the purchase, transfer, and distribution of equipment and supplies; the auditing of accounts; the provision of accommodations for the use of the courts; the preparation and submission of the budget of the courts, except the budget of the Supreme Court; and such other duties as may be assigned by the Supreme Court and the conference of the senior circuit judges. This Office is obviously not only useful for general administrative work in the judicial system, but also serves the judicial conference in helpful capacities.

---

[2] Title 28 U.S. Code sec. 218.

[3] N. J. Padelford, "The Federal Judicial Conference," *Am. Pol. Sci. Rev.*, XXVI, 482 (1932). See also "Report of the Judicial Conference" in the *Annual Report of the Attorney General of the United States.*

II. JURISDICTION OF THE FEDERAL COURTS [4]

Constitutional provisions. Article III of the Constitution stipulates that "the judicial power shall extend (1) to all cases, in law and equity, arising under this Constitution, the laws of the United States, and treaties made, or which shall be made, under their authority; (2) to all cases affecting ambassadors, other public ministers, and consuls; (3) to all cases of admiralty and maritime jurisdiction; (4) to controversies to which the United States shall be a party; (5) to controversies between two or more states; (6) between a state and citizens of another state; (7) between citizens of different states; (8) between citizens of the same state claiming lands under grants of different states; and (9) between a state, or the citizens thereof, and foreign states, citizens, or subjects." By the Eleventh Amendment (adopted 1798) the federal courts were deprived of their jurisdiction in cases brought against a state by citizens of another state or by citizens of a foreign state.

Jurisdiction determined by: 1. THE CHARACTER OF THE CASE. The provision of the Constitution quoted above makes clear that the federal courts acquire jurisdiction through the character of the *case* or the *parties*. Chief Justice Marshall pointed this out in Cohen v. Virginia (1821). All cases, regardless of who the parties may be, arising under the Constitution, federal laws (with a few exceptions in which Congress has given the state courts jurisdiction), and treaties fall under the jurisdiction of the federal courts. In like manner, all admiralty and maritime cases come under the jurisdiction of the federal courts. These types of cases may be clarified by examples. A state legislature or city council passes a measure that deprives some individual of his property without due process of law. Since this deprivation is prohibited by the Fourteenth Amendment, it is a matter over which the federal courts have jurisdiction. It is a case arising under the Constitution of the United States. Suppose an individual has some claim to a patent under the federal patent law, and one interpretation of that law will defeat his claim whereas another will sustain it. He has a case arising under the laws of the United States. Similarly, a trading privilege or some other right asserted under a treaty that involves the construction of that treaty is a proper case for the federal courts. A ship is taken as a prize in wartime by one of our vessels, a crime is committed aboard an American steamer on the high seas, a seaman is unable to collect his just wages—these are cases that, because of their character, go to the federal courts. To repeat, whatever the character of the parties, cases arising under the Constitution, laws, (with a few exceptions), and treaties of the

[4] C. N. Callender, *The American Courts* (1927), Ch. III; Mathews, *op. cit.,* Ch. XIV; Willoughby, *op. cit.,* Chs. LXI–LXII.

United States, and admiralty and maritime cases are all cases over which the federal courts have jurisdiction.

2. THE CHARACTER OF THE PARTIES. Other cases go to the federal courts because of the character of the parties. Cases of this type are: (1) those affecting ambassadors, other public ministers, and consuls (not American representatives abroad, but only foreign representatives in the United States); (2) controversies to which the United States is a party; (3) controversies between two or more states; (4) cases instituted by a state against citizens of another state (but not cases instituted against a state by a citizen of another state or by a citizen of a foreign state); and (5) cases between citizens of different states. To make this type of jurisdiction clear, we note that an ambassador carries his case to the federal courts, not because of the character of the case, but by reason of his status as an ambassador. Two citizens of the same state may have practically the same case, involving, let us say, an important contract, as do two other citizens of different states; but only the latter may carry their case before the federal courts, since they alone have the status (residence in different states in this instance) that entitles them to use these courts.

Exclusive and concurrent jurisdiction. Congress undoubtedly has the authority to vest federal judicial power exclusively in tribunals created by itself. In certain types of cases this allocation of power is necessary, and in other cases it seems advisable. Suits affecting ambassadors, other public ministers, and consuls, since these officers are accredited to the United States, naturally fall under the exclusive jurisdiction of the federal courts. Since the national government has the exclusive power to make war, prize cases are within the exclusive jurisdiction of its courts. Again, the federal courts are given exclusive jurisdiction in all cases in which the United States is a party, in controversies between the states, and in suits brought by a state against citizens of another state. This does not complete the list. On the other hand, in a number of very common cases, to be noted when we consider the jurisdiction of the federal district courts, Congress permits the state courts to exercise a concurrent jurisdiction with the federal courts.

Adjunct powers of the courts. Courts in general possess the powers necessary to maintain dignity and order in their proceedings, even without statutory authorization. Thus, they may punish persons for contempt. Congress has expressly authorized the federal courts to issue writs of habeas corpus and to issue other writs "not specifically provided for by statute, which may be necessary for the exercise of their respective jurisdictions, and agreeable to the usages and principles of law." [5]

THE GREAT WRITS. Of the writs that the courts may issue (state as well

[5] 28 U.S. Code 377, 451.

as federal), those of (1) habeas corpus, (2) mandamus, and (3) injunction are the most important.

1. The writ of *habeas corpus,* a common-law writ, may not be issued just because someone is in jail and wants to get out. It is issued by federal courts only when an individual is detained in connection with some matter over which such courts have jurisdiction. Thus, a person held on the suspicion that he has robbed a local filling station operator must apply to a state court for the writ; but either a person held for a violation of the federal narcotics act or a federal marshal charged with murder in defending the person of a federal judge may apply to a federal court for the writ. The procedure in connection with this writ has been sufficiently explained elsewhere.[6]

2. *Mandamus* is another common-law writ. It is used to compel some private person, or corporation, public official, or lower court to perform a particular duty imposed by law. A common carrier that fails to comply with certain sections of the transportation acts may be mandamused by a district court upon the application of the Attorney General at the request of the Interstate Commerce Commission. The most interesting cases in which the writ is used are those in which it applies to the acts of executive officers. The President is not subject to mandamus, nor may other executive officials be mandamused in connection with matters over which they are given discretion; but where the subordinate officials have a service to perform in which they are given no discretion (a mere ministerial service), the mandamus will be issued at the request of parties having a proper claim. For example, a citizen cannot mandamus the Secretary of the Treasury for refusing to consider him for an appointive position in his department; but if the citizen is legally entitled to funds from the United States, he could mandamus the disbursing officer should he withhold them.

3. The writ (or bill) of *injunction* is an equity remedy. Federal courts may enjoin parties from instituting proceedings in state courts, in order to preserve their own jurisdictional rights. In like manner, the federal tribunals may enjoin state officers from enforcing state laws that are in contravention to the national Constitution; a railroad company from laying its tracks until a franchise right has been determined; and striking workmen (until quite recently) from interfering with the business of their employers. Formerly the frequent use of the injunction in connection with labor troubles caused much political controversy and some bitterness on the part of labor leaders. The party who violates an injunction is guilty of contempt of court, and he may be brought in and summarily sent to jail without trial by jury.[7]

[6] See pages 131–132.

[7] On the writs, consult a law dictionary or the *Encyclopaedia of the Social Sciences.*

Specific jurisdiction of the several classes of federal courts. Up to this point we have been considering the question of the jurisdiction and powers of the federal courts in general. Now we shall see just what kind of jurisdiction each class of the federal courts—district courts, circuit courts of appeals, and the Supreme Court—possesses.

1. DISTRICT COURTS. The district courts have only original jurisdiction; that is, they are trial courts as distinguished from appellate courts. Chapter 2 of the *Judicial Code* details the original jurisdiction of these courts. Here we shall simply make a partial enumeration, as follows: crimes and offenses against the United States; admiralty and maritime cases; prize

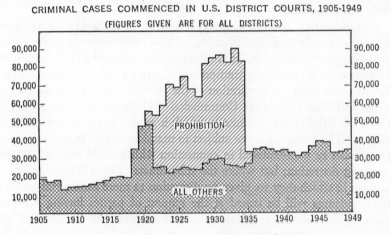

CRIMINAL CASES COMMENCED IN U.S. DISTRICT COURTS, 1905-1949
(FIGURES GIVEN ARE FOR ALL DISTRICTS)

From *Annual Report of the Director of the Administrative Office of the United States Courts* (1949), p. 100.

cases (cases of capture on the high seas in time of war); cases arising under the internal revenue and tariff laws, excepting certain tariff cases in which the Court of Customs and Patent Appeals has jurisdiction; suits under the postal, interstate commerce, patent, copyright, and trade-mark laws; suits respecting civil rights; suits and proceedings in bankruptcy; and concurrent jurisdiction with the Court of Claims in contract suits against the United States where the claim is not in excess of $10,000.

Until 1946 no one had the right to sue the United States for a tort (damage to property or personal injury). Such claims were submitted to Congress, where "hit or miss" damages were obtained through private bills. By the Federal Tort Claims Act (1946) district courts are authorized to render judgment on any claim against the United States "on account of damage to or loss of property or on account of personal injury or death caused by the negligent or wrongful act or omission of any employee of the Govern-

ment while acting within the scope of his office or employment, under circumstances where the United States, if a private person, would be liable."
Administrative agencies of the Government are given the authority, with
the consent of claimants, to settle cases for which claim is made for less than

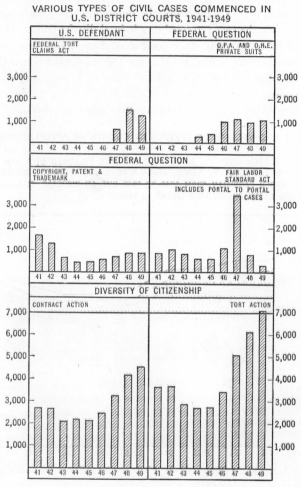

VARIOUS TYPES OF CIVIL CASES COMMENCED IN
U.S. DISTRICT COURTS, 1941-1949

From *Annual Report of the Director of the Administrative Office of the United States Courts*
(1949), p. 88.

$1,000. Thus Congress not only took the too-long-delayed action of re-
lieving itself of the chore of settling damage cases but also provided for
much more appropriate remedies.

The district courts have original jurisdiction "of all suits of a civil nature, at common law or equity, brought by the United States, or by any

officer thereof authorized by law to sue." In cases arising under the Constitution, laws, and treaties of the United States, and in cases between citizens of different states, and between citizens of a state and foreign states, citizens, or subjects, where the matter in controversy exceeds $3,000, they have concurrent jurisdiction with the state courts. But where an action is originally brought in a state court, the defendant may, under certain circumstances, have the case removed to a federal district court. If, however, the amount in controversy does not exceed $3,000, the state courts have exclusive jurisdiction. Thus, as far as the federal district courts have jurisdiction, it is original; but they fall far short of having original and exclusive jurisdiction in all cases, the state courts being given concurrent jurisdiction in many cases and exclusive jurisdiction in others.

SOURCE AND VOLUME OF APPEALS IN COURTS OF APPEALS, 1940-1949

A STEADY DECLINE UNTIL 1947 HAS BEEN FOLLOWED BY A SMALL RISE IN THE LAST TWO YEARS. APPEALS FROM ADMINISTRATIVE AGENCIES DECREASED RADICALLY FROM 1940 TO 1948, BUT AN INCREASE OF LABOR BOARD CASES CHANGED THE TREND IN 1949.

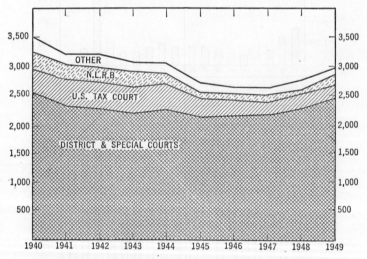

From *Annual Report of the Director of the Administrative Office of the United States Courts* (1949), p. 77.

2. CIRCUIT COURTS OF APPEALS. The circuit courts of appeals have no original jurisdiction. Their chief business is to hear numerous appeals from the district courts, although certain classes of appeals go direct from the district courts to the Supreme Court. In addition, the circuit courts have appellate jurisdiction in cases coming from the district courts in the territories; and they are empowered to enforce, set aside, or modify certain

orders of the Federal Trade Commission, the National Labor Relations Board, and a few other administrative agencies. The decisions of these courts are final in all cases between citizens of different states, in cases arising under the criminal, patent, copyright, bankruptcy, or revenue laws, and in a few other cases. Thus the primary purpose for which these courts were created, namely, to free the Supreme Court of a large number of appeals, has been accomplished. We should add, however, that the Supreme Court may have any of the cases mentioned above brought before it for final determination, if a party so petitions and if the Supreme Court deems it advisable.

3. THE SUPREME COURT. The Supreme Court has original jurisdiction only in two types of cases: (1) those affecting ambassadors, other public ministers, and consuls; and (2) cases in which states are parties. Congress has no authority to give the Supreme Court original jurisdiction in cases other than those enumerated. On the other hand, Congress has not hesitated to grant to inferior federal courts concurrent jurisdiction in some of these cases; for instance, cases between a state and citizens of another state. Congress has not, and may not, deprive the Supreme Court of its original jurisdiction. It has simply given other courts a concurrent original jurisdiction.

By far the largest part of the work of the Supreme Court is appellate and regulated by acts of Congress. A few cases may be appealed from district courts to the Supreme Court, but nearly all of the appeals come from circuit courts. As indicated above, many cases are decided finally by the circuit courts of appeals and may not be carried to the Supreme Court except by its order. But in important cases, such as those involving the construction of the Constitution of the United States, the constitutionality of acts of Congress and treaties, and cases in which state constitutions or laws are claimed to be in contravention to the Constitution of the United States, the Supreme Court has regular appellate jurisdiction.

Of particular importance in our system of government is the appellate jurisdiction of the Supreme Court in certain types of cases that have been decided in the highest state courts. It must be emphasized that not every case decided in a state supreme court may be so appealed. When no federal question is involved in a case, it is decided with finality by the supreme court of the state. But where a case arises under the Constitution, laws, or treaties of the United States, or in connection with some right or duty under the government of the United States, it may be appealed to the Supreme Court.[8]

[8] Strictly speaking, appeal lies only in those cases in which the state courts decide against a right claimed under federal law. Cases in which state courts uphold a right claimed under federal law are reviewed by the Supreme Court of the United States only at its discretion by *certiorari*, to use the legal term. Litigants have no *right* of appeal in such cases.

III. THE LAW ADMINISTERED BY THE FEDERAL COURTS

1. **Federal law.** It is understood, of course, that the Constitution itself is a law which the federal courts must apply, and that they must set aside any other "law" which contravenes its provisions. Treaties and acts of Congress passed in pursuance of the Constitution are laws. Thousands of cases come before the federal courts every year under provisions of acts of Congress. Thus, during the depression of the 'thirties, the federal bankruptcy statute was applied in the 60,000 or more bankruptcy cases (about three times the present number) that arose annually. Numerous cases now arise under the Fair Labor Standards Act, the Employers' Liability Act, and various penal statutes.

The only federal crimes are those specified in acts of Congress. There are quite a few such crimes, however, for Congress is authorized (1) to provide for the punishment of counterfeiting; (2) to define and punish piracies and felonies committed on the high seas, and offenses committed against international law; (3) to declare the punishment of treason; (4) to exercise *exclusive* legislation for the District of Columbia and places purchased for the erection of forts and arsenals; (5) to make *all* needful rules and regulations respecting the territories; and (6) above all, through its implied powers, to provide penalties for the violation of any law that it enacts. Illustrating the last-mentioned authority, the power to regulate interstate commerce and to establish post offices and post roads gives Congress the power to prescribe punishment for violation of laws with respect thereto. Before Prohibition repeal there were many criminal prosecutions under the dry laws, 56,992 of the 87,305 prosecutions in 1930 falling in the class of Prohibition cases.

2. **International law.** The federal courts frequently apply international law. Although the courts are bound by an act of Congress that may be contrary to international law, the Supreme Court early held that such "an act of Congress ought never to be construed to violate the law of nations if any other possible construction remains" [9] and that "till an act be passed, the court is bound by the law of nations, which is a part of the law of the land." [10] Prize cases, piracy cases, cases involving the interpretations of treaties, and boundary disputes between American states are but a few of the cases in which international law is applied.

3. **The common law.** The federal courts have jurisdiction in a large body of civil cases to which no federal law is applicable. These are the cases of "diversity of citizenship," cases between citizens of different states. A citizen of Illinois sues a citizen of Indiana, let us say, for damage to prop-

---

[9] The Charming Betsy, 2 Cranch 64 (1804).
[10] The Nereide, 9 Cranch 388 (1815).

erty or for personal injury. As made clear in the last section, the Illinois man may bring suit in a federal district court in Indiana. But no federal law covers such matters. What law or laws, then, will the federal court apply? The Federal Judiciary Act of 1789 gives the answer: "The laws of the several states . . . shall be regarded as rules of decision in trials at common law, in the courts of the United States, in cases where they apply." In the case just mentioned, the federal district court in Indiana would apply the laws of that state. For a hundred years or more there was confusion on this point. The courts of the United States applied the state statutes in such cases; but where there were no statutes, and if they happened not to approve of the common-law doctrines of a particular state, they formulated a sort of "general law" of their own. This situation is now clarified, however, by a recent decision of the Supreme Court; [11] and the federal courts are following state law, both common and statute, without exception.[12]

4. Equity. As noted above, the federal judicial power extends to cases in law and *equity*. Exploration of the origin and development of equity would be interesting and profitable, but here we must be content to observe that equity is that division or branch of the old English and American law which sometimes provides better remedies than the common law and protects certain rights not covered by that law. The courts of the United States have not been required by Congress to follow as "rules of decision" the equity rules of the several states. The Supreme Court, however, seems to have decided, of its own volition, to follow the practice of the states in equitable proceedings as well as in the common law cases.[13] It comes about, then, that in the diversity of citizenship cases the federal courts will follow state law, be it statutory, common law, or equity.

IV. PROCEDURE IN THE FEDERAL DISTRICT COURTS

The district courts are the trial courts, the courts of first instance, in the federal system. Uniformity of procedure in federal cases has been brought about by acts of Congress and, more recently, by the Supreme Court, which, acting under authority granted by Congress, has prescribed rules of procedure for the lower courts. Rules so prescribed now govern procedure in criminal and civil cases in the district courts, bankruptcy proceedings, admiralty cases, copyright cases, and appellate proceedings in criminal cases.

Criminal cases. Crimes of burglary, robbery, kidnaping, rape, and "singular murders in love triangles"—the types of crime that grab the

---

[11] Erie Railroad Co. v. Tompkins, 304 U.S. 64 (1938).
[12] W. F. Dodd, *Cases and Materials on Constitutional Law* (1949 ed.), pp. 358–359 n.
[13] Guaranty Trust Co. of N.Y. v. York, 326 U.S. 99 (1945).

headlines—are offenses over which state courts commonly have jurisdiction. As noted above, however, there is also a wide variety of federal crimes. If they are less interesting to the morbidly curious than the state crimes, that is an advantage to the federal courts, making it less difficult to maintain dignity and avoid sensationalism in their proceedings.

The Criminal Code of the United States defines a felony as any crime the punishment for which is death or imprisonment for more than one year. It classes as misdemeanors those offenses the penalty for which is not more than a year and not less than six months in jail, and as petty offenses those violations of law that may result in jail terms of not more than six months.[14] Indictment is not required for misdemeanors or petty offenses (lesser misdemeanors); and the latter, if the accused does not object, may be tried by a United States commissioner instead of a judge. But the Constitution prohibits the trial of any person for felony unless on the indictment of a grand jury. When it appears that a felony has been committed, the commissioner decides whether some individual or individuals shall be held for the grand jury. This jury consists of from 16 to 23 persons. It is advised and assisted by attorneys for the government, and with the concurrence of at least twelve of its members it may return an indictment naming the crime and the accused. The Constitution requires that the accused be given a speedy and public trial by an impartial jury of the state and district wherein the crime shall have been committed; that he shall be informed of the nature of the accusation; that he shall be confronted with the witnesses against him; that he shall have compulsory process for obtaining witnesses in his favor; that he shall have the assistance of counsel; that he shall not be compelled to be a witness against himself; that he shall not be deprived of life, liberty, or property without due process of law; and that he shall not be twice put in jeopardy for the same offense.[15]

Civil cases. The ordinary suits at common law are those in which parties seek to obtain possession of land from which they have been ousted or to which they have been denied access, suits for damages in cases of breaches of contracts, damage suits for injuries resulting from torts (trespasses, for example), and actions to recover personal property. The court of original jurisdiction, when sitting as a court of law, must, in conformity to the Seventh Amendment of the Constitution, try cases involving amounts in excess of twenty dollars before a jury, unless the jury is waived. Each party, of course, has counsel, and witnesses are examined and cross-examined.

[14] 18 Code of the United States, sec. 541.

[15] See Chapter 6, section III, for a fuller discussion of these Constitutional guaranties against arbitrary procedures. The Rules of Criminal Procedure cover some forty large pages in the Code of the United States (1946), title 18, Ch. 21A.

When all the evidence has been heard and the arguments have been made, the judge explains the law involved to the jury; but the facts are left for the jury to decide. The jury then deliberates and brings in the verdict, which in the federal courts must be unanimous. The judge may set aside the verdict if the jury has ignored his rulings on points of law, or if the jury's decision is clearly contrary to the evidence, or if the jury has reached its conclusion by some irregular means. However, if the judge sets aside the verdict, that does not mean that the other party wins, but only that a new trial must be held. This taking of cases from the jury is a much more common proceeding in the federal courts than it is in the state courts; and, considering the limitations of the jury system, it perhaps explains in part the higher confidence commonly reposed in the federal courts.

As has already been explained, equity affords relief in numerous cases not covered by the common law. Cases in equity are decided by a judge or judges alone, no juries being used. The equity proceeding with which most of us are familiar is that in which an injunction is sought. The great majority of civil cases, whether in law or equity, are cases which arise under state law and over which state courts have exclusive jurisdiction.

V. THE SUPREME COURT [16]

Sessions of the Court. The Supreme Court of the United States is an institution of such transcendent importance in our national life that we must make it a subject of special consideration. Each year it begins its session in October and continues until late in the spring. It is presided over by the Chief Justice, the prestige of whose position is only a little higher than that of an associate justice, and whose duties and powers differ from those of his eight associates only because he is the ceremonial head of the Court and directs certain administrative affairs of the body, as, for example, the naming of an associate to write the opinion of the Court after a case has been heard and discussed. Six of the justices constitute a quorum and a majority of the whole number is necessary for a decision.

OPENING OF THE COURT. "Oyez, Oyez, Oyez! [17] All persons having business before the honorable judges of the Supreme Court of the United States are admonished to draw near and give their attention, for the Court is now sitting. God save the United States and this honorable court."

---

[16] C. A. Beard, *The Supreme Court and the Constitution* (1912); L. B. Boudin, *Government by Judiciary* (1932); R. E. Cushman (ed.), "Ten Years of the Supreme Court, 1937–1947," *Am. Pol. Sci. Rev.*, XLI (1947), 1142–1181, and XLII (1948), 32–67; W. F. Dodd, "The United States Supreme Court, 1936–1946," *Am. Pol. Sci. Rev.*, XLI (1947), 1–11; F. Frankfurter and J. M. Landis, *Business of the Supreme Court* (1936 ed.); A. M. Schlesinger, Jr., "The Supreme Court: 1947," *Fortune*, January, 1947, p. 73; C. Warren, *Congress, the Constitution, and the Supreme Court* (1936 ed.).

[17] Old French, meaning "Hear Ye."

These words are uttered by the clerk in solemn tones entirely free from the perfunctory and commonplace qualities that ordinarily characterize such announcements. The audience in the grand structure where the Court now holds its sessions [18] is impressed with this regular midday announcement, and it rises to its feet as the nine distinguished men, wearing black silk robes, file in and take their places, the Chief Justice in the center and the associate justices on his right and left in the order of the length of their service in the Supreme Court. The Court is without question the most dignified, the most impressive, even awe-inspiring, body in America.[19] It has had its "off periods," but it is an institution one does not criticize with impunity.

PRESENTATION OF CASES. The preliminaries disposed of, the Court settles down to hearing cases. An attorney may talk for as much as an hour; and the judges listen attentively, especially if he is able, clear, and concise. Judges have been known to show some impatience with lawyers who did not have their cases well in hand. On occasion, an earnest young attorney may feel that a judge is not taking the trouble to follow his argument; but he may be agreeably surprised, perhaps embarrassed, by a question from the justice which proves that there was no lack of attention. Eloquent words count for little in this chamber, and perhaps sound a little hollow even to the inept attorney who speaks them. Jury-swaying arguments count for nothing at all. Oral argument is, in any event, only a part of the presentation. Printed briefs containing the arguments of counsel and the printed record of the case in the lower court often run into many pages.

Study and discussion. Ordinarily the Court spends four hours a day, five days a week, in hearing cases. But this no more represents the work of the judges than a few hours in the classroom constitute the work of a conscientious student. The printed records and arguments must be mastered after the case has been publicly presented. References must be consulted, and legal tangles must be straightened out. Then the judges must meet in private for discussion. Occasionally, when a majority cannot reach an agreement, a rearguing of the case is ordered, as instanced by the income tax case in 1895. So exacting and pressing is the work of the justices that they are usually busy both before and after each day's session and frequently have to labor far into the night. Occasionally there are short recesses to give them an opportunity to dispose of accumulated cases.[20]

[18] Until 1935 it sat in the old Senate Hall in the Capitol.

[19] For some of the material in this and the following paragraph, see the article by Mildred Adams, "In the Supreme Court Law Is Majesty," *New York Times Magazine*, Nov. 10, 1929. On the conservative lawyers' attitude toward this Court, the importance of its dignity, its stability, and so on, see Boudin, *op. cit.*, I, 1 ff. and II, 159 ff.

[20] The Court disposes of approximately 1,000 cases each year.

Decisions. When an agreement in a particular case has been reached, the Chief Justice himself, or an associate designated by him, writes the decision of the Court. Unanimity of agreement, or even majority agreement as to the principles that are applicable is not necessary; but that a majority reach the same conclusion is essential. As a result, therefore: (1) the nine justices may agree both as to the judgment and as to the principles of law on which it is based; (2) a majority may agree as to the judgment and principles, but a minority may dissent; and (3) both the majority and the minority may disagree among themselves as to the principles that govern their respective conclusions. In the event that a justice agrees with the conclusion of the Court but not with the reasons on which it is based, he may write a separate opinion. In like manner, a minority judge may write a dissenting opinion for his group; and if a justice in that minority does not accept the reasons assigned, he may write a dissenting opinion of his own. More will be said of the dissenting opinions presently.[21]

JUDGMENT, OPINIONS, AND OBITER DICTA. The judgment of the Court is usually stated in a brief sentence. *Examples:* "It follows that the district court erred in making the order appealed from, and the same is reversed." "There was no error in the judgment of the circuit court of appeals, and it is, therefore, affirmed." "The judgment of the state supreme court is therefore reversed and the case is remanded to that court for further proceedings not inconsistent with this opinion." "Our conclusion is that the petitioner is entitled to be discharged from custody, and it is so ordered." Judgments in such forms constitute the legal decisions of the Court.

The discussions, often covering many printed pages, setting forth the principles that control in the case, are designated as the opinions of the Court. Such opinions are accepted as declarations by which the Court will be guided subsequently in similar cases. But in giving its opinions, the Court does not always confine them to the points at issue in the case at hand. It may turn aside to related questions that it desires to see cleared up. Such digressions are known as *obiter dicta*. They are not accepted as stating the position of the Court in subsequent cases to the extent the ordinary opinions are, although they may be applied in proper cases if they happen to conform to the opinion of the Court.

[21] All the opinions in each case are, of course, published and distributed. Cases decided before 1882 are cited by the name of the court reporter charged with the duty of having them published. In order, these reporters were: Dallas (4 vols.), Cranch (9 vols.), Wheaton (12 vols.), Peters (16 vols.), Howard (24 vols.), Black (2 vols.), Wallace (23 vols.), and Otto (17 vols.). Thus, Marbury v. Madison is cited "1 Cranch 137," the numerals preceding the name indicating the volume and those following the name the page on which the decision begins. Since 1882, all volumes, beginning with 108, are numbered consecutively without mention of reporters' names, and cases decided since that date are cited "Buck v. Bell, 274 U.S. 200," "Finch & Co. v. McKittrick, 305 U.S. 395," etc. It is also a common practice (and a good one), to give the year of the decision as is done in this text.

DISSENTING OPINIONS. Of course, the conclusion of the majority settles a case; but not infrequently a minority opinion is received and discussed with as much interest as the majority opinion. The opinion of Justice Curtis in the Dred Scott Case (1857), of Justice Holmes in Lochner v. New York (1905), of Chief Justice Hughes in United States v. Macintosh (1931), and of Justice Stone in the United States v. Butler (1936), are a few of the outstanding dissenting opinions. Those who criticize the opinion of the Court may find much aid and comfort in the dissenting opinion. Thus did the foes of slavery use the minority opinion in the Dred Scott Case; the advocates of the rights of the states to use their police power without too much interference from the Supreme Court, the Holmes opinion in the Lochner case; the friends of a more liberal naturalization policy, the Hughes dissent in the Macintosh case. When Bryan was criticized for his condemnation of the income tax decision in 1895, he very cleverly replied, "If you want criticism, read the dissenting opinions of the Court."

"A dissent," said Charles Evans Hughes, "is an appeal to the brooding spirit of the law, to the intelligence of a future day. . . ." [22] The minority opinion of the Court today may become the majority opinion tomorrow. In 1936 the New York minimum wage law was held invalid in a five-to-four decision. In 1937 a similar law of the State of Washington was sustained by the same majority. And there had been no change in the personnel of the Court. Justice Roberts changed sides. This is simply one of many cases in which the Court has reversed itself.

FIVE-FOUR DECISIONS. A decision by a bare majority of five to four is likely to weaken popular confidence in the Court, for a time at least, especially if it is coincident with a political controversy over the subject to which it relates. Fortunately, these so-called "one-man" decisions have not been very common; but the vote was five to four in six of the twelve New Deal cases decided before June, 1936. Several constitutional amendments have been proposed that would require a more significant majority in cases in which a legislative act is declared unconstitutional. The wisdom of an amendment of this character is open to serious question. It seems best to leave the Court to work out this problem for itself. Former Associate Justice Clarke suggested that the Court voluntarily adopt a rule similar to the amendments proposed. No Chief Justice is proud of five-four decisions, and we may rest assured that earnest efforts are made to prevent them.

Judicial review. We are now to consider the most distinctive feature of the work of the Supreme Court and the one that has occasioned the greatest controversy, namely, its power to pass upon the constitutionality of legislation. The source of this power and the reasons for its exercise

---

[22] As quoted in Catherine D. Bowen's *Yankee from Olympus* (1944), p. 373.

are discussed in Chapter 3, section III. Here we shall simply refresh our memories with the statement that any part of a state constitution or law or any city charter or ordinance that contravenes any provision of the federal Constitution, laws, or treaties may be nullified by the Supreme Court of the United States, if it comes before the Court in a properly litigated case. Similarly, when acts of Congress and treaties contravene the Constitution, they may be nullified.

OPERATES ONLY IN LITIGATED CASES. Many persons seem to think that all acts of state legislatures are submitted to the Supreme Court for its approval, and that all of the statutes of Congress are immediately sent by special messenger to that eminent tribunal, where they are anxiously examined for taints of unconstitutionality. Of course this belief is absurd. The Court does not pass upon all legislative acts, as the President and governors are authorized to do; nor does it give advisory opinions, although the supreme courts in several of the states may do so.[23] The Supreme Court is a judicial tribunal, with the function of deciding only "cases and controversies." A statute of Congress or a state law comes to the Court, therefore, only when a party to a legal controversy tests the validity of the enactment under which it arises. For example, if an individual is held for a crime under an act of Congress, he may test the validity of that act; or if in a civil suit he claims that a right supposed to be enjoyed by the other party to the suit rests on a state law in conflict with the federal Constitution, he may test the validity of the state law. But persons not parties to a suit, who have only a general interest in its outcome, have no way of testing the constitutionality of a law. With these points in mind, it is easy to understand that the constitutionality of the great majority of legislative measures is never passed upon, although it is true that at some time or other the greater number of the more important acts are so reviewed. It is a matter of considerable interest that such a significant statute as the Missouri Compromise of 1820 was never judicially questioned until 1857, when it was declared void.[24]

OTHER LIMITATIONS ON JUDICIAL REVIEW. In addition to the rule that laws are not declared void except in actual litigation, there are several other limitations upon this power of judicial review. (1) It is agreed that the unconstitutionality of a statute should be clear beyond all reasonable doubt.[25] This rule of interpretation must be taken to mean beyond all reasonable doubt of the majority of the justices, for to allege that this

---

[23] In 1822 the Justices of the Supreme Court individually and informally gave an advisory opinion to President Monroe. See Charles Warren, *The Supreme Court in United States History* (1923), II, 55–57.

[24] J. M. Beck, *The Constitution of the United States* (1924), p. 226.

[25] See discussion in W. F. Dodd, *Cases and Materials on Constitutional Law* (1949 ed.), p. 58 n.

conviction governed the Court when five of the learned judges held a law void, and four no less learned judges held a contrary view, would be humorous to say the least. (2) Only that part of a statute which is unconstitutional is annulled, unless the parts are so interdependent that one may not be stricken out without doing violence to the others. Thus, when the Court held a federal corrupt practices act void as applied to senatorial primaries,[26] it was generally understood that other parts of the law still held, and a Republican committee concluded that wisdom and prudence dictated that candidates for the House of Representatives should continue to observe its provisions.[27] (3) The Court will not pass upon political questions, that is, questions which, in the opinion of the Court, the Constitution and the general scheme of American government leave to the President or Congress or both. When the State of Georgia questioned the constitutionality of the "Reconstruction Acts," the Supreme Court would take no action, stating that the statutes were political in character and did not involve personal or property rights.[28] Similarly, the Court will refuse to restrain the President by injunction from carrying into effect an act of Congress alleged to be unconstitutional.[29] (4) It is further stated that the Court will not declare void a law that does not violate constitutional provisions but that, in the opinion of the justices, is unwise or oppressive.[30] Yet it is difficult if not impossible, to free ourselves from the suspicion that the judges sometimes pronounce laws invalid under the claim that they violate constitutional provisions, when in reality they only violate the judges' economic or social theories. This suspicion may have become more general in the period 1935–1937, when the Court was nullifying so much New Deal legislation. Max Lerner writes that the public "began to see that judicial decisions were not babies brought by constitutional storks, but are born out of the travail of economic circumstances."[31]

Number and kinds of laws declared void. How many laws have been declared void? From some of the arguments that have been made against judicial review, one might get the impression that the justices do not feel that they have earned their lunch until they have invalidated some legislative act. In all its history the Supreme Court has declared invalid only about eighty acts of Congress, and the greater number of these were of small importance. Five or six times that number of acts have been contested

---

[26] Newberry v. United States, 256 U.S. 232 (1921).

[27] J. K. Pollock, Jr., *Party Campaign Funds* (1926), pp. 207–208.

[28] Georgia v. Stanton, 6 Wallace 50 (1868). See also Coleman v. Miller, 307 U.S. 433 (1939).

[29] Mississippi v. Johnson, 4 Wallace 475 (1867).

[30] In Ashwander v. Tennessee Valley Authority, 297 U.S. 288 (1936), some of these and certain other limitations are discussed.

[31] Quoted in C. Herman Pritchett, "The Roosevelt Court: Votes and Values," *Am. Pol. Sci. Rev.*, XLII (1948), 53, from Lerner's *Ideas for the Ice Age*.

before the Court, but their constitutionality has been upheld. The validity of well over a thousand state laws has been challenged, of which the Court has annulled about one fourth. Inasmuch as Congress enacts hundreds of laws annually and the state legislatures enact thousands, it is obvious not only that a very small percentage of them are declared void but also that relatively few laws ever come before the Supreme Court on the issue of constitutionality. It should be added, however, that both the number coming before the Court and the number annulled increased following the First World War until 1937. Since that date only one part of one act of Congress has been declared void.

More significant than the number of laws annulled are the kinds of laws annulled, particularly those that have incited popular criticism. In 1894 Congress passed an income tax law, which was declared void the next year on the ground that certain sections of it imposed a direct tax without apportionment among the states according to population, as required by the Constitution.[32] Under the provisions of the Agricultural Adjustment Act more than a billion dollars was collected through a processing tax, this money to be paid to farmers who accepted a program of crop reduction. This act, this hope of the farmer, said the Court, was invalid because it provided for expenditures for a regulation lying within the reserved powers of the states.[33] We take one other example of the nullification of acts of Congress. A minimum wage law for women and children in the District of Columbia was held to be a violation of the liberty of contract,[34] a right deduced from a provision of the Fifth Amendment that no person shall be deprived of life, liberty, or property without due process of law. A number of state laws have been nullified by the Court under the same clause of the Fourteenth Amendment; for example, the statute of the State of New York regulating the hours of employment in bakeries and the same state's minimum wage law for women and children.[35]

POPULAR CRITICISM RESULTING. When legislation of the character mentioned above is set aside, the decisions may be received with great protest, for a large part of the public has an interest, either direct or humanitarian, in seeing these laws upheld. The public is not capable of judging the fine points of constitutional construction involved; nor is it in the proper mood to judge, even if it were competent to do so under ordinary circumstances. Nevertheless, when the public feels that the judges have applied their own social philosophy to the cases at hand and that they have done so under the guise of interpreting the Constitution, we should not

[32] Pollock v. Farmers' Loan & Trust Co., 158 U.S. 601 (1895).
[33] United States v. Butler, 297 U.S. 1 (1936).
[34] Adkins v. Children's Hospital, 261 U.S. 525 (1923).
[35] Lochner v. New York, 198 U.S. 45 (1905); Morehead v. New York, 298 U.S. 587 (1936).

be too harsh in our judgment of that public, for frequently the minority of the justices take essentially the same view. Thus, in the New York bakery case just referred to, Justice Holmes, in dissenting, declared that the case was decided upon an economic theory which a large part of the country did not entertain, and that the word "liberty" in the Fourteenth Amendment was perverted when it was interpreted in such a way as to render invalid the New York statute.[36]

Judges cannot divest themselves of their background, their training, their philosophy much more successfully than the general run of mankind. Governor John Bricker, when a candidate for Vice President, was quoted in an AP dispatch as saying (Oct. 14, 1944), "A man cannot escape the impact of his economic and social environment by putting on a black robe." It would be marvelous indeed if judges were not influenced by their own social and economic theories when they come to interpret such broad and indefinite phrases of the Constitution as "due process of law" and the "equal protection of the laws." Clearly, when the Court holds that a ten-hour law for bakeshop employees is not "due process" and that a ten-hour law for women in industry is "due process," it may be plausibly asserted that the magic term is simply being interpreted to fit the judges' ideas of what police laws are needed and what are not needed; that the judges are exercising a power which rightly belongs to the legislators.

The Court and politics. As already indicated, the Supreme Court will not decide political questions. This statement is true, in a technical sense. For example, it will not decide which of two opposing governments in a foreign country is recognized by the United States, or whether the government of an American state is republican in form, or whether a state of war existed between the United States and some foreign country on a given date. Such questions are characterized by the Supreme Court (and by all other courts) as political, and are left to executive and legislative officers to decide.

But when we take a broader view of what constitutes a political question, we find that some of these questions are decided by the Court. In common parlance, labor laws, income tax laws, social security laws, public utility regulations, agricultural relief measures, currency legislation, in fact, any issues over which various groups of the people divide into more or less hostile camps are political in character. Such matters, affecting private rights so materially, properly come before the Court, and the decision in each case must please one political group and offend the other. This result is unavoidable, and any intelligent citizen can understand why it is so. As

---

[36] In dissenting in Morehead v. New York, 298 U.S. 587 (1936), Justice Stone said: "It is difficult to imagine any grounds, other than our own personal economic predilections," for holding invalid the New York minimum wage law.

long as the judges maintain a calm, objective view, the public should have no serious complaints.

On a few occasions, however, the judges have perhaps passed the bounds of judicial proprieties. In the Dred Scott Case, both the majority and the minority judges were influenced by political motives, as indicated by their written opinions in the case and particularly by their more recently available correspondence and papers relative to the decision.[37] In the income tax case a generation later, Joseph H. Choate, counsel for those who alleged the tax unconstitutional, told the justices in effect that they must stop the march of communism now or never.[38] Justice Field, in a concurring opinion, siding with the bare majority of the Court that held the statute unconstitutional, sounded hardly less like an advocate than a judge. Said he: "The present assault upon capital is but the beginning. It will be but the stepping-stone to others, larger and more sweeping, till our political contests will become a war of the poor against the rich; a war constantly growing in intensity and bitterness."[39] Happily, the justices have stepped into the political arena in this fashion in only a few cases, although in numerous instances they have been under the necessity of deciding cases in which powerful contending groups had vital interests.

Political parties and the Court. More frequently, perhaps, than the Court has willingly entered into politics, the political parties have made the Court or its decisions the subject of political controversy. Both wings of the Democratic party accepted the Dred Scott decision in 1860, while the Republicans denounced it as "a dangerous political heresy."[40] In 1896 the Democratic party denounced the income tax decision of the previous year, and declared it to be the duty of Congress to use all the constitutional power that remained after that decision, "to the end that wealth may bear its due proportion of the expense of the government." It further denounced "government by injunction as a new and highly dangerous form of oppression by which federal judges, in contempt of the laws of the states and rights of citizens, become at once legislators, judges, and executioners."[41] In 1924 the La Follette Progressives not only called for a constitutional amendment that would prohibit the Supreme Court from rendering acts of Congress invalid, but they advocated also a provision for the election of federal judges for a term not exceeding ten years.[42] Because the Court had overturned so much New Deal legislation, it was thought that the Court might be an issue in the campaign of 1936. But no responsible

[37] C. A. and Mary Beard, *Rise of American Civilization* (1930), II, 14 ff.
[38] *Ibid.*, pp. 335–336.
[39] 157 U.S. 429, 607 (1895).
[40] K. H. Porter, *National Party Platforms* (1924), pp. 53, 54, 57.
[41] *Ibid.*, pp. 184, 185.
[42] *Ibid.*, pp. 516–517, 519, 520.

leader, excepting Senator Norris, raised his voice during the campaign against judicial review or judicial conservatism.

Whatever the charge might be against the Supreme Court, that charge has been commonly regarded as a dangerous campaign issue—dangerous because millions who understand very little about the processes of government have a deep reverence for the Supreme Court. Indeed, they may not know the difference between the Supreme Court and the Constitution, and in that ignorance they have wisdom, for the Constitution is what the Court says it is; or, to use the words of an irreverent critic, "The Constitution is the Supreme Court's last guess."

President Franklin D. Roosevelt's proposal. With popular support for him at a new peak the President, on January 6, 1937, in an address to Congress, declared: "The judicial branch also is asked by the people to do its part in making democracy successful." Some of the people's representatives in Congress then busied themselves with plans to limit the jurisdiction of the Supreme Court, to require more than a mere majority of the Court to declare a law unconstitutional, and with other plans to restrain the Court. On February 5 the President announced his plan. There were several problems relating to the judiciary discussed in his message and embodied in the draft of a bill he sent to Congress, but the kernel of his plan was that he be authorized by law to appoint additional judges in all federal courts where there were incumbent judges of retirement age who did not choose to retire or resign. The President's main purpose, of course, was to reach the judges in the Supreme Court, and the draft bill provided that the number of judges in that tribunal might be increased from nine to as many as fifteen if its septuagenarians failed to retire. Six new justices named by the President would have assured New Deal measures a relatively safe passage through the Supreme Court.

The President's proposal immediately aroused a storm of controversy. Against his plan assembled the millions who believed that the Court decides all of its cases according to the clear meaning of the Constitution. This group was substantially reinforced by those who were satisfied with the decisions of the Court, although many in this group knew that the personal opinions and convictions of the judges entered into those decisions. Another opposition group, while agreeing with the President that the Court should be brought more into line with current developments, felt that his plan offered only a temporary solution. Still others opposed the plan because they considered it unfair, believing that it should have been disclosed during the preceding presidential campaign. The President had many sincere supporters and some who backed his proposal only for political reasons. The popular opposition was too strong, however, and he lost the battle.

THE NEW SUPREME COURT. But the President did not lose the "war." Time, "inexorable and remorseless," gave him the victory in the death or resignation of Justices who found in the Constitution clauses with which to entangle and choke some of the major statutes of the New Deal. Indeed, a few months after the President proposed his court plan, and before there had been any change in the personnel of the Supreme Court, that tribunal crossed over to the liberal side on the question of the constitutionality of minimum wage laws for women and children.[43]

To succeed Justice Van Devanter the President nominated Hugo L. Black, a Senator from Alabama, who was one of the leading advocates of Administration policies in the Upper House. The Department of Justice, following its usual practice, had prepared a list of some sixty men, eliminated about two thirds of them because in their private lives or public activities they had failed to measure up to the 1937 requirements for high judicial office, and submitted the remaining twenty names to the President, who had the official responsibility of choosing a name to submit to the Senate for confirmation or rejection. The President finally decided upon Hugo L. Black. Perhaps it was not generally known, or had been forgotten, that Senator Black had formerly been a member of the Ku Klux Klan. At any rate, a special brand of "senatorial courtesy" seems to presume that "every Senator is a witness to the irreproachable character of every other Senator" [44] and that any senator is therefore entitled to confirmation for any post to which he might be named by the Chief Executive. Following the confirmation, Justice Black's earlier association with the Klan became common knowledge, and there were many indignant protests against his taking a place on the Supreme Bench. It is fair to say, however, that Justice Black, by his work on the Court, appears to have lived down his regrettable affiliation with an "un-American" organization and that any blame for possible mistakes incident to his appointment should be apportioned between the Executive branch of the Government and the Senate.

President Roosevelt had occasion to appoint six other Associate Justices of the Supreme Court; and when Chief Justice Hughes resigned, the President named Associate Justice Stone as his successor. This last appointment is of interest when it is recalled that the late Chief Justice Stone was a Republican who had been appointed Associate Justice by his old friend Calvin Coolidge; but even a cursory glance at the record of Justice Stone makes his promotion quite understandable—his views on constitutional

[43] In Morehead v. New York, 298 U.S. 587 (1936) the decision was 5–4 against their constitutionality, and this was changed to 5–4 for constitutionality in West Hotel Co. v. Parrish, 300 U.S. 379 (1937). Mr. Justice Roberts changed sides.

[44] *Time*, August 23, 1937, p. 13.

questions were liberal enough for President Roosevelt. There is no doubt at all that the President secured a "friendly" Supreme Court. The New Deal had no judicial set-backs after 1936.

The preceding statement does not mean that all has been harmony in the Court since 1936. Justices still divide, and sometimes sharply, in their opinions. Justices Jackson and Frankfurter seem to adhere to a strict interpretation of the will of Congress as expressed in the statutes; and it is charged that Justices Black, Douglas, and one or two others interpret that will in such a way as to meet what they consider desirable social and economic goals. Professor C. Herman Pritchett has prepared some significant tables on divisions within the Court in recent years, and we are indebted to him for permission to reproduce one of them for this note. (The figures for the justices represent percentages and the + and — signs whether a particular justice's percentage was more "liberal" or less "liberal" than the Court majority.)

DEVIATION OF JUSTICES FROM POSITION OF COURT MAJORITY IN PERSONAL LIBERTY AND ECONOMIC CASES, 1941–46 TERMS [45]

	Personal liberty cases	Economic cases	Total cases
No. cases	82	191	273
Murphy	+45	+24	+31
Black	+17	+30	+26
Douglas	+14	+24	+22
Rutledge	+34	+17	+22
Reed	—21	— 6	—10
Frankfurter	—15	—19	—18
Jackson	—19	—20	—19
Stone	— 6	—24	—19
Burton	—33	—17	—23
Vinson	—49	—24	—31
Roberts	—20	—46	—38

What does it all come to? Simply this: Any party or faction in control of the political branches of the government for six or eight years will also be able to bring the Supreme Court into general accord with its policies. The Federalists had the Court in their day; the Southern slavocracy (the dominant wing of the Democratic party before 1860) had the Court in its day; powerful business interests who dominated the Republican party after the Civil War had the Court in their day; and at present the New Deal–Fair Deal wing of the Democratic party has it. This condition is not shocking. It could hardly be otherwise. As long as the Supreme Court decides questions of major policy (as it does through its power to pass upon

[45] From "The Roosevelt Court; Votes and Values," *Am. Pol. Sci. Rev.*, XLIII (1948), 66.

the constitutionality of laws), parties and interests in power will seek to control, and eventually will control, the Supreme Court. An intelligent man will not tear his hair when he finds the Supreme Court reflecting the general tone and spirit of the dominant political power. He will be concerned only when he observes political efforts to influence decisions in specific cases.

One of the wholesome developments of our time is that the Supreme Court has come, or is coming, to be recognized for what it is, for what acute foreign observers have always recognized it to be—a political-judicial tribunal. The Court itself recognizes its dual function. Its language is still legalistic (that is the tradition), but it does not pretend that grave questions of public policy are not inextricably associated with the issues of constitutionality. It has abandoned the judicial "prudery" that reminded one critic "of some Victorian virgin tubbing in a nightgown." [46] Neither physically nor figuratively does the Court sit on Mt. Olympus, but close to Congress, with which organ of government it shares a part of the responsibility for public policy. Accepting this fact, the Court can meet the issues with all their political and legal implications more squarely and more easily.[47] Perhaps some such realistic view of its functions explains why the present Court strikes down so few measures on the ground of unconstitutionality, why it is exercising self-restraint. In other words, frankly recognizing that judicial review makes it a negative political power, the Court is most reluctant to obstruct the positive (legislative) political power.

VI. FEDERAL JUDGES

Appointment of judges. Judges are appointed by the President with the advice and consent of the Senate.[48] A senator of the President's party from the state in which a district judge is to be appointed commonly names the person whom the President appoints. Various motives, personal and political, govern the senators in their selections; but they usually recommend men of character and competence. Occasionally the Attorney General may advise the President that a candidate so recommended does not measure up to the high standards required in the federal judiciary; but even then, a senator may stand on the rule of "senatorial courtesy," thus forcing the appointment of his own candidate or none at all.[49] A rather unusual case was presented in February, 1931, when President Hoover,

---

[46] Jerome Frank in *Courts on Trial* (1949), p. 311, quoting Karl Llewellyn.
[47] *Ibid.*, pp. 311 ff.
[48] See Chapter 11, section v.
[49] On Senator Glass's use of senatorial courtesy, see page 297.

acting upon the advice of the Attorney General and bar associations, refused to recommend to the Senate a candidate proposed for a Minnesota district by Senator Schall.[50]

In the appointment of judges for the higher courts, particularly for the Supreme Court, individual senators have less voice than in the district appointments. The Senate seldom fails to confirm a judicial appointment, and partly for this reason its rejection of John J. Parker [51] for the Supreme Bench in 1930 created the widest interest. The same year a number of senators expressed strong opposition to the confirmation of Charles Evans Hughes as Chief Justice, because they considered him too conservative; but the nomination was easily confirmed, and as Chief Justice he demonstrated that he was not so conservative as his critics supposed him to be. In nearly all cases, the judges appointed belong to the President's party,[52] and, what is more important, they usually belong to the school of political and economic thought that is dominant at that time.

Character of the judges. Although political considerations are by no means absent in the selection of judges, the baser political practices in connection with judicial appointments have been exceptionally few in number. Justices of the Supreme Court have usually been men of the highest integrity and ability and free from political (less commonly from economic) bias. A few of the judges of the inferior courts have failed in their trust—one was sent to the penitentiary for "selling" justice—but the percentage is very low, perhaps lower than one per cent. No position in America carries greater respect than a federal judgeship. Few indeed are the able lawyers who will decline an appointment as district judge, and a place on the Supreme Bench is most highly prized by the finest legal talent the country can produce. Our federal judges are quite superior to the general run of state judges, and compare most favorably with the judges in any country, not excepting Great Britain.

Yet legal talent and character, indispensable as they are, do not of themselves make great judges, not even able judges in this complex society. Judges should understand business, labor, social problems and every other major aspect of modern society. Few of them do. Law school training and legal practice do not give the whole picture of society, although it is a pleasure to report that some law schools are now making efforts to broaden their training. The successful lawyer who comes to the bench from his practice may know little of the broad fabric of life, and he may know well only one branch of the law. It is probable that men who have served as

[50] *Time,* Feb. 9, 1931, p. 13; and March 2, p. 11.

[51] He was charged with race prejudice, hostility to labor, and "conservatism."

[52] The latest exceptions to this rule occurred when President Hoover named Benjamin N. Cardozo, a Democrat, Associate Justice of the Supreme Court, and when Roosevelt named Associate Justice Stone, a Republican, Chief Justice.

professors of law, as administrative officials, or as legislators are better qualified for judicial office than railroad attorneys or mining lawyers. At any rate we are likely to find out, because the recent tendency has been to elevate to the bench men who have had the broader and more general training and experience.

SOME GREAT SUPREME COURT JUSTICES. Among the justices of the Supreme Court, Chief Justice Marshall (1801–1834) is commonly accorded first place. Presiding over the court before our national institutions had taken shape, he had free range to use his great talents in interpreting the Constitution in such a way as to give the national government wide powers. Firm in convictions, masterful in logic, and lucid in style, many of his decisions are not only great landmarks in constitutional law but classics in English prose as well. Chief Justice Roger B. Taney (1836–1864) does not hold a high place in the opinion of the average person because he was the author of the Dred Scott decision, but some students of constitutional law place him next to John Marshall.[53] Of the associate justices, certainly Joseph Story, John M. Harlan, and Benjamin N. Cardozo should be mentioned. Oliver Wendell Holmes, probably the most beloved man who ever sat in the Court, served from 1902 to 1932, resigning in his ninety-first year. As philosopher, statesman, and judge, he was famed throughout the English-speaking world.[54]

Salaries and retirement allowances. A district judge receives a salary of $15,000; a circuit judge, $17,500; an associate justice of the Supreme Court, $25,000; the Chief Justice, $25,500. The salaries are fixed by Congress, subject to the constitutional limitation that the compensation of no judge shall be decreased while he continues in office. In view of the quality of federal judges the salaries are rather low. It is easy to find judges who could make their judicial salaries several times over in the practice of law. Judges hold office for life[55] and may be removed only by impeachment. Liberal provision is made for the retirement of judges. Any judge who has served ten years may retire at the age of seventy on full pay, although retirement is not compulsory and can be made so only by Constitutional amendment.

Other court officers. For each federal district the President and the Senate appoint an attorney, who in turn, with the approval of the Department of Justice, appoints his own assistant attorneys. Their duties are to prosecute all delinquents for crimes and offenses under the laws of the

[53] See Chief Justice Hughes's tribute to Taney, New York *Times,* Sept. 27, 1931, p. 8, and editorial, same, Oct. 4, 1931.

[54] H. J. Laski, "Mr. Justice Holmes," *Harper's,* March, 1930, pp. 415–423.

[55] Judges not appointed under the judiciary article of the Constitution (judges in the territories, for example) may be appointed for a term of years.

United States and to represent the United States in all civil actions to which it is a party. In like manner, there is appointed for each district a marshal, who is required to attend the district court and execute its orders. Marshals and their deputies have the same powers in each state in executing the federal laws as the sheriffs and their deputies have in executing the state laws. Each court has also a clerk and necessary assistants, a commissioner (who conducts the preliminary hearing in criminal cases and decides whether an accused shall be held for grand jury), and probation and parole officers. Referees in bankruptcy are regularly appointed to handle the details of bankruptcy cases. The Supreme Court appoints a marshal, a clerk, a librarian, and a reporter of its decisions, and appoints or authorizes the appointment of necessary assistants to these officers. Each justice of the Supreme Court is allowed a law clerk.

VII. SPECIAL COURTS [56]

Courts for special areas. The Supreme Court, the circuit courts of appeals, and the district courts are the regular tribunals in the federal judicial system. They are sometimes called "constitutional courts" by way of emphasizing the fact that they were established under Article III of the Constitution and exercise the judicial powers enumerated in that article. Other courts have been established, not under the authority of the judiciary article, but under the authority of Congress to legislate exclusively for particular areas. Such courts are often designated "legislative courts." The United States Court of Appeals for the District of Columbia and the District Court of the United States for the District of Columbia derive their powers both from Article III and from the constitutional authority of Congress to make all laws for the District of Columbia.[57] Courts in the territories are established not under the provisions of Article III but under the authority of Congress to make all rules and regulations for the territories. Consular courts have been established by treaties with certain countries whose legal systems differ so materially from our own that our citizens experienced some difficulty in resorting to the foreign courts. Under the authority of our "extraterritorial" treaty with China (abrogated in 1943) Congress established a United States Court for China, giving it original jurisdiction in important cases and appellate jurisdiction with respect to the minor cases tried in the American consular courts in China. Judges of the courts named above, excepting those of the District of Columbia, not being judges within the meaning of the judiciary article, are not necessarily appointed, paid, and removed in accordance with the provisions of that

[56] W. G. Katz, "Federal Legislative Courts," *Harvard Law Review* (1930), XLIII, 894–924; Willoughby, *op. cit.,* pp. 529–532; *Am. Pol. Sci. Rev.* (1934), XXVIII, pp. 45–46.

[57] O'Donoghue v. United States, 289 U.S. 516 (1933).

article. They may have permanence of tenure and other safeguards of judicial status, but these depend upon Congress.

Courts for special cases: 1. COURT OF CLAIMS. There are certain legislative courts of special jurisdiction. One of these is the Court of Claims, established as long ago as 1855. Any contractual claim an individual may have against the United States may be brought to this court, although, if the amount involved is not more than $10,000, the district courts have concurrent jurisdiction. Cases may also be referred to the Court of Claims by Congress or by any of the executive departments. If a case so referred is one over which the court has jurisdiction by law, it disposes of it as it would handle a case brought by an individual; if not, the court simply makes a report to Congress or to the department that asked it to investigate a claim. As was explained in section 11 of this chapter, tort claims against the United States are brought in the district courts, with the right of appeal to the circuit courts or to the Court of Claims.

2. COURT OF CUSTOMS AND PATENT APPEALS. In 1909 the Court of Customs Appeals was created under the authority of Congress to regulate commerce. Its title was lengthened in 1929, when it was given jurisdiction to hear appeals from the Commissioner of Patents. In addition to this new duty of hearing patent appeals it has its old duty of hearing and deciding appeals made from the United States Customs Court.

3. CUSTOMS COURT. The Customs Court (known until 1926 as the Board of United States General Appraisers) has original jurisdiction over cases arising out of the collection of the customs revenue. It holds its sessions in New York City and other ports of entry.[58]

Reading List

C. A. Beard, *The Supreme Court and the Constitution* (1912).
Silas Bent, *Mr. Justice Oliver Wendell Holmes* (1932).
Albert J. Beveridge, *Life of John Marshall*, 4 vols. (1919).
L. B. Boudin, *Government by Judiciary*, 2 vols. (1932).
Catherine D. Bowen, *Yankee from Olympus* (1944).
C. N. Callender, *American Courts* (1927), Ch. III.
R. K. Carr, *Democracy and the Supreme Court* (1936).
E. S. Corwin, *The Doctrine of Judicial Review* (1914).
———, *Constitutional Revolution* (1941).
H. S. Cummings and C. McFarland, *Federal Justice* (1937).

[58] The Court of Claims has a chief judge and four associate judges—salary, $17,500; the Court of Customs and Patent Appeals, a chief judge and four other judges—salary, $17,500; the Customs Court, a chief judge and eight other judges—salary, $17,500. All these judges are appointed by the President with the consent of the Senate. Each court has the necessary marshals, clerks, and reporters. The Court of Claims has, in addition, eleven commissioners and certain other officers.

C. P. Curtis, *Lions Under the Throne* (1947).

R. E. Cushman (ed.), "Ten Years of the Supreme Court, 1937–1947," *Am. Pol. Sci. Rev.,* XLI (1947), 1142–1181 and XLII (1948), 32–67.

Jerome Frank, *Courts on Trial* (1949).

J. P. Frank, *Mr. Justice Black: The Man and His Opinions* (1948).

F. Frankfurter and J. M. Landis, *The Business of the Supreme Court* (1936 ed.).

P. A. Freund, *On Understanding the Supreme Court* (1949).

Morris Gall, *Judicial Decisions and Practical Judgment* (1946).

C. G. Haines, *American Doctrine of Judicial Supremacy* (1932 ed.).

Burton J. Hendrick, *Bulwark of the Republic: A Biography of the Constitution* (1937).

C. E. Hughes, *The Supreme Court of the United States* (1928).

Robert H. Jackson, *The Struggle for Judicial Supremacy* (1940).

S. J. Konefsky, *Chief Justice Stone and the Supreme Court* (1946).

J. M. Mathews, *The American Constitutional System* (1940 ed.), Chs. XIII–XV.

Wesley McCune, *The Nine Young Men* (1947).

C. H. Pritchett, *The Roosevelt Court* (1948).

J. C. Rose, *Jurisdiction and Procedure of the Federal Courts* (1926 ed.).

A. M. Schlesinger, Jr., "The Supreme Court: 1947," *Fortune,* January, 1947, p. 73.

K. B. Umbreit, *Our Eleven Chief Justices* (1938).

C. Warren, *Congress, the Constitution, and the Supreme Court* (1936 ed.).

———, *The Supreme Court in United States History,* 3 vols. (1923).

Mitchell Wendell, *The Relation Between Federal and State Courts* (1949).

W. W. Willoughby, *Principles of the Constitutional Law of the United States* (1930 ed.), Chs. LX–LXV.

Questions and Problems

1. Why was it deemed advisable to establish a system of federal courts as separate and distinct from those of the states?
2. Explain how the jurisdiction of the courts of the United States is determined by the character of *cases* and *parties.*
3. Show how cases arising under state law may come within the jurisdiction of the courts of the United States.
4. How does it happen that the courts of the United States may administer international law?   Common law?
5. What are the justifications, if any, for dissenting opinions?
6. Discuss the limitations on judicial review.
7. Define political questions.   What is the Supreme Court's position on them?
8. Would it be possible for the Supreme Court "to keep out of politics"?
9. Is the fact that the New Deal philosophy eventually became dominant in the Supreme Court in accordance with the history of the Court?
10. What is your estimate of the general quality and character of federal judges?
11. Explain the difference between "constitutional" and "legislative" courts.

☆ 18 ☆

The State Judicial System

THE state courts are much closer to the individual than are the federal courts. Practically all felonies and misdemeanors and the great majority of civil controversies over contracts, torts, property disputes, and domestic relations fall within the jurisdiction of the state tribunals. Certain legal procedures are technical and only those with special training can hope to understand them. It is, however, an error to assume that intelligent laymen, including the common garden variety of college and university students, cannot learn enough about the courts to enable them to make penetrating judgments on the judicial system and to make some contribution to the administration of justice. Furthermore, a review of our state judicial system is not a dreary assignment. The courts deal with life—sometimes in the raw. The judges themselves are human, and we need not hesitate to discuss them and their work."

I. ORGANIZATION AND JURISDICTION OF STATE COURTS [1]

Types of courts. In practically every state the courts are established by the state constitution and by legislative acts in pursuance thereof. Although the details of the judicial structure vary considerably from state to state, its fundamental aspects are essentially the same in all the states. Every state has a highest court of appeals, many have intermediate courts of appeals, all have various local courts of original jurisdiction, and all have minor courts.

1. The supreme court. The highest court in the state is ordinarily styled the "supreme court"; but it also goes under such titles as the "supreme judicial court," "supreme court of errors," and "court of appeals."

[1] C. N. Callender, *American Courts* (1927), Ch. II and Appendix; Bates, Field, and Others, *State Government* (1949 ed.), Ch. 18; W. B. Graves, American State Government (1946 ed.), Ch. XVI; *Book of the States, 1950–1951*, pp. 505–516.

The number of justices varies from three to nine. Because of the pressure of business before the courts, there is a tendency to increase the number and permit them to sit in separate divisions, thus expediting the handling of cases.

Supreme courts have very little original jurisdiction, their work being confined almost entirely to the hearing of appeals. In some states, appeals lie to the supreme court from the intermediate courts of appeals only; whereas in others, appeals may be made from some of the lower courts. It is a rather common practice in the states to allow appeals to the supreme court only if the amount involved exceeds a certain sum, final decision in lesser cases being made by the intermediate courts. Supreme courts are always given ultimate jurisdiction in all cases requiring an interpretation of the state constitution; and, subject to review by the Supreme Court of the United States, they may interpret such parts of the federal Constitution, laws, and treaties as may come before them. Indeed, it is the duty of all state courts to apply the federal Constitution and laws to appropriate cases.

Judicial review. In interpreting either the state or federal Constitution, the state supreme court [2] may exercise the power of judicial review; that is, it may pass upon the validity of a statute of the state legislature under either of these instruments. A state court may even pass upon the validity of provisions of the state constitution if the question of their being in violation of the federal Constitution is raised. This authority to declare null and void state laws and provisions of state constitutions has been used rather freely by the state courts, perhaps more freely than by the federal courts. Because of the detailed provisions of state constitutions and particularly because of the many restrictions they impose upon legislatures, those bodies should move with great circumspection in order to avoid the enactment of unconstitutional measures. They do not always so move. Indeed, sometimes they quite frankly pass a measure of questionable constitutionality and leave the responsibility with the courts.

The rather vague and indefinite provisions relative to "due process of law" and the "equal protection of the laws" appear in state constitutions as well as in the federal Constitution, and the state courts have voided many laws under these provisions. In so doing they have not infrequently been charged with conservatism, reaction, and reading their own theories into the constitutions—the charges made against federal judges. As a result of these criticisms, several states have by constitutional pro-

---

[2] The obligation of state courts to void state statutes that are in contravention to the federal Constitution is in its provision that "the judges in every state shall be bound thereby, anything in the constitution or laws of any state to the contrary notwithstanding" (Art. VI). See also People v. Western Union, 70 Colo. 90 (1921). All courts are bound to interpret the Constitution, but since the supreme courts have the final word, the practical result is that a law is not actually void until they so declare.

visions prohibited the supreme courts from nullifying a law unless two thirds, or even a higher fraction, of the judges concur.

Advisory opinions. By constitutional provision in six states and by custom in one or two others, the supreme court is required to give advisory opinions when requested to do so by the governor or legislature.[3] Such an opinion is not ordinarily requested except upon an important matter. When given, it is not considered as having the weight of a judicial precedent, inasmuch as the court hears no opposing arguments and decides no actual case.[4] These opinions are probably given a weight that falls between the opinions of an attorney general and court decisions in litigated cases. Eminent authorities differ on the wisdom of passing this function to the courts, and the legal profession very generally opposes it.

2. INTERMEDIATE COURTS OF APPEALS. The less populous states have no appellate courts except the supreme courts; but a number of the more densely populated states have established intermediate courts of appeals, which correspond somewhat to the federal circuit courts of appeals. Some of the states have just one such court, and others have several. They are known by various titles, such as "courts of appeals," "district courts of appeals," and "superior courts." Like the supreme courts, each of these courts has several judges.

Their jurisdiction varies greatly, but their purpose is always the same, namely, to carry a part of the burden of appeals for the supreme court. Sometimes their jurisdiction extends to appealed cases in which the amounts in controversy fall between a certain stipulated maximum and minimum (say, $4,000 and $200), cases above the maximum going to the supreme court and cases below the minimum being finally decided in a lower court. The decision may be final in some cases, and in others an appeal may lie to the supreme court. Appeals involving the constitutionality of laws, titles to state offices, felonies, and other important matters, in some states go directly from the lower courts to the supreme court, and in others must be carried first to the intermediate court of appeals.

3. COURTS OF ORIGINAL JURISDICTION. Local state courts have original jurisdiction in practically all cases of importance, and ordinarily an appellate jurisdiction in cases from minor courts. As a class they are often referred to as "trial courts" or "courts of first instance." The business before these courts may be divided into four types: civil cases at common law; equity suits; criminal prosecutions; and probate matters, that is, matters relating to wills and the estates of deceased persons.

---

[3] In Florida, South Dakota, and Vermont, when requested by the governor. In Colorado, Maine, and Massachusetts, when requested by the governor or legislature.

[4] In Colorado, however, such opinions have the same effect as opinions given in litigated cases. Graves, *op. cit.,* p. 707 note 4.

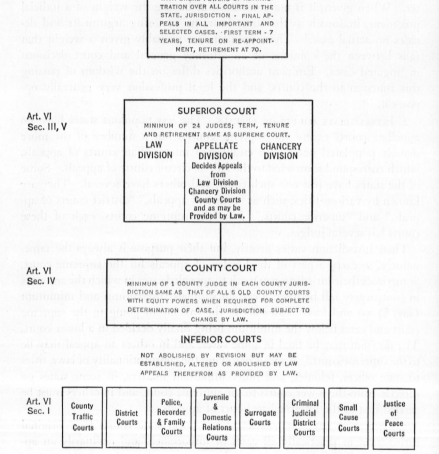

NEW JERSEY'S COURT SYSTEM
UNDER THE CONSTITUTION OF 1947

Art. VI
Sec. I, II, V,
VII

SUPREME COURT

Chief Justice and 6 Associates

WITH BROAD POWERS OF ADMINIS-
TRATION OVER ALL COURTS IN THE
STATE. JURISDICTION - FINAL AP-
PEALS IN ALL IMPORTANT AND
SELECTED CASES. ·FIRST TERM - 7
YEARS, TENURE ON RE-APPOINT-
MENT, RETIREMENT AT 70.

Art. VI
Sec. III, V

SUPERIOR COURT

MINIMUM OF 24 JUDGES; TERM, TENURE
AND RETIREMENT SAME AS SUPREME COURT.

LAW DIVISION	APPELLATE DIVISION	CHANCERY DIVISION
	Decides Appeals from Law Division Chancery Division County Courts and as may be Provided by Law.	

Art. VI
Sec. IV

COUNTY COURT

MINIMUM OF 1 COUNTY JUDGE IN EACH COUNTY JURIS-
DICTION SAME AS THAT OF ALL 5 OLD COUNTY COURTS
WITH EQUITY POWERS WHEN REQUIRED FOR COMPLETE
DETERMINATION OF CASE. JURISDICTION SUBJECT TO
CHANGE BY LAW.

INFERIOR COURTS

NOT ABOLISHED BY REVISION BUT MAY BE
ESTABLISHED, ALTERED OR ABOLISHED BY LAW
APPEALS THEREFROM AS PROVIDED BY LAW.

Art. VI
Sec. I

County Traffic Courts	District Courts	Police, Recorder & Family Courts	Juvenile & Domestic Relations Courts	Surrogate Courts	Criminal Judicial District Courts	Small Cause Courts	Justice of Peace Courts

Art. VI
Sec. VI

ALL JUDGES APPOINTED BY GOVERNOR WITH APPROVAL
OF SENATE, EXCEPT MUNICIPAL JUDGES AND SURROGATES

Prepared for the New Jersey Committee for Constitutional Revision by Joseph Harrison; Reproduced by Courtesy of
Joseph Harrison and the Editors of the Journal of the American Judicature Society.

In some states the same court may handle all types of litigation. In others several types of courts are established. Thus, Illinois has circuit courts of original jurisdiction in civil and criminal cases in each county; city courts having concurrent jurisdiction with the circuit courts; a Superior Court of Cook County (in which Chicago is located), having concurrent jurisdiction with the circuit courts; a Criminal Court of Cook County, which exercises in that area the ordinary criminal jurisdiction of the circuit courts; a Municipal Court of Chicago, having practically concurrent jurisdiction with the circuit courts except in equity suits and felonies; probate courts for counties of over 70,000 population; and county courts, with probate and certain other jurisdiction.[5] The courts of original jurisdiction have various titles—"superior," "circuit," "district," and others—which do not always indicate the nature of their jurisdiction.

4. MINOR COURTS. Below the ordinary courts of original jurisdiction there are courts that have original jurisdiction in petty cases. Although these may be designated as minor courts, they are not of minor importance, since the great majority of persons who go or are brought to court are concerned with trivial cases only. The office of justice of the peace had its origin in England centuries ago, and it has been an established institution in America from the beginning. In Britain the justice of the peace has jurisdiction in petty criminal cases only; but in America he may hear small civil cases as well, subject usually in both types of cases to appeal. In major criminal offenses, he may hold preliminary hearings and have accused persons held in custody. In addition to his judicial duties the justice of the peace may perform marriage ceremonies and attest formal documents. In some of the Southern states the justices as a group serve as county administrative boards.

Long since, the justices of the peace were found insufficient for the requirements of justice in the cities, and they have usually had to give way to city courts or at least share their jurisdiction with them. The city police court is now a well-known institution, which ordinarily has the power to dispose of cases of traffic regulation and other minor offenses. Often a separate court in a city, commonly designated a "municipal court," has jurisdiction in the smaller civil cases. In general, it may be said that the city courts are given wider jurisdiction than the justices of the peace. This is as it should be; the city magistrates are usually learned in the law, whereas the same cannot be said for the historic justices.

Several other courts—claims (against the state), juvenile, domestic relations, conciliation, and small (private) claims—have the rather special type of jurisdiction indicated by their titles. Some of these will receive brief mention in another section of this chapter.

The lack of judicial organization. State courts were originally organ-

[5] Callender, *op. cit.*, p. 246.

ized to meet the relatively simple needs of a rural society. As the country grew and an industrial civilization with all its complexities became established in most of the states, great changes in judicial organization were needed. There was a need for more courts, more judges, better systems of gathering and correlating judicial statistics, and, above all, for organization of the courts into a unified system. More courts were created and more judges were authorized from time to time, but that was as far as the legislatures usually went in meeting the new needs.

As a result of this halfway program the judicial system became more disorganized than ever. Some districts had more courts and judges than were needed; some had too few; and there was no higher court or administrative body with the authority to make proper adjustments. Furthermore, since there was no central judicial authority to make the rules of the courts, they were made by the legislatures, a task for which such bodies are not well fitted. In short, cumbersome and inflexible organization and rigid and ill-suited rules of procedure prevented, and to a large extent still prevent, the courts from performing their true function of administering justice speedily and free from unnecessary technicalities.

PROPOSED REMEDIES. A number of remedies have been designed for the improvement of judicial organization in the states. Here we shall give brief consideration to two of the most important of these—the unified court system and the judicial council.

The unified court system. Under this system all of the courts of the state would be organized as divisions or branches of a single, large judicial body. The chief justice or some other appropriate official would supervise the work of this consolidated court. Such a judicial system would make possible a division of judicial labor among various types of courts —civil, criminal, equity, and probate; the assignment of judges to tasks for which they are especially competent; dispatch in the settlement of cases; and the attainment of the goal that courts exist primarily for the benefit of litigants. A rather high degree of unity may be brought about without complete unification of the courts. This may be done through an administrative judge with power to assign judges to congested courts and to counsel with them on judicial problems. Massachusetts, New Jersey, Ohio, several other states, and a few large cities have made progress along this line.

The judicial council. Back in 1921 the Model State Constitution carried the significant proposal that the states set up judicial councils. What is more, the proposal has borne fruit, about thirty of the states having adopted it in some form. These councils are composed of representative judges of the various courts (the chief justice is commonly the head of the council), perhaps the attorney general, some practicing attorneys, probably a few members of the legislature, and often some laymen. The council is not a legislative or judicial body. It makes no laws, it decides no cases. Some of them have a few administrative powers, but the council must be considered primarily as an advisory and investigating body. Its administrative duties relate to the collection of statistics and other information essential to the efficient operation of the judicial system, and in some states the council may transfer judges from districts with light dockets to districts with crowded dockets.

Perhaps the chief duty of the council is to make rules of general practice. During the past century a number of states gave this power to the supreme court, but with the establishment of the judicial councils, it has been thought better to transfer the power to them. If a state should continue to vest this power in the supreme court, the authorities insist that the council should be assigned the task of taking the initiative, gathering data, drafting rules, and discussing their proposals with the bar, finally passing the rules up to the court for adoption. It seems to be very generally agreed that the legislature is not the body to make rules of general practice.[6]

II. STATE JUDGES AND OTHER COURT OFFICERS [7]

Selection. Federal judges, as everyone knows, are appointed by the President subject to confirmation by the Senate. A similar method of appointment was used in the colonies; but during the Revolution and immediately following it, the legislature took a larger part in the selection of judges. As the nineteenth century advanced, the democratic and pioneer influences led to the establishment of popular choice as the chief method of selection. At present only six or seven states have their judges chosen by the governor—or by the governor subject to legislative approval, or by the governor and the judicial council; some four or five leave this function to the legislature; more than three fourths of the states leave the choice of judges to the sovereign people.

SHOULD JUDGES BE APPOINTED OR ELECTED? Judges are supposed to stay out of politics, to be independent. The question arises as to what method of selection is least likely to bring the judiciary into politics. It is commonly agreed that choice by the legislative body is the most political of all the methods of selection, and there is no strong movement in its favor at present. The issue is rather between executive appointment and popu-

---

[6] Graves, *op. cit.,* pp. 690 ff. There is much literature on the subject of the judicial council and the reorganization of state judicial systems. The *Journal of the American Judicature Society* is most valuable. For example, among the articles in Vol. XXXI, No. 5 (February, 1948) are "New Jersey Goes to Head of Class" and "Judicial Article of New Jersey Constitution." See also Joseph Harrison, "Judicial Reform in New Jersey," *State Government,* Oct., 1949, pp. 232–236, 247.

[7] Bates, Field, and Others, *op. cit.,* pp. 537 ff.; Dodd, *op. cit.,* pp. 312–319; Bruce, *The American Judge* (1924), Ch. VII; M. Dawson, "Judging the Judges," *Harper's,* September, 1934, pp. 437–448; Graves, *op. cit.,* pp. 673 ff.; *Book of the States, 1950–1951,* pp. 505–516.

lar election. The advocates of the appointive system speak of the high quality of the English and of our own federal judges, obtained under that system; of the fact that only in the American states are judges elected. They allege that an elective judiciary must, of necessity, be a political judiciary; that candidates must descend from the bench and mount the rostrum or yield the judgeships to those who will do so. It is said that the people have no notion as to the competence of candidates for judicial office; and that in districts where so many judges are elected, popular choice is bound to be a farce.

But the advocates of the appointive system have perhaps overdrawn the picture. The facts are that the people have often made excellent choices, and that governors have not always made wise and nonpolitical appointments. Moreover, whether the elective or appointive method is used, the bar association, the best informed body on candidates for the judicial offices, exercises considerable influence with the voters or with the governor, as the case may be. Further, since the judges do decide political questions in passing upon the constitutionality of certain types of statutes, it is only proper that political considerations should enter into their selection. Then, too, it may be observed that the election of judges is not ordinarily attended by partisan appeals. At least a dozen states employ nonpartisan ballots for these elections, which, although they do not necessarily remove all partisan influences, nevertheless operate to reduce such influences. Not infrequently judges are re-elected solely on their records and without opposition. Yet we would be less than candid not to admit that, if partisan considerations are usually absent in the process of selecting judges, the personal interests of the candidates are almost always present, and it cannot be doubted that some candidates have made popular appeals, the effect of which has been to lower the prestige of the courts and even threaten the independence of the judiciary. It is even a fact that some judicial nominations have been bought and paid for. There are some methods of selecting judges that are decided improvements over those commonly employed. One of the best of these shall have attention.

The Missouri plan of judicial selection. In 1940 Missouri, following somewhat the system established six years earlier by California, adopted a new plan of judicial selection. This provides that whenever a vacancy exists in the supreme court, in the courts of appeals, and in certain other courts, a nominating commission, composed of both lawyers and laymen, shall nominate three candidates, and the governor must appoint one of these nominees. After serving twelve months this judge goes before the people upon his record and with no competing candidate. The question for the voters to decide is: Shall he continue in office? The people vote on the same question in reference to any judge whose term of office is about to expire. In the event a majority of the voters are against continuance in office, the nominating commission gives the governor a new list of nominees, the governor makes a new appointment, and after the judge has served for one year, the people vote on the question of his continuance in office. It will be noticed that this plan is designed to provide a method of appointment which is relatively free from politics and, at the same time, to reserve to the people the right of ultimate control. This method of selection is not greatly at variance with the plan proposed in the Model State Constitution, and it appears to meet with the warm approval of many leading members of the American Judicature Society.

The political struggle through which the state of Missouri passed in securing this plan should not be passed by. In 1940 the people adopted the amendment that provided for it by a majority of 95,000 votes. Near the end of the next session of the legislature, the time when deals are most commonly made and the will of the people flouted, the legislature proposed an amendment to repeal the amendment adopted in the previous election. In November, 1942, the people turned down this repeal amendment by a majority of 173,000. The increased majority by which the people of Missouri expressed themselves in favor of removing judges from politics was a tribute to their intelligence and their interest in good government, and it was also a testimonial to the effectiveness of civic leadership on that question.[8]

Terms of state judges. The independence of judges is commonly considered as being determined not only by the method of selection but also by the length of their terms. The terms vary a great deal in the several states and within the individual states. The highest justices almost invariably hold the longest terms. Their term is for life in Massachusetts and Rhode Island; to the age of seventy in New Hampshire; twenty-one years in Pennsylvania; fifteen years in Maryland; fourteen years in Louisiana and New York; and a lesser number of years in other states—six years being the most common. Judges of the lower courts commonly hold office for shorter terms than the higher judges. Thus in Illinois, justices of the peace and other members of the minor judiciary serve for four years, the judges of the regular trial courts for six years, and the supreme court judges for nine years. There is no doubt that the long term increases the independence and learning of a judge, and in a few of the states the terms have been lengthened in recent years. The practice of re-electing competent judges, which obtains in several states, serves as a fairly good substitute for the longer term.

Qualifications of state judges. State judges are almost invariably selected

[8] John Perry Wood, "Missouri Victory Speeds National Judicial Selection Reform," *Journal of the American Judicature Society*, XXVI, 142 (February, 1943). See also "Missouri and California Lawyers Appraise Judicial Selection Methods," *ibid.*, XXXI, 176 (April, 1948); "Missouri Bar to Supplement Court Plan," *ibid.*, XXXII, 23 (June, 1948); and L. M. Hyde, "Choosing Judges in Missouri," *National Municipal Review*, November, 1949, p. 491.

from the bar. The duties of the practitioner and the judge are really quite different, and in some countries there is a definite distinction between the two. In France, for example, young men are trained as lawyers or as judges, and the judicial profession is filled by those who have special training for it. No doubt our system has certain advantages over that of the French; but the fact remains that the duties of the advocate and the judge are different and that when a lawyer becomes a judge he must take himself in hand for some very important readjustments. As an attorney, he was a partisan, a talker, probably a specialist, and possibly unconcerned about the broader social problems of the state. As a judge, he must be an arbiter, a listener, learned in the whole field of the law and conversant with economics, history, and sociology. He must strive to gain a "full sense of the seamless web of life." He must become a "statesman as well as a jurist, thinker as well as lawyer." [9]

Manifestly it is exceedingly difficult, even under the most favorable circumstances, to find men who measure up to this standard; and it is not surprising that politics in selections, short terms, and inadequate salaries often produce state judges who are far below it. Indeed, in some states, judicial office, particularly that of trial judge, is not at all attractive to the best legal talent, and it not infrequently goes to second-class men or to young men who may hope to use it as a stepping-stone to a later lucrative practice. Although, broadly speaking, state judges are less likely than federal judges to be learned and independent, it should be said that a few states have maintained very good judicial standards. Cooley of Michigan, Doe of New Hampshire, Clark of North Carolina, Holmes (appointed to the Supreme Court of the United States in 1902) and Shaw of Massachusetts, Mitchell of Minnesota, Winslow of Wisconsin, and Kent and Cardozo (the latter appointed to succeed Justice Holmes in the Supreme Court of the United States in 1932) of New York, to mention only a few notable state judges, certainly belong to a select company of statesmen-jurists.

Salaries of state judges. In a few states the salary of judges is fixed by the constitution; but usually it is very sensibly left to the legislatures to decide, subject to a few constitutional limitations. Adequate salaries are paid in some states, but in others the scale of compensation is rather low. A salary of $10,000 for supreme court justices and $8,000 for the judges in the courts of original jurisdiction may be taken as a rough average. Federal judges and British judges receive more, and they have some additional compensation in the assurance of life tenure. It is fair to assume that more liberal salaries would elevate the standards of the state judiciary; for at present, in many states, competent men are loath to give up lucrative private practice for the relatively small compensation allowed judges. Some progress is being made in the direction of increasing the salaries,

[9] H. J. Laski, "Mr. Justice Holmes," *Harper's*, March, 1930, p. 415.

and two thirds of the states have made provision for pensions upon retirement.

Removal of state judges. Judges may be removed by impeachment in every state; but the political squabbles that commonly attend impeachment proceedings are so out of keeping with the nature of the judicial office that this method of removal is rarely used. Furthermore, impeachment requires a trial and a conviction for a specific offense. A more satisfactory method of removal, employed in a number of states, provides that the governor may at his option remove a judge upon address by both houses (usually a special majority) of the legislature. No trial or conviction is necessary, thus enabling the political authorities to remove a judge who for one reason or another may be incapacitated. One of the best examples of this type of procedure is provided for in the New Jersey Constitution of 1947. Under this provision the supreme court certifies to the governor that a particular judge is believed to be substantially incapacitated; the governor then appoints a commission of three persons to make inquiry; and on the recommendation of this commission the governor may retire the judge, "on pension as may be provided by law." In some states judges may be removed by a special majority of both houses of the legislature, the governor having no part in the matter.

In eight states [10] the people may remove a judge by recall; that is, by a special election ("diselection") held when 10–25 per cent of the voters officially request it. Back in Wilson's New Freedom era, when the recall was instituted, conservatives argued that the recall of judges would deal a terrible blow to the independence of the judiciary; that judges would be recalled every time they gave decisions which ran counter to the will of a bare majority of the voters; that the recall of judges meant, in effect, that the people would set themselves up as judges. As a matter of fact, the people have shown great restraint in the use of this emergency weapon. No supreme court justice has ever been recalled. Only a few inferior judges have been so removed and these almost without exception for personal delinquencies rather than for unpopular decisions. Whatever arguments may be advanced against the popular dismissal of judges, experience has demonstrated thus far that the judiciary is in no particular danger from this source.

Other court officers: 1. Clerk. The judges are, of course, the outstanding officers of the court, but there are certain other officers who are hardly less important.[11] There is always a clerk (sometimes elected, and sometimes appointed by the court), whose duty it is to keep the records, to issue

---

[10] They are: Arizona, California, Colorado, Kansas, Nevada, North Dakota, Oregon, and Wisconsin.

[11] On these officers, see J. A. Fairlie and C. M. Kneier, *County Government and Administration* (1930), Ch. VIII.

writs or other processes incident to litigation, to give certified copies of court documents, and to perform other court duties of a ministerial character.

2. PROSECUTING ATTORNEY. The prosecuting attorney (known also by various other titles, such as "state's attorney," "county attorney," and "prosecutor"), a county officer commonly elected, is a familiar figure about the trial courts. He serves as counsel for the grand jury, aiding it in preparing indictments; and in many states he may bring an accused person to trial without going through the formality of securing an indictment from a grand jury. He must conduct the prosecution of all offenders in the name of the state. Clearly the activity of this officer determines very largely the degree of law enforcement a county will attain. Some prosecutors have winked at lawlessness or at certain types of offenses; others, frequently young lawyers, have made records as prosecutors, and steadily climbed the political ladder from that first round. The prosecuting attorney also represents the state and the county in civil suits to which they happen to be parties, and he acts as a legal adviser to other county officers.

3. SHERIFF. The sheriff [12] is another important county officer usually elected by the people. A powerful and somewhat romantic figure in the English counties centuries ago, he now has only a few administrative duties to perform in that country. In the American county he must, as far as possible, prevent breaches of the peace, and arrest offenders; serve the writs issued by the courts; summon juries; execute the court's judgments; administer the county jail; and discharge other duties imposed by law. He is usually assisted by a number of deputies. A constable, commonly elected, serves the justice of the peace somewhat as the sheriff serves the ordinary courts of original jurisdiction.

4. CORONER. Still another ancient county officer, prevailingly elective, is that of coroner; but, unlike the sheriff's office, it has declined considerably in importance. Indeed, some states have transferred part or all of the coroner's duties to other officers, usually medical examiners. For example, Connecticut provides for examiners who shall be "able and discreet" men, learned in the science of medicine. The examiner shall "without delay repair to and take charge of the body" of any person who comes to "a sudden, violent, or untimely death." If the examiner believes such person has come to his death by a criminal act or through the fault of others, he notifies the coroner, who then holds an inquest. In most states, however, the whole matter is left to the coroner. He must investigate with the aid of a coroner's jury and perhaps a physician. The coroner instructs the jury as to the law; the jury decides the facts. The jury may thus officially accuse some person of murder; the coroner may then order the arrest, if such person is not already in custody. Clearly, the work of the coroner is

[12] From the old "shire-reeve," chief officer of the county in Saxon times.

of such a technical character that in those states which require no special qualifications for the office or give the coroner no expert assistance the duties are poorly performed.

III. THE LAW ADMINISTERED BY STATE COURTS [13]

The common law. The student is familiar with the fact that the laws of the states consist very largely of the common law (often called simply "law") and equity, which the colonists brought over from England. To be sure, this legal heritage has been changed by statute, more in some states than in others; but the basic principles of the English system still apply in the American states, except in Louisiana. It is highly desirable to have an understanding of just how this English law developed and how it came to be our law.

ITS ORIGIN. After the Norman Conquest and particularly during the reign of Henry II (1154–1189) the rather diverse systems of local law and judicial administration gave way to a centralized system. Justices were sent out from London "on circuits," and they held court in the various counties, acting under the authority of the king. In deciding the cases that came before them, they ascertained what the local customs were and ordinarily applied them in their decisions. Back in London, these justices no doubt related their experiences among themselves with mutual profit. On circuit again, a judge might have a case dissimilar to any he had decided before, and, furthermore, a controversy on which the customs of the community seemed conflicting, or, if uniform, contrary to justice. What did he do? He recalled that one of his brethren had a similar case a few months before; he followed the decision of his brother judge. And so it went on, the judges applying the customs of the communities where they seemed to do justice and using each other's decisions as precedents in other cases. In the course of time, a body of law *common* to the whole kingdom was developed. As the years passed, the judges came to rely much more upon earlier decisions than upon the customs of the communities. Finally, and long before the English colonies were planted in America, previous decisions rather rigidly established the principles to be followed in later cases. It must not be understood, however, that the law became absolutely fixed. One of the glories of the common law is that it has always submitted to gradual changes. But the trouble has been that the changes come just a little too gradually.

Equity. As already stated, the common law became too rigid. One could get redress only through the use of writs, which were limited in number and very technical in form. For many an injury there was no writ,

[13] Graves, *op. cit.,* Ch. XV; F. A. Ogg, *English Government and Politics* (1936 ed.), Ch. XXV; Roscoe Pound, "Common Law," *Encyclopaedia of the Social Sciences,* IV, 50.

and no writ meant no remedy. For example, there was no writ that
would cover a breach of an ordinary oral contract, leaving such contracts
to be broken with impunity. Again, if one lost title to his land by the
fraud of another, the common law afforded him no remedy. In any case,
the common law provided a remedy only after damage had been suffered.
This was a major defect, since for many injuries the payment of damages,
however large, obviously is no adequate compensation. Something was
needed to supplement the common law. This was found in *equity*. It
developed in this way. Since the courts were the king's courts and acted
under his authority, a person who failed to get justice in them turned to
the king with his complaint. As an act of grace, the king might grant the
relief prayed for. These petitions became so numerous that the king
referred most of them to his chancellor and chaplain, "the keeper of the
king's conscience." In the fourteenth century a special court, the court
of chancery or equity, was permanently established for such cases. But
let us not suppose that the chancellor and other equity judges had no other
guide than conscience. Very soon equity came to have its own system of
rules and remedies, and they are now hardly more elastic than those of the
common law. It nevertheless continues to supplement, and at certain
points to overlap, the common law. One other important fact should be
noted. It is, that "law" and "equity" combined long since fell short of the
needs of advancing civilization. They both remain, to be sure; but they
have been modified and supplemented by acts of Parliament as often as
that body has felt changes to be necessary.

Common law and equity in the states. As shown above, the English
colonists carried the English system of law to America and to all other
new lands in which they settled. The American Revolution did not
change the law in the states. Indeed, it may be said that our courts applied the common law more whole-heartedly after the Revolution than
before, although certain principles which seemed inapplicable in America
were never enforced here. Even now, our courts occasionally consult the
decisions of British courts in common law cases. A recent (October 24,
1949) example comes from Arkansas, where the supreme court, finding no
state law making the concealment of a dead body punishable, turned to the
English common law of 1607 and found that "indecent treatment" of a
body was a misdemeanor. In like manner, the courts of Britain sometimes
turn to American decisions. In neither case, however, are the decisions of
the courts of one country binding in the other; but they have great influence.
The principles of equity, with certain modifications, also came into our
legal system from Great Britain. In England law and equity are still administered in separate courts; in America they are administered by the
same courts except in a few states.

SOME EXAMPLES. In order to make the distinction between law and equity clear, we shall take a few examples of how the two operate in civil controversies in the states. Suppose A has been ousted from his land by B. A has a remedy at common law. He may recover his land through an action of ejectment. A may also claim damages from B because B temporarily deprived him of his rightful possession. Suppose C breaks a contract with D. For this breach of contract, C may be sued at common law. Taking one other example, suppose E has through his negligence caused F a personal injury. F may sue E for damages at common law. Now, suppose A conveys a piece of land to B, and in the deed the area of the land is incorrectly described. The common law does not afford an adequate remedy; but equity will compel A to execute a new deed correcting the mistake. Suppose C has secured a contract with D through fraudulent devices; the common law damage suit is again no adequate remedy. But in a court of equity D may prove the fraud and have the contract canceled. On the other hand, suppose E has entered into a perfectly valid contract with F to sell him a particular piece of property. If E fails to make delivery, F may sue him for damages at common law. Now, F may have a very special use for that particular piece of property— no other will serve his purpose. What he wants, therefore, is the property, not the insufficient damages he might get at law. He goes to a court of equity, and that court will command E to deliver the property in accordance with the contract. For the final illustration, take the case of a property owner who is about to extend his house beyond the building line and seems to be about to cut down one of his neighbor's fine trees. The neighbor will hasten to an equity court and secure an injunction against the adjoining property owner. He might wait until the damage is done and then sue at common law; but he wants his property preserved, not damages for its impairment or destruction. From these examples it should be clear that equity fills in two very big gaps in the common law: it provides for relief against threatened wrongs; and it redresses certain injuries not covered by the common law.

Statutes and codes. As the inadequacies of common law and equity led the British Parliament to supplement them by statutory law, so the American states have, in varying degrees, supplemented and changed them by statute. A number of states have enacted complete codes dealing with particular fields of law. It is sometimes said that the code abolishes the common law; but the code almost invariably draws very heavily from that law and is construed in the light of the common law. What the code actually does, in addition to making certain changes in the law, is to bring together all the laws on a given subject, as distinguished from the common law method of leaving them scattered about in thousands of judicial decisions. For example, many states have enacted criminal codes putting most of the old common law crimes on the statute books, dropping a few, and adding some entirely new crimes. Similarly, a number of states have established codes of criminal procedure and codes of civil procedure. Efforts are also made to secure uniform laws among the states on such subjects as negotiable instruments and sales. This movement is sponsored by the National Conference of Commissioners on Uniform State Laws, a body that has drafted about a hundred model statutes and has had the satisfaction of seeing at least a score of them quite generally adopted by state legislatures.[14] A few states have attempted to codify the whole body of law. Louisiana practically started her career as a state with a code modeled after the French civil law. In more recent years some other states of the South and some west of the Mississippi have adopted more or less complete codes.[15]

Is the code desirable? Although some advantages are to be gained by codifying certain branches of the law, particularly by revising and simplifying the rules of common law pleadings and enacting comprehensive statutes on subjects that the common law covers inadequately, there is some question as to the wisdom of codifying the whole field of law. One of the reputed advantages of the code system over the regular common law system is that the former brings all the law together, whereas the latter is found in thousands of judicial decisions—precedents. To this contention, the reply is often made that it is impossible to get every fragment of the common law in a code; that cases will arise that are not provided for in that compilation. To the argument that the code makes the law certain and definite, it is replied that the code itself requires judicial interpretation, because cases constantly arise that fall within the twilight zone of its provisions. Further, it is said that the code is less flexible than the common law; that under the code necessary changes must depend upon the legislature, whereas under the common law new cases may be fitted in and old precedents occasionally overruled by the courts themselves. Finally, it may be said that the members of the legal profession, who should know more than the rest of us about the relative merits of the code and the old common law system, generally look with disfavor upon the attempts to codify the whole domain of law.[16] Teachers of law, in particular, look with more favor upon the efforts of the American Law Institute, which is engaged in the good work of restating the common law and in formulating codes of procedure. The finished product will not

---

[14] Graves, *op. cit.*, pp. 627–632. See also his volume, *Uniform State Action: A Possible Substitute for Centralization* (1934); *Book of the States, 1950–1951*, pp. 147–150; and A. J. Harno, "Uniform State Laws and the Federal System," *State Government*, Nov. 1948, pp. 225–227, 236.

[15] C. A. Beard, *American Government and Politics* (1949 ed.), p. 640.

[16] *Ibid.*, pp. 640–641.

be an authorized code; but it will serve to guide lawyers and judges through the more controversial domains of the law, and also to give a more modern interpretation to many common law principles.

Other law. It seems hardly necessary to mention that state courts are bound by the state constitution, which is the highest law of a state, and by the still higher law of the nation—the Constitution, acts of Congress passed in pursuance thereof, and treaties. Furthermore, administrative rules and regulations issued by executive officers under the authority of the state constitution or of the legislature have the force of law.

IV. CIVIL LAW AND PROCEDURE [17]

Distinction between civil and criminal law. The law may be divided into two fields, civil and criminal. At the risk of stating the obvious, a brief distinction will be drawn between the two. A murder has been committed; a man has been robbed; a car has been stolen; a child has been kidnaped. These are a few examples of crime. The state assumes the duty of apprehending, prosecuting, and punishing those guilty of such offenses, although the victim of a crime or his relatives and friends may assist the state in some respects. A passenger has been killed in an accident; a car has been damaged through the carelessness of the driver of another car; a citizen has distracting noises and noxious fumes coming from his premises to such an extent as to disturb his neighbor in the use and enjoyment of his property; an individual has refused to pay his landlord, his grocer, or others who have performed services for him. Wrongs have been done in each case of the latter group, wrongs which are covered by law; but not wrongs of which the state will take cognizance unless the person wronged brings them to court. The distinction between criminal and civil cases is now clear. In criminal cases, the state is the plaintiff and judge; in civil cases, the aggrieved individual is the plaintiff and the state is the judge. The alleged wrongdoer in both types of cases is the defendant. It may happen that a wrong may be at the same time both civil and criminal. For example, if a grossly negligent driver injures another, the state may prosecute him for crime and the injured party may sue him for damages.

Many wrongful acts belong only in the realm of morals, not being recognized by either the criminal or civil law. Thus the ordinary town gossip seldom gets within the reaches of the law; and one may, like the Publican, pass by on the other side and refuse to succor a man in distress. However, moral wrongs are more and more being given by statute the status

---

[17] In the discussion of both the civil and criminal law the writer has followed the excellent summaries in C. A. Beard, *American Government and Politics* (1949 ed.), pp. 641 ff.; and in Bates, Field, and Others, *op. cit.,* pp. 560–565, 575–580. On procedure, Callender, *op. cit.,* Chs. V–IX, XII–XIII, has been followed. See also D. C. Lunt, *The Road to the Law* (1932).

of legal wrongs. In fact, many people think this tendency is altogether too strong.

Civil Law: 1. PROPERTY. Without going into too many technicalities, let us examine very briefly the content of the civil law. Private property is one of the basic factors of our civilization. The laws relating to it form the most important subdivision of the field of civil law. In legal theory there is no such thing as absolute ownership. For example, the state may take a piece of land from a private owner for a public building site or a road. The owner has a right to compensation and the state will compensate him, but he cannot hold "his" land against the needs of the state. What one has, then, are certain *rights* to use and dispose of property, not complete ownership. However, ownership is the term we use in common parlance, and it will suffice here. Property is divided into two main divisions, real and personal.

a) Real. Real property, generally speaking, consists of land and whatever is erected or growing upon it or affixed to it. An individual who buys a piece of land is said to have an *estate in fee simple.* This is the nearest thing to absolute ownership. He may use his estate as he sees fit, subject to the condition that he respect his neighbor's rights. Another form of estate is known as a *life estate.* A widower in most states has this right in the real property of his deceased wife. Similarly, a widow has a life estate in a part of her deceased husband's real property. One who has a life estate may not, of course, will it to another, that being a right held only by the owner in fee simple. Real property in lands and buildings is called *corporeal* or *tangible.* Certain other kinds of real property are designated as *incorporeal* or *intangible.* For example, the rights that one landowner may have to use the land of an adjoining owner for access to a highway, for pasture, for hunting, and for many other purposes belong in this class.

(b) Personal. Personal property consists primarily, though not exclusively, of movable things. This property is commonly classified as follows: (1) *real chattels,* for example, leases on land for terms of years; (2) *personal chattels*—ordinary movable property such as everyone owns—jewelry, clothing, books, and the like; (3) *choses in action,* which include bonds, stocks, claims one may have against debtors, and similar intangible rights; and (4) rights one may hold in patents and copyrights.

The law of inheritance. Property of deceased persons is inherited in accordance with the law, which differs somewhat in the several states. If the deceased has made a will that meets the requirements of the law, the executor, who is usually named in the will, after payment of the debts of the deceased, proceeds to distribute the property according to the stipulations of the will. If one dies intestate, that is, having made no will or one that is defective in form, the property is distributed to the heirs in accordance with the law and by an administrator appointed by a probate court. The law relating to wills and inheritance is exceedingly complex, and not infrequently there is prolonged litigation over the division of the decedent's estate. If one dies intestate without heirs, his property escheats, that is, reverts, to the state, the original and ultimate proprietor.

2. TORTS. Any violation of a wide group of individual rights, such as personal security, liberty, property, and reputation, is called a *tort,* and the injured party may institute a suit for damages. No definition of the term is satisfactory; it can be understood only by examples and explanations.

(*a*) *Against the person.* Certain torts are committed against the person. Arrest without probable cause belongs to this class. A homely illustration of this particular tort is furnished by a landlord who was forced to pay damages to a lodger whose arrest he had caused on a suspicion that she had stolen about half the feathers from a bed in her room.[18] A similar tort is the institution of legal proceedings against one with malice and without probable cause. The fact that the law affords protection against the institution of malicious proceedings must not be construed to mean that any time a defendant wins a judgment he may then collect damages from the unsuccessful plaintiff. The plaintiff must show that the suit was maliciously instituted. Another tort against the person is *assault,* which is an attempt, real or apparent, to do bodily harm. Thus, a threatening shake of a fist under another's nose or a rush toward another with intent to strike him constitutes assault. If bodily contact is made in such cases, another tort, *battery,* is committed. Of a number of other torts that are primarily against the person, we may mention enticing children away and alienating the affections of a wife or husband. *Slander* and *libel* constitute two well-known torts against the person. The former is a defamation of character published orally; the latter is the same published in writing, print, or figure.

(*b*) *Against property.* Certain torts are primarily connected with property. For example, A, without lawful excuse, interferes with B's attempts to secure contracts; or, A, having knowledge of a contract between B and C, influences C to break the contract. Again, A makes a fraudulent representation to B in a business deal, which B to his damage believes to be a truthful representation. *Trespass* covers a wide variety of torts, such as, the unlawful taking of personal property, forceful damage to such property, and nuisances to land. Indeed, the term is so broad that some of the torts mentioned under other headings, assault and battery, for example, are often classed as trespasses.

(*c*) *Against person and property.* Manifestly, a number of torts may affect both the person and property. Thus loud noises, noxious odors, or dense fumes, which discolor buildings and ruin the housewife's curtains,

[18] F. L. Simpson, *Cases on Torts* (1908), pp. 297–299.

are nuisances that not only disturb persons in their use and enjoyment of property but also lower the value of such property. Similarly, the many torts grouped under the familiar term *negligence,* such as careless or reckless driving, may cause both personal injury and damage to property.

No recovery of damages if injured party is at fault. Although damages may be recovered for a tort, it does not follow that damages will be paid every time one receives an injury. Suppose two negligent drivers have a collision, and one is injured. The injured party's "contributory negligence" bars him from collecting damages. By the same token, an employer is not liable at common law for the injuries of an employee who was negligent. Furthermore, the old common law doctrine of "fellow servant" prevented a workman from recovering damages if his injury was due to the negligence of another employee. In both these cases, however, the liability of the employer has been established by statute in most states, thanks to the efforts of socially minded citizens and labor organizations.[19]

3. CONTRACTS. The making and enforcing of contracts is an indispensable practice in business. An agreement to sell a piece of property for a specified sum, to pay at a specified time for value received the principal and a certain rate of interest on a note, to carry goods from one point to another for a consideration, to pay a stipulated premium in return for insurance protection, and many similar agreements are contracts. The important contracts must ordinarily be written in order to be enforceable in court. Others may be oral. An individual who has been shown a hat to his liking and walks out of a store with it without saying a word is understood to have made a contract, an implied contract, to take the hat and pay the price for it. For breach of contract one may collect damages at common law, and in certain cases, as already indicated, get an order for "specific performance" in an equity proceeding.[20]

4. BUSINESS ORGANIZATIONS. Another significant group of laws has to do with business organizations. Of particular interest are the partnership and the corporation.

(*a*) *Partnerships.* The partnership represents a relatively old form of business combination, but many small enterprises and some large ones are still carried on under this form. Its advantages are perhaps obvious enough, but it has certain disadvantages. For instance, it is dissolved when one of its members withdraws or dies. Also, the debts of the partnership are the debts of the individual members, which joint obligation means that a large debt may be saddled upon one solvent member, or that a too trusting individual may find himself ruined by the knavery of his partner.

(*b*) *Corporations.* The corporation is the institution through which

---

[19] See "Workmen's compensation," Chapter 24, sec. I.

[20] See Ch. 6, sec. v, on the prohibition upon the states against passing any laws impairing the obligation of contracts.

most large businesses have come to be conducted in the last hundred years. It comes into being through a charter issued by the state to a group of natural persons. This legal person so created may sue and be sued, buy and sell property, and exercise certain other rights, just as natural persons do. The term of its life is fixed by the charter, not by the death or withdrawal of a member or members. The membership may change, but the corporation goes on. This power of "perpetual succession" is one of the features of the corporation that make it superior to the partnership for business purposes. Another advantage it has over the partnership is that the individuals who hold the stock are liable only to the extent of the par value of that stock. Thus, a man who has $1,000 in the stock of a particular corporation will lose only that amount if the corporation should fail. His other property cannot be seized to pay the debts of the corporation.[21]

5. DOMESTIC RELATIONS. A word must be said about one other large body of private law, the law of domestic relations.

(*a*) *Marriage and divorce.* Marriage licenses are issued and weddings solemnized in accordance with state law. Persons below a certain age and within a certain degree of kinship are not permitted to marry. Certain types of marriages, for instance, those entered into under fraud or duress, may be annulled. Divorces are granted by the courts under the authority of a legislative act, although it was not until 1949 that South Carolina abandoned the old practice of leaving the granting of divorces entirely to the legislature. The only ground for divorce in some states is adultery; other states add such grounds as desertion, conviction of crime, and incurable insanity; and some states are very liberal, allowing dissolution of the marriage on such grounds as "mental cruelty" and "incompatibility of temperament." It is notorious that persons who live in states having strict divorce laws often go to more liberal states to obtain their "freedom." Not infrequently some difficulty arises over the refusal of the state in which the parties actually live to recognize the validity of a divorce which one of them obtained while residing temporarily in another state.[22]

(*b*) *Status of married women.* Some twenty-five hundred years ago King Ahasuerus laid it down as one of the laws of the Medes and the Persians "that every man should bear rule in his own house." The old common law was somewhat in accord with this rule. By that law the husband was the guardian and protector of his wife, and it followed more or less logically that her property became his, even her clothing. The wife could make no binding contracts, and her husband could recover damages for any injury done her. On the other hand, the husband was obliged to

---

[21] Only private corporations are discussed here. There are various other corporations, such as municipal corporations, which have governmental or quasi-governmental purposes.

[22] See Ch. 5, sec. 111, under "full faith and credit," for a brief discussion of this complicated problem.

support his wife and was held liable for any torts she might commit, for the necessities of life furnished her, and for the contracts she had entered into before marriage. Such, in substance, was the common law on the status of married women, a status that caused women struggling for emancipation to say they were "dead in the law."

During the last hundred years this status has been modified materially by liberal judges, and particularly by statutes. In some of the states, wives now enjoy practically the same rights as their husbands; but the forces that contend for absolute equality the nation over still have a few strongholds to take. In general, however, it can safely be said that such inequality of the sexes as remains is due to physiological, psychological, and social causes, rather than to legal discriminations. Justice Holmes is reported to have remarked that it took more than the Nineteenth Amendment to convince him that there was no difference between men and women.

(*c*) *Status of children.* In the old days a child was practically under the absolute control of the male parent, but modern law protects the child in various ways; for instance, in his right to support, and in guarding him against abuse. Children may be taken away from grossly incompetent parents and placed under guardians. The custody of children of divorced parents is left to the courts, subject only to very general statutory provisions. The courts consult the child's welfare, and as between the parents, allow the innocent rather than the guilty to have custody of the child. Occasionally, a child is placed in the custody of some third person. Children of divorced persons are commonly supported from the father's income or estate.

Civil procedure: The brief survey of the rules of substantive civil law must now be followed by a discussion of the rules by which this substantive law is enforced, the rules of civil procedure. A simple illustration will show the difference between substantive and procedural law. A is injured by the negligence of B. His right to damages is covered by substantive law; the method by which he legally recovers damages is a matter of procedure. Common law procedure was formerly used in all the states; but its technicalities were such that justice was often defeated, and, as a result, the states were led to modify the common law procedure by statutes, or by judges acting under the authority of statutes. At present the system of procedure differs somewhat in the several states, but a general discussion of it will suffice.

1. PLEADINGS: In some of the minor courts the parties to a suit simply go to court and tell their story, and the justice decides the case. This method has not been found satisfactory in the regular trial courts; consequently, they continue to use a rather formal system of pleadings.

(*a*) *Preliminaries.* The plaintiff goes to an attorney and tells his story, and the attorney directs the clerk of the court that has jurisdiction to issue a writ of summons. This writ summons the defendant to appear in court at a specified time to answer the plaintiff. It is given to the sheriff, whose duty it is to find the defendant or his attorney and serve the writ. Ordinarily, the action cannot proceed until actual service has been made; but in certain cases, for example, divorce actions, where the defendant is outside the jurisdiction or residing in parts unknown, publication in newspapers is deemed sufficient. If the defendant has not already engaged a lawyer, he should do so at once, for failure to enter appearance in connection with the suit will mean that judgment will be entered against him by default. The attorney "files an appearance" for his client with the clerk of the court. He then notifies the attorney for the plaintiff that the appearance has been filed, and the two attorneys thereafter notify each other of all the subsequent steps taken in the case.

(*b*) *The declaration and answer.* The next move is for the plaintiff to file a declaration (sometimes called a "complaint" or "petition"), setting forth his cause of action. It must be very carefully drawn, for it must show a cause of action sufficient in law to warrant a judgment for the plaintiff. This declaration is filed with the clerk of the court, and a copy of it is served on the defendant, together with a notice that he shall file an answer to the declaration within a certain date. The defendant, acting through his attorney, of course, may file a demurrer; that is, he may admit the facts as set forth by the plaintiff, but deny their legal sufficiency. In common parlance a demurer is, "Yes; but what of it?" This demurrer passes the question of the sufficiency of the declaration to the judge. If he adjudges it legally sufficient, he "overrules" the demurrer and the plaintiff wins his case, unless the court, as it generally does, allows the defendant to file an answer to the declaration. If the demurrer is sustained, the defendant wins this point and would have judgment in his favor but for the fact that the court then generally permits the plaintiff to remedy his declaration by amendment. Assume, now, that the defendant answers the declaration of the opposing party. This answer or plea may admit certain allegations of the plaintiff and deny others. The points on which the declaration and answer differ are the points which will be in issue at the trial. The nature of the defendant's answer may be such as to warrant a response by the plaintiff; and in a number of states this replication (or reply) is permitted, in order that all the points at issue may be brought out clearly. It often happens that the defendant's answer does not constitute a sufficient defense. It is now the plaintiff's privilege to demur, which he does by asking the court to enter judgment for him "for want of a sufficient answer" from the defendant.

Settlement out of court. After the parties have "agreed to disagree" on certain points, as shown in the declaration and answer, the case must be prepared for trial. The lawyers on both sides interview (the cynic might say "coach") their clients and witnesses, and make every legitimate effort to forge chains of evidence that cannot be broken. As the day of the trial draws near, both sides may feel somewhat uncertain and they may reach a settlement out of court, much to the relief of all parties. Occasionally, the judge suggests such a settlement when the case is called, with good effect. Experienced observers think that judges could frequently bring about such settlements if they were more inclined to extend their good offices in this way.

2. THE JURY. If no settlement is made, the case comes up for trial in due time. The judge presides over the court and passes on points of law, and a jury is usually called to decide the questions of fact. If both sides agree, the jury may be dispensed with, and the case is tried before the judge alone. Let us follow the steps of a case that is tried by jury. A number of citizens have been previously summoned for jury service; and when a particular case is to be tried, twelve persons (a smaller number in some states) are selected for this case. Counsel for either party may challenge any juror for cause; that is, on the ground that he is mentally defective, has business connections with the other party, is prejudiced, or on similar grounds. The judge will excuse such jurors as are shown to be unfitted for the service. Each party is also allowed several peremptory challenges, challenges for which no causes are assigned but which are made on the basis of "intelligent hunches" as to what jurors probably would be unfavorable to the party's case. Citizens ordinarily have an aversion to jury service, and they are often excused for rather flimsy reasons. Yet the average person will learn a great deal on a jury that he would never learn otherwise, and certainly a good citizen should be willing to make a temporary sacrifice for the good of society.

3. THE TRIAL. The jury having been secured and sworn, the judge orders the attorneys to proceed with the case. Thereupon the counsel for the plaintiff rises and makes the opening statement. He informs the court and the jury of the facts in the plaintiff's case, of the nature of the evidence he will offer to prove these facts, and of the damages he asks for his client. He does his best to create a favorable impression for his client with the jury. His case may be won or lost by this initial effort. In some courts this statement is immediately followed by the opening statement of the defendant's attorney, but in others this may be delayed until the evidence for the plaintiff has been offered. In any case the opening statement for the defendant has the same general purpose as that delivered for the plaintiff.

Examination of witnesses. The attorney for the plaintiff now proceeds to examine his witnesses, probably beginning with the plaintiff himself. He must be careful not to ask a witness a "leading question"; that is, a question that suggests to the witness the answer the attorney desires. Also, he must guard against asking questions that are not relevant to the issue; for instance, questions relating to the number of the defendant's dependent children, if the matter in controversy is the amount of damages to be allowed for a personal injury. When the plaintiff's lawyer has examined the witnesses for his side, the attorney for the defendant may then cross-examine them. His purpose is, of course, to expose the weak spots in their testimony and discredit them with the jury. This cross-examination often makes a good "show" in court; but if the attorney is not considerate in his treatment of witnesses, he is likely to turn the jury against his client's case. Witnesses for the defendant are examined and cross-examined in similar fashion. During the examination of witnesses one attorney may "object" to questions asked by the other, and the judge overrules or sustains the objection. In either case one of the lawyers is ruled against, and he may "take an exception" to the judge's ruling. These exceptions often constitute grounds for appealing the case.

4. THE VERDICT. If the evidence submitted indicates that one side or the other has failed to make out a case, the judge may, on motion of the attorney who considers his client entitled to the verdict, direct the jury to bring in a verdict for the defendant, or the plaintiff, as the case may be. The judge probably will decide, however, that sufficient evidence has been offered on each side to warrant the deliberation of the jury. If so, he directs the attorneys to "go to the jury." Each lawyer then makes an argument summarizing the points on which he rests his client's case. Following these, the judge delivers the "charge to the jury." In a number of the Western states the judge's charge precedes the arguments of the attorneys. This procedure has been criticized because it tends to leave the minds of the jurors on the eloquence of counsel rather than on the principles of law applicable to the case. The charge to the jury is often a rather long discourse. The judge explains the law applicable in the case, emphasizing that the jury must take his word for the law; that the jury is to decide the facts. He helps the jurors with this duty by reviewing the evidence offered and by giving them a great deal of good advice as to how evidence should be weighed, cautioning them at the same time that in reaching a verdict they must be governed by their own recollections of the evidence.

The jury then retires, somewhat bewildered, perhaps, by all the judge has told them, but having, in the ordinary case, a pretty good idea as to which party is entitled to a favorable verdict. The jurors deliberate, and usually compromise before reaching an agreement. The compromise is frequently necessary because twelve persons seldom see things alike and the majority of the states require a unanimous verdict. The jury may decide for the plaintiff or for the defendant; occasionally it is unable to reach an agreement. If it decides for the plaintiff, it must also fix the damages (the amount being another matter for compromise). In the event the jury disagrees, the case must be tried again with a new jury.

5. APPEALS. Sometimes both parties are disappointed in the verdict; usually one of them is, and he and his attorney may attempt to get a new trial. The argument for a new trial rests upon various grounds, such as judicial error in a ruling concerning the admissibility of evidence or in instructions to the jury, or a verdict contrary to the evidence. This argument will be heard by the judge who presided at the trial. If the judge refuses to grant a new trial, the losing party's next move in the fight is to take an appeal. Frequently there is no right of appeal in certain types of cases, such as those involving small amounts; but important cases, such as those in which the amounts in controversy are considerable or in which constitutional questions are involved, may be appealed as a matter of right.

Generally, in an appellate court, only points of law are at issue and there is no jury. Lawyers prepare their "briefs" and shape their arguments to convince the judges, reserving their oratorical and emotional efforts for the trial courts in which the jury is employed. The appellate court may sustain the judgment of the lower court, or it may point out certain errors in that court's proceedings and direct the court to hold a new trial. In a few cases, those requiring a construction of the Constitution of the United States being most common, appeal may be had from the highest state court to the Supreme Court at Washington. Trial, appeals, new trials, and perhaps more appeals, require a great deal of time. Sometimes a controversy may be in the courts for several years.[23]

Executing a judgment. Assume that in the course of time a plaintiff gets a judgment against a defendant. The defendant may be "judgment-proof," having no property with which to satisfy the judgment. In Dickens's day he was not "jail-proof," however, his creditor being permitted to cause him to languish in confinement until he paid or until the creditor was convinced that he could not pay. Imprisonment for debt is now abolished;[24] but, for obvious reasons, it was never a satisfactory method of collecting a debt from an insolvent debtor. Ordinarily the defendant has the means to satisfy the judgment, since the plaintiff and his attorney usually do not take the trouble to start suit against one who is insolvent. If the defendant should refuse to pay the damages allowed, the plaintiff's lawyer will get an order from the court directing the sheriff to sell certain properties of the defendant and to pay the plaintiff the amount of the judgment out of the proceeds.

Equity proceedings. The procedure as outlined above is that generally

[23] For the types of delays that occurred under the system employed in New Jersey before 1947, see Joseph Harrison, "Judicial Reform in New Jersey," *State Government,* Oct., 1949, p. 233.

[24] Individuals may still be imprisoned, however, for certain kinds of debts; for example, those involving fraud or willful disobedience of a court order. In Vermont an individual may be held in jail if he is unable to pay damages assessed by a court in a tort case.

followed in suits at common law. A brief discussion must now be devoted to proceedings in equity cases. The plaintiff files a "bill," stating his complaint and asking the court for relief. The defendant may demur, as in suits at common law, or he may answer the bill. The case goes to court on the points at issue shown by the bill and answer. A noteworthy feature of equity procedure is that a jury is seldom used. Occasionally a judge will direct that certain questions of fact be referred to a jury, although the verdict is advisory only, serving somewhat as a guide to the judicial conscience. A few states have granted by statute the right of jury trial in equity cases, and in such states the judge is bound by the jury findings in equity cases as in cases at common law.

Equity courts move more quickly than common law courts. Often no oral testimony is introduced, the bill, the answer, perhaps a replication, and depositions of witnesses being held sufficient. Not infrequently the judge will refer a complicated case to an examiner or master in chancery, who will investigate the case and make a report to the court. The court then makes its decree on the basis of this report although it is not bound to accept the findings of the examiner or master. As just indicated, equity courts give their decision in the form of decrees. The defendant may be ordered to execute a contract, cancel a mortgage, or to do or not to do various things. Failure to comply with the decree constitutes contempt of court and is punishable by fine or imprisonment.

Declaratory judgments.[25] It is understood that the common law provides remedies only after damage has been done, and that equity is often used to prevent an impending injury. But even equity stops short of the need in some cases. Parties often want to know, without the necessity of instituting ordinary suit, their rights under certain provisions of a will, a contract, or other instrument. Of course, one may consult a lawyer; but, valuable as his legal advice may be, it is often felt that something more in the nature of a judicial opinion is desirable. This is now provided for in a large majority of the states through the device known as the "declaratory judgment."[26] A party having an interest in such an instrument as mentioned above institutes the proceeding; the court then calls in the other party or parties and gives the declaratory judgment, thus settling the issue without giving a judgment for coercive relief. In 1933 declaratory judgment procedure received a decided impetus, when the Supreme Court of the United States held that it could review any such judgment of a state court if the facts of the case were such as to constitute a "case or

---

[25] C. S. Potts, "The Declaratory Judgment," *Journal of the American Judicature Society,* XXXVIII, 82 (October, 1944).

[26] Declaratory judgments must not be confused with advisory opinions, which are given in only a few states and only to executives and legislatures on such questions as the constitutionality of proposed legislation.

controversy" between the parties, thus bringing the case within the range of federal judicial authority.[27]

Conciliation and arbitration. Still less formal and less expensive than the declaratory judgment procedure, conciliation and arbitration have significant places in the administration of civil justice. Under conciliation procedure a duly authorized person, usually a court official, attempts to find a solution for an issue between two parties. He talks the matter over with them, quietly explaining the law and giving his opinion on its application in this case. He may mention the great expense of going through regular court procedure, and the case may be such as to prompt him to suggest that such a proceeding would be folly. The conciliator has no authority to bind the parties to the dispute, but tactful men, full of mellow wisdom, often suggest solutions that are mutually satisfactory to the disputants. Since 1913 the city of Cleveland has made extensive use of conciliation procedure, and New York City and several other cities have developed the practice. More than twenty years ago North Dakota adopted a state-wide conciliation plan.

Almost all the states have enacted some type of arbitration law, although only a few of the states measure up to the fairly adequate standards set by California, Massachusetts, New York, and one or two other states. The arbitration system works about as follows: Parties to a dispute, let us say over the fair value of services rendered, select an arbitrator, and, of equal importance, agree to abide by his decision. After appropriate hearings and deliberation, the arbitrator makes his decision, a decision that may be enforced as if it were a regular court judgment. An appeal lies to a court to determine whether the procedure was in accordance with law, but not as to the facts found by the arbitrator. This is the way the system operates in the states that have effective arbitration laws. In other states—in most of them, in fact—individuals may not be compelled to arbitrate, even though they agreed to do so in advance of any dispute, and appeals are permitted on both law and facts.

Arbitration has unquestionably demonstrated its feasibility. It only remains for legislatures in most of the states to rid themselves of the old idea that all cases should proceed, or should be allowed to proceed, to the stage of formal controversies, to be settled in the regular courts, where there are attorneys to argue, judges to rule and advise, and juries to deliberate. Perhaps we prefer to have our justice highly flavored with drama and cloaked in formality; or it may be that we are suspicious of an award that does not cost us a good round sum.[28]

[27] Nashville, C. & St. L. R. Co. v. Wallace, 288 U.S. 249 (1933). The next year Congress passed the Federal Declaratory Judgment Act.

[28] Dodd, *op. cit.*, 341–343; A. F. Macdonald, *American State Government and Administration* (1950 ed.), pp. 275–276; Emily Holt, "Justice Without Juries," *Harper's*, December, 1931, pp. 92–102.

V. CRIMINAL LAW AND PROCEDURE [29]

Crimes.   A crime is an act committed in violation of law and punishable by the state.   There are major offenses, or felonies, and minor offenses, or misdemeanors.

FELONIES.   The more common felonies are defined as follows: (1) *Treason* consists of levying war against a state or adhering to or aiding its enemies.   (2) *Murder* is the intentional killing of a human being by another.   A number of states distinguish between degrees of murder, deliberate and premeditated murder or murder that grows out of an attempt to commit another felony, such as burglary or robbery, being called "first degree"; and other types of murder, "second degree."   (3) *Manslaughter* is the unintentional killing of another.   This is also commonly divided into two or more degrees.   Taking another's life, even with intent, is usually classed as manslaughter rather than murder, if done under mitigating circumstances.   Indeed, one occasionally reads of a killing committed under such provocation that no indictment of any kind is made.   (4) *Arson* is the burning or partial burning of a building of another.   If a person should be burned to death in the building, the crime becomes murder as well as arson.   (5) *Burglary* consists of breaking into a building with the intention of committing therein a felony.   Stealing the family silver and jewelry is only one of a number of felonies that a burglar might intend to commit, although it is the most common.   (6) The unlawful taking of the property of another by force or threat of force is *robbery*.   (7) Taking property in sneak-thief and pickpocket fashion is *larceny,* a very common crime.   Stealing of personal property of considerable value is invariably a felony and it is often called "grand larceny," whereas small thefts are rated as misdemeanors and are known as "petty larcenies."   A number of other crimes, such as rape, forgery, embezzlement, taking property under false pretenses, kidnaping, and perjury, are commonly classed as felonies. The question as to whether a particular crime is a felony or misdemeanor is determined by the law of the state in which the act is committed.

MISDEMEANORS.   The typical justice of the peace and police court cases, punishable by small fines and short jail sentences, are classed as misdemeanors.   Defacing public property, illegal driving and parking, the use of profane or blasphemous language, the exhibiting of indecent pictures, the keeping of disorderly establishments, and the maintenance of various other nuisances go in this class.   A man who makes a great noise at night with a speaking trumpet, to the disturbance of the neighborhood, may find himself in the police court for creating such a nuisance.   A woman who had the habit of scolding on all occasions in such a manner as to con-

[29] See references for preceding section.

stitute a common nuisance was convicted some years ago in New Jersey.[30] But a devout worshiper in North Carolina, whose voice was heard at the end of each verse of a hymn after the congregation had ceased and whose peculiarity in this manner excited mirth in one portion of the congregation and indignation in the other, although held to be a proper subject for discipline in his church, was discharged by the court as being innocent of any public offense.[31] A number of offenses that were mentioned under torts may also be misdemeanors. Thus, assault and battery may give rise to civil action on the part of an injured person and at the same time be of such a nature as to constitute offenses against the public. The same may be said of libel and slander and some other wrongful acts.

WHAT CONSTITUTES A CRIME. Intent is the basic element in many crimes. Breaking and entering a house with the intention of committing a felony therein constitutes burglary, whether the felony be actually committed or not. A person seen thrusting his hand into the pocket of another and withdrawing it without the coveted wallet or watch may be convicted of an attempt to commit larceny. But one who takes property unlawfully under a *bona fide* claim of right is not guilty of larceny. Young children and insane persons cannot commit crimes in the technical sense, for they are irresponsible; intent cannot be shown. Drunkenness, however, is no excuse, though in some instances it may reduce the degree of the crime. A person who assists a felon is, of course, guilty of a crime also. He is designated as an "accessory before the fact," if, being absent at the time the crime was committed, he procures, counsels, or commands another to commit it; and he is an "accessory after the fact," if, knowing a felony to have been committed, he receives, relieves, or otherwise assists the felon. For treason and all offenses below the degree of felony there can be no accessories, all who would be classed as such in other crimes being treated as principals. In some jurisdictions there is no important distinction in any crime between an accessory before the fact and a principal, both being subject to the same penalty.

Criminal procedure. The public is much more interested in the trial of criminal cases than in the law respecting various crimes. This interest is not entirely misplaced, since the apprehension and prosecution of criminals is a matter of fundamental importance to society.[32]

1. WARRANTS AND ARRESTS. When a crime has been committed, the first thing, of course, is to arrest the guilty or suspected persons. Arrests may be made with or without a warrant, according to circumstances. In general it may be said that if one is seen in the act of committing a crime, or,

---

[30] Baker v. State, 53 N.J. Law 45 (1890).

[31] State v. Linkhaw, 69 N.C. 214 (1873).

[32] See National Commission on Law Observance and Enforcement, *Report* (No. 8) *on Criminal Procedure.*

if there is reasonable ground for belief that an individual has committed a felony, an arrest may be made without a warrant. In other cases a warrant must be had. It is usually issued when some person makes a sworn charge that a crime has been committed by another at a particular time and place. It should be stated here that the person making the charge must have reasonable grounds for it; otherwise the individual against whom complaint is lodged may sue him for causing his false arrest. When the complaint is duly made, a magistrate issues the warrant directing the apprehension of the individual named. Naturally, arrests are commonly made by officers; but individuals may make them also, acting upon their own initiative when they have witnessed a crime, or assisting an officer whenever called upon to do so.

Summary trials. If one is accused of a minor offense, of such a misdemeanor as exceeding the speed limit, parking in a prohibited area, or committing an ordinary nuisance, the trial is conducted by a magistrate or justice of the peace. This officer hears the case and decides questions of both law and fact, trial without jury in such cases not being held to violate the constitutional guaranty of trial by jury. The accused may have counsel if he desires it, and he may stand on his right to refuse to testify. The magistrate is commonly empowered to impose a small fine or a short jail sentence upon minor offenders. Appeals are allowed from the magistrate's court; but one convicted in such a court usually feels that there is more to be risked than gained by an appeal.

2. PRELIMINARY HEARINGS. When an arrest is made for a major offense, the individual is brought before a magistrate for a preliminary hearing. The magistrate does not conduct the trial; but rather, decides whether, considering the evidence against the accused, there are sufficient grounds to hold him for trial. The magistrate does not ordinarily hear evidence on both sides but hears only evidence against the accused. However, the accused must be allowed to testify on his own behalf if he cares to do so. If the evidence indicates probable guilt, the magistrate will hold the accused for the action of a grand jury or prosecuting attorney. In the meantime the accused may be released on bail, a right that the constitutions guarantee except for capital offenses. Furthermore, if he feels that he is being held in jail on insufficient grounds, or that he is forced to stay in jail because he cannot raise what he regards as an excessive bail, he may apply to a court for a writ of *habeas corpus.* He will then be brought into court, and a judge will determine the legality of his restraint. The judge's decision may result, of course, in his release, or in his being returned to jail to await further proceedings in his case.

3. INDICTMENT. On the basis of the magistrate's report of the preliminary hearing and from what other information the prosecuting attorney can gather, that officer prepares an indictment and presents it to a grand

jury. This body, carried over from English practice, was formerly used in all states for securing indictments, and it is still used in many of them. At common law it was composed of from 12 to 24 members, though in some states a smaller number is now provided. It considers the evidence presented by the prosecuting attorney, collects evidence for itself if so minded (it seldom is), and by majority vote decides what persons shall be held for trial. If it votes to hold a particular individual for trial, the foreman endorses "true bill" on the indictment. If a majority is convinced that a trial should not be held, the indictment is marked *"ignoramus"* (we ignore). The grand jury may not only pass upon cases presented to it by the prosecuting officer, but it may also direct him to prepare other indictments on the basis of evidence it uncovers.

Indictment by grand jury is often spoken of as a slow and cumbersome method of bringing an accused to trial. Some states no longer require it, and some others require it only for certain types of cases. In such states, indictment is by an "information" prepared by the district attorney and filed with the court having jurisdiction to try the case. Great care must always be taken in preparing an indictment. The offender and his victim must be named; the time, place, and character of the offense must be detailed; and it must be shown that the offense was contrary to law.[33] A defective indictment often results in the discharge of an accused on a "motion to quash." [34]

4. Arraignment. After the indictment, in due course the accused is arraigned; that is, he is brought to the bar of the court to answer the accusation, a copy of which has been furnished him. An officer of the court asks the accused to rise, states the charges, and then puts the question, "How say you, guilty or not guilty?" If the accused pleads "guilty," there is then no issue between him and the state, and the judge pronounces the sentence, although before doing so he may hear testimony and argument that may throw more light upon the case, thus aiding him in fixing a just sentence. The plea of "guilty" is often made when the defendant thinks he is quite likely to be convicted. Such a plea saves time and expense for the state, and usually results in a lighter sentence than the defendant would receive if found guilty by a jury. Not infrequently one reads of a defendant's changing his original plea of "not guilty" to "guilty." Occasionally, usually upon advice of counsel, a defendant changes his plea of "guilty" to "not guilty."

5. The trial. If the defendant pleads "not guilty" or refuses to plead at all (which is commonly treated as a plea of "not guilty"), he must then be tried by a jury. In a few states he may waive jury trial, but in most

---

[33] See Callender, *op. cit.,* pp. 177–178, for a typical indictment.

[34] Occasionally, a purely technical defect will spoil an indictment, as in West Virginia when "W. Virginia" was held insufficient to designate that state. 4 W. Va. 755 (1870).

states he has no option in this matter. The general rule is that the jury shall consist of twelve persons, although several states prescribe a smaller number for other than capital offenses. The jury is selected as in civil cases, the only differences being that a greater number of peremptory challenges are permitted and that great latitude is allowed in challenges for cause. The prejudices, the opinions, the knowledge, the associations, and what not, of each prospective juror are anxiously inquired into by counsel. It frequently happens that practically all intelligent persons in a community have knowledge of and an opinion concerning an important case that is brought to trial, the result being that they are disqualified as jurors and the box is filled with persons of a very low degree of intelligence. It is often suggested that alert citizens who would take an oath to return a verdict in accordance with the evidence presented at the trial would be much more likely to arrive at a correct decision than persons of low mentality who know nothing of a case previous to the trial, but there are many lawyers who are not impressed with the weight of this suggestion.

Court procedure. The prosecuting attorney opens the case for the state with a speech to the jury, outlining the charges against the defendant and the nature of the evidence he will offer to prove them. It is not the duty of this officer to secure a conviction of the accused unless he is guilty. It is his duty to see that justice is done. But, inasmuch as the prosecutor is judged by the number of conviction scalps he wears on his belt, he sometimes becomes overzealous in his efforts. After his opening speech, he examines his witnesses. These may be, and usually are, examined by counsel for the defendant. When the state's case has been thus presented, the defendant's counsel then makes his speech to the jury, examines his witnesses, and turns them over to the prosecutor for cross examination. Each attorney, as in civil cases, objects to certain questions asked of witnesses by the other and takes exceptions to unfavorable judicial rulings. The testimony concluded, the prosecutor attempts to show the jury that the accused stands convicted; and the defendant's attorney follows him in what is usually a still greater effort to show that the state has failed to prove the guilt of his client.

The attorneys are supposed to confine their addresses to the evidence in the case; but this rule is very liberally interpreted and it would seem that it is practically ignored in some cases, despite the fact that the better element in the legal profession insists upon its observance. To save the accused from the penitentiary or from death, counsel may paint for the jury a picture of a broken-hearted wife and mother and of children much worse than orphaned; and he may speak at length upon many similar points that have no bearing upon the question to be decided, namely, the guilt or innocence of the accused. Although prosecutors are not quite so likely to go to such lengths, there are a few cases in which their emotional appeals rival those of the defense counsel. In a famous murder case in North Carolina, a prosecutor shouted at the jury that a certain labor union headquarters was "a whole section of hell! There was immorality there. Yes, *immorality!* Hugging and kissing in public. I'm old-fashioned. I'm a Sunday school man." He said that he was defending his community, where "the dove of peace hovers around the vine-clad door and the kindly light of an autumn sun kisses the curly hair of happy children." He spoke of union organizers as "fiends incarnate, stript of their hoofs and horns . . . from the wild plains of Soviet Russia." He knelt before the jury, holding the hand of the slain man's widow. In conclusion he recited a poem to Mother, and, to show the breadth of his charity, shook hands with a communist.[35]

Following the closing speeches of the attorneys, the judge "charges" the jury. In this charge he informs them of the legal aspects of the case and tells them how to weigh the evidence that has been offered. The laws of most states prohibit the judge from commenting upon the evidence in such a way as to let the jury know his opinion concerning the guilt or innocence of the accused. The judge tells the jury that the accused is innocent unless the state has beyond a reasonable doubt proved him guilty. On the other hand, he cautions them that it is not necessary for the state to prove guilt beyond the possibility of a doubt. With these instructions, which in complicated cases may cover many pages, the jury retires to consider the verdict. Unanimity is almost invariably required for a decision in major offenses. Sometimes the verdict is quickly reached; but cases that make the newspaper headlines often hold the jury for hours, or even days. Sometimes it is impossible to reach any decision, in which case the jury is said to be "hung." For the less serious crimes, a number of states have modified the jury trial to the extent of requiring only a three-fourths or five-sixths majority for a verdict.

If a verdict of guilty is rendered and if the court overrules the frequently made motions in arrest of judgment and for a new trial, the judge pronounces the sentence. Before doing so, he may hear a plea for clemency from the attorney of the individual who stands convicted. If the unhappy man has a good record previous to the offense for which he is found guilty, the plea will probably not be in vain. The statutes commonly fix the maximum and minimum penalties, leaving the exact penalty for individual offenders to be determined by the judge, a discretion that a wise judge often applies on the side of clemency for persons who have fallen from grace but who are not past redemption.[36] The sentence ends the

---

[35] National Commission on Law Observance and Enforcement, *Report* (No. 11) on *Lawlessness in Law Enforcement*, pp. 319–320, and *Time*, October 28, 1929, p. 13.

[36] In a number of states the judge now imposes a maximum penitentiary sentence and an administrative board later fixes the exact time to be served.

work of the trial court, but on various grounds a subject of its adverse judgment may appeal to the higher state courts.[37]

Punishment for crime. Formerly, capital punishment was administered for a great variety of crimes. As late as the reign of George III there were about two hundred offenses punishable by death; among these offenses were cutting down a tree and stealing goods in a shop to the amount of five shillings. The same penalty was exacted for a number of crimes in the American colonies; but the number has steadily decreased, until now only five or six states have the death penalty for as many as four crimes, and in the majority of the states murder alone may carry that penalty. A number of states have abolished the death penalty altogether. Other punishments range from life imprisonment to short jail sentences and small fines, varying with the nature of the offense, the character of the offender, and, to some extent, according to the laws of the different states.

The criticism is often made that punishment as administered does not reform the criminal. Nearly every prison is crowded. The warden is by force of circumstances a custodian, who must operate the prison within his budget, rather than a reformer. Considering these facts, it would be surprising if a majority of the prisoners were reformed, although some of them undoubtedly are. Then, too, the trouble is not all within the prison walls. Prosecuting attorneys, who are often bent only on securing the severest penalty; judges, who sometimes lack human understanding or who are held to a rigid formula by statute; juries, who are not infrequently swayed by prejudice and emotion; and respectable citizens, who sometimes show an unwillingness to give an ex-convict a new start in life, all must bear a share of the blame.[38]

AMELIORATION OF PUNISHMENT. Punishments may be reduced in various ways. The most sweeping method is by the executive pardon, which, if unconditional, wipes away all legal consequences of the crime. In many jurisdictions a person convicted of a minor crime may be placed on proba-

---

[37] Appeal may be taken from the state supreme court to the Supreme Court of the United States only when a right under the federal Constitution has been claimed by a defendant and denied by the state court; for example, when it is claimed that "due process," a guaranty of the Fourteenth Amendment, is violated by state action.

Despite the safeguards surrounding an accused, it sometimes happens that an innocent person is convicted. The most celebrated of recent cases is that of Bertram M. Campbell, who, as the result of mistaken identification, served more than three years in Sing Sing for a forgery he did not commit. When his innocence was discovered, Governor Thomas E. Dewey, who had been the District Attorney under whose jurisdiction Campbell had been convicted, granted him a full pardon (August 28, 1945) and promised that he would ask the legislature to authorize liberal compensation for the innocent man. The legislature passed the necessary law, and the New York Court of Claims awarded Campbell $115,000 for his wrongful imprisonment.

[38] See Warden Lewis E. Lawes, "Why Our Prisons Fail," New York *Times,* Magazine Section, August 16, 1931. For an encouraging report on improvements in prison administration, see A. H. MacCormick, "Progress in American State Prisons," *State Government,* Apr., 1949, pp. 112–115.

tion and, if he maintains a proper standard of behavior, will not be required to serve a single day in prison. Nearly all the states now have a parole system, a system under which an individual who has served a part of his sentence and who has been a good prisoner may be released from prison. Such a person remains under the supervision of public authorities, however, and he may also receive assistance from them in obtaining employment and in "going straight." The effective administration of the parole system is seriously impaired in a number of states because too few parole officers are employed. The success of a parole system depends largely upon the work of these officers, a fact that governors and legislatures are slow to realize.

VI. "JUSTICE AND THE POOR" [39]

It is impossible to deal in this work with the whole field of judicial administration, but there are two other problems that must be briefly considered. These are: (1) justice and the poor; and (2) defects of legal procedure.

The theory and the fact. Equality of justice is accepted as a fundamental principle in America, and in general the substantive law confers no favors upon particular classes; but the principle of equality often vanishes when individuals must fight for the rights accorded them by law. Inability to pay court costs and fees and to buy the services of attorneys often separates the rich and the poor by a great gulf. Writing in 1919, R. H. Smith estimated that there were 35,000,000 persons in the United States unable to pay any appreciable amount for legal advice and assistance.[40] The loss of homes, savings, and wages for lack of adequate counsel in civil cases is tragic enough, but the position of the unfortunates who are accused of violating a criminal law is still more pitiable. Publicist Raymond Moley speaks of the great majority of the half million annually arraigned in the criminal courts of New York City as a helpless lot, constituting "not a problem of law enforcement as much as one of social welfare. They are, in large part, merely careless, defective, or unfortunate beggars, vagrants, degenerates, crap shooters, peddlers without licenses . . . sneak thieves, 'dopes,' and small-time cheats. . . . All are bewildered, frightened, blindly seeking relief from their difficulties." [41] Possibly the situation has been somewhat improved since those words were written,

---

[39] Raymond Moley, *Tribunes of the People* (1932); R. H. Smith, "Justice and the Poor," *Bulletin of the Carnegie Foundation for the Advancement of Teaching* (1919), No. XIII.

[40] *Ibid.*, p. 33.

[41] Quoted from "Justice for the Poor: A Task for New York," New York *Times*, May 3, 1931, sec. 9, p. 1, by permission of the author and the New York *Times*. Acknowledgment is also made to the Yale University Press, since it has published Professor Moley's *Tribunes of the People* in which the statement above is reproduced practically unchanged.

but certainly justice for the poor (and for the middle classes also, to a large degree) has not as yet been attained.

And this is not the whole story. The poor man's justice may cost him more than the rich man pays for his. Competent investigators made a survey of the cost of civil litigation in New York for the year 1930. It was found that the inhabitants of the City of New York paid through public revenues an average of eight cents each (not including lawyers' fees) for justice in the Municipal Court, the civil court that settles finally the vast majority of the poor man's cases. On the other hand, the inhabitants paid an average of fifty cents each in public revenues for justice in the higher courts, the courts to which men of large affairs go for civil justice. As a result, litigants in the Municipal Court paid 71.1 per cent of the cost of administering justice in that court while those who used the higher courts in New York City paid only about 10 per cent of the cost. It is thus apparent that in New York City, at least, those who can least afford to pay for justice are required to pay about seven times as much as those who can most easily afford to pay.[42] Another major item in the cost of litigation is counsel fees, an item so large that people of small means are often prevented from going to court, and down-and-outs who are brought to court on criminal charges commonly have grossly inadequate counsel.

Steps toward reform. Efforts are being made, however, to assist the "forgotten man" in obtaining justice. Kansas (1923) authorized cities and counties to set up small claims courts with authority to decide cases in which the amount involved does not exceed twenty dollars. Massachusetts, New Hampshire, California, and three or four other states have similar systems, and so do several of the larger cities, including Chicago, Philadelphia, and Cleveland. These courts proceed with a minimum of formality, discourage the participation of lawyers, hold costs to a very low figure, and narrowly restrict the right of appeal.[43]

Legal aid societies, both private and public, now flourish in eighty or more cities. A workman has a claim for a few dollars in wages; a hand laundress has not been paid because it is claimed that a shirt has not been returned; a divorced husband has ceased paying the ten dollars a week alimony ordered by the court, and his whereabouts is unknown; an injured laborer has encountered difficulties in collecting compensation due him; and a woman who rents one of her two plainly furnished rooms to a waitress has been arrested on her lodger's complaint that the landlady has stolen her clothes. Legal aid societies render assistance in such cases as these, and the best ones pride themselves upon serving their clients as efficiently as would a firm of private attorneys. The Legal Aid Society

---

[42] Summary in Graves, *op. cit.*, pp. 733–734.

[43] Macdonald, *op. cit.*, pp. 256–257; Leonard Sawyer, *Municipal Courts of New Hampshire* (Bureau of Govt. Research, U. of N.H., 1949).

in New York City has about a hundred clients a day bringing such problems as unpaid wages, domestic controversies, personal injuries, and unsettled estates. The cases of those who come seeking help are usually trivial and petty; yes, as trivial and petty as an empty stomach or weeks in jail! The equal protection of the laws is without meaning if it does not give the laundress her wages as it awards damages to a millionaire who was injured in an accident through the fault of a billion-dollar corporation.

The Office of Friend of the Court is authorized by law for every county in the State of Michigan. The Office enforces alimony decrees for the benefit of minor children, gives service in matters relating to land contracts and mortgage foreclosures, and co-operates with the juvenile courts and other social agencies in their work of rehabilitation.[44]

Luckless individuals without a "ten spot" in their possession who find themselves indicted for crime are, in most jurisdictions, assigned a lawyer by the court. Such lawyers are usually young men without experience or older men who have not succeeded in practice—in either case men who are no match for the public prosecutor, and certainly not to be compared with the able criminal lawyer whom the accused with modest means can afford. Now it is the obligation of the state to convict the guilty and release the innocent. It is therefore no less essential that the accused have counsel for his defense as energetic, as resourceful, and as effective as the state's attorney. In order to accomplish this socially desirable purpose a number of cities and counties have established the office of public defender. These include Los Angeles County, San Francisco, Cook County (Chicago), Minneapolis, and others. Connecticut and several other states have authorized state-wide systems. The defender is an officer of the state enjoying the same status in court as the prosecutor; but his duty is, as his title suggests, to defend the accused. In a number of jurisdictions he defends all the accused. Persons who are able to do so, pay the state a reasonable sum. In no case do they pay the defender. He is paid by the state at the end of each term of the court. Los Angeles has a slightly different public defender system. The salaried defender and his staff represent only those persons who are unable to pay for their defense (about fifty per cent of those who are brought to court). The success of this system, according to Moley,[45] is demonstrated by the fact that defendants regularly prefer the public defenders to the lawyers engaged in

[44] Graves, *op. cit.*, pp. 734 ff., John S. Bradway, *Legal Aid Bureaus* (1935); F. E. Cooper and J. P. Dawson, "The Office of the Friend of the Court in Wayne County, Michigan," *Annual Report of the Judicial Council of Michigan* (1935).

[45] *Op. cit.* See also Donald Freeman, "The Public Defender System," *Journal of the American Judicature Society*, XXXII, 74 (October, 1948), and for criticism of the Public Defender see W. S. Stewart, "The Public Defender System Is Unsound," *ibid.*, p. 115 (December, 1948).

the criminal practice. It is very doubtful whether any plans will or can be devised that will place the rich and the poor on the same footing in court; but the movements along the lines just indicated will place the poor in a more favorable position for gaining their rights.

Minorities and justice. Another wrong or inequity in our treatment of accused persons is that minorities, unpopular minorities, even if they have some money for attorneys' fees, may have difficulty in getting "equal justice." It is not easy to maintain that a Negro who in intelligence and economic status compares favorably with a white man can with equal ease secure his legal rights in all the courts of the land. He is certain to be under the necessity of winning a favorable verdict from a white jury, and the juries before which his case is commonly tried are quite likely to be prejudiced against him because of his race. Does a labor agitator on trial for murder have only the task of defending himself from that charge; or is he also under the handicap of having to overcome a prejudice the prosecutor, or the judge, or the jury may have against him because he is an agitator? A "radical" is on trial for robbery. Will the fact that he is a "radical" make it more or less difficult to convict him? Here is a despised religious minority, receiving the sort of contempt and scorn that was heaped upon another religious minority, the early Christians. Will the members of this sect who violate local ordinances be caught and arrested by the police with more zeal than they employ in dealing with the general body of inhabitants; and will local magistrates deal as leniently with them as they do with the general body of citizens who violate ordinances? Democracy is an ideal, and equal justice for all is a part of that ideal. The complete attainment of the ideal is not possible, but a constant striving toward it is the standing obligation of a democratic society.

VII. SOME PROBLEMS OF LEGAL PROCEDURE [46]

The system of judicial administration is often criticized by laymen, lawyers, and judges. It is criticized, not only by idealists, who take as their standard of justice the statute of the beauteous and unseeing lady who holds in her hands the scales on which all the elements of any dispute are nicely weighed, but also by those who "judge justice" by a relative standard, having due regard for the limitations of the human beings who must administer it. It is pointed out that lawyers, being advocates, cannot be expected to be disinterested; that juries often fail to reach a just verdict; and that judges sometimes display ineptitude in operating the

[46] Callender, *op. cit.,* Ch. XV; "A Program for Legal Reform in the United States," *The Consensus,* Vol. XVI, No. 3, October, 1931, and Vol. XVII, No. 2, October, 1932. Every issue of the *Journal of the American Judicature Society* has articles on this subject and suggestions for improving our judicial system.

scales. Legal terminology is characterized by some as being archaic, a characterization humorously illustrated by an indictment, repeatedly read in court, much to the merriment of spectators and jury and to the annoyance of judge and prosecutor, charging a slender and dignified youth with "riotously and routously" assaulting a powerful policeman.[47] In fact, almost every phase of legal procedure is criticized. It is said that from being a means of obtaining justice, procedure has become an end in itself; that attention is concentrated on form to such an extent that justice is often defeated.

The law's delay. The particular defect of procedure that is singled out for special attack, and that includes many of the other defects, is delay. Delay is not only the cause of prolonged annoyance and expense, but it is perhaps the most frequent cause of miscarriage of justice. It is an old grievance. Hamlet numbered among the thousand natural shocks that flesh is heir to "the pangs of dispriz'd love and the law's delay"; and the "head chancery," a hold by which a boxer clinches the head of his helpless opponent under his arm, is so named because it symbolizes the all but hopeless state of many cases that entered the British chancery courts in years gone by.[48]

"Delay resembles the many-headed hydra of mythology," writes Professor Callender.[49] "It is an evil of many phases and very difficult of extirpation. It may appear at any stage of a lawsuit, be slain by a judicial Hercules, and appear again at a later stage. The many forms which it may assume make it difficult to attack. It is not an isolated problem. The delay may be the result of the procrastination of lawyers; it may be the result of an archaic system of pleading; it may be occasioned by the overcrowded condition of a court's calendar; it may be a consequence of faulty trial procedure; it may be the outcome of inadequate processes for enforcing a judgment; it may be the result of a complex judicial structure; it may be the consequence of a complicated system of appellate procedure, and so on."

Witnesses change their residence, their memories grow dim, and some die before they are called to court. The patience and funds of an honest litigant may be exhausted while his unscrupulous opponent may finally win the case by artful dodges around the sinuosities of legal procedure. Some states have set about to correct this condition by revising the rules of judicial procedure and by establishing a more or less unified system of judicial administration. Although the progress is slow, with both professional and lay opinion agreed that procedure should be improved, it is reasonable to hope that the much needed overhauling is but fairly begun.

[47] A. Hamilton, M.D., "What about the Lawyers?" *Harper's,* Oct. 1931, p. 546.

[48] But cases do not remain so long in chancery since Britain reformed her court system (1873).

[49] *American Courts* (1927 ed.), pp. 220–221. By permission of McGraw-Hill Book Co., publishers.

Defects in the jury system. Common indeed is the complaint against the jury system. Judge Claude C. Coffin of Colorado draws up the following incisive indictment of juries.[50] "The jury poll, supposed to be a cross section of the county community, is at the outset by statutory exemptions purged of occupational types wherein we should find the highest degree of intelligence and integrity; then the panel is further purged of busy, first rate business and professional men by individual excuses. From the 'qualified' list of jurymen remaining are drawn the required number who in large majority have never before served as jurymen and who have little or no training or experience for the work at hand. But this is still not the end of the process of selecting 'qualified' jurors. Attorneys may then by peremptory challenge remove from the list a certain number of those who seem more likely to give heed to the cause, which they are supposed to do, than to mind the parties and the pleaders, which they are supposed not to do." The judge has several other counts in his indictment. Judge John J. Parker of the Circuit Court of Appeals of the United States (Fourth District) finds the chief weakness of the jury system in the fact that judges in most of the states are not permitted to give juries the assistance they need to understand and evaluate the evidence, an authority the federal judges possess and use to good advantage.[51]

Yet neither of these judges nor other intelligent critics of the jury system want to see it abolished. On the contrary, they are certain of its place in a democratic system of government. What they insist upon is the reform of the system. The essential features of this reform would be to improve the personnel of the jury by severely limiting classes, professions, and individuals who might be exempted or excused from service, and by giving the judge control of his court with the right and duty to assist jurors in weighing evidence. Other suggestions are that the number of jurors be reduced, that the unanimous verdict be abolished except perhaps in capital cases, that the jury be abolished for certain types of cases, and that jurors be made professional as are judges and lawyers. It has already been noted that a number of states have made some progress along one or more of these lines.

Pretrial conferences. A movement that gives promise of relieving congested dockets and simplifying the administration of justice is that of the pretrial conference. The judge meets the attorneys (and perhaps their clients) and they consider and analyze the case. Although the main purpose of the conference is to bring about adjustments that will simplify procedure in a case, it often results in the settlement of a case. An example

---

[50] "Jury Trial Tragic but Not Entirely Hopeless," *Journal of the American Judicature Society,* XXV, 13 (June, 1941).

[51] "Improvements of Jury System Must Come," *Journal of American Judicature Society,* XXVI, 71 (October, 1942).

of the functions of the pretrial conference is furnished by an Ohio court. In 1940 this court held 270 such conferences on jury cases. Of these cases 103 were either settled or otherwise disposed of; jury trial was waived in 12 cases; and in nearly all other cases arrangements were made that expedited the trials. The employment of pretrial procedure is now common in the federal courts and in many of the state courts. Leaders of the bench and bar very generally commend it.[52]

Defects peculiar to the criminal procedure. The same defects are generally apparent in both civil and criminal procedure, but certain procedural impediments are peculiar to the administration of criminal justice. A few of these demand serious attention. Sometimes, the magistrates who conduct the preliminary hearings are not properly qualified for their tasks, and there have been those who were corruptible. Failure to hold a hearing, or to conduct one properly, often means that the criminal goes free. It is proposed that the common practice of popular choice of magistrates give way to appointments, or that persons without legal training be declared ineligible for the office, or both. So far there has been little action upon these proposals. The grand jury is very generally conceded to have become a "venerable nuisance," a time-consuming method of determining what the committing magistrate and the prosecuting attorney have already decided; namely, that there is a *prima facie* case against an accused. Fortunately, many states have realized these facts, and some have abolished the grand jury completely; and a number of others have discontinued its use except for investigating general disorders and widespread conspiracies, a function that the grand jury may still usefully perform.

Should the right to refuse to testify be abolished? The elaborate system of rights of persons accused of crime not infrequently operates to free the professional criminal who knows how to use them. No one questions the necessity of some of these rights, such as the right of public trial, the privilege of counsel, and the right to compel the attendance of witnesses on behalf of the accused. But the same cannot be said so readily of the right of an accused to refuse to testify [53] or of the right of a witness to refuse to answer any question that would tend to incriminate him. In many civilized countries with superior systems of justice, this right does not exist. There is little doubt that it is an immunity which often prevents the uncovering of crime in this country. The criminal class jealously guards

---

[52] George E. Brand, " 'Mighty Oaks'—Pretrial," *Journal of the American Judicature Society*, XXVI, 36 (August, 1942); Judge Carl A. Weinman, "Give Pretrial a Trial," *ibid.*, XXV, 24 (June, 1941). Pretrial is used in criminal as well as civil cases; see Judge Luther B. Way, "New Technique Facilitates Criminal Trials," *ibid.*, XXV, 120 (December, 1941); "Use of Pretrial Procedure in State Courts," *ibid.*, XXVIII, 156 (February, 1945).

[53] It is generally held that comment by the prosecuting attorney upon the accused's failure to take the stand is a violation of his right to refuse to testify.

and frequently uses the right. Ordinarily the innocent man is willing, and often eager, to testify. The repeal of the right to refuse to testify would make it more difficult for the guilty to escape, without depriving the innocent of adequate means of defense.

Since the accused may not be forced to testify in court, it has long been the practice of many police investigators to make him give evidence following arrest, using threats and violence toward the accused if he refuses to talk. This "third degree" administered in jails and at police stations is roundly criticized by many authorities, particularly by the National Commission on Law Observance and Enforcement.[54] It would seem that if a person charged with a crime could be compelled to testify in court, there would no longer be any good excuse for permitting the often-winked-at lawlessness incident to the "third degree." Despite the arguments that may be made against retaining the right of refusal to testify, most criminal lawyers seem to want it retained, indeed may even have a professional interest in its retention. To many others it is a venerable object of reverence on which no impious hand should be laid.[55]

Viewing the subject of the administration of criminal law broadly, it may be said that there are too many survivals of mediaeval practice in our methods of attempting to cope with twentieth century criminals. True, there are isolated homicides, forgeries, and thefts; but the criminals who most seriously disturb the peace of society are organized and intelligent, as anyone knows who reads of the activities of gangs and racketeers.[56] The alertness and resourcefulness of the professional criminal is shown from the inception of crime to the last effort to evade punishment. Although considerable progress has been made in the direction of improved methods of apprehending criminals and some improvement in the legal machinery of prosecuting them is noticeable, the criminal class seems to manage to stay a few jumps ahead of the guardians of society. In combating the lawless, public officers must act lawfully, observing the niceties of constitutional and statutory restraints, a legal sieve designed to separate the innocent from the guilty, but through which the guilty often pass with the innocent. The best brains of the country are all but baffled in their attempt to cure procedural defects. When we add to the difficulties mentioned the well-known fact that officers of the law are sometimes allied with the criminals they are supposed to apprehend and prose-

---

[54] *Report* (No. 11) *on Lawlessness in Law Enforcement.*

[55] For both sides of this question see Claire B. Bird, "Our Constitutional Protection of Guilt," *Journal of the American Judicature Society*, XXV, 18 (June, 1941) and Abraham Wekstein, "The Constitutional Protection Against Self Incrimination," *ibid.*, XXVI, 154 (February, 1943).

[56] Moley, "War on the Gang," New York *Times*, sec. 9, Aug. 30, 1931; and "The Racket," *ibid.*, Aug. 9 and 16.

cute, the problem of "law enforcement" assumes an entirely new angle. Only an alert, if not outraged, public can rid itself of the traitors in its own house.

Reading List

American Municipal Association, *Formal Professional Qualification Requirement of Judges* (1938).

Annals of the American Academy of Political and Social Science, Vol. CLXVII, May, 1933, "The Administration of Justice," CCXVII, Sept., 1941, "Crime in the United States."

F. R. Aumann, *The Changing American Legal System* (1940).

S. E. Baldwin, *The American Judiciary* (1905), Chs. VIII–XXV.

F. G. Bates, O. P. Field, and Others, *State Government* (1949), Chs. 18–19.

H. Best, *Crime and Criminal Law in the United States* (1930).

A. A. Bruce, *The American Judge* (1924).

C. N. Callender, *American Courts* (1927).

Benjamin N. Cardozo, *The Nature of the Judicial Process* (1925).

W. S. Carpenter, *Judicial Tenure in the United States* (1918), Chs. III–IV.

W. F. Dodd, *State Government* (1928 ed.), Chs. X–XII.

J. A. Fairlie and C. M. Kneier, *County Government and Administration* (1930), Chs. VIII and XIII.

Jerome Frank, *Courts on Trial: Myth and Reality in American Justice* (1949).

Abraham L. Furman, *Chief Council: The Ordeal of a Public Defender* (1933).

J. L. Gillin, *Taming the Criminal* (1931).

L. P. Golberg and Eleanor Levinson, *Lawless Judges* (1935).

W. B. Graves, *American State Government* (1946 ed.), Chs. XV–XVIII.

W. E. Hannan and M. B. Csontos, *State Court Systems* (Council of State Governments (1940).

Evan Haynes, *Selection and Tenure of Judges* (1944).

A. G. Hays, *Trial by Prejudice* (1933).

A. N. Holcombe, *State Government in the United States* (1931 ed.), Chs. XIII–XIV.

Journal of the American Judicature Society (for current developments).

L. W. Lancaster and A. C. Breckenridge, *Readings in American State Government* (1950), Ch. VI.

A. Lepawsky, *Judicial System of Metropolitan Chicago* (1932).

Henry T. Lummus, *The Trial Judge* (1938).

D. C. Lunt, *The Road to the Law* (1932).

Austin F. Macdonald, *American State Government and Administration* (1950 ed.), Chs. XI–XII.

J. M. Maguire, "Poverty and Civil Litigation," *Harvard Law Rev.,* XXXVI, 361–404 (Feb., 1923).

R. Moley, *Our Criminal Courts* (1930).

———, *Politics and Criminal Prosecutions* (1930).

———, *Tribunes of the People* (1932).

E. N. Morgan, *Introduction to the Study of Law* (1926).

National Commission on Law Observance and Enforcement, *Reports* Nos. 4, 8–10 (1931).

Albert S. Osborn, *The Mind of the Juror* (1937).

Roscoe Pound, *Criminal Justice in America* (1945 ed.).

———, *Organization of Courts* (1940).

William A. Robson, *Civilization and the Growth of Law* (1934).

Gustav L. Schramm, *Piedpoudre or Small Claims Courts* (1928).

R. H. Smith, *Justice and the Poor* (1919).

——— and J. S. Bradway, "The Growth of Legal Aid Work in the United States," *Bull. U.S. Bureau of Labor Statistics,* No. 607 (1936 ed.).

C. F. Snider, *American State and Local Government* (1950), Chs. XI, XVII.

J. N. Ulman, *A Judge Takes the Stand* (1933).

Sam B. Warner and H. B. Cabot, *The Judges and Law Reform* (1936).

W. F. Willoughby, *Principles of Judicial Administration* (1929).

Questions and Problems

1. Draw a distinction between "advisory opinion" and "declaratory judgment."
2. Does your state have a unified court system? A judicial council? What improvements might be made in judicial organization in your state?
3. Discuss the various methods by which state judges are selected. What method of selection strikes the best balance between democratic and expert participation?
4. To what extent is the English law the law of the American states?
5. Make a list of the principal subjects with which our civil law deals.
6. Outline the main points of procedure in a civil case.
7. Explain the nature of an arbitration; a conciliation.
8. Define crime. Give the essential features of each of the principal felonies.
9. Indicate the steps in a typical criminal proceeding.
10. What are the principal shortcomings of the administration of criminal justice?
11. Discuss justice for the poor, the down-and-out, and minorities.

☆ 19 ☆

The National Administrative System

RECEDING chapters deal with the historic branches of the government—executive, legislative, and judicial. But little has been said about the daily work of the government as it affects the lives of citizens. In past generations our governments, along with most other governments, did not in fact touch the life of the ordinary citizen very closely. This condition has been greatly changed in the last century, especially during the last fifty years. The factory system, the concentration of population in small areas—indeed every feature of the Industrial Revolution has led governments to assume new functions. The depression that began in 1929 forced governments to assume unprecedented tasks. For a legislative body to decide that a particular government shall undertake the performance of certain services is a relatively simple matter, but the task of administering these functions is very complex. For this purpose elaborate administrative machinery has been devised and hundreds of thousands of men and women have been employed.

The remaining chapters of this volume deal with administrative organization and certain great functions of government. This chapter relates primarily to the administrative organization of the national government, although some reference is made to functions, particularly to the postal service. The next chapter (20) deals with state and local administrative organization, and Chapter 21 treats of administrative personnel—that great army of government employees. Taken together, these three chapters constitute a study of something approaching a fourth branch of government, the administrative branch. The remaining chapters relate to such important functions of government as the raising of revenues, budget preparation and administration, the regulation and promotion of commerce and business, the fostering of agriculture, the conservation of natural resources, labor legislation, the protection of health, social security, national defense, the conduct of foreign affairs, and international organization.

I. CONTROL OF THE ADMINISTRATIVE DEPARTMENTS [1]

The Constitution does not provide specifically for any administrative departments, although it assumes their establishment in the provision that the President "may require the opinion, in writing, of the principal officer in each of the executive departments, upon any subject relating to the duties of their respective offices," and gives authorization for their creation in the provision that Congress may "make all laws which shall be necessary and proper for carrying into execution the foregoing powers, and all other powers vested by this Constitution in the government of the United States, or in any department or officer thereof."

1. **Control by Congress.** Under this constitutional authority, Congress not only creates administrative agencies, but it also provides in great detail for their internal organization. It decides how many officers and employees shall be engaged, how they shall be chosen (with the exception of the heads of departments), and how much they shall be paid; what functions shall be performed by a department and each of its subdivisions; whether administrative officers shall have discretionary or only ministerial powers; and how much money shall be appropriated for the work of each department as a whole and for each of its branches. Furthermore, Congress may abolish a department or other administrative agency or any division thereof, or it may transfer a particular service from one agency to another. This is not a complete enumeration of the powers of Congress over administration; but it is sufficient to show something of the nature and wide extent of those powers.

2. **Control by the President.** The President also plays a leading part in controlling administration. He must "take care that the laws be faithfully executed"; that is, he must see that the work of the government is efficiently performed. Long ago we learned that he appoints the higher officers with the advice and consent of the Senate; that Congress has authorized the appointment of many "inferior" officers by the same method; that the President may at will remove officers so appointed.[2] Although the power to "hire and fire" in the public service must be exercised with some regard to political effect, it is, nevertheless, a powerful means of

---

[1] (Hoover) Commission on Organization of the Executive Branch of the Government, *General Management of the Executive Branch* (1949); John M. Pfiffner, *Public Administration* (1946 ed.), Chs. 4–6; Arthur W. Macmahon and John D. Millett, *Federal Administrators* (1939), Chs. 1–5; Leonard D. White, *An Introduction to the Study of Public Administration* (1948 ed.), Chs. III–VI.

[2] See Chapter 11, sec. v.

maintaining administrative standards. The constitutional powers to command the Army and Navy and to control foreign affairs, although the last-mentioned power is shared with the Senate, give the President an especially wide directing authority in these fields.

Further, in practically every phase of administrative activity, Congress has by statute conferred supervising and directing authority upon the President. The result is that although Congress, often upon presidential recommendation, determines what functions the government shall undertake, how much money shall be spent upon them, and what administrative agencies shall perform them, the President and his immediate subordinates are left to work out the details and to exercise constant supervision over the officers and employees engaged in the daily work of administering these functions. The President thus has the position of commander-in-chief of the administrative forces of the government.

Broad as his powers are, students of administration, as well as many statesmen, have felt that Congress should be even more liberal in delegating to him administrative powers, particularly in the direction of leaving him and his chief assistants more discretion with respect to administrative details. There is little doubt that the stoutest advocates of Executive power were fully satisfied by the action of Congress (1933) in granting to the President a wide range of powers to cope with the depression, or with the completeness and alacrity with which Congress delegated powers to the President during the two world wars.

3. Control by department heads. As everyone knows, Congress and the President rely chiefly upon the department heads for the performance of administrative duties. Congress is the board of directors, the President is the general manager, and the secretaries of the nine great executive departments are the heads of the different branches of the business of government. The powers and duties of a department head are numerous and important, but they are here summarized briefly.

(1) He supplies both the President and Congress with information, and often with advice. Acting as a group, the heads of departments serve as the President's Cabinet, assisting the Chief Executive in formulating policies.

(2) The head of each department appoints a number of subordinate officers and employees, subject to civil service rules, to be explained in Chapter 21. He has also a limited power of removal.

(3) The head of a department serves as a sort of buffer between the President and the public, interpreting the policies of the President to the public and calming the feelings of those who may be adversely affected by a particular administrative decision or policy.

(4) He "goes to the front" for the employees of his department, defending them against unjust criticism, and seeking for them better working conditions

and salary adjustments. He strives to keep up the morale of his employees by exercising just discipline, making fair promotions, encouraging study, and by any other means his ingenuity may suggest.

(5) In the chapter on "The President as Chief Legislator," mention is made of his rule-making, or ordinance, power. Often this power is exercised through the department heads. These officials (and the heads of most, if not all, other administrative agencies) are also authorized to issue rules and regulations for the conduct of their departments, and, in many cases, they are charged with the duty of filling in, in the form of administrative regulations, the details of statutes relating to broad functions of government, such as the regulation of immigration and the collection of customs and internal revenue.[3] It is probably not incorrect to say that a comprehensive statute on the books (the Social Security Act, for example) means little to the ordinary citizen until appropriate administrative authorities through their rules and regulations make the statute applicable to him in concrete form.

(6) Not only do department heads and other officials who help to determine policy act in a sort of legislative capacity by elaborating statutes, but they also have functions that are judicial in nature, in that they hear appeals from the rulings of minor officials and decide other cases that are brought directly to them. For example, the clerks in the land office make the original decision in matters connected with the entry into public lands, and the Secretary of the Interior will hear such cases on appeal; the Immigration officials at a port of entry make the original decisions concerning the right of a person to enter the United States, and the Attorney General is the final source of appeal; and the Postmaster General, acting upon information furnished him by subordinates, closes the mails to those who in his opinion are using them for fraudulent purposes.

II. THE ORGANIZATION AND FUNCTIONS OF THE DEPARTMENTS [4]

The First Congress under the Constitution, profiting from the experiences of the Confederation in attempting to manage executive affairs, established three executive departments, the Departments of State, Treasury, and War. Some congressmen thought that several other departments should have been created at that time; but the general fear in the states of the extension of the powers of the national government led the majority to hold the number of departments to the minimum and to group as many functions as possible within each department. As the work of the national government has increased, new departments have been added from time to time,

---

[3] J. P. Comer, *Legislative Function of National Administrative Authorities* (1927); James Hart, "The Exercise of Rule-making Power," in the Report of the President's Committee on Administrative Management, *Report with Special Studies* (1937), pp. 310–355.

[4] (Hoover) Commission on Organization of the Executive Branch of the Government (1949), *Reports;* Macmahon and Millet, *op. cit.,* Chs. 6–16; Pfiffner, *op. cit.,* Chs. 4–5; White, *op. cit.,* Chs. VI–VII; *U.S. Government Organization Manual* (1950–1951).

taking over duties that the older departments could no longer perform and administering new functions as well. The National Security Act, approved July 26, 1947, combined our defense departments, War and Navy, in the National Military Establishment headed by the Secretary of Defense. Included in the Establishment are the Departments of the Army, Navy, and Air Force, each with its secretary. Reserving for Chapter 27 the Military Establishment and for Chapter 28 the State Department and the Foreign Service, we shall now consider the organization and some of the functions of the other departments that, despite the extensive use of commissions and other agencies, still conduct the greater part of the national administration.

Departmental organization. One may think that an executive department is headed by a secretary who is responsible to the President; of an under secretary and assistant secretaries serving as a staff and otherwise aiding the secretary to whom they are responsible at all times and for all their actions; of a dozen or more chiefs of services or bureaus, each of whom is responsible to a particular assistant secretary or other officer near the secretary; of perhaps two score chiefs of divisions each of whom must report to a particular bureau chief; and so on down to the most lowly employee in a department. In other words, one may think of an organization in which the lines of authority have been carefully planned, the lines all running to the secretary through the administrative hierarchy. This picture is as inaccurate as it is attractive to the methodical mind. There is no such department. The organization charts of some of the departments look something like what has been described, but the charts do not tell the full story.

The Hoover Commission looked at the departments and found them wanting in effective organization. What is wrong with the executive departments? The Hoover Commission reported, in part, as follows:

1. Great confusion in the departments and agencies in their relations to the President and to each other.

2. Too many separate agencies and several of them not combined in accordance with major purposes.

3. Lack of departmental integration. Some bureau or division heads have independent authority granted by act of Congress. Line of authority is thus abridged, and the authority of both the President and the department head is undermined.

4. No uniformity in the method of appointing department subordinates. About one third of the bureau heads must be confirmed by the Senate, a bad practice.

5. Most department heads lack sufficient authority to assign responsibility within their departments.

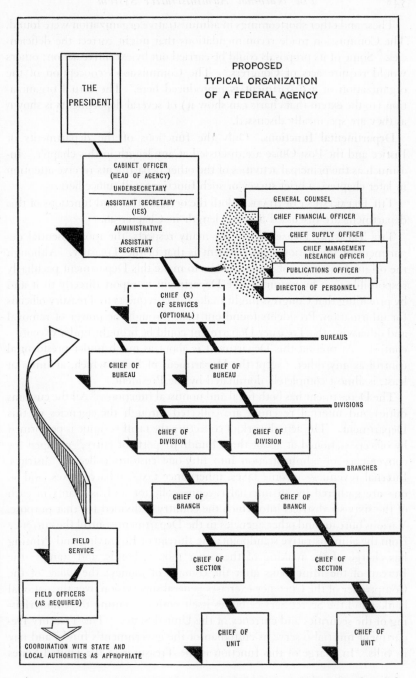

PROPOSED
TYPICAL ORGANIZATION
OF A FEDERAL AGENCY

THE PRESIDENT

CABINET OFFICER
(HEAD OF AGENCY)
UNDERSECRETARY
ASSISTANT SECRETARY
(IES)
ADMINISTRATIVE
ASSISTANT
SECRETARY

GENERAL COUNSEL
CHIEF FINANCIAL OFFICER
CHIEF SUPPLY OFFICER
CHIEF MANAGEMENT
RESEARCH OFFICER
PUBLICATIONS OFFICER
DIRECTOR OF PERSONNEL

CHIEF (S)
OF SERVICES
(OPTIONAL)

BUREAUS

CHIEF OF
BUREAU

CHIEF OF
BUREAU

DIVISIONS

CHIEF OF
DIVISION

CHIEF OF
DIVISION

BRANCHES

CHIEF OF
BRANCH

CHIEF OF
BRANCH

FIELD
SERVICE

CHIEF OF
SECTION

CHIEF OF
SECTION

FIELD OFFICERS
(AS REQUIRED)

CHIEF OF
UNIT

CHIEF OF
UNIT

COORDINATION WITH STATE AND
LOCAL AUTHORITIES AS APPROPRIATE

From the Hoover Commission's *Report on General Management of the Executive Branch.*

These and other shortcomings in administrative organization were found. The Commission made recommendations that might correct the deficiencies. Some of its proposals could be carried out by executive action; others would require acts of Congress.[5] The Commission's conception of the organization of a department is reproduced here. The actual organization (to the extent that charts can show it) of several departments is shown as they are specifically discussed.

Departmental functions. Only the functions of the departments of Justice and the Post Office are discussed at any length in this chapter. Inasmuch as the principal activities of the other departments receive attention in later chapters, a brief survey of such functions will suffice here.

THE DEPARTMENT OF STATE. Both the organization and functions of this department are discussed at some length in Chapter 28.

THE TREASURY DEPARTMENT. In many respects, the most essential department of the national government is that of the Treasury. Although the original intention of Congress was to make this Department peculiarly responsible to it by requiring the Department to report directly to it and by providing that Congress might make direct requests to Treasury officials for information, Presidents found out that, through the power of removal and otherwise, the Treasury Department could be brought under executive control. At present this Department is about as much under presidential control as any other, except the Department of State, which, at times at least, is almost completely dominated by the President.

The Department has both fiscal and nonfiscal functions. All the customs duties and internal revenues are collected through the agencies of this Department. The actual work of collecting the tariff revenue is performed by officers stationed at about three hundred "ports of entry," grouped for convenience of administration into fifty-one customs collection districts. Internal revenues—income taxes, inheritance taxes, tobacco taxes, and so on—are gathered by an internal revenue collector and assistants in each of the sixty-six districts into which the country is divided for that purpose. Various bureaus and other agencies in the Department control the currency from the administrative standpoint: the Bureau of Engraving and Printing has charge of the making of the paper money, bonds, and stamps; the Bureau of the Mint looks after the coinage of money; the Office of the Comptroller of the Currency exercises general supervision over the national banks; and the Secret Service busies itself with preventing the counterfeiting of the securities and currency of the United States. The Treasury Department must also serve as custodian of the government's funds, and pay its bills. In charge of this function is the Treasurer of the United States

[5] Report on *General Management of the Executive Branch*, pp. 31–33.

DEPARTMENT OF THE TREASURY

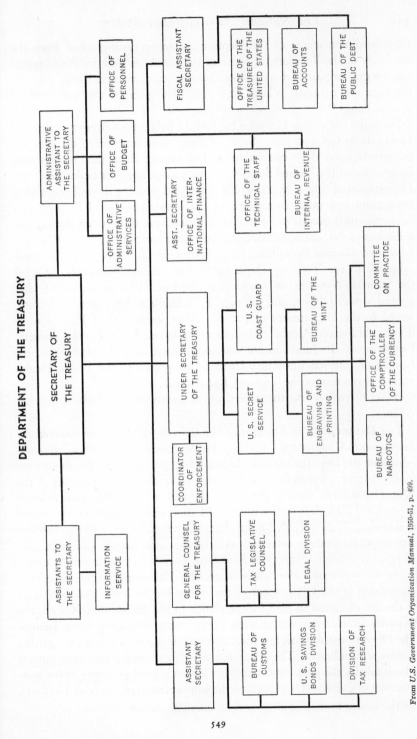

From *U.S. Government Organization Manual*, 1950–51, p. 499.

549

(a subordinate officer of the Department to be distinguished from the Secretary of the Treasury). Some of the money is kept in Washington; but the greater part of it is deposited for the government in banks scattered throughout the country, a large portion of it being kept in the twelve federal reserve banks.[6]

From the beginning, Congress has had the habit of assigning nonfinancial functions to the Treasury. Some of these were transferred to other departments upon their establishment, but among those that remain may be mentioned the United States Coast Guard (it operates under the Navy Department in time of war), which is charged with the duty of preventing smuggling and other infractions of the laws; the United States Secret Service, which guards our Presidents, in addition to its other duties; and a Bureau of Narcotics, which administers the narcotic statutes. With the advent of national Prohibition the enforcement of Prohibition laws naturally fell to the Treasury Department, since it had previously collected the internal revenues on intoxicating liquors. This arrangement later proved unsatisfactory, and in 1930 Prohibition enforcement was transferred to the Department of Justice. After the repeal of Prohibition a division of Federal Alcohol Administration was established in the Treasury Department. Its functions are now consolidated with the activities of the Bureau of Internal Revenue. Until a few years ago the Public Health Service was a unit of the Treasury Department, but under the Reorganization Act of 1939 it was transferred to the newly created Federal Security Agency.

THE DEPARTMENT OF DEFENSE. The defense functions are reserved for discussion in Chapter 27. At this point we consider briefly those responsibilities of the Department that do not relate directly or exclusively to national defense. Formerly, the Department of the Army (known as the War Department until 1947), as in the case of the other two original departments, administered a number of functions not particularly related to its title. These included naval defense, Indian affairs, and the distribution of public lands to veterans. All the functions named and practically all other nonmilitary functions have long since been transferred to appropriate departments. For many years the Philippines were under the supervision of the Department of the Army, but with the passage (1934) of the act designed to give independence to the Philippines in 1946, the Department was relieved of most of its duties respecting those Islands. The Department still has, however, two functions which might be regarded as only semimilitary. The Army has a highly trained group of engineers whose talents the government utilizes for such good purposes as the construction of dams and bridges, and the improvement of rivers and harbors.

[6] The financial functions of the Treasury are discussed more fully in Chapter 22.

As everyone knows, the Panama Canal, the "big ditch," is the work of Army engineers. And this leads to the second semimilitary (and the "semi" can be left out in time of war) function, the supervision of the Panama Canal and the Canal Zone. Serving under the direction of the Secretary of the Army, the Governor of the Panama Canal is responsible for the maintenance and operation of the Canal and for the government of the Canal Zone.

The Department of the Navy has never been charged with many responsibilities and duties other than those relating directly to the task of the Navy as an arm of the national defense. Yet it does administer certain functions which, although closely allied with the defense problem, have a somewhat broader significance. The Department of the Navy has supervision of civil governments in islands such as Guam, American Samoa, and other possessions of the United States when placed under naval administration. The Hydrographer of the Department makes surveys on the high seas and in foreign waters, collects and distributes information of hydrographic and navigational significance, prepares maps and charts, issues sailing directions, and in similar ways serves the United States Navy and navigators generally. The Naval Observatory at Washington, D.C., broadcasts time signals during the last five minutes of every hour. These signals are used by navigators to determine chronometer errors and positions, and by surveyors, and other scientific workers for the determination of position, the measurement of gravity, and for other purposes. Our standard time is determined by the Naval Observatory.

THE DEPARTMENT OF JUSTICE. The legal arm of the government from the executive standpoint is the Department of Justice. It must be carefully distinguished from the judiciary. The courts hear and decide only litigated cases; they give no legal advice to officers of the government and they do not prosecute offenders, two functions that constitute the principal duties of the Department of Justice.

The few duties that fell to the Attorney General in 1789 were held to be insufficient to warrant the creation of a special department for him. But, with the growth of the activities of the national government, particularly after the Civil War, the necessity for such a department was obvious, and it was duly constituted in 1870. Ranking next to the Attorney General is the Solicitor General, who represents the United States in court in certain important cases; six assistant attorneys general, each charged with the supervision of some phase of the activities of the Department; and a number of subordinate officials. The Federal Bureau of Investigation (Mr. J. Edgar Hoover and his G-men) is a unit of the Department of Justice, and so is the Immigration and Naturalization Service. In each of the ninety odd districts into which the country is divided for purposes of judicial administration, is a district attorney, who, with the necessary assistants, serves the United States as a prosecuting attorney serves a state. Also in each district there is a marshal, who is a "federal sheriff," and the requisite number of deputy marshals. These field officers are appointed by the President for a term of four years, and they serve under the supervision of the Department of Justice.

In performing one of its chief functions, that of giving legal advice or opinions, the Department limits itself to answering concrete legal questions presented by the President or other high administrative officials. Opinions of the Attorney General are, of course, somewhat in the nature of judicial decisions. They are commonly accepted as precedents in the executive departments, and they are often conclusive on the points of law involved, since many questions presented to the Attorney General never arise in courts of law. As already stated, the second important duty of the Department of Justice is to prosecute those who violate the laws of the United States. Action against violators of the revenue, immigration, antitrust, espionage, and other laws is regularly brought before the district courts by the district attorneys, representing the Department. Representatives of the Department must also defend the United States in the claims cases which may be brought against it in the district courts or in the Court of Claims. In addition to the duties mentioned, the Department administers the immigration and naturalization laws, the federal prisons, the federal parole system, and advises the President with respect to the granting of pardons.

This Department is much concerned in time of war with the problem of enforcing laws against sedition and sabotage and with the administration of laws respecting alien enemies. Wide powers are granted to the Department for these purposes, and they may be used in a most oppressive manner or they may be used with moderation. In 1917–1920 the Attorney General took vigorous action on all fronts, and was severely criticized by eminent members of the bar for his excessive zeal. With the entrance of the United States into the Second World War, the Attorney General made it clear that his office would use its powers with that restraint which should characterize any great government of the people, and this pledge was kept.

THE POST OFFICE DEPARTMENT. The Department with which the citizen is most familiar is that of the Post Office. It is the government's greatest business enterprise and it is a government monopoly. It employs about 500,000 persons, who receive and distribute millions of pieces of mail each day. In some forty-two thousand post offices and branches it does an annual business amounting to about two billion dollars. The cry often goes up, "Keep the government out of business"; but seldom, if ever, is

POST OFFICE DEPARTMENT

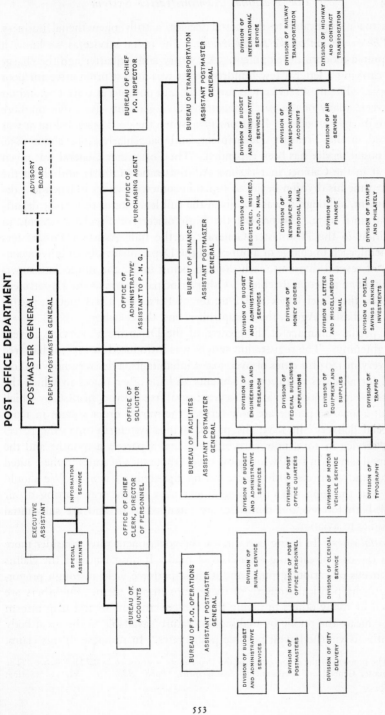

From *U.S. Government Organization Manual, 1950-51, p. 505.*

553

this made applicable to the postal service, a truly phenomenal business.

The expansion of the postal service. The postal service as we know it is quite a modern development. A century and a quarter ago the charge for carrying a letter a few hundred miles was almost prohibitive for poor people. The mail service was used little, and post offices were few and far between, many of the rural inhabitants living twenty-five miles or more from the nearest office. But from 1789, when the postal establishment was placed in the Treasury Department, and particularly since about 1850, the postal service has been expanded. The Postmaster General was given a seat in the Cabinet in Jackson's Administration (1829); and about the same time his division began to function somewhat as an independent department, although it was not given the full legal status of a great department until 1872. At present the high officers of the Department, in addition to the Postmaster General, are the four Assistant Postmasters General, each in charge of a bureau of the Department. Each bureau consists of several divisions, each division being under the immediate supervision of an appropriate chief.[7] Other principal officers of the Department include the Chief Clerk and Director of Personnel, the Chief Inspector, the Purchasing Agent, the Comptroller, and the Solicitor.

A partial summary of the growth of the Department's services is very enlightening. The registration system was introduced in 1855; urban free delivery in 1863 for cities of over 50,000 inhabitants, a delivery now authorized for all cities of 10,000 inhabitants and for other places in which the gross receipts amount to $10,000 a year; rural free delivery in 1896, by which about 25,000,000 people are now served; the money order system in 1864; "special delivery" in 1885; the postal savings system in 1911; the parcel post service in 1913, now carrying millions of parcels a month; and the air mail service in 1918, which now covers thousands of miles in the United States and connects with lines covering the civilized world. We should add that the high rates the government pays for the transporting of air mail, both foreign and domestic, are intended to be and are substantial subsidies to aviation.

Postal rates. In fixing postal rates, the government must consider more than the cost of carrying each class of mail. It must consider the claims and needs of various groups, and it must perforce yield in rough proportion to the political strength of the groups urging them. Publishers are joined by many others in saying that the government should help inform and educate the public by making "literature" available to the great body of citizens via the lowest possible postal rates. In response to this claim,

---

[7] The problem of the organization of the Department is discussed by C. H. Pritchett, "The Postmaster General and Departmental Management," *Public Adm. Rev.*, VI, 130 (Spring, 1946).

Congress has been rather generous. Educational, scientific, religious, and numerous other publications are distributed for a relatively low charge, and deficits from carrying such matter must be made up in profits from other classes of mail and from appropriations by Congress. Literature for the blind is carried free, and so are the publications of agricultural colleges and experiment stations. No charge is made, of course, for the billion pieces of mail carried each year for the national government. With

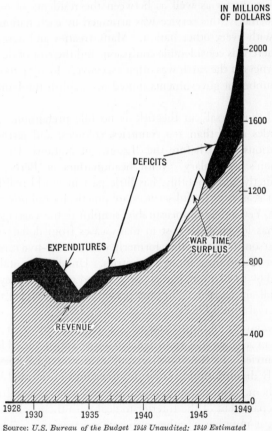

POST OFFICE DEFICITS 1928-1949

Source: *U.S. Bureau of the Budget 1948 Unaudited: 1949 Estimated*

From Hoover Commission's Report on *The Post Office*, p. 2.

these considerations in mind, one can understand why the Department's annual expenditures usually run well beyond its income.

The Hoover Commission recommended (Report on *The Post Office*) among other things for the postal service that: (1) all postmasters be brought completely under the merit system; (2) the service be decentralized for convenience of administration into 15 regions; (3) the subsidies to aviation paid through generous mail contracts be paid back to the Post Office Department by appropriations from tax funds and not be imposed upon the Post Office and mail users as at present; and (4) rates be increased for certain specified services to the point where they are self-supporting. The only one of these recommendations on which any progress has been made is the last.

The Universal Postal Union.   Mail must be carried between inhabitants of different countries as well as between the residents of any particular country.   Formerly, this service was arranged by each nation through an agreement with every other nation.   Many treaties and agreements were necessary, there was considerable confusion, and the cost of delivering mail to the far corners of the earth was often excessive.   In 1874, to remedy these defects, a number of governments united to establish the Universal Postal Union.

The word "universal" in the title is no idle pretension.   The Union, which includes more than 160 countries, colonies, and territories, was a "United Nations" even before the "League of Nations" had entered the common man's vocabulary.   With headquarters at Berne, this Union functions quietly and smoothly, has little part in world politics, and perhaps for that reason its useful services are practically unknown to the general public.   Yet it has immeasurably simplified the carriage of foreign mails, and has lowered the cost in many cases from dollars to cents.   A letter to a person in France that formerly cost seventy-five cents now costs five cents, the rate to most foreign countries.   Under the postal agreements administered by this Union, parcel post, insured matter, money orders, and other material are carried.   No sane person would advocate the abolition of the Universal Postal Union.[8]

THE DEPARTMENT OF THE INTERIOR.   The Department of the Interior corresponds in a general way to what is often called the "Home Office" in other countries.   Its functions, relating to matters of domestic concern, were formerly divided among other departments that seemed best fitted to administer them.   Not until 1849 did Congress collect these functions and create the Department of the Interior to deal with them.   Like most other departments, it now has a rather elaborate organization.   The Secretary, Under Secretary, and two Assistant Secretaries are in general charge of the offices, bureaus, and divisions that are immediately responsible for the several services of the Department.

This Department's principal assignment is to administer the laws relating to the public lands.   This function is discussed in Chapter 20, section 11.   The Department has a number of other duties, which cannot be easily

---

[8] N. L. Hill, *International Administration* (1931), pp. 12–13, 168–171; *U.S. Govt. Manual,* 1949, p. 570.

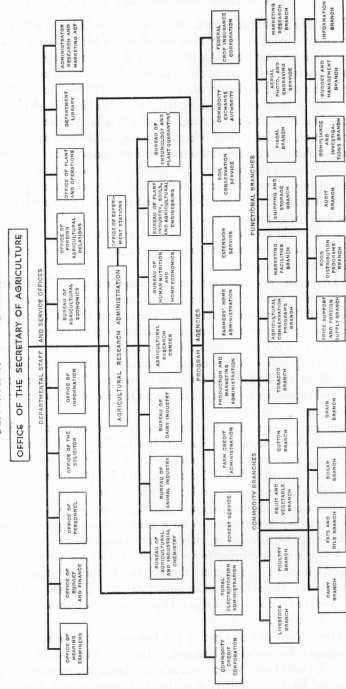

DEPARTMENT OF AGRICULTURE

OFFICE OF THE SECRETARY OF AGRICULTURE

DEPARTMENTAL STAFF AND SERVICE OFFICES

OFFICE OF HEARING EXAMINERS
OFFICE OF BUDGET AND FINANCE
OFFICE OF PERSONNEL
OFFICE OF THE SOLICITOR
OFFICE OF INFORMATION
BUREAU OF AGRICULTURAL ECONOMICS
OFFICE OF FOREIGN AGRICULTURAL RELATIONS
OFFICE OF PLANT AND OPERATIONS
DEPARTMENT LIBRARY
ADMINISTRATOR RESEARCH AND MARKETING ACT

AGRICULTURAL RESEARCH ADMINISTRATION

OFFICE OF EXPERIMENT STATIONS
BUREAU OF ANIMAL INDUSTRY
BUREAU OF DAIRY INDUSTRY
AGRICULTURAL RESEARCH CENTER
BUREAU OF HUMAN NUTRITION AND HOME ECONOMICS
BUREAU OF PLANT INDUSTRY, SOILS, AND AGRICULTURAL ENGINEERING
BUREAU OF ENTOMOLOGY AND PLANT QUARANTINE
BUREAU OF AGRICULTURAL AND INDUSTRIAL CHEMISTRY

PROGRAM AGENCIES

COMMODITY CREDIT CORPORATION
RURAL ELECTRIFICATION ADMINISTRATION
FOREST SERVICE
FARM CREDIT ADMINISTRATION
PRODUCTION AND MARKETING ADMINISTRATION
FARMERS' HOME ADMINISTRATION
EXTENSION SERVICE
SOIL CONSERVATION SERVICE
COMMODITY EXCHANGE AUTHORITY
FEDERAL CROP INSURANCE CORPORATION

COMMODITY BRANCHES

LIVESTOCK BRANCH
DAIRY BRANCH
POULTRY BRANCH
FATS AND OILS BRANCH
FRUIT AND VEGETABLE BRANCH
SUGAR BRANCH
COTTON BRANCH
GRAIN BRANCH
TOBACCO BRANCH

AGRICULTURAL CONSERVATION PROGRAMS BRANCH
PRICE SUPPORT AND FOREIGN SUPPLY BRANCH
MARKETING FACILITIES BRANCH
FOOD DISTRIBUTION PROGRAMS BRANCH
SHIPPING AND STORAGE BRANCH

FUNCTIONAL BRANCHES

FISCAL BRANCH
AUDIT BRANCH
AERIAL PHOTO. AND ENGRAVING SERVICE
COMPLIANCE AND INVESTIGATIONS BRANCH
BUDGET AND MANAGEMENT BRANCH
MARKETING RESEARCH BRANCH
INFORMATION BRANCH

From *U.S. Government Organization Manual*, 1949, p. 587.

classified. The health, education, and general supervision of our 400,000 Indian citizens living on many reservations is entrusted to the Bureau of Indian Affairs within this Department. The Department's Bureau of Mines is concerned with the safety of miners, the conservation of mineral resources, testing of fuels for the Government, and the production of helium gas, to mention four of its functions. Within this Department are located the National Park Service, Fish and Wildlife Service, the Bureau of Reclamation, the Division of (electric) Power, the Division of Territories and Island Possessions, and still other divisions and services. Originally the Office of Education was in this Department, but under the Reorganization Act of 1939 it was transferred to the Federal Security Agency. Some of the worst administrative scandals have arisen in this Department in connection with the administration of the public lands and in dealing with the Indians. It might not be too difficult to show that among the principal qualifications for its secretaryship are a suspicious nature, a reformer's zeal, and singleness of purpose.

THE DEPARTMENT OF AGRICULTURE. Although not given the full status of a department until 1889, a federal agricultural service was maintained by a so-called "department" after 1862. The present Department of Agriculture is one of the most efficient and satisfactory of all the executive departments. Its work is primarily scientific and technical. In its administration it is largely free from political interference, having a very high percentage of its employees under the merit system. The application of science and economics in agriculture has greatly increased its importance in recent years.

It maintains Bureaus of Animal Industry, Human Nutrition and Home Economics, Dairy Industry, Plant Industry, Soils, and Agricultural Engineering, Agricultural and Industrial Chemistry, Entomology and Plant Quarantine, Agricultural Economics, and a Soil Conservation Service, and several "administrations" conducting research and issuing bulletins on many phases of the farm problem. Although these services benefit the farmer primarily, they are also worth a great deal to the general public. The Department maintains an elaborate extension organization through which information is distributed to agricultural colleges, farm organizations, and directly to the farmers themselves. In this direct connection with the farmers the radio plays an important part. This is but a partial summary of the functions of this great Department, of which we shall learn more in Chapter 25.

THE DEPARTMENT OF COMMERCE. The Department of Commerce is next to the youngest, but one of the busiest departments. The joint Department of Commerce and Labor was created as a result of agitation on the part of business and labor, particularly after they had seen Congress bow to the will of the agricultural interests in 1889. Since the joint arrangement was not satisfactory to labor, Congress yielded in 1913 and established the Department of Labor.

The Department of Commerce is conducted, of course, by the Secretary, Under Secretary, Assistant Secretaries, and a number of directors, commissioners, and chiefs. This is the Department that Herbert Hoover directed for more than seven years preceding his elevation to the Presidency.

A general idea of the work of this Department may be gained by an enumeration of its bureaus, administrations, and corporations. Its bureaus are those of the Census, Foreign and Domestic Commerce, Standards, and Weather, the last of these having been transferred from the Department

DEPARTMENT OF LABOR

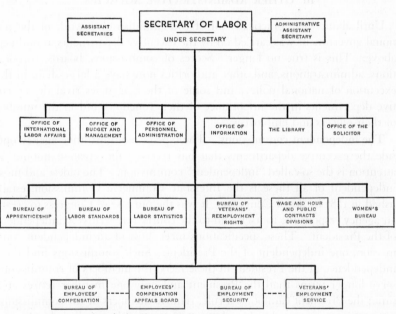

From *U.S. Government Organization Manual*, 1950-51, p. 509.

of Agriculture in 1940. To Commerce also belong the Patent Office, the Coast and Geodetic Survey, and the Civil Aeronautics Administration. In February, 1942, a number of other administrative agencies, chiefly those relating to the war program, were transferred to the Department. A partial list includes the Reconstruction Finance Corporation, the Defense Plant Corporation, the Rubber Reserve Company, the Metals Reserve Company, the Defense Supplies Corporation, and the Import-Export Bank of Washington. In 1945 this war accretion was taken from the Department as a condition of the confirmation of Henry A. Wallace as Secretary thereof. The principal services of the Department of Commerce are discussed in Chapter 23.

THE DEPARTMENT OF LABOR. The last of our great executive departments, the Department of Labor, was created to foster, promote, and
develop the welfare of American wage earners, by improving their working conditions and increasing their opportunities for profitable and productive employment. This Department administers the Bureau of Labor
Statistics, the Bureau of Labor Standards, the Women's Bureau, and several
other bureaus. Under its direction also function the Public Contracts
Division, the Wage and Hour Division, and the Office of International
Labor Affairs. The major services of the Department of Labor are discussed in Chapter 24.

III. OTHER ADMINISTRATIVE AGENCIES [9]

Until about 1880, practically all of the administrative work of the national government was carried on by the executive departments as outlined
above. This is true no longer. Scores of commissions, boards, corporations, administrations, and other authorities now have a large share in the
execution of national policy, and some of these agencies rival the executive departments in the importance of their functions and in the number
of their officers and employees.

The independent commissions. The type of administrative agency outside the executive departments that has received the greatest amount of
attention is the so-called "independent" commission. The oldest and most
independent of all these is the Interstate Commerce Commission, established in 1887 by act of Congress. It was the purpose of Congress to create
an agency responsible to itself and to the courts, but relatively independent
of the President. These specifications meet those of an independent commission, one independent of the President. Such commissions find their
independence of the President in these facts: the members of commissions
serve longer terms than the President and only one member retires at a
time; the President cannot, as a rule, remove members of the commissions
except for causes stipulated in the statutes (it will be recalled that he can
remove "executive officers" for any cause—for the good of the service); the
decisions of the independent commissions are independent—they do not
go to the White House for approval; and, finally, these commissions have
no channel of communication with the White House.[10] Other independent commissions than the ICC include the Federal Trade Commission

---

[9] (Hoover) Commission on Organization of the Executive Branch of the Government,
Federal Business Enterprises and *Independent Regulatory Commissions* (1949); R. E. Cushman,
The Independent Regulatory Commissions (1941); M. E. Dimock, "Government Corporations:
A Focus of Policy and Administration," *Am. Pol. Sci. Rev.,* XLIII (1949), 899–921, 1145–1164;
White, *op. cit.,* Chs. VIII–IX; *U.S. Govt. Manual.*

[10] White, *op. cit.,* pp. 103–105.

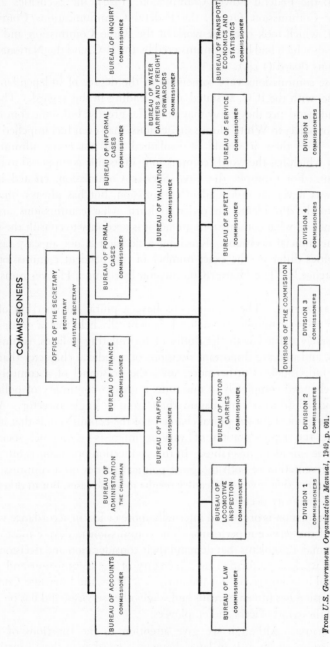

INTERSTATE COMMERCE COMMISSION

COMMISSIONERS

OFFICE OF THE SECRETARY
SECRETARY
ASSISTANT SECRETARY

BUREAU OF ACCOUNTS
COMMISSIONER

BUREAU OF ADMINISTRATION
THE CHAIRMAN

BUREAU OF FINANCE
COMMISSIONER

BUREAU OF FORMAL CASES
COMMISSIONER

BUREAU OF INFORMAL CASES
COMMISSIONER

BUREAU OF INQUIRY
COMMISSIONER

BUREAU OF LAW
COMMISSIONER

BUREAU OF LOCOMOTIVE INSPECTION
COMMISSIONER

BUREAU OF TRAFFIC
COMMISSIONER

BUREAU OF MOTOR CARRIES
COMMISSIONER

BUREAU OF VALUATION
COMMISSIONER

BUREAU OF SAFETY
COMMISSIONER

BUREAU OF WATER CARRIERS AND FREIGHT FORWARDERS
COMMISSIONER

BUREAU OF SERVICE
COMMISSIONER

BUREAU OF TRANSPORT ECONOMICS AND STATISTICS
COMMISSIONER

DIVISIONS OF THE COMMISSION

DIVISION 1
COMMISSIONERS

DIVISION 2
COMMISSIONERS

DIVISION 3
COMMISSIONERS

DIVISION 4
COMMISSIONERS

DIVISION 5
COMMISSIONERS

From *U.S. Government Organization Manual*, 1949, p. 601.

(1914), the Federal Power Commission (1920), the Securities and Exchange Commission (1934), the Federal Communications Commission (1934), which took over the work of the Radio Commission and certain functions which had been administered by the ICC, and the National Labor Relations Board (1935).

These commissions vary somewhat in the degree of independence they exercise, with the ICC, as stated above, leading in this regard. The statutory independence they enjoy may not differ greatly; but some commissions may not object to White House suggestions, may even feel impelled to seek them. And then, it should be explained that not every administrative agency which has the word "commission" in its title is supposed to be independent. For example, the Civil Service Commission, created back in 1883, was never an independent commission, but has always functioned close to the President. In order to learn what commissions are independent and what commissions are not it is necessary to consult the statutes and the judicial decisions. Reaching a decision is not an easy task, and authorities differ on the exact number of independent commissions now in existence.[11] The Hoover Commission listed nine; Hoover himself said eleven.

ORGANIZATION. The commissions have a plural membership of three, five, or a larger number of men. It is generally held that a group can be more safely trusted with the duties of formulating policies, issuing regulations, and making important decisions of a judicial character than can a single individual. Furthermore, since the personnel of a commission is never changed completely at one time, a greater continuity of policy may be expected from a commission than from a single director. Another strong argument for the plural character of the commission is that it makes possible the representation of various interests—economic, social, and otherwise—in its membership. In this connection provision is often made for representation of both the great political parties on a commission—an arrangement that gives satisfcatory results in some cases, but in others, only partisan majority decisions.

A commission is organized internally more or less in accordance with the needs of the service it performs. The commissioners devote most of their time to major problems that demand their consideration and decision. The routine work is performed by a secretary of the commission and various technical bureaus created for the purpose. Thus, the Interstate Commerce Commission has fifteen bureaus and some other services, and has on its rolls several thousand officers and employees.

FUNCTIONS. Although we give attention to the functions of specific commissions and boards in later chapters, a word as to their function and

---

[11] White, *op. cit.*, p. 103.

procedures in general is appropriate at this point. The independent agencies were not created with the idea that they should take over the regular work of the executive departments, but for the purpose of administering certain new and complex functions for which departmental organization was deemed (perhaps erroneously in a number of cases) to be inadequate. The departments are designed primarily to conduct work essentially of an administrative character, whereas the nature of the services performed by boards and commissions often requires that they be given a substantial allotment of quasi-legislative and quasi-judicial powers, as well as strictly administrative authority.

Administrative rulemaking and adjudication. The legislative and judicial powers just referred to require more than passing mention. Practically all administrative agencies have such powers, but since they appear most fully developed in the independent commissions, this is the appropriate point for a discussion of them. Technically, the commissions and other agencies do not have the power to make laws, for only Congress may make laws. But, Congress often passes broad and general acts, leaving the administrators to fill in the details with their rules and regulations—to serve as subordinate legislative bodies. Similarly, from the technical point of view, the administrators are not courts. Nevertheless, boards, commissions, and other agencies hear and determine questions relative to the rights, duties, privileges, and obligations of individuals and corporations under the laws, each such agency determining cases under the laws it administers. Administrative adjudication is provided for in the Federal Tort Claims Act, administrators being authorized to settle any claim, with certain exceptions, against the United States growing out of damage to property or personal injury where the amount of the claim does not exceed $1,000. To be sure, the jurisdiction of the administrators is limited to small claims, but it is well to remember that most claims are small. The majority of claims settled by these agencies are final, although, in accordance with the rather common practice, appeals may be made to the courts. It would be a mistake, however, to assume that only small or insignificant cases are permitted to go to administrative officers for settlement. This is the standard procedure for many types of cases, regardless of the amount involved or personal consequences to the individual. The individual finds protection against possible arbitrary decisions of the agencies through his right to carry his case from them to a court. It is true that it is by no means uncommon to find administrators with authority to determine finally all questions of fact, but the courts are always open to those who may charge that the administrators did not stay within the law, did not follow fair, just, and reasonable procedure—did not observe the requirements of due process of law.

Administrative rule-making and its close associate administrative adjudication have become quite unpopular among a fairly wide assortment of persons. There are no doubt those who want government to do little and who believe if the powers in question should be taken away from administrators, government could do but little (and they are right). Others believe that all laws should be made by legislatures and administered by courts. Still others recognize the need for placing these functions in the hands of the administrators, but they fear arbitrary action, and they often cite specific examples of it. The first group we will leave in their ox-carts, stuck in the mud. The second must be educated to the point where they understand that modern government cannot be conducted without a wide range of administrative action and discretion. The third group is entitled to a careful hearing. In fact they have had it, and Congress has given them a law—the Administrative Procedure Act of 1946. Under the provisions of this act a proposed rule must be outlined and published in the *Federal Register,* and interested parties must be furnished an opportunity to present data and arguments. All rules must be published or be made available for public inspection. A number of safeguards are thrown around the administrative adjudication process, all having the general purpose of standardizing the procedure and making it more like court procedure. Lawyers seem to be pleased with the Administrative Procedure Act; administrators and students of that science fear that it may too severely obstruct appropriate administrative action. The full effect of the law is not yet clearly revealed.[12]

The Hoover Commission, in its report on Independent Regulatory Commissions, recommended the improvement of their organization: by vesting all administrative responsibility in the chairman; delegating routine, preliminary, and less important work to the commission staffs; making bipartisan those commissions that are not now so constituted; and substituting removal for cause in the three commissions from which the President may now make removals at his pleasure. These recommendations seem to be administratively sound and in keeping with the general purposes of the independent commission.

Government corporations. An administrative device with which the public has become familiar in recent years is the government corporation. It is not, however, as new as the commission. Its increasing use rather than its novelty has made the public conscious of it. Even the old Continental Congress created a government corporation, the Bank of North America,

[12] Opposing views on the law: *for*—Willis Smith, "Drafting the Proposed Federal Administrative Procedure Act," *Journal of the American Judicature Society,* XXIX (1946), 133; *against*—Blachly and Oatman, "Sabotage of the Administrative Process," *Public Administration Review,* VI (1946), 213. See also Vincent M. Barnett, Jr., "Judicialization of the Administrative Process," *Pub. Adm. Rev.,* VIII (1948), 126.

and the First Congress under the Constitution chartered the Bank of the United States. Not until the First World War, however, did Congress find much use for the corporation, when it created the War Finance Corporation and several others for the period of the emergency. The depression of 1929 and succeeding years brought the government corporation to full flower. Who has not heard of the Reconstruction Finance Corporation (the first of these, chartered in 1932, before the New Deal), the Home Owners' Loan Corporation, the Federal Deposit Insurance Corporation, the Federal Public Housing Authority, the Tennessee Valley Authority, and perhaps others? At this time there are more than 100 government corporations, with an investment running to over twenty billions.

The corporation is supposed to have the following administrative advantages: its policy is controlled by a board of directors and its business is managed by an administrator; it enjoys more freedom from legislative interference than other types of administrative units because it usually has the authority to raise, spend, or save its own funds; its relationship with the Chief Executive is very flexible; and, until 1940, it usually had the privilege of selecting its personnel free from civil service restrictions. Some of these advantages are dubious, particularly the last one mentioned. And other types of administrative agencies may be set up in such a manner as to enjoy certain of the advantages claimed for the corporation.[13]

For these very reasons, plus the over-use of the corporate device (for an activity that was going to do a little buying or selling, or for an urgent service), the government corporation fell under suspicion, and its independence of action has been curtailed in various ways. For example, the Reorganization Act of 1939 brought nearly all the corporations (TVA and a few others were excepted) into a government department or "agency," thus bringing corporation policy under departmental influence, and to such an extent that some of the corporations have been "virtually obliterated." [14] Senator Harry F. Byrd's Joint Committee on Reduction of Nonessential Federal Expenditures brought in a bill that, on December 6, 1945, was approved as the Government Corporation Control Act. This measure goes far toward bringing the government corporation under the same type of control—budgetary, congressional, and accounting—as is imposed upon other administrative agencies. It is feared that the law went too far, depriving the corporation of its peculiar advantages as an instrument for the execution of government policy. What may be needed is a more carefully drawn statute, one designed not to make ineffective the corporation, but to regulate it in line with its purposes.[15] The Hoover Commission

---

[13] White, *op. cit.,* pp. 115 ff.; C. H. Pritchett, "The Government Corporation Control Act of 1945," *Am. Pol. Sci. Rev.,* XL, 495 (June, 1946).

[14] Dimock, *op. cit.,* 1156.

[15] Pritchett, *op. cit.*

seemed not unfriendly to the government corporation, and in its report on Federal Business Enterprises made a number of recommendations designed to systematize and standardize the operations of such corporations and to hold them responsible to Congress along such lines as those laid down in the Government Corporation Control Act.

Miscellaneous administrative agencies. There are yet other types of administrative organizations, units not in any executive department, and neither commissions nor corporations. These organizations are usually headed by executive officers who are very definitely responsible to the President. One such organization is the Federal Security Agency, which includes, among other administrative units, the Office of Education, the Public Health Service, the Social Security Administration (Board until 1946), the Food and Drug Administration, and the Office of Vocational Rehabilitation. Another is the Federal Works Agency, which includes the Public Buildings Administration, the Public Roads Administration, the Federal Fire Council, the Federal Real Estate Board, and the Bureau of Community Facilities. Then the Federal Reserve System is a well-known agency, and so is the Veterans Administration. It is quite unnecessary and it would be decidedly unprofitable to run through the entire list. The administrative agencies have an irritating way (to professors and students) of not staying put. Even while this is being written, reorganization is in progress.

War emergency agencies. Well over a hundred special administrative agencies were created during the Second World War. A few of these units operated within the executive departments, but the others either functioned directly under the President or reported to him. Among the agencies with which the public was familiar were the Office of War Information, the War Manpower Commission, the Office of Lend-Lease, the Office of Censorship, the Committee on Fair Employment Practice, the War Production Board, the Office of Price Administration, and the Selective Service System.

All the administrative war agencies combined employed approximately 200,000 individuals. When the shooting stopped, there began a rapid curtailment both in the number of agencies and in the number of persons employed by those that remained. At this writing we are fighting again in the Far East, and if we again organize for war we will have more emergency agencies. Chapter 27 deals at some length with the war and defense problems.

IV. THE PROBLEM OF REORGANIZING THE NATIONAL ADMINISTRATION [16]

Defects in the development of organization. No discussion of the national administrative system, however brief, is concluded without reference to the need for reorganization. It has been shown that new services have been added as demands for them became insistent; that these services have been frequently sandwiched into whatever existing department happened to be able to provide a place for them, with scant regard for the illogic or practical difficulties of the arrangement; and that, since 1913, this process has been greatly accelerated, not only by the establishment of bureaus and divisions in the departments, but particularly through the creation of numerous agencies independent of the executive departments. As a result of this policy (or lack of policy) several departments have been saddled with service bureaus whose functions have little or no relation to the primary work of such departments. For example, the Public Health Service was until recently in the Treasury Department and the Department of the Interior formerly had so many unrelated functions that it was sometimes characterized as a rag bag. A second result was that many services which should have been closely associated were located in different departments. A third result was manifest in the lack of an administrative organization with adequate powers to control the entire administrative branch. To be sure, the President has usually been empowered to control the administrative forces of the departments; but without a staff of assistants, this control could not be made effective and his authority over the various boards and commissions was only nominal.

Reorganization proposals. These defects and a number of others were clearly revealed in the elaborate report (1911) of President Taft's Efficiency and Economy Commission. This Commission recommended a number of changes in the administrative system, and the President passed them on to Congress with his approval; but as he had lost his leadership, the lawmakers on Capitol Hill practically ignored the recommendations. Wilson and his Congress were busy with other legislation and later with the conduct of the First World War.

The problem of administrative reorganization was not seriously tackled until 1920, when Congress created a Joint Committee on Reorganization,

---

[16] (Hoover) Commission on Organization of the Executive Branch of the Government, *Reports* (1949); President's Committee on Administrative Management, *Report with Special Studies* (1937); Herman Finer, "The Hoover Commission's Reports," *Pol. Sci. Qt.*, LXIV (1949), 405–419, 579–595; Louis W. Koenig (ed.), "The Hoover Commission: A Symposium," *Am. Pol. Sci. Rev.*, XLIII (1949), 933–1000; E. S. Redford, "The Value of the Hoover Commission Reports to the Educator," *Am. Pol. Sci. Rev.*, XLIV (1950), 283–298.

composed of three members of each House and (after 1921) a representative of the President. Responsible private research establishments immediately prepared plans for the consideration of the Joint Committee, the most comprehensive schemes being presented by the Institute of Government Research of Washington, D.C., and the National Budget Committee of New York City. Bills based somewhat upon these and other studies were introduced in Congress from time to time, but in the period of golden prosperity there was no general interest in such a dry subject as administrative reorganization. It probably sounded too much like reform. A few desirable adjustments were made, however, in Hoover's Administration. In 1933, when the country was at the bottom of the depression, Congress authorized the President to make sweeping changes in administrative organization. He did make a number of significant consolidations and transfers; but while this was being done, New Deal agencies were being created almost from day to day, so that reorganization did not keep pace with administrative expansion.

The Report of the President's (Brownlow) Committee on Administrative Management. In 1936 President Roosevelt appointed a committee of experts (Louis Brownlow, Chairman, Charles E. Merriam, and Luther Gulick) to make recommendations on the national administration. In January, 1937, the committee made its far-reaching (some have said daring) report to the President.

THE COMMITTEE'S RECOMMENDATIONS RESPECTING ADMINISTRATIVE ORGANIZATION. The committee proposed that a White House staff be established. The extent to which that proposal has been acted upon is discussed in Chapter 11. Respecting the executive departments, the committee recommended that the Department of the Interior be changed to a Department of Conservation, and that two new departments, Social Welfare and Public Works, be added. The main feature of the committee's proposals was that all the existing agencies of the Government—boards, commissions, authorities, and corporations, whether permanent or temporary—should be accommodated within the twelve departments.

How would the committee place in the executive departments the independent regulatory commissions with their combined administrative, sublegislative, and quasi-judicial powers? It would divide each such commission into an administrative section and judicial section. The administrative section would simply take its place as a regular bureau or division of the department and be made responsible to the Secretary. This section would do all the purely administrative and sublegislative work now performed by the independent commission. On the other hand, the judicial section would be placed in a department only for such purposes as the budget, personnel administration, and matériel. In its work it would be wholly independent of the department and the President. Its members would be appointed by the President with the approval of the Senate for long, staggered terms and would be subject to removal only under the terms stated in the laws. This judicial section would thus make decisions affecting the public interest and private rights in the same independent and impartial manner as the old regulatory commission.

The committee recommended, then, that every administrative agency of the Government be placed in a department, but it recognized the necessity for flexibility in the arrangement. Some of the boards or commissions could be located in the departments as ordinary bureaus; others would function relatively free of the departments except in matters of personnel, supplies, and budgeting; still others would be placed in the departments only for the purpose of permitting the secretaries to receive their reports and co-ordinate their policies with those of the departments. The committee's proposals were most comprehensive, and the journalist who wrote that they knocked the breath out of Congress was not far wrong.

From the Brownlow Committee to the Hoover Commission. The President approved the recommendations and sent them to Congress for the necessary legislation. The Government Reorganization Bill of 1938 (an Administration measure) embodied a number of the principal recommendations of the President's Committee, but the measure became associated with the President's unpopular plan (1937) to make the judiciary more responsive to the political branches of the government, and the charge of "dictator" was hurled at President Roosevelt from all sides—from senators and representatives, from Father Coughlin and Publisher Gannett, and from tens of thousands of others. There was some intelligent and patriotic opposition to the bill, but the opposition in general was more emotional than intelligent, more partisan than patriotic, and more effective than sound. Even after the President and his leaders in Congress had made a number of concessions, the bill, having passed the Senate, was beaten in the House after a bitter fight. The Reorganization Bill of 1939 was not sponsored by New Dealers but by moderates who were willing to exclude from it many of the provisions that had been points of attack against the bill of the previous year. After considerable parliamentary skirmishing this measure was passed.

The new law, effective until January, 1941, gave the President the authority to appoint as many as six executive assistants, the selfless six with "a passion for anonymity," as recommended by the Committee on Administrative Management. It gave him the authority, subject to Congressional veto, which must be exercised within a period of sixty days, to transfer the whole or a part of the work of any federal agency except that of twenty-one named agencies. Among these "untouchable" agencies we find the Civil Service Commission, the Federal Communications Commission, the Interstate Commerce Commission, the Securities and Exchange Commission, the National Labor Relations Board, the Tariff Commission, Veterans Administration, and the General Accounting Office. This last-named office includes the Comptroller General, whose functions the President's bill of the year before would have divided between the Budget Director and a new officer, the Auditor General. The President was denied the authority to abolish or create a new executive department; and, in exercising the powers of "bureau shuffling" which the act permitted, he was required to take care that no functions performed by any bureau or agency were "lost in the shuffle."

Under the authority of the act the President submitted five reorganization plans that, not having been disapproved by Congress within the sixty-day period, became effective. It would be tedious and unprofitable to enumerate all the changes made, but progress was not inconsiderable. In submitting Reorganization Plan No. IV (April 11, 1940) the President took the opportunity to recommend to Congress the extension of the reorganization law that was to expire January 20, 1941. Although Congress did not extend the life of the law, it did in that memorable December of 1941 authorize the President to redistribute functions among the rapidly growing and "more rapidly to grow" war agencies. The problem of administrative reorganization, of course, continued. After the war Congress passed the Reorganization Act of 1945, and President Truman proceeded to submit reorganization plans, winning the approval of Congress for some of them. But there was no reduction in Government expenses, and the complaints about all those "bureaucrats" and "wastrels" employed in Washington continued and increased. The Republicans captured Congress in 1946. Maybe the time had come for a different kind of reorganization.

The (Hoover) Commission on Organization of the Executive Branch of the Government. In 1947 Congress provided for a nonpartisan commission with authority to examine and make recommendations respecting the entire executive establishment with the purpose of (1) limiting expenditures, (2) eliminating duplication and overlapping of services, (3) consolidating services, (4) abolishing services, and (5) defining and limiting executive functions, services, and activities. Operating under the chairmanship of Herbert Hoover, the twelve commissioners attacked their assignment with enthusiasm and good will. They appointed "task forces," assigning to each a segment of the executive branch for study and report. Twenty-three such reports were made, some of a high order of excellence, others showing the results of special pressures and influences, the quality of each such report depending, of course, upon the composition of the task force that prepared it.   The Commission decided, not without some hesitation, that it should not recommend the abolishment of services, that its function was to help in making services better, not to determine whether or not they should exist.   In 1949 the Commission made nineteen reports —on General Management of the Executive Branch, Foreign Affairs, the Treasury Department, Federal Business Enterprises, and so on.   It is possible only to give some general comment respecting them.

The Commission would strengthen the President's position as chief of administration by placing in the Executive Office a Director of Personnel, who should be chairman of the Civil Service Commission, and would otherwise increase facilities in that office as indicated in Chapter 10, section IV of this volume.   It would group the numerous agencies of the executive branch into departments by major purpose, in order that each department might have a coherent mission.   It would give each department head full responsibility for the conduct of his department, leaving no subordinate with authority independent of his superior.   It would increase the powers and responsibilities of the Department of Labor by transferring to it several services from other agencies.   It would make the Department of Commerce an effective agent in the realm of transportation by placing several additional services under its jurisdiction, including a few now administered by the Interstate Commerce Commission.   It would create a new Department of Welfare.   It would have all administrative responsibility of any independent regulatory commission vested in the chairman of the commission.   It would correct defects in government corporation charters by seven specific amendments to the Government Corporation Control Act of 1945.   But we must stop.   The Commission made 277 recommendations.   A few of these are mentioned in preceding chapters.   Others receive attention later at appropriate points.

The reports are not in any sense revolutionary, a number of the proposals being very similar to those made twelve years ago by the Brownlow Committee.   But the Hoover Commission has had even more publicity than the Brownlow Committee.   The Hoover group may have had too much publicity, or the wrong kind.   Its reports have been widely heralded as blueprints for saving four billion dollars annually.   This claim may be unfortunate for two reasons: (1) there is no probability that any such sum can be saved, and (2) such a claim diverts attention from the significant recommendations of the Commission respecting improvement in administration.   Yet there will be some gain if the interest in reducing expenditures results in the adoption of a substantial number of the principal recommendations of the Commission.

The Bureau of the Budget estimates that 114 of the recommendations can be carried out by administrative action (orders of the President, for example) and that the others (163) would require legislation.[17] Congress has shown its interest in the passage of the Reorganization Act of 1949, an act that excepts from the President's reorganization recommendations only the General Accounting Office, thus giving the President a liberty of action not permitted in the earlier (1939) reorganization legislation. The President is authorized to submit plans to Congress, and the plan is approved if it does not receive a majority adverse vote in *either* House. Twenty-one Presidential Reorganization Plans have been submitted and sixteen approved. Congress passed the Unification Act of 1949 for the National Military Establishment, increased the salaries of civil servants, and has otherwise displayed interest in the Commission's recommendations.

Few students of government advocate the adoption of all the Hoover Commission's recommendations; some of them seem to go backward rather than forward. But even if all the good and none of the bad recommendations are carried out, the problem of administrative organization will remain. It should be and can be brought up to date, kept up to date, but reorganization will always be needed as the functions of government change and as new administrative techniques and procedures are developed.

Reading List

Annual reports of the heads of the several administrative departments and the
    other services.
P. H. Appleby, *Big Democracy* (1945).
Final Report of the Attorney General's Committee on Administrative Procedure
    (1941).
F. F. Blachly and M. E. Oatman, *Administrative Legislation and Adjudication*
    (1934).
———, *Federal Regulating Action and Control* (1940).
(Hoover) Commission on Organization of the Executive Branch of the Government, *Reports* (1949).
Robert E. Cushman, *The Independent Regulatory Commissions* (1941).
Marshall E. Dimock, "Government Corporations: A Focus of Policy and Administration," *Am. Pol. Sci. Rev.,* XLIII (1949), 899–921, 1145–1164.
———, *Modern Politics and Administration* (1937).
J. W. Fesler and Others, *Elements of Public Administration* (1946).
Herman Finer, "The Hoover Commission Reports," *Pol. Sci. Qt.,* LXIV (1949),
    405–419, 579–595.
G. A. Graham and Henry Reining, Jr., *Regulatory Administration* (1943).
W. B. Graves, *Public Administration in a Democratic Society* (1950).
E. P. Herring, *Federal Commissioners* (1936).
C. S. Hyneman, *Bureaucracy in a Democracy* (1950).

[17] Aiken and Koenig, *op. cit.,* 939.

Louis W. Koenig (ed.), "The Hoover Commission: A Symposium," *Am. Pol. Sci. Rev.,* XLIII (1949), 933–1000.

A. Langeluttig, *The Department of Justice of the United States* (1927).

D. E. Lilienthal and R. H. Marquis, "The Conduct of Business Enterprise by the Federal Government," *Harvard Law Review,* LIV (1941), 545–601.

A. W. Macmahon and J. D. Millett, *Federal Administrators* (1939).

F. M. Marks (ed.), *Elements of Public Administration* (1946).

L. Meriam and L. F. Schmeckebier, *Reorganization of the National Government* (1939).

J. M. Pfiffner, *Public Administration* (1946 ed.), Chs. IV–XII.

President's Committee on Administrative Management, *Report with Special Studies* (1937).

M. J. Pusey, *Big Government: Can We Control It?* (1945).

L. F. Schmeckebier, *New Federal Organizations: An Outline of Their Structure and Functions* (1943).

United States Government Manual.

United States News & World Report (weekly).

Harvey Walker, *Public Administration in the United States* (1937), Chs. I–V.

S. Wallace, *Federal Departmentalization* (1941).

L. D. White, *Public Administration* (1948 ed.), Chs. I–XII.

Questions and Problems

1. Outline the duties of the head of an administrative department.
2. Explain the administrative set-up in a typical department.
3. How would the Hoover Commission improve departmental organization?
4. Distinguish between the work of the Department of Justice and the courts of the United States.
5. Discuss the functions of the postal service, both economic and social.
6. Indicate the nature and functions of independent commissions. Evaluate their contributions to administration.
7. What are the reputed advantages of the government corporation? Could any of these advantages be retained in any other type of administrative organization?
8. What are the principal defects of federal administrative organization as seen by the experts?
9. Is it correct to say that administrative organization and reorganization is a continuous problem?

☆ *20* ☆

State and Local Administrative Organization

I NASMUCH as the problems of administrative organization are essentially the same for the states as for the national government, we shall be content to have a bird's-eye view of the state administrative set-up. Following the section on this topic, we shall give attention to county and city governmental and administrative organization.

I. STATE ADMINISTRATIVE ORGANIZATION [1]

The growth of the tasks of administration. A century and a half ago state administrative activities were few and far between. There were no railroad or other public utility commissions because practically no public utilities existed. There was no board of agriculture because land was plentiful and everybody was supposed to know the art of farming, which consisted of clearing the land, sowing, reaping, and then moving on to new and very cheap land when a farm was worn out. Few states did more than endorse education, for each community provided for the teaching of the three *R's* in its own little school, if it wanted one, and any education beyond that was strictly a private matter and was paid for accord-

---

[1] Bates, Field, and Others, *State Government* (1939), Ch. 12; J. C. Ballens, *Administrative Reorganization in the States since 1939* (Bureau of Pub. Adm., U. of Cal., 1947); A. W. Bromage, *State Government and Administration in the United States* (1936), Ch. XIV; A. E. Buck, *The Reorganization of State Governments in the United States* (1938); Council of State Governments, *Reorganizing State Government* (1950). J. A. Fairlie, "Studies on State and Rural Local Government," *Am. Pol. Sci. Rev.* (1933), XXVII, 317–329; W. B. Graves, *American State Government* (1946 ed.), Ch. X; A. N. Holcombe, *State Government in the United States* (1931 ed.), pp. 339–352, 434–445; Harvey Walker, *Public Administration in the United States* (1937), Ch. III.

ingly. There were no boards of health; for a few doctors scattered about over a commonwealth could "bleed and blister" the sick; and epidemics, since they were commonly regarded as manifestations of the wrath of God, could not be prevented. In those rugged days there were no factory inspectors, no mine rescue commissioners, and no body of any other description that looked after the interests of labor; for the majority of men worked for themselves or on farms, while the few who were employed in the more hazardous industries were deemed to have assumed all risks, and any attempt on the part of the state to protect them would have been considered an interference with their freedom.

Partly from lack of scientific knowledge, but chiefly because the need did not exist, state governments performed very few administrative functions before 1850. Industrialization, urbanization, science, and enlightenment along many lines have changed all this. The state now serves the public in scores of ways that were undreamed of by our agricultural civilization a hundred years ago, and it administers a few functions that were considered entirely outside the province of government twenty-five years ago. Administrative departments, boards, and commissions have been created by the dozens to take care of these services. The cost of operating the purely governmental organs of the state is not one tenth as much as the cost of maintaining the various public services. More than two thirds of all the state funds go to education, highways, and social security.

Creation of administrative agencies. The only state administrative officers one hundred and fifty years ago were the governor, lieutenant governor, secretary of state, attorney general, treasurer, and auditor (These are briefly discussed in Chapter 13). They were created by constitutional provision and remain constitutional officers. As the work of general administration grew, and, in particular, as the states seriously began to take on service functions, such as education, the construction and maintenance of highways, and the regulation of public utilities, new officers and agencies were created. About 1915 there were few states that could not boast of thirty or forty administrative organs, and some reached the hundred mark, and several multiplied this by two, producing a veritable administrative wilderness.

Two important differences are to be noted between the establishment of state and national administrative agencies. First, many officers, boards, and commissions are prescribed by the state constitutions, whereas the national administrative machinery is left entirely to congressional discretion. In the second place, although Congress has created a large number and several varieties of administrative agencies, it has made more successful efforts to keep them within the executive departments than have the states. State legislatures have shown a decided preference for boards and commissions. Each new need in the states has usually been met by the creation

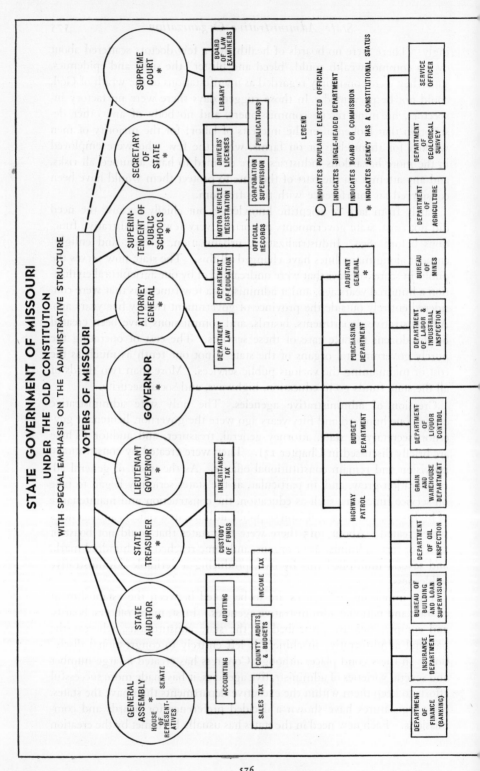

STATE GOVERNMENT OF MISSOURI
UNDER THE OLD CONSTITUTION
WITH SPECIAL EMPHASIS ON THE ADMINISTRATIVE STRUCTURE

VOTERS OF MISSOURI

- GENERAL ASSEMBLY *
  - HOUSE OF REPRESENTATIVES *
  - SENATE *
- STATE AUDITOR *
  - ACCOUNTING
  - AUDITING
  - SALES TAX
  - COUNTY AUDITS & BUDGETS
  - INCOME TAX
- STATE TREASURER *
  - CUSTODY OF FUNDS
  - INHERITANCE TAX
- LIEUTENANT GOVERNOR *
- GOVERNOR
  - HIGHWAY PATROL
  - BUDGET DEPARTMENT
  - PURCHASING DEPARTMENT
  - ADJUTANT GENERAL *
  - DEPARTMENT OF FINANCE (BANKING)
  - INSURANCE DEPARTMENT
  - BUREAU OF BUILDING AND LOAN SUPERVISION
  - DEPARTMENT OF OIL INSPECTION
  - GRAIN AND WAREHOUSE DEPARTMENT
  - DEPARTMENT OF LIQUOR CONTROL
  - DEPARTMENT OF LABOR & INDUSTRIAL INSPECTION
  - BUREAU OF MINES
  - DEPARTMENT OF AGRICULTURE
  - DEPARTMENT OF GEOLOGICAL SURVEY
  - SERVICE OFFICER
- ATTORNEY GENERAL *
  - DEPARTMENT OF LAW
- SUPERINTENDENT OF PUBLIC SCHOOLS *
  - DEPARTMENT OF EDUCATION
- SECRETARY OF STATE *
  - MOTOR VEHICLE REGISTRATION
  - DRIVERS' LICENSES
  - OFFICIAL RECORDS
  - CORPORATION SUPERVISION
  - PUBLICATIONS
- SUPREME COURT *
  - LIBRARY
  - BOARD OF LAW EXAMINERS

LEGEND
○ INDICATES POPULARLY ELECTED OFFICIAL
☐ INDICATES SINGLE-HEADED DEPARTMENT
☐ INDICATES BOARD OR COMMISSION
* INDICATES AGENCY HAS A CONSTITUTIONAL STATUS

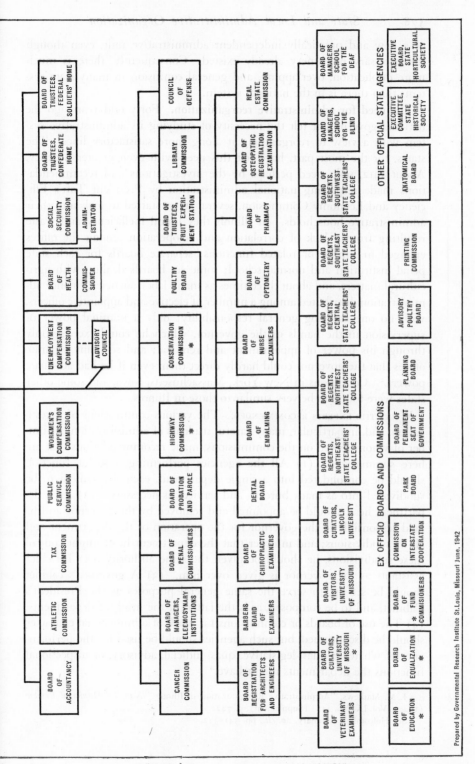

BOARD OF ACCOUNTANCY

ATHLETIC COMMISSION

TAX COMMISSION

PUBLIC SERVICE COMMISSION

WORKMEN'S COMPENSATION COMMISSION

UNEMPLOYMENT COMPENSATION COMMISSION

ADVISORY COUNCIL

BOARD OF HEALTH

COMMISSIONER

SOCIAL SECURITY COMMISSION

ADMINISTRATOR

BOARD OF TRUSTEES, CONFEDERATE HOME

BOARD OF TRUSTEES, FEDERAL SOLDIERS' HOME

CANCER COMMISSION

BOARD OF MANAGERS, ELEEMOSYNARY INSTITUTIONS

BOARD OF PENAL COMMISSIONERS

BOARD OF PROBATION AND PAROLE

HIGHWAY COMMISSION *

CONSERVATION COMMISSION *

POULTRY BOARD

BOARD OF TRUSTEES, FRUIT EXPERIMENT STATION

LIBRARY COMMISSION

COUNCIL OF DEFENSE

BOARD OF REGISTRATION FOR ARCHITECTS AND ENGINEERS

BARBERS BOARD OF EXAMINERS

BOARD OF CHIROPRACTIC EXAMINERS

DENTAL BOARD

BOARD OF EMBALMING

BOARD OF NURSE EXAMINERS

BOARD OF OPTOMETRY

BOARD OF PHARMACY

BOARD OF OSTEOPATHIC REGISTRATION & EXAMINATION

REAL ESTATE COMMISSION

BOARD OF VETERINARY EXAMINERS *

BOARD OF CURATORS, UNIVERSITY OF MISSOURI *

BOARD OF VISITORS, UNIVERSITY OF MISSOURI

BOARD OF CURATORS, LINCOLN UNIVERSITY

BOARD OF REGENTS, NORTHEAST STATE TEACHERS' COLLEGE

BOARD OF REGENTS, NORTHWEST STATE TEACHERS' COLLEGE

BOARD OF REGENTS, CENTRAL STATE TEACHERS' COLLEGE

BOARD OF REGENTS, SOUTHEAST STATE TEACHERS' COLLEGE

BOARD OF REGENTS, SOUTHWEST STATE TEACHERS' COLLEGE

BOARD OF MANAGERS, SCHOOL FOR THE BLIND

BOARD OF MANAGERS, SCHOOL FOR THE DEAF

EX OFFICIO BOARDS AND COMMISSIONS

BOARD OF EDUCATION *

BOARD OF EQUALIZATION *

BOARD OF FUND COMMISIONERS *

COMMISSION ON INTERSTATE COOPERATION

BOARD OF PERMANENT SEAT OF GOVERNMENT

PARK BOARD

PLANNING BOARD

ADVISORY POULTRY BOARD

PRINTING COMMISSION

ANATOMICAL BOARD

EXECUTIVE COMMITTEE, STATE HISTORICAL SOCIETY

EXECUTIVE BOARD, STATE HORTICULTURAL SOCIETY

OTHER OFFICIAL STATE AGENCIES

Prepared by Governmental Research Institute St.Louis, Missouri June, 1942

of a new and practically independent administrative unit, even though the necessary machinery already existed. Consequently, there is much more duplication, overlapping, and general confusion in many state systems than there is in the national system.

The need for administrative reorganization. Forty odd years ago the national government felt the necessity of studying its administrative system with a view to reorganizing it along more satisfactory lines. The states, for the most part, have felt this need with even greater urgency. About 1912, influenced perhaps by the investigations and recommendations made respecting national administration by President Taft's Efficiency and Economy Commission, several states started to look into their administrative households. In Illinois they found inefficiency and waste resulting from a lack of correlation and co-operation among the offices engaged in similar or related functions; separate boards for each state penal institution and normal school; some six boards dealing with agricultural matters, and about three times as many labor agencies; finance administration distributed among a number of elective and appointive officers, with no one carrying general responsibility; only a nominal power of supervision in the hands of the governor, which he could exercise only through his power of appointment and removal; and so many separate offices that the governor could hardly direct them even if he had adequate powers.[2] Conditions in New York, Massachusetts, Iowa, and some other states were found to be very similar to those in Illinois.

WHAT THE EXPERTS RECOMMENDED. The various commissions of investigation, and, in particular, many careful students of administration, a number of whom served on the commissions, made recommendations that are here summarized. (1) All the agencies performing a major function should be consolidated into a single department, each department to be subdivided into as many bureaus and services as necessary. (2) Each department head should be appointed and removed by the governor and be held responsible to the governor for the operation of the department and all its subdivisions; and in order that the department head might control these subdivisions, he should be given the same authority over his chief assistants as the governor is given over him. (3) A governor's cabinet should be set up, to serve the same general purposes as the President's Cabinet, and to be composed, as is the latter, of the heads of departments. (4) The use of boards or commissions for work of administerial character should be discontinued, but such agencies should be used for the performance of whatever quasi-legislative, quasi-judicial, advisory, or inspectional functions the departments might have.[3]

[2] J. M. Mathews, "Administrative Reorganization in Illinois," *National Municipal Review* (1920), Vol. IX, No. 11. (Supplement), p. 742.
[3] See Holcombe's summary, *op. cit.,* pp. 341–342.

The progress of reorganization. The fact that a particular system is generally recommended by experts does not secure its acceptance by state legislatures. "Why this change? Haven't we done well enough? The governor has too much power already." These and similar essentially thoughtless but politically effective questions are asked by legislators. Then there is an additional obstacle to reorganization in some states—it cannot be effected except by constitutional amendment. Nevertheless, some progress was and still is being made. Even before the comprehensive surveys by committees of experts had pitilessly exposed the weaknesses of state administrative organization, a few states had consolidated certain administrative functions.

MINOR READJUSTMENTS. Rearrangement of administrative agencies that hardly belongs in the class of administrative reorganization has been undertaken in a few states. The New Jersey legislature in 1915 and years following assembled many services into several departments. The general plan was to place a department under the control of a board, leaving the board the authority to appoint an executive officer. The terms of board members were usually made long and overlapping. This move did not represent reorganization on a large scale. On another page we shall note recent progress in New Jersey.

In 1921 Michigan created five new departments, placing many existing agencies in those departments, and set up an administrative board with the governor as chairman. A number of elective state officers sit on this board, thus leaving the governor in a position that cannot be described as that of chief administrator.[4] Other states that have made only piecemeal adjustments in recent years include North Carolina, Maine, and Wisconsin.

MORE COMPREHENSIVE PLANS. A number of states, of which Illinois, Missouri, Nebraska, Pennsylvania, and Washington are examples, have undertaken more ambitious programs of reorganization. Owing to the elaborate provisions of state constitutions, a complete reorganization plan ordinarily calls for a constitutional amendment, but nearly all these states have used the statutory method. Missouri and New Jersey were fortunate, however, in that they were able to provide for reorganization in their new constitutions (1945 and 1947, respectively).

The Illinois legislature, through its administrative code, adopted in 1917 and supplemented by later acts, brought some sixty administrative units into thirteen departments, each headed by a single director appointed by the governor with the consent of the senate (in practice the consent is little more than a formality) and removed by the governor practically at will. Individually, the directors are responsible to the governor for their departments; collectively, they serve as the governor's cabinet. The differ-

[4] Bromage, *op. cit.*, pp. 353-355.

ent functions of each department are administered by superintendents, bureau chiefs, or similarly titled assistants, who are responsible to the director, although appointed, like him, by the governor and the senate. For those services that require the exercise of considerable quasi-legislative or quasi-judicial power, paid boards are attached to the appropriate departments. An important feature of the system is found in the finance department, through which the governor is enabled to exercise a substantial control of activities in the other departments. Among other things, this department prepares the annual budget, examines and approves or disapproves vouchers and bills of the several departments, and ascertains whether the prices paid for labor and materials are fair, just, and reasonable.

New York, under the leadership of Governor Alfred E. Smith, adopted a plan of reorganization that placed the governor in very definite control of administration. Under the provisions of a constitutional amendment, approved in 1925, the legislature, with due regard for functional relationships, placed nearly two hundred administrative agencies in nineteen departments. Only the governor, lieutenant governor, comptroller, and attorney general remain elective officers. The governor, from his position as head of the "executive department" (the first of the nineteen departments), through his powers of appointment and removal, and through his cabinet conferences, has responsibility and authority sufficient to enable him to function as the chief administrator of the Empire State.[5]

Tennessee centered administrative powers in the office of governor two years before New York adopted the Smith plan. And still another state that has tied practically all the lines of administration in the executive chamber is Virginia (1927). Notwithstanding the fact that the movement was led in that State by a Jeffersonian Democrat, Governor Harry F. Byrd, the integration achieved would have scandalized the Sage of Monticello.[6]

New Jersey is the state most recently to undergo substantial administrative reorganization. The Constitution (Article V, Section iv) of 1947 provides, in part, that all executive and administrative offices, including the historic ones of secretary of state and attorney general, shall be allocated within not more than twenty principal departments; that each department shall be under the supervision of the governor; that the department head shall be a single executive unless otherwise provided by law, appointed by the governor with the advice and consent of the senate and removable at the pleasure of the governor; and that where a board or commission heads a department the members thereof shall be appointed by the governor with the advice and consent of the senate, and may be removed in a manner provided by law. The legislature, in carrying out the mandate of the

---

[5] F. D. Roosevelt, "Results in New York . . . ," *National Municipal Review* (1930), XIX, 224; *Manual for the Use of the Legislature of New York*, 1948, pp. 481 ff. ·

[6] Bromage, *op. cit.*, p. 350.

constitution, made extensive use of the reports of the Commission on State Reorganization, a body that had been functioning for four years. The legislative product might well be characterized as outstanding. Fourteen [7] principal departments were established, the scores of administrative agencies and instrumentalities of the state being distributed among the departments in accordance with their functions. Thus, the Department of Law and Public Safety, operating under the direction of the attorney general, includes the subdepartments of law, state police, motor vehicles, weights and measures, and alcoholic beverage control; such professional boards as dentistry, embalmers and funeral directors, engineers and land surveyors, nursing, and veterinary medical examiners; and several other administrative agencies of the public safety variety. In like manner, all fiscal functions are administered through one department, that of the Treasury. Under this system the governor is provided with a cabinet consisting of the fourteen department heads, persons appointed by him and directly responsible to him for the effective performance of the functions of their departments. This is administrative reorganization on a broad comprehensive scale, and it ought to produce satisfactory results.[8]

Despite some valiant undertakings at reorganization, the process throughout the nation has made only fair progress. Many elective public men and a few specialists in public administration fear the concentration of authority in the hands of the governor more than they deplore the probable waste and inefficiency of diffuse administration. Furthermore, an organized and integrated administration does not seem to stay that way. New functions are added to the tasks of administration and new machinery is established—and the not-so-long-ago reorganized system is again in need of reorganization.[9] Mention was just made of the Virginia administrative integration achieved under Governor Byrd. But twenty years later we read that the Old Dominion State has again undergone large-scale administrative reorganization.[10] And so it goes.

Control of state administration. Theoretically, the governor is the

---

[7] At the date of this writing the legislature had not yet approved the bill for the establishment of one of these departments, that of Education.

[8] C. Wesley Armstrong, Jr., "Administrative Reorganization in New Jersey," *State Government,* December, 1948, pp. 244–247, 254–255.

[9] A number of authorities are skeptical of reorganization plans and of accomplishments under these plans. See, for example, F. W. Coker, "Dogmas of Administrative Reform," *Am. Pol Sci. Rev.,* XVI, 399 (1922); W. H. Edwards, "Has State Reorganization Succeeded?" *State Government,* October, 1938, pp. 183 ff.; and Harvey Walker, "Theory and Practice in State Administrative Reorganization," *National Municipal Review,* April, 1930, pp. 249 ff.

[10] R. B. Pinchbeck, "Virginia Reorganizes Again," *National Municipal Review,* July, 1950, pp. 339–343. The Hoover Commission Report on the national administration has stimulated further study of administration in the states. *National Municipal Review,* July, 1949, p. 362.

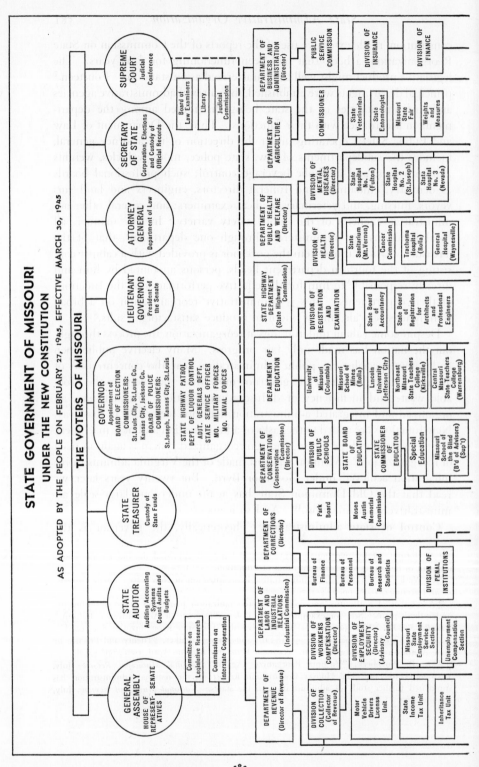

STATE GOVERNMENT OF MISSOURI
UNDER THE NEW CONSTITUTION

AS ADOPTED BY THE PEOPLE ON FEBRUARY 27, 1945, EFFECTIVE MARCH 30, 1945

THE VOTERS OF MISSOURI

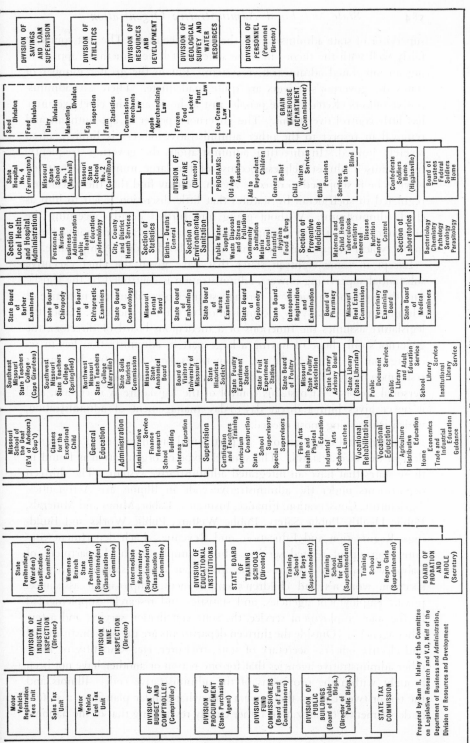

Courtesy of the *Legislative Research Committee*, Jefferson City, Missouri

Prepared by Sam R. Haley of the Committee
on Legislative Research and V.D. Neff of the
Department of Business and Administration,
Division of Resources and Development

583

supervisor of state administration, the chief executive. The fact coincides fairly well with the theory in those states that have something approaching an integrated administrative system. But in the greater number of states the governor's powers are quite inadequate. There are administrative officers elected by the people, just as he is, and the chief executive has little control over them. The governor's power of appointment and removal in respect to the other administrative officers is limited, often severely limited. In directing administration, the governor frequently finds himself almost helpless because of the large number of scattered services he is supposed to direct. Again, he may find that the officers are regulated in such detail by statutes that little discretion is left to him as chief administrator. Without going into further detail concerning the governor's difficulties in attempting to command the administrative forces in the typical state, we may say that his task borders on the impossible.

Except in some eighteen states that have given the chief executive substantial supervising powers, administration is controlled by the legislature through commissions or through statutes prescribing the minutiae of administration, usually by a combination of the two methods. Since the legislature assumes the functions of a meticulous board of directors, the governor's only hope of having a large part in administration lies in securing control of the legislature. Sometimes, he is successful; but success rests upon his place as party leader, his personality, and other political and personal factors. At best, his control of the legislature is uncertain, and it never gives him a direct day-to-day management of administration, which is the thing most needed.

Departmental organization. Departmental organization differs a great deal in the several states. The simplest type of organization is found in those states that have an integrated administrative system. The thirteen departments under the administrative code in Illinois are Aeronautics, Agriculture, Conservation, Finance, Insurance, Labor, Mines and Minerals, Public Health, Public Safety, Public Welfare, Public Works and Buildings, Registration and Education, and Revenue. Each department contains a group of related services. For example, in the Department of Labor we find six divisions—unemployment compensation, factory inspection, women's and children's employment, employment assistance, private employment agencies, and statistics and research—supplemented by the state employment service, the state conciliation service, and a few other agencies. Outside the thirteen departments are the old constitutional and elective officers—secretary of state, treasurer, etc.—and fifty or more other administrative agencies that for one reason or another have not been brought within the provisions of the administrative code. Illinois and the ten or twelve states that have a somewhat similar plan have a system of departmental organization rather closely resembling that of the national government. A few states, New Jersey and New York in particular, have highly departmentalized administrative systems, leaving very few agencies scattered here and there.

Disorganization, rather than organization, characterizes the organs of administration in the greater number of other states. They have more elective officers, officials practically independent of the governor, than have the states just described. They have scores of boards and commissions, many appointed by the governor, some appointed by other officers, and some elective. A few services are headed by individual officials; but the board system is prevalent, with scant regard to whether or not the service calls for this sort of direction. The kindred services are not ordinarily grouped into a department; each unit is a department in itself. The head or heads of units are usually made responsible to the governor; but his authority is not effective because of the weakness of his power of appointment and removal, the lack of adequate power of direction, and the large number of separate units. Some agencies are not even responsible in theory to the governor but are under the supervision of some other elective officer, or even a board.[11]

II. COUNTY ADMINISTRATIVE ORGANIZATION

Dependency of the states upon county administrative agencies. The states have administrative organization and personnel sufficient to perform only a minor fraction of the services they now offer. To a considerable extent they must rely upon local administrative agencies, particularly upon the counties, for the performance of routine state services. State law requires your birth certificate, but it is issued by a local official, probably by a county official. State law likewise requires a hunting license, a car license, a marriage license, but you go to the county courthouse to get them. State law regulates land transfers, wills, and divorces, but the counties take care of the administrative details. State law fixes certain standards for milk and other products on the market, but the county and city officers have the burden of enforcing these standards. The state establishes a minimum requirement for public education, but the county and city authorities are charged with the responsibility of enforcing them. Commit a crime (against the state), and you are arrested by a county or city officer, prosecuted by a county officer, before a judge elected by the county, and hear the verdict from a county jury. If found guilty, you may be sent to the *state* penitentiary. This process of illustration could be continued to monotony. To be sure, counties and cities, particularly the latter, have a number of local functions to perform, but a very significant phase of local

[11] See Graves, *op. cit.,* pp. 416, 418, 420 (facing), and 422 (facing), for instructive charts, tables, and maps on state administrative reorganization.

government is that of serving the state in an administrative capacity.

Legal status of counties. "While the county is an agency of the state, it is likewise a creature of the state."[12] It is created by the state, at all times subject to its control, and may be abolished by it. This complete power over counties was in earlier times held almost exclusively by the legislature; but it was not so long until some of the states started the practice of protecting counties from legislatures through constitutional provisions prohibiting the changing of boundaries, the moving of the county seat, and the like, without the assent of the people affected.

County officers. The county has no clear separation of powers along the traditional executive, legislative, and judicial lines. It has no chief executive; and a number of its officers, subject to no unified control, perform functions that are both judicial and administrative.

1. THE BOARD. The most important governing body in the county is the elective county board (known also by various other names), which functions in every state except Rhode Island, although neither the board nor the county as a unit of government is of any particular importance in the other New England states. Boards vary in size from three to as high as fifty members. They meet as actual needs and laws require, both of which vary among the states and counties within the same states. In some jurisdictions, the boards, during the time they are not in session, make a considerable use of committees. Board members are ordinarily paid on a per diem basis, although in a few large counties of some states fairly substantial salaries are provided.

These bodies have no powers other than those allowed by the constitution and legislature of the state. In general, they are empowered to control county finances, subject to restrictions as to the amount of taxes that may be levied and the purposes for which such taxes may be used and to like restrictions as to borrowing money; to construct county roads and bridges; to erect and maintain courthouses, jails, and other county buildings; to license and regulate dance halls, bathing beaches, and other places of recreation and amusement; to legislate on local matters (in a few states); to organize townships; to appoint a few officers, such as the county physician; to exercise a measure of supervision over the elective officers; to establish polling places and administer certain other features of the election laws; and to establish and maintain institutions for the care of the needy and, subject to national and state law, to make certain decisions on questions of social security administration.

2. OFFICERS ASSOCIATED WITH THE ADMINISTRATION OF JUSTICE. In all

[12] Cook County v. Chicago, 142 N.E. (Ill.) 512 (1924).

counties there are a number of officers whose chief function is the administration of justice. The more important ones are the sheriff, the coroner (or some other officer acting in that capacity), the prosecuting attorney, the clerk of the court, the justices of the peace, and constables. They have been sufficiently discussed, for our purposes, in Chapter 18, "The State Judicial System."

3. FINANCE OFFICERS. Several officers of the county are concerned with important matters of finance. The *assessor* is a familiar figure who goes from house to house fixing the value of personal and real property for purposes of state and local taxation. Commonly chosen by the people, the assessor is not always a man who knows how to evaluate property; nor is he always able to resist the tempting inducements held out to him by those who seek the favor of low assessments. In a few states assessors are appointed by state authorities, but this system involves a degree of trust in appointing officers that many people do not share. A more satisfactory plan of securing good assessors, which is used in a few jurisdictions, is found in the requirement that candidates shall pass an examination testing their fitness to be assessors before their names are placed upon the ballots. Assistants to assessors are ordinarily provided by appointment, and in some cities, notably New York and Baltimore, such assistants must demonstrate their qualifications by examination before receiving appointments. Assessment is not always a county matter. In a number of states assessors are township or district officers whose work is subject to review by some county authority.[13]

The county *treasurer,* like the assessor, is commonly elective. It is his duty to receive, deposit in banks, and disburse the county funds in accordance with the laws, which are usually so explicit that the treasurer has little discretion. Not so long ago it was quite common for the treasurer to receive for his own pocket the interest—sometimes a large amount—on county funds deposited in banks. This practice is now generally prohibited by law. Treasurers very commonly receive substantial salaries or even more substantial compensation in fees. Many scandals and shady transactions have been revealed in connection with the depositing of county funds. Banks have taken care of the treasurer's bond in return for the deposits; banks of political friends have been favored, even to the extent of being given deposits when known to be unsound. A number of states have sought to remedy these conditions by giving the county board the authority to select the depositaries, although a board as well as a treasurer might sometimes get off the straight and narrow path.

In addition to his work for the county the treasurer ordinarily acts as an agent for the collection of state funds, and in some states he receives

[13] State bodies in about forty states assess railroads and other special properties. In about thirty states state boards of equalization may review local assessments of other property.

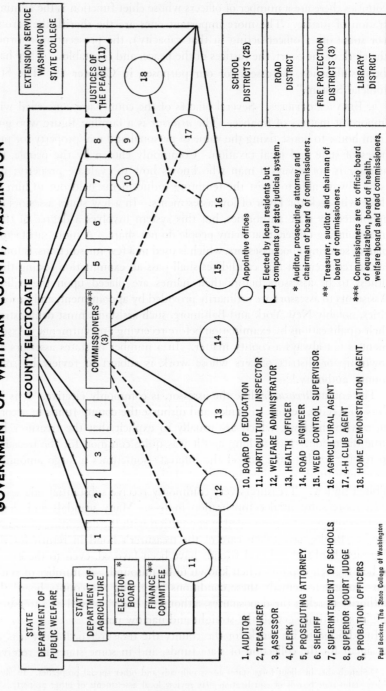

GOVERNMENT OF WHITMAN COUNTY, WASHINGTON

STATE DEPARTMENT OF PUBLIC WELFARE

STATE DEPARTMENT OF AGRICULTURE

ELECTION BOARD *

FINANCE COMMITTEE **

COUNTY ELECTORATE

EXTENSION SERVICE WASHINGTON STATE COLLEGE

JUSTICES OF THE PEACE (11)

COMMISSIONERS *** (3)

SCHOOL DISTRICTS (25)

ROAD DISTRICT

FIRE PROTECTION DISTRICTS (3)

LIBRARY DISTRICT

1. AUDITOR
2. TREASURER
3. ASSESSOR
4. CLERK
5. PROSECUTING ATTORNEY
6. SHERIFF
7. SUPERINTENDENT OF SCHOOLS
8. SUPERIOR COURT JUDGE
9. PROBATION OFFICERS
10. BOARD OF EDUCATION
11. HORTICULTURAL INSPECTOR
12. WELFARE ADMINISTRATOR
13. HEALTH OFFICER
14. ROAD ENGINEER
15. WEED CONTROL SUPERVISOR
16. AGRICULTURAL AGENT
17. 4-H CLUB AGENT
18. HOME DEMONSTRATION AGENT

○ Appointive offices

☐ Elected by local residents but components of state judicial system.

* Auditor, prosecuting attorney and chairman of board of commissioners.

** Treasurer, auditor and chairman of board of commissioners.

*** Commissioners are ex officio board of equalization, board of health, welfare board and road commissioners.

Paul Beckett, The State College of Washington

588

and passes on to local units of the county the moneys designated for them. A few states have a county officer known as the *tax collector;* in some others the assessor or sheriff does the collecting; in the majority the treasurer acts in that capacity, and very properly so.

The *auditor* is a county finance officer found in some sixteen of the states. His duties consist primarily of examining and approving bills and claims against the county. Following his favorable action, the county board ordinarily orders payment. Where there is no auditor, the county clerk, whose chief duties are described below, serves in somewhat the same capacity. Indeed, except perhaps in the very populous counties, there is no need for both auditor and clerk.

4. OTHER OFFICERS. Some twenty-five states have the office of county *clerk,* usually elective. The clerk keeps the records of the proceedings of the county board; prepares and distributes ballots for elections; issues certain licenses; makes reports as required by law; and performs numerous other ministerial and clerical tasks that vary considerably from state to state. Where there is no county clerk, these duties are discharged by the clerk of a court or other officer or officers.

A *register of deeds* is about as common in the counties as the county clerk. His chief duty is to keep the public records of the sale and transfer of real estate. This is an important function in a country where real property changes hands so frequently; and in those states that have no registers of deeds, some other county officer, usually the clerk, keeps these records. There are many other county officers—school, road, charity, etc., —varying in number, titles, and duties among the states and even among the counties of a particular state. The elective officers mentioned above are able to carry out the administrative work of the ordinary county; but in the more populous areas, hundreds or even thousands of assistants, deputies, and clerks are employed. In a few counties such assistants are engaged under the merit system.

Subdivisions of the county: 1. THE TOWN. For purposes of community government, counties are subdivided in one way or another in every state. In the New England states this subdivision is the town, a unit that dates from early colonial times. In these states it is an older and much more vital unit of government than the county. The term "town" has various meanings in different parts of the country and often several meanings in the same locality. The farmer says, "I am going to town," meaning to the little cluster of houses and stores, the village. The boy in the village says, "I am going up town," meaning that he is going a quarter of a mile to the point where the village trading is done. It is difficult for many Americans to understand that the New England town is a rural area averaging about twenty-five square miles, which usually includes a village. In theory, the town is governed by the whole body of citizens, who assemble at the town meetings, make the local laws, and elect a clerk and other town officials to carry out these laws and the many duties imposed by state authorities. This theory borders on the fact in those communities that are still chiefly agricultural and consequently not overburdened with population. But in industrial areas with more than 10,000 or 15,000 inhabitants, many of whom are nonnative or floaters, the system breaks down and most likely falls into the hands of a machine.

Ordinarily, city government is more competent for administering the affairs of the more populous communities, and that form is usually adopted when the town system becomes too unwieldy. The town or township system was adopted by a number of states outside of New England; but only in the Central states is there much resemblance to the New England system. Even in the Central states the town is of much less importance than in New England. This reduced significance came about because in the Middle West the town is subordinate to the county; because roads, schools, and some other local functions are usually administered by separate authorities; and because the town includes the rural population only.

2. County districts. In the Southern and Western states, counties are divided into administrative units known variously as magisterial districts, civil districts, and precincts. Ordinarily villages, and sometimes the smaller cities located within the district, are parts of the district organization. Such districts are convenient areas for the conduct of elections and the administration of petty justice, schools, and rural roads. An important characteristic of these districts is their almost complete subordination to the county. They were created for administrative purposes and their authority is exceedingly limited. Neither in the South, because of its earlier development along county lines, nor in the West, because of its wide, sparsely settled areas, has there been developed anything approximating the vigorous local government of the rural New England town.

3. Special districts. The regular county districts, particularly in the South and West, have not been found equal to the performance of a number of administrative functions. Consequently, special districts have been created for schools, highways, drainage, irrigation, and the like. Professor F. H. Guild has found forty-seven varieties of such districts under eighty-nine different titles.[14] Special districts may or may not have boundaries conforming to those of a county, regular district, or township. Their

[14] See reference to Guild's articles in J. A. Fairlie and C. M. Kneier, *County Government and Administration* (1930), p. 477. In 1936 Professor William Anderson placed the number of special districts at 8,580. Six years later his figure was 8,382, distributed as follows: water control, 2,911; rural road and bridge, 1,688; irrigation and conservation, 712; urban improvement, 277; urban utility, 702; housing, 525; soil conservation, 107; miscellaneous, 1,510. Anderson, *The Units of Government in the United States* (1942 ed.), p. 6. The appendix in Professor Anderson's 1949 reprint of the 1942 edition shows no significant changes since the latter date.

boundaries are determined by the area of need, not by the arbitrary lines of some pre-existing political unit. They have another advantage over the regular districts in that they are created to administer special functions—health, mosquito abatement, and so on. Still another advantage is in finance. Counties and the regular districts are commonly limited by law in the amount of taxes they may levy and the money they may borrow; but, by creating a special district, it is ordinarily possible to get funds sufficient for a given purpose. We might add that this circumvention is not always appreciated by the taxpayers. Officers of the special districts are appointed by county or state authorities in a number of instances, although popular election is the usual method of selection. Effort is made in a few states to guarantee that the appointed officials shall be qualified for the positions they hold; but there are few cases in which the requirement goes beyond the "suitable and competent person" generality.

Quite naturally several local government districts, sometimes coextensive and sometimes overlapping, with their special functions, and frequently with independent taxing powers, cause considerable confusion and waste. The problem here, as with the state administrative system, is one of co-ordination and consolidation, a problem that in rural areas has hardly been touched.

State control of local officers: 1. JUDICIAL CONTROL. Since counties and their subdivisions are concerned so largely with the administration of state laws, it is highly desirable that state officials be authorized to exercise some control over local officers. A degree of control is exercised by the courts, which, for example, by writ of mandamus may compel a county board to levy a tax to pay the amounts due on county bonds and by writ of injunction may restrain county officers from illegally changing the county seat or creating a debt in excess of that authorized by law. Courts are frequently empowered to remove local officers for corruption, incompetence, and similar causes; and in a few states judges have the duty of appointing certain county officers. But court control over officers corrects only the worst abuses and mistakes, and it is highly technical and cumbersome in any case.

2. ADMINISTRATIVE CONTROL. Any effective control or supervision over local officers must come from the central administrative authorities, as France and other countries of Continental Europe learned long ago. Control of our local officials, as far as such control was exercised at all, has been very largely in the hands of legislatures during the greater part of our history. This was the old English system, now considerably modified in favor of administrative control in that country and to a somewhat lesser extent in the American states. Administrative control in America takes several general forms. (1) Appointment of a few local officers is by state authorities. For example, the justice of the peace is appointed by the

governor in several states. (2) State authorities may fix the standard of attainment for certain employees who are selected by local authorities, as illustrated by the state standards set for teachers who are appointed by local boards and superintendents. (3) State officers may remove certain local officers in some states. The most conspicuous exercise of this authority occurred in New York in 1932, when Governor Franklin D. Roosevelt removed the Sheriff of New York County. (4) Local authorities may be required to make reports to state authorities. State officers may also have the power to inspect and advise, and, on occasion, command, local officers. (5) Payment of subsidies by the state to local communities for roads, schools, and other purposes, provided the communities meet standards fixed by the state, is a fairly effective scheme of central control. This type of control has been noticeably extended since 1933, the states having had to come to the aid of local communities in education, relief of unemployment, and other activities. (6) State authorities may also control through the review of local action. Examples of this are furnished in the approval of local health regulations by the state department of health and the adjustment of local tax assessments by state boards of equalization.[15] Although such powers may seem comprehensive, it must be remembered that the greater number of them apply only to particular matters in particular states. Students of administration generally hold that state administrative officers exercise only a fair control over local authorities and that legislatures depend too heavily on regulating the work of local officers by detailed statutory provisions.

Criticisms and proposals for improvements. For one hundred fifty years the American county has stood practically as it stands today. It was organized in colonial times to suit the needs of rural America and the states later admitted to the Union came with their counties organized to serve the needs of their rural civilization. The county still functions with some degree of success in rural areas, but it seldom achieves any noteworthy triumphs in urban communities. In small or sparsely populated rural counties the per capita cost of administration is usually high and in the metropolitan areas the county administrative system is often corrupt and almost always ineffective in dealing with the many technical activities it is supposed to assume. The stronghold of the spoilsman, with an organization that in truth belongs to the "ox cart" days, the county does not hold a place as a promising unit of government. Furthermore, the counties have fallen into financial difficulties and they have called loudly to the states for financial aid, bewailing at the same time their gradual loss of the power of self-government. In addition to these and many other criticisms of county government, we have the problem of special areas mentioned above.

[15] Fairlie and Kneier, *op. cit.,* pp. 92–104.

What solutions are offered? Abolish the counties; establish five or six or a dozen administrative areas in each state, is the answer efficiency men sometimes give. They say that the counties are much smaller than necessary in this day of rapid communication and transportation, and they show how money can be saved and services more efficiently performed by the larger units of administration. Carrying this proposal into execution presents just one difficulty—the people will not adopt it. It is proper also to raise the question of the desirability of such a plan. Would not democracy lose by this scrapping of the county? Rural democracy certainly would receive a blow. The economy of the proposal is readily admitted, but the price of going to the bargain basement for a governmental structure might prove to be a loss in civic consciousness.[16]

Retain the county system, but consolidate the counties to half their number, say some authorities. This is a perfectly sound proposal. Certainly there is no reason why an individual cannot travel forty miles to a county seat today if he could travel twenty miles to one fifty years ago. But the rural counties will not consolidate. The inhabitants of the county seat will vote against it to a man and so will all the other citizens of the county who feel that they might suffer some slight inconvenience. But the chief factor that will defeat such a proposal is the vague fear that this movement is but the beginning of a scheme to rob the counties of all power, a fear fed by all of the county politicians, who for obvious reasons are opposed to consolidation. So great is the opposition to consolidation that it has been found difficult or impossible to place an amendment in a state constitution that would *permit,* much less require, the people of counties to vote on the question.

Another type of consolidation that has been proposed and that has met with a little favor is the city-county combination. This is discussed in the next chapter.

There is still another type of consolidation, the consolidation of functions. For example, small and poor counties might combine for the purpose of maintaining a county hospital or a health unit or some other service. This is hardly as satisfactory as a complete consolidation, but it has some merit and it has been achieved in a few cases.

Considerable attention has been devoted to the problem of improving county administration by the introduction of some sort of executive management. There are those who believe that the county should adopt a manager system similar to the city-manager plan.[17] Although this plan has been advocated for some years and a few states have authorized its adoption, the number of counties that have installed it is relatively small.

[16] In a very readable volume, *Government in Rural America* (1937), Lane W. Lancaster sets forth in Chapter V and XV some of the obstacles to efficient county administration.

[17] See the National Municipal League's *County Manager Plan* (pamphlet, 1950).

It seems that the counties are more reluctant to accept a new system than are the cities. Besides, the functions of the county and the city are not the same. The city has many services that correspond rather closely to those of a business organization; the typical county has but few.

Perhaps Professor William Anderson is right in fixing his aim on the 165,049 units of government.[18] He would abolish the 118,308 school districts he found in 1941, leaving the schools to be administered by city or county authority, but under state control. Since 1941 a number of states have made considerable progress in reducing the number of such districts. In like manner he would abolish practically all the special districts. His blueprints call for the disappearance of the townships except in New England, where rural towns would be consolidated. The small villages he would deprive of their corporate existence. He would create city-counties in every area having a city of at least 50,000 population, giving such units of government the functions of the city, the county, and the school district. For rural areas he would leave the counties to administer state-wide services, such as schools, health, and welfare, and he would leave with these counties any purely rural functions. Of course, he advocates extensive consolidation for rural counties.

There are, then, many suggestions and plans for the improvement of county government, but very few of them have met with any enthusiasm from county and state officers or from the people. Counties continue for the most part to manage their affairs badly. They make increasing demands on the states for financial aid, while they proclaim, "never before has it been so necessary for counties to stand together in the preservation of local autonomy." Obviously it is not possible to receive funds from the state without at the same time giving the state a larger share in the administration of the services for which funds are advanced. In the last twenty years the trend toward state control of highways, education, public welfare, and health administration has been observed even by those who give these matters little attention. This result is inevitable. The states have the broader taxing powers, they have the technical staffs necessary for administration, and they are therefore better able to administer large functions. The counties should retain their purely local functions, but science and technology have made many local functions statewide functions. But this development towards centralization does not mean that the county is passing completely out of the picture. It does and should remain a vital administrative unit, subject of course to state supervision. In particular, the county should continue to play a large part in administering those services, such as education and social security, that so intimately touch the life of the individual.

[18] *Op. cit.,* pp. 45–47.

III. CITY GOVERNMENTAL ORGANIZATION [19]

A. The city's relation to state and national governments

The city to a lesser extent than the county discharges certain functions for the state and to a much greater extent than the county administers to local needs. Like the county, the city is a creature of the state. It was formerly the creature of the state legislature; but because the legislature often used its exclusive powers unwisely, constitutional restrictions were placed upon its authority over cities. These restrictions are now numerous and vary a great deal among the several states; but, in general, they are limitations on the authority of the legislature to do such things as grant charters to cities by special act, amend charters without the consent of the inhabitants of cities affected, and authorize cities to tax and borrow money beyond a stipulated percentage of the valuation of taxable property. It may be said that, although in theory the city is in essentially the same position of dependence upon the state as is the county, in actual fact the city is more independent than the county because of the constitutional limitations upon the legislature respecting its control of city affairs.

The city charter. Each city has a charter, a sort of constitution. It is acquired in various ways. In some states the legislature may still grant each city a charter by a special act, and each charter may be different. This power to grant charters by special act gives the legislature and the cities too much opportunity to play politics. There are states that have tried the expedient of requiring the legislatures to classify cities and give all in the same class the same charter. The trouble here is that cities may be so classified, as they were at one time in Ohio, that practically every city will be in a class to itself, and the special charter system will again prevail. A few states have a set of charters, allowing a city to adopt the one best suited to its needs. This is known as the "optional charter" system. Although it appears satisfactory, cities have often failed to find charters to meet their specifications.

Some years ago students of municipal problems pinned their faith on the home-rule charter as the solution of many of the city's ills. It is now authorized in sixteen or more states that include many of the largest cities.[20] A

[19] A. W. Bromage, *Introduction to Municipal Government and Administration* (1950); C. M. Kneier, *City Government in the United States* (1947 ed.); A. F. Macdonald, *American City Government and Administration* (1946 ed.), J. M. Pfiffner, *Municipal Administration* (1940); C. E. Ridley and O. F. Nolting, *The City-Manager Profession* (1934); C. P. Taft, *City Management: The Cincinnati Experiment* (1933).

[20] See the series of articles on "What Municipal Home Rule Means Today," *National Municipal Review*, 1932. J. D. McGoldrick, in his *Law and Practice of Municipal Home Rule* (1933), seems to think that the home-rule idea has been something of a fad that is now fading out, and there has been no strong movement for home-rule chapters since he published this volume.

small group of citizens, chosen by the voters or otherwise, drafts the charter for a city. It is then referred to the voters, whose approval puts it into effect, although in some states it must go through the formality of receiving legislative approval. The home-rule charter must not, of course, contain provisions contrary to the Constitution, statutes, or treaties of the United States, or to the constitution of the state, or to state laws. The home-rule principle is therefore subject to considerable modification.

Its CONTENT. By whatever method the charter may be acquired, it provides for the government of the city and the conduct of business, usually in great detail. It creates the municipal corporation (the city as a legal entity); provides for the framework of government; names the officials, the manner in which they shall be chosen, the length of their terms, and similar details; outlines the powers of the corporation and of its various officers; prescribes the method for letting contracts; lays down the rules to be observed in city finance; elaborates a municipal employment system; and makes detailed stipulations on scores of other subjects. The charter of any one of several of the larger cities fills a sizable volume. An important point to be noted is that the city has no powers except those delegated by state authority and found chiefly in the charter. Unlike the powers delegated to the national government in the federal Constitution, which are construed liberally by the federal courts, powers enumerated in the city charter are construed strictly by state judicial authority.

Types of state control. Cities are controlled by the state, although the amount of state "interference and obstruction" in city affairs varies in accordance with constitutional provisions affecting local government, the nature of the city charters, the composition of legislatures, and the attitude of the courts. This state control was formerly exercised almost exclusively by the legislatures, and it is still very largely in the hands of those bodies. Not only must the city look to the legislature for its authority but also, in a number of states, it must go to a legislature in which the rural communities have a majority of the representatives, although they have less than a majority of the population. This unequal representation exists because, as was explained in Chapter 16, the rural areas once had a large majority of the population and because their representatives, using their initial advantages, have refused to grant the cities their fair quota of representatives.

This struggle of the city against the legislature is nowhere better illustrated than in Illinois.[21] The city of Chicago bitterly protests against this discrimination, and it frequently raises the complaint that the legislature will not grant it the authority necessary to conduct its local affairs. In 1925 the Chicago Council unanimously passed a resolution of secession from the state! This bizarre gesture is indicative of the city reaction against rural-

21 Kneier, *op. cit.,* pp. 116 ff.

state domination. It may be that we shall come to the city-state (city a state unto itself) plan in time. This plan would be vigorously opposed by the "down-staters" or "up-staters" because the removal of the city from the state would mean an immense loss of revenue to the latter.

Legislative control of cities may not always mean unfriendly control, but it commonly means inflexible control. Laws are made applicable to all cities, or to cities in certain classes, without allowance for the special requirements of particular cities. Yet, if we are to have legislative control, it seems best to exercise it in this manner, for legislative acts for individual cities would produce a train of abuses, as they did before special legislation was prohibited.

Another type of control, administrative control, is used extensively in European countries and is growing in our own. The French and, to a lesser extent, the English grant through their central legislative bodies the very widest powers to local government units. But they provide also that these local units in exercising these powers shall be under very close administrative supervision imposed by the central administrative authority. The administrative officers in approving or vetoing a city budget or some proposed municipal undertaking are not limited to the consideration of legality, but they may consider the financial standing of the city, the usefulness of the proposed project, the effect on the surrounding community, and any number of other factors. Clearly the great advantage of administrative countrol is in its flexibility. It should be equally clear that unless the administrators who exercise this control are well trained, capable, thoroughly honest, and disinterested, the cities will suffer from discriminations and arbitrary acts to a number and degree beyond the capacity of an ordinary state legislature to impose. The European countries have been fairly successful in developing administrators who possess the necessary qualities.

There is not a great deal of state administrative control over cities in the United States, but there is a decided trend in that direction, particularly in the fields of education, health, public welfare, and finance. Since 1919 an Indiana law has authorized ten taxpayers to petition the State Board of Tax Commissioners to review either a local tax levy or a local bond issue proposal. The taxpapers have not failed to exercise the privileges conferred, nor has the State Board hesitated to order local authorities to make substantial reductions. North Carolina has taken what is commonly regarded as an extreme step. In 1931 it established a Local Government Commission composed of three state officers *ex officio* and six citizens appointed by the governor. The Commission is authorized to consider local bond issues from such angles as necessity, adequacy, their effect on the tax situation, and the condition of sinking funds. An issue of bonds not approved by the Commission may, however, be made with the approval of the voters. The state authority exercises a close supervision over the investment of sinking funds, and acts as virtual receiver over any unit of government that defaults on its bonds.[22] State grants-in-aid are very common now, and wherever there are such grants there are accompanying arrangements for state supervision.

Administrative control of the European type or of the North Carolina type is not likely to find wide acceptance in America, but there is good reason for a more general extension of state administrative control over the local administration of those functions in which the state has an essential interest. The purely local functions, of which there are still a goodly number in urban areas, should not be brought within the state regulatory framework.

Federal-city relations. Prior to 1933 the cities had only a very few direct associations with the federal government. But such relationships took a decided spurt in the depression years. The public works program of the federal government permitted federal grants to states, *cities,* and other public bodies. Large advances were made to cities for waterworks, sewerage systems, and schools. The money advanced was in gifts and loans in the 30–70 ratio. In 1935 the W.P.A. advanced large sums to cities for the purpose of providing work for employables on relief. On the application of cities the W.P.A. put men to work on athletic fields, parks, streets, and so on. These projects were financed almost entirely by federal funds and administered by federal officers. During the same year the P.W.A. made grants of 45 per cent of the total amount and loans of 55 per cent for approved local public works. This practice, with modifications, was continued for several years.

The Municipal Bankruptcy Act (1934), declared void in 1936, and its successor, which met the test of constitutionality, are discussed in another chapter of this volume.[23] Another municipal field into which the national government has entered is housing, discussed in Chapter 26.

These federal-city relations do not remove the city from the legal control of the state, but they are none the less significant. This process, if continued, is bound to cause the cities to rely more and more upon the central government and less upon the states. We have here a definite trend toward federal-city agreements and combinations, associations that will weaken the ties between the city and the state. The creation by the Conference of Mayors, in 1936, of a committee of fourteen to deal with federal legislation affecting the cities was not just an incidental matter.

---

[22] J. M. Pfiffner, *Public Administration* (1946 ed.), pp. 137–141, and his *Municipal Administration* (1940), pp. 124 ff.

[23] See page 757.

It was a recognition by the mayors of the place the federal government, upon their earnest solicitation, has assumed in their affairs.[24]

B. The conventional form of city government

The form of city government that brought us through the nineteenth century is the mayor-council plan. It is modeled largely after the structure of the national and state governments, emphasizing the separation of legislative and executive powers. Indeed, the cities followed these models even to the extent of establishing bicameral councils, although these have now been abandoned in every city in favor of the single chamber. Following the states again, the cities at first gave their chief executive officers few powers, but the trend for many years has been in the direction of strengthening the position of mayor. Since 1900 the mayor-council plan of city government has been challenged, first by the commission plan and later by the council-manager plan. Yet the mayor-council system, the only system our grandfathers knew, remains the leading type of municipal government. More than half the cities of over 30,000 population still employ it in varying forms.

The council. The council formerly exercised practically all the powers of government in the city. It still has a commanding place in some cities, but it has rather steadily lost power to the mayor in the others. It is always elected by the people, most commonly for a two-year term. Usually councilmen are chosen by wards, sometimes at large, and in a few instances by a combination method. Councils vary a great deal in size (not necessarily in accordance with the size of cities); but the tendency is to make them small, fifteen or twenty councilmen being considered sufficient in most cities. A few of the large cities pay councilmen fair salaries; usually they receive very little. Councils meet as often as necessary—weekly or fortnightly meetings being most common. They organize and proceed very much as state legislatures, relying upon standing committees for the greater part of the routine work.

The powers of the councils vary with charters and state laws, but every council has some legislative and administrative authority. Councils in general may pass ordinances (legislate) on such subjects as the following: the structure of city government, as far as the charter and general state law leave it unprescribed; street traffic, sanitation, health, fire prevention, and numerous other matters that fall under the broad "police" power of the city; revenue, appropriations, and other problems of city finance, always subject, of course, to limitations imposed by the state; the granting of franchises to streetcar and bus companies and other public utilities, again

---

[24] P. V. Betters and others, *Recent Federal-City Relations* (1936); Macdonald, *op. cit.,* Ch. V. See *Municipal Year Book* for recent developments.

under strict limitations prescribed by state law; and the management of city property.   On the administrative side the council has few powers, and these are properly declining in number.   Councils still make appointments to some offices, but appointments are usually made by the mayor subject to the approval of the council.   In a few cities offices are filled by the mayor alone.   However small the council's legal part in appointments may be, there are many individual members who by devious means and indefatigable efforts secure places for their friends and supporters in the city's vineyard.

The mayor.   The mayor far outshines the council in city government. A century ago he was chiefly a figurehead and the council had the power, but the success of mayors in handling affairs as compared with the councils' mediocre achievements and the rapid growth of administrative functions, particularly in the past fifty years, have placed the mayor in the ascendancy in most cities.   He is elected by the people; usually serves a two-year term, although the four-year term is growing in favor; receives a substantial salary in the larger cities—not infrequently more than the governor of his state.   Although some mayors have been conspicuous playboys, jokes, crooks, or frauds, the greater number of them are of higher caliber than councilmen.   A few mayors have gone on to high national office; but for one reason or another, mayors commonly do not seek, or at least fail to find, the favor of the voters outside the cities.

His powers.   The mayor is the official head of the city.   He handles communications between the city and outside governing authorities, issues proclamations, receives delegations, entertains distinguished visitors, and represents the city in other formal matters.   He is the city's chief administrator, being charged with the very broad duty, sometimes without adequate powers, of directing the various administrative units that perform the numerous services for the urban population.   As already stated, he usually has a wide appointing power, commonly and sometimes unfortunately shared with the council.

The preparation of a budget was formerly considered a legislative matter, but a number of cities now pass this responsibility to the mayor and other executive officers.   The financial program for revenues and expenditures prepared by the mayor and his staff is submitted to the council, which may both strike out and reduce items; but in a growing number of cities the council is not permitted to vote increases over the mayor's recommendations.   This restriction as to increases in the budget is singularly effective in preventing wasteful, "pork barrel" appropriations.

Just as the President and the governor, the mayor may recommend legislation to the co-ordinate governing body, the council, and often bring about its passage through his political influence and through a judicious use of the patronage. Following the national and state practice, the mayor is given the power to veto ordinances of the city council, a power that he uses frequently for good or ill, depending upon his qualifications and temperament. His veto is seldom overridden by the council, a two-thirds majority being commonly required for that purpose.

Growth of city functions. The council, the mayor, a few constables, some volunteer firemen, and perhaps a few other public-spirited individuals, were able to carry on the affairs of a city a hundred years ago; for in those days the city authorities were expected to do little besides pass an occasional ordinance, preserve the peace, keep the streets (often just dirt roads) passable, and make some crude efforts in the direction of sanitation. Now this is all changed. Large cities provide a hundred, or even two hundred services—libraries, schools, museums, playgrounds, bathing beaches, swimming pools, dispensaries, tuberculosis camps, and so on. Services have grown because the cities have grown, because science has made new services possible, and because the people demand them. The annual cost of these functions in any one of our largest cities runs into several hundred million dollars.

Administrative structure. Manifestly the work of the city can no longer be performed by the mayor and the council. The council serves as a board of directors, and the mayor is the general manager, or should be. The work is done through an elaborate administrative organization employing, in large cities, thousands of individuals. Functions are distributed among departments—five, ten, twenty, or more—as in the national and state systems. Departments are headed by single officials or boards, the former being preferred for most departments, the latter being used almost invariably for such departments as schools and charities. Some department heads are appointed by the mayor and some are elected, the practice varying among the cities and departments of the same city. Sometimes the mayor can control them and sometimes his authority is only nominal, his power depending upon the nature of the administrative structure and upon the mayor himself. Within each department there are as many bureaus, divisions, and sections as the several services of a department demand. These subdivisions are headed by officials who are commonly responsible to their immediate superiors. In a well-organized system the lines of responsibility run from subordinate to superior until they all finally reach the mayor, who is in a general way responsible to the people.

C. Newer forms of city government

Undisturbed for a century and a half was the American's devotion to the check and balance theory of government. The division of authority between executive and legislative branches, with all the attendant bicker-

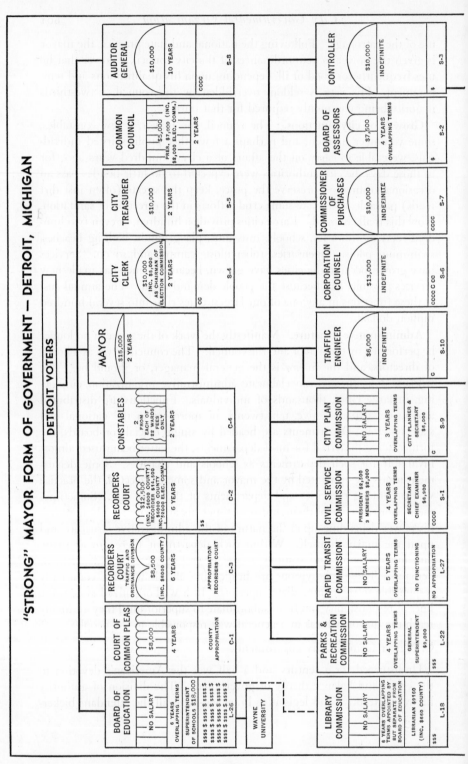

"STRONG" MAYOR FORM OF GOVERNMENT — DETROIT, MICHIGAN

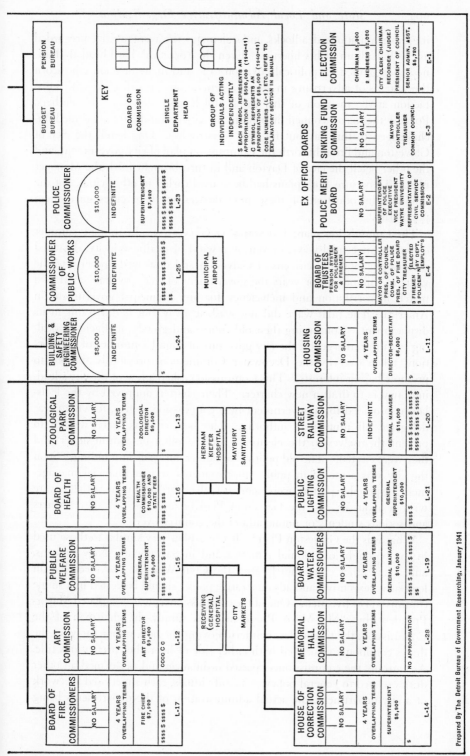

Prepared By The Detroit Bureau of Government Researching, January 1941

ings, recriminations, deadlocks, and stalemates, the average citizen regarded as the Palladium of his liberties. Even the "practical, hard-headed" business man pinned his political salvation to it, and many of them who scorn the systems of advertising in vogue a generation ago still glow with satisfaction at the mention of this check and balance device of the Fathers. Possibly the mayor-council division in the cities would have continued unchallenged to this day but for two catastrophes. One befell the city of Galveston and brought forth the Commission plan of city government, and the other befell the city of Dayton and in turn brought forth the Manager plan. To be sure, both plans had been used earlier in other cities, but the dramatic introduction of these new devices in these cities gave them popularity.

The Commission plan: Launched at Galveston. In the late summer of 1900 a huge tidal wave, driven by a wind of terrific velocity, drowned some seven thousand citizens of Galveston and destroyed property to the value of millions. For years the government of that city had stood as a match in corruption and inefficiency for any municipal government in America. The tidal wave did not wash it away, but it did result in its displacement. Continuing their old course and grossly negligent in dealing with the emergency, the city government found a number of its functions taken over by the Deepwater Commission, previously formed to promote harbor interests. This Commission asked a few of the city's leading lawyers to draft a new charter. Their charter, approved by the legislature, provided for a government by a commission of five, to whom was delegated all municipal authority. The best citizens were willing to present themselves to the electorate for the office of commissioner and they were elected. The old political organization went into hiding. Soon the city was a model in public improvements and in financial management. Special reporters were sent to Galveston; magazine articles were written about it; and the Galveston Plan became the talk of reformers and serious students of public affairs the country over.

What was the Galveston Plan? It was a plan very similar to those used in the boroughs of colonial America and in Sacramento, New Orleans, and a few other cities shortly after the Civil War. It provided that all legislative, executive, and administrative power should be vested in a single commission of five men. One of the commissioners was designated Mayor-President, but "Mr. Mayor-President" was simply the chairman of the Commission, the titleholder, neither enjoying the honors nor carrying the duties commonly associated with either side of his rather pretentious title. As a group, the commissioners passed ordinances and performed all other duties related to general policy. As individuals, each supervised the work of a city department, the actual administration of the departments being left to an officer with the proper technical qualifications. Here was in operation a plan of city government, enthusiastically acclaimed, that boldly set aside the traditional separation of powers.

THE DES MOINES REFINEMENTS. Although the Galveston experiment was admittedly a success, the rank and file of Americans hesitated to advocate it for general use. They were concerned about a five-man government with no "checks and balances," fearful of a government that might proceed quickly to an objective. The plan therefore spread slowly until Des Moines (1907) erected safeguards against the commission. The Des Moines Plan simply superimposed upon the earlier plan certain democratic institutions already in use—the recall, the initiative, and the referendum. Here were the checks against possible arbitrary authority.

The Des Moines Plan spread rapidly, receiving modifications as it spread. During the ten years following the action at Des Moines nearly every state authorized the use of the new system in some form or other, and about five hundred cities adopted it. Since 1917 very few cities have installed the commission system. Some cities have gone back to the mayor-council system; a larger number have abandoned the commission plan for the newer manager type of city government. In 1949 even Des Moines voted to shift to the manager plan, a fact that does not, however, lessen the value of the "Des Moines Plan" for illustrative purposes. Today the commission system is losing ground, although it is still in use in many small cities and a few larger ones, including Newark, New Orleans, and Portland, Oregon.

ADVANTAGES AND DEFECTS OF THE COMMISSION PLAN. Like every system or plan put forward as the solution of a problem of government, the commission system has revealed its good and bad points. It may be said that the principle of concentration of authority is distinctly good, as far as it goes, but it will presently be shown that there is a defect in this particular concentration. It may also be said that the simplification of city government, one of the main features of the commission plan, is greatly to be desired. Gone is the large number and bewildering variety of officers—some elected, some appointed; some responsible to one authority, some to another, and some only in a vague sort of way to the people.

Has the commission plan placed better men in office? For the first few years following its adoption the answer is very definitely "Yes." But after the cities have settled down to normal and the novelty of the plan has worn off, there is some question as to whether the caliber of their commissioners is higher than that of the old mayor-council officers. The new system is adopted as a reform, sometimes as the result of a popular uprising. The moral fervor of this movement results in the city's best being placed at the helm. The typical good citizen thinks that his duty is done. "We have a new form of government now, and everything will be all

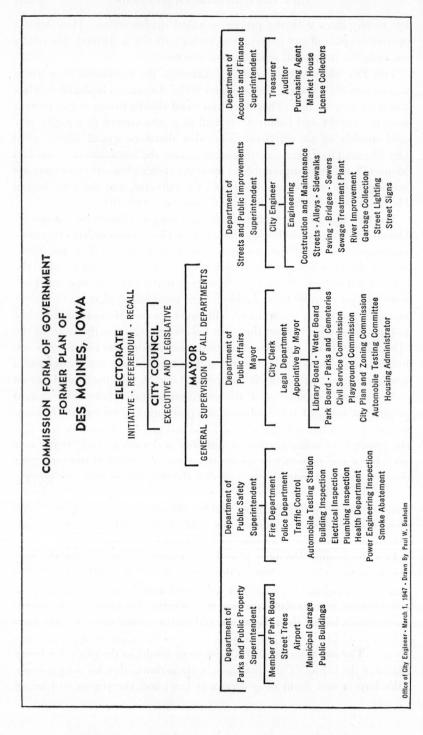

COMMISSION FORM OF GOVERNMENT
FORMER PLAN OF
DES MOINES, IOWA

ELECTORATE
INITIATIVE - REFERENDUM - RECALL

CITY COUNCIL
EXECUTIVE AND LEGISLATIVE

MAYOR
GENERAL SUPERVISION OF ALL DEPARTMENTS

Department of Parks and Public Property
Superintendent

Member of Park Board
Street Trees
Airport
Municipal Garage
Public Buildings

Department of Public Safety
Superintendent

Fire Department
Police Department
Traffic Control
Automobile Testing Station
Building Inspection
Electrical Inspection
Plumbing Inspection
Health Department
Power Engineering Inspection
Smoke Abatement

Department of Public Affairs
Mayor

City Clerk
Legal Department
Appointive by Mayor

Library Board - Water Board
Park Board - Parks and Cemeteries
Civil Service Commission
Playground Commission
City Plan and Zoning Commission
Automobile Testing Committee
Housing Administrator

Department of Streets and Public Improvements
Superintendent

City Engineer
Engineering
Construction and Maintenance
Streets - Alleys - Sidewalks
Paving - Bridges - Sewers
Sewage Treatment Plant
River Improvement
Garbage Collection
Street Lighting
Street Signs

Department of Accounts and Finance
Superintendent

Treasurer
Auditor
Purchasing Agent
Market House
License Collectors

Office of City Engineer - March 1, 1947 - Drawn By Paul W. Bosholm

606

right," he says. His interest lags. It is impossible for him to retain a civic revival spirit from year to year, even if he considered it necessary, which he does not. The old city politicians begin to come out from their hiding places. They are a bit chastened and say they are for the commission plan of government. They run for office and some of them are elected. Sometimes they get full control of the commission, and the old "happy days are here again."

Yet it is generally believed that the commission system has given the cities better government than they had under the conventional plan it succeeded. It has not lowered taxes, an achievement that its too optimistic proponents risked prophesying. However, since the cost of living was rising during the time the plan was flourishing most conspicuously, and since the people demanded more and more services from their governments, the failure to lower taxes is easily understood. As a matter of fact, tax levies were increased in commission-governed cities about as rapidly as they were in other cities. The advantage of the commission plan, if any, lies in the claim that it gives better service for the money, a claim that is subject to dispute but that careful students of government usually sustain with some degree of caution.

If we turn more definitely to the debit side of the ledger, we find several entries made against the commission plan. One is that it is not suited for larger cities. A commission of five, or seven, or nine could not be sufficiently representative of the interests of a great metropolis, nor could its administrative functions be distributed among so few departments of administration. A more damaging criticism (for it is one that applies to its operation in cities of any size) is that directed at the failure of the commission system to carry out to its limit the principle of concentration of administrative authority. It does mark an improvement over the ordinary mayor-council system, but it still leaves administrative responsibility in the hands of three, or five, or seven men. The commissioner of public safety may be blocked in his efforts because his plans are overridden by the other members of the commission. To the complaints of the public he replies that they should be carried to his colleagues who have tied his hands. His colleagues may reply that his proposals were unworkable.[25] The city's business will suffer materially while these charges and counter charges are passed back and forth.

Another major defect of the system is its requirement that commissioners serve as technical administrators. This development was not in the original plan. The Galveston Plan simply provided that the commissioners be supervisors of the several departments and left the details and

[25] It may happen, of course, that commissioners go to the other extreme and approve each other's proposals all too readily.

technicalities of administration to chiefs of departments. It soon became the common practice in other cities to require each commissioner to assume the duties of actual administrator of a department. Unfortunately a commissioner of high caliber often would not be competent to administer a department in which scientific and technical knowledge is required.

The situation was not improved when many cities took from the commissioners the power to assign members to departments and required candidates for the commission to run for specific administrative posts—finance, health, etc. Men with poor professional qualifications who had been through the form of training the jobs seem to require often presented themselves to the electorate, and they were often successful in their campaigns. The difficulty here is that the American has been slow to recognize the value of the professional and the expert in government. He does not understand why the amateur should not take direct charge of administration. He has required the commissioners to attempt to be both amateurs who form policies and professionals who administer policies. Few men can do both. When this became apparent, cities seeking to improve their systems of government turned to the manager plan rather than to the commission plan.[26]

The council-manager plan: Its ORIGIN. As a tidal wave almost literally washed away the wretched government of Galveston and started the commission government system on its course, so a flood at Dayton, Ohio, cleared out its wasteful and corrupt political hacks and brought the city manager, or council-manager form of government into existence. This statement is subject to some modification, for just as there had been commission governments before the Galveston storm, so also there were manager plans in operation before the Dayton flood. In 1908 Staunton, a small city in the Shenandoah Valley of Virginia, installed the first city manager plan. Three years later, the Lockport (N.Y.) Board of Trade presented to the legislature a draft of a charter embracing the manager system and asked that cities below 50,000 population be authorized to adopt it. The legislature did not act upon the suggestion, but the Lockport Plan was widely advertised. The next year (1912) several small cities in North Carolina and South Carolina adopted the city manager plan. While the Lockport Plan was receiving wide publicity, a committee in Dayton was busy studying charters. It recommended the city manager type of charter. Under the new home rule amendment to the state constitution

---

[26] On the commission plan see C. R. Woodruff (ed.), *City Government by Commission* (1911), and standard texts on municipal government by C. M. Kneier, T. H. Reed, A. F. Macdonald, W. B. Munro, J. M. Pfiffner, and others. Some of the weaknesses of the system are exposed in the decision of the voters of Des Moines to abandon it in favor of the Council-Manager Plan. See Katherine R. Stroud, "Des Moines Drops Own Plan," *National Municipal Review*, June, 1949, pp. 269–272, 277.

a city could have a charter of its own selection. Consequently, a large committee was appointed to push the campaign for a popular vote on the manager plan. While the campaign was in progress, the flood descended. A few months later the people voted for the manager plan. No doubt the flood had something to do with the popular vote on the question, but, coming as it did with the movement for the new charter, it probably had more to do with advertising the new city manager plan than with the favorable vote the plan received in Dayton.

Its GROWTH. The new plan spread rapidly from the time (1913) Dayton adopted it. It has maintained a steady growth to date, having, in 1948, about 800 cities operating under it. In about six cases out of seven the cities adopted a manager charter; in the others they simply installed it by ordinance. The latter procedure is commonly frowned upon because momentary dissatisfaction might lead to the repeal of the ordinance before the plan has had an opportunity to justify itself. Not only have adoptions grown steadily, but the friends of the system have found great encouragement in two other facts. It has been adopted by a number of the larger cities, by about one fifth of those with a population of over 100,000. The second encouraging fact is that it has been abandoned by few cities—about 30. Most of the backsliders were small cities, and half of them dropped the plan during the depression when whatever government that happened to be functioning was subject to attacks. Cleveland abandoned it in 1931, but the reasons were primarily political, having little relation to the merits of the manager system. It can be said, then, that the council-manager plan is still spreading and that it has demonstrated its suitability for larger cities, including Cincinnati, Dayton, Oakland, and Rochester. It remains to be tried in the very largest cities.

Its PRINCIPAL FEATURES. The council-manager form of government is a logical development from the commission form. Indeed considerable evidence indicates that the earliest designers of the manager system thought they were simply improving the existing commission plan. That improvement was in the concentration of executive authority in the hands of one man. The manager plan, as it was soon developed and as it stands today, passing over certain variations, provides for a small council of three, five, or seven members, who are elected at large on a nonpartisan ticket. This council has all the ordinance-making power, and it elects and removes the manager. The manager need not be, and usually is not, a resident of the city at the time of his appointment. This is a very fine feature of the plan, for it enables the council to pick the best man available and it makes possible a managership profession.

The manager is the chief administrator in every sense of the word. He appoints all administrative officers and employees; he directs their work;

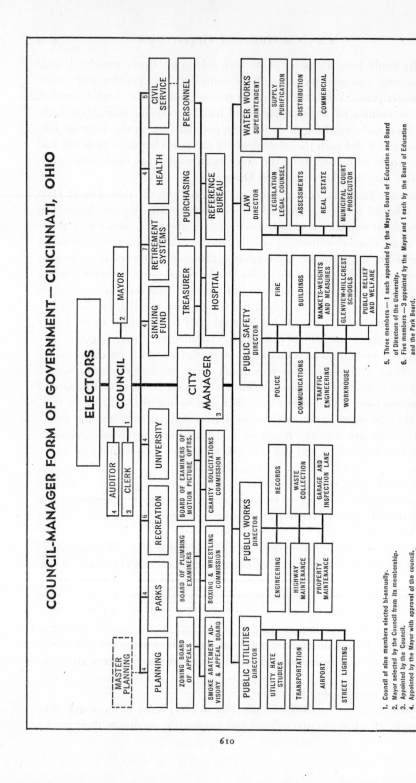

COUNCIL-MANAGER FORM OF GOVERNMENT—CINCINNATI, OHIO

ELECTORS

COUNCIL 1

AUDITOR 4
CLERK 3
MAYOR 2

CITY MANAGER 3

MASTER PLANNING 4

PLANNING 4
PARKS 4
RECREATION 6
UNIVERSITY 4

ZONING BOARD OF APPEALS
BOARD OF PLUMBING EXAMINERS
BOARD OF EXAMINERS OF MOTION PICTURE OPTRS.

SMOKE ABATEMENT ADVISORY & APPEAL BOARD
BOXING & WRESTLING COMMISSION
CHARITY SOLICITATIONS COMMISSION

PUBLIC UTILITIES DIRECTOR
UTILITY RATE STUDIES
TRANSPORTATION
AIRPORT
STREET LIGHTING

PUBLIC WORKS DIRECTOR
ENGINEERING
HIGHWAY MAINTENANCE
PROPERTY MAINTENANCE
RECORDS
WASTE COLLECTION
GARAGE AND INSPECTION LANE

PUBLIC SAFETY DIRECTOR
POLICE
COMMUNICATIONS
TRAFFIC ENGINEERING
WORKHOUSE
FIRE
BUILDINGS
MARKETS-WEIGHTS AND MEASURES
GLENVIEW-HILLCREST SCHOOLS
PUBLIC RELIEF AND WELFARE

SINKING FUND 4
RETIREMENT SYSTEMS 7
TREASURER
HOSPITAL

PURCHASING
REFERENCE BUREAU

LAW DIRECTOR
LEGISLATION LEGAL COUNSEL
ASSESSMENTS
REAL ESTATE
MUNICIPAL COURT PROSECUTOR

HEALTH 4
CIVIL SERVICE 5
PERSONNEL

WATER WORKS SUPERINTENDENT
SUPPLY PURIFICATION
DISTRIBUTION
COMMERCIAL

1. Council of nine members elected bi-annually.
2. Mayor selected by the Council from its membership.
3. Appointed by the Council.
4. Appointed by the Mayor with approval of the council.
5. Three members — 1 each appointed by the Mayor, Board of Education and Board of Directors of the University.
6. Five members — 3 appointed by the Mayor and 1 each by the Board of Education and the Park Board.
7. Make-up of ex-officio and other trustees elected by the memberships of the systems.

From the City Manager's Annual Report (1945)

610

and he promotes the industrious and capable and removes the inefficient. This ideal is not always attained, for in some cities a few elective officers remain and in others the council has a share, official or unofficial, in naming administrative officers. The manager is charged with the duty of keeping the council informed of the "state of the city" and of recommending to its consideration such measures as he shall deem necessary and expedient. It should be observed that nearly all of the cities with the manager plan continue the office of mayor, leaving that official the duty of presiding over the council and the pleasant ceremonial functions that commonly go with the office of mayor. The manager is thus left free for the real work of administration.

MANAGER AND COUNCIL. The council formulates and adopts policies, often upon the recommendation of the manager; the manager's duty is to see that the policies are executed, even if he does not approve of some of them. In some cases the council has paid little attention to the recommendations of the manager, and the manager usually interprets this situation to mean that he lacks the council's confidence and resigns. On occasion the council has interfered with the details of administration. This interference violates a basic principle of the plan, that the manager be unhampered in directing administration. It may indicate only a lack of confidence in a particular manager; but if it is chronic with the council, the manager plan will eventually fail.

When the plan is operating on a normal basis, the council commonly takes the advice of the manager on administrative matters and frequently follows his lead on questions of policy. This procedure is proper, for the manager is a trained professional giving all his time to his work and the councilmen are properly amateurs. Yet the council should never become a rubber stamp for the manager, certainly not on questions of policy. On what parks the city should lay out, what zoning ordinances it should enact, what hospitals should be erected, what streets should be opened up, and on other matters relating to plans and projects the council should hear the manager, but the decisions should be based upon the independent judgment of the council, the elected representatives of the people.

Under the mayor-council government the people are represented by both arms of the government. Under the manager-council type they are represented only by the council. It is important, therefore, that under the latter type of government, the council take its responsibilities seriously. If, as sometimes happens, the people look to the manager rather than to the council as the responsible authority on matters of city policy, that situation usually presages the beginning of the end of the manager system of government and almost certainly foreshadows the end of the career of a particular manager in a given city. The manager is on safe ground in urging the council to adopt a policy, but definitely overstepping the bounds if he should publicly advocate a policy before the council has approved it. But once the council has adopted a policy, the manager may support it publicly, unless, perchance, it should become an issue in the election of councilmen. In short, a manager may not only be a guide to the council but he may also be a discreet community leader.[27]

MANAGERSHIP AS A PROFESSION. Despite the fact that some managers have become involved in politics, sometimes because the local situation made it inevitable and sometimes because the managers made the mistake of assuming a political rôle, managership is developing as a profession. This rank it must attain if the council-manager plan is to be a continued success. Some of the evidences of the professional status of managership may be briefly indicated: (1) The salaries paid are such as to make the position of manager attractive. Managers are paid much more than mayors in cities of comparable size. Managers of cities between 50,000 and 100,000 population receive an average salary of nearly $9,000; mayors of cities in that class receive slightly more than half that amount. (2) The tenure of managers has steadily lengthened. In 1921 it was two years; at present it is approximately six years. (3) Successful managers are often promoted—offered positions in cities that pay higher salaries. This form of recognition was infrequent during the early years of the plan; now it is not at all uncommon. (4) The managers have developed a professional spirit. A City Managers' Association was formed in 1914, an association that has steadily grown in importance and that has, among other things, produced a code of ethics for managers. (5) In keeping with these developments, an interest in training managers has become very pronounced. The Managers' Association has given attention to this problem, and several educational institutions have outlined courses of training for those who hope to enter the profession. It may be said that the preparation generally considered desirable emphasizes engineering, public finance, accounting, municipal administration, and city-planning. Of course, a manager must be an executive, but there is some question as to what courses, if any, train one to be an executive. An essential feature of any such training should be a period of "internship" in a manager's office. Efforts have been made to provide for this, but not many managers will or can make room for an "apprentice," or "intern."

As a conclusion to this sketch of the council-manager plan, it may be said

---

[27] This is the view of the managers' function as expressed by Charles E. Ridley, Director of the City Managers' Association (letter to the author, October 31, 1949). A similar view is held by C. A. Harrell, manager of Norfolk, Va. See his "The City Manager as a Community Leader," *Public Management,* Oct., 1948, p. 290.

to have corrected the great weakness of the commission system by concentrating executive authority in the person of the manager; to have developed professional administration for cities; and to have given general satisfaction in its operation; in short, it has taken its place as an acceptable form of city government.[28]

D. The problem of metropolitan areas

Simultaneously with the growth of our great cities, the small cities and villages that were formerly some miles removed from them have extended their own boundaries until they are contiguous with those of the hub cities. New York, Chicago, and several other municipal leviathans are partially surrounded by satellite (one might almost say parasitic) cities. A great metropolitan area thus formed is physically, and to a large extent, economically and socially, a single urban unit; but governmentally the area is composed of a number of separate corporations.

Some years ago legal consolidation of surrounding cities with the greater city was quite common and the results were reasonably satisfactory; but the newer communities, because of the likelihood of a higher tax rate, a feeling of social superiority, or for other reasons, seem less inclined to be annexed now than a generation ago. Yet it seems fair to assume that fire and police protection, water supply, sanitation—in fact, that practically every important municipal function—could be more economically and more efficiently administered by one government than by half a dozen. Unity of action in certain functions is sometimes secured by the creation of special districts. Thus, thirteen cities of Southern California are included in a single district for water supply; and a sanitary district takes care of sewage disposal for the Chicago metropolitan area.[29] But the consolidation of a particular function of several contiguous cities is only a piece-meal method of attaining the desired administrative entity for metropolitan areas. It is a step in the right direction, but leaves too many functions to be independently administered by the authorities of the separate cities.

City-county consolidation. The city area is ordinarily a part of the territory of the county. County officers have authority in its urban as well as in its rural sections. Since county and city governments have some identical functions, their jurisdictions in respect to these functions over-

[28] On the council-manager plan, see E. S. Griffith, *Current Municipal Problems* (1933); C. E. Ridley and O. F. Nolting, *The City-Manager Profession* (1934); C. P. Taft, *City Management: The Cincinnati Experiment* (1933); L. D. White, *The City Manager* (1927); and standard texts on municipal government.

[29] Kneier, *op. cit.*, pp. 361–362. *Ibid.*, pp. 371 ff.; Macdonald, *op. cit.*, pp. 114 ff.; R. B. Pinchbeck, "City-County Separation in Virginia," *National Municipal Review*, July, 1940, p. 467.

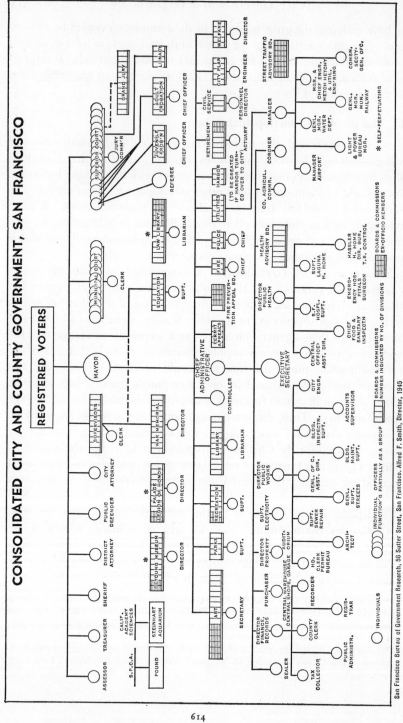

CONSOLIDATED CITY AND COUNTY GOVERNMENT, SAN FRANCISCO

REGISTERED VOTERS

San Francisco Bureau of Government Research, 50 Sutter Street, San Francisco, Alfred F. Smith, Director, 1945

lap. For example, the sheriff and the other law enforcement officers of the county may legally act in the city, despite the fact that the city has its own police officers. In actual practice the county enforcement officers usually confine their activities to the rural districts. Moreover, legal provision is sometimes made to give city authorities practically exclusive control within the city. This exclusive authority often appears in the domains of education and charity administration. Nevertheless, there is still too much duplication and confusion resulting from the overlapping authority of city and county officers.

A few states have attempted to correct these conditions by city-county consolidation. The city and county of Philadelphia were practically consolidated in 1854, although the county officers still have certain functions. San Francisco, Baltimore, St. Louis, and Denver are detached from counties and have governments independent of them. In Virginia all cities are closed to county authorities, the cities administering both municipal and county functions. Some other examples might be given, but the progress of such consolidations is slow. Rural communities frequently oppose a city-county consolidation because it means to them an increase in taxes, and they oppose the detachment of the cities from the counties because it means a heavy loss in taxable property. The opposition is logical enough in both cases.

The possibility of "regions." Even if counties and cities have the constitutional authority to consolidate or separate, and vote to do one or the other, the problem of the metropolitan area is left unsettled in many regions. This disorganized condition exists because an urban area may extend into several counties or into several states. The problem then becomes very complex. To meet this situation, a number of students of the metropolitan area are now recommending a new political unit to be called the "region." This unit would be given the authority to deal with such matters as sanitation, health, transportation, and planning for all areas of government within a designated metropolitan community. There is much to be said for the proposal, but before such a plan can be put into operation the electorate, the state legislatures, and Congress (to approve interstate compacts) must be converted to it. To be sure, as indicated above, government units in certain regions have united upon specific functions— water in the southern California area and sewage disposal in the Chicago area. The Boston region has a number of authorities whose jurisdiction extends over that metropolitan district. The Port of New York Authority, a shining example of regional co-operation, was established by compact between New York and New Jersey with the approval of Congress. Yet the big job remains to be done—the job of organizing the metropolitan region to exercise authority in all matters of common interest in the area.[30]

Reading List

STATE ADMINISTRATION

American Political Science Review. Articles on "State Administration" in practically every issue.

C. W. Armstrong, Jr., "Administrative Reorganization in New Jersey," *State Government,* Dec., 1948, pp. 244–247, 254–255.

A. W. Bromage, *State Government and Administration in the United States* (1936), Ch. XIV.

J. C. Bollens, *Administrative Reorganization in the States Since 1939* (Bureau of Pub. Adm., U. of Cal., 1947).

A. E. Buck, *The Reorganization of State Governments in the United States* (1938).

The Council of State Governments, *Reorganizing State Government* (1950).

W. D. Foulke, *Fighting the Spoilsmen* (1919).

W. B. Graves, *American State Government* (1946 ed.), Chs. X–XII.

A. N. Holcombe, *State Government in the United States* (1931 ed.), Chs. XI–XII, XVII–XVIII.

Illinois Legislative Reference Bureau, *Constitutional Convention Bulletins,* Nos. 5 and 9 (1920).

A. F. Macdonald, *American State Government and Administration* (1950 ed.), Ch. XIII–XVI, XX.

Commonwealth of Massachusetts, *Bulletins for the Constitutional Convention,* 1917–1918, Nos. 2, 3, 8, 10–14, 30.

———, Report of Commission on State Administration and Expenditures (1922).

J. M. Mathews, *American State Government* (1934 ed.), Ch. XIII.

Michigan Commission on Reform and Modernization of Government, *Documents and Proceedings* (1938) and *Report of a Preliminary Survey* (1938).

National Municipal Review. Articles on "State Administration" in many issues.

New York Bureau of Muncipal Research, *Organization and Management of State Government in Virginia* (1927).

New York, *Report of State Reorganization Commission* (1926).

New York State Constitutional Convention Committee, *Problems Relating to Executive Administration and Power* (1938).

Ohio, *Report of Joint Committee on Administrative Reorganization* (1921).

J. M. Pfiffner, *Public Administration* (1946 ed.), Chs. IV–IX, XV, XVII–XXI.

K. H. Porter, *State Administration* (1938).

C. F. Snider, *American State and Local Government* (1950), Chs. X, XII–XVI.

State Government (monthly).

L. D. White, *Introduction to the Study of Public Administration* (1948 ed.).

---

[30] C. E. Merriam, S. D. Parratt, and A. Lepawsky, *The Government of the Metropolitan Region of Chicago* (1933); New York State Constitutional Convention Committee, *New York City Government; Functions and Problems* (1938).

COUNTY ADMINISTRATION

A. W. Bromage, *American County Government* (1933).

Chicago Bureau of Public Efficiency, *The Nineteen Local Governments of Chicago* (1915); *Unification of Local Governments in Chicago* (1917); *Consolidation of Local Governments in Chicago* (1920).

Russell H. Ewing, *County Government and Administration, a Manual and Syllabus* (U. of Denver, 1940).

J. A. Fairlie and C. M. Kneier, *County Government and Administration* (1930).

H. S. Gilbertson, *The County: "The Dark Continent" in American Politics* (1917).

Florence S. Hellman, *County Government in the United States, a List of Recent References* (Lib. of Cong., 1940).

H. G. James, *Local Government in the United States* (1921).

W. Kilpatrick, *Problems in Contemporary County Government* (1930), and *State Supervision of Local Finance* (1940), pamphlet.

L. W. Lancaster, *Government in Rural America* (1937).

T. B. Manny, *Rural Municipalities* (1930).

National Municipal League, *The County Manager Plan,* pamphlet (1950).

National Municipal Review (monthly).

New York Bureau of Muncipal Research, *Report on County Government in Virginia* (1928).

K. H. Porter, *County and Township Government in the United States* (1922).

H. Quick, *A New Kind of County Government* (1925).

J. F. Sly, *Town Government in Massachusetts* (1930).

C. F. Snider and N. F. Garvey, "County and Township Government in 1947," *Am. Pol. Sci. Rev.* XLIII, 53 (Feb., 1949).

State-Local Relations: Report of the Committee on State-Local Relations. Council of State Governments (1946).

Tennessee Valley Authority, *County Government and Administration in the Tennessee Valley States* (1940).

G. A. Works and S. O. Lesser, *Rural America Today* (1942).

CITY ADMINISTRATION

The American City (monthly).

A. W. Bromage, *Introduction to Municipal Government and Administration* (1950).

The City of Des Moines, *The Des Moines Plan of Commission Government* (1939).

E. S. Griffith, *Current Municipal Problems* (1933).

H. G. Hodges, *City Management, Theory and Practice of Municipal Administration* (1939).

C. M. Kneier, *City Government in the United States* (1947 ed.).

A. F. Macdonald, *American City Government and Administration* (1946 ed.).

R. D. McKenzie, *The Metropolitan Community* (1933).

R. L. Mott, *Home Rule for American Cities* (1949).

The Municipal Yearbook.

National Municipal Review (monthly).

New York Bureau of Municipal Research, *City and County of Denver* (1914); *City and County of San Francisco* (1916); *City and County of Philadelphia* (1923).

J. M. Pfiffner, *Municipal Administration* (1940).

T. H. Reed, *Municipal Government in the United States* (1934 ed.).

C. E. Ridley and O. F. Nolting, *The City-Manager Profession* (1934).

Social Science Research Council, *City Manager Government in the United States* (1940).

———, *City Manager Government in Nine Cities* (1940).

———, *City Manager Government in Seven Cities* (1940).

P. Studensky, ed., *The Government of Metropolitan Areas in the United States* (1930).

C. P. Taft, *City Management: The Cincinnati Experiment* (1933).

L. D. White, *The City Manager* (1927).

C. R. Woodruff (ed.), *City Government by Commission* (1911).

H. B. Woolston, *Metropolis: A Study of Urban Communities* (1938).

Harold Zink, *Government of Cities in the United States* (1948 ed.).

Questions and Problems

1. Why is the state administrative structure designed a century ago entirely inadequate for present needs?
2. Write a brief sketch on the development of state administrative agencies.
3. Devise a plan of state administrative organization that will at the same time preserve democratic principles and provide the framework for effective administration.
4. What administrative reorganization has been undertaken in your state? What more is needed?
5. Can it be said that administrative organization is a continuous process?
6. Outline the main features of departmental organization.
7. What functions does your home county perform for the state?
8. How much discretion have your county officers over such matters as education, road construction, and public health?
9. Diagram the structure of your county government. Who is at the head of it?
10. Comment upon this statement: *If the people in every town, or township, or similar unit of local government displayed lively interest in that unit a happy future for the nation would be assured.*
11. What changes have been made in local rural government in your state since 1900? What trends are observable?
12. What types of city charters are permissible in your state?
13. Indicate the extent to which the cities are controlled by the state; the national government.
14. Explain the structure of the conventional type of city government. Do

you find in it any features which a state might use with profit in its own government?

15. Draw up a list of the best features of the commission plan of city government. What are its reputed weaknesses?

16. Diagram the structure of the council-manager type of government. What elements of this system stand out as particularly American?

17. Comment: *If we could find the best type of city government in respect to structure and organization, then we would have the best possible city government.*

☆ 21 ☆

The Civil Service

THE subject of this chapter is government personnel below the high executive and administrative officials, already discussed. Before the Second World War the number of civil employees of the national government ranged around one million. From 1941 to 1945 the number was increased to three million. With the coming of (what we hoped would be) peace and economy drives the number was reduced to about two million. State and local governments employ almost as many persons, not including teachers (see chart below). Although some of these employees hold places of considerable responsibility, the vast majority constitute the privates and noncommissioned officers of the forces of administration. They do the routine work, and they are the government agents with whom the humblest citizen comes into daily contact.

In exploring the government's civil servant problem, we must not lose sight of the servant himself. To express it concretely, we must interest ourselves in our postman: how he got his job, his pay, his chances for promotion, the manner in which he may be disciplined for failure to perform his duty, and his ultimate retirement on an annuity. The personnel problem is very much the same in any unit of government; so that our relatively complete treatment of the national civil service makes unnecessary more than a summary of state and local personnel problems.

I. A BRIEF HISTORY OF THE NATIONAL CIVIL SERVICE [1]

The period of efficiency. Not until 1883 were any serious restrictions placed upon those who appointed our minor federal officers and employees.

[1] C. R. Fish, *The Civil Service and the Patronage* (1905); W. D. Foulke, *Fighting the Spoilsman* (1919); L. Mayers, *The Federal Service* (1922); Chs. I–V; C. E. Merriam and

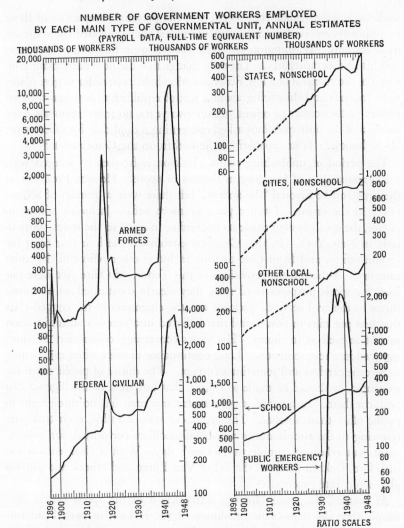

NUMBER OF GOVERNMENT WORKERS EMPLOYED
BY EACH MAIN TYPE OF GOVERNMENTAL UNIT, ANNUAL ESTIMATES
(PAYROLL DATA, FULL-TIME EQUIVALENT NUMBER)

From Solomon Fabricant's *The Rising Trend of Government Employment* (1949), p. 9, by the courtesy of the author and the National Bureau of Economic Research.

From Washington to John Quincy Adams (1829), Presidents and heads of departments usually picked for federal positions the best men available. Washington's appointments were without regard to party, although during his second administration he showed some preference for Federalists. Old

H. F. Gosnell, *The American Party System* (1949 ed.), Chs. X–XIII; W. E. Mosher, J. D. Kingsley and O. G. Stahl, *Public Personnel Administration* (1950 ed.), Chs. 1–3; L. D. White, *Public Administration* (1948 ed.), Chs. XXII–XXIII.

soldiers, however much they might win the personal sympathies of those in authority, received no appointments unless they possessed the requisite qualifications. Washington and John Adams were followed by Jefferson and his Democratic party. The only change that the new party made consisted in the removal of a few Federalist officeholders in order to give places to Democrats and thus bring about a sort of equilibrium between the two parties in the matter of offices. After two years, no more removals were made, and the only questions asked concerning a candidate for office were: "Is he honest? Is he capable? Is he faithful to the Constitution?" [2]

The period of unblushing spoils. Jackson is frequently charged with the responsibility of bringing in the era of spoils. He was President at the time and he favored "the system," but there were a number of accomplices in the crime. Twenty years or more before Jackson's advent to power, the spoils system made its beginning in some of the states, particularly in New York. In 1820 Congress established the four-year term for certain offices, and from time to time included other offices in the same category. Although the provisions of this Tenure of Office Act were not used for spoils purposes until 1829, they clearly constituted an alarming threat to the civil service. Jackson was the champion of the rugged class that had put him in power and that believed in a people's administration in fact as well as in theory. His views concerning offices may be summarized in a few sentences. Long continuance in office often causes men to become careless and sometimes corrupt. The duties of public office are so simple, or should be made so simple, that any man of intelligence can perform them. In a people's government one man has no more right to public office than another. The argument was plausible, even that part referring to the simple duties which officeholders performed, for government was relatively simple in Jackson's day. With a clear conscience, therefore, Jackson accepted the aid of Van Buren and others, and put his philosophy into practice.

At bottom, the reason for the introduction of the spoils system was simply this: the democratic revolution of the Jacksonian period put forward new leaders who, unlike the wellborn gentlemen who for the most part directed our political destinies during the first forty years of our national existence, were usually men of small means. They could not support themselves and give their time unselfishly to politics. They had to make politics pay. Elective offices took care of a few; but the rank and file, the local leaders, found sustenance in the postal service, the revenue service, or in other appointive positions. [3]

[2] Quoted from Jefferson's *Writings* in Fish, *op. cit.*, p. 36.
[3] Fish, *op. cit.*, pp. 156–157.

DECLINE OF THE SERVICE. Under the new system the efficiency of the federal service declined rapidly. Outright corruption was not uncommon. Swartwout, collector of the Port of New York, fled to Spain with over $1,250,000 which belonged to the federal treasury. Nor were "the people" particularly indignant. They smiled, marveled at the thief's boldness, and for years laughingly referred to any official who stole public funds as a "Swartwouter." The spoils system suited the rugged and none too scrupulous individualism of the times. The new Whig party criticized it severely; but when it came into power, it removed Democrats and installed Whigs, following spoils principles in good Jacksonian fashion. In short, the spoils system became an established institution. All Presidents from Jackson to Garfield were either its ardent supporters or its unresisting victims.

The age of reform. As early as 1853 Congress made some attempt to introduce the merit system by ordering the classification of clerks in the departments and by the requirement that only those who passed examinations should be appointed. This law was defective in several ways. It did not put selection on an open competitive basis; but left politicians to name their men, who then secured positions upon passing the examinations. Of course it provided no plan for establishing a roster of eligibles from which administrative authorities could choose the most competent. Furthermore, after the first few years of its existence the law was very indifferently enforced. Another civil service act was passed in 1871, but it was abandoned by President Grant two years later because of his own coolness toward the law and the lack of financial and moral support in Congress. Fortunately there was still some conscience in the land. George William Curtis and other advocates of civil service reform continued their work, with a slowly mounting public sentiment behind them. The assassination of Garfield, in 1881, by a disappointed office seeker gave the reform movement a decided stimulus. Two years later Congress passed the much-needed Pendleton Act, the main features of which are still in force.

THE PENDLETON ACT. Some of the principal provisions of the Pendleton Act are here summarized. (1) Certain groups of civil service employees are classified, that is, brought under the merit system, by the statute, and others may be so classified at the discretion of the President and the heads of departments. Other employees remain unclassified or outside the merit system. (2) Entrance into the classified service is by open, competitive examination, and recommendations from Congressmen "except as to the character or residence of the applicant" are not considered. (3) Preference in employment is to be given to war veterans. (4) Employees are free from assessment for party purposes and denied the privilege of active participation in politics. (5) The Act is carried into effect very largely by the President, acting through a bipartisan Civil Service Commission of three members.

Extension of the merit system. Perhaps the most fundamental provision of the Pendleton Act is the one that authorizes the President to increase the number of offices in the classified list. Only the classified offices are under the merit system, and the system is therefore a farce unless the Presidents generously exercise their powers to enlarge the list. How have they responded to this duty? When the law first went into effect (1883), only 13,924 of the 131,000 federal employees were placed in the classified service. This was a cautious beginning. But every President has added employees to the classified list. For example, Cleveland added the railway mail clerks; Harrison, the clerks and carriers of the free delivery post offices; McKinley, the Philippine service; Theodore Roosevelt, the rural free delivery men and a number of others; Wilson, income-tax employees and others; Hoover, employees of the District of Columbia; Franklin D. Roosevelt, certain employees of the Farm Credit Administration and of various other agencies. But Congress has not left to the Presidents the entire responsibility of extending the merit system. For example, in 1902 it placed the Census Bureau's employees under the system, and in 1927 did the same for those in the Prohibition Bureau.

For many years the "most prized prerogative" of each majority member of the House of Representatives was the right to name the first, second, and third class postmasters in his district. (Fourth class—rural—postmasters had been under the merit system since Taft's Administration.) Wilson gave congressmen a jolt by an order to the Civil Service Commission to hold an examination whenever a vacancy occurred in one of the three classes. Somewhat heroically the President named, for the four-year statutory term, the man who passed the best examination. With the change of administrations Wilson's order was practically nullified. In July, 1936, President Roosevelt issued an executive order making future postmasters subject to merit selection. But an act of Congress was required to abolish the four-year term. Backed by the prestige of his great victory in November and by the recommendations of his Committee on Administrative Management, the President achieved partial victory in the Ramspeck-O'Mahoney Postmaster Act (1938). By this legislation the first, second, and third class postmasters, nearly 15,000 of them, were placed under the classified service. The idea of abolishing senatorial confirmation, however, and the spoils that is bound to go with it, was too painful for congressmen to contemplate. Although the adoption of this limited merit system for the selection of postmasters has prevented the appointment of unqualified persons, it has not broken the virtual monopoly on such offices held by the majority party. Members of the minority party commonly believe that it is useless for them to compete in the examinations as long as the appointments are subject to senatorial confirmation. Authorities on the civil service in general and the Hoover Commission in particular recommend the abolishment of confirmation of postmasters by the Senate.[4]

In 1938 President Roosevelt extended the competitive service to all employees for whom the statutes authorized him to make such requirement. This brought about 45,000 more employees under the merit system. The number would have been practically doubled had not Congress excluded positions under the Works Projects Administration. The President, in the face of this and other anti-merit system action on the part of Congress continued to urge Congress to give him authority to place nearly all other federal employees under that system. In November, 1940, Congress, with "agony and groans," passed the Ramspeck Act, a measure of more promise for the merit system than any enacted since the passage of the original civil service act. It authorized the President to place within the classified service nearly all the federal employees, and provided that incumbents of 1940 should retain their positions, if they had served satisfactorily for six months and if they could pass a noncompetitive qualifying test. The President was not slow to begin the exercise of this authority, and the percentage of federal employees under the merit system soon reached an all-time high. About 93 per cent now hold this status.

But the spoilsmen die hard. The reformers have had to fight for the merit system every foot of the way; often they have had to retake lost ground. In times of emergency standards must be lowered somewhat, and that need is used as an excuse for a rush to the spoils system. During the First World War and immediately thereafter there was a lowering of standards and an increase in the number of "exempt" positions. The situation was even worse when the New Deal set up its many agencies to deal with the great depression. The recent demand for federal employees for war positions caused another setback, although it was milder than many observers were expecting. In any event, those who would improve the status and quality of public employees must fight continuously.

The good work started under President Arthur was partly undone by President Cleveland, who was hard pressed by Democrats whose appetites had been whetted by seeing the Republicans eat at the public crib for twenty-five years. When the Republicans came back into power, Cleveland's extensions of the merit system were partially set aside in order to make room for the faithful. The moral fervor that in part characterized the Democratic victory in 1912 did not deter President Wilson from yielding to the importunities of his followers, who had experienced six-

---

[4] Report on *The Post Office*, p. 10.

teen lean years. Flushing with triumph, in 1921 the Republican President and his advisers, starting the country on the road to "normalcy," had few qualms of conscience and followed hoary precedent when they removed some Democrats "for the good of the service." Why do Presidents backslide? It is because there are still many people who do not believe in the merit system. They are not often so outspoken in their opposition as its enemies of the 'seventies and 'eighties, who ridiculed "snivel" service reform and labeled it the "Chinese system"; but considerable opposition and a great deal of indifference remain—opposition on the part of politicians, and indifference on the part of the public.

In 1914 William Jennings Bryan, while Secretary of State, asked the Receiver-General of Customs at Santo Domingo to let him know what positions he had for "deserving Democrats." Speaking of the first Wilson administration, Vice President Marshall said his only regret was that they could not displace more Republicans and give their jobs to Democrats. Harding's Assistant Postmaster General, John M. Bartlett, regretted that offices which paid as high as $5,000 should be in the classified service. "What's wrong with the spoils system?" shouted a congressman from Oklahoma on the floor of the House in 1937. "America has grown great on spoils," he declared. "I can do a better job of picking the postmasters for my district than any Civil Service Commissioner." [5] It is a matter of regret that the Member spoke the sentiments of a large number of his colleagues.

Why the merit system anyway? The reader might raise the question, "Why, after all, should we be so insistent about the merit system? Why shouldn't the winning party have the offices?" The victorious party should have the political offices, the few offices in which policies are formulated, for, otherwise, the party would have some difficulty in carrying out the program it submitted to the people during the campaign. But the great majority of the offices, perhaps ninety-nine per cent of them, are nonpolitical. These should be under the merit system for the following reasons. (1) The merit system removes the demoralizing influence in the service that the partisan scuffle for office causes. (2) It very largely prevents the assessment of officeholders for political purposes. (3) It requires of the civil servants loyalty to the government rather than loyalty to a party. (4) It gives the employees security of tenure, without which no technical or professional officer can do his best work. (5) It elevates the civil service to a profession. (6) It makes possible a high degree of specialization within the service—an indispensable achievement if the government is to carry out the many technical duties it now assumes. No doubt other claims could be made for the merit system, but these will suf-

[5] *Time*, February 8, 1937.

fice. The President's Committee on Administrative Management recommended (1937) that all officers be selected and retained on the merit basis, excepting only those called to the highest positions and who have policies to determine. President Roosevelt's program of extending the merit system was, of course, based largely upon this recommendation.[6]

II. THE OPERATION OF THE NATIONAL CIVIL SERVICE LAWS[7]

The Civil Service Commission. As already mentioned, the Act of 1883 provided for a bipartisan Civil Service Commission of three persons, to be appointed by the President and Senate. Some very able men have served on this Commission. Theodore Roosevelt was a member from 1889 to 1895, and Professor Leonard D. White, one of the country's leading authorities on public administration, served from 1934 to 1937. Several times the Commission has passed through the fire of congressional investigation, and each investigation seems to have added to its good reputation. Acting under the original civil service law and other statutes and functioning under the general direction of the President, the Commission provides for open competitive examinations and certifies those who have passed with the highest grades to the appointing officers; administers statutory provisions and civil service regulations on the political activity of federal classified employees and certain state and local employees participating in federally financed activities; maintains service records and qualifications records of all federal employees; conducts investigations relating to the civil service; provides a system of promotion; establishes, in cooperation with other government agencies, training courses for federal employees; and administers the Classification Act of 1949, the Veterans Preference Act of 1944, and the Civil Service Retirement Act. These functions the Commission discharges through eleven divisions and several other units. For convenience in meeting the employment needs of federal administrative agencies scattered throughout the United States, the nation is divided into fourteen civil service regions, each with headquarters in some principal city. Under the supervision of the regional offices are approximately 5,000 local boards of examiners. From 1941 to 1945, much of the effort of the Commission and these district offices was directed to meeting the unprecedented needs of the government for employees in numerous war agencies.

[6] *Report*, p. 9.

[7] *Annual Reports of the U.S. Civil Service Commission;* (Hoover) Commission on Organization of the Executive Branch of the Government, *Personnel Management* (1949); Herman Finer, "The Hoover Commission Reports," II, *Pol. Sci. Qt.,* LXIV (1949), 584 ff.; Mayers, *op. cit.,* Chs. VI–XVI; Mosher, Kingsley, and Stahl, *op. cit.;* F. W. Reeves, "Civil Service as Usual," *Pub. Adm. Rev.,* IV, 327 (Autumn, 1944); F. W. Reeves and P. T. David, *Personnel Administration in the Federal Government* (1937); White, *op. cit.,* Chs. XXII–XXXI.

Variety of civil service examinations. There is no such thing as *the* civil service examination. Different work calls for different qualifications, and there are as many different examinations as there are different positions to be filled. The idea that the average person has, of a single civil service clerical examination that most high school graduates could pass, is all wrong. Of course, there are many examinations for clerkships paying from, say, $2,400 to $3,500 a year; but there are thousands of positions requiring the highest training and paying $6,000, $7,000, $9,000, or even more. Looking through the list of civil service "offerings," we find that our government wants, among many other experts, poultry geneticists; several grades of guidance and placement officers; senior olericulturists; assistant and associate fisheries economists; assistant pomologists; experts in social service administration; varying grades of home economics specialists; sugar beet pathologists; radio engineers, from assistants to seniors; toxicologists; research assistants for the Civil Service Commission; educationists; and principal agronomists for wheat investigations. Applicants for positions of the type mentioned are given "unassembled" examinations, which are explained below.

The civil service has places also, with appropriate salaries, for elevator conductors, elevator mechanics, antinarcotic agents, woodworker helpers, junior foresters and range examiners, junior mathematicians, assistant accountants, junior observers in meteorology, assistant inspectors for radio enforcement, radio operators, reservation protectors of mammals and birds, dairymen, junior microanalysts, computers, stenographers, and typists, to mention only a few. Positions of these and similar classes are filled from the list of applicants who pass "assembled" examinations, presently to be explained. If the student is unfamiliar with some of the titles named above, he is in the same class as the writer; but the random selection nevertheless gives us some idea of the more than 1,700 varieties of civil service examinations. From 1933 to 1940 the annual average number of applicants examined was well over a half million, and the number has been much higher since the latter date.

"Unassembled" and "assembled" examinations. Applicants for the higher class positions in the civil service are not usually required to report at any place for examination. Hence, the term "unassembled" is applied to such examinations. Competitors for the kinds of positions just mentioned really take no examination at all; but they must forward material showing their qualifications to the Civil Service Commission, where it is passed upon by designated officers. Thus, a man who wishes to qualify for the position of associate fisheries economist must show that he is a college graduate; that he has had experience in matters related to fisheries; and must submit a thesis or publication on the subject. With all the

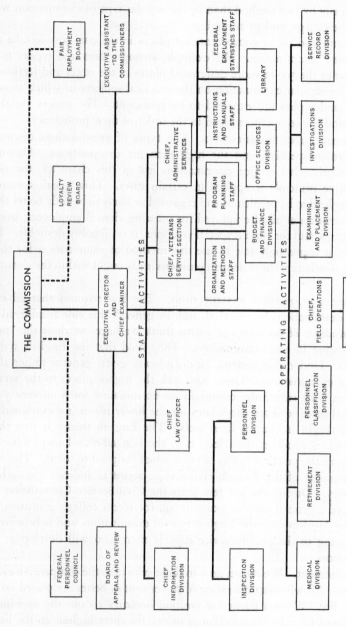

UNITED STATES CIVIL SERVICE COMMISSION

THE COMMISSION

FAIR EMPLOYMENT BOARD

EXECUTIVE ASSISTANT TO THE COMMISSIONERS

LOYALTY REVIEW BOARD

FEDERAL PERSONNEL COUNCIL

BOARD OF APPEALS AND REVIEW

EXECUTIVE DIRECTOR AND CHIEF EXAMINER

STAFF ACTIVITIES

CHIEF, ADMINISTRATIVE SERVICES

CHIEF, VETERANS SERVICE SECTION

CHIEF LAW OFFICER

CHIEF INFORMATION DIVISION

FEDERAL EMPLOYMENT STATISTICS STAFF

INSTRUCTIONS AND MANUALS STAFF

PROGRAM PLANNING STAFF

ORGANIZATION AND METHODS STAFF

LIBRARY

OFFICE SERVICES DIVISION

BUDGET AND FINANCE DIVISION

PERSONNEL DIVISION

RETIREMENT DIVISION

INSPECTION DIVISION

MEDICAL DIVISION

OPERATING ACTIVITIES

INVESTIGATIONS DIVISION

EXAMINING AND PLACEMENT DIVISION

CHIEF, FIELD OPERATIONS

PERSONNEL CLASSIFICATION DIVISION

SERVICE RECORD DIVISION

14 REGIONAL OFFICES

From U.S. Government Organization Manual, 1949, p. 609.

629

relevant facts before the examining committee, he can be graded more satisfactorily by this method than by the regular type of examination with which the college student is familiar.

The rank and file of competitors for places in the civil service take the "assembled" examination. For example, stenographers and typists must go to one of the 500 or more designated places in the states and territories and take a regular examination on the practical subjects in which stenographers and typists are expected to be proficient. The papers are then graded and the competitors listed in the order of their proficiency.

NONCOMPETITIVE EXAMINATIONS. The types of examinations discussed above are competitive, and the high men get the positions. Although nearly all the civil service examinations are of this character, the noncompetitive principle is applied in certain cases. This "pass" system is generally held to be pernicious and regarded as likely to be little better than no examination at all, if employed for securing clerical employees; but in special cases, and for certain special positions, it is probably desirable. For example, it seems only fair to use this method of examination for those holding positions at the time such positions are brought within the classified service.

PRACTICAL VS. GENERAL EXAMINATIONS. The law requires that all civil service examinations be practical, and, in general, this rule is adhered to. Many students of personnel problems think we have overdone the "practical" feature in our examinations. They hold that the English system is better. Under that system, candidates are given general rather than practical examinations. Those who seek the higher places in the service are given what constitutes essentially an examination for a university degree, and those who are candidates for the lower places are examined on subjects taught in the public schools. The English theory is that these examinations result in the selection of the best all-round men, who can easily learn the practical duties of office when assigned to them. The very high character of the English civil service seems to indicate strength in the theory. During the last few years the Civil Service Commission has developed a general-purpose examination for recent college graduates. It has some kinship with the English type of examination, and is believed to be bringing to the public service capable men who will develop as administrators.

Appointment. We return now to those who take the competitive examinations. All who obtain a rating of 70 per cent or better are placed on the eligible list. When a particular position becomes vacant, the appointing officer must fill it by the selection of one of the three highest on the list of eligibles for that position. The department head or other high administrative officer who makes the appointment is allowed to choose one of three, in order that he may consider personality and special qualifications in making the selection. Even though this discretion may at times be abused, it is undoubtedly used to good advantage by conscientious officials.

A civil service rule requires that "as nearly as the conditions of good administration will warrant" the appointments shall be made among the states and territories upon the basis of population. Very close adherence to this rule has, however, not been possible. Some states do not furnish their quotas of eligibles, and some, particularly the North Atlantic states, furnish an excess. Furthermore, fair apportionment is difficult if not impossible to maintain, owing to the fact that veterans and their wives or widows are appointed without regard to apportionment principles, although such apportionments are charged to the state quotas.

VETERAN PREFERENCE. Our civil service has long followed the practice of making concessions to war veterans. The ex-service men of the First World War were thus able to gain about one fourth of the appointments in the civil service. Recent legislation is designed to continue this favored status for the former soldiers and sailors of the Second World War. The Veterans Preference Act of 1944 contains the following significant provisions: (1) veterans are to be exclusively employed in a number of minor civil service positions; (2) five points are to be added to the earned examination ratings of all honorably discharged ex-service men and women; (3) ten points are to be added to the examination rating of candidates having service-connected disabilities, wives of disabled ex-service men, unmarried widows of ex-service men and (by an act of January 19, 1948) widowed, divorced, and separated mothers of ex-service men and women who died in the service or were totally and permanently disabled; (4) persons entitled to veterans preference under "(3)" are to be placed at the *top* of the appropriate lists of eligibles, except on the registers of professional or scientific positions paying more than $3,000 a year. Soon after the end of the Second World War veterans entered the Civil Service at the rate of thousands a week, and the Civil Service Commission almost leaned over backwards to extend to them their privileges under the law.[8] Nearly half of the federal employees now have veteran status.[9]

Is VETERAN PREFERENCE FAIR TO THE SERVICE? There is no reason why the veterans should not have some of the privileges mentioned. But, should ablebodied veterans be given five extra points, and should disabled veterans, wives of incapacitated veterans, veterans' widows, and widowed mothers of deceased veterans be given ten extra points and, in addition, be placed at the top of the list of eligibles, regardless of their ratings? The basis for the civil service is merit—the appointment of candidates best qualified for

[8] *Report of the Civil Service Commission*, 1945, pp. 13–29.
[9] *Ibid.*, 1948, p. 62.

the positions. Having regard to the purpose of the merit system, to answer in the affirmative the question just raised, one must argue somewhat as follows: "Ablebodied veterans are five points more competent to fill civil service positions than are nonveterans possessing the same qualifications. Disabled veterans, their wives and widows, and their widowed mothers are ten points more competent than nonveterans, and five points more competent than physically fit veterans. Not only that, but those in the '10-point' class are so competent that they must be appointed before any other eligibles may be selected." This "argument" is absurd. Veterans preference does not rest upon the merit system, but it is based upon the theory that the government should take proper care of the veterans. This theory is not disputed; but many students of public personnel problems maintain that the government already discharges its obligations through other means, such as pensions, hospital privileges, rehabilitation, and the like. The Hoover Commission recommended a significant modification in the present practice. Under the Commission's plan all applicants would be grouped into such categories as "outstanding," "well qualified," "qualified," and "unqualified"; and candidates in each class with veteran status would simply be listed ahead of nonveterans.[10] To date no action has been taken on this recommendation.

Salaries and classification. Salaries in the civil service may not be characterized as either low or high. Office boys, stenographers, typists, clerks, guards, and persons in related categories are somewhat better paid than are their friends holding similar positions in private employment. But federal employees who hold the managerial and professional positions must look with envy at the salaries (if they are salary conscious) or other income received by persons in comparable positions in industry and elsewhere. Salary adjustments provided between 1940 and 1948 continued and increased the advantage of federal employees in the lower positions over those in the higher places, increases of from 43 to 56 per cent being voted to employees in the lowest pay grades, whereas those in the highest grade received only a 15 per cent increase. The increases provided in the Classification Act of 1949, somewhat as recommended by the Hoover Commission, were substantial, even for the higher grades, but bureau chiefs, heads of divisions, doctors, lawyers, and scientists are still not so well paid as they would be in private life. The higher degree of security and permanence one enjoys in the public service over that in private employment may be some justification for the lower compensation in the former, but the fact remains that it is most difficult for the Government to retain in the service some of the best men because of the competition from industry, banks, and other private enterprises.

[10] Report on *Personnel Management*, pp. 18–19.

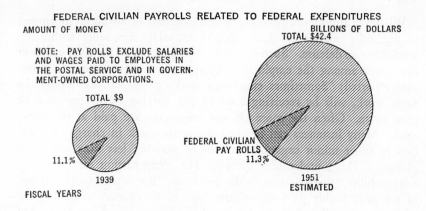

FEDERAL CIVILIAN PAYROLLS RELATED TO FEDERAL EXPENDITURES

AMOUNT OF MONEY

BILLIONS OF DOLLARS
TOTAL $42.4

NOTE: PAY ROLLS EXCLUDE SALARIES
AND WAGES PAID TO EMPLOYEES IN
THE POSTAL SERVICE AND IN GOVERN-
MENT-OWNED CORPORATIONS.

TOTAL $9

11.1%

1939

FISCAL YEARS

FEDERAL CIVILIAN
PAY ROLLS
11.3%

1951
ESTIMATED

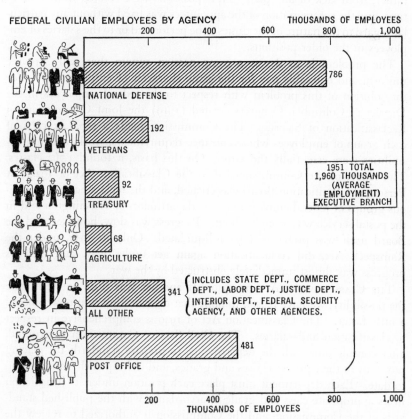

FEDERAL CIVILIAN EMPLOYEES BY AGENCY   THOUSANDS OF EMPLOYEES

                    200   400   600   800   1,000

NATIONAL DEFENSE   786

VETERANS   192

TREASURY   92

AGRICULTURE   68

ALL OTHER   341 { INCLUDES STATE DEPT., COMMERCE
                          DEPT., LABOR DEPT., JUSTICE DEPT.,
                          INTERIOR DEPT., FEDERAL SECURITY
                          AGENCY, AND OTHER AGENCIES.

POST OFFICE   481

1951 TOTAL
1,960 THOUSANDS
(AVERAGE
EMPLOYMENT)
EXECUTIVE BRANCH

                    200   400   600   800   1,000
                    THOUSANDS OF EMPLOYEES

From Bureau of the Budget, *The Federal Budget in Brief,* Fiscal Year 1951, p. 39.

Whatever arguments, plausible or specious, may be advanced in support of niggardly salaries for public employees, salary inequality within the service has no defense. Such inequality was long one of the chief causes of discontent among the employees. In 1920 the Reclassification Commission reported: "Sometimes employees working side by side, doing the same work, will be receiving rates of pay varying by 50 per cent, or even more. Often the more efficient employees are paid at the lower rates. Many instances can be cited where the clerk in charge of a section or other minor organization unit is receiving less than other employees working under his direction. His compensation for the added responsibility," the report ironically continues, "lies in the fact that if one of his more highly paid subordinates resigns his chances of getting the vacancy are excellent." [11] Such inequalities did not arise from design, but rather, from lack of any plan. New positions were created from time to time, and the compensation of the appointees was fixed without any particular regard to the nature of the duties to be performed or to the salaries of employees in the older positions.

The problem is to devise a compensation system that will "provide uniform and equitable pay for the same character of employment." For the solution of this problem with respect to the federal employees in the District of Columbia, Congress created (1919) the Joint Commission on Reclassification of Salaries. The Commission made a separate class of each group of employees whose entrance requirements, work, and responsibilities were essentially the same. On this basis, it found 1,762 classes. The report of the Commission led to the Classification Act of 1923. A Personnel Classification Board was created, and the reclassification of various groups of federal employees in the departments at Washington and in the postal service was brought about. Progress was slow, however, and the Board itself was presently (1932) liquidated. Only in 1940, under the Ramspeck Act, did reclassification again get under way, and then its progress was almost immediately obstructed by the war.

THE CLASSIFICATION ACT OF 1949. If another war does not terminate the possibility, we have reason to hope that classification will now proceed a little faster. The Classification Act of 1949 is comprehensive in respect to classification and salaries. The Civil Service Commission is required, after consultation with the departments, to prepare standards for placing positions in their proper classes and grades, and to keep such standards up to date. Each department must place each position under its jurisdiction in its appropriate class and grade in accordance with the published standards of the Commission, and the Commission is authorized to review the

---

[11] Quoted in Mayers, *op. cit.*, pp. 190–191.

classification of positions in the departments in order to determine whether the standards are being observed.

The act of 1949 fixes compensation rates for a General Schedule (GS) that includes professional and scientific service, the clerical, administrative, fiscal and subprofessional service; and a Crafts, Protective, and Custodial Schedule (CPC) that includes the types of employees indicated. Grades in the GS run from 1 to 18, from positions the duties of which consist of the simplest routine or elementary work to those the duties of which are of the widest scope and complexity and require originality, planning ability, a thorough knowledge of administrative problems and techniques, or other exceptional qualities. The act limits to 25 the number of positions in Grade GS–18. Grades in the CPC run from 1 to 10, from errand boys and parcel checkers to supervisors of maintenance personnel. A look at the accompanying chart of grades and salaries will be helpful.

COMPENSATION FOR THE GENERAL SCHEDULE *

Grade	Per annum rates						
GS-1	$2,200	$2,280	$2,360	$2,440	$2,520	$2,600	$2,680
GS-2	$2,450	$2,530	$2,610	$2,690	$2,770	$2,850	$2,930
GS-3	$2,650	$2,730	$2,810	$2,890	$2,970	$3,050	$3,130
GS-4	$2,875	$2,955	$3,035	$3,115	$3,195	$3,275	$3,355
GS-5	$3,100	$3,225	$3,350	$3,475	$3,600	$3,725	$3,850
GS-6	$3,450	$3,575	$3,700	$3,825	$3,950	$4,075	$4,200
GS-7	$3,825	$3,950	$4,075	$4,200	$4,325	$4,450	$4,575
GS-8	$4,200	$4,325	$4,450	$4,575	$4,700	$4,825	$4,950
GS-9	$4,600	$4,725	$4,850	$4,975	$5,100	$5,225	$5,350
GS-10	$5,000	$5,125	$5,250	$5,375	$5,500	$5,625	$5,750
GS-11	$5,400	$5,600	$5,800	$6,000	$6,200	$6,400	
GS-12	$6,400	$6,600	$6,800	$7,000	$7,200	$7,400	
GS-13	$7,600	$7,800	$8,000	$8,200	$8,400	$8,600	
GS-14	$8,800	$9,000	$9,200	$9,400	$9,600	$9,800	
GS-15	$10,000	$10,250	$10,500	$10,750	$11,000		
GS-16	$11,200	$11,400	$11,600	$11,800	$12,000		
GS-17	$12,200	$12,400	$12,600	$12,800	$13,000		
GS-18	$14,000						

COMPENSATION FOR THE CRAFTS, PROTECTIVE, AND CUSTODIAL SCHEDULE *

Grade	Per annum rates						
CPS-1	$1,510	$1,570	$1,630	$1,690	$1,750	$1,810	$1,870
CPC-2	$2,120	$2,190	$2,260	$2,330	$2,400	$2,470	$2,540
CPC-3	$2,252	$2,332	$2,412	$2,492	$2,572	$2,652	$2,732
CPC-4	$2,420	$2,530	$2,610	$2,690	$2,770	$2,850	$2,930
CPC-5	$2,674	$2,754	$2,834	$2,914	$2,994	$3,074	$3,154
CPC-6	$2,900	$2,980	$3,060	$3,140	$3,220	$3,300	$3,380
CPC-7	$3,125	$3,225	$3,325	$3,425	$3,525	$3,625	$3,725
CPC-8	$3,400	$3,525	$3,650	$3,775	$3,900	$4,025	$4,150
CPC-9	$3,775	$3,900	$4,025	$4,150	$4,275	$4,400	$4,525
CPC-10	$4,150	$4,275	$4,400	$4,525	$4,650	$4,775	$4,900

* As provided by the Classification Act of 1949, sec. 601.

Promotion. Under the merit system the new employee is on probation for six months. If he serves satisfactorily through this period, he becomes a regular member of the great body of civil servants; and, if he is a normal human being, he hopes to receive promotions from time to time. His chances are not so good in some branches of the federal service as they are in private business because relatively few men are needed in the higher positions and because too many of these positions are filled by political appointment rather than by promotion of "career" men. The Civil Service Commission has done very little about promotions, leaving that important phase of personnel administration very largely to the appointing officers in the departments.

THE QUESTION OF OPEN OR CLOSED SERVICES. Congress has by statute required that the higher places in certain branches of the service, for example, in the medical corps of the Public Health Service, be filled by promotion from the lower positions. In some other administrative units the appointing officers, of their own volition, have followed the system of filling the upper grades by promotion from within the service rather than by recruitment from without. This is a tradition in the postal service. All the 500,000 postal employees, except the chief officers in the Department at Washington and the first-, second-, and third-class postmasters,[12] enter the service as clerks or carriers. From this humble beginning, a clerk or carrier with the requisite qualifications may be promoted by successive stages until he becomes postmaster of a large city, division superintendent of railway mail, or receives some other responsible position. In 1947 President Truman won the applause of students of public personnel and others when he named as Postmaster General Jesse M. Donaldson, who had worked his way up from the bottom of the ladder. Many positions in the federal service above the lowest grade must be or may be filled by recruitment. Such positions are said to be "open," as distinguished from the places filled by promotion, which are designated as "closed."

Authorities on personnel generally favor the closed system, on the grounds that it offers strong inducement to competent and ambitious persons to enter the service at an early age, increases the opportunity for advancement, and improves the morale of the employees. Few will deny, however, that the open system often makes possible better selections for special and important positions; and a rigid use of the closed system in all lines of the civil service is seldom advocated. We somewhat cautiously conclude, then, that promotion is the more desirable method of filling positions above the lower grade if training for the higher positions can be readily acquired by experience in the service, and that recruitment from

[12] Although now within the classified service postmasterships may still be filled by recruitment.

the outside is advisable if the positions require broad general education or special technical training.[13]

THE BASIS OF PROMOTION. One of the most perplexing questions in the field of personnel administration, is that of the method of selection for promotion. In some of the smaller organizations, the administrative officer has sufficient contact with his force to know who should be promoted. But even in those cases, some formal method of selection is usually recommended. Such a method furnishes the officer responsible for promotions with a fairly high degree of protection from pressure, and gives the rank and file of employees the feeling that they are receiving fair treatment in the matter of advancement—a most important factor in keeping up the morale of the service.

Higher administrative officials, department heads and others, make the promotions, but they are supposed to be guided by the principle of seniority, examinations, and efficiency records. Employees are likely to prefer the rule of seniority, and students of public administration and officers responsible for promotions favor examinations or efficiency records or both. Promotion examinations have been long required (and often evaded) in the federal service. Efficiency records have also been used, several kinds, and without any convincing proof that they are the answer to the promotion question. Keeping adequate efficiency records is difficult and a chore likely to be neglected. The Hoover Commission found that the efficiency rating system was too complicated, and the Commission also criticized its use as a basis for both rewards and penalties. It would substitute for efficiency rating "ability and service record" ratings, a substitution that might not prove to be any particular improvement over the efficiency rating.[14] In concluding their discussion on the problem of promotion Mosher, Kingsley, and Stahl express the conviction that the relative value of competitive examinations, service records, and seniority as bases for promotion are much less vital to good administration than the judicious use of such methods in combination. These authorities also emphasize the point that every appointing officer in the service should have a whole philosophy of promotion—have it permeate his thinking and his belief—and should know that promotion is an essential phase of filling positions with capable persons and is a significant instrument for maintaining morale.[15]

Discipline and removal. In any business organization the maintenance of effective forms of discipline and removal is most important; otherwise

---

[13] On this topic, see Mayers, *op. cit.*, Ch. VIII; Mosher, Kingsley, and Stahl, *op. cit.*, Chs. 7 and 14; and White, *op. cit.*, Ch. XXVII.

[14] Report on *The Post Office*, pp. 5, 33.

[15] Mosher, Kingsley, and Stahl, *op. cit.*, p. 184.

a satisfactory standard of service from all employees cannot be secured. Private business ordinarily has no difficulty in applying rather drastic and summary disciplinary principles, but governments are often charged, perhaps thoughtlessly, with "going easy" with their employees. Public employees may often have influence with some legislator or other official, and, to avoid difficulty, disciplinary officers occasionally put up with an employee who is far below the standard. Then too, since the element of profit is absent from the public service, one of the strong incentives for weeding out those who function at a loss is absent. Also, the civil service officer who has immediate supervision of an employee usually lacks the authority to remove him, that form of execution being reserved for the department head or some other high official. The higher officers of the federal service do have adequate powers of discipline and removal, but, for the reasons just given, the powers are perhaps not so freely exercised as they should be. Too often, administrators seem to transfer to other agencies employees who should be removed.[16]

What are the legal requirements respecting removals? A federal statute of 1912, which has served as a model in a number of states and cities, provides that no person in the classified service shall be removed "except for such cause as will promote the efficiency of said service"; that the reasons for a removal must be given in writing to the person whose removal is sought; that such person shall be given time to answer these reasons in writing; "but no examination of witnesses nor any trial or hearing shall be required except in the discretion of the officer making the removal." The act also provides that "in making removals or reductions, and in other punishments, like penalties shall be imposed for like offenses, and no discrimination shall be exercised for political or religious reasons." [17] Public Law 623 of 1948 provides back pay for employees whose removal or suspension is found upon appeal to be unwarranted. The original Civil Service Act forbids any officer or employee of the United States mentioned in the act to "discharge or promote, or degrade, or in any manner change the official rank or compensation of any other officer or employee, or promise or threaten so to do, for giving or withholding or neglecting to make any contribution of money or other valuable for any political purpose."

Manifestly, the power of administrative officers to make removals is not seriously restricted by laws and rules. But conscience and the traditions of the service are usually, although not always, sufficient to protect employees from unjust removal. Removals and other forms of disciplinary action are relatively few in number, the employee usually receiving the benefit of any doubt.

[16] John Fisher, "Let's Go Back to the Spoils System," *Harper's,* Oct., 1945, p. 362.
[17] 37 Stat. 555, sec. 13.

Prohibition of partisan activity. Various efforts are made to protect those under the merit system from political pressure on the one hand, and to restrain them from voluntary partisan activity, on the other. The Civil Service Act prohibits any officer of the United States, except the President, from soliciting or receiving a contribution from any other officer or employee for a political purpose. The Civil Service Commission is authorized to investigate violations of this provision, and it has shown considerable energy in exercising this power. The act further states that no person in the public service is for that reason under any obligation to render any political service, and that no person in the service has any right to coerce the political action of any other person. Although no penalties are prescribed for the violation of this provision, it is generally believed that it is fairly well observed.[18] The federal employee does not enjoy full protection from political pressure, however. Persons not holding any office may solicit him anywhere except at the place of his employment. It requires no stretch of the imagination to realize that a non-officeholder active in politics may, almost as easily as an official superior, coerce an employee. The law should, therefore, be broadened to prohibit solicitation by any person.

May an employee of his own free will engage in partisan activities? Rule I of the civil service regulations states that he retains the right to vote and to express privately his opinions on all political subjects, but that he shall take no active part in political management or political campaigns. In practice, this rule means that an employee may do such things as attend party meetings and vote in the same, if he takes no active part; hold membership, but not office, in political clubs; and make party contributions through any person not employed by the United States. The rule is interpreted to prohibit him from doing such things as serving as a delegate to a convention, offering himself as a candidate for office, distributing campaign literature, transporting voters to and from the polls, and betting upon the results of elections. Those in the competitive classified civil service are thus rather severely limited with respect to political conduct—some say to the point where they cannot exercise their rights as citizens. But as long as so many superior administrative officers hold their positions as political appointees, it is doubtful if the rank and file of the employees responsible to them could find adequate protection from political coercion but for this rule. We have, then, an interesting case of a rule apparently designed to curb the partisan activities of the general run of employees, but that serves the much more useful purpose of protecting them from the partisan influence of their superiors.

THE HATCH ACTS. The Hatch Acts of 1939 and 1940 were explained

18 Mayers, *op. cit.,* p. 158.

in part in Chapter 10, section VII, but a paragraph on their prohibitions regarding partisan activity in the civil service is necessary here. The first of these acts was designed to curb the political activity of unclassified (these had been the worst offenders) as well as classified civil servants. With the exception of a few score high officials, all civil servants are prohibited from engaging in "pernicious political activities." The law does not, however, apply to unclassified employees with the same severity with which it applies to those who are classified, the former still having the "privilege" of being solicited for campaign funds and the right to express publicly (classified employees only privately) their opinions, providing such public utterance does not constitute a part of an organized campaign. The act of 1940 forbids any person employed by a state or local government, in a service financed wholly or principally by the federal government, to participate in party management and political campaigns, to solicit party funds, and otherwise to engage in political activities.

The Civil Service Commission carries a large part of the difficult assignment of enforcing these acts. If classified employees of the federal service violate the first Hatch Act, the Commission sees to it that they are removed from office; if unclassified employees violate it, the Commission reports to the federal agencies to which such employees are assigned, and the agencies are supposed to make the removals. In the case of the second Hatch Act, federal agencies having charge of disbursements to state and local agencies report all violations to the Commission, and the Commission may make investigations of its own. A state or local government, upon being informed of the delinquency of an employee, must remove him; and if it does not do so, the federal agency through which the funds are supplied for the project on which he is employed withholds a sum of money double the culprit's salary. Such laws do not mark the beginning of a millennium of politically clean public employees. They rather mark another, and belated, attempt to remove some of the worst features of politics from administration.[19]

THE LOYALTY PROGRAM. If civil servants may be dropped from the rolls for positive and aggressive action that characterizes a good party worker, persons who are disloyal to the United States most certainly should be excluded from public employment. We used to think that character was enough; that it included loyalty. It is not necessarily so. In this day in which totalitarian ideologies compete with democratic concepts, an individual who might meet the ordinary test of character may have affiliations and plans incompatible with loyalty to his country. Since about 1940, statutes and independent executive policy have called for the exclusion from public employment of Communists, Fascists, and Nazis. Until 1947 this

[19] For a critical analysis of the Hatch Act see Leon D. Epstein, "Political Sterilization of Civil Servants: U.S. and Great Britain," *Pub. Adm. Rev.*, X (Autumn, 1950), 281–290.

particular type of security consisted chiefly of pre-employment investigations that resulted in weeding from the list of eligibles those whose loyalty was a matter of "reasonable doubt."

But our concern to keep the Atomic "secret" and our general state of jitters, as best exemplified by the activities of the Dies Committee on Un-American Activities, led to an order for an intensive check on all employees.[20] They were fingerprinted and checked against FBI files. Employees were given certain safeguards against arbitrary removal. These included the right to a hearing before a loyalty board of the department or agency in which he was employed and the right of appeal to the Loyalty Review Board, a sort of "loyalty supreme court" established by the Civil Service Commission. This Review Board was composed of distinguished private citizens, and it early declared that it would not consider disloyal the "advocacy of change in the form of government or the economic system of the United States, or both, however far-reaching such change may be," unless that advocacy also included the use of unconstitutional means to bring about the change. The Review Board's powers were only advisory to department heads, but the Board's anti-witch hunting policy seems to have met with the approval of all officers responsible for removals. Only a few hundred employees have been removed or have resigned under investigation. Yet the standard for refusal of employment and making removals—"that, on all the evidence, reasonable grounds exist for belief that the person involved is disloyal"—is subject to various interpretations and could be used arbitrarily. We should always bear in mind that tyrants and dictators have made much of loyalty, valuing it more than any other good quality in a citizen, even to the practical exclusion of every other quality.

Professor Emeritus Charles E. Merriam, a member of the Loyalty Review Board (but not speaking as a member), suggests a positive approach to the promotion of loyalty among government employees. He would give closer attention to their compensation and their working and living conditions; give them broader opportunities through in-service training to improve their competence and enrich their lives; and halt the "stream of bitter, smearing attacks upon public servants and service. Bureaucrats, barnacles, taxeaters, loafers—these terms constantly applied to public servants do not tend to improve the morale of the workers or to promote attachment to the government they serve. To say that 'the best public servant is the worst' comes close to the line of disloyalty." [21]

---

[20] Executive Order 9835, March 22, 1947.

[21] "Some Aspects of Loyalty," *Pub. Adm. Rev.*, VIII (1948), 83–84. Senator Joseph R. McCarthy's particularly sensational charges of disloyalty in the State Department, and general concern respecting both loyalty and personal liberty, led the President (January, 1951) to appoint the (Nimitz) Commission on Internal Security and Individual Rights, giving it authority to study all federal loyalty programs.

Employees' organizations. Related to the matter of the political activities and affiliations of employees is the problem of employees' organizations.[22] Just as laborers and professional men not in government employment have their unions and associations for vocational and professional purposes, so the civil servants have developed their organizations with similar ends in view. Although public employees adopted the plan of organization later than private employees, since about 1900 the former have shown a growing tendency to organize, and this movement undoubtedly will continue. There are a number of such organizations within the postal service. Of these, the National Federation of Post Office Clerks and the Railway Mail Association may be mentioned. A National Federation of Federal Employees (founded in 1917), with locals throughout the country, receives practically all civil servants who desire membership except postal employees. In 1931 a dispute within the American Federation of Labor led to the formation of the American Federation of Government Employees, an organization that has had an active if short history. Still later, in 1937, the AFL and the CIO controversy led to the formation of the United Federal Workers of America, an organization that affiliated with the CIO. In 1946 the UFWA combined with another CIO affiliate, the State, County, and Municipal Workers of America, to form the United Public Workers of America.

Employees' organizations are naturally concerned with such matters as the maintenance of the merit system, the improvement of working conditions, salary increases and standardization, and pensions; and sometimes they show genuine interest in improving the quality of the services they render. Although such associations are not always unselfish and their programs with respect to salaries, pensions, and some other phases of public employment may run counter to the public interest, their general influence is on the credit side of the ledger. They do not ordinarily claim the right to strike, and the Taft-Hartley Act (sec. 305) prohibits it "just in case." They almost invariably support the merit system, collectively present their grievances, and otherwise build up the morale of the service. They also serve as units through which the higher administrative officers may effectively reach the whole body of employees. Technically, of course, there is no reason why this may not be done through regular official channels; practically, however, it is often much easier to secure wholehearted co-operation through a conference with the leaders of the employees.

AFFILIATION WITH OUTSIDE GROUPS. Since 1912 the government employees have been permitted to affiliate with the American Federation of Labor

---

[22] On this topic see Mosher, Kingsley, and Stahl, *op. cit.*, Ch. 13; Sterling Spero, *Government as Employer* (1948); White, *op. cit.*, Chs. XXIX–XXX.

and other unions. Employees' organizations may not, however, affiliate with outside associations that impose upon them the obligation to strike. Despite the strike restriction, which materially weakens federal employees' organizations as allies of labor, the unions have welcomed affiliation. Not all the civil service organizations desire to affiliate, however, and in 1931 the National Federation of Federal Employees withdrew from affiliation.

Advantages of affiliation to government employees. The National Federation of Federal Employees by its own account profited immensely through co-operation with the AFL. The unions seek to prevent the imposition of "gag" rules upon the civil servants, work for their repeal where they have already been applied, and champion the cause of these employees in the matter of hours of labor and wages. The seven-hour day for government clerks and the eight-hour day for workers under federal jurisdiction are achievements for which the AFL claims a large share of credit. The interest of the unions in the wages and conditions of employment in the civil service is twofold. First, they have a direct interest in those so employed; and, second, they recognize that the standards of government employment will very materially influence standards in private employment. The unions are equally interested and influential in the treatment of state and local employees, particularly city employees. Private labor has been a powerful ally, because it can act militantly and has millions of votes at its command. Support is not mutual, however, for, as already implied, the restrictions upon the activities of civil service organizations prevent them from giving any considerable assistance to the unions. Furthermore, government employees, excepting craftsmen and unskilled workers, are not particularly "union-minded."

TVA MANAGEMENT-EMPLOYEE RELATIONS. Mosher, Kingsley, and Stahl find very high promise in the system of management-employee relations established by the Tennessee Valley Authority.[23] Employees may bargain collectively, through representatives of their own choosing, without any restrictions. All matters of concern to the employees are submitted to their representatives before action is taken. The rights of workers and management are set forth clearly and in detail, and the procedures by which these rights are to be maintained are determined with the full approval of all concerned. Here, say the authorities, is pioneering in industrial citizenship, democracy in action on the economic front, where it really counts. The Authority has been able to deal with various labor organizations (some affiliated with AFL, others with CIO, and still others having no affiliation at all) in seven states. This enlightened policy, recognizing as it does that men should have more responsibility for

[23] *Op. cit.,* pp. 326–327. See also White, *op. cit.,* p. 465.

their jobs than "doing what they are told" and more interest in them than is measured by a salary check, has been suggested as a model for other government agencies. Certainly it is worth their careful study.

The retirement system: Its PURPOSE. A retirement system is very generally recognized as highly desirable for the permanent civil servants. Their salaries are low; and, without a retirement allowance, many of them, upon release from the service in old age, would be dependent upon relatives or become public charges. More important than this consideration from the standpoint of the efficiency of the service is the fact that if there is no provision for retirement allowance, administrative officers will be reluctant to dismiss employees whose age has rendered them inefficient. A former Commissioner of Pensions, Eugene Ware, was about to dismiss a thoroughly inefficient old man over eighty years of age. Before the order was issued the old fellow dropped dead. The Commissioner reflected that had he dismissed the man he would have been charged with inhumanly murdering him. After that he was not able to bring his courage to the point of dismissing any of the old people in his bureau.[24] From the number of old men employed in many offices in Washington twenty years ago, it may be assumed that other high administrative officers were restrained by considerations similar to those which stayed the hand of the Commissioner of Pensions.

Its PROVISIONS. Despite our liberality in respect to pensions for soldiers and sailors and the need for a retirement system for civil employees, no retirement law for the latter was enacted until 1920. Features of the act of that date and the amending acts of 1926, 1930, and 1942 are here briefly summarized.

(1) For some years all employees in the classified civil service of the United States, and several groups of unclassified employees, including permanent laborers, have been within the retirement provisions. Not until 1942, however, was complete retirement coverage provided for all employees.

(2) The retirement age, formerly fixed at 70, 65, or 62, depending upon the nature of the work in which the employee was engaged, is now uniformly established at 70. Employees who have served thirty years may retire voluntarily at 60; if for fifteen years, at 62.

(3) Five per cent of the salary of each employee is deducted from his pay and is added to the retirement fund. This fund is further supplemented by the Government.

(4) The amount of the annuity depends upon length of service and the salary of the annuitant, but it may not exceed three fourths of the average

[24] J. T. Doyle, "The Federal Civil Service Retirement Law," *Annals of the American Acad. of Pol. and Soc. Sci.* (1924), CXIII, 334.

salary received for any five consecutive years of service, and in no case may it exceed $1,600.

(5) If an employee voluntarily leaves the service before he has reached the age of retirement, the amount he has paid into the fund, with interest at 4 per cent, is returned to him. In case of death or involuntary separation from the service, unless upon charges of delinquency, he or his legal representative receives certain funds in addition to the amount accumulated in the individual account. It should be noted that the retirement system as here outlined is not a pension system, strictly speaking. The employees contribute from their salaries a large part of the fund from which annuities are paid.

Compensation for death or injury. In 1916 Congress passed an act authorizing compensation for federal employees killed or injured in the discharge of their duties. Civil servants or their dependents are not required to establish their claims before a court, but must do it before an administrative body—the Bureau of Employees' Compensation.

Possible improvements in the civil service. Not only is the civil service in need of steady protection against the threats of spoilsmen, but constantly in need of positive means of improvement. It is no less in danger from the dry rot of faulty internal organization, outmoded procedures, and unimaginative leadership than it is from congressmen, who would fell it to the earth with their broad axe of senatorial confirmation of all appointees in the better-salaried government positions. Some, if not the majority, of leading authorities on personnel administration very seriously question the effectiveness of the Civil Service Commission. It is commended for its administration of assembled examinations for large groups of standardized positions, of personnel classification, and of the retirement system; but the point is raised as to whether the Commission, because of the plural nature of its membership, can make a positive approach to the personnel problem.

The authorities who make this and other criticisms recommend that the Civil Service Commission be abolished, and that a single well-qualified nonpolitical administrator be designated to head the personnel agency, such administrator to have the duty of assisting the President and the heads of the various administrative agencies in developing and executing an up-to-date personnel program. In short, it is believed that the Commission is good only at routine matters, that it spends its time and energy chiefly on such questions, and that an administrator, definitely recognized as an essential member of the President's staff, would be much better fitted than the Commission to develop personnel administration along positive and imaginative lines. The experts would not, however, leave everything to the administrator. They would establish a Civil Service Board of nonsalaried members, which board would represent the public, keep an eye on the merit system, advise the President and Congress on matters related thereto, and render such other assistance as might be appropriate.[25]

The Hoover Commission recommended somewhat less drastic reorganization of the Civil Service Commission. Considering that the President is, in the final analysis, responsible for the solution of personnel problems, the Hoover group recommended that there be established in the Executive Office an Office of Personnel, headed by a director who should also be chairman of the Civil Service Commission.[26] This director, keeping in constant touch with the personnel officers of the several departments, would be the principal staff adviser to the President on personnel problems. Among other recommendations of the Hoover Commission respecting the civil service are the following: that the Civil Service Commission concern itself with setting personnel standards and keeping a watchful eye upon their maintenance by the departments rather than (as now) processing a multitude of personnel transactions; that the chairman should take care of all the administrative work of the Commission; that each department should have a personnel director; and that a career service be developed to attract and hold in responsible administrative positions (those nearest the secretaries and under secretaries of departments) men of high competence.[27]

Perhaps one of the principal shortcomings of our personnel system lies in the failure to achieve the purpose stated in the last-mentioned recommendation. It is easy to say that we need permanent officials of high rank and prestige, on salaries of from $12,000 to $16,000 a year, to advise and counsel and serve the temporary and political officers who head the departments—to bridge the gap between politics and administration. But we have not yet succeeded in identifying these top permanent administrative positions; and, of course, career men are in the dark as to the manner in which such heights may be reached, and many potential career men, in the face of all the uncertainties, prefer to remain in private life.[28]

A word for the federal employee. Perhaps the public does not fully appreciate the federal employee. He is often thought of as an individual of only moderate intelligence who has no particular ambition or initiative; who performs his work rather indifferently, not feeling the necessity of trying to outdo his fellow employee nor standing in constant fear of being "jacked up" by the boss; and who is reasonably content to work for a

---

[25] Reeves, *op. cit.* The author gives not only his own views, but also very helpful summaries of other views and proposals.

[26] *General Management of the Executive Branch*, pp. 13–14.

[27] *Personnel Management*, pp. 9, 22–26.

[28] For a rather severe and well-considered criticism of the Hoover Commission for the "poverty" of its Personnel Management Report, see Herman Finer, "The Hoover Commission Reports," *Pol. Sci. Qt.*, LXIV (1949), 584 ff.

small salary and hopes someday to retire on a still smaller annuity. But in reply it may be said that moderate intelligence is all that is needed for the performance of most of the duties of the service, just as the great majority of positions in private business enterprise call for no more. There are positions in the civil service that call for a high degree of intelligence and professional training, and the service has had a little success in attracting capable men for such places, often for much smaller salaries than they could demand in private employment. As for ambition—not all men desire to be merchant princes, or captains of industry, or insurance salesmen. Some have the ambition to serve the public as its employees. Concerning the reputed indifference of the federal employee, it may be said that those accustomed to the hustle of private business may mistake the calm of the civil service for lack of interest. But, granting that there is some basis for the charge, one might argue that the fundamental integrity of those in the classified service entitles them to some indulgence in other particulars. Of course the caliber of the employees should and perhaps can be improved; but even now they are for the most part honest, industrious, and capable. Back in Hoover's administration, Secretary Ogden Mills, speaking of the permanent employees in the key positions in the Treasury Department, declared:

Those men who receive no recognition, are never mentioned in the press, are the men to whom the country owes a great debt of gratitude and they are underpaid. There are men in the Treasury Department without whom the Treasury could not function. You never hear of them. Their services would command greater salaries in the commercial world, very much greater salaries in some cases. They get their satisfaction out of the work performed. They go on year in and year out, working ten and twelve hours a day in order to get the job well done.[29]

This praise is no less merited today than it was in 1931.

III. THE CIVIL SERVICE IN STATE AND LOCAL AREAS [30]

The extent of the merit system. The spoils practice raged for years in the state and local civil service, as it did in the federal service from 1829 to 1883. Indeed, it may be said that the spoils poison spread into the federal administration from some of the states, notably from New York. Merit

---

[29] In *The Consensus,* Vol. XVI, No. 4, p. 38.

[30] *The Book of the States, 1950–1951,* pp. 192–221; A. W. Bromage, *Introduction to Municipal Government and Administration* (1950), Ch. XXI; Graves, *American State Government* (1946 ed.), Ch. XII; C. M. Kneier, *City Government in the U.S.* (1947 ed.), Ch. XXVI; A. F, Macdonald, *American State Government and Administration* (1950 ed.), Ch. XVII; W. E. Mosher, J. D. Kingsley, and O. G. Stahl, *Public Personnel Administration* (1950 ed.); L. D. White, *Introduction to Public Administration* (1948 ed.), Chs. XXII–XXXI.

system acts were passed in New York and Massachusetts about the same time the first permanent merit system act was passed by the federal government (1883). About twenty years later, Illinois and Wisconsin followed their example, and at the present time some twenty states [31] are listed as having comprehensive merit system programs. In all the other states a minimum merit program operates in conformity with the requirements of an amendment (1939) of the Federal Social Security Act. Those state departments that receive federal funds for public assistance and employment security must be operated under a merit system. The non-civil-service states commonly set up "merit system councils" to administer personnel policies of those state agencies that take part in the federal security program. A number of states that do not have "service-wide" coverage under a merit system, nevertheless provide for coverage in certain departments or services in addition to the social security agencies. Kentucky, Nebraska, and Washington, to mention just three states, have established such limited merit systems.

Practically all of the larger cities and a few of the small ones have adopted the merit system. In the big municipalities the large number of employees and the technical nature of much of the work made this reform imperative. Only about 10 per cent of the counties are under a merit plan. This lagging behind is due in part to the fact that counties, except in a few urban areas, have few employees and in part to the fact that counties are the last stronghold of the spoilsmen. In 1941 New York State attracted wide attention by becoming the first to make the merit system applicable to all counties, townships, villages, and school districts. A few other states have general civil service laws for local governments, but none of them approach New York's complete coverage.

Formal adoption of the merit system does not necessarily mean that it is actually established. Politicians are forever finding short cuts to jobs for their friends, through securing the appointment of "reasonable" civil service commissioners, or by other means. Not infrequently the civil service laws are repealed, as in Arkansas (1939), and New Mexico (1941). Even those states that seek to protect the system by constitutional provision are not safe. The Michigan civil service law of 1937 rested upon a constitutional amendment, but that did not prevent the repeal of a number of its most excellent provisions (1939). The basic reason for the slow progress of the merit system is that the public is not decidedly averse to spoils. Often one hears heated deunnunciation of "politics" in the public service. It usually develops that a good Republican or an equally good

[31] *Good Government* (January–February, 1951) lists eighteen, as follows: Alabama, California, Colorado, Connecticut, Illinois, Kansas, Maine, Maryland, Massachusettes, Michigan, Minnesota, New Jersey, New York, Ohio, Oregon, Rhode Island, Vermont, Wisconsin.

FUNCTIONAL DISTRIBUTION OF STATE EMPLOYMENT: APRIL, 1949 AND 1948 *

Function	1949 Employees Number (in thousands)	1949 Employees Per cent	1949 Pay roll Amount (in millions)	1949 Pay roll Per cent	1948 Employees Number (in thousands)	1948 Employees Per cent	1948 Pay roll Amount (in millions)	1948 Pay roll Per cent	Per cent change (a) April 1948–April 1949 Number of employees	Per cent change (a) April 1948–April 1949 Monthly pay roll
Total	982	100.0	$196.9	100.0	926	100.0	$171.2	100.0	6.1	15.0
General governmental functions	964	98.2	193.1	98.1	908	98.1	167.4	98.0	6.1	15.1
General control	78	8.0	17.8	9.0	71	7.6	15.5	9.0	10.9	14.7
Public safety	56	5.7	13.9	7.1	56	6.0	12.2	7.1	1.2	14.1
Police	17	1.7	4.1	2.1	16	1.7	3.5	2.0	5.7	16.9
Highways	164	16.7	32.2	16.3	151	16.3	28.4	16.6	9.0	13.3
Natural resources	66	6.8	12.8	6.5	61	6.6	11.1	6.5	8.4	15.0
Health	25	2.6	5.4	2.7	26	2.8	5.1	3.0	—2.3	5.2
Hospitals and institutions for the handicapped	158	16.1	27.7	14.1	145	15.6	23.3	13.7	9.2	18.8
Public welfare	34	3.5	6.7	3.4	32	3.4	5.9	3.4	7.1	13.6
Correction	31	3.2	7.0	3.6	34	3.7	6.1	3.6	—8.2	14.2
Schools	294	29.9	56.7	28.8	277	29.9	47.5	27.8	6.2	19.4
Employment security administration	46	4.6	10.9	5.6	47	5.1	10.1	5.9	—3.0	8.2
Other general government	11	1.1	2.0	1.0	10	1.0	2.1	1.2	9.0	—5.5
State government enterprises	18	1.8	3.8	1.9	17	1.9	3.4	2.0	3.1	11.4
Alcoholic-beverage monopoly systems	13	1.3	2.7	1.4	13	1.4	2.5	1.4	1.8	8.4
Other	5	.5	1.1	.6	5	.5	1.0	.6	6.8	19.0

Note: Because of rounding, detail may not add to totals.   (a) Per cent changes computed from unrounded figures.
* Reproduced by courtesy of the Council of State Governments from *The Book of the States, 1950–1951,* p. 200.

STATE PERSONNEL AGENCIES *

(As of June, 1949)

State	Name of Agency	Established [a]	Coverage [b]
Alabama	State Personnel Board	1939	General
Arizona	Merit System Council	1940 1949	Grant-in-Aid Programs State Patrol
Arkansas	Merit System Council	1940	Grant-in-Aid Programs
California	State Personnel Board	1913	General
Colorado	Civil Service Commission	1907	General
Connecticut	State Personnel Dept.	1937	General
Delaware	Merit System Council	1938	Grant-in-Aid Programs
Florida	Merit System Council	1940	Grant-in-Aid Programs
Georgia	State Personnel Board	1939	Grant-in-Aid Programs, several other services
Idaho	Merit System Council	1937	Grant-in-Aid Programs, Fish and Game Commission
Illinois	Civil Service Commission	1905	General
Indiana	State Personnel Division	1941	Grant-in-Aid Programs, several other services
Iowa	Merit System Council	1939	Grant-in-Aid Programs
Kansas	Dept. of Civil Service	1941	General
Kentucky	Personnel Council	1940 1941	Dept. of Econ. Security Dept. of Health
Louisiana	Merit System Council	1940	Grant-in-Aid, Division of Vocational Rehabilitation
Maine	State Personnel Board	1937	General
Maryland	Dept. of State Employment	1921	General
Massachusetts	Dept. of Civil Service	1885	General
Michigan	Civil Service Commission	1937	General
Minnesota	Department of Civil Service	1939	General
Mississippi	Merit System Council	1938	Several services
Missouri	Division of Personnel	1940	Grant-in-Aid Programs, Dept. of Corrections
Montana	Joint Merit System Council	1940	Grant-in-Aid Programs
Nebraska	Merit System Council	1940	Grant-in-Aid Programs, Clerical employees of "code" depts.

State	Name of Agency	Established a	Coverage b
Nevada	State Merit Board	1937	Grant-in-Aid Programs
New Hampshire	Merit System Council	1940	Grant-in-Aid Programs
New Jersey	Civil Service Commission	1908	General
New Mexico	Merit System Council	1940	Grant-in-Aid Programs
New York	Department of Civil Service	1883	General
North Carolina	State Personnel Department	1949	General
North Dakota	Merit System Council	1940	Several services
Ohio	Civil Service Commission	1913	General
Oklahoma	State Personnel Board	1940	Grant-in-Aid Programs
Oregon	Civil Service Commission	1940	General
Pennsylvania	Civil Service Commission	1941	Grant-in-Aid Programs, several other services
Rhode Island	Dept. of Civil Service	1939	General
South Carolina	Merit System Council	1936	Several services
South Dakota	Merit System Council	1940	Grant-in-Aid Programs, several other services
Tennessee	Department of Personnel	1937	General
Texas	Merit System Council	1941	Public Welfare, two other services
Utah	Merit System Council	1942	Grant-in-Aid Programs, two other services
Vermont	Merit System Council	1939	Grant-in-Aid Programs
Virginia	State Personnel Department	1942	General
Washington	State Personnel Board	1937	Grant-in-Aid Programs, Dept. of Fisheries
West Virginia	Merit System Council	1940	Grant-in-Aid Programs, two other services
Wisconsin	Bureau of Personnel	1905	General
Wyoming	Joint Merit System	1940	Grant-in-Aid Programs

* Adapted from *Book of the States, 1950–1951,* pp. 195–196.

a The year shown in this column is the year in which a merit system program was first established in the state. In a number of states, subsequent changes, consolidations, or extensions of coverage have occurred.

b Coverage: The pattern of merit system coverage differs from state to state. In those states where coverage is shown as "general," employees in most state agencies are included in the merit system program. In those states where coverage is shown as "Grant-in-Aid Programs," coverage tyuically includes such functions as public welfare, employment security, public health, and related activities administered by state agencies participating in various aspects of the federal aid program. (See the 1949 Federal Security Agency publication, *Directory of State Merit Systems.*)

Democrat is venting his spleen at an administration of the other party. Only when partisans criticize their own party for corrupting the civil service is there evidence of sincere devotion to the merit system.

Long ago the American public discarded its tolerance in the matter of the political selection and removal of school teachers. This relatively successful effort to remove politics from the schools would seem to indicate that the people could have the merit principle in operation in all lines of administrative activity if they really wanted it. It may be said, however, that the public is being slowly awakened to the necessity for improving personnel standards in the public service, and that, despite a number of instances of back-sliding on the part of states and local communities which have adopted merit system laws, the general program for an improved civil service has distinctly advanced, particularly since 1935.[32] Mention has already been made of the significance of the federal requirement that state administrative agencies receiving social security funds from the national government shall administer them under a merit system. If, as a result of compliance with this requirement, the administration of the social security services is substantially improved, there is reason to hope that the public demand for state-wide merit system laws will become insistent.[33]

Operation of the civil service laws. State and local civil service laws are administered by a civil service commission, a personnel board, a department of civil service, or by an agency with some such title, the members of which are commonly appointed by the chief executive officer of the area. The commission, or whatever the personnel agency may be called, has general charge of the administration of the civil service laws, and the steady work for which it holds the legal responsibility is performed by an executive officer and staff.

The state and local service agencies have not, as a rule, attained the high standard set by the federal commission. Furthermore, civil service commissions often have a common fault—that of giving too much attention to compliance with laws, rules, and regulations and not enough to the operational problems of department heads and other officers who must "get the work done." All too often state and local commissions have been under political domination, striving to do the will of the appointing officer rather than to enforce the merit principles faithfully. It seems that state and

---

[32] The progress of the merit system can be followed by reference to current issues of such publications as the *National Municipal Review* and *Good Government*.

[33] In connection with the improvements in state personnel administration as a result of federal pressure it might be worth while to note, on the other hand, that there is some complaint among state personnel officers to the effect that the federal service operates as a bit of a drain upon the state service. State authorities, some of them at least, say that the federal civil service steadily, if slowly, draws from the states some of the best administrators and employees. If this charge is true, it is probably because of the wider opportunities in the federal service, its prestige, and stability.

local governments are unable to recruit for their service persons with as good qualifications as those who enter the federal service. This inability is due to various factors, among which may be mentioned the prestige of the federal service and its relative freedom from political interference.

Salaries in the state and local areas are often inequitable. "Equal pay for equal work" is still a goal to be attained in many jurisdictions. Labor is usually better paid than the clerical and scientific forces, for powerful local labor organizations see to it that laborers in the public service receive the "going rate." Satisfactory salary adjustments depend upon scientific classification of positions. Although a number of studies of classification or standardization have been made, the results of such studies have not been put into effect as rapidly as the needs require; and where reclassifications have been made, considerable difficulty is always experienced in maintaining them against interested persons who present "special cases."

Promotion is based upon seniority, efficiency ratings, promotional examinations, or the discretion of the administrative officer—usually upon a combination of these. All too often the opinion prevails that only a political "pull" will bring a promotion, and in many cases there is enough basis for this opinion to discourage the civil service reformer as well as the capable employee who waits in vain for his promotion.

Discipline is imposed in a number of forms—deprivation of seniority, demerits, suspension, and others. The method of removal varies in form from removal at the discretion of a high administrative officer, as in the federal service, to removal upon the initiative of such officers, subject to the right of the employee to a judicial review. There is some dispute as to what form of removal best secures the interest of the employee and the public. The weight of authority seems to be on the side of the federal system, although it is conceded that more attention to recruitment might well lead to additional protection of the employee against removal.

As for retirement or pension systems, a number of our governments have in the last twenty years adopted some kind of plan. A few have liberal plans, but more commonly the annuity falls somewhat below this standard.

Problems and trends in the state and local civil service. A poser of long standing has been that of how to get capable, alert, dynamic personnel in the administrative services. It is an old story that in the contest for talent, government has often lost to business. But the situation has been greatly improved for government since the Great Depression. Although the change has been more noticeable in the federal service, other services have shared somewhat in this development. Yet the fact remains that government must meet business as a rival for capable administrators, and government can do this rather effectively if it puts its best foot forward, emphasizing the many attractions of a public career.

Another problem of the civil service is that of reducing the number of amateurs and politicians in key administrative posts and turning the posts over to trained administrators. The tendency among legislators and elected administrative officials is to exempt the higher and better paid positions from the merit system. This tendency has been in part supported by the failure of our educational institutions to train adequately a sufficient number of general and expert administrators. During the last twenty years, however, political officials have shown evidence of receding somewhat from their position that the best administrative posts should be reserved for faithful party workers, and the same score of years has witnessed a most encouraging growth of schools of public administration in nearly all of our best universities.

Of a number of other problems that might be mentioned, one concerns the civil service commission. As noted above, these agencies have in the past been concerned with the important (but nevertheless negative) function of keeping spoils out of the civil service, with enforcing the laws and rules and regulations to that end. More recently an encouraging development has appeared—the commissions are giving more attention to the positive side of their responsibilities. They are evolving comprehensive programs of personnel management, giving careful consideration to conditions of work, classification, salaries, improvement in the service, promotion, and various other factors that build morale and *esprit de corps,* without which employees have a humdrum existence and the public their listless service.

Although we take due notice of the opposition to the merit principle and note certain back-slidings and discouraging delays, it may be said that the merit system is moving forward. That is the trend. Evidence of this is found in the continued and increased activity of merit system study groups and citizens' leagues in those states that have only a part of their administrative personnel under the system. And bills designed to strengthen or extend the merit principle commonly attract strong support, both in and out of the legislature.[34]

IV. TRAINING FOR THE PUBLIC SERVICE [35]

One of the chief causes of the failure of government employees to meet and attain the best standards is the lack of adequate training *for* and *in* the civil service. Pre-entry training for government administrators was

[34] *Book of the States,* 1950–1951, p. 194.

[35] Franklin G. Connor and R. H. Landis, "The Federal Administrative Intern Program," *Personnel Adm.,* VII (1945), 11; G. A. Graham, *Education for Public Administration* (1941); Milton Hall, *Employee Training in the Public Service* (1941); M. B. Lambie, *Training for the Public Service* (1935); Mosher, Kingsley, and Stahl, *op. cit.,* Ch. 15; K. E. Stromsen and M. Dreese, "Attitude of NIPA Interns Toward a Career in the Federal Service," *Pub. Adm. Rev.,* X (Autumn, 1950), 254–261; L. D. White, *op. cit.,* Ch. XXVI.

long practically ignored by all except a few universities. But after the New Deal revealed a shortage in qualified administrators, a number of other universities joined the pioneers in offering courses designed to prepare young men and women for administrative work. Some institutions emphasize the British idea that a broad liberal education is the best pre-entry training and maintain that men with flexible minds and breadth of vision will learn the science of administration after they enter the service. Others hold that the "science" of administration can be taught to carefully picked graduate students. Perhaps there is room for training in both directions, and it might be said that institutions which admit only graduates for instruction in the science of public administration achieve this double objective. At any rate, colleges and universities, in striking contrast to their attitude thirty years ago, now show a very lively interest in encouraging young people to prepare for careers in the public service.

Before leaving the question of pre-entry training, mention should be made of the National Institute of Public Affairs, which annually selects a small number of college graduates for internships in the departments in Washington. Note should also be taken of the fact that a number of educational institutions have arranged with state and local authorities for brief internships for promising students. For example, since 1937, Wisconsin has authorized its executives to hire, through the Civil Service Commission, highly qualified college seniors and graduate students to serve as apprentices in the departments, a plan that is reported to operate very successfully.

However satisfactory the pre-entry training may be (and there is still much room for its improvement and expansion), post-entry training, direction as to how knowledge may be applied to concrete and specific duties to be performed in particular government services, is imperatively demanded if there is to be efficiency and economy in those services. Mosher and Kingsley give special attention to this problem, showing what has been done to solve it and what ought to be done before it may be said that a relatively satisfactory program of training is in operation.[36] They emphasize the necessity of selecting trainers who do not lose themselves in details and who appreciate the relation of theory and broad treatment to practical problems. Post-entry training should begin on the day the new employees are inducted into the service, and a number of agencies can now be found that do not neglect the inductees. The Social Security Administration has arranged for a series of orientation lectures for all new employees; another federal agency supplies its inductees with a handbook entitled *Your Job and the Farm Credit Administration*. This kind of attention to those entering the public service helps to make them feel at home

[36] *Op. cit.*, pp. 279 ff.

and starts building their morale, without which there can be no energetic and alert civil service.

Apprenticeship or internship is a phase of the induction program. Apprenticeship is the term used in reference to training for the skilled trades. It is unusual in the public service, although the Government Printing Office, the Tennessee Valley Authority, and a few other agencies maintain such programs. Internship is the term used rather loosely to designate the training course for those who are entering the professional fields of administration, such as accounting, personnel, and engineering. Here again TVA is one of the pioneers, as is also the Rural Electrification Administration. Various administrative agencies have established "vestibule schools" in which employees are trained before they are assigned to duty. The public is not unfamiliar with the intensive training provided by the Department of Justice for the G-men. The Treasury Department trains its revenue agents and the State Department its foreign service officers. But only a few government agencies have comprehensive training programs aimed at the improvement of their personnel from the time of induction to the period of full maturity in the service. Perhaps the Department of Agriculture with its graduate school approaches this ideal. The most encouraging feature in the movement for post-entry training is not the extent and effectiveness of present programs, but rather the fact that in recent years government officials as well as professors of public administration have become conscious of the need for it.

Reading List

Roger S. Abbott, "The Federal Loyalty Program: Background and Problems," *Am. Pol. Sci. Rev.,* XLII (1948), 486–499.

Annual Reports of the United States Civil Service Commission.

Paul H. Appleby, "A Reappraisal of Federal Employment as a Career," *Pub. Adm. Rev.,* VIII (1948), 85–90.

G. C. S. Benson, *The Administration of the Civil Service in Massachusetts* (1937).

A. W. Bromage, *Introduction to Municipal Government and Administration* (1950), Ch. XXI.

Commission of Inquiry on Public Service Personnel, *Better Government Personnel* (1935).

The Federal Employee (monthly).

Herman Finer, "The Hoover Commission Reports," II, *Pol. Sci. Qt.,* LXIV (1949), 584 ff.

C. R. Fish, *The Civil Service and the Patronage* (1904).

W. D. Foulke, *Fighting the Spoilsmen* (1919).

C. J. Friedrich and others, *Problems of the American Public Service* (1935).

Walter W. Gellhorn, *Security, Loyalty, and Science* (1950).

Good Government (bi-monthly).

W. B. Graves, *Public Administration in a Democratic Society* (1950), Chs. 7–14.

Milton Hall, *Employee Training in the Public Service* (1941).

M. F. Halloran, *Romance of the Merit System* (1929 ed.).

H. F. Hubbard, *Elements of a Comprehensive Personnel Program* (Civil Service Assembly, 1947).

Randolph J. Jouno, "Efficiency Rating Boards of Review in the Federal Service," *Western Pol. Qt.,* II (1949), 610–614.

C. M. Kneier, *City Government in the United States* (1947), Ch. XXVI.

M. B. Lambie, *Training for the Public Services* (1935).

A. F. Macdonald, *American State Government and Administration* (1950 ed.), Ch. 17.

L. Mayers, *The Federal Service* (1922).

J. E. McLean (ed.), *The Public Service and University Education* (1949).

L. Meriam, *Personnel Administration in the Federal Government: An Examination of Some Pending Proposals* (1937).

———, *Public Service and Special Training* (1936).

C. E. Merriam, "Some Aspects of Loyalty," *Pub. Adm. Rev.,* VIII (1948), 81–84.

A Model State Civil Service Law (Civil Service Assembly, 1946).

W. E. Mosher, J. D. Kingsley, and O. G. Stahl, *Public Personnel Administration* (1950 ed.).

J. M. Pfiffner, *Public Administration* (1946 ed.), Chs. XV, XVII–XXI.

Public Personnel Review (quarterly).

F. W. Reeves, "Civil Service as Usual," *Pub. Adm. Rev.,* IV (1944), 327–340.

F. W. Reeves and P. T. David, *Personnel Administration in the Federal Government* (1937).

Sterling Spero, *Government as Employer* (1948).

F. M. Stewart, *The National Civil Service Reform League* (1929).

L. D. White, *Introduction to the Study of Public Administration* (1948 ed.), Chs. XXII–XXXI.

———, *Civil Service in Wartime* (1945).

Questions and Problems

1. How was it possible before 1820 to maintain an efficient national civil service without a law requiring the merit system?
2. Trace the course of civil service reform in the national government.
3. Suggest the chief current obstacles to an entirely adequate merit system.
4. Give a critical estimate of the relative advantages and disadvantages of British and American types of civil service examinations.
5. How do you justify the "unassembled" examinations for candidates for the higher posts in the civil service?
6. Discuss the problem of veteran preference.
7. Outline a plan of promotion that would be at once fair to the civil servants and tend to maintain high standards in the service.

8. What problems are involved in government employees' affiliation with labor unions?
9. How might the national civil service be improved from the standpoint of its administration?
10. Discuss the progress of the merit system in state civil service.
11. Distinguish between the older (negative) functions and the newer (positive) functions of the personnel agency. Is there any necessary conflict between the two?
12. Assuming an adequate civil service law, what more is needed to assure the operation of the merit system?

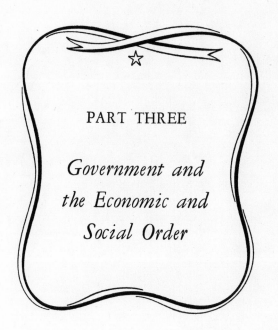

PART THREE

*Government and
the Economic and
Social Order*

☆ 22 ☆

Government Finance

IN the preceding chapters covering constitutions, civil and political rights, parties and the electoral processes, the executive, legislative, and judicial powers, and administrative organization and personnel, the chief concern is with the powers, structure, and procedure of government. However, the *functions* of government are touched upon at certain points: for example, the protection of personal and property rights, in Chapter 6, and the administration of justice, in Chapters 17 and 18. But in the remaining chapters, the purpose is to consider *functions* primarily, concentrating upon government activities relating to such important matters as finance, commerce, business, labor, agriculture, safety, health, social security, national defense, foreign relations, and international co-operation. The final chapter may be said to relate to the "functions" of citizens, their obligations.

Government finance—taxes, spending, and so on—the subject of the present chapter, is naturally a matter of transcendent importance. Tied up with every phase of government activity, it is the function upon which all other functions depend. For what purposes shall a government appropriate money? From what sources shall the revenue be drawn? How much of the income of the rich should government take—half, three fourths, practically all? And how much of the income of the largest income producers could the government take before such individuals would go on a sit-down strike against producing and earning? What is the fair balance between rates for rich and poor in a tax program? When and to what extent should public debts be incurred? How should the currency be regulated? What should be done to protect bank depositors? These and many other questions arise under the general title of government finance. There are few scientific answers. Here, as in most cases, there are powerful conflicting and often selfish interests harassing our legislators and adding more confusion to problems already seething with complexities.

I. LIMITATIONS UPON THE FISCAL POWERS OF CONGRESS [1]

The first clause in section VIII, Article I, of the Constitution gives Congress the power "to lay and collect taxes, duties, imposts, [2] and excises, to pay the debts and provide for the common defense and general welfare of the United States." This is a very concise statement of the power of the national government to tax and to appropriate money. Before examining the very wide taxing power that this clause conveys, we should note that it is subject to certain limitations.

1. **Duties, imposts, and excises must be uniform.** One of the limitations on the power of Congress to lay taxes is contained in the same clause in which the taxing power is granted. It reads: ". . . but all duties, imposts, and excises shall be uniform throughout the United States." This restriction means, for example, that the duty or tariff on coffee shall be the same at the port of New York as at the port of San Francisco, and that the federal excise tax on a pack of cigarettes shall be the same in Maine and New Mexico. Is the uniformity rule violated when American citizens who own foreign-built pleasure yachts are required to pay an excise upon their use, while their fellow citizens who own domestic yachts are not so taxed? The courts have held that this does not violate the rule, since foreign-built yachts are uniformly taxed and domestic yachts are uniformly taxed. [3] An act of Congress provided that those who paid federal inheritance taxes should have a part of such tax refunded if the states in which they lived also imposed an inheritance tax. This act was attacked as being in contravention to the uniformity clause, since those living in states with no inheritance tax law would pay a higher federal inheritance tax than those who resided in states having such a law. But the Supreme Court held that the act did no violence to the uniformity principle; that the rule of liability to pay the tax was the same in all parts of the United States. [4]

From these illustrations we reach the conclusion that persons and property may be classified, very strictly classified, for levies of duties, imposts, and excises, and that as long as the tax falls with equal force upon all persons within a class or all property within a class it is uniform within the meaning of the constitutional requirement. Thus, an inheritance of $50,000 may be taxed at a higher rate than an inheritance of half that amount, since per-

---

[1] R. E. Cushman, *Leading Constitutional Decisions* (1950 ed.), pp. 287–298, 383–388; Walter F. Dodd, *Cases and Materials on Constitutional Law* (1949 ed.), pp. 478–506; J. M. Mathews, *The American Constitutional System* (1940 ed.), Ch. XVI.

[2] "Imposts" are duties on imported goods. "Duties" are ordinarily understood to include both import and export duties. Since another section of the Constitution prohibits export duties, the term "duties" in the clause quoted above is without significance.

[3] Billings v. U.S., 232 U.S. 261 (1914).

[4] Florida v. Mellon, 273 U.S. 12 (1927).

sons are classified according to the amount of the inheritance. Similarly, a five-dollar tax might be imposed upon the use of each motor car of a given class, whereas the use of those in another class might be taxed at a lower rate or not at all.

2. Direct taxes must be apportioned according to population. What has been said respecting uniformity in the taxes laid by Congress applies only to indirect taxes and to taxes on incomes. Direct taxes must be apportioned among the states according to their population.[5] What are direct and what are indirect taxes? The terms are not defined in the Constitution, but the courts have made the distinction. A direct tax is a capitation tax (so much per individual), a tax on land, or a general property tax. A tax on income from certain sources is also held to be a direct tax. This tax stands in a class to itself and will be discussed presently. Among the indirect taxes may be mentioned import duties, the inheritance tax, taxes on various specific articles, on occupations, on theater tickets, and on playing cards. If Congress lays a direct tax, it must decide how much revenue it wants from the tax and then divide the amount among the states according to population. A state with one twentieth of the total populaion, regardless of its wealth or lack of it, will have to pay one twentieth of the tax. Congress has levied direct taxes only a few times and not at all since the Civil War. The indirect tax, which needs only be uniform throughout the United States, is much simpler to levy and collect, more satisfactory as a source of revenue, and distributes the tax burden more fairly.

THE INCOME TAX. It was just observed that the income tax stands in a class to itself. During the Civil War the first income tax was levied, and, since it was generally understood at that time to be an indirect tax, Congress did not apportion it among the states according to population. The Supreme Court upheld the validity of this tax.[6] In 1894 Congress passed a much more comprehensive income tax law. The Civil War measure had been applied only to incomes from salaries and wages; the new law levied taxes on incomes from practically all sources, lands and personal property included. No time was lost in contesting the validity of this act before the Supreme Court. After the Court had heard the case argued twice, it decided, five to four, that such sections of the law as applied to incomes from real and personal property imposed direct taxes and were therefore void, and that, with the provisions relating to these two important classes stricken out, the entire law should be held void.[7] This decision was greeted with inordinate praise by large property holders and conservatives, and with intense condemnation from other quarters.

[5] Constitution, Art. I, sec. 1, cl. 3.
[6] Springer v. U.S., 102 U.S. 586 (1881).
[7] Pollock v. Farmers' Loan, etc., 158 U.S. 601 (1895).

A movement was set on foot for a constitutional amendment, which was finally adopted in 1913, eighteen years after the decision. The Sixteenth Amendment reads: "The Congress shall have power to lay and collect taxes on incomes, from whatever source derived, without apportionment among the several states, and without regard to any census or enumeration." The tax on incomes from real and personal property remains a direct tax, under the memorable decision just mentioned; but the Amendment authorizes its levy and collection as an indirect tax. That is, it is subject only to the uniformity limitation. Persons in a few states in which most of the wealth of the country is located pay 90 per cent of the income taxes, but no one can raise an objection that has legal validity. Much higher rates are levied upon large incomes than upon small incomes. If the tax applies equally to all persons in each income class, it is valid.

3. **Revenue laws shall not favor ports of one state over those of another.** A third limitation on the taxing power is that "no preference shall be given by any regulation of commerce or revenue to the ports of one state over those of another." [8] So far as this clause restricts Congress in the enactment of revenue measures, it supplements the requirement that all duties, imposts, and excises shall be uniform throughout the United States. The "no preference" restriction is not interpreted to mean that *a* port in one state shall not be given preference over *a* port in another. Such preference is shown whenever Congress makes a port in one state a "port of entry" and refuses to make another port in another state a port of entry. What is forbidden is discrimination against the ports of one state or of several states.[9]

4. **Interstate duties prohibited.** The clause in the Constitution containing the "no preference" restriction also provides that vessels bound to, or from, one state, shall not be required to enter, clear, or pay duties in another. It is not likely that Congress would ever establish trade barriers between the states, by duties or otherwise, even if there were no such prohibition in the Constitution.

5. **Export duties prohibited.** A more important limitation upon the taxing power of Congress than either of the last two mentioned is the prohibition that "no tax or duty shall be laid on articles exported from any state." [10] This provision was included in the Constitution because the Southern delegates at the Philadelphia Convention were afraid Congress might levy an export duty on raw materials—the principal products of the Southern states. This clause lays the only positive prohibition upon the power of Congress to tax. The other restrictions are limitations, not upon the

---

[8] Constitution, Art. I, sec. ix, cl. 6.

[9] Pennsylvania v. Wheeling, etc., 18 Howard 421 (1855).

[10] Constitution, Art. I, sec. ix, cl. 5.

power of taxation, but upon the manner of its exercise. For example, Congress may levy direct taxes to any amount, but they must be apportioned according to the population of the states. Coming now to the meaning of the export prohibition, we find that the word "exports" applies only to articles shipped to foreign countries. Congress is not only prohibited from laying a duty on such articles, but the Supreme Court has held that Congress is prohibited from imposing a stamp tax on foreign bills of lading, a stamp tax upon charter parties for the carriage of cargo to foreign ports, and a similar tax upon marine insurance policies covering exported goods. On the other hand, the Court has decided that the requirement that all packages of tobacco intended for export be stamped, the object being to prevent fraud, is not an export tax. A general tax that falls upon all property alike and that just happens to hit some property intended for exportation is a valid tax, despite the intent of exportation. It has been judicially determined also that the income tax is valid as applied to the incomes of exporters. What is prohibited is the singling out and taxing of articles intended for export and the taxing of export transactions. General taxes, taxes that do not lay a special or direct burden upon exports, are not within the prohibition under discussion.[11]

6. **The implied prohibition.** There is one prohibition upon the power of Congress to tax that is not mentioned in the Constitution. It is implied from the nature of our federal system of government. The Constitution contemplates two governments, the national and the state, each supreme in its own sphere. Following this line of reasoning, the Supreme Court early held that a state was not permitted to tax the national government or its instrumentalities. At a later date, it declared that the same prohibition saved the states and their instrumentalities from being taxed by Congress. This point was discussed at some length in Chapter 5, section 1, under the sub-title "Intergovernmental taxation."

7. **A tax must not violate due process.** A general limitation upon the powers of Congress, which therefore applies to tax legislation, is imposed by the Fifth Amendment in the provision that no person shall be deprived of life, liberty or property, without due process of law. A tax levied upon property that for the purposes of taxation is not located within the jurisdiction of the government, is invalid. Similarly, a tax imposed to secure revenues for a purely private purpose is invalid. The taxing power must be exercised for a public purpose. Nor may the public purpose be a demoralizing one.

Breadth of the taxing power: 1. TAXATION FOR THE GENERAL WELFARE. Congress is authorized to levy taxes "to pay the debts and provide for the

---

[11] *The Constitution of the United States to Jan. 1, 1938* (annotated), pp. 287–288.

common defense and general welfare of the United States." Notice that Congress is empowered to levy taxes for the general welfare. It is not, however, authorized to legislate for the general welfare. The power to tax and to appropriate money is thus broader than the power to legislate. Congress has appropriated money to the states for various purposes; often for projects over which Congress has hardly a shadow of legislative power. The money is commonly granted to the state subject to conditions. The meeting of these conditions by the states means, of course, that the national government secures, in effect, legislative control over the objects for which appropriations are made. This subject was discussed in Chapter 5, section IV, under the title "Federal aid." Other appropriations for objects over which Congress is given no clear legislative powers include grants for the relief of earthquake, drought, and flood sufferers in this country and abroad, and for the promotion of world fairs.

2. TAXATION FOR THE PURPOSE OF REGULATION. Not the slightest question exists concerning the power of Congress to tax for revenue; but an important question, that may not be entirely settled even yet, arises over the authority of that body to use the taxing power for other than revenue purposes. Tariffs have been enacted for many years with the avowed purpose of protecting American products, revenue being only an incidental consideration or no consideration at all. Very few have raised as their objection to the protective tariff the claim that it is an unconstitutional use of the revenue power. This argument is no longer taken seriously. It might be added that Congress could restrict importations directly through its power to control foreign commerce. As it has this power, there is no reason why it should not be permitted to accomplish the same purpose indirectly through the taxing power.

In 1866 Congress levied a 10 per cent tax upon the circulating notes of state banks (private banks chartered by the states). This tax was contested as being excessive and as having been levied for the purpose of driving such notes out of circulation. The Supreme Court held that the high rate of the tax did not render it unconstitutional. It laid special stress upon the fact that, since Congress had the authority to regulate the national currency, no valid legal objection could be raised to the act of Congress that sought to accomplish this end indirectly through the medium of the taxing power.[12]

But, can Congress accomplish, through its taxing power alone, a purpose it has no authority to accomplish through any other provision of the Constitution? In other words, may Congress, under the guise of the taxing power, pass restrictive and prohibitive measures on subjects not committed to its authority by the Constitution? The answer is "Yes," up to

---

[12] Veazie Bank v. Fenno, 8 Wallace 533 (1869).

a certain point. It has been done a number of times. In order to discourage butter substitutes, Congress taxed yellow oleomargarine 10 cents per pound. The Court held that the motive to discourage the sale or manufacture of one article over another did not invalidate the tax. Opium has been made the object of a very high tax, and the tax provision is accompanied by regulations respecting its sale and distribution. The tax was sustained in spite of the regulations, these being held to be reasonably related to the enforcement of the tax.

The expansion of this principle. Having failed to receive judicial support in its attempt to restrict child labor through the use of its power over interstate commerce, and being encouraged by the liberality with which the Court had upheld its use of the taxing power, Congress made an effort to exercise this power for the purpose of discouraging the employment of children in industry. The act provided that those who knowingly employed children under specified ages in mines, mills, and similar industrial establishments should pay, in addition to all other taxes, an excise of 10 per cent on all net profits. Observe that the excise was made the same, regardless of what percentage the number of children employed might be of the whole number of employees. This, coupled with the word "knowingly," led the Court to hold the act void. The tax was not a tax, said the Court, but a penalty designed to restrict the employment of children.[13]

The Agricultural Adjustment Act of 1933 provided for a processing tax, the revenues from which were to go to farmers who agreed to limit their production of certain commodities. There was no question of the power of Congress to impose this tax. The question arose over the spending of the money. Could it not be spent for the "general welfare"—the improvement of the lot of the farmers? The Supreme Court of the United States did not meet the question from this angle, but held that Congress in *spending* money for the purpose of *regulating* agricultural production, a regulation it had no power to exercise through its *legislative* power, was encroaching upon the reserved powers (Tenth Amendment) of the states.[14] The six judges who gave this decision did not deny the right of Congress to levy the tax or to spend the money. The spending of the money for a regulatory purpose was the basis of their objection. But Justice Stone, in a vigorous dissent for the minority, said that "the power of Congress to spend is inseparable from persuasion to action over which Congress has no legislative control." He gave a number of examples of such persuasion. As he saw it, the majority decision led to "absurd consequences. The government may give seeds to farmers, but may not condition the gift upon their being planted in places where they are most needed, or even planted

[13] Bailey v. Drexel Furniture Company, 259 U.S. 20 (1922).
[14] United States v. Butler, 297 U.S. 1 (1936).

at all. The government may give money to the unemployed, but may not ask that those who get it shall give labor in return, or even to use it to support their families . . . All that, because it is purchased regulation infringing state powers, must be left for the states, who are unable or unwilling to supply the necessary relief."

But the triple-A case is history. No longer is the Tenth Amendment an obstruction to the exercise of national power. The Court is now much less strict in interpreting the powers of Congress. Doubtless Congress could still, in the opinion of the Court, exceed its constitutional authority to spend for the general welfare, but almost certainly the Court will take a liberal view of such spending. In 1937 Justice Cardozo, in upholding old age benefits under the Social Security Act, stated that it was necessary to distinguish between one welfare and another, between a particular welfare and the general welfare; and the discretion of Congress in this matter would not be disturbed by the Court unless Congress acted arbitrarily.[15]

II. THE SOURCES OF NATIONAL REVENUE AND THE OBJECTS OF EXPENDITURES [16]

The government of the United States collects and expends funds of colossal proportions. A century ago a few million dollars was sufficient to keep the national government's machinery in motion for a year. In 1900 more than half a billion was required; in the 'twenties the amount fluctuated around the four billion mark; and since 1933 the expenditures and revenues, the latter running considerably behind the former, have continued to rise. With the Second World War came the fiscal sky-rocket, expenditures for the fiscal year ending June 30, 1945, being nearly $100,-000,000,000, and revenues a little less than half that amount.

Sources of revenue: CUSTOMS RECEIPTS. Customs receipts constitute a small source of revenue and internal revenues the large source. Until the Civil War the national government relied chiefly upon its customs receipts. As late as the nineteen 'twenties this source was substantial, but by no means the main source, representing only about one seventh of the total revenue. The depression years cut the amount in half, to approximately $300,000-000 per annum. It is now around the half billion mark, constituting hardly a "drop in the bucket" of the total revenue.

INTERNAL REVENUE. Excise taxes, levies on the manufacture, sale, and use of various articles, provide a fairly tidy sum for the national government. The excise law of 1791, which laid a tax upon distilled liquors and which provoked an uprising in western Pennsylvania, imposed the best

[15] Helvering v. Davis, 301 U.S. 619.
[16] *Annual Reports of the Secretary of the Treasury.*

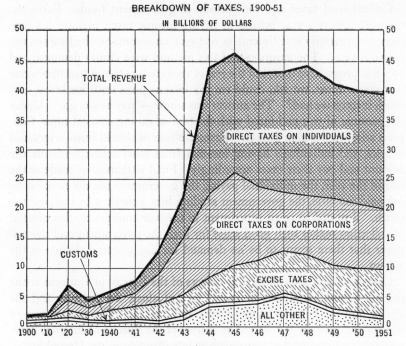

BREAKDOWN OF TAXES, 1900-51
IN BILLIONS OF DOLLARS

From *The New York Times*, Jan. 29, 1950.

known of the earlier excise taxes. In 1797 the first estate tax was levied. This tax, commonly called an inheritance tax, is an excise upon the transmission of property at the death of the owner. Since the Civil War, Congress has made steady use of the power to levy excises. The estate, gas, liquor, tobacco, and retailers' excise taxes now yield approximately $7,500,-000,000. Naturally, in time of war the excise taxes are levied at a higher rate, and many privileges and transactions other than those mentioned are made subject to such taxes.

Income taxes. The internal revenue "jack pot" is the corporation and individual income tax. During the First World War this source yielded some $4,000,000,000 annually. It was soon reduced, however, and did not reach that figure again until we were about to plunge into the second world struggle. Persons on relatively small incomes are now on the list of federal income tax payers, and the rates are steeply graduated so as to recover for the government the major part of the larger incomes. In 1945 receipts from corporation and individual incomes totaled slightly more than $35,000,000,000. Following that date, there was some tax reduction, and the yield from this source fell to about $31,000,000,000. With the war drums sounding once more, income taxes have again begun to mount.

Collection of taxes and the custody of government funds. Formerly, we were always a year behind in paying income taxes, making tax payments in quarterly installments in one year on income we had earned the previous year. The absurdities of this method were clearly demonstrated by a few progressive men, but the rest of us were sure that it had to be done that way. How, we ask, could we pay income taxes until we knew how much income we had? The answer was simple—"pay as you go." Under the pressure of war and faced with the task of raising colossal sums, Congress adopted the plan (1943). Taxes are now withheld from wages and salaries, and individuals having incomes from other sources estimate the amount and pay their taxes accordingly. Final settlement is made at the end of the year, the individual paying the government the difference if he has paid too little, the government sending him a check if he has paid too much. Resorted to as an experiment in the war emergency, this method of collection makes such good sense for both the government and the taxpayer that there seems to be no demand for any essential change in the system.

Customs duties are collected by officers of the Bureau of Customs at the three hundred odd "ports of entry" located along the Atlantic and the Pacific and the boundaries of Canada and Mexico. The greater part of the internal revenue is collected by officers of the Bureau of Internal Revenue, who are stationed at convenient points throughout the United States. Miscellaneous funds of the type mentioned in a preceding paragraph are collected by the appropriate government units in the ordinary course of their work. The federal funds are stored in vaults at Washington, in the twelve federal reserve banks, and in national banks that meet the requirements of depositaries as laid down by the Treasury Department.

National expenditures. Where does the money go? Much of it is appropriated for the maintenance of the Army, the Navy, the Air Force, for pensions and the care of veterans, and for payments on the public debt, interest and principal. Prior to 1933, about 70 per cent of all appropriations were for these purposes. But from 1933 to 1940 Congress annually appropriated several billions for relief and recovery enterprises, spending amounts approximating those it voted for the conduct of the war (1917-1918) with the Central Powers. Roughly a fifth of the total is appropriated for Congress, the Executive Office, and the executive departments and services not mentioned above. Following the Second World War, we find again that about 70 per cent of all the federal revenues are used for war, past or future.

A look at the chart on page 673 will show that, even before the 1950 crisis in Korea, our national expenditures were running over $40,000,000,-000 per annum. With the cold war against communism turned into armed conflict what will our budgets become—$80-$90,000,000,000? No one

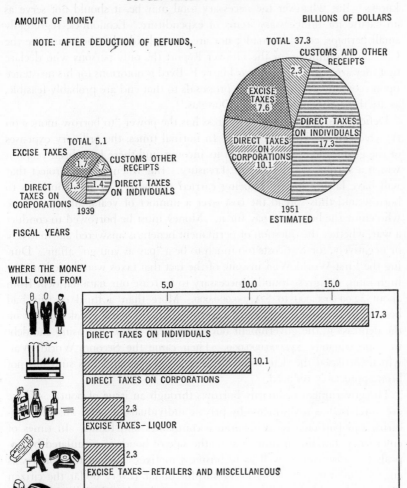

BUDGET RECEIPTS: SUMMARY

AMOUNT OF MONEY

BILLIONS OF DOLLARS

NOTE: AFTER DEDUCTION OF REFUNDS,

TOTAL 37.3

CUSTOMS AND OTHER
RECEIPTS

2.3

EXCISE
TAXES
7.6

DIRECT TAXES
ON INDIVIDUALS
17.3

DIRECT TAXES
ON
CORPORATIONS
10.1

TOTAL 5.1

EXCISE TAXES

1.7   .7   CUSTOMS OTHER
RECEIPTS

DIRECT
TAXES ON
CORPORATIONS

1.3   1.4   DIRECT TAXES
ON INDIVIDUALS

1939

1951
ESTIMATED

FISCAL YEARS

WHERE THE MONEY
WILL COME FROM

	5.0	10.0	15.0	
DIRECT TAXES ON INDIVIDUALS				17.3
DIRECT TAXES ON CORPORATIONS			10.1	
EXCISE TAXES – LIQUOR	2.3			
EXCISE TAXES – RETAILERS AND MISCELLANEOUS	2.3			
EXCISE TAXES – MANUFACTURERS	1.7			
EXCISE TAXES – TOBACCO	1.3			
CUSTOMS AND OTHER RECEIPTS	2.3			

5.0   10.0   15.0

From Bureau of the Budget, *The Federal Budget in Brief, Fiscal Year 1951*, p. 7.

knows. But whatever the necessary total may be, it should not serve as an excuse for unnecessary items of expenditure. Economies, regrettably small perhaps, could be made; nor are the individuals who constitute the Citizens Committee for the Hoover Report the only persons who declare that they are possible. Senator Harry F. Byrd is notorious for his insistence upon economy and some of his proposals to that end are probably feasible, as are those of Senator Paul H. Douglas.[17]

Deficits and borrowing. Congress has the power "to borrow money on the credit of the United States." In normal times, the ordinary expenses of the government are paid from its income, and there have been years in which a surplus was left in the Treasury. But when a great project that will have lasting benefit is being carried through, it is good business to borrow and thus spread the cost over a number of years, allowing those who enjoy the benefit to pay for it. Money must be borrowed to conduct a war, whether the question of permanent benefit is answered affirmatively or negatively, for war costs too much to be a "pay as you go" affair. During the First World War, in spite of the fact that taxes were levied at very high rates, Congress found it necessary to increase our national debt from about $2,000,000,000 to $25,500,000,000. More than a third of this had been repaid before the financial reverses of the 'thirties. Making war on the depression, the government borrowed large sums, increasing the debt to approximately $42,000,000,000. Then came the Second World War, which increased the debt to about $264,000,000,000, and this sum has not been appreciably reduced.

The government ordinarily borrows through an issue of bonds. These are purchased as investments by private individuals, general business concerns, and particularly by insurance companies and banks. In times of emergency, notably in time of war, the sale of bonds is stimulated by appeals to patriotism as well as to business motives. When the country is engaged in war, practically every surplus dollar (every dollar the citizen need not spend) should go into government bonds. A dollar that goes into a bond, like the dollar the government absorbs in taxes, is another dollar taken out of the market as a competitor for scarce goods. It is one more dollar taken out of the trend toward inflation. To be sure, the government can borrow all the money it needs from banks. Moreover, the government could simply print all the money it wants. But when the government prints money, or when it borrows money from banks (except when it borrows from the people's savings in the banks), it is creating more money and thus causing inflation. On the other hand, when it borrows from the

[17] For years Byrd has insisted upon the elimination of waste and extravagance, and Douglas has recently annoyed his colleagues with his persistent attacks upon the "pork barrel," presently to be considered.

BUDGET EXPENDITURES: SUMMARY

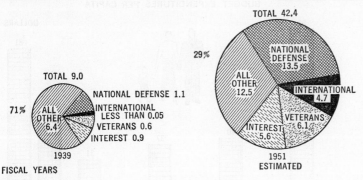

AMOUNT OF MONEY

BILLIONS OF DOLLARS

TOTAL 42.4

29%

NATIONAL DEFENSE 13.5

ALL OTHER 12.5

INTERNATIONAL 4.7

VETERANS 6.1

INTEREST 5.6

TOTAL 9.0

NATIONAL DEFENSE 1.1

INTERNATIONAL LESS THAN 0.05

VETERANS 0.6

INTEREST 0.9

71%

ALL OTHER 6.4

1939

1951 ESTIMATED

FISCAL YEARS

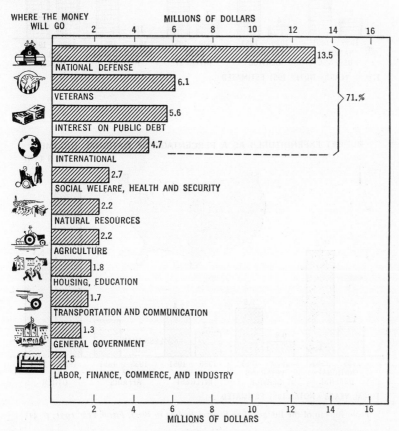

WHERE THE MONEY WILL GO

MILLIONS OF DOLLARS

| | 2 | 4 | 6 | 8 | 10 | 12 | 14 | 16 |

NATIONAL DEFENSE — 13.5

VETERANS — 6.1

INTEREST ON PUBLIC DEBT — 5.6

INTERNATIONAL — 4.7

71.%

SOCIAL WELFARE, HEALTH AND SECURITY — 2.7

NATURAL RESOURCES — 2.2

AGRICULTURE — 2.2

HOUSING, EDUCATION — 1.8

TRANSPORTATION AND COMMUNICATION — 1.7

GENERAL GOVERNMENT — 1.3

LABOR, FINANCE, COMMERCE, AND INDUSTRY — .5

MILLIONS OF DOLLARS

From Bureau of the Budget, *The Federal Budget in Brief, Fiscal Year 1951*, p. 9. (The President's budget for 1952 is almost $72 billions, the increase being for national defense.)

BUDGET EXPENDITURES PER CAPITA

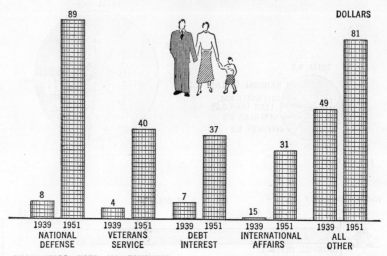

DOLLARS

FISCAL YEARS—NOTE: 1951 ESTIMATED

	1939	1951
NATIONAL DEFENSE	8	89
VETERANS SERVICE	4	40
DEBT INTEREST	7	37
INTERNATIONAL AFFAIRS	15	31
ALL OTHER	49	81

BUDGET EXPENDITURES AS A PERCENTAGE OF NATIONAL INCOME

PER CENT

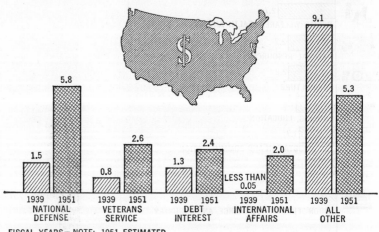

FISCAL YEARS— NOTE: 1951 ESTIMATED

	1939	1951
NATIONAL DEFENSE	1.5	5.8
VETERANS SERVICE	0.8	2.6
DEBT INTEREST	1.3	2.4
INTERNATIONAL AFFAIRS	LESS THAN 0.05	2.0
ALL OTHER	9.1	5.3

From Bureau of the Budget, *The Federal Budget in Brief, Fiscal Year 1951*, p. 41.

incomes of citizens, it simply transfers purchasing power from them to it-self, and thus gets money to finance the war without causing inflation. Taxation and citizen bond-buying are twin virtues in financing a war, and it is a pleasure to record that during the Second World War the United States did not stray entirely from the path of either virtue.

FEDERAL GOVERNMENT BUDGET RECEIPTS AND EXPENDITURES

FISCAL YEARS 1915 THROUGH 1951

[IN MILLIONS]

Fiscal year	Total budget receipts	Total budget expenditures	Surplus or deficit	Fiscal year	Total budget receipts	Total budget expenditures	Surplus or deficit
1915	$683	$746	—$63	1934	$3,065	$6,694	—$3,630
1916	762	713	+48	1935	3,729	6,521	—2,791
1917	1,100	1,954	—853	1936	4,069	8,494	—4,425
1918	3,630	12,662	—9,032	1937	4,979	7,756	—2,777
1919	5,085	18,448	—13,363	1938	5,803	6,979	—1,177
1920	6,649	6,357	+291	1939	5,104	8,966	—3,862
1921	5,567	5,058	+509	1940	5,264	9,183	—3,918
1922	4,021	3,285	+736	1941	7,227	13,387	—6,159
1923	3,849	3,137	+713	1942	12,696	34,187	—21,490
1924	3,853	2,890	+963	1943	22,201	79,622	—57,420
1925	3,598	2,881	+717	1944	43,892	95,315	—51,423
1926	3,753	2,888	+865	1945	44,762	98,703	—53,941
1927	3,992	2,837	+1,155	1946	40,027	60,703	—20,676
1928	3,872	2,933	+939	1947	40,043	39,289	+754
1929	3,861	3,127	+734	1948	42,211	33,791	+8,419
1930	4,058	3,320	+738	1949	38,246	40,057	—1,811
1931	3,116	3,578	—462	1950 [1]	37,763	43,297	—5,533
1932	1,924	4,659	—2,735	1951 [1]	37,306	42,439	—5,133
1933	2,022	4,623	—2,602				

[1] Estimated.

From the Bureau of the Budget, *The Federal Budget in Brief, Fiscal Year 1951*, p. 44.

In the postwar years 1946–1949 there was concern over our failure to balance the budget, our resort to more borrowing in a period of prosperity. It is a matter of common knowledge that this situation develped primarily because of large military expenditures and aid to Western European countries (also essentially a military expense); but the fact of deficit financing was regrettable, nevertheless. If we were unable to balance the budget in "good times," what would we do in "hard times"? At the time of his resignation (October 19, 1949) as Chairman of the President's Council of Economic Advisers, Dr. Edwin G. Nourse stated, among other things: "I am not happy when I see government slipping back into deficits as a way of life in a period when production and employment are high, instead of putting its financial house in order and husbanding reserves to support the economy if less prosperous times overtake us." He readily conceded, however, that he had hardly more than stated a problem; that balancing a

FEDERAL GOVERNMENT BUDGET EXPENDITURES BY FUNCTION

FISCAL YEARS 1939, 1943 THROUGH 1951

[IN MILLIONS OF DOLLARS]

Function	1939	1943	1944	1945	1946	1947	1948	1949	1950 (est.)	1951 (est.)
National defense	1,077	70,267	83,766	84,569	45,134	14,316	10,961	11,914	13,148	13,545
Veterans' services and benefits	559	605	744	2,094	4,414	7,370	6,567	6,669	6,905	6,080
International affairs and finance	19	166	244	677	1,462	6,542	4,782	6,462	5,964	4,711
Social welfare, health, and security	3,946	1,190	1,013	1,046	1,048	1,314	1,869	1,907	2,297	2,714
Housing and community development	ª 154	302	308	ª 193	ª 199	348	82	282	1,006	1,329
Education and general research	36	46	88	150	80	64	63	70	125	434
Agriculture and agricultural resources	1,198	593	1,203	1,610	749	1,244	574	2,512	2,671	2,206
Natural resources not primarily agricultural	228	409	326	243	247	622	1,099	1,512	1,845	2,218
Transportation and communication	498	3,576	4,311	3,367	789	548	1,224	1,622	1,894	1,682
Finance, commerce, and industry	51	264	171	106	30	102	88	120	225	212
Labor	70	240	225	204	174	194	183	193	219	243
General government	560	349	665	955	950	1,361	1,499	1,170	1,223	1,267
Interest on the public debt	941	1,813	2,610	3,622	4,747	4,958	5,188	5,352	5,725	5,625
Reserve for contingencies									50	175
Total	9,028	79,819	95,675	98,451	59,626	38,983	34,179	39,785	43,297	42,439
Adjustment to daily Treasury statement basis	−63	−197	−360	252	1,077	305	−388	272		
Total Budget expenditures	8,966	79,622	95,315	98,703	60,703	39,289	33,791	40,057	43,297	42,439

ª Deduct, excess of repayments and collections over expenditures.
From the Bureau of the Budget, The Federal Budget in Brief, Fiscal Year 1951, p. 44.

budget in the face of postwar demands was next to impossible; that the issues raised were not those of black and white. What the Doctor was really worried about (and he was not alone in his worry) was the easy declarations that "the size of the national debt does not matter." [18]

Dr. Nourse's words of caution are well worth considering, even as our budget grows to meet the demands of another military threat. Taxes could be increased to Second World War rates, or possibly above those rates, and citizen purchase of bonds could be established on a broader and more compelling basis than it was during that struggle. By such noninflationary financing the dollar could be held at a point near its 1950 value and the debt would be held to a minimum.

III. PREPARATION AND ADMINISTRATION OF THE FISCAL PROGRAM [19]

Our concern here is with the methods by which the fiscal program is prepared, voted, and administered. Such activities were long a hit-or-miss game, but the amounts now involved and the attending strain upon our national economy have forced the government authorities to follow a plan, although it is less than perfect.

The Bureau of the Budget. As the cost of government increased and the call for efficiency became louder, the idea of a budget system gained support in Congress. The first budget bill, passed in 1920, was vetoed by President Wilson, not because he was opposed to the budget system (quite the contrary), but on the grounds that this particular bill unconstitutionally restricted the President's power to remove the Comptroller General.[20] But in 1921 Congress passed and President Harding approved the present Budget and Accounting Act. The provisions of this act that relate to the budget proper require the President to transmit to Congress at the beginning of each regular session:

(1) Estimates of the expenditures and appropriations necessary for the support of the government for the ensuing fiscal year.

(2) Estimates of the receipts of the government during the ensuing fiscal year, under existing revenue laws and such revenue proposals as he shall make.

18 *New York Times,* November 3, 1949.

19 M. E. Dimock, *Business and Government* (1949), Ch. 20; H. M. Groves, *Financing Government* (1945 ed.); F. M. Marx, "The Bureau of the Budget . . . ," *Am. Pol. Sci. Rev.,* XXXIX (1945), 653, 869; E. E. Naylor, *The Federal Budget System in Operation* (1941); J. M. Pfiffner, *Public Administration* (1946 ed.), Chs. XXII–XXVII; D. T. Selko, *The Federal Financial System* (1940); H. D. Smith, *The Management of Your Government* (1945); L. D. White, *Public Administration* (1948 ed.), Chs. XVIII–XXI.

20 In the Humphrey case, 295 U.S. 602 (1935), it was held that Congress had the power to restrict the right of the President to remove such independent officers.

(3) Estimates of the expenditures and receipts of the government during the fiscal year in progress.

(4) A list of the expenditures and receipts of the government during the last completed fiscal year.

(5) Statements showing the condition of the treasury at the end of the last fiscal year and estimates of that condition for the year in progress and the ensuing year.

(6) Facts regarding the indebtedness of the United States.

(7) Such other financial statements as he may deem necessary to give full knowledge of the financial condition of the government.

Manifestly, the President cannot personally prepare these facts and estimates for Congress. This work is done by the Bureau of the Budget created by the act. This Bureau was formerly located in the Treasury Department, but it was actually responsible only to the President, and under a reorganization plan of 1939 it was transferred to his Executive Office. At the same time the functions of the Central Statistical Board were transferred to the Bureau of the Budget. The chief officers of the Bureau are the Director, six Assistant Directors, and the General Counsel. Under Executive Order 8248, of September 8, 1939, the functions of the Bureau include the following:

1. To assist the President in the fiscal program of the government.

2. To supervise and control the administration of the Budget.

3. To conduct research in the development of improved plans of administrative management, and to advise the executive departments and agencies of the Government with respect to improved administrative organization and practice.

4. To aid the President to bring about more efficient and economical conduct of Government service.

5. To assist the President by clearing and co-ordinating departmental advice on proposed legislation. . . .

6. To assist in the consideration and clearance and, where necessary, in the preparation of proposed Executive orders and proclamations . . .

7. To plan and promote the improvement, development, and coordination of . . . statistical services.

8. To keep the President informed of the progress of activities by agencies of the Government with respect to work proposed, work actually initiated, and work completed, together with the relative timing of work between the several agencies of the Government; all to the end that the work programs of the several agencies . . . may be co-ordinated and that the moneys appropriated by the Congress may be expended in the most economical manner possible with the least possible overlapping and duplication of effort.[21]

The foregoing makes apparent that the functions of the Bureau of the Budget are broader than the assembling of numbers preceded by dollar

[21] *United States Government Manual*, 1949, p. 56.

signs. Its functions were more comprehensive than that from the beginning of its history. But in the days of Charles G. Dawes, the first Director of the Budget, the Bureau was viewed primarily as an agency for assisting the President in the preparation of the Budget and in keeping government expenses at a minimum. It still performs these functions, but it also has the much broader one of planning for the efficient administration of all the services of the government. It is concerned with keeping expenses down, yes, but it views the entire administrative process. In preparing an intelligent financial program, it must consider all the policies Congress has established, the President's purposes, and what apportionment of funds will accomplish the desired results most economically and efficiently.

Preparing the budget. Each annual budget is in preparation for at least six months. The spending program for any fiscal year has its inception in June, more than twelve months before that fiscal year begins. For example, in June, 1949, the Bureau of the Budget asked each spending agency, including corporations wholly owned by the government, to submit its estimates of appropriations required for the fiscal year July 1, 1950–June 30, 1951. The budget officer in each department or other agency has the various bureaus submit their estimates to him. He reviews these estimates, taking into account the policy of the department head and the departmental program as a whole. He confers often with the department head and with the bureau chiefs. The departmental estimates are thus revised and made ready for the Bureau of the Budget.

About the middle of September the Bureau of the Budget has all the departmental estimates assembled and it begins an intensive examination of them. The estimates of each department are critically studied and sifted by budget examiners who have comprehensive knowledge of the laws, programs, practices, and problems relating to its services. The examiners also hold hearings in which the operating departments have an opportunity to supplement their written requests with oral explanations and in which the examiners ask pertinent and penetrating questions of the operating heads. This consideration of the estimates by the Bureau may go on for several months—the study, the hearings, the conferences, particularly the conversations between the Director and the department heads and between the Director and the President. The Presidnt is, of course, the final authority on what is to go into the budget, but in most matters he will follow the advice of the Director.[22]

22 Harold D. Smith, *The Management of Your Government* (1945), Ch. VI. Smith was Director of the Budget during and for several years before the Second World War. Through him the Bureau became an effective tool for the execution of government policy—a positive, constructive agency rather than simply a "hold expenses down" organization.

When the estimates are accepted by the President (usually late in December), he transmits them to Congress (ordinarily the next day after he has delivered his annual "State of the Union" message to that body). The Budget, which is a huge volume weighing five or six pounds and covering from 1,200 to 1,600 pages, should be distinguished from the Budget Message that accompanies it. The estimates thus submitted are the only lawful estimates. Officers of the various departments and establishments are forbidden to appear before Congress or its committees in an attempt to secure increases over the President's estimates except at the request of either House of Congress.

Congress and the fiscal program. A good budget system requires the cooperation of the legislative body with the executive department. What has Congress done to bring itself into line with the budget system it has established? For one thing, each House has conferred upon its Committee on Appropriations the sole authority to prepare such bills. This plan is a distinct improvement over the old method of allowing several different committees to bring in appropriation measures. A feature of the old system that has certain obvious advantages is retained by the Senate in the provision that the committees on Agriculture, Post Office, Armed Services, and some other important committees may havê members sit with the Committee on Appropriations when it is considering appropriations for the services mentioned. When the House of Representatives receives the budget from the President, it is referred to the Committee on Appropriations, which divides itself into subcommittees in order to consider appropriations for the several activities of the government. Although the President's estimates may be changed as the Committee sees fit, in practice they are not changed a great deal and the total recommended by the Committee is usually about what is requested by the President. The House may change the bills recommended by the Committee, but ordinarily it follows the Committee's lead.

The Senate and its Appropriations Committee show somewhat less restraint than the House in voting funds; but when the appropriations are finally through both Houses, the total money granted does not ordinarily vary greatly from the amount requested by the President. It would seem, therefore, that Congress has entered into the spirit of the budget program and that it has in effect imposed upon itself the obligation not to vote appropriations in excess of the President's estimates. It is still possible, of course, to distribute a little pork.

THE "PORK BARREL" AND "LOGROLLING." The haphazard way in which appropriations were formerly prepared and voted led to a pernicious system of indirect or "honest" graft, a system from which we have not yet entirely escaped. Funds in the federal treasury or to accrue to it were thought of as a barrel of pork, and each congressman was expected to get his share for his constituency, just as the head of each "darky" household in slavery times was expected to get his portion of real pork when the barrel was open in the planter's backyard. Congressmen and the leading citizens of their districts talked both seriously and jokingly of "pork," but seldom with any sense of shame. About 1915, John N. Garner, then an inconspicuous representative from Texas, is reported to have said: "Every time one of these Yankees gets a ham, I'm going to do my best to get a hog." [23] As already intimated, congressmen were not solely responsible for this attitude. They were intimidated by the political organizations in their districts, entreated by letters and personal calls from individual voters, and urgently wired by local chambers of commerce (which at the same time dolefully complained of the rising cost of government) to secure appropriations for such purposes as the erection of a local post office or other federal building, the dredging of a river, and a project of irrigation. Regardless of whether these things were actually needed or feasible, the representative was judged in congressional campaigns by the amount of money he had obtained for his district.

How was it possible for one representative or senator to get the entire Congress to vote for unnecessary expenditures in his district? That was easy. Other congressmen wanted similar things for their districts, and they supported each other's demands. This mutual backing was called "logrolling," a term borrowed from the frontier, where the pioneers often joined forces in the rugged physical enterprise of rolling logs.[24] Of course there were always some congressmen who disdained the unseemly scramble around the pork barrel and who reproached their brethren for the unworthy motives that prompted the figurative logrolling.

If the odor of pork does not fill the halls of Congress to the extent it did forty years ago, it must nevertheless be sadly recorded that pork still holds a place as a congressional diet. Even most of the economy-minded congressmen either partake thereof or allow their colleagues to indulge. One exception is Senator Paul H. Douglas. In the spring of 1950 he named 64 projects costing $830,000,000 that he labeled as non-essential or wasteful. One item called for the improvement of a small-boat harbor close to the U.S. Naval Academy. The harbor was for pleasure boats; there were two other anchorage facilities available near by; and the Bureau of the Budget had declared the project not in accord with the President's program. Nev-

---

[23] Quoted by G. Milburn, in an article in *Harper's*, November, 1932, pp. 669–682.

[24] C. A. and Wm. Beard, *The American Leviathan* (1930), pp. 178–179 contains a good account of the "system" in its palmiest days.

ertheless, Senator Douglas' motion to omit the item was shouted down. His motions to eliminate other items were also defeated.[25] A few months later, when the Korean crisis made necessary larger military appropriations and should have encouraged economy in every appropriation, Senator Douglas returned to his attack on the pork barrel, but was voted down 47 to 28.[26]

REVENUE MEASURES. Congress does not enact a broad revenue measure annually, but almost every session it has the task of revising or amending the revenue laws. The Ways and Means Committee in the House and the Finance Committee in the Senate, perhaps the most important legislative committees, are in charge of the preparation of all revenue bills. Under ordinary circumstances the minority party members of these committees are given scant consideration by the majority; but in times of emergency, partisan politics may be laid aside temporarily and a fair degree of co-operation may be obtained.

Directing our attention to the House Committee, we find that it receives advice and suggestions from all quarters, particularly and properly from the Secretary of the Treasury, the President, and the Speaker. Someone advocates a higher rate of tax on big incomes; another, an income tax that will include the small incomes; another, a sales tax; another proposes revenues from undivided profits. The Committee adopts this, discards that, lays something else aside for future consideration, and then may decide to start all over again. The press gives full publicity to the progress of the Committee, to the extent that it is made available. The Committee watches the press in order to learn the reaction of the public to the facts reported and the rumors discussed, for he is a rare congressman who does not heed the voting public.[27]

Working often in small groups or subcommittees, holding hearings, conferring among themselves, meeting members of the Senate Finance Committee for informal discussion, receiving an urgent suggestion from the President or the Speaker, the Committee on Ways and Means finally has its bill ready for the House. Here it is debated, amended, and, in the course

---

[25] Robert Wallace, "A Look Inside the Pork Barrel," *New Republic,* May 29, 1950, pp. 10–12.

[26] *Time,* August 7, 1950, p. 15.

[27] It is not often that a congressman feels free to take the bold stand assumed by Charles R. Crisp, Acting Chairman of the Ways and Means Committee, in February, 1932. "I have burned every bridge behind me," he declared, in a speech in the House. "No matter what the personal political consequences may be, I'm going to advocate levying sufficient taxes to balance the budget. It means nothing to the United States whether I remain in Congress or not, but it means much to the United States government that its honor, its credit, its security be maintained at par. . . . I want you and the country to gird yourselves with stamina, with backbone and with courage to meet this emergency. All must make tremendous sacrifices. For the budget must be balanced either through a manufacturers' sales tax or excise taxes on commodities and industries." *Time,* Feb. 22, 1932, p. 15.

of time, adopted. Then the bill must pass through the Senate Finance Committee and the whole body of senators. It is almost certain to receive many amendments, and it is returned to the House, where these amendments must be considered. If the House fails to approve all the amendments, then a "conference" is arranged between members of the two Houses, as described under congressional procedure. The time is short now, and the agreement reached by the conference is quite likely to receive formal approval in both Houses. However dissatisfied the President may be with the revenue bill, he almost invariably signs it, for the government must have money on which to operate and private business can proceed with more certainty when a revenue bill becomes a law.

The tariff. Formerly, a tariff measure, a bill designed to produce some revenue and protect American industry from foreign competition, furnished the occasion for lobbying on a grand scale. The problem of the tariff was complicated enough of itself, but it was further confused by the aggressive claims of selfish interests and the exigencies of politics. The Trade Agreements Act of 1934 (to be discussed in the next chapter) has transferred a great deal of the tariff detail to the Executive department, but Congress is still the place of last resort and modern illustrations of old tariff-making procedures are still to be found. "I've been coming here for thirty years," said a woolgrowers' lobbyist in 1947; "and the way you get bills through is to go up and grab the fellows and talk to them. A speech never changed a vote yet." Another point on his method of operation: ". . . The way you get bills passed is—you scratch my back and I'll scratch yours." The same idea was put in more detail by a member of the House from Georgia. Said he: "So far as I know, there is not a sheep living in the Third Congressional District of Georgia. . . . But . . . I do not feel I have any right to ask the Congress to do any more for the cotton producer, for the tobacco producer, for the peanut producer . . . than the wool producers have to ask the Congress to do for the producers of wool and the other commodities of the great West." [28]

ATTEMPTS TO IMPROVE CONGRESSIONAL CONSIDERATION OF FISCAL MEASURES. The foregoing paragraphs indicate that congressional consideration and decision on revenues and expenditures are lengthy and somewhat complicated processes. Congressmen themselves often do not know exactly what the situation is, for while revenue and appropriations bills are being considered by the appropriate committees of the two houses, no committee has any responsibility for the complete fiscal program of the government—for the balancing of revenues and expenditures, for increasing or decreasing the public debt. The Legislative Reorganization Act of 1946 (sec. 138) was designed to correct that defect by the following plan:

[28] Tris Coffin, "No Speech Ever Changed a Vote," *New Republic,* July 14, 1947, pp. 16–18.

The Committee on Ways and Means and the Committee on Appropriations of the House of Representatives, and the Committee on Finance and the Committee on Appropriations of the Senate, or duly authorized subcommittees thereof, are authorized and directed to meet jointly at the beginning of each regular session of Congress and after study and consultation, giving due consideration to the budget recommendations of the President, report to their respective Houses a legislative budget for the ensuing fiscal year, including the estimated over-all federal receipts and expenditures for such year. Such report shall contain a recommendation for the maximum amount to be appropriated for expenditure in such year. . . . If the estimated receipts exceed the estimated expenditures, such report shall contain a recommendation for a reduction in the public debt.

If the estimated expenditures exceed the estimated receipts, then the joint committee shall recommend that the national debt be increased by the amount of the difference.

Here may be the solution to a problem, some legislators and others thought; this "legislative budget" is the answer. They have been disappointed. "The legislative budget," writes Professor Jesse W. Burkhead, "has been a failure," and chiefly because Congress or committees thereof are unable to determine early in a session what the fiscal program should be.[29]

Some improvement in appropriations procedure is looked for in a plan adopted in 1950. Instead of the usual ten or more appropriations bills a consolidated bill was enacted, a bill covering 431 pages, calling for some 36 billions in appropriations for about 40 agencies. The chief omissions were items for international relations and for the interest on the national debt. Events in Korea of course upset this orderly plan. Large supplemental emergency appropriations had to be made.

Administering the budget. Of hardly less importance than the method of preparing and voting the budget is the system by which expenditures of the departments are controlled after the money has been appropriated. Formerly a Comptroller of the Treasury and auditors attached to the Treasury Department performed this function, but their only duty was to pass upon the legality of expenditures. The Budget and Accounting Act of 1921 abolished the office of Comptroller of the Treasury and created an independent establishment, the General Accounting Office. This Office is headed by the Comptroller General of the United States, who is appointed by the President and the Senate for a period of fifteen years and who may not be removed except by Congress and then only for certain specified causes. The Office is thus intended to be free from executive control.

The Comptroller General was given the authority to prescribe a system

[29] "Federal Budgetary Developments, 1947–1948," *Pub. Adm. Rev.*, VIII (1948), 267.

of accounts for the departments and establishments; and although some progress has been made in improving departmental accounting procedures, the improvement has been along lines designed to assist the General Accounting Office rather than the President, the Treasury Department, or the Bureau of the Budget. Another function of the Office is that of settling claims by or against the United States, such settlements being made independent of the administrative departments. But the chief functions are those of accounting and auditing. Through its accounting authority the Office makes decisions as to proposed expenditures and the availability of funds. Through its auditing authority it examines and verifies accounts after the transactions have been made in order to discover any illegality or irregularity in the expenditures.

These two functions of accounting and auditing should not be exercised by the same organization, for the control of expenditures through accounting is an executive function and should be under executive direction, whereas auditing is for the purpose of giving Congress a check on the Executive and it is therefore a function that should be exercised free from executive control. The President's Committee on Administrative Management (1937) pointed out the anomalous situation created by the association of the two functions in the Accounting Office, and the Committee recommended that the powers to determine the use of appropriations, to settle accounts and claims, and to prescribe administrative accounting systems be transferred to the Treasury Department, where they would be under executive control. The Committee maintained that, with the auditing function left in the independent Auditor General's Office (the Committee would have his title changed from Comptroller to Auditor), Congress would have proper and sufficient means for holding the administrative forces to accountability. Since the President has been frequently vexed by decisions of the Comptroller, he was more than pleased to transmit the Committee's recommendations to Congress. That body, however, was unfavorable to the proposals; and it must be added that it was supported in this attitude by some fiscal authorities hardly less eminent than those who urged the change.[30]

The Hoover Commission's Recommendations (1949) did not go quite so far as those of the President's Committee. The Hoover report on *Budgeting and Accounting* did, however, recommend the establishment in the Treasury Department of an Accountant General who should be given authority to prescribe accounting methods for the administrative departments, subject to the approval of the Comptroller General.[31] This leaving the final say-so respecting accounting methods and procedures to

[30] The Brookings Institution among others. See White, *op. cit.*, pp. 307–308.
[31] Pp. 35–41.

the Comptroller may win the votes of congressmen for the Accountant General plan. The Commission was careful to point out that such an arrangement would not undermine the powers of the Comptroller.

In conclusion it must be stated that administrative reorganization between 1939 and 1949 brought about a greater degree of executive control in the administration of the budget. As already explained, the Bureau of the Budget was moved to the White House establishment, and it was charged by the Executive with the duty of supervising, controlling, and *administering* the Budget. Acting through the Director of the Budget, the President requires the spending agencies of the government to submit monthly statements of amounts they propose to spend; and after approval by the Director, such monthly apportionments become the maxima that may be expended. Thus, an appropriation by Congress does not become an order to spend, but only permission to spend, subject to Executive approval. The Director may use his power to prevent excessive and wasteful expenditures and for other fiscal reasons. Although Executive restraints could be and were laid upon spending before 1939, the rearrangement of that date gave more emphasis to the system. The new arrangement also places the Bureau of the Budget in a better position to perform general services in the interest of economy and efficiency, services it was always supposed to perform but did not. The reference here is to research on administrative management, the co-ordination of departmental advice on proposed legislation, the improvement and development of the statistical services, the preparation of executive orders, and advice to the President on the progress of administrative activities. In other words, the Bureau is now a part of the White House administrative staff.

IV. THE CURRENCY AND BANKING [32]

Congress has the power "to borrow money, . . . to coin money, regulate the value thereof, and of foreign coin." [33] Its power to charter and regulate banks is implied from these and other enumerated powers. [34]

The currency. Congress may coin money and regulate its value; but the states are forbidden to coin money, emit bills of credit, or make anything but gold or silver coin a tender in payment of debts. [35] The states

---

[32] Dimock, *op. cit.*, Chs. 21–22; M. B. Foster and Raymond Rodgers, *Money and Banking* (1947 ed.); E. W. Kemmerer, *The A. B. C. of the Federal Reserve System* (1938 ed.); W. B. Munro, *The Government of the United States* (1946 ed.), Ch. XXVI; Clark Warburton, "Monetary Control under the Federal Reserve Act," *Pol. Sci. Qt.*, LXI (1946), 505–534; H. White, *Money and Banking* (1935).

[33] Constitution, Art. I, sec. VIII, cls. 2 and 5.

[34] See pp. 41–44.

[35] Constitution, Art. I, sec. X, cl. 1.

may charter banks and these banks may issue paper money, but such paper money may not be used as legal tender; that is, as money which must be accepted in payment of a debt. As indicated in the first part of this chapter, Congress effectively removed state bank notes from the currency field when (1866) it placed a heavy tax upon them. From the beginning, Congress coined gold and silver, and in 1791 it chartered a national bank with the authority to issue bank notes, although such notes were not made legal tender. Under the pressure of the Civil War, however, Congress made United States notes legal tender. Not being redeemable at the Treasury in coin, the notes depreciated to less than half their face value. In 1867 the issue was attacked as unconstitutional, and the Supreme Court so held. But later, with a partial change in personnel, the Supreme Court decided that the issue of the legal tender notes was valid, basing its decision primarily upon the theory that the issue was a reasonable method of financing the war.[36]

Congress reissued the legal tender notes or "greenbacks," as they were commonly called, after the war emergency had passed. The authority to do so could no longer be found in the exigencies of war; but, in 1884, the Supreme Court held that Congress could issue legal tender notes, even in time of peace, under authority implied from its general power over finance.[37]

The gold standard. During the greater part of our history gold and silver were coined independently. From the 'seventies until 1900 there was a very strong movement for the coinage of silver and gold at a fixed ratio. Bryan proposed a ratio of 16 to 1 and went down to defeat. From 1896 until 1933 we were thoroughly committed to the gold standard. To be sure, silver and various types of paper money constituted the chief media of circulation, but the Gold Standard Act of 1900 required the Secretary of the Treasury to keep all kinds of money at a parity with gold, a provision which meant that any kind of money upon presentation at the Treasury should be redeemed in gold. Thus the gold standard was maintained, making every dollar the equivalent of a gold dollar. To the average man, money was simply money, whether it was gold, silver, or some form of paper currency. He was not likely to complain unless someone handed him a quantity of coin, when he might good-naturedly ask for paper. The gold standard may have been a "cross of gold" to Bryan, but to bankers, businessmen, and the investing public it became a "golden calf."

But times can change. With nearly all the great nations driven off the gold standard by disturbed economic conditions following the First

[36] Legal Tender Cases, 12 Wallace 457 (1871).
[37] Juilliard v. Greenman, 110 U.S. 421.

World War and with the business decline in this country going well below what we had previously considered the bottom of the economic trough, many voices were raised for inflation. As prices continued to fall, we abandoned the gold standard (April, 1933), not because the country's gold holdings were low (they were quite the reverse), but because it was hoped that by cutting loose from gold the value of the dollar would decline, thus raising the price of goods. The plan seemed to work.

In May, 1933, Congress, when considering farm relief, took other steps toward inflation. Further inflation does not seem to have been a part of the program of the Democratic leaders, but the "inflationary" element staged a successful revolt in Congress and only by a compromise engineered by the President were several types of inflation not made mandatory. What the bill did provide for was *permissive* inflation, leaving the President to exercise at his discretion several inflationary powers, among which was the power to reduce the gold content of the dollar by as much as 50 per cent.

In January, 1934, the President reduced the gold content of the dollar by about 41 per cent. Prior to that time the President had ordered holders of gold and gold certificates to turn them over to the federal reserve banks and accept other money for them; and Congress had canceled the "gold clause" in contracts, clauses that stipulated payment in gold coin of the weight and fineness of the gold dollar before 1933. Although we may be said to have gone back to the gold standard, gold no longer circulates as money. It is a gold standard with qualifications. All the monetary gold is owned by the government and held by the Treasury (physically the gold is in large bars and is kept in a deep stronghold in Kentucky). This gold, worth about $24,000,000,000 in terms of the devalued dollar and representing approximately half the world supply, serves as the metallic base for our paper currency.

Silver also serves as a base for our money. By the terms of the Silver Purchase Act of 1934 the Secretary of the Treasury is required to purchase silver from time to time until one fourth of the monetary stock shall consist of that metal. With certain exceptions the government has assumed ownership of all silver, some of which it keeps in bullion and some of which it circulates in the form of silver coins. The problem of 1933 of how to bring about a decline in the value of the dollar and thus raise prices was solved all too well by our entrance into the Second World War. The insatiable demands of the war machine caused prices to rise, and they continued to rise in the postwar period.

Early history of banking: 1. THE BANKS OF THE UNITED STATES. A good banking system is considered an essential for an industrial society; but it cannot be said that our own system has always kept pace with our needs.

In 1791 Congress chartered the First Bank of the United States and gave it the power to issue notes to serve as paper money. It was a great aid, not only to business but also to the government; for it was of material service in collecting the revenues, in advancing loans to the government, and in serving as its depositary. Although Jefferson and others who stood for a strict construction of the Constitution maintained that Congress had no authority to establish such an institution, the courts were not called upon to settle the issue. In 1811 the Bank's charter expired; but after the War of 1812 the financial situation was such that Congress chartered the Second Bank of the United States. This Bank had a somewhat stormy history. The constitutionality of its charter was attacked but upheld (McCulloch v. Maryland). The state banks resented the fact that it competed with them in what they and the local politicians considered their exclusive field of operation. Also, there was a general desire for higher prices, for inflation, which the central bank resisted. Then, too, frontier people generally feared and hated it as a sort of monster that drew to itself the wealth they had earned by the sweat of their brows. Jackson made it a paramount question, and won a great victory on the issue in the presidential campaign of 1832. When its charter expired in 1836, the Bank came to an end as a national institution.

2. THE STATE BANK MONOPOLY. For nearly thirty years thereafter, banks operating under state laws had a monopoly of the business. Banking laws were very liberal, altogether too liberal in the majority of the states. The states were prohibited by the Constitution from issuing bills of credit, but the Supreme Court held that they could authorize banks to issue such bills. A few states permitted banks to issue no more notes than they were able to redeem in gold, and a few banks in states with lax laws followed conservative policies and restricted the issue of notes. But the states and the banks commonly responded to the popular demand for cheap money. In circulation were notes as "good as gold," notes worth fifty cents on the dollar, and notes worth little or nothing, depending upon the bank of issue.

The national banking system. The Civil War brought the present national banking system into being. To the obvious need for a national currency system was added the urgent need of the government for a market for its bonds. The Act of 1863 and later amendments required each national bank to issue notes up to the amount of the capital stock of the bank, such notes to be secured by federal bonds owned by the bank and deposited with the United States Treasury. Shortly after the Banking Act was passed, Congress taxed the notes of the state banks out of existence, thus leaving the national banks a monopoly on the privilege of issuing notes. Although the new system brought about marked improvement in banking and currency, defects were revealed in the course of time.

ITS PRINCIPAL DEFECTS. If a single word can characterize the defects of the new national banking system, that word is *inelasticity*. The cash reserves of the banks were largely concentrated in New York. This concentration of reserves was not in itself bad; but since there was no agency controlling the banking reserves of the country, they could not be quickly shifted to meet the credit needs of other localities. Again, both local and central banks were subject to a rigid requirement to retain certain percentages of their deposits as reserves, so that when the reserves reached these points on the downgrade there could be no extension of credit, a situation that is likely to bring disaster to business. Another defect was in the restriction that no notes should be issued except those covered by government bonds. Notes issued on the general assets of the banks would have provided a more elastic currency to meet the varying needs of business—more notes when business was active, and fewer when business was "off." Various "depressions" and "panics," particularly that of 1907, exposed these and other limitations of the system.

The Federal Reserve System. The Federal Reserve Act of 1913 (as amended in 1935) brought about fundamental changes in the banking system. The country was divided into twelve districts, and a federal reserve bank was established in each. The stock of these banks is owned by the local "member banks." All national banks must be members, and state banks may become members by complying with certain requirements. An individual has very few business transactions with a federal reserve bank. They are the "bankers' banks," although the individual, banking with a member bank, benefits indirectly.

FUNCTIONS OF THE FEDERAL RESERVE BANKS. Just what are the functions of the federal reserve banks? In the first place, they hold practically all of the reserves of the member banks. Although banking reserves are thus more highly centralized than before, the discretion allowed federal reserve officers is such that these reserves can be made available for credit needs in various parts of the country much more freely than under the old system.

As a second essential function, the reserve banks purchase from member banks the promissory notes or commercial paper of persons to whom the member banks have loaned money. This procedure is called "rediscounting." With the receipts from this "commercial paper" the member banks can make loans to other individuals and thus continue to serve the needs of local business.

A third important service performed by the reserve banks is the issue of notes. The notes now in circulation are for the most part *federal reserve notes*. They must have a backing of at least 40 per cent in certificates covered by the government's gold stock, the remaining 60 per cent or less being covered by eligible commercial paper (notes), which the reserve banks have obtained by rediscounting or otherwise. Member banks may secure this currency for their customers by taking commercial paper to the reserve banks and bringing back borrowings in the form of federal reserve notes.

Among other important functions performed by the federal reserve banks may be mentioned their service as the national government's bankers. Through these banks the government receives and makes payments, sells its bonds, and makes other business transactions. This use of the federal reserve banks made possible the closing of the nine subtreasuries the government had formerly maintained in convenient centers.

Still another service is performed by the System through its "open-market" committee. This committee consists of the members of the Board of Governors of the Federal Reserve System and five representatives chosen by the reserve banks. This committee has the duty of exercising control over the buying and selling of the notes and bonds of the United States by the reserve banks. These banks, by dealing in the obligations of the government, very largely determine the supply of bank credit available for commercial purposes at a given time. If more money is needed for business purposes, the open-market committee may permit the reserve banks to purchase government obligations to the amount of a billion or two, thus putting money into business channels. This procedure also helps keep up the price of government bonds. If the committee wishes to check credit expansion, it may authorize the sale of government obligations by the reserve banks, thus taking money out of ordinary investment channels.

THE BOARD OF GOVERNORS. One of the defects of the banking system before the Federal Reserve Act was the absence of central control. This is now secured through the Board of Governors, which is composed of seven members appointed by the President and Senate for terms of fourteen years. The President also designates the members of the Board who are to serve as chairman and vice-chairman. Each reserve bank has its own board of directors, who name a president and vice-president subject to the approval of the Board of Governors in Washington. The president of a reserve bank is its responsible executive officer.

This centralized system made possible the expansion of credit necessitated by the world wars. No irredeemable paper was issued, as during the Civil War. After the First World War, federal reserve authorities, through the rediscount rate and open-market operations, managed to control credit conditions and thus keep business on a fairly even keel; but after 1928 their efforts were not so successful. It should be observed, however, that the business disasters of the 'thirties were caused by a variety of factors, the greater number of them entirely outside the sphere of activity of the Federal Reserve System. If the System did not prevent inflation in the war and postwar years (1941–1950) it was not so much for lack of authority as for the difficulty, even impossibility, of resisting the Treasury program that called for such inflationary practices as the sale of government bonds (tens of billions worth) to banks and Federal Reserve support (under Treasury pressure) of the price of such bonds through open market purchases. Such purchases have made available too much credit, a condition that contributes substantially to inflation.

The banking crisis of 1932–1933. The collapse of our banking system in 1933 is, unfortunately, not fresh in our memories. One of its principal causes was speculation. Instead of making their loans exclusively for self-liquidating commercial transactions, as commercial banks do in England and Canada, our banks eagerly entered the field of investment loans, buying bonds and then more bonds of many varieties in the golden age of 1921–1929. High authorities in Washington encouraged commercial banks to embark upon this enterprise. With the business decline, bond values declined; and as business continued "down the chute," bonds went along with it. When large withdrawals of deposits were made, banks had to sell their bonds regardless of the demoralized market. Banks failed by the hundred, 522 in the month of October, 1931. The National Credit Corporation was formed, an organization through which strong banks would help weak banks. Success was only temporary. In January, 1932, the Reconstruction Finance Corporation was created to make liberal advances to hard pressed banks. This was a success for a few months. But it was becoming obvious by this time that farm mortgages would have to be written down and that the real estate situation in the cities was also threatening the banks. There came another spurt of bank failures, and in February and early March of 1933, governors of a number of states closed banks. There was another Black Friday (March 3) in New York, $100,000,000 in gold being withdrawn from the banks in the nation's financial capital in a single day. At 4:30 a. m. the next day, Governor Lehman closed all the banks in the state, having the solemn declaration of the bankers that they could not remain open another half day. On March 6 President Roosevelt closed all the banks in the country. With the utter collapse of the banking system in a country that had well over four billions in gold, the nation had witnessed the "greatest débâcle in banking history."

The banking acts of 1933 and 1935. After the collapse of the banking system the country breathed more easily. The worst had happened at last. Called into special session, Congress immediately approved the President's proclamation closing the banks and placing an embargo on gold exportation and authorized him to take similar action in future emergencies. Congress further empowered the President and the Secretary of the Treasury to regulate banking during such emergencies; authorized the Secretary of the Treasury to prohibit the hoarding of gold or gold certificates; gave the Comptroller of the Currency power to appoint "conservators" for national banks whose assets were in danger; and provided for the emergency issue of currency against the security of obligations of the United States or notes, drafts, bills of exchange, or bankers' acceptances. With the passage of this act, solvent banks were reopened by national and state authorities and the country took on a genuine spirit of optimism.

A few months after these emergency acts, a comprehensive banking law was passed. The act was designed to correct the weaknesses of the banking system in a number of particulars, but its most important sections are those designed to prevent speculative use of bank funds and to guarantee deposits. A curb on the speculative use of funds is sought through the significant requirement that banks which are members of the federal reserve system must divorce their security affiliates. Private banks that receive deposits must do likewise; and if such banks elect to continue to receive deposits, they must submit to state or federal examinations. Among other provisions aimed at the same purpose are those that require the federal reserve banks to keep advised on the loans and investments of member banks, prohibit member banks from accepting funds that are to be loaned to brokers, forbid interlocking directorates with security firms, and make officers of a member bank ineligible for loans by that bank.

The act provided for a deposit guaranty (strongly opposed by many banking authorities) varying from 100 to 50 per cent, depending upon the amount of the deposit. The Banking Act of 1935, as amended, requires complete insurance up to $10,000, but that is the maximum which may be insured. The insurance fund is raised by annual levies of one twelfth of one per cent on the average deposits of the insured banks, and it is administered by the Federal Deposit Insurance Corporation. All banks in the Federal Reserve System must accept the guaranty plan. Other banks may have their deposits insured also, but any state bank that has deposits of more than a million dollars must become a member of the Federal Reserve System in order to retain the insurance feature. Thus, through the Federal Reserve System and the Federal Deposit Insurance Corporation the national government is reaching into the far corners of the country and greatly strengthening a banking system that has long needed more unity and control. Yet we are still some distance away from absolute central control of banking.

Government banking institutions. No discussion of banks would be at all adequate that fails to make mention of the credit agencies the government has established since 1930. These agencies do not have all of the attributes of ordinary banks, but they perform many of the functions of banks, supplementing and perhaps competing with them, and they may in time crowd them considerably. There are the Farm Credit Administration, the Federal Home Loan Banks, the Federal Savings and Loan Insurance Corporation, and perhaps a score of others.

The first, the best known, and the giant of all these is the Reconstruction Finance Corporation. It was established in 1932 and authorized to advance money to banks, trust companies, building and loan associations, railroads, and certain other institutions. Presently it was authorized to make loans to general business, and it entered the field in a large way but not without caution. In its first years it made some loans for relief, loans no one expected it to recover, but by far the largest share of its loans have been to business enterprises on a business basis. Billions were loaned in a few years, billions that were of inestimable benefit to commerce and industry and on which the government took no loss. In 1937 it was thought that it had served its purpose and might withdraw from the field, and Congress actually took steps to terminate its activities. But then came the "recession" of 1938, and on its heels the Second World War. The RFC was deeply involved in furthering the war program. Under the authority of five or six acts of Congress and various executive orders, it engaged in such war activities as making loans to, and purchasing the obligations of, any business enterprise for any purpose advantageous to the national defense; purchasing, for the same purpose, the capital stock of any business corporation; the creation and organization of corporations, such as the Defense Plant Corporation and the Rubber Reserve Company, to aid the government in its defense program; the purchase of various strategic materials; the erection and expansion of plants for the production of arms and other instruments of war; the provision of facilities for aviation training; and a host of other undertakings.[38] The RFC continues to function, but it seems to have become susceptible to "pressures" and "influence," and has lost its high standing.

The state banks. There are still about 10,000 state banks, which is nearly double the number of national banks. Unless state banks are members of the Federal Reserve System, or have accepted the deposit insurance plan (the greater number of them have), they are not subject to any federal control. The states supervise their banks through a department of banking,

[38] *Reconstruction Finance Corporation Act, as Amended, and Other Laws Pertaining to RFC* (pamphlet, 1941); "The War Goes to Mr. Jesse Jones," *Fortune,* Dec., 1941, p. 91; Reconstruction Finance Corporation, *Annual Report, 1949;* Merle Fainsod and Lincoln Gordon, *Government and the American Economy* (1949 ed.), pp. 715–721.

or through a combined department of banking and insurance. Such department or commission, by requiring reports and making inspections, enforces the state law respecting accounts, bank investments, ordinary loans, and so on.

The chief criticism of state banks is that they have failed in alarming numbers. They are frequently poorly administered, often too dependent upon a single industry, and usually too small. "What will the little banks do in the little county seats?" inquired the late Senator Huey Long of the Senate banking authority, the late Carter Glass. "'Little banks!'" answered Senator Glass scornfully. "Little corner grocerymen who get together $10,000 or $15,000 and then invite the deposits of their community and then at the very first gust of disaster topple over and ruin their depositors! What we need in this country are real banks and real bankers." Many another person agrees with Senator Glass that the day of the small bank has passed and harbors the minimum hope that those which cannot enter the Federal Reserve System will close their doors. What the country needs is a unified banking system, a system that the national legislation of the 'thirties tends to establish.

Protection of investors. Although not in the class of banking legislation, certain acts of recent years may receive appropriate mention at this point because they are designed primarily to protect investors. The Securities Act of 1933 requires that all new issues of securities, with a few exceptions, be submitted to the Securities and Exchange Commission before being offered for sale in interstate commerce or through the mails. The promoters must give to the Commission all essential information regarding the securities, the promoters being held responsible for the truthfulness of this information. The Securities Exchange Act of 1934 attempts to regulate stock exchanges through this same Commission. The act requires such procedures as the submission of exchange by-laws to the Commission for approval, registration with the Commission of securities listed on the exchanges, and presentation to the Commission of the financial conditions of firms and corporations whose securities are to be so listed. The Public Utility Holding Company Act of 1935 imposes upon the Securities and Exchange Commission the duty of supervising various activities of holding companies and subsidiaries, such as security transactions, intercompany loans, proxies, and dividends. The act is designed, of course, to protect consumers and investors. The Trust Indenture Act of 1939 requires that bonds, notes, debentures, and similar securities offered for sale be issued under standards satisfactory to the SEC. The Investment Company Act and the Investment Advisers Act of 1940 afford further protection to investors and confer additional duties upon the Commission. The former act provides for the regulation of investment trusts and investment companies, and the latter for the registration of all persons engaged in the investment advisory business and prohibits certain abuses that had existed in this business. Although the Commission has the power to control in some degree the issuance of securities by public utility holding companies, no statute that it administers guarantees an investor against loss. What the Commission does is to require adequate disclosure of information about securities. The investor is left to form his own opinion and to assume the risks incident to investment.

V. STATE FINANCE [39]

The cost of state government (and of all other government) has increased by leaps and bounds in the last fifty years. This increase is explained in part by the decline in the value of the dollar, but the major explanation is that the states have tremendously increased their expenditures by vast expansion of old functions, such as highway construction and education, and the addition of new and expensive functions, particularly social security. After the national government takes its fifty billions or so in taxes the states must find roughly one seventh of that amount for their functions and leave local governments sources to tap for a somewhat larger amount. A review of state finance must include such matters as the limitations on taxing powers, sources of revenue, budgeting, and borrowing money.

Limitations upon the taxing power. There are three important limitations upon the state legislatures' power to tax. *First,* there is the limitation with respect to the taxing of commerce. The federal Constitution prohibits the states from levying import, export, or tonnage duties. Control of interstate commerce by the national government means that the states cannot tax interstate commerce. The states may, however, tax property as such, even though it is used in interstate or foreign commerce. Thus, the states may and do impose general property taxes upon railroad and steamship companies. What is prohibited is the taxing of an *act* of interstate or foreign commerce. *Second,* the state may not tax the national government or its instrumentalities.[40]

Third, state tax laws must satisfy a provision of the Fourteenth Amendment of the federal Constitution that reads: No state shall "deprive any person of life, liberty, or property, without due process of law; nor deny to any person within its jurdisiction the equal protection of the laws."

[39] R. G. and Gladys C. Blakey, *Sales Taxes and Other Excises* (1945); A. G. Buehler, *Public Finance* (1948 ed.); Federation of Tax Administrators, *Recent Trends in State Finance* (1948); H. M. Groves, *Financing Government* (1945 ed.); M. S. Kendrick, *Public Finance* (1950).

[40] On limitations *one* and *two* see Ch. 5, sec. I.

As judicially interpreted, this clause means that a state may levy no taxes on property or rights not within its jurisdiction. This interpretation can get very technical, especially in relation to the taxing of intangible property. For example, it has been held that the State of Utah may impose a tax upon a transfer by death of shares of stock in the Union Pacific Railroad Company, a Utah corporation, even though the decedent resided in New York and kept his stock certificates there. Utah had the right to tax because the corporation owed its existence to that state.[41] The provision of the Amendment quoted above means also, among other things, that taxes may be levied only for public purposes (not for the special benefit of particular persons or corporations), and that they shall bear equally upon the same types of property. It should be noted, however, that the Supreme Court of the United States now construes these tax limitations rather liberally in favor of the states, the Utah case just cited furnishing a good example of this generous attitude. In the greater number of state constitutions are limitations very similar to the "due process" and "equal protection" restraints of the federal Constitution, and it is not unusual to find a state court more severe in holding the legislature in check than is the Supreme Court of the United States.

Sources of revenue. States draw their income from various sources. Probably no two states have identical tax systems; but nearly all of them levy a general property tax, an inheritance tax, a corporation tax, unemployment compensation taxes, and certain others.[42]

1. THE GENERAL PROPERTY TAX. The general property tax is the oldest state tax, and the one from which practically all the revenue was formerly derived, but from which only about five per cent (excluding unemployment compensation) is derived at present. It still carries by far the largest share of the revenue burden in most cities and counties. The theory of the general property tax is simple. Each person pays a tax determined by the value of his house, lands, horses, cattle, machinery, furniture, jewelry, stocks, bonds, mortgages, and so on. This is an *ad valorem* tax—so much per hundred dollars of assessed valuation. It falls alike upon all property owners, supposedly. It was fairly satisfactory in the days when governments did not need much money, and when the earthly goods of most men consisted of real property and tangible personal property. The farmer could not hide his buildings, fields, and live stock from the assessor; nor could he conceal easily the great hall clock or the "parlor" sofa. Furthermore, the ordinary assessor had little difficulty in arriving at a fair valuation of these properties. But the concentration of property in cities and

---

[41] State Tax Commission of Utah v. Aldrich, 316 U.S. 174 (1942).

[42] *Book of the States* (*1950–1951*), pp. 230 ff.; W. B. Graves, *American State Government* (1946 ed.), Ch. XIII, and C. F. Snider, *American State and Local Government* (1950), Chs. XXIV–XXV, contain excellent discussions of the state revenue system. See also "The States' Scramble for Taxes," *Tax Outlook*, August, 1949, pp. 12–16.

the revolutionary increase in the amount of intangible property (securities of various kinds) since the Civil War have changed all this. City property is ordinarily much more difficult to evaluate than rural property; and intangible property locked in the owner's strong box, whether held by rural or urban inhabitants, often escapes the assessor's rolls. Indeed, the kindly assessor may rather encourage a timid individual to make no mention of his intangibles, since the general property tax rate in some states is almost confiscatory when applied to them.

Assessment. The problem of assessing real and personal property for purposes of taxation calls for more than passing mention, for unscientific assessment constitutes a fundamental shortcoming in the administration of the general property tax. The assessors are local officers, usually elected, and seldom have any training for their important work. In most states the assessors are given written instructions, and in a few, some additional aids; but no amount of such help will reduce assessment to routine or give impartial valuations to property unless the assessors are honest and intelligent. The taxpayer often makes his own assessment, particularly his personal property or assessment.

The assessor walks into the home of a wealthy individual and makes dutiful inquiry about pianos, washing machines, electric refrigerators, and clocks; but he hardly notices the fine paintings on the wall or the oriental rug on the floor (unless he becomes conscious of not having properly cleaned his shoes before entering). Yet the rugs and the paintings are probably worth much more than the other articles enumerated. If the assessor places them on his list, he gives them the very low value that the owner mentions. The assessor moves on, feeling perhaps that justice has not been done, but not knowing just what he can do about it. He goes next to a home presided over by a proud but unsophisticated bride. Hardly realizing that she is talking to an assessor, she lists their modest properties at something approximating their full value. A more cheering version of this story has the husband, who is on friendly terms with the assessor, meeting that gentleman as he is leaving the house and setting him right as to the "real" value of the property. At any rate these fictitious cases illustrate the very common fact that assessments of personal property are made largely by the owners rather than by the assessor.

Equalization. Manifestly, assessments will vary greatly even among individuals visited by the same assessor, and they vary still more among the districts canvassed by different assessors. In order to reduce these inequalities, county or other district boards of review or equalization are authorized to hear complaints of individual taxpayers and to correct material injustices in assessments. These boards are also required to equalize assessments among the several districts or townships of a county, to the end that all may be equitably taxed. Ordinarily, however, only the grosser inequalities are corrected. When county authorities have passed upon assessments, the rolls are placed before a state tax commission or other state officers serving as a board of equalization. This board may order reassessments in particular counties or districts, or reassessments of particular kinds of property. It is also the duty of this board, or of some other state authority, to assess public utilities, such as railroad, telegraph, and telephone systems—properties that, because of their nature and extent, are not easily or equitably assessed by local authorities. A number of states have wisely entrusted the central tax commission with the power to supervise local assessments and to make investigations of the general conditions of taxation. Such commissions have greatly improved the taxation systems in several states.

. *Criticisms of the general property tax.* It has already been shown that it is very difficult to get fair assessment of property. Ordinarily, real property and the general run of tangible personal property are not assessed in an equitable manner, and there are still wider disproportions in the assessment of other properties. The luxuries of the wealthy are usually assessed too low and intangibles are frequently not assessed at all. Taxes based upon unfair assessments are, of course, unfair. The burden falls with particular force upon the owners of real estate and tangible property, hitting the farmer as a class harder than any other.

But suppose all property is assessed alike—the tax is still subject to criticism, for the reason that some forms of property yield much greater income than others. A number of states have frankly recognized this, and they have provided for the classification of property for purposes of taxation. For example, intangibles have been placed in a special class and taxed at a lower rate than tangibles. What drove the intangibles into hiding originally was that the general property tax on their actual value was practically confiscatory. With the lower tax rate there is less urge to conceal them and less leniency for those who do conceal them. The result is that intangibles are now more commonly declared, the state gets more return for the lower rate than it did for the higher, and the owner of real estate and tangible personal property has some aid in supporting the government. But classification of property, although affording some relief, does not solve the tax problem. Recognizing the unsatisfactory results of this general property tax, a number of states have abandoned it, leaving it for local government units. In desperation farmers and taxpayers' associations have compelled some states to place a limit on the rate of the general property tax. All the states have sought other sources of revenue.

2. INCOME AND INHERITANCE TAXES. One of the newer forms of taxation is the income tax. Several states had tried it before the Sixteenth Amendment made it possible for the national government to levy taxes on incomes from whatever source derived. About thirty states, a num-

STATE TAX COLLECTIONS, BY MAJOR SOURCE:* 1940–1947 a

(Dollar amounts in millions)

Tax Source	1947 b (Preliminary)	1946	1945	1944	1943	1942	1941	1940
Total tax collections:								
Including unemployment compensation	$6,767	$6,014	$5,603	$5,425 c	$5,131	$5,011	$4,507	$4,157
Excluding unemployment compensation	5,798	4,980	4,350 c	4,106 c	3,959	3,935	3,606	3,313
General sales, use, or gross receipts	1,179	900	776	721	671	633	575	499
Motor vehicle fuel sales	1,124	887	696	685	776	942	913	839
Alcoholic beverage sales	412	402	310	267	280	256	216	193
Tobacco product sales	245	199	145	160	141	131	106	97
Motor vehicle and operator licenses	540	461	414	413 c	414	451	434	387
Alcoholic beverage licenses	70	67	58	55	55	56	56	62
Individual income	418	389	357 c	316	293	249	225	206
Corporation income	461	442	453 c	446	340	269 c	197	155
Property	262	253	276	247	258	271	268	260
Death and gift	166	146	136	114	109	112	118	113
Severance	94	90	83	71	75	62	53	53
Other, except unemployment compensation d	827	744	643	608	547	503 c	445	449
Unemployment compensation tax	969	1,034	1,254	1,319	1,172	1,076	901	844

Note: Because of rounding to nearest million, detail does not always add to total.

a The amounts for 1947 through 1942 consist of collections for the fiscal years of the respective states ended within the twelve months prior to July 1; for prior years the data pertain to fiscal years ended within the respective calendar years.

b Amounts consist of actual collections and estimates.

c Revised.

d Includes revenues from the following sources: sales and gross receipts taxes on insurance companies, public utilities, parimutuels, admissions and amusements; licenses for corporations in general, alcoholic beverages, hunting and fishing, occupations, chain stores, and amusement and race tracks; poll, documentary and stock transfers, and miscellaneous taxes.

* Reproduced by courtesy of the Council of State Governments from *The Book of the States, 1948–1949,* p. 237.

ber of them encouraged by the example of the national government, now levy income taxes, usually on both individuals and corporations. The state systems, like the national, are progressive—with the smallest incomes exempt, low rates for modest incomes, and higher rates for the bigger incomes. The highest rate is low (usually about 6 per cent) as compared with the national tax rate. Naturally enough, the income tax does not meet with universal acclaim. For instance, it is not popular with those who would pay little or no taxes under the general property tax requirement. Nevertheless, it is commonly considered fair, being based on the ability to pay. Since 1942 high federal income taxes have naturally reduced enthusiasm for the state income tax, definitely slowing up the movement for such a tax in those states that are without it.

The inheritance tax is employed in every state except Nevada. The rate of this excise on the privilege of a beneficiary to inherit property varies with the amount of the inheritance and with the beneficiary's degree of relationship to the deceased. The inheritance tax has a great deal to commend it. Often, but not always, an heir has done little to build up the fortune he inherits and thus has no very strong ground of complaint when the state takes a share of it. There are even strong individualists who have said that income and inheritance taxes help to bring about a more desirable distribution of wealth. It should be noted that income and inheritance taxes are not the state "gold mines" some people imagine them to be. Although in two or three states they may yield one third or more of the state revenue, taking the country as a whole, they yield only about one sixth of it.

3. BUSINESS TAXES. Some special form of tax is commonly levied upon many types of businesses. These taxes take various and often complicated forms. One of the simpler forms is the corporation income tax, noted above, which is levied in about two thirds of the states. Corporations are often subject to a franchise tax (a tax on the privilege of doing business in the state), which tax is usually a small percentage of the value of the capital stock of the corporation, or a percentage of dividends paid, or some other fair basis of measurement. Incorporation fees represent another form of tax. Of course states may tax foreign corporations (those chartered in other states) as well as domestic corporations, provided they are taxed in proportion to the amount of business they transact in particular states. Even corporations engaged in interstate commerce—railroads and telegraph companies, for example—may be taxed by a state. In taxing such business, the state must be careful, however, that the tax bears a fair proportion to the value of the business carried on in the state. For example, a tax of 2 per cent on every Pullman ticket sold in a state would be invalid, because it would have practically no relation to the value of the Pullman business in that state; but a tax on Pullman tickets based on

the number of miles such passengers travel within the state would be valid, because it would obviously bear a fair relationship to the value of the business in that state.[43]

In addition to the corporation tax, many states levy taxes upon business conducted by individuals. Taxes upon professions and occupations are particularly popular as sources of revenue in the South. Several states have put chain stores in a special class and have levied much higher taxes upon them than upon the "home-owned" stores. The purpose of this tax law is undoubtedly to aid the local stores as well as to bring in revenue.

4. THE SALES TAX. There are various forms of this tax, but the principal one is the retail sales tax.[44] It was not in general use until 1933, when the depression brought it in as an emergency source of revenue. Although depression-born, it has shown no signs of departing with a partial restoration of normal times. It has been found to be a very productive source of revenue. Furthermore, it is very popular with tax-payers' associations, whose chief concern is to keep down taxes on real property. One often hears the statement that the sales tax broadens the base of taxation. Of course it does, but this means that many very poor people are brought within the ranks of taxpayers. There is little doubt that this tax bears much more heavily upon the poor than it does upon others, for the poor have to spend a very substantial part of their income for the bare necessities of life. It is true that this tax is no great burden in times of full employment and high wages; and it is, of course, possible to exempt, as some states do, such items as medicine and food from the tax. It now yields about one fifth of the revenue of the states (excluding unemployment compensation taxes).

5. EXCISE TAXES. Taxes on liquor and tobacco yield considerable revenue for the states. A gasoline tax, varying in rate but rather commonly 5 cents per gallon, is imposed in practically every state. Originally, funds derived from this source were earmarked (a questionable policy) for highway construction and maintenance, but in periods of financial stringency, periods in which the gas tax still produced a handsome revenue, legislatures diverted some of these funds to other uses, a procedure that with some justification (because of the established earmarking practice) was roundly denounced by automobile associations.

6. UNEMPLOYMENT COMPENSATION TAXES. The payroll tax, imposed by the federal government and the laws of every state, is not always considered a state tax because the money is deposited in a federal trust account. This money is used for an essential part of the federal-state social security program. The payroll tax now amounts to about a billion dollars a year.

[43] Pullman Co. v. Richardson, 261 U.S. 330 (1923).
[44] R. G. and G. C. Blakey, *Sales Taxes and Other Excises* (1945).

7. OTHER REVENUES. The foregoing list includes the principal sources from which the states derive revenue by taxation. Certain other revenues are derived from fees for particular services. The various court fees connected with legal procedure furnish a familiar example. Various license fees are collected for the enjoyment of specific privileges, such as, hunting, fishing, owning a dog, running a pool hall, selling beer, and the like. The license is required primarily because it furnishes the state with a convenient means of regulating the thing licensed. The fee charged may or may not be based on the cost of regulating the privilege or business. Some states still receive revenues from the lands granted by the national government for public education. A few states have some returns from their own business enterprises, such as docks, canals, warehouses and more recently, the liquor business. Of course the taxpayers are ultimately responsible for these ventures, which sometimes turn out to be liabilities rather than assets. Fines supply a little revenue in every state, but the amount is probably much smaller than the average citizen realizes. In enumerating the sources of revenue we should by no means forget the various federal-aid funds and the outright grants the national government makes to the states in depression periods.

Where the money goes. From these sources of revenue, including the payroll tax but not taking into account the federal grants, the states now receive approximately six and one half billions annually. Naturally, their expenses ought to be about the same, although they may be slightly less than the revenue in times of prosperity and in excess of the revenue in "lean" years. Schools, highways, and various forms of social security absorb the lion's share of state income. Something must be set aside each year for payment of interest and principal on debts. Health, sanitation, conservation, libraries, correctional institutions, and similar services each get small shares.

It has already been noted that the cost of state government has increased greatly in the past thirty-five years. This increase, with two exceptions, has been fairly evenly distributed over the various services. The exceptions are the highway and public welfare departments, expenditures in the former having advanced about twice as rapidly as in the other services and in the latter (only since 1932) many times more rapidly.[45]

Early haphazard appropriation methods. In former times the state legislatures passed their revenue and appropriation bills with the same general absence of system that characterized congressional conduct in such matters before the national budget system was inaugurated (1921). Each spending service, acting with little or no regard for the other services or for any superior administrative officer, would submit a statement of its needs, usually very much exaggerated, to the committee on appropriations.

[45] See tables in *Book of the States*, pp. 249 ff.

The most influential or most insistent administrators might get as much as or more than they needed from the committee; others would probably get less.

The "pork barrel" and "logrolling" evils flourished in state legislatures as in Congress, resulting in additional extravagance and waste. Occasionally, a legislature would make a gesture of economy, either by reducing appropriations all around, without considering the needs of particular services, or, perhaps more likely, by reducing the appropriations for those services the curtailment of which would bring the least adverse political reaction. Frequently, the committee (or committees) on appropriations paid little attention to the state revenues with which the appropriations should balance. Almost invariably a number of appropriation measures, some of them smelling strongly of pork, would pass the legislature in the last hectic days of its session. The bills then went to the governor, who, in most states, could veto and reduce separate items. The typical governor was a little more frugal than the legislature, and he usually wielded the pruning knife somewhat vigorously, although not always wisely. In any case, the governor's veto could operate only as a negative correction upon the "program" of expenditure proposed by the legislature.

Budget systems. With the rising cost of government, taxpayers very naturally became insistent that something be done to stem the tide. Students of public administration, particularly Dr. F. A. Cleveland, pointed out very clearly that order could be brought into state finances and some economies could be effected by the adoption of a budget system. Beginning before the First World War period, the idea spread rapidly among the lawmakers, and within twenty years every state had a budget system of one sort or another. A few states have not carried the idea very far, entrusting the preparation of the budget to a legislative committee. This legislative budget system may secure unified action with respect to revenue and appropriations in the legislature; but it fails to give the high executive officers who must administer the expenditures a sufficient voice in proposing them. Nearly a third of the states have the budget prepared by a commission, which commonly consists of the governor, several other administrative officers, and a few members of the legislature. The administrative budget plan is designed to bring about greater harmony between administrative officers and members of the legislature. Legislators, having helped prepare a budget, will feel under some obligation to defend it in the legislature.

The plan that meets with the most general favor and is employed in about two thirds of the states is the executive budget system. It varies, of course, among the states; but broadly speaking, it follows the budget practice of the national government. The governor, like the President, is individually responsible for preparation of the financial program. One-man responsibility seems to work better than group responsibility. Of course, the concentration of the budget authority in the hands of the chief executive greatly increases his power, but despite occasional abuses this is generally held to be desirable. Reforms in American government have very commonly proceeded along the line of increasing executive power.[46]

The legislature and the budget. Regardless of how the budget is prepared, the legislature has the authority to do with it as it sees fit. It may accept it as it stands, reduce it as a whole, increase it as a whole, strike out items, or add new items. But with a program of expenditures presented along with the estimates of revenue, the legislature is not in position to "run wild" in enacting fiscal measures. The budget gives the people something definite to insist upon; and if the legislature changes the budget materially, it must justify itself for doing so. It has turned out, therefore, that in spite of the legal authority of the legislature to play havoc with the budget, there is less irresponsibility and more system in voting appropriations now than formerly. Pork barrels have become smaller and logrolling has become a more hazardous legislative occupation. Particularly is this improvement noticeable where organized bodies of taxpayers are vigilant when the legislature is in session. In Maryland the legislature has less freedom with the budget than in other states. There, as in other states, the legislature may strike out or decrease (with a few exceptions) items in the governor's budget; but it is prohibited by the state constitution from making any increases except for legislative and judicial expenses. This rule rather effectively limits the distribution of pork, and some authorities recommend its general adoption.

Supervision of expenditures. The state's financial house cannot be set in order simply by the adoption of a system for making appropriations. The expending of the money should be supervised at all times. Formerly, legislatures attempted to control the expenditures of the various administrative services by listing in a separate item of appropriation the amount that might be used for each purpose of a service. This system was too rigid. It did not secure the greatest wisdom in the use of funds, because the legislature could not look a year or more ahead and determine exactly what expenditures should be made. It is well enough for the legislature to decide what projects shall be undertaken and how much shall be allowed for these projects; but the detailed control of expenditures within a service can be exercised much more satisfactorily by the higher executive officers.

A number of states have adopted the plan of making appropriations for each department and commission under several main headings, such as salaries, supplies, and capital outlays, leaving the chief administrative officers some discretion as to the details of expenditure under each heading.

---

[46] One of the latest and best discussions on budget procedure is by L. D. White in his *Introduction to the Study of Public Administration* (1948 ed.), Ch. XIX.

In these states it is ordinarily provided that funds may be transferred from one heading to another when an emergency exists and when the permission of the governor has been obtained. Some states go still further and require the spending officers to secure the approval of the governor for their monthly or quarterly expense program. Such systems as these give a very desirable flexibility in the matter of expenditures. But this sort of supervision in itself is not sufficient. An up-to-date system of accounting, which most of the states have failed to adopt, is necessary. It would show exactly where all the state's money has gone, reveal bad contracts and excessive costs, and thus lead in some measure to the stoppage of waste.

The methods of control here outlined are executive devices. They are the means by which the chief administrator may enforce economies and develop efficiency. By what means may the legislature satisfy itself that the appropriations it makes are legally expended? This service is the function of the auditor. He is the servant of the legislature as the director of the budget, or the director of finance is the agent of the chief executive. Rather commonly the auditor may pass upon the legality of a proposed expenditure and disallow it, if in his opinion it is contrary to law. Authorities take sides and give each other some stout blows on this question, some holding that the true function of an auditor is not to disallow proposed expenditures but to call to the attention of administrative officials any irregularities in their proposed expenditures and, if the warning is unheeded, report the situation to the legislature. This is the executive view of the matter. Those who view it from the legislative standpoint are convinced that nothing less than the power to disallow can make the auditor an effective agent of the legislature.[47]

Borrowing money. Any government must occasionally borrow money. A number of the early state legislatures displayed considerable prodigality on this score, and, as a result, nearly all the states have placed limits upon the amounts the legislatures may borrow. The federal Constitution imposes only one limitation—that the states may not borrow through the expedient of issuing bills of credit (paper money). State constitutions contain such types of limitations as: a fixed sum; a sum that may not be exceeded except for certain specified purposes; a sum that may be exceeded only with the approval of the voters; and specifications with respect to the purposes for which money may be borrowed. A few states have practically no debt; some have considerable indebtedness, but in no state is the per capita debt more than a very small fraction of that of the national government. From 1941 through 1946 the states rather steadily reduced their debts, bringing them to less than two and one half billion dollars;[48] but since the latter

---

[47] See White, *op. cit.*, Ch. XXI, especially at p. 308. See also J. W. Martin and Robt. Sawyer, "The Independent State Post-Audit," *State Government*, May, 1941, p. 107.

[48] *Book of the States*, pp. 243 ff.

date they have started to rise again, and now stand near the three billion mark.

Debts have been incurred in times past for various internal improvements, chiefly for waterways. During the last thirty years soldiers' bonuses and highways have been the principal objects for which debts have been contracted. States borrow by issuing interest-bearing bonds, which are bought by investors. The period for which bonds are issued ordinarily varies with the duration of the benefit to be secured by the proposed expenditures— ten, twenty, or more years. An entire issue of bonds may be retired on a specified date of maturity. The state sets aside, or is supposed to set aside, a fund each year so that the entire principal will be on hand when the bonds mature. This is called the "sinking fund system." It is all right in theory, but in practice the states sometimes fail to build up the fund or lose part of it by bad investments. Hence, when the bonds mature, it becomes necessary to borrow again. A system that works better in practice and that many cities and some states now employ is the "serial bond system." By this system some bonds mature each year and are retired from current revenue.

VI. LOCAL FINANCE [49]

The story of increasing expenditures for local government is essentially the same as that of the states. In 1900 local expenditures were less than $1 billion; in 1942 more than $7 billion; and the estimates for 1950 range around $11 billion, the cities spending the largest amount, the schools and counties running a rough tie for second place. Local debts just about doubled between 1922 and 1932, remained relatively stable until 1946, when they advanced again, and now stand at about $17 billion, of which amount the cities are obligated for more than half. The increased cost of local government is due primarily to improved and expanded services and the decline in the value of the dollar.

State control of local finance. The financial powers of local governments are limited by the state. Only such taxes may be imposed as are authorized by the state government. Ordinarily, the state specifies a certain maximum rate beyond which local authorities may not tax general property, and prescribes the exact rates of other taxes and licenses. In the matter of borrowing, the counties and cities are also limited by the state, the maximum amount usually being fixed at a certain percentage—five, eight, or some such figure—of the assessed valuation of taxable property.

[49] A. W. Bromage, *Introduction to Municipal Government and Administration* (1950), Chs. XXII–XXIII; L. W. Lancaster, *Government in Rural America* (1937), Chs. VI–VII; C. M. Kneier, *City Government in the United States* (1947 ed.), Chs. XXVIII–XXX; A. F. Macdonald, *American City Government and Administration* (1951 ed.), Chs. 19–20; C. F. Snider, *American State and Local Government* (1950), Chs. XXIV–XXV.

It is often provided, however, that the amount of indebtedness may be increased with the approval of the voters. These limitations are not always effective; for a number of special governing bodies, each with the power to tax and borrow money, may have authority over a part or all of the county or city area. Indeed, it is often for the purpose of circumventing financial limitations that these special authorities are created. Neither these nor any other attempts to establish rigid control over local finance are altogether satisfactory. Flexibility is the thing needed. This can better be secured by general limitations imposed by law and applied by state administrative authorities according to the demands of particular cases. A few states are making some progress in this direction.

Sources of local revenues. Counties and school districts derive their revenues chiefly from the general property tax, around 95 per cent of the tax revenue coming from this source. As indicated in the discussion of state taxes, local officers assess general property for purposes of state taxation. This same assessment serves local taxing bodies as a basis of taxation. Tax officials simply add the rates imposed by the various local taxing authorities to the rate of the state tax, and the property owner receives a bill for the total. Counties draw some revenue from licenses, fees, and fines. In several southern states the poll tax is a small source of county revenue. It is not uncommon for a state to apportion to counties a part of the state receipts from motor vehicle licenses, the gas tax, or from some other tax. Many states make direct grants to counties for specific purposes, particularly for schools and highways.

Cities rely somewhat less upon the general property tax than do the counties receiving on the average about 80 per cent of their revenue from that source. A number of cities are authorized to tax occupations and professions, such taxes being based, for example, upon the volume of a business or upon average individual earnings in a particular profession. Street railways, bus lines, and other public utility companies must pay something into the city's treasury for the use of the streets. Often this tax is in the form of a small percentage of the companies' gross receipts. Some utilities are usually operated by the city itself. Water is very commonly supplied in this way. Municipal revenue from such services, over and above the cost of maintaining them, is seldom very large. There is usually some controversy as to whether the city is making or losing money on its public utilities, the conclusion depending upon one's attitude toward the "government in business" and upon the method of accounting. Other sources of municipal funds include grants from the state and national governments. In recent years grants from these governments have been sizable, and we may expect the practice to continue and expand because sources of revenue may be more easily tapped by the nation and the states than by municipalities.

SPECIAL ASSESSMENTS. Cities often make special assessments for particular improvements. For example, a street is to be paved, a sewer is to be laid, or a new park is to be opened up. Property owners near by will receive the greatest benefit, and they are accordingly required to pay a substantial part of the cost of the improvement. In the case of street paving, they are sometimes obliged to pay the entire cost. Obviously, special assessments will operate unfairly if the assessment does not bear a direct proportion to the benefit received, a proportion exceedingly difficult to calculate.

Appropriation methods. County budget systems worthy of the name are probably employed in only about a third of the counties. In a few states the budget is prepared by an administrative officer of the county, usually the auditor. In others, it is prepared by the county board. In any case, the appropriation must be voted by the board. The absence of a financial program in the majority of counties no doubt leads to a great deal of waste. This waste is likely to pass unnoticed (in times of prosperity), for the reason that the expenditures of the average county are not large. But there are many counties, and, when the total cost is figured, we find that it is roughly $2 billion. Effective county budget systems, with some state supervision and control, would probably reduce expenditures without impairing county services.

Cities spend a great deal more money than counties, and, since they are also watched a little more closely by taxpayers, it is not surprising that most of them have adopted some sort of budget system. In fact, the cities deserve the credit for having introduced the budget system. The states adopted it later, and the national government finally followed suit.[50] In some cities the term "budget" is used in an attempt to conceal the fact that appropriations are prepared and voted in the same old careless and extravagant way. Other cities have budget systems to the extent that there is a budget-making authority standing between the departments which make the requests for funds and the councils which appropriate them; but only a few cities have taken another step, generally considered desirable, and have vested final budget-framing authority with the chief executive—mayor or manager.

Other taxing areas. Perhaps it seems enough when one has been taxed by the nation, the state, the county, the city and the school district; but few taxpaying individuals escape so easily. Authority to tax, make expenditures, and borrow money is vested in officials of various other units of government. The towns of New England, the towns or townships of the

50 W. F. Willoughby, *Movement for Budgetary Reform in the States* (1918), pp. 5–8.

West, and villages (commonly called "towns" in the South) everywhere have financial powers. Special districts have become common in recent years, particularly in the West and South. As stated in the chapter on "Administration," there are special districts for highways, drainage, irrigation, sanitation, diking, mosquito abatement, and other purposes, each with the authority to tax. Often these districts are coterminous or overlapping, creating no little confusion and irritation with respect to administration in general and taxation in particular. Nearly all the revenue for such districts is derived from the general property tax; although special assessments sometimes carry a substantial part of the cost of drainage, irrigation, roads, and some other improvements.

The tax problem remains. Despite the fact that there probably never has been a time when politicians, businessmen, farmers, the press, and assorted orators have not proclaimed that the limit in taxation has been reached, that the people could pay no more, their assertions have been followed, and with increasing frequency, by the imposition of new and by an increase in old levies. Somehow the people have been able to take it, so far. Very literally they have asked for more—for more public services necessitating higher taxes. In the few years of jittery peace following the Second World War, about a fourth of our national income went for taxes, and as the international crises of 1950 culminated in shooting, our expenditures and our tax bill took another spurt. Surely, if we are to avoid chaos, we must pay as we go to the extent that it is possible to do so. Americans will have to learn to pay even higher taxes than they are now paying and "like it," if they are going to be happy.

The necessity for very high taxes does not preclude improvements in our tax structure. On the contrary, that necessity makes such improvements all the more imperative. Back in 1900 (at least a thousand years ago considering what the next half century brought) taxation was a relatively simple matter. The national government did very well on customs duties and liquor and tobacco excises; the states managed to get along with taxes on general property, inheritances, and corporations; and local governments drew their revenue almost wholly from general property taxes. Only the last-mentioned tax supplied an appreciable source of income for more than one of the three areas of government. But today, with the strenuous competition for revenue between the national government and the states, the tacit agreement concerning the allocation of sources of revenue has broken down. The federal government taxes income and so do many of the states. For a long time it was understood that tobacco and liquor excises would be levied exclusively by Uncle Sam; but the states eventually tapped the same sources. The gasoline tax was at first exclusively imposed by the states, but the Congress, presumably to even up the score with them for invading the liquor and tobacco domains, also levied a gasoline tax.[51]   And so the search for taxable sources goes on and with it the competition between governments for those sources.

More significant perhaps than intergovernmental duplications in respect to sources of revenue is the matter of the tax structure in particular areas of government.   Are the federal personal income tax rates equitable, or are they fixed arbitrarily?   What are the proper rates for a corporation income tax, and what are the merits of an excess profits tax?   Is the state general property tax fair as between large and small owners, or as between owners of residence and business property?   Is the sales tax or an increased sales tax the answer to the need for more state revenue, or is it simply an easy answer (it produces the revenue)?   Again, is the sales tax fair as between persons of wealth who hold large properties and who spend much less than their income and persons of very moderate income who must spend it all (and pay sales taxes on practically all of it) in order to live?   These and other questions that might be raised have no clear, ready answers, and some of them probably have no answer; but they may be taken as cautions and warnings in relation to tax structures, present and prospective.

"What kind of tax is the best?" a politician of long ago was asked. "What is the best way to pick a goose?" he asked by way of reply.   "Why— why the best way to pick a goose is the way that brings the least squawk." It may be that the people's representatives in this democratic country have on occasion unjustifiably imposed a tax on a certain class of persons whose squawk would be feeble or need not be heeded.

Reading List

E. D. Allen and O. H. Brownlee, *Economics of Public Finance* (1947)
American Year Book, see chapter on "Public Finance and Taxation."
T. J. Anderson, *Federal and State Control of Banking* (1934).
P. Blackwell, *Past and Present Facts About Money in the United States* (1936).
R. G. Blakey and Gladys Blakey, *Sales Taxes and Other Excises* (1945).
A. W. Bromage, *Introduction to Municipal Government and Administration* (1950), Chs. XXII–XXIII.
A. E. Buck, *The Budget in Governments of Today* (1934).
Alfred G. Buehler (ed.), "Government Finance in a Stable and Growing Economy," *The Annals,* 266 (Nov., 1949).
———, *Public Finance* (1948 ed.)
Council of Economic Advisers, *Annual Reports.*
D. R. Dewey, *Financial History of the United States* (1934 ed.).
Marshall E. Dimock, *Business and Government* (1949), Chs. 20–22.
Federation of Tax Administrators, *Recent Trends in State Finance* (1948).

[51] W. B. Graves, *American State Government* (1946 ed.), pp. 561 ff.

M. B. Foster and R. Rodgers, eds., *Money and Banking* (1947 ed.).

W. B. Graves, *Public Administration in a Democratic Society* (1950), Chs. 15–23.

H. M. Groves, *Financing Government* (1945 ed.).

Alvin H. Hansen, *Monetary Theory and Fiscal Policy* (1949).

———, and H. S. Perloff, *State and Local Finance in the National Economy* (1944).

E. W. Kemmerer, *The A.B.C. of the Federal Reserve System* (1938 ed.).

———, *Money* (1936).

M. S. Kendrick, *Public Finance* (1950).

C. M. Kneier, *City Government in the United States* (1947 ed.), Chs. XXVIII–XXIX.

L. W. Lancaster, *Government in Rural America* (1937), Chs. VI–VII.

H. L. Lutz, *Public Finance* (1947 ed.).

Fritz Morstein Marx, "The Bureau of the Budget . . ." *Am. Pol. Sci. Rev.,* XXXIX (1945), 653, 869.

D. T. Selko, *The Federal Financial System* (1940).

H. D. Smith, *The Management of Your Government* (1945).

C. F. Snider, *American State and Local Government* (1950), Chs. XIV–XXV.

P. Studensky, *Public Borrowing* (1930).

———, *Chapters in Public Finance* (1935).

Tax Institute, *Financing the War* (1942).

U.S. Treasury Department, *Annual Reports*.

H. Walker, *Public Administration in the United States* (1937), Chs. VI, VII, X.

Clark Warburton, "Monetary Control Under the Federal Reserve Act," *Pol. Sci. Qt.,* LXI (1946), 505–534.

H. White, *Money and Banking* (1935).

L. D. White, *Introduction to Public Administration* (1948 ed.), Chs. XVIII–XXI.

Questions and Problems

1. Is there any constitutional prohibition upon the amount that Congress may tax?
2. Show that the power of Congress to tax and appropriate money is broader than its power to legislate.
3. Explain the controversy over the constitutionality of the income tax.
4. What are the main points at issue at this time in relation to national taxation?
5. Outline the procedure in the enactment of a national revenue bill.
6. Indicate the significant changes in the methods of handling federal finances since 1921.
7. Trace the history of national banking legislation.
8. To what extent has the Federal Reserve System helped in solving the banking problem?

9. What limitations does the federal Constitution impose upon the taxing powers of the states?
10. Outline the history of the general property tax as a source of revenue. What use does your state now make of it?
11. What features of the state income and inheritance taxes commonly commend them?
12. List the arguments for and against the sales tax.
13. Would you recommend that a single "best source of revenue" bear practically all of the state's tax burden?
14. Indicate the appropriate functions of state and local executive officers and the legislature in budget-making.
15. What control should the chief executive have over funds after they have been appropriated by the legislature? What control should the legislature retain?
16. Under what conditions may a state or local government appropriately borrow money? For what purposes have your state and local governments recently borrowed?
17. Give the "pros" and "cons" on the proposition that the national government only should levy an income tax. Would your reasoning be the same if the national government agreed to distribute a fixed percentage (say 10 per cent) of the amount collected to the states on the basis of wealth?

☆ 23 ☆

Commerce and Business:
Their Regulation and Promotion

MODERN government has as one of its major responsibilities the regulation and promotion of commerce and business. Our national government has always exercised exclusive control over foreign trade and commerce; and, although it has by no means crowded the states out of the field of regulation and promotion of domestic commerce, it has more and more drawn upon its power to regulate interstate commerce, entering fields that were formerly unregulated or left entirely to state authority.

Power of Congress over foreign and interstate commerce. Congress is given the power "to regulate commerce with foreign nations and among the several states, and with the Indian tribes." This power is subject to only one specific limitation—that no duty shall be levied on exports.[1] It is important to note the extent of this power. Manufacturing is not commerce, but the instant a manufacturer in one state places an article in the hands of a carrier to be shipped into another state or to a foreign country, the article becomes the subject of interstate or foreign commerce and remains so until the carrier delivers it. A person who boards a train in Chicago for New York is an interstate passenger from the beginning of the journey until its end, not simply at points where the train crosses state lines. As long ago as 1871 it was held that a steamer plying entirely within the state of Michigan was engaged in interstate commerce because it carried some goods destined for points *outside* the state. All persons and things (including radio communications) in interstate and foreign commerce and the agencies conducting that commerce fall under the regulatory power of Congress.

[1] Gibbons v. Ogden, 9 Wheaton 1 (1824) is still a leading case on the authority of Congress to regulate commerce.

Since 1935, acts of Congress and decisions of the Supreme Court have extended the national power over commerce. In order to come within the sphere of national regulation, a transaction does not have to be one in interstate or foreign commerce. Thus, the federal power may be extended to regulate the price of coal sold in, or the sale of which directly affects, interstate commerce; [2] and Congress may legislate on labor disputes and hours and wages in these mining industries. Similarly, Congress may regulate the hours and wages of labor in those manufacturing establishments that make goods for shipment in interstate commerce.[3] In the Southeastern Underwriters Association case,[4] the Supreme Court held that fire insurance companies, operating under noncompetitive agreements in six states, were subject to the Sherman Antitrust Act, which prohibits contracts in restraint of interstate trade.

The decisions of the Court on these questions of commerce regulation were practically revolutionary, overruling several earlier and significant decisions that had limited the national authority over commerce. Although Congress has made wide use of its commerce power in recent years, it still sees fit to leave many details of that commerce unregulated, or to allow the states to exercise the regulatory authority.

I. FOREIGN COMMERCE AND BUSINESS [5]

How has Congress exercised its plenary powers over foreign commerce and how has it aided American business in foreign countries? It has passed laws for the protection and convenience of shippers, seamen, and passengers; has fostered a merchant marine; has found business opportunities abroad for Americans and extended them protection in such business; and has attempted, through tariff laws, to strengthen American industry at home. It is observed that much more is done for the promotion of commerce than is done in the way of restrictive regulation.

Protection of passengers and seamen. Various laws have been made for the protection of passengers and seamen. American ships must be inspected; and their masters, pilots, and other officers must be examined and licensed. Sailing for a foreign port, a vessel must carry a passport,

---

[2] Sunshine Anthracite Coal Co. v. Adkins, 310 U.S. 381 (1940).

[3] United States v. Darby Lumber Co., 312 U.S. 100 (1941).

[4] 322 U.S. 533 (1944).

[5] Stuart Chase, *Tomorrow's Trade* (1945); J. G. B. Hutchins, "One Hundred and Fifty Years of American Navigation Policy," *Quarterly Journal of Economics* (Feb., 1939), LIII, 238; R. L. Kramer, ed., "Our Foreign Commerce in Peace and War," *The Annals,* CCXI (Sept., 1940); W. H. Reeves and P. D. Dickens, "Private Foreign Investments: A Means of World Economic Development," *Pol. Sci. Qt.,* LXIV (1949), 211–244; U.S. Maritime Commission, *Economic Survey of the American Merchant Marine* (1937); *Annual Reports of the Secretary of Commerce.*

which it deposits with the American consul upon its arrival. Incidentally, consular officers are given considerable authority in applying our navigation laws to American merchantmen abroad. Passengers are protected by legal limitations as to the number a ship may carry, and by requirements as to health precautions and safety appliances. Thus, by a statute of 1882, Congress provided in some detail for the accommodations of steerage passengers, in such particulars as the space to be allotted to each passenger, ventilation, cleanliness, medical facilities, and the like. Elaborate regulations have been made respecting the rights and duties of officers and seamen, particularly concerning the conditions of employment and wages of seamen.

Aids to navigation. Numerous aids to navigation are provided by the services that chart and patrol the seas, both within our territorial waters and on the high seas. The Coast and Geodetic Survey of the Department of Commerce makes hydrographic and topographic studies of the coasts of the United States and the territories, observes the behavior of tides and currents, prepares charts, and performs similar useful services. The Coast Guard maintains about 36,000 aids to navigation, ranging from the unlighted wooden buoys to lightships and electronic long-range aids. The Coast Guard also maintains an ice patrol. In the spring and early summer it is particularly active along the transatlantic steamship lanes, finding and keeping charted icebergs and field ice, and reporting its observations for the protection of shipping. These are but a few of the efforts made by the national government to gain scientific knowledge of the seas and keep them safe for commerce.

Merchant marine policy. In the early days of the Republic, American ships were common sights in foreign ports, and they carried their legitimate share of the world's commerce. With the advent of the steamer, Americans found competition more difficult to meet, and to add to their difficulties, on the eve of the Civil War, Congress repealed a subsidy it had previously granted them. For some time thereafter American ships did not play an important part in world trade, despite some attempt to encourage them by levying tonnage duties upon foreign vessels coming into American ports and by imposing higher duties upon goods brought in by foreign vessels than upon goods imported in American vessels.

The First World War drew many foreign ships out of the American carrying trade, and we found ourselves with excellent markets in Europe and with not enough vessels to carry the goods to them. In order to meet this emergency, Congress created (1916) the Shipping Board and endowed it with the power to purchase, construct, lease, and operate merchant ships, and to encourage and promote American shipping generally. Upon our entrance into that war, Congress set up the Emergency Fleet Corporation, which, under the general supervision of the Shipping Board, and generously aided from the national treasury, built ships with such astonishing rapidity that in a few years we possessed a great merchant fleet.

With the war emergency passed, what should the government do with these ships? "Sell them to private interests at a small fraction of their cost and pay them a subsidy to operate them," said those who wanted to get the government out of the shipping business as soon as possible. This proposal was opposed by progressives, but in the end it was substantially adopted. By an act of 1920, Congress, while directing the Shipping Board to continue and expand its activities, also directed it to sell its ships as soon as possible to American companies. The Board still continued to operate a number of ships; but it sold its finest vessels to private interests at rather low figures. Private companies were also aided by the government through loans for the construction and improvement of vessels and by mail contracts so generous in their terms that they amounted in effect to liberal subsidies.

The Merchant Marine Act of 1936. The Merchant Marine Act of 1936 created the United States Maritime Commission and transferred to it the functions of the Shipping Board. The policy declared in the act is as follows:

It is necessary for the national defense and development of its foreign and domestic commerce that the United States shall have a merchant marine (1) sufficient to carry its domestic water-borne commerce and a substantial portion of the water-borne export and import foreign commerce of the United States . . . (2) capable of serving as a naval and military auxiliary in time of war or national emergency, (3) owned and operated . . . by citizens of the United States insofar as may be practicable, and (4) composed of the best-equipped, safest, and most suitable types of vessels, constructed in the United States and manned with a trained and efficient citizen personnel.

The Maritime Commission is charged with the duty of creating an adequate and well-balanced merchant fleet to provide for the needs of all routes essential for the flow of the foreign commerce of the United States. Of particular significance is the power of the Commission to administer construction and operating subsidies. To aid a citizen in the construction of a new vessel to be used on a desirable route in foreign commerce, the Commission is empowered to have the vessel constructed in the United States, to pay the cost of construction, and then sell the vessel to the citizen for an amount equal to the estimated cost of the construction of the vessel if it were constructed abroad. In no case, however, may this "construction-differential subsidy," as it is called, exceed 50 per cent of the cost of the vessel. On a somewhat similar plan, the Commission is authorized to administer an "operating-differential subsidy," designed to place the operation of American ships on a parity with those of foreign competitors. The arrangement made in these cases is that the American owner be paid a subsidy equal to the amount it costs to operate, less the amount it costs his foreign competitor to operate. In 1942 the operating subsidy was virtually suspended because merchant vessels were requisitioned by the government.

Before the outbreak of the Second World War the Commission had provided for a ship-construction program that called for 500 ships in ten years. During the war that program was accelerated many fold, to 5,300 vessels and 54,000,000 deadweight tons. The speed of construction was little short of incredible (and the cost almost matched it). About half the vessels built were Liberty ships, useful in war but of little value in the fast peacetime trades. Fast, modern, dry cargo ships, tankers, the speedy Victory ships, large transports, and a variety of others were constructed. Our merchant marine became the greatest in the world, and it is doubtful whether the last war could have been won without it. There is evidence that certain shipping companies made enormous profits from their war contracts,[6] but this regrettable phase of the story should not close our eyes to the fact that a job was done, well done.

Today the merchant marine consists of thousands of vessels, plenty of ships to carry our part of the world's commerce and more. We should keep our place on the sea, both as a means of strengthening our economy (and that of the world) and of maintaining a merchant marine as an indispensable arm of defense in another possible war. The Merchant Ship Sales Act of 1946 was designed to hold the Liberty ships as a reserve fleet and to sell the vessels suitable for peacetime trade to private companies. Over a period of five years the Federal Maritime Administrator sold nearly 2,000 surplus ships to foreign and American buyers. If American operators purchased 847 of the best of the carriers, the C-type freighters, at bargain prices, there is some additional compensation to the public in the fact that we hold a substantial part of the carrying trade.

The coasting trade. Strictly speaking, the coasting trade is not a part of our foreign commerce; but it is at least sea trade, and it may be appropriately mentioned at this point. Congress has appropriated enormous sums for the improvement of harbors, rivers, channels, and the like. The Panama Canal, a great benefit to both foreign and coasting trade, is the most familiar example of such enterprises. All of these improvements except the Panama Canal are open to American vessels without charge. Congress planned to allow our vessels free use of the Canal; but a treaty with Great Britain obligated us to open it to the vessels of all nations on the same terms, and President Wilson persuaded Congress to repeal the provision

---

[6] Allen Bernard, "Operation Plunder," a series of articles in *The New Republic*, beginning May 13, 1946.

exempting Americans from the payment of tolls. Not only has Congress generously opened improved waterways to Americans, but the domestic trade has been reserved to American vessels during the greater part of our history. This exclusive privilege gives American vessels a greater advantage than might at first appear, for the coasting trade includes not only trade between points on the coasts of continental United States but trade with the overseas possessions as well. It should be added, however, that vessels of certain foreign countries may still engage in this overseas trade.[7]

Promotion of American business abroad. Closely associated with the development of American shipping is the policy of finding opportunities abroad for American business. In order to remove the restrictions that surrounded our trade in China and with an altruistic belief that "it was commerce that republicanized and civilized men," as one congressman expressed it, we sent thither in 1844, Caleb Cushing, who secured rights of trade and tariff concessions for Americans. Then followed, a decade later, Commodore Perry's picturesque negotiations with the Japanese, which resulted in opening up trade with that Empire. Even before those days American diplomats and consuls were often busy with negotiations, investigations, and other activities in the interest of American trade. As we grew into a great commercial nation following the Civil War, these activities increased. Active on behalf of American trade in all countries, the State Department has at times taken aggressive action for American interests in China and certain countries to the south of us. On occasion the President himself has offered a hand, as when Mr. Taft communicated directly with the Prince Regent in China urging the use of American capital for the development of China. The diplomatic service has rapidly expanded its commercial functions since 1900, and the consular service has always made such functions its chief concern.

FOREIGN SERVICE OF THE DEPARTMENT OF COMMERCE. Supplementing the diplomatic and consular officials is the Office of International Trade of the Bureau of Foreign and Domestic Commerce. Its representatives collect and distribute information on foreign markets, assist in adjusting misunderstandings arising over commercial transactions, explain foreign tariff classifications, give advice concerning the integrity and financial standing of foreign buyers, and so on. The Office is credited with having opened up markets abroad that American business hardly hoped to enter.

[7] Inland water transportation likewise receives marked encouragement from Congress. The best example of this is furnished by the government's operation of a barge line from Illinois and Minnesota to the Gulf of Mexico. This enterprise is opposed by certain railroad interests and in general by those who want to "get the government out of business." In 1932 the United States and Canada signed a treaty (not yet ratified) in which they agreed to develop jointly the St. Lawrence, so that ocean-going vessels might enter the Lake ports.

CHANGES IN OUR FOREIGN TRADE

EXPORTS

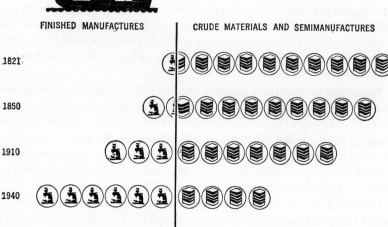

FINISHED MANUFACTURES | CRUDE MATERIALS AND SEMIMANUFACTURES

1821
1850
1910
1940

EACH SYMBOL REPRESENTS 10 PER CENT OF ALL EXPORTS

IMPORTS

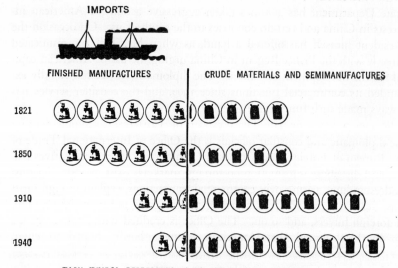

FINISHED MANUFACTURES | CRUDE MATERIALS AND SEMIMANUFACTURES

1821
1850
1910
1940

EACH SYMBOL REPRESENTS 10 PER CENT OF ALL IMPORTS

From Twentieth Century Fund, *U.S.A.: Measure of a Nation* (Macmillan).

Through its recommendations an American exporter might find an outlet for electric refrigerators in Paris and a manufacturer of cosmetics a market for his products in Indonesia. During the last war much of the activity of the Office of International Trade was in watching, measuring, and reporting the dislocations of established trade and exchange arising as a result of the war. In the postwar years it has been occupied with the restoration of its peacetime trade functions. The Office was particularly active in lending assistance to the European Recovery Program during its early stages and before the Economic Co-operation Administration became a full-fledged agency. The Recovery Program has, of course, given American business market opportunities in Europe, and the Office of International Trade has extended its services to our producers and exporters in order that they might use such opportunities to the best advantage.[8]

OTHER AIDS TO FOREIGN COMMERCE. In its efforts to promote foreign trade, Congress, through the Webb-Pomerene Act of 1918, practically exempted export associations from the operation of the antitrust laws. About the same time Congress authorized national banking associations to establish branches in foreign countries, and authorized the chartering of private corporations for the purpose of engaging in international and foreign banking. In 1934 the Export-Import Bank of Washington was created by executive order, and later continued by act of Congress. Its purpose is to supplement private capital in financing trade between the United States or its territories and any foreign country. In the same year foreign-trade zones (called "free ports" in Europe) were authorized for American ports of entry. These zones are small areas in which foreign goods intended for trans-shipment to other foreign countries may be stored and processed, free of duty. The Foreign Trade Zones Board, which consists of the Secretaries of Commerce, the Treasury, and the Army, must pass upon the application of a city for a zone. It is believed that this arrangement might prove to be a decided aid to foreign trade; but because of the exigencies of war, only two or three zones have as yet been established.

Value of foreign trade. The prosperity of the country depends a great deal upon our exports. Basic products that must rely rather heavily upon export trade include iron and steel in Pennsylvania, automobiles in Michigan, meat packing and milling in the Northwest (both very definitely affecting the prosperity of the farmer), lumber in the Far Northwest, petroleum in the Southwest, tobacco and cotton in the South, and fruits in Florida and the Far West. The capitalist, the industrial laborer, and the farmer in practically every section of the country clearly have a definite interest in the state of the export trade. In 1929 this trade amounted to

[8] *Report of the Secretary of Commerce* (1948), pp. 167 ff.

about five billion dollars.   The general business decline that started almost imperceptibly in the summer of 1929 reduced this amount to less than half in 1932.   There is no question that this falling off in foreign sales caused some factories to close, increased the number of idle workmen, and decreased the price of farm products.   These facts indicate something of the relation of foreign trade to general prosperity.   We may object to government activity that unduly favors the export business of particular groups at the expense of others, but an objection to a broad and fair policy of finding markets abroad is hardly in order.

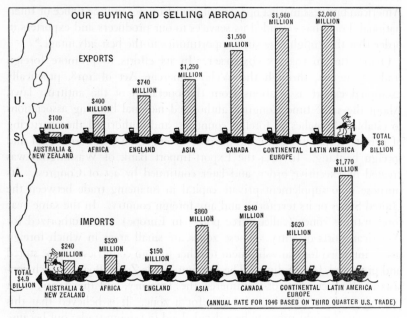

Reprinted from the *U.S. News & World Report* (Jan. 31, 1947), an independent weekly magazine on national and international affairs, published at Washington.   Copyright, 1947, United States News Publishing Corporation.

Tariffs and world trade.   The tariff is at the heart of the problem of foreign trade.   Although the government makes vigorous efforts to promote American exports, at the behest of various interests it often severely restricts imports.   This restriction is imposed through the "protective tariff," long the main plank in Republican platforms, but resisted in varying degrees by the Democrats.   The idea is, of course, to keep the home market for American producers; to give American industries a reasonable profit and American labor high wages.   Experts find it impossible to agree as to what tariff rates are necessary to bring about these results, and manufacturers seeking the "reasonable profit" through the aid of the tariff exert tremendous pressure upon congressmen, making the problem still more difficult. The tendency is for tariffs to go up, each nation maneuvering to get a position favorable to its industry and commerce. For example, our Hawley-Smoot Tariff Act of 1930 raised the duty on about 650 articles of international commerce. This tariff, of course, made it more difficult for foreign business to export to the United States.

Partly in retaliation for our high tariff rates and partly in the hope of improving their domestic commercial activity, many countries proceeded to increase their tariff rates and to impose other commercial restrictions. Canada shaped her tariff laws so as to transfer to Great Britain purchases that had previously been made in the United States. Mexico increased the duties on wheat and flour, products imported largely from the United States. Twenty-nine nations in Europe and Latin America revised their tariffs upward in 1930, and Great Britain deserted her historic free-trade policy the next year. In addition to increasing the tariff rates, a number of countries resorted to other restrictions, such as the quota system, by which only limited quantities of certain commodities may be imported. Thus, each country tries to keep the home market for its own industry, with the rather natural result that world trade is severely handicapped.

UNITED STATES EXPORTS AND IMPORTS OF GOODS AND SERVICES

(BILLIONS OF DOLLARS)

Period	Exports of goods and services [1]	Imports of goods and services [1]	Surplus of exports of goods and services [1]
1936–38 average	4.1	3.6	0.5
1946	15.0	7.2	7.8
1947	19.7	8.5	11.2
1948	16.8	10.5	6.3
1949 [2]	15.8	10.0	5.8
Annual rates:			
1948—First quarter	17.7	10.1	7.6
Second quarter	16.9	10.1	6.8
Third quarter	15.8	11.0	4.8
Fourth quarter	16.8	10.7	6.1
1949—First quarter	17.0	10.4	6.6
Second quarter	17.7	9.7	8.0
Third quarter	14.5	9.9	4.6
Fourth quarter [2]	14.1	10.3	3.8

[1] Includes income on investments.
[2] Estimates based on incomplete data.
Reproduced from Council of Economic Advisers, *The Annual Economic Review*, Jan. 3, 1950, Table 7.

TRADE AGREEMENTS. Faced with rapid fluctuations in international trade conditions, President Roosevelt (1934) asked Congress for authority to make executive trade agreements with the foreign powers. After considerable debate (in the Senate) on the subject of constitutional limitations concerning the delegation of so much power, Congress voted him the authority.

The Trade Agreements Act of 1934 (an amendment to the Hawley-Smoot Tariff Act) authorizes trade agreements with foreign countries that may reduce import duties as much as 50 per cent, provided the other contracting powers make similar concessions respecting their imports from the United States. Secretary of State Cordell Hull proceeded with enthusiasm and energy in the negotiation of agreements, and a number were concluded. The plan proved to be popular with growers of export crops, manufacturers looking for foreign markets, and with many others who wanted a revival of foreign trade. It was opposed, of course, by certain industrial and agricultural interests who want a protected market, and by a few sincere souls who have not yet learned that if Americans are to sell goods abroad they must also, in the long run at least, buy goods from abroad. The "Ayes" had it, however, and still have it. The Trade Agreements Act is still in force, Congress having five times voted to extend the period for making trade agreements.

Foreign loans. Lending and borrowing money is not commerce within the meaning of the commerce clause of the Constitution, but foreign loans are very definitely connected with foreign trade. Before the First World War Americans were making some investments abroad and during the war and for a short time after its conclusion the United States advanced huge sums to our military associates. This money was used to purchase goods in the United States. Since only a very small part of these loans were ever repaid, the American taxpayer has really carried the burden. For several years following 1921, the State Department exercised some scrutiny over private loans to foreign countries. In 1922 it announced that

the flotation of foreign bond issues in the American market is assuming an increasing importance, and on account of the bearing of such operations upon the proper conduct of affairs it is hoped that American concerns that contemplate making foreign loans will inform the Department of State in due time of the essential facts and of subsequent developments of importance. . . . The Department of State cannot, of course, require American bankers to consult it, [but] the Department believes that in view of the possible national interests involved it should have the opportunity of saying to the underwriters concerned, should it appear advisable to do so, that there is or is not objection to any particular issue.[9]

[9] Quoted in J. C. Malin, *The United States After the World War* (1930), p. 326.

Following this policy, the administration sometimes withheld its approval from proposed private loans to countries that had not funded their war debts to the United States. In February, 1928, the Department of State, in disapproving a proposed private loan to Russia, took occasion to announce that it did not "view with favor financial arrangements designated to facilitate in any way the sale of Soviet bonds in the United States." The Department scrutinized private loans to several countries in the Caribbean area, and its approval was given in such a way as to indicate its strong support.[10] These loans to foreign countries were often used to buy goods in the United States. The statement was made a moment ago that one country cannot export goods to another unless it imports from that other country. It is possible, however, to export without importing, for a time, if credits are available for the country buying our goods. This was the situation for a few years preceding the world economic collapse, when it was discovered that those who had financed these purchases had lost a large part of their loans. There are many occasions when private foreign loans are advisable, but in the future more caution may be exercised in making such investments.

The tens of billions that the United States poured into foreign countries through loans and lend-lease agreements during the Second World War came not from private lenders but from the federal treasury (the American taxpayers). These funds were investments for winning the war, and they should not be evaluated as commercial transactions. With the end of the war and the hope of peace ahead, the question of reconstruction loans to certain friendly foreign governments became urgent. They could not reconstruct their economy without help from us, for the materials they needed for rebuilding were for the most part in America and they had no dollars with which to buy them. In 1947 we advanced $4,400,000,000 to Great Britain, and in the same year we inaugurated the European Recovery Program (Marshall Plan) that has thus far involved the expenditure of several times the amount advanced to Britain. Up to June 30, 1950, about nine and one half billions had been expended under that Plan. The purpose of the program is to aid participating countries in promoting industrial and agricultural production, maintaining the soundness of their currency and finances, and stimulating the growth of international trade. Most of the money advanced for this program is being spent in the United States (see chart), thus stimulating our industry and trade. The restoration of prosperity in Western Europe would without a doubt be economically profitable to the United States, and it would almost certainly help prevent the rise or spread of anti-democratic governments, thus pro-

[10] *Ibid.,* pp. 326 ff.

moting a measure of peace. Such a program, even if it is not completely successful, will be worth the investment. About four fifths of the amount shown on the accompanying chart of budget expenditures for international affairs (1951) represents Marshall Plan funds.

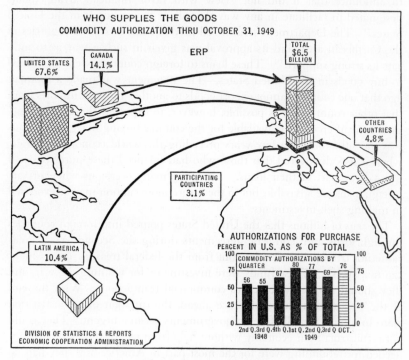

WHO SUPPLIES THE GOODS
COMMODITY AUTHORIZATION THRU OCTOBER 31, 1949

ERP

TOTAL
$6.5
BILLION

UNITED STATES
67.6%

CANADA
14.1%

OTHER
COUNTRIES
4.8%

PARTICIPATING
COUNTRIES
3.1%

LATIN AMERICA
10.4%

AUTHORIZATIONS FOR PURCHASE
PERCENT IN U.S. AS % OF TOTAL

COMMODITY AUTHORIZATIONS BY
QUARTER

DIVISION OF STATISTICS & REPORTS
ECONOMIC COOPERATION ADMINISTRATION

From *The New York Times*, Jan. 4, 1950.

II. THE REGULATION AND PROMOTION OF DOMESTIC TRANSPORTATION AND COMMUNICATIONS

A. Railroads [11]

Transportation before the railroads. Commerce, interstate and intrastate, was very primitive in the early days of the Republic. Transportation by land was hardly any further advanced than it was in the medieval times. The question of regulation did not present itself. The task was

[11] *Annual Reports of the Interstate Commerce Commission;* Marshall E. Dimock, *Business and Government* (1949), Chs. 17–19; C. D. Drayton, *Transportation under Two Masters* (1946); Merle Fainsod and Lincoln Gordon, *Government and the American Economy* (1948 ed.), Ch. IX; D. P. Locklin, *Economics of Transportation* (1947 ed.); I. L. Sharfman, *The Interstate Commerce Commission,* 5 vols. (1931–1937); G. L. Wilson, ed., "Railroads and Government," *The Annals,* CLXXXVII (September, 1936).

BUDGET EXPENDITURES: INTERNATIONAL AFFAIRS AND FINANCE

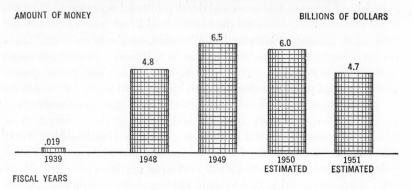

AMOUNT OF MONEY

BILLIONS OF DOLLARS

6.5

6.0

4.8

4.7

.019

| 1939 | 1948 | 1949 | 1950 ESTIMATED | 1951 ESTIMATED |

FISCAL YEARS

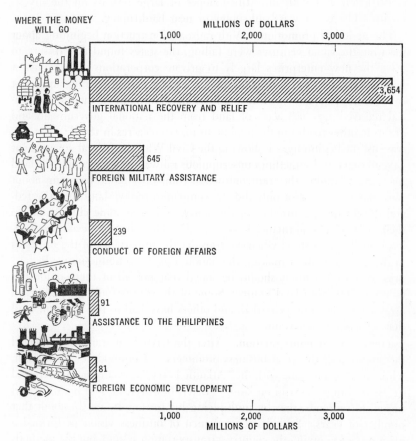

WHERE THE MONEY WILL GO

MILLIONS OF DOLLARS

1,000   2,000   3,000

3,654

INTERNATIONAL RECOVERY AND RELIEF

645

FOREIGN MILITARY ASSISTANCE

239

CONDUCT OF FOREIGN AFFAIRS

91

ASSISTANCE TO THE PHILIPPINES

81

FOREIGN ECONOMIC DEVELOPMENT

1,000   2,000   3,000

MILLIONS OF DOLLARS

From Bureau of the Budget, *The Federal Budget in Brief, Fiscal Year 1951*, p. 11.

to build and improve highways and develop internal waterways. The national government constructed the Cumberland Road, which ran from the town of that name in Maryland to Wheeling, on the Ohio River. This road was finally (1840) extended to Vandalia, Illinois. Despite continued agitation for national road construction, states' rights and states' responsibility theories prompted those in authority to resist further demands on the federal treasury. Left to themselves, the states gave some attention to highways, but much more attention and money to the construction of canals. The most successful of these was the Erie Canal in New York, which before its completion (1825) was paying dividends and which cut freight rates from New York City to Buffalo by nearly 90 per cent. Many other states proceeded to build canals, often without counting the cost of construction and with unjustified hopes of large returns on the investments. The result was bankruptcy or near bankruptcy.

The period of promotion. With railroad construction beginning about the time the canal ventures were failing, the states found it necessary to leave the new enterprises largely to private corporations. But when it became clear that railroads could play a leading part in opening up a vast continent, federal government supplied aid. Thus, in 1850 the Illinois Central received 2,500,000 acres of land from the national government, and grants to other roads ran the total up to 19,000,000 acres in 1856.[12] But this was just the beginning. Following the Civil War, the federal government gave to eager and sometimes unscrupulous railway promoters enough land for a great empire, the transcontinental companies alone receiving about 100,000,000 acres. Not only did the companies receive land; but the federal government, a number of the states, and even some cities, came to their aid with liberal financial assistance.[13] This liberality, even prodigality, is easily understood when we consider the importance of the railroads in the general plan of making the nation a great economic unit. In fairness to the railroads it should be stated that not all of them made immense profits from land grants. Some of them practically gave the land away to get the country settled, and others have had to pay taxes on land that settlers did not want.

The period of nonregulation. After the Civil War, railroads engaged the attention of the great business promoters. "Commodore" Vanderbilt, while making a fortune with the "Atlantic Ferry," contemptuously referred to "them things that run on land." Later, however, he sold his ships and turned to railroads, thereby multiplying his fortune by ten in about that number of years. Such hard-fisted men of business vision performed a great service in giving the country a transportation system, but the methods

---

[12] R. V. Harlow, *The Growth of the United States* (1925), p. 382.
[13] C. A. and Wm. Beard, *The American Leviathan* (1930), pp. 398–399.

they employed sometimes corresponded more closely to the practices of the medieval robber barons than to modern ethical standards. A few big men on the inside manipulated stocks with a total disregard for the interests of the ordinary stockholder. And, what was much worse, the rank and file of shippers were at the mercy of the roads, both in respect to service and rates. The published rates meant little, since the policy of the roads was to charge the ordinary shippers all they could pay and to grant to the biggest patrons whatever concessions seemed necessary. For example, three great railway companies held small oil men to regular freight rates, but they gave a rebate to a colossal oil company. Not only that, but they paid over to the large oil company a commission on every barrel of oil they carried for the small oil concerns! A shipper might be charged more for a 100-mile haul than for a 200-mile haul. This discrepancy came about because a railway company ordinarily had no competitor for short hauls.

Competition among the roads often led to rate wars in which both sides sometimes lost. Being practical men, the railway officials soon came to see that they could better further their interests by reaching an understanding. Competing roads formed pools, dividing the traffic on a percentage basis and apportioning the profits and losses accordingly. Against this monopoly the general public was helpless. Formerly, shippers might profit occasionally by a rate war; now the railroads, no longer fighting each other, could concentrate upon their common objective—collecting all the traffic would bear, all the time.[14]

RAILROADS AND STATE POLITICS. The foregoing and many other abuses were known to exist, but little could be done to stop them because of the alliance of railroad men and politicians. Railroads were most liberal in furnishing passes to public men. They went to state legislatures and almost openly bribed the members. Sometimes competing companies sought legislative favors, occasions that offered the greatest financial opportunities to legislators. Railroad financiers contributed handsomely to the coffers of both political parties. Said Jay Gould of the Erie Railroad: "In a Republican district I was a Republican; in a Democratic district I was a Democrat; in a doubtful district I was doubtful; but I was always Erie." [15]

The corrupt alliance of railroads and politicians was profitable to both parties. Private pockets and party war chests received the funds, and the railroads had immunity from governmental interference. A number of states did manage to pass regulatory laws, but these were often evaded. When an associate told "Commodore" Vanderbilt that his transactions were forbidden by the laws of New York, he replied: "My God, John, you don't

[14] Harlow, *op. cit.*, pp. 588–589.
[15] Quoted in E. M. Sait, *American Parties and Elections* (H. R. Penniman's ed., 1948), p. 287.

suppose you can run a railroad in accordance with the statutes of New York, do you?" [16]   The railroads were entirely too big and powerful for the states to handle, and the great promoters understood this thoroughly.

National regulation.   For some time, various progressive groups had urged the need of national regulation of railroads.   Following an investigation that revealed the conditions outlined above and many other abuses, Congress passed the Interstate Commerce Act of 1887.   This was an important step.   For one thing, it introduced the principle of national control of interstate railways.   The act declared that rates should be just and reasonable, prohibited pooling, forbade rebates and special privileges to particular shippers, and contained other provisions designed to prevent unjust practices.   It established the Interstate Commerce Commission, with powers to conduct investigations and to issue orders to carry the act into effect.   But the railroad companies were actively hostile to the Commission and the courts were often unfriendly to it; and since no railroad was obligated to obey an order of the Commission until the courts had sustained the order, the Commission was, for the time being, relatively ineffective.

The year 1906 is the next significant date in railway legislation.   The Hepburn Act of that year extended the Interstate Commerce Act to express and sleeping car companies, enlarged the personnel of the Commission, and increased and broadened its power in many respects, especially in the matter of fixing rates and issuing orders.   Under the Hepburn Act a policy of vigorous regulation of common carriers was undertaken.   No longer could it be said that the national government was only toying with the idea of regulation.

We mention yet five other commerce acts.   The Transportation Act of 1920 still further extended the scope of federal regulation, but it was also affirmative and constructive in that its aim was "to build up a system of railways prepared to handle promptly all the interstate traffic of the country."   The Emergency Transportation Act of 1933 had the same general purpose, but it went much farther.   The Motor Carrier Act of 1935 brought interstate motor transportation within the field of regulation, and the Transportation Act of 1940 did the same for inland and coastal water transportation.   Both of these acts emphasize the unity of transportation—water, highway, and rail.   Still another Interstate Commerce Act (1942) brought freight forwarders (express companies, etc.) under federal regulation.

Present status of regulation.   In the next few paragraphs we shall consider present-day railroad regulation.   The pages that conclude this sec-

[16] Quoted in Harlow, *op. cit.*, p. 584.

tion deal with the newer aspects of the problem—government encouragement and assistance.

1. GENERAL REGULATIONS. No longer may railway companies issue passes to petty politicians and others who have no legitimate claim upon the railroads. Persons and firms who formerly received rebates and other special transportation favors now find that they are forbidden by law. Then, of course, there is the requirement that rates shall be just and reasonable. Pooling is on the list of prohibitions, although the Interstate Commerce Commission may allow it when it seems to be in the interest of better service. Railway promoters may no longer play fast and loose in issuing securities. Such issues must have the consent of the Commission. By an act of 1933, railway holding companies, which long thwarted the Commission, are brought under its control. If a railroad has a direct financial interest in a product, it is forbidden to transport it, although timber and its products are excepted from this rule. Railroads are also forbidden to have an interest in a competing water carrier; but, here again, a few exceptions are permitted. These and other restrictions are accompanied by more or less appropriate penalties for their violation. Affirmative regulations are found in the requirements that the carriers shall publish their rates, make annual reports to the Interstate Commerce Commission, and keep their accounts on forms prescribed by the Commission.

2. SAFETY LEGISLATION. A field of railway legislation that assumed great importance years ago is that of safety. When the railroads became interstate, the states could no longer deal with this problem, for uniformity was essential, and each state had its own peculiar safety requirements. Beginning with the Safety Appliance Act of 1893, Congress enacted a series of measures that very largely superseded existing state legislation and practically prevented the enactment of additional state laws on the subject. The first act required that cars be equipped with secure grab irons or handholds, automatic couplers, and continuous brakes, and prescribed driving-wheel brakes for locomotives. These and similar safety requirements were made applicable not only to interstate commerce trains, but to all cars and locomotives used on railroads engaged in interstate commerce. In 1911 Congress interested itself in locomotive boilers, establishing the requirement that steam boilers must be inspected and tested from time to time to the end that no one be placed in "unnecessary peril to life and limb." Four years later boiler inspection was expanded to inspection and regulation of the entire locomotive, and the states were held to be completely excluded from this field of regulation. By the Transportation Act of 1920 the Interstate Commerce Commission was given authority to require railroads to install some automatic system of train control. Just when any particular railroad should be required to install such a device

was left to the discretion of the Commission.   Thousands of miles of track have been placed under an automatic control system.

Not only has Congress sought to insure the safety of railroad employees and travelers by requiring the use of various safety devices of a mechanical nature, but it has also promoted safety through legislation designed to reduce human error in the operation of trains.   Thus, to avoid accidents growing out of great fatigue of employees, railroads are forbidden, by an act of 1907, to keep trainmen on duty more than sixteen hours in any day. Under the Motor Carrier Act the Commission is authorized to establish reasonable requirements for the safe operation of such carriers, including maximum hours of service of employees whose activities affect safety of operation.   Other acts, although not aimed primarily at promoting safety, have at least improved relations between employees and employers and thus brought about a better service for the public.   Among these acts may be mentioned the Second Employers' Liability Act (1908), the Adamson Act (1916), the Railway Labor Act of 1926 (amended 1934), the Railway Pension Acts of 1934 and 1935, and the Railroad Unemployment Insurance Act of 1938.[17]

The Interstate Commerce Commission.   It is manifestly impossible for Congress itself to exercise any minute control over the railroads.   Congress passes general laws, and wisely leaves the details of their application to the Interstate Commerce Commission.   This body of eleven men, with its large staff of technical assistants, is one of the most important administrative agencies of the national government.   The comprehensive powers of the Commission are well illustrated by a few provisions of the Transportation Act of 1920.   The consolidation of railroads into a limited number of systems is authorized, subject to the approval of the Commission.   Incidentally, this authority to consolidate marks a very definite turn from restrictive to constructive regulation of railroads.   The act prohibits the issue of railroad securities except under authority granted by the Commission.   It empowers the Commission, under normal conditions, to establish rules and regulations in respect to car service, and, in emergencies, to direct such service in whatever manner best promotes the interest of the public.

Furthermore, the Commission is given far-reaching powers over rates. This power is exceedingly difficult to administer.   Until 1933 just and reasonable rates were determined by the value of railway properties, and wise men seemed to differ fundamentally as to just how they should be evaluated.   In the year mentioned a significant change was made in rate-making.   As amended, the Interstate Commerce Act requires the ICC to give "due consideration, among other factors, to the effect of rates on the

[17] See Chapter 24.

movement of traffic; to the need, in the public interest, of adequate and efficient railway transportation service at the lowest cost consistent with the furnishing of such service; and to the need of revenues sufficient to enable the carriers under honest, economical, and efficient management, to provide such service." In the exercise of its far-reaching authority, the Commission is empowered to make extensive investigations, to compel the attendance of witnesses and the production of records, to direct the federal district attorneys to prosecute violators of the interstate commerce acts, and to issue various orders. Although the Commission is often spoken of as the "supreme court of American transportation," this title is subject to some modification in view of the fact that its orders are subject to review by the regular federal courts.

Decline of state control over railroads. As the national government has exercised its interstate commerce power in respect to the railroads, state regulation has been considerably restricted. To be sure, the states still have the authority to control intrastate commerce; but where there is a substantial relation between interstate and intrastate commerce, the national regulation of the former supersedes state regulation of the latter. Thus, the national safety requirements are applicable to intrastate trains operating on through-state lines, since such trains, if not equipped with proper safety appliances, constitute a clear and present danger to interstate commerce. The same principle is applied to rates. Texas fixed freight rates within that state in such a way as to favor certain of her cities and to discriminate against Shreveport, Louisiana. The Interstate Commerce Commission ordered the railroads to cease making these discriminatory charges, and the order was sustained by the Supreme Court of the United States.[18]

State power was further limited by a decision that grew out of the Transportation Act of 1920. In conformity with the purpose of this act to give the railroads a fair return on their properties, the Interstate Commerce Commission granted an increase in rates. Wisconsin claimed that she could still control local rates, and refused to adopt the rates fixed by the Commission. The Supreme Court held that an adequate national transportation system with a fair return to the railroads on their property value could not be secured with each state fixing local rates, and therefore upheld the Commission's order that all intrastate rates which affected interstate commerce should conform to the rates for the latter.[19]

It should not be assumed, however, that the states have been completely ousted from the domain of railroad legislation. In the case just cited, the Supreme Court declared that it was not depriving the states of their power over intrastate commerce, except where Congress must control such com-

[18] Houston Ry. v. U.S., 234 U.S. 342 (1914).
[19] Wisconsin v. C. B. & Q. Ry., 257 U.S. 563 (1922)

merce in order to exercise effective control over interstate commerce. We should note also that, in the interest of the health and safty of the public, the states may impose certain minor regulations upon interstate trains, such as the requirement that they shall slow down at grade crossings.[20]

Newer aspects of the railroad problem. About 1900 "railways were collectively represented as an ogre, a vicous monopoly, the farmers' foe, and the shady stock speculator's darling."[21] In our time regulation has reduced abuses to such an extent that we commonly think of railroads as trusted public servants. The problem of regulation is no longer the burning issue. Our chief concern is keeping the railroads out of financial straits and aiding them with organization plans, to the end that the nation may have an adequate system of transportation.

From 1929 until recently, when war business strained their capacity, the railroads were in a very unsatisfactory financial condition. The Reconstruction Finance Corporation, although established (1932) primarily for the purpose of helping banks and similar financial institutions, during the first few months of its existence extended $170,000,000 of its $2,000,000,000 credit fund to needy railroads. The general business decline probably accounted in a large measure for the falling off in railroad earnings, but other factors played a part. Water carriers, pipe lines, airplanes, and motor carriers, particularly the latter, had developed very rapidly as competitors of the railroads. In 1932 the Interstate Commerce Commission made an investigation of motor vehicle operations and recommended federal regulation of motor vehicles engaged in interstate commerce. As noted above, this legislation was enacted in 1935, and the Transportation Act of 1940 brought inland and coastal water carriers into the system.

Viewing the railroad problem broadly, we may say that unrestrained competition, either as between railroads or as between them on the one hand and water and motor carriers on the other, is no longer considered in the public interest. The idea of consolidation and co-ordination, under close government supervision, is now the line of approach to the transportation problem. The act of 1940 emphasized this approach. It created a temporary Board of Investigation and Research and charged it with the duty of investigating the relative economy and fitness of railroad, motor vehicle, and water carriers for transportation service, in order to determine the type of service each form of carrier is best fitted to perform, and the methods that should be encouraged and developed for each, to the end that there may be provided a *national* transportation system adequate for commerce and the national defense.

The railroads in the Second World War. The record of the railroads

[20] See p. 84.
[21] *Time,* January 11, 1932, p. 14.

in the Second World War is outstanding. Their services on land were no less significant than those of the merchant marine on the seas. In the spring of 1942 the Nazi submarine campaign off the Atlantic coast was a sweeping success, but the railroads prevented it from being a catastrophe for America. They hauled 900,000 barrels of oil and gas a day from the Southwest to the East, when only the most optimistic transportation experts believed they could carry more than 200,000 barrels. By speeding up their trains, by loading their cars more heavily, and by not sending the empty cars in opposite directions at the same time, they succeeded to a remarkable degree in hauling the millions of carloads of raw materials to the industrial plants; the troops, the provisions, and the instruments of war to the ports of embarkation. No doubt one explanation of the wartime efficiency of the railway carriers is found in the Office of Defense Transportation, a war agency with wide powers that were used with keen discretion and judicious restraint by a most capable transportation authority, Joseph B. Eastman.

The postwar years find the railroads facing another crisis. They still have much business, but they are in danger of going in the red again. The trouble is that their operating costs have risen by at least 50 per cent. The problem now is to get the consent of the Interstate Commerce Commission for necessary increases in freight rates. Another problem that the roads must solve is how to attract passengers. The answer might well be in a *reduction* in passenger rates.

B. Highway Construction and Motor Transportation [22]

When motor vehicles came into general use, the country became more highway conscious than it had been since the possibilities of canals and railroads had diverted attention from the problem of improving the primitive roads and paths a century earlier. To be sure, there has always been some interest in highway extension and improvement; but as the number of registered motor cars reached 10,000,000, then 20,000,000 (in 1950 the number was 43,000,000), the problem of the construction of highways— national, state, and local—suitable for this new form of transportation increasingly engaged the powerful interest of automobile associations and chambers of commerce, as well as the interest of farmers and car owners in general. The automobile is not only responsible for our $50,000,000,000 highway investment; but being a fast, dangerous, and very common means of transportation, it laid at the doors of all governments the prob-

---

[22] J. J. George, "The Federal Motor Carrier Act of 1935," *Cornell Law Quarterly* (1936), XXI, 249–275; Council of State Governments, *Highway Safety and Motor Transportation* (1950); Locklin, *op. cit.*, Chs. XXVIII–XXIX; *U.S. Govt. Org. Manual*, 1950–1951, pp. 258–260, 377, 381.

lem of its regulation. We shall deal first with the matter of roads; then with the problem of regulation of motor vehicles.

Highway construction: 1. LOCAL. Road construction was primarily a local enterprise until a generation ago, and such work as was done on roads was often performed in a careless and indifferent manner by the male residents of a community as they gossiped and smoked and had a good time generally in the day or two they worked to pay their "road tax." Local communities still play an important part in the building and care of roads, especially those roads that serve as feeders to the main high-ways. In the Eastern states the town, and in the majority of other states the county, is the unit for local road administration. The obligation to provide a county with a system of roads belongs to the county board; but there is a commendable and growing tendency to place an engineer in actual charge of road construction.

Highway costs are met from the ordinary property tax, the poll and labor tax (in a few states), special assessments of property owners bene-fited, the gasoline tax, and wheel and vehicle taxes. No state collects road revenues from all these sources. The present tendency is to rely more upon the gasoline tax and automobile license fees, the state collecting the money and passing part of it down to the counties.

2. STATE. Even before the advent of the automobile a few states adopted a policy of financing and improving highways, and with the growth of motor transportation other states rapidly joined their ranks. States have granted funds to counties for highways on condition that the counties pay a substantial part of the cost (often half) and on another important condi-tion that the counties build the roads in accordance with standards fixed by the state. This plan of state aid has usually operated successfully. It has the merits of improving the quality of the highways, of imposing state control without completely depriving the counties of the road function, and of spreading the cost a little more widely.

State-wide highway systems under the exclusive control of the state are becoming more and more common. Under such systems the main roads are selected and designated as state highways, and the county or other local authorities are left to administer farm-to-market roads and byways. In discharging road functions, the states have found it necessary to estab-lish highway commissions or authorities with similar titles. These agencies not only direct state highway construction and maintenance and supervise the local expenditure of state-aid funds, but they also frequently serve as general advisers to county road authorities and in a few cases they have some power of appointment and removal of such authorities. Because of the technical character of highway administration and because the auto-mobile has made the county relatively much smaller than it used to be, the state is now recognized as the proper unit of administration for arterial highways, and experts are generally of the opinion that considerable state control over local highway matters is highly desirable. Indeed, at least four states, Delaware, North Carolina, Virginia, and West Virginia, now assume full responsibility for the construction and maintenance of all roads.

3. NATIONAL. The fight that raged a hundred years ago over the question as to whether the national government should build roads resulted in the retirement of that government from this branch of activity. But with the coming of the automobile and the realization that roads played an important part in national defense, the old question was reintroduced and answered in the affirmative. In 1916 Congress passed the Federal Aid Road Act, by which it authorized the Secretary of Agriculture to spend, in co-operation with the states, over a five-year period, the sum of $75,000,000 on roads over which the mails were being carried. Five years later the Federal Highway Act authorized expenditures for trunk lines (those forming interstate highway systems) and important connecting highways. From 1921 to 1930 the annual grant was $75,000,000, and in 1931 it was increased to $125,000,000. Some grants were made for other than trunk line highways, bringing the total above the last-named figure.[23]

The greater part of these appropriations is divided among the states according to area, population, and the mileage of rural delivery routes, each basis of measurement determining the distribution of a third of the funds. Then there are certain strings attached to the appropriations. Although there has been some relaxation of the requirement since 1932, the general rule has been that no state may receive this federal aid unless it matches the federal dollar. It is a fifty-fifty proposition. In the second place the states must accept a considerable degree of federal supervision in highway construction. The results have been generally satisfactory. A national highway system is being developed through the pooling of funds and expert information on the part of the federal government and the states.

Postwar highway program. Highways were much used by heavy traffic during the war and they were not kept in the best state of repair. Even a large proportion of the money available for construction and repair was not expended, owing to labor and material shortages. Before the end of the war elaborate plans were made for a new spurt in highway development. The Federal Aid Highway Act of 1944 deserves to rank beside the acts of 1916 and 1921 in the history of highway legislation. It authorized $500,000,000 for the construction of highways in each of the first three postwar years. Of the annual appropriation, $225,000,000 was for the federal-aid system, $150,000,000 for secondary roads, and $125,000,000 for the federal-aid highway system in urban areas. Money that accumulated

[23] *Report of the Secretary of the Treasury,* 1941, p. 648.

for highways during the war was to be added to the new appropriations. Two new highway systems are being created, the national system of interstate highways, which will connect great cities and industrial areas and tap the routes of strategic importance for national defense, and a secondary system, which will be made up of feeder roads, rural mail routes, and school bus routes. The Federal Aid Highway Act of 1948 authorized $450,000,000 for each of the fiscal years 1950 and 1951, the funds to be assigned to the three classes of construction in the same proportions as were provided by the act of 1944. National support of highway development will undoubtedly continue on a large scale.

Motor vehicle regulation. The governments have not completed their task when they have collected the money from the motorists and have built the highways. There remains the very important matter of the regulation of traffic. The chief problem is that of safety. As many as 40,000 persons have been killed in a single year on the highways and in the streets, and the number of injured annually is many times 40,000. Aside from the suffering caused by motor accidents, the economic loss reaches a staggering figure. From the little hamlet that imposes a speed limit of fifteen miles an hour to the national government that prepares broad advisory plans of traffic regulation, the civil authorities are concerned with reducing the hazards of motor traffic. Occasionally, the motorist suspects that the regulations imposed by the councils of some villages are more the result of resentment at the seeming lack of respect that city folks show for the town as they sail gaily through it than of a genuine desire to make the town safe for pedestrians, but certainly only a few traffic regulations are not designed primarily for safety and convenience. State motor vehicle regulations and supplementary municipal ordinances cover what seems to the ordinary individual every possible phase of the subject.

Indeed, the subject is so fully covered that the typical motorist in the typical community probably violates some regulation nearly every time he takes a drive. Laws require that vehicles be registered and that drivers be licensed. They prescribe speed limits, types of lights, drivers' signals, and mufflers. They specify in detail the manner in which trailers may be used, prohibit parking on highways, and fix penalties for the reckless driver—a class that in some states includes the car operator who has in "his or her embrace another person." These and numerous similar regulations conspicuously fail to bring the accident rate down to that minimum number that might be considered unavoidable. The United States Department of Commerce has given assistance to states and cities by sponsoring the National Conference on Street and Highway Safety. Every one of the states has adopted some part or parts of the Uniform Vehicle Code prepared by the Conference, and a number of cities have put its Municipal

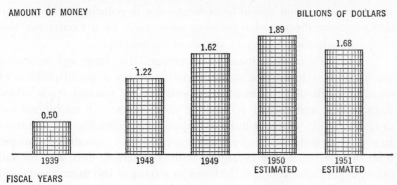

BUDGET EXPENDITURES: TRANSPORTATION AND COMMUNICATION

AMOUNT OF MONEY

BILLIONS OF DOLLARS

1.89

1.62

1.68

1.22

0.50

| 1939 | 1948 | 1949 | 1950 ESTIMATED | 1951 ESTIMATED |

FISCAL YEARS

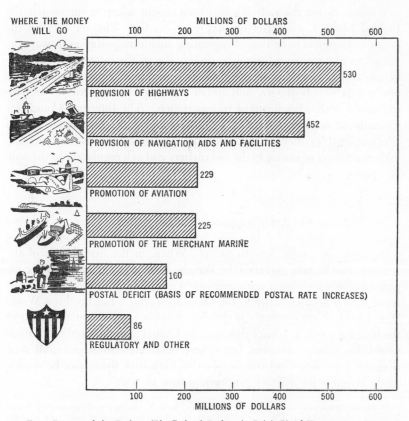

WHERE THE MONEY WILL GO

MILLIONS OF DOLLARS

100   200   300   400   500   600

530
PROVISION OF HIGHWAYS

452
PROVISION OF NAVIGATION AIDS AND FACILITIES

229
PROMOTION OF AVIATION

225
PROMOTION OF THE MERCHANT MARINE

160
POSTAL DEFICIT (BASIS OF RECOMMENDED POSTAL RATE INCREASES)

86
REGULATORY AND OTHER

100   200   300   400   500   600
MILLIONS OF DOLLARS

From Bureau of the Budget, *The Federal Budget in Brief, Fiscal Year 1951*, p. 27.

Traffic Ordinance into effect. This not-too-encouraging degree of uniformity in regulation should be of some value in reducing accidents, particularly since the model regulations were made by a Conference that pooled the experience of every section of the country.

THE PROBLEM OF THE COMMERCIAL VEHICLE. The large and increasing use of motor vehicles as common carriers presents a special problem of regulation. In 1934 this motor transportation had reached 45,000 inland communities, and created very telling competition with established rail carriers. While passenger miles of the railroads declined 40 per cent from 1930 to 1934, common carrier buses increased their operation by 10 per cent. Of course, it may be argued with considerable force that the rail carriers lost much business to the buses on account of bad management and high rates. Yet the buses had a great advantage in their relatively small cost of operation and in their freedom from federal regulation.

Whether or not the railroads had been caught asleep at the switch, the Federal Motor Carrier Act of 1935 was overdue. The act declares the policy of Congress to be that of regulating such transportation in ways designed to preserve its advantages, protect the public interest, promote efficient and economical service "without unjust discriminations, undue preferences or advantages, and unfair or destructive practices," and coordinate it with other forms of transportation. The Interstate Commerce Commission is given a long list of powers and duties for the purpose of effectuating this policy. Unquestionably this legislation was much needed, both as a matter of justice to the rail carriers and as a regulation in the public interest.

C. Aviation [24]

No doubt men of lively imagination in all periods of history reflected upon the possibility of flying; and legend has it that a Greek, Dædalus, using artificial wings, flew to Sicily! When, in the first decade of the century, two bicycle makers (the Wright Brothers) and others were experimenting with 'planes, our government gave them little more encouragement than it gave credence to the Dædalus legend. But the First World War forced all governments to develop aviation as an essential branch of the fighting services. After that war the United States not only continued to develop military aviation, but it very definitely encouraged civil aviation, for experience and training in this branch of flying can be readily made available for military purposes in time of war.

[24] *Annual Reports of the Secretary of Commerce;* Kent T. Healy, *The Economics of Transportation in America* (1940), Ch. 9; H. S. Leroy, "Civil Aeronautics Authority," *Air Law Review,* IX, 315 (Oct., 1938); C. E. Puffer, *Air Transportation* (1941); *U.S. Govt. Org. Manual, 1949,* pp. 312–315, 335–337.

As early as 1918 air mail service was established between Washington and New York, and in the course of a few years nearly all of the principal cities were given this service. Now about 700 cities are included in various routes. Originally, the government owned and operated the air mail facilities; but in accordance with the general policy to "keep the government out of business," the service was soon transferred to private concerns. For some years these companies were awarded very liberal mail contracts, the announced purpose being that of encouraging commercial aviation. Aided by such subsidies, air transport companies developed a passenger service, one that now measurably competes with the railroads.

Not only has the government aided air transportation through its mail contracts, but it has stimulated aviation in various other ways. The Air Commerce Act of 1926 placed civil aviation under the fostering care of the Department of Commerce, whose Bureau of Air Commerce administered the act. The Civil Aeronautics Act of 1938 created a new authority, and under the present set-up civil aviation is regulated and promoted by the Civil Aeronautics Administration and by the Civil Aeronautics Board. The Administration, operating in the Department of Commerce, encourages the establishment of civil airways, landing areas, and other navigation facilities; designates federal airways (the Federal Airways System now comprises a network of nearly 60,000 miles); makes provision for the control of air traffic; examines and rates airmen; inspects aircraft; issues safety certificates; and performs a wide variety of other duties, including the training of citizens of foreign countries in the operation and maintenance of aeronautical equipment. The Civil Aeronautics Board, an independent agency, prescribes safety rules and regulations; reviews reports of all accidents and determines their probable cause; denies or grants "certificates of public convenience and necessity" to carriers; prescribes or approves rates and fixes the mail rate compensation; approves or disapproves business relationships between air carriers; assists the State Department in the negotiation of agreements with foreign governments for the development of air transportation; and otherwise serves as an "interstate and foreign commerce commission" for the air services.

D. Communications [25]

Telegraph, telephone, and cable lines. Electric communications have been developed primarily by private initiative, although government aid and encouragement have usually been forthcoming. During the First

[25] *Annual Reports of the Federal Communications Commission;* Dimock, *Business and Government,* Ch. 19; Fainsod and Gordon, *op. cit.,* Ch. XI; H. S. Hettinger, Ed., "New Horizons in Radio," *The Annals,* CCXIII (January, 1941); C. A. Siepmann, *Radio's Second Chance* (1946); and *Radio, Television, and Society* (1950).

World War the national government took over all such communications and the railroads as well, but returned them to their owners shortly after the conclusion of hostilities. During the Second World War ample powers were granted to the President to take over telephone, telegraph, and cable facilities.

Telephone and telegraph companies, having many lines in interstate commerce, are subject to the Federal Communications Commission, which must see that their rates are "just and reasonable" and that they make no unjust discriminations between customers. Another important function of the Commission is to grant hearings for the consolidation of telephone companies and to authorize such consolidations when they are "in the public interest." A considerable number of consolidations have been allowed. Since better telephone service can be provided by monopolies, the program of consolidation under regulation is considered entirely satisfactory. Telegraph communication has been practically monopolistic in character for some time. As for cable lines, none may connect the United States with any foreign country unless licensed by the President. He may withhold or revoke such licenses for the purpose of securing cable rights for Americans in foreign countries or for the purpose of preserving the security of the United States. He has the further duty of enforcing the requirement that cable companies shall charge only just and reasonable rates and maintain adequate service.

Radio. Although radio had been used on ships for some years, citizens in general were not particularly conscious of this revolutionary means of transmitting intelligence until the First World War, and the rush to install receiving sets in millions of American homes is almost within the memory of present-day college students. There are now some two hundred important broadcasting stations and a number of less powerful stations. Tens of thousands of people are employed in various phases of the radio business, and large sums of money are invested in it. Stretching its network through the entire country, extending its waves across international boundaries, possessing the greatest possibilities for good or ill in the life of our people, in 1927 it was subjected to national regulation. Present regulations are under the comprehensive Communications Act of 1934, and its amendments. Among other significant provisions of the regulatory act are those applying the antitrust laws to service and apparatus; the requirement that all candidates for the same public office shall be allowed the same use of radio facilities; and the stipulation that all advertising shall be broadcast as such.

The act is administered by the Federal Communications Commission. The Commission has the responsibility of granting licenses to stations, fixing their wave-lengths, and allotting the time during which they may

broadcast.   Perhaps the broadest power of the Commission is that of granting and renewing licenses under the guiding principles of "public interest,
convenience, or necessity."   Although the Commission is forbidden to exercise censorship over communications, it is by no means inconceivable that
stations in fear of losing their license, or in panic at the thought of the
government's taking over broadcasting, may impose a censorship of their
own.   Each invention or discovery that confers a blessing upon man
seems to leave some problems on his doorstep, and not the least of the
problems the radio has brought is the old problem (in a new form) of
maintaining free speech.

III. THE REGULATION AND PROMOTION OF GENERAL BUSINESS

The subject matter for this section includes the regulation of corporations (other than those engaged in transportation and communications),
the protection and development of markets, and scientific aids to business.

A. State Regulation [26]

1. **The regulation of ordinary corporations.**   As corporate business developed, regulation in the states became essential, much more imperative
in the highly industrialized states than in the others, but insistent in all
of them.

Issuance of charters.   Certain types of business concerns may be chartered by the federal government, but the great majority of corporations
have always had to look to the states for charters.   The charter is the
corporation's authorization to do business.   It sets forth the manner in
which the corporation shall be organized and the general methods by
which it may conduct its business.   A century ago legislatures commonly
granted charters by special acts, but this practice has been generally abandoned.   Under the present system, states have general corporation laws,
and charters are issued in pursuance of these laws.   A group applies to
the secretary of state (or whatever authority is empowered to issue charters),
who examines the application, makes sure that all terms of law are complied with, and then issues a charter upon receipt of a fee.   A corporation
is known as "domestic" in the state that issues the charter, and as "foreign" in other states.   It is a very common practice for states to admit
foreign corporations, a privilege for which they not infrequently exact
a higher fee than they require of domestic corporations engaged in the
same business.   A state may not, however, prevent a corporate or natural

[26] F. G. Crawford, *State Government* (1931) Chs. XXI–XXIII; A. F. Macdonald, *American State Government and Administration* (1950 ed.), Ch. XXVIII; C. F. Snider, *American
State and Local Government* (1950), Ch. XXII; *Book of the States, 1950–1951,* pp. 469–
489.   See also "Blue Books" of various states.

person from engaging in interstate commerce, or burden such commerce by requiring a license for its conduct.

CONTINUOUS SUPERVISION. But the states do not issue charters of incorporation or grant foreign corporations the privilege of doing business and then let them pursue their merry course. Most of the states were satisfied with this procedure two generations ago; but in our time they exercise a continuous supervision over business organizations. Corporations are required to make various reports to the secretary of state or, better, to a corporation commission. Through an examination of these reports and by other checks the extent to which a corporation is observing the laws may be determined, and in the case of major violations the privilege of carrying on business may be revoked.

In order to protect the public from security frauds a great many states have enacted "blue-sky" laws. These statutes prohibit the issue of securities unless approved by state authority, which approval is given only when a company furnishes complete information concerning its financial condition and the nature of the securities it proposes to offer, and designates the property upon which the securities are to be based. These laws do no more than protect the investor against fraud. He may still make very unwise purchases of securities. If the investor is a "sucker," the laws can not remove him from that class.

2. Regulation of corporations affected with a public interest. Certain types of business are very close to the public, in that practically every citizen must depend upon them. In particular, banks, insurance companies, and public utilities come within this group. Such business is said to be "affected with a public interest." It would be absurd to expect each person to determine the soundness of a bank or an insurance company. Government must do what it can to make these concerns safe.

(*a*) BANKS. Inasmuch as the federal government has assumed ever-increasing (but not exclusive) responsibility for the regulation of banks, that subject is more appropriately considered in a treatise on the federal government.[27]

(*b*) INSURANCE. The public must put its trust and savings in insurance companies as in the banks; and, for the same reason, the states must regulate the business of insurance. Although, in 1944, the Supreme Court held that the national government might through its power over interstate commerce reach certain transactions of insurance companies, the states are still and with the approval of Congress (Act of March 9, 1945), essentially in control of the business. Most of the states have exercised this power with considerable energy since New York (1905) investigated the practices of insurance companies. A state administrative authority, often

---

[27] See the preceding chapter, sec. IV.

the superintendent of insurance, is required to keep an eye on the assets of the companies, to see that their funds are invested in sound securities, and otherwise to enforce the state laws designed for the protection of policy-holders. Some states of the Central West have themselves gone into the insurance business. For example, Wisconsin issues life insurance policies for small amounts; North Dakota and two or three other states insure the farmers' crops against hail; and a larger number insure against industrial accidents. Whether insurance is undertaken by states or by companies chartered by them, it is a business that calls not only for honesty but for technical talent of a high order.

(c) PUBLIC UTILITIES. Certain other businesses, monopolistic in character, call for special regulation by the states. To this class belong the railroads, bus lines, and telegraph and telephone systems. Concerning these utilities, it may be said that, although the states continue to regulate them in their intrastate business, the federal government, through its power over interstate commerce, has rather effectively entered the field of regulation. Other important utilities, and these are regulated almost exclusively by the states and their local subdivisions, included electric power and gas. State laws govern such subjects as the granting of franchises, the issuing of stocks and bonds, the quality of the service rendered, the rates to be charged, and, in addition, require reports from the companies.

These matters cannot possibly be regulated in detail by law. For specific application of the laws the states have created state and local public utility commissions, endowing them with powers similar to those held by the national Interstate Commerce Commission. These commissions hold extensive hearings in respect to rates and other matters brought before them by utility companies or the public. Their decisions are always subject to judicial review on points of law, and in many jurisdictions on facts as well. Manifestly the commissions' duties require a high degree of talent and integrity. There has been some difficulty in finding men with sufficient qualifications to fill these positions. Complaint is made that they are much more likely to side with the companies than with the public. This condition may exist because men holding the view of the companies are often appointed commissioners, or possibly because the companies are usually represented by better legal talent than is the public. There is complaint also that the courts are sometimes unfriendly to the decisions of commissions that favor the public. Granted that the commissions do not and cannot always satisfy the public and that the courts may occasionally block their best efforts, it is generally agreed that commission regulation is superior to the old system, which was essentially that of nonregulation.

A number of cities own their utilities, particularly gas and electric plants. Since small electric plants cannot be conducted economically, a few states have authorized communities to combine in "utility regions." This authorization offers a sort of standing threat to power companies to give better rates and services. It does not mean that these communities will immediately enter the power business. The great body of Americans, until recently at least, have looked with disfavor upon public ownership and operation of utilities, preferring to solve the problem by official regulation and informal adjustments with private companies.

B. Federal Regulation [28]

During Washington's Administration the new federal government put American credit on a solid basis, established a sound monetary system, chartered a federal bank, levied a tariff, and passed a tonnage act. Such measures were designed not only for the advantage of the government itself, but also for the improvement of business. This policy of business promotion has continued to our own time. Of the policy of promotion more will be said a little later. For the present we shall consider the government's attitude toward business from the standpoint of regulation.

Federal regulation became necessary when the states found themselves unable to check effectively the great corporations, trusts, and holding companies that grew up in the generation following the Civil War. Often guilty of practices similar to those that had brought many railroads into bad repute, these great business combines shared with the railroads a widespread and often merited public hostility. To be sure, the state authorities did not always attempt to limit the operations of the "soulless" corporations and "unspeakable" trusts, for corporation officers or agents not infrequently "had a way" with legislators. But even with an honest desire to do so, legislatures usually found their powers inadequate, for big business was commonly interstate business and very incompletely subject to state regulation. The solution was to get Congress to undertake the task, using its power over interstate and foreign commerce.

The Sherman Antitrust Act (1890). After considerable deliberation Congress finally passed the now well-known Sherman Antitrust Act, forbidding "every contract, combination in the form of trust or otherwise, or conspiracy, in restraint of trade or commerce among the several states" and prescribing heavy penalties for violations of the law. This act was heralded by some almost as a relief from bondage, but there was to be a great deal more wandering in the wilderness on the problem of trusts. Supported by the best legal talent against the somewhat indifferent at-

[28] *Annual Reports of the Federal Trade Commission; Annual Reports of the Attorney General;* "The Antitrust Campaign," *Fortune,* July, 1948, p. 63; T. C. Blaisdell, *The Federal Trade Commission* (1932); Fainsod and Gordon, *op. cit.,* Chs. XIII–XV; H. D. Koontz, *Government Control of Business* (1941).

torneys who represented the government, the trusts won a victory in the first case that came before the Supreme Court. In that case, certain sugar refineries in Pennsylvania were charged with having combined to secure a monopoly. The government's case was not well prepared, in that it failed to show that the trust controlled the prices and sale of sugar beyond the state line and thus restrained interstate commerce. The court therefore held that the combination complained of was one of manufacturers and that since manufacturing was not interstate commerce the Sherman Act did not apply.[29]

The enforcement of the antitrust law lay not heavily upon the conscience of Presidents or federal attorneys in the decade following this decision. The first President to establish a reputation as a "trust buster" was Theodore Roosevelt, who distinguished between "good" and "bad" trusts and proclaimed his hostility for the latter in a manner highly approved by their victims. Yet his record for dissolving trusts is not particularly impressive, although a notable victory was won when the Supreme Court dissolved the Northern Securities Company, an organization that held the securities of the Great Northern and the Northern Pacific railroads in order to eliminate competition between them.

THE "RULE OF REASON." In disbanding two great combinations in 1911, the Supreme Court laid down the "rule of reason," a rule that occasioned considerable comment and criticism. It will be recalled that the Sherman Act forbade *every* contract in restraint of interstate trade. The Court's rule of reason was that Congress had not intended to forbid every such contract, but had simply meant to embody in statute form the common law, which recognized as illegal only those contracts that "unreasonably" restrained trade. In arriving at this decision the Court may have taken some liberties with the statute. Indeed, one member, Justice Harlan, in a vigorous dissenting opinion declared that the Court had usurped the powers of Congress and legislated this meaning into the law. At any rate, the decision made a sweeping classification of business combinations into two groups: those reasonable and within the law; and those unreasonable and without the law.

But just what contracts were "unreasonable"? Many businessmen felt, with some justification, that the law itself was unreasonable in that it did not name in clear terms the practices that would subject them to its penalties. This uncertainty as to the application of the law, combined with

[29] United States v. E. C. Knight Co., U.S. 1 (1895). But in 1937, in the Jones and Laughlin Steel Co. case, the Supreme Court held that industry, although intrastate when separately considered, might have activities so closely and substantially related to interstate commerce as to bring it under the regulatory power of Congress (301 U.S. 1). In 1948 the Knight case was clearly reversed, Mandeville Is. v. Am. Crystal Sugar, 334 U.S. 219.

the constant growth of business combinations since its enactment, clearly indicated a need for additional and more specific legislation.

The Clayton Act (1914). In his campaign for the presidency Wilson had stressed the need for the regulation of trusts, and his first Congress passed the Clayton Antitrust Law. Rather more specific than the Sherman Act, it prohibits, among other objectionable practices, discriminating charges to purchasers of identical articles, a practice clearly in restraint of trade. Also prohibited is the practice of making a reduction in price to one purchaser on condition that he make no purchase from a competing firm, where the agreement is of such a nature as to reduce competition materially or tend to establish a monopoly. The act also contains various provisions designed to prevent interlocking arrangements among large banks operating under the laws of the United States, manufacturing concerns, and common carriers. Another important provision of the act enables an individual to secure an injunction against firms following prohibited practices, a form of legal action that could be taken only by the government under the Sherman Act. The Clayton Act was also designed to restrict the use of injunctions in labor disputes, a purpose that, as the next chapter will show, was not fully accomplished.

The Federal Trade Commission Act (1914). About a month before it passed the Clayton Act, Congress placed on the statute books the Federal Trade Commission Act, a measure declaring unlawful price-fixing agreements, boycotts, combinations in restraint of trade, and other unfair methods of competition. Perhaps the most significant provision of the act was that establishing the Federal Trade Commission, presently to be discussed.

Fair-practices legislation since 1914. Under the National Industrial Recovery Act of 1933 the antitrust laws were practically suspended. When the NIRA was declared unconstitutional, the antitrust laws were restored, and congressional interest in their revival was manifested in the Robinson-Patman Act of 1936. That legislation amended the Clayton Act and restated in more inclusive form the basic principle prohibiting price discriminations. It forbids the seller of a commodity to discriminate in price between different purchasers "where the effect of such discrimination may be substantially to lessen competition or tend to create a monopoly in any line of commerce, or to injure, destroy, or prevent competition with any person who either grants or knowingly receives the benefit of such discrimination, or with customers of either of them."

The Wheeler-Lea Act of 1938 is incorporated into the Federal Trade Commission Act and broadens that act in several particulars. As earlier legislation prohibits unfair methods of competition, so the Wheeler-Lea amendment prohibits "unfair or deceptive acts or practices in commerce."

The dissemination of false advertising of foods, drugs, devices (for use in the diagnosis, prevention, or treatment of disease), or cosmetics is made unlawful, and criminal penalties are prescribed for advertising relative to any such commodity, the use of which may be injurious to health, or where there is intent to defraud or mislead.

Reference should be made to two other recent acts. The Wool Products Labeling Act of 1939 provides for the protection of producers, manufacturers, distributors, and consumers from the unrevealed presence of substitutes and mixtures in wool products. The Trade-Mark Act of 1946 authorizes the cancellation of trademarks when they had been fraudulently procured, illegally used, and under certain other circumstances.

Enforcement of the antitrust laws; the Federal Trade Commission. The antitrust measures are enforced by appropriate arms of the federal government—the provisions respecting banks by the Federal Reserve Board, those applying to common carriers by the Interstate Commerce Commission, and those applying to commerce in general by the Federal Trade Commission, the courts having a final word to say in cases duly before them. The chief agency for administering the antitrust laws is the FTC. It is composed of five members, appointed by the President with the consent of the Senate for terms of seven years. On the staff of the FTC are administrative officers, attorneys, economists, accountants, and clerks, bringing the total number to about 600. The duties of the FTC may be divided into two main classes—law enforcement and investigation.

1. LAW ENFORCEMENT. The FTC administers the Federal Trade Commission Act, a section of the Clayton Act, and some more recent acts, including the Robinson-Patman Act (1936), the Wheeler-Lea Act (1938), the Wool Products Labeling Act (1939), and the Trade-Mark Act (1946). The act creating the FTC makes the general declaration that unfair methods of competition in commerce are unlawful, and leaves the FTC to decide just what methods of competition are unfair. From time to time it has branded various practices as unfair, until the accumulated list occupies six pages in its annual report for 1949. Specific practices thus forbidden include the use of false or misleading advertising; procuring the business secrets of competitors by bribing their employees, or by similar means; using merchandising schemes based on lot or chance; the use of the "free" goods device to create an impression that something is being given away when its price is actually included in the amount paid for other articles; and misrepresenting the interest rate on deferred payments.[30]

A practice may be investigated by the FTC upon its own initiative or, more commonly, upon complaint of a party that a particular practice of some concern is unfair. Thus, in 1942, the FTC investigated the case of a

[30] *Annual Report of the Federal Trade Commission* (1949), pp. 90 ff.

firm that represented its face powder and creams to be germicidal by reason of their vitamin content, and the case of a company engaged in the sale of tennis, badminton, and squash rackets, imported in an unfinished state from Japan, which importation was concealed by obliterating the legend "made in Japan." [31]

The FTC always gives the party against whom complaint is made a copy of the charges. The next step is the hearing at which all parties are fully represented. If the FTC finds unfair the practice complained of, it issues a "cease and desist" order. In 1949 such orders were issued in 47 cases. It may happen that the original notice of a complaint is sufficient to cause a party to stop an unfair practice. But ordinarily the party against whom complaint is made will make a defense before the FTC. When ordered to cease and desist, a party not infrequently contests the FTC's order in the federal courts.

The FTC may proceed in a United States district court by injunction to prevent the dissemination of matter prohibited, pending the final disposition of a complaint under the law. One such order enjoined an urban drug chain from advertising the efficacy of a weight-reducing compound while neglecting to suggest that some stout matrons might prefer obesity and good eyesight to slimness and blindness, a blackout in vision being a possible effect of this particular miracle worker.[32] If one has doubts of the value of the work of the FTC, or of the cupidity and rapacity of a segment of the human race, let him thumb through a list of the practices attempted by promoters and prohibited by the Commission.

The prevention of unfair practices is sought not only through these prohibitory orders of the FTC, but also through co-operation of the FTC with various lines of business. The FTC sponsors trade-practice conferences, in which those engaged in a particular industry may arrive at an agreement as to what constitutes unfair practice within the industry and have such agreement approved by the FTC.

2. INVESTIGATION. Another important group of powers belonging to the FTC, and not entirely dissociated from those of law enforcement, are those relating to investigations. Upon its own initiative, or upon application of the Attorney General, the FTC investigates the manner in which corporations are carrying out court decrees issued against them under the antitrust laws. Under the direction of the President or either House of Congress, it must investigate and report alleged violations of the antitrust acts: and upon the request of the Attorney General, it must "investigate and make recommendations for the readjustment of the business of any corporation alleged to be violating the antitrust acts." The FTC is authorized to investigate from time to time the conditions of foreign trade and to make such

---

[31] *Annual Report of the FTC* (1942), p. 42.
[32] *Ibid.* (1939), p. 111.

recommendations to Congress thereon as it deems advisable. It is further authorized to gather information concerning the organization, business, conduct, practices, and management of any corporation engaged in commerce (excepting banks and common carriers), and its relation to other corporations and individuals. Under its power of investigation and research, the FTC has made numerous studies of the highest value, useful not only in an academic sense but of very immediate service to Congress in the preparation of needed legislation. Some of the more recent research activities of the FTC include investigations of the power and gas utilities and chain stores. During the Second World War it conducted surveys of 4,300 companies operating in essential industries to ascertain the facts of their compliance with priority orders of the War Production Board.[33]

The judicial trend in antitrust decisions. Two recent and notable antitrust decisions of the Supreme Court of the United States must receive attention. Reference was made on page 126 to Associated Press v. United States,[34] in which it was held that the AP could not claim that freedom of the press gave it the right to fix discriminatory conditions for the admission of a new member (the Chicago *Sun*) where the applicant had as a competitor an old AP member (the Chicago *Tribune*). The point to be made here is that the Associated Press was, through its restrictive by-laws, promoting arrangements and combinations which restrained the flow of news in interstate commerce, and that it was maintaining a restraint of trade which the Sherman Antitrust Act was designed to prevent. This decision gave the Sherman Act a new and interesting turn; and, considering that three judges dissented and that the Associated Press is very powerful, we may not have heard the last of the point at issue.

In the United States v. Southeastern Underwriters Association,[35] the Sherman Act was given another interesting application. In 1869 the Supreme Court had held that "issuing a policy of insurance is not commerce."[36] This opinion was pronounced at a time when insurance companies were attempting to evade state regulation on the claim that insurance was interstate commerce. For seventy-five years the Court held to its "not commerce" decision. In the meantime insurance companies spread their operations across state boundaries, and prospered and expanded to the point where certain of the state regulations were no longer very effective. They formed combinations and agreements across state lines on premium rates and agents' commissions, and they employed boycotts and other types of intimidation to enforce their agreements. At least these practices were followed by the two hundred private stock fire insurance companies that constituted the Southeastern Underwriters Association. The Court decided that such combinations and agreements, reaching into six states, were in restraint of trade and prohibited by the Sherman Act. Following this decision, the Seventy-ninth Congress, by Public Law 15, brought the interstate insurance business under the antitrust acts to the extent that such business is not regulated by state law. The date fixed for beginning the application of these laws to insurance was June 30, 1948, and the FTC found itself with one more area of law enforcement.

Regulation a continuous problem. It may be said that by far the greater part of the antitrust and fair trade legislation has been aimed in the right direction. It would be a great mistake, however, to assume that the field has been adequately covered. Business combinations and concentrations are actually on the increase, and many are the arrangements in restraint of trade that the law does not cover. The emergency of the Second World War served as a decided stimulus for such combinations because the need for supplies was so urgent that manufacturers were left a wide range of discretion as to business arrangements. Indeed, during the Second World War, at the request of the military departments, the FTC deferred proceedings against firms engaged in war production.[37] War has never been a time for insistence upon meticulous observation of customary restraints; and if the restraints are those which in normal times are accepted only grudgingly and of necessity, we may be assured that they rest lightly upon the wartime conscience.

Even before the United States entered the Second World War there was a marked trend toward business concentration. The President (1938) called attention to this fact, and Congress set up the Temporary National Economic Committee, composed of a few members of each House and some high administrative officials. The Committee took its assignment seriously, hearing hundreds of witnesses and studying numerous reports, but its members were divided in their recommendations, as men usually are when they consider large problems. But the post-war era has called for renewed activity in the enforcement of antitrust laws,[38] and it will probably call for new laws also. Of one thing there is abundant assurance—the problem of regulation will remain.

C. Federal Aids to Business [39]

From what has already been stated, it is clear that the federal government has encouraged and promoted business as well as regulated it. Pro-

---

[37] *U.S. Govt. Manual,* First Ed., 1946, p. 450.

[38] See *Fortune,* July, 1948, p. 63 and *U.S. News,* Dec. 17, 1948, p. 34.

[39] *Annual Reports of the Department of Commerce;* C. A. and Wm. Beard, "The Public

motion came first, then restrictive regulation combined with promotion, and finally came enlightened regulation and promotion in close co-operation with business. Government encouragement and support for business is particularly outstanding in the domains of foreign commerce, railroad transportation, and aviation, already reviewed. The same co-operative principle is apparent in the work of the Federal Trade Commission, which, while enforcing the restrictive antitrust laws, is, as we have already learned, nevertheless empowered to work in harmony with business and to encourage it in every way possible. Business, of course, receives invaluable support through the maintenance of a stable currency system, the regulation of banking, and the far-flung operations of the Post Office Department. Indeed, practically every function the government performs serves business in one way or another. A few of these aids not already discussed may be briefly considered.

   1. **Domestic marketing service.**   In addition to the promotion of foreign commerce, noted in the first part of this chapter, the Department of Commerce is actively engaged in several ways in assisting business in general. It makes studies of the national income; collects, tabulates, analyzes, and releases to the public various data widely used by business firms, government officials, and others whose interests and duties call for an understanding of business conditions; co-operates with university schools of business administration and departments of economics; gathers information and makes reports on such matters as operating conditions in the wholesale grocery trade and accounting methods for small retailers; and publishes the *Survey of Current Business* (monthly), and, from time to time, special circulars, such as *How Manufacturers Reduce Their Distribution Costs; State, Regional, and Local Market Indicators, 1939–1946;* and *Selecting a Store Location.*

   2. **Commercial standards.**   A set of standards being indispensable for business practice, the Constitution gives Congress the power "to fix the standard of weights and measures." Congress has legalized two standards—the somewhat cumbersome English system, with which everyone is familiar, and the simple metric system, which the student uses in laboratories and occasionally sees employed in industry. The original units of weights and measures are kept by the National Bureau of Standards in the Department of Commerce. From this Bureau the states may procure copies of the standards for use in testing local weights and measures. To the Bureau public agencies and private individuals may send instruments and materials, and, for small fees, have them tested by federal standards.

Be Served," *Scribner's Magazine,* April, 1933, and by the same authors, *The American Leviathan,* Ch. XIV; E. L. Graham, and F. W. Harris, *Patents, Trademarks, and Copyrights* (1921); J. A. Dienner, *The United States Patent System* (1941).

Electric batteries, weights and balances, airplane engines, pottery and china-ware, fusible boiler plugs, rubber, clinical thermometers, and a host of other things are tested annually.

FEDERAL SPECIFICATIONS. As a part of the standardization process, the national government has developed, primarily through the Commerce and Treasury departments, federal specifications for various materials regularly purchased by that government. Close to 2,000 purchase specifications have now been promulgated. The states, learning by experience that they can trust the scientists who prepare the federal specifications, have come to insist that materials sold to them shall conform to those specifications. The public is also aware of these specifications, and manufacturers often advertise that their products are prepared according to such specifications. Thus good service is performed by the national government for itself, other government units, producers, and consumers. Everyone should be happy. In addition to the type of specification that originated in connection with government purchases, the Bureau of Standards now encourages trades, whether they sell to the government or not, to agree upon standards in their respective lines of production. When a sufficient percentage of those engaged in a particular business agree upon a set of rules, they are published by the government as "commercial standards" for that business. Many firms have requested to be listed "willing to certify" that their abrasives, insecticides, padlocks, soaps, towels, and what not, conform either to the federal specifications or to the commercial standards.

SIMPLIFIED PRACTICE RECOMMENDATIONS. The late Henry Ford is reported to have said some years ago that the buyer could have a car of any color he desired as long as it was black. He wanted to make as many cars as possible as cheaply as possible, and this program had no place for variety. Manufacturers of articles designed to be ornamental as well as useful must heed the call for varieties, but those who make things designed primarily to stand wear and tear should limit sizes and styles to a minimum. Realizing the great economic waste that comes from manufacturers' over-indulgence in the matter of varieties, the Bureau of Standards has assumed the task of assisting producers in reaching agreements to reduce the number to actual requirements. From time to time the Bureau brings together manufacturers of a particular class of articles, and it is often successful in securing a "simplified practice recommendation." Several hundred such recommendations have been secured. Numerous and unnecessary varieties in size and style have been eliminated at great saving to manufacturers and consumers. Although the fact that simplified practices have been adopted for such common matters as wrapping and packing supplies, the size of milk bottles, and the width of beds may not interest the reader, it indicates the practical nature of the service rendered by the Bureau.

3. Patents, trade-marks, and copyrights.   Under its authority to "promote the progress of science and useful arts by securing for limited times to authors and inventors the exclusive right to their respective writings and discoveries" Congress has enacted patent and copyright laws.

PATENTS.   The patent laws are administered by the Patent Office in the Department of Commerce.   When an inventor pays a fee and satisfies the examiners of patents that he has something different and useful—a mechanism, a design, or even a growing plant—he receives a patent that entitles him to exclusive rights in his product for a period of seventeen years.   He may even secure privileges in foreign countries by having his patent registered in those countries with which the United States has patent agreements.   The holder of a new patent may meet with difficulties, however, for the grant of a patent does not protect him from suits brought by competitors who claim that their patents have been infringed.   Very fine distinctions must be made in patent litigation, and some of the best legal talent in the country is engaged in this practice.   The number of patents issued annually by the United States varies between 25,000 and 50,000, and the total issued is approximately 2,400,000—about the number granted by all other countries combined.

It is a matter of serious concern that the patent privilege has not served exclusively its original purpose of protecting inventors and encouraging technology.   Some authorities charge that patents are acquired by monopolies and tightly held by them for the promotion of their own business and to the disadvantage of inventors and the public.   The engineers employed by large business concerns invent minor improvements on a patented product, the improvement is in turn patented, and the manufacturing process secures a complicated legal protection that insures a monopoly.   Monopolies are alleged often to purchase patents for no other purpose than to prevent others from acquiring them, and thus breaking the monopoly.[40]   Amendments to the patent law have been recommended from time to time, but to date no action has been taken.

TRADE-MARKS.   In addition to granting patents, the Patent Office registers trade-marks.   The federal government has no specific grant of authority to perform this service; but under the commerce clause, Congress has provided for the registration of trade-marks that are employed in interstate and foreign commerce.   Since large business is seldom confined within the boundaries of any state, the registration privilege has considerable value.   Before a trade-mark is registered, the Patent Office checks over prior registrations to make sure that existing rights will not be infringed.   A registration is good for twenty years, and renewal is granted without limit.   The

---

[40] See Thurman Arnold, "We Must Reform the Patent Laws," *Atlantic Monthly*, CLXX, 47 (September, 1942); G. W. Stocking and M. W. Watkins, *Monopoly and Free Enterprise* (1951), Ch. 14.

owner of a registered trade-mark may use it or sell it as he sees fit. If his rights are infringed by a competitor, the courts afford him ample remedies. In order to give trade-marks international protection, the United States and several other powers have an agreement whereby the citizens of any one of these countries may register their trade-marks with an international bureau and thus receive the same protection against infringements in the other countries as in their own.

COPYRIGHTS. A division of the Library of Congress is charged with the duty of issuing copyrights for books, cartoons, charts, maps, labels, prints, musical compositions, and similar productions. A copyright is granted to anyone who makes the request. Unlike the procedure in granting patents and registering trade-marks, the Register of Copyrights makes no search to determine whether the desired copyright infringes upon other such rights previously granted. If there is any infringement, the injured party must go to the federal courts for relief. The owner of the copyright has exclusive privileges with respect to his production for a period of twenty-eight years, and his rights may be renewed for a like period.

For a long time the holders of copyrights had no protection from their infringement in foreign countries. American publishers "pirated" English works; that is, reproduced them on this side without the consent of either the authors or their publishers and without paying royalties. Dickens and his publishers were special victims of this unethical practice. English publishers often displayed a similar lack of restraint and reproduced American publications. Finally, by appropriate laws and treaties, the United States secured protection for American copyrights abroad by granting to foreign authors and publishers similar protection against infringement in the United States. There is a proviso, however, that books in the English language must be printed in the United States in order to get the benefit of our copyright laws.

4. **Bankruptcy laws.** Although the national government and the states have concurrent powers to make bankruptcy laws, the national act of 1898 was so inclusive as practically to exclude the states from the field. Under this law an individual or corporation, excepting railroads, banks, insurance companies, and municipal corporations, may voluntarily institute bankruptcy proceedings. In like manner, involuntary proceedings may be instituted against persons or corporations, with the exceptions named above and with the additional exceptions of farmers and laborers. In any bankruptcy case the purpose is to distribute the bankrupt's assets among his creditors and discharge him from further obligations to them. The bankruptcy law is administered by referees in bankruptcy, men who are appointed by federal district judges and who are responsible to the judges.

The depression of the 'thirties led to liberal amendments of the act of 1898. Persons and corporations failed by the tens of thousands, many of them not because they were not basically solvent but simply because valuable assets could not be turned into cash except at ruinous prices. An amendment of 1933 authorized persons in such straits to go not as bankrupts but as "debtors" and, under proper court supervision, arrange settlements with their creditors. The harassed railroads were also given relief by a plan that authorized any group owning 5 per cent of a carrier's indebtedness to propose a plan of reorganization, which should become effective when approved by the appropriate court, the Interstate Commerce Commission, and the holders of at least two thirds (the old requirement was all) of the road's indebtedness. Other corporations were, by an act of 1934, given the right to reorganize as "debtors" with the consent of the majority of their creditors and under court supervision.

Farmers were given consideration in the general act of 1933 and special attention in the later farm mortgage moratoria laws. The first of these, the Frazier-Lemke Act of 1934, was declared unconstitutional as being in violation of due process of law,[41] but the next year the statutory craftsmen in Congress were able to fashion a measure that overcame this objection.[42] Municipal corporations no less than private ones and individuals had their financial difficulties in the 'thirties. Thousands of cities, counties, and other local government units could not pay their obligations on bonds. In 1934 Congress enacted the Municipal Bankruptcy Act. Two years later it was held void by the Supreme Court on the ground that it deprived the states of their authority over local governments.[43] But later and modified legislation, scrutinized by a more friendly Supreme Court, met the test of constitutionality,[44] and local governments at last had the authority to make adjustments with their creditors. These changes in the bankruptcy law make it less rigid and bring it within the realities of our times.

The President's Economic Reports. Basic aids to government and business and the people generally are provided by the terms of the Employment Act of 1946. Grim fears of depressions, recessions, and chaos had produced strong demands for government action to head them off. This measure, regarded by many observers at the time as a very feeble response to an obvious necessity, has in its broad general terms possibilities of considerable magnitude. It requires the President to submit to Congress an annual Economic Report (and such other economic reports as he may care to submit) setting forth (1) the levels of employment, production, and pur-

[41] Louisville Joint Stock Bank Co. v. Radford, 295 U.S. 555 (1935).
[42] Wright v. Vinton Branch, Mountain Trust Bank of Roanoke, 300 U.S. 440 (1937).
[43] Ashton v. Cameron County Water Improvement District No. 1, 298 U.S. 513 (1936).
[44] United States v. Bekins, 304 U.S. 27 (1938).

chasing power; (2) current and foreseeable trends in the same; (3) a review of the economic program of the government and of economic conditions in the United States; and (4) a program for promoting employment opportunities, production, and purchasing power. How is the President to prepare such reports? The act gives him a Council of Economic Advisers, three persons "exceptionally qualified to analyze and interpret economic developments, to appraise programs and activities of the government" in the light of the purposes of the act, and to formulate policy "to promote employment, production, and purchasing power under free competitive enterprise."

The Council has entered upon its one and sufficiently exacting duty, that of supplying the President with economic advice, with energy, wisdom, and imagination tempered with realism. Although some of its members have on occasion "gone off on their own," forgetting that their function is to advise the President, and although some authorities (including the Hoover Commission) think the function could be better performed by a single individual, the fact remains that the annual Economic Review which the Council submits to the President is an economic document of significance. The Council also makes other reports from time to time. Employment, production, wages, prices, and pensions; money and credit; the flow of goods and purchasing power; the short- and long-range economic outlook; business investment needs; the housing problem; and many other economic and fiscal problems constitute one of their reports, a report that is given clarity and emphasis by many appropriate charts and graphs.

Following the Council's report as much or as little as he likes, the President prepares his Economic Report for Congress. In view of the variety of subjects with which this report may deal, it is a relatively brief document. In it the President gives a summary of the current economic situation, announces policies, and recommends legislation. The Council's work is in the realm of economics not politics (at least it is not supposed to be). The President presumably translates the Council's economic advice into terms of the politically possible and feasible. Anyhow, business, labor, and the rest of us have the benefit of the work of the Council and the advantage of a statement from the President respecting his economic policies. And we have the further advantage of the findings and recommendations of the Congressional Joint Committee on the Economic Report, both the committee and the recommendations being required by the Employment Act.[45]

Emergency aid. In the decade 1929-1939 the federal government established the Reconstruction Finance Corporation which loaned billions

[45] Fritz Morstein Marx (ed.), "Formulating the Government's Economic Program: A Symposium," *Am. Pol. Sci. Rev.,* XLII (1948), 272-336; *The Economic Reports of the President* (Harcourt, Brace & Co., 1949). Annual reports are released about Jan. 10.

to banks, trust companies, insurance companies, and similar enterprises. The government also advanced large sums for construction projects such as dams, sewage and garbage disposal plants, housing projects, and so on. In the same period it came to the aid of home owners, assisting them with financing their loans. In addition the government appropriated several billions for direct relief. Such wide-scale government activities were an assistance to business no less than very present aids to the unemployed.[46]

Reading List

"The American Foreign Aid Program," *Proceedings of the Academy of Pol. Sci.,* XXIII (Jan., 1950).

T. W. Arnold, *The Bottlenecks of Business* (1940).

I. R. Barnes, *Public Utility Control in Massachusetts* (1930).

G. Beckett, *The Reciprocal Trade Agreements Program* (1941).

P. W. Bidwell, *Tariff Policy of the United States* (1936).

Stuart Chase, *Tomorrow's Trade* (1945).

Council of State Governments, *Highway Safety and Motor Truck Regulation* (1950).

J. A. Dienner, *The United States Patent System* (1940).

Marshall E. Dimock, *Business and Government* (1949).

C. D. Drayton, *Transportation Under Two Masters* (1946).

H. S. Ellis, *The Economics of Freedom: The Program and Future of Aid to Europe* (1950).

Annual Reports of the Federal Communications Commission.

Annual Reports of the Federal Trade Commission.

The Economic Reports of the President (1949).

Merle Fainsod and Lincoln Gordon, *Government and the American Economy* (1948 ed.).

F. P. Hall, *Government and Business* (1939 ed.).

Alvin H. Hansen, *Economic Policy and Full Employment* (1947).

Kent T. Healy, *The Economics of Transportation in America* (1940).

C. B. Hoover, *International Trade and Domestic Employment* (1945).

H. L. Ickes, *Back to Work: The Story of the W.P.A.* (1935).

Annual Reports of the Interstate Commerce Commission.

J. W. Jenks and W. E. Clark, *The Trust Problem* (1929 ed.).

J. E. Kallenbach, *Federal Co-operation with the States under the Commerce Clause* (1942).

J. D. Larkin, *Trade Agreements: A Study in Democratic Methods* (1940).

David Lasser, *Private Monopoly, the Enemy at Home* (1945).

D. P. Locklin, *Economics of Transportation* (1947 ed.).

Abba P. Lerner (ed.), *Planning and Paying for Full Employment* (1946).

---

[46] Dimock, *op. cit.,* Chs. 7–8; Fainsod and Gordon, *op. cit.,* Ch. XVI; H. L. Ickes, *Back to Work: The Story of P.W.A.* (1935); D. Lawrence, *Beyond the New Deal* (1934); G. H. E. Smith and C. A. Beard, *The Recovery Program* (1935).

A. F. Macdonald, *American State Government and Administration* (1950 ed.), Chs. 26, 28.

Fritz Morstein Marx (ed.), "Formulating the Federal Government's Economic Program: A Symposium," *Am. Pol. Sci. Rev.,* XLII (1948), 272–336.

W. E. Mosher and F. G. Crawford, *Public Utility Regulation* (1933).

C. E. Puffer, *Air Transportation* (1941).

F. D. G. Ribble, *State and National Power Over Commerce* (1937).

C. C. Rohlfing and others, *Business and Government* (1949).

F. B. Sayre, *The Protection of American Export Trade* (1940).

Annual Reports of the Securities and Exchange Commission.

I. L. Sharfman, *The Interstate Commerce Commission,* 5 vols. (1931–1937).

Charles Siepmann, *Radio's Second Chance* (1946).

C. F. Snider, *American State and Local Government* (1950), Chs. XXI–XXII.

G. W. Stocking and M. W. Watkins, *Monopoly and Free Enterprise* (1951).

C. Warren, *Bankruptcy in United States History* (1935).

Dixon Wecter, *The Age of the Great Depression, 1929–1941* (1948).

P. M. Zeis, *American Shipping Policy* (1939).

Questions and Problems

1. Would you say that, in recent decisions on what constitutes commerce, the Supreme Court has gone back to John Marshall or has departed further from him?
2. Write a sketch of the merchant marine policy of the United States.
3. Can you reason that the activities of our government in expanding American business opportunities abroad are not for the special interest of a particular group?
4. Discuss the relation of the tariff and foreign loans to our foreign trade.
5. Outline the history of the regulation of railroads in the United States.
6. What is the relation of motor transportation to highway construction?
7. Show the nature of the problems of regulation that are presented by aviation; by wireless communications.
8. Review the history of the federal antitrust laws and their enforcement.
9. Write a critical essay on federal aids to business.
10. Compare the powers of the state and national governments to regulate corporations.
11. Discuss the trends of the states in relation to the regulation of public utilities.

☆ 24 ☆

Government and Labor

UNTIL about 1900, a large percentage of workers were their own masters on farms and in small shops. The farmer could eat regardless of hard times, and many of those who had left the farm in prosperous years could retrace their steps when the wheels of commerce slowed down. In those days governments concerned themselves little with such matters as conditions of employment, hours of labor, and wages.

·Although a few people still cling to the idea that "individualism" and the "dignity of labor" demand that governments pursue a "noninterference" policy, the high percentage of industrial workers, the hazards of industrial employment, the concentration of workers in large cities, and other employment factors have made such a laissez-faire policy impossible. And the fact that labor may insist upon the employment of two men for a one-man job (featherbedding), limit production quotas (the slow down), call unjustified strikes, and engage in other activities that inconvenience, annoy, irritate, and even bring hardship upon the population reinforces the argument that governments must recognize that labor relations concern the general public. State labor legislation came first—laws for the protection of workers in the hazardous industries. Later, the national government entered the field, and, following 1933, it set the pace.

I. THE STATES AND LABOR [1]

Unless labor is employed by the national government, or engaged in foreign or interstate commerce, or occupied with activities that feed commerce, or with some other activity within the scope of national authority,

[1] A. W. Bromage, *State Government and Administration in the United States* (1936), pp. 478–495; A. F. Macdonald, *American State Government and Administration* (1950 ed.), Ch. XXIX; J. T. Young, *The New American Government and Its Work* (1933 ed.), Ch. XXVII; *Book of the States, 1950–1951*, pp. 441–468.

it must look to the states for protection. Before the national government interested itself in labor's welfare, the more progressive industrial states were providing a minimum of protection for labor. At the present time a number of states have rather elaborate sets of labor laws. Naturally these vary a great deal from state to state; but they commonly apply to such subjects as collective bargaining, hours and conditions of work, wages, labor disputes, and workmen's compensation.

The status of trade unions. The right of labor to organize and bargain collectively with employers is now generally recognized. The right of a particular craft to strike for such purposes as an increase in wages or to prevent a reduction is also recognized, but striking simply to assist another union is generally held to be illegal.

The methods that the strikers may employ are limited. The "sit-down" strike was declared illegal by the Supreme Court of the United States.[2] Picketing is usually permissible if it consists only of attempts to persuade others not to take the strikers' jobs. Intimidation by threats or violence is illegal. The difficulty of drawing a line between persuasion and intimidation is at once apparent. Employers often seek injunctive relief against strikers and they frequently obtain it. Some states have attempted to limit this form of action in labor disputes, but an act of the Arizona Legislature prohibiting the courts of that state from granting injunctions to employers was held by the Supreme Court of the United States to be in violation of the "equal protection" clause of the Fourteenth Amendment.[3] Anti-injunction laws not so sweeping in their provisions as the Arizona law are, however, commonly upheld, and half the states now have such statutes on their books. The primary boycott (the refusal of a union group to patronize an "unfair" employer) and the secondary boycott (the attempt of a union to prevent third parties from patronizing an employer) are both illegal in many states, being considered conspiracies to injure the employer's business. These are but general statements concerning the status of unions, and they must necessarily be of that type because of variations among the states both as to legislative acts and judicial decisions.

Hours of labor: 1. MEN. A few decades ago, the hours of work, like all other problems of labor, were left entirely to the employer and the employee to determine. But the great advantage of the employer over the employee has led many states to come to the assistance of the latter. Men are still expected to be able to take care of themselves, but there are certain exceptions to be noted. Quite a few states have fixed the eight-

[2] National Labor Relations Board v. Fansteel Metallurgical Corporation, 306 U.S. 240 (1939).
[3] Truax v. Corrigan, 257 U.S. 312 (1921).

hour day for those employed by them or by local governments. It seems also that states may require contractors on public works to observe the eight-hour day. Such laws exert an appreciable influence over private employment.

There is no question of a state's authority to fix the hours of labor for its own employees. How far can it go in fixing a limit for private employees? Such laws interfere with the freedom of contract and may be judicially stricken down as being in violation of constitutional provisions that no person shall be deprived of life, *liberty* (of contract in such cases), or property without due process of law. But where the courts are convinced that labor is in actual need of protection, they hold that the freedom of contract must give way to the police power of the state. Thus, as long ago as 1898 the Supreme Court sustained a Utah statute limiting labor in mines to eight hours a day.[4] A few years later it held invalid a New York statute limiting labor in bakeries to ten hours,[5] although in 1917 this decision was practically overruled when the Oregon ten-hour factory law was sustained.[6] There is now no doubt that the states may limit the hours of labor of men in dangerous or unhealthful employment; and it is generally believed that, in keeping with the policy of the national government to limit hours, they may limit the hours of employment in industry generally.

2. WOMEN AND CHILDREN. Recognizing the difference between the physical capacity of men and women, the courts have generally upheld statutes for the protection of women that would have been declared invalid if applied to men. "Due process" has been made to yield to the obligation of the states to safeguard their women. Child labor legislation easily passes judicial scrutiny. Children are wards of the state, and the state owes them special protection. In many states, children under fourteen, or perhaps fifteen or sixteen, may not be employed in mines and factories, and children within a specified age group above this limit may not be employed beyond a stipulated number of hours. The hours of labor for children often are limited in other types of employment. Not infrequently night work is prohibited altogether. Compulsory school attendance laws also have the effect of limiting child labor. It should be added that child labor laws, like any others, are sometimes indifferently enforced.

Conditions of work. Some years ago a miner, humorously fatalistic, told the writer that he always examined his lunch before going into the

[4] Holden v. Hardy, 169 U.S. 366.
[5] Lochner v. New York, 198 U.S. 45 (1905).
[6] Bunting v. Oregon, 243 U.S. 246 (1917). On the application of "due process" to this and the cases mentioned in notes 4 and 5, see pages 139–140.

mines and that if he found articles of diet for which he had a particular weakness, he ate them at once, not risking the chance of being deprived of them by being killed before twelve o'clock! The hazards of mining are not so great now as they were, for the states have made serious attempts to lessen them. The requirements for ventilation, safety lamps, and various other safety appliances, enforced by inspection officers, have added somewhat to the miner's allotment of years. Factories are similarly required to provide for the safety of their employees. Whizzing saws and other dangerous machinery must be covered as far as possible. Suction pipes must be installed to take up the dust that would otherwise go into workmen's lungs. The manufacturing of articles in the home of workers, commonly called "sweating," is prohibited or restricted in many states. Laundries and bakeries must conform to standards of sanitation fixed in the interest of the health of employees and the public. These are but a few typical health, safety, and comfort measures that the states have enacted for employees. Usually they are upheld as being proper exercises of the states' police power, due process of law being reserved to strike down those measures that, in the opinion of the courts, are improper or arbitrary uses of that power.

Wages. The freedom of contract gives way in certain particulars to the urgent necessity of protecting labor in the collection of wages. The Supreme Court of the United States has held valid a Tennessee statute which required that store orders issued in payment of wages must be redeemed in cash.[7] The same Court upheld an Arkansas statute providing that, where miners were being paid by the ton for their output, coal should be weighed before being screened.[8] Of course it was argued that such statutes deprived employers and employees of their freedom to make the kind of labor contracts they desired, and that the statutes were therefore contrary to "due process"; but the Court said in the latter case: "laws . . . enacted for the protection of the public health, safety, or welfare . . . may be valid notwithstanding they have the effect to curtail or limit the freedom of contract."

Formerly, when states attempted to fix minimum wages, they soon ran against the constitutional snag of "due process." Of course the states may fix wages for those employed on public works, but fixing wages for private employment is another matter entirely. At first they attempted to do so only for women and children. Congress, the legislatures in a third of the states, and the legislative bodies in nearly all of the European countries at one time or another, have enacted such laws. The supreme courts in several of the states sustained them, and the Supreme Court of the

[7] Knoxville Iron Co. v. Harbison, 183 U.S. 13 (1901).
[8] McLean v. Arkansas, 211 U.S. 539 (1909).

United States, by an equal division (Mr. Justice Brandeis not sitting), affirmed the favorable decision of the Supreme Court of Oregon.[9] A few years later, however, the Supreme Court held invalid the act of Congress that provided for the minimum wage for women and children in the District of Columbia.[10]

In 1933 the New York legislature passed a carefully drafted minimum wage law designed to overcome the objections the Supreme Court had made to the law Congress had enacted for the District of Columbia. But the Court found, five to four, the New York Act to be an oppressive exercise of the police power, an infringement upon the "freedom of contract" of workers and employers, and therefore in violation of the due process provision of the Fourteenth Amendment.[11] "It is difficult to imagine any grounds," said Justice Stone, in dissent, "other than our own personal economic predilections, for saying that the contract of employment is any the less an appropriate subject of legislation than are scores of others in dealing with which this Court has held that legislatures may curtail individual freedom in the public interest." Ten months later, the five-four majority against minimum wages changed to five-four for minimum wages, Justice Roberts shifting his position. Speaking for the new majority, Chief Justice Hughes declared: "The Constitution does not speak of freedom of contract. It speaks of liberty and prohibits the deprivation of liberty without due process of law. . . . But the liberty safeguarded is liberty in a social organization which requires the protection of law against the evils which menace the health, safety, morals, and welfare of the people." [12] There is no doubt that the states may now have their minimum wage laws for women and children. Furthermore, since the authority of Congress to fix minimum wages for *men* engaged in or making goods to be shipped in interstate commerce (Fair Labor Standards Act of 1938) has been sustained as being within the commerce power and not in violation of due process of law,[13] it is to be assumed that state minimum wage laws for men will in like manner meet the test of due process. New York and several other states have enacted minimum wage laws for men.

Restricting the sale of products of convict labor. In order that convicts may earn a part of their keep, receive the disciplinary benefits of labor, and learn a trade that will help them take an honorable place in society upon their discharge, the states commonly put them to work. Formerly, the services of convicts were often contracted to private individuals on a per diem or piece-work basis. As this practice was subject to grave abuses,

[9] 243 U.S. 629 (1917).
[10] Adkins v. Children's Hospital, 261 U.S. 525 (1923).
[11] Morehead v. New York, 298 U.S. 587 (1936).
[12] West Coast Hotel Company v. Parrish, 300 U.S. 379 (1937).
[13] United States v. Darby Lumber Co., 312 U.S. 100 (1941).

nearly all the states have given it up and now furnish employment directly for their convicts. In a number of jurisdictions they are employed on public roads. In practically all prisons there are shops in which articles are made for state use or for sale by the state. In either case, particularly in the latter, the state is competing with private business and free labor. Organized labor is especially hostile to this form of competition, and, in response to labor's insistence, some states have limited the articles that may be produced by prison industry to those that are needed in state institutions. But whatever a state may do respecting its own prison labor, it could not, without authority from Congress, interfere with interstate commerce to the extent of preventing the shipment into it and the sale within its borders of goods manufactured in the prisons of other states. Heeding the demands of labor, Congress, by an act of 1935, granted the states the substance of this authority.

Settlement of industrial disputes. The great waste caused by industrial disputes, usually differences between employers and employees over wages, has led a number of states to provide means of mediation and arbitration for the contending parties. A board or commission is created that may, upon its own motion or upon request of one or both parties, attempt to settle the points at issue. Sometimes, where both parties have agreed to arbitration, the terms of the settlement are binding upon the disputants; but more commonly the acceptance of a suggested settlement depends upon their mutual satisfaction with the results obtained. In 1932 a rather typical settlement was reached in New York. When 27,000 garment workers and their employers failed to reach an agreement over wages and other matters, Lieutenant Governor Lehman was called in to act as mediator. After a week of conferences with the various groups, he obtained the acceptance of terms that averted a strike and were announced by those most vitally concerned as a "victory for all parties." [14] Without troops, without police, and, more significant, without the support of an arbitration law, Governor Gardner of North Carolina went to High Point and settled a wage strike in twenty-four hosiery mills. Said he, "A strike like this is war and war is insanity." He persuaded both sides to appoint a board of arbitration and to agree to accept the decision of the board. Headed by the Governor, the board reported its findings—compromises—at the end of four hours. "Let's get closer together," exclaimed the Governor, being photographed with leaders of the recent strike.[15]

Many disputes are not settled by such voluntary co-operation. To save losses to employers, employees, and the public that result from strikes, some states have added mandatory features to laws relating to such dis-

[14] *New York Times,* July 24, 1932, p. 1.
[15] *Time,* August 15, 1932, p. 11.

putes. For example, Colorado (1915) empowered its industrial commission to compel a hearing in labor disputes and to prohibit strikes and lockouts until after the commission had made its report. Kansas went a great deal further. An act of 1920 created a court of industrial relations and authorized it to investigate and make compulsory settlements of labor disputes in various essential industries, including public utilities, mining, food, fuel, and clothing. The statute created the widest interest and was a common subject of debate for a few years. It was not long, however, until the legal features of the debate were settled by the Supreme Court of the United States. A section of the statute was declared unconstitutional on the ground that it was a limitation upon the freedom of contract protected by the due process provision of the Fourteenth Amendment,[16] and, later, the whole statute was declared void because, in the opinion of the Court, the food, clothing and fuel industries were not sufficiently affected with a public interest to justify compulsory arbitration.[17]

Workmen's compensation for accidents. Tens of thousands of workmen are killed and injured in line of duty every year. Formerly, the only method by which they or their relatives could obtain compensation was to institute suit against the employers. Occasionally, handsome damages would be collected by a lawyer who impressed a jury with his pleas for a wife, or widow, and six dependent children of the victim of an industrial accident. But more often the employers were saved by the old common-law defenses of "contributory negligence," "fellow servant," and "assumption of risk." [18] Nearly all the states have abolished these defenses in industrial accident cases, thus placing employees in a much more favorable legal position. But many states have gone further. They have provided for systems of industrial insurance.

This is the way a typical system works: Employers are required to establish funds from which compensation shall be paid to injured workmen. Such workmen no longer go to court for compensation, but an industrial commission hears their cases and fixes the amount of compensation for each in proportion to the extent of the injury. The procedure is relatively speedy and free from technicalities, the employer being no longer allowed to set up the old common-law defenses noted above. These laws in the interest of the disabled veterans of industry who had been engaged in developing the wealth of the state may be sustained upon the same theory as pensions for soldiers wounded in defending it. "A machine as well as a bullet may produce a wound and the disabling effect may be the same," said the Supreme Court of the United States in upholding a statute

[16] Wolff Packing Co. v. Court of Industrial Relations, 262 U.S. 525 (1923).
[17] *Ibid.*, 267 U.S. 552 (1925).
[18] For explanation of these defenses see page 770.

of the State of Washington.[19] Sickness, as well as accidents, may arise from causes directly traceable to employment. Accepting this fact, a number of states have extended the provisions of their compensation acts to cover diseases attributable to occupations.

One other method of offering relief to disabled industrial workmen deserves mention. A man may be incapacitated for his own trade, but he may be trained for another. This is called vocational rehabilitation, and Congress has recognized its importance to the extent of providing federal aid to the states for the purpose.

Recent trends in state labor legislation. An indication of our present direction with labor legislation may be found by taking a few samples. In 1949 twenty-four states were extending full coverage to workmen against the hazards of occupational disease, and a number of other states were covering specific occupational diseases. In the same year thirty-six states increased benefits or extended coverage under workmen's compensation laws. A new development in workmen's compensation legislation is the "second-injury fund." This covers the case of an employee who, having lost a member of the body, loses another in an industrial accident. If the total cost of compensation (likely to be for total disability) is imposed upon the latest employer, physically handicapped persons would commonly be refused employment. The second-injury fund meets this problem by taking care of all the cost incident to the first injury, leaving the second employer responsible only for compensation for the last. In 1949 two more states joined the ranks of those having established second-injury funds, bringing the total number to forty-one. In 1945 New York and New Jersey enacted fair employment practices laws and the next year they were joined by Massachusetts. At the same time New Jersey enacted a measure that bespoke a conscience that more states might make manifest. The law referred to is one designed to protect the health and living conditions of migratory workers, toilers who at times seem to be outside the bounds of protection, despitefully used and shamefully abused.

But not all the recent legislation has been pro-labor. Since 1932 labor has had relatively friendly government. It cannot be said that labor has always employed moderation in the use of its older rights or in the exercise of the privileges it has won under the new laws. Consequently, a tendency to put the brakes on labor has become apparent. In 1947 fourteen states passed anti-closed-shop ("right to work") laws, twelve states enacted legislation restricting strike activity, and eleven states prohibited the secondary boycott. It seems, however, that this restrictive tendency was checked in 1949.

[19] Mountain Timber Co. v. Washington, 242 U.S. 219 (1917).

II. NATIONAL LABOR LEGISLATION

A. Protection of labor on the common carriers [20]

Through its authority to regulate interstate and foreign commerce and to appropriate money for various purposes not listed in the Constitution, Congress exercises a rather wide range of powers to do good or ill for labor. The first labor legislation, naturally enough, had to do with seamen; then came the railway employees.

Seamen. Men employed on our merchant ships in earlier times were subject to rather rough treatment. Only about a century ago, the Boston Marine Society petitioned the government to restore the right to flog sailors to their work. Exemption from flogging seems to have been one of the few rights that seamen enjoyed at that time. Long after Negro slavery was abolished, the Supreme Court of the United States held that a seaman who broke his contract could be imprisoned for desertion, although such imprisonment was held to be contrary to the Thirteenth Amendment when imposed for the breaking of ordinary labor contracts.[21] Now seamen have what appear to be quite adequate legal safeguards.

Various statutes running over a long period show concern for the seamen. The most significant of these is the La Follette Seamen's Act, which became a law (1915) largely through the insistence of the Seamen's Union strongly backed by the American Federation of Labor. The seaman's diet must include specified quantities of water, rice, beans, pickles, bread, salt pork, potatoes, coffee, tea, sugar, and so on. Clothing, tobacco, and blankets must be kept in the "slop chest" and sold to the crew at not more than a 10 per cent increase over the wholesale prices. Seamen must be furnished with safe and warm quarters. Their wages must be paid in legal tender, regularly, and part payment must be made in every port. The hours of labor are prescribed, and the crews are not to be required to do unnecessary work on Sundays and holidays. Furthermore, the act provides that all vessels shall have in their crews a high percentage of able seamen—a concession to the demands of skilled labor and a safety precaution as well.

But the greatest triumph for seamen is found in the relaxation of penalties for offenses. Punishment for desertion is specifically limited to "forfeiture of all or any part of the clothes or effects he leaves on board and of all or any part of the wages or emoluments which he has then earned," a penalty considerably less severe than the sentence of imprisonment noted

[20] Kent T. Healy, *The Economics of Transportation in America* (1940), Chs. 16–17; H. R. Northrup, "Industrial Relations on the Railroads," in C. E. Warne and others (eds.), *Labor in Postwar America* (1949); Julius H. Parmelee, *The Modern Railway* (1940), Chs. XXI–XXIV.

[21] See page 120.

in the preceding paragraph. Penalties for other offenses are equally mild, that for assaulting any master or mate being imprisonment for not more than two years.[22] But a strike on the high seas or even in a foreign port may still be designated mutiny, it seems.[23]

Relatively generous provision is made for sick or injured seamen by the terms of the Longshoremen's and Harbor Workers' Compensation Act of 1927. About the only type of injury in which compensation is not allowed is that occasioned solely by the intoxication of the employee. If an injury to an employee results in death, then liberal death benefits are paid to his dependents.

Railway employees. A few of the acts passed for the safety of passengers and train crews were discussed under "Railroads" in the last chapter. At this point, brief attention is to be given to some of those laws that have been enacted primarily for the benefit of railroad laborers and their employers, although public interest and convenience are by no means absent from them.

1. HOURS OF LABOR. The Hours of Service Act of 1907, limiting the employment of persons engaged in the movement of trains to sixteen consecutive hours, was a safety measure designed to reduce accidents caused by the fatigue of overworked employees. It is a rather far cry from this act to the Adamson Act of 1916, which established the eight-hour day for trainmen employed on interstate railways. To be sure, the Adamson Act had some relation to safety; but the main purpose was to limit the working day to hours advocated by the labor unions. Indeed, the bill became a law through the threat of a nation-wide strike of railway employees. The passage of the bill was a great victory for organized labor and the occasion of a very loud public protest; but its constitutionality was sustained by the Supreme Court, despite the fact that in those days the Court was putting a strict construction upon the powers of Congress under the commerce clause.

2. EMPLOYERS' LIABILITY. For a long time, employees on interstate trains and other employees under federal jurisdiction could not recover damages for injuries received in the course of employment except under the old common-law rules, which were entirely inadequate to meet the needs of an industrial civilization. For example, if a laborer was injured through the negligence of a "fellow servant," his employer was not liable. Again, the employer escaped liability if a laborer's injury was caused in part by his own "contributory negligence." Another rule that stood in the way of his claim for damages was that of "assumption of risks," which in everyday language meant that a workman assumed all the ordinary hazards of his employment.

[22] 46 U.S. Code 701.
[23] 18 U.S. Code 483, 484 and Southern Steamship Co. v. NLRB, 316 U.S. 31 (1942).

The Second Employers' Liability Act (1908) [24] abrogated the first of these rules and greatly modified the second and third. It applies to all employees actually engaged in interstate commerce. The company no longer escapes liability by attaching the blame to a "fellow servant." If the accident is due in part to the "contributory negligence" of the injured employee, the company is liable for that portion of the damages not chargeable to such neglect. As for the "assumption of risks," the company may no longer make that defense unless it can prove that the injury occurred despite the fact that the company was observing all provisions of law designed to prevent it. The act also provides that relatives may recover damages when railway employees are killed—elementary justice achieved by the abrogation of the common-law rule that one person should not be awarded damages for the wrongful death of another.

3. SETTLEMENT OF RAILWAY LABOR DISPUTES. In the interest of employers, employees, and the public, the adjustment of labor disputes with a minimum of friction is highly desirable. The first effective act to this end was passed in 1898. Under the system of mediation and arbitration that it provided, a number of labor troubles were satisfactorily settled. The system was strengthened by a later act; but it broke down in 1916 when the railroad brotherhoods refused to submit to arbitration. During the war period of 1917–1918, when the government operated the railroads, it set up a Railway Wage Board and various boards of adjustment. These functioned smoothly, owing to the liberal attitude of the government, the temporary employer. With the return of the railroads to their owners, the machinery for settling disputes was necessarily changed.

The Transportation Act of 1920 established a Railroad Labor Board and authorized, but did not require, the establishment of railroad boards of labor adjustment. Few of the latter were ever set up, and most of the work of adjustment was left to the Labor Board. This Board, composed of three representatives each of employers, employees, and the public, was given jurisdiction in various types of labor disputes, including wage disputes. Its decisions were not always observed, and it was frequently charged with partiality to the employers.

The Railway Labor Act of 1926 abolished this board and placed great emphasis upon conferences between employees and employers for the settlement of disputes. The act, as amended in 1934, established the National Mediation Board and the National Railroad Adjustment Board. The first of these bodies, which consists of three members appointed by the President, has as its principal duty the mediation (not settlement by com-

---

[24] The First Employers' Liability Act was declared void because its provisions extended to all employees of interstate carriers whether or not such employees were actually engaged in interstate commerce functions.

pulsion) of differences between railroads, express and Pullman companies, and airlines on the one hand and their employees on the other. The differences are, of course, commonly those relating to rates of pay and rules (working conditions). The Adjustment Board consists of four large divisions, each representing an equal number of employers and employees, and in case of a deadlock the Mediation Board may appoint a referee to sit with a division for the purpose of making an award. The Mediation Board is also authorized to appoint arbitrators in cases where arbitration has been agreed upon and the parties are unable to agree on the neutral arbitrators. The Adjustment Board disposes of the vast majority of cases without fuss or difficulty, hundreds of them every year. Only the major cases come before the Mediation Board. By an act of 1936 the jurisdiction of the Mediation Board was extended to air carriers engaged in interstate commerce or under mail contracts.

The law provides that if a dispute is not adjusted by mediation or arbitration, a strike vote may be taken. In the event the strike is voted, an emergency investigating board is designated by the President to get the facts and report to him. Usually these reports have been of such impartial nature and so strongly backed by public opinion that the parties to the dispute have accepted them. For the period of the war emergency an act of Congress (1943) authorized the President to establish a National Railway Labor Panel. In case a dispute was not adjusted by normal procedures, the Panel was authorized to set up emergency boards that should seek settlement.

Thousands of railroad labor disputes have been settled by conciliation, mediation, and voluntary arbitration. And it is still correct to say that railway labor relations set a fairly good standard. The failure (primarily the responsibility of certain unions), in the spring of 1946, of all efforts to settle wage disputes and other points at issue between the railroads and the trainmen and the resulting brief but paralyzing strike, and the less serious failure, in 1950, of a union to accept the report of a fact-finding board, should not lead us to the hasty conclusion that mediation and voluntary arbitration will not work, to insist that we must have coercion.

4. RAILWAY WORKERS RETIREMENT SYSTEM. In 1934 Congress passed the Railway Pensions Act. That act required contributions from the railroads and the employees for the purpose of establishing a pension fund for the latter. But the next year the Supreme Court, in a five to four decision, declared that the establishment of a retirement system for railroad workers was "in no proper sense a regulation of the activity of interstate transportation." [25] Congress followed this decision with the Railroad Re-

[25] Railroad Retirement Board v. Alton R. Co., 295 U.S. 330 (1935).

tirement Act and the Carriers Taxing Act (1937). These acts were framed in close consultation with employees and employers, and, in 1946, the validity of the retirement act seems to have been assumed in R.R. Retirement Board v. Duquesne Warehouse Company (326 U.S. 446). Annuities are paid up to a maximum of $144 per month.

Railroad unemployment insurance is provided by acts of 1938, 1939, and 1946. The daily benefit scale ranges from $1.75 to $5 and maximum benefits for any year range from $227.50 to $650, according to earnings.

B. Protection of employees feeding Interstate Commerce [26]

Formerly, national labor legislation was enacted almost exclusively for persons actually engaged in interstate and foreign commerce; but the New Deal Administration gave the commerce clause a much broader interpretation, and pushed through legislation in the interest of labor that was employed in mining, manufacturing, or other enterprises, provided their activities affected interstate commerce.

The National Industrial Recovery Act (1933). The depression measure, the National Recovery Act, extended a friendly hand to labor in various ways. Child labor in industry was prohibited. Section 7a, around which there was so much controversy, gave labor the right to organize and bargain collectively through representatives of their own choosing. In 1933 the President created the National Labor Board and the next year supplanted it with the National Labor Relations Board. These and other labor boards found that union recognition was the most vital labor question and the one that was submitted to them most frequently. Conducting elections in which employers' unions and the regular unions were competing for collective bargaining representatives gave the labor boards severe tests and involved them in some law suits. Of course the Supreme Court's decision against NRA in May, 1935, ended employer-employee relationships under that organization.[27] The Guffey Coal Act, passed after the NRA decision, gave labor essentially the old NRA rights in the soft coal industry, but the Supreme Court held it invalid also.

The National Labor Relations Act. Passed in June, 1935, in response to labor's demands for something to take the place of section 7a under the now defunct NRA, the National Labor Relations Act renewed the guaranty of collective bargaining and made a new advance in its provision that specifically forbids interference by an employer in the organization of his employees. The act set up a National Labor Relations Board, which

[26] Acts of Congress as cited: *Reports of the Secretary of Labor* and of the *National Labor Relations Board*.

[27] Schechter v. United States, 295 U.S. 495 (1935).

was charged with the duties of enforcing the rights of labor. It was not limited in its application to business clearly of interstate commerce character, but brought within its scope business that affects interstate commerce. On April 12, 1937, the Supreme Court in a far-reaching five-four decision sustained its constitutionality. Said Chief Justice Hughes, speaking for the majority of the Court:

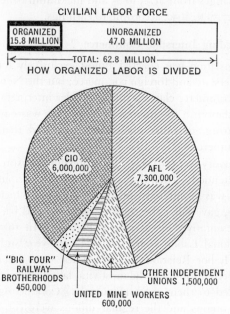

CIVILIAN LABOR FORCE

ORGANIZED 15.8 MILLION

UNORGANIZED 47.0 MILLION

|←————TOTAL: 62.8 MILLION————→|

HOW ORGANIZED LABOR IS DIVIDED

CIO 6,000,000

AFL 7,300,000

"BIG FOUR" RAILWAY BROTHERHOODS 450,000

OTHER INDEPENDENT UNIONS 1,500,000

UNITED MINE WORKERS 600,000

From *The New York Times*, Oct. 31, 1949.

Although activities [of an industry] may be intrastate in character when separately considered, if they have such a close and substantial relation to interstate commerce that their control is essential or appropriate to protect that commerce from burdens and obstructions, Congress cannot be denied the power to exercise that control. . . . When industries organize themselves on a national scale making their relation to interstate commerce the dominant factor in their activities, how can it be maintained that their industrial labor relations constitute a forbidden field into which Congress may not enter when it is necessary to protect interstate commerce from the paralyzing consequences of industrial war? [28]

This decision was significant not only because it upheld the rights of labor but also because it made a historic reinterpretation of the power of Congress to legislate under the commerce clause of the Constitution. It suggested Chief Justice Marshall's interpretation of that clause in the case of Gibbons v. Ogden.

The National Labor Relations Act and the board that administered it were severely criticized. Employers included in their charges against the legislation its failure to make trade unions "responsible" through compulsory incorporation and its failure to list "unfair practices" by labor unions, such as coercion to join unions and the sit-down strike.[29] Em-

[28] National Labor Relations Board v. Jones and Laughlin Steel Corporation, 301 U.S. 1 (1937).

[29] Selig Perlman, "The United States of America," in H. A. Marquand, and Others, *Organized Labour in Four Continents* (1939), p. 387. For a complete study of the Labor Board, see D. O. Bowman, *Public Control of Labor Relations* (1942).

ployees said also that the Board was unfair to them, and the AF of L fired some heavy bolts at the Board for alleged partiality to the CIO. A large segment of the public seemed to accept the view that the Wagner Act gave too much to labor and exacted too little in return and that it stimulated rather than retarded industrial conflicts. Such criticisms of the act and its administration, combined no doubt with the desire in some quarters to limit the legitimate rights of labor, led the House of Representatives to authorize (1939) an investigation by a committee whose leading members were no friends of labor. This committee recommended a number of amendments to the law, some of which would have weakened it fundamentally. But the defenders of the original legislation, particularly Senator Wagner, while admitting that certain administrative defects should be corrected, ably defended it by showing that the Board had made a remarkably good record in adjusting cases without formal proceedings, in securing judicial vindication of its rulings against which appeals had been made, and in reducing, to some extent, the number of strikes.

The Labor-Management Relations (Taft-Hartley) Act of 1947. During the Second World War industry made good, and largely restored itself to popular favor. Labor did well also, but a few strikes during the war and several serious ones immediately after it headed labor toward the doghouse. The arrogance of John L. Lewis was not mitigated through his mastery of Elizabethan phraseology, nor was the autocracy of James C. Petrillo less irksome because of his appreciation of classical music. In the popular mind labor was "at it again," demonstrating its irresponsibility. Republican success in the congressional elections of 1946 meant a new labor relations law.

With the support of many Democrats, particularly Southerners, the Republican leadership succeeded in passing over a vigorous presidential veto the Taft-Hartley Act. As this legislation would cover more than thirty pages of this text, only a few of its high spots can be touched on here. More than half of the act is a restatement of the National Labor Relations Act as amended by the new legislation. Unions may prescribe their own rules for membership, but it is made an unlawful practice for an employer to deny employment under a union-shop agreement if such employer has reasonable grounds to believe that membership is not available to a prospective employee (for example, a Negro) on the same terms as others. It is an unfair labor practice for unions to require "excessive" or "discriminatory" initiation fees, such unfair fees to be determined by the Labor Relations Board. Unions no less than employers are guilty of an unfair practice if they refuse to bargain, once the representative agencies have been certified. Employers are prohibited from interfering with employees' right to organize, but "the expressing of any views, arguments, or opinion, or the dissemination thereof, whether in written, printed, graphic, or visual form, shall not constitute or be evidence of an unfair labor practice." The closed-shop is prohibited, and the union-shop is permitted only when the majority of the employees in the bargaining unit favor it. Strikes and boy-cotts are prohibited for such purposes as forcing an employer or a self-employed person to join a union; requiring an employer to cease using, selling, or transporting the products of another producer; and requiring an employer to bargain with a labor organization that has not been certified by the Labor Board.

To put it shortly, the most significant changes made by the Taft-Hartley law are in the practices of labor that are made unfair and illegal. Every-one knows, of course, about the anti- or non-Communist affidavit that a labor leader must sign if he wishes to use the services of the Board. The provision of the law relating to political contributions was discussed in the section on party finance, in the Chapter on Campaigns and Elections. The provisions of the act relating to the settlement of labor disputes will be noted presently. No doubt the legislation contains a number of provisions that are entirely fair and proper; but there is much evidence that the act was conceived in an anti-labor spirit, and some students of labor problems think a few of its provisions, such as those authorizing private suit for damages and the use of the injunction, will in a recession period stand re-vealed as formidable weapons in the hands of employers. Even some in-dustrialists admit that the act goes too far. There will no doubt be amend-ments, and the "final" product will lie somewhere between Wagner-Connery and Taft-Hartley.[30]

The Fair Labor Standards Acts. The first Fair Labor Standards (Wage and Hour) Act was passed in 1938. It applies to employment in interstate commerce and in the production of goods intended for interstate commerce, but makes certain exceptions, the most important being farm and retail service grades. The law fixed normal hours at forty-four per week for the first year of its operation, but provided that it should be reduced to forty hours within three years. Some exceptions to the hour maximum are permitted, for example, in the seasonal industries. Twenty-five cents (it seems a long time ago!) an hour was fixed as the minimum wage for the first year, the minimum to be increased to forty cents in 1945. Variations in the minimum wage were permitted in the different industries, but no minimum wage was to be fixed "solely on a regional basis." Yet sub-stantially this basis is used when, for example, a lower rate is fixed for seamless hosiery workers, mostly Southern, than for full-fashioned hosiery workers, mostly Northern.

[30] See W. S. Hopkins, *Labor in the American Economy* (1949), p. 300; Joseph Shister, *Economics of the Labor Market* (1949), pp. 305 ff.

In general employers did not quarrel with the "objectives" of this law, but they claimed that in its administration there had been too much rigidity. In rush seasons they said payroll costs mount (time and a half must be paid for overtime) too high for profits to be made. Also they complained because maximum hour provisions applied to workers whose incomes were substantial. Farmers raised a considerable outcry against the legislation. To be sure, farm labor was exempt from its provisions and so was the processor who first handled a farm product, but others who handled farm products were not exempt. Then, as might be expected, there was difficulty in enforcing the law, difficulty due primarily to industrial opposition and insufficient staff in the enforcement agency, the Wage and Hour and Public Contracts Divisions of the Department of Labor.

Many amendments to the Fair Standards Act were proposed, but the Administration successfully resisted them all with one exception—in 1943 it agreed to a forty-eight hour week in the war industries. Considering the rising cost of living in postwar years, the forty cents an hour minimum wage looked silly, but in 1946 an Administration amendment to increase the minimum to sixty-five cents failed to get out of the Rules Committee in the House of Representatives. Not until 1949 was the legal minimum increased to seventy-five cents. About 22,000,000 employees are under the provisions of these laws.

The Government Contracts (Walsh-Healey) Act (1936). The Walsh-Healey Act is not based on the commerce power but rather on the authority of a government to prescribe conditions in its contracts. All persons and firms who get contracts from the national government in excess of $10,000 must conform to labor standards very similar to those imposed by the old National Recovery Act. The new act, the "Little NRA," requires all such contractors to pay not less than the prevailing minimum wage in the locality in which the work is being done, which minimum is determined by the Secretary of Labor; it fixes the eight-hour day and the forty-hour week for labor employed by these contractors; it prohibits the employment of convict labor, male persons under sixteen, and female persons under eighteen; it prohibits the employment of labor on contracts in buildings or under working conditions that are unsanitary or hazardous or dangerous to health and safety; and it prescribes appropriate penalties for its violation. It is generally believed that the improvement in labor standards on government contract work will have a decided influence in improving labor standards generally. Of course these standards were of necessity relaxed during the war, but they have since been restored.

Employment Service. Even in the prosperous years of the Coolidge era hundreds of thousands of workers were unemployed. In the spring of 1933 the number was commonly estimated at about 13,000,000, and it remained high until the war industries were in full operation (1943). The President's Council of Economic Advisers reported that there was an average of 3,400,000 unemployed during the relatively prosperous year of 1949.[31] How can jobs be found for these persons, nearly all of whom are eager to work? Work must be made available first, and after that there must be some agency to assist the workers in finding it.

Employment services have been operated by a number of states for years and by the national government since the First World War. But they have been rather feeble efforts in normal times and wholly inadequate to meet large-scale unemployment. The state and federal agencies have usually failed to co-operate, and in some cases they have actually been in rivalry. After about eight years of agitation in Congress and a pocket veto by President Hoover, the important Wagner-Peyser Bill finally became a law with President Roosevelt's approval in June, 1933. It is administered by the Bureau of Employment Security. It brings about close co-operation between state agencies and the federal agency through the allotment of federal funds to states that make an appropriation and meet the federal standard of efficiency. During the Second World War the state employment agencies were brought directly under federal operation, and the United States Employment Service (the then responsible office) carried the chief responsibility for the manpower program.

Since an adequate program for the placement of workers must be both local and national in scope and since many workers out of employment must accept employment in lines other than those in which they have been engaged, the normal job of the Bureau of Employment Security is perplexing and stupendous. Some aid to the employment service comes from the Bureau of Labor Statistics, the government's indispensable fact-finding agency on all matters relating to labor economics. The Bureau collects and distributes information on labor supply, hours, wages, cost of living, industrial accidents, and similar factors affecting labor. It is a truism that, in meeting any situation, we must know first what the situation is.

Under the terms of the Employment Act of 1946 the President's Economic Report and the studies and reviews upon which the Report is based relate, in final analysis, to the subject of promoting and maintaining employment, developing and keeping jobs for all who are able, willing, and seeking to work. But inasmuch as the studies and reports under the provisions of the act have covered, and properly so, practically the entire national economy, they were discussed in the preceding chapter under the subtitle of "Aids to business."

[31] In their *Annual Economic Review,* Jan. 3, 1950.

LABOR FORCE

THE LABOR FORCE INCREASED BY ABOUT 800,000 FROM 1948 TO 1949 AND CIVILIAN EMPLOYMENT DROPPED ABOUT 700,000.

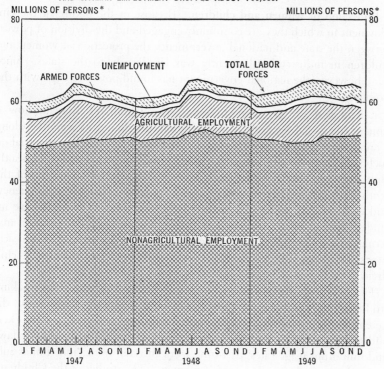

MILLIONS OF PERSONS*

MILLIONS OF PERSONS*

ARMED FORCES

UNEMPLOYMENT

TOTAL LABOR FORCES

AGRICULTURAL EMPLOYMENT

NONAGRICULTURAL EMPLOYMENT

1947   1948   1949

UNEMPLOYMENT THROUGHOUT 1949 WAS MUCH HIGHER THAN IN 1948.

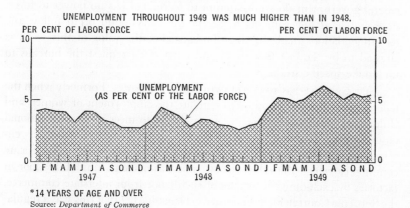

PER CENT OF LABOR FORCE

PER CENT OF LABOR FORCE

UNEMPLOYMENT
(AS PER CENT OF THE LABOR FORCE)

1947   1948   1949

*14 YEARS OF AGE AND OVER

Source: *Department of Commerce*

From Council of Economic Advisers, *The Annual Economic Review,* Jan. 3, 1950, Chart 2.

C. The protection of women and children and minorities in industry

Protection of women and children. Because of the nature of the employment in which they are commonly engaged and the division of powers between the state and national governments, the protection of women and children in industry until recently was left largely to the states. Since 1933, however, the national government has found power to cope with the problem.

1. RESEARCH AND RECOMMENDATIONS. The Children's Bureau, now a unit of the Social Security Administration, distributes its activities along a fairly wide front of investigation and research. It assembles material on such subjects as the children of the unemployed, maternal and child health, child labor, industrial home work (which often deprives children of the mother's care), children in industrialized agriculture, juvenile delinquency, and child welfare and social security. Specific research projects have included, among others, neonatal mortality and moribundity studies, maternal care in Hartford, Connecticut, rickets studies, studies of physical fitness of school children, and institutional treatment of delinquent children.

The Women's Bureau is also largely a research organization, making studies on technological changes in relation to women's employment, the potential earning power of Southern mountaineer handicraft, pieceworkers and their production and earnings in the dress industry, state hour laws and minimum wage rates, part-time work in retail trade, and similar subjects relating to the employment of women. The studies of the Children's and Women's Bureaus are available for both public and private use. The federal government does not attempt to force, and has no power to force, state and local governments to accept the facts found or to follow the recommendations made by these bureaus; but the value of this work is attested to by the fact that states and cities often request the bureaus to undertake specific studies.

2. ATTEMPTS AT POSITIVE REGULATION: (*a*) *Failures.* Formerly when the federal government attempted to regulate the employment of women and children by positive enactments, it was likely to meet with constitutional obstructions. Through its power over interstate commerce Congress enacted various laws respecting employees (principally male) of interstate common carriers. But when the attempt was made to limit child labor in factories by excluding the articles of such labor from interstate commerce, the Supreme Court held, in Hammer v. Dagenhart,[32] that this was a regulation of manufacturing, which is not commerce, under the guise of the

[32] 247 U.S. 251 (1918).

commerce power. It stated that the power to regulate commerce did not include the right to forbid commerce in particular commodities, unless such commodities were in themselves harmful; for example, lottery tickets and liquor. The Court was not impressed with the argument that there was an essential similarity in the injury done to children employed in manufacturing articles otherwise harmless and the injury done to the consumer of harmful articles. In the former case the injury occurs before the articles have been placed in interstate commerce; in the latter, after transportation is completed—a point that impresses some laymen as being a distinction without a difference. The case was decided by a five-four division of the Court, and public opinion on the question was perhaps divided in reverse proportions. It is a pleasure to record that in 1941 the Court expressly overruled Hammer v. Dagenhart.[33]

But having been thwarted in 1916 in its attempt to employ the commerce power in this way, Congress made another attempt to restrict child labor in the states. This time (1919) it relied upon its power to tax. It levied a 10 per cent tax upon the net profits of all firms and establishments that knowingly employed children below certain specified ages in factories, mills, and similar industrial establishments. We have previously learned that this act was declared unconstitutional because it was more of a penal statute than a revenue measure.[34] Following its second failure to meet the judicial requirements of constitutionality, Congress proposed an amendment to the Constitution that would in clear terms give it the power to regulate child labor; but the amendment has not yet been ratified by the necessary three-fourths majority of the states.

What authority has Congress to enact labor laws for the protection of women and children in territory over which it has sole jurisdiction? The answer is, of course, that it is fundamentally the same as that which may be exercised in the states by state and congressional authority combined. But here again there are constitutional limits. For example, the "due process" clause of the Fifth Amendment may stand in the way, as it did when Congress enacted a minimum wage law for women and children in the District of Columbia and found that the Supreme Court held it to be a deprivation of liberty (insofar as it applied to adult women) within the meaning of that clause.[35]

(*b*) *Recent successes.* No longer does the Supreme Court of the United States hold that Congress or the state legislatures, in enacting wage and hour laws for women and children, are depriving them and those who

---

[33] United States v. Darby Lumber Company, 312 U.S. 100 (1941).

[34] Bailey v. Drexel Furniture Company, 259 U.S. 20 (1922).

[35] Adkins v. Children's Hospital, 261 U.S. 525 (1923).

would employ them of the liberty of contract under the "due process" clause of the Fifth or Fourteenth Amendment. In 1937 those earlier decisions were explicitly overruled.[36]

The Government Contracts Act of 1936 prohibits the employment of boys under sixteen and girls under eighteen years of age by any company fulfilling a contract with the federal government. The Jones Sugar Act of the following year excludes from the benefits of a subsidy any beet grower who "utilized" children under fourteen, except where the parents own at least 40 per cent of the crop. Encouraged by the broader definitions given by the Supreme Court in 1937 to the term "interstate commerce," Congress inserted a child labor provision in the Fair Labor Standards Act of 1938. This provision forbids the shipment in interstate commerce of goods mined or manufactured by firms employing children under sixteen years of age, or under eighteen, if the Children's Bureau declares the occupation to be hazardous. But children may be employed in agriculture if the employment does not interfere with a legal requirement to attend school, and children under sixteen may be employed by parents or guardians except in mining and manufacturing, if schooling and health are safeguarded. This statute is estimated to reach not more than 25 per cent of the working children, since a large portion of child labor has no relation to interstate commerce. The full national prohibition of child labor would be possible only under the authority of the Child Labor Amendment.

Protection of minorities. In the matter of employment the rank discrimination against certain races, particularly the Negro race, is notorious. The minority races are usually assigned to the less skilled (even when they have the skill), the menial, the lower-paid jobs. This unfair distinction holds true even in periods of full employment; and when jobs become scarce, the members of such races are likely to be among the first to be without them. Ordinarily, the selection of employees is a private matter, and governments have made little or no effort to prevent discrimination in the selection. During the depression of the 'thirties, however, the national government, in administering work relief, made an effort to see that the minorities had their fair share. During the Second World War the problem of racial discrimination came to public attention in two forms: first, since we were at war for democracy, for freedom, against powers that practiced the worst forms of racial discrimination, consistency and decency demanded that we abate some of our own discriminatory practices; and, second, since we were so hard-pressed for manpower, we could ill-afford the waste that resulted from non-use of a large available supply of labor.

These and other considerations prompted the President to establish a Committee on Fair Employment Practice. An executive order provided

[36] West Coast Hotel Co. v. Parrish, 300 U.S. 379.

that all agencies of the government should include in every contract a provision obligating contractors not to discriminate against persons of any race, color, creed, or nationality in the matter of employment. It provided further that the Committee should receive and investigate all complaints regarding discrimination, take appropriate steps to eliminate the same, make reports and recommendations to the President with respect to discriminations in war industries, and so on. Considering the amount of anti-Negro, anti-Jew, and anti-sentiments generally that many otherwise good Americans possess, it is not surprising that the efforts of the FEPC were less than 100 per cent effective. Rather we should be encouraged that the government seriously attempted to reduce the discrimination.

Since the war a permanent FEPC law has been advocated. The type of measure sought is one that would prohibit various types of employers— employers of persons whose operations affect interstate or foreign commerce, contractors performing services for the government, and the government itself—and labor unions from discriminations in employment because of race, color, creed, national origin, or ancestry. It is proposed that such legislation be enforced by procedures similar to those employed by the war FEPC and by permanent commissions, such as the Interstate Commerce Commission and the Federal Trade Commission—that is, by informal negotiations, formal conferences, public hearings, "cease and desist" orders, and, finally, by appeal to a federal court to enforce an order.

Despite strong Administrative backing for fair employment legislation, no bill has been passed. Strategically placed "minorities" on congressional committees block the way.

Southern congressmen do not want equal treatment of the Negroes and the Mexicans (neither do many non-Southerners); others think a little discrimination against Jews is a "good thing"; still others, while favoring equal treatment, think that the problem is one for churches and schools— that prejudice is no subject for legislation. It should be added here that not all employers are guilty of racial discrimination and that the leadership of the unions is for the most part against discrimination, although it is true that certain unions, particularly locals, have a record of discrimination that would do "credit" to the Ku Klux Klan.

D. The settlement of labor disputes [37]

One of the unsolved problems of our time is that of the settlement of disputes between employees and employers. The old method was largely by injunction, which was often just a scheme of suppression, suppression

[37] Marshall E. Dimock, *Business and Government* (1949), Ch. 10; Lloyd S. Reynolds, *Labor Economics and Labor Relations* (1949), pp. 255 ff. and Ch. XIV; Joseph Shister, *Economics of the Labor Market* (1949), Ch. 12.

THE BASES OF JOB DISCRIMINATION
(COMPLAINTS TO FEPC, FISCAL YEAR 1943-44)

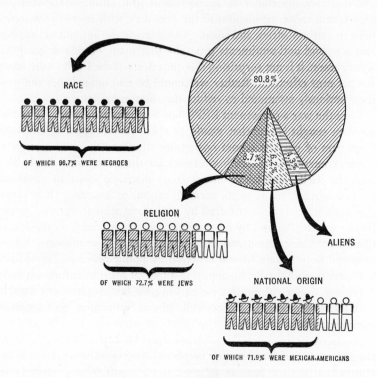

RACE

OF WHICH 96.7% WERE NEGROES

80.8%

3.7% 6.2% 4.3%

RELIGION

OF WHICH 72.7% WERE JEWS

ALIENS

NATIONAL ORIGIN

OF WHICH 71.9% WERE MEXICAN-AMERICANS

THOSE CHARGED WITH DISCRIMINATION

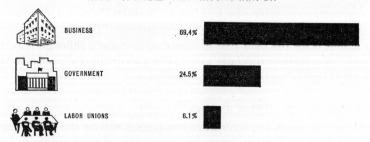

BUSINESS 69.4%

GOVERNMENT 24.5%

LABOR UNIONS 6.1%

Source: *First Report, FEPC, based on 4,081 complaints for fiscal year 1943-44*

From *Report of the President's Committee on Civil Rights* (1947), p. 54.

of labor. Lately, we have found more appropriate means, but we have no sure and reliable means, no system under which all parties can be assured of justice, much less of satisfaction.

The injunction. Employees of a plant are on strike and they seek to get the scabs off the job by singing militant hymns, threatening bodily harm, and using numerous other devices. The employers go before a judge (there is no jury), tell him their troubles, and ask him to issue an injunction prohibiting the strikers from doing a number of specific things that are, in the opinion of the operators, interfering with plant production. If the judge issues the injunction (formerly he did so more frequently than now), it is an order to the strikers to desist and refrain from doing particular things in maintaining their strike. If the strikers violate the injunction, they are brought into court on a contempt proceeding (again there is no jury), fined or jailed or both.

The use of the injunction in labor disputes first came to be a burning issue in 1894, at the time of the Pullman strike in Chicago. For violating an injunction against interfering with the transmission of the mails or with interstate commerce, Eugene V. Debs, the leader of the strike, was cited for contempt of court, tried without jury (the feature of the injunction process at which labor particularly rebels), fined, and imprisoned. The case, which made Debs famous, marked the beginning of organized labor's long fight against the injunction, or, to use labor's term, "government by injunction." But in the succeeding years, injunctions were sought and obtained with increasing frequency by organized capital against organized labor. Strikes were frequently broken by means of the injunction, and labor and many others felt that the courts were allied with capital against labor. In 1908 the Supreme Court held that labor boycotts were combinations in restraint of trade and were thus in violation of the Sherman Antitrust Act, an unexpected decision that further stimulated the efforts of labor for remedial legislation.

Anti-injunction laws: The labor clauses of the Clayton Act. Not until 1914 did labor find a friendly Congress and win what at the time appeared to be valuable concessions. The Clayton Act declared that "the labor of a human being is not a commodity or article of commerce"; that the anti-trust laws shall not be construed to forbid the existence of labor organizations or to forbid the members of such organizations from carrying out the legitimate objects thereof; and that labor organizations shall not be construed to be combinations or conspiracies in restraint of trade. The statute severely restricted the use of injunctions in industrial disputes, and prescribed the jury trial, if requested, for those cited for violating certain types of injunctions.

Although proclaimed as the Magna Charta of labor, the charter prac-

tically vanished item by item as the federal tribunals passed upon its meaning. Thus, in 1922, Attorney General Daugherty obtained an injunction
against striking railway employees, prohibiting them from using, among
other things, threats, violent or abusive language, opprobrious epithets,
jeers, taunts, entreaties, argument, persuasion, and reward in their attempt
to induce the scabs to leave their jobs. The recital of activities from which
the strikers should "absolutely desist and refrain" occupied several pages,
and left them no ground upon which effective action could be taken. This
and similar injunctions left labor with but a shadow of what the labor
clauses in the Clayton Act seemed to give them. Strikes were frequently
broken by injunctions charging labor with interstate conspiracies and
monopolies. Labor agitators were still jailed without trial by jury for violating these injunctions. The "yellow dog" contract—an agreement of
employment wherein the employee promises his employer that he will not
join a trade union—spread in use and was upheld by the courts. In bitter
disappointment, labor renewed its efforts to get legislative relief.

Finally, in 1932, many of the grievances of labor were removed by the
Norris-LaGuardia Act. It is significant that at the time of the passage of
the Clayton Act a considerable proportion of the public was hostile to the
demands of labor and that twenty years later a more comprehensive act
met with general approval. The Norris-LaGuardia Act passed both
Houses of Congress by overwhelming majorities, with only a few spokesmen of the industrial states issuing warnings about "making a long march
toward Moscow." This change in attitude was observed also in a number of states, where anti-injunction bills similar to the federal legislation
were enacted. Indeed, the Wisconsin legislature passed such a law a year
before Congress placed the Norris-LaGuardia bill on the statute books.

THE NORRIS-LAGUARDIA ACT. Under the provisions of the Norris-
LaGuardia Act the "yellow dog" contract, as objectionable to labor as its
cryptic title indicates, was banished into legal exile—declared to be unenforceable in the courts of the United States. Federal courts are forbidden
to issue injunctions against workers for: striking; using union funds to
aid the strike; furthering the strike by advertising, speaking, and picketing;
holding mass meetings; and urging others to join the strike. Only two
limitations are placed upon labor: in giving publicity to facts involved in
a labor dispute, there must be no violence and no fraud. The employer
may still get his injunction if he can show that he has made "every reasonable effort" to settle the strike and if he shows that unlawful acts have been
committed or threatened against him and that failure to enjoin the strikers
will cause him "substantial and irreparable" injury. He is further required
to deposit a bond to recompense the strikers in the event the court causes
them damage by the erroneous issuance of a temporary injunction. An-

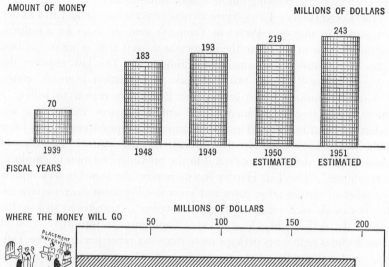

BUDGET EXPENDITURES: LABOR

AMOUNT OF MONEY

MILLIONS OF DOLLARS

70 — 1939
183 — 1948
193 — 1949
219 — 1950 ESTIMATED
243 — 1951 ESTIMATED

FISCAL YEARS

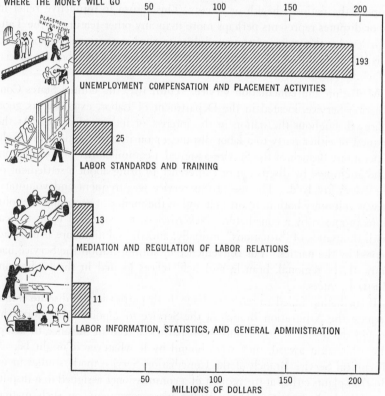

WHERE THE MONEY WILL GO

MILLIONS OF DOLLARS

193 — UNEMPLOYMENT COMPENSATION AND PLACEMENT ACTIVITIES

25 — LABOR STANDARDS AND TRAINING

13 — MEDIATION AND REGULATION OF LABOR RELATIONS

11 — LABOR INFORMATION, STATISTICS, AND GENERAL ADMINISTRATION

MILLIONS OF DOLLARS

From Bureau of the Budget, *The Federal Budget in Brief, Fiscal Year 1951*, p. 31.

other provision of the bill gives the defendant the right of trial by jury in any contempt case growing out of a labor injunction.

THE TAFT-HARTLEY LAW—MORE INJUNCTIVE RELIEF. The Taft-Hartley Act, passed in 1947 over President Truman's veto, provides for a tightening up on labor in respect to the injunction as well as in other particulars. Labor again fears "government by injunction." The law *requires* the National Labor Relations Board to seek an injunction from the courts if, after preliminary investigation, the Board has reason to believe a union is engaging in certain specified unfair practices, including a secondary strike or boycott. This provision repeals a provision dear to labor in the Norris-LaGuardia Act that injunctions were banned "regardless of whether or not the disputants stand in the proximate relation of employer or employee." The Taft-Hartley Act authorizes the Board to seek injunctive relief in certain other cases and gives the President discretionary authority to seek such relief in the case of strikes or threatened strikes that imperil the national health or safety. This return to injunctive relief in labor disputes represents perhaps more than any other feature of the Taft-Hartley Act the swing of the pendulum toward restrictions on labor, and it is but natural that this feature should be singled out by labor for special attack.[38]

Mediation and conciliation service. Until 1947 the United States Conciliation Service, located in the Department of Labor, extended its good offices throughout the nation in the interest of industrial peace. At the request of either party to a labor dispute, or on its own motion, the Field Operations Branch of the Service assigned a commissioner of conciliation, who attempted by discussion or conference to bring about a settlement of the issues involved. The use of this service was frequent and voluntary. It was voluntary both in resort to it and in the matter of accepting the solutions proposed by a conciliator. Nevertheless, it was called upon to deal with thousands of "situations" annually, and the solutions are usually accepted by the parties. For convenience in administration the Service had some thirty regional, branch, and field offices located in the leading industrial centers.

If mediation failed to settle an issue, both parties to the dispute might request the Arbitration Branch of the Service to appoint arbitrators who would make the award. Since both parties agreed in advance to accept the arbitration award, they were bound by it whatever it might be. A Technical Service Branch of the Conciliation Service made studies in industrial plants either at the request of a commissioner assigned to a dispute or of both the parties. These studies were commonly on such matters as wage incentive, job evaluation and classification, and other rather tech-

[38] Florence Peterson, *Supplement to Survey of Labor Economics* (1948), pp. 10–12.

nical matters. Such studies obviously play a significant part in clearing up the points at issue and enabling a commissioner to arrive at a fair proposal or decision.

The Taft-Hartley Act created a new organization, the Federal Mediation and Conciliation Service. Its functions are similar but more limited than those of the U.S. Conciliation Service that it displaced. For example, the new agency is directed to avoid intervening in disputes having only a minor effect on interstate commerce, and in disputes arising over the interpretation of an existing agreement it is cautioned against intervening except as a last resort.

The settlement of labor disputes in wartime. The normal facilities for mediation and arbitration, although used extensively, were inadequate to the demands of the war period. To prevent and settle labor disputes—to the end that there might be uninterrupted production in the war industries—the National War Labor Board was established. The Board was authorized to take over any labor controversy that the Secretary of Labor might certify could not be settled by conciliation; and the Board was also empowered, after consultation with the Secretary of Labor, to assume jurisdiction over a dispute on its own motion. The Board was given final authority to decide the question at issue, using mediation or arbitration, as it saw fit. The National Board in Washington kept its hands on policy and sat as a sort of supreme court to hear appeals from the twelve regional boards; and the latter, through their numerous tripartite panels, carried the burden of settling most of the disputes, chiefly wage and salary adjustment cases.

An essential feature of the organization of the War Labor Board, its regional boards, and its tripartite panels was the equal representation of the public, labor, and industry on each board and panel. The successes of the War Labor Board were numerous, but they did not capture any newspaper headlines nor attract public attention. The Board stood determinedly against rapid increases in wages, and it is entitled, therefore, to a fair share of the credit for holding in check the forces of inflation.

Nevertheless, the Board was sometimes ignored. Strikes, particularly coal miners' strikes, in violation of labor's wartime agreement not to strike, indicated the necessity of supplementing the authority of the Board. In June, 1943, Congress, not without a show of temper, passed the War Labor Disputes (Smith-Connally) Act. This measure authorized the President to take over any war industry when he found that a labor disturbance interfered with production; and, as long as the government remained in control of a plant or industry, strikes and other interruptions growing out of labor disputes were prohibited. In those plants not under government control strikes were not prohibited; but before a strike could become legal, a union was required to give notice of a dispute to the Secretary of Labor, the War Labor Board, and the Labor Relations Board, then "cool off" for at least thirty days before taking a strike vote. This measure angered labor, and it did not prevent strikes, although there were relatively few strikes during the war.

National emergency cases. The Taft-Hartley Act provides that in case of disputes affecting an entire industry, or a substantial part of it, in which a stoppage would imperil the national health or safety, the President may appoint a board of inquiry to investigate and report the facts (no recommendations) to him. The President may then direct the Attorney General to seek an injunction against the strike, and this the court is to grant, if it appears to the court that the national health or safety is in danger. It then becomes the duty of the parties to the dispute to make every effort to settle, using, if they will, the Mediation and Conciliation Service. And it is the concurrent duty of the President to reconvene the board of inquiry.

At the end of a sixty-day period (if the dispute has not been settled), the board reports to the President on the positions of the parties and in particular on the details of the employer's last offer of settlement. It is then the duty of the National Labor Relations Board to take a vote among the employees to learn their wish respecting the employer's last offer. When the results of this ballot are known, or upon a settlement being reached, the injunction is discharged. Finally, after four or five months, it appears, the President reports to Congress with such recommendations as he may care to make. Not the least impressive feature of this provision is its cumbersomeness.

At this writing the President has invoked the Act eight times, twice in coal strike situations. For defying an injunction issued in 1948 John L. Lewis and the United Mine Workers were fined $1,420,000. Stoppages and strikes ran from May, 1949, to March, 1950, while Lewis and the operators engaged in "fencing" operations, the former using the weapon "oppressors" and the latter the weapon "dictator." As the sham negotiations continued, the miners and the whole country suffered. Finally, the President invoked Taft-Hartley, naming a board of inquiry, the first step required by the Act. A few days later the board reported what was rather common knowledge —that the two sides were not allowing collective bargaining to flow "freely and effectively." At this point an injunction was obtained directing the UMW to send the men back to work. Mr. Lewis complied by sending out the appropriate directives, but the miners refused to obey the order, uttering such defiances as, "Let 'em dig coal with the injunction." Making its last practical move under the Act, the government went to court to have the injunction enforced. But since Lewis had twice ordered the miners back to work, the court failed to find UMW in contempt of its order. This exhausted the resources of Taft-Hartley. The President then asked Congress for authority to take over the mines, at which juncture the operators and the union found that they could negotiate "freely and effectively" for a new work contract.

The Taft-Hartley Act does not by its terms prohibit strikes, but it may have a restraining influence. It is probably one of the factors that has reduced the number of labor-industrial conflicts since 1946.

III. LAWS ARE NOT ENOUGH

The laws of themselves will not fully meet the problem of labor relations. The Wagner-Connery Act pleased one group; others called it a challenge to freedom. The Taft-Hartley Act was satisfactory to industrialists; union men dubbed it the "slave labor" law. Whether or not the Taft-Hartley law is a "conglomeration of unintelligible provisions," as one labor economist characterized it,[39] the law is not the solution. Nor will the next law contain the solution. No statute can be drafted that will with equal justice distribute favors and rewards and pains and penalties between contenders in a complicated economic struggle.[40] Any such statute will contain some injustice, and the very best of them will be only temporary. A change in attitudes, however, would make possible more perfect laws.

Labor must become responsible, must learn that it has duties no less than rights and privileges. It must learn to practice moderation. Labor must grow up, stop considering itself a youth and entitled to special consideration. It must recognize that the public has an interest in seeing that labor and management function together on a productive basis. The rest of us must learn also. We criticize labor for its insistence upon the 40-hour week, for its efforts to enforce the closed shop, for work stoppages, for wage increase demands, for high initiation fees, for spending so much money, for drinking too much, and even for political activity. It is not possible to examine each of these charges (some of them are without merit), but it would probably not overtax our energy to find charges against other groups in our society to match those made against labor.

Why, then, is the criticism directed primarily at labor? It may be because a large segment of American industry and perhaps an equally large part of the public has not yet accepted labor as one of the dominant forces in society. Originally, American civilization was primarily agricultural; later, manufacturing, mining, and business dominated our thinking, al-

[39] W. S. Hopkins, *Labor in the American Economy* (1948), p. 300.

[40] Eric Johnston, former President of the United States Chamber of Commerce and a man of moderate views, says that labor and management should and could get together and write a labor law fair to both sides. *New York Times Magazine*, Jan. 29, 1950, p. 7.

though the farmer was not forced out of the picture. A generation ago organized labor entered the scene. It is new; it is fighting for a place, sometimes almost as aggressively and as ruthlessly as the "robber barons" of industry fought in the generation following the Civil War. The "captains of industry" and "the admirals of commerce" made their millions and gave some of them to schools and libraries. Today we "tut-tut" their piratical methods, but we speak of the men tolerantly, and label them as great Americans of the frontier days. Labor is with us right now. It is roughly pushing its way into the American economic and political system and to some extent weakening the businessman's control of government.

Labor is not therefore popular with the businessman or with the public that accepts him as a model. Furthermore, the excesses of labor are so obvious. When it strikes, it does not attempt to keep it secret; on the contrary it stages a parade. Contrast this with the industrial combinations in restraint of trade, worked out in secret by highly paid legal talent and secretly put into operation. If a laborer manages to make four or five hundred dollars a month, he probably spends a lot of it lavishly and in what "nice people" call bad taste. This same public does not, however, particularly object when it hears of a farmer making thousands while the laborer makes his hundreds; nor does it receive with pleasure the news that salaries have been limited to $25,000 for the duration of a war. To make an end of this discussion, it is suggested that when the general body of employers and citizens arrive at the day on which they concede that labor is entitled not simply to subsistence, but also to a large share of the good things, many of which it makes with its own hands, the labor problem will be well on the road to solution.

Reading List

R. C. Atkinson and Others, *Public Employment Service in the United States* (1938).

D. O. Bowman, *Public Control of Labor Relations: A Study of the National Labor Relations Board* (1942).

Kurt Brown, *The Right to Organize and Its Limits* (1950).

H. L. Childs, *Labor and Capital in National Politics* (1930).

J. R. Commons and J. B. Andrews, *Principles of Labor Legislation* (1936 ed.).

Marshall E. Dimock, *Business and Government* (1949), Chs. 9–11.

W. F. Dodd, *Administration of Workmen's Compensation* (1936).

F. Frankfurter and N. Greene, *The Labor Injunction* (1930).

T. R. Fisher, *Industrial Disputes and Federal Legislation* (1940).

Eli Ginzberg, *The Labor Leader* (1948).

C. S. Golden and Harry Ruellenburg, *The Dynamics of Industrial Democracy* (1942).

R. L. Greenman, *The Worker, the Foreman, and the Wagner Act* (1939).

H. Harris, *American Labor* (1938).

W. S. Hopkins, *Labor in the American Economy* (1948).

L. C. Kesselman, *The Social Politics of FEPC* (1948).

C. C. Killingsworth, *State Labor Relations Acts* (1948).

Annual Reports of the National Labor Relations Board.

Annual Reports of the Secretary of Labor.

Aaron Levenstein, *Labor Today and Tomorrow* (1945).

C. E. Lindblom, *Unions and Capitalism* (1949).

A. F. Macdonald, *American State Government and Administration* (1950 ed.), Ch. 29.

H. A. Marquand and Others, *Organized Labor in Four Continents* (1939).

H. W. Metz, *Labor Policy of the Federal Government* (1945).

C. W. Mills, *The New Men of Power* (1948).

Florence Peterson, Supplement to *Survey of Economics* (1948).

Lloyd S. Reynolds, *Labor Economics and Labor Relations* (1949).

Malcolm Ross, *All Manner of Men* (1948).

Joseph Shister, *Economics of the Labor Market* (1949).

S. H. Slichter, *The Challenge of Industrial Relations* (1947).

C. F. Snider, *American State and Local Government* (1950), Ch. XXIII.

C. E. Warne and Others, *Labor in Postwar America* (1949).

G. S. Watkins and P. A. Dodd, *Labor Problems* (1940 ed.).

S. T. Williamson and Herbert Harris, *Trends in Collective Bargaining* (1945).

Questions and Problems

1. Trace the efforts of the states to protect women and children in industry. How does it happen that "due process of law" no longer operates as a primary obstacle to such legislation?

2. How have the states attempted to protect workmen from accidents and disease and to compensate incapacitated workmen?

3. Indicate the trends in labor legislation in your state during the last 20 years.

4. How did it happen that the first comprehensive national labor laws related to railway workers and seamen?

5. Outline the stages in the development of means for the settlement of railway labor disputes. What facilities are still lacking?

6. Show how the national government has entered the field to protect employees feeding interstate commerce.

7. What is labor's particular objection to the injunction and how has this objection been met?

8. Discuss the provisions of the Taft-Hartley Act relating to the settlement of labor disputes.

9. Trace the efforts of the national government to protect women and children in industry.

10. Discuss this statement: *The employment rights of minorities hold an importance equal to their civil liberties.*

11. Write a 200-word essay on the present trend of national labor legislation.
12. Give your considered opinion of what labor should do in order to win a widespread public confidence.
13. What, in your opinion, are the common faults of the public in its attitude toward labor? The faults of labor in its attitude toward the public?

☆ *25* ☆

Agriculture and Conservation

THE farmer has sometimes felt that he has not received his share of government favors; that industry and labor have been heeded while the tillers of the soil have been largely ignored. Probably industry did have greater influence than agriculture in the councils of state prior to 1933, but only since that date has labor's influence rivaled that of agriculture. In any event, the government has not ignored the farmer. This chapter shows that whatever the burdens of the American husbandman have been, they have not been caused by chronic government neglect. Taking the long view we may say that the conservation of natural resources is of no less concern to Americans than the well-being of the farmer. Consequently conservation is treated as something more than an annex to this chapter.

I. GOVERNMENT ASSISTANCE TO AGRICULTURE [1]

Occupation and reclamation. From the time of its creation the federal government has aided the farmer by letting him have its lands at practically no cost. In the past forty years it has further aided him by using its resources to redeem vast arid regions for agriculture. Both of these policies are briefly discussed in section II of this chapter.

Scientific research. No department of the national government makes more use of science than the Department of Agriculture, which employs numerous experts in many lines to make studies and conduct experiments and pass the information on to the general body of farmers. Here are some samples of this interesting and valuable work.

[1] J. S. Davis, *On Agricultural Policy, 1926–1938* (1939); Marshall E. Dimock, *Business and Government* (1949), Chs. 12–13; E. F. Dummeier and R. B. Heflebower, *Economics with Applications to Agriculture* (1940 ed.), Chs. XIX–XXIX; Merle Fainsod and Lincoln Gordon, *Government and the American Economy* (1948 ed.), Ch. 5; E. S. Sparks, *History and Theory of Agricultural Credit in the United States* (1932); *Annual Reports of the Secretary of Agriculture.*

1. CHEMISTRY AND SOILS. Perhaps the reader is not especially concerned about any loss that may result from the decrease in weight and nutritive value of hay which occurs during spontaneous heating. Nevertheless, the Bureau of Agricultural and Industrial Chemistry has told us that spontaneous heating takes well over $100,000,000 from the value of our national hay crop each year; and, to find practical means of reducing this lose, the Bureau has conducted researches in experimental barns. In an important strawberry-growing district of North Carolina, growers customarily put down their fertilizer in two applications, one after the berries were picked and the other during the winter. Following experiments by our scientific Bureau, the growers put down all the fertilizer in one application, in the early fall, and the next spring picked from 400 to 500 more quarts of berries per acre than formerly. As other examples of the Bureau's work, its laboratories have developed cork substitutes from peanut hulls, an adhesive from soybean flakes, a portable flavor-recovery unit for obtaining essences in the field from fruits and berries and many another such product or device.

2. SOIL CONSERVATION. Mistaken land-use practices in the United States have caused the ruin by erosion of nearly 300,000,000 acres of land and seriously damaged as many more.

Erosion dissipates fertile soil in dust storms, piles up soil on lower slopes, covers rich bottom land with poor subsoil, destroys food and cover for wildlife, and increases flood hazards. Furthermore, it causes the silting and sedimentation of stream channels, reservoirs, dams, ditches, and harbors, and damages roads, railways, irrigation works, power plants, and public water supplies.

The picture is dark, but not overdrawn. The Soil Conservation Service of the Department of Agriculture is studying this problem on scores of demonstration projects and has prepared a soil conservation plan for each demonstration area. It recommends contouring, strip cropping, terracing, crop rotation, and other conservation practices. This Service encourages the organization among farmers of voluntary soil conservation associations, of which there are now about 2,100. Among the other duties of the Service are those of making investigations of watersheds and proposing measures for the prevention of soil erosion on watersheds and of acquiring by purchase submarginal farm lands and putting them to more productive use, such as grazing.

3. PLANT INDUSTRY DEVELOPMENT. The Bureau of Plant Industry, Soils, and Agricultural Engineering, is equally busy and scientific in its domain. In North Carolina corn yields average only about 20 bushels to the acre under traditional farm practices. That is very poor. The Bureau proceeded to experiment, and found that yields of more than 70 bushels per acre were consistently obtained by combining heavy applications of nitrogen, properly placed, with growing corn hybrids, increasing the number

of plants per acre, and controlling weeds by means of shallow cultivation.[2]

4. ANIMAL AND DAIRY INDUSTRY. The Department of Agriculture is equally as devoted to research in the animal industry and dairying as in the other fields described above. The Bureau of Animal Industry tells the farmer that experiments have demonstrated, contrary to general belief, that a hog should not have all he can eat. True, hogs fed a limited ration make less rapid gains and require longer feeding periods than those fed a full ration, but the former are more efficient in utilizing their ration and require much less feed per hundred pounds of gain than do those fed a full ration. Furthermore, limited feeding produces somewhat leaner carcasses, an advantage to the hog raiser, since the American consumer is now willing to pay higher prices for leaner pork. For years the Bureau has been cooperating with state authorities in the eradication of bovine tuberculosis, and has reduced infection among cattle to a marked degree. The elimination of tuberculosis from poultry and swine has also received the attention of the Bureau.

Dairy research is conducted by the Bureau of Dairy Industry. Its studies include various phases of such problems as dairy-cattle breeding, improving the quality of milk, and the manufacturing of dairy products. It makes particular efforts to learn and place at the disposal of manufacturers improved methods of manufacturing cheese, certain types of imported cheese still being preferred to competing American brands.[3] How may dairymen produce more milk to meet consumer demands? Feed the cows heavier; give them more grain, advises the Bureau of Dairy Industry.[4]

5. SCIENTIFIC WARFARE AGAINST PESTS. The farmer has many foes in the kingdom of animals, insects, fungi, and bacteria. In his wars with them the United States government is his powerful scientific ally. Predatory animals such as wolves raid his stock; rats and other rodents devour his garnered crops. The Fish and Wildlife Service (of the Department of the Interior) lends various types of assistance in their extermination. Particularly effective is science in the eradication of rodents. Armed with chemicals recommended by the Service and using them according to directions, any farmer may march forth against rats and other rodents as effectively, if not so picturesquely, as the Pied Piper of Hamlin.

Insect pests, doing the farmers an annual damage running into hundreds of millions through attacks on their crops and flocks, exist in hundreds of species, each species occurring in myriads. The European corn borer, the Mexican bean beetle, the oriental fruit fly, the plum curculio, grasshoppers, chinch bugs, buffalo gnats, common cattle grubs, southern pine

[2] *Report of the Department of Agriculture,* 1948, pp. 119-120.
[3] *Ibid.,* 1937, pp. 56 ff.
[4] *Ibid.,* 1941, pp. 117-118.

beetles, Japanese beetles, Thurberia weevils, Mormon crickets, screw-worms, gypsy and brown-tail moths, black flies, and cattle-fever ticks are but a few destructive varieties. Even a farmer's tobacco stored in a warehouse is not safe from pests. An army of cosmopolitan moths may go forth and destroy it. Drought, which of itself spells loss or even privation for the farmer, may further distress him because it is favorable to the multiplication of certain insect pests, reducing disease among them and aiding their hibernation. The Bureau of Entomology and Plant Quarantine is busy studying insect pests of all kinds, learning their life history to find the most favorable time for attack, and testing ammunition to discover the most effective charges that may be used against them. The disastrous grasshopper outbreak of 1931 was predicted by the entomologists. They pointed out that effective control was "possible chiefly against the 'egg beds' and against the newly hatched hoppers"; that eggs could be destroyed by cultivating the spots where grasshoppers had collected for oviposition; and that the young insects could be destroyed by poisoned bran baits. Unfortunately, this advice was not heeded to the extent of taking adequate steps to control the grasshoppers.[5]

The Bureau of Plant Industry, Soils, and Agricultural Engineering, in addition to its work mentioned under paragraph 3, is engaged in the study of plant diseases. For example, in 1931 it reported distinct progress in the control of stem rust of wheat through the eradication of some 18,000,000 barberry bushes, and in 1948 that such rust had been brought under almost complete control. A rapid and devastating spread of the white pine blister rust was discovered in Montana, Idaho, and Washington. How could the disease be controlled? By a systematic eradication of currant and gooseberry bushes, advised the Bureau.[6] The Bureau of Agricultural and Industrial Chemistry comes to the aid of sick plants by experimenting with fumigants and insecticides. Those having knowledge of the toxic powers of nicotine may be impressed with the news that experts in the Bureau have developed a synthetic organic compound, *neonicotine,* which is much more toxic than nicotine when sprayed upon plant lice.

As civilized man seems to pick up more diseases, so scientifically nurtured plants appear to develop new ones. In 1946 a new disease, *helminthosporium blight,* struck the oat crop; and the scientists proceeded at once to develop blight-resistant varieties of oats. But the introduction of new and resistant varieties do not end the struggle. The human factor sometimes enters. For instance, the use of resistant varieties of wheat brought stinking smut or bunt under control. The bunt-resistant varieties did not, however, yield as many bushels as the bunt-susceptible varieties, and some

[5] *Report of the Secretary of Agriculture,* 1931, pp. 66 ff.; *U.S. Govt. Org. Manual,* 1950–1951, pp. 213–214.

[6] *Report of the Secretary of Agriculture,* 1931, p. 65, and *ibid.,* 1948, p. 123.

of the farmers went back to the cultivation of the latter. As a consequence, in one year an eighth of the wheat marketed in the Pacific Northwest was graded "smutty." [7]

Quarantines. To fight an insect or fungus outbreak successfully and to protect the country from its ravages, the conflict must be localized. Consequently, the Secretary of Agriculture is authorized by an act of Congress to place a plague area under quarantine. He may not issue such an order, however, until after state officers and interested private parties have been heard. The state affected, often with the aid of federal funds and federal employees, then undertakes measures of eradication. The Mediterranean fruit fly outbreak in Florida made necessary a quarantine there from May 1, 1929, to November 15, 1930. During the greater part of this period, state and federal agents were locating and destroying infestations, the last one being found in a dooryard in St. Augustine, July 25, 1930. The quarantine prevented the spread of the insect to other states, and although it resulted in some temporary losses to Floridians, these losses were offset many times by the assurance of open markets for their pest-free products. A Japanese beetle quarantine during 1930–1931 was similarly successful. While nurserymen and other interested parties were co-operating with federal agents in preventing the spread of the pest, federal inspectors were issuing clearance certificates for plants not infested, thus assuring their acceptance at their destination without fear of infestation. [8]

6. SCIENCE AND THE WEATHER. A college janitor, one of whose many duties was to hoist the indication flags for a weather forecaster, often piously observed, "I wish Professor Simeon would let the Lord regulate the weather." Of course the forecasters cannot "do anything about the weather"; but they can tell us within a fair degree of accuracy what the weather is going to do for us. This information is invaluable to navigators on the sea and in the air. It is hardly less valuable to the farmer. The navigator must have it to bring his ship and passengers safely to port; the farmer must have it to save his stock and crops, although at times he may not be able to meet adverse weather conditions with sufficient defenses.

The Weather Bureau was formerly located in the Department of Agriculture, but it is now in the Department of Commerce. With its stations all over the country, connected by the most improved methods of communication, the Bureau is able through the press, flags, whistles, and, most important of all, radio, to advise the farmers in each locality of coming changes in the weather. Warned of approaching frost, the wise fruit grower lights his "smudge pots" in his orchards; warned of floods, the stockman drives his cattle and sheep from the lowlands; and so on.

[7] *Ibid.,* 1948, p. 123.
[8] *Report of the Secretary of Agriculture* (1931), pp. 71–72.

7. ELECTRICITY ON THE FARM. In 1933 the Electric Farm and Home Authority was created for the purpose of aiding in the distribution, sale, and installation of electrical apparatus in such a manner as to enable home and farm owners to use electricity at low cost. It was authorized to extend credit facilities for the purchase of such apparatus and to co-operate with publicly and privately owned utilities and dealers in electrical appliances to facilitate the use of electricity on a sound and economical basis. In May, 1936, a Rural Electrification Administration was established by act of Congress. The Administration was allotted a sum of money for a ten-year program, and it was authorized to supervise a program of approved projects with respect to the generation and distribution of electric energy in rural areas. Under certain conditions it may lend the entire cost of power lines in areas that are without them. An act of September, 1944, liberalized the terms of loans, and rapid progress has since been made in rural electrification. It should be mentioned that farm areas in some parts of the country have long been served by private light and power companies. The federal action was designed to supplement such services. About two thirds of farm homes now receive electrical energy, and the number of rural consumers is increasing at the rate of about 40,000 per month.[9]

Agricultural education. Although much of the scientific information gathered by the Department of Agriculture passes directly to farmers, a great deal more of it does not. "Middlemen" are needed to help pass the facts on to the farmers and to assist them in their interpretation. These men are found on the faculties of colleges established under the terms of the Morrill Act, and in agricultural extension work.

1. COLLEGES. Under the provisions of the Morrill Act of 1862 and later supplementary legislation, nearly 11,000,000 acres of public land, much of it very valuable, have been set aside for the states, each state sharing the land in proportion to its representation in Congress, and each assuming the obligation to use the proceeds from such lands to maintain one or more colleges in which shall be taught "without excluding other scientific and classical studies and including military tactics, . . . such branches of learning as are related to agriculture and the mechanic arts." Colleges and universities established under the terms of this act are the familiar land-grant colleges. Under an act of 1890, additional aid came to the colleges in the form of annual appropriations from the federal treasury. The Nelson Act (1907) and the Bankhead-Jones Act (1935) further increased the appropriations.

In the original grant the federal government made practically no attempt to supervise the states in their use of the funds, but it developed that some control was desirable. A number of the states sold their land

[9] *Report of the Secretary of Agriculture,* 1948, pp. 152–154 and *U.S. Govt. Org. Manual,* 1950–51, pp. 233–234.

grants and at such low prices as to suggest scandal. Consequently, in 1889, Congress decreed that no state admitted to the Union thereafter should sell the land for less than ten dollars an acre. In 1890, with the beginning of annual appropriations, Congress directed the Secretary of the Interior to see that the colleges were fulfilling their purposes before he approved the annual allotments. Central control, inevitable in such cases, has increased a bit in recent years. Through its appropriations of funds for education in agriculture and the mechanic arts and through ever-increasing stipulations as to their specific uses, the federal government is able to carry out a national educational policy.

2. EXPERIMENT STATIONS. To give instruction in the principles of scientific agriculture, leaders in this type of education early recognized the necessity of adequate facilities for experimentation. In response to their demands Congress, in 1887, passed the Hatch Act, establishing an experiment station in every A. and M. college, allowing each state a lump sum for that purpose. Allowances were later increased, and with them, as in the case of the colleges proper, came an increase in federal control. Funds for these stations now total around $20,000,000 annually. About one third of this comes from the federal government, the remainder from state and local governments and private sources.

Thousands of research projects are under way at the stations every year. The Department of Agriculture, through its Office of Experiment Stations, co-operates in such experiments as are of general importance. The projects have to do with production, distribution, and sale of farm products, with the needs of the farm home, and with rural community matters. Results of experiments and investigations, such as hybrid tomatoes, potato-breeding, smut-resistant wheat, cobalt deficiencies in dairy cattle, and home-mixed calf starter rations, are disseminated by colleges, books, bulletins, the press, and the radio. In carrying them to the farmer for practical use, the extension services are of particular value.

3. EXTENSION SERVICE. Though many farmers may send their sons and daughters to the agricultural colleges, only a few farmers themselves can arrange to attend. Besides, the farmer wants his particular problems met a little more directly than is possible in a general college course. In 1914, in recognition of this situation, Congress passed the Smith-Lever Act, which provides for instruction and practical demonstrations in agriculture and home economics for persons not attending college. This act was not just a federal "hand-out" to the states. There were strings attached. The money was not to be divided equally among the states; but, excepting a sum of $10,000, each state was to receive a sum that bore the same relation to the total sum appropriated as its rural inhabitants bore to the total rural population of the United States. More important, each state receiving

the federal funds was required to "match the federal dollar," that is, appropriate a like sum from its own treasury for the same purpose. Furthermore, the states were required to submit their plans for using the funds to the Department of Agriculture for its approval. Thus, to secure federal funds for extension work, the states must not only assume financial obligations, but they must also allow the federal government an important voice in determining the details of their expenditure. This is now a common arrangement respecting any "federal aid" money.

Under the Smith-Lever and four other extension acts (the Bankhead-Flannagan Act of 1945 is the latest), Congress appropriated about $26,-000,000 for the fiscal year 1948. The states, counties, and other agencies appropriated varying amounts. The extension service now includes hundreds of specialists stationed usually at the state colleges of agriculture, and a much larger field force of county agents, home demonstration agents, and others. These agents lend assistance wherever possible, both to the individual farmer and to the farm community. During the Second World War they were particularly active in aiding farmers in meeting crop goals and in recruiting emergency farm labor. Not the least important work of the extension service is in contact with boys and girls. Under expert supervision, they are organized into "4-H" clubs and encouraged to grow vegetables, raise stock and poultry, can fruit, and so on.

We may conclude, then, that the federal government gives very material support to agricultural education, and that, in promoting such education, the national and state governments co-operate both in finances and functions in such a way as to cause an individual concerned about the division of powers between the two governments to scratch his head in bewilderment.

Agricultural credit. Large-scale farming and expensive farm equipment, necessitating larger capital outlays than formerly, led the federal government to come to the assistance of agriculture in the matter of credit. President Theodore Roosevelt's Country Life Commission and a commission appointed by President Wilson to study rural credits explored the field, and the report of the latter commission had great weight in shaping a farm loan system.

Beginning in 1916, credit agencies were created from time to time, and as their number and duties increased, the need for a unified system became apparent. This need was met in 1933 by the establishment of the Farm Credit Administration, whose administrative head holds the title of Governor. Functioning since 1939 as a unit of the Department of Agriculture, this Administration supervises and co-ordinates the activities of land banks and other corporations and organizations authorized to extend agricultural credit. On occasion it takes a direct part in loan activities.

1. FEDERAL LAND BANKS. The Federal Farm Loan Act (1916) established the federal land banks and created the Federal Farm Loan Board to administer them. In response to great pressure from those interested in joint-stock land banks, Congress permitted them to continue to operate, but they were required to come under the supervision of the Farm Loan Board. In 1933 Congress withdrew the authority of the joint-stock banks to make additional loans. At the same time Congress transferred the functions of the Board to a single Commissioner. There are twelve federal land banks located with due regard for the agricultural interests of the country.

How does the farmer borrow from these banks? Ordinarily, a farmer must present his request for a loan to the secretary-treasurer of the local farm loan association and an appraiser for the land bank. If the request is approved, the farmer may borrow, at a relatively low rate of interest and for from five to forty years, up to 65 per cent of the appraised value of his farm. He gives the association a first mortgage, which is endorsed by it and forwarded to the district land bank. This mortgage, along with many others, is used as security for bonds sold to the investing public by the land bank to get more money to lend to other farmers. Coming back to our particular mortgage—the land bank sends the loan to the local association, which is required to subscribe to the capital stock of the land bank in an amount equal to 5 per cent of the loan. The farmer is required to subscribe to an equal amount of stock in the local farm loan association. This is the common procedure, but in recent years it has been possible for farmers to borrow directly from the land banks.

2. FEDERAL FARM MORTGAGE CORPORATION. Many farm mortgages went into default during 1930–1933, and the central government was forced to extend aid to the farmers and the land banks. In January, 1934, the Federal Farm Mortgage Corporation was created for the purpose of refinancing these farm mortgages. This Corporation could issue bonds to the amount of $2,000,000,000, the principal and interest of which were fully guaranteed by the United States. These bonds were given to the land banks in exchange for their bonds. By this procedure the land banks were placed in a position to extend more credit to the farmers. The Land Bank Commissioner could make farm mortgage loans of an emergency character, the federal land banks acting as his agents. The Commissioner acquired the money for this purpose from the Farm Mortgage Corporation. Authority to make loans of this character expired in 1947.

3. INTERMEDIATE CREDIT BANKS. The federal land banks take farmers' land mortgages and give long-term credit. Often the farmers want credit for shorter terms than these banks can extend it and they want to offer other security than land. They want loans for a few months or a year or

two on wheat, cotton, apples, hogs, and other products and live stock.
In 1923 Congress came to their aid with the Agricultural Credits Act, an
omnibus measure combining the more important parts of several bills introduced to meet the farmers' demands. The principal features of the act
are those relating to the intermediate credit banks. Twelve such banks
were established as separate divisions of the federal land banks. The
farmer who wants money on his crops or livestock may get it from a local
loan institution, such as a bank, an agricultural credit corporation, or a
livestock loan company. The local institution may then go to an intermediate credit bank and discount the paper the farmer has given as security for his loan. The intermediate credit banks also serve the farmer by
making loans to agricultural and livestock co-operative associations, associations formed by the farmers for the purpose of obtaining loans.

4. Banks for co-operatives. The Farm Credit Act of 1933 set up banks
in each of the twelve farm credit districts for the purpose of making loans to
farmers' co-operative associations. Loans may be made for the purpose of
financing the handling of readily marketable commodities, for financing
the operations of the co-operatives, for the construction or purchase of
physical facilities, for merchandising agricultural products, and for similar
purposes.

5. Production credit corporations. The Farm Credit Act also set up
production credit corporations. Through combined action with the intermediate credit bank in each district, the credit corporations form a short-
term credit system for general agricultural purposes. Loans are advanced
for such purposes as raising livestock and improving farm equipment and
buildings. The farmer must submit his application for a loan through his
local production credit association. The production credit corporation in
each farm credit district assists in the organization of these associations and
provides most of their capital.

6. The Farmers Home Administration. Since 1935 provision has been
made for extending loans to the operator of a family-type farm and to other
farm people not so well situated. The Bankhead-Jones Farm Tenant Act
of 1937 and the Farmers Home Administration Act of 1946 specifically
authorize such aid. Operating loans are made to small farm owners,
tenants, and sharecroppers. These loans are not only authorized for farm
operations but also for family living needs, including medical care. Loans
are also made to farm tenants, sharecroppers, laborers, and veterans to buy
a family-type farm, or to improve and enlarge a farm to bring it up to that
class. These farm ownership loans are not available for the purchase or
improvement of a farm that is above the average of family-type farms in
the county. Operating loans in any one year may not exceed $3,500, and
farm ownership loans may not exceed $12,000. Other types of loans avail-

able are water facility loans (for seventeen Western states) and flood and disaster loans. Each year several hundred thousand farmers obtain loans from the Farmers Home Administration. Considering that loans from this service are not available unless the farmer is unable to obtain adequate credit elsewhere, the record for repayment—nearly 90 per cent—is remarkably high.[10]

7. THE COMMODITY CREDIT CORPORATION. Chartered in 1933 under the laws of Delaware and rechartered in 1948 by the United States Government, the Commodity Credit Corporation (CCC) is empowered to buy and sell and otherwise deal in agricultural commodities. It is authorized to have outstanding as much as $4,750,000,000 in bonds and notes, which obligations are fully and unconditionally guaranteed by the United States. The major program of the CCC is price support for farm commodities, and to this end it makes loans on or purchases such commodities. This activity comes in for further discussion under the general title of "agricultural marketing."

The exigencies of war led the Commodity Credit Corporation to employ its funds for the protection of the farmers from the results of abrupt dislocations of export trade and for the expansion of scarce and essential agricultural products. In "prosecuting the war" the CCC bought foreign agricultural commodities required by the United States and its allies; and, in helping to effectuate the program of hemispheric solidarity, it purchased and stored in Latin-American countries commodities to which war closed the possibility for exportation.

Agricultural marketing. The government services in respect to soils, plants, the weather, and other matters that particularly lend themselves to scientific investigation materially aid the farmer in producing better and larger crops. The credit facilities just discussed similarly aid the farmer, especially in the direction of large-scale production. When the crops are harvested and the livestock is ready for slaughter, the farmer must find a market. Here, again, the federal government offers a variety of services. There is special need for them. The farmer has often been the victim of sharp market practices, and there is often a surplus of farm produce. Perhaps it may be said also that the government is under a special obligation to furnish marketing assistance, since its scientific aid is partly responsible for the farmers' surplus. There is space only for a bare enumeration of the more significant marketing services.

1. CROP AND MARKET NEWS. Growers and buyers must have information concerning crops and markets the country over in order to proceed intelligently. The Bureau of Agricultural Economics keeps a watchful

[10] *Report of the Secretary of Agriculture*, 1948, pp. 147–150; *U.S. Govt. Org. Manual*, 1950–51, pp. 225–227.

eye on growing crops, makes calculations as to probable yields, and issues reports thereon. The Production and Marketing Administration gathers information on the market supply and demand conditions on cereals, fruits, vegetables, poultry and dairy products, and other farm commodities. It obtains this information at the large terminal markets and at important receiving centers and shipping points. By wire, radio, newspapers, and mail this information is disseminated to all interested parties.

2. FARM PRODUCE STANDARDS. Since buyers in distant cities cannot visit farms and sample the products the farmer has to sell, standards must be made uniform in order that all interested parties will use the same terms and specifications in grading farm products. To some extent this uniformity of standards can be brought about by private arrangement or by state law; but only the national government has the constitutional authority and sufficient resources at its command to establish uniform standards for commodities sold in interstate and foreign commerce. The Production and Marketing Administration arrives at its standards through co-operation with growers and buyers, and does not ordinarily make them obligatory until general voluntary acceptance of them has demonstrated their satisfactory character. Acts of Congress make the standards mandatory for grain, cotton, and certain other commodities when they are shipped in interstate or foreign commerce. An inspection service is maintained in the principal producing areas and receiving centers on fruits, vegetables, hay, beans, and other products. A permissive service is provided upon request for dairy and poultry products, rice, meats, wool, and canned fruits and vegetables. Mandatory and free inspection of tobacco is provided at those auction markets where a two-thirds majority of producers have voted for it. During the war the inspection service passed upon huge quantities of food purchased for the armed forces of the United States, for shipment by the Red Cross, and for transfer to other countries under the Lend-Lease Act.

3. PROTECTION AGAINST FRAUD AND DISCRIMINATION. Several acts have been passed to protect the growers against unfair practices of buyers and of owners of warehouses. By an act of 1916 owners of warehouses storing farm produce entering interstate or foreign commerce are required to obtain licenses from the Secretary of Agriculture. He issues such licenses only to those who have adequate plants and who post satisfactory bonds. These "bonded warehouses" must treat all growers alike, accepting their goods on the same terms as long as storage space is available. Receipts for goods stored must be given on a specified form, and all commodities received must be graded by licensed inspectors employing the standards mentioned in 2 above.

A report from a commission merchant that produce reached its destination in bad condition, or was totally spoiled, is an old story with farmers. One farmer was even notified that his white sand had failed to stand the trip! By the terms of the Produce Agency Act of 1927 such merchants are forbidden to throw away, unless actually spoiled, perishable goods shipped in interstate commerce, or to make false reports of the conditions of such produce on arrival. An act of 1930 further strengthens federal control over marketing. Commission merchants, dealers, and brokers in perishable farm products must now obtain licenses from the Secretary of Agriculture. He may also revoke them for violations of the law. Holders of these permits must order their business in accordance with the details of the statute and keep complete records of all transactions. Upon complaint by an aggrieved producer, hearings are held and relief and damages awarded, if the complaint is well founded.

In marketing his livestock through the channels of interstate or foreign commerce, the farmer receives protection under the Packers and Stockyards Act of 1921. Packers risk severe penalties when they attempt price manipulation and certain other unfair practices. Owners of stockyards are also under supervision as to rates and practices. Although the official approval of the Secretary of Agriculture is needed for some of the actions that are taken, the administration of these and similar acts is the responsibility of the Production and Marketing Administration.

4. REGULATION OF TRADING IN FUTURES. The prices of agricultural commodities are often the subject of market speculation, to the disadvantage of the farmers. Take wheat, as a familiar example. An operator may agree to deliver 100,000 bushels to a miller six months later at a dollar a bushel. This is called "trading in futures." Now the operator hopes that the price of wheat will fall before the time for delivery, for his profit is measured by the decline in price from the time of the agreement to the date of delivery. Obviously, such traders thrive in a falling market and their manipulations will be to this end, the farmer being the chief loser. Back in 1916 Congress took a cautious step in the enactment of the Cotton Futures Act. It levies a tax of 2 cents per pound on all contracts for future deliveries of cotton, unless they stipulate the grade of cotton to be delivered. This measure could hardly be expected to prevent speculation injurious to the farmer.

The Grain Futures Act of 1922 went further. With the exception of producers' associations, all dealers in wheat, corn, and certain other grains must operate under federal supervision and through "contract markets" designated by the Secretary of Agriculture. Such markets must be conducted by boards of trade acting under definite regulations; records must be kept open to federal inspection; measures must be taken to prevent price manipulation; and so on. A dealer on such exchanges who fails to comply with regulations may be deprived of the right to transact interstate business. The Secretary of Agriculture may close the entire market when its board acts unlawfully.[11]

The Research and Marketing Act of 1946. The most recent marketing legislation indicates that there is no letup in the purpose of Congress to give the farmer a large assortment of marketing assistance. Noting only section 203 of the act of 1946 we find that the Secretary of Agriculture is authorized and directed to investigate to determine improved methods of preparing, processing, packing, handling, transporting, storing, distributing, and marketing agricultural products; determine costs of marketing such products and assist in the development of more efficient marketing methods, practices, and facilities for more orderly marketing and reducing spread between producer and consumer; develop and improve standards of quality, condition, quantity, grade and packing, and to recommend and demonstrate such standards to encourage commercial adoption of them; conduct, assist, foster, and direct studies and informational programs designed to eliminate artificial barriers to the free movement of agricultural products; conduct and co-operate in consumer education for more effective utilization and greater consumption of agricultural products; and in nine other related ways bestir himself and the forces at his command to the end that the farmer might have better markets.

Government efforts to improve farm prices. Despite all of the government services extending help to the farmer, his economic lot was not enviable between 1921 and 1941. Even in the happy days of general plenty immediately preceding the inauguration of President Hoover, the farmer failed to reap prosperity. During the campaign of 1928 it was rather commonly assumed that the government must do something out of the ordinary for him.

THE AGRICULTURAL MARKETING ACT OF 1929. In a move to relieve the farmer Congress passed the Agricultural Marketing Act, which was designed to aid him in a big way and in new ways, particularly through a section aimed at the prevention and control of surplus products. The Federal Farm Board was established and charged with the duty of administering this and other sections of the act. Its most staggering task was to stabilize the prices of certain farm commodities. To accomplish this aim it set up stabilization corporations for cotton, grain, and other farm products. These corporations bought the farmer's surplus in an attempt to

---

[11] The services of the Production and Marketing Administration are briefly stated in the *United States Govt. Org. Manual,* 1950–51, pp. 229–233. An excellent discussion of the marketing aids supplied by the government, although somewhat out of date, is found in C. A. and Wm. Beard, *The American Leviathan* (1930), pp. 533–545.

keep prices up. But with the general economic decline of 1930–1932 the attempts at stabilization failed miserably.

THE AGRICULTURAL ADJUSTMENT ACT OF 1933. With farmers in the Middle West rioting because of mortgage foreclosures and tragically low prices for their products and with Senator David A. Reed asserting that if the people of industrial Pennsylvania knew what the bill before Congress contained, "they'd riot in the streets," the Agricultural Adjustment Act became a law. It was the purpose of the act to raise the prices of wheat, corn, cotton, milk, and several other agricultural products to a point where they would bear a fair relationship to the prices the farmer had to pay for the goods he bought. Of course some standard had to be agreed upon, and the relationship between the price of farm commodities and the price of goods purchased by the farmer during the period of 1909–1914 was fixed as the standard. Applying the standard for a particular commodity, wheat, it was found that on the basis of what the farmer had to pay for his purchases in June, 1933, he should have 89 cents per bushel for his wheat in order to attain the prewar "parity." Now in June, 1933, the farmer was getting 59 cents per bushel for his wheat. The price was 30 cents too low. This amount the government paid to wheat farmers who signed contracts to reduce their wheat acreage by 15 per cent. Along with dollar revaluation, business recovery, and other influences, the agricultural adjustment program had its part in restoring the farmers' purchasing power to approximately what it had been in 1929. But, in January, 1936, the Supreme Court of the United States, in a six-to-three decision, declared the Adjustment Act unconstitutional.[12]

THE SOIL CONSERVATION AND DOMESTIC ALLOTMENT ACT OF 1936. Even before the invalidation of the first Agricultural Adjustment Act, those responsible for its administration had begun to place less emphasis on flat reductions in crop acreage and more on differential adjustments to the requirements of local and national conditions. Several acts have been passed to accomplish what could not be done under the act of 1933. The first of these is the Soil Conservation and Domestic Allotment Act. This act contains important provisions on conservation, a subject on which Congress has undoubted power to legislate, and thus avoids the shoals on which the first adjustment act was wrecked. Incidentally, and this is the main point, the Conservation Act provides for the payment of rewards to farmers who divert a part of their land from such soil-depleting crops as corn, cotton, tobacco, and wheat to such soil-building crops as alfalfa, clover, and peas.

THE AGRICULTURAL ADJUSTMENT ACT OF 1938. Big crops during the recession of 1937 and 1938 piled up on the agricultural surpluses of the de-

[12] See United States v. Butler, 297 U.S. 1. Also this volume, p. 667.

pression. Farmers were saying again, and bitterly, "Bumper crops, yes, the bigger the crop the harder the bump." Something more than the Conservation Act of 1936 was necessary to hold up the price of farm commodities. The solution offered was the Agricultural Adjustment Act of 1938, a very comprehensive, "all aid to the farmer short of war," piece of legislation. Payments to farmers who participate in the soil conservation program continue. More significant, when approved by two thirds of the growers, acreage quotas for states, counties, and individual farmers are fixed for any particular crop, and marketing quotas for the crop are fixed for any year in which that crop promises to exceed the normal crop by a certain percentage. For complying with this plan farmers receive their parity payments; that is, by mortgaging a crop to the Commodity Credit Corporation they can get a check up to 90 per cent of the parity value of their crop (under the Second World War amendment to the Adjustment Act they were allowed that much), parity being determined by the price of the crop during the period 1909–1914 plus the rise in the cost of living since that date. Notice that parity payments are not determined by dollars as of the date mentioned but by what the dollars would buy at that time. Thus, if prices are up 50 per cent, the farmer gets 50 per cent more dollars in parity payments than he would have received for his crop in "noninflated" dollars in 1909–1914. If the price of the commodity later goes above the amount of the loan, the farmer may repay the loan and sell his goods on the market. If the price goes below the amount of the loan, the farmer is glad to forget it, and the Commodity Credit Corporation takes the loss. This is the nonrecourse (heads I win, tails you lose) feature of the loan.

Under the Steagall (wartime) Amendment to the Adjustment Act farmers were guaranteed the liberal price supports indicated above until December 31, 1948. The same generous policy has been followed by Congress in later farm legislation. The most recent measure, the Agricultural Act of 1949, changes some formulas, but the basic principle remains—liberal price supports for farm commodities.

In bumper-crop years prices obviously will tend to be low, and the Commodity Credit Corporation will, therefore, purchase large quantities of farm commodities. These it will store up for the years of scarcity, when it will sell them on the market. This is the way the ever-normal granary is supposed to be maintained. Of course, if there are too many bumper crops the granary might burst its sides and the government would find itself suffering considerable loss on these price support payments. Indeed it seems quite certain that large losses are now being incurred. The potato price support program, one of the most uneconomical, cost the government about $500,000,000 up to January 1, 1950. At the time the Secretary of Agriculture published this figure, he announced that he would dump be-

BUDGET EXPENDITURES: AGRICULTURE AND AGRICULTURAL RESOURCES

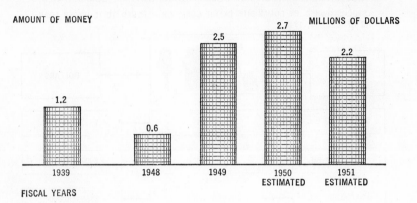

AMOUNT OF MONEY

MILLIONS OF DOLLARS

FISCAL YEARS

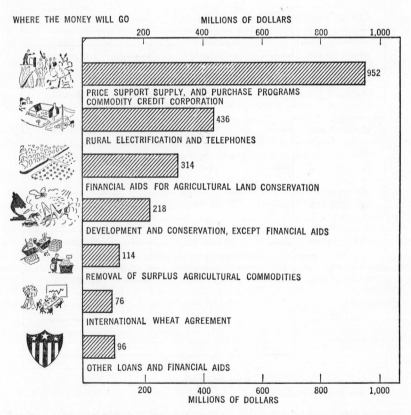

WHERE THE MONEY WILL GO

MILLIONS OF DOLLARS

952

PRICE SUPPORT SUPPLY, AND PURCHASE PROGRAMS
COMMODITY CREDIT CORPORATION

436

RURAL ELECTRIFICATION AND TELEPHONES

314

FINANCIAL AIDS FOR AGRICULTURAL LAND CONSERVATION

218

DEVELOPMENT AND CONSERVATION, EXCEPT FINANCIAL AIDS

114

REMOVAL OF SURPLUS AGRICULTURAL COMMODITIES

76

INTERNATIONAL WHEAT AGREEMENT

96

OTHER LOANS AND FINANCIAL AIDS

MILLIONS OF DOLLARS

From Bureau of the Budget, *The Federal Budget in Brief, Fiscal Year 1951*, p. 23.

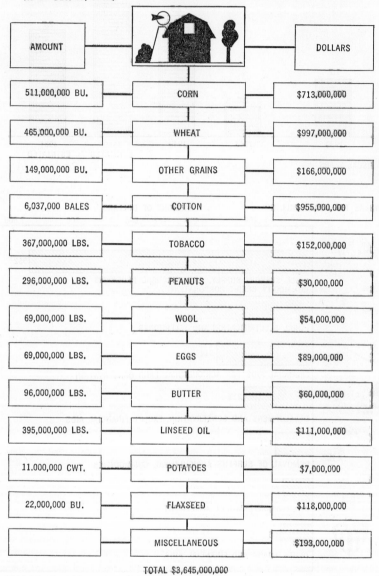

GOVERNMENT'S 3.6-BILLION-DOLLAR STAKE IN FARM COMMODITIES

(STOCKS OWNED BY COMMODITY CREDIT CORP. OR PLEDGED TO IT UNDER LOAN, AS OF DEC. 31, 1949.)

AMOUNT		DOLLARS
511,000,000 BU.	CORN	$713,000,000
465,000,000 BU.	WHEAT	$997,000,000
149,000,000 BU.	OTHER GRAINS	$166,000,000
6,037,000 BALES	COTTON	$955,000,000
367,000,000 LBS.	TOBACCO	$152,000,000
296,000,000 LBS.	PEANUTS	$30,000,000
69,000,000 LBS.	WOOL	$54,000,000
69,000,000 LBS.	EGGS	$89,000,000
96,000,000 LBS.	BUTTER	$60,000,000
395,000,000 LBS.	LINSEED OIL	$111,000,000
11.000,000 CWT.	POTATOES	$7,000,000
22,000,000 BU.	FLAXSEED	$118,000,000
	MISCELLANEOUS	$193,000,000

TOTAL $3,645,000,000

Basic data: *Agriculture Dept.*

tween 25,000,000 and 40,000,000 bushels back on the farmer. Now these potatoes had cost the government an average of $1.25 a bushel in price supports, but the farmer was to get them for one cent a hundred pounds. He could use them for fertilizer or livestock feed, but none could be sold for human consumption. The potatoes would be dyed to prevent that. The consumers and taxpayers, having lost $500,000,000 in supporting the farmers' prices for potatoes, still had to pay 5 or 6 cents a pound for them at the market.[13]

KEEPING UP POTATO PRICES: COST TO THE GOVERNMENT

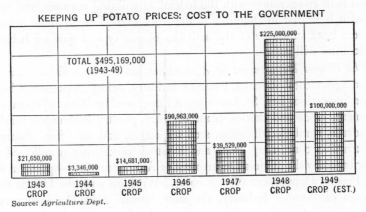

Source: *Agriculture Dept.*

Reprinted from the *U.S. News & World Report* (Feb. 17, 1950), an independent weekly magazine on national and international affairs, published at Washington. Copyright, 1950, United States News Publishing Corporation.

THE BRANNAN PLAN. Large producers (those who are sometimes referred to as factory-type farmers), their principal organization—The American Farm Bureau Federation—most congressmen, and the majority of conservatives prefer the price support system to other forms of aid to farmers. Although many family-type farmers are members of the Farm Bureau, small farmers in the main prefer some other method of assistance, as do the workers in the cities and some other people. Charles F. Brannan, the Secretary of Agriculture, has proposed a different plan. Technicalities aside, the Brannan Plan proposes that farmers accept soil-conservation practices, acreage allotments, and marketing quotas. There is nothing new in these. It would give the farmer the income to make his purchasing power what it was during the past ten years. There is nothing revolutionary about that either. But then the plan would reduce its subsidy benefits as farm operations became larger. That is something different. And it would let the eggs, the cheese, the butter, and other commodities find their own price level on store shelves. The idea seems to be that if the taxpayer

[13] See news releases of Feb. 3, 1950.

is to bear the cost of higher farm income, let him be compensated in lower prices. This may be too simple as explained. It may not be the answer to the question, "How can we help the farmer and at the same time reap some benefit for others?" But the system now in operation is not the answer either.

State services to agriculture. Every state has an executive department, or board, fully occupied with carrying out numerous statutes enacted primarily for the purpose of benefiting the farmer.[14]   A great deal of this state effort is in co-operation with the federal agricultural agencies, and nearly all of it is similar in character to the work carried on by those agencies. Here a brief summary of the activities of one typical state on behalf of agriculture will suffice.

The Illinois Department of Agriculture has fourteen divisions, as follows: agricultural statistics, livestock industry, apiary inspection, Chicago grain inspection, East St. Louis grain inspection, institutional farm management, foods and dairies, plant industry, poultry husbandry, markets, standards, rural electrification, seed inspection, and state fair. Statistical information concerning crops and livestock production is collected and distributed by the Illinois Department of Agriculture in co-operation with the Federal Department of that name. Working with the United States Bureau of Animal Industry, the state bureau assists herd owners in emergencies, disseminates information on the diseases of animals, promotes cattle testing, and in various other ways makes itself useful to stockmen of the state. The 30,000 beekeepers of the state are served by the division of apiary inspection, a division operated primarily for the eradication of the bee disease known as "American foulbrood." The division of foods and dairies administers the licensing law applicable to those industries engaged in various types of food business, and it is charged with the duty of enforcing the laws applicable to food products, concentrated feeding stuffs, fertilizers, cold storage plants, paints and oils, commission merchants, poultry dealers, egg dealers, and wood alcohol labeling. It battles the roadside sale of impure milk, destroys cream unfit for consumption, and stops livestock rackets at county fairs.

The division of plant industry co-operates with the United States Department in appropriate ways, and seeks to prevent the introduction into, and the dissemination within, the state of insect pests and plant diseases. It inspects all plant nurseries in the state, gives certificates to nurseries found to be free from harmful pests, abates infestation nuisances of plant pests, enforces the plant quarantine laws, and in other ways seeks to protect plant life. The poultry industry of Illinois is served by the division of that name. It lays particular stress upon its regulation of the Illinois

[14] See *Book of the States, 1950–1951,* pp. 398–440.

Hatchery Plan, a plan designed to build a high standard for hatchery chicks and to serve as a protection to the farmer who purchases baby chicks. It assists the state institution farms with their poultry projects and promotes the "Illinois egg laying contest." The principal duties of the division of markets consist of enforcing the grading and packing features of the state's standardization law; the administration of the agricultural co-operative act and the law governing the storage of grain; and providing shipping point inspection service on fruits and vegetables, and butter and egg grading services under State-Federal inspection agreements. No mention has been made of the work of several other divisions of the Illinois Department of Agriculture, but the summaries of the principal responsibilities and duties of those mentioned serve to indicate the wide variety of activities the state undertakes in the interest of agriculture and, to some extent, in the interest of the consumer.[15]

II. CONSERVATION OF NATURAL RESOURCES [16]

The natural resources of the United States, as to variety, quantity, and quality, are not equaled by those of any other country. Formerly, we thought the supply would never be exhausted; that Mother Earth would replenish her treasures as fast as we took them from her. Not a few still seem to be guided by this faith. But the more intelligent, many of whom are in official places, belong to a "faithless" generation as far as natural resources are concerned. They believe that future (and futile) mourning over their loss can be avoided only by heroic measures of conservation in this generation.

Land settlement. We started our national existence with untold acres of public land. Even now there are several hundred millions of acres of such land, and one of the principal functions of the Department of the Interior is to administer the laws respecting it. Two of the pressing problems of the new nation were to get money with which to pay its debts and to get settlers on the land. The sale of public lands at very low prices brought in some revenue, and it was an important factor in the rapid economic and social development of the country; but it was not infrequently attended by the gravest scandals. Land speculation was very common, relatively perhaps as common as speculation in stocks in the nineteen twenties. The land companies bought and sold land, often tainting both

---

[15] *Illinois Blue Book, 1947–1948*, pp. 445 ff.

[16] E. G. Cheyney and T. Schantz-Hansen, *This Is Our Land: The Story of Conservation in the United States* (1940); Dimock, *Business and Government*, Chs. 23–24; Fainsod and Gordon, *Government and the American Economy*, Ch. 20; C. H. Pritchett, *The Tennessee Valley Authority* (1943); *Reports of the Secretary of Agriculture and of the Secretary of the Interior.*

transactions with fraud and corruption. In 1862 a new policy was introduced—land would be given away to homesteaders, one hundred sixty acres
to go to any American citizen who would pay a small fee for the registration
of his claim and do a little work on the land for a period of five years.
Tens of millions of acres were taken up in this way, a plan that resulted in
placing many settlers in the territories. But speculators still had their
innings, securing lands from homesteaders, bona fide and often not, for less
than their actual value. Despite the abuses, the system was largely justified,
for it was certainly a speedy means of building our national empire.

Reclamation. When relatively little of the public land naturally suitable for agriculture remained, a policy of reclaiming desert land was instituted. There are millions of acres of such land in the United States.
Some of it is very rich. All it needs is water. At first Congress encouraged irrigation projects by extending aid to the states and private concerns;
but since 1902 it has authorized federal construction on the public domain,
the government to be repaid from funds raised by the sale of lands, royalties from oil leases, and later, receipts from irrigation and power contracts.
The Bureau of Reclamation, located in the Department of the Interior, has
general charge of this service. About 5,000,000 acres now receive water
from government irrigation projects, and the annual value of crops produced on these lands is above $400,000,000.

When we consider irrigation, the question naturally comes to mind,
Why should the government continue to reclaim land when, with the
land now under cultivation, the farmer in normal times is able to produce much more than he is able to sell at a fair price? Even before 1941,
irrigation frequently cost as much as $150 per acre, sometimes $200. Obviously, large benefits must be found before projects on such lands can be
made to pay. Several of the projects constructed have practically failed,
the settlers not being able to meet the very generous terms of their water
contracts. But there is another angle to the problem. Some of the Western states must rely heavily upon irrigation. Should the central government be willing to risk a loss in order to develop their resources? The
answer has often been "No," but very naturally it is not cheerfully accepted by the states concerned, and in recent years the federal government
has been more accommodating.

Then, too, irrigation does not stand by itself. Land reclamation is
only one phase of the great problem of conservation. Viewed broadly,
as the National Resources Planning Board viewed it, the problem is to
devise a plan that takes into consideration the "use of land, water, and
other national resources, in their physical, social, governmental, and economic aspects." Thus viewed, an irrigation project that might not prove

CROP VALUES ON RECLAMATION PROJECTS 1906-47 (CUMULATIVE)

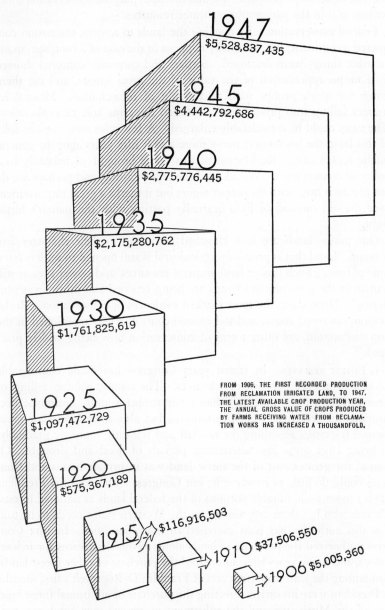

1947 $5,528,837,435

1945 $4,442,792,686

1940 $2,775,776,445

1935 $2,175,280,762

1930 $1,761,825,619

1925 $1,097,472,729

1920 $575,367,189

1915 $116,916,503

1910 $37,506,550

1906 $5,005,360

FROM 1906, THE FIRST RECORDED PRODUCTION FROM RECLAMATION IRRIGATED LAND, TO 1947, THE LATEST AVAILABLE CROP PRODUCTION YEAR, THE ANNUAL GROSS VALUE OF CROPS PRODUCED BY FARMS RECEIVING WATER FROM RECLAMATION WORKS HAS INCREASED A THOUSANDFOLD.

From the *Annual Report of the Secretary of the Interior,* 1948, p. 72.

to be a good economic venture for the government might yet be desirable because of its social benefits. Of this multiple purpose conservation more will be said in the paragraphs on water resources.

Federal conservation. By opening the lands to settlers, the nation conquered a continent; but, as usually happens in the case of a conquest, many valuable things were destroyed. Settlers and corporate concerns showed little or no appreciation of the value of the great forests, and cut them down for quick profits, with no thought of reforestation. Mineral resources falling into private hands suffered the same sort of exploitation. The story could be considerably enlarged. A few wise men saw the folly of this from the beginning; many more saw it fifty years ago; the general public sees it now. Realization of this waste brought us belatedly to a policy of conservation. We adopted the policy tardily, and perhaps we do not pursue it now with the proper vigor; but it marks a great improvement over the old method of light-heartedly parting with the nation's birthright.

Our public lands are now classified according to their character and content. Land that is primarily agricultural is still opened to settlers from time to time. Such timber land, mineral resources, and power sites as still remain in the government's hands are being retained and other areas purchased. These show the most marked evidences of conservation. Reclamation, discussed above, and soil erosion control, briefly mentioned in the previous section, are other forms of conservation now being widely practiced.[17]

1. FOREST RESERVES. In recent years Congress has made considerable effort to conserve our timber resources. The almost wanton felling of trees threatened not only to exhaust our timber supply, optimistic declarations to the contrary notwithstanding, but also, since forests are great natural reservoirs absorbing the rainfall and releasing moisture gradually, to bring large areas into alternating periods of flood and drought. Of course, the greater part of the forest land was in private hands and Congress could do little to conserve it; but Congress authorized the President (1891) to set aside suitable portions of the federal lands as national forests. No one who has done any touring in the Western states needs to be told that this authority has been exercised in many localities. In 1911 Congress authorized the purchase of lands along navigable streams for federal forests, and a few years later authorized the purchase of other forest lands. Not among the least important acts of Franklin D. Roosevelt's first months as President were his orders directing the purchase of additional forest land east of the Mississippi and the enlistment of 275,000 men for forest conservation projects.

[17] Great national parks, such as Yellowstone and Glacier, also represent a form of conservation.

The Forest Service, formerly in the Department of the Interior but now in the Department of Agriculture, administers 152 national forests covering approximately 200,000,000 acres. It protects the forests from insects and disease and, but for careless hunters, fishermen, loggers, and campers, would succeed much better than it does in fire prevention and control. It scientifically regulates the grazing of livestock on the range; manages water-

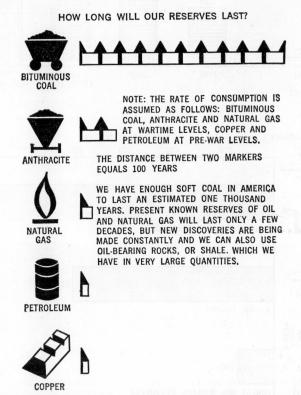

HOW LONG WILL OUR RESERVES LAST?

BITUMINOUS COAL

NOTE: THE RATE OF CONSUMPTION IS ASSUMED AS FOLLOWS: BITUMINOUS COAL, ANTHRACITE AND NATURAL GAS AT WARTIME LEVELS, COPPER AND PETROLEUM AT PRE-WAR LEVELS.

ANTHRACITE

THE DISTANCE BETWEEN TWO MARKERS EQUALS 100 YEARS

WE HAVE ENOUGH SOFT COAL IN AMERICA TO LAST AN ESTIMATED ONE THOUSAND YEARS. PRESENT KNOWN RESERVES OF OIL AND NATURAL GAS WILL LAST ONLY A FEW DECADES, BUT NEW DISCOVERIES ARE BEING MADE CONSTANTLY AND WE CAN ALSO USE OIL-BEARING ROCKS, OR SHALE. WHICH WE HAVE IN VERY LARGE QUANTITIES.

NATURAL GAS

PETROLEUM

COPPER

From Twentieth Century Fund, *U.S.A.: Measure of a Nation* (Macmillan, 1949), p. 85.

sheds so as to reduce flood damage and soil erosion and protect the sources of water for domestic supply and other purposes; takes some responsibility for the development of wildlife; and makes provision for outdoor recreation for "human life." At its forest and range experiment stations it conducts research and investigations on the many phases of forestry; and through these stations and the main office it co-operates with state and private owners of forest lands in the application of sound management practices, in the distribution of planting stock to farmers for windbreaks, shelterbelts, and farm woodlands, in organized protection against fire, and in other ways.[18]

[18] *U.S. Govt. Org. Manual*, 1950–51, pp. 228–229.

BUDGET EXPENDITURES: NATURAL RESOURCES NOT PRIMARILY AGRICULTURAL

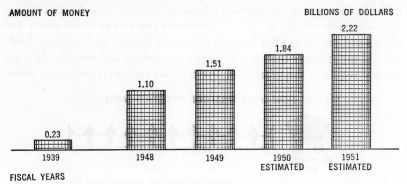

AMOUNT OF MONEY   BILLIONS OF DOLLARS

1939	1948	1949	1950 ESTIMATED	1951 ESTIMATED
0.23	1.10	1.51	1.84	2.22

FISCAL YEARS

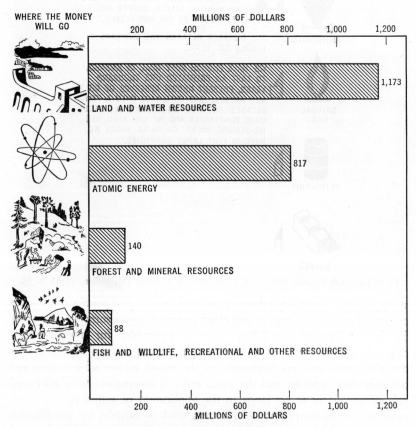

WHERE THE MONEY WILL GO   MILLIONS OF DOLLARS

LAND AND WATER RESOURCES — 1,173

ATOMIC ENERGY — 817

FOREST AND MINERAL RESOURCES — 140

FISH AND WILDLIFE, RECREATIONAL AND OTHER RESOURCES — 88

MILLIONS OF DOLLARS

From Bureau of the Budget, *The Federal Budget in Brief, Fiscal Year 1951*, p. 25.

Wars take a heavy toll of forests as they do of all other resources. They use up material at a terrific rate. Before the Second World War the best scientific estimate of the annual timber growth, after deductions for losses by fire, insects, and disease, placed it just over nine billion cubic feet. The annual timber cut was estimated at over eleven billion cubic feet, thus exceeding the growth by two billion cubic feet. The annual cut during the war was about 30 per cent above the prewar cut, thus giving foresters and all the rest of us something to worry about. More growth, more fire and disease prevention, more economical use of forest resources comprise the answer.[19]

2. MINERALS. Just as the national government had freely parted with our timber lands prior to 1891, so it disposed of our mineral lands. The result in both cases was the same—prodigality, shameless waste. But since 1910, following the policy earlier initiated with respect to forests, the government has shown more disposition to conserve its mineral resources. No longer are mineral lands sold or given away. The government expressly reserves for itself the minerals under the soils that it sells for agricultural purposes. Mineral lands may be leased for mining by private companies, but such exploitation must be under government control and royalties must be paid into the national treasury. Whatever the merits of unhindered private ownership and development may be, Congress decreed by an act of 1920 that ownership of the public mineral lands should remain with the government. The Bureau of Mines, now back in its original Department, the Interior Department, performs most important functions for the government and the mining industry by conducting experiments and distributing information on various phases of mining. During the last war this Bureau examined hundreds of deposits of strategic and critical materials in 48 states and discovered new reserves of iron, antimony, chromium, manganese, tungsten, and other ores.[20]

Petroleum resources. The difficulties of preserving our natural resources are well illustrated by the reckless exploitation of the petroleum supply. According to Harold L. Ickes, former Secretary of the Interior, "compared with oil, we have been as frugal as a Scotsman in the management of our other natural resources."[21] Oil has been taken from the ground with little thought of future needs. Conservationists have warned that the supply is limited; that in 40, 50, or 60 years it will be seriously depleted. But oil kings have replied that when "such prophets of disaster as Pinchot and his faction" have died and are forgotten, there will be plenty of oil for our children's children. They also denounce the conservationists for "hurting

---

[19] *Report of the Secretary of Agriculture,* 1945, pp. 141 ff.
[20] *U.S. Government Manual,* First Edition, 1946, p. 264.
[21] In *The New York Times,* June 11, 1933, sec. 8, p. 1.

business." In normal times it is good business—good temporary business—to believe that the "cruse of oil will never fail," for that belief justifies rapid exploitation. But nearly all of our reputable geologists tell us that this is a vain hope born of a burning desire for quick profits. Indeed, many petroleum refiners know that the oil resources in the United States, large as they are, are very definitely limited. Proof of this is found in the very active efforts made by officials of great oil companies to secure the backing of the government in their exploitations of foreign oil fields.[22]

In recent years the oilmen have learned that too much oil can be produced. New gushing wells flooded the market during depression years, bringing the price so low that wells were operated at a loss. The wells in east Texas alone, flowing at full capacity, could supply the nation's normal demand. With the great surplus (accompanied by much greater waste) created by the 400,000 wells in the country, it is not difficult to understand why oil has sold for 25 cents per barrel—in at least one case for as low as 4 cents. The representatives of this industry, the second in the land, tried to reach agreements to limit production, but a minority group always nullified such voluntary plans of co-operation. Some states legislated, but this legislation proved ineffective because the oil industry is too big and powerful to be handled by the action of individual states.

In the spring of 1933 the President, the Secretary of the Interior, and Congress were asked to act. The result was that the oil industry received special attention in the National Industrial Recovery Act. Among other powers given the President to regulate the industry was a very significant one authorizing him to prohibit the transportation in interstate and foreign commerce of petroleum and its products produced in excess of the amount permitted by state law. But the first New Deal legislation to receive the judicial veto was the oil control section of NIRA. The Supreme Court held that the power to prohibit the shipment of "hot oil," which the oil control section gave the President, was a delegation of legislative power and therefore unconstitutional.[23] Congress then passed another law. This time it delegated no authority, but went straight to the heart of the matter by prohibiting the shipment in interstate and foreign commerce of oil produced in excess of the quotas permitted under state law.

If the Second World War did not teach us that the supply of oil is exhaustible, it at least brought home to the most selfish and thoughtless the fact that demands on oil resources and transportation may produce a temporary scarcity, and very quickly. In 1942 the President established the Petroleum Administration for War and designated the Secretary of the

---

[22] See J. Ise, *The United States Oil Policy* (1927).
[23] Panama Refining Co. v. Ryan, 293 U.S. 388 (1935).

Interior as Administrator. This war agency was given the assignment of co-ordinating the government's petroleum policies and providing oil for the prosecution of the war and other essential purposes. To carry out these functions it was given broad authority respecting conservation, rationing, and shipment of petroleum. Most of our cars stayed off the highways, a few of us shivered a bit in our homes, but no one suffered as the armed forces and the essential industries were receiving their oil.

3. WATER RESOURCES.[24] If our forest and mineral resources have been wasted by extravagant use, our water resources have been wasted by lack of use. Our rivers can be used for domestic, industrial, and commercial purposes—to produce electric power; to irrigate arid lands; to provide a highway for water-borne trade; to supply a home for commercially valuable fish, such as salmon; and to provide recreation. Uncontrolled and unprotected, rivers are subject to pollution, and occasionally they devastate the country with floods.

Federal regulation respecting power sites. Although Congress gave some attention to water uses from the earliest times and started its irrigation projects as long ago as 1902, its first major concern with water use in the modern sense was indicated in respect to hydroelectric power, an industry that was rapidly growing to large proportions even before the First World War. Most of this development was directed by private concerns. In 1920, in the interest of power conservation, Congress passed the Federal Water Power Act, a comprehensive measure relating to the use of water power on public lands and navigable streams and creating a Federal Power Commission composed of the Secretaries of Agriculture, the Interior, and War. An act of 1930 created a new commission with enlarged powers, its five members to be appointed by the President and the Senate. When hydroelectric construction, whether private or municipal, is proposed on a location within the scope of the Power Act, a license must be secured from the Commission, such license to run not more than fifty years. The Commission is empowered to regulate rates, services, and the issue of securities by companies so licensed, provided state regulatory bodies lack the necessary powers.

The authority of the Commission has been considerably widened by recent legislation. The Public Utility Act of 1935 gives it jurisdiction not only over water-power projects on navigable streams or affecting interstate or foreign commerce, as previously provided, but also over the interstate movement of all electric energy. In other words, the Power Commission became a sort of interstate commerce commission for the regulation of rates and services of interstate electric-power companies. The Natural

[24] Nearly all the material on water resources was prepared by my colleague Doctor Daniel M. Ogden, Jr., who has made an extensive study of the subject.

Gas Act of 1938 extends the power of the Commission to that commodity as the act of 1935 extended to the Commission the authority to regulate electric energy moving in interstate commerce. The Commission is also given certain supervisory duties in respect to the administration of the Tennessee Valley Authority, Bonneville Dam, and Fort Peck Dam. The Commission had the tremendous task of mobilizing the electric power of the United States to meet the demands of the war industries.

Federal multiple-purpose projects. The regulation undertaken by the Federal Power Commission is of minor importance when compared with the government's multiple-purpose projects, developments that include irrigation, flood control, navigation, hydroelectric power, and other water uses. The first multiple-purpose (really only dual purpose, but that was significant) project was constructed in 1906 by the Reclamation Service on the Salt River. There some water was diverted for irrigation, and other water was used to generate electric power for pumping and for commercial sale to help pay for the project. To dispose of the power, Congress provided that preference should be given to electric-distribution bodies that were publicly or co-operatively owned.

The Tennessee Valley Development, the first major multiple-purpose effort had its inception during the First World War, in the construction of Wilson Dam at Muscle Shoals on the Tennessee River. The project was designed to generate power for the manufacture of nitrates for explosives and to improve navigation. Built by the Army Engineers, it was completed in 1925. Since nitrates were then no longer in heavy demand by the Army, it sold the power for whatever it could get to the nearest privately owned electric-distribution companies. Efforts were made in the 'twenties to induce the federal government to lease the dam, to lease the power generating facilities, or otherwise to step out of the power-generating field. Even Henry Ford bid for the plant. But all such proposals were stoutly resisted by Senator George W. Norris and his supporters. At Senator Norris' insistence, Congress twice enacted legislation providing for permanent federal operation of the plant, but the idea of "the government in business" brought prompt vetoes from Presidents Coolidge and Hoover.

In May, 1933, Senator Norris saw his hopes brought to fruition. With the strong backing of the Roosevelt Administration, Congress established a conservation project embracing the entire Tennessee River and its six principal tributaries, which included parts of seven states. Instead of assigning conservation duties to functional agencies, such as forest conservation to the Forest Service and navigation to the Army Engineers, Congress created the Tennessee Valley Authority to administer all federal natural resource development activities in the Tennessee Valley. An

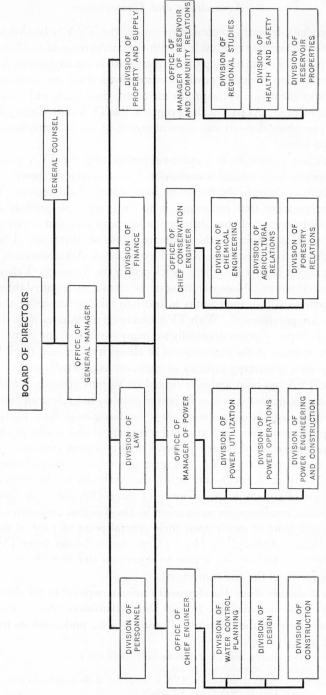

TENNESSEE VALLEY AUTHORITY

BOARD OF DIRECTORS

GENERAL COUNSEL

OFFICE OF GENERAL MANAGER

DIVISION OF PERSONNEL

DIVISION OF LAW

DIVISION OF FINANCE

DIVISION OF PROPERTY AND SUPPLY

OFFICE OF CHIEF ENGINEER

OFFICE OF MANAGER OF POWER

OFFICE OF CHIEF CONSERVATION ENGINEER

OFFICE OF MANAGER OF RESERVOIR AND COMMUNITY RELATIONS

DIVISION OF WATER CONTROL PLANNING

DIVISION OF DESIGN

DIVISION OF CONSTRUCTION

DIVISION OF POWER UTILIZATION

DIVISION OF POWER OPERATIONS

DIVISION OF POWER ENGINEERING AND CONSTRUCTION

DIVISION OF CHEMICAL ENGINEERING

DIVISION OF AGRICULTURAL RELATIONS

DIVISION OF FORESTRY RELATIONS

DIVISION OF REGIONAL STUDIES

DIVISION OF HEALTH AND SAFETY

DIVISION OF RESERVOIR PROPERTIES

From *U.S. Government Organization Manual,* 1950-51, p. 528.

independent, federally owned corporation, the TVA is headed by three directors chosen by the President with the concurrence of the Senate. Its main purposes are to develop the Tennessee River for navigation, flood control, generation of electric power consistent with flood and navigation control, experimentation in the proper use of marginal lands, and reforestation development.[25] As part of this program, the TVA is producing fertilizer from phosphate deposits and is encouraging its use by demonstrations on selected farms.

Especially significant is a provision authorizing the TVA to construct and operate high-voltage transmission lines to carry the power from its twenty-three dams to the important load centers of the region. The law further provides that preference is to be granted to publicly and co-operatively owned electric distribution agencies and that a rate is to be established to encourage the widespread use of electricity. Under the stimulus of loans from the Rural Electrification Administration, farmer co-operatives rapidly have been developed in the Tennessee Valley to buy the federal power. Moreover, most of the cities have acquired the distribution systems within their limits in order to take advantage of the public preference provisions.[26] With TVA encouragement, rates were fixed that slashed electricity prices drastically for many customers, and there followed a huge upsurge in the consumption of electricity. In 1949 the TVA had an installed generating capacity of 2,500,000 kilowatts.[27]

The TVA has been and is criticized on various grounds, but the principal charge against it is that its power rates do not reflect all costs. The Authority allocates costs among those for navigation, flood control, electric power, and other purposes; and it is charged that it allocates too little for the generation of electric power. In 1939 a joint committee of Congress investigated the TVA and gave a somewhat inconclusive report, the majority substantially sustaining the Authority in the matter of the allocation of costs, but the minority of three (Republicans) dissented.[28] The debate continues, the sides taken by the different authorities seeming to depend quite as much upon their general point of view as upon any other factor. Although the Hoover Commission did not slight TVA in its investigations and reports, it may be significant that it made no comment on the merits of the rate controversy.

The Colorado River Development came in response to the demands of the West for reclamation. In 1928 the Reclamation Service, which had been advanced to the status of a Bureau in 1923, undertook its most am-

[25] 48 *Stat.* 58 (1933).
[26] See C. Herman Pritchett, *The Tennessee Valley Authority* (1943).
[27] *U.S. Govt. Org. Manual,* 1949, p. 496.
[28] Joint Committee to Investigate the TVA, *Investigation of the Tennessee Valley Authority, Report* . . . Sen. Doc. 56, 76th Cong., 1st Sess.

bitious project, a power-irrigation development at Boulder Canyon on the Colorado River. This entailed the construction of the highest dam ever built by man, the Hoover Dam, to generate 1,322,000 kilowatts of electricity. Incidental benefits include flood control, recreation, and navigation improvement. Irrigation for California, Arizona, and Nevada, and domestic water for Los Angeles and vicinity have been provided by this and other projects, such as the Davis Dam farther downstream.

The Columbia River Power System had its origin in 1933, when the Public Works Administration authorized the Columbia Basin Reclamation Project, including the construction of Grand Coulee Dam on the upper Columbia River. The largest concrete structure ever built, Grand Coulee Dam proved to be the backbone of American aluminum production during the Second World War. When its eighteenth 108,000 kilowatt generator is installed in 1952, it will provide 1,944,000 kilowatts of hydroelectric power for commercial and irrigation use. Eventually, 1,200,000 acres in central Washington will be irrigated by water pumped from the dam.

In 1933 the Public Works Administration also authorized money with which the Army Engineers constructed a second dam, Bonneville Dam, on the Columbia River forty miles above Portland at Cascade Rapids in the scenic Columbia Gorge. This dam was to provide 518,400 kilowatts of electricity and, in response to rural and business demands of more than sixty years' standing, create slack water to The Dalles, a city in Oregon, as an aid to navigation on the Columbia River. In 1935, as Bonneville Dam neared completion, a major power-disposal question faced Congress. The Army Engineers were constructing one dam, the Bureau of Reclamation of the Department of the Interior another, on the same river. The dams were within easy transmission distance of each other, and serious doubt was being raised about the market for a block of power that more than doubled regional generating capacities. Moreover, engineers agreed that new transmission lines had to be built to carry the huge additional power supply, for the two dams then under construction would skim only the surface of the 25,000,000 kilowatt power potential of the Columbia River.[29]

After considerable debate over whether the dams should be operated separately or together for power purposes, whether the rates should be uniform everywhere power was sold or reflect transmission distance from the dams, whether the federal government should construct the needed new transmission lines, and what sort of agency should be assigned the task, Congress finally decided upon the same power policy as prevailed in the

[29] This constitutes approximately 40 per cent of the potential water power of the continental United States. Note that it is ten times greater than the TVA.

Tennessee Valley: federal transmission, a uniform low rate to encourage widespread use, and preference to publicly and co-operatively owned distribution agencies.[30] But to administer the law a "temporary" administrative compromise was worked out. The Army Engineers were to run Bonneville Dam and generate the electricity. The Army would then turn the power over to a new agency, the Bonneville Power Administration, to be established in the Department of the Interior, which would transmit and sell the power at wholesale to retail distribution agencies.[31] In 1940 the President extended this compromise to Grand Coulee Dam by Executive Order 8526, so that the Bureau of Reclamation generates power there which the Bonneville Power Administration also sells.[32]

The heavy demand for power caused by the development of aluminum industries in the Pacific Northwest and the erection of the federal plutonium plant at Hanford, Washington, during the war led to a critical regional power shortage and encouraged rapid expansion of federal power production. New dams are now under construction by both the Army Engineers and the Bureau of Reclamation, which will more than double the federal generating capacity in the region by 1956 and dwarf federal power production on the Tennessee River system.

During the Second World War, competition between the Army Engineers and the Bureau of Reclamation increased, partly because of mutual expansion and the extension of general flood control and drainage powers to the Army Engineers. Consequently, beginning in 1945, agitation developed in the Pacific Northwest for the creation of a Columbia Valley Authority patterned on the Tennessee model to unify water resource development for the region. In January, 1949, President Truman endorsed the plan and directed the interested agencies to draft a bill for regional unification of water-resource development responsibilities. As a proposal to create a Columbia Valley Administration, it was introduced April 16 of that year. Earnest and lengthy debate over its merits followed.

The Missouri Basin Development represents another multiple use of rivers. On the Missouri River, which flows through dehydrated eastern Montana, North Dakota, and South Dakota, the Army Engineers erected Fort Peck Dam in Montana during Roosevelt's first Administration. With the water made available by this project the Bureau of Reclamation has undertaken an ambitious program of irrigation. In its lower reaches

[30] See Daniel M. Ogden, Jr., "The Development of Federal Power Policy in the Pacific Northwest," (Unpublished Ph.D. Dissertation, Department of Political Science, University of Chicago, 1949), Ch. VII.

[31] *U.S. Statutes at Large,* Vol. L, Part I, p. 731 (1937) as amended.

[32] U.S. Congress, Senate and House, *Columbia Power Administration,* Joint Hearings before Subcommittees of the Committee on Commerce, U.S. Senate, and the Committee on Rivers and Harbors, House of Representatives, 77th Cong., 2d Sess., on S. bill 2430 and H.R. bills 6889 and 6890, June 3–19, 1942, pp. 68–69.

the Missouri is being developed for navigation, flood control, and power by the Army Engineers. The clashing needs of navigation and reclamation led to another interagency wrangle during the closing years of the Second World War and to a proposal that a Missouri Valley Authority be created to unify water-resource development administration in that region. Similar proposals have been recommended to end the clashes apparently caused by divided responsibility in the Central Valley in California, and on the Arkansas River.

Inter-agency committees have been organized to bring harmony among the agencies having conflicting powers in important river basins. Such committees were set up in the Missouri basin in 1944 and in the Columbia basin in 1946. But inefficiency is inherent in a system that delegates functional responsibility for different aspects of the development of each river to more than one agency, especially when such agencies are divided not only among bureaus but among several departments and independent commissions as well. This problem engaged the attention of the Hoover Commission, which offered this comment and recommendation:

> The [inter-agency] committees have failed to solve any important aspects of the problem . . . because the dominant members, the Corps and the Bureau, have been unwilling to permit inter-agency committees to settle their differences. The result has been neglect or avoidance by the committees of virtually all major areas of inter-agency conflict, and concentration instead on technical studies and publicity. . . .
>
> There is simply no escaping the fact that so long as the present over-lapping of functions exists with respect to the Corps of Engineers, the Bureau of Reclamation, and the Federal Power Commission, costly duplication, confusion, and competition are bound to result. It has been demonstrated time and again that neither by voluntary cooperation nor by executive coordination can the major conflicts be ironed out. . . .
>
> We recommend that the rivers and harbors and flood control activities of the Corps of Engineers be transferred to the Department of the Interior.[33]

Since the federal power-disposal policy decisions taken in the TVA Act and the Bonneville Act and reiterated in the Flood Control Act of 1944 as general nation-wide policy have been sustained despite recent attempts to reverse them,[34] and since the Department of the Interior is now uniformly responsible for power disposal except in the Tennessee Valley, future struggles over federal water-resource development seem destined to center on the

[33] The Commission on Organization of the Executive Branch of the Government, *Reorganization of the Department of the Interior* (1949), pp. 29–35.

[34] See U.S. Congress, House, *Amending Section 5 of the Flood Control Act of 1944 Transferring Jurisdiction of Hydroelectric Power Projects to War Department and Federal Power Commission*, Hearings before Committee on Public Works, House of Representatives, 80th Congress, 1st Sess., on H.R. 3036, June 4–July 7, 1947.

type of administrative organization—river valley authorities or other agencies—best suited to give maximum efficiency.

Federal planning. Although Americans have had some experience with planning, especially in cities, we have been very slow to come to the realization that the best use of our national resources can be brought about only after careful studies of those resources have been made and plans for their development have been formulated and adopted. With this idea in mind the President, in 1934, established the National Resources Board. This agency, later designated the National Resources Planning Board, had only advisory functions, but they were comprehensive. Its duties, among others, were: (1) to prepare and make available to the President, with recommendations, data and plans that might be helpful to a planned development and use of land, water, mineral, and other national resources, and such related subjects as might be referred to it by the President; (2) to co-operate with governmental agencies, federal, state, and local, and with any public or private planning or research agencies, in carrying out any of its duties; (3) to record all proposed federal projects involving the acquisition of land and land research projects and to provide the agencies concerned with information pertinent to the projects.

POSTWAR EFFORTS. In 1942–1943 the National Resources Planning Board, naturally enough, began to devote its major efforts to war and postwar problems. Its comprehensive reports—*National Resources Development Report for 1943* and *Security, Work, and Relief*—surveying the postwar scene and making recommendations, created some discussion among serious people, but with the general public they were widely *unread* documents. As for congressmen, they had been growing more and more suspicious of plans and planners as the depression grew dimmer in their memories. And here were these reports dealing with such topics as full employment, social security, health, and recreation—"more New Deal stuff." As a matter of fact, the reports were essentially conservative; at no point did they denounce "free enterprise" or the "American way." In any event, one might think that congressmen would not object to having before them the results of the research of the National Resources Planning Board. But their response to the Board's reports was to abolish the Board at the end of 1943 by cutting off its funds, and to make certain that they would hear no more of planning they specifically declared that the functions of the Board should not be transferred to any other agency! [35] Of course congressmen recognize the necessity for at least a minimum of planning, but they seem to prefer to do it through their own committees and without the aid of experts who belong, as the members of the National Resources Planning Board did, to the Executive Office of the President.

[35] 57 Stat. 169.

State conservation. Supplementing the work of the national government and co-operating with it in a number of functions, the state conservation services are not insignificant. In a number of states such services are gathered into a single department in accordance with the national plan of placing most of these functions in the Department of the Interior. In other states they may be scattered among various boards and commissions. Whatever the organization may be, the administrators are charged with numerous duties and powers respecting irrigation, drainage, mineral resources, forests, fish and game, parks, and so on.

THE NORTH CAROLINA SYSTEM. A suitable example of a state conservation program is found in North Carolina. It has a Department of Conservation and Development, headed by a Director who is advised by a Board. For convenience of administration the work of the Department is divided among several divisions. The Forestry Division is concerned with the 21,000,000 acres of land (most of it privately owned) in timber of some kind or best adapted to the growth of timber. Specifically, this service engages in the work of forest protection, including fire prevention, fire fighting, and the enlistment of "minute men" for the latter purpose; has charge of the forest nursery, from which it annually distributes to farmers at cost several hundred thousand seedlings for reforestation; administers the state parks and forests; and collects and distributes information on forest resources. For forest protection each state receives federal aid under the Clarke-McNary Act.

The Game Division protects the supply of bird and animal life and rehabilitates the wild life of the state by contributing to its increase. These functions it seeks to accomplish through education, the establishment of game refuges and sanctuaries, limiting the open seasons, and the like. The Division of Inland Fisheries is charged with the enforcement of laws applying primarily to sport fishermen, and the Commercial Fisheries Division with the enforcement of laws appropriate to its title. Both divisions co-operate with the United States Bureau of Fisheries in maintaining fish hatcheries.

The Water Resources Division makes surveys, keeps a close watch on power developments, gives special attention to future hydroelectric needs of the state, and co-operates with the Federal Power Commission, to mention only a few of its duties.

Certainly no less important than several other divisions named is the Division of Mineral Resources, which conducts geological surveys, identifies samples of minerals sent in from any section of the state, and publishes scientific bulletins.

To aid commerce and industry generally, a division under that title was established. It makes business surveys in various industries, keeps in close contact with chambers of commerce, and co-operates with the Federal Bureau of Foreign and Domestic Commerce where practicable. Finally, the Division of Public Relations advertises the state, not brazenly or at great expense, but commonly through news articles and photographs that are printed in papers and journals without expense to the commonwealth.

State planning. In the 'thirties planning boards or councils were established by nearly all the states, and some of these states united in forming regional planning commissions. The idea of planning was even adopted in some counties. State planning boards, largely through their full-time research staffs, made studies and recommendations on such subjects as population and population trends, land-use, housing, water resources, fiscal policies, and governmental organization.

Nearly all the states have a planning or development agency giving particular attention to the postwar period. The state planners seem to have less of a prophetic light in their eyes than the national planners of a few years ago; consequently, the former do not commonly arouse the fears of the legislatures. Furthermore, a state planning organization is often designated "economic board," "industrial commission," or "re-employment commission," terms that are familiar and down to earth. The states have developed plans for public works, and they have surveyed industrial opportunties, potential manpower, physical resources, and other factors. Although state plans have been directed primarily toward industrial expansion and re-employment, not excluded from such plans are education, medical care, and similar social services—subjects that in the National Resources Planning Board reports aroused the ire of Congress. Reports recommend the extension of a forest-park program and the re-organization of a public school system; a more intelligent utilization of agricultural and forest land and the extension of welfare activities; and means by which textile industries may be attracted to a state and ways by which housing may be improved. Planning we surely must have, government planning. Every business plans or goes to pot.

Reading List

Annual Reports of the Secretary of Agriculture; and *of the Secretary of the Interior.*

Department of Agriculture, *Miscellaneous Publications* No. 88 (1934), "The United States Department of Agriculture; Its Structure and Functions."

J. Cameron, *Development of Government Forest Control in the United States* (1928).

E. G. Cheyney and T. Schantz-Hansen, *This Is Our Land; The Story of Conservation in the United States* (1940).

Marshall E. Dimock, *Business and Government* (1949), Chs. 12–13, 23–24.

R. L. Duffus and C. Krutch, *The Valley and Its People: A Portrait of T.V.A.* (1944).

E. F. Dummeier and R. B. Heflebower, *Economics with Application to Agriculture* (1940 ed.).

Merle Fainsod and Lincoln Gordon, *Government and the American Economy* (1948 ed.), Chs. 5 and 20.

Herman Finer, *The T.V.A.: Lessons for International Application* (1944).

J. M. Gaus and L. O. Wolcott, *Public Administration and the U.S. Department of Agriculture* (1940).

T. S. Harding, *Two Blades of Grass . . .* (1947).

J. Ise, *United States Oil Policy* (1927).

J. E. Johnsen, comp., *Federal and State Control of Water Power* (1928).

P. L. Kleinsorge, *The Boulder Canyon Project; History and Economic Aspects* (1941).

J. D. Lewis, "Democratic Planning in Agriculture," *Am. Pol. Sci. Rev.,* XXXV, 232–249, 454–469 (April, June, 1941).

David Lilienthal, *T.V.A.—Democracy on the March* (1944).

S. G. McLendon, *History of the Public Domain of America* (1924).

C. E. Merriam, "The National Resources Planning Board: A Chapter in American Planning Experience," *Am. Pol. Sci. Rev.,* XXXVIII, 1075 (Dec., 1944).

C. H. Pritchett, *The Tennessee Valley Authority* (1943).

R. R. Renne, *Land Economics* (1947).

R. M. Robbins, *Our Landed Heritage: The Public Domain, 1776–1936* (1942).

T. W. Schultz, *Agriculture in an Unstable Economy* (1945).

D. H. Smith, *The Forest Service* (1930).

R. P. Teele, *The Economics of Land Reclamation* (1927).

Twentieth Century Fund, *Electric Power and Government Policy* (1948).

P. A. Waring and W. M. Teller, *Roots in the Earth* (1943).

A Water Policy for the American People. Summary of Recommendations from the Report of the President's Water Resources Policy Committee (1950).

W. W. Wilcox, *The Farmer and the Second World War* (1947).

Questions and Problems

1. Consult the latest *United States Government Organization Manual* and prepare a list of the government's scientific services for agriculture.
2. In view of the normal problem of agricultural surpluses, how can you justify aids to the farmer that result in his growing more?
3. Can it be said that the government has been relatively liberal in making credit available to the farmer?
4. Organize the story of agricultural marketing legislation since 1933.
5. What evidences are there that, despite our industrial civilization, the farmer still exercises a powerful influence upon government?
6. What is the government doing for the small farmer?

7. List the services to agriculture provided by your state.
8. Indicate some of the problems involved in the reclamation of arid lands.
9. What would constitute a fairly satisfactory forest conservation program?
10. *Have I not a right to do what I will with my own?* Answer this question in relation to the conservation of natural resources.
11. Discuss the economic and social implications of TVA.
12. Does your state or local government have a planning board or commission? If so, what has it (or they) achieved?
13. *America grew great without plans, and we don't want any plans now.* Subject this statement to careful analysis.

☆ 26 ☆

Security and Social Welfare

A MONG the functions of government that have been greatly expanded during the past century are police, fire, and health protection. A function of longer standing, and one that is ever present and baffling, is that of protecting the public morals. The social security function, essentially a new one, now takes much of our attention and a large share of our government budgets. Education as a public function had its beginning in some states in early colonial times, but the American public schools as we now know them are largely the product of the last seventy-five years. In this chapter we shall briefly review the above-named services.

I. POLICE AND FIRE PROTECTION [1]

Although other government jurisdictions are not unconcerned with the problems, the city has the primary responsibility for giving us police and fire protection.

The city police system: DEVELOPMENT OF THE POLICE SYSTEM. The great cities of the ancient world had fairly adequate police protection, but its almost complete absence in the mediaeval cities was one of the principal reasons why life in them was precarious. Indeed, the same lack of protection made the day unsafe and the night hideous in English cities until well into modern times. The only guardians of the law were the residents, who took turns walking the unlighted streets, perhaps whistling in futile attempts to hide their fear. Substantial citizens busy with their private affairs hired loafers and disabled men to take their turn as watchmen.

---

[1] A. W. Bromage, *Introduction to Municipal Government and Administration* (1950), Chs. XXV–XXVI; Federal Bureau of Investigation, *Standards of Police Training* (1939); Institute of Training in Municipal Administration (Chicago), *Municipal Fire Administration* (1942 ed.) and *Municipal Police Administration* (1943 ed.); A. F. Macdonald, *American City Government and Administration* (1946 ed.), Chs. 21–23.

In London, bellmen were chosen to supplement the watchmen, but they proved no more efficient. Both were the common subjects of jests, and rowdies often made them the victims of rough practical jokes. Crime flourished to such a degree that the London gentleman who had to be abroad at night took a guard with him. All this went on until 1839, when Robert Peel,[2] the Home Secretary in the British Cabinet, persuaded Parliament to create a professional police system. Hooted and jeered, occasionally violently assaulted, early policemen did not have a pleasant life, but it was not long until the high character of their work earned them the respect, even the affection, of the public.

Until after the middle of the nineteenth century American cities attempted to preserve order in the old English way, and with as little success. A group of students, having taken their examinations and "out to make an evening of it," might conclude the celebrations by beating up "the watch." A legislative investigation of conditions in New York City led to the adoption, in 1844, of a police system patterned after the new British model. As the New York force soon displayed greater energy in suppressing crime than the unorganized and undisciplined peace officers had shown, in the course of a few years practically all the larger cities followed the new model.

MODERN POLICE ORGANIZATION. The police in a few of the large cities are under state control. This arrangement is not unreasonable, since the policemen are engaged chiefly in enforcing state laws. But the cities bear the cost, and they usually resent state "interference" in their affairs. Consequently, municipal authorities are allowed to direct the police in nearly all cities. A board or a single commissioner has general charge of the city's police. The commissioner method, because it offers less opportunity for political manipulations and provides full-time service and unity of command, is commonly employed. Commissioners are rarely appointed from the force, men of broader experience and more general qualifications being preferred. Lawyers, doctors, real estate men, barbers, bankers, undertakers, and others are appointed to the post in rapid succession, two years being about the average tenure. The board or commissioner is charged with the broad duties of determining policy and organizing and managing the police force. In some cities the chief administrators must be guided by civil service rules in such matters as making appointments and promotions.

In immediate command of the police force is a chief of police, commonly selected from the force. Smaller cities usually do not feel the need of both commissioner and chief, and, in consequence, they frequently com-

---

2 Policemen were first called "Peelers" and "Bobbies," and later, because of their copper buttons, "coppers"—shortened to "cops" in America.

bine the functions of both officers in that of the chief of police. Attached to the headquarters of the chief are various inspectors, sergeants, and patrolmen. Stationed in precincts or districts are captains, with their lieutenants, sergeants, and patrolmen, each captain being a sort of chief in his district but very definitely responsible to the big chief at the central station. Large cities usually have intermediate units, divisions, one for every four or five precincts. The chief officer of a division is usually known as "inspector."

Police training. Formerly it was thought that policemen needed no special training. It was believed that physical strength and common sense, backed up by a club, a gun, and a pocket manual, made a patrolman. One commissioner explained how he fitted a man for the task: "I say to him that now he is a policeman, and I hope he will be a credit to the force. I tell him that he doesn't need anybody to tell him how to enforce the law; that all he needs to do is to go out on the street and keep his eyes open. I say 'You know the Ten Commandments, don't you? Well, if you know the Ten Commandments and you go out on your beat and you see somebody violating one of those Commandments, you can be sure that he is also violating some law.'"[3] Such grossly inadequate "training" gives us policemen as unprepared for ordinary patrol duty as the commissioner who gave it.

Years ago the Europeans learned that policemen should be trained, and they provided facilities for such training; but only in the past thirty years have American cities responded to this crying need. Many cities still leave their officers to follow their common sense and the Ten Commandments, although some of these easy-going municipalities select their men under civil service rules. Other cities, not discounting the importance of common sense or a knowledge of the Commandments, select their recruits by competitive examinations, and then give them instruction in police powers and duties, elementary law, rules of evidence, legal procedure, first aid, the handling of prisoners, criminal identification, report writing, and other subjects. The comprehensive three-year curriculum for police officers at Berkeley, California, has attracted wide attention, and it is commonly rated as among the best in the country, certainly as one of the few in-service curricula that represents a broad conception of desirable qualities in a police officer and an ambitious program to develop them.

But the best in-service training may fail to provide the best possible police officers. Modern police problems are so varied, so complicated, and the knowledge that can be brought to their solution so woven into the total fabric of our society that education in the arts and sciences no less than

[3] Quoted in Macdonald, *op. cit.,* p. 458 from *Report of the Sub-Committee on Police to the Crime Commission of New York State,* p. 27.

training in specific skills is now often recommended for future police officers. At least eight colleges and universities [4] now recognize this need to the extent that they offer degree programs in police science and administration.

Police duties. As the private soldier does the fighting for an army, so the patrolman is the principal law enforcer for the police department. He is on active duty eight hours a day, on reserve for another eight hours, and free the remaining time. On duty he may walk or use a motorcycle or an automobile, his means of transportation depending upon the character and length of his beat. He must cover his patrol within a certain designated time, keep his eyes open for violations of law, give particular attention to suspicious characters and disreputable places, and make arrests when necessary. Often a law is violated in such a trivial manner that an official warning accompanied by a smile is sufficient; another infraction may be of such a nature as to call for a stern reprimand; a third may be properly dealt with only by a prompt arrest. The patrolman is therefore a walking judge, handing out decisions in very minor cases and determining what cases are sufficiently grave to warrant regular legal prosecution. The patrolman must also serve as a sort of information bureau, report accidents, and carry out any special orders of his superiors. In recent years traffic regulation has become a special police problem. Bells, lights, "one-way streets," and "no U turns" all help; but personal supervision is necessary. Patrolmen are detailed from the regular force for this work, often after special training for it. To the average citizen the traffic officer is now a more familiar figure than the patrolman.

Major crimes are commonly committed by experts. The trails they leave can be followed only by officers of the law whose skill at detection is equal to the professional criminals' art of concealment. Patrolmen who seem to have an aptitude for this highly scientific work of investigation and detection are sometimes detailed for it, but the selection of the detective force by special civil service tests should give a better qualified personnel. The latter method is now used in a number of cities. Whatever the method of selection may be, the necessity for special training for this service is now generally recognized. Despite improvement in recent years, we are still behind the great European cities in the type of personnel attracted to the service and, following somewhat logically from this, in the application of science to detection.

CRITICISM OF THE POLICE SYSTEM. The police force of a typical American city is grossly inefficient. Crime flourishes, and few arrests are made. "The American professional criminal," says Professor A. F. Macdonald,

---

[4] Including the University of California, the University of Southern California, Indiana University, and the State College of Washington.

"soon learns that his occupation is safe as well as lucrative." [5] What is the reason for this? In 1931 the National Commission on Law Observance and Enforcement offered a number of reasons.[6] They are worth reproducing at some length:

(1) "The short and insecure term of office of the chief"—2.41 years in the great cities; "his control by the politicians whether linked in alliance with the criminals or not in his appointment and conduct of the office; his lack of independence; and frequently his incompetence for the place." No other city has such a fine record as Milwaukee for speedy detection, arrest, and trial of criminals. "The citizens there lay it to the fact that the city has had only two chiefs of police in 46 years and no control over the chief is ever attempted by the politicians."

(2) "The second outstanding evil of such poor police administration is the lack of competent, efficient, and honest patrolmen and subordinate officers. The latter are with rare exceptions selected or promoted from the rank and file of the patrolmen, possibly by reason of seniority, but more likely by direction of politicians whose private interests are to be subserved. Even where there are civil service examinations, the hand of the politician is all too plainly visible in such promotions." The patrolmen are selected "because of their partisan political activities or by civil service examinations, which can only remotely make certain of their qualifications for the discharge of their duties." Practically no effort is made to educate, train, and discipline them and to eliminate the incompetents. The patrolmen look to their political backers for retention and promotion in the service.[7]

(3) "The lack of efficient communication systems whereby intelligence of the commission of a crime and descriptions of the criminals may be quickly spread over a wide territory. . . . The tools for the detection, pursuit, and arrest of the criminal should be better than the equipment of the criminal in his commission of the crime and escape from the scene of it." The need for faster automobiles and especially for teletype and radio is emphasized. "We venture to state . . . that, with perhaps two exceptions, not a single police force of cities above 300,000 population has an adequate communication system and equipment essential in these days to meet the criminal on even equal terms." [8]

[5] *Op. cit.,* pp. 454–456.
[6] *Report* No. 14, pp. 1–9.
[7] It is fair to add that, since 1931 (the date of the Report), some cities have substantially raised entrance requirements and improved selection procedures.
[8] Beginning in 1930 the number of police radio systems increased rapidly. It can now be said that the police department of almost every community above 25,000 population in the United States is equipped with radio communication facilities or teletype, or both. In many cities, however, operating procedure is poorly organized and operational planning almost unknown.

(4) "The well-known and oft proven alliance between criminals and corrupt politicians which controls, in part, at least, where it does not wholly do so, the police force of our large cities, might well be taken as a primary cause for police inefficiency, since it rules the head and every subordinate, and lays a paralyzing hand upon determined action against such major criminals."

(5) "The excessively rapid growth of our cities in the past half century, together with the incoming of so many millions of immigrants, ignorant of our language, laws, and customs, and necessarily adhering, in their racial segregation in large cities, to the language and customs of their native lands, has immeasurably increased the difficulties of the police in detecting crime among the foreign born." (Notice that the Commission states only that it is difficult to detect crime among the foreign born. The charge commonly made that this element of the population is more given to crime than the native population is shown to be *false* by the same Commission in its tenth report, entitled "Crime and the Foreign Born.") For better detection of foreign-born criminals, the Commission suggests more policemen of non-English speaking nationalities and a force of secret service officers known only to the chief and reporting only to him.

(6) Finally, the Commission reports that "there are too many duties cast upon each officer and patrolman. This is the outcome of the transition from rural or small-town policing to city communities." It recommends "segregations of patrolmen under designated officers who would have charge of prevention and detection of specific crimes."

The Federal Bureau of Investigation. Other units of the government investigate postal violations, counterfeiting, and a few other crimes, but the FBI investigates alleged violations of some 120 federal statutes including the National Bank Act, the National Motor Vehicle Theft Act, the White Slave Traffic Act, and the Federal Kidnaping Statute. Since the passage of the kidnaping act in 1932, the Bureau has investigated several hundred cases of kidnaping and solved all but two. In 1949 it brought about 9,000 cases to court and won convictions in more than 97 per cent of them. During the Second World War, and in succeeding years that brought no peace, the FBI has been giving much of its attention to internal security, having the responsibility of investigating violations of the Atomic Energy Act of 1946, rounding up Communist conspirators, and checking the "loyalty record" of more than 2,000,000 federal employees. Despite its efficiency (and perhaps even because of it) the FBI is viewed with concern by some citizens who are neither ordinary criminals nor disloyal Americans. Such disapprobation comes at least in part from the fact that the Bureau has in its files trivia, gossip, and hearsay on nobody knows how many Americans who are probably no less patriotic than its Director.[9]

[9] *Time*, Aug. 8, 1949, pp. 10–13; *New Republic*, Dec. 4, 1950, p. 18.

State police. The Texas Rangers, celebrated in song and story, were established by the Republic of Texas as a border patrol. Although as early as 1865 Massachusetts had a number of state constables, the idea of a state police system did not definitely take shape in any American state until 1905, Pennsylvania leading the way in that year. The reasons for the establishment of the "state constabulary" in Pennsylvania were the break-down of the sheriff-constable system in rural communities and the disturbed industrial conditions in the coal and iron regions. Although Pennsylvania is still in the lead with some 2,000 police officers, all the states now have a police system. In about one fourth of the states the authority of the state officer is limited to enforcement of the highway code. In the other states these officers have general police authority. State police are usually better trained, organized, directed, and disciplined than the city forces. They are usually unpopular with city police forces, out of jealousy perhaps, and labor hates and fears them because of their availability for service in strike areas. The principal function of the state police has been that of exercising general police authority in rural areas, supplementing the work of rural peace officers. The local officers are practically help-less in combating motorized crime, while the state police is equipped to apprehend the fast moving criminals. A few states even have "air cops." Other duties of the state officers consist of enforcing state statutes relating to fishing, hunting, fire prevention, gambling, and the like. It is said that the state police in some of the Eastern states have set a new standard in police administration and will acquire a larger significance in the future. With criminals recognizing no local boundaries and moving swiftly from one area to another, it seems very logical that the officers of detection should be no less free to ignore boundaries.

Fire protection: THE IMPORTANCE OF FIRE PREVENTION. Fire losses in the United States amount to about a million dollars a day. Our per capita losses are much higher than those of any European country. Yet we have the best fire-fighting forces and equipment in the world. In 1917–1919 our soldiers in France often remarked that medium-sized French cities seemed to have no force or apparatus for fighting fires, whereas in American cities of the same size there was the daily drama of shrieking sirens, roaring motors loaded with equipment and firemen, and pedestrians scurrying to places of safety. Asked to state how much property he had seen destroyed by fire in France, the doughboy often admitted he had seen no fires. Now the French do have an occasional fire and they do have an organized system of fire fighting; but this is not their major line. Their efforts are concentrated upon *preventing* the occurrence of fires, rather than in fighting them. So well does this policy succeed in European countries generally that they have not felt the necessity of developing the fire-fighting art to the point of American efficiency. They are willing to concede that we are the champion fire fighters of the world. How do the Europeans prevent fires? In the first place, lumber is so expensive that few persons want to erect frame buildings. In the second place, their laws prohibit frame structures in any area where they will constitute a fire menace. And, in the third place, the use of fire in dwellings and places of business is thoroughly regulated by law. In recent decades American cities have seen the wisdom of fire prevention. Although they may still lay disproportionate emphasis upon fire fighting, the matter of prevention has been seriously undertaken.

AMERICAN METHODS OF PREVENTION. All our large cities have rather elaborate regulations respecting fire prevention, and nearly all other cities have rules more or less suited to their needs. The rules commonly fix fire limits; that is, areas in which only buildings of a certain fire-resisting type may be constructed. There is a lot of talk about fireproof buildings, but there is no such building. There are buildings that will not burn, but no buildings that will not crumble when subjected to high temperatures, temperatures that may be developed by neighboring buildings in conflagration. Hence, even the so-called fireproof (actually only fire-resisting) buildings are not safe unless all buildings in the same area are constructed of noncombustible materials. Of course, some flexibility is provided for in the fire-prevention rules. Buildings such as theaters, in which a fire would likely cause loss of human life, may have no wood materials except for trimmings. Stores and shops are ordinarily allowed wood floors and partitions, but no other use of timber is permitted. Still more wood may be allowed in the structure of other buildings. It should be noted that these ordinances prescribing the type of building materials that may be used are not retroactive—they apply only for buildings to be erected; they do not require the demolition of structures standing at the time such ordinances are passed.

Equal in importance to the rules themselves is their enforcement. A staff of trained inspectors must be provided. Cities have commonly failed to engage a sufficiently large and competent staff. They have not always found honest men. It costs a little more to conform to the building material requirements, and it has been found that inspectors are sometimes lenient in this matter. Contractors who have good standing at the city hall know that the inspectors are not going to bother them overmuch. Then, too, the people who risk their lives in unsafe buildings are not particularly concerned about the enforcement of the fire-prevention ordinances. They are not sufficiently educated on the subject of fire prevention either to demand that fire ordinances be enforced or to refrain from acts of individual carelessness that often cause fires. Perhaps, after all, we Americans enjoy our fires! [10]

10 Macdonald, *op. cit.,* pp. 467–470.

THE FIRE DEPARTMENT. Fire fighting will always be necessary; prevention will only lessen the need for it. Until around 1850, American cities relied upon volunteer fire brigades for this function. Boys about town who wanted some excitement or who saw fire fighting as an avenue of approach to politics were quite willing to "run," and they did it very well, although rival companies, arriving at a conflagration about the same time, occasionally fought each other and almost forgot the fire. All cities of any considerable size now have full-time, professional firemen. The chief of the fire department is commonly appointed by the mayor, and the other officers of the department are selected in about the same manner as police officers. The ordinary firemen are usually selected under civil service rules requiring competitive examinations. When appointed, they are given a little training, very little in some cities, and assigned to places as engineers and hosemen. The fire-fighting force, like the police force, is distributed over the city at conveniently located stations, a captain being in charge of each station. It may be of some interest to note here that, although an American city has fewer policemen than a European city of the same size, it has about twice as many firemen, and pays three times as much for fire protection.

Fire-fighting equipment. Cities usually keep their fire-fighting equipment up to date. Horses and steam engines have given way to motors, and ladder trucks now have ladders of the quick-lifting aërial type. Chemical extinguishers are in use everywhere. Heavy streams of water are forced through turret pipes and deluge sets. High pressure systems are installed for the business districts, the pressure sometimes being as much as 300 pounds per square inch. Smoke helmets and gas masks enable firemen to go where they never went before and come out alive. Pulmotors enable them to resuscitate persons who have been overcome by smoke. Within three minutes after an alarm has sounded, a company is usually at the scene of the fire, a stream is turned on, and, says one chief, "in a few minutes the furniture goes floating out of the window." [11] This remark indicates that in extinguishing a fire more damage may be done than is caused by the fire itself. Many fire-fighting units do not seem to be concerned about this, but the more progressive ones carry waterproof covers, brooms, mops, and so on, and do systematic salvage work.

PRIVATE FIRE PROTECTION. Factories, department stores, and other large commercial establishments do not rely solely upon the city for fire protection. They have their watchmen, who make the rounds and punch clocks to give proof that periodic inspection was actually made. Mechanical watchmen and fire extinguishers in the form of automatic sprinklers are usually installed, frequently under legal requirement. These are sealed with a substance that melts when a fire breaks out, thereby re-

[11] Quoted in Munro, *Municipal Government and Administration* (1923), Vol. II, p. 254.

leasing the water to deluge the affected area and to sound an alarm attached to the sprinkler-head. Some years ago it was estimated that private persons and establishments pay about one third as much for fire protection as the cities spend on their fire departments.[12]

II. PUBLIC HEALTH [13]

Much more progress has been made in guarding society against disease than in protecting it from the violence of its own members and the ravages of fire. Advances in health protection are particularly noteworthy along the lines of prevention, the very lines on which our police and fire systems are weakest. All the governments—national, state, and local—play an important part in preserving the health of the people.

Federal health activities. In addition to maintaining numerous hospitals for its soldiers, sailors, ex-service men, sailors of the merchant marine, civilian government employees, and lepers, the federal government performs a number of other health services.

1. QUARANTINE REGULATIONS. The immigration officials see to it that diseased immigrants do not enter the United States; but disease may be carried by general passengers, crews, unsanitary ships and their accompanying pests, particularly rats, as well as by the lowly immigrant in the steerage. Congress has succeeded in lessening this danger by appropriate legislation. Any ship from a foreign port desiring to dock in an American port must procure from an American consul at the port from which it sailed a certificate attesting to its sanitary condition and the health of its crew and passengers. Upon arrival at quarantine, a ship is given another inspection by our domestic health officers before she is allowed to dock. Clearly the authority of the national government to make and enforce regulations of the type described arises under its power over foreign commerce.

2. THE PURE FOOD AND DRUGS ACTS. The interstate commerce power has been still more useful in the hands of the national government in safeguarding the health of the public. It has not been used so much to restrict the travel of diseased persons between the states, but chiefly in respect to foods and drugs. In the latter part of the last century the market was flooded

---

[12] Munro, *op. cit.*, pp. 255–256.

[13] F. G. Bates, O. P. Field, and Others, *State Government* (1949 ed.), pp. 422–431; C. A. and Wm. Beard, *The American Leviathan* (1930), pp. 578–593; Merle Fainsod and Lincoln Gordon, *Government and the American Economy* (1948 ed.), Ch. 7; *Annual Reports of the Public Health Service* and of the *Federal Security Agency*; A. F. Macdonald, *American State Government and Administration* (1950 ed.), Ch. 25; W. G. Smillie, *Public Health Administration in the United States* (1947 ed.); *Book of the States, 1950–1951*, pp. 325 ff.

with adulterated food, diseased meat, and all kinds of remedies guaranteed to cure any kind of disease. The people were not only the victims of deception, but many of the products sold them were very injurious to health. In response to what amounted almost to a popular uprising, Congress enacted the Food and Drugs Act and the Meat Inspection Act in 1906. Despite the strenuous opposition of business most affected by these laws and the lingering resentment a few individuals still bear toward the government for its efforts to protect them from stimulating "cure-alls" concocted by their favorite quack—mail-order doctors—the food and drug laws are rated among the most beneficial statutes of the past fifty years. They close the channels of interstate and foreign commerce to unhealthful, adulterated, or misbranded foods, meat, beverages, and drugs. Specifically, the Meat Inspection Act, administered by the Department of Agriculture, requires approval by federal officers of all slaughterhouses preparing meat for interstate trade; the inspection of animals before slaughter; and the inspection of meat for packing or canning.

With respect to other foods, the Food and Drugs Act prohibits such practices as the use of harmful preservatives, the adulteration of a food, unless the label faithfully reveals such adulteration, and the selling of one product under the name of another. The same rules apply to beverages. As for drugs, those medicines that contain such ingredients as alcohol and laudanum must have the percentage indicated on the label. Other drugs must conform to standards recognized by the *United States Pharmacopoeia,* that is, the directory of medical chemicals.

The reader is aware that not everything that can be purchased at a drug store is a drug. For example, cosmetics are not, at least not within the meaning of the act under discussion; for they are not "intended to be used for the cure, mitigation, or prevention of disease of man or animals." Thus it happened that cosmetics with acid content could be sold in interstate trade, despite the occasional tragedies attending their use. Lotions containing wood alcohol, which may cause blindness, and mercury of lead, which may produce inflammation, making an entrance for bacteria into the system, were formerly legally available in great quantities to beauty seekers.

The Wheeler-Lea Act of 1938 may have corrected some of these abuses, for it prohibits the dissemination of false advertising of food, drugs, cosmetics, and devices (meaning those for use in the diagnosis, prevention, or treatment of disease), and empowers the Federal Trade Commission to require advertisers of the four named products, in any case where they might cause bodily injury, to reveal that fact affirmatively. "It cleans your breath while it cleans your teeth." "A safe, sure way to correct bad breath is through the regular use of the thorough, cleansing action provided only by the special ingredients" in the World's Best. The federal Trade Commission required the "World's Best" to cease making this claim because such ingredients could aid only in the elimination of bad breath originating in the mouth and because most bad breath originates not in the mouth but arises from other sources—faulty digestion, for example.[14]

The Food and Drug Administration. The enforcement of the pure food and drug acts (excepting the provisions relating to advertising) is largely in the hands of a unit in the Federal Security Agency, the Food and Drug Administration. For enforcement purposes the country is divided into 16 districts, each with testing laboratories, chemists, and inspectors. Factories are inspected for sanitary conditions, raw materials used, and relevant practices. When violations are suspected, shipments are reported for destination sampling. Primary attention is directed, of course, to violations most serious to the public welfare. Constructive enforcement is provided for manufacturers who request it, and it consists of suggestions concerning manufacturing processes, labeling, improvements in sanitation, and so on. Before any new drug may be placed on the market, the Administration must be satisfied respecting the adequacy of manufacturing controls and safety for use. Insulin, penicillin, and certain other drugs receive predistribution control, each batch manufactured being sampled before it is certified for distribution. If processors desire it, the Administration furnishes continuous inspection in oyster and shrimp canneries, and the plants may then label their products as so supervised.

More specialized and highly scientific work for the Administration is performed in its Washington laboratories. Much of the work here is in developing methods of detection and proof of adulteration that will "stand up" in court actions. Another principal function of the laboratories is that of research to form a groundwork for enforcement policy. For example, they study the toxicity of ingredients used in the manufacture of foods, drugs, and cosmetics, the composition of products that come within the provisions of the acts enforced, and the potency of drugs and vitamins.[15]

These protective activities, combined with those of the Federal Trade Commission against fraudulent advertising, would seem to give the public rather full protection. But they do not—not yet. In 1947 the government convicted an individual who had a simple and wonderful device that he called the Spectro-Chrome. They sold for $90 and he had distributed 9,000 of them. The device was a box containing an electric light bulb (a strong one) and glass panes of different colors. One color, the light shin-

---

[14] See an interesting and entertaining article by R. M. Cunningham, Jr., "Toothpaste Ads v. the Truth," *New Republic*, March 4, 1946, p. 313.
[15] *U.S. Government Manual*, 1949, pp. 378–80.

ing through it on the patient, would cure cancer, another stomach ulcers—it was that easy. Defense witnesses at the trial testified that the machine had cured constipation in a dachshund and made calving easy for cows if their heads were pointed to the north during treatment. But the government had more witnesses who testified that numerous victims of serious diseases had died while taking the treatments. One defense witness who had been "cured" of epilepsy by the Spectro-Chrome involuntarily turned government witness when he had an attack while on the stand and would probably have strangled to death had not a government medical witness saved him.

It took the government almost twenty years to "get" the distributor of the Spectro-Chrome. How many others does it not get? Those responsible for law enforcement estimate that for every one convicted there are two or three more at large. And this is not all. Frauds of the type mentioned for which people pay from $100 to $1,000 or $1,500 are not the most common. The garden variety of fake is what an individual buys in a bottle for a dollar or two. Many of the patent medicines are entirely lawful, some are unlawful but proof is difficult, and only a few are easily demonstrated as being without the law. There are some 70,000 manufacturers of foods, drugs, and cosmetics in the United States, and at least one authority claims that the Food and Drug Administration has only about one sixth the staff and facilities necessary to do the checking and inspecting that ought to be done in the public interest.[16]

Still another obstacle to enforcement is that of the attitude of the people the laws are intended to protect. They love their patent medicines, and some individuals even seem to want to be fooled. All these factors complicate the task of enforcing the drug laws. Let it be said finally, in all fairness, that many of the patent medicines are beneficial, and many others that are not beneficial are harmless.

3. THE PUBLIC HEALTH SERVICE. The few activities noted above by no means indicate the breadth of federal activities in making and keeping the nation healthy. A broader view of these activities may be gained by taking a few samples from the work of the Public Health Service, formerly located in the Treasury Department, but now with the Federal Security Agency.

(1) It seeks through the inspection of ships and airplanes to prevent the introduction of diseases from abroad. The degree of efficiency with which this service is performed may be indicated by the fact that, despite the rising

---

[16] Carl Malmberg, "No Good for What Ails You," *New Republic*, August 25, 1947, p. 23. See also his *Diet and Die* (1935) and A. Kallet and F. J. Schlink, *100,000,000 Guinea Pigs* (1933).

incidence of small pox, cholera, typhus, and plague in foreign countries in 1948, no such disease was introduced into the United States during that year.

(2) It co-operates with the state and local health units and private organizations in safeguarding environmental sanitation. Its activities in this realm include work on such health engineering problems as swimming-pool sanitation, sewage disposal, water-supply, and housing sanitation. It aids the state and local communities in the control and inspection of milk and food handling in restaurants. Its recommended milk ordinance is in effect throughout a number of states and in many counties and cities in the other states, reaching nearly a fourth of the nation's population. Its restaurant standards are in effect in communities that contain nearly half the population. The Water Pollution Control Act of 1948 establishes a federal-state-municipal co-operative program for the control of pollution of interstate waters. This program calls for the expenditure of well over $100,000,000; and $10,000,000 is earmarked for the Health Service for its research, survey, and administrative functions respecting water-pollution control.

(3) It encourages the establishment and extension of local health departments throughout the country. Such departments have a significant part to play in the field of environmental sanitation, and they provide public-health nursing service, collect vital statistics, administer disease-control programs and maternal and child-welfare services. The Health Service finds that only about 7,000,000 people live in areas where the local health units are adequately staffed, although some local health activity is undertaken in communities that contain nearly half the population.

(4) It has waged a long and continuous battle to forestall disease, co-operating with state and local agencies. Particular attention has been directed to combating venereal disease, heart disease, tuberculosis, diabetes, and communicable disease, and to improving dental health, nutrition, industrial hygiene, and health education. The most recent disease-control programs are for cancer and mental health. Some idea of the value of this type of service is indicated by the fact that the mortality from syphilis has been cut in half since 1938, when the co-operative program of combating it was started.

(5) It has developed and is expanding scientific research on the diseases mentioned above and on leprosy, malaria, Rocky Mountain spotted fever, relapsing fever, and other diseases. The National Institutes of Health co-ordinates all the research programs, a number of which have available for use the large and up-to-date clinical and laboratory research center at Bethesda, Maryland.

The preceding list gives only a partial outline of the regular work of the

DISCRIMINATION CONTRIBUTES TO POOR HEALTH

LIFE EXPECTANCY OF NEGROES
10 YEARS LESS THAN WHITES
(1940)

WHITE
10 20 30 40 50 62.8 67.3

NEGRO
10 20 30 40 52.3 55.6

MATERNAL DEATH RATES OF NEGROES
IS MORE THAN DOUBLE THAT OF WHITES
(1940)

3.5 PER 1000   8.0 PER 1000

SOME UNDERLYING CAUSES

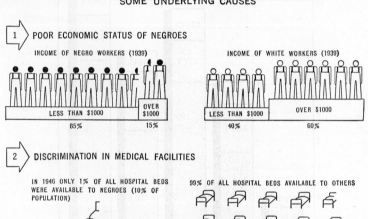

1 > POOR ECONOMIC STATUS OF NEGROES

INCOME OF NEGRO WORKERS (1939)

| LESS THAN $1000 | OVER $1000 |
| 85% | 15% |

INCOME OF WHITE WORKERS (1939)

| LESS THAN $1000 | OVER $1000 |
| 40% | 60% |

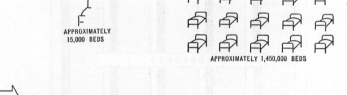

2 > DISCRIMINATION IN MEDICAL FACILITIES

IN 1946 ONLY 1% OF ALL HOSPITAL BEDS
WERE AVAILABLE TO NEGROES (10% OF
POPULATION)

APPROXIMATELY
15,000 BEDS

99% OF ALL HOSPITAL BEDS AVAILABLE TO OTHERS

APPROXIMATELY 1,450,000 BEDS

3 > SHORTAGE OF TRAINED NEGRO PERSONNEL
(1942)

1 NEGRO DOCTOR FOR EVERY 3,377 NEGROES

IN 1940 THERE WERE ONLY 7,192 TRAINED
AND STUDENT NEGRO NURSES

RATIO OF DOCTORS TO GENERAL POPULATION
1 TO EVERY 750 PERSONS

AND ONLY 1,471 NEGRO DENTISTS

TO SERVE A NEGRO POPULATION OF 13,000,000

Source: *U.S. Bureau of the Census and U.S. Public Health Service*

From *Report of the President's Committee on Civil Rights* (1947), p. 72.

849

Public Health Service. For it and through it the national government appropriates about $200,000,000 a year, more than half of which goes as grants-in-aid to the states for their health progams. More than $12,000,000 go to universities and other institutions for research work, and more than $3,000,000 to schools of nursing.

MEDICAL CARE NEEDED AND WHAT WE ARE LIKELY TO SPEND

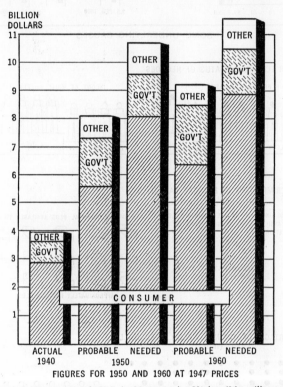

FIGURES FOR 1950 AND 1960 AT 1947 PRICES

From Twentieth Century Fund, *U.S.A.: Measure of a Nation* (Macmillan, 1949), p. 39.

The public health work is usually done very quietly and very efficiently. The war against disease that goes on constantly at a relatively low cost and without loud patriotic appeals to do this or that is nevertheless a war, a war in which strategy must be used against the hidden enemies of the human race and in which strategy must sometimes be used to convince the race that it has so many invisible enemies. There are still many individuals in our own country who, in effect, insist upon their right to have a disease (and, of course, upon their right to pass it on to their neighbors). Not the least of the tasks of the public health officers is that of persuading the public to accept for its own benefit certain health services.

THE SUGGESTION OF NATIONAL HEALTH INSURANCE. In May, 1948, following a request of the President to prepare a report setting forth a ten-year health program, a National Health Assembly was convened in Washington for the purpose of forming a "grass roots" basis for future progress. More than 800 representatives of public and private agencies and health organizations participated in the deliberations of the Assembly, and its recommendations, looking to the next decade, were significant. It saw a need for 40 to 50 per cent more doctors, including an increase in the national investment in health education and financial assistance for qualified men and women who undertake this long and expensive training. It would increase the number of hospital beds by two thirds, giving special emphasis to rural and small town areas. It would extend basic public health service to some 40,000,000 people, chiefly in rural areas. And the recommendations ran on with "We must provide," "We must extend," "We must double or triple," "We must delve more deeply," and last, "We must apply the principles of insurance to provide prepaid adequate medical care for substantially all the people." Here we have the recommendation for what people who do not like it call "socialized medicine." The Assembly "was unanimous in recognizing that the application of insurance principles is the most practicable answer to this problem. It differed only as to whether it should take a voluntary or compulsory form, and no specific recommendation was made." [17]

President Truman has recommended a national compulsory health insurance program. At this writing Congress seems unlikely to enact the legislation necessary for launching such a plan, at least not in the immediate future. The question as to the best means of providing adequate medical care is likely to remain an issue for some time. The fact remains, however, that the national health could be greatly improved. Twenty-five million people have a chronic disease; 8 million need help for their mental disorders; 68 million would find their budgets "knocked into a cocked hat" by hospitalization; and there are no registered general hospitals in 40 per cent of the counties where 15 million people live.

State public health activities. Although the protection of health has always been a state function, until some sixty years ago the states did very little in this direction because scientific knowledge upon which to base action was quite limited. But since the days of our grandparents medical science has advanced rapidly, and the great majority of the states have taken positive measures to secure some of its benefits for the public. The entrance of the national government into this field in a large way a generation ago has not caused the states to withdraw from it. On the contrary,

[17] As summarized in the *Report of the Federal Security Agency*, 1948, pp. 39–41. See also FSA, *The Nation's Health—A Ten-Year Plan* (1948).

it has stimulated state activity. Besides, the health functions of the two governments are complementary rather than overlapping.

ORGANIZATION OF STATE HEALTH AGENCIES. What have the states done? They have established state boards of health, often giving them the power to issue important orders and regulations for the purpose of carrying into effect general statutes relative to the public health, and always giving them the authority to investigate health conditions and to supervise the work of subordinate health officers. Not infrequently a state board of health is given a considerable degree of control over local agencies. Of course, a board cannot carry on the routine work of health protection. This is carried on by administrative officials and employees, subject to the general supervision of the board. The executive head of the administrative forces has some such title as "state health officer" or "director of public health." The administrative services of the typical department of health are divided into appropriate bureaus, with doctors, chemists, engineers, and other scientists and technicians assigned to each according to the need. It should be stated here that not all the public health functions are monopolized by the department of that name. Departments of agriculture, education, social security, or other administrative agencies usually have a good share.

FUNCTIONS OF STATE HEALTH AGENCIES. Space permits only a partial enumeration of the functions of the health agencies.[18]

(1) The collection of vital statistics and the assembling of other information contributing to a knowledge of health conditions and trends.

(2) A very old service is that of quarantine, the compulsory isolation of persons with contagious diseases.

(3) Hygienic laboratories are commonly maintained for the purpose of making bacteriological examinations of various kinds.

(4) Hospitals are established for the care of persons unable to pay for private treatment, a number of states making special efforts to provide treatment for the tuberculous.

(5) The administration of the vaccination laws and the distribution of vaccines are other important functions.

(6) The medical examination of school children is now a general and splendid service, often leading to correction of defects that if undiscovered until later life might not yield to treatment.

(7) Some states maintain a bureau of child hygiene, which reaches the preschool child, giving physical and mental examinations, advising parents, and so on.

(8) Still another service comes in the enforcement of laws relative to sewage disposal and water supplies.

(9) Inspections of factories, canneries, packing plants, and similar es-

---

[18] For a fuller discussion see Bates, Field, and Others, *op. cit.*, pp. 427 ff.

tablishments are health functions with respect to employees, or the public, or both.

(10) The enforcement of state food and drug acts is another very important duty of the health administration.

(11) In more recent years the states have joined with the national government in scientific efforts to reduce the number of cases of venereal disease and to cure existing cases. Their aim is accomplished chiefly by the dissemination of information, consultation services for health officers and private physicians, and free distribution of drugs.

(12) The treatment of the mentally ill is a responsibility that states have long assumed but that they have often negligently discharged. As ignorance has grudgingly given way to science, the states have improved their services; but in many states the application of science still lags woefully behind knowledge, and legislatures are all-too-reluctant to make appropriations for the proper care of the mentally ill.

(13) Our final reference is to a most fundamental health service, that of educating the public in elementary health precautions, a program many states have carried forward in a very satisfactory manner, the schools serving as the principal media.

Licensing professions and trades affecting the public health. In addition to their provision of the types of services mentioned, the states regulate the practice of professions and trades that touch the public health. This regulation is carried out chiefly by examining applicants and licensing those of good character and demonstrated competence and by the revocation of licenses for cause. Subject to such regulations are physicians, surgeons, psychiatrists, dentists, optometrists, chiropractors, chiropodists, osteopaths, pharmacists, veterinarians, embalmers, plumbers, barbers, hairdressers, cosmeticians, electrologists, manicurists, permanent wave operators, and others. The fitness of a person to practice any particular profession or trade of the type named is determined by a state board of examiners chosen from the list of established practitioners.

County health administration. Much poetry has been written about the country, mostly by people who no longer live in it; some fiction has a rural setting, but hosts of people believe more fiction about farm and country than reputable writers would be guilty of endorsing. One of these fictions has it that the country, being such a healthful place in which to live, has little or no public health problem. The truth is, however, that rural communities have their full share of measles, whooping cough, diphtheria, influenza, lobar pneumonia, and diarrhea, and almost a monopoly on diseases traceable to polluted water, food, or soil—such diseases as hookworm, malaria, dysentery, and typhoid. Furthermore, although the death rate in the country is slightly lower than in the city, physical defects of a debilitating kind are more common in the country. This evidence is abundantly sufficient to show that rural areas have their health problem, a problem made difficult of solution in part because of the widespread ignorance of the nature of disease among rural populations.[19]

Health organization in rural communities was established in the day when diseases were believed to be transmitted largely, if not exclusively, from personal contact and smells. Consequently, the unit of administration (such as it was) was small—the town, a county district, and, less often, the county. Even when knowledge of disease transmission became more general, the smaller units of administration were commonly retained. Small communities are usually unable to provide health services worthy of the name because the cost is beyond their means. The county is now regarded as the smallest area populous enough and wealthy enough to provide those preventive and educational services that constitute the modern public health program. Such a program calls for full-time, permanent organization for health services; for at least one medical health officer, a nurse, a sanitary inspector, and a clerk. The minimum services to be rendered include the recording of vital statistics, the assembling of data on and the control of communicable diseases; the inspection of water and food supplies and the enforcement of hygienic regulations applicable thereto; the maintenance of nursing service for mothers and infants.[20]

Very few rural counties have established these services. Country people generally do not see any great need for them; moreover, even the minimum standard outlined above would be a heavy financial drain on a number of the rural counties. What progress has been made in rural health protection has come largely from the educational activities and financial support offered by private organizations like the Rockefeller Foundation and the Commonwealth Fund and by the state and national governments. Indeed, adequate health protection can hardly be expected to reach the majority of rural communities without education, supervision, and financial subsidies from the state or national government. And in recent years these state and national aids have been increasing.

City health services. The cities are now very much alive to their responsibilities respecting the health of their inhabitants. The states fix the health standards that municipalities must attain, and they ordinarily exercise sufficient control to make sure that the standards are maintained; but many cities go far beyond the standards required by state law and, in addition, include functions not mentioned in the law.

ADMINISTRATIVE ORGANIZATION. Many cities still have boards of health for general supervisory purposes; but a number of authorities feel that

[19] Lane W. Lancaster, *Government in Rural America* (1937), pp. 329 ff.
[20] *Ibid.*, p. 339.

the board of health is unnecessary and sometimes in the way—that, in any case, regular administrative officers, who are quite competent to take over the duties of the board, must be employed. Whether a city makes use of a board or not, a health officer is in direct charge of the administrative activities. In large cities the department of health is divided into several divisions or bureaus, each charged with particular functions and having assigned to it the necessary physicians, laboratory experts, inspectors, and other specialists.

FUNCTIONS. With certain exceptions the work of the city's health forces is similar to that performed by state agencies. Of course, city authorities have no subordinate agencies to supervise, and they must intensify some activities that do not engage the major attention of state authorities and add a few that concern those authorities only incidentally. Working in congested areas, city authorities must be most vigilant for communicable diseases, quick to impose quarantines when such diseases are found or reported, and careful to disinfect the premises when an illness has terminated. Eternal vigilance is one of the prices of a city's pure milk supply. Used by practically everyone and an especially fine food for children, milk and its products are unfortunately very easily subject to contamination and therefore often bring disease and death. Many cities have the most stringent regulations respecting the testing and quality of milk sold to their inhabitants. Samples of milk are constantly being taken from wagons on the streets and tested in laboratories. Inspection of the dairies that ship milk to the city is also a regular proceeding.

The "smoke nuisance" is entirely a city problem. It is not, as a student once told the writer, the problem of preventing individuals from smoking tobacco, but the problem of forcing manufacturers and others maintaining smokestacks belching forth clouds of ugly, dirty smoke, often laden with poisonous gases, to abate the smoke nuisance. Many cities have successfully met the situation by requiring all large users of soft coal to install smoke consumers. Other regulations and activities of city health authorities, being of a character similar to those mentioned under state and county health functions, are omitted from this discussion.[21]

The health phases of other services. Several services vitally connected with health are administered by other than health departments, or by health and other authorities combined. Among these may be mentioned housing, sanitation, water supply, and recreation. The health phases of these services are fundamental, and they are here treated to the practical exclusion of the others.

HOUSING. Housing conditions in nearly all of our large cities and in

[21] For fuller discussion, see Munro, *Municipal Administration*, Chs. XXXIV–XXXVI; Macdonald, *American City Government and Administration* (1951 ed.), Ch. 28.

some of the small industrial cities and towns have for years amounted almost to a national scandal. Lacking sufficient light, air, living space, and toilet facilities, living in crowded rooms, or a room, often with a lodger or two to help piece out an existence, the unskilled worker's family has a hard and not infrequently losing fight against disease and moral deterioration. Some would lay all the blame on the shiftlessness of the laborer and dismiss the subject. No doubt some of the fault lies there; but city governments have generally recognized that not all the circumstances are under his control, and consequently have come to his aid with housing regulations, some cities with elaborate ones. These codes contain a number of provisions respecting such matters as building materials, fire escapes, and stairs—provisions designed to lessen the fire hazard. But requirements respecting light, air and sanitation—predominantly health regulations— are treated even more extensively. Such regulations limit the amount of lot space a building may occupy; state the minimum requirements for floor space and windows; and prescribe the minimum standards for water, toilet facilities, drainage, and so on. Often the regulations are meager enough, as instanced by the requirement that there shall be running water on every floor, accessible to every family; but they do afford some protection to tenants. The laws are also designed to bring the tenants up to certain standards. For example, the keeping of poultry and swine in tenements is prohibited. "They kept the pig in the parlor" was found to be very near a reality, not just the words of a song.[22]

Promotion of housing. The difficulties involved in devising just the right sort of legal regulations and enforcing them have caused many authorities to approach the housing problem from another angle, the angle of promotion. This phase of housing was by no means lost sight of in the President's Conference on Home Building and Home Ownership (1931). This Conference published eleven volumes of reports, which constitute the most comprehensive publication yet made in housing science. To date not a great deal has been done to promote housing. Certain private corporations in New York, Newark, Chicago, and a few other cities have erected tenements that are let to workers at reasonable rates; but relatively few families are accommodated and the rent is still above what the unskilled wage-earners are able to pay. Many European cities have adopted the scheme of municipal housing; but, with the present state of political control in practically all branches of American city government, authorities generally issue warning against the undertaking on this side of the Atlantic. As an encouragement for the erection of model apartments, New York grants tax exemption on those that do not rent for more than a stipulated maximum per month. A few housing organizations have

[22] Macdonald, *op. cit.,* Chapter 26.

constructed tenements under this law. Another means of aiding housing is through cheap government credit. This method is common in European countries, but until recently its acceptance made but little headway in our own.

Federal housing projects. Since 1932 the federal government has taken a very active interest in housing development, this being one of several problems that that government, almost ignoring the states, has approached through direct relationship with the cities. In 1932 Congress authorized the R.F.C. "to make loans to corporations formed wholly for the purpose of providing housing for families of low income, or for reconstruction of slum areas, which are regulated by state or municipal law as to rents, charges, capital structure, rate of return, and areas and methods of operation," provided such undertakings were self-liquidating in character. This idea was something new. Then came the New Deal with its National Industrial Recovery Act, under Title II of which loans were offered to private housing corporations and federal administrative authorities were authorized to undertake public housing projects. Later, additional appropriations were made for the same purposes. The Housing Division of the Public Works Administration assisted several limited-dividend corporations with the financing of housing projects, and it let contracts for work on approximately fifty public housing enterprises. Federal housing construction was slowed up, however, by some legal tangles, including a district court decision denying the government the authority to condemn land for slum clearance.

The national public housing program really got under way with the passage of the National Housing Act of 1937. This legislation leaves the state and municipal authorities the initiative, but it provides for federal loans and subsidies for low-rent housing and slum clearance programs. The local authority submits plans for construction to the national authority; and if such plans meet the federal requirement that cost shall not exceed a stipulated sum ($4,000 per family unit in all except the large cities), the federal government will make loans, at low rates of interest, covering 90 per cent of the cost. The federal government also makes outright grants for the construction of low-rent units to be occupied by families who would be otherwise obliged to live in the slums.

The federal housing program is tied up with slum clearance, the standard plan (to which exceptions are permitted) being that for each modern unit constructed a slum unit must be demolished. Such projects cost a great deal of money in large cities, where slum dwellings may stand on land valued at four or five dollars per square foot. Not a few housing authorities suggested that new construction be undertaken in areas where land is less costly, and that slum clearance be retarded for the time being. The program was pushed forward, however, as originally planned. The states with large urban communities were almost unanimous in permitting such areas to engage in public housing under the federal plan. Before 1942 many cities had taken advantage of this privilege, and the Federal Public Housing Authority had approved housing projects costing hundreds of millions. Of course this development was suspended or given new direction by the war.

War and postwar housing problems. Even before the attack on Pearl Harbor, laborers started for defense plants in the industrial centers. After the attack they literally overran those centers—half a million in the Los Angeles area, another half million around San Francisco, hundreds of thousands in other cities, perhaps nine million in all. They had to be housed in some way. The government placed all of its housing activities within one organization, the National Housing Agency. Working with state and local authorities and private builders, this agency managed to erect some 165,000 permanent dwellings, 75,000 demountable ones, and various dormitories and temporary shelters. These, plus trailers, plus "share the home," solved the problem about as well as it could be solved.

Immediately after the war the housing situation seemed more acute than it was during the war. Between 1942 and 1946 there was practically no construction of dwellings except in the defense areas. Many of those were of no value for peacetime; some were too flimsy, and others were in the wrong place. Furthermore, there were many more families in 1946 than there were in 1942. Following the war it was estimated that about three million low and moderate cost houses were urgently needed for veterans and others, and that some twelve million dwelling units would be needed in the next ten years. The National Housing Agency made comprehensive recommendations as to ways and means, and Congress made some effort to relieve the situation, particularly by an appropriation of $400,000,000 to be used as premium payments to makers of new materials required in unconventional types of construction. The program lagged, however, because of a shortage of building materials (nonresidential construction perhaps getting more than its share), plumbing equipment, and other essentials, and because of rising costs.[23] In the meantime war veterans lived in trailers or doubled-up with relatives and friends or total strangers, and concocted fantastic schemes for getting a place of their own or even a little privacy. Such glaring housing inadequacies mean not only inconvenient, unsanitary, and unhealthful living, but they may also cause divorce and broken homes. In Congress and out, discussion and agitation of the housing situation continued for several years, and the Housing Act of 1949 was the result. This measure provides, among other

[23] *United States News,* Sept. 6, 1946, p. 54, and Oct. 25, p. 26.

things, for loans and grants to local public agencies for locally planned and managed slum-clearance, $1,500,000,000 being authorized for loans over a 5-year period, for national contributions and loans for 810,000 low-rent public housing units over a 6-year period, and for aids for farm housing and for housing research. The measure does not constitute a comprehensive housing program, but, even if it did, some years would be required for its fulfillment. The housing problem contains construction difficulties as well as financial ones.

SANITATION. A few centuries ago the pedestrian picking his way down a slimy street was much less on the lookout for street traffic than for dishwater and similar refuse that might be thrown at any time from a window or door of a city dwelling. Rubbish and garbage also took their places in gutters, and swine and dogs came to help themselves. Occasionally a good rain would come and sweep some of the noisome mess out of the city. Sewage disposal was almost as primitive. One of the chief reasons for the good health record of modern cities is found in their progress in sanitation, in the collection and removal of wastes under the direction of sanitary engineers. It must be said, however, that sanitation is more than a branch of public health; a great deal of it, the removal of ashes and rubbish, for example, simply contributes to public convenience.

Garbage would probably be a menace to public health, and unquestionably a nuisance, if not properly disposed of. It is ordinarily collected by city employees, but sometimes by private contractors. It is disposed of in various ways, a number of which are quite satisfactory. These are: towing it to sea, if far enough out; feeding it to hogs; burning it or reducing it, that is, cooking the grease out to be used for such purposes as the manufacture of soap. The residue makes a good fertilizer base.

Quick and effective collection and disposal of sewage is absolutely essential to the public health. A soldier in the front line or even in no man's land is in less danger than his civilian brother would be in a city without a sewage system. Every city must have this type of subway service, and the spent water supply, carrying human, household, and industrial wastes, must be kept moving to avoid trouble. In large cities the trunk mains are six or eight feet in diameter. Not the least of the marvelous things in Paris is its sewage system, its great horseshoe-shaped main tunnels being from fifteen to twenty feet in diameter. The sewage flows in a trough beneath a projecting footpath, and above this path there are galleries that carry the city water mains, electric lighting, telegraph, and telephone wires, pneumatic postal tubes, and pipes containing compressed air to be used as power. A properly identified visitor may have an instructive and entirely pleasant motor boat trip through the mains in company with the inspector.

Cities dispose of their sewage in various ways. Those near the sea run the sewage into it—at a point several miles from land, to avoid polluting the beach. A number of cities on the Great Lakes empty sewage into them; cities on rivers usually make use of them, the Mississippi getting about two billion gallons a day. Sufficient water renders the sewage harmless, but in those areas of rapid growth the amount of sewage deposited has sometimes polluted the water. Cities not having this natural means for disposal must take care of their sewage by filtering or other processes.[24]

WATER SUPPLY. Every city must have an abundant supply of water. It is essential to safety, convenience, and health. Ancient Rome was well supplied through her great aqueducts. The inhabitants of mediaeval cities used but little, and that was often impure, coming chiefly from rivers and wells. The modern city gets its water from various sources—springs, lakes, rivers, and mountains. Water unfit for use in the condition the city finds it, is carried through water-treatment plants, where it is filtered, chlorinized, or given other treatment necessary to make it harmless.[25] A few still prefer the "cold, pure, wholesome water" from the farmhouse well (which may be located in a little valley with the pigpen on one side and the stable on the other), but people of moderate intelligence know that the health risk as between it and city water is easily ten to one.

RECREATION. Realizing that recreation facilities are essential to the physical and mental health of both young and old, every city has made some provision for them. Young people must play in order to use up surplus energy; and if the opportunity for play is not given, they often get into mischief and land in the juvenile court. Occasionally they make mischief even of their play, if it is unsupervised. Progressive cities, therefore, not only provide large playgrounds in every section where there are a few hundred children, but they engage playground supervisors as well. Many cities, however, furnish inadequate playgrounds and maintain no supervision over them. The value of economy is not underestimated, but there is some doubt as to the wisdom of this particular economy. Parks are places of recreation and play for all classes and ages. A few decades ago one might see in a park a sign, "five dollars fine for walking on the grass." Fortunately, we have learned that parks are made for the people, not the people for the parks. Although all the cities have parks, only a small proportion of them have park systems—parks of different types, in the different sections of the city, or even outside, connected with tree-lined boulevards. Although we might wish that more cities would turn their

---

[24] Munro, *Municipal Administration*, Chs. XXII–XXIII; J. M. Pfiffner, *Municipal Administration* (1940), pp. 453–463.

[25] A. W. Bromage, *Introduction to Municipal Government and Administration* (1950), pp. 583–585; Munro, *op. cit.*, Ch. XLI.

attention to the need for additional playground facilities and more enlightened planning for parks, there is no great reason for discouragement, considering what has been accomplished in these directions in recent decades. During the depression years, however, shortsighted economy cut very heavily into the recreational program in some cities.

III. PUBLIC MORALS [26]

We shall now deal briefly with a topic upon practically every phase of which there is strong disagreement; around which sentiment, tradition, prejudice, and religion form strange alliances and wage deadly combats. One man knows he is right and he wants his convictions expressed in a rule of law for all. The gentleman who takes a diametrically opposite view wants his law. A third man—some would call him nonmoral —wishes they would both "mind their own business" and leave the public alone. But as long as human nature, or American nature, is what it is, agitation on moral questions will probably continue. A few of these questions are discussed here. Perhaps they are not all moral questions per se; but moral considerations have always entered strongly into the debate, making them moral questions for the purposes of this discussion.

Federal regulation. The power of the national government to put morals on a statutory basis comes primarily from its commerce, postal, and taxing powers, and, for a time, from the Eighteenth Amendment. Reserving this Amendment for the moment, let us take a few samples of what has been done under other authority.

From the mails are excluded lottery tickets, obscene or indecent writings or pictures, contraceptive information or devices, matter designed to promote frauds and swindles, "literature" tending to incite crime, prize fight films, and certain other matter. It may happen that a postal censorship may not pass judicial scrutiny, as Postmaster General Frank Walker discovered when he attempted to exclude *Esquire's* "Varga Girls" from the mails. Persons denied the use of the mail would naturally turn to other means of communication; but Congress using its commerce power, has blocked these channels also.

Considerable debate and some occasional merriment have arisen over the exclusion of "obscene or immoral" books. What is an obscene or immoral book? Until a short time ago this question was left to the decision of customs officials. They could decide just what "foreign" books were

---

[26] M. S. Callcott, *Principles of Social Legislation* (1932), Ch. VII; L. M. Hacker, "The Rise and Fall of Prohibition," *Current History*, September, 1932, pp. 662–672; A. C. Millspaugh, *Crime Control by the National Government* (1937), Chs. VII, X; National Commission on Law Observance and Enforcement, *Report on the Enforcement of the Prohibition Laws* (No. 2, January, 1931).

"bad" and prevent professors of literature from using them in class instruction! Congressional debates on this question in connection with the tariff act of 1930 entertained some citizens and scandalized others. The result was a compromise. Obscene or immoral matter or objects are still barred; but one may appeal a case of customs censorship to the Secretary of the Treasury, who may let down the bars for classics and scientific works imported for noncommercial purposes. Furthermore, a federal district court may pass upon the merits of a book found by customs officials to be "immoral and obscene." In 1934 a district court held that James Joyce's *Ulysses* was not obscene, overruling the findings of the customs officials.[27]

The commerce power is further used to prevent the transportation of women for immoral purposes. Long ago, prostitutes were denied admission to the United States; and the Mann Act (1910) prescribes a heavy fine and imprisonment for any person who transports a woman or girl in foreign or interstate commerce for an immoral purpose, thus striking commercialized vice an effective but by no means a fatal blow.

The commerce, taxing, and treaty-making powers are all invoked to regulate traffic in narcotics. Both their importation and exportation are definitely restricted by law, and we co-operate with other countries in exchanging information necessary for intelligent regulation. Producers of opium in the United States must pay a very high excise tax and furnish a proportionately high bond. Dealers must pay a small license tax and submit to elaborate sales regulations. These regulations are designed ostensibly to prevent the dealers from escaping the payment of the tax, actually for the purpose of securing a degree of control over a devastating evil.

The Prohibition experiment. Many states "went dry" before the Eighteenth Amendment was adopted. But intoxicating liquors were still legitimate articles of interstate commerce, and states could not prevent them from being shipped in. Congress came to the aid of the dry states, however, particularly with the Webb-Kenyon Act of 1913. This act forbade the interstate transportation of liquor intended to be used in violation of state laws, a notable concession to the dry states. In 1919, with the adoption of the Eighteenth Amendment, legal prohibition came for the entire nation. "The manufacture, sale, or transportation of intoxicating liquors within, the importation thereof into, or the exportation thereof from the United States and all territory subject to the jurisdiction thereof for beverage purposes" was prohibited, and Congress and the states were given concurrent power to enforce the Amendment by appropriate legislation.

THE PROBLEM OF ENFORCEMENT. Practically all of the state legislatures passed enforcement measures, some of which were very drastic. Congress

[27] *Time,* January 29, 1934, p. 49.

passed the Volstead Act, which defined as intoxicating any liquid fit for beverage which contained as much as one half of one per cent of alcohol. The act also contained numerous regulations for enforcement, prescribed penalties for violations (not more than six months' imprisonment or $1,000 fine for the first offense), and set up enforcement machinery. Enforcement was not successful in every part of the country, being especially difficult in large cities and industrial centers. A few states repealed their enforcement laws. In 1927, in the hope of improving enforcement, Congress put Prohibition officers under the merit system, and three years later moved the enforcement unit from the Treasury Department to the Department of Justice and reorganized the enforcement agency as the Bureau of Prohibition. In 1929 the Jones-Stalker "five and ten" Act was passed. Aimed at commercial violations of the law, the maximum penalty was fixed at five years' imprisonment, or a $10,000 fine, or both.

PROHIBITION REPEAL. In the meantime, Congress and the President decided that the whole question of Prohibition enforcement, as well as law enforcement in general, should be studied. The President appointed a National Commission on Law Observance and Enforcement, composed of very distinguished citizens and headed by George W. Wickersham. After eighteen months of investigation, they submitted an 80,000 word *Report on the Enforcement of the Prohibition Laws.* The commissioners were divided in their views, and their report could hardly be expected to "stimulate the clarification of the public mind," as President Hoover stated it should. The report did, however, stimulate public discussion, and the more the subject was discussed the more apparent it became that the country was ready to abandon the Prohibition experiment.

The Twenty-first Amendment was put through Congress while we were at the bottom of the depression (February, 1933), and it was ratified by conventions in the states before the end of the year. In addition to the repeal of the Eighteenth Amendment the Twenty-first prohibits the transportation or importation of liquor into any state in violation of the laws thereof. This simply puts the old Webb-Kenyon Act into the Constitution. There was some difficulty attending the enforcement of that act in the days when automobiles were few and slow and there were no airplanes. The obligation to protect dry states is even more difficult to meet in this new era of speed. The problem is simple at this time, however, for there are only two dry states—Oklahoma and Mississippi.

State regulations affecting morals: 1. LIQUOR. Although the national government, through its powers expressed and implied, does take a hand in regulating public morals, the subject is one that in the main still belongs to the states. The control of the liquor business was almost entirely a state function until the adoption of the Eighteenth Amendment, and since the repeal of that Amendment the states again have the chief responsibility. Only Mississippi and Oklahoma remain dry. About a third of the states have made the sale of liquor a state monopoly. Such a monopoly, properly administered, has proved one of the best means of handling the sale of liquor. Incidentally, it has yielded some states considerable revenue. A majority of the states regulate the traffic by the licensing system. A liquor control board in practically every state administers the liquor laws. This central system of control ought to give better results than were obtained under the old pre-Prohibition system, which left very wide discretion to local authorities.

2. Gambling. One of the "besetting sins" of mankind is gambling. The states undertake to prohibit, restrict, or localize its various forms; but it is generally conceded that it cannot be absolutely eradicated. Common gamblers, under most criminal codes, come within the classifications of vagrants and vagabonds. Gambling is usually prohibited in public conveyances and certain other public places. Keeping places for gambling is ordinarily a criminal offense. The familiar slot machine falls under the ban in many states. Horse racing is the subject of legislation largely because of the betting connected with it, but everyone knows that the laws have not stopped "playing the ponies." The lottery was formerly in good standing, both legally and morally. Now it may be necessary to explain that a lottery is a scheme for the distribution of money or property by chance among persons who give a valuable consideration for the chance. Some of our very fine, even denominational, colleges obtained funds a century and a quarter ago through lotteries. But their demoralizing effect seemed to grow, or the conscience of the nation was awakened, with the result that they are now forbidden in every state.[28]

3. Sexual vice. Sexual vice has been a problem in all periods of recorded history. Although generally admitted to be ineradicable, prostitution is given the sanction of law in but few countries. Some foreign governments regulate prostitution, thereby implying a legalization of it within limits; but in other countries and in practically all of the American states it exists only by sufferance. Measures of repression and restraint are taken against both prostitutes and places of prostitution, the measures being vigorous or mild, depending upon the instructions to and the attitude of the police. A common proceeding against the women is to arrest them as vagrants; that is, as persons without legitimate means of support and likely to conduct themselves offensively in securing a livelihood. A house of ill-fame may be closed as a nuisance. The states also

[28] E. Freund, *The Police Power* (1904), Ch. VII.

have their laws against lewd and lascivious conduct, obscene publications and performances, and similar conduct or practices conducive to vice.[29]

The problem of enforcing laws relating to morals. It is one thing to get a law on the statute books and another thing to have it enforced. That statement is as true as it is trite. It holds especially true for laws respecting public morals. Lawmaking is national or state (leaving out of consideration municipal ordinances of regulatory nature); law enforcement is local. Here a good deal of the trouble lies. A legislative body in which rural representatives hold a majority passes a law prohibiting, let us say, betting on horse races. In the cities those who promote horse races, those who attend them, and those who police them may think the law against betting is absurd. Consequently, the law will not be enforced in those localities. It will probably not be enforced anywhere except where there are no horse races! The same story applies to a number of other laws. Another type of law is indifferently enforced, not because of the practice against which it is directed is not a recognized evil, but because local opinion considers attempts at prevention futile.

The question naturally arises, "Why pass laws which are not or cannot be enforced in communities that seem to need them most?" Well, in the first place, a legislative body responds to the will of the best organized and most persistent group, the group that controls the most votes. Moral reformers often have many votes behind them. But why do the reformers want a law that cannot be enforced? They will seldom admit that it cannot be enforced; they assert that where enforcement fails, it is because the proper efforts were not made. Furthermore, the reformer seems to think that, even if enforcement is not possible, a moral gesture in statutory terms should be made against an evil practice; otherwise the surrender to the powers of darkness is complete. The writer does not mean to imply that there should be no legislation against moral evils. But he does mean to say that in so legislating we should be sure to direct our efforts only against practices generally recognized as immoral and that the statutes should be so shaped that their enforcement would be practicable. For those practices which we regard as demoralizing but with which the law cannot cope, we should be content with denunciation and education.

IV. SOCIAL SECURITY [30]

A century ago the insane, the feeble-minded, the crippled, the blind, to say nothing of the unemployed, the sick, and the aged, were left to find

[29] *Ibid.,* Ch. IX.

[30] Grace Abbott, *From Relief to Social Security* (1942); Isabel G. Carter (ed.), "Appraising the Social Security Program," *The Annals,* 202 (1939); P. H. Douglas, *Social Security in the*

what succor they might from private sources. The state assumed practically no obligation for these unfortunate millions. But scientific knowledge, perhaps a growing sentiment of humanity, and in particular the change from an agricultural civilization to an industrial one have wrought a great change. Private charity still flourishes and should continue to function, but governments have had to assume the major rôle in caring for the helpless. To encourage and assist the state and local governments in the performance of these functions the federal government now offers plans, money, and supervision.

County welfare administration. One of the oldest responsibilities of local government is the care of the indigent—"poor relief." Until recently the needy were commonly regarded as unworthy, shiftless nuisances, and treated accordingly. Local officials granted the minimum of food, clothing, and fuel to certain applicants and often denied it to others who were equally in want. The indigent sick, the aged, the feebleminded, deserted wives and children, and other unfortunates were given indoor relief; that is, they were sent to an institution known as the poorhouse, almshouse, county farm, or county home. Whatever its name, the place was about the same, a poorhouse, "a perfect testimonial of man's inhumanity to man, as well as a conspicuous example of inefficient and reactionary government," [31] stated the Virginia Board of Public Welfare in reference to the almshouses of that state. The same characterization would have applied (and still may apply) to a few of these "homes" in a number of other states. The authorities suggested that substantial improvements could be made, both in economy of administration and in the treatment accorded the inmates, by co-operation among the counties in materially reducing the number of institutions. Virginia has made significant progress in this direction, and some other states have followed the same procedure.

But outdoor aid, doled out in groceries and clothing, and even well-administered homes for the aged and broken do not quiet the modern social conscience, which is quickened to the conviction that the poor may be worthy and deserve assistance that will enable them to maintain their self-respect. The ill who are without funds should receive proper medical care, the aged might be pensioned and thus be enabled to remain in their own homes, and dependent mothers and children might be given financial assistance. That is the thinking of our time; it is fast becoming the prac-

United States (1939 ed.); Fainsod and Gordon, *Government and the American Economy,* Ch. 21; A. F. Macdonald, *American State Government and Administration* (1950 ed.), Ch. 23; C. F. Snider, *American State and Local Government* (1950), Ch. XVIII; M. S. Stewart, *Social Security* (1939 ed.); *Reports of the Social Security Administration.*

[31] Quoted in J. A. Fairlie and C. M. Kneier, *County Government and Administration* (1930), p. 283.

tice also; and it is closing many almshouses and well on its way toward abolishing the old "grocery order" type of relief.

This modern and humane philosophy was not born of the Great Depression, but it gained general acceptance during that period. Not only did the 'thirties witness a wide change in attitude toward the unfortunate on the part of the general population but they also saw the abandonment of the idea that relief was a local problem. Indeed, we practically stopped talking about "relief," preferring the term *social welfare* or *social security,* and on a national basis. The national government through its Social Security Act (1935) pretty well fixes the minimum standards of assistance and the states, even the reluctant ones, conform in order to get a share of the federal social security grant. But the state-federal welfare program does not remove the counties from the picture. The operation of the program where it really counts, the granting of financial assistance to the blind, to dependent children, to the aged—is in the hands of the county. The nation and the state wisely hold the county to merit system personnel in welfare administration, and inspectors and supervisors keep a check on what the county is doing, but the fact remains that the county is the basic unit in the administration of several features of the social security program. It could not well be otherwise; units of administration there must be, and if the counties were not in existence to provide them, somewhat similar areas of local administration would have to be provided.

State institutions for dependents. In the rugged days of a century ago dependents of almost every description and condition were often sent to county poorhouses. A more enlightened society has gradually segregated the various classes and established separate state institutions for them. About the first class to be thus segregated was the insane. The harmless insane were brought from the poorhouses and the violent insane from the jails, and were given appropriate care, sometimes in private asylums subsidized by the state and sometimes in state hospitals. The latter method of care is at present almost universal. Mental defectives now constitute the largest class of public dependents. Somewhat in keeping with the advance of knowledge concerning the feeble-minded, the epileptic, and other classes of unfortunates, nearly all of the states have established separate institutions for them. Educational institutions are maintained at state expense for the deaf, the dumb, and the blind. These individuals are not charity cases. They receive their training under the sound theory that they are entitled to public education, just as the other youths in the state. Furthermore, if the state did not educate them, many of them would become its dependents. Another type of state institution, the hospital for the indigent sick and for those afflicted with certain diseases, was mentioned under the section on health protection.

THE PROBLEM OF ADMINISTRATION. The management of these institutions, including the difficult tasks of selecting properly qualified personnel, purchasing large quantities of supplies, and keeping "politics" out of both duties, is full of perplexities. Formerly, the practice was to create a board for each institution, but the newer tendency is to put all similar establishments under the same board. In some states this movement has gone so far that all correctional institutions, including prisons, as well as the charitable establishments, are placed under a single, general agency. It is generally thought that a centralized plan is the better; that it makes for uniform practices, secures a higher quality of service, and effects economy in management and in the purchase of supplies. But it is usually found difficult to keep the spoils system out of the managements of institutions, whatever the plan of supervision may be. In any case of mismanagement the inmates of charitable institutions are the chief sufferers. Every little while we hear of brutal treatment, impure food, or some other indefensible condition (always promptly denied by those in authority) at a charitable institution. Although the condition complained of sometimes exists only in the imagination of some soft-hearted or excitable person, all too often there is much truth in the charge.

Poor relief. The duty of taking care of the poor is still largely a local function; but the states care for those whose maintenance is not properly chargeable to any local community, and customarily also provide accommodations for the poor who need special treatment, regardless of residence. In the latter case the county of residence is commonly charged for the service. States sometimes maintain orphans' homes, a service in which religious and other private organizations long led, and still lead, the way.

Mothers' pensions. The type of relief mentioned above is commonly called institutional or "indoor" relief. "Outdoor" relief, or home relief, that is, the giving of aid without commitment to an institution, is now becoming more common than the older form. It is socially more desirable because it avoids breaking up homes, but it is perhaps a little more costly. A form of this type of relief that is generally recommended is the mother's pension. Beginning with Illinois and Missouri in 1911, nearly all the states and the District of Columbia now provide allowances for widows and deserted wives who have not adequate means for the support of their small children. With the coming of social security under the sponsorship of the national government, mothers' pensions and other forms of state relief have been greatly augmented by the federal treasury.

Reasons for national social security. Incomes of most workers have always been very low. They are low now (see chart and figures on "lower-income families" and "money income"). Any appreciable saving is impossible for tens of millions in the labor force. Only national programs of aid can provide the needed assistance. Able-bodied factory and white-collar workers, even in normal times and through no fault of their own,

AMERICA'S LOWER-INCOME FAMILIES

OUT OF 39.200,000 FAMILIES IN THE U.S. THERE ARE
9,700,000 WITH INCOME OF LESS THAN $2,000 A YEAR

OF THOSE FAMILIES

6,300,000 ARE IN CITY AREAS

3,400,000 ARE ON FARMS

2,900,000 ARE HEADED BY PERSONS WITH ONLY GRADE SCHOOLING

2,800,000 ARE HEADED BY PERSONS IN UNSKILLED OCCUPATIONS

2,400,000 ARE HEADED BY PERSONS 65 YEARS OR OLDER

1,400,000 ARE HEADED BY WOMEN

1,200,000 ARE HEADED BY NONWHITES

ESTIMATES BASED ON 1950 POPULATION AND INCOME PROJECTIONS, FROM OFFICIAL DATA FOR 1948.

Reprinted from *U.S. News & World Report* (Jan. 20, 1950), an independent weekly magazine on national and international affairs, published at Washington. Copyright, 1950, United States News Publishing Corporation.

often find themselves without employment. In 1929 the number of unemployed was 2,000,000; in 1933, 13,500,000; and in 1936, although there were many signs of returning prosperity, 12,000,000.[32] It seems that only a

[32] AFL estimates.

major war can give us full employment, or bring us up to the "standard" of 2,000,000 unemployed.

Then there is the problem of the aged worker, or, more broadly speaking, the problem of security for the aged. In 1900 there were 3,000,000 persons over 65 years of age in the United States; in 1930, 7,500,000; and it is estimated that there will be at least 15,000,000 such persons in 1970. The number of men and women over 65 years of age thus increases in much more rapid proportion than the population as a whole. Not only that, but the percentage of unemployed aged persons steadily increases. Only about 25 per cent were unemployed in 1890, but more than 40 per cent were in that class in 1930. The problems of unemployment and security for the aged are the two most urgent problems the industrial civilization has left on our doorstep.

MONEY INCOME RECEIVED BY EACH FIFTH OF FAMILIES AND SINGLE PERSONS,
1935-36, 1941 AND 1948 *

Families and single persons ranked from lowest to highest income	Percentage of money income			Average money income in dollars of 1948 purchasing power [1]			Per cent increase in average income	
	1935-36	1941	1948	1935-36	1941	1948	1935-36 to 1948	1941 to 1948
Lowest fifth	4.0	3.5	4.2	$ 534	$ 592	$ 893	67	51
Second fifth	8.7	9.1	10.5	1,159	1,546	2,232	93	44
Third fifth	13.6	15.3	16.1	1,810	2,597	3,410	88	31
Fourth fifth	20.5	22.5	22.3	2,734	3,816	4,711	72	23
Highest fifth	53.2	49.6	46.9	7,083	8,418	9,911	40	18
All groups	100.0	100.0	100.0	2,664	3,396	4,231	59	25

* From Council of Economic Advisers, *The Annual Economic Review*, Jan. 3, 1950, Table 14.

[1] Current dollars divided by the consumers' price index on the base 1948 = 100 to give a rough measure of changes in purchasing power of income.

Note.—Adjustments have been made in basic survey data for each year. Detail will not necessarily add to totals because of rounding.

Sources: National Resources Planning Board (1935-36), Department of Labor (1941), and Council of Economic Advisers (1948).

Long before governments assumed any responsibility for the unemployed, labor organizations established funds that were distributed to members who were out of work. But these funds protected only a small percentage of the workers, and they were wholly inadequate to meet any prolonged or wide-spread unemployment. Governments came to the rescue, beginning about 1900. Belgium, France, Holland, Finland, Great Britain, and others assumed this new obligation. Wisconsin was the first American state to pass an unemployment insurance act (1932).

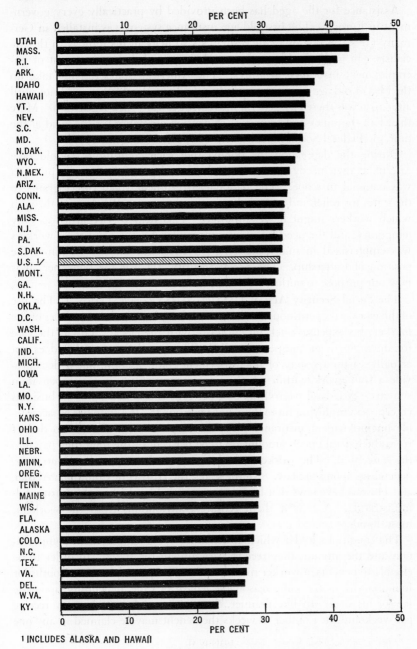

1 INCLUDES ALASKA AND HAWAII

From *Annual Report of the Social Security Administration*, 1948, p. 148.

Assistance for the aged has been provided by practically every government in Europe. The first old-age insurance system was installed in Germany (1889) as one phase of Bismarck's strategy in his fight with the Socialists. In general, old-age pension laws preceded the enactment of unemployment insurance measures. The American states did not take up the idea of old-age pensions until after the First World War, and not until after 1930 was there any general movement toward such legislation. More than half the states had some sort of pension assistance for the aged at the time the Federal Social Security Act was passed (August, 1935).

During the depression the dogma that each community should take care of its own needy gave way to the sound principle that the problem was national in scope. The national government voted direct grants to the states for relief and provided numerous agencies (PWA, etc.) through which workers might be re-employed. This help was regarded as only temporary, and the need for a permanent plan for the security of workers was emphasized in many quarters, the President himself assuming the position of leadership. The Social Security Act was the outcome. It is now our purpose to outline its main provisions.

The Social Security Act: 1. Unemployment compensation. "The life of the worker is continuous. The income from his job obeys the tides of the market; his expenses click on endlessly with the clock. This is the case for unemployment compensation." [33] The Social Security Act does not actually set up a system of unemployment compensation, but it does provide a framework within which states may establish such compensation systems. A federal payroll tax of 3 per cent is imposed upon all business enterprises employing more than eight persons.[34] If a state has an acceptable unemployment insurance plan, the employers are allowed to deduct from the federal tax an amount up to 90 per cent of the total they pay into the state fund. The workers may or may not be required to contribute, depending upon state law. All the states, the District of Columbia, Alaska, and Hawaii have laws that have been approved by the Social Security Administration. A few of them require contributions from the workers; most do not.

The conditions under which workers receive unemployment compensation and the amount they receive vary among the states. In order to be eligible to benefits, a worker must have been employed for two months, or four months, or for some reasonable length of time, depending upon the law of his state. In like manner, the amount of benefit he may receive per week and the number of weeks the benefit may be claimed in any one

---

[33] *Report of the Social Security Board,* 1936, p. vi.

[34] Farm labor, domestic servants, and a few other classes are not included.

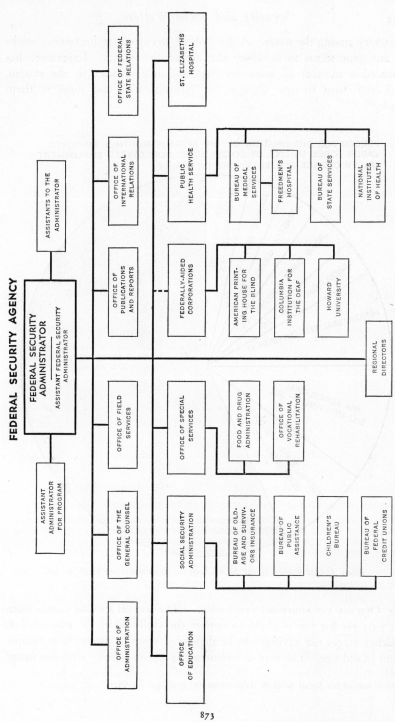

FEDERAL SECURITY AGENCY

From *U.S. Government Organization Manual*, 1950-51, p. 616.

year vary among the states. A third of the weekly wage for twenty weeks in any year seems to be about the average allowance. Experience has revealed a number of inconsistencies and inadequacies in the system, and from time to time changes are recommended and some of them made.[35]

PERCENTAGE DISTRIBUTION OF THE AVERAGE MONTHLY EMPLOYED LABOR FORCE IN 1947, BY COVERED AND NONCOVERED EMPLOYMENT UNDER OLD-AGE AND SURVIVORS INSURANCE.

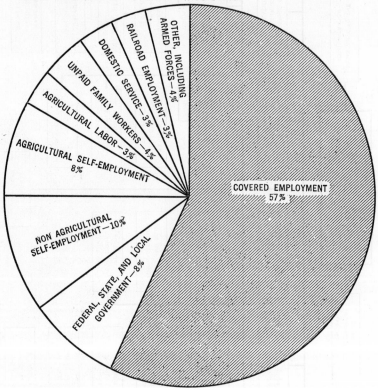

OTHER, INCLUDING ARMED FORCES—4%

RAILROAD EMPLOYMENT—3%

DOMESTIC SERVICE—3%

UNPAID FAMILY WORKERS—4%

AGRICULTURAL LABOR—3%

AGRICULTURAL SELF-EMPLOYMENT 8%

NON AGRICULTURAL SELF-EMPLOYMENT—10%

FEDERAL, STATE, AND LOCAL GOVERNMENT—8%

COVERED EMPLOYMENT 57%

From *Annual Report of the Social Security Administration*, 1948, p. 90.

2. OLD-AGE AND SURVIVORS INSURANCE. "The worker's living comes from his job; yet his life is likely to outlast the skills which he can market. Neither wages nor savings can be depended upon to protect him against want in old age. The way of industrial provision is beset with too many

[35] *Report of the Social Security Administration*, 1948, pp. 64–65.

NUMBER OF AGED PERSONS RECEIVING BENEFITS UNDER OLD-AGE AND SURVIVORS INSURANCE[1] AND NUMBER RECEIVING OLD-AGE ASSISTANCE PER 1,000 PERSONS 65 YEARS AND OVER IN EACH STATE[2] JUNE 1948

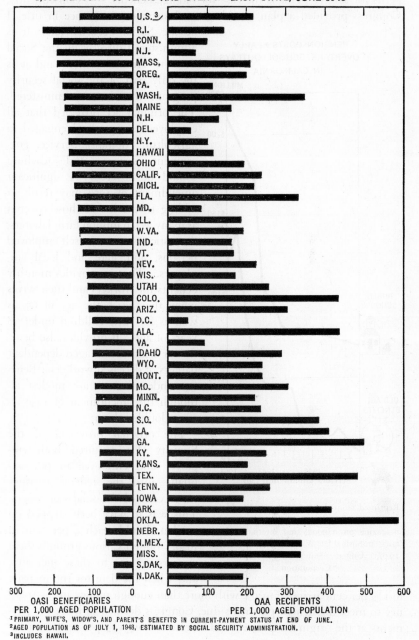

OASI BENEFICIARIES
PER 1,000 AGED POPULATION

OAA RECIPIENTS
PER 1,000 AGED POPULATION

[1] PRIMARY, WIFE'S, WIDOW'S, AND PARENT'S BENEFITS IN CURRENT-PAYMENT STATUS AT END OF JUNE.
[2] AGED POPULATION AS OF JULY 1, 1948, ESTIMATED BY SOCIAL SECURITY ADMINISTRATION.
[3] INCLUDES HAWAII.

From *Annual Report of the Social Security Administration,* 1948, p. 70.

perils for safety. This is the case for old-age benefits." [36] Consequently,
Congress provided a plan of old-age and survivors insurance in title II
of the Social Security Act. It is
administered directly by the Social
Security Administration, and it is
the only part of the social security
program that is so administered.
The original act provided that all
employees except those engaged in
agriculture, domestic service, government service, and teaching
should be covered. A significant
amendment of 1950 may result in
adding to the list of those covered
as many as ten million farm laborers,
domestic servants, self-employed
persons, and state and local employees. The act provides monthly
benefits for workers and their wives
when they reach the age of 65, as
well as for their children under 18
years of age. It provides also benefits for widows and aged dependent
parents of deceased workers. Benefits under the act are modest although the amendment of 1950 almost doubled them.

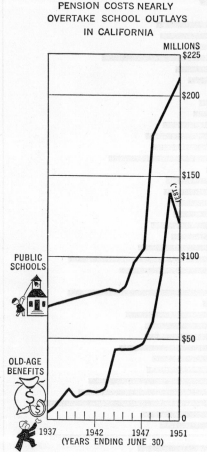

PENSION COSTS NEARLY
OVERTAKE SCHOOL OUTLAYS
IN CALIFORNIA

Reprinted from the *U.S. News & World Report* (Nov. 18, 1949), an independent weekly
magazine on national and international affairs, published at Washington. Copyright,
1949, United States News Publishing
Corporation.

The original provision of the
Security Act required both employer and employee to pay annually into the federal treasury
1 per cent of the salary or wages.
This was to have been stepped up
until it should reach 3 per cent in
1949. But on various grounds there
were objections to these increases,
and when the date for the increase
to 1½ per cent arrived (1940), with more than enough money in the treasury to meet the benefit payments due, Congress decided to leave the payments at the original 1 per cent. The rate is now 1½ per cent each for

[36] 1936, p. vi.

NUMBER OF CHILDREN RECEIVING BENEFITS UNDER OLD-AGE AND SURVIVORS
INSURANCE[1] AND NUMBER RECEIVING AID TO DEPENDENT CHILDREN PER 1,000
CHILDREN UNDER 18 YEARS OF AGE,[2] JUNE 1948

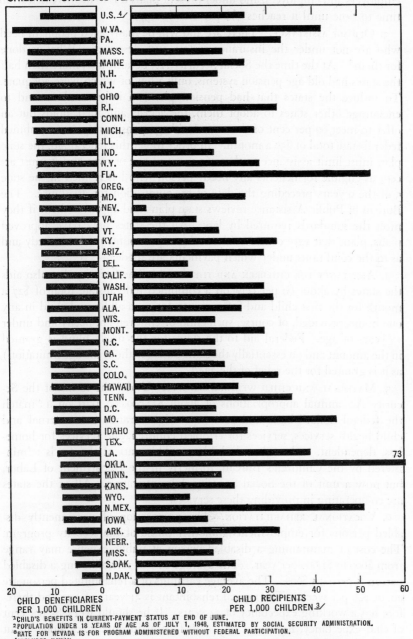

CHILD BENEFICIARIES
PER 1,000 CHILDREN

CHILD RECIPIENTS
PER 1,000 CHILDREN[3]

[1] CHILD'S BENEFITS IN CURRENT-PAYMENT STATUS AT END OF JUNE.
[2] POPULATION UNDER 18 YEARS OF AGE AS OF JULY 1, 1948, ESTIMATED BY SOCIAL SECURITY ADMINISTRATION.
[3] RATE FOR NEVADA IS FOR PROGRAM ADMINISTERED WITHOUT FEDERAL PARTICIPATION.
[4] INCLUDES HAWAII.

From *Annual Report of the Social Security Administration*, 1948, p. 74.

employers and employees, and under present plans it is to be increased from time to time until it reaches 3¼ per cent in 1970.

3. OLD-AGE ASSISTANCE. There are and will be many aged people in need who are not under the insurance system just described. What is done for them? At the time the Social Security Act became law, more than half the states had old-age pension systems, only a few of which were adequate. To induce the states that had pension plans to improve them and to encourage other states to adopt them, the act, as amended, holds out an offer to meet 60 per cent of the cost of old-age pensions up to a combined federal-state total of $50 a month. In order to get this federal aid, the state plan must limit assistance to those 65 years of age or over and it must accept as eligible for benefits any needy person who has resided in the state 5 of the 9 years preceding the date of his application for assistance. The Bureau of Public Assistance reviews state plans and approves them if they meet the standards required by law. All the states now have approved plans, plans that vary considerably, both as to amounts paid the needy and as to the conditions under which payments are made.

4. ASSISTANCE FOR CHILDREN AND THE BLIND. The Security Act also aids the states by about 60 per cent on a combined federal-state total of $27 a month for the first child and $18 a month for each additional child in any one home, provided, of course, such child or children are needy and under 18 years of age. Federal aid to the states for the needy blind is granted in the amount and on essentially the same basis (without the age limitation) as it is granted for the relief of the aged.

5. MATERNAL AND CHILD WELFARE SERVICES. Under the terms of the Security Act annual appropriations of about $22,000,000, part on a "match the federal dollar" basis and part in outright grants, for maternal and child health services, services for crippled children, and services for homeless, dependent, and neglected children. This part of the act is administered by the Children's Bureau, formerly in the Department of Labor, but now a unit of the Social Security Administration. All of the states are co-operating in providing these services.

6. VOCATIONAL REHABILITATION. The preparation of permanently disabled persons for employment is another phase of the security program. The cost of maintaining a disabled person at public expense may range from $600 to $1,000 per year. The average cost of rehabilitating a disabled person is perhaps $600. The average earnings of a rehabilitated person are about $40 per week. The typical rehabilitant is 31 years of age and therefore has a working expectancy of 34 years. If he should work 85 per cent of that expectancy, he would return in federal income taxes alone about $10 for every $1 expended on his rehabilitation.[37] Not only is rehabilita-

[37] *Report of the Federal Security Agency,* 1948, p. 17.

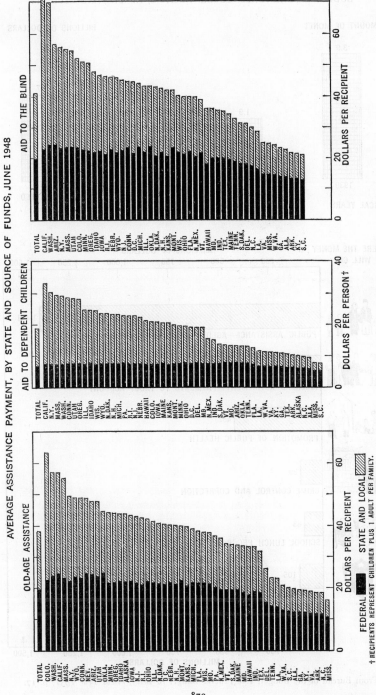

AVERAGE ASSISTANCE PAYMENT, BY STATE AND SOURCE OF FUNDS, JUNE 1948

OLD-AGE ASSISTANCE

AID TO DEPENDENT CHILDREN

AID TO THE BLIND

FEDERAL · STATE AND LOCAL

† RECIPIENTS REPRESENT CHILDREN PLUS 1 ADULT PER FAMILY.

From *Annual Report of the Social Security Administration, 1948*, p. 167.

879

BUDGET EXPENDITURES: SOCIAL WELFARE, HEALTH, AND SECURITY

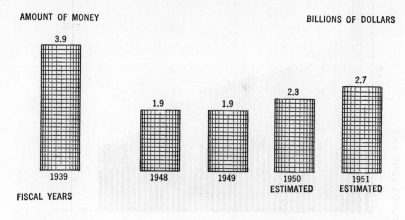

AMOUNT OF MONEY

BILLIONS OF DOLLARS

3.9 — 1939
1.9 — 1948
1.9 — 1949
2.3 — 1950 ESTIMATED
2.7 — 1951 ESTIMATED

FISCAL YEARS

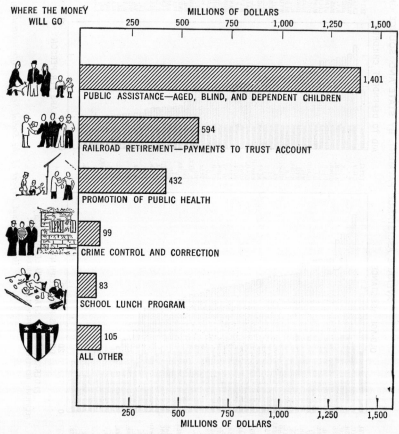

WHERE THE MONEY WILL GO

MILLIONS OF DOLLARS

PUBLIC ASSISTANCE—AGED, BLIND, AND DEPENDENT CHILDREN — 1,401

RAILROAD RETIREMENT—PAYMENTS TO TRUST ACCOUNT — 594

PROMOTION OF PUBLIC HEALTH — 432

CRIME CONTROL AND CORRECTION — 99

SCHOOL LUNCH PROGRAM — 83

ALL OTHER — 105

MILLIONS OF DOLLARS

From Bureau of the Budget, *The Federal Budget in Brief, Fiscal Year 1951*, p. 17.

tion economically sound from the government's standpoint, but it is also economically profitable for society as a whole, and no one can estimate its value to the rehabilitant in restored independence and morale. It is not surprising that as long ago as 1920 Congress passed the Vocational Rehabilitation Act, thus establishing this particular type of security before the general social security program was seriously considered. The annual appropriation for rehabilitation, most of it on a federal-aid basis, is now more than $25,000,000.

Viewing the social security program as a whole, one may conclude that it is more than a cautious approach to the security problem. It is in no sense a complete solution, but the advance made is a distinct achievement, one that in the complacent 'twenties seemed remote indeed. It is criticized from two quarters, by those who say it is grossly inadequate and by those who claim it goes too far. No doubt difficulties will continue to arise in its administration, and no doubt there will be need from time to time for amendments. No legislation of this type could possibly be drafted that would not later need revision and correction. Debates attending the enactment of the amendment of 1950 clearly indicated that congressmen are fully aware of the need for constant reconsideration of the social security problem.

Private pensions and annuities. Retirement systems have been provided in rapidly increasing numbers by industry and business. It is estimated that only about 600,000 employees were so covered in 1940 and that some 7,200,000 are now covered, by 13,000 enterprises. The majority of these plans are financed by the employers; others operate under joint employer-employee contributions. Payments under these plans supplement government social security benefits, bringing total monthly annuities to between $100 and $125 for some 55 per cent of the retired workers, over $125 for 20 per cent, but under $100 for 25 per cent. The minimum goal of the workers seems to be $100 per month in retirement benefits. The agreement reached between the Ford Motor Company and the UAW in 1949 was at that figure, the Company paying the difference between the retired worker's social security benefits and $100. Employers and employees in general approve the principle of retirement payments, the workers primarily for reasons of security and the employers primarily because such funds give the workers an incentive to stay on the job. The workers prefer pensions—that the employers pay all the cost, as in the Ford Motor case; the employers very naturally have a hankering for the annuity plan, the system that calls for some employee contributions. Big Steel and labor fought this issue of employee contributions in 1949, and labor won, although labor agreed to contribute a part of certain other benefit funds.

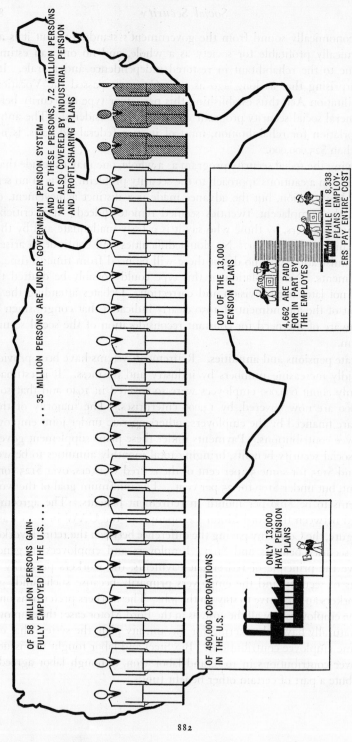

PENSIONS FOR WORKERS: INDUSTRY COVERAGE VS GOVERNMENT

Reprinted from the *U.S. News & World Report* (Nov. 11, 1949), an independent weekly magazine on national and international affairs, published at Washington. Copyright, 1949, United States News Publishing Corporation.

V. EDUCATION [38]

Although some encouragement and aid for education come from the national government (and more is constantly being sought), schooling from kindergarten through the university is primarily a state function.

State educational policy. With a few exceptions the colonies left education to private individuals and institutions. But following the Revolution the idea of elementary education at public expense gained rapidly, and in the course of time this became the practice in every nook and corner of the country.[39] Secondary schools and state universities were added to the state program; but not always in logical sequence, the university sometimes being established first. In our own time we find that the constitution and laws of a state usually call for elementary, secondary, and vocational schools, teachers' colleges, an A. and M. college, a university, and certain other institutions of learning. State laws also prescribe in considerable detail the methods by which education shall be financed, stipulating, for example, the manner in which funds shall be raised for the higher institutions, what part of the total cost, if any, of secondary and elementary education shall be chargeable to the state, and how the local units shall raise their quotas of the cost. The laws also commonly provide for a state school board and a superintendent of schools, charging them jointly or separately with the duties of making rules and regulations respecting the state public school system, conducting inspections, licensing teachers, collecting statistics, and similar responsibilities. Ordinarily, the board determines questions of policy, and the administrative work is done by the superintendent. The state colleges and universities are very commonly left free of the state school board and the superintendent of schools. A separate board, often a separate board for each institution, administers them.

HIGHER EDUCATION. Although a few of the Eastern states with very old privately endowed universities have no state institution by that name, all the other states have. Attendance in the universities and state colleges, as well as in the private institutions of higher learning, has increased most remarkably in the past generation. In the old days the favored few went to college to acquire the learning and culture a "gentleman" was supposed

[38] W. H. Burton, *Introduction to Education* (1934); The Council of State Governments, *The Forty-Eight State School System* (1949); Newton Edwards and H. G. Richey, *The School in the American Social Order* (1947); J. D. Russell and C. H. Judd, *American Educational System* (1940); R. M. Hutchins, *Higher Learning in America* (1936); H. D. Gideonse, *Higher Learning in a Democracy* (1937); J. D. Russell, "The States in Higher Education," *State Government*, May, 1949, pp. 135–139, 147.

[39] Long after their establishment, however, the "free schools" in some sections of the country, particularly the South, were looked upon as schools for the poor and were sometimes openly referred to as such.

to have; the masses now go for the purpose of receiving training that will enable them to make a living. The colleges have responded to this new demand, particularly the state institutions, by offering vocational courses in an array of subjects never dreamed of by the pedagogues of a hundred years ago and which amaze the European and bring forth some adverse criticism in our own country. Liberal education is not omitted from the curricula, but critics say that undue emphasis is given the vocational subjects. Still, there is a great deal to be said both for the democracy that provides it and for the system itself, the system that prepares students to make a living. Another feature of our higher educational system is the opportunity it "gives a poor boy to work his way through college." This opportunity, which does not exist in many other countries, is often referred to as one of the glories of the American system. The "poor boy" does not always eventually triumph, as in the story, but he is given his chance. Those who cannot attend college have their chance also. The college goes to them through its extension professors sent to give courses at local centers and through the correspondence courses that can be taken wherever mail is delivered.

PUBLIC SCHOOLS. The state usually fixes a minimum standard for the public schools, exercises some general supervision to see that those standards are maintained, grants a subsidy for the support of the schools of each district, and leaves the rest to local initiative and enterprise. Each county, city, township, or whatever the unit may be has its school board of laymen, and the larger units have their professional superintendents also. The board has general authority in school matters and quite often has the power, within certain limits, to fix the school levy. Communities almost invariably take great pride in and often make considerable sacrifice for their public schools. We take it as a matter of course that the school building shall be the best and most conspicuous structure in a small town. A number of distinguished foreigners who have found many features of American culture about which to make caustic comment are favorably impressed with the dominance of our public schools. In the town and to some extent in the cities the school is not just the school, but it furnishes a public forum and is a center for recreation and social life as well.

As for courses of instruction, preparation for college is not forgotten; but the "practical" courses are emphasized more and more—courses that will fit the students to become breadwinners. Nearly all the larger cities have special vocational schools for training students in electrical installation, plumbing, printing, stenography, cooking, sewing, and a host of other trades and callings. Night schools are now commonly provided for youths who must earn a living during the day and for adults who did not have advantages earlier. A number of cities provide junior colleges and a few have established municipal universities. Schools for such classes of unfortunates as the tuberculous have been founded in some areas.

In a discussion of education, the public library, the handmaiden of education, should always be mentioned. Practically every city of any consequence now has a well-equipped free public library. Rural communities sometimes receive a lesser service through the "traveling" library. An economy of the depression years that people of vision generally condemned was the very severe reduction made in appropriations for libraries.

The problem of finance. The schools cost a great deal of money. Approximately one fourth of the state and local revenue goes for education. It is generally thought that the schools are worth the money and that less waste and extravagance occur with school expenditures than with most other public expenditures. However, in times of retrenchment, the schools have sometimes been the special target of attack. The small salary of the thrifty teacher now appears very large to the deflated business man. The whole school system is attacked as extravagant. It is right that the schools should be asked to reduce costs; but straight percentage reductions, easy to calculate and often employed, often result in the curtailment of a particular school service that we should be most anxious to preserve.

Another financial problem is that of the rural school. The cost is high and many rural communities are poor, even in relatively prosperous times. Since the funds must be raised primarily from taxable property in the district, it follows that taxpayers in a poor area will have to pay much higher school taxes for the same type of school than are paid by their more favored brethren in a wealthy district. A partial solution lies in the consolidation of schools. But, while consolidation gives better schools, it does not improve the financial situation a great deal for the impoverished areas forming the larger district. A better solution is for the state to assume more financial responsibility for the schools and give aid to local communities in proportion to their needs and deserts. Who objects to this? Naturally the taxpayers in the more prosperous areas of the state, who say that each township should educate its own children, a theory that is just one step ahead of the one held before the dawn of this Republic, namely, that each family should educate its own. Nevertheless, a number of states have come to the aid of the rural communities in the manner here suggested.

Even the great cities have their problem of school financing. It is that the school board, the largest spender in the city, is usually empowered to fix a school tax rate and spend the money as it sees fit. This plan makes it impossible to treat city finances as a unit. While the council may be retrenching in the services for which it votes appropriations, the board of education may be increasing appropriations for the schools. It is perhaps desirable that the school budget be approved by the council, thus making it possible for all the city services to be considered on an equal footing, the needs of each being considered in relation to all the others and total appropriations being limited to an amount not unduly burdensome on the taxpayers.

Reading List

Grace Abbott, *From Relief to Social Security* (1942).

Annual Reports of the Social Security Administration and the *Federal Security Agency.*

G. W. Bachman and Lewis Merriam, *The Issue of Compulsory Health Insurance* (1948).

C. A. and Wm. Beard, *The American Leviathan* (1930), Ch. XVIII.

A. W. Bromage, *State Government and Administration in the United States* (1936), Chs. XVII–XVIII.

———, *Introduction to Municipal Government and Administration* (1950), Chs. XXV–XXXI.

M. S. Callcott, *Principles of Social Legislation* (1932).

Isabel G. Carter (ed.), "Appraising the Social Security Program," *The Annals,* 202 (1939).

J. M. Clark, *Alternative to Serfdom* (1948).

M. L. Colean, *American Housing* (1944).

The (Hoover) Commission on Organization of the Executive Branch of the Government, *Social Security and Education* (1949).

The Council of State Governments, *The Forty-Eight State School Systems* (1949).

P. H. Douglas, *Social Security in the United States* (1939 ed.).

H. G. Epsy, *Public Secondary School* (1939).

Merle Fainsod and Lincoln Gordon, *Government and the American Economy* (1948 ed.), Ch. 21.

Nathaniel W. Faxon (ed.), *The Hospital in Contemporary Life* (1949).

Federal Bureau of Investigation, *Standards in Police Training* (1939).

H. D. Gideonse, *Higher Learning in a Democracy* (1937).

R. M. Hutchins, *Higher Learning in America* (1936).

Federal Security Agency, *The Nation's Health—A Ten-Year Plan* (1948).

Institutes for Training in Municipal Administration (Chicago), *Municipal Fire Administration* (1942 ed.) and *Municipal Police Administration* (1943 ed.).

A. F. Macdonald, *American State Government and Administration* (1950 ed.), Chs. XXIII–XXIX.

Carl Malmberg, *140 Million Patients* (1947).

Lewis Merriam, *Relief and Social Security* (1946).

A. C. Millspaugh, *Crime Control by the National Government* (1937).

H. S. Mustard, *Government in Public Health* (1945).

National Commission on Law Observance and Enforcement (Wickersham Commission), *Report on the Enforcement of the Prohibition Laws of the United States* (No. 2, January, 1931).

J. M. Pfiffner, *Municipal Administration* (1940).

Report of the President's Committee on Social Trends, *Recent Social Trends* (1933), Researches 7, 8, 11, 18, 21, 23, and 24.

J. D. Russell, "The States in Higher Education," *State Government,* May, 1949, p. 135 ff.

J. D. Russell and C. H. Judd, *American Educational System* (1940).

James S. Simmons (ed.), *Public Health in the World Today* (1949).

W. G. Smillie, *Public Health Administration in the United States* (1947 ed.).

C. F. Snider, *American State and Local Government* (1950) Chs. XVII–XX.

M. S. Stewart, *Social Security* (1939 ed.).

H. H. Waite, *Disease Prevention* (1928).

G. A. Weber, *Food, Drug, and Insecticide Administration* (1928).

H. W. Wiley, *History of a Crime Against the Food Law* (1929).

Helen R. Wright (ed.), *Social Service in Wartime* (1945).

Questions and Problems

1. Write a 200-word essay on city police problems, with particular reference to your own city (if you live in one).
2. Can you show that American methods of protection from fire indicate both the strength and weakness of our skills and methods?
3. How do you explain the fact that public health protection in the cities has made more rapid progress than rural health protection?
4. What are the chief obstacles to the enactment and enforcement of pure food and drug acts?
5. Outline the work of the U.S. Public Health Service.
6. How would you meet the problem of providing adequate medical service for all the American people?
7. Discuss public education in relation to the successful operation of a health program.
8. How do the states protect the public health?
9. Show how legislation with respect to the public morals may illustrate the limitations of law.
10. Comment upon the economic and social implications of this statement: *Each family should take care of its own dependents.* And this: *Each community should take care of its own indigent.*
11. State the case for unemployment insurance.
12. Discuss the social and economic considerations involved in the proposition that everyone should retire at 65 on a pension or an annuity equal to 40 per cent of his annual earnings at the time he reached the retirement age.
13. Why do we not reason that it is just socialism—communism—to educate children at public expense?

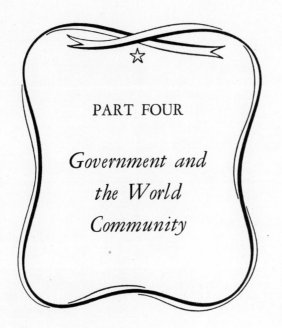

PART FOUR

*Government and
the World
Community*

☆ 27 ☆

National Defense

"THEY cannot harm us; we are too far away. Besides, someone may assassinate their leader. We hear that his people are 'fed up' with him. Even if they get here, something will turn up to prevent their attacking us. And if the attack should actually take place, 10 million men will spring to arms and drive them into the sea." The speaker is the typical American of practically any period of our history indulging in one of his favorite pastimes, the enjoyment of his "immunity complex." The "bonehead" of the comic strips gets out of all his scrapes; Superman never fails to annihilate his enemies; and, whatever her mishaps and misadventures may be along the way, the girl in the magazine story invariably gets her man. So it has been and so it will be with our country —danger may be imminent, neglect and incompetence may invite disaster, but we will find, or good luck will provide, a happy end to every crisis.[1] Thus reasons the American. Only the atomic bomb has given him pause.

Geographical position, economic resources, the enterprise of our people, and good luck have thus far brought us safely through every military threat. But in these days of rapid transportation geography does not vouchsafe to us the immunity of old; our continental economic resources are found to be less than sufficient for the conduct of total war; and, luck, although at times a very present help in the time of need, has ever been wholly unreliable as an ally. We have fought a number of wars, each in the hope, and sometimes in the rather firm belief, that it would be the last. But crises in other lands fade our hopes, and bombs dropping on our ships and soil shatter our beliefs. Once more war has come.

War is all that General William T. Sherman said it is, and more. Its modern atomic horrors have not made it improbable, much less impossible. Blindly hating it is likely to lead only to military inadequacy and ineffi-

[1] This analogy is suggested by Norman Cousins in his "The Immunity Complex in America," *Saturday Review of Literature*, October 18, 1941.

ciency. We must face the problem of national defense and war, and we must consider their impact upon democratic society.

I. WAR POWERS OF THE PRESIDENT AND OF CONGRESS [2]

The war powers granted by the Constitution. Congress has the power to (1) declare war; (2) to raise and support armies; (3) to provide and maintain a navy; (4) to make rules for the government and regulation of the land and naval forces; (5) to provide for calling forth the militia, and for organizing, arming, and disciplining the militia when it is in the service of the United States; (6) to levy taxes and appropriate money for the common defense; and (7) to make any laws that may be necessary for carrying any of these powers into execution. The war power of Congress is, therefore, comprehensive.

The Constitution makes the President the Commander-in-Chief of the Army and Navy and of the state militia when it is called into the service of the United States. Certain other powers and duties that relate to the war power are conferred upon the President by the Constitution. They are as follows: the duty to execute the laws of the United States; the obligation (which he shares with Congress) to guarantee to every state a republican form of government and to protect each of them against invasion and domestic violence; and the right and duty to make recommendations to Congress. From the evidence Congress apparently has the greater part of the war power, and so it seemed to Alexander Hamilton, one of the framers of the Constitution. The truth is, however, that the President holds the center of the stage in the grim drama of war.

How Congress legislates for defense. The theory underlying the Constitutional distribution of war powers is that Congress should fix the broad outlines of military policy and that the President and other administrative officials should carry it into execution. In order to determine a policy Congress should decide what we will defend, where we will defend it, and when we will defend it. Shall we defend this nation, its outlying possessions, the Western Hemisphere, or the whole world? Where shall we meet the possible foe or foes? Shall we sit and wait for them to attack us, go meet them, or attack them before they start? It cannot be said that these questions have ever been decided. We have been divided in Congress and out between collective security and isolation, between preparedness and pacifism, between Anglophobes and Anglophiles, to mention only a few causes of divided counsels. Another difficulty

---

[2] E. S. Corwin, *The President: Office and Powers* (1948 ed.), Ch. VI; and *Total War and the Constitution* (1947); P. Herring, *The Impact of War: Our American Democracy under Arms* (1941), Chs. V–VI; D. O. Walter, *American Government at War* (1942), Ch. III.

in the way of formulating policy is the unpredictable action of other countries.

Yet some fairly respectable peacetime planning and legislation have been effected. The National Defense Act of 1916 deserves mention. It was the main feature of our very modest "preparedness" program prior to our European adventure of 1917–1918. Following that war, the country was again divided on the question of a military establishment. There were many fine pacifists of the type of Jane Addams, there were extreme militarists of the Prussian variety, and there were varieties between these extremes. But the professional soldiers, the administrators, and the military affairs committees of Congress evolved a compromise plan that was embodied in a notable piece of legislation, the National Defense Act of 1920. It provided for a standing army, which might be expanded as the national defense might require, the organized reserves, and the Reserve Officers' Training Corps and the Civilians' Military Training Corps. It organized the United States into corps areas. And it established the principle of mobilization as against volunteering, and the principle of industrial mobilization.

Our reliance on the British Navy as a part of our defense force in the Atlantic and our failure, for at least a decade, to notice that we might be the losers in a program for the limitation of naval armaments brought us up to 1933 with a Navy far from first class. That year found another Roosevelt who loved navies in the White House, and Congress responded to his demands to enlarge and strengthen the Navy. In 1940, in response to the fall of France and the fear that Britain might be overcome and her Navy turned against us, Congress authorized the construction of a two-ocean Navy, the Navy we might have had years before had we followed the construction program begun during the First World War. Although Congress and the President must carry a large share of the blame for any lack of preparedness, either military or naval, the professional soldiers and sailors have a share of the blame. They have often been accused of planning for the "last war," that is, for a war that had been fought with weapons that had since been outmoded, of overlooking the possibilities of such instruments as tanks and planes and atomic bombs in future wars.

How wars are declared. The Constitution clearly confers the authority to declare war upon Congress. But as a matter of fact the President has much more to do with it than Congress. He is in a position to force the hand of Congress. He may, as Commander-in-Chief, order troops to occupy disputed territory, as did President Polk, and when they are fired upon by opposing forces, announce to Congress that war exists. Or he may, as did President McKinley, send a battleship into "troubled waters" where it might be sunk (or sink from internal causes), with the result that war becomes inevitable. More important, the President, through his control of foreign relations, has the power, not perhaps to lead the country into war or away from war, but certainly to "graze the edge of war," to steer us about its treacherous sinuosities, and, subject to the unpredictable acts of probable enemies, to pick the spot and time at which we might enter. Our entrance into both the First and the Second World Wars was largely determined by the respective foreign policies of Presidents Woodrow Wilson and Franklin D. Roosevelt. Congress has, of course, declared war in all of the cases mentioned, but that was only a detail and not even that in the case of the declaration against Japan after its attack on Pearl Harbor.[3] In 1950 our "police action" in Korea was undertaken on the authority of the President acting with the Security Council of the United Nations.

The President as Commander-in-Chief. Although the President is a civilian,[4] it is conceivable that as Commander-in-Chief of the Army and Navy he might take the field and assume direct charge of military operations, as did many kings, ancient and medieval, and the Emperor Napoleon. Washington did in fact take the field to suppress the Whiskey Rebellion, but other Presidents have wisely stayed at the seat of govment. Lincoln, exasperated with his slow-moving generals, did issue some strictly military orders, but he regretted doing so and refrained from issuing more after Grant took command of the Union forces. General of the Army George C. Marshall, Chief of Staff during the Second World War, gratefully records that, at the most critical periods of the conflict, President Roosevelt even refrained from asking questions of the generals.[5] Doubtless some of the Presidents have entertained some notion that they were military strategists and they may have exerted influence in this direction; but, with the exceptions noted, they have left military orders to the generals. Jefferson Davis was a trained soldier, and once he gave Lee a military order—to which the latter responded with the tender of his sword. No important questions have arisen over the President's purely military powers—he seldom, if ever, exercises them. But controversies have raged around his use of his powers as Chief Executive and Commander-in-Chief to determine broad questions of war policy and to regiment the life of the nation.

During the period of the war between the states, responsible men did not scruple to call President Lincoln "absolute," "uncontrollable," "tyrant," "usurper," and "despot." Why? Because Lincoln, upon his inaugura-

[3] New York Life Ins. Co. v. Bennion, U.S. Circuit Ct. of App., Tenth Cir., Nov. 6, 1946. See also "When Did the War Begin?" *Am. Jour. of Int. Law,* July, 1947, p. 621.

[4] The Surrogate of Dutchess County, N.Y., so held in July, 1950, and there is little doubt that his holding is correct.

[5] *Biennial Report of the Chief of Staff, 1943–1945,* p. 114.

tion, finding no plans for saving the imperiled Union, took such action as he deemed necessary to save it. He did not wait for Congress to legislate. In fact, he did not call Congress into special session until ten weeks after the fall of Fort Sumter. He reasoned that as Chief Executive and Commander-in-Chief he had the duty and he ought to have the power to take any action against forces hostile to the United States. He embodied the militia into a volunteer army, added thousands of men to the regular Army and to the Navy, incurred for the United States a debt of a quarter of a billion dollars (a very large sum in those days), paid money from the Treasury to persons unauthorized to receive it, excluded "treasonable correspondence" from the mails, ordered a blockade of Southern ports, suspended the writ of habeas corpus, and detained under military guard persons suspected of treasonable acts or of contemplating such acts—"and all of this for the most part," writes Professor E. S. Corwin, "without the least statutory authorization." [6] Congress and the courts (the latter with some reservations) later approved these acts of the President, and the Commander-in-Chief was thus encouraged to issue other orders and proclamations for which there was no clear authority in the statutes.

War powers delegated to the President. In the First World War Wilson followed, as far as they were applicable, the precedents established by Lincoln. But the First World War was something new, a war of populations, not simply a contest of armies. It called not only for soldiers, but also for the complete mobilization of the manpower and resources of the nations involved. Within three months of its outbreak the British Parliament found it necessary to authorize the executive power to conduct the war and regulate the life of civilians without much reference to Parliament. Although the United States was in that war but a short time and it never really touched our shores, Congress found it necessary to follow the example of our European associates and delegate wide powers to the Chief Executive.

The Food and Fuel Control Act authorized the President to regulate by license the importation, manufacture, storage, mining, or distribution of necessities; to take over factories, packing houses, pipe lines, mines or other plants; and to exercise similar powers in relation to foods and war materials. Numerous other statutes gave the President far-reaching powers. For example, the Trading with the Enemy Act authorized him to license trade with the enemy, and to censor all communications with foreign countries, and the Espionage Act authorized him to declare unlawful the exportation of certain goods. The powers thus delegated to the President were, in turn, usually redelegated by him to administrative agents serving under his direction. These officers issued in the President's name

[6] Corwin, *The President*, p. 278.

thousands of orders and regulations relating to every aspect of the war program. Both Lincoln and Wilson exercised "dictatorial" powers, and the difference was only in this: Lincoln used his powers of Commander-in-Chief to the fullest, expecting and receiving approval of Congress, whereas Wilson was given wide powers by acts of Congress and therefore relied somewhat less than Lincoln upon his authority as Commander-in-Chief.[7]

Governmentally speaking, the Second World War was conducted much as was the First World War. Congress again generously delegated powers to the Chief Executive, more generously than in 1917–1918. He was allowed the widest discretion in the application of the war-power statutes —the First War Powers Act (1941), the Second War Powers Act (1942), the Emergency Price Control Act (1942), and others. These acts were elaborated into specific policy first by the President's orders (often themselves grants of wide discretion) to administrative officials, and second by orders promulgated by these officials. A relatively new administrative device called the "directive" (at least the term was new) was frequently used by the President and other high officials to explain, modify, or amplify an order or orders. It is less formal than the administrative order, much easier to prepare, and seems to be more flexible in its uses.

It is noteworthy that the Chief Executive frequently issued executive orders "as President and as Commander-in-Chief." This is a clear indication that he rested his authority not only upon acts of Congress but also, as did Lincoln and Wilson, upon his inherent powers as President. Indeed, on one occasion at least (September 7, 1942) the President told Congress that if it did not repeal a certain section of the Emergency Price Control Act and thus enable him to fix maximum prices on farm commodities, he would act without such authorization. In other words, he would ignore a provision of a law that Congress had full authority under the Constitution to enact, and he would do this on the theory that it was his duty to do what the emergency required, law or no law.[8] Congress responded to a part of his demand, and he did not carry out his threat. In a future atomic war we may find a President acting contrary to the law and the Constitution to avert disaster for his imperiled country!

II. THE NATIONAL SECURITY ORGANIZATION [9]

We have fought and won our wars through two defense organizations, the War Department and the Department of the Navy, fed and supported

---

[7] Corwin, *op. cit.*, pp. 283–287.

[8] *Ibid.*, pp. 303–304.

[9] Robert H. Connery, "Unification of the Armed Forces—The First Year," *Am. Pol. Sci. Rev.*, XLIII (1949), 38–52; Gus C. Lee, "The Organization for National Security," *Pub. Adm.*

by various emergency organizations that were created just prior to the outbreak of hostilities or soon after such outbreak. We have always had time, time to rectify mistakes made because of lack of co-ordination between the State Department and the fighting services and between the fighting services themselves, time to reorganize, time to improvise, time to build ships and planes, manufacture weapons, and train defense forces. But in the Second World War we had very little margin; we might have lost it. Hardly any person who gives national defense a thought now believes that we can win another war unless we are fundamentally prepared for it, organized for it, before it begins. We have no strong allies in sight to contain the possible enemy while we are preparing to meet him, and even if we had such allies they would not be able to save us from devastating attacks by atomic weapons. All of this and more was perfectly clear to our defense experts at the end of the Second World War. Congress was convinced also and provided for very significant changes in our defense establishment in the National Security Acts of 1947 and 1949, the latter act coming after the Hoover Commission had put its finger upon some weak spots in the former. The discussion that follows is based primarily upon the act of 1949.

Co-ordination for national security: THE NATIONAL SECURITY COUNCIL. At the head of our defense system, on the high policy level, we find the National Security Council the membership of which consists of the President (who is Chairman), the Vice President, the Secretary of State, the Secretary of Defense, the Chairman of the National Security Resources Board, and, at the request of the President, certain other high executives, such as the Secretaries of the Army, the Navy, and the Air Force. This is a policy-making and co-ordinating body, in no sense an executive or operating group. It is charged with the weighty responsibility of assessing and appraising "the objectives, commitments, and risks of the United States in relation to our actual and potential military power. . . ." Thus the Council considers as a single question foreign and military policy, an indispensable procedure for intelligent action. Clearly this Council is a "Cabinet" with a specialized function that logically could be handled by the regular Cabinet, but, as that body has developed, would not be.

THE CENTRAL INTELLIGENCE AGENCY. Serving under the Council and headed by a Director is the Central Intelligence Agency. Foreknowledge of the intentions of possible enemies is not obtained so much by "cloak and dagger" work, so breathlessly entertaining in fiction, as by the careful analysis of readily available information respecting crops, factories,

---

Rev., IX (1949), 36–44; Fritz Morstein Marx (ed.), "National Defense and Democratic Society: A Symposium," *Am. Pol. Sci. Rev.,* XLIII (1949), 524–563; Marquis W. Childs, "The Battle of the Pentagon," *Harper's,* Aug., 1949, pp. 47–53.

and laboratories in foreign countries. This is the assignment of the Intelligence Agency. Our defense establishments have always had personnel engaged in collecting and interpreting information respecting the potentialities and intentions of foreign countries, and they will continue these activities, working for Central Intelligence.

THE NATIONAL SECURITY RESOURCES BOARD. In mobilizing for and playing our part in winning the two World Wars we created various emergency agencies as noted above. The National Security Resources Board, a civilian agency established in the Executive Office of the President, is designed to do, in advance of emergency, a great many things that the emergency war agencies did, and to do it better. The Board advises the President concerning "the co-ordination of military, industrial, and civilian mobilization," including "programs for the effective use in time of war of the nation's natural and industrial resources for military and civilian needs, for the maintenance and stabilization of the civilian economy in time of war." Here is a clear recognition of the problem of total war, of the necessity of balancing military necessity and civilian economy. We cannot feed everything to the defense forces. Hitler did not support his home front properly, and thus weakened his defenses no less seriously, if less obviously, than if he had skimped the fighters. The Board then has the task of advising the President on how to keep the economy in balance and at the same time acquire the materials and manpower necessary for waging war. In carrying out its functions the Board makes extensive use of the facilities of the executive departments and other agencies of the government. Through its own staff the Board has made studies on such subjects as stockpiling, strategic relocation of industries, and electric-power problems.

The Department of Defense. The agencies and organizations considered above are advisory to the President and outside the National Military Establishment. In 1949 this Establishment was named the Department of Defense and given the status of second in rank of the nine executive departments. Within the Department of Defense is the Department of the Army, the Department of the Navy, the Department of the Air Force, and certain other agencies. The three subordinate departments are not designated as "executive" departments but as "military" departments.

THE SECRETARY OF DEFENSE. Appointed from civilian life (the emergency of 1950 that prompted the appointment of General of the Army George C. Marshall constitutes an exception), the Secretary of Defense is the President's principal assistant in all matters relating to defense. Under his direction the three military departments function, although each of these is administered by its own secretary. The Secretary of Defense is required to submit written reports to the President at least twice a year, accompanied by such recommendations as he may care to make and by separate reports from the three military departments. Despite the superior position of the Secretary of Defense the secretary of any military department or any member of the Joint Chiefs of Staff may on his own initiative, after informing the Secretary of Defense, present to Congress his recommendation on any matter relating to defense. The law setting up the Department of Defense provides also for a Deputy Secretary and Assistant Secretaries of Defense.

THE DEPARTMENT OF THE ARMY. Although the Department of the Army has other duties (discussed in the chapter on the National Administrative System), its principal responsibilities are those of organizing, training, and maintaining the Army. The Secretary of the Army is charged with such duties as are required of him by law or as may be referred to him by the President. His specific duties include the supervision of all estimates of appropriations for the expenses of the Department; of the procurement of all military supplies; and of all expenditures for the support, transportation, and maintenance of the Army. He is responsible for the improvement of weapons, for proper instruction of military personnel, and for discipline and morale in the Army.

The Secretary of the Army is seldom a soldier by profession, although, like Henry L. Stimson, he may have had military experience. At least three great Secretaries of War, Elihu Root, Newton D. Baker, and Henry L. Stimson, were men whose interest in peace was whole-hearted and who earnestly labored to promote it through international courts and other institutions for the pacific settlement of disputes. The Secretary should be, and usually is, a man of wide administrative experience who is capable of harmonizing civilian interests and military needs. He must interpret the civilian to the soldier and the soldier to the civilian. Aiding the Secretary is an Under Secretary and Assistant Secretaries, to whom are delegated general administrative duties.

The General Staff. The General Staff, so much needed for the efficient administration of military affairs, was not established until 1903, when Secretary of War Root finally convinced Congress of its importance. The General Staff is charged with the duty of planning for recruiting, mobilizing, organizing, supplying, equipping, and training the Army. It is headed by the Chief of Staff, who is the adviser to the President, the Secretary of Defense, and the Secretary of the Army on all military matters. The Secretaries are not expected to act contrary to his advice, and if they do not like their military expert they may ask the President to appoint another. A good Chief of Staff should not only work easily with the Secretary of the Army but he should also know how to approach committees of Congress, how, for example, to engage their interest with football metaphors should they not be convinced by the maxims of Napoleon or Frederick the Great. In time of peace the Chief of Staff is the Commanding General of the field forces, and he continues in that capacity in war until such time as the President may designate a commanding general.

THE DEPARTMENT OF THE NAVY. Every schoolboy knows that the President is the Commander-in-Chief of the Navy and that the Department of the Navy is headed by a civilian Secretary. The other principal civilian officers of the department are the Under Secretary of the Navy and two Assistant Secretaries of the Navy, one of whom has general administrative control over naval aviation (the Navy still has air forces). The activities of the department are carried on largely through offices and bureaus, headed invariably by naval officers. Administered by the Department of the Navy also is the Marine Corps, known from the "halls of Montezuma to the shores of Tripoli." In time of war the United States Coast Guard likewise functions under the Department of the Navy. The Coast Guard is the federal maritime police, and its functions as such include maritime law enforcement, saving and protecting life and property, establishing and maintaining lighthouses, radio beacons, radio direction-finder stations, and buoys, and making preparations for national defense.

The Office of the Chief of Naval Operations. The Office of the Chief of Naval Operations is somewhat similar to the General Staff of the Army. The Chief of Naval Operations advises the President and the Secretary of the Navy on the conduct of war; serves as military executive to the Secretary of the Navy on the activities of the Naval Establishment; commands the operating forces of the Navy; and is responsible for the readiness of the Navy for war. He is concerned with such matters as the alteration, repair, and design of ships, the location of naval stations and naval yards, fuel reservations and depots, personnel, and numerous other matters. Obviously one man cannot discharge all these duties. He is assisted by a staff—a Vice Chief of Naval Operations and six Deputy Chiefs—and he utilizes the services of various bureaus and officers. If it cannot be said that the top naval officers in Washington planned with imagination, vision, and foresight to meet the problems that faced the Navy in 1941, it may be cheerfully conceded that they redeemed themselves by their action when the crisis was upon them.

THE DEPARTMENT OF THE AIR FORCE. The third military department, the new one, is the Department of the Air Force, with its Secretary, Under Secretary, and two Assistant Secretaries. It took over from the Army the Army Air Forces, and they became the United States Air Force. Like the Army, the Air Force has its Chief of Staff, who holds the same rank as the Army Chief of Staff and the Chief of Naval Operations. This department has, of course, the responsibility "for the preparation of the air forces necessary for the effective prosecution of war."

STAFF AGENCIES OF THE DEPARTMENT OF DEFENSE. Under the Security Act of 1947 the Secretary of Defense was given very little authority. He was given "general" direction over the military departments, but not the administrative power necessary to exact compliance. He could request, ask, urge, beg, entreaty, advise, and be consulted, but the reports that came out of Washington were full of his difficulties, although they were doubtless exaggerated. The legislation of 1949, although it clarified somewhat the position of the Secretary of Defense, did not appreciably add to his powers. He is still primarily a general supervisor without much authority. His importance in the defense picture may develop through the qualities of men who hold the place and the value of the work of the staff agencies that the law of 1947, as amended in 1949, provides. These agencies are the Armed Forces Policy Council, the Joint Chiefs of Staff (and Joint Staff), a Munitions Board, and a Research and Development Board.

The Armed Forces Policy Council. To advise the Secretary of Defense on matters of broad policy relating to the armed forces there is established within the Department of Defense the Armed Forces Policy Council, composed of the Secretary of Defense (who is Chairman and has the power of decision), the Deputy Secretary, the secretaries of the three military departments, and the highest ranking staff officers of the three military departments. The Council meets frequently, often with other top officials present, and it is understood that it gives full consideration and discussion to most of the basic issues of national defense.

Joint Chiefs of Staff. An organization without which any unification of the armed services would be hopeless is that of the Joint Chiefs of Staff. It consists of an armed service officer of high rank, named by the President, who is chairman and has no vote, and the three highest ranking staff officers of the military departments, who do have votes. The members of this staff are the top military advisers to the President, the National Security Council, and the Secretary of Defense. It has the specific duties, among others, to prepare strategic plans and make provision for the strategic direction of the military forces. The Joint Chiefs of Staff is served by a Joint Staff, consisting of not more than 210 officers of the three armed services. It is in the deliberations of the Joint Chiefs of Staff respecting what forces to employ for what, and similar questions of high policy that the so-called "Battle of the Pentagon" has been fought.

The Munitions Board. In support of strategic and logistic plans prepared by the Joint Chiefs of Staff the Munitions Board is given a wide variety of responsibilities, including planning for the military aspects of industrial mobilization, the determination of relative priorities of the various segments of the military procurement programs, and the assembly and review of material and personnel requirements presented by the Joint Chiefs of Staff. Even the rigid words of a statute fail to conceal the fact that the responsibilities of the Board are fundamental.

The Research and Development Board. Headed by a civilian chairman and having two members from each of the military departments, the Research and Development Board has the responsibilities indicated by its title. It prepares programs of research for military purposes, advises with regard to scientific trends relating to national security, co-ordinates research and development among the military departments, and performs similar duties. This Board more than any other organization in the Department of Defense brings the talents of the scientists to the defense program. It is a matter for regret, perhaps for grave concern, that "loyalty checks" have caused some of our ablest scientists to decline employment with the Board.

These summary and arid words are intended to give the briefest possible explanation of recent attempts to strengthen and unify our armed forces. The reorganization was designed to increase the efficiency of those services, develop a team, and to eliminate waste. It cannot be said that much progress has been made as yet. Each arm of the service is proud of its history, its traditions, and fearful that it may lose some of its importance, some of its prestige. The habits formed and made almost inflexible by a hundred and sixty years of single blessedness will be only slowly changed in a marriage of expediency. Essential unification of the military forces will probably be brought about as younger officers, educated in the new era of unification, begin to crowd the older men in the higher positions.

The armed forces. Indispensable as are the organizations outlined above and as are the men who administer them, the officials who plan and think defense, who go to Capitol Hill—to the "legislative front"—for personnel, money, and equipment, they do not constitute our defense. Our fighting forces consist of the hundreds of thousands of officers and enlisted men in camps and forts, on ships, in airplanes, on training grounds and in training stations, and elsewhere. And by no means are these forces all fighting forces in the literal sense. Many of them "service" the fighting units, providing them with food, clothing, weapons, and other supplies. The service of supply is just exactly as important as the actual fighting service. "Mother take down your service flag—your son is in the fighting SOS," shows nothing more than good-natured ignorance of what constitutes a proper defense force.

Everyone knows that we had a very large and effective military force at the end of the last war and that immediately after the end of the struggle we disbanded the greater part of it. With our "police action" adventure now in progress in Korea and with the international picture in general very threatening, we find it necessary to rearm. On January 1, 1950, our Regular Army consisted of about 650,000 men, a force that is now being expanded to perhaps two or three times that number. Another unit of our defense is the National Guard, some divisions of which are being called into active service as these lines are being written. Another peacetime group whose members are more nearly ready for active military service than other civilians is the Organized Reserve Corps. To this group belongs the Reserve Officers' Training Corps with which most college students are familiar. During the Second World War provision was made for a Women's Auxiliary Corps, and it functioned so successfully that a permanent Women's Army Corps has been authorized. At the date mentioned above, the Army probably had at its more or less immediate call for duty not more than a million and a half men. But the availability of that number did not signify by any means that they were organized in combat divisions and ready to meet an enemy. The crisis in Korea proved all too well that we had only a small combat force immediately available.

The striking power of the Navy at the end of the Second World War may be characterized by language no less restrained than that used for the latest movie sensation. Its peacetime, or rather cold war, strength has been a great deal less, to put it mildly. On January 1, 1950, the Naval personnel consisted of some 45,000 officers and approximately 375,000 enlisted men. The strength of the Navy is maintained in part by a Naval Reserve, the members of which are kept in a partial state of readiness by training courses and other instructional work. Emergencies of 1950 called for strengthening the Navy, although perhaps less urgently than they called for strengthening the Army. The Marine Corps, an integral part of the Naval Establishment, has demonstrated time and time again that it is the type of fighting unit best adapted to such service as the 1950 "police action" in Korea requires. Consequently, in that year the Corps' unorganized reserves were called up, and these plus enlistments were expected to bring the number of Marines up to about 200,000.

The Air Force, the newest arm of defense, had more than 43,000 combat planes at its peak in May, 1945, and a personnel of about 2,280,000 officers and enlisted men. The decline of its strength is indicated by the fact that its personnel had been reduced to approximately 420,000 on January 1, 1950. It seems that the emergencies of this mid-century year will force marked increases in personnel and in planes.

The year 1950 found us once more pouring out billions in money (the chart below represents expenditures before the Korean crisis, and we may expect the amounts to be trebled) and feverishly hurrying to assemble men and weapons. For ten years we have not had any real peace, and there is no indication that we shall have a satisfactory peace for years to come. Perhaps this generation must learn to live with crises, to consider them the nearest approach we have to "normalcy." This may be, and probably is, one of those long periods of world upheaval, and men must adjust themselves to it as best they may.

The North Atlantic Treaty. In these very threatening days, with no strong nations standing between the United States and its strongest potential foe, we have abandoned our long-standing policy of avoiding alliances. In the spring of 1948, presumably in fear of encroachment from the Soviet Union, five nations of Western Europe, including Britain and France, signed a treaty of military alliance and let it be known that they should like to have the co-operation of the United States. In response our government proposed the North Atlantic Treaty, a pact under which "The parties agree that an armed attack against one or more of them in Europe or North America shall be considered an attack against them all. . . ." The treaty further provides that in case of such attack each nation shall take "such action as it deems necessary, including the use of armed force." There was considerable discussion of the treaty in the Senate, particularly on the point as to how far the United States was committing itself. The consensus seems to be that we are committed to aid in some way in case a signatory power should be attacked, but that the precise question as to whether we should go to war in any particular case could be decided only by Congress, the body that has the authority to declare war. On July 21, 1949, the treaty was ratified by a large (82 to 13) and nonpartisan majority. Eleven other nations are now parties to it.

By way of implementing the treaty, Congress passed (1949) the Mutual Defense Assistance Act, approving a military aid program that included an appropriation of $1,314,010,000 for the first year. The original program under that act called for "integrated" North Atlantic defense, which could mean simply balanced national forces. It soon became clear, however, that the nations could not each develop a full military defense, and a plan was developed under which a sort of international force might be created, a force to be established by a division of labor and military functions among the signatory powers. As the international situation became more critical we increased our appropriations to support this collective system. Our European allies have, of course, contributed also, but the United States is spending a much higher percentage of its total appropriations on armaments than are the Europeans.

In January, 1951 the North Atlantic Council (under American chairman-

BUDGET EXPENDITURES: NATIONAL DEFENSE

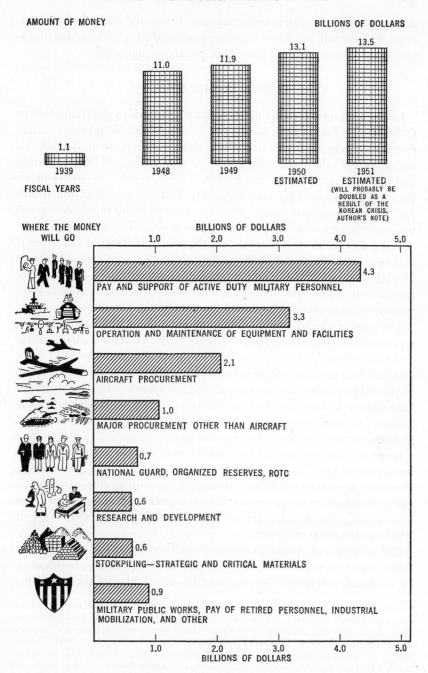

AMOUNT OF MONEY   BILLIONS OF DOLLARS

13.5
13.1
11.9
11.0

1.1
1939   1948   1949   1950   1951
                                    ESTIMATED   ESTIMATED
FISCAL YEARS   (WILL PROBABLY BE
                                                  DOUBLED AS A
                                                  RESULT OF THE
                                                  KOREAN CRISIS.
                                                  AUTHOR'S NOTE)

WHERE THE MONEY   BILLIONS OF DOLLARS
WILL GO   1.0   2.0   3.0   4.0   5.0

4.3
PAY AND SUPPORT OF ACTIVE DUTY MILITARY PERSONNEL

3.3
OPERATION AND MAINTENANCE OF EQUIPMENT AND FACILITIES

2.1
AIRCRAFT PROCUREMENT

1.0
MAJOR PROCUREMENT OTHER THAN AIRCRAFT

0.7
NATIONAL GUARD, ORGANIZED RESERVES, ROTC

0.6
RESEARCH AND DEVELOPMENT

0.6
STOCKPILING—STRATEGIC AND CRITICAL MATERIALS

0.9
MILITARY PUBLIC WORKS, PAY OF RETIRED PERSONNEL, INDUSTRIAL
MOBILIZATION, AND OTHER

                     1.0   2.0   3.0   4.0   5.0
                          BILLIONS OF DOLLARS

From Bureau of the Budget, *The Federal Budget in Brief, Fiscal Year 1951*, p. 13.

ship) gave General Eisenhower Supreme Command of its international army, and the will of Western Europe to defend itself and the determination of the United States to assist were greatly strengthened.

III. THE ATOMIC BOMB [10]

In war nothing is certain but uncertainty. General of the Army George C. Marshall, Chief of Staff during the Second World War, makes it clear that victory was not due to our efforts alone. Indeed, he thinks that this nation should take little credit for its part in staving off disaster during the first years we were in the conflict. "It is certain," he writes in his Biennial Report for 1943-1945 (page 1), "that the refusal of the British and Russian peoples to accept what appeared to be inevitable defeat was the great factor in the salvage of our civilization." For the success of the Allied resistance in those fateful days the General also gives "full credit" to the miscalculations and plain blunders of the German General Staff and High Command. The Nazis were neither supermen in the field nor master planners in their underground fortresses, nor was their total economy as well administered as that of Britain and the United States.

The race of the scientists. When, in 1944, the Allies had built up a superiority in men and equipment, many of the German leaders realized that only a miracle of science could save them. But miracles can happen in a war, and the Nazis were hopeful of one that might prolong this one indefinitely or even win it. During the last months of the struggle the Germans with their new and terrible buzz-bombs made life hideous in Britain. German scientists were feverishly working on other weapons, including atomic ones; but they lost the race.

It appears that we could have won the war without the atomic bomb, but we might have lost it had our enemies developed it first. Fortunately, President Roosevelt and Prime Minister Churchill, neither of them scientists, but both of them men of vision, orators, leaders, put their heads together on a gamble, a two-billion-dollar scientific gamble; and they won. This was *the* secret of the war.

The British and American scientists had been smashing the atom for some years. In 1941 the British were certain that an atomic bomb could be produced, and their scientists went to work. Shortly thereafter they

[10] Department of State, *A Report on the International Control of Atomic Energy,* Publication 2498 (March 16, 1946) and *United States Atomic Energy Proposals,* Publication 2560 (June 14, 1946); War Department, *Effects of Atomic Bombs on Hiroshima and Nagasaki* (1946); D. Masters and K. Way (eds.), *One World or None* (1946); H. D. Smyth, *Atomic Energy for Military Purposes* (1945); Henry L. Stimson, "The Decision to Use the Atomic Bomb," *Harpers Magazine,* February, 1947, pp. 97-107; Gerald Wendt, "A New Job for the Atom," *Harper's,* May, 1949, pp. 21-27.

learned that the Germans might be ahead of them. At this point Roosevelt and Churchill agreed to pool their atomic scientists, to push the experiments in the United States, which had the facilities and which was presumably safe from enemy attack. The Manhattan Project; Oak Ridge, Tennessee; Hanford, Washington; Los Alamos, New Mexico are known to all of us. And so is Hiroshima, upon which (August 6, 1945) the harnessed "basic power of the universe" was released. Then Churchill spoke again (Roosevelt was dead): "We must indeed pray that these awful agencies will be made to conduce to peace among nations and that, instead of wreaking measureless havoc upon the entire globe, they may become the perennial fountain of world prosperity."

President Truman spoke of the "awful responsibility" that rested upon Canada, Great Britain, and the United States, the possessors, for the time being, of the dread secret. The President and the rest of us began to consider with alarm what we had done and to imagine, all too feebly, the terror of the day when an enemy might release this "final judgment" over London or New York City. Uninformed indeed is that person who does not know that misused atomic energy may destroy the world.

The control of atomic energy. To President Truman should go all credit for reasonably prompt action on control of atomic energy. On October 3, 1945, he asked Congress to establish a commission to control atomic fission domestically and at the same time he suggested discussion of international control. On January 24, 1946, the United Nations Atomic Energy Commission was created. Then came (March 16) the Acheson-Lilienthal Report on the International Control of Atomic Energy, prepared under the auspices of the State Department. This document foreshadowed the Baruch proposals, which, on June 14, on behalf of the United States, he laid before the Atomic Energy Commission of the United Nations. These recommendations call for an International Atomic Development Authority that should have, among other powers, (1) complete control of the world's supplies of uranium and thorium, the sources of atomic power; (2) "complete managerial control of the production of fissionable materials"; (3) "absolute control" over atomic research; (4) the authority to inspect atomic activities in all countries. Mr. Baruch stressed the point that the powers that had the atomic secret could not give it up without a guarantee of safety; that safety could come only through international cooperation. Perhaps the most significant proposal was this—the activities of the Atomic Authority must not be hampered by the veto power of any nation, "regardless of its strength." Russia made a somewhat different set of proposals, and the discussion went on, but no progress was made. In the meantime Russia developed the bomb, and we now think that we can produce an H-bomb. (For further discussion of attempts to get international agreement on the regulation of atomic energy, see pages 969–971.)

Domestic control of atomic energy has proceeded along satisfactory lines. In the summer of 1946 Congress enacted the McMahon Bill, which creates an Atomic Energy Commission and places control primarily in the hands of civilians. Military men had strenuously argued that they should have control, but they lost the argument by a narrow congressional vote. As the international situation has steadily worsened since the establishment of the commission, there is no doubt that its chief energies have been in the direction of improving and multiplying atomic bombs, a large stockpile of which is said to be on hand.

Of all the words that have been spoken and written on the atomic bomb, perhaps the most foolish are these: it is so terrible that it will probably prevent war—no nation will dare use it for fear of retaliation. No weapon yet devised has prevented war. Weapons are made for war, not to prevent war. In his report referred to above, Bernard M. Baruch said, "Peace is never long preserved by weight of metal or by an armament race." Yet he does not despair: "Behind the black portent of the new atomic age lies a hope which, seized upon with faith, can work our salvation. If we fail, then we have damned every man to be the slave of Fear. Let us not deceive ourselves: We must elect World Peace or World Destruction. . . . We must embrace international co-operation or international disintegration." Of this general topic Chapter 29 treats at some length.

IV. THE NATIONAL ECONOMY IN THE SECOND WORLD WAR [11]

It is worth our while to analyze the manner in which we organized our economy and produced the materials that won the Second World War because such analysis shows how effectively we used our resources and because the measures taken give us a mild preview of what we shall have to do to meet a greater threat.

The task of production. More than a year before Pearl Harbor the government was setting up emergency defense agencies charged with the duty of stimulating and co-ordinating the manufacture of weapons and other implements of war. There was considerable confusion in these days, however, and the going was slow. Shortly after the declarations of war the President announced that in 1942 there should be produced 60,000 planes, 45,000 tanks, 20,000 antiaircraft guns, and 8,000,000 dead weight tons of merchant ships, and that 1943 should see a significant improvement

[11] Marshall E. Dimock, *Business and Government* (1949), Ch. 25; Merle Fainsod and Lincoln Gordon, *Government and the American Economy* (1948 ed.), Chs. 22–23; Herring, *op. cit.,* Ch. 9; Donald M. Nelson, *Arsenal of Democracy: the Story of American War Production* (1946); H. W. Spiegel, *The Economics of Total War* (1942); Walter, *op. cit.,* Chs. 1–2.

WHERE WARTIME WORKERS CAME FROM

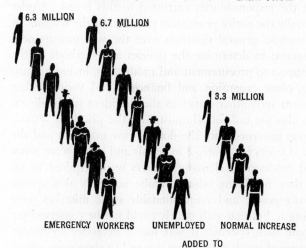

6.3 MILLION   6.7 MILLION   3.3 MILLION

EMERGENCY WORKERS   UNEMPLOYED   NORMAL INCREASE

ADDED TO

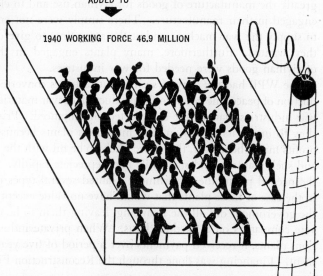

1940 WORKING FORCE 46.9 MILLION

GAVE US 63.2 MILLION PEOPLE AT WORK IN 1944
(FIGURES INCLUDE MEMBERS OF THE ARMED FORCES)

From Twentieth Century Fund, *U.S.A.: Measure of a Nation* (Macmillan, 1949), p. 7.

over these figures. He established the War Production Board and designated as its head Donald M. Nelson, an able and experienced industrial
executive.

Vast indeed were the responsibilities entrusted to this board. Under
its control went virtually the entire productive potential of the nation. It
was authorized to exercise general direction over the war procurement
and production program; to determine the policies and methods of the
federal agencies in respect to procurement and production, including purchasing, contracting, plant expansion and financing, and various other
factors; and to perform such other duties as the President might direct.
To this board went also the task of administering the priorities system.
Under this system was governed both the flow of raw materials and the
processing of goods. Orders for strategic materials and goods were given
priority ratings, and producers and manufacturers were required to fill
such orders before they filled any others. Quite naturally this system
irritated a great many people and unquestionably some mistakes were
made in administering it, but materials clearly could not be conserved for
war use without some such system. It was found necessary to restrict
greatly the manufacture of goods for civilian use and to close some plants
engaged in their manufacture. There simply were not enough materials
to supply the war machine and at the same time to give civilians all that
they wanted. Furthermore, many plants engaged in the manufacture
of civilian goods were needed for war industries.

The WPB had the duty of seeing that factories converted from the production of peacetime goods to the production of war materials and that new
war industries plants were constructed and financed. Private capital was
slow to invest its money in new munitions plants because, whatever the
profits might be in war, they were likely to be nil with the return of peace,
and such plants would stand idle and depreciate rapidly. In order to get
the needed plants the government granted several types of aid. Indeed,
in the case of those plants that would have no value except in time of war,
the government did all the financing, leaving them to be operated by private companies on a fixed-fee basis. When private industry built munitions plants, it received payments over a period of five years for its investment. Financing was done through the Reconstruction Finance Corporation.

Mass production won the war; but before we had planes and tanks rolling off the assembly line, we had to build the machines necessary for their
manufacture. The machines used to make automobiles, electric refrigerators, typewriters, or vacuum cleaners could not be used to make airplanes, tanks, shells, or bomb cases. Entirely different machines were re-

quired; and when these were built, we were well on the road toward mass production. But we had not gone all the way until we had every possible plant, large and small, feeding the war machine. Ordinarily, contracts were let to large firms, and the small firms were brought into the war industries through subcontracting. The contracting firm made the princi-

THE WARTIME "MIRACLE OF PRODUCTION"

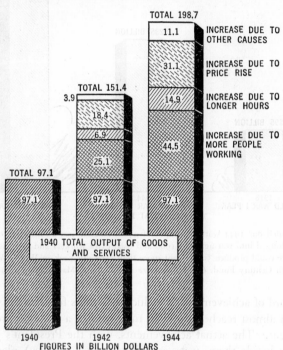

TOTAL 198.7

11.1 — INCREASE DUE TO OTHER CAUSES

31.1 — INCREASE DUE TO PRICE RISE

TOTAL 151.4

3.9

14.9 — INCREASE DUE TO LONGER HOURS

18.4

6.9

44.5 — INCREASE DUE TO MORE PEOPLE WORKING

25.1

TOTAL 97.1

97.1   97.1   97.1

1940 TOTAL OUTPUT OF GOODS AND SERVICES

1940   1942   1944

FIGURES IN BILLION DOLLARS

WE DOUBLED OUR DOLLAR VOLUME OF GOODS AND SERVICES DURING THE WAR LARGELY BECAUSE OF MORE PEOPLE WORKING; LONGER HOURS; AND HIGHER PRICES.

From Twentieth Century Fund, *U.S.A.: Measure of a Nation* (Macmillan, 1949), p. 5.

pal parts of a weapon and subcontracted with ten or twenty or even more small firms for the other parts. The large firm had the responsibility of keeping the subcontractors moving at the right speed with the work "farmed-out" to them, so that the many parts flowed back to the main plant in good time to be joined together into an intricate machine on the assembly line.

All this integration of efforts required organization and co-operation of the highest order. In making arrangements for mass production, American industrialists led all the world; and our assembly lines were no less a threat to our enemies than were our forces that carried the arms fashioned by American industry.

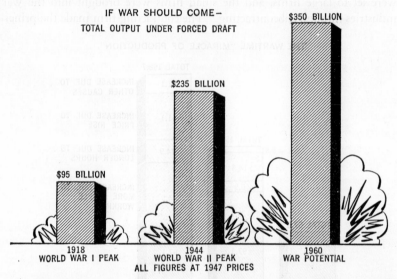

IF WAR SHOULD COME—
TOTAL OUTPUT UNDER FORCED DRAFT

$350 BILLION

$235 BILLION

$95 BILLION

| 1918 | 1944 | 1960 |
| WORLD WAR I PEAK | WORLD WAR II PEAK | WAR POTENTIAL |

ALL FIGURES AT 1947 PRICES

The world called our 1944 wartime output of goods and services a "miracle" of production. If we were plunged into war again in 1960 and used extra workers and extra working hours as in 1944, we could produce 50 per cent more than even our peak in World War II. From Twentieth Century Fund, *U.S.A.: Measure of a Nation* (Macmillan, 1949), p. 100.

The record of achievement. Production figures for the first year of the war (1942) almost reached what, in 1941, seemed a fantastic prediction of the President. The actual achievements, with the President's goal set in parentheses beside them, were as follows: 49,000 (60,000) planes, 32,000 (45,000) tanks, 17,000 (20,000) antiaircraft guns, and 8,200,000 (8,000,000) tons of merchant ships. The Office of War Information pointed out that an increasing proportion of the planes being built were of the heavy bomber type, and that thousands of essential scout cars and track carriers, in addition to tanks, had been manufactured. In succeeding years our output became a veritable avalanche, engulfing our enemies. In 1944 we outproduced the Axis in munitions by more than 50 per cent, and our output accounted for more than 40 per cent of the armament production by all belligerents. And the miracle is that, while this was being done, the American standard of living attained or rose close to the highest level ever reached.

Rationing and price control. With approximately half of our manpower in the fighting services or on the industrial front processing foods, materials, and weapons to supply those services the quantity of the goods available for civilian consumption was, of necessity, greatly reduced. Under the circumstances civilians obviously would rush to purchase the goods that were available. Persons with the most money and the least patriotic restraint would get more than their share of the goods, and producers and sellers of those goods would reap a rich harvest by advancing prices. In order to prevent these deplorable conditions the government instituted a system of rationing and price control.

Even before the outbreak of war gasoline was rationed to dealers, and in 1942 it was rationed to consumers also, partly to conserve gasoline, partly to solve the transportation problem, but primarily to save automobile tires. Another commodity that was rationed early was sugar, and as the American people and their leaders learned the meaning of total war other goods were rationed in rapid succession. Some volunteer rationing was attempted, but that was only partially successful. Only compulsory rationing is fair—will defeat the "chiselers" and "fudgers" who insist upon special privileges and favors in the face of the gravest national emergency.

Despite the hesitation with which less than the most courageous and scientific measures were taken to hold down prices, the record of achievement is good, very good. In 1944 federal taxes picked up the neat little sum of $44,000,000,000. At the same time, individual (as distinguished from bank) purchases of war bonds absorbed other billions. These huge sums, taken from the national income of $150,000,000,000 plus, greatly reduced the amount left in the hands of the American people to spend, thus definitely aiding in the fight against inflation. Although the other expedients designed to control prices were commonly thought to be "too little and too late," they worked out much better than was expected. The proof is that we came through the Second World War with a rise in the cost of living only a fraction of the rise we experienced in the less than two years we were engaged in the First World War. After 1945 only half-hearted efforts were made to control inflation, and the rearmament program, beginning in 1950, gives us more inflation.

V. THE WAR VETERANS [12]

After every war we have the veterans whose interest in public affairs is commendable, whose share of the offices and public positions is out of all proportion to their numbers, and whose care is the nation's responsibility.

[12] K. Durham, *Billions for Veterans: an Analysis of Bonus Problems Yesterday, Today and Tomorrow* (1932); Charles Hurd, *The Veterans' Program* (1946); T. Powell, *Tattered Banners* (1933).

The influence of ex-service men in postwar politics and administration.
For a long generation following the Civil War military heroes and just
plain veterans, Confederate as well as Union, exerted a tremendous influence upon American government, national, state, and local. Elective offices they filled by the thousands, and appointive offices (the low qualifications for which were lowered still further for veterans) they manned by
the tens of thousands. The GAR won liberal pensions from the federal
government, and the ex-Confederates secured less substantial ones from
their own states.

Veterans of the First World War, by all accounts, have been very successful in securing adequate care for their disabled or sick comrades, pensions for certain groups, and a bonus for every man who wore the uniform
of his country in that war. Furthermore, the national government and
some of the state and local governments lowered the civil service requirements for veteran candidates for all appointive positions. Although a
considerable number of these veterans were elected to public office, they
did not equal in number or influence the record of their grandfathers in
post-Civil War days, when both houses of Congress were practically
swamped with ex-officers, Northern and Southern, and three generals, a
colonel, and a major were elected President. In 1920 General Pershing's
boom for the presidency did not get started, and the only officer of the
First World War who has been a serious contender for the nomination
was Leonard Wood, a politician-general whom Pershing would not permit
to serve under him in France. "Captain" Truman's election to the Presidency came via the Vice Presidency. Probably the veterans of 1917–1918
failed to match the political power of the boys in blue and gray because the
First World War was not for America a great struggle in which the life
of the nation was at stake and, in consequence, its veterans failed to capture the imagination, the hearts, and the votes of the electors.

What will be the place of the veterans of the Second World War in
American politics? There are approximately three times as many veterans of the Second World War as there were of the First. Furthermore,
the Second World War was a national crisis of proportions comparable
to the Civil War. Add these two facts and the sum may be ex-servicemen's
influence and participation in politics to match that of the Civil War
veterans. Our new veterans have already entered public office in large
numbers. In years to come they may "take over." Let us hope that they
will be as good as our civilian-soldier statesmen Hayes, Garfield, Harrison,
and McKinley, and certainly that none will be as bad in civil office as
Grant, the trained soldier. Appointive office also beckons the veteran,
and it was noted in an earlier chapter (21, section 11) that generous provisions have been made for him in the federal civil service. States and

BUDGET EXPENDITURES: VETERANS SERVICES AND BENEFITS

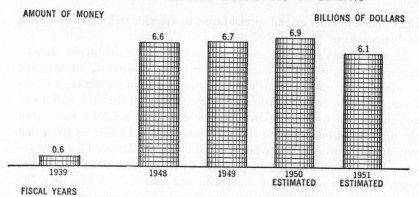

AMOUNT OF MONEY   BILLIONS OF DOLLARS

1939	1948	1949	1950 ESTIMATED	1951 ESTIMATED
0.6	6.6	6.7	6.9	6.1

FISCAL YEARS

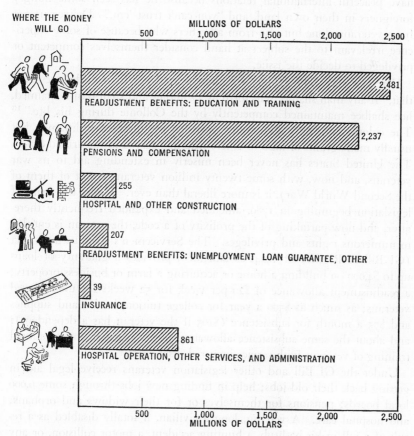

WHERE THE MONEY WILL GO — MILLIONS OF DOLLARS

READJUSTMENT BENEFITS: EDUCATION AND TRAINING — 2,481

PENSIONS AND COMPENSATION — 2,237

HOSPITAL AND OTHER CONSTRUCTION — 255

READJUSTMENT BENEFITS: UNEMPLOYMENT LOAN GUARANTEE, OTHER — 207

INSURANCE — 39

HOSPITAL OPERATION, OTHER SERVICES, AND ADMINISTRATION — 861

MILLIONS OF DOLLARS

From Bureau of the Budget, *The Federal Budget in Brief,* Fiscal Year 1951, p. 15.

cities in like manner extend special favors to veterans seeking employment in their services.

Many veterans have the good habit of interesting themselves in government policy, particularly in matters of national defense, international relations, immigration, labor, and education. Except on the topic of defense, they may know as little about these subjects as the rank and file of citizens, but at times their attitude has seemed to be: "We have worn the uniform of our country; therefore we know." Deliver us from that veteran (or anyone else) who is certain that he knows Germany because he once had a very brief glimpse of it; who knows that the inhabitants of a certain island in the Pacific are immoral because they "go neckid," or practically so (he has seen them); who knows that we can't have peaceful international relations because he has seen some hungry foreigners in their own land, and "you can't trust 'em." Deliver us not from veterans alone but also from all others who because of some experience irrelevant to the subject at hand consider themselves competent or privileged to decide the issue.

Veterans' care. The Pilgrim Fathers started it. In 1636 they resolved that, "If any man shalbee sent forth as a souldier and shall return maimed, hee shalbee maintained competently by the Collonie during his life." [13] The colonies not only commonly provided for disabled militiamen but usually made grants of land to others who had served in the armed forces. The United States has never been miserly in extending aid to its war veterans, and now, with some twenty million veterans (most of them of the Second World War), it is more liberal than ever. Under the terms of legislation beginning in 1789, amended and expanded frequently thereafter, and now partaking of the prolixity of a code, the veteran is entitled to numerous rights and privileges. The Servicemen's Readjustment Act (GI Bill of Rights) of 1944, as amended, provides a guaranty of loans up to $4,000 on building a home or acquiring a farm or business property; a readjustment allowance of $20 per week for 52 weeks for unemployed veterans; as much as $500 a year for college tuition, books, and supplies and $75 a month for subsistence ($105 if the veteran has a dependent); and about the same subsistence allowance, plus a pension, for vocational training of veterans with service-incurred disabilities.

Under the GI Bill and other legislation veterans receive legal aid in getting back their old jobs; help in finding new jobs through some 6,000 local boards; pensions for themselves or for their widows and orphans; and hospital care. A veteran, long a civilian, if totally disabled as a result of a fall in his bathtub, a hunting accident, a motor collision, or any one of a thousand civilian mishaps, may receive a pension as high as $60

[13] Quoted in *Time*, April 1, 1946, p. 22.

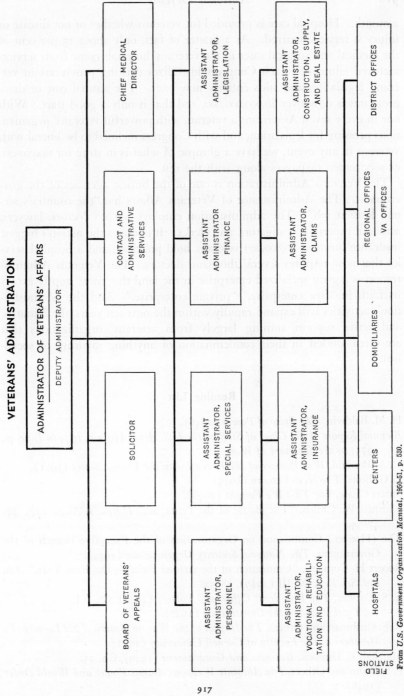

VETERANS' ADMINISTRATION

ADMINISTRATOR OF VETERANS' AFFAIRS

DEPUTY ADMINISTRATOR

BOARD OF VETERANS' APPEALS

SOLICITOR

CONTACT AND ADMINISTRATIVE SERVICES

CHIEF MEDICAL DIRECTOR

ASSISTANT ADMINISTRATOR, PERSONNEL

ASSISTANT ADMINISTRATOR, SPECIAL SERVICES

ASSISTANT ADMINISTRATOR FINANCE

ASSISTANT ADMINISTRATOR, LEGISLATION

ASSISTANT ADMINISTRATOR, VOCATIONAL REHABILITATION AND EDUCATION

ASSISTANT ADMINISTRATOR, INSURANCE

ASSISTANT ADMINISTRATOR, CLAIMS

ASSISTANT ADMINISTRATOR, CONSTRUCTION, SUPPLY, AND REAL ESTATE

HOSPITALS

CENTERS

DOMICILIARIES

REGIONAL OFFICES   VA OFFICES

DISTRICT OFFICES

FIELD STATIONS

From *U.S. Government Organization Manual,* 1950-51, p. 580.

a month. Hospital care is provided for veterans whether or not disease or injury is service-incurred. As a matter of fact, only about 15 per cent of the medical and surgical cases in the veterans' hospitals come from service-incurred ailments. Each Congress liberalizes existing provisions in veterans' legislation and adds entirely new ones. The annual cost of these programs is now over $6,000,000,000, and that is only a good start. With one in every seven Americans a veteran, with powerful veterans' organizations pressing for legislation, and with Congress inclined to be liberal with veterans in any event, we have a glimpse of what is in store for taxpayers, ex-servicemen taxpayers along with the rest.

The Veterans Administration is one of the busiest agencies of the government. The Administrator of Veterans Affairs has "the country's second lousiest job." The administration employs 200,000 doctors, lawyers, actuarial experts, investigators, and clerks. It operates the nation's biggest insurance business (6,800,000 veterans hold policies), and a hospital service that now requires several thousand doctors. The Veterans Administration is a great socialized enterprise in the land that most stoutly avows its faith in "free enterprise," "private enterprise." And the administration's activities will expand rapidly within the next ten years, the initiative and active support coming largely from veterans' organizations that are often loudest in their condemnation of anything savoring of socialism.

Reading List

H. M. Baldwin, *The Price of Power* (1948).

Biennial Report of the Chief of Staff of the U.S. Army (July 1, 1943 to June 30, 1945) to the Secretary of War.

C. A. Berdahl, *War Powers of the Executive in the United States* (1921).

C. G. Bolte, *The New Veteran* (1945).

Stuart Chase, *For This We Fought* (1946).

Marquis W. Childs, "The Battle of the Pentagon," *Harper's,* Aug., 1949, pp. 47–53.

The (Hoover) Commission on Organization of the Executive Branch of the Government, *The National-Security Organization* (1949).

Robert H. Connery, "Unification of the Armed Forces—The First Year," *Am. Pol. Sci. Rev.,* XLIII (1949), 38–52.

E. S. Corwin, *The President: Office and Powers* (1948), Ch. VI.

——, *Total War and the Constitution* (1947).

R. E. Cushman and Others, *The Impact of the War on America: Six Lectures by Members of the Faculty of Cornell University* (1942).

Marshall E. Dimock, *Business and Government* (1949), Ch. 25.

F. S. Dunn and Others, *The Absolute Weapon: Atomic Power and World Order* (1946).

K. Durham, *Billions for Veterans; an Analysis of Bonus Problems Yesterday, Today and Tomorrow* (1932).

Merle Fainsod and Lincoln Gordon, *Government and the American Economy* (1948 ed.), Chs. 22–23.

S. E. Harris, *The Economics of America at War* (1943).

Pendleton Herring, *The Impact of War: Our American Democracy under Arms* (1941).

Charles Hurd, *The Veterans' Program* (1946).

J. G. Kerwin (ed.), *Civil-Military Relationships in American Life* (1948).

Fleet Admiral Ernest J. King, *The United States Navy at War. Final Official Report to the Secretary of the Navy* (covering the period March 1, 1945 to October 1, 1945).

Gus C. Lee, "The Organization for National Security," *Pub. Adm. Rev.,* IX (1949), 36–44.

Fritz Morstein Marx (ed.), "National Defense and Democratic Society: A Symposium," *Am. Pol. Sci. Rev.,* XLIII (1949), 524–563.

Agnes E. Meyer, *Journey through Chaos* (1944).

Donald M. Nelson, *Arsenal of Democracy* (1946).

Richard O. Niehoff, "Organization and Administration of the United States Atomic Energy Commission," *Pub. Adm. Rev.,* VIII (1948), 91–102.

W. F. Ogburn, ed., *American Society in Wartime* (1945).

John Dos Passos, *State of the Nation* (1944).

T. Powell, *Tattered Banners* (1933).

President's Advisory Commission on Universal Training, *A Program for National Security* (1947).

T. Sellin (ed.), *Universal Military Training* (1945).

H. D. Smyth, *Atomic Energy for Military Purposes* (1945).

H. W. Spiegel, *The Economics of Total War* (1942).

N. J. Spykman, *America's Strategy in World Politics* (1942).

E. R. Stettinius, *Lend-Lease: Weapon for Victory* (1944).

D. O. Walter, *American Government at War* (1942).

War Department, *Effects of Atomic Bombs on Hiroshima and Nagasaki* (1946).

Gerald Wendt, "A New Job for the Atom," *Harper's,* May, 1949, pp. 21–27.

R. D. Wilson, *Jim Crow Joins Up* (1944).

C. W. Wright, ed., *Economic Problems of the War and Its Aftermath* (1945).

Questions and Problems

1. Give a realistic description of how the United States enters into war.
2. Of what war powers may Congress not deprive the President? To what extent may Congress delegate war powers to him?
3. Indicate the functions of defense agencies that serve in an advisory capacity to the President.
4. Explore some of the problems involved in unifying the military departments. To what extent did the creation of a Department of Defense solve these problems?

5. Examine at least three problems presented by the development of atomic energy.
6. How was war production achieved during the Second World War?
7. Show what place rationing and price control have in a war economy.
8. Prepare a considered statement on our obligations to war veterans.
9. Estimate the place of war veterans in American public life during the next forty years.

☆ 28 ☆

The Conduct of Foreign Relations

A MERICAN government has no subject more vital to its operation than the conduct of foreign affairs. This subject and military defense are often closely intertwined. Wise foreign policy substantially supplements a defense program; the best defense system may prove entirely inadequate if associated with inept foreign policy. Any great power should shape its defense largely in terms of its foreign policy. Often they do not; sometimes the two seem to have little relation. It is not the purpose of the writer to pass many judgments on American foreign policy, but rather to present a discussion of the manner in which foreign relations are conducted. Chapter 29, dealing with international organization, is essentially a continuation of the present chapter.

I. THE PRESIDENT'S CONTROL OF FOREIGN AFFAIRS [1]

The conduct of our foreign relations is very largely in the hands of the President. This is true, despite the fact that for the approval of policy he must depend to a considerable extent upon the Senate and to an increasing degree upon the whole Congress. Of course, the President does not personally administer the details of our official intercourse with foreign nations. Much of the work is left to the Secretary of State, the President's right-hand man in all diplomatic matters, and to subordinate officers in the diplomatic service. But the President is the responsible official, and he often takes a direct part in international affairs.

The extent to which the President actively participates in diplomatic negotiations depends upon the Chief Executive's interest. Wilson and

[1] E. M. Borchard, "Treaties and Executive Agreements," *Am. Pol. Sci. Rev.*, XL (1946), 729 ff.; E. S. Corwin, *The President* (1948 ed.), Ch. V; H. J. Laski, *The American Presidency* (1940), Ch. IV; J. M. Mathews, *American Foreign Relations* (1938 ed.); Q. Wright, *The Control of American Foreign Relations* (1922); H. M. Macdonald and others, *Outside Readings in American Government* (1949), Ch. XXI.

perhaps Franklin D. Roosevelt represent one extreme. They took personal control of nearly all international matters of any consequence. Wilson was in reality his own Secretary of State. Perhaps the other extreme is represented by Harding, who relied chiefly upon his Secretary of State, the very capable and indefatigable Charles Evans Hughes. In any case, directly or indirectly, the President controls the foreign service personnel, serves as our sole official international spokesman, recognizes new governments and states, makes treaties (subject to the approval of the Senate), and, consequently, has the power to determine very largely our foreign policy. In this section we consider the President's part in these matters, reserving the organization and activities of the State Department and the foreign service for the following section.

Control of foreign service personnel. The Constitution authorizes the President, with the consent of a majority of the senators present, to appoint ambassadors, other public ministers, and consuls. Those who hold the lower and intermediate positions in these services are now appointed subject to civil service rules, but the President has a relatively free hand (the Senate almost invariably confirms his nominees) in the appointment of ambassadors and ministers. He may, of course, remove diplomatic and consular officers at any time. Not only does the President have a wide controlling authority over the personnel of our foreign service; but, through his constitutional authority to receive diplomats and other public ministers from foreign countries, he may, in a negative sense at least, exert some control over them. He need not receive persons against whom he has objections, nor is he bound to receive anyone from governments with which he does not wish to establish friendly relations. Having received a diplomat, he may for various reasons request the foreign government to recall him. He may even dismiss a foreign representative, as President Cleveland dismissed the British Minister, Sackville-West, for interference in the presidential campaign of 1888.

Sole official spokesman on foreign affairs. The President is the only official who may communicate with a foreign government. Private negotiations with foreign governments would clearly be out of order in any case; but, following the attempt of a Quaker to make peace with France in 1799, Congress stipulated a fine and imprisonment for such interference. Congress itself may not address a foreign power. Even a resolution in response to congratulations extended by a prince is held to violate the Constitution and practice of the United States respecting intercourse with foreign powers. When the House of Representatives by resolution protested against the Maximilian government in Mexico, Secretary of State Seward advised the French government that the question was purely executive, and that the decision rested, not with the House, or even with Congress, but with the President of the United States.

If the President is the only official spokesman for the United States, it follows that to him alone may be addressed communications from foreign powers. As early as 1793, Jefferson, then Secretary of State, told Citizen Gênet that the President was the only authority with whom foreign nations could communicate. When German Ambassador Bernstorff warned the American people, through the press, against sailing on the *Lusitania,* Secretary of State Lansing referred to the proceeding as a "surprising irregularity." Bernstorff should have advised the President of the plans of the German government and left the matter of warning American citizens to the President's discretion. These illustrations are sufficient to show that only the President or his representatives may officially receive or send foreign communications.[2]

The power of recognition. The power of recognition of foreign governments and foreign states rests entirely in the hands of the President. The Constitution makes no provision for it; but by international practice and as an incident to the power to send (subject, of course, to confirmation of appointments by the Senate) and receive diplomats, it has long been considered a purely executive function. Suppose a revolt in a foreign country leads to the overthrow of the government and the revolutionists get control. Whether we shall recognize the new government, or continue to recognize the old, or eventually recognize no government at all is for the President to decide, although advice sought and unsought will come to him, both from official and unofficial quarters.

The question of recognizing new governments has been a very vital one in our relations with the Latin-American countries and with Soviet Russia. Recognition, either long delayed or premature, may seriously affect new governments and injure the standing of the United States with them. Recent examples of recognition are furnished by the President's recognition of De Gaulle's Government of France (1944) and of a number of "Governments in Exile" (1940–1942)—governments that fled to Britain or America as the Axis powers were occupying their home lands.

The President may also recognize new states. This is an affair of much more consequence than recognizing a new government; for new states are carved from the territory of old states, and recognition of the newcomer is, therefore, a recognition of the parent state's loss of territory. Thus President Theodore Roosevelt grievously offended Colombia when he recognized Panama as a new state after the inhabitants of the Isthmus had staged a brief revolt. President Truman was on less controversial ground when,

[2] Wright, *op. cit.,* Ch. III.

in 1948, he recognized the new state of Israel, established in pursuance of a resolution of the General Assembly of the United Nations.[3]

Treaty and agreement-making power.   The Constitution authorizes the President to make treaties, but places rather strict limitations upon his power in this respect, requiring that treaties shall be approved by two thirds of the senators present.[4]   Indeed, some members of the Constitutional Convention wished to limit the treaty-making power of the President even further, by requiring the consent of the House of Representatives in addition to that of the Senate, or by requiring a two-thirds majority of the entire Senate.   Approval by a majority of the Senate and the House is often advocated today, because consent of a simple majority in both Houses would be easier to obtain than the two-thirds majority in the Senate and because, in most cases, the House must co-operate in putting a treaty in force.[5]

STAGES IN TREATY-MAKING: *1. Negotiation.*   The process of treaty-making may conveniently be divided into a number of separate stages, the first of which is negotiation.   Although negotiations are sometimes suggested by resolution of Congress, the initiative is commonly taken by the President. In any case he appoints the negotiators, outlines the provisions they are to strive to incorporate in the treaty, gives them additional instructions from time to time while the negotiations are in progress, and passes upon their finished product.   In these actions the President is legally free from senatorial interference; but considerations of practical politics may lead him to consult with the Senate, or at least with members of the Foreign Relations Committee, during the course of the negotiations, or even to appoint members of the Senate on the commission of negotiation.[6]

2. Senatorial consideration.   When the treaty has been negotiated, the President transmits it to the Senate for its consent to ratification.   At this stage the Senate may consent to the treaty as drafted, refuse its consent entirely, or consent on condition that certain specified changes (amendments or reservations) be made in the document.   In the latter case the President must then reopen negotiations with the foreign government with a view to securing its consent to the proposed changes, or he may allow the treaty to be dropped.   After the treaty has been sent to the Senate for approval, the President may at any time withdraw it from further consider-

---

[3] The President may also recognize, by a proclamation of neutrality, that war exists between nations.   In like manner he may recognize the "insurgency" or "belligerency" of a revolting faction within a nation.

[4] Art. II, sec. II, cl. 2.

[5] See New York *Times,* Sept. 25, 1932, for Newton D. Baker's proposal.   On May 9, 1945, the House passed H.J. Res. 60 to amend the Constitution so as to provide for the consent to the ratification of treaties by a majority vote of the two Houses.

[6] Wright, *op. cit.,* pp. 248–251.

ation, after which he may resubmit it in its original form or with such changes as the foreign government has agreed to, or which he himself suggests, or he may drop it entirely.[7]

3. Ratification and exchange of ratifications. The stages of treaty-making after senatorial approval of the document has been secured are in the hands of the President alone. He informs the foreign nation (or nations) of the American acceptance and proceeds to make arrangements for the exchange of ratifications, which makes the treaty internationally binding. After the exchange of ratifications the President proclaims the treaty in force as a part of the law of the land.

AGREEMENT-MAKING POWER: *1. On the authority of a treaty or an act of Congress.* Many executive agreements are made under authorization of treaties to which the United States is a party, or under the authority of an act of Congress either prior or subsequent to the agreement. These agreements usually relate to such subjects as boundary settlements, extradition of fugitives from justice, arbitration, trade-marks, patents, copyrights, postal service, and commercial privileges.[8] More recently, however, agreements have included not only subjects that, like those just mentioned, belong in the area of international administration, but also matters of high policy, broad questions that a few years ago would have been considered as falling distinctly under the treaty power. Indeed, there are those who are of the firm opinion that the treaty-making authority is being circumvented by the increasing use of the agreement-making procedure.

The reciprocal trade agreements (in progress since 1934) are made by the President under the authority of the Trade Agreements Act. Agreements under the wartime Lend-Lease Act furnish another illustration. The transfer of destroyers to Great Britain in return for rights with respect to naval and air bases represents an executive agreement in the days "of all aid to Britain short of war." The Attorney General found that the transfer of the vessels was authorized by an act of Congress and that the use of the bases was for the future determination of Congress. The agreement of the United States to participate in the United Nations Relief and Rehabilitation Administration came about by the following stages: a draft plan proposed by the State Department, conferences between officials of that Department and appropriate committees of Congress and individual congressmen (which resulted in numerous changes in the original plan), signing of the agreement by forty-four nations, approval by both houses of Congress. This was an "executive-congressional agreement," to use the language of Senator Taft. This case makes clear that, the agreement-

---

[7] *Ibid.,* pp. 254–255; S. B. Crandall, *Treaties, Their Making and Enforcement* (1916 ed.), pp. 81–97.

[8] Wright, *op. cit.,* pp. 237 ff.

making power of President and Congress acting together is far-reaching, that it is a means by which the Senate's authority over treaty-making may be circumvented. But the procedure in making agreements is much more flexible than that prescribed for treaties, and the former will probably continue in extensive use.[9]

2. *On the President's sole authority.* The President possesses the power to make certain agreements with foreign nations on his own authority. Probably the most outstanding example of this type of agreement is that made in 1933 between President Franklin D. Roosevelt and Maxim Litvinov, in which American recognition of Soviet Russia was accompanied by the assignment to the United States of all amounts due to the Soviet Government from American nationals. The President, through his power of recognition and his authority as Commander-in-Chief, clearly is in a position to make many such agreements on his sole authority.

The problem of secret and personal diplomacy. Not all agreements are openly arrived at or publicly announced. There is the "agreed memorandum" of July 29, 1905, of an exchange of opinion between Count Katsura, representing the Emperor of Japan, and William Howard Taft (then Secretary of War), acting as the personal representative of President Theodore Roosevelt. The memorandum, discovered among the first Roosevelt's unpublished papers some twenty years later, may be summarized as follows: Mr. Taft suggested that the Japanese did not want to take the Philippines from the United States, and Count Katsura assured him that they did not. The Count then observed that it would be advantageous to all parties if the United States, Great Britain, and Japan could enter a secret agreement to preserve peace in the Far East. Mr. Taft replied that a secret agreement would be impossible, but he "thought he could assure" the Japanese that the American people would be pleased to join with them and the British for the preservation of peace in the Far East. The Japanese representative then asked the American representative what Japan should do about Korea, and he was informed that Japan would be fully justified in establishing a military protectorate over Korea. This memorandum was approved by Theodore Roosevelt twelve days before the publication of the terms of the second Anglo-Japanese alliance.[10]

It probably did not escape the notice of the reader that Taft was not our Secretary of State at the time nor was he our ambassador to Japan. He was the Secretary of War and the personal and special representative of the President. This circumvention of regular diplomatic channels, this personalized method of handling foreign relations—"presidential ad-

[9] See Borchard, *op. cit.*

[10] See Tyler Dennett, *Roosevelt and the Russo-Japanese War* (1925), pp. 112–114 and Corwin, *op. cit.,* p. 480.

venturing" as Professor Edward S. Corwin calls it—did not begin with President Theodore Roosevelt, nor did it end with him. Cleveland used it, and Presidents before him did. Wilson had his Colonel E. M. House, and Franklin D. Roosevelt his Harry Hopkins. This method of conducting foreign relations is not unconstitutional, but it makes for secrecy and intrigue. The second Roosevelt handled many international matters personally, by conversations with the leaders of other powers. Who has not heard or read of his conferences at Cairo, Teheran, Yalta, and other points. Agreements reached at such conferences were primarily military but with strong political implications. "I just have a hunch," this Roosevelt would say, and he might negotiate on that basis. At Teheran, Roosevelt, in conference with Churchill and Stalin, casually agreed that the Russians ought to have one third of the surrendered Italian fleet. This oral promise was unknown to practically all his advisers. A few months later the officers of the Military Establishment were dumfounded upon being asked by the Russian representatives in Washington when they might have "their share of the Italian Fleet." [11] There seems to be no question of the power of the President, through his authority to conduct foreign relations and his authority as Commander-in-Chief, to follow a purely personal line and one that may result in secret agreements.

Shaping foreign policy. The aggregate of diplomatic powers discussed above makes apparent that the President is the principal agent in the government for determining foreign policy. To be sure, the Senate may block his efforts by withholding consent to a treaty, and Congress may embarrass or even tie the hands of the President by enacting legislation that conflicts with his plans or by failing to enact laws or authorize agreements necessary for perfecting his plans. The Senate's adverse action with respect to Wilson's League of Nations proposal is well known. The act of Congress (1924) that abrogated the "Gentlemen's Agreement" (the understanding by which Japanese immigration had been regulated for nearly twenty years) over the protest of President Coolidge and Secretary Hughes, and that caused serious friction between the two countries, is a familiar example of what Congress may do. These and similar illustrations that might be offered of the thwarting of the President's policy prove only that he does not always have clear sailing. He is still the guiding force in determining our relations with the foreign powers.

The proclamation of neutrality issued by Washington in 1793, at the time the nations of Europe were entering upon a general war, not only laid down a course that this country has since followed, but also had great

---

[11] Hanson W. Baldwin, "Our Worst Blunders in the War," *Atlantic*, Jan. 1950, p. 31. The Russians did not get their "third." They were persuaded to accept some British and American vessels.

influence in fixing the standard that other nations have followed. In his Farewell Address, Washington announced the policy of isolation. Admitting the wisdom of this policy for a young republic, and without considering the equally wise variations from it in the days of national adolescence and manhood, we simply add that it has had and still has a very pronounced influence in the conduct of American foreign relations. The Monroe Doctrine, announced by the President in 1823 and interpreted by each succeeding President according to his own notions of what it should be, has had an incalculable influence both in our official actions and in the minds of the people sanctioning those actions.

The conciliatory policy of Lincoln and Seward brought us safely through serious international difficulties during the Civil War. Wilson's policy kept us out of the First World War for a time and determined almost the exact date of our entrance into it. The brief period of isolation, due largely to the Senate's opposition to Wilson's foreign policy of international co-operation at the end of the war, gave way to a new era of executive leadership that might be characterized as one of cautious co-operation with the foreign powers. We took an important part in the negotiations that resulted in the Pact of Paris (1928) renouncing war as an instrument of national policy, and we assumed leadership in interpreting its obligations. Then came the dictators, singly and in combinations, and the new series of crises supplied numerous illustrations of the tremendous power of the President in guiding our foreign relations. Under the President's leadership we extended all aid to Britain "short of war," took down the "silly-fool dollar sign," promoted hemispheric solidarity, appeased Japan, and finally went to war.

The most recent examples of the shaping of foreign policy are furnished by the Truman Doctrine and the Marshall Plan. The information that the British would withdraw from Greece led to the somewhat hastily announced Truman Doctrine. On March 12, 1947, the President recommended to Congress the extension of financial and military aid to Greece and Turkey as a means of preventing the spread of Communism. This doctrine was hurriedly conceived and promptly and loudly criticized as being at best a negative approach to the problem and at its worst a commitment that would inevitably lead to war. The Marshall Plan soon followed, and further discussion of the Truman Doctrine practically ceased. The Marshall Plan (explained on page 725), represents a positive approach to the basic European postwar problem, the restoration of the industrial plant.

The primacy of the President in foreign affairs. Proof of the primacy of the President in the conduct of foreign relations is hardly less than overwhelming. This place of awful responsibility comes to him through his authority to send ambassadors and ministers on regular missions and his personal and special representatives on particular missions and on roving missions, to recognize new governments and new states, and to make treaties and agreements, the agreements often being made on his sole authority as head of foreign relations or as Commander-in-Chief of the armed forces, the same agreements sometimes being secret. Nor should we fail to notice that his authority to move the Army and Navy about has often been a significant factor in the direction of foreign relations. The Senate or the Congress may from time to time apply a brake, even effectively block a plan or project of the President; but obstruction is negative. The President has the positive power. The actions of the Chief Executive, even his secret agreements, commonly bind the nation. Whether other nations respect us or hold us in contempt, trust us or suspect us, seek our friendship or arm against us, depends largely upon the intelligence and judgment the President brings to the discharge of his weighty duties as head of our foreign relations.

II. THE DEPARTMENT OF STATE AND THE FOREIGN SERVICE [12]

Whatever the President's powers and responsibilities may be, he cannot single-handedly conduct foreign relations. In some specific matter and on some occasion, dramatic or otherwise, he may, for good or ill, take a direct hand, but the State Department and thousands of Foreign Service officers and employees scattered throughout the world carry on the bulk of the work.

The Department of State: THE SECRETARY. The Department of State is the first of the executive departments, and the Secretary of State is the ranking member of the President's Cabinet. He is usually a man in whom the President and the country have great confidence, although on occasion he is one who has been elevated to the post because of his place as a leader in the party. The list of Secretaries compares rather favorably with the roster of Presidents. A number of them, including Jefferson and John Quincy Adams, have become President; and among those who were probably qualified for the Presidency we find Clay, Webster, Hay, Root, Hughes, Stimson, Hull, and George C. Marshall.

ORGANIZATION. For some years the Department has lacked adequate organization and personnel for performing its functions. Often we read such indictments as "Our Anachronistic Foreign Office" and "The Riddle

[12] Robert Bendiner, *The Riddle of the State Department* (1942); J. R. Childs, *American Foreign Service* (1948); (Hoover) Commission on Organization of the Executive Branch of the Government, *Foreign Affairs* (1949); G. H. Stuart, *The Department of State* (1949); Department of State, *The Foreign Service* (Publication 3612, 1949); *U.S. Govt. Org. Manual* (1949), pp. 84–103.

of the State Department." The Hoover Commission took due notice of the need for better organization, more personnel, and higher salaries, and some of its recommendations have been carried into effect.

Next to the Secretary of State stands the Under Secretary, who serves as his superior's principal adviser, and, in the absence of the Secretary, takes over as Acting Secretary of State. There are two Deputy Under Secretaries (as recommended by the Hoover Commission), one supervises the departmental and Foreign Service administration and the other supervising policies and procedures of the other areas of the Department. The Counselor, holding the rank of Assistant Secretary of State, assists the Secretary in the solution of problems and in other work of a highly responsible character. Eight Assistant Secretaries of State have particular services for which they are responsible, as follows: International Organization (UN) Affairs, international economic affairs, liaison with Congress and the Bureau of the Budget, international information and educational exchange, and the other four Assistant Secretaries have the assignment for the development and implementation of policy with respect to the American republics, Europe, the Near East and Africa, and the Far East, each Secretary being responsible for one of these areas. The Legal Adviser, who has equal rank with the Assistant Secretaries, is responsible for all departmental and Foreign Service matters of a legal character.

A sort of general staff consisting of the higher officers of the Department advises the Secretary on developments and assists in planning policy. Nineteen directors of "Offices," each having a segment of the Department's work under his supervision, report to the Secretary directly or through higher officers. Below the "Offices" function some seventy-five divisions, each headed by a "chief." This organization as briefly outlined carries out the many headquarters services without which the Department, extending its lines to the uttermost parts of the earth, could not function. To the Washington office our diplomatic representatives, consuls, and other foreign service officers must look for information and instructions, and to it belongs the heavy responsibility of formulating (with the President) and implementing American foreign policy.

GENERAL FUNCTIONS. The chief duties of the Department, as already indicated, are centered around the conduct of foreign affairs. Always subject to the President's direction, it has general charge of the negotiation of treaties; prepares instructions for our ambassadors and other representatives in foreign countries; issues passports to American citizens and extends protection to them when abroad; hears complaints of American citizens concerning alleged commercial discrimination in foreign lands, and seeks redress for them where such complaints are valid; receives similar complaints from foreigners, and offers redress where it is due;

DEPARTMENT OF STATE

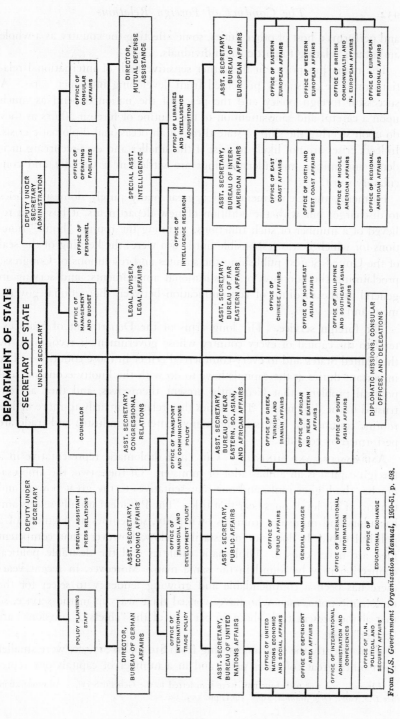

From *U.S. Government Organization Manual*, 1950–51, p. 498.

and performs a host of other duties, some affecting the country as a whole and others relating to particular individuals.

The many pin pricks in the rather sensitive flesh of international relations must be constantly prevented from developing into open sores. A successful foreign policy and the peace of the nation depend as much upon a careful and sane attention to the routine of foreign affairs as they do upon steering the ship of state through an occasional diplomatic crisis. Indeed, crises are not likely to arise if the smaller and ever-recurring incidents and minor misunderstandings are settled in a friendly and conciliatory spirit.

Formerly, the Department had a great many purely domestic duties to discharge; but with the addition of new departments, it has been relieved of a number of such functions. Among the routine "home" functions for which it was responsible until 1950 were: the keeping of the seal of the United States; publishing the statutes and resolutions of Congress; proclaiming the adoption of constitutional amendments; and serving in general as the medium of communication between the national government and the states.[13]

The foreign service. The long arms of the Department of State extend to the capital of every country whose government is recognized by the United States and to every commercial center in those countries. The important duties at the capitals have to do with the knotty economic and political problems that frequently present themselves, and they are entrusted to the diplomats. The duties that relate primarily to more or less routine commercial affairs in the many centers of industry and trade are performed by consuls.

AMBASSADORS AND MINISTERS. Our chief diplomatic representative in a foreign capital is an ambassador or minister. Of these two, the ambassador has the higher rank, and our representatives to the great powers and to most of the lesser ones bear that title. The President usually selects ambassadors and ministers from his own party, sometimes as payment of a political debt. It does not necessarily follow, however, that competent men are never chosen. Diplomatic qualities and the desirable political connection may be found in the same man. Moreover, in recent years there has been a commendable and growing tendency to select for the diplomatic posts, men who have worked their way up in the service, so that at the present time about 60 per cent of the "chiefs of missions" are "career" men.

Until recently the salaries, varying from $10,000 to $17,500, were smaller than other great countries paid; and in a number of capitals our repre-

13 In 1950 most of such functions were transferred to the General Services Administration. See *U.S. Govt. Org. Manual*, 1950–1951, pp. 355, 356.

sentatives were compelled to draw liberally from their private incomes. It was impossible for anyone who was without a private fortune to represent us, for example, in London. This condition has been partially rectified by the Foreign Service Act of 1946, which fixes the salary range from $15,000 to $25,000.

Their duties. Broadly speaking, the chief of mission carries out all the instructions of his government and keeps his eyes and ears open for anything that may be of interest to it. He negotiates protocols, conventions, and treaties especially regarding international intercourse, tariffs, shipping, commerce, and the preservation of peace. He reports on political and economic conditions and trends of significance to the United States. He makes representations to the authorities of foreign governments concerning the protection of American citizens, their rights, and their property. He establishes and utilizes personal contacts for the benefit of his government and of American citizens. Above all, he is supposed to create good will and common understanding, and use these as instruments for enhancing international confidence and co-operation. He must, of course, manage his office efficiently and apportion work and responsibility among his assistants in such a manner as to obtain the best results. Speechmaking he cannot avoid; but he must always be careful of his utterances, embarrassing his government at no time, and at all times maintaining his personal dignity. These are a few of his duties.[14] It is hardly necessary to add that in discharging them he must exercise the greatest caution and tact—he must be a diplomat.

FOREIGN SERVICE OFFICERS. The top diplomats, the chiefs of mission, constitute only a small fraction of the personnel engaged in the foreign service. Associated with each chief of mission are experienced Foreign Service officers upon whom he must rely very much as the Secretary of State must depend upon the Under- and Assistant Secretaries in the Department in Washington. These Foreign Service officers hold such ranks as minister (ranking next to the ambassador at the embassy in London, for example), counselor, and first, second, and third secretary. Foreign Service officers of lower rank and Foreign Service Staff officers and employees perform work of a less responsible and routine character. Foreign Service Reserve officers who are usually specialists in some economic or cultural subject are often attached to a mission. The total number of officers and employees about our London and Paris embassies runs to several hundred. In some 185 cities of the world the United States operates

14 For a lively account of the duties of an ambassador, see B. J. Hendrick, *Life and Letters of Walter H. Page,* Vol. I, pp. 159-161, or a quotation from these pages in C. A. and Wm. Beard, *The American Leviathan,* pp. 715-717. For an account of the work of a particularly alert diplomat see W. E. Dodd, Jr. and Martha Dodd, *Ambassador Dodd's Diary* (1941).

a consular service. The Foreign Service officers, holding the ranks of consul general, consul, and vice consul, are responsible for the work at the consular posts. They are assisted by various specialists, clerks, typists, and so on.

Their duties. The duties of the Foreign Service officers and other personnel about the embassy or legation have already been touched upon. The work of a consulate is primarily, although not exclusively, commercial. It is no less important than the diplomatic work, and the Foreign Service officers are ordinarily commissioned to do both and are transferred from one to the other. Here is a partial list of a consul's duties: He analyzes and makes reports on market conditions, statistics of trade, systems of production, and similar economic matters in his district. He replies to trade inquiries from American citizens, always aiming to promote good will and to help present and future trade relations. He certifies invoices of all goods shipped to the United States and makes reports on undervaluation, in order that our government may not be deprived of lawful revenue. He assists in preventing the importation of prohibited articles. He "enters and clears" American ships, administers relief of seamen, signs on and discharges seamen, settles disputes between them and their masters, and takes charge of shipwrecked vessels. He visas passports for foreigners who wish to travel in the United States, and issues visas to immigrants. He witnesses marriage ceremonies where one of the participants is an American citizen. As still further duties, he performs various notarial services and administers and settles the estates of American citizens and sailors who have died abroad. The consul, especially the consul in a seaport, leads a busy life.

A CAREER IN THE FOREIGN SERVICE. Some mild attempts were made by Cleveland, Roosevelt, and Taft to put the diplomatic and the consular services on the merit basis; but the Rogers Act of 1924, as amended by an act of 1931, reorganized and greatly improved both services in several particulars. This legislation has been superseded by the Foreign Service Act of 1946, upon which the following discussion is based.

All persons in the foreign service are classified. There are the chiefs of mission (ambassadors and ministers) in four classes, with salaries ranging from $15,000 to $25,000. The Foreign Service officers (our particular concern here) are of seven classes, with salaries ranging from $3,630 to $13,500. Foreign Service Staff officers and employees are distributed among twenty-two classes, with salaries ranging from $1,050 to $10,000.

A college or university graduate, if interested in a career in the foreign service, would ordinarily desire to become a Foreign Service officer. To become such an officer, class 6, the beginner's class, he must pass written, oral, and physical examinations. The written examination on English, government, history, economics, and modern language extends over a period of three days and is one that even the best of candidates respect. Perhaps not one in five who take the examination passes it. But passing the written examination is only the first hurdle. The Oral, taking about an hour, is *the* examination, so it is reported. Only a fraction of those who pass the Written survive the Oral. At this final weed-out the candidate faces five men, each of whom has been through his record thoroughly. They make mental notes on his presentability, his manner, his diction, his readiness, and other qualities that constitute a well-rounded man, an effective personality. If successful in the examinations, a candidate is placed on the eligible list from which the President makes his nominations to the Senate. Few appointments are made, however, for there are only some 1,400 Foreign Service officers, and within this select group the annual turnover is small.

Once appointed, a new officer spends several months at the State Department's Foreign Service Institute, where he learns the rules and regulations of the service, how to prepare reports, and many other things. It is reported that at the turn of the century they were told such things as "take snuff often and slowly" and to "sit with your back to the light." Now they have such advice as "don't shade your reports to make yourself important," and "remember that you're not supposed to stand on a bar and lead a community sing . . . and please don't become a stuffed shirt with a swelled head." [15]

A new appointee will probably serve for a time at some consular post, then have a period at an embassy, perform some duty with the State Department in Washington, then go back to a consulate or embassy, and so on. He does not enter the consular service or the diplomatic service— he enters the Foreign Service and he is assigned to serve where he is most needed or performs best. An officer is supposed to advance in the service according to his ability and achievements. The regulation now is that he must win promotion from class to class in a specified time or be dropped. This is the "promotion up or selection out" plan long in use in the United States Navy.

In the paragraphs on ambassadors and ministers it was observed that it is possible for a Foreign Service officer to advance to the rank of minister. This promotion policy is now followed with more than flagging perseverance. It should be further noted that a Foreign Service officer may be promoted to the rank of "career minister" without being the chief of a mission. For example, the second ranking man at our London embassy and certain directors in the State Department are career ministers.

CRITICISM OF THE FOREIGN SERVICE. Our foreign service, both as it op-

15 Ralph G. Martin, "So You Want To Be a Diplomat," *New Republic*, Oct. 27, 1947, p. 17.

erates in Washington and abroad, has been criticized on various grounds, some frivolous and some worthy of attention. There are too many "cookie pushers," too many "pink tea fellows," too many pairs of spats in the foreign service. To this last-named indictment, a career man is reported to have retorted, "Diplomats are more spat upon than spatted." It is not to be denied that foreign service personnel has been recruited too much from among eastern persons of means, from Harvard, Yale, and Princeton, the "Ivy League." This practice was followed because the service attracted such persons and because the compensation for it was so low that only those individuals who had private income could afford to accept appointment. Conditions have steadily improved since the passage of the Rogers Act (1924) and the further strengthening of the service by the Foreign Service Act of 1946. Salaries are now fairly adequate and every effort is being made, and with some success, to attract a more representative group of Americans to the Foreign Service. Of course, there are a number of men in the service who belong to the so-called Pre-Rogers Age, but gradually the old restrictive traditions are being left behind.

"Diplomacy is easy on the head but hard on the feet," cracked a political ambassador at a press conference after a round of receptions. "That depends upon which one uses the more," counter-cracked a more experienced diplomat. Of course, a foreign service officer must be a socially acceptable person, must spend time and even energy at parties, but he must also use his head. The present program of selection and training gives assurance that his head is making some progress over his feet. A few years ago, one of the most serious charges leveled at the foreign service was that it was out of touch with democratic trends, too conservative, too "fascist-minded." This general charge has, or had, this much substance: diplomacy has generally been the domain of conservatives, and even in democratic countries the "status quo" groups have always filled a large number of berths in the foreign service. It is not too much to hope that under present plans of operation this criticism will become less valid.

In 1950 Senator Joseph R. McCarthy made the sensational charge that the State Department was employing Communists, just how many the Senator did not make clear. To date the charge and a resulting investigation have not revealed that any Communist is so employed. The charge seems to rest upon the fact that certain officers, employees, and advisers of the State Department had or have opinions respecting American foreign policy in Asia that are inacceptable to Senator McCarthy, his articulate backers, and perhaps to many others. A policy that failed to stop Communism in China does not necessarily make Communists of its authors.

Reading List

S. F. Bemis, *The Latin-American Policy of the United States* (1943).

The Brookings Institution, *Major Problems of United States Foreign Policy, 1949-1950* (1949).

L. H. Chamberlain and R. C. Snyder (eds.), *American Foreign Policy* (1948).

J. R. Childs, *American Foreign Service* (1948).

The (Hoover) Commission on Organization of the Executive Branch of the Government, *Foreign Affairs* (1949).

E. S. Corwin, *The President: Office and Powers* (1948 ed.), Ch. V.

C. G. Dawes, *Journal as Ambassador to Great Britain* (1939).

Tyler Dennett, *Roosevelt and the Russo-Japanese War* (1925).

W. E. Dodd, Jr., and Martha Dodd, *Ambassador Dodd's Diary* (1941).

E. M. Earl, "A Half-Century of American Foreign Policy: Our Stake in Europe, 1898-1948," *Pol. Sci. Qt.*, LXIV (1949), 168-188.

E. O. Guerrant, *Roosevelt's Good Neighbor Policy* (1949).

The Memoirs of Cordell Hull, 2 vols. (1948).

Philip Jessup, Elihu Root, 2 vols. (1938).

J. M. Mathews, *American Foreign Relations: Conduct and Policies* (1938 ed.).

Wallace McClure, *International Executive Agreements* (1941).

Elmer Plischke, *Conduct of American Diplomacy* (1949).

R. E. Sherwood, *Roosevelt and Hopkins* (1948).

Department of State, *The Foreign Service* (Publication 3612, 1949).

E. R. Stettinius, *Roosevelt and the Russians* (1949).

G. H. Stuart, *American Diplomatic and Consular Practice* (1936).

————, *The Department of State* (1949).

R. W. Van Alstyne, *American Diplomacy in Action* (1946).

Quincy Wright, *The Control of American Foreign Relations* (1922).

Questions and Problems

1. What provisions of the Constitution relate to the President's power to conduct foreign affairs?
2. Show why the treaty-making power is essentially an executive function.
3. Explain how agreements may be made under the Constitution; under the authority of a treaty; under the authority of an act of Congress.
4. Discuss this statement: *Secret agreements are prohibited under the American system.*
5. Could you say that, in the conduct of foreign relations the President's discretion is more significant than his constitutional powers and limitations?
6. How is the Department of State organized to discharge its functions?
7. Outline the duties of ambassadors and other chiefs of mission.
8. Discuss the qualifications and duties of Foreign Service officers.
9. Review some of the criticisms of our foreign service and indicate what steps have been taken to meet them since the First World War.

☆ 29 ☆

The United States and International Organization*

T HIS chapter deals with the vitally pressing problem of establishing and maintaining international peace and justice. Upon the solution of this problem may depend the very physical existence of American and Western civilization.

In the slow and hesitating evolution of organization designed to promote international security the United States has played a strange and vacillating role. Before the First World War we promoted the small beginnings of such machinery. After that war and for two decades following we refused all responsibility for supporting a world-wide League of Nations that had come into being largely as the result of the personal leadership of an American President. During the Second World War and in the postwar period, however, we assumed world leadership in bringing into being the United Nations, the most comprehensive plan yet adopted for international organization. Our continued support will contribute materially to whatever successes the United Nations achieves under the present Charter and to the building of a more effective system of world organization.

The pre-League era. It would be interesting and instructive to review the progress of international organization prior to the establishment of the League of Nations, but the limits of space require us to resist the temptation to trace this historical development and to salve the conscience by reference to authorities who have delved into this history.[1] A

---

* This chapter was written in 1947 by the late Winston B. Thorson, Associate Professor of History, The State College of Washington, and revised for this edition by H. Paul Castleberry, Assistant Professor of Political Science in the same institution.

[1] F. J. Brown, C. Hodges, and J. S. Roucek, *Contemporary World Politics* (1939), Chs. XVII–XVIII; Clyde Eagleton, *International Government* (1948 ed.), Chs. I, II, VII–X; T. V. Kalijarvi (ed.), *Modern World Politics* (1945 ed.), pp. 25–41, 98–125; Hans J. Morgenthau,

thumbnail sketch of such development must have reference to the dreamers and thinkers like Hugo Grotius of Holland and our own William Penn, whose proposals for an international organization to preserve peace and promote justice among the nations went unheeded. Not until 1815, after a quarter century of devastating warfare, did Europe make a significant attempt to establish an organization to keep the peace. This arrangement was the Holy Alliance, a very loose organization of victors—England, Austria, Russia, and Prussia—that held "congresses" from time to time to preserve the *status quo* in Europe,[2] and that failed within a decade largely because England would not go along with the other powers in their pro-absolutist interpretation of the functions of the Alliance. The European powers continued, however, as crises arose to hold conferences in the interest of peace. This so-called Concert of Europe met with some success, for there was no general war for a century. It failed, nevertheless, to prevent the First World War.

The United States had no part in the political associations just mentioned, but it took a position of leadership in promoting international arbitration, both in resort to arbitration for the settlement of its own international disputes and in the establishment (1899 and 1907) of the Permanent Court of Arbitration at The Hague.[3] In like manner the United States played its part in promoting the work of international administrative organizations, such as the Universal Postal Union and the International Bureau of Weights and Measures. These organizations were not concerned with "high politics," but with such prosaic and at the same time essential matters as the movement of mails across national boundaries, uniformity in weights and measures, and other nonpolitical matters.

This pre-League organization was insufficient to preserve international order and ensure justice, as was demonstrated in 1914, when the assassination of an Austrian archduke and the train of events it precipitated plunged the world into war. Shortly thereafter, however, efforts were begun to establish a more effective international organization. In this undertaking the United States made gestures toward assuming a more important

---

Politics among Nations (1948), Chs. XXIII, XXV; Pitman B. Potter, *An Introduction to the Study of International Organization* (1948 ed.), Chs. VI–IX; F. L. Schuman, *International Politics* (1941 ed.), pp. 99–141, 171–211; W. R. Sharp and D. Kirk, *Contemporary International Politics* (1944 ed.), Chs. I–II, VIII–IX, XX; H. M. Vinacke, *International Organization* (1934), Chs. I–VII, IX, XIV.

[2] The attempt at international government called the Holy Alliance was based on a series of treaties negotiated between 1814 and 1815. Of these the Treaty of the Holy Alliance itself was only one. See Morgenthau, *op. cit.,* pp. 361–367. The system lacked any kind of permanent organization.

[3] The so-called Hague Court was not a court at all, but was simply a panel of jurists from which courts of arbitration could be set up when needed by the states agreeing to its use. Some forty nations accepted the Hague Court plan, but in the years before the First World War only fifteen controversies were settled by the Court.

role than had been its custom in the past. That it failed to assume responsibilities commensurate with its power is well known.

I. THE LEAGUE OF NATIONS [4]

Planning for peace. Well before the entrance of the United States into the First World War numerous persons here and in other countries became convinced that the only means of rescuing mankind from the scourge of war was through some universal organization to maintain peace. This idea won the support of President Woodrow Wilson, who was determined that the victory of the Allies in the war must be used as the opportunity to create a "league of nations," an organization with powers of enforcement to put down aggression and to bring the anarchical political organization of the world into conformity with the growing economic and cultural unity. In his address to Congress in 1917, asking for a declaration of war against Germany, he stated that this country would fight for "a universal dominion of right by such a concert of free peoples as shall bring peace and safety to all nations and make the world at last free." In the months following, Wilson became the leader of world opinion seeking to make the creation of such a new international system the primary war aim of the Allied Powers. This position was emphasized in 1918 by the last of Wilson's famous Fourteen Points, which asserted as the major war objective the establishment of "a general association of nations" to afford "mutual guarantees of political independence and territorial integrity to great and small states alike."

When the Fourteen Points became the basis for the armistice of November, 1918, the chance had arrived to bring into being a structure for international co-operation based on a new concept of international morality. President Wilson himself led the American delegation to Paris to take part in making the peace settlement with Germany (January–June, 1919). There he insisted successfully that the Covenant (or constitution) of the League of Nations should be made an integral part of the peace treaty. In fact, the Covenant, written by a committee of the Conference under Wilson's chairmanship, became the first section of the Treaty of Versailles and of the separate treaties written afterward for the four lesser states that had been allied with Germany.[5]

[4] Brown, Hodges, and Roucek, *op. cit.*, Chs. XX–XXIII; H. E. Davis (ed.), *Pioneers in World Order* (1944); Eagleton, *op. cit.*, Chs. X–XI; Institute on World Organization, *World Organization: A Balance Sheet of the First Great Experiment* (1943); Kalijarvi, *op. cit.*, pp. 125–134; League of Nations Association, *Essential Facts Underlying World Organization* (1941); Schuman, *op. cit.*, pp. 211–247; Sharp and Kirk, *op. cit.*, Chs. XXI–XXVIII; Vinacke, *op. cit.*, Chs. VII, X–XIII, XV.

[5] For a discussion of Wilson's difficulties in securing the kind of covenant he desired see T. A. Bailey, *Wilson and the Lost Peace* (1944).

The organs of the League. The preamble of the Covenant declared that the basic purpose of the League was "to promote international co-operation and to achieve international peace and security." Toward these ends there was established an international organization that went far beyond that which had preceded it a century before. Unlike the Holy Alliance, the League could be described as "a real organization with a legal personality, agents, and agencies of its own." [6] Its principal agencies were the Assembly, the Council, and a Secretariat. These and certain other instruments of the League require brief examination.

(1) The Assembly. Members of the League met annually and in occasional special sessions to constitute the Assembly. Each member state was entitled to three delegates but only one vote. In general, the rule of unanimity prevailed in voting, though in decisions concerning the settlement of international disputes the votes of the parties to the dispute were not to be counted.[7]

Although Article 3 of the Covenant provided that "the Assembly may deal at its meetings with any matter within the sphere of action of the League or affecting the peace of the world," it did not possess legislative power. The work of the Assembly usually issued either in the form of a resolution or a draft treaty for ratification by members. Nevertheless, certain of the Assembly's exclusive powers,[8] such as its control of finances, together with its aggressive approach to world problems, contributed to its becoming the dominant organ of the League.

(2) The Council. The second principal organ of the League was the Council, the composition of which reflected the claims of the great powers for special representation. It was to be composed of nine members. Five powers were to be given permanent membership, but the absence of the United States reduced the number to four—Great Britain, France, Italy, and Japan. Four lesser powers, selected by the Assembly, constituted non-permanent members. Over the years Germany became the fifth permanent member, and the number of non-permanent members was increased to eleven.

The Council was required by the Covenant to meet at least once a year, and in practice it met much more often. Voting was largely restricted by the rule of unanimity, as in the case of the Assembly.

Like the Assembly, the Council was given the right to deal with any matter within the scope of the League, and any circumstance that threatened to disturb the peace could be presented to it as well as to the As-

---

[6] Morgenthau, *op. cit.,* p. 369.

[7] Another exception to the rule of unanimity was provided in Art. 15, par. 10 of the Covenant.

[8] Eagleton, *op. cit.,* p. 278.

sembly. Although some few powers were delegated by the Covenant exclusively to the Council,[9] there was no general differentiation of functions between the Council and the Assembly to be found. In general, it may be said "they were simply two cogs designed to work closely together in the same machinery," representing a compromise between the demands of state equality and the claims of special responsibility put forth by the big powers.[10] Although the Council was neither a legislative nor an executive body, certain provisions of the Covenant, together with such practices of the Assembly as agreeing upon a line of action and calling upon the Council to carry it into effect, permits us to say that the Council tended to assume executive functions.

(3) THE SECRETARIAT. The civil service of the League of Nations, permanently located at League headquarters in Geneva, Switzerland, was charged with keeping records, preparing agenda for meetings of the Assembly and the Council, receiving reports from League agencies, publishing documents, and the performance of related duties. Under the direction of the Secretary-General, who was chosen for an indefinite term by the Assembly and the Council, the Secretariat was the backbone of the League. It furnished co-ordination, continuity, information, and experience to support the efforts of the shifting delegates of nations through whom the work of the League ostensibly was done.

(4) OTHER AGENCIES. Besides the three principal organs of the League, the Covenant provided for bringing various older international administrative agencies under the direction of the League, and for the creation of technical organizations to advance international understanding and co-operation in the fields of health, communications and transit, economics and finance, and intellectual matters.[11] The Covenant further laid down the terms of a new system for control of colonial areas, whereby former German and Turkish territories became mandates under the League. The areas in question, which were assigned to certain of the victors by the peace treaties, were to be administered according to the principles laid down in the Covenant and under limited supervision of the League Council.[12]

The Covenant also recognized two companion agencies, each created, however, by a separate constitution of its own. The first of these, the Permanent Court of International Justice—often called the World Court—was constituted to handle international legal questions. All members of the League were automatically members of the Court, and other nations

[9] Eagleton, *op. cit.*, p. 278.

[10] *Ibid.*, p. 277.

[11] *Ibid.*, pp. 282 ff.

[12] See Art. 22 of the Covenant.

might join if they chose. The Court itself consisted of fifteen judges elected by the Assembly and the Council.[13] In part its work involved the giving of advisory opinions upon the request of the League Assembly or Council. Beyond this, the activity of the Court consisted of the actual settlement of disputes. It should be noted that under the terms of the Statute, or constitution, of the Court only states could be parties before the Court. No state, even though it had joined the Court, could be compelled to submit to judicial settlement except of its own volition. There was, of course, compulsory jurisdiction in certain instances, but this resulted from special agreements between nations that wished to extend the jurisdiction of the Court among themselves.

The other companion agency recognized in the Covenant was the International Labor Organization. It consisted of all League members and any other states that wished to join, and was directed to make studies and to recommend action by the member states on international labor problems.

The record of the League. The League of Nations began to function in 1920, developed markedly during the first decade of its existence, but went rapidly into eclipse after 1931 and into virtual suspension in the late 'thirties. The League was not finally liquidated until 1946, when the member states voted it out of existence, transferring its assets to the new United Nations.

During its lifetime the record of the League of Nations was checkered but its accomplishments were by no means insignificant. Certainly its major successes were in the nonpolitical fields. It arranged financial assistance to several small nations; it aided in handling the European refugee problem; it convoked the Geneva Disarmament Conference in 1932; it developed programs for international health and disease control, for curtailing international dealings in narcotics and prostitution, for expanding world-wide intellectual co-operation, and for registration and publication of over four thousand international agreements. It carried on the administration of the Free City of Danzig and the Saar Basin, and it supervised the mandate system. By 1941 the International Labor Organization had submitted to its members some sixty-seven draft conventions on labor matters, and a total of eight hundred and eighty-one ratifications were returned. The Permanent Court of International Justice by 1940 had rendered thirty-one judgments on cases brought before it, and twenty-seven advisory opinions on international legal questions submitted by League agencies. All this nonpolitical activity by the League and its companion

[13] Though the United States was never a member, four American jurists served as judges of the Court: John Bassett Moore, 1922–1928; Charles Evans Hughes, 1928–1930; Frank B. Kellogg, 1930–1935; Manley O. Hudson, 1936–1939.

agencies, greatly expanding the areas of international co-operation, warrants the statement that the League of Nations completely justified its existence, quite apart from its successes or failures on political matters.

Unquestionably the major task of the League was the peaceful settlement of disputes and the prevention of war, and final judgment on the League must be based upon its failure in this area. Over thirty political disputes were settled or adjusted by the League. Among the most satisfactory settlements were those between Sweden and Finland over control of the Aaland islands (1921), between Greece and Bulgaria after a border clash (1925), between Great Britain and Turkey over possession of the Mosul oil area (1926), between Colombia and Peru over rival frontier claims (1933), and between Yugoslavia and Hungary after the assassination of the Yugoslav king (1934). Less satisfactory were the settlements of the controversy over Vilna (1920–1923) and the Corfu episode (1923), in which Poland and Italy respectively imposed the decisions they wished through the League. Wholly unsatisfactory and, in fact, destructive of the League as an effective force were the failures to deter and to punish the Japanese aggression in Manchuria (1931) and the Italian attack upon Ethiopia (1935). To be sure, in the latter case, the League did declare Italy an aggressor and did half-heartedly impose sanctions—the only time in the League's history—but to no avail. After that, through the remaining years of peace, through the crises precipitated by the Japanese attack on China, the intervention of Hitler and Mussolini in the Spanish civil war, and Hitler's seizures of central European territories, the League was almost wholly ignored. Although it continued its empty sessions in its then recently completed magnificent palace at Geneva, it had become impotent, a failure in its primary task.

Reasons for the failure of the League. The causes of the failure of the League to prevent war and maintain international order are of special significance at present, for they demonstrate clearly the dangers faced by the United Nations. Some of the major causes for the League's failure as a system of collective security are the following:

(1) Psychological and sociological factors were paramount in the demise of the League. The League's institutions and procedures were unable to invoke the fundamental loyalties of people. The organization was unable to create a lasting expectation of peace or confidence in its guaranties.[14]

(2) The lack of a direct relationship between the League of Nations and the people of the world is another important factor leading to the failure of the League. The organization was built upon the prevailing doctrine of international law that sovereign states are the only subjects of that law and that individuals are subjects of the sovereign state and not citizens of

[14] Quincy Wright, *A Study of War* (1942), Vol. II, pp. 1060 ff.

the world community. The result has been summarized as follows: "The League could reach people only indirectly through the medium of national governments. Consequently, popular insistence upon the observance of League procedures was at the mercy of government policies, and reciprocally government policies were at the mercy of nationally minded publics." [15]

(3) Inadequate membership is a further reason for the failure of the League. Although an international organization whose main purpose is the maintenance of world stability does not need to be universal in the sense that all nations of the world belong to it, nevertheless, it must be universal in the sense that all powerful nations, which are the ones most likely to disturb the peace of the world, are under its jurisdiction. The League never had such a basis or such support.

Although Saudi Arabia, Nepal, and the United States were the only nations that were never at some time members of the League, by 1939 the number of members had decreased by about one third. Withdrawals from membership included such powerful nations as Germany, Japan, and Italy.[16] The expulsion of Russia in 1939 for its attack on Finland removed another great power from the roster. Of the two nations that were potentially the most powerful in the world—the United States and the Soviet Union—one was never a member, and the other was a member only during the League's declining years from 1934–1939.

(4) The League of Nations was committed to principles of justice defined in terms of the *status quo* that several of the great powers would not or could not support. The fact that the League Covenant was written into the peace treaties and that it bound the members "to respect and preserve against external aggression the territorial integrity and existing political independence of all members of the League" made the League a guarantor of the *status quo* created in 1919. In the views of France, which became the dominant power on the European continent as a result of the war, and other countries—such as Poland, Rumania, Czechoslovakia—that had benefited greatly by the peace treaties, the primary task of the League was the preservation of that settlement. Under these circumstances the full and unconstrained co-operation of the German Republic, Italy, Japan, or of Soviet Russia [17] was difficult and, in the end, impossible. The article of the Covenant calling for reconsideration and revision of treaties that had become "inapplicable" was a dead letter from the beginning, and the Wilsonian plan of the League as an organization readily adaptable to changing conditions was completely lost. Divergent national interests

---

[15] *Ibid.*, Vol. II, pp. 938–939.

[16] Ten of the twenty Latin American republics withdrew between 1924 and 1939.

[17] Soviet Russia, not France or Great Britain, however, took the lead at Geneva from 1934 to 1938 in trying to make the League effective as a system of collective security against Hitlerite Germany. See F. L. Schuman, *Soviet Politics at Home and Abroad* (1946), pp. 274–281.

thus prevailed over the principles of justice defined by the League in terms of the *status quo*.[18]

(5) Another reason the power of the League was insufficient to assure international equilibrium was the divergent policy of Great Britain and France toward the fundamental requirements of stability. One of the principal requisites of order was to ensure the permanent inability of Germany to wage war, and the essential prerequisite of success was the continuing unity of France and Great Britain in maintaining the hegemony of France on the continent. Great Britain, however, sought to regain the controlling influence it had exerted over the affairs of Europe during the nineteenth century. This objective meant the restoration of the previous balance of power on the continent, with Britain as its holder. Because of the superior power of the British, this policy prevailed and was reflected in the activities of the League of Nations.[19]

(6) Finally, the League suffered from serious constitutional weaknesses. One of the principal defects was failure fully to outlaw war. Instead, members were forbidden to go to war only under certain conditions.[20] The obligations not to go to war were presented in the Covenant only as exceptions, and once the exceptions were complied with, it could be argued that recourse to war was not unlawful. As one authority puts it: "Even if the members had lived up to the provisions of the Covenant, they would have found in the fundamental law of the League an instrument for the prevention of some wars and the legalization of others." [21]

There were, then, significant weaknesses in the League structure, but no amount of "tinkering with the machinery" of the League, no evolving of a perfect constitutional mechanism, could in itself have made the League effective, unless the member states wished it to be so and would co-operate to that end. The League was not an entity in itself. It was only an instrument to facilitate whatever degree of co-operation the national states wished to undertake. The experience of the League makes crystal clear that the success of an international organization for peace depends much less upon high-sounding paper commitments and perfected procedures, and much more upon the readiness of the nations and the peoples of the world to assume and to be bound by certain basic international obligations. Without this willingness, no international organization can work.

---

[18] See Morgenthau, *op. cit.,* pp. 377–378.
[19] For a full account see Morgenthau, *op. cit.,* pp. 371–373.
[20] See Art. 12; Art. 13, par. 4; Art. 15, par. 6, Covenant of the League of Nations.
[21] Morgenthau, *op. cit.,* pp. 374–375.

II. THE UNITED NATIONS [22]

The Second World War hurled the United States again into the affairs of other nations and other continents. Even before Pearl Harbor, this conflict awakened some understanding of the rôle this country must play in international affairs, simply because it is a powerful nation in a world that economics, science, and technology have made "one world." By one of those remarkable shifts of American public opinion, this nation, which for the most part during two decades had turned its back upon the League of Nations, became the leader first in the discussion and later in the preparation and implementation of plans for a postwar international organization.[23]

Steps toward a new international organization. During the Second World War many Americans brought forward proposals for a new organization. Multitudes of theories and plans were expounded, some by experts and some by the rankest amateurs in international affairs.[24] Discussion of these proposals helped to crystallize opinion and paved the way for official action.

More significant than the proposed plans were the actual steps for a new international organization subsequently taken by our government under the personal direction of President Roosevelt. Taking care to enlist the participation and co-operation of members of Congress, he was especially solicitous of the sensibilities of the opposition Republicans in working out his plans. In 1943 the House of Representatives in the Fulbright Resolution, and the Senate in the Connally Resolution, by overwhelming majorities approved participation in a postwar organization to ensure international security. At Moscow, during the month separating the Fulbright and Connally Resolutions, Secretary of State Cordell Hull definitely committed the United States to co-operate in establishing "at the earliest

[22] S. Arne, *The United Nations Primer* (1945); V. M. Dean, *The Four Cornerstones of Peace* (1946); A. W. Dulles and B. P. Lamb, *The United Nations*—Foreign Policy Association Headline Series No. 59 (1946); "Developing a Working International Order—Political, Economic and Social," *Proceedings of the Academy of Political Science,* Vol. XXII, Jan., 1947; Eagleton, *op. cit.,* Chs. XII–XIV, XVII–XVIII; L. M. Goodrich and E. Hambro, *Charter of the United Nations* (1949 ed.); "Making the United Nations Work," *The Annals . . .* Vol. CCXLVI, July, 1946; "The United Nations Charter," *International Conciliation*—no. 413, September, 1945, pp. 441–479; Kalijarvi, *op. cit.,* pp. 134–142.

[23] Gallup polls of public opinion revealed that, while in 1937 only 26 per cent of the American people had approved joining a world league, 72 per cent did in July, 1944, and 81 per cent in April, 1945. However, a 1944 poll revealed that only 44 per cent knew that the United States had never been a member of the League of Nations! T. A. Bailey, *A Diplomatic History of the American People* (1946 ed.), pp. 837, 839.

[24] E. Culbertson, *Total Peace* (1943); O. Newfang, *World Government* (1942); C. K. Streit, *Union Now* (1939 ed.) and *Union Now with Britain* (1941). See also E. Wynner and G. Lloyd, *Searchlight on Peace Plans* (1944), pp. 129–185.

practicable date a general international organization for the maintenance of international peace and security." In 1944 the representatives of the United States, Great Britain, Russia, and China, meeting at Dumbarton Oaks, drew up an outline for the general world organization. This became the subject of much discussion, both by governments and by the people in general. At Yalta early in 1945, at the last meeting of Roosevelt, Stalin, and Churchill, a decision was reached that the time had come for final action.

According to agreement, the conference to draft the Charter of the United Nations met at San Francisco on April 25, 1945, convening two weeks before the capitulation of Germany and three and one-half months before the surrender of Japan.[25] Despite certain prior understandings, some matters of serious difference at the San Francisco Conference divided Russia on one side and the United States and Britain on the other. Likewise, the medium and smaller nations made determined efforts to augment their position within the organization. In the end, settlement of these and other issues was effected, usually by compromise, and the Charter of the United Nations, a document of one hundred and eleven articles, well over twice the length of the League Covenant, was agreed upon. In the light of the strength of national loyalties, the diversity of culture, and the different political and economic systems of the nations represented, the document represented a major achievement.[26]

The beginning of the United Nations. There was a minimum of delay in bringing the organization into actual operation. The United States was the first major nation to act. President Truman presented the Charter to the Senate immediately after the Conference closed, and it was ratified by 89 to 2 on July 28, 1945. By October, with the war over, the required number of ratifications from the participating nations had been deposited, and the American Secretary of State declared the Charter in force. The first session of the General Assembly, which had the tasks of creating the other agencies and of selecting personnel, met in London in January, and in New

[25] There were over fourteen hundred delegates present at San Francisco. The personnel of the American delegation, selected by President Roosevelt shortly before his death, demonstrated how carefully efforts were made to give the widest possible representation. The delegation was made up of Secretary of State Edward R. Stettinius, Chairman; ex-Secretary of State Cordell Hull (who did not attend because of illness); Senators Tom Connally (Democrat) and Arthur H. Vandenberg (Republican); Representatives Sol Bloom (Democrat) and Charles A. Eaton (Republican); Commander Harold E. Stassen (Republican), and Virginia C. Gildersleeve (independent Democrat).

[26] An official report of the San Francisco Conference containing all documents, debates, and committee reports, was published as *Documents of the United Nations Conference on International Organization* (1945). Fifteen volumes.

For a condensed version of the Charter, see Appendix, pp. 1031–1040.

York in October, 1946. Subsequently, as all are aware, it was decided that the United Nations would establish permanent headquarters in the United States.

Significant features. The purposes of the United Nations as set forth in the Preamble and in Article 1 of the Charter are to maintain peace, secure fundamental human rights, advance social and economic welfare, and establish conditions under which justice and respect for obligations arising from international law can be maintained. To accomplish these ends the Charter provides for six principal organs: a General Assembly, a Security Council, an Economic and Social Council, a Trusteeship Council, an International Court of Justice, and a Secretariat. Before examining these specific institutions, however, we should offer a brief comment on a few of the features of the UN of general significance.

(1) MEMBERSHIP. Although the value system of the UN is set forth by the Preamble in the name of "We the peoples of the United Nations," the organization is a league of *states,* and in no sense a union of *individuals.* Furthermore, the organization agreed upon at San Francisco was essentially a league of the victors in the Second World War. No nations were invited to participate in the Conference except those that had formally joined in the struggle against the Axis. Both enemies and neutrals were excluded. In consequence, nations constituting the original members were virtually the same as the signatories at San Francisco, since all fifty had ratified the Charter before the meeting of the first Assembly.[27] Unlike the League Covenant, the Charter makes no provision for withdrawal, although states may be expelled by the General Assembly upon recommendation of the Security Council.

Besides the original members the Charter makes provision for the admission of "other peace-loving states" that accept the obligations of the organization. Such states may be admitted by the General Assembly upon recommendation of the Security Council. At this writing, nine additional states have been admitted to the UN, making the total membership 60.[28] The applications of 14 other states, however, have been pending, in some cases for more than two years. Discussions by the Security Council of the admission of the states in question are entangled with the struggle between East and West usually designated as the "cold war." Those states whose admission is supported by the West have been blocked by use of the veto; and those supported by the Soviet Union have failed to receive the

[27] Poland was the fifty-first member. It was not a participant at San Francisco, but was eligible to original membership since it had signed the Declaration by the United Nations in 1942.

[28] States admitted since the UN began to function are Afghanistan, Iceland, Sweden, and Siam in 1946; Pakistan and Yemen in 1947; Burma in 1948; Israel in 1949; Indonesia in 1950.

necessary votes.[29]   Though Secretary-General Trygve Lie has repeatedly urged the admission of all 14, and though the International Court of Justice has ruled that criteria other than that laid down in the Charter should not block the admission of new states, there is no indication that the stalemate will soon be broken.[30]

(2) SOVEREIGNTY OF MEMBERS UNIMPAIRED.   A second important feature of the UN that requires notice here is its relationship to the national states that constitute the international community.   That the independent status of its members was not to be impaired is made abundantly clear by the provision of the Charter that bases the United Nations upon the principle of the "sovereign equality of all its Members." [31]   Each *member* is thus carefully protected against interference.   Furthermore, the UN is expressly forbidden "to intervene in matters which are essentially within the domestic jurisdiction of any state." [32]   Both of these clauses, fully supported at San Francisco by the United States, were intended to emphasize the fact that the UN is only an organization to facilitate voluntary co-operation among its members and is devoid of legislative powers.

Only in the case of enforcement action against an aggressor may members be bound to action without their consent.   Even then the enforcement agency can give no final decision.   After putting down an aggression it can only make recommendations for settling the dispute that had caused the UN to take enforcement action.

Yet, for *non-members* these immunities are not so clear.   It is provided in the Charter that the organization shall ensure that states which are not members of the UN act in accordance with its principles "so far as may be necessary for the maintenance of international peace and security." [33] Shades of national sovereignty!   Under this clause the organization clearly might assume authority not based on the consent of the states affected.

(3) GREAT POWER UNANIMITY.[34]   A third significant feature of the United Nations is the principle of great power unanimity.   The unwritten

---

[29] The Soviet Union has vetoed the applications of Austria, Ceylon, Eire, Finland, Italy, South Korea, Nepal, Portugal, and Trans-Jordan.   Opposition by the United States and its supporters has been responsible for the rejection of Albania, Bulgaria, Hungary, North Korea, Outer Mongolia, and Rumania.

[30] *See Admission of a State to the United Nations (Charter Art. 4), Advisory Opinion*, I. C. J. Reports, 1947–1948, p. 65; reprinted in *Amer. Journal of Inter. Law*, Vol. 42 (1948), p. 627. Late in 1949 the International Court of Justice was asked for an advisory opinion on the question whether states not recommended by the Security Council can be admitted by the General Assembly.   In March, 1950, the Court decided that this action would be contrary to the Charter.

[31] Art. 2, par. 2.

[32] Art. 2, par. 7.

[33] Art. 2, par. 6.

[34] Art. 27.

assumption running throughout the Charter is that peace depends on agreement of the Great Powers. In consequence, those powers enjoy a special status. Any one of the five permanent members of the eleven-member Security Council—the United States, the Soviet Union, China, France, and Great Britain—may prevent the adoption of amendments to the Charter. With one exception, each may block any *non-procedural* (substantive) actions of the Security Council. Furthermore, on the basis of a "Statement" of the Big Five at San Francisco, any question as to whether a matter before the Council is procedural and thus not subject to veto must be treated by the Council as a substantive question, which, of course, is subject to veto.[35] This Statement of the Big Five is in no sense a part of the Charter. Nevertheless, it has been respected by the Council on several occasions, and has served to narrow the range of procedural questions and to increase the range of questions subject to veto.

The only exception to the principle of Great Power unanimity in non-procedural matters applies to action taken under Chapter VI of the Charter, that is, action to achieve the pacific settlement of disputes. In a case of that kind a Great Power may not use the veto if it is a party to the dispute. However, others of the Big Five remain free to block substantive action even here. This veto means, for example, that if a nation friendly to the United States is having difficulty with a state not friendly to the United States, our country—if it desired—could prevent the Security Council from making any recommendations.

All substantive action under Chapter VII, on the other hand, is subject to the rule of unanimity, a rule that permits a state to be the judge in its own case. Thus, if the United States were accused in the Security Council of aggression or of conduct representing a threat to the peace, it has power to veto a resolution containing the accusation, directing an investigation of the matter, or ordering the use of coercion.

These are only a few of the many features of the UN that recognize the special claims of the Great Powers. In part, their special privileges result from the argument that the nations that will have to assume most of the responsibility for curtailing an aggressor should be given special protection from involvement by nations that have little to contribute. Also important were demands in the United States and elsewhere that the nation must not be submerged to a "super-state." In the words of Senator Vandenberg: "The veto is our defense against what I venture to believe would be bitterly condemned in many quarters as our 'involuntary servitude' if our veto power did not exist. It is the complete answer to any rational fears that we may be subordinating our destiny to alien com-

[35] See Goodrich and Hambro, *op. cit.*, pp. 219 ff.

mands. . . . It guarantees our perpetuated independence of international dictation." [36] Still another ground for the special claims of the Great Powers has been that frequently called "realism." According to this viewpoint, the only hope for peace lies in unanimous agreement among the great states, particularly the United States and the Soviet Union. When they can agree, runs this argument, their power will make the UN invincible. If, on the other hand, they cannot agree to coercive measures it would be hopeless to try to resort to force. Such an effort would mean the beginning of the very war the Charter is intended to prevent. Basically for these reasons the UN was not geared to prevent the use of force by a Great Power, or even by a small power that has the support of a Great Power. It has frequently been urged, however, that the veto as actually applied goes beyond the needs of "realism" and might advantageously be restricted to fewer matters than it has.[37]

(4) Decentralization. A final characteristic of the United Nations (for which there is space for only a brief comment) is its decentralization. It may be said to be decentralized both because of the encouragement it gives to the separate establishment of specialized international organizations, such as the World Health Organization, and because of its recognition of regional political organizations, such as the Organization of American States.

Having summarized the principal and general characteristics of the UN, we turn now to an examination of the composition and functions of its six main organs.

The General Assembly. One of the chief organs of the UN is the General Assembly, of which all the nations in the organization are members. In its annual meetings and occasional special sessions [38] each member is represented equally and has one vote. The powers and duties of the Assembly are broad. It elects the non-permanent members of the Security Council, all the members of the Economic and Social Council, and some members of the Trusteeship Council. It shares with the Security Council the election of the Secretary-General and the judges of the International Court of Justice; the admission, suspension, and expulsion of members; and the power to call a General Conference for the purpose of revising the

---

[36] Senate Document 59, 79th Cong., 1st Sess., p. 10.

[37] See *Report of the Interim Committee of the General Assembly on the Problem of Voting in the Security Council*, United Nations Document No. A/578, July 15, 1948; reprinted in *International Organization*, Vol. 3 (1949), p. 190. For an account of the favorable action taken by the General Assembly on recommendations respecting limitation of the veto, see Yuen-li Liang, "Notes on Legal Questions Concerning the United Nations," *Amer. Journal of Inter. Law,* Vol. 43 (1949), pp. 705–706.

[38] Special sessions may be called by the Secretary General at the request of the Security Council or by a majority of the members of the UN. See Art. 20.

THE UNITED NATIONS

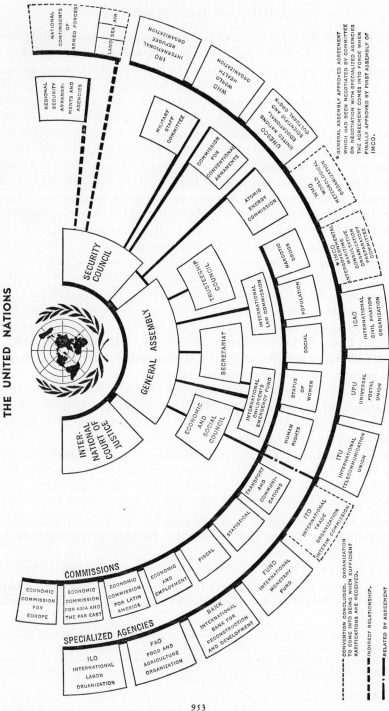

From Office of Public Affairs, Department of State, *Economic and Social Problems in the United Nations*, July, 1950.

Charter.   The Assembly possesses exclusive power to propose amendments to the Charter; to establish rules governing the selection of the staff of the Secretariat; to approve the budget, and to apportion the expenses among the members; and to approve agreements bringing the so-called "Specialized Agencies" into relationship with the UN.   Furthermore, the Assembly is directed to receive and consider annual and special reports from the other bodies of the organization.   Functions of the UN with respect to the negotiation, alteration, and enforcement of trusteeship agreements—other than agreements for strategic areas [39]—are exercised by the General Assembly.   Finally, both the Trusteeship Council and the Economic and Social Council are subordinate to the Assembly and act under its authority.   Thus, the Assembly emerges somewhat as the central and co-ordinating organ of the UN.   In an important departure from the unanimity rule of the League, action in the Assembly on "important questions" is by two-thirds of those voting; on other matters only a simple majority is required.[40]

The functions of the General Assembly are essentially those of initiative, of discussion, of study, and of recommendation.[41]   The Assembly may discuss any matters within the scope of the Charter.   It may call any situations likely to endanger international peace and security to the attention of the Security Council.   Or, if it chooses, the Assembly may make recommendations with regard to such questions to the states concerned or to the Security Council or to both.   Its power to make recommendations on matters within the general authority of the UN is limited only by a prohibition barring recommendations on disputes actually before the Security Council.   None of these powers, however, are legislative, for the Charter confers no legislative powers upon the Assembly.   Nevertheless, the Assembly is the substitute for an international legislature; and although its recommendations are not legally binding, they provide an important instrument for making the weight of the public opinion of the world bear upon the members of the UN.

NONPOLITICAL ACTIVITIES.   Virtually every power possessed by the Assembly has been used with vigor and dispatch.   In the nonpolitical field its accomplishments have been formidable.   Some of the highlights of its work in nonpolitical areas are these:

(*1*) *Human rights.*   The Assembly has adopted a Universal Declaration of Human Rights setting forth the rights to which most of the members of the UN believe all men and women everywhere should be entitled.

---

[39] Whether an area is "strategic," in effect, is decided by the nation holding it; and if the Security Council agrees, a Trusteeship agreement is negotiated with the Security Council accordingly.

[40] Some questions require two-thirds vote because of specific provisions in the Charter. Otherwise, the Assembly determines for itself what questions before it are "important questions."

[41] Arts. 10–17.

This may be followed by the submission of treaties implementing the Declaration. A similar contribution in the human rights field is the treaty on "genocide" recently submitted to the members of UN by the Assembly. This agreement outlaws the kind of thing that happened in the Nazis' gas chambers. Human rights accomplishments also include the adoption by the Assembly of a treaty covering the gathering and international transmission of news, and setting forth a procedure by which official correction of false news reports may be circulated.

(2) *Development of international law.* The human rights work of the Assembly is directly related to the development of the law of nations. In proportion as such agreements as those mentioned are adopted by the nations of the world there will have been a substantial addition to international law. Similar contributions may be expected to result from the studies and recommendations of the International Law Commission,[42] created by the Assembly in 1947. What is most needed in the meantime is adoption by national Congresses and Parliaments of the various declarations and treaties that have already been submitted to them by the Assembly. Here the achievement to date is not far above zero.

(3) *Social and humanitarian work.* Important accomplishments of the Assembly in the social and humanitarian fields have resulted from the implementation it has given the work of the various Commissions operating under its authority from the support it has given the various Specialized Agencies and from programs it has initiated directly. This work has been tremendous, and ranges from the adoption of a draft convention for the suppression of traffic in persons, to emergency relief for almost a million Arabs and Jews made refugees by the recent war in Palestine. Under another program initiated by the Assembly the UN has provided food and medical care for millions of expectant mothers in Europe and Asia. By the end of 1949 it was giving a daily supplementary feeding to nearly 5,000,000 hungry children in countries devastated by the war and was administering a large-scale anti-tuberculosis project under which 17,500,000 children and adolescents in Europe had already been examined and over 8,000,000 vaccinated. These are only a few samples of the character and scope of the record of the Assembly in the social and humanitarian fields.

(4) *Economic action.* In the economic field the work of the Assembly has been equally vigorous. Agencies working directly or indirectly under its direction have actively been seeking to improve the standard of living of the people of the world and to reduce trade barriers between their governments. In 1949 an expanded program of technical assistance for under-

---

[42] The first session of the Commission was held April–June, 1949. See Clyde Eagleton, "First Session of the International Law Commission," *Amer. Journal of Inter. Law,* Vol. 43 (1949), p. 758.

developed countries was unanimously approved by the Assembly. It provides for sending experts to economically backward areas at the request of member governments.[43] Funds are largely to be drawn from voluntary contributions by UN members. Total expenditures during the first two years of the new program are to be small, however, and will only approximate the cost of converting an old American cruiser into a guided-missile carrier.

POLITICAL ACTIVITIES. Although the activity of the Assembly in non-political matters has been of increasing breadth and vigor, it is development in the political field that has usually made the headlines. During the brief period of its existence the Assembly has been almost as active in political matters, including conflicts among the victors of the Second World War, as the Security Council. In fact, almost every important political issue presented to the UN has at one time or another been before the Assembly. In numerous instances it has been able to take important action when the Security Council was unable to reach agreement. Its work has been facilitated by the practice, tending to evade the veto, of removing matters from the agenda of the Security Council by a procedural vote, that is, by the vote of any seven members of the Council. Once removed from the Security Council, the Assembly can make recommendations on any conflict; otherwise, it would be limited to mere discussion. To facilitate its work the Assembly has made wide use of visiting commissions for investigation purposes. By means of broad interpretations of the Charter it has avoided being restrained by the clause excepting "domestic" questions from the purview of the organization. It has also been active in elaborating the machinery of the UN. In its 1949 session the Assembly authorized the creation of a reserve panel of assistants designed to provide the world organization with qualified persons ready to serve as on-the-spot observers. At the same session it voted to establish the first international guard force—a trained and uniformed corps of 300 persons to assist UN missions in every part of the world by ensuring their safety and by providing communications service. Finally, utilizing its power to "establish such subsidiary organs as it deems necessary for the performance of its functions," [44] the Assembly in 1947 created the Interim Committee, or "Little Assembly." By this means provision has been made for the continuous operation of the Assembly through a committee on which each member of the UN is entitled to one representative.[45]

The most significant action of the General Assembly in elaborating the

---

[43] See Thomas J. Hamilton, *N.Y. Times*, Oct. 16, 1949.

[44] Art. 22.

[45] For an account of the powers and limitations of the Interim Committee, see Goodrich and Hambro, *op. cit.*, pp. 196–198.

machinery of the UN and in developing its power to deal with international conflict came late in 1950 when the Assembly adopted a plan to enable it to cope readily with aggression. The major provisions of the plan are the results of Secretary Acheson's efforts:

(1) If the Security Council is unable to take action against aggression because one of its members uses the veto, the Assembly can be called into emergency session on twenty-four hours' notice to deal with the aggression.

(2) The Assembly can make "appropriate recommendations to members for collective measures including . . . use of armed force."

(3) Each UN member is asked to "maintain within its national armed forces elements so trained and organized and equipped that they could promptly be made available . . . for service as a United Nations unit or units."

Thus, the Assembly is geared to act in the future whenever the principal enforcement agency of the UN—the Security Council—is blocked by use of the veto.

The Security Council. Unlike the General Assembly, which is largely a deliberative organ concerned with the totality of matters coming within the scope of the UN, the Security Council is concerned primarily with preserving and maintaining international peace and security. In this area its power exceeds that of the Assembly, since all members are bound by its decisions and since it has exclusive jurisdiction over any dispute or situation as long as it chooses to keep such matters before it.

As already indicated, the Council is composed of five permanent and six non-permanent members. Permanent members are China, France, the Soviet Union, Great Britain, and the United States. The non-permanent members are elected by the General Assembly for a period of two years. Those elected are not eligible for immediate re-election. In sessions of the Council each member is represented by only one delegate. The Charter provides that any member of the UN which is not a member of the Council may be invited by the Council to participate, without vote, in the discussion of any question that in the opinion of the Council affects its interest. Furthermore, the Charter directs that any such member or any state not a member, shall be invited to participate, without vote, in any discussion before the Council concerned with a dispute to which it is a party.

The Security Council is organized in a manner permitting it to function continuously. Most of its activity is at the permanent headquarters of the organization, but it may meet elsewhere if it desires. Its powers include participation with the General Assembly in the admission, expulsion and suspension of members; in the election of the judges of the International Court of Justice; and in the appointment of the Secretary-General. In its own right it may restore the rights and privileges of members that have been suspended by the UN. These are all examples of the powers of the Council relating to the working of the UN as a whole.

Undoubtedly the most important powers of the Security Council relate to (1) the pacific settlement of disputes, and (2) action with respect to threats to the peace, breaches of the peace, and acts of aggression. Subject to the limitation that it act within the purposes and principles of the Charter, and subject to the requirements of the voting regulations, the powers of the Council are circumscribed by no restraints. As we have seen,[46] action on substantive matters requires the affirmative vote of seven members, including the Big Five. On procedural matters action may be taken on the vote of any seven members. Subject to these limitations, the members of the UN have conferred upon the Council primary responsibility for the maintenance of international peace and security, and have agreed to accept and to carry out its decisions.

(1) PACIFIC SETTLEMENT. With respect to "pacific settlement of disputes" action of the Security Council is governed by the provisions of Chapter VI of the Charter. Whenever it desires, the Council may call upon the parties to a dispute, the continuance of which is likely to endanger international peace and security, to seek a solution by negotiation, enquiry, mediation, conciliation, arbitration, adjudication, resort to regional agencies, or other peaceful means. It has power to "investigate any dispute, or any situation which might lead to international friction or give rise to a dispute."[47] Disputants by mutual agreement may request the Council to recommend terms of settlement.[48] Furthermore, when the parties to a dispute have been unable to settle it by peaceful means, the Charter directs them to refer the matter to the Council. After either party does so, the Council may recommend such terms of settlement as it considers appropriate.[49] In all this, a party to a dispute—even one of the Big Five— must refrain from voting.

Plagued by the establishment of the principle that even a decision to launch an investigation is subject to veto by members of the Big Five that are not parties to the dispute, the Council, nevertheless, has interpreted the chapter on pacific settlement very broadly. Its investigating committees have made valuable on-the-spot studies, as in the cases of the Greek frontier and the dispute between India and Pakistan over the status of Kashmir. It has provided mediatory and conciliatory functions, as in setting up a Committee of Good Offices to assist in the settlement of the dispute between The Netherlands and Indonesia, instructing the United Nations

---

[46] See above, pages 950–951.

[47] Art. 34. This power of investigation is seriously limited by the clause that follows it, but the practice of the Council has been to ignore the limitation.

[48] Art. 38.

[49] Art. 37.

Mediator to perform mediatory functions in Palestine, and establishing a Commission of Investigation and Mediation in connection with the dispute between India and Pakistan. It has successfully furthered judicial settlement, as in its recommendation that Great Britain and Albania submit to the International Court of Justice disputes resulting from damage to British ships and the loss of forty-four of their personnel in the Corfu Channel due to the explosion of mines allegedly laid by Albania. These are only representative examples of the broad activities of the Security Council based on the pacific settlement chapter of the Charter.

(2) THREATS TO THE PEACE, BREACHES OF THE PEACE, AND ACTS OF AGGRESSION. With respect to action other than pacific settlement, the Security Council acts under Chapter VII of the Charter. In these matters the permanent members, unrestrained as under Chapter VI, are free to be judges in their own case. The Charter provides that "the Security Council shall determine the existence of any threat to the peace, breach of the peace, or act of aggression." [50] To prevent the aggravation of such situations, it is authorized to "call upon the parties concerned to comply with such provisional measures as it deems necessary or desirable." [51] It may also make recommendations designed to maintain or restore international peace and security.[52]

These powers are the only powers conferred by Chapter VII which the Council, until the Korean crisis in 1950, had invoked. They were at the basis of its "cease-fire order" and subsequent efforts in 1947 to achieve settlement in the Dutch-Indonesian dispute. Another order to curtail military action was issued in the Arab-Jewish conflict in Palestine in 1948. In both instances emphasis was on provisional measures intended to prevent the aggravation of the situation and to bring hostilities to an end.[53]

Although the Council has stressed measures intended to prevent breaches of the peace and to restore peace on the basis of agreement, the Council is authorized to order the use of coercion. To give effect to its coercive orders, it may call upon members to apply such measures short of force as complete or partial interruption of economic relations and of rail, sea, air, postal, telegraphic, radio, and other means of communication. It may also call upon them to sever diplomatic relations.[54]

It should be remembered that all members by signing the Charter have assumed the obligation to obey all Security Council orders. However, if the Council considers measures short of force inadequate, it may take such action by air, sea, or land forces as may be necessary to maintain or resume

[50] Art. 39.
[51] Art. 40.
[52] Art. 39.
[53] See Goodrich and Hambro, *op. cit.*, pp. 266–276.
[54] Art. 41.

international peace and security.[55] The Charter directs the Council to conclude agreements with the members of the UN to make available armed forces, assistance, and facilities necessary for the purpose of maintaining international peace and security. The chiefs of staff of the Big Five are designated as a Military Staff Committee to advise and assist the Security Council on all questions relating to its military requirements, and to be responsible for the strategic direction of any armed forces placed at its disposal. Establishment of the forces contemplated, as all are aware, has been impossible because of the world-wide struggle for power between the American bloc and the Soviet bloc. Meanwhile, under the Charter, the Big Five shall constitute the enforcement agency of the UN.[56]

The strongest action in its history was taken by the Security Council in June and July of 1950. On June 24 the Soviet-backed regime in North Korea launched an attack on the Republic of Korea, the southern portion of the peninsula governed by a regime established under the auspices of the General Assembly of the UN in 1949 and recognized by it as the only government of Korea. On June 25 the Security Council called on the North Koreans to "cease hostilities" and to withdraw invasion forces. Two days later the Council recommended "that the members of the United Nations furnish such assistance to the Republic of Korea as may be necessary to repel the armed attack and to restore international peace and security in the area." Twenty-four hours earlier President Truman had ordered General MacArthur to send American air and sea forces into action, and on July 7 the Security Council by a vote of 7 to 0 made the United States its agent in organizing and directing the United Nations armed forces in the area. The UN's decision to make the United States its agent finds support in Article 46 of the Charter which provides that "the action required to carry out the decisions of the Security Council for the maintenance of international peace and security shall be taken by all the Members of the United Nations or by some of them, as the Security Council may determine."

These spectacular actions of the Security Council were made possible by a Soviet boycott of the UN that began in January, 1950. The Power that almost certainly would have used the veto had not chosen to be present. At the end of July, however, the Soviet Union announced its return to the UN. With the involvement of the Chinese Communists in the Korean conflict late in 1950, Security Council efforts to take action were effectively stymied. In December, 1950, the Soviet Union vetoed a resolution ordering the Chinese back across the Manchurian border. In consequence, the non-Communist world resorted once again to the General

[55] Art. 42.
[56] Art. 106.

Assembly, recently empowered to take more effective action in such matters.

The Economic and Social Council. In seeking to bring about friendly relations among nations, members of the UN have pledged to co-operate for the achievement of a number of broad social and economic objectives. These objectives are the promotion (1) of higher standards of living, of full employment, and of conditions of social and economic progress; (2) of the solution of international, economic, social, and health problems; (3) of international cultural and educational co-operation; and (4) of universal respect for, and observance of, human rights and fundamental freedoms.[57] The agency charged with promoting and coordinating these activities is ECOSOC, the Economic and Social Council. It consists of eighteen members of the UN elected by the General Assembly. The Charter secures both continuity and change in the composition of the Council by providing that six members shall be elected each year for a term of three years.

FUNCTIONS OF ECOSOC. The principal functions of the Economic and Social Council are described in Article 62 of the Charter, which authorizes ECOSOC to make studies and call international conferences on economic, social, and related matters. ECOSOC is also empowered to make recommendations in these fields and to prepare draft conventions for submission to the General Assembly. Its functions also include assistance to the Security Council and the carrying out of duties assigned by the General Assembly.

In addition, ECOSOC is charged with the task of co-ordinating the activities of the various Specialized Agencies established by separate agreements outside the UN. If it desires, it may, subject to the approval of the General Assembly, conclude agreements with the Specialized Agencies bringing them into relationship with the UN. Such agreements have been concluded with ten Specialized Agencies, and prospective agreements with three others await the full establishment of those Agencies.[58]

Although much co-operative work in the economic, social, health, educational, and cultural fields is carried out by national governments through

[57] Art. 55.

[58] See chart, page 963. Some of the Specialized Agencies date to pre-League of Nations days, and others are of recent origin. The ten that have been brought under the UN are Universal Postal Union (UPU); International Labor Organization (ILO); International Telecommunication Union (ITU); Food and Agriculture Organization (FAO); International Monetary Fund; International Civil Aviation Organization (ICAO); United Nations Educational, Scientific and Cultural Organization (UNESCO); World Health Organization (WHO); International Refugee Organization (IRO); and International Bank for Reconstruction and Development. Of these, IRO is temporary and due for extinction by 1951.

The three agencies not yet fully established are International Trade Organization (ITO); Inter-governmental Maritime Consultative Organization (IMCO); and World Meteorological Organization (WMO).

the Specialized Agencies, the Charter directs ECOSOC to set up Commissions in the economic and social fields and for the promotion of human rights. Twelve such Commissions have already been constituted,[59] and serve the important functions of fact-finding and consultation on problems within their respective fields.

The Commission reports have served in many cases as the basis for action. The Commission on Human Rights, for example, did the preliminary work on the Universal Declaration of Human Rights, adopted by the Assembly on the recommendation of ECOSOC in 1948 by a majority of 48 votes. It also did the spade work on the draft convention on the international transmission of news and the right of correction adopted by the Assembly in 1949. It is presently working on a treaty that, when adopted by the members of the UN, will undertake to ensure the international protection of human rights. Commissions in such fields as health and economic problems have done work of similar magnitude.

TECHNICAL ASSISTANCE AND AMERICA'S "POINT FOUR." A major problem in improving world economic and political stability is posed by the vast underdeveloped areas of the earth, which act as a drag upon the world economy and a source of political and social disorder. ECOSOC and the Specialized Agencies during the past two and one-half years have undertaken a technical assistance program, including economic surveys of underdeveloped areas, expert advice to member countries, and a large-scale publications program for disseminating current technical knowledge.

This work early in 1949 received a considerable boost from President Truman's "Point Four" program. In his inaugural address on January 20, 1949, President Truman announced that the United States would embark on a co-operative program to extend technical assistance to the underdeveloped areas of the world, and that this program would be one of the four major pillars of the United States foreign policy. The purpose of the program, he said, was "to help the free peoples of the world, through their own efforts, to produce more food, more clothing, more materials for housing, and more mechanical power to lighten their burdens," and by so doing to promote peace and enable all men to attain "freedom and dignity and the fullness of life."

Assurances were given that Point Four was intended to strengthen the UN system. In fact, on the urging of the United States delegate, the Economic and Social Council instituted a study that resulted in the General Assembly's decision late in 1949 to launch an expanded global program of technical assistance for underdeveloped countries. This is the UN program to which we have already referred; it called for the expenditure of between $25,000,000 and $50,000,000 during the first two years. Mean-

[59] For a list of these Commissions, see charts, pages 953, 963.

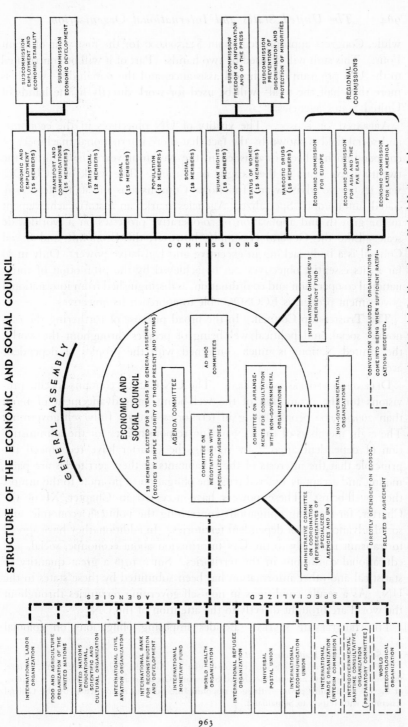

STRUCTURE OF THE ECONOMIC AND SOCIAL COUNCIL

GENERAL ASSEMBLY

COMMISSIONS

SUBCOMMISSION EMPLOYMENT AND ECONOMIC STABILITY

SUBCOMMISSION ECONOMIC DEVELOPMENT

SUBCOMMISSION FREEDOM OF INFORMATION AND OF THE PRESS

SUBCOMMISSION PREVENTION OF DISCRIMINATION AND PROTECTION OF MINORITIES

ECONOMIC AND EMPLOYMENT (15 MEMBERS)

TRANSPORT AND COMMUNICATIONS (15 MEMBERS)

STATISTICAL (12 MEMBERS)

FISCAL (15 MEMBERS)

POPULATION (12 MEMBERS)

SOCIAL (18 MEMBERS)

HUMAN RIGHTS (18 MEMBERS)

STATUS OF WOMEN (15 MEMBERS)

NARCOTIC DRUGS (15 MEMBERS)

REGIONAL COMMISSIONS

ECONOMIC COMMISSION FOR EUROPE

ECONOMIC COMMISSION FOR ASIA AND THE FAR EAST

ECONOMIC COMMISSION FOR LATIN AMERICA

ECONOMIC AND SOCIAL COUNCIL
18 MEMBERS ELECTED FOR 3 YEARS BY GENERAL ASSEMBLY (DECIDES BY SIMPLE MAJORITY OF THOSE PRESENT AND VOTING)

AGENDA COMMITTEE

AD HOC COMMITTEES

COMMITTEE ON NEGOTIATIONS WITH SPECIALIZED AGENCIES

COMMITTEE ON ARRANGEMENTS FOR CONSULTATION WITH NON-GOVERNMENTAL ORGANIZATIONS

NON-GOVERNMENTAL ORGANIZATIONS

ADMINISTRATIVE COMMITTEE ON COORDINATION (REPRESENTATIVES OF SPECIALIZED AGENCIES AND UN)

INTERNATIONAL CHILDREN'S EMERGENCY FUND

DIRECTLY DEPENDENT ON ECOSOC.

RELATED BY AGREEMENT

CONVENTION CONCLUDED, ORGANIZATIONS TO COME INTO BEING WHEN SUFFICIENT RATIFICATIONS RECEIVED.

SPECIALIZED AGENCIES

INTERNATIONAL LABOR ORGANIZATION

FOOD AND AGRICULTURE ORGANIZATION OF THE UNITED NATIONS

UNITED NATIONS EDUCATIONAL, SCIENTIFIC AND CULTURAL ORGANIZATION

INTERNATIONAL CIVIL AVIATION ORGANIZATION

INTERNATIONAL BANK FOR RECONSTRUCTION AND DEVELOPMENT

INTERNATIONAL MONETARY FUND

WORLD HEALTH ORGANIZATION

INTERNATIONAL REFUGEE ORGANIZATION

UNIVERSAL POSTAL UNION

INTERNATIONAL TELECOMMUNICATION UNION

INTERNATIONAL TRADE ORGANIZATION (INTERIM COMMISSION)

INTERGOVERNMENTAL MARITIME CONSULTATIVE ORGANIZATION (PREPARATORY COMMITTEE)

WORLD METEOROLOGICAL ORGANIZATION

From Office of Public Affairs, Department of State, *Economic and Social Problems in the United Nations,* July, 1950.

963

while, Congress appropriated about $34,500,000 for the first year of Point Four. This sum will be used by two hands. Part of it will be contributed to the UN program of technical assistance, and the remainder—which is more than half the total—will be used for work directly in the hands of United States agencies.[60]

APPRAISAL OF ECOSOC. The virility of UN objectives in the economic and social field is shown by the fact that more international machinery of co-operation has been established in the past four years than during the twenty active years of the League of Nations. The work of ECOSOC, with its twelve advisory and functional Commissions and its thirteen associated autonomous Specialized Agencies marks an historic achievement in the growth and application of co-operative processes on a world-wide scale. Like the General Assembly, however, the Economic and Social Council is a body lacking in executive and legislative power. Only in so far as its essential objectives can be achieved by the promotion of international co-operation and co-ordination, as distinguished from international government proper, is ECOSOC able to approach its objectives.

The Trusteeship Council. In the broad purpose of furthering the economic, social, and political well-being of peoples throughout the world, the United Nations is much concerned with the peoples of dependent areas.

DEPENDENT PEOPLES IN GENERAL. The UN Charter contains specific provisions for the promotion of the well-being and advancement of more than 200,000,000 people living in territories not yet fully self-governing. The eight members of the UN having responsibilities for the administration of dependent areas [61] by signing the Charter have recognized the principle that the interests of the inhabitants of these territories are paramount, and accept as a sacred trust the obligation to promote to the utmost their well-being. These powers have accepted in Chapter XI of the Charter, far-reaching obligations concerning the political, economic, and social advancement of dependent territories. In addition, they have agreed to transmit regularly to the UN information about economic, social, and educational conditions in the territories. Since 1946 a great quantity of statistical and other information has been submitted by these states to the UN. As a result, conditions in non-self-governing territories throughout the world are brought directly to the attention of the UN.

THE TRUSTEESHIP SYSTEM. Besides imposing obligations on colonial

---

[60] See Thomas J. Hamilton, *op. cit.*

[61] The eight powers having such responsibilities are Australia, Belgium, Denmark, France, the Netherlands, New Zealand, the United States, and Great Britain. Italy, not yet a member of the UN, is a ninth power with such responsibilities, due to recent action by the General Assembly with respect to Somaliland.

powers in general, the Charter provides for the establishment of international trusteeships for territories placed under that system by means of agreements between colonial powers and the General Assembly. Each such power is free to decide whether it will bring its colonies under trusteeship. Of some sixty colonial territories, about ten are now within the trusteeship system. Six of these trust territories are in Africa; four are in the Pacific area. They include approximately 15,000,000 people.

States administering territories placed under trusteeship carry out their work under the watchful eye of the Trusteeship Council, which is under the aegis of the Assembly. The Council consists of the following members of the UN: (1) those members administering trust territories; (2) members of the UN that are permanent members of the Security Council and that are not administering trust territories; (3) as many additional members elected for three-year terms by the General Assembly as may be necessary to equalize the number of members administering trust territories and the number of members that do not. The result is a balanced membership of six states that administer trust territories and six other states that do not.

In order to ascertain whether the nations actually administering trust territories carry out the principles of the Charter, the Trusteeship Council has been making full use of the powers conferred by the Charter. These include the authority to visit areas under trusteeship, to require annual reports from administering powers, and to receive petitions from the natives. Petitions have been numerous and effective. In response to one, for example, the Council sent a mission to Western Samoa, and its report in favor of greater self-government was quickly put into effect by the administering power, New Zealand.

TRUST TERRITORY OF THE UNITED STATES. The United States has placed only one of its dependent territories under UN trusteeship. This is the Trust Territory of the Pacific Islands, consisting of the Marshall, Caroline, and Mariana Islands (except Guam), formerly under Japanese mandate. The United States has designated this area a "strategic area," which the Charter places under supervision of the Security Council aided by the Trusteeship Council, instead of under the General Assembly. This arrangement was made possible by the Charter on the theory that some areas should be regarded as part of the international security system and as available for enforcement action by the Security Council.

Although the agreement with the Security Council that made the area "strategic" makes detailed provisions for the political, economic, social, and educational advancement of the native people, the real purpose in making it "strategic" undoubtedly was *national* rather than *international*. Although one of the basic objectives of the trusteeship system, according to the Charter, is "to ensure equal treatment in social, economic, and commercial matters for all Members of the United Nations and their nationals, and also equal treatment for the latter in the administration of justice," [62] the United States in the trust agreement reserved the right to discriminate in favor of its own nationals.[63]   Furthermore, the United States reserved the right to decide how far the Trusteeship Council might exercise its usual powers—receiving petitions from the natives, making visits, requiring reports from the administering power—if the United States chooses to close the area for "security reasons."   Commenting on this arrangement, one authority has said: "The control which the United States may exercise in this area is almost as complete as if the islands had been taken in full sovereignty.   The agreement was approved by the Security Council with little debate, and an inviting precedent was thus established for other nations to follow." [64]

The Secretariat.   Another principal organ of the United Nations is the Secretariat—the civil service of the organization.   The provisions of the Charter relating to the Secretariat give expression to the importance that attaches both to the office of its head, the Secretary-General, and to the maintenance of an efficient and reliable international civil service.[65]

The Secretary-General is appointed by the General Assembly upon the recommendation of the Security Council.   He is entrusted with the ordinary administrative functions of the principal organs of the UN, other than the International Court of Justice, and with the preparation of annual reports to the General Assembly on the working of the UN.   Furthermore, unlike his predecessor in the League of Nations, he is authorized to bring to the attention of the Security Council any matter that in his opinion may threaten the maintenance of international peace and security.   This is a task of great responsibility, and one that the first Secretary-General, Mr. Trygve Lie, has used unhesitatingly.

The Charter contains detailed provisions for securing the efficiency and the independence of the Secretariat.   It provides that the Secretary-General and his staff shall not seek or receive any instructions from any government or from any other authority outside the organization.   Members of the UN have undertaken to respect the exclusively international character of the responsibilities of the Secretary-General and the staff and not to seek to influence them in the discharge of their responsibilities.   Detailed provisions on the organization of the Secretariat have been adopted by the Assembly, which has primary responsibility for matters of that kind.

[62] Art. 76, par. d.
[63] See Goodrich and Hambro, *op. cit.*, p. 454.
[64] Eagleton, *International Government, op. cit.*, p. 344.
[65] See Chapter XV of the Charter.

The work of the UN Secretariat is as varied as it is important. In addition to the secretarial services, translations, record keeping, and other duties that form the more routine aspects of its work, the Secretariat has undertaken complex tasks of analysis, study, and publication in many fields at the request of the various UN organs and on its own initiative. Under the active leadership of the Secretary-General, the Secretariat has exhibited marked resourcefulness. During the past year it has carried on studies designed to increase the efficiency of the United Nations as a whole, and upon request of the General Assembly has undertaken to recommend solutions for specific problems, such as the use of the veto power and the development of additional means of achieving closer international co-operation. The successful achievement of an effective Secretariat, numbering some 3,000 persons from the fifty-nine member nations, stands as a clear accomplishment on a practical work-a-day basis of the kind of co-operation the UN was designed to achieve in the broader relations between nations.

The International Court of Justice. The last of the principal organs of the United Nations that must be considered here is the International Court of Justice. All members of the UN are *ipso facto* parties to the Statute (constitution) of the Court. Others may be parties to the Statute in accordance with conditions determined by the General Assembly upon recommendation of the Security Council.

The Statute of the Court is almost identical to the Statute of its predecessor, the Permanent Court of International Justice. Unlike the League Covenant, however, the Charter makes the Court an integral part of the UN—its "principal judicial organ." Furthermore, since the power to request advisory opinions is not confined to the General Assembly and the Security Council, the new Court offers further possibilities outside the range of its predecessor. Other organs of the UN, including the Specialized Agencies brought into relationship with it, may at any time be authorized by the General Assembly to request advisory opinions of the Court on legal questions arising within the scope of their activities.

ORGANIZATION. The Court consists of fifteen judges selected by the General Assembly and the Security Council. Headquarters is at The Hague, the seat of the Court's predecessor. The term of office for judges is nine years, and there is no prohibition on reelection. A judge may be dismissed only by unanimous vote of the other judges. To prevent any one state from dominating the Court, the Charter provides that no more than two of the judges may be from the same state. To ensure impartiality, it provides that no member of the Court may exercise any political or administrative function, or engage in any other occupation of a professional nature.

FUNCTIONS: *Advisory opinions.* Much of the activity of the Court has consisted of handing down advisory opinions on legal questions submitted by the General Assembly. These, however, have not been numerous because the tendency has been toward the political interpretation of the Charter. That is, such controversies as those concerning the meaning of the Charter have been settled largely by the General Assembly and the Security Council without reference to the Court. In fact, the General Assembly is the only organ of the UN that has asked the Court for advisory opinions and up to the time of this writing the Court had been presented with only five such requests.

Observers have frequently urged that more and more of the disputes in the UN should be referred to the Court. Unless the Court were sprinkled with John Marshalls, however, it may be that in such matters as interpretation of the Charter greater growth will result in the UN from political interpretation than would be possible were all such controversies referred to the Court. It is difficult to imagine, for example, what the Court might have done with the numerous disputes concerning the meaning of the phrase "domestic questions." According to the Charter, such questions are outside the competence of the UN. Legal tests of the meaning of "domestic questions" might easily have resulted in restricting materially the competence of the UN. As it is, the clause means no more than the members of the political organs permit it to mean.

Settlement of legal controversies; the United States and the optional clause. Besides advisory opinions on legal aspects of disputes submitted by the various organs of the UN, the International Court of Justice serves as a means of settling legal controversies between nations. No dispute may be settled unless both parties (nations) have agreed to the jurisdiction of the Court. This agreement is normally a special and specific one between the parties to each dispute. In order to give the Court more opportunity to decide on legal disputes between them, however, many states have signed a special declaration called "the optional clause." [66] They thus give *advance* consent to the jurisdiction of the Court in legal disputes with other states that have also signed the optional clause. By this means the Court may be said to have a certain area of compulsory jurisdiction.

At the present time thirty-four states are signatories of the optional clause. When the United States Senate accepted the clause by a vote of 60 to 2 in 1946, it added various damaging reservations, among which was one withholding from consideration by the Court "disputes with regard to matters which are essentially within the jurisdiction of the United States *as determined by the United States.*" (Italics mine.) This qualification shocked many people in the United States and elsewhere, for it is capable of retarding considerably the procedures of international adjudication. It

[66] Art. 36, par. 2, Statute of the Int. Court of Justice.

demonstrates, however, how far our own people are from supporting one of the requirements of international government.

Until 1949 only one dispute had been submitted to the Court. In 1949, however, four new cases involving minor disputes between various nations were presented to the Court, so the process of judicial settlement appears to be receiving a new stimulus.

The United Nations and International Security. By the end of five years' operation, the UN—despite the numerous achievements pointed out in this discussion—appears to be regarded less and less as an effective instrument of international security. One of the basic causes is the struggle between the communist world led by the Soviet Union and the democratic world led by the United States. Each would like to fill the power vacuum left by the Second World War. Peace treaties with Germany and Japan have neither been written nor are in immediate prospect. The Soviet Union would prefer a communist Europe and a communist Asia; the United States and those who share its values would prefer that these areas be democratic. Except in Europe, where action initiated by the United States in the form of the Truman Doctrine, the Marshall Plan, and the Atlantic Pact has stemmed the tide, time has served the communist cause well. The year 1949 saw China's 450,000,000 people brought into the orbit of the hammer and the sickle. Southeast Asia—Indo-China, Burma, the Malay States, the Philippines, Thailand—hang in the balance.

In the contemporary scene even small states have been able to defy important actions of the UN. The Fourth Assembly, for example, in 1949 resolved that the city of Jerusalem should be administered by the UN. Both Arabs and Jews defied the resolution. Israel rejected the plan, and Jordan refused even to discuss the matter! On June 12, 1950 the Trusteeship Council voted to return the proposal to the Assembly and to report its failure in the attempt at internationalization.[67]

This is only the most recent of other such defiances of the UN by small powers.[68] Such defiance is possible while the major powers remain unable to prevent it. Disagreement among the great powers on effective action, however, may be expected to be frequent, so long as the sovereign nations of the world are not governed by either a common superior or a common morality. Not only is there absent a universally accepted standard of justice today, but no nation appears to be prepared to accept and submit itself to such a standard.

Failure to regulate atomic energy. Despite the basic difficulties recounted above, the problem of international security is becoming more

[67] See The Brookings Institution, *Current Developments in United States Foreign Policy,* (December, 1949), pp. 37–40; and (May–June, 1950), p. 53.

[68] See Goodrich and Hambro, *op. cit.,* pp. 159–161, for an account of South Africa's defeat of Assembly action to protect the Indian minority in South Africa.

and more pressing because of the increasing ability of civilization to destroy itself. To end the war with Japan in 1945, the United States dropped the first atomic bombs. On August 6 the target was Hiroshima, population 300,000. One bomb caused an explosion equal to 20,000 tons of TNT. Flash burns, blast, falling debris, and conflagrations killed 78,150 people, with 13,983 missing, 37,425 injured, of whom many died later of radiation sickness, and 176,987 rendered ill, homeless, hungry, or indigent. Almost five square miles of the city were leveled by the blast and by the subsequent fire. Out of 90,000 buildings, 62,000 were destroyed and 6,000 were severely damaged.[69]   Three days after dropping the first atomic bomb the American forces released another—this time over Nagasaki, Japan—causing similar damage and ending the war. Since that time the weapon is reported to have been vastly improved. Also, research in bacteriological warfare has made such amazing progress that scientists have suggested that if the Third World War comes, it will be a war in which most people may die from silent, insidious weapons that make no sound and give no warning, but wipe out human beings by the millions.[70]

With a monopoly on the production of the atomic bomb, however, the United States for four years after Hiroshima enjoyed a relative amount of security. It developed a plan for the international control of atomic energy that became the basis of a plan adopted in 1948 by vote of most of the nations in the General Assembly. This American-backed scheme called for setting up an international control agency with broad powers to own, operate, and manage all mines and dangerous plants; to control production and use of uranium and thorium (basic raw materials for atomic bombs); to conduct research and to license projects for the peaceful uses of atomic energy. As soon as this agency began to work, the United States would dispose of its bombs and share atomic "know-how." There would be international management of all atomic energy development. The control agency would have full powers of inspection within the borders of any UN member nation, and a ban would be placed on the use of the veto power in the United Nations on questions involving atomic energy.

The plan outlined above did not, however, secure full support. Six members of the General Assembly in 1948 supported Soviet counter-proposals, treaties proposing control and outlawing of the bomb. One treaty would outlaw the atomic bomb, provide for destruction of all existing bombs, and prevent manufacture of any new bombs; the other, becoming effective at the same time as the first, would provide for international control of atomic energy. Instead of international management, there would be national responsibility for manufacture and development

[69] F. L. Schuman, *International Politics* (1948 ed.), pp. 922 ff.
[70] *Ibid.*, p. 384.

of nuclear fuels, with limited international inspection. The veto power would be maintained on atomic energy as well as on other security matters to avoid undermining the unanimity of the Big Five.

Opposition by the United States to the Soviet plan was based on the argument that this meant that controls would be ineffective. Americans could also argue that the disarmament proposal would weaken the United States far more than the Soviet Union, since the latter possessed greater power in conventional armaments. The Soviet Union, on the other hand, said it opposed the American-backed proposal because it would permit too much interference with Soviet internal development.

The West and the East were thus unable to work out a system for the international control of atomic energy at the Third Assembly in 1948. Subsequent efforts of the UN Atomic Energy Commission also have been without avail. Meanwhile, the power picture has changed drastically. In the autumn of 1949 President Truman announced that the Soviet Union had exploded an atomic bomb. The American monopoly was broken. Shortly thereafter at the Fourth General Assembly the East and the West stood firmly on their respective plans for atomic control, and the result was no agreement. Soon afterward, early in 1950, President Truman announced that the United States would begin work on the hydrogen bomb.

Twelve of the country's leading physicists have declared that New York or any of the greatest cities of the world could be destroyed by the blast of a single hydrogen bomb.[71] Dr. Albert Einstein has warned that annihilation of all life on earth has been brought within the range of technical possibilities. This prediction has been supported by other eminent scientists. Four atomic scientists recently warned that the H-bomb could be rigged to set off clouds of radioactive dust that would kill most plant and animal life in the world. The dusts would be carried around the world by the winds. Dr. Leo Szilard, famous bio-physicist, has said it would take only 500 tons of heavy hydrogen in one H-bomb to make a dust that would be lethal for five years and that would kill everyone in the world. A larger number of H-bombs used in a war could create a carbon dust that would be active for 5,000 years, making life impossible.[72] The problem of survival has thus reached unprecedented proportions. How much time it will take the United States and the Soviet Union to develop this new instrument of destruction cannot be said. Since Russia was able to develop the A-bomb in the minimum time predicted by United States scientists, it would be naive to think that our country will long enjoy a new monopoly. Who, in fact, can say with certainty that we will be the first to produce an H-bomb?

[71] *The New York Times,* Feb. 5, 1950.
[72] *Ibid.,* Feb. 27, 1950.

World government. The inability of the UN to end the cold war has given renewed impetus to proposals for change. Some of the most important of these are proposals for the establishment of a world state.[73] Advocates of this approach hold that the maintenance of peace is possible only through the transference of the sovereignties of individual states to a world authority that would be as sovereign over the individual nations as the individual nations are sovereign within their respective territories. Most call for an international constitutional convention to set up a new world organization that will establish world law and maintain world order.

There is no shirking the conclusion that international peace would be more safely assured with the establishment of a world state. On the other hand, such a state seems impossible of establishment under the present moral, social, and political conditions of the world.

BARRIERS TO WORLD GOVERNMENT. Several reasons exist for taking a dim view of the prospects for establishing a world state, three of which have been forcibly outlined by Professor Hans J. Morgenthau:[74]

(1) No society exists that is coextensive with the presumed range of a world state. There is no supra-national society comparable in cohesive bonds to domestic societies and comprising all individuals of all states. On the contrary, the nation continues to be the recipient of man's highest earthly loyalties.

(2) The peoples of the world are not willing and able to do what is necessary to keep world government standing. They are not prepared to give an international government their highest loyalty. Rather, they remain willing and able to sacrifice and die in order that national governments may be kept standing. Men who would do otherwise would by the conditions of the world be forced to act as partisans of another nation and as traitors to their own. This loyalty to national government exists because above one's own nation there is nothing on behalf of which a man could act. There are only other nations besides one's own.

(3) The peoples of the world are not willing and able to do what the world state requires of them in order that it may fulfill its purpose of maintaining peace.

The first result of this fact has bearing on enforcement machinery. In

---

[73] See Commission to Frame a World Constitution, *Preliminary Draft of a World Constitution* (1949); Norman Cousins, *Modern Man is Obsolete* (1945); Ely Culbertson, *Total Peace* (1943); Cord Meyer, Jr., *Peace or Anarchy* (1947); Emery Reves, *The Anatomy of Peace* (1945). For a well-known regional approach see C. K. Streit, *Union Now* (1949 ed.).

[74] See Morgenthau, *op. cit.*, pp. 391–402. See the arguments of Reinhold Neibuhr, "Myth of World Government," *Nation* (March 16, 1946), pp. 312–314; N. A. Pelcovits, "World Government Now?" *Harper's Magazine* (November, 1946), pp. 396–403; and Sumner Welles, "The Only Way to World Government," *Reader's Digest* (March, 1946), pp. 97–100.

a poll of public opinion in 1947, 75 per cent of the people answered in the affirmative the question: "Would you like to see the United States join in a movement to establish an international police force to maintain world peace?" Only 13 per cent, however, wanted the United States to join in an international police force that outnumbered the armed forces of this country.

Besides establishing enforcement agencies able to meet any threat to the peace with overwhelming strength, however, a world state would also have to create and keep in motion agencies for social and political change of a world-wide character that might allow all groups of mankind to expect at least some satisfaction for their conflicting claims. Here, too, the people of the world are not willing and able to do what the world state requires of them in order that it might fulfill its purpose of maintaining peace. How could the different peoples of the world be represented in legislative agencies for social change? Even if this problem could be solved, a parliament representing peoples of such different moral convictions, political interests, and abilities for self-government as the Americans, the Chinese, the Indians, and the Russians would find it well-nigh impossible to create out of these differences an operating whole.

Although in no period of modern history has civilization been more in need of permanent peace and, hence of a world state, it is equally clear that in no period of modern history have the moral, social, and political conditions of the world been less favorable for its establishment. Just as there can be no state without a society willing and able to support it, there can be no world state without a world community willing and able to support it.

Working for peace through the UN. The foregoing discussion should suffice to warn against relying on any simple and fascinating formula or mechanism for ensuring international peace. Even the UN, like the League of Nations before it, has frequently been oversold. Masses of people have innocently been led to expect more from the existing organization than it was ever equipped to achieve, for the organization was not designed to coerce one of the Big Five. Furthermore, expectations have frequently presupposed the existence of an integrated international society that actually does not exist. The best solution for the problem of peace appears to be to seek slowly to bring into being the kind of integrated international society that will make possible a world state sometime in an unknown number of generations hence.

If we can think of the UN, not as a world parliament, but as a place for continuous negotiation and compromise between sovereign states, further progress may best be made, not by junking the strongest organization we could devise at the height of a wartime alliance, but by various slow and gradual steps through the existing mechanism directed toward making better use of the UN as it is now. This organization and the Specialized Agencies are competent to do much of the work now being accomplished under the Marshall Plan and the current Point Four technical assistance program. Member states, the United States included, might more vigorously carry out the recommendations of the General Assembly and the Economic and Social Council. There might be more abundant use of the Optional Clause to further judicial settlement of disputes. Further use of the International Trusteeship system by the members of the UN is to be encouraged. Certain highly controversial areas—the Dardanelles, the Antarctic regions, certain of the Italian colonies—might profitably be placed directly under UN administration.

It is even possible to think in terms of some modification of the use of the veto. Any such change will require the approval of the Soviet Union, and dealing with the Russians has proved to be extremely difficult. Furthermore, it is not certain that our own country would be able to make sufficient concessions to win agreement from the Russians.

From another angle, the UN can be provided with armed forces within the present framework. Although the Military Staff Commission has been deadlocked with regard to the type and size of forces to be assigned to the Security Council, it is not necessary to wait for agreement in the Council and its agent, the Commission. This fact was fully demonstrated in the Korean conflict by the establishment of a UN armed force despite the absence of prior agreement.

Nothing in the Charter forbids states from assigning armed force to the UN. Furthermore, the General Assembly has full authority to appropriate money to recruit a thoroughly independent force. Some students of the Charter hold that such forces could not be used except under the direction of the Security Council, which, in turn, is likely to be stymied with the veto. Recent developments in UN practice, however, suggest that the veto is easily by-passed. As we have seen, the 1950 revolution in the Assembly authorized that body to make "appropriate recommendations to members for collective measures including . . . use of armed force," and each UN member was asked to maintain within its national armed forces elements so trained and organized that they can promptly be made available for service as UN units.

Measures such as this—like many of the other proposals to strengthen the organization outlined above—are fraught with grave danger and should be approached with extreme caution. If changes or "reforms" served to drive the Soviet Union out of the UN—as well they could—the price might be greater than the gain. In the event the Soviet Union withdrew, any number of other nations not now in the Soviet vest pocket might also withdraw in an effort to avoid being parties to what they could regard as an American military alliance against the East. Furthermore, one authority recently suggested an additional important consideration:

It is a great advantage to us and one which we often overlook to keep the Russians inside the framework of a permanent political organization where we can meet with them continuously, where we can hammer out our arguments, where we can, if necessary, shout defiance at each other because as long as we have this mechanism of continuous conference we have the possibility of working out such areas of agreement as can possibly be found to exist.[75]

As already suggested, it is difficult to think that international peace can be made as secure as domestic peace without a world state. However, it seems doubtful that a world state can be created without relying on the peace-preserving and community-building processes made possible by skilled application of persuasion, negotiation, pressure, and honest compromise inside and outside the UN. These were the tools of those who made possible many of the past successes of the UN. Those who will provide its future direction must be equally well equipped. Although we have suggested that many constructive steps are possible to strengthen the UN, the world cannot move more rapidly, if it is to move peacefully, than general consent can be obtained. Peoples and statesmen must combine imagination and patience if the UN is to contribute to the needs of the times.

Security may occasionally require rearmament, mobilization, and alliances for purposes that cannot yet be met by the UN. Catastrophe is certain, however, only if either the East or the West is wedded to a political religion aiming at universal dominion. This goal would make impossible the mutual accommodation and compromise essential to peace in our time and to the building of a more highly integrated world society for the future.

Reading List

Annals of the American Academy of Political and Social Science, Vol. CCXLVI, July, 1946, "Making the United Nations Work."

S. Arne, *The United Nations Primer* (1948 ed.).

T. A. Bailey, *A Diplomatic History of the American People* (1946 ed.), Chs. XXV, XXVII, XXXV, XXXIX, XL, XLVIII.

F. L. Benns, *Europe since 1914 in Its World Setting* (1945 ed.), Chs. VI, XIX, XXII.

A. Boyd, *The United Nations Organization Handbook* (1946).

F. J. Brown, C. Hodges, J. S. Roucek, *Contemporary World Politics* (1939), Chs. XVII–XXIII.

[75] Grayson Kirk in *U.S.M.A. Student Conference on U.S. Affairs* (1949), p. 33.

Commission to Frame a World Constitution, *Preliminary Draft of a World Constitution* (1949).

V. M. Dean, *The Four Cornerstones of Peace* (1946).

H. E. Davis (ed.), *Pioneers in World Order* (1944).

L. Dolivet, *The United Nations* (1946).

Clyde Eagleton, *International Government* (1948 ed.).

H. O. Eaton (ed.), *Federation, the Coming Structure of World Government* (1943).

H. V. Evatt, *The United Nations* (1949 ed.).

————, *The Task of the United Nations* (1949).

D. F. Fleming, *The United States and the World Court* (1945).

Foreign Policy Association Headline Series:

    A. W. Dulles and B. P. Lamb, *The United Nations.* No. 59 (1946).

    Thomas J. Hamilton and V. M. Dean, *Report on the UN.* No. 75 (1949).

    M. Lerner, *World of the Great Powers.* No. 61 (1947).

W. T. R. Fox, *The Super Powers: The United States, Britain, and the Soviet Union—Their Responsibility for the Peace* (1944).

L. M. Goodrich and E. Hambro, *The Charter of the United Nations* (1949 ed.).

J. B. Harrison, L. A. Mander, N. H. Engel (eds.), *If Men Want Peace* (1946).

T. V. Kalijarvi (ed.), *Modern World Politics* (1945), Chs. II, VI, VII.

L. A. Mander, *Foundations of Modern World Society* (1947 ed.).

D. Masters and K. Way (eds.), *One World or None* (1946).

Cord Meyer, Jr., *Peace or Anarchy* (1947).

H. J. Morgenthau, *Peace, Security, and the United Nations* (1946).

————, *Politics among Nations* (1948).

Pitman B. Potter, *An Introduction to the Study of International Organization* (1948 ed.).

Proceedings of the Academy of Political Science, Vol. XXI, No. 3, May, 1945, "World Organization—Economic, Political, and Social" and Vol. XXII, No. 2, January, 1947, "Developing a Working International Order—Political, Economic and Social."

E. Reves, *The Anatomy of Peace* (1945).

L. F. Schmeckebier, *International Organizations in Which the United States Participates* (1935).

F. L. Schuman, *International Politics* (1948 ed.).

W. R. Sharp and G. Kirk, *Contemporary International Politics* (1944), Chs. I, II, VII, IX, XX–XXVIII.

J. T. Shotwell, *The Great Decision* (1945 ed.).

Clarence K. Streit, *Union Now* (1949 ed.).

H. M. Vinacke, *International Organization* (1934), Chs. I–XV.

S. Welles, *The Time for Decision* (1944).

W. L. Willkie, *One World* (1943).

E. Wynner and G. Lloyd, *Searchlight on Peace Plans* (1944).

Publications of The United Nations agencies, the State Department, The American Association for the United Nations, The Carnegie Endowment for International Peace, The Foreign Policy Association, The Woodrow Wilson Foundation, The World Peace Foundation, The University of Chicago Round Table, The NBC University of the Air, Americans United for World Government.

Periodicals devoted wholly or in large part to The United Nations and international affairs: *International Conciliation, Foreign Policy Bulletin, Foreign Policy Reports, American Journal of International Law, United Nations News, Corps Diplomatique* (in English), *Foreign Affairs, World Report, Freedom and Union, United Nations World, United Nations Bulletin, International Organization, World Politics.*

Questions and Problems

1. It has frequently been said that the League of Nations would have been able to preserve peace in the 'thirties if the Covenant had been more carefully written. Comment critically.

2. Discuss the meaning of and the justification for the principle of great power unanimity in the organization of the UN.

3. Describe the obligations of members of the UN with respect to their colonies not under trusteeship.

4. List the important powers of the Trusteeship Council relating to trust territories. Evaluate the contribution of the United States to the development of the principle of international trusteeship.

5. Outline the arguments for world government. What are the principal obstacles? Discuss fully.

6. Distinguish carefully between the two principal kinds of cases decided by the International Court of Justice. Point out the basis and extent of its compulsory jurisdiction, and comment on the contribution of the United States thereto.

7. How is the work of ECOSOC and the various Specialized Agencies made effective? Discuss fully.

8. What are the causes for the failure of the members of the UN to agree on a plan for the international control of atomic energy?

9. Distinguish carefully between the procedures, powers, and limitations of the Security Council in the matters of (1) the pacific settlement of disputes; (2) "action with respect to threats to the peace, breaches of the peace, and acts of aggression."

10. The Constitution of UNESCO says that "a peace based exclusively upon the political and economic arrangements of government" cannot be adequate, and that "peace must therefore be founded, if it is not to fail, upon the intellectual and moral solidarity of mankind." What are the principal obstacles to the building of such "intellectual and moral solidarity"? What practical measures may be taken toward that end?

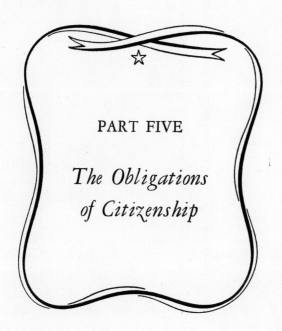

PART FIVE

*The Obligations
of Citizenship*

The Obligations of Citizenship

"WE, therefore, the Representatives of the United States of America, in General Congress, Assembled, appealing to the Supreme Judge of the world for the rectitude of our intentions, do, in the Name, and by Authority of the good People of these Colonies, solemnly publish and declare, That these United Colonies are, and of Right ought to be Free and Independent States . . . And for the support of this Declaration, with a firm reliance on the Protection of Divine Providence, we mutually pledge to each other our Lives, our Fortunes and our sacred Honor." *Our Lives, our Fortunes and our sacred Honor!* These were no empty words. Having defied an empire and called forth a new nation, the Signers were in honor bound to go forward until their purpose was accomplished, and the penalties for failure were the penalties for treason—the confiscation of their estates and death by hanging.

I. THE AMERICAN HERITAGE

The bequest of liberty. Washington's Army met with reverses, men and supplies came in slowly, and in the late fall of 1776 Thomas Paine, the great agitator and pamphleteer of the Revolution, wrote one of his classics.

These are the times that try men's souls. The summer soldier and the sunshine patriot will, in this crisis, shrink from the service of their country; but he that stands it *now,* deserves the love and thanks of man and woman. Tyranny, like hell, is not easily conquered; yet we have this consolation with us, that the harder the conflict, the more glorious the triumph. What we obtain too cheap, we esteem too lightly; it is dearness only that gives everything its value. Heaven knows how to put a proper price upon its goods; and it would be strange indeed if so celestial an article as FREEDOM should not be highly rated.

These words warmed the hearts of the thinly-clad and ragged soldiers of the Continental Army. The patriots may have irreverently agreed that they could make good use of a moderate quantity of what is reputed to be the chief ingredient of hell; and as they left their bloody footprints on the snow and shivered in their bunks they must have commented, perhaps in language less celestial but no less picturesque and vigorous than that of Thomas Paine, that freedom was being contended for at great cost. Indeed, the statesmen who guided the infant country and the soldiers who fought for her existence knew the price of a nation's freedom.

No less heroically, and, on occasion, no less dramatically, men and women have assumed great risks to win personal liberties for themselves, their children, and their fellow-men. In the chapter on Civil Liberties attention was given to a provision of the First Amendment of the federal Constitution and similar provisions in our state constitutions—the guaranties of freedom of religion, of speech, and of the press. Who fathered the principle of religious freedom? Roger Williams, whose leading tenet was that "no one should be bound to worship or to maintain a worship against his own consent." For his heresy he was banished from Massachusetts Bay Colony and, after spending a winter of privation in the forests, founded a small colony at Providence in which applied, for the most part, his conception of religious liberty. Anne Hutchinson, "of ready wit and bold spirit," "like Roger Williams or worse," to use the language of the exasperated Governor Winthrop, was also voted the honor of banishment from Massachusetts, after which she contributed her part toward establishing religious freedom in Rhode Island. These two heroes of independent thought and deed; John Bunyan writing in the Bedford jail; ministers of other dissident groups who, jailed in Virginia for preaching contrary to law, continued their exhortations from their cells; and many others of equally stout convictions—men and women who paid the price of freedom of conscience—are the people to whom we owe our religious liberty.

Among many other jewels of freedom that we now take for granted is the right to the writ of habeas corpus. It was not always so. James I and Charles I, for reasons that seemed sufficient to themselves, but that were not in accordance with law, arbitrarily committed to the Tower troublesome members of the Puritan gentry. In 1627 the court held that the "special command of His Majesty," without regard to the law of the land, was sufficient reason for retaining men in prison. Accordingly, some of the choice spirits of England languished behind bars for no other cause than that they had incurred a king's displeasure. But there came a day when the sufferings of these men bore the fruit of freedom. In 1679

Parliament passed the Habeas Corpus Act prohibiting imprisonment except for cause expressed in law. The privilege of the writ of habeas corpus thus established in Britain became the heritage of Englishmen in America.

Essentially the same story could be told of practically every liberty we now enjoy. Nearly every clause of freedom written into our constitutions has in it something of a biography of lonely mental pioneering, moral courage, and physical suffering. For centuries gone by, men and women of original mind and noble purpose have borne the ridicule of their neighbors, heard the contumelious taunts of their opponents, sometimes experienced the loss of their estates, on occasion groaned on the rack and rotted in dungeons, and in not a few instances died gloriously on the scaffold. We have our liberties because our progenitors knew what it was to be without them, because they thought they were worth the cost in terms of effort and sacrifice.

The bequest of democracy. Our forefathers established the democratic framework for our system of government. They did not set up a pure democracy. They understood and we understand that such a government would have been impossible, for a pure democracy is that form of government in which all the adults meet in a hall or grove and elect their officers, levy taxes, vote appropriations, and enact laws. Such a system is suitable only for small, homogeneous communities. The framers did, however, establish a democratic republic, a system of government under which the people in an area of continental dimensions may govern themselves through representatives of their own choosing. The framers of the state constitutions did exactly the same thing—established representative governments, democratic republics. Some of the states took unusual precautions to insure the functioning of democracy, calling for annual elections. It doesn't matter what the men of the seventeen-seventies or eighties called their creations. Today we call them democratic republics or, for short, democracies.

It should be emphasized that the framers of the federal Constitution, in addition to providing for representative democracy, left the question of who might vote to the states. They were worried about what the states might do with other matters, but they were quite willing to trust them to fix the suffrage qualifications. Furthermore, the framers of the Constitution established no privileged class; they expressly declared that there should be none. The republic that was fairly launched on its way in 1789 was democratic enough to accommodate Jefferson, Jackson, and Lincoln.

It is hardly more than a quibble, therefore, to assert that America is a

republic, not a democracy.[1]   Those who insist that the United States is
just and *only* a republic never tell us exactly what they have in mind.
They solemnly proclaim that we have a republic, but they do not clearly
explain what their main point is.   One might take the liberty of guessing
what they are up to.   They are opposed to modern democratic practices
as represented by the initiative and referendum (although they have
learned to use them to their advantage) and the recall, primary elections,
popular election of United States senators, corrupt (elections) practices
acts (except as applied to certain "democratic" or "communistic" organizations), antilobbying laws, antitrust laws, persons on relief or old-age pensions exercising the elective franchise, "starry-eyed visionary planners," and
"young whipper-snapper lawyers" who draft administrative regulations.
Of course these peculiar "republicans" do not expect the country to make
a sharp turn from its evil democratic ways, but by reiterating, "the framers
established a republic, not a democracy," they may hope to check the democratic process.

We have, then, our heritage of liberty—civil, religious, democratic.
What shall we do with it?   What can the citizens do to make American
democratic government more effective?   In the foregoing chapters the
obligations and duties of the citizen frequently became apparent.   This
final chapter has the sole purpose of stressing these obligations.

II. THE QUEST FOR INFORMATION

The search for facts is the citizen's first obligation because without them
he will be able to perform few, if any, of his other obligations.   Candor
compels us to admit that this is a difficult assignment, one impossible to
complete with scientific accuracy.   We derive some encouragement, however, from the reflection that there are very few "hundred percenters" in
any performance and that much less than perfect knowledge serves in
most cases as a satisfactory basis for the judgment and action of the citizen.

General sources of information: Radio.   Turning on the radio one learns
that he has only one choice among pens if he wishes to write satisfactorily; that his wife can be sure of holding his love by using the only
love-holding hand lotion; that he will find just one brand of cigarette
that will give him exquisite pleasure and do him no harm; that he will
enjoy early rising if his wife serves the only breakfast food fit for human
consumption.   Momentarily he may wish for a dictator who would keep
some of this annoying advertising off the air; but then he reflects that
the dictator would probably prohibit the broadcasting of many good pro-

[1] See an interesting article by Sidney Hook, "Is the U.S. a Republic or Democracy?" *New
York Times Magazine,* Oct. 19, 1947, p. 17.

grams and reserve the air exclusively for his own purposes. In any event, with all of its irritating practices, the radio does furnish us with news and with many worth-while opinions. Through a little "shopping around" by means of the radio dial any person of ordinary intelligence can soon learn when and from what station or stations good news broadcasts come. By continued attention he can learn who gives the news and who mixes opinions with the news, and with the help of some of the better news programs he can form some intelligent opinions of his own.

NEWSPAPERS. The newspaper is, of course, a much older source of information than the radio. Despite well-founded criticisms of the modern daily paper, it is probably a better source of news today than it was fifty years ago. In those days journalism was largely personal, some of it brilliantly personal and sincerely devoted to the public good; but it was common to find, even in the best of these earlier papers, personal and partisan bias not only in the editorials but also in the news columns. The criticisms most frequently heard of the newspaper in our generation is that it is primarily a business enterprise, often a corporation, and as such it is concerned chiefly with profits for the owners. It is argued that, since advertising is the largest source of income for the newspaper publishers, the temptation to publish only such news as will please the advertisers is not always resisted. Certainly it can hardly be denied that, all too commonly, significant news is suppressed, published as inconspicuously as possible, or colored by misleading headlines. But there is no ground for despair. There are nonpartisan newspapers that "doctor" the news hardly at all, and some of these are cleared of any charge of knowingly distorting the news. Furthermore, there are partisan journals that, according to workable standards in an imperfect world, acceptably present the news, however biased they may be in their editorial columns.

Yet it is perhaps not unfair to say that the newspapers that come into the homes of the majority of citizens fail to give the news in unbiased fashion. If citizens "know their newspapers"—and an encouraging proportion of them do—it is possible for them to learn much from the news columns without being led astray. An individual should be on his guard against becoming a constant reader of one partisan newspaper and accepting its diluted news and fortified editorials as "law and gospel." No less indiscriminating and no more serviceable in democratic society, however, is the individual who, exasperated with the partisan appeals of the only newspaper to which he can conveniently subscribe, blindly sets his course against anything that particular publication might advocate.

MAGAZINES. If one is not particularly concerned about the news of the day and hour, he can shun the radio and the newspaper (the late Justice Oliver Wendell Holmes, one of democracy's noblemen, did not read newspapers) and still be sufficiently informed for a fairly intelligent discharge of the obligations that democracy imposes. There are a number of so-called weekly news magazines that provide, in popular language, very satisfactory summaries, often with interpretative comment, of the important events and developments. Available to persons of most modest income are well-established, seriously-purposed, monthly periodicals, presenting timely articles on current problems. Although these publications may be rather roughly classified as conservative, liberal, and radical, there is seldom an issue of any magazine devoted to public questions that does not present some new facts and stimulating suggestions.

CAUTION AGAINST PROPAGANDA. It goes without saying that one must be constantly on guard against propaganda. Over the radio and in the press propaganda is often mixed with the news, and the news itself may be so presented that it is nothing more than propaganda. By comparing and checking different sources of information one may eliminate a certain amount of misinformation. One can develop a critical listening or reading attitude that will enable him to discount much that is brought to his attention. Such statements as "it is alleged," "a high official of the government who desires not to be quoted is reported to have said," and "it is the opinion in informed circles that" should heavily discount the accuracy and value of any statement that follows.

It is freely admitted, however, that no suggestions that might be given can render the responsible citizen's task of seeking information a simple one. Yet we must shout from the housetops that it is a responsibility he must not shirk. The most tragic course he could take is to abandon the effort to inform himself and retreat into a shell of cynicism. This is abdication, the abject surrender, of a public trust reposed in every citizen.

Special sources of information. The preceding paragraphs carry some suggestions for all citizens. Those that follow are addressed more especially to those who will soon be college graduates, both men and women, those who because of their opportunities must assume positions of leadership in civic affairs. They should be ready to participate actively in dealing with such proposals as the council-manager system of government for their city, a judicial council for their state, the merit system for government employees in any area of government, interstate trade barriers, the bases of foreign trade, the control of atomic energy, the United Nations, and so on. Of course no one is prepared on a moment's notice to take a leading part in the disposal of such questions, but a college graduate should be able, on occasion, to study a particular issue and make a contribution to its solution.

"BACK TO COLLEGE." The problem facing those who wish to be prepared for active participation in civic affairs is to assemble the information on public issues. How is that done? Let us look at the solution from the point of view of one whose college days are already behind him. Quite probably his interest in specific public questions may have been aroused in college days. The responsible citizen faced now with an old question presented in unacademic form may find that his college books, even some of his old notes, may take on a new significance. The sources suggested might give him some leads and hints as to the location of more complete information. Again perhaps he may, when faced with a civic problem, believe it or not, write to his former professors for suggestions and references to other authorities. It is not recorded that any professors have objected to assisting in this way in the development of their former students; on the contrary, they are usually pleased and flattered that their aid is sought.

THE LIBRARY. Much more helpful than the old professor in acquiring information on public issues is the library. Nearly all cities have fairly good public libraries, and few large cities are without an educational institution that has a library containing a wealth of information for the inquiring citizen. All too frequently he asks for books, and only for books, on a particular subject. To be sure, there is no objection to the use of books, but books seldom tell the whole story. For one thing, books are seldom up to date; and for another, no books may appear on a question for several years after it has become a subject of public discussion. Further, on many pertinent questions no book is ever written. On current problems, periodicals of various professional societies are commonly much more fruitful sources of information than books.

Does a citizen seek information on a point of international law or foreign policy? Let him examine the current issues of the *American Journal of International Law* and *Foreign Affairs*. Is his interest for the time being on some phase of city government? Let him refer to the files of the *National Municipal Review* or *Public Management*. If he is concerned with a problem of administrative organization or procedure, let him refer to the *Public Administration Review*. Perhaps also it would not be amiss to mention one other professional publication, the *American Political Science Review*, which has a rather wide and general range in the whole field of government. These are but samples, and the publications listed as containing helpful information on the questions raised are taken almost at random, with no intention of intimating that there are not others that might be equally helpful. In all of this seeking for information one must be alert, must learn to tap all possible sources. On occasion the spoken word of a workman may contain more good sense than a learned article.

III. INTELLIGENT VOTING

In the lush 'twenties there was such a falling off in participation in elections that a number of organizations solemnly warned us of our duty to exercise the elective franchise. More strenuous times have awakened us politically to the point where general "get out the vote" movements hardly seem necessary (if they ever were). Much more important than the mere fact of voting is the exercise of an intelligent choice; and if an election stimulates so little interest that an individual has no basis for a judgment on candidates and issues, democracy suffers no more when he stays at home than when he votes. What is wanted and what we do not always get is discriminating voting.

Types of voters: 1. THE IRATE. "Will you please tell me," asks a character of the cartoons, "how I can mark my ballot so that I'll be voting against the present administration?" This picture is a gross exaggeration of the situation, of course, but there is enough sad truth in it to curdle its humor. All too often the voters are "mad" and vote against a candidate they dislike rather than for a man of their choice. Norman Thomas tells the story of a man who, after having heard him speak (1932), said: "Mr. Thomas, I agree with all you say, but I must vote for Roosevelt because we must 'get' Hoover."

2. THE FAINT-HEARTED. The man who wanted to "get" Hoover illustrates another shortcoming of voters, a weakness especially common to faint-hearted third-party adherents. This is their belief that their candidates will not win and their desire to cast a vote for candidates of a major party who have a chance of winning, even though they dislike those candidates or their principles only less than they abhor the standard bearers of the other major party. Such voters justify their action by saying that they do not want to "throw their votes away." The late Eugene V. Debs, believing, perhaps for good reason, that he suffered a loss of votes by the application of this theory, tersely commented: "The only man who throws his vote away is the man who votes for a candidate he does not want and gets him." Surely it can be said that a person who to "save" his vote marks his ballot for candidates not of his choice has thrown away his political principles.

3. THE BLIND PARTISAN. The partisan who votes a straight ticket when another party may have superior candidates for some offices is simply a cog in a wheel of a party machine. There always have been those who refused to cross the party line even if it meant supporting a fire hydrant for mayor or a manhole for councilman. Around 1900 a candidate's name was often placed in nomination at a convention with the statement that he was a Republican or a Democrat who had never "scratched

the ticket" in all his life. (Before the introduction of the Australian ballot one could vote for a candidate of another party only by drawing a line through the name of a nominee of his own party, thus "scratching the ticket," and writing in the name of his choice.) In grandfather's time voters of only mild partisan faith were loath to perform this drastic operation on the party's ticket. It may well be that the failure of the voters to engage in this type of grafting on their ballots had some relation to the forms of political graft that brought American politics into disrepute.

4. THE DISCRIMINATING. Fortunately, in recent years, the number of voters who "scratch," or "split," the ticket has been on the increase. For one thing, splitting the ticket is now only a minor operation, requiring simply that the voter mark a cross opposite the name of each candidate of his choice, regardless of the party affiliation of the candidates. There is no more "scratching" (although the term is still used); no more "writing-in," unless the voter desires to support an individual who has not been nominated by any party. Much more significant than the mechanical improvement of the ballot is the decline of blind partisanship on the part of the average voter. That this change has taken place is difficult to prove, but many observers are insistent that the trend is away from partisan allegiance and toward independent voting. In the opinion of the writer a few figures from three recent elections indicate a healthy degree of independence on the part of the electorate:

STATE OF IDAHO, GENERAL ELECTION, 1936

Republican votes	Office	Democratic votes
66,232	President	125,683
128,723	U.S. Senator	74,444
83,430	Governor	115,098

STATE OF WASHINGTON, GENERAL ELECTION, 1940

Republican votes	Office	Democratic votes
322,123	President	462,145
342,589	U.S.Senator	404,718
392,522	Governor	386,706

STATE OF WASHINGTON, GENERAL ELECTION, 1948

Republican votes	Office	Democratic votes
386,315	President	476,165
445,958	Governor	417,035

Significance of the primaries. It is no less essential that voters participate intelligently in primary elections than in general elections. Fifty years ago the political machine frequently controlled the party through manipulating conventions. Since the advent of the direct primary the machine attempts to capture this nominating system. All too often it succeeds in doing so, and it succeeds because in many areas the rank and file of voters do not participate in the primaries. Partisanship will bring a majority of party members out for a general election, but it does not cause them to see the importance of nominating the best possible candidates. Is not the selection of candidates of competence and integrity a mark of the most enlightened partisanship and citizenship?

Perhaps the principal reason for the voter's sluggish interest in the direct primary is that he has failed to grasp the fact that his part in choos-

EXTENT OF VOTERS' POLITICAL INFORMATION *

KNOWLEDGE AS TO VICE-PRESIDENTIAL CANDIDATES
(October, 1944)

	Could Name Correctly	Could Not Name
	%	%
Bricker	67	33
Truman	62	38

IDENTIFICATION OF SENATORS OF VOTER'S STATE
(January, 1945)

Could Name Both Senators Correctly	Could Name Only One Senator Correctly	Could Not Name Either Senator
%	%	%
42	24	34

KNOWLEDGE AS TO NUMBER OF SENATORS IN VOTER'S STATE
(August, 1945)

Correct	Incorrect
%	%
58	42

IDENTIFICATION OF THE GOVERNOR OF VOTER'S STATE
(August, 1945)

Named Correctly	Named Incorrectly or No Knowledge
%	%
89	11

ELECTION INFORMATION
(January, 1946)

Knew That Congressional Elections Were to be Held in 1946	Did Not Know That Congressional Elections Were to be Held in 1946
%	%
31	69

IDENTIFICATION OF MEMBER OF THE HOUSE OF REPRESENTATIVES FROM VOTER'S DISTRICT

Named Correctly	Could Not Name Correctly
%	%
51	49

* From *The Gallup Political Almanac for 1946*, p. 212.

ing elective personnel consists of two fundamental steps—nomination and election, and nomination no less than election. It is no answer for the nonpartisan voter to say that his independent political status debars him from participating in the primaries, for the election laws of most states are not so rigid as to exclude him from such participation and his conscience is unduly sensitive if it stands in his way.[2]

KNOWLEDGE OF PRESIDENTIAL AND VICE-PRESIDENTIAL CANDIDATES, AUGUST 25, 1948 **

			Could name correctly	Could not name
			%	%
Democratic	Harry S. Truman		91	9
	Alben Barkley		49	51
Republican	Thomas E. Dewey		88	12
	Earl Warren		58	42
Progressive	Henry A. Wallace		67	33
	Glen Taylor		30	70
States Rights	J. Strom Thurmond		11	89
	Fielding Wright		3	97
Socialist	Norman Thomas		21	79
	Tucker P. Smith	less than ½		99½ plus

** From the Gallup (American Institute of Public Opinion) Poll.

Voters' leagues. The voters obviously need all the help they can get. The figures given above on the "Extent of Voters' Political Information" are anything but reassuring. If the voters know so little about the higher officers, how little indeed they must know about local officers and candidates. Is there any means by which they may be informed concerning candidates for the state legislature, the county commission, and the city council? Voters' leagues suggest a possible answer. A community might find that its leading citizens are willing to associate on a nonpartisan basis for the purpose of investigating and recommending candidates.

Mr. A, a candidate for the legislature on the Democratic ticket, is a successful automobile dealer. He has served a term on the city council and has shown special interest in developing the city playgrounds and parks. Mr. B, a candidate for the legislature on the Republican ticket, is a lawyer and a former member of the school board. He has served two terms in the legislature and is the author of the Workmen's Compensation Act. Either candidate is worthy of support.

Or,

Mr. C, a candidate for county superintendent of schools, is a graduate of Y university, has been a high school teacher for five years, is active in promoting

---

[2] Governor Chester Bowles of Connecticut argues rather persuasively that "The Independent Voter Isn't Independent" anyhow, *New York Times Magazine,* Nov. 13, 1949, p. 13. Bowles' point is that in order to be effective one must work in a party, in the primaries and pre-primaries.

a plan to improve teaching standards. Mr. D, a candidate for the same position, is a graduate of Z university, has taught in high schools for fifteen years, but never more than two years in the same place, and was principal for one year. Mr. C is considered the better candidate.

And so the voters' league might go on through the list. It would perhaps be better for the league to mention only the candidates it endorses. It might get into difficulties in outlining the experience and qualities of candidates it does not recommend. An organization of this type, under broad-minded leadership, might grow to be very helpful and have considerable influence. The great danger is, of course, that it might become partisan, or too conservative, or too radical. That is why citizens of breadth and tolerance are essential for its leadership. Such organizations have met with some success in a few of the cities, notably in New York and Chicago.

IV. ACTIVE PARTICIPATION IN POLITICS AND PUBLIC AFFAIRS

Voting, even voting regularly and intelligently, is not enough. A citizen who has had the advantage of a high school or college education should take his place on the active list in the discussion of public questions, in political campaigns, and in urging upon government officials programs in the public interest. If we sleep through sewer scandals, oil steals, social security agitation, tax reform debates, and city, state, and national election campaigns, democracy will die as we slumber. It is fatal to say that politics is dirty, and no place for a lady or gentleman. This attitude will only make true what is now less than half true. It will turn politics over to the self-seekers, the spoilsmen, and the underworld. The "cleaner than thou" heirs of American democracy must come forth and take their place on the firing line and, if need be, in the mud. They will probably be surprised at the number of powder-begrimed and mud-besplattered persons who remain clean within, and their experience will certainly be broadened and their dispositions will probably be enlivened.

Four types of political activities. The late President A. T. Hadley of Yale once suggested that there were at least four different types of political activities in which American citizens might appropriately engage: one man might desire to enter politics as a career; another might prefer general part-time activity in good government movements, such as civil service reform; a third may reserve his activity for emergencies and crises; a fourth —and he has by far the largest company—may content himself with the exercise of general influence on the conduct of public affairs.[3] As there is

---

[3] Cited in R. C. Brooks, *Political Parties and Electoral Problems* (1933 ed.), p. 576.

usually no great difficulty in engaging the service of citizens in time of emergency, we shall center our discussion on the other suggestions.

EXERCISE OF GENERAL INFLUENCE. Mr. John Civis is what one would call a substantial citizen. He has no political "axes to grind" and no burning zeal for any particular political reform, but he has a laudable desire to make his weight felt on the side of honest and efficient government. How does he accomplish his aim? Of course, he keeps himself informed. He arrives at his conclusions independently and he does not hesitate to voice them, giving the ground upon which they are based. He will write to or call upon the City Engineer, the Director of Public Health, or the Mayor in connection with an important matter that, in his opinion, ought to be adjusted or pressed. He will write an original letter (not simply sign one handed to him by a pressure group), suggesting to his United States senator or any other representative official a course of action in reference to any issue involving public policy on which he (Mr. Civis) has an opinion he desires to have considered.[4] In these and numerous other ways he will make his influence felt among public officials, party leaders, newspaper editors, and those who like himself maintain an intelligent and somewhat general interest in government. The weight of the opinions of this one citizen will not be in any sense decisive, but if a small percentage of the disinterested voters, say 5 per cent, should do likewise, a major part of the reason for writing this chapter on the obligations of the citizen would no longer exist. The trouble is that we have left cranks and those seeking special favors as the almost exclusive users of the avenues through which those who conduct government may be reached. Instead of criticizing and ridiculing old "fuss-budgets" who write, phone, and wire public men, we should get busy ourselves. The recipients of our communications have no particular difficulty in recognizing a bona fide, disinterested, intelligent approach.

Our same John Civis will find that he can improve his mind and broaden his usefulness as a citizen by participation in public discussions of current problems. Town halls and forums, an encouraging development of recent years, admirably serve the purpose of discussion. To be sure, such discussion often "gets nowhere," but that ineffectiveness is usually because the leaders have not taken the pains to prepare for their function. If the leaders have the matter in hand, the forum is informative, interesting, and often lively. There is no better proof of the vitality of democracy in any community than the existence of well-managed forums where not too many holds are barred.

AFFILIATION WITH GOOD GOVERNMENT MOVEMENTS. If John Civis prefers

[4] See Tom Page, "Ten Pointers on How to Write to Your Congressman," *Tax Outlook,* June, 1948, p. 10.

to concentrate his efforts on specific points of civic improvement, he will find no dearth of good government movements and organizations with which he may affiliate. President Hadley mentioned civil service reform as an example of such a movement, and he doubtless did so because this is not only one of the oldest but also one of the most effective of the better government movements. For eighty years the National Civil Service Reform League has waged unselfishly with dignity, understanding, and confidence an unremitting fight against the spoils system in politics. Its achievements are noteworthy, but its work is not finished. Those who are attracted to its banner will be following in the footsteps of such eminent citizens as George William Curtis, Theodore Roosevelt, Woodrow Wilson, and Charles W. Eliot. Scores of other organizations, national in scope, also devote themselves to the public interest. Among these we mention the National Municipal League and the National League of Women Voters. The former is a professional or semiprofessional organization that devotes its efforts in a very practical way primarily, although not exclusively, to the improvement of city government. Any citizens in a local community who want to "do something about their city government" will find no difficulty in engaging the interest of the League and in securing specific aids from it. The Women Voters are nonprofessional and interested in every government from the United Nations to the village. It publishes informative and readable pamphlets on such subjects as *Building World Security*, *The Citizen and the United Nations*, *What's the U.S. to You?*, *The 40 Billion Dollar Question: What Does the Government Budget Mean to the Citizen?*, and *Know Your Town Government*.

Nearly every community has a variety of organizations concerned with government problems.[5] Some of these groups are interested primarily in matters that directly affect their members, others are quite disinterestedly devoted to the public good, but the greater number of them represent a combination of these two motivating factors. There is no city of any size in which an individual with normal concern about his own and civic affairs will not find a congenial organization or two in which he can enroll as a worker.[6]

To those who would find their place in government reform organizations this writer makes bold to offer a suggestion. Keep your sense of humor, your balance, your imagination. You will need them. Who has not seen the unimaginative, humorless, fanatic reformer, characterized by Theodore Roosevelt as belonging to the "lunatic fringe," who drives

[5] For an outstanding example (in Cincinnati) of one such organization, see National Municipal League, *Citizen Organization for Political Activity* (pamphlet, 1949 ed.).

[6] See Brooks, *op. cit.*, pp. 579 ff., for an interesting discussion on active participation in politics; also W. E. Mosher and others, *Responsible Citizenship* (1941), pp. 842 ff.; J. T. Salter, *The Pattern of Politics* (1940).

more people away from the camp than a well-balanced recruiter can draw to it? The good reformer must be a politician in the sense that he must know when to press his point, how hard to press it, and when to give the public a "breathing spell."

POLITICS AS A CAREER. There are those who have the entirely laudable ambition of entering politics as a career. How shall they proceed? There is no fixed rule of action; no set plan. The writer knows of one young man who, residing in a tough urban district in Prohibition days, sought entrance to public life via bartending in a speakeasy. It is hoped, however, that others will make their start within the framework of the law. It is relatively easy to make a beginning. Those who have not found it so have started out by demonstrating that they were not very promising politicians. That is, they have tried to start too fast, too high, or condescendingly. A young person must in practically every case begin at the bottom, in his precinct. First, he should ascertain whether or not the local organization of his party is such as to command his loyalty. If it does, he can then approach his precinct committeeman with every prospect of a welcome. The committeeman will give him work, without pay, distributing "literature," interviewing voters, talking to young people who are not yet old enough to vote, and helping in various other ways to build up the party in the precinct. The young recruit will not, in all probability, be asked to make any speeches, write any articles, or participate in matters of major strategy; but if he carries out his humble tasks with modest, cheerful efficiency, the day will probably come when he will be a leading political figure not only in his precinct but also in larger areas.

In an earlier chapter the importance of the precinct as a political unit was emphasized. All political workers and organizers recognize this fact. They do not scorn the lowly unit cell of party life, nor those who tend the cell. Votes come from precincts and from nowhere else. It might be said with a great deal of truth that a party is no stronger than its precinct workers. There have been successful party workers who have gone on to membership on state and even national committees of their party who took pains to retain the post of committeemen in their precincts. Such men recognize the importance of holding their local bailiwicks to the fulfillment of their ambition to ascend the scale of the party hierarchy. They feel that they are weakened in their claims for larger things if they are not "solid" in their own precincts.

Although party workers usually start in the precinct, there are possibilities of beginning at a higher point. A young woman who has made a study of social legislation might find that she is in demand as a speaker on a particular social issue throughout a city or even a state. An active young member of the Chamber of Commerce may become interested in problems of taxation and take his place as one of the leaders in a community effort to introduce a better tax system and set out to do something about it. Such opportunities are numerous and varied and present special, although not exclusive, opportunities to college graduates. From the springboard of interest in some significant issue an individual who may not have had any idea of entering politics may find himself "up to the neck" in politics, the very best kind of politics. And it might take most of his time and start him on a career in public office.

Hints to the would-be politician. There are words of caution for those who would enter politics as a career. Politics is one of the most unstable of all callings or professions. The worthy candidate may not be elected, or, having been elected, may soon be rejected. It seems desirable therefore that an individual with political ambitions should have independent means, or a business connection, or a profession, or a job to which he can retire in times of political reverses. The early political successes of Theodore and Franklin D. Roosevelt are often attributed to the fact that they had no financial worries and could give themselves unreservedly, without concern about financing the education of their children or about old age security, to the fascinating game of politics.

It is sometimes said that public men without independent sources of income are less to be trusted as public servants than are those in the more favored economic group, that poor men are likely to sacrifice their principles in order to continue in office. At least within the knowledge of this writer this proposition has no basis in fact. Rich men and poor men have abandoned their principles, have betrayed the public to serve themselves or their party or faction. Certainly men of small means and large ideas ornament many pages of American history. Although poor men who enter politics are under a decided personal handicap, the suggestion that they are less likely than others to prove themselves worthy agents of the people is inadmissible.

Politics is of course a gamble. The best-laid plans of the most meritorious aspirant may fail to materialize. Party leaders may set him aside for reasons of geography; or he may be passed over as a result of a change in the factional control within his party; or, if nominated, he may fail of election because he is on a ticket with others who do not inspire confidence; or he may go down to defeat because his nomination comes at a time when the popular trend is against his party. For these and many reasons beyond his control and for which he is in no way responsible he may fail to achieve his goal. His chance may come again; it may not. In any event, he should be able to smile, to "take it."

Those who find the political field inviting may not resent a statement concerning decency in politics. Scandals and skulduggery make newspaper headlines; integrity and respectability do not. The exploits of blemished political characters have often entertained the populace, whereas men of probity have failed to arouse any particular enthusiasm. As is intimated on an earlier page, public life is probably not so devoid of respectability as is commonly imagined, and the newcomer may be surprised at the number of serious, hardworking, passably upright men with whom he is associated. The standard of the average politician is probably every whit as high as that of the familiar campus "framer" and "fixer." Indeed, a campus politician of this variety who plans later to make politics a career might be warned not to attempt to carry with him all of his campus practices, at least not without first consulting the penal code. If we elevate our vision above the ward boss and the rural courthouse gang, we find, on the whole, a fairly honorable company. Ballot box thieves, racketeers, grafters, bribetakers, and similar criminals are far outnumbered by men who, possessing perhaps a little less than their share of human selfishness, prejudice, and folly, take seriously their obligations as representatives of the people. Surely this is an attainable standard, an indispensable standard.

V. ACCEPTANCE OF THE BASES OF REPRESENTATIVE GOVERNMENT

As our democracy functions through representatives, we must accept the bases upon which representative government rests. No doubt good authorities would vigorously debate the validity of certain principles on any complete list that other authorities might present; but this writer, without making any pretense of presenting an exhaustive list, suggests just three principles that he believes most authorities would accept. They are (1) a habit on the part of the voters of respecting the judgment of their representatives; (2) tolerance on the part of the party or faction that happens to have the responsibility for conducting the government; and (3) compliance (not necessarily cheerful or uncritical) on the part of minority groups.

Burke on the representative's relation to his constituents. In a day when we sometimes seem inclined to place our casual judgment, or simply a desire based upon community or personal interest, against the more considered judgment of our representative and demand that he serve us simply as an errand boy, the words of Edmund Burke, one of the most gifted of all the men who ever sat in the English House of Commons and a warm friend of America, are singularly appropriate. Addressing the electors of Bristol, November 3, 1774, he said:

It ought to be the happiness and glory of a representative to live in the strictest union, the closest correspondence, and the most unreserved communication with his constituents. Their wishes ought to have great weight with him; their opinion high respect; their business unremitted attention. It is his duty to sacrifice his repose, his pleasures, his satisfaction, to theirs; and above all, ever, and in all cases, to prefer their interests to his own. But his unbiased opinion, his mature judgment, his enlightened conscience, he ought not to sacrifice to you, to any man, or to any set of men living. . . . Your representative owes you, not his industry only, but his judgment; and he betrays instead of serving you if he sacrifices it to your opinion.[7]

Six years later, he addressed the same electors, as follows:

I did not obey your instructions: No. I conformed to the instructions of truth and nature, and maintained your interest, against your own opinions, with a constancy that became me. A representative worthy of you ought to be a person of stability. I am to look, indeed, to your opinions; but to such opinions as you and I *must* have five years hence. I was not to look to the flash of the day. I knew that you chose me, in my place, along with others, to be a pillar of the state, and not a weathercock on the top of the edifice, exalted for my levity and versatility, and of no use but to indicate the shifting of every fashionable gale.[8]

Voiced over a hundred and fifty years ago, these words are no less applicable to our own day. Indeed, in view of the demand upon modern government, the numerous details and complexities of its functioning, Burke's theory may be more imperative in our time than it was in his own. Our elected representatives are above the average in intelligence. They are at the center of government, giving the major part of their time to shaping its policies. We have the right to advise them and to retire them to private life if they do not accept our counsel. But should we not, upon reflection, praise, rather than condemn, those representatives who do their own studying, consult their own conscience, and arrive at their own independent judgment? Their ability is worth little to us if we will not suffer them to exercise their own judgment. It should be a matter of pride to us that we have had and now have a few public officers who have met Burke's high standard. One associates with Burke such senators as William E. Borah, Carter Glass, and George W. Norris; and one would have no difficulty in making a short list of contemporary public men who belong in this class. Our confidence in representative government is greatly strengthened as we record the fact that a man of independent character, even when in disagreement with his constituents, has often won triumphant re-election, sometimes because the representative brought the voters to his way of thinking and at other times simply because the voters wanted to retain an independent spirit in office.

The need for a tolerant majority. We have said that the party responsible

[7] Edmund Burke, *Works*, I, 446–447.

[8] *Ibid.*, II, 138. The electors were not quite ready to accept this version of a representative's obligations, and Burke had to seek another constituency.

for the conduct of government must be tolerant. Majority rule does not mean majority tyranny. The majority must be willing to argue peaceably with the minority, to hear its objections, to submit to its criticism, to heed its warnings, and to welcome its suggestions. A majority that outrages a minority by imposing upon it discriminatory or unjust legislation is striking a blow at the foundations of representative government.[9] It might seem that this warning should be addressed to government authorities rather than to citizens, but a moment's reflection will show the justification for its wider application. The general tone and temper and direction of a government is shaped in the long run by the whole citizenry, and if the people are impatient and would deal unjustly with minorities, hateful government measures are likely to be enacted. Antiparochial school laws are examples of legislation likely to be enacted and fair employment practices "laws" are examples of legislation likely to fail of enactment when a democracy forgets its obligations to minorities.

Americans have most need for tolerance. Approximately 35,000,000 of us are foreign born or children of foreign born or mixed parents—5,000,000 Germans, nearly as many Italians, and so on. Then there are 14,000,000 Negroes. Nearly all of these people are good Americans, and one who disbelieves this statement might give it more credence upon hearing alien parents sadly lament the complete and voluntary Americanization of their children. However, the offspring are not so American as their parents believe them to be; and this fact, on the whole, is no loss to the Republic. Indeed, the language, the literature, the ideas, and the ideals of peoples of different nationalities are well worth preserving as a part of American culture. It is superfluous to inquire what each of the races and nationalities mentioned have contributed to our national life. It is no less a work of supererogation to say that intolerance, whether manifested in discriminatory legislation or in laws that would impose upon peoples of divergent cultures a strait-jacket Americanism, would lessen their opportunity and desire to contribute their portion of that variety which enriches our civilization. Furthermore, just as we have need for moderation in dealing with races and nationalities, so also we need it no less in solving the problems peculiar to the social and economic areas into which our continental empire is naturally divided.

Americans can afford to be tolerant. Abundantly endowed with natural resources, fortunate in our national frontiers, and some distance removed (even yet) from potential enemies, we are more secure than the people of any other nation. Our relative security has made it possible for us to carry on our debates and to fashion our domestic legislation, with some

---

[9] H. J. Laski, *Parliamentary Government in England* (1938), pp. 4 ff., contains an interesting analysis of the prerequisites of representative government.

exceptions, along moderate lines. Times of emergency include most of the exceptions; and with the passing of any emergency we have returned, if somewhat haltingly, to rational arguments and even-handed laws. During recent years our foreign relations have been on a rather continuous emergency basis, and restrictive measures, like the Internal Security Act of 1950, are doubtless here for the period of the emergency, a period that may cover a generation. The hope for democracy is that repeal of the rigorous measures designed to meet a crisis follows its passing.

The need for minority co-operation. If representative government presupposes consideration for minorities, by the same token it presupposes minority compliance with the government's established policies. On the whole, American minorities, save a few small ones, have not been resistant to this requirement. During most of its history our country has had two major political parties holding remarkably similar principles on matters of major concern. The "never-ending din of political conflict," to use Lord Balfour's expression, may have caused us to believe that great issues were at stake, but we confused the bare-fisted fight over office with what was in reality only a pillow fight over principles. This last sentence is somewhat of an exaggeration, yet not a gross exaggeration. Our Republicans and Democrats are in fundamental agreement on private property, the profit motive, public schools, the conservation of national resources, and a host of other subjects. One party may believe in a little less regulation of business, a little less social security, slightly higher taxes on lower incomes, bigger or more battleships than another, but the fact remains that the major parties usually differ in degree and in method, rather than on principles. Professor Arthur W. Macmahon expressed it very well in his Presidential Address before the American Political Science Association, December 28, 1947. "Electoral campaigns," said he, "are concerned with the tempo rather than the trend—in other words, the main course of development or the direction—of public policy." [10] And thus our great political parties march along, arm-in-arm as it were; and the vast majority of us accommodate ourselves, often hesitantly but seldom with serious misgivings, to the program of whichever party happens to be in power.

The day may come when two major parties take to the field to battle to the death not only for offices but also for fundamental principles upon which they hold uncompromising and diametrically opposite views. A few years ago some authorities thought this situation was arising in Great Britain, where the Conservative and Labor parties seemed to hold irreconcilable positions on the basic question of the ownership of the means of production.[11] When in power, however, the Labor party proceeded with

[10] *Am. Pol. Sci. Rev.*, XLII (1948), 3.
[11] Laski, *op. cit.*, 148 ff.

some caution, and the Conservative party came more and more to modify its views respecting "free enterprise" and social security. It now appears that the British people can easily accommodate themselves to change brought about by a shift in control from one of these parties to the other. If British and American history is a guide to the future (and it must be admitted that history is not a perfect guide), a change by legislative enactment in either country, in a particular month or year, from one economic system to another, is hardly to be expected. Changes we have had in our own country, sometimes so rapidly, as during the past twenty years, that they have been accompanied by bitter denunciations and recriminations. Yet they have proceeded within the framework of fairly familiar economic and political patterns, and we have some reason to assume that future changes will follow a similar course. But however the changes may come, as long as they fall within the clauses of the Constitution, we must accept them. Resistance is revolution, and revolution is not representative government.

No one should draw the inference from the foregoing paragraphs that it is the intention of the author to suggest that an individual should not offer legal resistance to any act of any government that, in his opinion, violates one of his rights. On the contrary, it is asserted to be the duty of the individual to offer such resistance, for by so doing he not only protects himself from the operation of discriminatory measures but he also performs a public service. Thus the man who goes to court to contest the validity of a "restrictive covenant," a speech gag regulation, a special assessment, a subsidy, or compulsory insurance law represents his neighbors, even the whole nation, as well as himself. One of the healthy restraints upon a government that would be inconsiderate or arbitrary is the sure knowledge that individuals will resist, with every constitutional and legal means at their command, the application of unfair and unjust legislation. What is meant, then, when we say that the acts of government must be accepted is that, after legal means of contesting the validity of a law or policy have been exhausted, citizens have the obligation to comply, regardless of what that law or policy might be.

Organizations inimical to representative government. Threats to representative government have always been present and are now present in new and varied forms. The business organization that formerly secured its special privilege from legislators by a bribe now pours its millions into propaganda to win a favorable public opinion; the city boss, fighting a dogged retreat, finds that the old method of buying voters direct is giving way to purchase through the promise of large grants from the government; the labor leader now rivals the businessman as a seeker after privilege; the old-age pensioners give promise of rivaling the farmers in political

power; and an infinite variety of arrogant and selfish majorities and screaming and grabbing minorities make the progress of representative government hazardous.　But these activities threaten our system only incidentally,
not directly; they are not aimed at its destruction.　More recently, organizations have sprung up that would make the direct attack.　Their
names, often patriotic and inviting, may not reveal their true character
and purpose.　Not infrequently, good citizens desiring to assist in some
worthy cause may innocently become affiliated with an organization the
plans and purposes of which he abhors.　The suggestion is made that an
individual should carefully check the status of an organization in which
he is considering membership if he is in any degree uncertain respecting
its activities.　The Department of Justice has prepared a list of organizations membership in which is deemed incompatible with employment by
the United States.　The list includes such well-known organizations as
the German-American Bund and the Communist Party, and such less
well-known groups as the Citizens Protective League, the American
Peace Mobilization, and scores of others.　A glance at the Attorney
General's list might save well-meaning and worthy American citizens
from embarrassment.

VI. RELIANCE UPON ESTABLISHED AUTHORITY

How did the Italians and the Germans lose their liberties to dictators?
There are many explanations, to be sure, but a significant one is that
vicious private bands, organized practically as armies, set about to rectify
conditions.　There were, to be sure, sore spots in these two unhappy
countries, but their existence and the desirability for their eradication does
not alter the fact that the exchange of the boils of democracy for the leprosy of totalitarianism was effected by armed forces operating outside the
sphere of governmental authority.　If this turn of events is a grim warning to every democracy to put its house in order, it is no less a warning of
how not to achieve that desirable end.　Totalitarianism is but the ultimate
fate of a democracy that trusts too little in duly constituted authority, a fate
that we hope is a long way from overtaking us in the United States.　Yet,
even if we make the comforting assumption, possibly a fool's assumption,
that we are in no danger of the final disaster, we cannot flatter ourselves
that we are free from the baneful effect of forces operating without the
sanction of law.

The vigilante menace.　In frontier days we had our vigilantes who,
maintaining a crude form of "law and order" where there was no legal
authority, perhaps justified their existence.　The South, suffering under a
vindictive and capricious Reconstruction, resorted to the familiar Ku Klux

Klan (a special type of vigilante organization), and historians have not judged her too harshly. Both the vigilantes and the Klan have captured the popular imagination to such an extent that whenever there occurs a local disorder excited citizens are quick to suggest the old vigilante remedy; and whenever certain anxious souls decide that the aliens are a menace, that spies are out everywhere, or that their fellow citizens have strayed too far from the path of rectitude and that the nation is in peril, the Klan or some variation of it is suggested as the instrument by which we might be saved.

Concerning the use of vigilantes in contemporary local disorders, the following might be said: *First,* the duly constituted authorities are usually quite competent to handle the situation. *Second,* if they are not able to hold the disruptive forces in check, they can easily call to other duly constituted authorities for help, or they can swear in special officers from the local population. *Third,* there is the ever-present possibility that vigilantes may be made the dupes of clever men who have very personal (economic) reasons for advocating a vicious course of action. *Fourth,* vigilantes are largely irresponsible, and are ignorant and careless of the rights of persons against whom they act. *Fifth,* vigilantes are more likely to represent the physical strength and emotional instability of a community than its enlightened conscience and balanced judgment.

It seems axiomatic that good citizens should bear testimony against vigilantism of any kind. Yet its manifestation in labor troubles and in reference to "radical" speakers are so frequent as to cause grave concern to thoughtful persons. Particularly is this true in times of emergency and in the no less hectic periods of emergency's aftermath. Groups of the vigilante type have stoned pickers from strawberry patches, "roughed" an individual who stated that a particular act of Congress was unconstitutional, threatened, rotten-egged, and kidnaped champions of unpopular causes, and intimidated ministers who preached in a foreign language. In some cases such things have been done with the connivance of city or county authorities, a fact that indicates the extent to which the vigilante spirit has taken possession of us. College men and women have the opportunity and the obligation in their respective communities to take the lead against these misdirected efforts. One may be greatly encouraged at discovering the calming effects of a few words of quiet caution diplomatically spoken.

LYNCHING. Occasionally a group of vigilantes disgraces America with a lynching. This crime is not confined to offenses against the Negro in the South, but it does have its most frequent visitations on that race and in that region. Not only do a number of states have laws listing it specifically as a crime—in any case it is murder—but also, because of failure in the enforcement of these laws, there has been repeated agitation for a national law. Federal legislation on the subject, however, has been found to be politically impossible because of Southern opposition. Furthermore, an effective federal statute would be exceedingly difficult to draft because of constitutional limitations on the powers of Congress. Moreover, this crime is a social disease and there is doubt as to the possibility of a statutory cure.

The sad fact is that lynching has been enthusiastically, sometimes gaily, approved by millions of ignorant people and condoned by thousands of intelligent ones. It is significant that Governor Ritchie, who seemed to have a life interest in the governorship of Maryland, was defeated in the campaign for a fifth term, just after he had acted courageously and vigorously in an unsuccessful attempt to bring to justice the leaders of a lynching mob. Governor Rolph's public approval of lynching in California brought a storm of protest from a number of editors and public men, but there is grave doubt as to whether his offer to pardon the lynchers, if convicted, caused him to lose standing with the "man in the street." Indeed, there were many men who were not in the street who agreed with Rolph, although they thought he erred in making a public statement.

An encouraging sign of progress toward the eradication of the crime of lynching comes from a group of progressive women in the South who denounce the men of that region who say that lynching must be condoned because it is one method of protecting womanhood. There are, in fact, few cases of lynching for rape, but a much higher number for trivial offenses to "keep the Negro in his place." An organization of great promise is the Commission on Interracial Co-operation, whose headquarters are at Atlanta. This Commission has directed thorough studies of lynching. The educational value of these studies and the other activities of the Commission may eventually sift down to some of the vicious and thoughtless persons of the variety who invariably participate in lynchings.[12]

The hood-shirt threats. Vigilante groups are commonly local and sporadic; the various "hooded" or "shirted" organizations cover wider areas and are set up on a more or less permanent basis with national officers, sometimes quite a little money, and always an ambitious program. Democracy, to be consistent, may not object to the presentation and advocacy of a program; but it probably has the right to compel its sponsors to go unmasked and ununiformed, and it assuredly has the duty to prevent them from resorting to violence. It is common knowledge that the type of organization under discussion usually advocates such principles as the abolition of free speech and religious liberty, and some of the proponents

---

[12] *State Government*, March, 1934, pp. 58–61; L. T. Nordyke, "Ladies and the Lynchers," *Survey Graphic*, November, 1939.

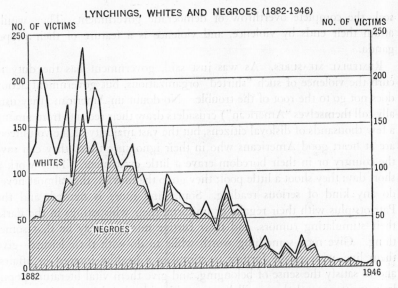

LYNCHINGS, WHITES AND NEGROES (1882-1946)

From *The Report of the President's Committee on Civil Rights* (1947), p. 21.

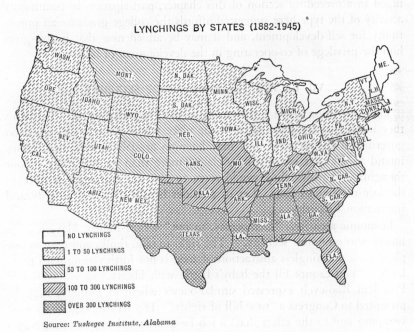

LYNCHINGS BY STATES (1882-1945)

NO LYNCHINGS
1 TO 50 LYNCHINGS
50 TO 100 LYNCHINGS
100 TO 300 LYNCHINGS
OVER 300 LYNCHINGS

Source: *Tuskegee Institute, Alabama*

From *The Report of the President's Committee on Civil Rights* (1949), p. 21.

seek the complete overthrow of democratic government. They would attain their ends by violence, and violence is a feature of their propaganda.

REMEDIAL MEASURES. As was just said, government has the duty to curb the violence of such "shirted" organizations, but government action does not go to the root of the trouble. No doubt un-American (they usually call themselves "American") crusaders draw their recruits from among a few thousands of disloyal citizens, but the vast majority of the volunteers are at heart good Americans who in their ignorance think they can save the country or in their boredom crave a little excitement. They work a short day; they shoot a little pool; they go to the movies; they almost never do any kind of serious reading. Something more is needed, and the Patriots-plus with their regalia or uniform, their whisperings in the dark, their stimulating rumors, and their furtive missions may be that something. Give men something worth while to do with their leisure—give them live, wide-awake forums to stimulate a healthy interest in affairs, and to satisfy the sense of belonging, and give them vital literature popularly written—and there will be a considerable shrinkage in the recruiting ground for organizations representing a perverted Americanism. As noted in a preceding section of this chapter, participation in community activity of the type here suggested affords the college graduate an opportunity for self-development, and it may be added now that it also gives him the privilege of co-operating in the development of others.

VII. FACING THE PROBLEM OF SECURITY

There are those who say that we have gone "security crazy." If by this they mean that we have come to the place where we rely too much on government for security, they may have an arguable point; but if they intend to say that security now claims more than its fair share of our thoughts and plans, they would seem to lose the argument at once in the face of obvious facts. Let us consider briefly economic security and international security.

Economic security. "Democracy, to me," writes Maury Maverick, "is liberty *plus* economic security." The right to talk, think, and pray as one pleases are meaningless abstractions if food is not forthcoming with regularity. "You cannot fill the baby's bottle with liberty," says Maverick.[13] President Roosevelt expressed similar views when, in January, 1944, he presented to Congress a "new bill of rights." His recommendations were sweeping and to the effect that: a job be guaranteed to everyone; wages

[13] In *Blood and Iron* (1939). Quoted in *Teaching the Civil Liberties,* p. 15, by Howard B. Wilson and others, National Council for the Social Studies, bulletin 16 (May, 1941).

he complete overthrow of democratic government. They would
their ends by violence, and violence is a feature of their propa-
.

MEDIAL MEASURES. As was just said, government has the duty to
he violence of such "shirted" organizations, but government action
not go to the root of the trouble. No doubt un-American (they usu-
all themselves "American") crusaders draw their recruits from among
thousands of disloyal citizens, but the vast majority of the volunteers
heart good Americans who in their ignorance think they can save
ountry or in their boredom crave a little excitement. They work a
day; they shoot a little pool; they go to the movies; they almost never
ny kind of serious reading. Something more is needed, and the
ots-plus with their regalia or uniform, their whisperings in the dark,
stimulating rumors, and their furtive missions may be that some-
. Give men something worth while to do with their leisure—give
live, wide-awake forums to stimulate a healthy interest in affairs,
o satisfy the sense of belonging, and give them vital literature popu-
written—and there will be a considerable shrinkage in the recruit-
round for organizations representing a perverted Americanism. As
in a preceding section of this chapter, participation in community
ty of the type here suggested affords the college graduate an oppor-
y for self-development, and it may be added now that it also gives
he privilege of co-operating in the development of others.

VII. FACING THE PROBLEM OF SECURITY

ere are those who say that we have gone "security crazy." If by this
mean that we have come to the place where we rely too much on
rnment for security, they may have an arguable point; but if they
d to say that security now claims more than its fair share of our
ghts and plans, they would seem to lose the argument at once in
ace of obvious facts. Let us consider briefly economic security and
national security.

onomic security. "Democracy, to me," writes Maury Maverick, "is
ty *plus* economic security." The right to talk, think, and pray as one
es are meaningless abstractions if food is not forthcoming with regu-
y. "You cannot fill the baby's bottle with liberty," says Maverick.[13]
ident Roosevelt expressed similar views when, in January, 1944, he
ented to Congress a "new bill of rights." His recommendations were
ping and to the effect that: a job be guaranteed to everyone; wages

n *Blood and Iron* (1939). Quoted in *Teaching the Civil Liberties*, p. 15, by Howard
lson and others, National Council for the Social Studies, bulletin 16 (May, 1941).

Klan (a special type of vigilante organization), and historians have
not judged her too harshly. Both the vigilantes and the Klan have captured the popular imagination to such an extent that whenever there occurs a local disorder excited citizens are quick to suggest the old vigilante
remedy; and whenever certain anxious souls decide that the aliens are a
menace, that spies are out everywhere, or that their fellow citizens have
strayed too far from the path of rectitude and that the nation is in peril,
the Klan or some variation of it is suggested as the instrument by which
we might be saved.

Concerning the use of vigilantes in contemporary local disorders, the
following might be said: *First,* the duly constituted authorities are usually
quite competent to handle the situation. *Second,* if they are not able to
hold the disruptive forces in check, they can easily call to other duly constituted authorities for help, or they can swear in special officers from the
local population. *Third,* there is the ever-present possibility that vigilantes may be made the dupes of clever men who have very personal
(economic) reasons for advocating a vicious course of action. *Fourth,*
vigilantes are largely irresponsible, and are ignorant and careless of the
rights of persons against whom they act. *Fifth,* vigilantes are more likely
to represent the physical strength and emotional instability of a community
than its enlightened conscience and balanced judgment.

It seems axiomatic that good citizens should bear testimony against
vigilantism of any kind. Yet its manifestation in labor troubles and in
reference to "radical" speakers are so frequent as to cause grave concern
to thoughtful persons. Particularly is this true in times of emergency and
in the no less hectic periods of emergency's aftermath. Groups of the
vigilante type have stoned pickers from strawberry patches, "roughed"
an individual who stated that a particular act of Congress was unconstitutional, threatened, rotten-egged, and kidnaped champions of unpopular
causes, and intimidated ministers who preached in a foreign language.
In some cases such things have been done with the connivance of city or
county authorities, a fact that indicates the extent to which the vigilante
spirit has taken possession of us. College men and women have the opportunity and the obligation in their respective communities to take the
lead against these misdirected efforts. One may be greatly encouraged
at discovering the calming effects of a few words of quiet caution diplomatically spoken.

LYNCHING. Occasionally a group of vigilantes disgraces America with
a lynching. This crime is not confined to offenses against the Negro in the
South, but it does have its most frequent visitations on that race and in
that region. Not only do a number of states have laws listing it specifically
as a crime—in any case it is murder—but also, because of failure in the en-

forcement of these laws, there has been repeated agitation for a national law. Federal legislation on the subject, however, has been found to be politically impossible because of Southern opposition. Furthermore, an effective federal statute would be exceedingly difficult to draft because of constitutional limitations on the powers of Congress. Moreover, this crime is a social disease and there is doubt as to the possibility of a statutory cure.

The sad fact is that lynching has been enthusiastically, sometimes gaily, approved by millions of ignorant people and condoned by thousands of intelligent ones. It is significant that Governor Ritchie, who seemed to have a life interest in the governorship of Maryland, was defeated in the campaign for a fifth term, just after he had acted courageously and vigorously in an unsuccessful attempt to bring to justice the leaders of a lynching mob. Governor Rolph's public approval of lynching in California brought a storm of protest from a number of editors and public men, but there is grave doubt as to whether his offer to pardon the lynchers, if convicted, caused him to lose standing with the "man in the street." Indeed, there were many men who were not in the street who agreed with Rolph, although they thought he erred in making a public statement.

An encouraging sign of progress toward the eradication of the crime of lynching comes from a group of progressive women in the South who denounce the men of that region who say that lynching must be condoned because it is one method of protecting womanhood. There are, in fact, few cases of lynching for rape, but a much higher number for trivial offenses to "keep the Negro in his place." An organization of great promise is the Commission on Interracial Co-operation, whose headquarters are at Atlanta. This Commission has directed thorough studies of lynching. The educational value of these studies and the other activities of the Commission may eventually sift down to some of the vicious and thoughtless persons of the variety who invariably participate in lynchings.[12]

The hood-shirt threats. Vigilante groups are commonly local and sporadic; the various "hooded" or "shirted" organizations cover wider areas and are set up on a more or less permanent basis with national officers, sometimes quite a little money, and always an ambitious program. Democracy, to be consistent, may not object to the presentation and advocacy of a program; but it probably has the right to compel its sponsors to go unmasked and ununiformed, and it assuredly has the duty to prevent them from resorting to violence. It is common knowledge that the type of organization under discussion usually advocates such principles as the abolition of free speech and religious liberty, and some of the proponents

[12] *State Government*, March, 1934, pp. 58–61; L. T. Nordyke, "Ladies and the Lynchers," *Survey Graphic*, November, 1939.

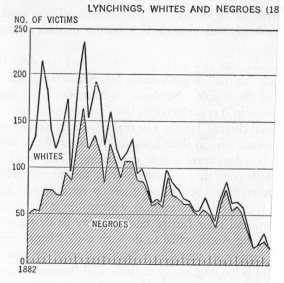

LYNCHINGS, WHITES AND NEGROES (18

From *The Report of the President's Committee on Civil*

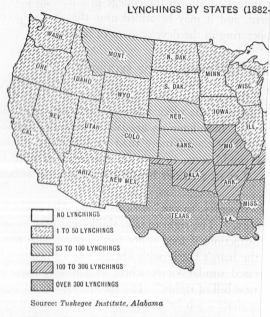

LYNCHINGS BY STATES (1882–

NO LYNCHINGS
1 TO 50 LYNCHINGS
50 TO 100 LYNCHINGS
100 TO 300 LYNCHINGS
OVER 300 LYNCHINGS

Source: *Tuskegee Institute, Alabama*

From *The Report of the President's Committee on Ci*

be maintained at a level high enough to provide adequate food, clothing, and shelter; farm prices be held high enough to give farmers a decent standard of living; adequate homes be provided for all; and compensation be paid to those who are idle because of illness or accident. He even asked that businessmen's markets be protected from monopolies at home and from cartels in foreign countries. Whatever one may think of the possibility of attaining Roosevelt's goals, the listing of them outlines some of the principal hazards to economic security.

UNEMPLOYMENT. True it is that most men suffer temporary hardships with fortitude and, if they have reasonable hope that the necessities of life will not be cut off, endure with infinite patience a submarginal existence. But they react with rebellious bitterness or debilitating hopelessness when there is no prospect of employment, no hope of improving their economic condition, no security from want. Economic insecurity is thus a double danger to democracy in that it renders freedom a mockery to those in distress and brings near to all the threat of revolution. It may be argued with considerable force that personal economic insecurity was one of the chief causes for the failure of democracy in certain European countries and that its persistence in some little countries on that continent is possible because of the relatively high degree of economic security enjoyed by the inhabitants.

In the past two decades, excepting the war years, millions of American citizens have been unemployed and in want. Some would solve the problem by saying that there is plenty of work for all and that the unemployed should get jobs and go to work. Although a few very capable and resourceful people can always find some kind of employment, the average man cannot go from one employment to another, certainly not in a period of declining industrial activity. Governments, particularly the national government, have made efforts through doles, government work projects, and unemployment insurance to provide relief for those in distress, but the problem of unemployment has not yet been solved. It requires more faith than is good for us or our democracy to believe that, without heroic measures, the future will not have its years of acute distress caused by industrial dislocation and unemployment.

OTHER HAZARDS. Economic insecurity arises not only from unemployment but also from the hazards of employment, illness, and old age. Much has been done in recent years to banish these specters from the lives of working men, but much remains to be done; and some of this remedial legislation has perhaps been prompted as much by political pressures as it has by the needs of those for whom it was designed. In slaying the dragon of insecurity our legislators need the support of all good citizens no less to enable them to resist unfair demands than to strengthen them in their efforts to provide a minimum of security for all. It must be admitted that this whole subject is full of unsolved problems, but no reasonable person can doubt that economic insecurity is one of democracy's most insistent challengers, a challenger that must be met and worsted.

International security. "For ages lost in the drifts of time, some of the most mysterious eyes on earth have stared cryptically toward tiny Bikini Atoll. On Easter Island, outrigger of the fleets of archipelagoes that ride the Pacific Ocean, a long file of stone colossi rear cold, immortal faces. No one knows what men carved these gigantic symbols, what hands, what primitive technology raised them, with what devotion or what fears. Whether they are gods or images of human greatness, they are menacing. They are monuments to the fact that man's history can perish utterly from the earth.

"Of all strange things that Easter Island idols have looked out upon through the ages, the strangest was prepared last week" (late June, 1946). "A world, with the power of universal suicide at last within its grasp, was about to make its first scientific test of that power." [14] That is it, "universal suicide"—unless . . . Albert Einstein, shy, childlike, and saintly, whose equation made the atomic bomb theoretically possible and whose letter to President Roosevelt led to the Manhattan Project and the bomb, is the first to cry "unless." "There is no foreseeable defense against atomic bombs," he wrote in the *New York Times.* "Scientists do not even know of any field which promises us any hope of adequate defense." [15] And the Emergency Committee of Atomic Scientists, of which Einstein is chairman, declared that the people must do "a new type of thinking . . . if mankind is to survive and move toward higher levels." The possibility of the H-bomb now reinforces the warning of the men who developed the A-bomb. Scientists who understand such forces know that they can blow up the earth. We will do well to take the judgment of the scientists, and bring nuclear products under control in a world organized for peace and security.

VIII. ADHERENCE TO THE PRINCIPLE OF ACCOMMODATION

In his justly famed speech on conciliation with America, Edmund Burke made the declaration that "All governments, indeed, every human benefit and enjoyment, every virtue, and every prudent act is founded on compromise and barter. We balance inconveniences; we give and take; we permit some rights that we may enjoy others; and we choose rather to

[14] *Time,* July 1, 1946, p. 52. The entire "Crossroads" article is well worth reading.
[15] Quoted in *Time,* July 1, 1946, p. 58. On February 9, 1950, Dr. Vannevar Bush repeated, in substance, the warning of Dr. Einstein, *New York Times,* Feb. 10.

be happy citizens than subtle disputants." [16] Great Britain, acting rather imperiously toward her American colonies at the time, learned a bitter lesson from that experience and later, in a spirit of compromise and accommodation, met with success in dealing with some of her other colonies.

Perfectionist souls there are who can see no compromise on any question, and the rank and file of honorable men will not compromise on certain issues; but the typical issue that presents itself to the public for solution can and must be met by compromise. Some want a very limited social security program, others want full coverage of all groups; some advocate a high tariff, others none at all; some wish only a mild regulation of public utilities, others would control them in meticulous detail. The reader may continue this listing of opposing forces, and he knows that the answer in each case, as expressed in terms of government policy, is compromise. Few, if any, know the perfect answer; and the extremists, who are most likely to think they have it, may be fanatical, or selfish, or both. The moderate solution commends itself to moderate men.

The leading members of the Philadelphia Constitutional Convention knew what they wanted, and they were pretty sure that what they wanted would be good for the country. There was a grave difficulty attending their deliberations, however, for they disagreed rather strongly on several points. They had to compromise, to agree upon a Constitution that practically every member of the Convention thought he could improve. Of the instrument of government upon which the members of the Convention, not without misgivings, agreed, Alexander Hamilton, speaking before the New York ratification convention, said: "The truth is that the plan in all its parts, was a plan of accommodation." [17] Washington, writing to his favorite nephew and heir, Bushrod Washington, made this statement: "The warmest friends and the best supporters the Constitution has do not contend that it is free from imperfections; but they have found them unavoidable and are sensible, if evil is likely to arise therefrom, the remedy must come hereafter. . . . I do not think we are more inspired, have more wisdom, or possess more virtue, than those who will come after us." [18]

These words of Washington not only strengthen the proposition that government is compromise, but also express a confidence in the American people, in their wisdom and character. Democracy can flourish on the wisdom of a few, if that wisdom is supported by the character of many. A few spirits like Abraham Lincoln and Justice Oliver Wendell Holmes,

[16] Edmund Burke, *Works*, I, 500.
[17] Quoted in Burton J. Hendrick, *Bulwark of the Republic* (1937), p. 90.
[18] Quoted, *ibid.*, p. 99.

and others less known to fame but fit to be associated with them in wisdom, breadth of view, and tolerance, supported by men of good will, can make democracy work.

Reading List

Louis Adamic, *A Nation of Nations* (1945).

J. T. Adams, *The American: The Making of a New Man* (1943).

Dewey Anderson and P. E. Davidson, *Ballots and the Democratic Class Struggle* (1943).

Norman Angell, *Let the People Know* (1943).

Max Ascoli, *Intelligence in Politics* (1936).

E. S. Bates, *American Faith* (1940).

C. L. Becker, *Freedom and Responsibility in the American Way of Life* (1945).

R. Benedict, *Race, Science, and Politics* (1940).

Alfred Bingham, *Techniques of Democracy* (1942).

B. Bliven and A. G. Mezerik, eds., *What the Informed Citizen Needs to Know* (1945).

E. S. Bogardus, *Democracy by Discussion* (1945).

Catherine Drinker Bowen, *Yankee from Olympus: Justice Holmes and His Family* (1944).

D. W. Brogan, *The American Character* (1944).

Vannevar Bush, *Modern Arms and Free Men* (1949).

Thomas R. Carskadon, *U.S.A.: Measure of a Nation* (1949).

A. R. Chandler, ed., *The Clash of Political Ideals* (1941).

M. R. Cohen, *The Faith of a Liberal* (1946).

H. S. Commager, *The American Mind: An Interpretation of American Thought and Character since the 1880's* (1950).

G. S. Counts, *The Prospects of American Democracy* (1938).

N. Cousins, *A Treasury of Democracy* (1942).

———, *Modern Man Is Obsolete* (1945).

A. Craven, *Democracy in American Life* (1941).

B. Croce, *Politics and Morals* (1945).

John Dewey, *Freedom and Culture* (1939).

M. H. Dorr and E. H. Litchfield, *Facts about Your Job as a Voting Citizen* (1940).

John Dos Passos, *The Ground We Stand On* (1941).

F. R. Dulles, *Labor in America* (1949).

Herman Finer, *America's Destiny* (1947).

E. F. Frazier, *The Negro in the United States* (1949).

Douglas Southall Freeman, *George Washington* (1948), 2 vols.

C. J. Friedrich, *Constitutional Government and Democracy* (1941).

———, *The New Belief in the Common Man* (1943).

H. F. Gosnell, *Getting Out the Vote* (1927).

L. Gulick, *Votes in New York City on Referenda, 1920–1934, Inclusive* (1936).

A. G. Hays, *Democracy Works* (1939).

M. P. Heavenrich, *The Participation of Flint Citizens in Elections* (1938).

John Hersey, *Hiroshima* (1946).

Harold L. Ickes, *The Autobiography of a Curmudgeon* (1943).

H. J. Laski, *Reflections on the Revolution of Our Time* (1943).

Alfred Lief, *Democracy's Norris* (1939).

David Lilienthal, *This I Do Believe* (1949).

R. W. Logan, ed., *What the Negro Wants* (1944).

R. S. and Helen Lynd, *Middletown* (1929).

———, *Middletown in Transition* (1937).

R. M. MacIver, *The Ramparts We Guard* (1950).

James Marshall, *The Freedom to Be Free* (1943).

Helen E. Martz, *Citizen Participation in Government* (1948).

Carey McWilliams, *Brothers Under the Skin* (1943).

———, *A Mask for Privilege: Anti-Semitism in America* (1948).

Dumas Malone, *Jefferson the Virginian* (1948).

C. E. Merriam, *On the Agenda of Democracy* (1941).

———, *The Making of Citizens* (1931).

———, *Systematic Politics* (1945).

———, *What Is Democracy?* (1941).

Gustavus Myers, *History of Bigotry in the United States* (1943).

Gunnar Myrdal, *American Dilemma: The Negro Problem and Modern Democracy* (1943).

J. N. Nathanson, *Forerunners of Freedom: The Re-Creation of the American Spirit* (1941).

Allen Nevins, *Heritage of America* (1930).

George William Norris, *Fighting Liberal* (autobiography, 1943).

H. W. Odum, *American Social Problems* (1939).

W. A. Orton, *The Liberal Tradition* (1946).

H. A. Overstreet, *The Mature Mind* (1949).

V. Parrington, *Main Currents in American Thought* (1927–1930).

C. W. Patten, *The Battle for Municipal Reform* (1941).

J. T. Salter, *The Pattern of Politics* (1940).

J. A. Schumpeter, *Capitalism, Socialism, and Democracy* (1943).

Gilbert Seldes, *Proclaim Liberty* (1942).

T. V. Smith, *The Democratic Way of Life* (1939 ed.).

———, *The Democratic Tradition in America* (1941).

W. T. Stace, *The Destiny of Western Man* (1942).

W. H. Rogers and Others, *Explorations in Living: A Record of the Democratic Spirit* (1941).

W. H. Stead, *Democracy Against Unemployment* (1942).

Lincoln Steffens, *Autobiography* (1931).

D. S. Strong, *Organized Anti-Semitism in the United States* (1941).

R. G. Swing, *Calling America* (1939).

Ordway Tead, *New Adventures in Democracy* (1939).

H. A. Wallace, *The Century of the Common Man* (1943).

W. L. Warner and others, *Color and Human Nature* (1924).

Dixon Wecter, *The Age of the Great Depression, 1929–1941* (1948).

Richard Welling, *As the Twig Is Bent* (1942).

Morton W. White, *Social Thought in America: The Revolt against Formalism* (1950).

W. A. White, *Politics: The Citizens Business* (1924).

———, *Autobiography* (1946).

Brand Whitlock, *Forty Years of It* (1914).

C. F. Wittke, *We Who Built America* (1939).

Questions and Problems

1. Explain the means by which you keep abreast of "what's going on in the world."

2. Discuss this: *Persons who vote the straight party ticket contribute more to party responsibility and good government than do those voters who "scratch" their tickets.*

3. List at least four current issues in your community. How are civic organizations meeting them? How might they improve their approach to these problems?

4. How does it happen that active participation in politics is so often frowned upon in America?

5. Discuss: *Most men and women who enter public life are entitled to the gratitude of the Republic.*

6. Strike a balance between a representative's obligation to his immediate constituents and to the whole people.

7. Discuss the principle of compromise and accommodation in the operation of democratic government.

8. Analyze this statement: *The "sheet and pillow-case" and "shirt" types of organizations are composed largely of those who do not believe in or who do not understand the basic principles of democracy.*

9. Have you any explanation of the fact that some intelligent and well-educated Americans have been members of organizations supporting communist doctrines?

10. Show the relationship of domestic security to international peace.

Appendixes
and Index

APPENDIX 1

The Constitution of the United States

WE, the people of the United States, in order to form a more perfect union, establish justice, insure domestic tranquillity, provide for the common defense, promote the general welfare, and secure the blessings of liberty to ourselves and our posterity, do ordain and establish this Constitution for the United States of America.

Article I

Section I.   All legislative powers herein granted shall be vested in a Congress of the United States, which shall consist of a Senate and House of Representatives.

Section II.   1. The House of Representatives shall be composed of members chosen every second year by the people of the several States, and the electors in each State shall have the qualifications requisite for electors of the most numerous branch of the State legislature.

2. No person shall be a Representative who shall not have attained the age of twenty-five years, and been seven years a citizen of the United States, and who shall not, when elected, be an inhabitant of that State in which he shall be chosen.

3. Representatives and direct taxes [1] shall be apportioned among the several States which may be included within this Union, according to their respective numbers, which shall be determined by adding to the whole number of free persons, including those bound to service for a term of years, and excluding Indians not taxed, three fifths of all other persons. [2]   The actual enumeration shall be made within three years after the first meeting of the Congress of the United States, and within every subsequent term of ten years, in such manner

[1] See the Sixteenth Amendment.
[2] "Three fifths of all other persons" referred to the slaves. See Thirteenth and Fourteenth Amendments.

as they shall by law direct. The number of Representatives shall not exceed one for every thirty thousand, but each State shall have at least one Representative; and until such enumeration shall be made, the State of *New Hampshire* shall be entitled to choose three, *Massachusetts* eight, *Rhode Island and Providence Plantations* one, *Connecticut* five, *New York* six, *New Jersey* four, *Pennsylvania* eight, *Delaware* one, *Maryland* six, *Virginia* ten, *North Carolina* five, *South Carolina* five, and *Georgia* three.

4. When vacancies happen in the representation from any State the executive authority thereof shall issue writs of election to fill such vacancies.

5. The House of Representatives shall choose their Speaker and other officers, and shall have the sole power of impeachment.

Section III. 1. The Senate of the United States shall be composed of two Senators from each State, chosen by the legislature thereof, for six years; and each Senator shall have one vote.

2. Immediately after they shall be assembled in consequence of the first election, they shall be divided as equally as may be into three classes. The seats of the Senators of the first class shall be vacated at the expiration of the second year; of the second class, at the expiration of the fourth year, and of the third class, at the expiration of the sixth year, so that one third may be chosen every second year; and if vacancies happen by resignation or otherwise during the recess of the legislature of any State, the executive thereof may make temporary appointments until the next meeting of the legislature, which shall then fill such vacancies.[3]

3. No person shall be a Senator who shall not have attained to the age of thirty years, and been nine years a citizen of the United States, and who shall not, when elected, be an inhabitant of that State for which he shall be chosen.

4. The Vice-President of the United States shall be President of the Senate, but shall have no vote, unless they be equally divided.

5. The Senate shall choose their other officers, and also a President *pro tempore* in the absence of the Vice-President, or when he shall exercise the office of President of the United States.

6. The Senate shall have the sole power to try all impeachments. When sitting for that purpose, they shall be on oath or affirmation. When the President of the United States is tried, the Chief Justice shall preside: and no person shall be convicted without the concurrence of two thirds of the members present.

7. Judgment in cases of impeachment shall not extend further than to removal from office, and disqualification to hold and enjoy any office of honor, trust, or profit under the United States; but the party convicted shall, nevertheless, be liable and subject to indictment, trial, judgment, and punishment, according to law.

Section IV. 1. The times, places, and manner of holding elections for Senators and Representatives shall be prescribed in each State by the legislature

---

[3] See the Seventeenth Amendment.

thereof; but the Congress may at any time by law make or alter such regulations except as to the places of choosing Senators.

2. The Congress shall assemble at least once in every year, and such meeting shall be on the first Monday in December, unless they shall by law appoint a different day.[4]

Section V. 1. Each house shall be the judge of the elections, returns, and qualifications of its own members, and a majority of each shall constitute a quorum to do business; but a smaller number may adjourn from day to day, and may be authorized to compel the attendance of absent members, in such manner, and under such penalties, as each house may provide.

2. Each house may determine the rules of its proceedings, punish its members for disorderly behavior, and with the concurrence of two thirds, expel a member.

3. Each house shall keep a journal of its proceedings, and from time to time publish the same, excepting such parts as may in their judgment require secrecy, and the yeas and nays of the members of either house on any question shall, at the desire of one fifth of those present, be entered on the journal.

4. Neither house, during the session of Congress, shall, without the consent of the other, adjourn for more than three days, nor to any other place than that in which the two houses shall be sitting.

Section VI. 1. The Senators and Representatives shall receive a compensation for their services, to be ascertained by law and paid out of the Treasury of the United States. They shall, in all cases except treason, felony, and breach of the peace, be privileged from arrest during their attendance at the session of their respective houses, and in going to and returning from the same; and for any speech or debate in either house they shall not be questioned in any other place.

2. No Senator or Representative shall, during the time for which he was elected, be appointed to any civil office under the authority of the United States, which shall have been created, or the emoluments whereof shall have been increased during such time; and no person holding any office under the United States shall be a member of either house during his continuance in office.

Section VII. 1. All bills for raising revenue shall originate in the House of Representatives; but the Senate may propose or concur with amendments as on other bills.

2. Every bill which shall have passed the House of Representatives and the Senate shall, before it become a law, be presented to the President of the United States; if he approve he shall sign it, but if not he shall return it, with his objections, to that house in which it shall have originated, who shall enter the objections at large on their journal and proceed to reconsider it. If after such reconsideration two thirds of that house shall agree to pass the bill, it shall be sent, together with the objections, to the other house, by which it shall likewise be re-

4 See the Twentieth Amendment, sec. 2.

considered, and if approved by two thirds of that house it shall become a law. But in all such cases the votes of both houses shall be determined by yeas and nays, and the names of the persons voting for and against the bill shall be entered on the journal of each house respectively. If any bill shall not be returned by the President within ten days (Sundays excepted) after it shall have been presented to him, the same shall be a law, in like manner as if he had signed it, unless the Congress by their adjournment prevent its return, in which case it shall not be a law.

3. Every order, resolution, or vote to which the concurrence of the Senate and House of Representatives may be necessary (except on a question of adjournment) shall be presented to the President of the United States; and before the same shall take effect, shall be approved by him, or being disapproved by him, shall be repassed by two thirds of the Senate and House of Representatives, according to the rules and limitations prescribed in the case of a bill.

Section VIII. 1. The Congress shall have power to lay and collect taxes, duties, imposts, and excise, to pay the debts and provide for the common defense and general welfare of the United States; but all duties, imposts, and excises shall be uniform throughout the United States;

2. To borrow money on the credit of the United States;

3. To regulate commerce with foreign nations and among the several States, and with the Indian tribes;

4. To establish an uniform rule of naturalization, and uniform laws on the subject of bankruptcies throughout the United States;

5. To coin money, regulate the value thereof, and of foreign coin, and fix the standard of weights and measures;

6. To provide for the punishment of counterfeiting the securities and current coin of the United States;

7. To establish post-offices and post-roads;

8. To promote the progress of science and useful arts by securing for limited times to authors and inventors the exclusive right to their respective writings and discoveries;

9. To constitute tribunals inferior to the Supreme Court;

10. To define and punish piracies and felonies committed on the high seas and offenses against the law of nations;

11. To declare war, grant letters of marque and reprisal, and make rules concerning captures on land and water;

12. To raise and support armies, but no appropriation of money to that use shall be for a longer term than two years;

13. To provide and maintain a navy;

14. To make rules for the government and regulation of the land and naval forces;

15. To provide for calling forth the militia to execute the laws of the Union, suppress insurrections, and repel invasions;

16. To provide for organizing, arming, and disciplining the militia, and for governing such part of them as may be employed in the service of the United

States, reserving to the States respectively the appointment of the officers, and the authority of training the militia according to the discipline prescribed by Congress;

17. To exercise exclusive legislation in all cases whatsoever over such district (not exceeding ten miles square) as may, by cession of particular States and the acceptance of Congress, become the seat of the Government of the United States, and to exercise like authority over all places purchased by the consent of the legislature of the State in which the same shall be, for the erection of forts, magazines, arsenals, dockyards, and other needful buildings; and

18. To make all laws which shall be necessary and proper for carrying into execution the foregoing powers, and all other powers vested by this Constitution in the Government of the United States, or in any department or officer thereof.

Section IX. 1. The migration or importation of such persons as any of the States now existing shall think proper to admit shall not be prohibited by the Congress prior to the year one thousand eight hundred and eight, but a tax or duty may be imposed on such importation, not exceeding ten dollars for each person.

2. The privilege of the writ of habeas corpus shall not be suspended, unless when in cases of rebellion or invasion the public safety may require it.

3. No bill of attainder or ex post facto law shall be passed.

4. No capitation or other direct tax shall be laid, unless in proportion to the census or enumeration hereinbefore directed to be taken.[5]

5. No tax or duty shall be laid on articles exported from any State.

6. No preference shall be given by any regulation of commerce or revenue to the ports of one State over those of another; nor shall vessels bound to or from one State be obliged to enter, clear, or pay duties in another.

7. No money shall be drawn from the Treasury but in consequence of appropriations made by law; and a regular statement and account of the receipts and expenditures of all public money shall be published from time to time.

8. No title of nobility shall be granted by the United States; and no person holding any office of profit or trust under them shall, without the consent of the Congress, accept of any present, emolument, office, or title, of any kind whatever, from any king, prince, or foreign State.

Section X. 1. No State shall enter into any treaty, alliance, or confederation; grant letters of marque and reprisal; coin money; emit bills of credit; make anything but gold and silver coin a tender in payment of debts; pass any bill of attainder, ex post facto law or law impairing the obligation of contracts, or grant any title of nobility.

2. No State shall, without the consent of Congress, lay any imposts or duties on imports or exports, except what may be absolutely necessary for executing its inspection laws; and the net produce of all duties and imposts, laid by any State on imports or exports, shall be for the use of the Treasury of the United

---

[5] See the Sixteenth Amendment.

States; and all such laws shall be subject to the revision and control of the Congress.

3. No State shall, without the consent of Congress, lay any duty of tonnage, keep troops or ships of war in time of peace, enter into any agreement or compact with another State or with a foreign power, or engage in war, unless actually invaded or in such imminent danger as will not admit of delay.

Article II

Section I. 1. The executive power shall be vested in a President of the United States of America. He shall hold his office during the term of four years, and together with the Vice-President, chosen for the same term, be elected as follows:

2. Each State shall appoint, in such manner as the legislature thereof may direct, a number of electors, equal to the whole number of Senators and Representatives to which the State may be entitled in the Congress; but no Senator or Representative, or person holding an office of trust or profit under the United States, shall be appointed an elector.

[The electors shall meet in the respective States and vote by ballot for two persons, of whom one at least shall not be an inhabitant of the same State with themselves. And they shall make a list of all the persons voted for, and of the number of votes for each; which list they shall sign and certify, and transmit sealed to the seat of government of the United States, directed to the President of the Senate. The President of the Senate shall, in the presence of the Senate and House of Representatives, open all the certificates, and the votes shall then be counted. The person having the greatest number of votes shall be the President, if such a number be a majority of the whole number of electors appointed; and if there be more than one who have such majority, and have an equal number of votes, then the House of Representatives shall immediately choose by ballot one of them for President; and if no person have a majority, then from the five highest on the list the said House shall in like manner choose the President. But in choosing the President the votes shall be taken by States, the representation from each State having one vote; a quorum for this purpose shall consist of a member or members from two thirds of the States, and a majority of all the States shall be necessary to a choice. In every case, after the choice of the President, the person having the greatest number of votes of the electors shall be the Vice-President. But if there should remain two or more who have equal votes, the Senate shall choose from them by ballot the Vice-President.] [6]

3. The Congress may determine the time of choosing the electors and the day on which they shall give their votes, which day shall be the same throughout the United States.

4. No person except a natural-born citizen, or a citizen of the United States at the time of the adoption of this Constitution, shall be eligible to the office of President; neither shall any person be eligible to that office who shall not have

[6] This paragraph was superseded by the Twelfth Amendment adopted in 1804.

attained to the age of thirty-five years, and been fourteen years a resident within the United States.

5. In case of the removal of the President from office, or of his death, resignation, or inability to discharge the powers and duties of the said office, the same shall devolve on the Vice-President, and the Congress may by law provide for the case of removal, death, resignation, or inability, both of the President and Vice-President, declaring what officer shall then act as President, and such officer shall act accordingly until the disability be removed or a President shall be elected.

6. The President shall, at stated times, receive for his services a compensation, which shall neither be increased nor diminished during the period for which he may have been elected, and he shall not receive within that period any other emolument from the United States or any of them.

7. Before he enter on the execution of his office he shall take the following oath or affirmation:

"I do solemnly swear (or affirm) that I will faithfully execute the office of President of the United States, and will to the best of my ability preserve, protect, and defend the Constitution of the United States."

Section II. 1. The President shall be Commander-in-chief of the Army and Navy of the United States, and of the militia of the several States when called into the actual service of the United States; he may require the opinion, in writing, of the principal officer in each of the executive departments, upon any subject relating to the duties of their respective offices, and he shall have power to grant reprieves and pardons for offenses against the United States, except in cases of impeachment.

2. He shall have power, by and with the advice and consent of the Senate, to make treaties, provided two thirds of the Senators present concur; and he shall nominate, and, by and with the advice and consent of the Senate, shall appoint ambassadors, other public ministers and consuls, judges of the Supreme Court, and all other officers of the United States, whose appointments are not herein otherwise provided for, and which shall be established by law; but the Congress may by law vest the appointment of such inferior officers, as they think proper, in the President alone, in the courts of law, or in the heads of departments.

3. The President shall have power to fill up all vacancies that may happen during the recess of the Senate, by granting commissions which shall expire at the end of their next session.

Section III. He shall from time to time give to the Congress information of the state of the Union, and recommend to their consideration such measures as he shall judge necessary and expedient; he may, on extraordinary occasions, convene both houses, or either of them, and in case of disagreement between them with respect to the time of adjournment, he may adjourn them to such time as he shall think proper; he shall receive ambassadors and other public ministers; he shall take care that the laws be faithfully executed, and shall commission all the officers of the United States.

Section IV. The President, Vice-President, and all civil officers of the United States shall be removed from office on impeachment for and conviction of treason, bribery, or other high crimes and misdemeanors.

Article III

Section I. The judicial power of the United States shall be vested in one Supreme Court, and in such inferior courts as the Congress may from time to time ordain and establish. The judges, both of the supreme and inferior courts, shall hold their offices during good behavior, and shall, at stated times, receive for their services a compensation which shall not be diminished during their continuance in office.

Section II. 1. The judicial power shall extend to all cases, in law and equity, arising under this Constitution, the laws of the United States, and treaties made, or which shall be made, under their authority; to all cases affecting ambassadors, other public ministers, and consuls; to all cases of admiralty and maritime jurisdiction; to controversies to which the United States shall be a party; to controversies between two or more States; between a State and citizens of another State;[7] between citizens of different States; between citizens of the same State claiming lands under grants of different States, and between a State, or the citizens thereof, and foreign States, citizens or subjects.

2. In all cases affecting ambassadors, or other public ministers and consuls, and those in which a State shall be a party, the Supreme Court shall have original jurisdiction. In all the other cases before mentioned the Supreme Court shall have appellate jurisdiction, both as to law and fact, with such exceptions and under such regulations as the Congress shall make.

3. The trial of all crimes, except in cases of impeachment, shall be by jury; and such trial shall be held in the State where the said crimes shall have been committed; but when not committed within any State, the trial shall be at such place or places as the Congress may by law have directed.

Section III. 1. Treason against the United States shall consist only in levying war against them, or in adhering to their enemies, giving them aid and comfort. No person shall be convicted of treason unless on the testimony of two witnesses to the same overt act, or on confession in open court.

2. The Congress shall have power to declare the punishment of treason, but no attainder of treason shall work corruption of blood or forfeiture except during the life of the person attained.

Article IV

Section I. Full faith and credit shall be given in each State to the public acts, records, and judicial proceedings of every other State. And the Congress may by general laws prescribe the manner in which such acts, records, and proceedings shall be proved, and the effect thereof.

[7] See the Eleventh Amendment.

Section II. 1. The citizens of each State shall be entitled to all privileges and immunities of citizens in the several States.

2. A person charged in any State with treason, felony, or other crime, who shall flee from justice, and be found in another State, shall, on demand of the executive authority of the State from which he fled, be delivered up, to be removed to the State having jurisdiction of the crime.

3. No person held to service or labor in one State, under the laws thereof, escaping into another, shall, in consequence of any law or regulation, be discharged from such service or labor, but shall be delivered up on claim of the party to whom such service or labor may be due.[8]

Section III. 1. New States may be admitted by the Congress into this Union; but no new State shall be formed or erected within the jurisdiction of any other State; nor any State be formed by the junction of two or more States or parts of States, without the consent of the legislatures of the States concerned as well as of the Congress.

2. The Congress shall have power to dispose of and make all needful rules and regulations respecting the territory or other property belonging to the United States; and nothing in this Constitution shall be so constructed as to prejudice any claims of the United States or of any particular State.

Section IV. The United States shall guarantee to every State in this Union a republican form of government, and shall protect each of them against invasion, and on application of the legislature, or of the executive (when the legislature cannot be convened), against domestic violence.

Article V

The Congress, whenever two thirds of both houses shall deem it necessary, shall propose amendments to this Constitution, or, on the application of the legislatures of two thirds of the several States, shall call a convention for proposing amendments, which in either case shall be valid to all intents and purposes as part of this Constitution, when ratified by the legislatures of three fourths of the several States, or by conventions in three fourths thereof, as the one or the other mode of ratification may be proposed by the Congress, provided that no amendments which may be made prior to the year one thousand eight hundred and eight shall in any manner affect the first and fourth clauses in the ninth section of the first article; and that no State, without its consent, shall be deprived of its equal suffrage in the Senate.

Article VI

1. All debts contracted and engagements entered into, before the adoption of this Constitution, shall be as valid against the United States under this Constitution as under the confederation.

2. This Constitution, and the laws of the United States which shall be made

---

[8] This was the constitutional requirement respecting the return of fugitive slaves.

in pursuance thereof, and all treaties made, or which shall be made, under the authority of the United States, shall be the supreme law of the land; and the judges in every State shall be bound thereby, anything in the Constitution or laws of any State to the contrary notwithstanding.

3. The Senators and Representatives before mentioned, and the members of the several State legislatures, and all executive and judicial officers both of the United States and of the several States, shall be bound by oath or affirmation to support this Constitution; but no religious test shall ever be required as a qualification to any office or public trust under the United States.

Article VII

The ratification of the conventions of nine States shall be sufficient for the establishment of this Constitution between the States so ratifying the same.

Done in convention by the unanimous consent of the States present, the seventeenth day of September, in the year of our Lord one thousand seven hundred and eighty-seven, and of the independence of the United States of America the twelfth. In witness whereof, we have hereunto subscribed our names.

AMENDMENTS

Article I [9]

Congress shall make no law respecting an establishment of religion, or prohibiting the free exercise thereof; or abridging the freedom of speech or of the press; or the right of the people peaceably to assemble, and to petition the government for a redress of grievances.

Article II

A well-regulated militia being necessary to the security of a free State, the right of the people to keep and bear arms shall not be infringed.

Article III

No soldier shall, in time of peace, be quartered in any house without the consent of the owner, nor in time of war, but in a manner to be prescribed by law.

Article IV

The right of the people to be secure in their persons, houses, papers, and effects, against unreasonable searches and seizures, shall not be violated, and no warrants shall issue but upon probable cause, supported by oath or affirma-

[9] The first ten amendments were proposed in 1789, and adopted in 1791.

tion, and particularly describing the place to be searched, and the person or things to be seized.

Article V

No person shall be held to answer for a capital or otherwise infamous crime, unless on a presentment or indictment of a grand jury, except in cases arising in the land or naval forces, or in the militia, when in actual service in time of war or public danger; nor shall any person be subject for the same offense to be twice put in jeopardy of life or limb; nor shall be compelled in any criminal case to be a witness against himself, nor be deprived of life, liberty, or property, without due process of law; nor shall private property be taken for public use without just compensation.

Article VI

In all criminal prosecutions the accused shall enjoy the right to a speedy and public trial, by an impartial jury of the State and district wherein the crime shall have been committed, which district shall have been previously ascertained by law, and to be informed of the nature and cause of the accusation; to be confronted with the witnesses against him; to have compulsory process for obtaining witnesses in his favor, and to have the assistance of counsel for his defense.

Article VII

In suits at common law, where the value in controversy shall exceed twenty dollars, the right of trial by jury shall be preserved, and no fact tried by a jury shall be otherwise re-examined in any court of the United States, than according to the rules of the common law.

Article VIII

Excessive bail shall not be required, nor excessive fines imposed, nor cruel and unusual punishments inflicted.

Article IX

The enumeration in the Constitution of certain rights shall not be construed to deny or disparage others retained by the people.

Article X

The powers not delegated to the United States by the Constitution, nor prohibited by it to the States, are reserved to the States respectively or to the people.

Article XI [10]

The judicial power of the United States shall not be construed to extend to any suit in law or equity, commenced or prosecuted against one of the United States by citizens of another State, or by citizens or subjects of any foreign State.

Article XII [11]

The electors shall meet in their respective States and vote by ballot for President and Vice-President, one of whom, at least, shall not be an inhabitant of the same State with themselves; they shall name in their ballots the person voted for as President, and in distinct ballots the persons voted for as Vice-President, and they shall make distinct lists of all persons voted for as President and of all persons voted for as Vice-President, and of the number of votes for each; which lists they shall sign and certify, and transmit sealed to the seat of the government of the United States, directed to the President of the Senate. The President of the Senate shall, in the presence of the Senate and House of Representatives, open all the certificates and the votes shall then be counted. The person having the greatest number of votes for President shall be the President, if such number be a majority of the whole number of electors appointed; and if no person have such majority, then from the persons having the highest numbers not exceeding three on the list of those voted for as President, the House of Representatives shall choose immediately, by ballot, the President. But in choosing the President the votes shall be taken by States, the representation from each State having one vote; a quorum for this purpose shall consist of a member or members from two thirds of the States, and a majority of all the States shall be necessary to a choice. And if the House of Representatives shall not choose a President whenever the right of choice shall devolve upon them, before the fourth day of March next following, then the Vice-President shall act as President, as in the case of the death or other constitutional disability of the President. [12]

The person having the greatest number of votes as Vice-President shall be the Vice-President, if such number be a majority of the whole number of electors appointed; and if no person have a majority, then from the two highest numbers on the list the Senate shall choose the Vice-President; a quorum for the purpose shall consist of two thirds of the whole number of Senators, and a majority of the whole number shall be necessary to a choice. But no person constitutionally ineligible to the office of President shall be eligible to that of Vice-President of the United States.

10 Proposed in 1794, adopted in 1798.
11 Proposed in 1803, adopted in 1804.
12 See the Twentieth Amendment.

Article XIII [13]

Section I. Neither slavery nor involuntary servitude, except as a punishment for crime whereof the party shall have been duly convicted, shall exist within the United States or any place subject to their jurisdiction.

Section II. Congress shall have power to enforce this article by appropriate legislation.

Article XIV [14]

Section I. All persons born or naturalized in the United States, and subject to the jurisdiction thereof, are citizens of the United States and of the State wherein they reside. No State shall make or enforce any law which shall abridge the privileges or immunities of citizens of the United States; nor shall any State deprive any person of life, liberty, or property, without due process of law; nor deny to any person within its jurisdiction the equal protection of the laws.

Section II. Representatives shall be apportioned among the several States according to their respective numbers, counting the whole number of persons in each State, excluding Indians not taxed. But when the right to vote at any election for the choice of electors for President and Vice-President of the United States, Representatives in Congress, the executive and judicial officers of a State, or the members of the legislature thereof, is denied to any of the male inhabitants of such State, being twenty-one years of age, and citizens of the United States, or in any way abridged, except for participation in rebellion, or other crime, the basis of representation therein shall be reduced in the proportion which the number of such male citizens shall bear to the whole number of male citizens twenty-one years of age in such State.

Section III. No person shall be a Senator or Representative in Congress, or elector of President and Vice-President, or hold any office, civil or military, under the United States or under any State, who, having previously taken an oath as a member of Congress, or as an officer of the United States, or as a member of any State legislature, or as an executive or judicial officer of any State, to support the Constitution of the United States, shall have engaged in insurrection or rebellion against the same, or given aid or comfort to the enemies thereof. But Congress may, by a vote of two thirds of each house, remove such disability.

Section IV. The validity of the public debt of the United States, authorized by law, including debts incurred for payment of pensions and bounties for services in suppressing insurrection or rebellion, shall not be questioned. But neither the United States nor any State shall assume or pay any debt or obliga-

[13] Proposed and adopted in 1865.
[14] Proposed in 1866, adopted in 1868.

tion incurred in aid of insurrection or rebellion against the United States, or any claim for the loss or emancipation of any slave; but all such debts, obligations, and claims shall be held illegal and void.

Section V. The Congress shall have power to enforce, by appropriate legislation, the provisions of this article.

Article XV [15]

Section I. The right of citizens of the United States to vote shall not be denied or abridged by the United States or by any State on account of race, color, or previous condition of servitude.

Section II. The Congress shall have power to enforce this article by appropriate legislation.

Article XVI [16]

The Congress shall have power to lay and collect taxes on incomes, from whatever source derived, without apportionment among the several States, and without regard to any census or enumeration.

Article XVII [17]

The Senate of the United States shall be composed of two Senators from each State, elected by the people thereof, for six years; and each Senator shall have one vote. The electors in each State shall have the qualifications requisite for electors of the most numerous branch of the State legislatures.

When vacancies happen in the representation of any State in the Senate, the executive authority of such State shall issue writs of election to fill such vacancies: *Provided,* That the legislature of any State may empower the executive thereof to make temporary appointments until the people fill the vacancies by election as the legislature may direct.

This amendment shall not be so construed as to affect the election or term of any Senator chosen before it becomes valid as part of the Constitution.

Article XVIII [18]

Section I. After one year from the ratification of this article the manufacture, sale, or transportation of intoxicating liquors within, the importation thereof into, or the exportation thereof from the United States and all territory subject to the jurisdiction thereof for beverage purposes is hereby prohibited.

Section II. The Congress and the several States shall have concurrent power to enforce this article by appropriate legislation.

[15] Proposed in 1869, adopted in 1870.
[16] Proposed in 1909, adopted in 1913.
[17] Proposed in 1912, adopted in 1913.
[18] Proposed in 1917, adopted in 1919.

Section III. This article shall be inoperative unless it shall have been ratified as an amendment to the Constitution by the legislatures of the several States, as provided in the Constitution, within seven years from the date of the submission hereof to the States by the Congress.

Article XIX [19]

The right of citizens of the United States to vote shall not be denied or abridged by the United States or by any State on account of sex.

Congress shall have power to enforce this article by appropriate legislation.

Article XX [20]

Section I. The terms of the President and Vice-President shall end at noon on the 20th day of January, and the terms of Senators and Representatives at noon on the 3d day of January, of the years in which such terms would have ended if this article had not been ratified; and the terms of their successors shall then begin.

Section II. The Congress shall assemble at least once in every year, and such meeting shall begin at noon on the 3d day of January, unless they shall by law appoint a different day.

Section III. If, at the time fixed for the beginning of the term of the President, the President elect shall have died, the Vice-President elect shall become President. If a President shall not have been chosen before the time fixed for the beginning of his term, or if the President elect shall have failed to qualify, then the Vice-President elect shall act as President until a President shall have qualified; and the Congress may by law provide for the case wherein neither a President elect nor a Vice-President elect shall have qualified, declaring who shall then act as President, or the manner in which one who is to act shall be selected, and such person shall act accordingly until a President or Vice-President shall have qualified.

Section IV. The Congress may by law provide for the case of the death of any of the persons from whom the House of Representatives may choose a President whenever the right of choice shall have devolved upon them, and for the case of the death of any of the persons from whom the Senate may choose a Vice-President whenever the right of choice shall have devolved upon them.

Section V. Sections 1 and 2 shall take effect on the 15th day of October following the ratification of this article.

Section VI. This article shall be inoperative unless it shall have been ratified as an amendment to the Constitution by the legislatures of three fourths of the several States within seven years from the date of its submission.

[19] Proposed in 1918, adopted in 1920.
[20] Proposed in 1932, adopted in 1933.

Article XXI [21]

Section I. The eighteenth article of amendment to the Constitution of the United States is hereby repealed.

Section II. The transportation or importation into any state, territory, or possession of the United States for delivery or use therein of intoxicating liquors, in violation of the laws thereof, is hereby prohibited.

Section III. This article shall be inoperative unless it shall have been ratified as an amendment to the Constitution by convention in the several States, as provided in the Constitution, within seven years from the date of the submission hereof to the States by the Congress.

Article XXII [22]

Section I. No person shall be elected to the office of the President more than twice, and no person who has held the office of President, or acted as President, for more than two years of a term to which some other person was elected President shall be elected to the office of the President more than once. But this Article shall not apply to any person holding the office of President when this Article was proposed by the Congress, and shall not prevent any person who may be holding the office of President, or acting as President, during the term within which this Article becomes operative from holding the office of President, or acting as President during the remainder of such term.

Section II. This Article shall be inoperative unless it shall have been ratified as an amendment to the Constitution by the legislatures of three-fourths of the several States within seven years from the date of its submission to the States by the Congress.

[21] Proposed in February, 1933, and adopted in November, 1933.
[22] Proposed in March, 1947, and adopted in February, 1951.

APPENDIX 2

Charter of the United Nations[1]

WE, the peoples of the United Nations

Determined to save succeeding generations from the scourge of war, which twice in our lifetime has brought untold sorrow to mankind, and

To reaffirm faith in fundamental human rights, in dignity and worth of the human person, in the equal rights of men and women and of nations large and small, and

To establish conditions under which justice and respect for the obligations arising from treaties and other sources of international law can be maintained, and

To promote social progress and better standards of life in larger freedom, and for these ends

To practice tolerance and live together in peace with one another as good neighbors, and

To unite our strength to maintain international peace and security, and

To insure, by the acceptance of the principles and the institution of methods, that armed force shall not be used, save in the common interest, and

To employ international machinery for the promotion of the economic and social advancement of all peoples, have resolved to combine our efforts to accomplish these aims.

Accordingly, our respective governments, through representatives assembled in the city of San Francisco, who have exhibited their full powers found to be in good and due form, have agreed to the present Charter of the United Nations and do hereby establish an international organization to be known as the United Nations.

Chapter I

PURPOSES

(Art. 1) 1. To maintain international peace and security, and to that end: to take effective collective measures for the prevention and removal of threats

[1] Condensation reproduced by permission from *Facts on File*, Vol. V., No. 271, December 23–31, 1945.

to the peace and for the suppression of acts of aggression . . . , and to bring about by peaceful means, and in conformity with the principles of justice and international law, adjustment or settlement of international disputes . . . which might lead to a breach of the peace;

2. To develop friendly relations among nations . . .

3. To achieve international co-operation in solving international problems of an economic, social, cultural or humanitarian character, and . . . encouraging respect for human rights [irrespective of] . . . race, sex, language or religion; . . .

PRINCIPLES

(Art. 2) 1. The organization is based on the principle of the sovereign equality of all its members. 2. . . . [they] shall fulfill in good faith [their] obligations . . . 3. . . . settle their . . . disputes by peaceful means . . . 4. . . . refrain . . . from threat or use of force . . . 5. . . . give the United Nations every assistance in any action . . . 6. The Organization shall ensure that states not members act in accordance with these principles . . . 7. [Restrains jurisdiction from domestic matters.]

Chapter II

MEMBERSHIP

(Art. 3) [Original members defined.]

(Art. 4) [Opens membership to all other peace-loving nations which accept obligations and by decision of the General Assembly on recommendation of Security Council.]

(Art. 5) A member . . . against which preventive or enforcement action has been taken . . . may be suspended from the exercise of [its] rights and privileges . . . by the General Assembly upon the recommendation of the Security Council . . .

(Art. 6) A member . . . which has persistently violated [Charter] principles . . . may be expelled . . . by the General Assembly upon the recommendation of the Security Council.

Chapter III

ORGANS

(Art. 7) [There are established as principal organs: General Assembly, Security Council, Economic and Social Council, International Court of Justice, Trusteeship Council, Secretariat and such subsidiaries as necessary.]

(Art. 8) [No restrictions on eligibility of men and women to participate in any capacity in the above agencies.]

Chapter IV

THE GENERAL ASSEMBLY

Composition

(**Art. 9**) [Shall consist of all the members with not more than five representatives each.]

Functions and Powers

(**Art. 10**) . . . may discuss any questions . . . within the scope of the charter or relating to the powers and functions of any organ provided in the Charter, and, except as provided in Art. 12, may make recommendations to the members . . . or to the Security Council, or both . . .

(**Art. 11**) 1. . . . may consider the general principles of co-operation in the maintenance of peace . . . and may make recommendations . . . to members or to the Security Council or both. 2. . . . may discuss any questions relating to the maintenance of . . . peace . . . [see Arts. 12, 35] . . . A question on which action is necessary shall be referred to the Security Council . . . 3. . . . may call the attention of the Security Council to situations which are likely to endanger . . . peace . . .

(**Art. 12**) 1. While the Security Council is exercising [jurisdiction] in respect of any dispute . . . the General Assembly shall not make any recommendation with regard to that dispute . . . unless the Security Council so requests . . .

(**Art. 13**) [Authorizes study and recommendations in international law and economic, social, cultural, educational and health progress.]

(**Art. 14**) [Authorizes recommendations to solve threatening situations regardless of origin.]

(**Art. 15**) [Authorizes reports.]

(**Art. 16**) [Authorizes trusteeships—see Chaps. XII, XIII.]

(**Art. 17**) [Places responsibility for budgets.]

Voting

(**Art. 18**) 1. [Each member shall have one vote.] 2. Decisions . . . shall be made by a two-thirds majority of those present and voting. [Subjects specified such as keeping peace, election of members to organs, admission of new members, expulsions, suspensions.]

(**Art. 19**) [Suspends votes of members behind in payments.]

Procedure

(**Art. 20**) . . . shall meet in regular annual sessions and in . . . special sessions . . . convoked by the Secretary General at the request of the Security Council or of a majority of the members . . .

(Art. 21) . . . shall adopt its own rules of procedure. It shall elect its president for each session.

(Art. 22) [May establish necessary subsidiaries.]

Chapter V

THE SECURITY COUNCIL

Composition

(Art. 23) 1. . . . shall consist of 11 members . . . [The U.S., the U.K., the U.S.S.R., China and France shall be permanent members.] The General Assembly shall elect six other members . . . 2. [Non-permanent members shall serve two years.] 3. Each member . . . shall have one representative.

Primary Responsibility

(Art. 24) 1. In order to insure prompt and effective action . . . its members confer on the Security Council primary responsibility for the maintenance of international peace and security, and agree that in carrying out its duties . . . the Security Council acts in their behalf. 2. [Powers specified in Chaps. VI, VII, VIII, and XII.]

(Art. 25) The members of the United Nations agree to accept and carry out the decisions of the Security Council in accordance with the provisions of the present Charter.

(Art. 26) [To promote peace] the Security Council shall be responsible for formulating . . . a system for the regulation of armaments.

Voting

(Art. 27) 1. Each member . . . shall have one vote. 2. Decisions . . . on procedural matters shall be made by an affirmative vote of seven members . . . 3. Decisions . . . on all other matters shall be made by an affirmative vote of seven members including the concurring votes of the permanent members . . .

Procedure

(Art. 28) 1. . . . shall be so organized as to be able to function continuously. Each member . . . shall for this purpose be represented at all times . . .

(Art. 29) [May establish subsidiary organs.]

(Art. 30) [Shall adopt own rules of procedure.]

(Art. 31) Any member of the United Nations which is not a member of the Security Council may participate without a vote in the discussion of any question . . .

(Art. 32) Any member [see Art. 31] . . . or any State not a member of the United Nations, if it is party to a dispute . . . , shall be invited to participate in the discussion . . .

Chapter VI

PACIFIC SETTLEMENT OF DISPUTES

(Art. 33) 1. The parties to any dispute . . . shall . . . seek a solution by negotiation . . . 2. The Security Council shall . . . call upon the parties to settle their dispute . . .

(Art. 34) The Security Council may investigate any dispute . . . which might lead to international friction . . .

(Art. 35) 1. Any member of the United Nations may bring any dispute . . . [under Art. 34] to the attention of the Security Council or of the General Assembly. 2. A State . . . not a member of the United Nations may bring to the attention of the . . . Council or . . . Assembly any dispute to which it is a party, if it accepts in advance, . . . obligations of pacific settlement . . .

(Art. 36) 1. The Security Council may, at any stage of the dispute . . . [under Art. 33] . . . recommend . . . adjustment. 2. The . . . Council should [consider] . . . any procedures . . . already . . . adopted by the parties. 3. In making recommendations . . . the . . . Council should [consider] . . . that legal disputes should . . . be referred to the International Court of Justice . . .

(Art. 37) 1. Should the parties to a dispute . . . [see Art. 33] fail to settle . . . they shall refer it to the Security Council . . . [to] decide whether to take action under Art. 36 . . .

(Art. 38) Without prejudice to . . . Arts. 33–37 . . . the . . . Council may, if all the parties to any dispute so request, make recommendations to the parties . . .

Chapter VII

ACTION WITH RESPECT TO THREATS TO THE PEACE, BREACHES OF THE PEACE AND ACTS OF AGGRESSION

(Art. 39) The Council shall determine the existence of any threat to the peace . . . and decide . . . measures . . .

(Art. 40) [Council may call upon parties to comply with provisional measures.]

(Art. 41) . . . may decide what measures not involving . . . force are to be employed to give effect to its decisions . . .

(Art. 42) Should . . . measures [in Art. 41] be inadequate . . . it may take action by . . . [force].

(Art. 43) All members . . . undertake to make available . . . armed forces, assistance and facilities, including rights of passage . . .

(Art. 44) When . . . Council has decided to use force, it shall, before calling upon a member not represented on it to provide forces . . . invite that member, if . . . [he desires] to participate in the decisions . . .

(Art. 45) . . . members shall hold immediately available national air force contingents . . . for enforcement . . .

(Art. 46) Plans for . . . force shall be made by . . . Council . . .

(Art. 47) [A Military Staff shall advise.]

(Art. 48) 1. The action . . . shall be . . . by all members, or by some . . . as [determined].

(Art. 49) [Members shall offer mutual assistance in carrying out measures.]

(Art. 50) [If enforcement creates special economic problems States may consult the Security Council.]

(Art. 51) Nothing . . . shall impair the inherent right of . . . self-defense . . .

Chapter VIII

REGIONAL ARRANGEMENTS

(Art. 52) 1. [Nothing in the Charter precludes regional arrangements for peace.] 2. [Parties to such shall seek peaceful settlement of local disputes before referring them to the Security Council.]

(Art. 53) 1. The . . . Council shall . . . utilize such arrangements . . . for enforcement . . . But no . . . action will be taken . . . without authorization . . . except . . . against any enemy state . . . 2. . . . "enemy state" . . . applies to any state which during the second World War has been an enemy of any signatory of the present Charter.

(Art. 54) The Security Council shall . . . be kept fully informed of activities undertaken or in contemplation . . .

Chapter IX

INTERNATIONAL ECONOMIC AND SOCIAL CO-OPERATION

(Art. 55) . . . the United Nations shall promote (A) Higher standards of living . . . (B) Solutions of . . . problems . . . (C) . . . respect for . . . human rights and . . . freedoms . . .

(Art. 56) [All members pledge action to achieve Art. 55.]

(Art. 57) [Relations with specialized agencies.]

(Art. 58) [Co-ordinates special agencies.]

(Art. 59) [Initiates new agencies.]

(Art. 60) [Fixes responsibility under Assembly.]

Chapter X

ECONOMIC AND SOCIAL COUNCIL

Composition

(Art. 61) [Shall consist of 18 members.]

Functions and Powers

(Art. 62) [May make studies, recommendations, prepare draft conventions, call conferences.]

(Art. 63) [May enter into an agreement with special agencies and co-ordinate their activities.]

(Art. 64) [May obtain reports from them and make reports.]

(Art. 65) [May furnish information to the Council.]

(Art. 66) [May carry out Assembly recommendations.]

Voting

(Art. 67) 1. Each member . . . shall have one vote. 2. Decisions . . . by a majority present and voting.

Procedure

(Art. 68) [It] . . . shall set up commissions . . .

(Art. 69) . . . any member [invited] . . . to participate . . .

(Art. 70) [Agencies may participate in deliberations.]

(Art. 71) [Consultations permitted sometimes.]

(Art. 72) [It shall adopt its own rules of procedure.]

Chapter XI

DECLARATION REGARDING NON-SELF-GOVERNING TERRITORIES

(Art. 73) Members . . . recognize . . . interests of the inhabitants of these territories are paramount . . .

(Art. 74) [Their policy must be based on good neighborliness.]

Chapter XII

INTERNATIONAL TRUSTEESHIP SYSTEM

(Art. 75) . . . established for the . . . supervision of such territories as may be placed thereunder . . .

(Art. 76) . . . objectives [are] in accordance with . . . Art. 1.

(Art. 77) . . . shall apply to (a) Territories now . . . under mandate; (b) . . . which may be detached from enemy states . . . ; (c) . . . voluntarily placed under system by [administrators] . . .

(Art. 78) . . . shall not apply to members . . .

(Art. 79) [Terms shall be agreed upon by parties concerned.]

(Art. 80) [Except as agreed upon nothing shall alter rights of states or peoples or agreements.]

(Art. 81) [Agreements shall include terms and designate the authority, which may be a member.]

(Art. 82) There may be designated . . . a strategic area . . . which may include part or all of the trust territory . . .

(Art. 83) 1. All functions . . . relating to the strategic area . . . shall be exercised by the Security Council. 2. . . . objectives . . . in Art. 76 shall be applicable . . .

(Art. 84) . . . the trust territory shall play its part in the maintenance of international peace and security . . .

(Art. 85) [Functions of trusteeship agreements for all areas not strategic come under the Assembly.]

Chapter XIII

THE TRUSTEESHIP COUNCIL COMPOSITION

(Art. 86) . . . shall consist of (A) Those members administering trust territories; (B) Such . . . mentioned by name in Art. 23 as are not administering [trusts]; and (C) As . . . elected . . .

Functions and Powers

(Art. 87) The General Assembly and . . . the Trusteeship Council . . . may: Consider reports . . . accept petitions . . . provide for periodic visits . . .

(Art. 88) . . . shall formulate a questionnaire on . . . each trust territory, and the administering authority [shall report annually].

Voting

(Art. 89) [Members have one vote each. Decisions by a majority present and voting.]

Procedure

(Art. 90) . . . shall adopt own rules of procedure . . .

(Art. 91) . . . shall avail itself of assistance . . .

Chapter XIV

THE INTERNATIONAL COURT OF JUSTICE

(Art. 92) . . . shall be the judicial organ . . .

(Art. 93) All members of the United Nations are ipso facto parties to the statute of the . . . Court of Justice . . . A State . . . not a member . . . may become a party . . .

(Art. 94) Each member . . . undertakes to comply with the decision of the . . . Court . . . if any party to a case fails to perform . . . under judgment . . . the other . . . [has] recourse to the Security Council . . .

(Art. 95) [Nothing herein prevents use of other tribunals.]

(Art. 96) [Advisory opinion may be requested.]

Chapter XV

THE SECRETARIAT

(Art. 97) There shall be a secretariat . . . a secretary general and . . . staff . . . appointed by the General Assembly . . .

(Art. 98) [Duties.]

(Art. 99) . . . [He] may bring to the attention of the Security Council any matter . . . [threatening peace].

(Art. 100) [He and his staff] . . . shall not seek or receive instructions from any government . . . [and] shall refrain from any action . . . [compromising internationality]. Each nation undertakes to respect [their internationality] . . .

(Art. 101) [The Secretary General shall appoint the staff.]

Chapter XVI

MISCELLANEOUS PROVISIONS

(Art. 102) Every treaty . . . shall be registered . . .

(Art. 103) [Charter obligations take precedence over others.]

(Art. 104) [The Organization is promised legal freedom.]

(Art. 105) [The Organization is guaranteed privileges and immunities.]

Chapter XVII

TRANSITIONAL SECURITY ARRANGEMENTS

(Art. 106) [Until special agreements in Art. 43 are completed, the Big 5 powers shall consult and take necessary action to maintain peace.]

(Art. 107) [The Charter shall not hinder the prosecution of the war still going on.]

Chapter XVIII

AMENDMENTS

(Art. 108) [Charter may be amended by two-thirds vote and ratification by two-thirds of members, including all permanent Council members.]

(Art. 109) [A conference to review the Charter may be called by two-thirds vote of the Assembly and by seven Council members. If not held within 10 years, it may then be called by majority vote of Assembly and by seven Council members.]

Chapter XIX

RATIFICATION AND SIGNATURE

(Art. 110) [Charter shall be ratified and deposited with the U.S. Government by members and shall take effect upon deposit of ratifications by the Big 5 and a majority of the others.]

(Art. 111) The present Charter, of which the Chinese, English, French, Russian and Spanish texts are equally authentic, shall remain deposited in [U.S. Government archives] . . . [Done in San Francisco, June 26, 1945.]

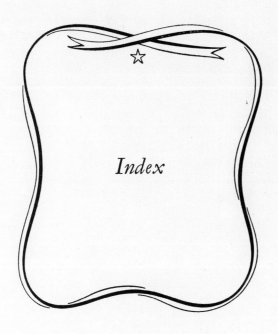

Index

Index